FORD | FULL SIZE VANS
1989-91 REPAIR MANUAL

President	Gary R. Ingersoll
Senior Vice President	Ronald A. Hoxter
Publisher	Kerry A. Freeman, S.A.E.
Editor-In-Chief	Dean F. Morgantini, S.A.E.
Managing Editor	David H. Lee, A.S.E., S.A.E.
Manager of Manufacturing	John J. Cantwell
Production Manager	W. Calvin Settle, Jr., S.A.E.
Senior Editor	Richard J. Rivele, S.A.E.
Senior Editor	Nick D'Andrea
Senior Editor	Ron Webb
Editor	Richard J. Rivele, S.A.E.

CHILTON BOOK COMPANY

ONE OF THE *ABC PUBLISHING COMPANIES,*
A PART OF CAPITAL CITIES/ABC, INC.

Manufactured in USA
© 1991 Chilton Book Company
Chilton Way, Radnor, PA 19089
ISBN 0–8019–8157-3
Library of Congress Catalog Card No. 90–056091
1234567890   0987654321

Contents

Contents

SAFETY NOTICE

Proper service and repair procedures are vital to the safe, reliable operation of all motor vehicles, as well as the personal safety of those performing repairs. This manual outlines procedures for servicing and repairing vehicles using safe, effective methods. The procedures contain many NOTES, CAUTIONS and WARNINGS which should be followed along with standard safety procedures to eliminate the possibility of personal injury or improper service which could damage the vehicle or compromise its safety.

It is important to note that the repair procedures and techniques, tools and parts for servicing motor vehicles, as well as the skill and experience of the individual performing the work vary widely. It is not possible to anticipate all of the conceivable ways or conditions under which vehicles may be serviced, or to provide cautions as to all of the possible hazards that may result. Standard and accepted safety precautions and equipment should be used when handling toxic or flammable fluids, and safety goggles or other protection should be used during cutting, grinding, chiseling, prying, or any other process that can cause material removal or projectiles.

Some procedures require the use of tools specially designed for a specific purpose. Before substituting another tool or procedure, you must be completely satisfied that neither your personal safety, nor the performance of the vehicle will be endangered

Although information in this manual is based on industry sources and is complete as possible at the time of publication, the possibility exists that some car manufacturers made later changes which could not be included here. While striving for total accuracy, Chilton Book Company cannot assume responsibility for any errors, changes or omissions that may occur in the compilation of this data.

PART NUMBERS

Part numbers listed in this reference are not recommendations by Chilton for any product by brand name. They are references that can be used with interchange manuals and aftermarket supplier catalogs to locate each brand supplier's discrete part number.

SPECIAL TOOLS

Special tools are recommended by the vehicle manufacturer to perform their specific job. Use has been kept to a minimum, but where absolutely necessary, they are referred to in the text by the part number of the tool manufacturer. These tools can be purchased under the appropriate part number, from Ford Dealer or regional distributor or an equivalent tool can be purchased locally from a tool supplier or parts outlet. Before substituting any tool for the recommended one, read the SAFETY NOTICE at the top of this page.

ACKNOWLEDGMENTS

The Chilton Book Company expresses its appreciation to Ford Motor Co., Dearborn, Michigan for their generous assistance.

General Information and Maintenance

HOW TO USE THIS BOOK

Chilton's Total Car Care Manual for 1989–91 Ford Full-Size Vans and Motor Home chassis is intended to help you learn more about the inner workings of your vehicle and save you money on its upkeep and operation.

The first two sections will be the most used, since they contain maintenance and tune-up information and procedures. Studies have shown that a properly tuned and maintained van can get at least 10% better gas mileage than an out-of-tune van. The other sections deal with the more complex systems of your van. Operating systems from engine through brakes are covered to the extent that the average do-it-yourselfer becomes mechanically involved. It will give you detailed instructions to help you change your own brake pads and shoes, replace spark plugs, and do many more jobs that will save you money, give you personal satisfaction, and help you avoid expensive problems.

A secondary purpose of this book is a reference for owners who want to understand their van and/or their mechanics better. In this case, no tools at all are required.

Before removing any bolts, read through the entire procedure. This will give you the overall view of what tools and supplies will be required. There is nothing more frustrating than having to walk to the bus stop on Monday morning because you were short one bolt on Sunday afternoon. So read ahead and plan ahead. Each operation should be approached logically and all procedures thoroughly understood before attempting any work.

All sections contain adjustments, maintenance, removal and installation procedures, and repair or overhaul procedures. When repair is not considered practical, we tell you how to remove the part and then how to install the new or rebuilt replacement. In this way, you at least save the labor costs. Backyard repair of such components as the alternator is just not practical.

Two basic mechanic's rules should be mentioned here. One, whenever the left side of the van or engine is referred to, it is meant to specify the driver's side of the van. Conversely, the right side of the van means the passenger's side. Secondly, most screws and bolt are removed by turning counterclockwise, and tightened by turning clockwise.

Safety is always the most important rule. Constantly be aware of the dangers involved in working on an automobile and take the proper precautions. (See the procedure in this section Servicing Your Vehicle Safely and the SAFETY NOTICE on the acknowledgement page.)

Pay attention to the instructions provided. There are 3 common mistakes in mechanical work:

1. Incorrect order of assembly, disassembly or adjustment. When taking something apart or putting it together, doing things in the wrong order usually justs cost you extra time; however, it CAN break something. Read the entire procedure before beginning disassembly. Do everything in the order in which the instructions say you should do it, even if you can't immediately see a reason for it. When you're taking apart something that is very intricate, you might want to draw a picture of how it looks when assembled at one point in order to make sure you get everything back in its proper position. (We will supply exploded view whenever possible). When making adjustments, especially tune-up adjustments, do them in order; often, one adjustment affects another, and you cannot expect even satisfactory results unless each adjustment is made only when it cannot be changed by any order.

2. Overtorquing (or undertorquing). While it is more common for over-torquing to cause damage, undertorquing can cause a fastener to vibrate loose causing serious damage. Especially when dealing with aluminum parts, pay attention to torque specifications and utilize a torque wrench in assembly. If a torque figure is not available, remember that if you are using the right tool to do the job, you will probably not have to strain yourself to get a fastener tight enough. The pitch of most threads is so slight that the tension you put on the wrench will be multiplied many, many times in actual force on what you are tightening. A good example of how critical torque is can be seen in the case of spark plug installation, especially where you are putting the plug into an aluminum cylinder head. Too little torque can fail to crush the gasket, causing leakage of combustion gases and consequent overheating of the plug and engine parts. Too much torque can damage the threads, or distort the plug which changes the spark gap.

There are many commercial products available for ensuring that fasteners won't come loose, even if they are not torqued just right (a very common brand is Loctite®). If you're worried about getting something together tight enough to hold, but loose enough to avoid mechanical damage during assembly, one of these products might offer substantial insurance. Read the label on the package and make sure the products is compatible with the materials, fluids, etc. involved before choosing one.

3. Crossthreading. This occurs when a part such as a bolt is screwed into a nut or casting at the wrong angle and forced. Cross threading is more likely to occur if access is difficult. It helps to clean and lubricate fasteners, and to start threading with the part to be installed going straight in. Then, start the bolt, spark plug, etc. with your fingers. If you encounter resistance, unscrew the part and start over again at a different angle until it can be inserted and turned several turns without much effort. Keep in mind that many parts, especially spark plugs, used tapered threads so that gentle turning will automatically bring the part you're threading to the proper angle if you don't force it or resist a change in angle. Don't put a wrench on the part until its's been turned a couple of turns by hand. If you suddenly encounter resistance, and the part has not seated fully, don't force it. Pull it back out and make sure it's clean and threading properly.

Always take your time and be patient; once you have some experience, working on your van will become an enjoyable hobby.

TOOLS AND EQUIPMENT

Naturally, without the proper tools and equipment it is impossible to properly service you vehicle. It would be impossible to catalog each tool that you would need to perform each or any operation in this book. It would also be unwise for the amateur to rush out and buy an expensive set of tool on the theory that he may need on or more of them at sometime.

The best approach is to proceed slowly gathering together a good quality set of those tools that are used most frequently. Don't be misled by the low cost of bargain tools. It is far better to spend a little more for better quality. Forged wrenches, 6- or 12-point sockets and fine tooth ratchets are by far preferable to their less expensive counterparts. As any good mechanic can tell

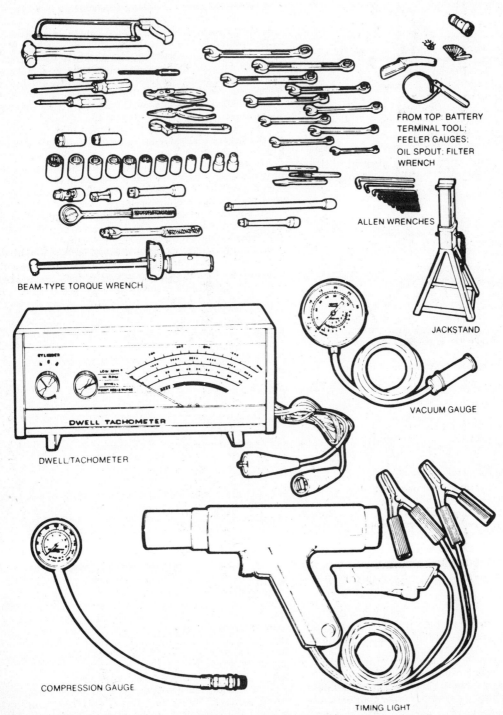

FROM TOP: BATTERY TERMINAL TOOL; FEELER GAUGES; OIL SPOUT; FILTER WRENCH

ALLEN WRENCHES

BEAM-TYPE TORQUE WRENCH

JACKSTAND

VACUUM GAUGE

DWELL/TACHOMETER

COMPRESSION GAUGE

TIMING LIGHT

The basic collection of tools and test instruments is all you need for most maintenance on your truck

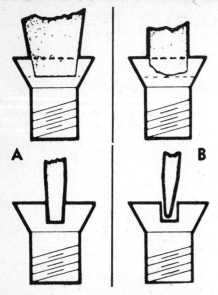

Keep screwdriver in good shape. They should fit the slot as shown "A". If they look like those shown in "B", they need grinding or replacing

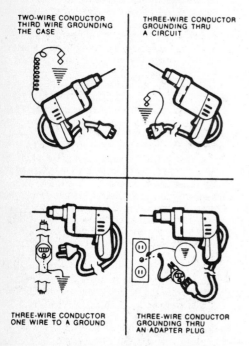

When using electric tools, make sure they are properly grounded

you, there are few worse experiences than trying to work on a van with bad tools. Your monetary savings will be far outweighed by frustration and mangled knuckles.

Begin accumulating those tools that are used most frequently; those associated with routine maintenance and tune-up.

In addition to the normal assortment of screwdrivers and pliers you should have the following tools for routine maintenance jobs:

1. SAE (or Metric) or SAE/Metric wrenches-sockets and com-

bination open end-box end wrenches in sizes from ⅛ in. (3mm) to ¾ in. (19mm) and a spark plug socket (¹³⁄₁₆ in. or ⅝ in. depending on plug type).

If possible, buy various length socket drive extensions. One break in this department is that the metric sockets available in the U.S. will all fit the ratchet handles and extensions you may already have (¼ in., ⅜ in., and ½ in. drive).

2. Jackstands for support.
3. Oil filter wrench.
4. Oil filler spout for pouring oil.
5. Grease gun for chassis lubrication.
6. Hydrometer for checking the battery.
7. A container for draining oil.
8. Many rags for wiping up the inevitable mess.

In addition to the above items there are several others that are not absolutely necessary, but handy to have around. these include oil dry, a transmission funnel and the usual supply of lubricants, antifreeze and fluids, although these can be purchased as needed. This is a basic list for routine maintenance, but only your personal needs and desire can accurately determine you list of tools.

The second list of tools is for tune-ups. While the tools involved here are slightly more sophisticated, they need not be outrageously expensive. There are several inexpensive tach/dwell meters on the market that are every bit as good for the average mechanic as a $100.00 professional model. Just be sure that it goes to a least 1,200–1,500 rpm on the tach scale and that it works on 4, 6, 8 cylinder engines. (A special tach is needed for diesel engines). A basic list of tune-up equipment could include:

1. Tach/dwell meter.
2. Spark plug wrench.
3. Timing light (a DC light that works from the van's battery is best, although an AC light that plugs into 110V house current will suffice at some sacrifice in brightness).
4. Wire spark plug gauge/adjusting tools.
5. Set of feeler blades.

Here again, be guided by your own needs. A feeler blade will set the points as easily as a dwell meter will read well, but slightly less accurately. And since you will need a tachometer anyway. . . well, make your own decision.

In addition to these basic tools, there are several other tools and gauges you may find useful. These include:

1. A compression gauge. The screw-in type is slower to use, but eliminates the possibility of a faulty reading due to escaping pressure.
2. A manifold vacuum gauge.
3. A test light.
4. An induction meter. This is used for determining whether or not there is current in a wire. These are handy for use if a wire is broken somewhere in a wiring harness.

As a final not, you will probably find a torque wrench necessary for all but the most basic work. The beam type models are perfectly adequate, although the newer click type are more precise.

Special Tools

Normally, the use of special factory tools is avoided for repair procedures, since these are not readily available for the do-it-yourself mechanic. When it is possible to preform the job with more commonly available tools, it will be pointed out, but occasionally, a special tool was designed to perform a specific function and should be used. Before substituting another tool, you should be convinced that neither your safety nor the performance of the vehicle will be compromised.

Some special tools are available commercially from major tool manufacturers. Others can be purchased from your Ford Dealer or from the Owatonna Tool Company, Owatonna, Minnesota 55060.

SERVICING YOUR VEHICLE SAFELY

It is virtually impossible to anticipate all of the hazards involved with automotive maintenance and service but care and common sense will prevent most accidents.

The rules of safety for mechanics range from "don't smoke around gasoline" to "use the proper tool for the job." The trick to avoiding injuries is to develop safe work habits and take every possible precaution.

Do's

● Do keep a fire extinguisher and first aid kit within easy reach.

● Do wear safety glasses or goggles when cutting, drilling, grinding, or prying, even if you have 20/20 vision. If you wear glasses for the sake of vision, then they should be made of hardened glass that can serve also as safety glasses, or wear safety glasses over your regular glasses.

● Do shield your eyes whenever you work around the battery. Batteries contain sulphuric acid; in case of contact with the eyes or skin, flush the area with water or a mixture of water and baking soda and get medical attention immediately.

● Do use safety stands for any under-van service. Jacks are for raising vehicles; safety stands are for making sure the vehicle stays raised until you want it to come down. Whenever the vehicle is raised, block the wheels remaining on the ground and set the parking brake.

● Do use adequate ventilation when working with any chemicals. Like carbon monoxide, the asbestos dust resulting from brake lining wear can be poisonous in sufficient quantities.

● Do disconnect the negative battery cable when working on the electrical system. The primary ignition system can contain up to 40,000 volts.

● Do follow manufacturer's directions whenever working with potentially hazardous materials. Both brake fluid and antifreeze are poisonous if taken internally.

● Do properly maintain your tools. Loose hammerheads, mushroomed punches and chisels, frayed or poorly grounded electrical cords, excessively worn screwdrivers, spread wrenches (open end), cracked sockets, slipping ratchets, or faulty droplight sockets can cause accidents.

● Do use the proper size and type of tool for the job being done.

● Do when possible, pull on a wrench handle rather than push on it, and adjust your stance to prevent a fall.

● Do be sure that adjustable wrenches are tightly adjusted on the nut or bolt and pulled so that the face is on the side of the fixed jaw.

● Do select a wrench or socket that fits the nut or bolt. The wrench or socket should sit straight, not cocked.

● Do strike squarely with a hammer. Avoid glancing blows.

● Do set the parking brake and block the drive wheels if the work requires that the engine be running.

Don't's

● Don't run an engine in a garage or anywhere else without

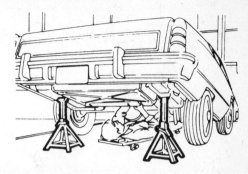

Always use jackstands when working under your truck

proper ventilation — EVER! Carbon monoxide is poisonous; it takes a long time to leave the human body and you can build up a deadly supply of it in your system by simply breathing in a little every day. You may not realize you are slowly poisoning yourself. Always use proper vents, window, fans or open the garage door.

● Don't work around moving parts while wearing a necktie or other loose clothing. Short sleeves are much safer than long, loose sleeves and hard-toed shoes with neoprene soles protect your toes and give a better grip on slippery surfaces. Jewelry such as watches, fancy belt buckles, beads or body adornment of any kind is not safe working around a van. Long hair should be hidden under a hat or cap.

● Don't use pockets for toolboxes. A fall or bump can drive a screwdriver deep into your body. Even a wiping cloth hanging from the back pocket can wrap around a spinning shaft or fan.

● Don't smoke when working around gasoline, cleaning solvent or other flammable material.

● Don't smoke when working around the battery. When the battery is being charged, it gives off explosive hydrogen gas.

● Don't use gasoline to wash your hands; there are excellent soaps available. Gasoline may contain lead, and lead can enter the body through a cut, accumulating in the body until you are very ill. Gasoline also removes all the natural oils from the skin so that bone dry hands will such up oil and grease.

● Don't service the air conditioning system unless you are equipped with the necessary tools and training. The refrigerant, R-12, is extremely cold and when exposed to the air, will instantly freeze any surface it comes in contact with, including your eyes. Although the refrigerant is normally non-toxic, R-12 becomes a deadly poisonous gas in the presence of an open flame. One good whiff of the vapors from burning refrigerant can be fatal.

● Don't ever use a bumper jack (the jack that comes with the vehicle) for anything other than changing tires! If you are serious about maintaining your van yourself, invest in a hydraulic floor jack of at least 1½ ton capacity. It will pay for itself many times over through the years.

1 GENERAL INFORMATION AND MAINTENANCE

SERIAL NUMBER IDENTIFICATION

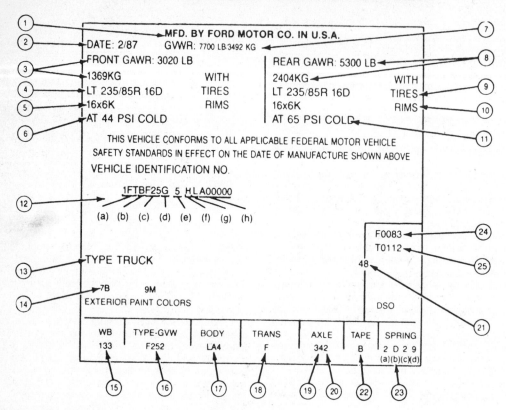

Truck safety compliance certification label

① Name and Location of Manufacturer

② Date of Manufacture

③ Front Gross Axle Weight Ratings in Pounds (LB) and Kilograms (KG)

④ Front Tire Size

⑤ Rim Size

⑥ Front Tire Cold PSI

⑦ Gross Vehicle Weight Rating in Pounds (LB) and Kilograms (KG)

⑧ Rear Gross Axle Weight Rating in Pounds (LB) and Kilograms (KG)

⑨ Rear Tire Size

⑩ Rim Size

⑪ Rear Tire Cold PSI

⑫ Vehicle Identification Number
 (a) World Manufacturer Identifier
 (b) Brake System and Gross Vehicle Weight Rating (GVWR) Class for Ford completed Trucks and MPV's. For Buses and Incomplete Vehicles, the fourth digit determines the brake system (only).
 (c) Model or Line, Series, Chassis, Cab or Body Type
 (d) Engine Type
 (e) Check Digit
 (f) Model Year (Ford-Complete Trucks and MPV's)
 (g) Assembly Plant Code
 (h) Sequence Number

⑬ Type Vehicle

⑭ Exterior Paint Codes (two sets of figures designates a two-tone)

⑮ Wheelbase in Inches

⑯ Model Code and GVW

⑰ Interior Trim, Seat and Body/Cab Type

⑱ Transmission Code

⑲ Rear Axle Code

⑳ Front Axle Code if so Equipped

㉑ District/Special Order Codes

㉒ External Body Tape Stripe Code

㉓ Suspension Identification Codes
 (a) Aux. Opt. Usage Code (Front)
 (b) Front Spring Code
 (c) Aux. Opt. Usage Code (Rear)
 (d) Rear Spring Code

㉔ Front Axle Accessory Reserve Capacity in Pounds

㉕ Total Accessory Reserve Capacity in Pounds

Vehicle

The vehicle identification number is located on the left side of the dash panel behind the windshield.

A seventeen digit combination of numbers and letters forms the Vehicle Identification Number (VIN). Refer to the illustration for VIN details.

Vehicle Safety Compliance Certification Label

The label is attached to the driver's door lock pillar. The label contains the name of the manufacturer, the month and year of the vehicle, certification statement and VIN. The label also contains gross vehicle weight and tire data.

Engine

The engine identification tag identifies the cubic inch displacement of the engine, the model year, the year and month in which the engine was built, where it was built and the change level number. The change level is usually the number one (1), unless there are parts on the engine that will not be completely interchangeable and will require minor modification.

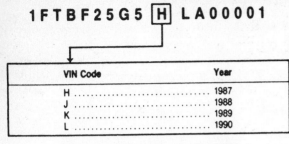

1FTBF25G5 [H] **LA00001**

VIN Code	Year
H	1987
J	1988
K	1989
L	1990

Year code location in the VIN

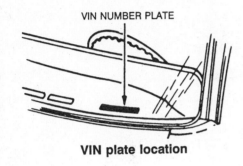

VIN NUMBER PLATE

VIN plate location

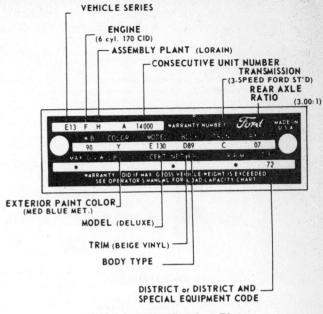

VEHICLE SERIES

ENGINE
(6 cyl. 170 CID)

ASSEMBLY PLANT (LORAIN)

CONSECUTIVE UNIT NUMBER

TRANSMISSION
(3-SPEED FORD ST'D)

REAR AXLE RATIO
(3.00:1)

EXTERIOR PAINT COLOR
(MED BLUE MET.)

MODEL (DELUXE)

TRIM (BEIGE VINYL)

BODY TYPE

DISTRICT or DISTRICT AND
SPECIAL EQUIPMENT CODE

Vehicle Identification Plate

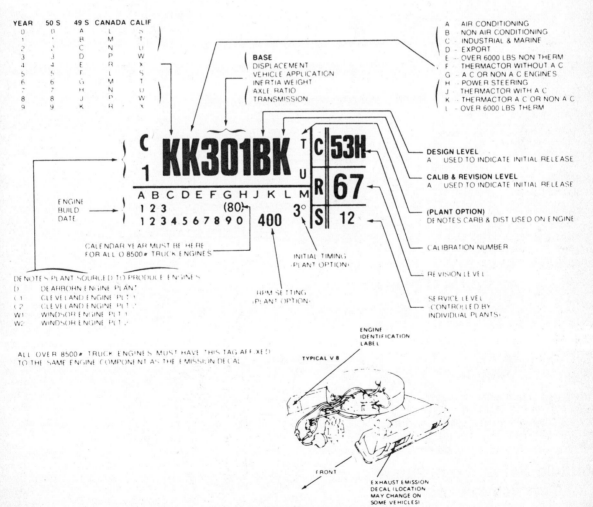

YEAR	50 S	49 S	CANADA	CALIF
0	0	A	L	S
1	1	B	M	T
2	2	C	N	U
3	3	D	P	W
4	4	E	R	X
5	5	F	L	S
6	6	G	M	T
7	7	H	N	U
8	8	J	P	W
9	9	K	R	X

A - AIR CONDITIONING
B - NON AIR CONDITIONING
C - INDUSTRIAL & MARINE
D - EXPORT
E - OVER 6000 LBS NON THERM
F - THERMACTOR WITHOUT A C
G - A C OR NON A C ENGINES
H - POWER STEERING
J - THERMACTOR WITH A C
K - THERMACTOR A C OR NON A C
L - OVER 6000 LBS THERM

BASE
DISPLACEMENT
VEHICLE APPLICATION
INERTIA WEIGHT
AXLE RATIO
TRANSMISSION

DESIGN LEVEL
A USED TO INDICATE INITIAL RELEASE

CALIB & REVISION LEVEL
A USED TO INDICATE INITIAL RELEASE

(PLANT OPTION)
DENOTES CARB & DIST USED ON ENGINE

CALIBRATION NUMBER

REVISION LEVEL

SERVICE LEVEL
CONTROLLED BY
INDIVIDUAL PLANTS

ENGINE BUILD DATE

CALENDAR YEAR MUST BE HERE
FOR ALL O 8500# TRUCK ENGINES

DENOTES PLANT SOURCED TO PRODUCE ENGINES
D   DEARBORN ENGINE PLANT
C1   CLEVELAND ENGINE PLT 1
C2   CLEVELAND ENGINE PLT 2
W1   WINDSOR ENGINE PLT 1
W2   WINDSOR ENGINE PLT 2

INITIAL TIMING
(PLANT OPTION)

RPM SETTING
(PLANT OPTION)

ALL OVER 8500# TRUCK ENGINES MUST HAVE THIS TAG AFFIXED
TO THE SAME ENGINE COMPONENT AS THE EMISSION DECAL

ENGINE IDENTIFICATION LABEL

TYPICAL V 8

FRONT

EXHAUST EMISSION
DECAL (LOCATION
MAY CHANGE ON
SOME VEHICLES)

Engine Identification Label

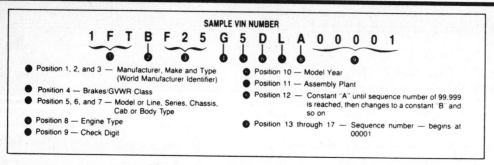

SAMPLE VIN NUMBER

1 F T B F 2 5 G 5 D L A 0 0 0 0 1

● Position 1, 2, and 3 — Manufacturer, Make and Type (World Manufacturer Identifier)

● Position 4 — Brakes/GVWR Class

● Position 5, 6, and 7 — Model or Line, Series, Chassis, Cab or Body Type

● Position 8 — Engine Type

● Position 9 — Check Digit

● Position 10 — Model Year

● Position 11 — Assembly Plant

● Position 12 — Constant "A" until sequence number of 99,999 is reached, then changes to a constant "B" and so on

● Position 13 through 17 — Sequence number — begins at 00001

VIN Code Plate

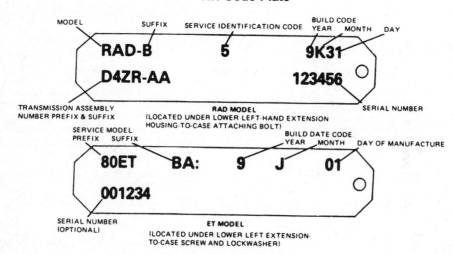

MODEL   SUFFIX   SERVICE IDENTIFICATION CODE   BUILD CODE
YEAR   MONTH   DAY

RAD-B   5   9K31

D4ZR-AA   123456

TRANSMISSION ASSEMBLY NUMBER PREFIX & SUFFIX

RAD MODEL
(LOCATED UNDER LOWER LEFT-HAND EXTENSION HOUSING-TO-CASE ATTACHING BOLT)

SERIAL NUMBER

SERVICE MODEL
PREFIX   SUFFIX

BUILD DATE CODE
YEAR   MONTH   DAY OF MANUFACTURE

80ET   BA: 9   J   01

001234

SERIAL NUMBER
(OPTIONAL)

ET MODEL
(LOCATED UNDER LOWER LEFT EXTENSION-TO-CASE SCREW AND LOCKWASHER)

Manual transmission identification tag

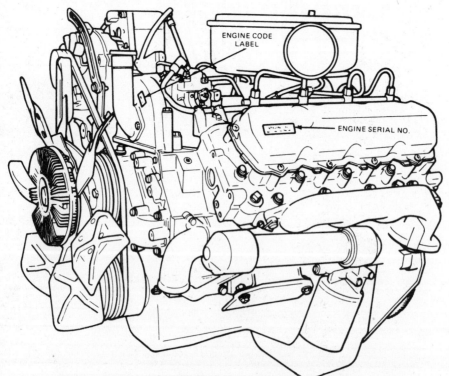

ENGINE CODE LABEL

ENGINE SERIAL NO.

Diesel engine serial number and identification label locations

ENGINE IDENTIFICATION CHART

No. of Cylinders and Liters Displacement	Actual Displacement		Fuel System	Type	Built by	Engine Code	Years
	Cu. In.	CC					
6-4.9	300.1	4,917.5	EFI	OHV	Ford	Y	1989–91
8-5.0	301.5	4,942.2	EFI	OHV	Ford	N	1989–91
8-5.8W	351.9	5,765.9	EFI	OHV	Ford	H	1989–91
8-7.3	443.6	7,270.0	Diesel	OHV	Nav.	M	1989–91
8-7.5	459.8	7,535.5	EFI	OHV	Ford	G	1989–91

Nav.: Navistar International Corp.

The engine identification tag is located under the ignition coil attaching bolt on all engines except the 7.3L diesels. The diesel engine I.D. number is stamped on the front of the block in front of the left cylinder head.

The engine identification code is located in the VIN at the eighth digit. The VIN can be found in the safety certification decal and the VIN plate at the upper left side of the dash panel. Refer to the "Engine Application" chart for engine VIN codes.

Transmission

The transmission identification letter is located on a metal tag or plate attached to the case or it is stamped directly on the transmission case. Also, the transmission code is located on the Safety Certification Decal. Refer to the "Transmission Application" chart in this section.

Drive Axle

The drive axle code is found stamped on a flat surface on the axle tube, next to the differential housing, or, on a tag secured by one of the differential housing cover bolts. A separate limited-slip tag is attached to the differential housing cover bolt. The letters L-S signifies a limited-slip differential.

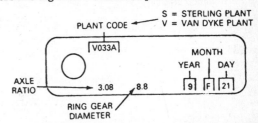

Differential identification tag. Limited slip units have a separate tag secured by a cover bolt

MANUAL TRANSMISSION APPLICATION CHART

Transmission Types	Years	Models
Mazda M50D 5-sp Overdrive	1989–91	All
ZF S5-42 5-speed Overdrive	1989–91	All

AUTOMATIC TRANSMISSION APPLICATION CHART

Transmission	Years	Models
Ford C6 3-speed	1989–91	All models; all engines
Ford AOD 4-speed	1989–91	E-150, 250
Ford E40D	1989–91	1989 E-250, 350 8500 lb. GVW 1990–91 E-250, 350 All

DRIVE AXLE APPLICATION CHART

Axle	Model	Years
Ford 8.8 inch	E-150	1989–91
Dana 60	E-250, 350 SRW	1989–91
Dana 70	E-350 DRW	1989–91

SRW: Single rear wheels
DRW: Dual rear wheels

CAPACITIES CHART

Years	Engine	Engine Oil Inc. Filter (qt.)	Transmission (pt.) Manual	Transmission (pt.) Auto*	Drive Axle (pt.)	Fuel Tank (gal.)	Cooling System (qt.) std.	Cooling System (qt.) w/AC	Cooling System (qt.) ExtraCool
1989–91	6-4.9	6.0	①	②	③	④	15.0	18.0	18.0
	8-5.0	6.0	①	②	③	④	17.5	17.5	18.5
	8-5.7	6.0	①	②	③	④	20.0	21.0	21.0
	8-7.3	10.0	①	②	③	④	31.0	31.0	—
	8-7.5	6.0	①	②	③	④	28.0	28.0	28.0

*Includes torque converter
① M5 OD: 7.6
  ZF FS-42: 6.8
② C6: 23.8
  AOD: 24.0
  E40D: 31.0
③ Ford 8.8 in.: 5.5
  Dana 60: 6.0
  Dana 70: 6.5
④ 124 in. W.B.: 18.0
  All other vans and club wagons: 22.0 standard;
  16.0 auxiliary
  Cutaway and stripped chassis: 36.0

PREVENTIVE MAINTENANCE SCHEDULE

Model/Interval	Item	Service
Gasoline Engine Models		
Every 6 months or 6,000 miles	Crankcase	change oil & filter
	Cooling system	change coolant
	Idle speed and TSP-off speed	adjust
	Ignition timing	adjust
	Decel throttle control system	check
	Chassis fittings	lubricate
	Clutch linkage	inspect and oil
	Exhaust system heat shields	inspect
	Transmission, automatic	adjust bands, check level
Every 15 months or 15,000 miles	Spark plugs	replace
	Exhaust control valve	check & lubricate
	Drive belts	check and adjust
	Air cleaner temperature control	check
	Choke system	check
	Thermactor system	check
	Crankcase breathe cap	clean
	EGR system	clean and inspect
	PCV system	clean and inspect
Every 30 months or 30,000 miles	PCV valve	replace
	Air cleaner element	replace
	Air cleaner crankcase filter	replace
	Fuel vapor system	replace
	Brake master cylinder	check
	Brakes	inspect
	Rear wheel bearings, Dana axles	clean and repack
Diesel Engine Models		
Every 6 months or 5,000 miles	Crankcase	change oil and filter
	Idle speed	check and adjust
	Throttle linkage	check operation
	Fuel/water separator	drain water
	U-joints	lubricate
	Front axle spindles	lubricate
Every 6 months or 15,000 miles	Fuel filter	replace
	Drive belts	check/adjust
	Steering linkage	lubricate
Every year	Coolant	check condition/replace
	Cooling hoses, clamps	check condition/replace

ROUTINE MAINTENANCE

NOTE: All maintenance procedures included in this Section refer to both gasoline and diesel engines except where noted.

Air Cleaner

The air cleaner is a paper element type.

The paper cartridge should be replaced according to the Preventive Maintenance Schedule at the end of this Section.

NOTE: Check the air filter more often if the vehicle is operated under severe dusty conditions and replace or clean it as necessary.

REPLACEMENT

Gasoline Engines

1. Loosen the two clamps that secure the hose assembly to the air cleaner.
2. Remove the two screws that attach the air cleaner to the bracket.
3. Disconnect the hose and inlet tube from the air cleaner.
4. Remove the screws attaching the air cleaner cover.
5. Remove the air filter and tubes.

To install:
1. Install the air filter and tubes.
2. Install the screws attaching the air cleaner cover. Don't overtighten the hose clamps! A torque of 12–15 inch lbs. is sufficient.

3. Connect the hose and inlet tube to the air cleaner.
4. Install the two screws that attach the air cleaner to the bracket.
5. Tighten the two clamps that secure the hose assembly to the air cleaner.

Diesel Engines

1. Open the engine compartment hood.
2. Remove the wing nut holding the air cleaner assembly.
3. Remove and discard the old filter element, and inspect the condition of the air cleaner mounting gasket. Replace the gasket as necessary.
4. Place the new filter element in the air cleaner body and install the cover and tighten the wing nut.

Fuel Filter

REPLACEMENT

――――――― CAUTION ―――――――
NEVER SMOKE WHEN WORKING AROUND OR NEAR GASOLINE! MAKE SURE THAT THERE IS NO IGNITION SOURCE NEAR YOUR WORK AREA!
――――――――――――――――――――

Fuel Injected Gasoline Engines

The inline filter is mounted on the same bracket as the fuel supply pump on the frame rail under the van, back by the fuel tank. To replace the filter:

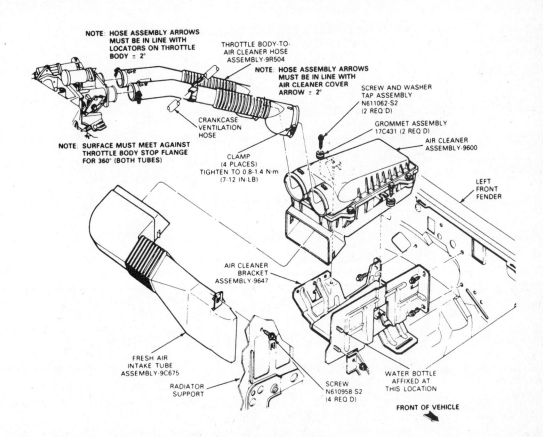

6-4.9L air cleaner

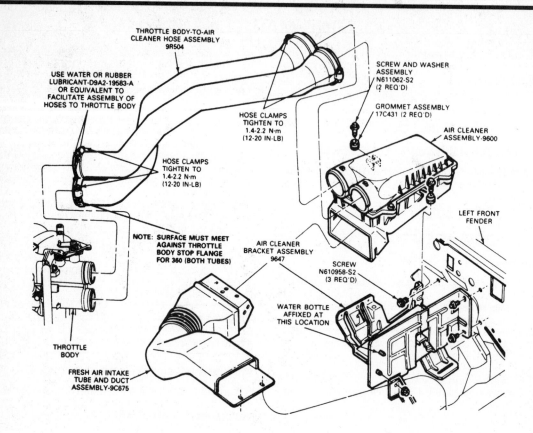

THROTTLE BODY-TO-AIR
CLEANER HOSE ASSEMBLY
9R504

USE WATER OR RUBBER
LUBRICANT-D9A2-19583-A
OR EQUIVALENT TO
FACILITATE ASSEMBLY OF
HOSES TO THROTTLE BODY

SCREW AND WASHER
ASSEMBLY
N611062-S2
(2 REQ'D)

GROMMET ASSEMBLY
17C431 (2 REQ'D)

HOSE CLAMPS
TIGHTEN TO
1.4-2.2 N·m
(12-20 IN-LB)

AIR CLEANER
ASSEMBLY-9600

HOSE CLAMPS
TIGHTEN TO
1.4-2.2 N·m
(12-20 IN-LB)

LEFT FRONT
FENDER

NOTE: SURFACE MUST MEET
AGAINST THROTTLE
BODY STOP FLANGE
FOR 360 (BOTH TUBES)

AIR CLEANER
BRACKET ASSEMBLY
9647

SCREW
N610958-S2
(3 REQ'D)

WATER BOTTLE
AFFIXED AT
THIS LOCATION

THROTTLE
BODY

FRESH AIR INTAKE
TUBE AND DUCT
ASSEMBLY-9C675

Air cleaner for E-150, E-250 with 8-5.0L and 8-5.8L engines

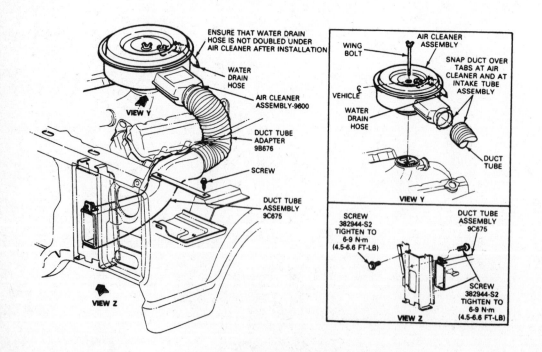

ENSURE THAT WATER DRAIN
HOSE IS NOT DOUBLED UNDER
AIR CLEANER AFTER INSTALLATION

WATER
DRAIN
HOSE

AIR CLEANER
ASSEMBLY-9600

VIEW Y

DUCT TUBE
ADAPTER
9B676

SCREW

DUCT TUBE
ASSEMBLY
9C675

VIEW Z

WING
BOLT

AIR CLEANER
ASSEMBLY

SNAP DUCT OVER
TABS AT AIR
CLEANER AND AT
INTAKE TUBE
ASSEMBLY

VEHICLE

WATER
DRAIN
HOSE

DUCT
TUBE

VIEW Y

SCREW
382944-S2
TIGHTEN TO
6-9 N·m
(4.5-6.6 FT-LB)

DUCT TUBE
ASSEMBLY
9C675

SCREW
382944-S2
TIGHTEN TO
6-9 N·m
(4.5-6.6 FT-LB)

VIEW Z

Diesel air cleaner

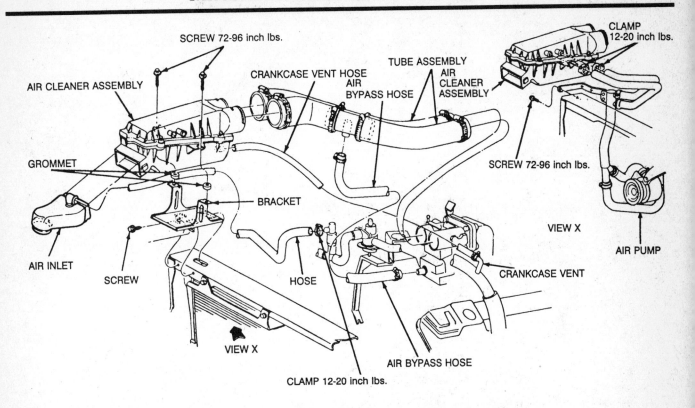

SCREW 72-96 inch lbs.

CLAMP 12-20 inch lbs.

AIR CLEANER ASSEMBLY

CRANKCASE VENT HOSE
AIR BYPASS HOSE

TUBE ASSEMBLY AIR CLEANER ASSEMBLY

GROMMET

SCREW 72-96 inch lbs.

BRACKET

VIEW X

AIR INLET

SCREW

HOSE

AIR PUMP

CRANKCASE VENT

VIEW X

AIR BYPASS HOSE

CLAMP 12-20 inch lbs.

8-7.5L engine air cleaner used on the motor home chassis

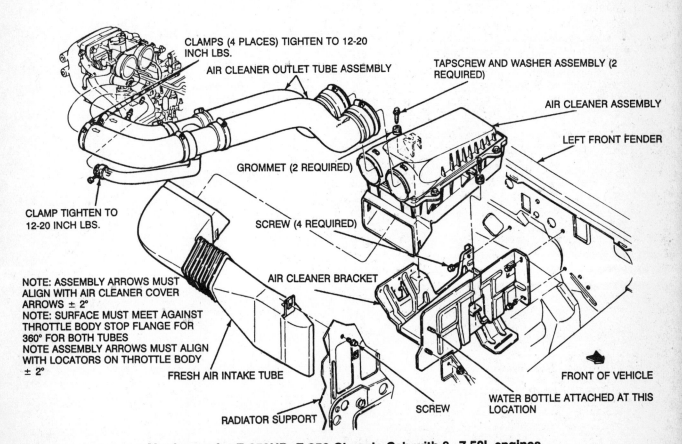

CLAMPS (4 PLACES) TIGHTEN TO 12-20 INCH LBS.

AIR CLEANER OUTLET TUBE ASSEMBLY

TAPSCREW AND WASHER ASSEMBLY (2 REQUIRED)

AIR CLEANER ASSEMBLY

LEFT FRONT FENDER

GROMMET (2 REQUIRED)

CLAMP TIGHTEN TO 12-20 INCH LBS.

SCREW (4 REQUIRED)

AIR CLEANER BRACKET

NOTE: ASSEMBLY ARROWS MUST ALIGN WITH AIR CLEANER COVER ARROWS ± 2°
NOTE: SURFACE MUST MEET AGAINST THROTTLE BODY STOP FLANGE FOR 360° FOR BOTH TUBES
NOTE ASSEMBLY ARROWS MUST ALIGN WITH LOCATORS ON THROTTLE BODY ± 2°

FRESH AIR INTAKE TUBE

FRONT OF VEHICLE

WATER BOTTLE ATTACHED AT THIS LOCATION

RADIATOR SUPPORT

SCREW

Air cleaner for E-250HD, E-350 Chassis Cab with 8- 7.50L engines

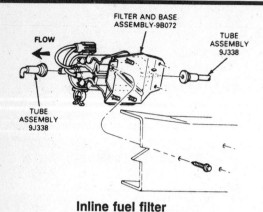

Inline fuel filter

1. Raise and support the rear end on jackstands.
2. With the engine off, depressurize the fuel system. See Section 5.
3. Remove the quick-disconnect fittings at both ends of the filter. See Section 5.
4. Remove the filter and retainer from the bracket.
5. Remove the rubber insulator ring from the filter.
6. Remove the filter from the retainer.
7. Install the new filter into the retainer, noting the direction of the flow arrow.
8. Install a new rubber insulator ring.
9. Install the retainer and filter on the bracket and tighten the screws to 60 inch lbs.
10. Install the fuel lines using new retainer clips.
11. Start the engine and check for leaks.

Diesel Engines

The 7.3L diesel engines use a one-piece spin-on fuel filter. Do not add fuel to the new fuel filter. Allow the engine to draw fuel through the filter.

1. Remove the spin-on filter by unscrewing it counterclockwise with your hands or a strap wrench.
2. Clean the filter mounting surface.

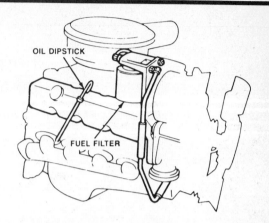

Diesel fuel filter location; filter screws on

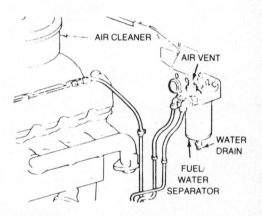

Open the drain screw on the bottom of the water separator to drain

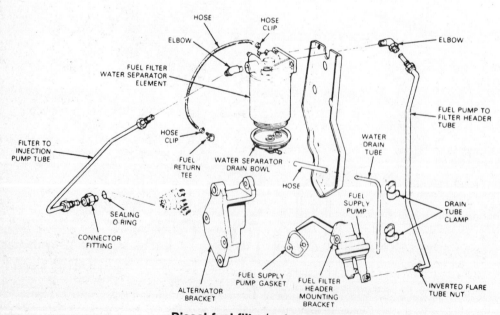

Diesel fuel filter/water separator

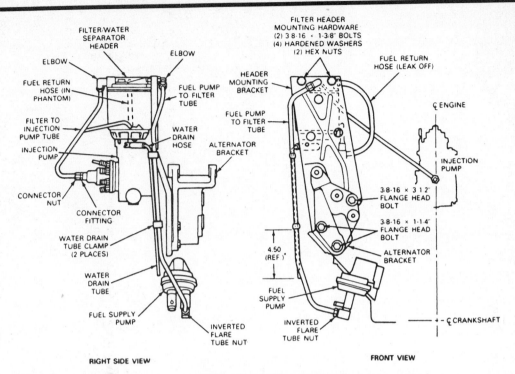

Diesel fuel filter removal

3. Coat the gasket or the replacement filter with clean diesel fuel. This helps ensure a good seal.
4. Tighten the filter by hand until the gasket touches the filter mounting surface.
5. Tighten the filter an additional ½ turn.

NOTE: After changing the fuel filter, the engine will purge the trapped air as it runs. The engine may run roughly and smoke excessively until the air is cleared from the system.

Fuel/Water Separator

Diesel Engines

The 7.3L diesel engines are equipped with a fuel/water separator in the fuel supply line. A Water in Fuel indicator light is provided on the instrument panel to alert the driver. The light should glow when the ignition switch is in the Start position to indicate proper light and water sensor function. If the light glows continuously while the engine is running, the water must be drained from the separator as soon as possible to prevent damage to the fuel injection system.

1. Shut off the engine. Failure to shut the engine off before draining the separator will cause air to enter the system.
2. Unscrew the vent on the top center of the separator unit 2½ to 3 turns.
3. Unscrew the drain screw on the bottom of the separator 1½ to 2 turns and drain the water into an appropriate container.
4. After the water is completely drained, close the water drain fingertight.
5. Tighten the vent until snug, then turn it an additional ¼ turn.
6. Start the engine and check the Water in Fuel indicator light; it should not be lit. If it is lit and continues to stay so, there is a problem somewhere else in the fuel system.

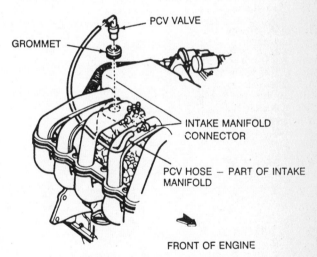

6-4.9L PCV valve location

NOTE: All but very early production models have a drain hose connected to separator which allows water to drain directly into a container placed underneath the vehicle.

PCV Valve

Gasoline Engines Only

Check the PCV valve according to the Preventive Maintenance Schedule at the end of this Section to see if it is free and not gummed up, stuck or blocked. To check the valve, remove it from the engine and work the valve by sticking a screwdriver in the crankcase side of the valve. It should move. It is possible to clean the PCV valve by soaking it in a solvent and blowing it out with compressed air. This can restore the valve to some level of

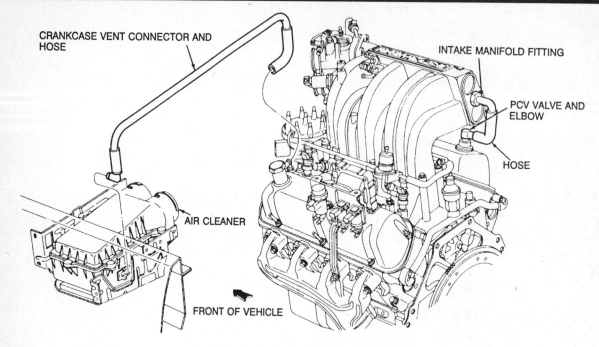

CRANKCASE VENT CONNECTOR AND HOSE

INTAKE MANIFOLD FITTING

PCV VALVE AND ELBOW

HOSE

AIR CLEANER

FRONT OF VEHICLE

8-5.0L and 8-5.8L PCV valve location

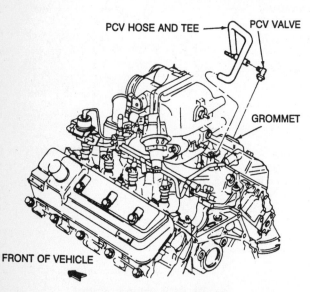

PCV HOSE AND TEE

PCV VALVE

GROMMET

FRONT OF VEHICLE

8-7.5L PCV valve location

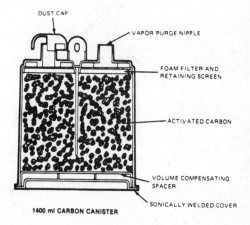

DUST CAP

VAPOR PURGE NIPPLE

FOAM FILTER AND RETAINING SCREEN

ACTIVATED CARBON

VOLUME COMPENSATING SPACER

SONICALLY WELDED COVER

1400 ml CARBON CANISTER

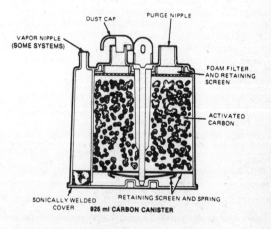

DUST CAP

PURGE NIPPLE

VAPOR NIPPLE (SOME SYSTEMS)

FOAM FILTER AND RETAINING SCREEN

ACTIVATED CARBON

SONICALLY WELDED COVER

RETAINING SCREEN AND SPRING

925 ml CARBON CANISTER

Carbon canister cross-sections

operating order. This should be used only as an emergency measure. Otherwise the valve should be replaced.

Evaporative Canister

Gasoline Engines Only

The fuel evaporative emission control canister should be inspected for damage or leaks at the hose fittings every 24,000 miles. Repair or replace any old or cracked hoses. Replace the canister if it is damaged in any way. The canister is located under the hood, to the right of the engine.

For more detailed canister service, see Section 4.

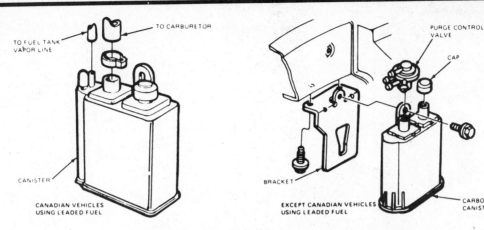

Carbon canisters are mounted on the inner fender

Battery

Loose, dirty, or corroded battery terminals are a major cause of "no-start." Every 3 months or so, remove the battery terminals and clean them, giving them a light coating of petroleum jelly when you are finished. This will help to retard corrosion.

Check the battery cables for signs of wear or chafing and replace any cable or terminal that looks marginal. Battery terminals can be easily cleaned and inexpensive terminal cleaning tools are an excellent investment that will pay for themselves many times over. They can usually be purchased from any well-equipped auto store or parts department. Side terminal batteries require a different tool to clean the threads in the battery case. The accumulated white powder and corrosion can be cleaned from the top of the battery with an old toothbrush and a solution of baking soda and water.

Unless you have a maintenance-free battery, check the electrolyte level (see Battery under Fluid Level Checks in this Section) and check the specific gravity of each cell. Be sure that the vent holes in each cell cap are not blocked by grease or dirt. The vent holes allow hydrogen gas, formed by the chemical reaction in the battery, to escape safely.

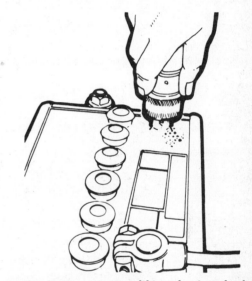

Clean the battery posts with a wire terminal cleaner

REPLACEMENT BATTERIES

The cold power rating of a battery measures battery starting

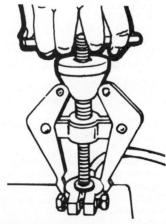

Top terminal battery cables are easily removed with this inexpensive puller

Clean the cable ends with a stiff cable cleaning tool (male end)

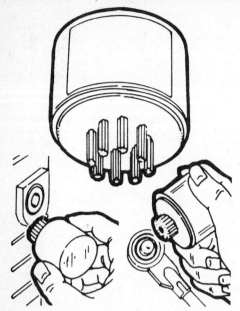

Side terminal batteries require a special wire brush for cleaning

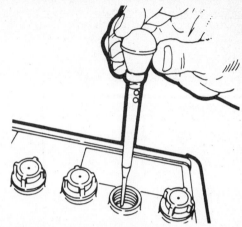

The specific gravity of the battery can be checked with a simple float-type hydrometer

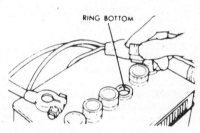

Fill each battery cell to the bottom of the spill ring with distilled water

SPECIFIC GRAVITY (@ 80°F.) AND CHARGE Specific Gravity Reading (use the minimum figure for testing)	
Minimum	**Battery Charge**
1.260	100% Charged
1.230	75% Charged
1.200	50% Charged
1.170	25% Charged
1.140	Very Little Power Left
1.110	Completely Discharged

Battery specific gravity. Some testers have colored balls which correspond to the numerical values in the left column

Specific Gravity Reading	Charged Condition
1.260–1.280	Fully Charged
1.230–1.250	¾ Charged
1.200–1.220	½ Charged
1.170–1.190	¼ Charged
1.140–1.160	Almost no Charge
1.110–1.130	No Charge

performance and provides an approximate relationship between battery size and engine size. The cold power rating of a replacement battery should match or exceed your engine size in cubic inches.

FLUID LEVEL (EXCEPT MAINTENANCE FREE BATTERIES)

Check the battery electrolyte level at least once a month, or more often in hot weather or during periods of extended van operation. The level can be checked through the case on translucent polypropylene batteries; the cell caps must be removed on other models. The electrolyte level in each cell should be kept filled to the split ring inside, or the line marked on the outside of the case.

If the level is low, add only distilled water, or colorless, odorless drinking water, through the opening until the level is correct. Each cell is completely separate from the others, so each must be checked and filled individually.

If water is added in freezing weather, the van should be driven several miles to allow the water to mix with the electrolyte. Otherwise, the battery could freeze.

SPECIFIC GRAVITY (EXCEPT MAINTENANCE FREE BATTERIES)

At least once a year, check the specific gravity of the battery. It should be between 1.20 in.Hg and 1.26 in.Hg at room temperature.

The specific gravity can be check with the use of an hydrometer, an inexpensive instrument available from many sources, including auto parts stores. The hydrometer has a squeeze bulb at one end and a nozzle at the other. Battery electrolyte is sucked into the hydrometer until the float is lifted from its seat. The specific gravity is then read by noting the position of the float. Generally, if after charging, the specific gravity between any two cells varies more than 50 points (0.50), the battery is bad and should be replaced.

It is not possible to check the specific gravity in this manner on sealed (maintenance free) batteries. Instead, the indicator built into the top of the case must be relied on to display any signs of battery deterioration. If the indicator is dark, the battery can be assumed to be OK. If the indicator is light, the specific gravity is low, and the battery should be charged or replaced.

CABLES AND CLAMPS

Once a year, the battery terminals and the cable clamps should be cleaned. Loosen the clamps and remove the cables, negative cable first. On batteries with posts on top, the use of a puller specially made for the purpose is recommended. These are inexpensive, and available in auto parts stores. Side terminal battery cables are secured with a bolt.

Clean the cable lamps and the battery terminal with a wire brush, until all corrosion, grease, etc., is removed and the metal is shiny. It is especially important to clean the inside of the clamp thoroughly, since a small deposit of foreign material or oxidation there will prevent a sound electrical connection and inhibit either starting or charging. Special tools are available for cleaning these parts, one type for conventional batteries and another type for side terminal batteries.

Before installing the cables, loosen the battery holddown clamp or strap, remove the battery and check the battery tray. Clear it of any debris, and check it for soundness. Rust should be wire brushed away, and the metal given a coat of anti-rust paint. Replace the battery and tighten the holddown clamp or strap securely, but be careful not to overtighten, which will crack the battery case.

After the clamps and terminals are clean, reinstall the cables, negative cable last; do not hammer on the clamps to install.

Tighten the clamps securely, but do not distort them. Give the clamps and terminals a thin external coat of grease after installation, to retard corrosion.

Check the cables at the same time that the terminals are cleaned. If the cable insulation is cracked or broken, or if the ends are frayed, the cable should be replaced with a new cable of the same length and gauge.

—————————— CAUTION ——————————
Keep flame or sparks away from the battery; it gives off explosive hydrogen gas. Battery electrolyte contains sulphuric acid. If you should splash any on your skin or in your eyes, flush the affected area with plenty of clear water. If it lands in your eyes, get medical help immediately.
—————————————————————————————

Belts

Once a year or at 12,000 mile intervals, the tension (and condition) of the alternator, power steering (if so equipped), air conditioning (if so equipped), and Thermactor® air pump drive belts should be checked, and, if necessary, adjusted. Loose accessory drive belts can lead to poor engine cooling and diminish alternator, power steering pump, air conditioning compressor or Thermactor® air pump output. A belt that is too tight places a severe strain on the water pump, alternator, power steering pump, compressor or air pump bearings.

Replace any belt that is so glazed, worn or stretched that it cannot be tightened sufficiently.

NOTE: The material used in late model drive belts is such that the belts do not show wear. Replace belts at least every three years.

On vehicles with matched belts, replace both belts. New ½ in. (13mm), ⅜ in. (10mm) and $^{15}\!/_{32}$ in. (12mm) wide belts are to be adjusted to a tension of 140 lbs.; ¼ in. (6mm) wide belts are ad-

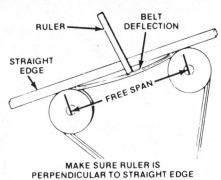

Measuring belt deflection

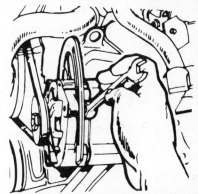

To adjust belt tension or to change belts, first loosen the component's mounting and adjusting bolts slightly.

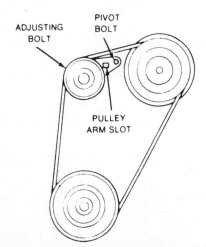

Some pulleys have a rectangular slot to aid in moving the accessory to be tightened

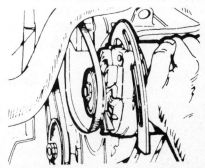

Push the component towards the engine and slip off the belt

HOW TO SPOT WORN V-BELTS

V-Belts are vital to efficient engine operation—they drive the fan, water pump and other accessories. They require little maintenance (occasional tightening) but they will not last forever. Slipping or failure of the V-belt will lead to overheating. If your V-belt looks like any of these, it should be replaced.

Cracking or Weathering

This belt has deep cracks, which cause it to flex. Too much flexing leads to heat build-up and premature failure. These cracks can be caused by using the belt on a pulley that is too small. Notched belts are available for small diameter pulleys.

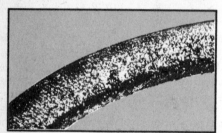

Softening (Grease and Oil)

Oil and grease on a belt can cause the belt's rubber compounds to soften and separate from the reinforcing cords that hold the belt together. The belt will first slip, then finally fail altogether.

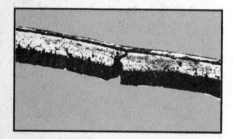

Glazing

Glazing is caused by a belt that is slipping. A slipping belt can cause a run-down battery, erratic power steering, overheating or poor accessory performance. The more the belt slips, the more glazing will be built up on the surface of the belt. The more the belt is glazed, the more it will slip. If the glazing is light, tighten the belt.

Worn Cover

The cover of this belt is worn off and is peeling away. The reinforcing cords will begin to wear and the belt will shortly break. When the belt cover wears in spots or has a rough jagged appearance, check the pulley grooves for roughness.

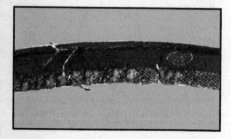

Separation

This belt is on the verge of breaking and leaving you stranded. The layers of the belt are separating and the reinforcing cords are exposed. It's just a matter of time before it breaks completely.

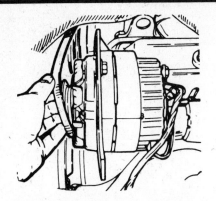

Slip the new belt over the pulley

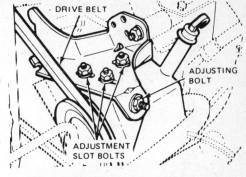

Power steering pump adjustment

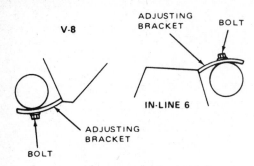

Pull outward on the component and tighten the mounting bolts

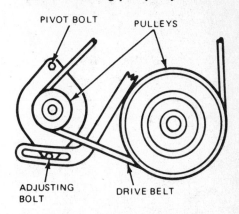

Alternator belt adjustment

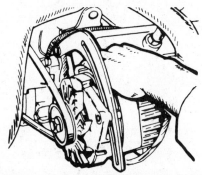

Air pump adjustment points

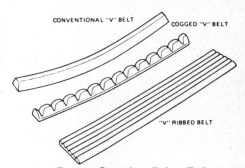

Power Steering Drive Belt

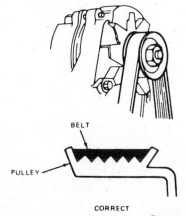

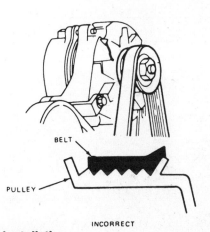

Serpentine belt installation

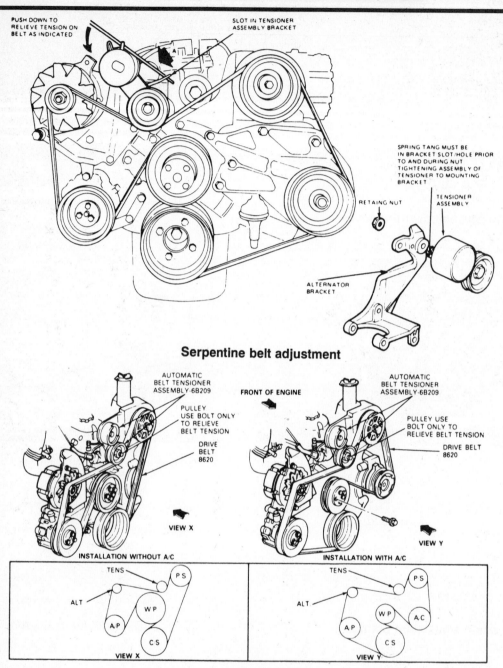

PUSH DOWN TO RELIEVE TENSION ON BELT AS INDICATED

SLOT IN TENSIONER ASSEMBLY BRACKET

SPRING TANG MUST BE IN BRACKET SLOT/HOLE PRIOR TO AND DURING NUT TIGHTENING ASSEMBLY OF TENSIONER TO MOUNTING BRACKET

RETAING NUT

TENSIONER ASSEMBLY

ALTERNATOR BRACKET

Serpentine belt adjustment

AUTOMATIC BELT TENSIONER ASSEMBLY-6B209

FRONT OF ENGINE

PULLEY USE BOLT ONLY TO RELIEVE BELT TENSION

DRIVE BELT 8620

VIEW X

INSTALLATION WITHOUT A/C

AUTOMATIC BELT TENSIONER ASSEMBLY-6B209

PULLEY USE BOLT ONLY TO RELIEVE BELT TENSION

DRIVE BELT 8620

VIEW Y

INSTALLATION WITH A/C

TENS | PS
ALT
A/P | WP
CS

VIEW X

TENS | PS
ALT
A/P | WP | AC
CS

VIEW Y

6-4.9L drive belts

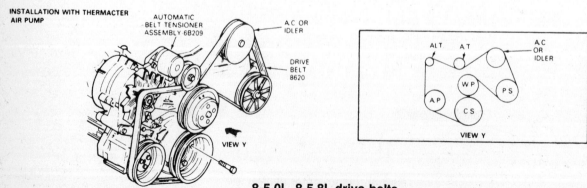

INSTALLATION WITH THERMACTER AIR PUMP

AUTOMATIC BELT TENSIONER ASSEMBLY-6B209

AC OR IDLER

DRIVE BELT 8620

VIEW Y

ALT | AT | AC OR IDLER
A/P | WP | PS
CS

VIEW Y

8-5.0L, 8-5.8L drive belts

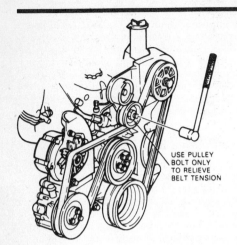

NOTE: THE SINGLE BELT, SERPENTINE DRIVE ARRANGEMENT OF THE 4.9L, 5.0L AND 5.8L EFI ENGINES USE AN AUTOMATIC BELT TENSIONER. NO BELT TENSION ADJUSTMENT IS REQUIRED.

SPECIAL INSTRUCTIONS:

1. LIFT AUTO TENSIONER PULLEY BY APPLYING TORQUE TO IDLER PULLEY PIVOT BOLT WITH WRENCH AND SOCKET

2. INSTALL DRIVE BELT OVER PULLEYS PER APPROPRIATE BELT ROUTING

3. CHECK BELT TENSION. REFERENCE TENSION CODE (4.9L), (5.0L) OR (5.8L)

4. IF BELT TENSION IS TOO LOW CHECK WITH NEW BELT BEFORE REPLACING TENSIONER.

5. IF TENSION IS NOT WITHIN SPECIFICATION INSTALL A NEW AUTOMATIC TENSIONER. LOCATE PIN AS SHOWN IN VIEW A.

NOTE:
LOCATING PIN MUST BE IN BRACKET HOLE PRIOR TO AND DURING BOLT TORQUING ASSEMBLY OF TENSIONER TO MOUNTING BRACKET

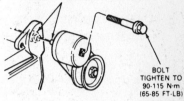

USE PULLEY BOLT ONLY TO RELIEVE BELT TENSION

BOLT TIGHTEN TO 90-115 N·m (65-85 FT-LB)

VIEW A

Drive belt adjustments on the 6-4.9L, 8-5.0L and 8- 5.8L engines

BELT TENSION SPECIFICATION INSTALLATION
667-845N (150-190 LB)
REINSTALLED 622-711N (140-160 LB)
MINIMUM 400N (90 LB)

A/C OR IDLER PULLEY

TENSIONER

DRIVE BELT 8620

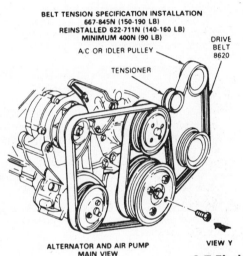

ALTERNATOR AND AIR PUMP MAIN VIEW

VIEW Y

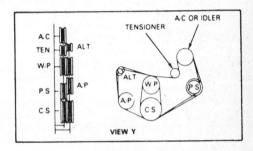

8-7.5L drive belts

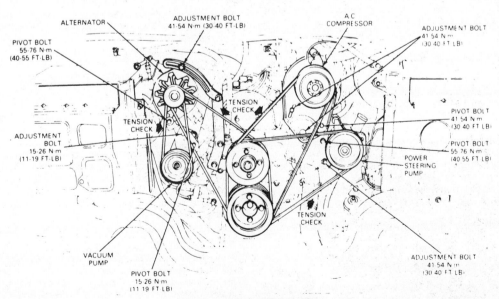

8-7.3L diesel drive belts

justed to 80 lbs., measured on a belt tension gauge. Any belt that has been operating for a minimum of 10 minutes is considered a used belt. In the first 10 minutes, the belt should stretch to its maximum extent. After 10 minutes, stop the engine and recheck the belt tension. Belt tension for a used belt should be maintained at 110 lbs. (all except ¼ in. wide belts) or 60 lbs. (¼ in. wide belts). If a belt tension gauge is not available, the following procedures may be used.

ADJUSTMENTS FOR ALL EXCEPT THE SERPENTINE (SINGLE) BELT

--- CAUTION ---

On models equipped with an electric cooling fan, disconnect the negative battery cable or fan motor wiring harness connector before replacing or adjusting drive belts. The fan may come on, under certain circumstances, even though the ignition is off.

Alternator (Fan Drive) Belt

1. Position the ruler perpendicular to the drive belt at its longest straight run. Test the tightness of the belt by pressing it firmly with your thumb. The deflection should not exceed ¼ in. (6mm).
2. If the deflection exceeds ¼ in. (6mm), loosen the alternator mounting and adjusting arm bolts.
3. Place a 1 in. open-end or adjustable wrench on the adjusting ridge cast on the body, and pull on the wrench until the proper tension is achieved.
4. Holding the alternator in place to maintain tension, tighten the adjusting arm bolt. Recheck the belt tension. When the belt is properly tensioned, tighten the alternator mounting bolt.

Power Steering Drive Belt

6-4.9L

1. Hold a ruler perpendicularly to the drive belt at its longest run, test the tightness of the belt by pressing it firmly with your thumb. The deflection should not exceed ¼ in. (6mm).
2. To adjust the belt tension, loosen the adjusting and mounting bolts on the front face of the steering pump cover plate (hub side).
3. Using a pry bar or broom handle on the pump hub, move the power steering pump toward or away from the engine until the proper tension is reached. Do not pry against the reservoir as it is relatively soft and easily deformed.
4. Holding the pump in place, tighten the adjusting arm bolt and then recheck the belt tension. When the belt is properly tensioned tighten the mounting bolts.

V8 MODELS

1. Position a ruler perpendicular to the drive belt at its longest run. Test the tightness of the belt by pressing it firmly with your thumb. The deflection should be about ¼ in. (6mm).
2. To adjust the belt tension, loosen the three bolts in the three elongated adjusting slots at the power steering pump attaching bracket.
3. Turn the steering pump drive belt adjusting nut as required until the proper deflection is obtained. Turning the adjusting nut clockwise will increase tension and decrease deflection; counterclockwise will decrease tension and increase deflection.
4. Without disturbing the pump, tighten the three attaching bolts.

Air Conditioning Compressor Drive Belt

1. Position a ruler perpendicular to the drive belt at its longest run. Test the tightness of the belt by pressing it firmly with your thumb. The deflection should not exceed ¼ in. (6mm).

2. If the engine is equipped with an idler pulley, loosen the idler pulley adjusting bolt, insert a pry bar between the pulley and the engine (or in the idler pulley adjusting slot), and adjust the tension accordingly. If the engine is not equipped with an idler pulley, the alternator must be moved to accomplish this adjustment, as outlined under Alternator (Fan Drive) Belt.
3. When the proper tension is reached, tighten the idler pulley adjusting bolt (if so equipped) or the alternator adjusting and mounting bolts.

Thermactor® Air Pump Drive Belt

1. Position a ruler perpendicular to the drive belt at its longest run. Test the tightness of the belt by pressing it firmly with your thumb. The deflection should be about ¼ in. (6mm).
2. To adjust the belt tension, loosen the adjusting arm bolt slightly. If necessary, also loosen the mounting belt slightly.
3. Using a pry bar or broom handle, pry against the pump rear cover to move the pump toward or away from the engine as necessary.

--- CAUTION ---

Do not pry against the pump housing itself, as damage to the housing may result.

4. Holding the pump in place, tighten the adjusting arm bolt and recheck the tension. When the belt is properly tensioned, tighten the mounting bolt.

SERPENTINE (SINGLE) DRIVE BELT MODELS

Most models feature a single, wide, ribbed V-belt that drives the water pump, alternator, and (on some models) the air conditioner compressor. To install a new belt, loosen the bracket lock bolt, retract the belt tensioner with a pry bar and slide the old belt off of the pulleys. Slip on a new belt and release the tensioner and tighten the lock bolt. The spring powered tensioner eliminates the need for periodic adjustments.

WARNING: Check to make sure that the V-ribbed belt is located properly in all drive pulleys before applying tensioner pressure.

Hoses

--- CAUTION ---

On models equipped with an electric cooling fan, disconnect the negative battery cable, or fan motor wiring harness connector before replacing any radiator/heater hose. The fan may come on, under certain circumstances, even though the ignition is Off.

REPLACEMENT

Inspect the condition of the radiator and heater hoses periodically. Early spring and at the beginning of the fall or winter, when you are performing other maintenance, are good times. Make sure the engine and cooling system are cold. Visually inspect for cracking, rotting or collapsed hoses, replace as necessary. Run your hand along the length of the hose. If a weak or swollen spot is noted when squeezing the hose wall, replace the hose.

1. Drain the cooling system into a suitable container (if the coolant is to be reused).

--- CAUTION ---

When draining the coolant, keep in mind that cats and dogs are attracted by the ethylene glycol antifreeze, and are quite likely to drink any that is left in an uncovered container or in puddles on the ground. This will prove fatal in sufficient quantity. Always drain the coolant into a sealable container. Coolant should be reused unless it is contaminated or several years old.

HOW TO SPOT BAD HOSES

Both the upper and lower radiator hoses are called upon to perform difficult jobs in an inhospitable environment. They are subject to nearly 18 psi at under hood temperatures often over 280°F, and must circulate nearly 7500 gallons of coolant an hour — 3 good reasons to have good hoses.

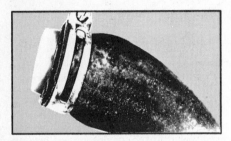

Swollen Hose

A good test for any hose is to feel it for soft or spongy spots. Frequently these will appear as swollen areas of the hose. The most likely cause is oil soaking. This hose could burst at any time, when hot or under pressure.

Cracked Hose

Cracked hoses can usually be seen but feel the hoses to be sure they have not hardened; a prime cause of cracking. This hose has cracked down to the reinforcing cords and could split at any of the cracks.

Frayed Hose End (Due to Weak Clamp)

Weakened clamps frequently are the cause of hose and cooling system failure. The connection between the pipe and hose has deteriorated enough to allow coolant to escape when the engine is hot.

Debris In Cooling System

Debris, rust and scale in the cooling system can cause the inside of a hose to weaken. This can usually be felt on the outside of the hose as soft or thinner areas.

2. Loosen the hose clamps at each end of the hose that requires replacement.

3. Twist, pull and slide the hose off the radiator, water pump, thermostat or heater connection.

4. Clean the hose mounting connections. Position the hose clamps on the new hose.

5. Coat the connection surfaces with a water resistant sealer and slide the hose into position. Make sure the hose clamps are located beyond the raised bead of the connector (if equipped) and centered in the clamping area of the connection.

6. Tighten the clamps to 20–30 inch lbs. Do not overtighten.

7. Fill the cooling system.

8. Start the engine and allow it to reach normal operating temperature. Check for leaks.

Cooling System

———— CAUTION ————

Never remove the radiator cap under any conditions while the engine is running! Failure to follow these instructions could result in damage to the cooling system or engine and/or personal injury. To avoid having scalding hot coolant or steam blow out of the radiator, use extreme care when removing the radiator cap from a hot radiator. Wait until the engine has cooled, then wrap a thick cloth around the radiator cap and turn it slowly to the first stop. Step back while the pressure is released from the cooling system. When you are sure the pressure has been released, press down on the radiator cap (still have the cloth in position) turn and remove the radiator cap.

At least once every 2 years, the engine cooling system should be inspected, flushed, and refilled with fresh coolant. If the coolant is left in the system too long, it loses its ability to prevent rust and corrosion. If the coolant has too much water, it won't protect against freezing.

The pressure cap should be looked at for signs of age or deterioration. Fan belt and other drive belts should be inspected and adjusted to the proper tension. (See checking belt tension).

Hose clamps should be tightened, and soft or cracked hoses replaced. Damp spots, or accumulations of rust or dye near hos-

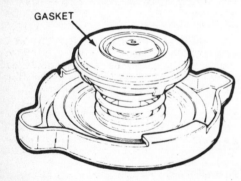

GASKET

Check the radiator cap gasket for cracks or wear

Keep the radiator fins clear of debris for maximum cooling

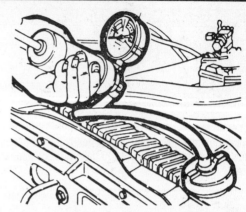

The system should be pressure tested once a year

es, water pump or other areas, indicate possible leakage, which must be corrected before filling the system with fresh coolant.

CHECK THE RADIATOR CAP

While you are checking the coolant level, check the radiator cap for a worn or cracked gasket. It the cap doesn't seal properly, fluid will be lost and the engine will overheat.

Worn caps should be replaced with a new one.

CLEAN RADIATOR OF DEBRIS

Periodically clean any debris — leaves, paper, insects, etc. — from the radiator fins. Pick the large pieces off by hand. The smaller pieces can be washed away with water pressure from a hose.

Carefully straighten any bent radiator fins with a pair of needle nose pliers. Be careful — the fins are very soft. Don't wiggle the fins back and forth too much. Straighten them once and try not to move them again.

DRAIN AND REFILL THE COOLING SYSTEM

Completely draining and refilling the cooling system every two years at least will remove accumulated rust, scale and other deposits. Coolant in late model vans is a 50/50 mixture of ethylene glycol and water for year round use. Use a good quality antifreeze with water pump lubricants, rust inhibitors and other corrosion inhibitors along with acid neutralizers.

1. Drain the existing antifreeze and coolant. Open the radiator and engine drain petcocks, or disconnect the bottom radiator hose, at the radiator outlet.

NOTE: Before opening the radiator petcock, spray it with some penetrating lubricant.

2. Close the petcock or reconnect the lower hose and fill the system with water.

3. Add a can of quality radiator flush.

4. Idle the engine until the upper radiator hose gets hot.

5. Drain the system again.

6. Repeat this process until the drained water is clear and free of scale.

7. Close all petcocks and connect all the hoses.

8. If equipped with a coolant recovery system, flush the reservoir with water and leave empty.

9. Determine the capacity of your coolant system (see capacities specifications). Add a 50/50 mix of quality antifreeze (ethylene glycol) and water to provide the desired protection.

10. Run the engine to operating temperature.

11. Stop the engine and check the coolant level.

12. Check the level of protection with an antifreeze tester, replace the cap and check for leaks.

Air Conditioning

GENERAL SERVICING PROCEDURES

The most important aspect of air conditioning service is the maintenance of pure and adequate charge of refrigerant in the system. A refrigeration system cannot function properly if a significant percentage of the charge is lost. Leaks are common because the severe vibration encountered in an automobile can easily cause a sufficient cracking or loosening of the air conditioning fittings. As a result, the extreme operating pressures of the system force refrigerant out.

The problem can be understood by considering what happens to the system as it is operated with a continuous leak. Because the expansion valve regulates the flow of refrigerant to the evaporator, the level of refrigerant there is fairly constant. The receiver/drier stores any excess of refrigerant, and so a loss will first appear there as a reduction in the level of liquid. As this level nears the bottom of the vessel, some refrigerant vapor bubbles will begin to appear in the stream of liquid supplied to the expansion valve. This vapor decreases the capacity of the expansion valve very little as the valve opens to compensate for its presence. As the quantity of liquid in the condenser decreases, the operating pressure will drop there and throughout the high side of the system. As the R-12 continues to be expelled, the pressure available to force the liquid through the expansion valve will continue to decrease, and, eventually, the valve's orifice will prove to be too much of a restriction for adequate flow even with the needle fully withdrawn.

At this point, low side pressure will start to drop, and severe reduction in cooling capacity, marked by freeze-up of the evaporator coil, will result. Eventually, the operating pressure of the evaporator will be lower than the pressure of the atmosphere surrounding it, and air will be drawn into the system wherever there are leaks in the low side.

Because all atmospheric air contains at least some moisture, water will enter the system and mix with the R-12 and the oil. Trace amounts of moisture will cause sludging of the oil, and corrosion of the system. Saturation and clogging of the filter/drier, and freezing of the expansion valve orifice will eventually result. As air fills the system to a greater and greater extend, it will interfere more and more with the normal flows of refrigerant and heat.

A list of general precautions that should be observed while doing this follows:

1. Keep all tools as clean and dry as possible.
2. Thoroughly purge the service gauges and hoses of air and moisture before connecting them to the system. Keep them capped when not in use.
3. Thoroughly clean any refrigerant fitting before disconnecting it, in order to minimize the entrance of dirt into the system.
4. Plan any operation that requires opening the system beforehand in order to minimize the length of time it will be exposed to open air. Cap or seal the open ends to minimize the entrance of foreign material.
5. When adding oil, pour it through an extremely clean and dry tube or funnel. Keep the oil capped whenever possible. Do not use oil that has not been kept tightly sealed.
6. Use only refrigerant 12. Purchase refrigerant intended for use in only automotive air conditioning system. Avoid the use of refrigerant 12 that may be packaged for another use, such as cleaning, or powering a horn, as it is impure.
7. Completely evacuate any system that has been opened to replace a component, other than when isolating the compressor, or that has leaked sufficiently to draw in moisture and air. This requires evacuating air and moisture with a good vacuum pump for at least one hour.

If a system has been open for a considerable length of time it may be advisable to evacuate the system for up to 12 hours (overnight).

8. Use a wrench on both halves of a fitting that is to be disconnected, so as to avoid placing torque on any of the refrigerant lines.

ADDITIONAL PREVENTIVE MAINTENANCE CHECKS

Antifreeze

In order to prevent heater core freeze-up during A/C operation, it is necessary to maintain permanent type antifreeze protection of $+15°F$ ($-9°C$) or lower. A reading of $-15°F$ ($-26°C$) is ideal since this protection also supplies sufficient corrosion inhibitors for the protection of the engine cooling system.

WARNING: Do not use antifreeze longer than specified by the manufacturer.

Radiator Cap

For efficient operation of an air conditioned van's cooling system, the radiator cap should have a holding pressure which meets manufacturer's specifications. A cap which fails to hold these pressure should be replaced.

Condenser

Any obstruction of or damage to the condenser configuration will restrict the air flow which is essential to its efficient operation. It is therefore, a good rule to keep this unit clean and in proper physical shape.

NOTE: Bug screens are regarded as obstructions.

Condensation Drain Tube

This single molded drain tube expels the condensation, which accumulates on the bottom of the evaporator housing, into the engine compartment.

If this tube is obstructed, the air conditioning performance can be restricted and condensation buildup can spill over onto the vehicle's floor.

SAFETY PRECAUTIONS

Because of the importance of the necessary safety precautions that must be exercised when working with air conditioning systems and R-12 refrigerant, a recap of the safety precautions are outlined.

1. Avoid contact with a charged refrigeration system, even when working on another part of the air conditioning system or vehicle. If a heavy tool comes into contact with a section of copper tubing or a heat exchanger, it can easily cause the relatively soft material to rupture.
2. When it is necessary to apply force to a fitting which contains refrigerant, as when checking that all system couplings are securely tightened, use a wrench on both parts of the fitting involved, if possible. This will avoid putting torque on the refrigerant tubing. (It is advisable, when possible, to use tube or line wrenches when tightening these flare nut fittings.)
3. Do not attempt to discharge the system by merely loosening a fitting, or removing the service valve caps and cracking these valves. Precise control is possibly only when using the service gauges. Place a rag under the open end of the center charging hose while discharging the system to catch any drops of liquid that might escape. Wear protective gloves when connecting or disconnecting service gauge hoses.
4. Discharge the system only in a well ventilated area, as high concentrations of the gas can exclude oxygen and act as an anesthetic. When leak testing or soldering this is particularly important, as toxic gas is formed when R-12 contacts any flame.

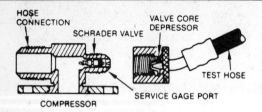

Schrader valve

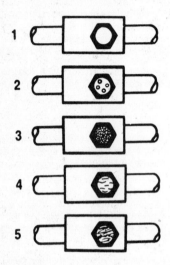

1 Clear sight glass — system correctly charged or over-charged

2 Occasional bubbles — refrigerant charge slightly low

3 Oil streaks on sight glass — total lack of refrigerant

4 Heavy stream of bubbles — serious shortage of refrigerant

5 Dark or clouded sight glass — contaminent present

Sight glass inspection

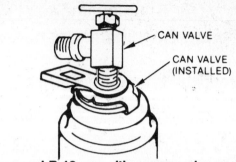

One pound R-12 can with opener valve connected

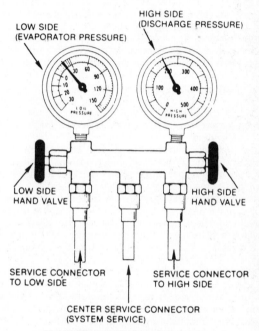

Typical manifold gauge set

5. Never start a system without first verifying that both service valves are backseated, if equipped, and that all fittings are throughout the system are snugly connected.

6. Avoid applying heat to any refrigerant line or storage vessel. Charging may be aided by using water heated to less than 125°F (52°C) to warm the refrigerant container. Never allow a refrigerant storage container to sit out in the sun, or near any other source of heat, such as a radiator.

7. Always wear goggles when working on a system to protect the eyes. If refrigerant contacts the eye, it is advisable in all cases to see a physician as soon as possible.

8. Frostbite from liquid refrigerant should be treated by first gradually warming the area with cool water, and then gently applying petroleum jelly. A physician should be consulted.

9. Always keep refrigerant can fittings capped when not in use. Avoid sudden shock to the can which might occur from dropping it, or from banging a heavy tool against it. Never carry a refrigerant can in the passenger compartment of a van.

10. Always completely discharge the system before painting the vehicle (if the paint is to be baked on), or before welding anywhere near the refrigerant lines.

TEST GAUGES

Most of the service work performed in air conditioning requires the use of a set of two gauges, one for the high (head) pressure side of the system, the other for the low (suction) side.

The low side gauge records both pressure and vacuum. Vacuum readings are calibrated from 0 to 30 inches Hg and the pressure graduations read from 0 to no less than 60 psi.

The high side gauge measures pressure from 0 to at last 600 psi.

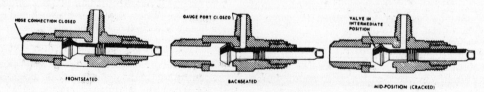

Manual service valve positions

Both gauges are threaded into a manifold that contains two hand shut-off valves. Proper manipulation of these valves and the use of the attached test hoses allow the user to perform the following services:
1. Test high and low side pressures.
2. Remove air, moisture, and contaminated refrigerant.
3. Purge the system (of refrigerant).

4. Charge the system (with refrigerant).

The manifold valves are designed so that they have no direct effect on gauge readings, but serve only to provide for, or cut off, flow of refrigerant through the manifold. During all testing and hook-up operations, the valves are kept in a close position to avoid disturbing the refrigeration system. The valves are opened only to purge the system or refrigerant or to charge it.

Troubleshooting Basic Air Conditioning Problems

Problem	Cause	Solution
There's little or no air coming from the vents (and you're sure it's on)	• The A/C fuse is blown • Broken or loose wires or connections • The on/off switch is defective	• Check and/or replace fuse • Check and/or repair connections • Replace switch
The air coming from the vents is not cool enough	• Windows and air vent wings open • The compressor belt is slipping • Heater is on • Condenser is clogged with debris • Refrigerant has escaped through a leak in the system • Receiver/drier is plugged	• Close windows and vent wings • Tighten or replace compressor belt • Shut heater off • Clean the condenser • Check system • Service system
The air has an odor	• Vacuum system is disrupted • Odor producing substances on the evaporator case • Condensation has collected in the bottom of the evaporator housing	• Have the system checked/repaired • Clean the evaporator case • Clean the evaporator housing drains
System is noisy or vibrating	• Compressor belt or mountings loose • Air in the system	• Tighten or replace belt; tighten mounting bolts • Have the system serviced

Sight glass condition
  Constant bubbles, foam or oil streaks
  Clear sight glass, but no cold air
  Clear sight glass, but air is cold
  Clouded with milky fluid
	
	• Undercharged system
	
	• No refrigerant at all
	• System is OK
	• Receiver drier is leaking dessicant
		
		• Charge the system
		
		• Check and charge the system
		
		• Have system checked

Large difference in temperature of lines	• System undercharged	• Charge and leak test the system
Compressor noise	• Broken valves • Overcharged • Incorrect oil level • Piston slap • Broken rings • Drive belt pulley bolts are loose	• Replace the valve plate • Discharge, evacuate and install the correct charge • Isolate the compressor and check the oil level. Correct as necessary. • Replace the compressor • Replace the compressor • Tighten with the correct torque specification

Troubleshooting Basic Air Conditioning Problems (cont.)

Problem	Cause	Solution
Excessive vibration	· Incorrect belt tension · Clutch loose · Overcharged · Pulley is misaligned	· Adjust the belt tension · Tighten the clutch · Discharge, evacuate and install the correct charge · Align the pulley
Condensation dripping in the passenger compartment	· Drain hose plugged or improperly positioned · Insulation removed or improperly installed	· Clean the drain hose and check for proper installation · Replace the insulation on the expansion valve and hoses
Frozen evaporator coil	· Faulty thermostat · Thermostat capillary tube improperly installed · Thermostat not adjusted properly	· Replace the thermostat · Install the capillary tube correctly · Adjust the thermostat
Low side low—high side low	· System refrigerant is low · Expansion valve is restricted	· Evacuate, leak test and charge the system · Replace the expansion valve
Low side high—high side low	· Internal leak in the compressor—worn	· Remove the compressor cylinder head and inspect the compressor. Replace the valve plate assembly if necessary. If the compressor pistons, rings or
Low side high—high side low (cont.)	 · Cylinder head gasket is leaking · Expansion valve is defective · Drive belt slipping	cylinders are excessively worn or scored replace the compressor · Install a replacement cylinder head gasket · Replace the expansion valve · Adjust the belt tension
Low side high—high side high	· Condenser fins obstructed · Air in the system · Expansion valve is defective · Loose or worn fan belts	· Clean the condenser fins · Evacuate, leak test and charge the system · Replace the expansion valve · Adjust or replace the belts as necessary
Low side low—high side high	· Expansion valve is defective · Restriction in the refrigerant hose	· Replace the expansion valve · Check the hose for kinks—replace if necessary
Low side low—high side high	· Restriction in the receiver/drier · Restriction in the condenser	· Replace the receiver/drier · Replace the condenser
Low side and high normal (inadequate cooling)	· Air in the system · Moisture in the system	· Evacuate, leak test and charge the system · Evacuate, leak test and charge the system

INSPECTION

—— CAUTION ——

The compressed refrigerant used in the air conditioning system expands into the atmosphere at a temperature of –21.7°F (–30°C) or lower. This will freeze any surface, including your eyes, that it contacts. In addition, the refrigerant decomposes into a poisonous gas in the presence of a flame. Do not open or disconnect any part of the air conditioning system.

Sight Glass Check

You can safely make a few simple checks to determine if your air conditioning system needs service. The tests work best if the temperature is warm (about 70°F [21.1°C]).

NOTE: If your vehicle is equipped with an aftermarket air conditioner, the following system check may not apply. You should contact the manufacturer of the unit for instructions on systems checks.

1. Place the automatic transmission in Park or the manual transmission in Neutral. Set the parking brake.
2. Run the engine at a fast idle (about 1,500 rpm) either with the help of a friend or by temporarily readjusting the idle speed screw.
3. Set the controls for maximum cold with the blower on High.
4. Locate the sight glass in one of the system lines. Usually it is on the left alongside the top of the radiator.
5. If you see bubbles, the system must be recharged. Very likely there is a leak at some point.
6. If there are no bubbles, there is either no refrigerant at all or the system is fully charged. Feel the two hoses going to the belt driven compressor. If they are both at the same temperature, the system is empty and must be recharged.
7. If one hose (high pressure) is warm and the other (low pressure) is cold, the system may be all right. However, you are probably making these tests because you think there is something wrong, so proceed to the next step.
8. Have an assistant in the van turn the fan control on and off to operate the compressor clutch. Watch the sight glass.
9. If bubbles appear when the clutch is disengaged and disappear when it is engaged, the system is properly charged.
10. If the refrigerant takes more than 45 seconds to bubble when the clutch is disengaged, the system is overcharged. This usually causes poor cooling at low speeds.

WARNING: If it is determined that the system has a leak, it should be corrected as soon as possible. Leaks may allow moisture to enter and cause a very expensive rust problem.

Exercise the air conditioner for a few minutes, every two weeks or so, during the cold months. This avoids the possibility of the compressor seals drying out from lack of lubrication.

TESTING THE SYSTEM

1. Park the van in the shade, at least 5 feet from any walls.
2. Connect a gauge set.
3. Close (clockwise) both gauge set valves.
4. Start the engine, set the parking brake, place the transmission in NEUTRAL and establish an idle of 1,100–1,300 rpm.
5. Run the air conditioning system for full cooling, in the MAX or COLD mode.
6. The low pressure gauge should read 5–20 psi; the high pressure gauge should indicate 120–180 psi.

WARNING: These pressures are the norm for an ambient temperature of 70–80°F (21–27°C). Higher air temperatures along with high humidity will cause higher

system pressures. At idle speed and an ambient temperature of 110°F (43°C), the high pressure reading can exceed 300 psi.

Under these extreme conditions, you can keep the pressures down by directing a large electric floor fan through the condenser.

DISCHARGING THE SYSTEM

1. Remove the caps from the high and low pressure charging valves in the high and low pressure lines.
2. Turn both manifold gauge set hand valves to the fully closed (clockwise) position.
3. Connect the manifold gauge set.
4. If the gauge set hoses do not have the gauge port actuating pins, install fitting adapters T71P–19703–S and R on the manifold gauge set hoses. If the van does not have a service access gauge port valve, connect the gauge set low pressure hose to the evaporator service access gauge port valve. A special adapter, T77L–19703–A, is required to attach the manifold gauge set to the high pressure service access gauge port valve.
5. Place the end of the center hose away from you and the van.
6. Open the low pressure gauge valve slightly and allow the system pressure to bleed off.
7. When the system is just about empty, open the high pressure valve very slowly to avoid losing an excessive amount of refrigerant oil. Allow any remaining refrigerant to escape.

EVACUATING THE SYSTEM

NOTE: This procedure requires the use of a vacuum pump.

1. Connect the manifold gauge set.
2. Discharge the system.
3. Make sure that the low pressure gauge set hose is connected to the low pressure service gauge port on the top center of the accumulator/drier assembly and the high pressure hose connected to the high pressure service gauge port on the compressor discharge line.
4. Connect the center service hose to the inlet fitting of the vacuum pump.
5. Turn both gauge set valves to the wide open position.
6. Start the pump and note the low side gauge reading.
7. Operate the pump until the low pressure gauge reads 25–30 in.Hg. Continue running the vacuum pump for 10 minutes more. If you've replaced some component in the system, run the pump for an additional 20–30 minutes.
8. Leak test the system. Close both gauge set valves. Turn off the pump. The needle should remain stationary at the point at which the pump was turned off. If the needle drops to zero rapidly, there is a leak in the system which must be repaired.

LEAK TESTING

Some leak tests can be performed with a soapy water solution. There must be at least a ½ lb. charge in the system for a leak to be detected. The most extensive leak tests are performed with either a Halide flame type leak tester or the more preferable electronic leak tester.

In either case, the equipment is expensive, and, the use of a Halide detector can be **extremely** hazardous!

CHARGING THE SYSTEM

—— CAUTION ——

NEVER OPEN THE HIGH PRESSURE SIDE WITH A CAN OF REFRIGERANT CONNECTED TO THE SYSTEM! OPENING THE HIGH PRESSURE SIDE WILL OVERPRESSURIZE THE CAN, CAUSING IT TO EXPLODE!

1. Connect the gauge set.
2. Close (clockwise) both gauge set valves.
3. Connect the center hose to the refrigerant can opener valve.
4. Make sure the can opener valve is closed, that is, the needle is raised, and connect the valve to the can. Open the valve, puncturing the can with the needle.
5. Loosen the center hose fitting at the pressure gauge, allowing refrigerant to purge the hose of air. When the air is bled, tighten the fitting.

CAUTION

IF THE LOW PRESSURE GAUGE SET HOSE IS NOT CONNECTED TO THE ACCUMULATOR/DRIER, KEEP THE CAN IN AN UPRIGHT POSITION!

6. Disconnect the wire harness snap-lock connector from the clutch cycling pressure switch and install a jumper wire across the two terminals of the connector.
7. Open the low side gauge set valve and the can valve.
8. Allow refrigerant to be drawn into the system.
9. When no more refrigerant is drawn into the system, start the engine and run it at about 1,500 rpm. Turn on the system and operate it at the full high position. The compressor will operate and pull refrigerant gas into the system.

NOTE: To help speed the process, the can may be placed, upright, in a pan of warm water, not exceeding 125°F (52°C).

10. If more than one can of refrigerant is needed, close the can valve and gauge set low side valve when the can is empty and connect a new can to the opener. Repeat the charging process until the sight glass indicates a full charge. The frost line on the outside of the can will indicate what portion of the can has been used.

CAUTION

NEVER ALLOW THE HIGH PRESSURE SIDE READING TO EXCEED 240 psi.

11. When the charging process has been completed, close the gauge set valve and can valve. Remove the jumper wire and reconnect the cycling clutch wire. Run the system for at least five minutes to allow it to normalize. Low pressure side reading should be 4–25 psi; high pressure reading should be 120–210 psi at an ambient temperature of 70–90°F (21–32°C).
12. Loosen both service hoses at the gauges to allow any refrigerant to escape. Remove the gauge set and install the dust caps on the service valves.

NOTE: Multi-can dispensers are available which allow a simultaneous hook-up of up to four 1 lb. cans of R-12.

CAUTION

Never exceed the recommended maximum charge for the system. The maximum charge for systems is 3 lb.

Windshield Wipers

Intense heat from the sun, snow, and ice, road oils and the chemicals used in windshield washer solvent combine to deteriorate the rubber wiper refills. The refills should be replaced about twice a year or whenever the blades begin to streak or chatter.

WIPER REFILL REPLACEMENT

Normally, if the wipers are not cleaning the windshield properly, only the refill has to be replaced. The blade and arm usually require replacement only in the event of damage. It is not neces-

sary (except on new Tridon® refills) to remove the arm or the blade to replace the refill (rubber part), though you may have to position the arm higher on the glass. You can do this turning the ignition switch on and operating the wipers. When they are positioned where they are accessible, turn the ignition switch off.

There are several types of refills and your vehicle could have any kind, since aftermarket blades and arms may not use exactly the same type refill as the original equipment.

Most Anco® styles use a release button that is pushed down to allow the refill to slide out of the yoke jaws. The new refill slides in and locks in place.

Some Trico® refills are removed by locating where the metal backing strip or the refill is wider. Insert a small screwdriver blade between the frame and metal backing strip. Press down to release the refill from the retaining tab.

Other Trico® blades are unlocked at one end by squeezing 2 metal tabs, and the refill is slid out of the frame jaws. When the new refill is installed, the tabs will click into place, locking the refill.

The polycarbonate type is held in place by a locking lever that is pushed downward out of the groove in the arm to free the refill. When the new refill is installed, it will lock in place automatically.

The Tridon® refill has a plastic backing strip with a notch about 1 in. (25mm) from the end. Hold the blade (frame) on a hard surface so that the frame is tightly bowed. Grip the tip of the backing strip and pull up while twisting counterclockwise. The backing strip will snap out of the retaining tab. Do this for the remaining tabs until the refill is free of the arm. The length of these refills is molded into the end and they should be replaced with identical types.

No matter which type of refill you use, be sure that all of the frame claws engage the refill. Before operating the wipers, be sure that no part of the metal frame is contacting the windshield.

Ckecking tread with an inexpensive depth gauge

Tread wear indicators are built into all new tires. When they appear, it's time to trash that old rubber for some new skins

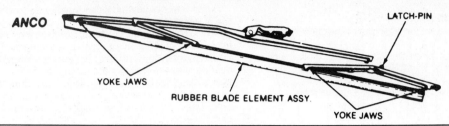

ANCO

LATCH-PIN

YOKE JAWS

RUBBER BLADE ELEMENT ASSY.

YOKE JAWS

TRIDON

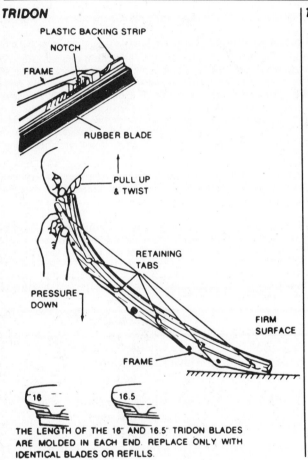

PLASTIC BACKING STRIP

NOTCH

FRAME

RUBBER BLADE

PULL UP & TWIST

RETAINING TABS

PRESSURE DOWN

FIRM SURFACE

FRAME

THE LENGTH OF THE 16" AND 16.5" TRIDON BLADES ARE MOLDED IN EACH END. REPLACE ONLY WITH IDENTICAL BLADES OR REFILLS.

TRICO

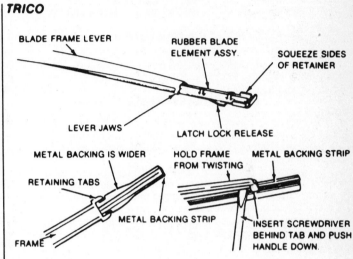

BLADE FRAME LEVER

RUBBER BLADE ELEMENT ASSY.

SQUEEZE SIDES OF RETAINER

LEVER JAWS

LATCH LOCK RELEASE

METAL BACKING IS WIDER

HOLD FRAME FROM TWISTING

METAL BACKING STRIP

RETAINING TABS

FRAME

METAL BACKING STRIP

INSERT SCREWDRIVER BEHIND TAB AND PUSH HANDLE DOWN.

POLYCARBONATE

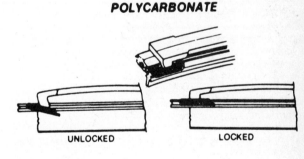

UNLOCKED

LOCKED

Popular styles of wiper refills

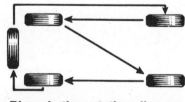

Bias-ply tire rotation diagram

Tread depth can be checked with a penny; when the top of Lincoln's head is visible, it's time for new tires

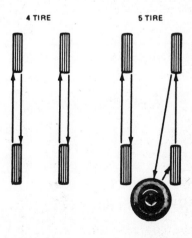

4 TIRE   5 TIRE

Radial-ply tire rotation diagram

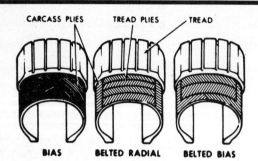

CARCASS PLIES TREAD PLIES TREAD

BIAS BELTED RADIAL BELTED BIAS

Types of tire construction

Tires and Wheels

The tires should be rotated as specified in the Maintenance Intervals Chart. Refer to the accompanying illustrations for the recommended rotation patterns.

The tires on your van should have built-in tread wear indicators, which appear as ½ in. (13mm) bands when the tread depth gets as low as ¹⁄₁₆ in. (1.5mm). When the indicators appear in 2 or more adjacent grooves, it's time for new tires.

For optimum tire life, you should keep the tires properly inflated, rotate them often and have the wheel alignment checked periodically.

Some late models have the maximum load pressures listed in the V.I.N. plate on the left door frame. In general, pressure of 28–32 psi would be suitable for highway use with moderate loads and passenger van type tires (load range B, non-flotation) of original equipment size. Pressures should be checked before driving, since pressure can increase as much as 6 psi due to heat. It is a good idea to have an accurate gauge and to check pressures weekly. Not all gauges on service station air pumps are to be trusted. In general, van type tires require higher pressures and flotation type tires, lower pressures.

TIRE ROTATION

It is recommended that you have the tires rotated every 6,000 miles. There is no way to give a tire rotation diagram for every combination of tires and vehicles, but the accompanying diagrams are a general rule to follow. Radial tires should not be cross-switched; they last longer if their direction of rotation is not changed. Truck tires sometimes have directional tread, indicated by arrows on the sidewalls; the arrow shows the direction of rotation. They will wear very rapidly if reversed. Studded snow tires will lose their studs if their direction of rotation is reversed.

NOTE: Mark the wheel position or direction of rotation on radial tires or studded snow tires before removing them.

If your van is equipped with tires having different load ratings on the front and the rear, the tires should not be rotated front to rear. Rotating these tires could affect tire life (the tires with the

Troubleshooting Basic Wheel Problems

Problem	Cause	Solution
The car's front end vibrates at high speed	• The wheels are out of balance • Wheels are out of alignment	• Have wheels balanced • Have wheel alignment checked/adjusted
Car pulls to either side	• Wheels are out of alignment • Unequal tire pressure • Different size tires or wheels	• Have wheel alignment checked/adjusted • Check/adjust tire pressure • Change tires or wheels to same size
The car's wheel(s) wobbles	• Loose wheel lug nuts • Wheels out of balance • Damaged wheel • Wheels are out of alignment • Worn or damaged ball joint • Excessive play in the steering linkage (usually due to worn parts) • Defective shock absorber	• Tighten wheel lug nuts • Have tires balanced • Raise car and spin the wheel. If the wheel is bent, it should be replaced • Have wheel alignment checked/adjusted • Check ball joints • Check steering linkage • Check shock absorbers
Tires wear unevenly or prematurely	• Incorrect wheel size • Wheels are out of balance • Wheels are out of alignment	• Check if wheel and tire size are compatible • Have wheels balanced • Have wheel alignment checked/adjusted

Troubleshooting Basic Tire Problems

Problem	Cause	Solution
The car's front end vibrates at high speeds and the steering wheel shakes	• Wheels out of balance • Front end needs aligning	• Have wheels balanced • Have front end alignment checked
The car pulls to one side while cruising	• Unequal tire pressure (car will usually pull to the low side) • Mismatched tires • Front end needs aligning	• Check/adjust tire pressure • Be sure tires are of the same type and size • Have front end alignment checked
Abnormal, excessive or uneven tire wear See "How to Read Tire Wear"	• Infrequent tire rotation • Improper tire pressure • Sudden stops/starts or high speed on curves	• Rotate tires more frequently to equalize wear • Check/adjust pressure • Correct driving habits
Tire squeals	• Improper tire pressure • Front end needs aligning	• Check/adjust tire pressure • Have front end alignment checked

Tire Size Comparison Chart

"Letter" sizes			Inch Sizes	Metric-inch Sizes		
"60 Series"	"70 Series"	"78 Series"	1965–77	"60 Series"	"70 Series"	"80 Series"
			5.50-12, 5.60-12	165/60-12	165/70-12	155-12
		Y78-12	6.00-12			
		W78-13	5.20-13	165/60-13	145/70-13	135-13
		Y78-13	5.60-13	175/60-13	155/70-13	145-13
			6.15-13	185/60-13	165/70-13	155-13, P155/80-13
A60-13	A70-13	A78-13	6.40-13	195/60-13	175/70-13	165-13
B60-13	B70-13	B78-13	6.70-13	205/60-13	185/70-13	175-13
			6.90-13			
C60-13	C70-13	C78-13	7.00-13	215/60-13	195/70-13	185-13
D60-13	D70-13	D78-13	7.25-13			
E60-13	E70-13	E78-13	7.75-13			195-13
			5.20-14	165/60-14	145/70-14	135-14
			5.60-14	175/60-14	155/70-14	145-14
			5.90-14			
A60-14	A70-14	A78-14	6.15-14	185/60-14	165/70-14	155-14
	B70-14	B78-14	6.45-14	195/60-14	175/70-14	165-14
	C70-14	C78-14	6.95-14	205/60-14	185/70-14	175-14
D60-14	D70-14	D78-14				
E60-14	E70-14	E78-14	7.35-14	215/60-14	195/70-14	185-14
F60-14	F70-14	F78-14, F83-14	7.75-14	225/60-14	200/70-14	195-14
G60-14	G70-14	G77-14, G78-14	8.25-14	235/60-14	205/70-14	205-14
H60-14	H70-14	H78-14	8.55-14	245/60-14	215/70-14	215-14
J60-14	J70-14	J78-14	8.85-14	255/60-14	225/70-14	225-14
L60-14	L70-14		9.15-14	265/60-14	235/70-14	

Tire Size Comparison Chart

"Letter" sizes			Inch Sizes	Metric-inch Sizes		
"60 Series"	"70 Series"	"78 Series"	1965–77	"60 Series"	"70 Series"	"80 Series"
	A70-15	A78-15	5.60-15	185/60-15	165/70-15	155-15
B60-15	B70-15	B78-15	6.35-15	195/60-15	175/70-15	165-15
C60-15	C70-15	C78-15	6.85-15	205/60-15	185/70-15	175-15
	D70-15	D78-15				
E60-15	E70-15	E78-15	7.35-15	215/60-15	195/70-15	185-15
F60-15	F70-15	F78-15	7.75-15	225/60-15	205/70-15	195-15
G60-15	G70-15	G78-15	8.15-15/8.25-15	235/60-15	215/70-15	205-15
H60-15	H70-15	H78-15	8.45-15/8.55-15	245/60-15	225/70-15	215-15
J60-15	J70-15	J78-15	8.85-15/8.90-15	255/60-15	235/70-15	225-15
	K70-15		9.00-15	265/60-15	245/70-15	230-15
L60-15	L70-15	L78-15, L84-15	9.15-15			235-15
	M70-15	M78-15				255-15
		N78-15				

NOTE: Every size tire is not listed and many size comaprisons are approximate, based on load ratings. Wider tires than those supplied new with the vehicle should always be checked for clearance

lower rating will wear faster, and could become overloaded), and upset the handling of the van.

TIRE USAGE

The tires on your van were selected to provide the best all around performance for normal operation when inflated as specified. Oversize tires (Load Range D) will not increase the maximum carrying capacity of the vehicle, although they will provide an extra margin of tread life. Be sure to check overall height before using larger size tires which may cause interference with suspension components or wheel wells. When replacing conventional tire sizes with other tire size designations, be sure to check the manufacturer's recommendations. Interchangeability is not always possible because of differences in load ratings, tire dimensions, wheel well clearances, and rim size. Also due to differences in handling characteristics, 70 Series and 60 Series tires should be used only in pairs on the same axle; radial tires should be used only in sets of four.

The wheels must be the correct width for the tire. Tire dealers have charts of tire and rim compatibility. A mismatch can cause sloppy handling and rapid tread wear. The old rule of thumb is that the tread width should match the rim width (inside bead to inside bead) within an inch. For radial tires, the rim width should be 80% or less of the tire (not tread) width.

The height (mounted diameter) of the new tires can greatly change speedometer accuracy, engine speed at a given road speed, fuel mileage, acceleration, and ground clearance. Tire manufacturers furnish full measurement specifications. Speedometer drive gears are available for correction.

NOTE: Dimensions of tires marked the same size may vary significantly, even among tires from the same manufacturer.

The spare tire should be usable, at least for low speed operation, with the new tires.

TIRE DESIGN

For maximum satisfaction, tires should be used in sets of five. Mixing or different types (radial, bias-belted, fiberglass belted) should be avoided. Conventional bias tires are constructed so that the cords run bead-to-bead at an angle. Alternate plies run at an opposite angle. This type of construction gives rigidity to both tread and sidewall. Bias-belted tires are similar in construction to conventional bias ply tires. Belts run at an angle and also at a 90° angle to the bead, as in the radial tire. Tread life is improved considerably over the conventional bias tire. The radial tire differs in construction, but instead of the carcass plies running at an angle of 90° to each other, they run at an angle of 90° to the bead. This gives the tread a great deal of rigidity and the sidewall a great deal of flexibility and accounts for the characteristic bulge associated with radial tires.

Radial tire are recommended for use on all Ford vans. If they are used, tire sizes and wheel diameters should be selected to maintain ground clearance and tire load capacity equivalent to the minimum specified tire. Radial tires should always be used in sets of five, but in an emergency radial tires can be used with caution on the rear axle only. If this is done, both tires on the rear should be of radial design.

NOTE: Radial tires should never be used on only the front axle.

FLUIDS AND LUBRICANTS

Oil and Fuel Recommendations

Gasoline Engines

All 1989–91 Ford vans must use lead-free gasoline.

The recommended oil viscosities for sustained temperatures ranging from below 0°F (–18°C) to above 32°F (0°C) are listed in this Section. They are broken down into multiviscosities and single viscosities. Multiviscosity oils are recommended because of their wider range of acceptable temperatures and driving conditions.

When adding oil to the crankcase or changing the oil or filter, it is important that oil of an equal quality to original equipment be used in your van. The use of inferior oils may void the warranty, damage your engine, or both.

The SAE (Society of Automotive Engineers) grade number of oil indicates the viscosity of the oil (its ability to lubricate at a given temperature). The lower the SAE number, the lighter the oil; the lower the viscosity, the easier it is to crank the engine in cold weather but the less the oil will lubricate and protect the engine in high temperatures. This number is marked on every oil container.

Oil viscosities should be chosen from those oils recommended for the lowest anticipated temperatures during the oil change interval. Due to the need for an oil that embodies both good lubrication at high temperatures and easy cranking in cold weather, multigrade oils have been developed. Basically, a multigrade oil is thinner at low temperatures and thicker at high temperatures. For example, a 10W–40 oil (the W stands for winter) exhibits the characteristics of a 10 weight (SAE 10) oil when the van is first started and the oil is cold. Its lighter weight allows it to travel to the lubricating surfaces quicker and offer less resistance to starter motor cranking than, say, a straight 30 weight (SAE 30) oil. But after the engine reaches operating temperature, the 10W–40 oil begins acting like straight 40 weight (SAE 40) oil, its heavier weight providing greater lubrication with less chance of foaming than a straight 30 weight oil.

The API (American Petroleum Institute) designations, also found on the oil container, indicates the classification of engine oil used under certain given operating conditions. Only oils designated for use Service SG heavy duty detergent should be used in your van. Oils of the SG type perform may functions inside the engine besides their basic lubrication. Through a balanced system of metallic detergents and polymeric dispersants, the oil prevents high and low temperature deposits and also keeps sludge and dirt particles in suspension. Acids, particularly sulphuric acid, as well as other by-products of engine combustion are neutralized by the oil. If these acids are allowed to concentrate, they can cause corrosion and rapid wear of the internal engine parts.

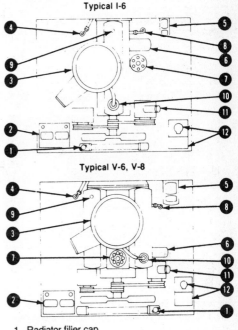

Typical I-6

Typical V-6, V-8

1. Radiator filler cap
2. Battery
3. Air cleaner
4. Automatic transmission dipstick
5. Brake master cylinder
6. Engine oil filter
7. Distributor
8. Engine oil dipstick
9. PCV valve
10. Engine oil filler cap
11. Power steering reservoir
12. Windshield washer reservoir and radiator overflow bottle

Engine compartment service points

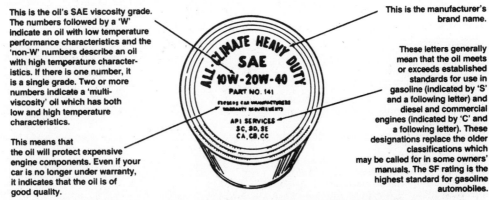

This is the oil's SAE viscosity grade. The numbers followed by a 'W' indicate an oil with low temperature performance characteristics and the 'non-W' numbers describe an oil with high temperature characteristics. If there is one number, it is a single grade. Two or more numbers indicate a 'multi-viscosity' oil which has both low and high temperature characteristics.

This means that the oil will protect expensive engine components. Even if your car is no longer under warranty, it indicates that the oil is of good quality.

This is the manufacturer's brand name.

These letters generally mean that the oil meets or exceeds established standards for use in gasoline (indicated by 'S' and a following letter) and diesel and commercial engines (indicated by 'C' and a following letter). These designations replace the older classifications which may be called for in some owners' manuals. The SF rating is the highest standard for gasoline automobiles.

ALL CLIMATE HEAVY DUTY
SAE
10W–20W–40
PART NO. 141
(SUZUKI CAR MANUFACTURES WARRANTY REQUIREMENTS)
API SERVICES
SC, SD, SE
CA, CB, CC

The top of the oil can will tell you all you need to know about the oil

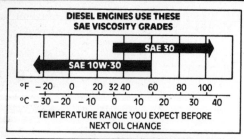

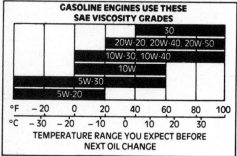

Engine oil viscosities

───────────── CAUTION ─────────────

Non-detergent motor oils or straight mineral oils should not be used in your Ford gasoline engine.

Diesel Engines

Diesel engines require different engine oil from those used in gasoline engines. Besides doing the things gasoline engine oil does, diesel oil must also deal with increased engine heat and the diesel blow-by gases, which create sulphuric acid, a high corrosive.

Under the American Petroleum Institute (API) classifications, gasoline engine oil codes begin with an **S**, and diesel engine oil codes begin with a **C**. This first letter designation is followed by a second letter code which explains what type of service (heavy, moderate, light) the oil is meant for. For example, the top of a typical oil can will include: API SERVICES SG, CD. This means the oil in the can is a superior, heavy duty engine oil when used in a diesel engine.

Many diesel manufacturers recommend an oil with both gasoline and diesel engine API classifications.

NOTE: Ford specifies the use of an engine oil conforming to API service categories of both SG and CD. DO NOT use oils labeled as only SG or only CD as they could cause engine damage.

FUEL

Fuel makers produce two grades of diesel fuel, No. 1 and No. 2, for use in automotive diesel engines. Generally speaking, No. 2 fuel is recommended over No. 1 for driving in temperatures above 20°F (–7°C). In fact, in many areas, No. 2 diesel is the only fuel available. By comparison, No. 2 diesel fuel is less volatile than No. 1 fuel, and gives better fuel economy. No. 2 fuel is also a better injection pump lubricant.

Two important characteristics of diesel fuel are its cetane number and its viscosity.

The cetane number of a diesel fuel refers to the ease with which a diesel fuel ignites. High cetane numbers mean that the fuel will ignite with relative ease or that it ignites well at low temperatures. Naturally, the lower the cetane number, the higher the temperature must be to ignite the fuel. Most com-

mercial fuels have cetane numbers that range from 35 to 65. No. 1 diesel fuel generally has a higher cetane rating than No. 2 fuel.

Viscosity is the ability of a liquid, in this case diesel fuel, to flow. Using straight No. 2 diesel fuel below 20°F (–7°C) can cause problems, because this fuel tends to become cloudy, meaning wax crystals begin forming in the fuel. 20°F (–7°C) is often call the cloud point for No. 2 fuel. In extremely cold weather, No. 2 fuel can stop flowing altogether. In either case, fuel flow is restricted, which can result in no start condition or poor engine performance. Fuel manufacturers often winterize No. 2 diesel fuel by using various fuel additives and blends (no. 1 diesel fuel, kerosene, etc.) to lower its winter time viscosity. Generally speaking, though, No. 1 diesel fuel is more satisfactory in extremely cold weather.

NOTE: No. 1 and No. 2 diesel fuels will mix and burn with no ill effects, although the engine manufacturer recommends one or the other. Consult the owner's manual for information.

Depending on local climate, most fuel manufacturers make winterized No. 2 fuel available seasonally.

Many automobile manufacturers publish pamphlets giving the locations of diesel fuel stations nationwide. Contact the local dealer for information.

Do not substitute home heating oil for automotive diesel fuel. While in some cases, home heating oil refinement levels equal those of diesel fuel, many times they are far below diesel engine requirements. The result of using dirty home heating oil will be a clogged fuel system, in which case the entire system may have to be dismantled and cleaned.

One more word on diesel fuels. Don't thin diesel fuel with gasoline in cold weather. The lighter gasoline, which is more explosive, will cause rough running at the very least, and may cause extensive damage to the fuel system if enough is used.

OIL LEVEL CHECK

Check the engine oil level every time you fill the gas tank. The oil level should be above the ADD mark and not above the FULL mark on the dipstick. Make sure that the dipstick is inserted into the crankcase as far as possible and that the vehicle is resting on level ground. Also, allow a few minutes after turning off the engine for the oil to drain into the pan or an inaccurate reading will result.

1. Open the hood and remove the engine oil dipstick.

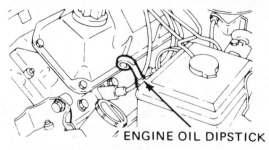

ENGINE OIL DIPSTICK

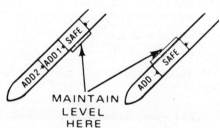

Checking engine oil level

2. Wipe the dipstick with a clean, lint-free rag and reinsert it. Be sure to insert it all the way.

3. Pull out the dipstick and note the oil level. It should be between the **SAFE** (MAX) mark and the **ADD** (MIN) mark.

4. If the level is below the lower mark, replace the dipstick and add fresh oil to bring the level within the proper range. Do not overfill.

5. Recheck the oil level and close the hood.

NOTE: Use a multi-grade oil with API classification SG.

OIL AND FILTER CHANGE

NOTE: The engine oil and oil filter should be changed at the same time, at the recommended intervals on the maintenance schedule chart.

The oil should be changed more frequently if the vehicle is being operated in very dusty areas. Before draining the oil, make sure that the engine is at operating temperature. Hot oil will hold more impurities in suspension and will flow better, allowing the removal of more oil and dirt.

Loosen the drain plug with a wrench, then, unscrew the plug with your fingers, using a rag to shield your fingers from the heat. Push in on the plug as you unscrew it so you can feel when all of the screw threads are out of the hole. You can then remove the plug quickly with the minimum amount of oil running down your arm and you will also have the plug in your hand and not in

the bottom of a pan of hot oil. Drain the oil into a suitable receptacle. Be careful of the oil. If it is at operating temperatures it is hot enough to burn you.

The oil filter is located on the left side of all the engines installed in Ford vans, for longest engine life, it should be changed every time the oil is changed. To remove the filter, you may need an oil filter wrench since the filter may have been fitted too tightly and the heat from the engine may have made it even tighter. A filter wrench can be obtained at an auto parts store and is well worth the investment, since it will save you a lot of grief. Loosen the filter with the filter wrench. With a rag wrapped around the filter, unscrew the filter from the boss on the side of the engine. Be careful of hot oil that will run down the side of the filter. Make sure that you have a pan under the filter before you start to remove it from the engine; should some of the hot oil happen to get on you, you will have a place to dump the filter in a hurry. Wipe the base of the mounting boss with a clean, dry cloth. When you install the new filter, smear a small amount of oil on the gasket with your finger, just enough to coat the entire surface, where it comes in contact with the mounting plate. When you tighten the filter, rotate if only a half turn after it comes in contact with the mounting boss.

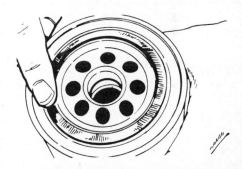

Wipe clean engine oil around the rubber gasket on the new filter. This helps ensure a good seal

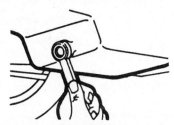

Loosen, but do not remove, the drain plug on the bottom of the oil pan. Get your drain pan ready

Install the new filter by hand only; DO NOT use a strap wrench to install

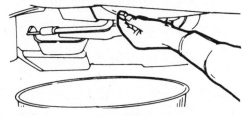

Unscrew the plug by hand. Keep an inward pressure on the plug as you unscrew it, so the oil won't escape until you pull the plug away

Move the drain pan underneath the oil filter. Use a strap wrench to remove the oil filter — remember it is still filled with about a quart of hot, dirty oil

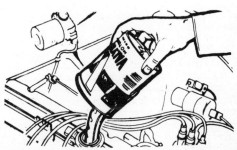

Don't forget to install the drain plug before refilling the engine with fresh oil

Transmission

FLUID RECOMMENDATIONS

Manual Transmissions:
- All models – Dexron®II ATF

Automatic Transmissions:
- All models – Dexron®II ATF

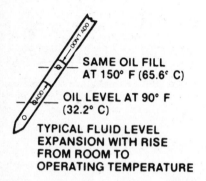

_____ SAME OIL FILL
AT 150° F (65.6° C)

_____ OIL LEVEL AT 90° F
(32.2° C)

TYPICAL FLUID LEVEL
EXPANSION WITH RISE
FROM ROOM TO
OPERATING TEMPERATURE

Checking automatic transmission fluid level. Check transmission when it is warmed to operating temperature

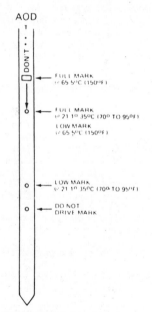

AOD

FULL MARK
(@ 65.5°C (150°F)

FULL MARK
(@ 21.1° 35°C (70° TO 95°F)
LOW MARK
(@ 65.5°C (150°F)

LOW MARK
(@ 21.1° 35°C (70° TO 95°F)

DO NOT
DRIVE MARK

AOD dipstick marks

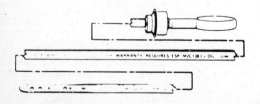

C6 automatic transmission dipstick (note the special fluid designation)

LEVEL CHECK

Automatic Transmissions

It is very important to maintain the proper fluid level in an automatic transmission. If the level is either too high or too low, poor shifting operation and internal damage are likely to occur. For this reason a regular check of the fluid level is essential.

1. Drive the vehicle for 15–20 minutes to allow the transmission to reach operating temperature.
2. Park the van on a level surface, apply the parking brake and leave the engine idling. Shift the transmission and engage each gear, then place the gear selector in **P** (PARK).
3. Wipe away any dirt in the areas of the transmission dipstick to prevent it from falling into the filler tube. Withdraw the dipstick, wipe it with a clean, lint-free rag and reinsert it until it seats.
4. Withdraw the dipstick and note the fluid level. It should be between the upper (FULL) mark and the lower (ADD) mark.
5. If the level is below the lower mark, use a funnel and add fluid in small quantities through the dipstick filler neck. Keep the engine running while adding fluid and check the level after each small amount. Do not overfill.

Manual Transmission

The fluid level should be checked every 6 months/6,000 miles, whichever comes first.

1. Park the van on a level surface, turn off the engine, apply the parking brake and block the wheels.
2. Remove the filler plug from the side of the transmission case with a proper size wrench. The fluid level should be even with the bottom of the filler hole.
3. If additional fluid is necessary, add it through the filler hole using a siphon pump or squeeze bottle.
4. Replace the filler plug; do not overtighten.

DRAIN AND REFILL

Automatic Transmission

1. Raise the van and support on jackstands.

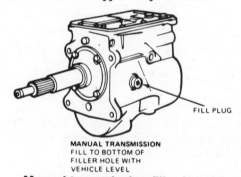

FILL PLUG

MANUAL TRANSMISSION
FILL TO BOTTOM OF
FILLER HOLE WITH
VEHICLE LEVEL

Manual transmission filler location

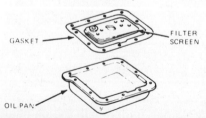

GASKET

FILTER
SCREEN

OIL PAN

Automatic transmission filters are found above the transmission oil pan

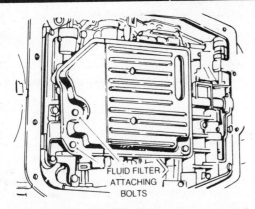

Fluid filter, automatic overdrive (AOD)

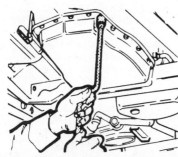

Many late model vehicles have no drain plug. Loosen the pan bolts and allow one corner of the pan to hang, so that the fluid will drain out

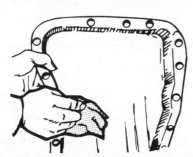

Clean the pan thoroughly with a safe solvent and allow it to air dry

2. Place a drain pan under the transmission.

3. Loosen the pan attaching bolts and drain the fluid from the transmission.

4. When the fluid has drained to the level of the pan flange, remove the remaining pan bolts working from the rear and both sides of the pan to allow it to drop and drain slowly.

5. When all of the fluid has drained, remove the pan and clean it thoroughly. Discard the pan gasket.

6. Place a new gasket on the pan, and install the pan on the transmission. Tighten the attaching bolts to 12–16 ft. lbs.

7. Add three 3 quarts of fluid to the transmission through the filler tube.

8. Lower the vehicle. Start the engine and move the gear selector through shift pattern. Allow the engine to reach normal operating temperature.

9. Check the transmission fluid. Add fluid, if necessary, to maintain correct level.

Install a new pan gasket

Fill the transmission with required amount of fluid. Do not overfill!

Manual Transmission

1. Place a suitable drain pan under the transmission.

2. Remove the drain plug and allow the gear lube to drain out.

3. Replace the drain plug, remove the filler plug and fill the transmission to the proper level with the required fluid.

4. Reinstall the filler plug.

Rear Axles

FLUID LEVEL CHECK

Clean the area around the fill plug, which is located in the housing cover, before removing the plug. The lubricant level should be maintained to the bottom of the fill hole with the axle in its normal running position. If lubricant does not appear at the hole when the plug is removed, additional lubricant should be added. Use hypoid gear lubricant SAE 80 or 90.

NOTE: If the differential is of the limited slip type, be sure and use special limited slip differential additive.

DRAIN AND REFILL

Drain and refill the rear axle housing every 24,000 miles, or every day if the vehicle is operated in deep water. Remove the oil with a suction gun. Refill the axle housings with the proper oil. Be sure and clean the area around the drain plug before removing the plug. See the section on level checks.

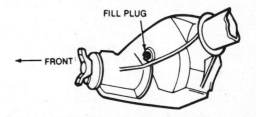

Differential fill plug location

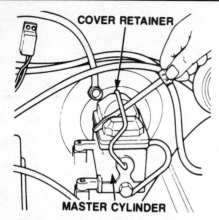

Prying off the master cylinder retaining wire

Brake Master Cylinder

The master cylinder reservoir is located under the hood, on the left side firewall. Before removing the master cylinder reservoir cap, make sure the vehicle is resting on level ground and clean all dirt away from the top of the master cylinder. Pry off the retaining clip or unscrew the holddown bolt and remove the cap. The brake fluid level should be within ¼ in. (6mm) of the top of the reservoir.

If the level of the brake fluid is less than half the volume of the reservoir, it is advised that you check the brake system for leaks. Leaks in the hydraulic brake system most commonly occur at the wheel cylinder.

There is a rubber diaphragm in the top of the master cylinder cap. As the fluid level lowers in the reservoir due to normal brake shoe wear or leakage, the diaphragm takes up the space. This is to prevent the loss of brake fluid out the vented cap and contamination by dirt. After filling the master cylinder to the proper level with heavy duty brake fluid, but before replacing the cap, fold the rubber diaphragm up into the cap, then replace the cap in the reservoir and tighten the retaining bolt or snap the retaining clip into place.

Hydraulic Clutch Reservoir

The hydraulic fluid reservoirs on these systems are mounted on the firewall. Fluid level checks are performed like those on the brake hydraulic system. The proper fluid level is indicated by a step on the reservoir. Keep the reservoir topped up with DOT-3 Heavy-Duty Brake fluid; do not overfill.

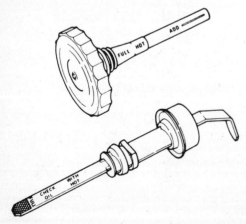

Typical power steering pump reservoir dipsticks

— CAUTION —

Carefully clean the top and sides of the reservoir before opening, to prevent contamination of the system with dirt, etc. Remove the reservoir diaphragm before adding fluid, and replace after filling.

See the illustration of the hydraulic clutch assembly in Section 7.

Power Steering Reservoir

Position the vehicle on level ground. Run the engine until the fluid is at normal operating temperature. Turn the steering wheel all the way to the left and right several times. Position the wheels in the straight ahead position, then shut off the engine. Check the fluid level on the dipstick which is attached to the reservoir cap. The level should be between the ADD and FULL marks on the dipstick. Add fluid accordingly. Do not overfill. Use power steering fluid.

Chassis Greasing

The lubrication chart indicates where the grease fittings are located. The vehicle should be greased according to the intervals in the Preventive Maintenance Schedule at the end of this Section.

Front Wheel Bearings

ADJUSTMENT

The front wheels each rotate on a set of opposed, tapered roller bearings as shown in the accompanying illustration. The grease retainer at the inside of the hub prevents lubricant from leaking into the brake drum.

1989

1. Raise and support the front end on jackstands.
2. Remove the grease cap and remove excess grease from the end of the spindle.
3. Remove the cotter pin and nut lock shown in the illustration.
4. Back off the adjusting nut 2-3 turns.
5. Rotate the wheel, hub and rotor assembly while tightening the adjusting nut to 22–25 ft. lbs. in order to seat the bearings.
6. Back off the adjusting nut ⅛ turn.
7. Locate the nut lock on the adjusting nut so that the castellations on the lock are lined up with the cotter pin hole in the spindle. Try to avoid turning the adjusting nut.
8. Install the new cotter pin, bending the ends of the cotter pin around the castellated flange of the nut lock. If possible, check the bearing endplay. Proper endplay should be 0.001–0.010 in. (O.025–0.254mm).
9. Check the wheel for proper rotation, then install the grease cap. If the wheel still does not rotate properly, inspect and clean or replace the wheel bearings and cups.

1990–91 Except Motor Home Chassis and Stripped Commercial Chassis

1. Raise and support the front end on jackstands.
2. Remove the grease cap and remove excess grease from the end of the spindle.
3. Remove the cotter pin and nut lock shown in the illustration.
4. Loosen the adjusting nut 3 full turns. Obtain a clearance between the brake rotor and brake pads by rocking the wheel in and out several times to push the pads away from the rotor. If that doesn't work, you'll have to remove the caliper (see Section 9). The rotor must turn freely.

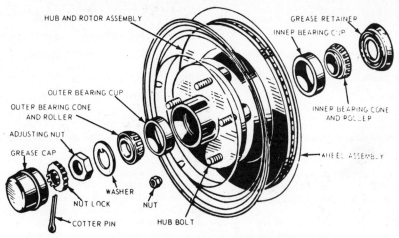

Front hub, bearing, and grease seal

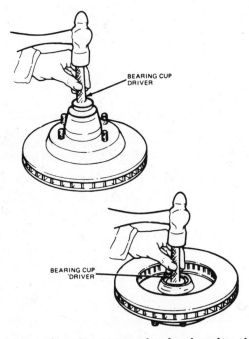

Front wheel bearing removal using bearing driver

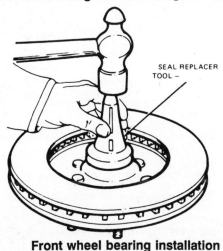

Front wheel bearing installation

5. Tighten the adjusting nut to 17–25 ft. lbs. while rotating the rotor in opposite directions.

6. Back off the adjusting nut 120–180° (⅓–½ turn).

7. Install the retainer and cotter pin without additional movement of the locknut.

8. If a dial indicator is available, check the endplay at the hub. Endplay should be 0.00024–0.0050 in. (0.006–0.127mm).

9. Install the grease cap.

10. If removed, install the caliper.

Motor Home Chassis
Stripped Commercial Chassis

1. Raise and support the front end on jackstands.

2. Remove the grease cap and remove excess grease from the end of the spindle.

3. Remove the cotter pin and nut lock shown in the illustration.

4. Loosen the adjusting nut 3 full turns. Obtain a clearance between the brake rotor and brake pads by rocking the wheel in and out several times to push the pads away from the rotor. If that doesn't work, you'll have to remove the caliper (see Section 9). The rotor must turn freely.

5. Tighten the adjusting nut to 17–25 ft. lbs. while rotating the rotor in the opposite direction.

6. Back off the adjusting nut 120–180° (⅓–½ turn).

7. Tighten the adjusting nut to 18–20 inch lbs. while rotating the rotor.

8. If a dial indicator is available, check the endplay at the hub. Endplay should be 0.00024–0.0050 in. (0.006–0.127mm). The torque required to turn the hub should be 10–25 inch lbs.

9. Install the locknut, cotter pin and grease cap.

10. If removed, install the caliper.

11. Install the wheel. Torque the lug nuts to 140 ft. lbs. After 500 miles, retorque the lug nuts.

REMOVAL, REPACKING, AND INSTALLATION

Before handling the bearings, there are a few things that you should remember to do and not to do.

Remember to DO the following:

- Remove all outside dirt from the housing before exposing the bearing.
- Treat a used bearing as gently as you would a new one.
- Work with clean tools in clean surroundings.
- Use clean, dry canvas gloves, or at least clean, dry hands.
- Clean solvents and flushing fluids are a must.

- Use clean paper when laying out the bearings to dry.
- Protect disassembled bearings from rust and dirt. Cover them up.
- Use clean rags to wipe bearings.
- Keep the bearings in oil-proof paper when they are to be stored or are not in use.
- Clean the inside of the housing before replacing the bearing.

Do NOT do the following:

- Don't work in dirty surroundings.
- Don't use dirty, chipped or damaged tools.
- Try not to work on wooden work benches or use wooden mallets.
- Don't handle bearings with dirty or moist hands.
- Do not use gasoline for cleaning; use a safe solvent.
- Do not spin-dry bearings with compressed air. They will be damaged.
- Do not spin dirty bearings.
- Avoid using cotton waste or dirty cloths to wipe bearings.
- Try not to scratch or nick bearing surfaces.
- Do not allow the bearing to come in contact with dirt or rust at any time.

1. Raise and support the front end on jackstands.
2. Remove the wheel cover. Remove the wheel.
3. Remove the caliper from the disc and wire it to the underbody to prevent damage to the brake hose. See Section 9
4. Remove the grease cap from the hub. Then, remove the cotter pin, nut lock, adjusting nut and flat washer from the spindle. Remove the outer bearing assembly from the hub.
5. Pull the hub and disc assembly off the wheel spindle.
6. Remove and discard the old grease retainer. Remove the inner bearing cone and roller assembly from the hub.
7. Clean all grease from the inner and outer bearing cups with solvent. Inspect the cups for pits, scratches, or excessive wear. If the cups are damaged, remove them with a drift.
8. Clean the inner and outer cone and roller assemblies with solvent and shake them dry. If the cone and roller assemblies show excessive wear or damage, replace them with the bearing cups as a unit.
9. Clean the spindle and the inside of the hub with solvent to thoroughly remove all old grease.
10. Covering the spindle with a clean cloth, brush all loose dirt and dust from the brake assembly. Remove the cloth carefully so as to not get dirt on the spindle.
11. If the inner and/or outer bearing cups were removed, install the replacement cups on the hub. Be sure that the cups seat properly in the hub.
12. It is imperative that all old grease be removed from the bearings and surrounding surfaces before repacking. The new lithium-based grease is not compatible with the sodium base grease used in the past.
13. Install the hub and disc on the wheel spindle. To prevent damage to the grease retainer and spindle threads, keep the hub centered on the spindle.
14. Install the outer bearing cone and roller assembly and the flat washer on the spindle. Install the adjusting nut.
15. Adjust the wheel bearings by torquing the adjusting nut to 17–25 ft. lbs. with the wheel rotating to seat the bearing. Then back off the adjusting nut ½ turn. Retighten the adjusting nut to 10–15 inch lbs. Install the locknut so that the castellations are aligned with the cotter pin hole. Install the cotter pin. Bend the ends of the cotter pin around the castellations of the locknut to prevent interference with the radio static collector in the grease cap. Install the grease cap.

WARNING: New bolts must be used when servicing floating caliper units. The upper bolt must be tightened first. For caliper service see Section 9.

11. Install the wheels.
12. Install the wheel cover.

Full Floating Rear Axle Bearings

REMOVAL, REPACKING AND INSTALLATION

1989

The wheel bearings on Dana full floating rear axles are packed with wheel bearing grease. Axle lubricant can also flow into the wheel hubs and bearings, however, wheel bearing grease is the primary lubricant. The wheel bearing grease provides lubrication until the axle lubricant reaches the bearings during normal operation.

1. Set the parking brake and loosen — do not remove — the axle shaft bolts.
2. Raise the rear wheels off the floor and place jackstands under the rear axle housing so that the axle is parallel with the floor. Release the parking brake.
3. Remove the axle shaft bolts and lockwashers. They should not be re-used.
4. Place a heavy duty wheel dolly under the wheels and raise them so that all weight is off the wheel bearings.
5. Remove the axle shaft and gasket(s).
6. Remove the caliper. See Section 9.
7. Using a special hub nut wrench, remove the hub nut.

NOTE: The hub nut on the right spindle is right hand thread; the one on the left spindle is left hand thread. They are marked RH and LH. NEVER use an impact wrench on the hub nut!

8. Remove the outer bearing cone and pull the wheel straight off the axle.
9. With a piece of hardwood or a brass drift which will just clear the outer bearing cup, drive the inner bearing cone and inner seal out of the wheel hub.
10. Wash all the old grease or axle lubricant out of the wheel hub, using a suitable solvent.
11. Wash the bearing cups and rollers and inspect them for pitting, galling, and uneven wear patterns. Inspect the roller for end wear.
12. If the bearing cups are to be replaced, drive them out with a brass drift. Install the new cups with a block of wood and hammer or press them in.
13. If the bearing cups are properly seated, a 0.0015 in. (0.038mm) feeler gauge will not fit between the cup and the wheel hub. The gauge should not fit beneath the cup. Check several places to make sure the cups are squarely seated.
14. Pack each bearing cone and roller with a bearing packer or in the manner previously outlined for the front wheel bearings. Use a multi-purpose wheel bearing grease.

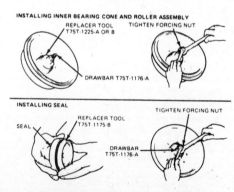

Rear wheel bearing and seal installation. Seal installation tools are very helpful here

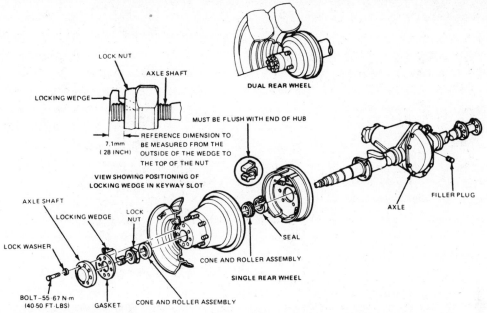

Rear wheel hub showing wedge positioning — E-350 with dual rear wheels shown

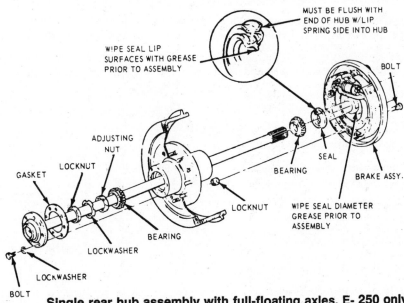

Single rear hub assembly with full-floating axles, E- 250 only

15. Place the inner bearing cone and roller assembly in the wheel hub. Install a new inner seal in the hub with a seal installation tool.

16. Wrap the threads of the spindle with tape and carefully slide the hub straight on the spindle. Take care to avoid damaging the seal! Remove the tape.

17. Install the outer bearing. Start the hub nut, making sure that the hub tab is engaged with the keyway prior to threading.

18. Tighten the nut to 65–75 ft.lbs. while rotating the wheel.

NOTE: The hub will ratchet at torque is applied. This ratcheting can be avoided by using Ford tool No. T88T-4252-A. Avoiding ratcheting will give more even bearing preloads.

19. Back off (loosen) the adjusting nut 90° (¼ turn). Then, tighten it to 15–20 ft. lbs.

20. Using a dial indicator, check endplay of the hub. No endplay is permitted.

21. Clean the hub bolt holes thoroughly. Replace the hub if any cracks are found around the holes or if the threads in the holes are in any way damaged.

22. Install the axle shaft, new flange gasket, lock washers and *new* shaft retaining bolts. Coat the bolt threads with thread adhesive. Tighten them snugly, but not completely.

23. Install the caliper.

24. Install the wheels.

25. Lower the van to the ground.

26. Tighten the wheel lug nuts.

27. Tighten the axle shaft bolts to 70–85 ft. lbs.

1990–91

The wheel bearings on full floating rear axles are packed with

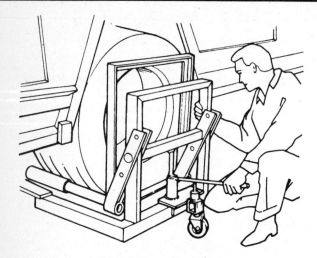

Heavy duty wheel dolly

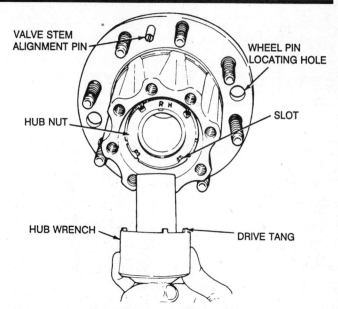

Hub wrench engagement

wheel bearing grease. Axle lubricant can also flow into the wheel hubs and bearings, however, wheel bearing grease is the primary lubricant. The wheel bearing grease provides lubrication until the axle lubricant reaches the bearings during normal operation.

1. Set the parking brake and loosen — do not remove — the axle shaft bolts.

2. Raise the rear wheels off the floor and place jackstands under the rear axle housing so that the axle is parallel with the floor. The axle shafts must turn freely, so release the parking brake.

3. Remove the axle shaft bolts and lockwashers. They should not be re-used.

4. Place a heavy duty wheel dolly under the wheels and raise them so that all weight is off the wheel bearings.

5. Remove the axle shaft and gasket(s).

6. Remove the brake caliper. See Section 9.

7. Using a special hub nut wrench, remove the hub nut.

NOTE: The hub nuts for both sides are right hand thread and marked RH.

8. Remove the outer bearing cone and pull the wheel straight off the axle.

9. With a piece of hardwood or a brass drift which will just clear the outer bearing cup, drive the inner bearing cone and inner seal out of the wheel hub.

10. Wash all the old grease or axle lubricant out of the wheel hub, using a suitable solvent.

11. Wash the bearing cups and rollers and inspect them for pitting, galling, and uneven wear patterns. Inspect the roller for end wear.

12. If the bearing cups are to be replaced, drive them out with a brass drift. Install the new cups with a block of wood and hammer or press them in.

13. If the bearing cups are properly seated, a 0.0015 in. (0.038mm) feeler gauge will not fit between the cup and the wheel hub. The gauge should not fit beneath the cup. Check several places to make sure the cups are squarely seated.

14. Pack each bearing cone and roller with a bearing packer or in the manner previously outlined for the front wheel bearings. Use a multi-purpose wheel bearing grease.

15. Place the inner bearing cone and roller assembly in the wheel hub. Install a new inner seal in the hub with a seal installation tool.

16. Wrap the threads of the spindle with tape and carefully slide the hub straight on the spindle. Take care to avoid damaging the seal! Remove the tape.

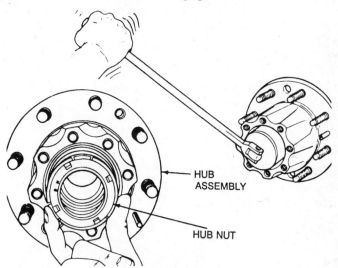

Tightening the hub nut

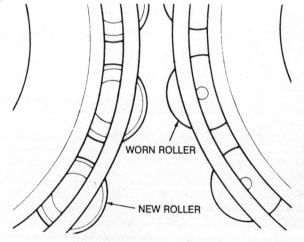

Roller bearing end wear

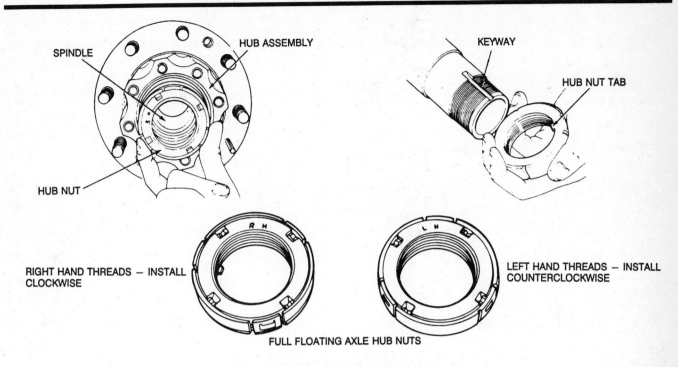

Hub nut installation

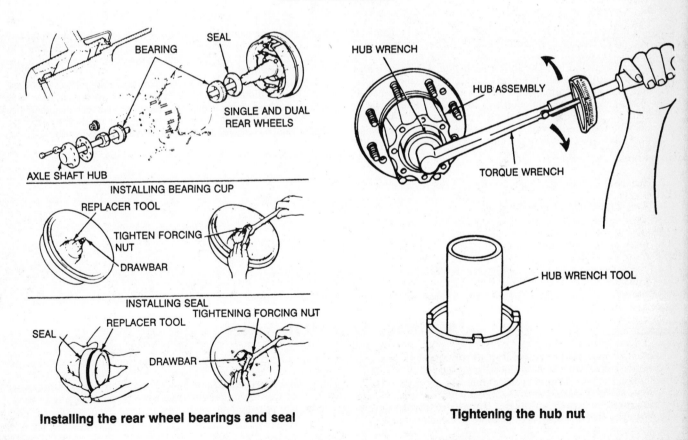

Installing the rear wheel bearings and seal

Tightening the hub nut

17. Install the outer bearing. Start the hub nut, making sure that the hub tab is engaged with the keyway prior to threading.
18. Tighten the nut to 65–75 ft.lbs. while rotating the wheel.

NOTE: The hub will ratchet at torque is applied. This ratcheting can be avoided by using Ford tool No. T88T-4252-A. Avoiding ratcheting will give more even bearing preloads.

19. Back off (loosen) the adjusting nut 90° (¼ turn). Then, tighten it to 15–20 ft. lbs.

20. Using a dial indicator, check endplay of the hub. No endplay is permitted.
21. Clean the hub bolt holes thoroughly. Replace the hub if any cracks are found around the holes or if the threads in the holes are in any way damaged.
22. Install the axle shaft, new flange gasket, lock washers and *new* shaft retaining bolts. Coat the bolt threads with thread adhesive. Tighten them snugly, but not completely.
23. Install the caliper.
24. Install the wheels.
25. Lower the van to the ground.
26. Tighten the wheel lug nuts.
27. Tighten the axle shaft bolts to 40–55 ft. lbs.

PUSHING AND TOWING

To push-start your vehicle, (manual transmission only), check to make sure that bumpers of both vehicles are aligned so neither will be damaged. Be sure that all electrical system components are turned off (headlight, heater, blower, etc.). Turn on the ignition switch. Place the shift lever in Third or Fourth and push in the clutch pedal. At about 15 mph, signal the driver of the pushing vehicle to fall back, depress the accelerator pedal, and release the clutch pedal slowly. The engine should start.

When you are doing the pushing, make sure that the two bumpers match so you won't damage the vehicle you are to push. Another good idea is to put an old tire between the two vehicles. Try to keep your van right up against the other vehicle while you are pushing. If the two vehicles do separate, stop and start over again instead of trying to catch up and ramming the other vehicle. Also try, as much as possible, to avoid riding or slipping the clutch.

If your van has to be towed by a tow truck, it can be towed forward for any distance with the driveshaft connected as long as it is done fairly slowly. Otherwise disconnect the driveshaft at the rear axle and tie it up. On full-floating rear axles, the rear axle shafts can be removed and the hub covered to prevent lubricant loss.

JACKING AND HOISTING

It is very important to be careful about running the engine, on vehicles equipped with limited slip differentials, while the vehicle is up on the jack. This is because when the drive train is engaged, power is transmitted to the wheel with the best traction and the vehicle will drive off the jack if one drive wheel is in contact with the floor, resulting in possible damage or injury.

Jack a Ford van from under the axles, radius arms, or spring hangers and the frame. Be sure and block the diagonally opposite wheel. Place jackstands under the vehicle at the points mentioned or directly under the frame when you are going to work under the vehicle.

JUMP STARTING A DEAD BATTERY

The chemical reaction in a battery produces explosive hydrogen gas. This is the safe way to jump start a dead battery, reducing the chances of an accidental spark that could cause an explosion.

Jump Starting Precautions

1. Be sure both batteries are of the same voltage.
2. Be sure both batteries are of the same polarity (have the same grounded terminal).
3. Be sure the vehicles are not touching.
4. Be sure the vent cap holes are not obstructed.
5. Do not smoke or allow sparks around the battery.
6. In cold weather, check for frozen electrolyte in the battery. Do not jump start a frozen battery.
7. Do not allow electrolyte on your skin or clothing.
8. Be sure the electrolyte is not frozen.

CAUTION: Make certin that the ignition key, in the vehicle with the dead battery, is in the OFF position. Connecting cables to vehicles with on-board computers will result in computer destruction if the key is not in the OFF position.

Jump Starting Procedure

1. Determine voltages of the two batteries; they must be the same.
2. Bring the starting vehicle close (they must not touch) so that the batteries can be reached easily.
3. Turn off all accessories and both engines. Put both vehicles in Neutral or Park and set the handbrake.
4. Cover the cell caps with a rag—do not cover terminals.
5. If the terminals on the run-down battery are heavily corroded, clean them.
6. Identify the positive and negative posts on both batteries and connect the cables in the order shown.
7. Start the engine of the starting vehicle and run it at fast idle. Try to start the car with the dead battery. Crank it for no more than 10 seconds at a time and let it cool for 20 seconds in between tries.
8. If it doesn't start in 3 tries, there is something else wrong.
9. Disconnect the cables in the reverse order.
10. Replace the cell covers and dispose of the rags.

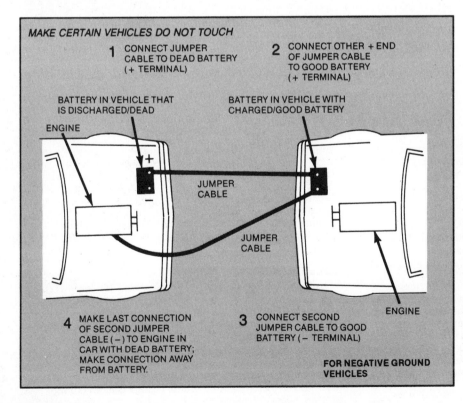

MAKE CERTAIN VEHICLES DO NOT TOUCH

1 CONNECT JUMPER CABLE TO DEAD BATTERY (+ TERMINAL)

2 CONNECT OTHER + END OF JUMPER CABLE TO GOOD BATTERY (+ TERMINAL)

BATTERY IN VEHICLE THAT IS DISCHARGED/DEAD

BATTERY IN VEHICLE WITH CHARGED/GOOD BATTERY

ENGINE

JUMPER CABLE

JUMPER CABLE

ENGINE

4 MAKE LAST CONNECTION OF SECOND JUMPER CABLE (−) TO ENGINE IN CAR WITH DEAD BATTERY; MAKE CONNECTION AWAY FROM BATTERY.

3 CONNECT SECOND JUMPER CABLE TO GOOD BATTERY (− TERMINAL)

FOR NEGATIVE GROUND VEHICLES

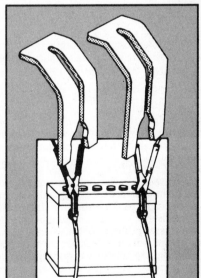

Side terminal batteries occasionally pose a problem when connecting jumper cables. There frequently isn't enough room to clamp the cables without touching sheet metal. Side terminal adaptors are available to alleviate this problem and should be removed after use

JUMP STARTING A DUAL-BATTERY DIESEL

Ford vans equipped with the 7.3L V8 diesel utilize two 12 volt batteries, one on either side of the engine compartment. The batteries are connected in a parallel circuit (positive terminal to positive terminal, negative terminal to negative terminal). Hooking the batteries up in parallel circuit increases battery cranking power without increasing total battery voltage output. Output remains at 12 volts. On the other hand, hooking two 12 volt batteries up in a series circuit (positive terminal to negative terminal, positive terminal to negative terminal) increases total battery output to 24 volts (12 volts plus 12 volts).

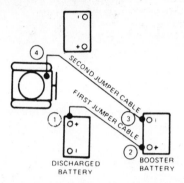

Diesel dual-battery jump starting diagram

— CAUTION —

NEVER hook the batteries up in a series circuit or the entire electrical system will go up in smoke, especially the starter.

In the event that a diesel van needs to be jump started, use the following procedure.
1. Turn all lights off.
2. Turn on the heater blower motor to remove transient voltage.
3. Connect one jumper cable to the passenger side battery positive (+) terminal and the other cable clamp to the positive (+) terminal to the booster (good) battery.
4. Connect one end of the other jumper cable to the negative (–) terminal of the booster (good) battery and the other cable clamp to an engine bolt head, alternator bracket or other solid, metallic point on the diesel engine. DO NOT connect this clamp to the negative (–) terminal of the bad battery.

— CAUTION —

Be very careful to keep the jumper cables away from moving parts (cooling fan, belts, etc.) on both engines.

5. Start the engine of the donor truck and run it at moderate speed.
6. Start the engine of the diesel.
7. When the diesel starts, remove the cable from the engine block before disconnecting the positive terminal.

TRAILER TOWING

Factory trailer towing packages are available on most vans. However, if you are installing a trailer hitch and wiring on your van, there are a few thing that you ought to know.

Trailer Weight

Trailer weight is the first, and most important, factor in determining whether or not your vehicle is suitable for towing the trailer you have in mind. The horsepower-to-weight ratio should be calculated. The basic standard is a ratio of 35:1. That is, 35 pounds of GVW for every horsepower.

To calculate this ratio, multiply you engine's rated horsepower by 35, then subtract the weight of the vehicle, including passengers and luggage. The resulting figure is the ideal maximum trailer weight that you can tow. One point to consider: a numerically higher axle ratio can offset what appears to be a low trailer weight. If the weight of the trailer that you have in mind is somewhat higher than the weight you just calculated, you might consider changing your rear axle ratio to compensate.

Hitch Weight

There are three kinds of hitches: bumper mounted, frame mounted, and load equalizing.

Bumper mounted hitches are those which attach solely to the vehicle's bumper. Many states prohibit towing with this type of hitch, when it attaches to the vehicle's stock bumper, since it subjects the bumper to stresses for which it was not designed. Aftermarket rear step bumpers, designed for trailer towing, are acceptable for use with bumper mounted hitches.

Frame mounted hitches can be of the type which bolts to two or more points on the frame, plus the bumper, or just to several points on the frame. Frame mounted hitches can also be of the tongue type, for Class I towing, or, of the receiver type, for Classes II and III.

Load equalizing hitches are usually used for large trailers. Most equalizing hitches are welded in place and use equalizing bars and chains to level the vehicle after the trailer is hooked up.

The bolt-on hitches are the most common, since they are relatively easy to install.

Check the gross weight rating of your trailer. Tongue weight is usually figured as 10% of gross trailer weight. Therefore, a trailer with a maximum gross weight of 2,000 lb. will have a maximum tongue weight of 200 lb. Class I trailers fall into this category. Class II trailers are those with a gross weight rating of 2,000–3,500 lb., while Class III trailers fall into the 3,500–6,000 lb. category. Class IV trailers are those over 6,000 lb. and are for use with fifth wheel trucks, only.

When you've determined the hitch that you'll need, follow the manufacturer's installation instructions, exactly, especially when it comes to fastener torques. The hitch will subjected to a lot of stress and good hitches come with hardened bolts. Never substitute an inferior bolt for a hardened bolt.

Wiring

Wiring the van for towing is fairly easy. There are a number of good wiring kits available and these should be used, rather than trying to design your own. All trailers will need brake lights and turn signals as well as tail lights and side marker lights. Most states require extra marker lights for overly wide trailers. Also, most states have recently required backup lights for trailers, and most trailer manufacturers have been building trailers with backup lights for several years.

Additionally, some Class I, most Class II and just about all Class III trailers will have electric brakes.

Add to this number an accessories wire, to operate trailer internal equipment or to charge the trailer's battery, and you can have as many as seven wires in the harness.

Determine the equipment on your trailer and buy the wiring kit necessary. The kit will contain all the wires needed, plus a plug adapter set which included the female plug, mounted on the bumper or hitch, and the male plug, wired into, or plugged into the trailer harness.

When installing the kit, follow the manufacturer's instructions. The color coding of the wires is standard throughout the industry.

One point to note, some domestic vehicles, and most imported vehicles, have separate turn signals. On most domestic vehicles, the brake lights and rear turn signals operate with the same bulb. For those vehicles with separate turn signals, you can purchase an isolation unit so that the brake lights won't blink whenever the turn signals are operated, or, you can go to your local electronics supply house and buy four diodes to wire in series with the brake and turn signal bulbs. Diodes will isolate the brake and turn signals. The choice is yours. The isolation units are simple and quick to install, but far more expensive than the diodes. The diodes, however, require more work to install properly, since they require the cutting of each bulb's wire and soldering in place of the diode.

One final point, the best kits are those with a spring loaded cover on the vehicle mounted socket. This cover prevents dirt and moisture from corroding the terminals. Never let the vehicle socket hang loosely. Always mount it securely to the bumper or hitch.

Cooling

ENGINE

One of the most common, if not THE most common, problem associated with trailer towing is engine overheating.

With factory installed trailer towing packages, a heavy duty cooling system is usually included. Heavy duty cooling systems are available as optional equipment on most vans, with or without a trailer package. If you have one of these extra-capacity systems, you shouldn't have any overheating problems.

If you have a standard cooling system, without an expansion tank, you'll definitely need to get an aftermarket expansion tank kit, preferably one with at least a 2 quart capacity. These kits are easily installed on the radiator's overflow hose, and come with a pressure cap designed for expansion tanks.

Another helpful accessory is a Flex Fan. These fan are large diameter units are designed to provide more airflow at low speeds, with blades that have deeply cupped surfaces. The blades then flex, or flatten out, at high speed, when less cooling air is needed. These fans are far lighter in weight than stock fans, requiring less horsepower to drive them. Also, they are far quieter than stock fans.

If you do decide to replace your stock fan with a flex fan, note that if your van has a fan clutch, a spacer between the flex fan and water pump hub will be needed.

Aftermarket engine oil coolers are helpful for prolonging engine oil life and reducing overall engine temperatures. Both of these factors increase engine life.

While not absolutely necessary in towing Class I and some Class II trailers, they are recommended for heavier Class II and all Class III towing.

Engine oil cooler systems consist of an adapter, screwed on in place of the oil filter, a remote filter mounting and a multi-tube, finned heat exchanger, which is mounted in front of the radiator or air conditioning condenser.

TRANSMISSION

An automatic transmission is usually recommended for trailer towing. Modern automatics have proven reliable and, of course, easy to operate, in trailer towing.

The increased load of a trailer, however, causes an increase in the temperature of the automatic transmission fluid. Heat is the worst enemy of an automatic transmission. As the temperature of the fluid increases, the life of the fluid decreases.

It is essential, therefore, that you install an automatic transmission cooler.

The cooler, which consists of a multi-tube, finned heat exchanger, is usually installed in front of the radiator or air conditioning compressor, and hooked inline with the transmission cooler tank inlet line. Follow the cooler manufacturer's installation instructions.

Select a cooler of at least adequate capacity, based upon the combined gross weights of the van and trailer.

Cooler manufacturers recommend that you use an aftermarket cooler in addition to, and not instead of, the present cooling tank in your van's radiator. If you do want to use it in place of the radiator cooling tank, get a cooler at least two sizes larger than normally necessary.

NOTE: A transmission cooler can, sometimes, cause slow or harsh shifting in the transmission during cold weather, until the fluid has a chance to come up to normal operating temperature. Some coolers can be purchased with or retrofitted with a temperature bypass valve which will allow fluid flow through the cooler only when the fluid has reached operating temperature, or above.

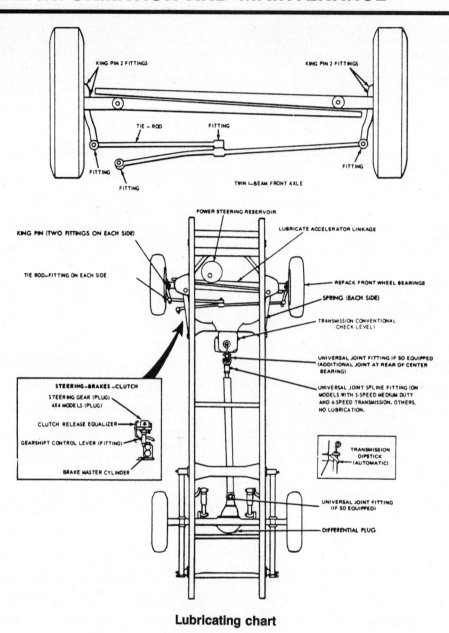

Lubricating chart

Engine Performance and Tune-Up

2

QUICK REFERENCE INDEX

GENERAL INDEX

In order to extract the full measure of performance and economy from your engine it is essential that it be properly tuned at regular intervals. A regular tune-up will keep your vehicle's engine running smoothly and will prevent the annoying minor breakdowns and poor performance associated with an untuned engine.

A complete tune-up should be performed every 12,000 miles or twelve months, whichever comes first. This interval should be halved if the vehicle is operated under severe conditions, such as trailer towing, prolonged idling, continual stop and start driving, or if starting or running problems are noticed. It is assumed that the routine maintenance described in Section 1 has been kept up, as this will have a decided effect on the results of a tune-up. All of the applicable steps of a tune-up should be followed in order, as the result is a cumulative one.

If the specifications on the tune-up sticker in the engine compartment disagree with the Tune-Up Specifications chart in this Section, the figures on the sticker must be used. The sticker often reflects changes made during the production run.

Spark Plugs

A typical spark plug consists of a metal shell surrounding a ceramic insulator. A metal electrode extends downward through the center of the insulator and protrudes a small distance. Located at the end of the plug and attached to the side of the outer metal shell is the side electrode. The side electrode bends in at a 90° angle so that its tip is even with, and parallel to, the tip of the center electrode. The distance between these two electrodes (measured in thousandths of an inch) is called the spark plug

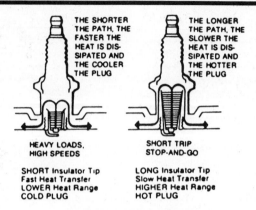

THE SHORTER THE PATH, THE FASTER THE HEAT IS DISSIPATED AND THE COOLER THE PLUG

THE LONGER THE PATH, THE SLOWER THE HEAT IS DISSIPATED AND THE HOTTER THE PLUG

HEAVY LOADS. HIGH SPEEDS.

SHORT TRIP STOP-AND-GO

SHORT Insulator Tip
Fast Heat Transfer
LOWER Heat Range
COLD PLUG

LONG Insulator Tip
Slow Heat Transfer
HIGHER Heat Range
HOT PLUG

Spark plug heat range

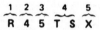

$$\underbrace{R}_{1}\ \underbrace{4}_{2}\ \underbrace{5}_{3}\ \underbrace{T\ S}_{4}\ \underbrace{X}_{5}$$

1 – R--INDICATES RESISTOR-TYPE PLUG.
2 – "4" INDICATES 14 mm THREADS.
3 – HEAT RANGE
4 – TS--TAPERED SEAT
    S--EXTENDED TIP
5 – SPECIAL GAP

Spark plug type number chart, using the R45TSX as an example

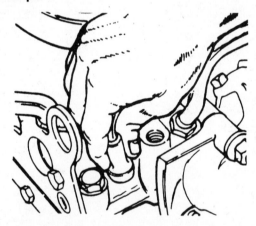

Twist and pull on the rubber boot to remove the spark wires; never pull on the wire itself

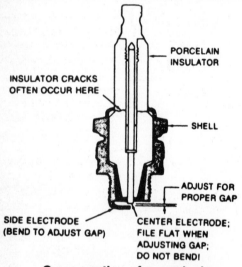

PORCELAIN INSULATOR

INSULATOR CRACKS OFTEN OCCUR HERE

SHELL

ADJUST FOR PROPER GAP

SIDE ELECTRODE (BEND TO ADJUST GAP)

CENTER ELECTRODE; FILE FLAT WHEN ADJUSTING GAP; DO NOT BEND!

Cross section of a spark plug

Always use a wire gauge to check the electrode gap; a flat feeler gauge may not give the proper reading

Adjust the electrode gap by bending the side electrode

Diagnosis of Spark Plugs

Problem	Possible Cause	Correction
Brown to grayish-tan deposits and slight electrode wear.	• Normal wear.	• Clean, regap, reinstall.
Dry, fluffy black carbon deposits.	• Poor ignition output.	• Check distributor to coil connections.
Wet, oily deposits with very little electrode wear.	• "Break-in" of new or recently overhauled engine. • Excessive valve stem guide clearances. • Worn intake valve seals.	• Degrease, clean and reinstall the plugs. • Refer to Section 3. • Replace the seals.
Red, brown, yellow and white colored coatings on the insulator. Engine misses intermittently under severe operating conditions.	• By-products of combustion.	• Clean, regap, and reinstall. If heavily coated, replace.
Colored coatings heavily deposited on the portion of the plug projecting into the chamber and on the side facing the intake valve.	• Leaking seals if condition is found in only one or two cylinders.	• Check the seals. Replace if necessary. Clean, regap, and reinstall the plugs.
Shiny yellow glaze coating on the insulator.	• Melted by-products of combustion.	• Avoid sudden acceleration with wide-open throttle after long periods of low speed driving. Replace the plugs.
Burned or blistered insulator tips and badly eroded electrodes.	• Overheating.	• Check the cooling system. • Check for sticking heat riser valves. Refer to Section 1. • Lean air-fuel mixture. • Check the heat range of the plugs. May be too hot. • Check ignition timing. May be over-advanced. • Check the torque value of the plugs to ensure good plug-engine seat contact.
Broken or cracked insulator tips.	• Heat shock from sudden rise in tip temperature under severe operating conditions. Improper gapping of plugs.	• Replace the plugs. Gap correctly.

gap. The spark plug in no way produces a spark but merely provides a gap across which the current can arc. The coil produces anywhere from 20,000 to 40,000 volts which travels to the distributor where it is distributed through the spark plug wires to the spark plugs. The current passes along the center electrode and jumps the gap to the side electrode, and, in do doing, ignites the air/fuel mixture in the combustion chamber.

SPARK PLUG HEAT RANGE

Spark plug heat range is the ability of the plug to dissipate heat. The longer the insulator (or the farther it extends into the engine), the hotter the plug will operate; the shorter the insulator the cooler it will operate. A plug that absorbs little heat and remains too cool will quickly accumulate deposits of oil and carbon since it is not hot enough to burn them off. This leads to plug fouling and consequently to misfiring. A plug that absorbs too much heat will have no deposits, but, due to the excessive heat, the electrodes will burn away quickly and in some instances, preignition may result. Preignition takes place when plug tips get so hot that they glow sufficiently to ignite the fuel/air mixture before the actual spark occurs. This early ignition will usually cause a pinging during low speeds and heavy loads.

TUNE-UP SPECIFICATIONS
Diesel Engines

Years	Engine No. Cyl. Liters	Static Timing	Dynamic Timing	Nozzle Opening Pressure (psi)	Curb Idle Speed (rpm)	Fast Idle Speed (rpm)	Maximum Compression Pressure (psi)
1989–91	8-7.3	Index	①	1,850	650–700	850–900	440

Static timing is set by aligning the index mark on the pump mounting flange with the index mark on the pump mounting adapter.

① Cetane rating of 38–42: Up to 3,000 ft.—6° ATDC ± 1° Over 3,000 ft.—7° ATDC ± 1°

Cetane rating of 43–46: Up to 3,000 ft.—5° ATDC ± 1° Over 3,000 ft.—6° ATDC ± 1°

Cetane rating of 47–50: Up to 3,000 ft.—4° ATDC ± 1° Over 3,000 ft.—5° ATDC ± 1°

TUNE-UP SPECIFICATIONS
Gasoline Engines

Years	Engine No. Cyl. Liters	Spark Plugs Type	Gap (in.)	Distributor Point Gap (in.)	Dwell (deg.)	Ignition timing (deg.) Man. Trans.	Auto. Trans.	Valve Clearance In.	Exh.	Idle Speed Man. Trans.	Auto. Trans.
1989–91	6-4.9	BSF-44C	0.044	Electronic		①	①	Hyd.	Hyd.	①	①
	8-5.0	ASF-42C	0.044	Electronic		①	①	Hyd.	Hyd.	①	①
	8-5.8	ASF-32C	0.044	Electronic		①	①	Hyd.	Hyd.	①	①
	8-7.5	ASF-42C	0.044	Electronic		①	①	Hyd.	Hyd.	①	①

① See underhood sticker

The general rule of thumb for choosing the correct heat range when picking a spark plug is: if most of your driving is long distance, high speed travel, use a colder plug; if most of your driving is stop and go, use a hotter plug. Original equipment plugs are compromise plugs, but most people never have occasion to change their plugs from the factory-recommended heat range.

REPLACING SPARK PLUGS

A set of spark plugs usually requires replacement after about 20,000 to 30,000 miles, depending on your style of driving. In normal operation, plug gap increases about 0.001 in. (0.025mm) for every 1,000–2,500 miles. As the gap increases, the plug's voltage requirement also increases. It requires a greater voltage to jump the wider gap and about two to three times as much voltage to fire a plug at high speeds than at idle.

When you're removing spark plugs, you should work on one at a time. Don't start by removing the plug wires all at once, because unless you number them, they may become mixed up. Take a minute before you begin and number the wires with tape. The best location for numbering is near where the wires come out of the cap.

NOTE: Apply a small amount of silicone dielectric compound (D7AZ-19A331-A or the equivalent) to the inside of the terminal boots whenever an ignition wire is disconnected from the plug, or coil/distributor cap connection.

1. Twist the spark plug boot and remove the boot and wire from the plug. Do not pull on the wire itself as this will ruin the wire.

2. If possible, use a brush or gag to clean the area around the spark plug. Make sure that all the dirt is removed so that none will enter the cylinder after the plug is removed.

3. Remove the spark plug using the proper size socket. Truck models use either a ⅝ in. or ¹³⁄₁₆ in. size socket depending on the engine. Turn the socket counterclockwise to remove the plug.

Be sure to hold the socket straight on the plug to avoid breaking the plug, or rounding off the hex on the plug.

4. Once the plug is out, check it against the plugs shown in the Color section to determine engine condition. This is crucial since plug readings are vital signs of engine condition.

5. Use a round wire feeler gauge to check the plug gap. The correct size gauge should pass through the electrode gap with a slight drag. If you're in doubt, try one size smaller and one larger. The smaller gauge should go through easily while the larger one shouldn't go through at all. If the gap is incorrect, use the electrode bending tool on the end of the gauge to adjust the gap. When adjusting the gap, always bend the side electrode. The center electrode is non-adjustable.

6. Squirt a drop of penetrating oil on the threads of the new plug and install it. Don't oil the threads too heavily. Turn the plug in clockwise by hand until it is snug.

7. When the plug is finger tight, tighten it with a wrench. If you don't have a torque wrench, tighten the plug as shown.

8. Install the plug boot firmly over the plug. Proceed to the next plug.

CHECKING AND REPLACING SPARK PLUG CABLES

Visually inspect the spark plug cables for burns, cuts, or breaks in the insulation. Check the spark plug boots and the nipples on the distributor cap and coil. Replace any damaged wiring. If no physical damage is obvious, the wires can be checked with an ohmmeter for excessive resistance. (See the tune-up and troubleshooting section.)

When installing a new set of spark plug cables, replace the cables on at a time so there will be no mixup. Start by replacing the longest cable first. Install the boot firmly over the spark plug. Route the wire exactly the same as the original. Insert the nipple firmly into the tower on the distributor cap. Repeat the process for each cable.

FIRING ORDERS

To avoid confusion, replace spark plug wires one at a time.

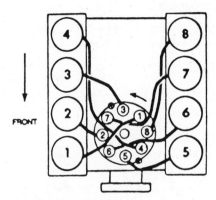

351 (5.8L) V8 engine
Firing order: 1-3-7-2-6-5-4-8
Distributor rotation: clockwise

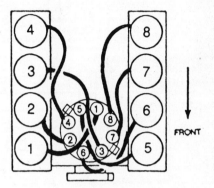

302 (5.0L) and 460 (7.5L) V8 engines
Firing order: 1-5-4-2-6-3-7-8
Distributor rotation: clockwise

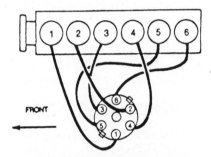

300 (4.9L) 6 cylinder engine
Firing order: 1-5-3-6-2-4
Distributor rotation: clockwise

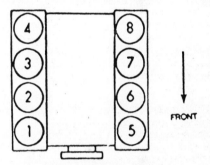

445 (7.3L) Diesel engines
Firing order: 1-2-7-3-4-5-6-8

ELECTRONIC IGNITION SYSTEMS

TFI-IV System

SYSTEM OPERATION

The TFI-IV ignition system features a universal distributor using no centrifugal or vacuum advance. The distributor has a die cast base which incorporates an integrally mounted TFI (Thick Film Integrated) ignition module, a "Hall Effect" vane switch stator assembly and provision for fixed octane adjust-

ment. The TFI system uses an E-Core ignition coil. No distributor calibration is required and initial timing is not a normal adjustment, since advance etc. is controlled by the EEC-IV system.

GENERAL TESTING

Ignition Coil Test

The ignition coil must be diagnosed separately from the rest of the ignition system.

1. Primary resistance is measured between the two primary

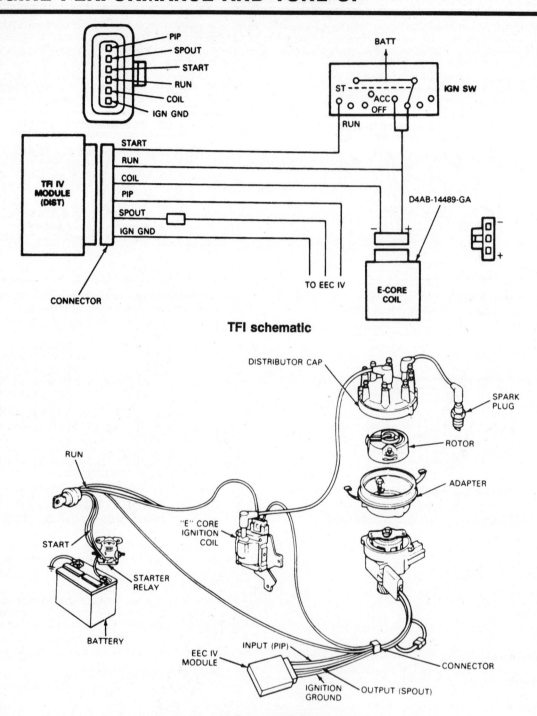

TFI schematic

TFI components

(low voltage) coil terminals, with the coil connector disconnected and the ignition switch off. Primary resistance should be 0.3–1.0Ω.

2. The secondary resistance is measured between the BATT and high voltage (secondary) terminals of the ignition coil with the ignition off, and the wiring from the coil disconnected. Secondary resistance must be 8,000–11,500Ω.

3. If resistance tests are okay, but the coil is still suspected, test the coil on a coil tester by following the test equipment manufacturer's instructions for a standard coil. If the reading differs from the original test, check for a defective harness.

Spark Plug Wire Resistance

Resistance on these wires must not exceed 5,000Ω per foot. To properly measure this, remove the wires from the plugs, and remove the distributor cap. Measure the resistance through the distributor cap at that end. Do not pierce any ignition wire for any reason. Measure only from the two ends.

NOTE: Silicone grease must be re-applied to the spark plug wires whenever they are removed. When removing the wires from the spark plugs, a special tool should be used. do not pull on the wires. Grasp and twist the boot

to remove the wire. Whenever the high tension wires are removed from the plugs, coil, or distributor, silicone grease must be applied to the boot before reconnection. Use a clean small screwdriver blade to coat the entire interior surface with Ford silicone grease D7AZ–19A331–A, Dow Corning #111, or General Electric G–627.

Adjustments

The air gap between the armature and magnetic pick-up coil in the distributor is not adjustable, nor are there any adjustment for the amplifier module. Inoperative components are simply replaced. Any attempt to connect components outside the vehicle may result in component failure.

TROUBLESHOOTING THE TFI-IV SYSTEM

NOTE: After performing any test which requires piercing a wire with a straight pin, remove the straight pin and seal the holes in the wire with silicone sealer.

Ignition Coil Secondary Voltage

1. Disconnect the secondary (high voltage) coil wire from the distributor cap and install a spark tester between the coil wire and ground.
2. Crank the engine. A good, strong spark should be noted at the spark tester. If spark is noted, but the engine will not start, check the spark plugs, spark plug wiring, and fuel system. If there is no spark at the tester: Check the ignition coil secondary wire resistance; it should be no more than $5,000\Omega$ per foot. Inspect the ignition coil for damage and/or carbon tracking. With the distributor cap removed, verify that the distributor shaft turns with the engine; if it does not, repair the engine as required. If the fault was not found proceed to the next test.

Ignition Coil Primary Circuit Switching

1. Insert a small straight pin in the wire which runs from the coil negative (–) terminal to the TFI module, about 1 in. (25mm) from the module.

WARNING: The pin must not touch ground!

2. Connect a 12 VDC test lamp between the straight pin and an engine ground.
3. Crank the engine, noting the operation of the test lamp. If the test lamp flashes, proceed to the next test. If the test lamp lights but does not flash, proceed to the Wiring Harness test. If the test lamp does not light at all, proceed to the Primary Circuit Continuity test.

Ignition Coil Resistance

Refer to the General Testing for an explanation of the resistance tests. Replace the ignition coil if the resistance is out of the specification range.

Wiring Harness

1. Disconnect the wiring harness connector from the TFI module; the connector tabs must be PUSHED to disengage the connector. Inspect the connector for damage, dirt, and corrosion.
2. Attach the negative lead of a voltmeter to the base of the distributor. Attach the other voltmeter lead to a small straight pin. With the ignition switch in the RUN position, insert the straight pin into the No. 1 terminal of the TFI module connector. Note the voltage reading. With the ignition switch in the RUN position, move the straight pin to the No. 2 connector terminal. Again, note the voltage reading. Move the straight pin to the No. 3 connector terminal, then turn the ignition switch to the START position. Note the voltage reading then turn the ignition OFF.

3. The voltage readings should all be at least 90% of the available battery voltage. If the readings are okay, proceed to the Stator Assembly and Module test. If any reading is less than 90% of the battery voltage, inspect the wiring, connectors, and/or ignition switch for defects. if the voltage is low only at the No. 1 terminal, proceed to the ignition coil primary voltage test.

Stator Assembly and Module

1. Remove the distributor from the engine.
2. Remove the TFI module from the distributor.
3. Inspect the distributor terminals, ground screw, and stator wiring for damage. Repair as necessary.
4. Measure the resistance of the stator assembly, using an ohmmeter. If the ohmmeter reading is $800–975\Omega$, the stator is okay, but the TFI module must be replaced. If the ohmmeter reading is less than 800Ω or more than 975Ω; the TFI module is okay, but the stator module must be replaced.
5. Repair as necessary and install the TFI module and the distributor.

TFI Module

1. Remove the distributor cap from the distributor, and set it aside (spark plug wires intact).
2. Disconnect the TFI harness connector.
3. Remove the distributor.
4. Remove the two TFI module retaining screws.
5. To disengage the modules terminals from the distributor base connector, pull the right side of the module down the distributor mounting flange and then back up. Carefully pull the module toward the flange and away from the distributor.

WARNING: Step 5 must be followed EXACTLY; failure to do so will result in damage to the distributor module connector pins.

6. Coat the TFI module baseplate with a thin layer of silicone grease (FD7AZ–19A331–A or its equivalent).
7. Place the TFI module on the distributor base mounting flange. Position the module assembly toward the distributor bowl and carefully engage the distributor connector pins. Install and torque the two TFI module retaining screws to 9–16 inch lbs.
8. Install the distributor assembly.
9. Install the distributor cap and check the engine timing.

Primary Circuit Continuity

This test is performed in the same manner as the previous Wiring Harness test, but only the No. 1 terminal conductor is tested (ignition switch in Run position). If the voltage is less than 90% of the available battery voltage, proceed to the coil primary voltage test.

Ignition Coil Primary Voltage

1. Attach the negative lead of a voltmeter to the distributor base.
2. Turn the ignition switch ON and connect the positive voltmeter lead to the negative (–) ignition coil terminal. Note the voltage reading and turn the ignition OFF. If the voltmeter reading is less than 90% of the available battery voltage, inspect the wiring between the ignition module and the negative (–) coil terminal, then proceed to the last test, which follows.

Ignition Coil Supply Voltage

1. Attach the negative lead of a voltmeter to the distributor base.
2. Turn the ignition switch ON and connect the positive voltmeter lead to the positive (+) ignition coil terminal. Note the voltage reading then turn the ignition OFF. If the voltage reading is at least 90% of the battery voltage, yet the engine will still

not run; first, check the ignition coil connector and terminals for corrosion, dirt, and/or damage; second, replace the ignition switch if the connectors and terminal are okay.

3. Connect any remaining wiring.

IGNITION TIMING ADJUSTMENT

With the TFI-IV system no ignition timing adjustment is possible and none should be attempted.

IDLE SPEED ADJUSTMENT

Gasoline Engines

These engines have idle speed controlled by the TFI-IV/EEC-IV system and no adjustment is possible.

7.3L V8 Diesel

CURB IDLE ADJUSTMENT

1. Place the transmission in neutral or park.
2. Bring the engine up to normal operating temperature.
3. Idle speed is measured with manual transmission in neutral and automatic transmission in Drive with the wheels blocked and parking brake ON.
4. Check the curb idle speed, using a magnetic pickup tachometer suitable for diesel engines. The part number of the Ford tachometer is Rotunda 99–0001. Adjust the idle speed to 600–700 rpm.

NOTE: Always check the underhood emissions control information sticker for the latest idle and adjustment specifications.

5. Place the transmission in neutral or park and momentarily speed up the engine. Allow the rpm to drop to idle and recheck the idle speed. Readjust if necessary.

FAST IDLE ADJUSTMENT

1. Place the transmission in neutral or park.
2. Start the engine and bring up to normal operating temperatures.

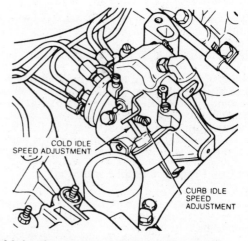

Diesel injection pump showing idle speed adjustment. Pump is mounted on top (front) of the intake manifold

3. Disconnect the wire from the fast idle solenoid.
4. Apply battery voltage to activate the solenoid plunger.
5. Speed up the engine momentarily to set the plunger.
6. The fast idle should be between 850–900 rpm. Adjust the fast idle by turning the solenoid plunger in or out.
7. Speed up the engine momentarily and recheck the fast idle. Readjust if necessary.
8. Remove the battery voltage from the solenoid and reconnect the solenoid wire.

VALVE LASH

Valve adjustment determines how far the valves enter the cylinder and how long they stay open and closed.

If the valve clearance is too large, part of the lift of the camshaft will be used in removing the excessive clearance. Consequently, the valve will not be opening as far as it should. This condition has two effects: the valve train components will emit a tapping sound as they take up the excessive clearance and the engine will perform poorly because the valves don't open fully and allow the proper amount of gases to flow into and out of the engine.

If the valve clearance is too small, the intake valve and the exhaust valves will open too far and they will not fully seal on the cylinder head when they close. When a valve seats itself on the cylinder head, it does two things: it seals the combustion chamber so that none of the gases in the cylinder escape and it cools itself by transferring some of the heat it absorbs from the combustion in the cylinder to the cylinder head and to the engine's cooling system. If the valve clearance is too small, the engine will run poorly because of the gases escaping from the combustion chamber. The valves will also become overheated and will warp, since they cannot transfer heat unless they are touching the valve seat in the cylinder head.

NOTE: While all valve adjustments must be made as accurately as possible, it is better to have the valve adjustment slightly loose than slightly tight as a burned valve may result from overly tight adjustments.

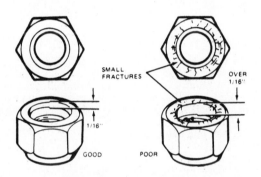

Checking the rotor stud nut

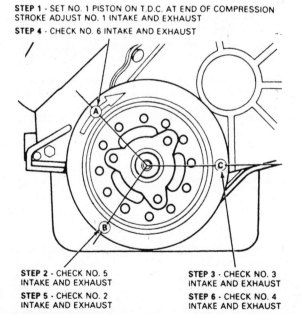

6-4.9L engine hydraulic valve clearance adjustment

ADJUSTMENT

6-4.9L Engine

1. Rotate the crankshaft by hand so that No.1 piston is at TDC of the compression stroke. Make a chalk mark on the damper at that point, then, make 2 more chalk marks about 120° apart, dividing the damper into 3 equal parts. See the accompanying illustration.

2. With No.1 at TDC, tighten the rocker arm bolts on No.1 cylinder intake and exhaust to 17–23 ft. lbs. Then, slowly apply pressure, using Lifter Bleed-down wrench T70P-6513-A, or equivalent, to completely bottom the lifter. Take care to avoid excessive pressure that might bend the pushrod. Hold the lifter in this position and check the clearance between the rocker arm and the valve stem tip. Allowable clearance is 2.5–5.0mm (0.10–0.20 in.) with a desired clearance of 3.0–4.5mm (0.125–0.175 in.).

3. If the clearance is less than specified, install a shorter pushrod. If the clearance is greater than specified, install a longer pushrod.

4. Rotate the crankshaft clockwise — viewed from the front — until the next chalk mark is aligned with the timing pointer. Repeat the procedure for No.5 intake and exhaust.

5. Rotate the crankshaft to the next chalk mark and repeat the procedure for No.3 intake and exhaust.

6. Repeat the rotation/checking procedure for the remaining valves in firing order, that is: 6–2–4.

8-5.0L Engine

1. Rotate the crankshaft by hand so that No.1 piston is at TDC of the compression stroke. Make a chalk mark on the damper at that point, then, make 2 more chalk marks about 90° apart in a clockwise direction. See the accompanying illustration.

2. With No.1 at TDC, slowly apply pressure, using Lifter Bleed-down wrench T70P-6513-A, or equivalent, to completely bottom the lifter, on the following valves:
- No.1 intake and exhaust
- No.7 intake

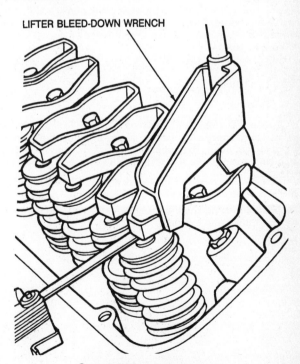

Special bleed-down tool

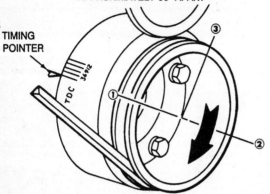

WITH NO. 1 AT TDC AT THE END OF THE COMPRESSION STROKE, MAKE CHALK MARKS AT POINTS 2 AND 3, APPROXIMATELY 90° APART

TIMING POINTER

Marking the damper on the 8-5.0L and 8-5.8L engines

- No.5 exhaust
- No.8 intake
- No.4 exhaust

Take care to avoid excessive pressure that might bend the pushrod. Hold the lifter in this position and check the clearance between the rocker arm and the valve stem tip. Allowable clearance is 1.8–4.9mm (0.071–0.193 in.) with a desired clearance of 2.4–4.2mm (0.096–0.165 in.).

3. If the clearance is less than specified, install a shorter pushrod. If the clearance is greater than specified, install a longer pushrod.

4. Rotate the crankshaft clockwise — viewed from the front — 180°, until the next chalk mark is aligned with the timing pointer. Repeat the procedure for:
- No.5 intake
- No.2 exhaust
- No.4 intake
- No.6 exhaust

5. Rotate the crankshaft to the next chalk mark — 90° — and repeat the procedure for:
- No.2 intake
- No.7 exhaust
- No.3 intake and exhaust
- No.6 intake
- No.8 exhaust

8-5.8L Engine

1. Rotate the crankshaft by hand so that No.1 piston is at TDC of the compression stroke. Make a chalk mark on the damper at that point, then, make 2 more chalk marks about 90° apart in a clockwise direction. See the accompanying illustration.

2. With No.1 at TDC, slowly apply pressure, using Lifter Bleed-down wrench T70P-6513-A, or equivalent, to completely bottom the lifter, on the following valves:
- No.1 intake and exhaust

- No.4 intake
- No.3 exhaust
- No.8 intake
- No.7 exhaust

Take care to avoid excessive pressure that might bend the pushrod. Hold the lifter in this position and check the clearance between the rocker arm and the valve stem tip. Allowable clearance is 2.5–5.0mm (0.098–0.198 in.) with a desired clearance of 3.1–4.4mm (0.123–0.173 in.).

3. If the clearance is less than specified, install a shorter pushrod. If the clearance is greater than specified, install a longer pushrod.

4. Rotate the crankshaft clockwise — viewed from the front — 180°, until the next chalk mark is aligned with the timing pointer. Repeat the procedure for:
- No.3 intake
- No.2 exhaust
- No.7 intake
- No.6 exhaust

5. Rotate the crankshaft to the next chalk mark — 90° — and repeat the procedure for:
- No.2 intake
- No.4 exhaust
- No.5 intake and exhaust
- No.6 intake
- No.8 exhaust

8-7.5L Engine

1. Rotate the crankshaft by hand so that No.1 piston is at TDC of the compression stroke. Make a chalk mark on the damper at that point. See the accompanying illustration.

2. With No.1 at TDC, slowly apply pressure, using Lifter Bleed-down wrench T70P-6513-A, or equivalent, to completely bottom the lifter, on the following valves:
- No.1 intake and exhaust
- No.3 intake
- No.4 exhaust
- No.7 intake
- No.5 exhaust
- No.8 intake and exhaust

Take care to avoid excessive pressure that might bend the pushrod. Hold the lifter in this position and check the clearance between the rocker arm and the valve stem tip. Allowable clearance is 1.9–4.4mm (0.075–0.175 in.) with a desired clearance of 2.5–3.8mm (0.100-0.150 in.).

3. If the clearance is less than specified, install a shorter pushrod. If the clearance is greater than specified, install a longer pushrod.

4. Rotate the crankshaft clockwise — viewed from the front — 360°, until the chalk mark is once again aligned with the timing pointer. Repeat the procedure for:
- No.2 intake and exhaust
- No.4 intake
- No.3 exhaust
- No.5 intake
- No.7 exhaust
- No.6 intake and exhaust

CHILTON'S THREE "C's"
DIESEL ENGINE DIAGNOSIS PROCEDURE

Condition	Cause	Correction
Rough Idle	Improper adjustment	Adjust idle
	Accelerator control cable binding	Repair or lubricate
	Air or water in the fuel system	Clear air or water from fuel system
	Injection nozzle clogged	Check and clean injector nozzles
	Injection pump malfunction	Check injection pump
Poor Performance	Air cleaner clogged	Check element
	Accelerator control cable binding	Check control cable for free movement
	Restricted fuel flow (water or air)	Check lines and filter
	Incorrect injection timing	Check injection timing
	Injection nozzle clogged	Check and clean injector nozzles
	Injection pump malfunction	Replace injection pump
Excessive Exhaust Smoke	Restricted air cleaner	Check element
	Air or water in fuel filter	Remove air or water from fuel system
	Improper grade fuel	Check fuel in tank
	Incorrect injection timing	Check injection timing
	Injection pump malfunction	Replace injection pump
	Injection nozzle stuck open	Check injector nozzles
Excessive Fuel Consumption	Restricted air cleaner	Check element
	Leak in fuel lines	Check for leaks
	Incorrect idle speed	Check idle
	Restricted exhaust system	Check exhaust
	Improper grade of fuel	Check fuel in tank
	Injection pump malfunction	Check injection pump operation
Loud Knocking in Engine	Defective fuel injector	Replace fuel injector

NOTE: If the problem persists after performing these preliminary checks, disassembly and inspection of internal engine components may be necessary for further diagnosis.

Typical Thick Film Integrated (TFI) Ignition System and Closed Bowl Distributor

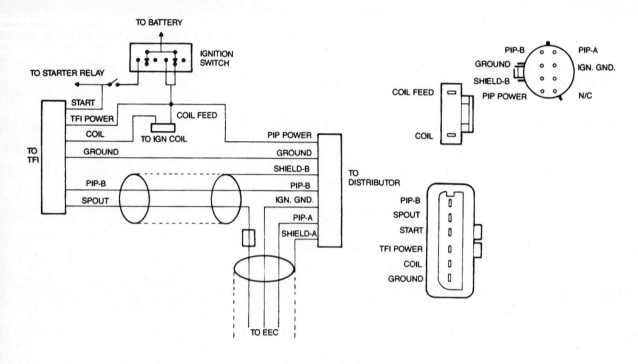

Typical Thick Film Integrated (TFI) Ignition System with Open Bowl Distributor

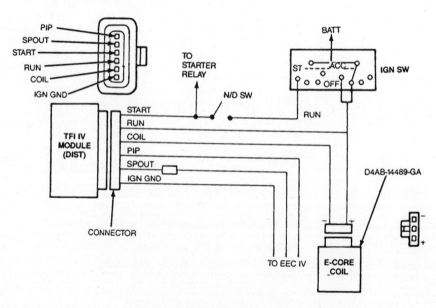

Engine and Engine Overhaul

3

GENERAL ENGINE SPECIFICATIONS

Engine No. Cyl. Liters	Years	Fuel System Type	SAE net Horsepower @ rpm	SAE net Torque ft. lbs. @ rpm	Bore × Stroke (in.)	Comp. Ratio	Oil Pres. (psi.) @ 2000 rpm
6-4.9	1989–91	EFI	150 @ 3,400	265 @ 2,000	4.00 × 3.98	8.8:1	40–60
8-5.0	1989–91	EFI	185 @ 3,800	270 @ 2,400	4.00 × 3.00	9.0:1	40–60
8-5.8W	1989–91	EFI	210 @ 3,800	315 @ 2,800	4.00 × 3.50	8.8:1	40–60
8-7.3	1989–91	Diesel	180 @ 3,300	345 @ 1,400	4.11 × 4.18	21.5:1	40–70
8-7.5	1989–91	EFI	245 @ 4,000	380 @ 2,800	4.36 × 3.85	8.5:1	40–65

EFI: Electronic fuel injection

VALVE SPECIFICATIONS

Engines No. Cyl. Liters	Years	Seat Angle (deg)	Face Angle (deg)	Spring Test Pressure (lbs. @ in.)	Spring Installed Height (in.)	Stem-to-Guide Clearance (in.) Intake	Exhaust	Stem Diameter (in.) Intake	Exhaust
6-4.9	1989–91	45	44	①	②	0.0010–0.0027	0.0010–0.0027	0.3416–0.3423	0.3416–0.3423
8-5.0	1989–91	45	44	③	④	0.0010–0.0027	0.0015–0.0032	0.3416–0.3423	0.3411–0.3418
8-5.8W	1989–91	45	44	200 @ 1.20	⑤	0.0010–0.0027	0.0015–0.0032	0.3416–0.3423	0.3411–0.3418
8-7.3	1989–91	⑥	⑥	80 @ 1.833	⑦	0.0055	0.0055	0.3717–0.3724	0.3717–0.3724
8-7.5	1989–91	45	44	229 @ 1.330	1.813	0.0010–0.0027	0.0010–0.0027	0.3415–0.3423	0.3415–0.3423

① Intake: 166–184 @ 1.240
Exhaust: 166–184 @ 1.070
② Intake: 1.640
Exhaust: 1.470
③ Intake: 196–212 @ 1.360
Exhaust: 190–210 @ 1.200
④ Intake: 1.78
Exhaust: 1.60
⑤ Intake: 1.782
Exhaust: 1.594
⑥ Intake: 30
Exhaust: 37.5
⑦ Intake: 1.767
Exhaust: 1.833

CAMSHAFT SPECIFICATIONS

(All specifications in inches)

Engine No. Cyl. Liters	Journal Diameter 1	2	3	4	5	Bearing Clearance	Lobe Lift Int.	Exh.	End Play
6-4.9	2.0175	2.0175	2.0175	2.0175	—	0.0020	0.2490 ①	0.2490 ①	0.004
8-5.0	2.0810	2.0660	2.0510	2.0360	2.0210	0.0020	0.2375	0.2474	0.004
8-5.8W	2.0810	2.0660	2.0510	2.0360	2.0210	0.0020	0.2780	0.2830	0.004
8-7.3	2.0995	2.0995	2.0995	2.0995	2.0995	0.0025	0.2535	0.2530	0.005
8-7.5	2.1243	2.1243	2.1243	2.1243	2.1243	0.0020	0.2520	0.2780	0.004

① E-150 w/2.47:1 or 2.75:1 axle & man. trans.
49S: 0.2470

CRANKSHAFT AND CONNECTING ROD SPECIFICATIONS

(All specifications in inches)

Engines No. Cyl. Liters	Years	Crankshaft Main Bearing Journal Dia.	Main Bearing Oil Clearance	Shaft End Play	Thrust on No.	Connecting Rod Journal Dia.	Oil Clearance	Side Clearance
6-4.9	1989–91	2.3982–2.3990	0.0008–0.0015	0.004–0.008	5	2.1228–2.1236	0.0008–0.0015	0.0060–0.0130

CRANKSHAFT AND CONNECTING ROD SPECIFICATIONS

(All specifications in inches)

Engines No. Cyl. Liters	Years	Crankshaft					Connecting Rod		
		Main Bearing Journal Dia.	Main Bearing Oil Clearance	Shaft End Play	Thrust on No.		Journal Dia.	Oil Clearance	Side Clearance
8-5.0	**1989-91**	2.2482–2.2490	①	0.004–0.008	3		2.1228–2.1236	0.0008–0.0015	0.0100–0.0200
8-5.8W	**1989-91**	2.9994–3.0002	①	0.004–0.008	3		2.3103–2.3111	0.0008–0.0015	0.0100–0.0200
8-7.3	**1989-91**	3.1228–3.1236	0.0018–0.0036	0.0020–② 0.0090	3		2.4980–2.4990	0.0011–0.0036	0.0120–0.0240
8-7.5	**1989-91**	2.9994–3.0002	0.0008–0.0015	0.004–0.008	3		2.4992–2.5000	0.0008–0.0015	0.0100–0.0200

① #1: 0.0001–0.0015
All others: 0.0005–0.0015
② 1991: 0.0025–0.0085

PISTON AND RING SPECIFICATIONS

(All specifications in inches)

Engines No. Cyl. Liters	Years	Ring Gap		Ring Side Clearance			Oil Control	Piston-to-Bore Clearance
		#1 Compr.	#2 Compr.	Oil Control	#1 Compr.	#2 Compr.		
6-4.9	**1989-91**	0.0100–0.0200	0.0100–0.0200	0.015–0.055	0.0019–0.0036	0.0020–0.0040	snug	0.0010–0.0018
8-5.0	**1989-91**	0.0100–0.0200	0.0100–0.0200	0.015–0.055	0.0013–0.0033	0.0020–0.0040	snug	0.0013–② 0.0030
8-5.8W	**1989-91**	0.0100–0.0200	0.0100–0.0200	0.015–0.055	0.0013–③ 0.0033	0.0020–0.0040	snug	0.0018–0.0026
8-7.3	**1989-91**	0.0130–0.0450	0.0600–0.0850	0.0100–0.0240	0.0020–0.0040	0.0020–0.0040	0.0010–0.0030	①
8-7.5	**1989-91**	0.0100–0.0200	0.0100–0.0200	0.010–0.035	0.0025–0.0045	0.0025–0.0045	snug	0.0022–0.0030

① Nos. 1–6: 0.0055–0.0085
Nos. 7, 8: 0.0060–0.0085
② 1991: 0.0014–0.0022
③ 1991: 0.0020–0.0040

TORQUE SPECIFICATIONS

(All specifications in ft. lb.)

Engine Liters	Years	Cyl. Head	Conn. Rod	Main Bearing	Crankshaft Damper	Flywheel	Manifold	
							Intake	Exhaust
6-4.9	**1989-91**	①	40–45	60–70	130–150	75–85	22–32	22–32
8-5.0	**1989-91**	②	19–24	60–70	70–90	75–85	23–25	18–24
8-5.8W	**1989-91**	③	40–45	95–105	70–90	75–85	23–25	18–24
8-7.3	**1989-91**	⑧	④	⑤	90	44–50	⑥	⑦
8-7.5	**1989-91**	⑪	45–50 ⑫	95–105	70–90	75–85	⑩	⑨

① Step 1: 50–55 ft. lb.
Step 2: 60–65 ft. lb.
Step 3: 70–85 ft. lb.
② Step 1: 55–65 ft. lb.
Step 2: 65–72 ft. lb.
③ Step 1: 85 ft. lb.
Step 2: 95 ft. lb.
Step 3: 105–112 ft. lb.
④ Step 1: 38 ft. lb.
Step 2: 48–53 ft. lb.

⑤ Step 1: 75 ft. lb.
Step 2: 95 ft. lb.
⑥ Step 1: Tighten to 24 ft. lb.
Step 2: Run engine to normal operating temperature
Step 3: Retorque to 24 ft. lb. hot
⑦ Step 1: Tighten to 35 ft. lb.
Step 2: Run engine to normal operating temperature
Step 3: Retorque to 35 ft. lb. hot
⑧ Step 1: 65 ft. lb.

Step 2: 90 ft. lb.
Step 3: 100 ft. lb.
⑨ 1988–90: 22–30
1991: 22–45
⑩ Step 1: 8–12 ft. lb.
Step 2: 12–22 ft. lb.
Step 3: 22–35 ft. lb.
⑪ Step 1: 70–80 ft. lb.
Step 2: 100–110 ft. lb.
Step 3: 130–140 ft. lb.
⑫ 1991: 41–45

ENGINE ELECTRICAL

Understanding the Engine Electrical System

The engine electrical system can be broken down into three separate and distinct systems:
1. The starting system.
2. The charging system.
3. The ignition system.

BATTERY AND STARTING SYSTEM

Basic Operating Principles

The battery is the first link in the chain of mechanisms which work together to provide cranking of the automobile engine. In most modern vans, the battery is a lead/acid electrochemical device consisting of six 2v subsections connected in series so the unit is capable of producing approximately 12v of electrical pressure. Each subsection, or cell, consists of a series of positive and negative plates held a short distance apart in a solution of sulfuric acid and water. The two types of plates are of dissimilar metals. This causes a chemical reaction to be set up, and it is this reaction which produces current flow from the battery when its positive and negative terminals are connected to an electrical appliance such as a lamp or motor. The continued transfer of electrons would eventually convert the sulfuric acid in the electrolyte to water, and make the two plates identical in chemical composition. As electrical energy is removed from the battery, its voltage output tends to drop. Thus, measuring battery voltage and battery electrolyte composition are two ways of checking the ability of the unit to supply power. During the starting of the engine, electrical energy is removed from the battery. However, if the charging circuit is in good condition and the operating conditions are normal, the power removed from the battery will be replaced by the generator (or alternator) which will force electrons back through the battery, reversing the normal flow, and restoring the battery to its original chemical state.

The battery and starting motor are linked by very heavy electrical cables designed to minimize resistance to the flow of current. Generally, the major power supply cable that leaves the battery goes directly to the starter, while other electrical system needs are supplied by a smaller cable. During starter operation, power flows from the battery to the starter and is grounded through the van's frame and the battery's negative ground strap.

The starting motor is a specially designed, direct current electric motor capable of producing a very great amount of power for its size. One thing that allows the motor to produce a great deal of power is its tremendous rotating speed. It drives the engine through a tiny pinion gear (attached to the starter's armature), which drives the very large flywheel ring gear at a greatly reduced speed. Another factor allowing it to produce so much power is that only intermittent operation is required of it. This, little allowance for air circulation is required, and the windings can be built into a very small space.

The starter solenoid is a magnetic device which employs the small current supplied by the starting switch circuit of the ignition switch. This magnetic action moves a plunger which mechanically engages the starter and electrically closes the heavy switch which connects it to the battery. The starting switch circuit consists of the starting switch contained within the ignition switch, a transmission neutral safety switch or clutch pedal switch, and the wiring necessary to connect these in series with the starter solenoid or relay.

A pinion, which is a small gear, is mounted to a one-way drive clutch. This clutch is splined to the starter armature shaft. When the ignition switch is moved to the **start** position, the solenoid plunger slides the pinion toward the flywheel ring gear via a collar and spring. If the teeth on the pinion and flywheel match properly, the pinion will engage the flywheel immediately. If the gear teeth butt one another, the spring will be compressed and will force the gears to mesh as soon as the starter turns far enough to allow them to do so. As the solenoid plunger reaches the end of its travel, it closes the contacts that connect the battery and starter and then the engine is cranked.

As soon as the engine starts, the flywheel ring gear begins turning fast enough to drive the pinion at an extremely high rate of speed. At this point, the one-way clutch begins allowing the pinion to spin faster than the starter shaft so that the starter will not operate at excessive speed. When the ignition switch is released from the starter position, the solenoid is de-energized, and a spring contained within the solenoid assembly pulls the gear out of mesh and interrupts the current flow to the starter.

Some starter employ a separate relay, mounted away from the starter, to switch the motor and solenoid current on and off. The relay thus replaces the solenoid electrical switch, buy does not eliminate the need for a solenoid mounted on the starter used to mechanically engage the starter drive gears. The relay is used to reduce the amount of current the starting switch must carry.

THE CHARGING SYSTEM

Basic Operating Principles

The automobile charging system provides electrical power for operation of the vehicle's ignition and starting systems and all the electrical accessories. The battery services as an electrical surge or storage tank, storing (in chemical form) the energy originally produced by the engine driven generator. The system also provides a means of regulating generator output to protect the battery from being overcharged and to avoid excessive voltage to the accessories.

The storage battery is a chemical device incorporating parallel lead plates in a tank containing a sulfuric acid/water solution. Adjacent plates are slightly dissimilar, and the chemical reaction of the two dissimilar plates produces electrical energy when the battery is connected to a load such as the starter motor. The chemical reaction is reversible, so that when the generator is producing a voltage (electrical pressure) greater than that produced by the battery, electricity is forced into the battery, and the battery is returned to its fully charged state.

The vehicle's generator is driven mechanically, through V-belts, by the engine crankshaft. It consists of two coils of fine wire, one stationary (the stator), and one movable (the rotor). The rotor may also be known as the armature, and consists of fine wire wrapped around an iron core which is mounted on a shaft. The electricity which flows through the two coils of wire (provided initially by the battery in some cases) creates an intense magnetic field around both rotor and stator, and the interaction between the two fields creates voltage, allowing the generator to power the accessories and charge the battery.

There are two types of generators: the earlier is the direct current (DC) type. The current produced by the DC generator is generated in the armature and carried off the spinning armature by stationary brushes contacting the commutator. The commutator is a series of smooth metal contact plates on the end of the armature. The commutator is a series of smooth metal contact plates on the end of the armature. The commutator plates, which are separated from one another by a very short gap, are connected to the armature circuits so that current will flow in one directions only in the wires carrying the generator output. The generator stator consists of two stationary coils of wire which draw some of the output current of the generator to form a powerful magnetic field and create the interaction of fields which generates the voltage. The generator field is wired in series with the regulator.

Newer automobiles use alternating current generators or alternators, because they are more efficient, can be rotated at higher speeds, and have fewer brush problems. In an alternator, the field rotates while all the current produced passes only through the stator winding. The brushes bear against continuous slip rings rather than a commutator. This causes the current produced to periodically reverse the direction of its flow. Diodes (electrical one-way switches) block the flow of current from traveling in the wrong direction. A series of diodes is wired together to permit the alternating flow of the stator to be converted to a pulsating, but unidirectional flow at the alternator output. The alternator's field is wired in series with the voltage regulator.

The regulator consists of several circuits. Each circuit has a core, or magnetic coil of wire, which operates a switch. Each switch is connected to ground through one or more resistors. The coil of wire responds directly to system voltage. When the voltage reaches the required level, the magnetic field created by the winding of wire closes the switch and inserts a resistance into the generator field circuit, thus reducing the output. The contacts of the switch cycle open and close many times each second to precisely control voltage.

While alternators are self-limiting as far as maximum current is concerned, DC generators employ a current regulating circuit which responds directly to the total amount of current flowing through the generator circuit rather than to the output voltage. The current regulator is similar to the voltage regulator except that all system current must flow through the energizing coil on its way to the various accessories.

Ignition Coil

REMOVAL AND INSTALLATION

1. Disconnect the battery ground.
2. Disconnect the two small and one large wires from the coil.
3. Disconnect the condenser connector from the coil, if equipped.
4. Unbolt and remove the coil.
5. Installation is the reverse of removal.

Ignition Module

REMOVAL AND INSTALLATION

Removing the module, on all models, is a matter of simply removing the fasteners that attach it to the fender or firewall and pulling apart the connectors. When unplugging the connectors, pull them apart with a firm, straight pull. NEVER PRY THEM APART! To pry them will cause damage. When reconnecting them, coat the mating ends with silicone dielectric grease to waterproof the connection. Press the connectors together firmly to overcome any vacuum lock caused by the grease.

NOTE: If the locking tabs weaken or break, don't replace the unit. Just secure the connection with electrical tape or tie straps.

Distributor

REMOVAL

1. Disconnect the primary wiring connector from the distributor.
2. Mark the position of the cap's No.1 terminal on the distributor base.
3. Unclip and remove the cap. Remove the adapter.

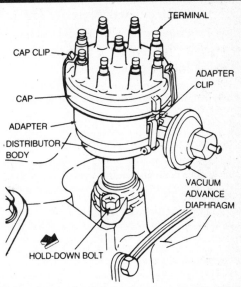

Distributor assembly. Arrow points to front

4. Remove the rotor.
5. Remove the TFI connector.
6. Matchmark the distributor base and engine for installation reference.
7. Remove the holddown bolt and lift out the distributor.

INSTALLATION

1. Rotate the engine so that the No.1 piston is at TDC of the compression stroke.
2. Align the timing marks so that the engine is set at the initial timing shown on the underhood sticker.
3. Install the rotor on the shaft and rotate the shaft so that the rotor tip points to the No.1 mark made on the distributor base.
4. Continue rotating the shaft so that the leading edge of the vane is centered on the vane switch assembly.
5. Position the distributor in the block and rotate the distributor body to align the leading edge of the vane and vane switch. Verify that the rotor tip points to the No.1 mark on the body.

NOTE: If the vane and vane switch cannot be aligned by rotating the distributor body in the engine, pull the distributor out just far enough to disengage the gears and rotate the shaft to engage a different gear tooth. Repeat Steps 3, 4 and 5.

6. Install and finger tighten the holddown bolt.
7. Connect the TFI and primary wiring.
8. Install the rotor, if not already done.

NOTE: Coat the brass portions of the rotor with a $\frac{1}{32}$ in. (0.8mm) thick coating of silicone dielectric compound.

9. Install the cap and adapter (as necessary). Install the wires and start the engine.
10. Check and set the initial timing.
11. Tighten the holddown bolt to 25 ft. lbs.

Alternator

IDENTIFICATION

There are 2 different types of alternators found on the year and model range covered in this book. They are:

Ford Side Terminal, Internal Regulator Alternator

This unit is standard equipment. The regulator in integrated within the alternator body and is not adjustable.

Leece-Neville 165 Ampere

This unit is optional equipment on some 1989–91 vans. A separate, electronic, fully adjustable regulator is employed in this system.

OPERATION

The alternator charging system is a negative (–) ground system which consists of an alternator, a regulator, a charge indicator, a storage battery and wiring connecting the components, and fuse link wire.

The alternator is belt-driven from the engine. Energy is supplied from the alternator/regulator system to the rotating field through two brushes to two slip-rings. The slip-rings are mounted on the rotor shaft and are connected to the field coil. This energy supplied to the rotating field from the battery is called excitation current and is used to initially energize the field to begin the generation of electricity. Once the alternator starts to generate electricity, the excitation current comes from its own output rather than the battery.

The alternator produces power in the form of alternating current. The alternating current is rectified by 6 diodes into direct current. The direct current is used to charge the battery and power the rest of the electrical system.

When the ignition key is turned on, current flows from the battery, through the charging system indicator light on the instrument panel, to the voltage regulator, and to the alternator. Since the alternator is not producing any current, the alternator warning light comes on. When the engine is started, the alternator begins to produce current and turns the alternator light off. As the alternator turns and produces current, the current is divided in two ways: part to the battery to charge the battery and power the electrical components of the vehicle, and part is returned to the alternator to enable it to increase its output. In this situation, the alternator is receiving current from the battery and from itself. A voltage regulator is wired into the current supply to the alternator to prevent it from receiving too much current which would cause it to put out too much current. Conversely, if the voltage regulator does not allow the alternator to receive enough current, the battery will not be fully charged and will eventually go dead.

The battery is connected to the alternator at all times, whether the ignition key is turned on or not. If the battery were shorted to ground, the alternator would also be shorted. This would damage the alternator. To prevent this, a fuse link is installed in the wiring between the battery and the alternator. If the battery is shorted, the fuse link is melted, protecting the alternator.

ALTERNATOR PRECAUTIONS

To prevent damage to the alternator and regulator, the following precautions should be taken when working with the electrical system.
1. Never reverse the battery connections.
2. Booster batteries for starting must be connected properly: positive-to-positive and negative-to-ground.
3. Disconnect the battery cables before using a fast charger; the charger has a tendency to force current through the diodes in the opposite direction for which they were designed. This burns out the diodes.
4. Never use a fast charger as a booster for starting the vehicle.
5. Never disconnect the voltage regulator while the engine is running.
6. Avoid long soldering times when replacing diodes or transistors. Prolonged heat is damaging to AC generators.
7. Do not use test lamps of more than 12 volts (V) for checking diode continuity.
8. Do not short across or ground any of the terminals on the AC generator.
9. The polarity of the battery, generator, and regulator must be matched and considered before making any electrical connections within the system.
10. Never operate the alternator on an open circuit. make sure that all connections within the circuit are clean and tight.
11. Disconnect the battery terminals when performing any service on the electrical system. This will eliminate the possibility of accidental reversal of polarity.
12. Disconnect the battery ground cable if arc welding is to be done on any part of the car.

CHARGING SYSTEM TROUBLESHOOTING

There are many possible ways in which the charging system can malfunction. Often the source of a problem is difficult to diagnose, requiring special equipment and a good deal of experi-

Troubleshooting Basic Charging System Problems

Problem	Cause	Solution
Noisy alternator	• Loose mountings • Loose drive pulley • Worn bearings • Brush noise • Internal circuits shorted (High pitched whine)	• Tighten mounting bolts • Tighten pulley • Replace alternator • Replace alternator • Replace alternator
Squeal when starting engine or accelerating	• Glazed or loose belt	• Replace or adjust belt
Indicator light remains on or ammeter indicates discharge (engine running)	• Broken fan belt • Broken or disconnected wires • Internal alternator problems • Defective voltage regulator	• Install belt • Repair or connect wiring • Replace alternator • Replace voltage regulator

Troubleshooting Basic Charging System Problems

Problem	Cause	Solution
Car light bulbs continually burn out— battery needs water continually	• Alternator/regulator overcharging	• Replace voltage regulator/alternator
Car lights flare on acceleration	• Battery low • Internal alternator/regulator problems	• Charge or replace battery • Replace alternator/regulator
Low voltage output (alternator light flickers continually or ammeter needle wanders)	• Loose or worn belt • Dirty or corroded connections • Internal alternator/regulator problems	• Replace or adjust belt • Clean or replace connections • Replace alternator or regulator

ence. This is usually not the case, however, where the charging system fails completely and causes the dash board warning light to come on or the battery to become dead. To troubleshoot a complete system failure only two pieces of equipment are needed: a test light, to determine that current is reaching a certain point; and a current indicator (ammeter), to determine the direction of the current flow and its measurement in amps. This test works under three assumptions:

1. The battery is known to be good and fully charged.

2. The alternator belt is in good condition and adjusted to the proper tension.

3. All connections in the system are clean and tight.

NOTE: In order for the current indicator to give a valid reading, the car must be equipped with battery cables which are of the same gauge size and quality as original equipment battery cables.

1. Turn off all electrical components on the car. Make sure the doors of the car are closed. If the car is equipped with a clock, disconnect the clock by removing the lead wire from the rear of the clock. Disconnect the positive battery cable from the battery and connect the ground wire on a test light to the disconnected positive battery cable. Touch the probe end of the test light to the positive battery post. The test light should not light. If the test light does light, there is a short or open circuit on the car.

2. Disconnect the voltage regulator wiring harness connector at the voltage regulator. Turn on the ignition key. Connect the wire on a test light to a good ground (engine bolt). Touch the probe end of a test light to the ignition wire connector into the voltage regulator wiring connector. This wire corresponds to the **I** terminal on the regulator. If the test light goes on, the charging system warning light circuit is complete. If the test light does not come on and the warning light on the instrument panel is on, either the resistor wire, which is parallel with the warning light, or the wiring to the voltage regulator, is defective. If the test light does not come on and the warning light is not on, either the bulb is defective or the power supply wire form the battery through the ignition switch to the bulb has an open circuit. Connect the wiring harness to the regulator.

3. Examine the fuse link wire in the wiring harness from the starter relay to the alternator. If the insulation on the wire is cracked or split, the fuse link may be melted. Connect a test light to the fuse link by attaching the ground wire on the test light to an engine bolt and touching the probe end of the light to the bottom of the fuse link wire where it splices into the alternator output wire. If the bulb in the test light does not light, the fuse link is melted.

4. Start the engine and place a current indicator on the positive battery cable. Turn off all electrical accessories and make sure the doors are closed. If the charging system is working properly, the gauge will show a draw of less than 5 amps. If the system is not working properly, the gauge will show a draw of more than 5 amps. A charge moves the needle toward the battery, a draw moves the needle away from the battery. Turn the engine off.

5. Disconnect the wiring harness from the voltage regulator at the regulator at the regulator connector. Connect a male spade terminal (solderless connector) to each end of a jumper wire. Insert one end of the wire into the wiring harness connector which corresponds to the **A** terminal on the regulator. Insert the other end of the wire into the wiring harness connector which corresponds to the **F** terminal on the regulator. Position the connector with the jumper wire installed so that it cannot contact any metal surface under the hood. Position a current indicator gauge on the positive battery cable. Have an assistant start the engine. Observe the reading on the current indicator. Have your assistant slowly raise the speed of the engine to about 2,000 rpm or until the current indicator needle stops moving, whichever comes first. Do not run the engine for more than a short period of time in this condition. If the wiring harness connector or jumper wire becomes excessively hot during this test, turn off the engine and check for a grounded wire in the regulator wiring harness. If the current indicator shows a charge of about three amps less than the output of the alternator, the alternator is working properly. If the previous tests showed a draw, the voltage regulator is defective. If the gauge does not show the proper charging rate, the alternator is defective.

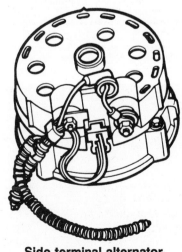

Side terminal alternator

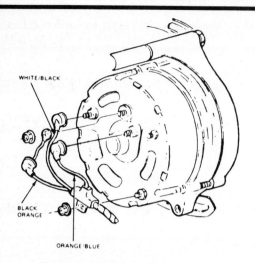

Rear terminal alternator

REMOVAL AND INSTALLATION

1. Open the hood and disconnect the battery ground cable.
2. Remove the adjusting arm bolt.
3. Remove the alternator through-bolt. Remove the drive belt from the alternator pulley and lower the alternator.

NOTE: Some engines are equipped with a ribbed, K-section belt and automatic tensioner. A special tool must be made to remove the tension from the tensioner arm. Loosen the idler pulley pivot and adjuster bolts before using the tool. See the accompanying illustration for tool details.

4. Label all of the leads to the alternator so that you can install them correctly and disconnect the leads from the alternator.
5. Remove the alternator from the vehicle.
6. To install, reverse the above procedure. Observe the following torques:
- Pivot bolt: 58 ft. lbs.
- Adjusting bolt: 25 ft. lbs.
- Wire terminal nuts: 60–90 inch lbs.

BELT TENSION ADJUSTMENT

The fan belt drives the alternator and water pump. if the belt is too loose, it will slip and the alternator will not be able to produce it rated current. Also, the water pump will not operate efficiently and the engine could overheat.

Check the tension of the belt by pushing your thumb down on the longest span of the belt, midway between the pulleys. Belt deflection should be approximately ½ in. (13mm).

To adjust the belt tension, proceed as follows:

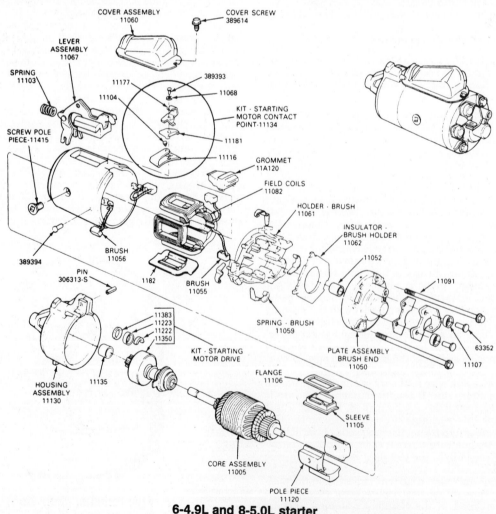

6-4.9L and 8-5.0L starter

1. Loosen the alternator mounting bolt and the adjusting arm bolts.

2. Apply pressure on the alternator front housing only, moving the alternator away from the engine to tighten the belt. Do not apply pressure to the rear of the cast aluminum housing of an alternator; damage to the housing could result.

3. Tighten the alternator mounting bolt and the adjusting arm bolts when the correct tension is reached.

Regulator

REMOVAL AND INSTALLATION

Leece-Neville Alternator

The regulator is mounted on the back of the alternator.
1. Disconnect the diode trio lead from the regulator terminal.
2. Remove the 2 nuts retaining the regulator and the jumper leads.
3. Carefully pull the regulator from its holder.

NOTE: The brushes will snap together when the regulator is removed. They can now be checked for length. Brush length minimum is 4.76mm (0.188 in.).

To install:
4. Push the brushes back into their holders and insert a $\frac{1}{32}$ in. pin. through the hole provided in the housing. This will hold the brushes in place.
5. Carefully push the regulator into place and *just start* the retaining nuts. Remove the brush holding pin and *then* tighten the retaining nuts.
6. Connect the diode trio leads.

Starter Motor

REMOVAL AND INSTALLATION

Except Diesel

1. Disconnect the negative battery cable.
2. Raise the front of the van and install jackstands beneath

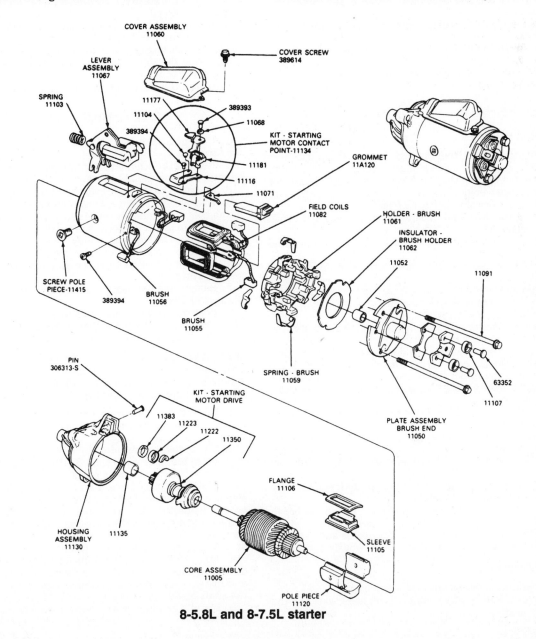

8-5.8L and 8-7.5L starter

the frame. Firmly apply the parking brake and place blocks in back of the rear wheels.

3. Tag and disconnect the wiring at the starter.

4. Turn the front wheels fully to the right. On some later models it will be necessary to remove the frame brace. On many models, it will be necessary to remove the two bolts retaining the steering idler arm to the frame to gain access to the starter.

5. Remove the starter mounting bolts and remove the starter.

6. Reverse the above procedure to install. Observe the following torques:
- Mounting bolts: 12–15 ft. lbs. on starters with 3 mounting bolts and 15–20 ft. lbs. on starters with 2 mounting bolts.
- Idler arm retaining bolts to 28–35 ft. lbs. (if removed).

Make sure that the nut securing the heavy cable to the starter is snugged down tightly.

8-7.3L Diesel

1. Disconnect the battery ground cable.

2. Raise the vehicle and disconnect the cables and wires at the starter solenoid.

3. Turn the front wheels to the right and remove the two bolts attaching the steering idler arm to the frame.

4. Remove the starter mounting bolts and remove the starter.

5. Installation is the reverse of removal. Torque the mounting bolts to 20 ft. lbs.

OVERHAUL — EXCEPT DIESEL

Brush Replacement

1. Remove the starter from the engine as previously outlined.

2. Remove the starter drive plunger lever cover and gasket.

3. Loosen and remove the brush cover band and remove the brushes from their holder.

4. Remove the two through-bolts from the starter frame.

5. Separate the drive end housing, starter frame and brush end plate assemblies.

6. Remove the starter drive plunger lever and pivot pin, and remove the armature.

7. Remove the ground brush retaining screws from the frame and remove the brushes.

8. Cut the insulated brush leads from the field coils, as close to the field connection point as possible.

9. Clean and inspect the starter motor.

10. Replace the brush end plate if the insulator between the field brush holder and the end plate is cracked or broken.

11. Position the new insulated field brushes lead on the field coil connection. Position and crimp the clip provided with the brushes to hold the brush lead to the connection. Solder the lead, clip, and connection together using resin core solder. Use a 300 watt soldering iron.

12. Install the ground brush leads to the frame with the retaining screws.

13. Install the starter drive plunger lever and pivot pin, and install the armature.

14. Assemble the drive end housing, starter frame and brush end plate assemblies.

15. Install the two through-bolts in the starter frame. Torque the through-bolts to 55–75 inch lbs.

16. Install the brushes in their holders and install the brush cover band.

17. Install the starter drive plunger lever cover and gasket.

18. Install the starter on the engine as previously outlined.

Drive Replacement

1. Remove the starter as outlined previously.

2. Remove the starter drive plunger lever and gasket and the brush cover band.

3. Remove the two through-bolts from the starter frame.

4. Separate the drive end housing from the starter frame.

5. The starter drive plunger lever return spring may fall out after detaching the drive end housing. If not, remove it.

6. Remove the pivot pin which attaches the starter drive plunger lever to the starter frame and remove the lever.

7. Remove the stop ring retainer and stop ring from the armature shaft.

8. Slide the starter drive off the armature shaft.

9. Examine the wear pattern on the starter drive teeth. There should be evidence of full contact between the starter drive teeth and the flywheel ring gear teeth. If there is evidence of irregular wear, examine the flywheel ring gear for damage and replace if necessary.

10. Apply a thin coat of white grease to the armature shaft before installing the drive gear. Place a small amount of grease in the drive end housing bearing. Slide the starter drive on the armature shaft.

11. Install the stop ring retainer and stop ring on the armature shaft.

12. Install the starter drive plunger lever on the starter frame and install the pin.

13. Assemble the drive end housing on the starter frame.

14. install the two through-bolts in the starter frame. Tighten the starter through bolts to 55–75 inch lbs.

15. Install the starter drive plunger lever and gasket and the brush cover band.

16. Install the starter as outlined previously.

OVERHAUL — DIESEL

1. Disconnect the field coil connection from the solenoid motor terminal.

2. Remove the solenoid attaching screws, solenoid and plunger return spring. Rotate the solenoid 90° to remove it.

3. Remove the through-bolts and brush end plate.

4. Remove the brush springs and brushes from the plastic brush holder and remove the brush holder. Keep track of the location of the brush holder with regard to the brush terminals.

5. Remove the frame assembly.

6. Remove the armature assembly.

7. Remove the screw from the gear housing and remove the gear housing.

8. Remove the plunger and lever pivot screw and remove the plunger and lever.

9. Remove the gear, output shaft and drive assembly.

10. Remove the thrust washer, retainer, drive stop ring and slide the drive assembly off of the output shaft.

WARNING: Don't wash the drive because the solvent will wash out the lubricant, causing the drive to slip. Use a brush or compressed air to clean the drive, field coils, armature, gear and housing.

11. Inspect the armature windings for broken or burned insulation, and open connections at the commutator. Check for any signs of grounding.

12. Check the commutator for excessive runout. If the commutator is rough or more than 0.127mm out-of-round, replace it or correct the problem as necessary.

13. Check the plastic brush holder for cracks or broken pads. Replace the brushes if worn to a length less than ¼ in. (6mm) in length. Inspect the field coils and plastic bobbins for burned or damaged areas. Check the continuity of the coil and brush connections. A brush replacement kit is available. Any other worn or damaged parts should be replaced.

14. Apply a thin coating of Lubriplate 777®, or equivalent on the output shaft splines. Slide the drive assembly onto the shaft and install a new stopring, retainer and thrust washer. Install the shaft and drive assembly into the drive end housing.

15. Install the plunger and lever assembly making sure that

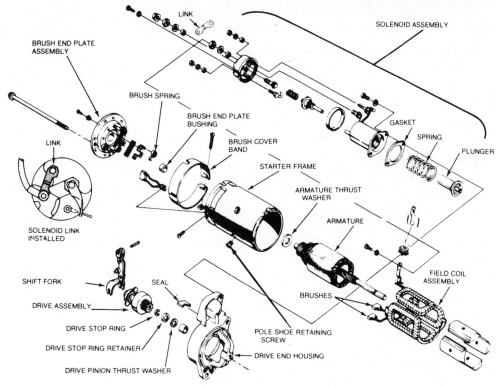

Solenoid actuated type starter

the lever notches engage the flange ears of the starter drive. Attach the lever pin screw and tighten it to 10 ft. lbs.

16. Lubricate the gear and washer. Install the gear and washer on the end of the output shaft.

17. Install the gear housing and tighten the mounting screw to 84 inch lbs.

18. After lubricating the pinion, install the armature and washer on the end of the shaft.

19. Position the grommet around the field lead and press it into the starter frame notch. Install the frame assembly on the gear housing, making sure that the grommet is positioned in the notch in the housing.

20. Install the brush holder on the end of the frame, lining up the notches in the brush holder with the ground brush terminals. The brush holder is symmetrical and can be installed with either notch and brush terminal.

21. Install the brush springs and brushes. The positive brush leads must be placed in their respective slots to prevent grounding.

22. Install the brush endplate, making sure that the insulator is properly positioned. Install and tighten the through-bolts to 84 inch lbs.

NOTE: The brush endplate has a threaded hole in the protruding ear which must be oriented properly so the starter-to-vacuum pump support bracket can be installed.

23. Install the return spring on the solenoid plunger and install the solenoid. Attach the 2 solenoid attaching screws and tighten them to 84 inch lbs. Apply a sealing compound to the junction of the solenoid case flange, gear and drive end housings.

24. Attach the motor field terminal to the **M** terminal of the solenoid, and tighten the fasteners to 30 inch lbs.

25. Check the starter no-load current draw. Maximum draw should be 190 amps.

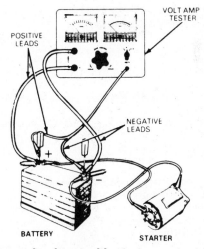

Starter no-load test with starter on test bench

Starter Relay

REMOVAL AND INSTALLATION

Gasoline Engines

1. Disconnect the positive battery cable from the battery terminal. With dual batteries, disconnect the connecting cable at both ends.

2. Remove the nut securing the positive battery cable to the relay.

3. Remove the positive cable and any other wiring under that cable.

Troubleshooting Basic Starting System Problems

Problem	Cause	Solution
Starter motor rotates engine slowly	• Battery charge low or battery defective	• Charge or replace battery
	• Defective circuit between battery and starter motor	• Clean and tighten, or replace cables
	• Low load current	• Bench-test starter motor. Inspect for worn brushes and weak brush springs.
	• High load current	• Bench-test starter motor. Check engine for friction, drag or coolant in cylinders. Check ring gear-to-pinion gear clearance.
Starter motor will not rotate engine	• Battery charge low or battery defective	• Charge or replace battery
	• Faulty solenoid	• Check solenoid ground. Repair or replace as necessary.
	• Damage drive pinion gear or ring gear	• Replace damaged gear(s)
	• Starter motor engagement weak	• Bench-test starter motor
	• Starter motor rotates slowly with high load current	• Inspect drive yoke pull-down and point gap, check for worn end bushings, check ring gear clearance
	• Engine seized	• Repair engine
Starter motor drive will not engage (solenoid known to be good)	• Defective contact point assembly	• Repair or replace contact point assembly
	• Inadequate contact point assembly ground	• Repair connection at ground screw
	• Defective hold-in coil	• Replace field winding assembly
Starter motor drive will not disengage	• Starter motor loose on flywheel housing	• Tighten mounting bolts
	• Worn drive end busing	• Replace bushing
	• Damaged ring gear teeth	• Replace ring gear or driveplate
	• Drive yoke return spring broken or missing	• Replace spring
Starter motor drive disengages prematurely	• Weak drive assembly thrust spring	• Replace drive mechanism
	• Hold-in coil defective	• Replace field winding assembly
Low load current	• Worn brushes	• Replace brushes
	• Weak brush springs	• Replace springs

4. Tag and remove the push-on wires from the front of the relay.

5. Remove the nut and disconnect the cable from the starter side of the relay.

6. Remove the relay attaching bolts and remove the relay.

7. Installation is the reverse of removal.

Battery

REMOVAL AND INSTALLATION

1. Loosen the nuts which secure the cable ends to the battery terminals. Lift the negative battery cables from the terminals first with a twisting motion, then the positive cables.

If there is a battery cable puller available, make use of it.

WARNING: On vehicles with dual batteries, take great care to avoid ground the disconnected end of the positive cable linking the two batteries, before the other end is disconnected.

2. Remove the holddown nuts from the battery holddown bracket and remove the bracket and the battery. Lift the battery straight up and out of the vehicle, being sure to keep the battery level to avoid spilling the battery acid.

3. Before installing the battery in the vehicle, make sure that the battery terminals are clean and free from corrosion. Use a battery terminal cleaner on the terminals and on the inside of the battery cable ends. If a cleaner is not available, use coarse grade sandpaper to remove the corrosion. A mixture of baking soda and water poured over the terminals and cable ends will help remove and neutralize any acid buildup.

WARNING: Take great care to avoid getting any of the baking soda solution inside the battery. If any solution gets inside the battery a violent reaction will take place and/or the battery will be damaged.

4. Before installing the cables onto the terminals, cut a piece of felt cloth, or something similar into a circle about 3 in. (76mm) across. Cut a hole in the middle about the size of the battery terminals at their base. Push the cloth pieces over the terminals so that they lay flat on the top of the battery. Soak the pieces of cloth with oil. This will keep oxidation to a minimum.

5. Place the battery in the vehicle. Install the cables onto the terminals.

WARNING: On vehicles with dual batteries, take great care to avoid grounding the disconnected end of the positive cable linking the two batteries, after the other end is connected.

6. Tighten the nuts on the cable ends.

NOTE: See Section 1 for battery maintenance illustrations.

7. Smear a light coating of grease on the cable ends and tops of the terminals. This will further prevent the buildup of oxidation on the terminals and the cable ends.

8. Install and tighten the nuts of the battery holddown bracket.

Troubleshooting Engine Mechanical Problems

Problem	Cause	Solution
External oil leaks	• Fuel pump gasket broken or improperly seated	• Replace gasket
	• Cylinder head cover RTV sealant broken or improperly seated	• Replace sealant; inspect cylinder head cover sealant flange and cylinder head sealant surface for distortion and cracks
	• Oil filler cap leaking or missing	• Replace cap
External oil leaks	• Oil filter gasket broken or improperly seated	• Replace oil filter
	• Oil pan side gasket broken, improperly seated or opening in RTV sealant	• Replace gasket or repair opening in sealant; inspect oil pan gasket flange for distortion
	• Oil pan front oil seal broken or improperly seated	• Replace seal; inspect timing case cover and oil pan seal flange for distortion
	• Oil pan rear oil seal broken or improperly seated	• Replace seal; inspect oil pan rear oil seal flange; inspect rear main bearing cap for cracks, plugged oil return channels, or distortion in seal groove
	• Timing case cover oil seal broken or improperly seated	• Replace seal
	• Excess oil pressure because of restricted PCV valve	• Replace PCV valve
	• Oil pan drain plug loose or has stripped threads	• Repair as necessary and tighten
	• Rear oil gallery plug loose	• Use appropriate sealant on gallery plug and tighten
	• Rear camshaft plug loose or improperly seated	• Seat camshaft plug or replace and seal, as necessary
	• Distributor base gasket damaged	• Replace gasket

Troubleshooting Engine Mechanical Problems (cont.)

Problem	Cause	Solution
Excessive oil consumption	• Oil level too high	• Drain oil to specified level
	• Oil with wrong viscosity being used	• Replace with specified oil
	• PCV valve stuck closed	• Replace PCV valve
	• Valve stem oil deflectors (or seals) are damaged, missing, or incorrect type	• Replace valve stem oil deflectors
	• Valve stems or valve guides worn	• Measure stem-to-guide clearance and repair as necessary
	• Poorly fitted or missing valve cover baffles	• Replace valve cover
	• Piston rings broken or missing	• Replace broken or missing rings
	• Scuffed piston	• Replace piston
	• Incorrect piston ring gap	• Measure ring gap, repair as necessary
	• Piston rings sticking or excessively loose in grooves	• Measure ring side clearance, repair as necessary
	• Compression rings installed upside down	• Repair as necessary
	• Cylinder walls worn, scored, or glazed	• Repair as necessary
	• Piston ring gaps not properly staggered	• Repair as necessary
	• Excessive main or connecting rod bearing clearance	• Measure bearing clearance, repair as necessary
No oil pressure	• Low oil level	• Add oil to correct level
	• Oil pressure gauge, warning lamp or sending unit inaccurate	• Replace oil pressure gauge or warning lamp
	• Oil pump malfunction	• Replace oil pump
	• Oil pressure relief valve sticking	• Remove and inspect oil pressure relief valve assembly
	• Oil passages on pressure side of pump obstructed	• Inspect oil passages for obstruction
	• Oil pickup screen or tube obstructed	• Inspect oil pickup for obstruction
	• Loose oil inlet tube	• Tighten or seal inlet tube
Low oil pressure	• Low oil level	• Add oil to correct level
	• Inaccurate gauge, warning lamp or sending unit	• Replace oil pressure gauge or warning lamp
	• Oil excessively thin because of dilution, poor quality, or improper grade	• Drain and refill crankcase with recommended oil
	• Excessive oil temperature	• Correct cause of overheating engine
	• Oil pressure relief spring weak or sticking	• Remove and inspect oil pressure relief valve assembly
	• Oil inlet tube and screen assembly has restriction or air leak	• Remove and inspect oil inlet tube and screen assembly. (Fill inlet tube with lacquer thinner to locate leaks.)
	• Excessive oil pump clearance	• Measure clearances
	• Excessive main, rod, or camshaft bearing clearance	• Measure bearing clearances, repair as necessary

Troubleshooting Engine Mechanical Problems (cont.)

Problem	Cause	Solution
Connecting rod bearing noise	• Insufficient oil supply	• Inspect for low oil level and low oil pressure
	• Carbon build-up on piston	• Remove carbon from piston crown
	• Bearing clearance excessive or bearing missing	• Measure clearance, repair as necessary
	• Crankshaft connecting rod journal out-of-round	• Measure journal dimensions, repair or replace as necessary
	• Misaligned connecting rod or cap	• Repair as necessary
	• Connecting rod bolts tightened improperly	• Tighten bolts with specified torque
Piston noise	• Piston-to-cylinder wall clearance excessive (scuffed piston)	• Measure clearance and examine piston
	• Cylinder walls excessively tapered or out-of-round	• Measure cylinder wall dimensions, rebore cylinder
	• Piston ring broken	• Replace all rings on piston
	• Loose or seized piston pin	• Measure piston-to-pin clearance, repair as necessary
	• Connecting rods misaligned	• Measure rod alignment, straighten or replace
	• Piston ring side clearance excessively loose or tight	• Measure ring side clearance, repair as necessary
	• Carbon build-up on piston is excessive	• Remove carbon from piston
Valve actuating component noise	• Insufficient oil supply	• Check for: (a) Low oil level (b) Low oil pressure (c) Plugged push rods (d) Wrong hydraulic tappets (e) Restricted oil gallery (f) Excessive tappet to bore clearance
	• Push rods worn or bent	• Replace worn or bent push rods
	• Rocker arms or pivots worn	• Replace worn rocker arms or pivots
	• Foreign objects or chips in hydraulic tappets	• Clean tappets
	• Excessive tappet leak-down	• Replace valve tappet
	• Tappet face worn	• Replace tappet; inspect corresponding cam lobe for wear
	• Broken or cocked valve springs	• Properly seat cocked springs; replace broken springs
	• Stem-to-guide clearance excessive	• Measure stem-to-guide clearance, repair as required
	• Valve bent	• Replace valve
	• Loose rocker arms	• Tighten bolts with specified torque
	• Valve seat runout excessive	• Regrind valve seat/valves
	• Missing valve lock	• Install valve lock
	• Push rod rubbing or contacting cylinder head	• Remove cylinder head and remove obstruction in head
	• Excessive engine oil (four-cylinder engine)	• Correct oil level

Troubleshooting Engine Mechanical Problems (cont.)

Problem	Cause	Solution
High oil pressure	• Improper oil viscosity	• Drain and refill crankcase with correct viscosity oil
	• Oil pressure gauge or sending unit inaccurate	• Replace oil pressure gauge
	• Oil pressure relief valve sticking closed	• Remove and inspect oil pressure relief valve assembly
Main bearing noise	• Insufficient oil supply	• Inspect for low oil level and low oil pressure
	• Main bearing clearance excessive	• Measure main bearing clearance, repair as necessary
	• Bearing insert missing	• Replace missing insert
	• Crankshaft end play excessive	• Measure end play, repair as necessary
	• Improperly tightened main bearing cap bolts	• Tighten bolts with specified torque
	• Loose flywheel or drive plate	• Tighten flywheel or drive plate attaching bolts
	• Loose or damaged vibration damper	• Repair as necessary

Troubleshooting the Cooling System

Problem	Cause	Solution
High temperature gauge indication— overheating	• Coolant level low	• Replenish coolant
	• Fan belt loose	• Adjust fan belt tension
	• Radiator hose(s) collapsed	• Replace hose(s)
	• Radiator airflow blocked	• Remove restriction (bug screen, fog lamps, etc.)
	• Faulty radiator cap	• Replace radiator cap
	• Ignition timing incorrect	• Adjust ignition timing
	• Idle speed low	• Adjust idle speed
	• Air trapped in cooling system	• Purge air
	• Heavy traffic driving	• Operate at fast idle in neutral intermittently to cool engine
	• Incorrect cooling system component(s) installed	• Install proper component(s)
	• Faulty thermostat	• Replace thermostat
	• Water pump shaft broken or impeller loose	• Replace water pump
	• Radiator tubes clogged	• Flush radiator
	• Cooling system clogged	• Flush system
	• Casting flash in cooling passages	• Repair or replace as necessary. Flash may be visible by removing cooling system components or removing core plugs.
	• Brakes dragging	• Repair brakes
	• Excessive engine friction	• Repair engine
	• Antifreeze concentration over 68%	• Lower antifreeze concentration percentage

Troubleshooting the Cooling System (cont.)

Problem	Cause	Solution
High temperature gauge indication— overheating	• Missing air seals • Faulty gauge or sending unit • Loss of coolant flow caused by leakage or foaming • Viscous fan drive failed	• Replace air seals • Repair or replace faulty component • Repair or replace leaking component, replace coolant • Replace unit
Low temperature indication— undercooling	• Thermostat stuck open • Faulty gauge or sending unit	• Replace thermostat • Repair or replace faulty component
Coolant loss—boilover	• Overfilled cooling system • Quick shutdown after hard (hot) run • Air in system resulting in occasional "burping" of coolant • Insufficient antifreeze allowing coolant boiling point to be too low • Antifreeze deteriorated because of age or contamination • Leaks due to loose hose clamps, loose nuts, bolts, drain plugs, faulty hoses, or defective radiator • Faulty head gasket • Cracked head, manifold, or block • Faulty radiator cap	• Reduce coolant level to proper specification • Allow engine to run at fast idle prior to shutdown • Purge system • Add antifreeze to raise boiling point • Replace coolant • Pressure test system to locate source of leak(s) then repair as necessary • Replace head gasket • Replace as necessary • Replace cap
Coolant entry into crankcase or cylinder(s)	• Faulty head gasket • Crack in head, manifold or block	• Replace head gasket • Replace as necessary
Coolant recovery system inoperative	• Coolant level low • Leak in system • Pressure cap not tight or seal missing, or leaking • Pressure cap defective • Overflow tube clogged or leaking • Recovery bottle vent restricted	• Replenish coolant to FULL mark • Pressure test to isolate leak and repair as necessary • Repair as necessary • Replace cap • Repair as necessary • Remove restriction
Noise	• Fan contacting shroud • Loose water pump impeller • Glazed fan belt • Loose fan belt • Rough surface on drive pulley • Water pump bearing worn • Belt alignment	• Reposition shroud and inspect engine mounts • Replace pump • Apply silicone or replace belt • Adjust fan belt tension • Replace pulley • Remove belt to isolate. Replace pump. • Check pulley alignment. Repair as necessary.

3 ENGINE AND ENGINE OVERHAUL

Troubleshooting the Cooling System

Problem	Cause	Solution
No coolant flow through heater core	• Restricted return inlet in water pump	• Remove restriction
	• Heater hose collapsed or restricted	• Remove restriction or replace hose
	• Restricted heater core	• Remove restriction or replace core
	• Restricted outlet in thermostat housing	• Remove flash or restriction
	• Intake manifold bypass hole in cylinder head restricted	• Remove restriction
	• Faulty heater control valve	• Replace valve
	• Intake manifold coolant passage restricted	• Remove restriction or replace intake manifold

NOTE: *Immediately after shutdown, the engine enters a condition known as heat soak. This is caused by the cooling system being inoperative while engine temperature is still high. If coolant temperature rises above boiling point, expansion and pressure may push some coolant out of the radiator overflow tube. If this does not occur frequently it is considered normal.*

Troubleshooting the Serpentine Drive Belt

Problem	Cause	Solution
Tension sheeting fabric failure (woven fabric on outside circumference of belt has cracked or separated from body of belt)	• Grooved or backside idler pulley diameters are less than minimum recommended	• Replace pulley(s) not conforming to specification
	• Tension sheeting contacting (rubbing) stationary object	• Correct rubbing condition
	• Excessive heat causing woven fabric to age	• Replace belt
	• Tension sheeting splice has fractured	• Replace belt
Noise (objectional squeal, squeak, or rumble is heard or felt while drive belt is in operation)	• Belt slippage	• Adjust belt
	• Bearing noise	• Locate and repair
	• Belt misalignment	• Align belt/pulley(s)
	• Belt-to-pulley mismatch	• Install correct belt
	• Driven component inducing vibration	• Locate defective driven component and repair
	• System resonant frequency inducing vibration	• Vary belt tension within specifications. Replace belt.
Rib chunking (one or more ribs has separated from belt body)	• Foreign objects imbedded in pulley grooves	• Remove foreign objects from pulley grooves
	• Installation damage	• Replace belt
	• Drive loads in excess of design specifications	• Adjust belt tension
	• Insufficient internal belt adhesion	• Replace belt
Rib or belt wear (belt ribs contact bottom of pulley grooves)	• Pulley(s) misaligned	• Align pulley(s)
	• Mismatch of belt and pulley groove widths	• Replace belt
	• Abrasive environment	• Replace belt
	• Rusted pulley(s)	• Clean rust from pulley(s)
	• Sharp or jagged pulley groove tips	• Replace pulley
	• Rubber deteriorated	• Replace belt

Troubleshooting the Serpentine Drive Belt (cont.)

Problem	Cause	Solution
Longitudinal belt cracking (cracks between two ribs)	• Belt has mistracked from pulley groove • Pulley groove tip has worn away rubber-to-tensile member	• Replace belt • Replace belt
Belt slips	• Belt slipping because of insufficient tension • Belt or pulley subjected to substance (belt dressing, oil, ethylene glycol) that has reduced friction • Driven component bearing failure • Belt glazed and hardened from heat and excessive slippage	• Adjust tension • Replace belt and clean pulleys • Replace faulty component bearing • Replace belt
"Groove jumping" (belt does not maintain correct position on pulley, or turns over and/or runs off pulleys)	• Insufficient belt tension • Pulley(s) not within design tolerance • Foreign object(s) in grooves • Excessive belt speed • Pulley misalignment • Belt-to-pulley profile mismatched • Belt cordline is distorted	• Adjust belt tension • Replace pulley(s) • Remove foreign objects from grooves • Avoid excessive engine acceleration • Align pulley(s) • Install correct belt • Replace belt
Belt broken (Note: identify and correct problem before replacement belt is installed)	• Excessive tension • Tensile members damaged during belt installation • Belt turnover • Severe pulley misalignment • Bracket, pulley, or bearing failure	• Replace belt and adjust tension to specification • Replace belt • Replace belt • Align pulley(s) • Replace defective component and belt
Cord edge failure (tensile member exposed at edges of belt or separated from belt body)	• Excessive tension • Drive pulley misalignment • Belt contacting stationary object • Pulley irregularities • Improper pulley construction • Insufficient adhesion between tensile member and rubber matrix	• Adjust belt tension • Align pulley • Correct as necessary • Replace pulley • Replace pulley • Replace belt and adjust tension to specifications
Sporadic rib cracking (multiple cracks in belt ribs at random intervals)	• Ribbed pulley(s) diameter less than minimum specification • Backside bend flat pulley(s) diameter less than minimum • Excessive heat condition causing rubber to harden • Excessive belt thickness • Belt overcured • Excessive tension	• Replace pulley(s) • Replace pulley(s) • Correct heat condition as necessary • Replace belt • Replace belt • Adjust belt tension

ENGINE MECHANICAL

Engine Overhaul Tips

Most engine overhaul procedures are fairly standard. In addition to specific parts replacement procedures and complete specifications for your individual engine, this section also is a guide to accept rebuilding procedures. Examples of standard rebuilding practice are shown and should be used along with specific details concerning your particular engine.

Competent and accurate machine shop services will ensure maximum performance, reliability and engine life.

In most instances it is more profitable for the do-it-yourself mechanic to remove, clean and inspect the component, buy the necessary parts and deliver these to a shop for actual machine work.

On the other hand, much of the rebuilding work (crankshaft, block, bearings, piston rods, and other components) is well within the scope of the do-it-yourself mechanic.

TOOLS

The tools required for an engine overhaul or parts replacement will depend on the depth of your involvement. With a few exceptions, they will be the tools found in a mechanic's tool kit. More in-depth work will require any or all of the following:
- a dial indicator (reading in thousandths) mounted on a universal base
- micrometers and telescope gauges
- jaw and screw-type pullers
- scraper
- valve spring compressor
- ring groove cleaner
- piston ring expander and compressor
- ridge reamer
- cylinder hone or glaze breaker
- Plastigage®
- engine stand

The use of most of these tools is illustrated in this section. Many can be rented for a one-time use from a local parts jobber or tool supply house specializing in automotive work.

Occasionally, the use of special tools is called for. See the information on Special Tools and Safety Notice in the front of this book before substituting another tool.

INSPECTION TECHNIQUES

Procedures and specifications are given in this section for inspecting, cleaning and assessing the wear limits of most major components. Other procedures such as Magnaflux® and Zyglo® can be used to locate material flaws and stress cracks. Magnaflux® is a magnetic process applicable only to ferrous materials. The Zyglo® process coats the material with a fluorescent dye penetrant and can be used on any material Check for suspected surface cracks can be more readily made using spot check dye. The dye is sprayed onto the suspected area, wiped off and the area sprayed with a developer. Cracks will show up brightly.

OVERHAUL TIPS

Aluminum has become extremely popular for use in engines, due to its low weight. Observe the following precautions when handling aluminum parts:
- Never hot tank aluminum parts (the caustic hot tank solution will eat the aluminum.
- Remove all aluminum parts (identification tag, etc.) from engine parts prior to the tanking.
- Always coat threads lightly with engine oil or anti-seize compounds before installation, to prevent seizure.

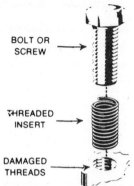

Thread repair insert kits can restore damaged threads

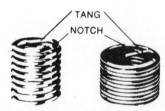

Damaged bolt holes can be repaired with Standard thread repair insert (left) and spark plug thread insert (right)

Drill out the damaged threads with the specified drill bit. Drill completely through the hole or to the bottom of the blind hole

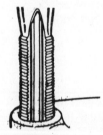

With the tap supplied, tap the hole to receive the insert. Keep the tap well oiled and back it out frequently to avoid clogging he threads

- Never overtorque bolts or spark plugs especially in aluminum threads.

Stripped threads in any component can be repaired using any of several commercial repair kits (Heli-Coil®, Microdot®, Keenserts®, etc.).

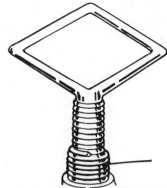

Screw the inert onto the installation tool until the tang engages the slot. Screw the insert into the tapped hole until it is 1/4 to 1/2 turn below the top surface. After installation, break off the tang with a hammer and punch

When assembling the engine, any parts that will be frictional contact must be prelubed to provide lubrication at initial start-up. Any product specifically formulated for this purpose can be used, but engine oil is not recommended as a prelube.

When semi-permanent (locked, but removable) installation of bolts or nuts is desired, threads should be cleaned and coated with Loctite® or other similar, commercial non-hardening sealant.

REPAIRING DAMAGED THREADS

Several methods of repairing damaged threads are available. Heli-Coil® (shown here), Keenserts® and Microdot® are among the most widely used. All involve basically the same principle—drilling out stripped threads, tapping the hole and installing a prewound insert—making welding, plugging and oversize fasteners unnecessary.

Two types of thread repair inserts are usually supplied: a standard type for most Inch Coarse, Inch Fine, Metric Course and Metric Fine thread sizes and a spark lug type to fit most spark plug port sizes. Consult the individual manufacturer's catalog to determine exact applications. Typical thread repair kits will contain a selection of prewound threaded inserts, a tap (corresponding to the outside diameter threads of the insert) and an installation tool. Spark plug inserts usually differ because they require a tap equipped with pilot threads and a combined reamer/tap section. Most manufacturers also supply blister-packed thread repair inserts separately in addition to a master kit containing a variety of taps and inserts plus installation tools.

Before effecting a repair to a threaded hole, remove any snapped, broken or damaged bolts or studs. Penetrating oil can be used to free frozen threads. The offending item can be removed with locking pliers or with a screw or stud extractor. After the hole is clear, the thread can be repaired, as shown in the series of accompanying illustrations.

Checking Engine Compression

A noticeable lack of engine power, excessive oil consumption and/or poor fuel mileage measured over an extended period are all indicators of internal engine war. Worn piston rings, scored or worn cylinder bores, blown head gaskets, sticking or burnt valves and worn valve seats are all possible culprits here. A check of each cylinder's compression will help you locate the problems.

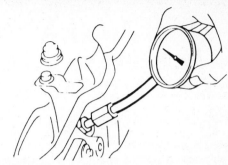

The screw-in type compression gauge is more accurate

As mentioned earlier, a screw-in type compression gauge is more accurate that the type you simply hold against the spark plug hole, although it takes slightly longer to use. It's worth it to obtain a more accurate reading. Follow the procedures below.

Gasoline Engines

1. Warm up the engine to normal operating temperature.
2. Remove all the spark plugs.
3. Disconnect the high tension lead from the ignition coil.
4. On fully open the throttle either by operating the throttle linkage by hand or by having an assistant floor the accelerator pedal.
5. Screw the compression gauge into the no.1 spark plug hole until the fitting is snug.

WARNING: Be careful not to crossthread the plug hole. On aluminum cylinder heads use extra care, as the threads in these heads are easily ruined.

6. Ask an assistant to depress the accelerator pedal fully. Then, while you read the compression gauge, ask the assistant to crank the engine two or three times in short bursts using the ignition switch.
7. Read the compression gauge at the end of each series of cranks, and record the highest of these readings. Repeat this procedure for each of the engine's cylinders. Compare the highest reading to the reading in each cylinder.

A cylinder's compression pressure is usually acceptable if it is not less than 80% of of the highest reading. For example, if the highest reading is 150 psi, the lowest should be no lower than 120 psi.

No cylinder should have a reading below 100 psi.

8. If a cylinder is unusually low, pour a tablespoon of clean engine oil into the cylinder through the spark plug hole and repeat the compression test. If the compression comes up after adding the oil, it appears that the cylinder's piston rings or bore are damaged or worn. If the pressure remains low, the valves may not be seating properly (a valve job is needed), or the head gasket may be blown near that cylinder. If compression in any two adjacent cylinders is low, and if the addition of oil doesn't help the compression, there is leakage past the head gasket. Oil and coolant water in the combustion chamber can result from this problem. There may be evidence of water droplets on the engine dipstick when a head gasket has blown.

Diesel Engines

Checking cylinder compression on diesel engines is basically the same procedure as on gasoline engines except for the following:

1. A special compression gauge adaptor suitable for diesel engines (because these engines have much greater compression pressures) must be used.
2. Remove the injector tubes and remove the injectors from each cylinder.

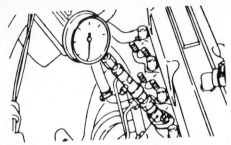

Diesel engines require a special compression gauge adapter

WARNING: Don't forget to remove the washer underneath each injector. Otherwise, it may get lost when the engine is cranked.

3. When fitting the compression gauge adaptor to the cylinder head, make sure the bleeder of the gauge (if equipped) is closed.

4. When reinstalling the injector assemblies, install new washers underneath each injector.

Engine

REMOVAL AND INSTALLATION

WARNING: Disconnect the negative battery cable(s) before beginning any work. Always label all disconnected hoses, vacuum lines and wires, to prevent incorrect reassembly. Do not disconnect any air conditioning lines unless you are thoroughly familiar with air conditioning systems and the hazards involved; escaping refrigerant (Freon®) will freeze any surface it contacts, including skin and eyes. Have the system discharged professionally before required repairs are started.

6–4.9L

1. Drain the cooling system and the crankcase.

─────── CAUTION ───────

When draining the coolant, keep in mind that cats and dogs are attracted by the ethylene glycol antifreeze, and are quite likely to drink any that is left in an uncovered container or in puddles on the ground. This will prove fatal in sufficient quantity. Always drain the coolant into a sealable container. Coolant should be reused unless it is contaminated or several years old.

The EPA warns that prolonged contact with used engine oil may cause a number of skin disorders, including cancer! You should make every effort to minimize your exposure to used engine oil. Protective gloves should be worn when changing the oil. Wash your hands and any other exposed skin areas as soon as possible after exposure to used engine oil. Soap and water, or waterless hand cleaner should be used.

2. Remove the engine cover.
3. Remove the throttle body inlet tubes.
4. Disconnect the positive battery cable.
5. Discharge the air conditioning system. See Section 1.
6. Disconnect the refrigerant lines at the compressor. Cap all openings at once.
7. Remove the compressor.
8. Disconnect the refrigerant lines at the condenser. Cap all openings at once.
9. Remove the condenser.
10. Disconnect the heater hose from the water pump and coolant outlet housing.
11. Disconnect the flexible fuel line from the fuel pump.
12. Remove the radiator.

13. Remove the bumper.
14. Remove the grille.
15. Remove the gravel deflector.
16. Remove the fan, water pump pulley, and fan belt.
17. Disconnect the accelerator cable.
18. Disconnect the brake booster vacuum hose at the intake manifold.
19. On vans with automatic transmission, disconnect the transmission kickdown rod at the bellcrank assembly.
20. Disconnect the exhaust pipe from the exhaust manifold.
21. Disconnect the Electronic Engine Control (EEC) harness from all the sensors.
22. Disconnect the body ground strap and the battery ground cable from the engine.
23. Disconnect the engine wiring harness at the ignition coil, the coolant temperature sending unit, and the oil pressure sensing unit. Position the wiring harness out of the way.
24. Remove the alternator mounting bolts and position the alternator out of the way.
25. Remove the power steering pump from the mounting brackets and move it to one side, leaving the lines attached.
26. Raise and support the van on jackstands.
27. Remove the starter.
28. Remove the automatic transmission filler tube bracket, if so equipped.
29. Remove the rear engine plate upper right bolt.
30. On manual transmission equipped vans:
    a. Remove the flywheel housing lower attaching bolts.
    b. Disconnect the clutch return spring.
31. On automatic transmission equipped vans:
    a. Remove the converter housing access cover assembly.
    b. Remove the flywheel-to-converter attaching nuts.
    c. Secure the converter in the housing.
    d. Remove the transmission oil cooler lines from the retaining clip at the engine.
    e. Remove the lower converter housing-to-engine attaching bolts.
32. Remove the nut from each of the two front engine mounts.
33. Lower the vehicle and position a jack under the transmission and support it.
34. Remove the remaining bellhousing-to-engine attaching bolts.
35. Attach an engine lifting device and raise the engine slightly and carefully pull it from the transmission. Lift the engine out of the vehicle.

To install the engine:
36. Place a new gasket on the muffler inlet pipe.
37. Carefully lower the engine into the van. Make sure that the dowels in the engine block engage the holes in the bellhousing.

38. On manual transmission equipped vans, start the transmission input shaft into the clutch disc. It may be necessary to adjust the position of the engine or transmission in order for the input shaft to enter the clutch disc. If necessary, turn the crankshaft until the input shaft splines mesh with the clutch disc splines.
39. On automatic transmission equipped vans, start the converter pilot into the crankshaft. Secure the converter in the housing.
40. Install the bellhousing upper attaching bolts. Torque the bolts to 50 ft. lbs.
41. Remove the jack supporting the transmission.
42. Remove the lifting device.
43. Install the engine mount nuts and tighten them to 70 ft. lbs.
44. Install the automatic transmission coil cooler lines bracket, if equipped.
45. Install the remaining bellhousing attaching bolts. Torque them to 50 ft. lbs.
46. Connect the clutch return spring, if so equipped.

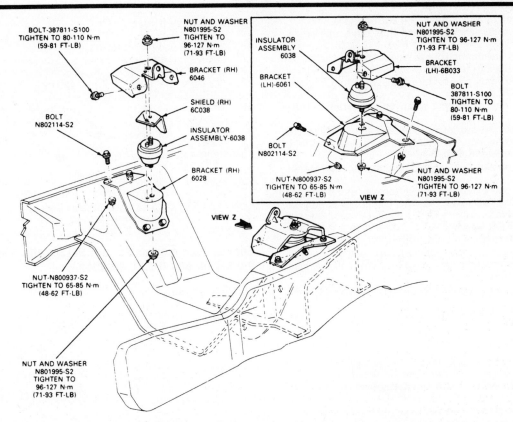

Engine front mounts for the E-150 and E-250 with the 6-4.9L engine

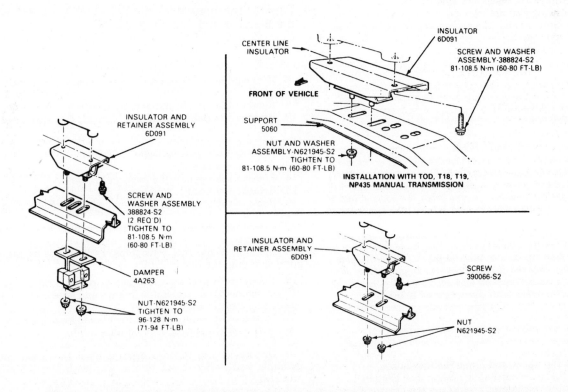

Engine rear mounts for the E-150, 250 and 350 with the 6-4.9L engine

47. Install the starter and connect the starter cable.
48. Attach the automatic transmission fluid filler tube bracket, if so equipped.
49. On vans with automatic transmissions, install the transmission oil cooler lines in the bracket at the cylinder block.
50. Connect the exhaust pipe to the exhaust manifold. Tighten the nuts to 25–35 ft. lbs.
51. Connect the engine ground strap and negative battery cable.
52. On a van with an automatic transmission, connect the kickdown rod to the bellcrank assembly on the intake manifold.
53. Connect the accelerator linkage.
54. Connect the brake booster vacuum line to the intake manifold.
55. Connect the coil primary wire, oil pressure and coolant temperature sending unit wires, fuel line, heater hoses, and the battery positive cable.
56. Connect the EEC sensors.
57. Install the alternator on its mounting bracket.
58. Install the power steering pump on its bracket.
59. Install the water pump pulley, spacer, fan, and fan belt. Adjust the belt tension.
60. Install the air conditioning compressor. Connect the refrigerant lines.
61. Install the gravel deflector.
62. Install the grille.
63. Install the bumper.
64. Install the radiator.
65. Install the condenser and connect the refrigerant lines.
66. Charge the refrigerant system. See Section 1.
67. Connect the upper and lower radiator hoses to the radiator and engine.
68. Connect the automatic transmission oil cooler lines, if so equipped.
69. Install the engien cover.
70. Fill the cooling system.
71. Fill the crankcase.
72. Start the engine and check for leaks.
73. Bleed the cooling system.
74. Adjust the clutch pedal free-play or the automatic transmission control linkage.
75. Install the air cleaner.

8–5.0L
8–5.7L

1. Remove the engine cover.
2. Drain the cooling system and crankcase.

——————— CAUTION ———————
When draining the coolant, keep in mind that cats and dogs are attracted by the ethylene glycol antifreeze, and are quite likely to drink any that is left in an uncovered container or in puddles on the ground. This will prove fatal in sufficient quantity. Always drain the coolant into a sealable container. Coolant should be reused unless it is contaminated or several years old.

The EPA warns that prolonged contact with used engine oil may cause a number of skin disorders, including cancer! You should make every effort to minimize your exposure to used engine oil. Protective gloves should be worn when changing the oil. Wash your hands and any other exposed skin areas as soon as possible after exposure to used engine oil. Soap and water, or waterless hand cleaner should be used.

3. Disconnect the battery and alternator cables.
4. Remove the air intake hoses, PCV tube and carbon canister hose.
5. Disconnect the upper and lower radiator hoses.
6. Discharge the air conditioning system. See Section 1.
7. Disconnect the refrigerant lines at the compressor. Cap all openings immediately.

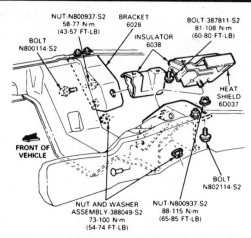

Engine front mounts for the E-150, 250 and 350 with the 8-5.0L and 8-5.8L engines

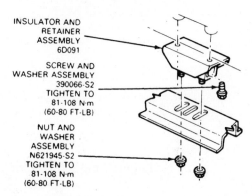

Engine rear mounts for the E-150, 250 and 350 with the 8-5.0L and 8-5.8L engine

8. If so equipped, disconnect the automatic transmission oil cooler lines.
9. Remove the fan shroud and lay it over the fan.
10. Remove the radiator and fan, shroud, fan, spacer, pulley and belt.
11. Remove the grille.
12. Remove the gravel deflector.
13. Remove the bumper.
14. Remove the upper grille support bracket.
15. Remove the hood lock support.
16. Remove the alternator pivot and adjusting bolts. Remove the alternator.
17. Disconnect the oil pressure sending unit lead from the sending unit.
18. Disconnect the fuel tank-to-pump fuel line at the fuel pump and plug the line.
19. Disconnect the chassis fuel line at the fuel rails.
20. Disconnect the accelerator linkage and speed control linkage at the throttle body.
21. Disconnect the automatic transmission kick-down rod and remove the return spring, if so equipped.
22. Disconnect the power brake booster vacuum hose.
23. Disconnect the throttle bracket from the upper intake manifold and swing it out of the way with the cables still attached.
19. Disconnect the heater hoses from the water pump and intake manifold or tee.

24. Disconnect the temperature sending unit wire from the sending unit.
25. Remove the upper bellhousing-to-engine attaching bolts.
26. Remove the wiring harness from the left rocker arm cover and position the wires out of the way.
27. Disconnect the ground strap from the cylinder block.
28. Disconnect the air conditioning compressor clutch wire.
29. Raise the front of the van and disconnect the starter cable from the starter.
30. Remove the starter.
31. Disconnect the exhaust pipe from the exhaust manifolds.
32. Disconnect the engine mounts from the brackets on the frame.
33. On vans with automatic transmissions, remove the converter inspection plate and remove the torque converter-to-flywheel attaching bolts.
34. Remove the remaining bellhousing-to-engine attaching bolts.
35. Lower the vehicle and support the transmission with a jack.
36. Install an engine lifting device.
37. Raise the engine slightly and carefully pull it out of the transmission. Lift the engine out of the engine compartment.

To install:

38. Lower the engine carefully into the transmission. Make sure that the dowel in the engine block engage the holes in the bellhousing through the rear cover plate. If the engine hangs up after the transmission input shaft enters the clutch disc (manual transmission only), turn the crankshaft with the transmission in gear until the input shaft splines mesh with the clutch disc splines.
39. Install the engine mount nuts and washers. Torque the nuts to 80 ft. lbs.
40. Remove the engine lifting device.
41. Install the lower bellhousing-to-engine attaching bolts. Torque the bolts to 50 ft. lbs.
42. Remove the transmission support jack.
43. On vans with automatic transmissions, install the torque converter-to-flywheel attaching bolts. Torque the bolts to 30 ft. lbs.
44. Install the converter inspection plate. Torque the bolts to 60 inch lbs.
45. Connect the exhaust pipe to the exhaust manifolds. Tighten the exhaust pipe-to-exhaust manifold nuts to 25–35 ft. lbs.
46. Install the starter. Torque the mounting bolts to 20 ft. lbs.
47. Connect the starter cable to the starter.
48. Lower the van.
49. Install the upper bellhousing-to-engine attaching bolts. Torque the bolts to 50 ft. lbs.
50. Connect the wiring harness at the left rocker arm cover.
51. Connect the ground strap to the cylinder block.
52. Connect the air conditioning compressor clutch wire.
53. Connect the heater hoses at the water pump and intake manifold or tee.
54. Connect the temperature sending unit wire at the sending unit.
55. Connect the accelerator linkage and speed control linkage at the throttle body.
56. Connect the automatic transmission kick-down rod and install the return spring, if so equipped.
57. Connect the power brake booster vacuum hose.
58. Connect the throttle bracket to the upper intake manifold.
59. Connect the fuel tank-to-pump fuel line at the fuel pump. Disconnect the chassis fuel line at the fuel rails.
60. Connect the oil pressure sending unit lead to the sending unit.
61. Install the alternator.
62. Connect the refrigerant lines to the compressor.
63. Install the hood lock support.
64. Install the upper grille support bracket.

65. Install the bumper.
66. Install the gravel deflector.
67. Install the grille.
68. Install the radiator and fan, shroud, fan, spacer, pulley and belt.
69. Connect the upper and lower radiator hoses, and, if so equipped, the automatic transmission oil cooler lines.
70. Install the air intake hoses, PCV tube and carbon canister hose.
71. Connect the battery and alternator cables.
72. Fill the cooling system and crankcase.
73. Charge the air conditioning system. See Section 1.
74. Install the engine cover.

If the torque for a particular fastener was not mentioned above, use the following torque values as a guide:
- $\frac{1}{4}$ in.–20: 6–9 ft. lbs.
- $\frac{5}{16}$ in.–18: 12–18 ft. lbs.
- $\frac{3}{8}$ in.–16: 22–32 ft. lbs.
- $\frac{7}{16}$ in.–14: 45–57 ft. lbs.
- $\frac{1}{2}$ in.–13: 55–80 ft. lbs.
- $\frac{9}{16}$ in.: 85–120 ft. lbs.

8–7.5L

1. Remove the hood and engine cover.
2. Drain the cooling system.

--- CAUTION ---

When draining the coolant, keep in mind that cats and dogs are attracted by the ethylene glycol antifreeze, and are quite likely to drink any that is left in an uncovered container or in puddles on the ground. This will prove fatal in sufficient quantity. Always drain the coolant into a sealable container. Coolant should be reused unless it is contaminated or several years old.

3. Disconnect the negative battery cable from the block.
4. Remove the air cleaner assembly.
5. Remove the crankcase ventilation hose.
6. Remove the canister hose.
7. Disconnect the upper and lower radiator hoses.
8. Disconnect the transmission oil cooler lines from the radiator.
9. Disconnect the engine oil cooler lines at the oil filter adapter.

WARNING: Don't disconnect the lines at the quick-connect fittings behind or at the oil cooler. Disconnecting them may permanently damage them.

10. Discharge the air conditioning system. See Section 1.
11. Disconnect the refrigerant lines at the compressor. Cap the openings at once!
12. Disconnect the refrigerant lines at the condenser. Cap the openings at once!
13. Remove the condenser.
14. Remove the fan shroud from the radiator and position it up, over the fan.
15. Remove the radiator.
16. Remove the fan shroud.
17. Remove the bumper and grille.
18. Remove the fan, belts and pulley from the water pump.
19. Remove the compressor.
20. Remove the power steering pump from the engine, if so equipped, and position it to one side. Do not disconnect the fluid lines.
21. Disconnect the fuel pump inlet line from the pump and plug the line.
22. Disconnect the oil pressure sending unit wire at the sending unit.
23. Remove the alternator drive belts and disconnect the alternator from the engine, positioning it aside.
24. Disconnect the ground cable from the right front corner of the engine.

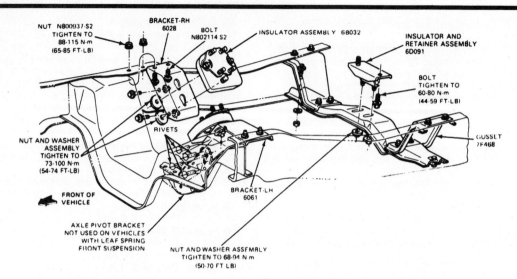

Engine supports for the E-250 and 350 with the 8- 7.5L engine

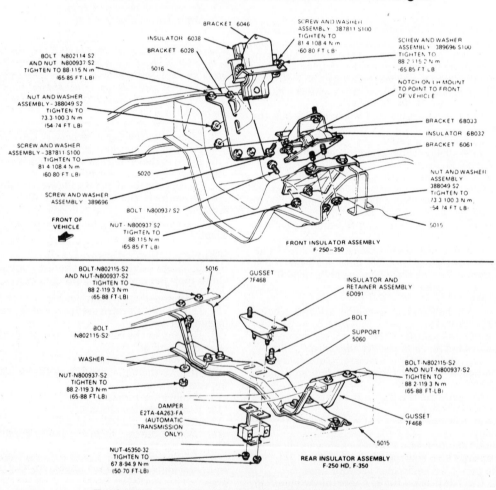

Engine supports for the E-250, 350 with the diesel

25. Disconnect the heater hoses.
26. Remove the transmission fluid filler tube attaching bolt from the right side valve cover and position the tube out of the way.
27. Disconnect all vacuum lines at the rear of the intake manifold.

28. Disconnect the speed control cable, if so equipped.
29. Disconnect the accelerator rod and the transmission kickdown rod and secure them out of the way.
30. Disconnect the engine wiring harness at the connector on the fire wall. Disconnect the primary wire at the coil.
31. Remove the upper flywheel housing-to-engine bolts.

32. Raise the vehicle and disconnect the exhaust pipes at the exhaust manifolds.

33. Disconnect the starter cable and remove the starter. Bring the starter forward and rotate the solenoid outward to remove the assembly.

34. Remove the access cover from the converter housing and remove the flywheel-to-converter attaching nuts.

35. Remove the lower the converter housing-to-engine attaching bolts.

36. Remove the engine mount through bolts attaching the rubber insulator to the frame brackets.

37. Lower the vehicle and place a jack under the transmission to support it.

38. Remove the converter housing-to-engine block attaching bolts (left side).

39. Remove the coil and bracket assembly from the intake manifold.

40. Attach an engine lifting device and carefully take up the weight of the engine.

41. Move the engine forward to disengage it from the transmission and slowly lift it from the van.

To install:

42. Lower the engine slowly into the van.

43. Slide the engine rearward to engage it with the transmission and slowly lower it onto the supports.

44. Install the engine support nuts and torque them to 74 ft. lbs.

45. Remove the engine lifting device.

46. Install the converter housing-to-engine block upper and left side attaching bolts. Torque the bolts to 50 ft. lbs.

47. Install the coil and bracket assembly on the intake manifold.

48. Remove the jack from under the transmission.

49. Lower the van.

50. Install the upper converter housing-to-engine attaching bolts. Torque the bolts to 50 ft. lbs.

51. Install the flywheel-to-converter attaching nuts. Torque the nuts to 34 ft. lbs.

52. Install the access cover on the converter housing. Torque the bolts to 60–90 inch lbs.

53. Install the starter.

54. Connect the starter cable.

55. Raise the vehicle and connect the exhaust pipes at the exhaust manifolds.

56. Connect the engine wiring harness at the connector on the fire wall.

57. Connect the primary wire at the coil.

58. Connect the accelerator rod and the transmission kickdown rod.

59. Connect the speed control cable.

60. Connect all vacuum lines at the rear of the intake manifold.

61. Install the transmission fluid filler tube attaching bolt from the right side valve cover and position the tube out of the way.

62. Connect the heater hoses.

63. Connect the ground cable at the right front corner of the engine.

64. Install the alternator and drive belts.

65. Connect the oil pressure sending unit wire at the sending unit.

66. Connect the fuel pump inlet line at the pump and plug the line.

67. Install the power steering pump and belt.

68. Install air conditioning compressor. Connect the refrigerant lines.

69. Install the fan, belts and pulley on the water pump.

70. Position the fan shroud over the fan.

71. Install the radiator.

72. Attach the fan shroud.

73. Install the condenser.

74. Connect the refrigerant lines at the condenser.

75. Charge the air conditioning system. See Section 1.

76. Connect the engine oil cooler lines at the oil filter adapter.

77. Connect the transmission oil cooler lines at the radiator.

78. Connect the upper and lower radiator hoses.

79. Connect the canister hose.

80. Install the grille and bumper.

81. Connect the crankcase ventilation hose.

82. Connect the negative battery cable from the block.

83. Fill the cooling system.

84. Install the air cleaner assembly.

85. Install the hood and engine cover.

If the torque for a particular fastener was not mentioned above, use the following torque values as a guide:

- ¼ in.–20: 6–9 ft. lbs.
- $\frac{5}{16}$ in.–18: 12–18 ft. lbs.
- ⅜ in.–16: 22–32 ft. lbs.
- $\frac{7}{16}$ in.–14: 45–57 ft. lbs.
- ½ in.–13: 55–80 ft. lbs.
- $\frac{9}{16}$ in.: 85–120 ft. lbs.

8-7.3L Diesel Engines

1. Remove the hood and engine cover.
2. Drain the coolant.

——————————— **CAUTION** ———————————

When draining the coolant, keep in mind that cats and dogs are attracted by the ethylene glycol antifreeze, and are quite likely to drink any that is left in an uncovered container or in puddles on the ground. This will prove fatal in sufficient quantity. Always drain the coolant into a sealable container. Coolant should be reused unless it is contaminated or several years old.

3. Remove the air cleaner and intake duct assembly and cover the air intake opening with a clean rag to keep out the dirt.

4. Remove the upper grille support bracket and upper air conditioning condenser mounting bracket.

5. On vehicles equipped with air conditioning, the system MUST be discharged to remove the condenser.

WARNING: DO NOT attempt to do this yourself, unless you are familiar with air conditioning repair. See Section 1.

6. Remove the radiator fan shroud halves.

7. Remove the fan and clutch assembly as described under water pump removal in this Section.

8. Detach the radiator hoses and the transmission cooler lines, if so equipped.

9. Remove the condenser. Cap all openings at once!

10. Remove the radiator.

11. Remove the grille and bumper.

12. Remove the power steering pump and position it out of the way.

13. Disconnect the fuel supply line heater and alternator wires at the alternator.

14. Disconnect the oil pressure sending unit wire at the sending unit, remove the sender from the firewall and lay it on the engine.

15. Disconnect the accelerator cable and the speed control cable, if so equipped, from the injection pump. Remove the cable bracket with the cables attached, from the intake manifold and position it out of the way.

16. Disconnect the transmission kickdown rod from the injection pump, if so equipped.

17. Disconnect the main wiring harness connector from the right side of the engine and the ground strap from the rear of the engine.

18. Remove the fuel return hose from the left rear of the engine.

19. Remove the two upper transmission-to-engine attaching bolts.
20. Disconnect the heater hoses.
21. Disconnect the water temperature sender wire.
22. Disconnect the overheat light switch wire and position the wire out of the way.
23. Raise the van and support on it on jackstands.
24. Disconnect the battery ground cables from the front of the engine and the starter cables from the starter.
25. Remove the fuel inlet line and plug the fuel line at the fuel pump.
26. Detach the exhaust pipe at the exhaust manifold.
27. Disconnect the engine insulators from the no. 1 crossmember.
28. Remove the flywheel inspection plate and the four converter-to-flywheel attaching nuts, if equipped with automatic transmission.
29. Remove the jackstands and lower the van.
30. Support the transmission on a jack.
31. Remove the four lower transmission attaching bolts.
32. Attach an engine lifting sling and remove the engine from the van.

To install:
33. Lower the engine into van.
34. Align the converter to the flex plate and the engine dowels to the transmission.
35. Install the engine mount bolts and torque them to 80 ft. lbs.
36. Remove the engine lifting sling.
37. Install the four lower transmission attaching bolts. Torque the bolts to 65 ft. lbs.
38. Remove transmission jack.
39. Raise and support the front end on jackstands.
40. If equipped with automatic transmission, install the four converter-to-flywheel attaching nuts. Torque the nuts to 34 ft. lbs.
41. Install the flywheel inspection plate. Torque the bolts to 60–90 inch lbs.
42. Attach the exhaust pipe at the exhaust manifold.
43. Connect the fuel inlet line.
44. Connect the battery ground cables to the front of the engine.
45. Connect the starter cables at the starter.
46. Lower the van.
47. Connect the overheat light switch wire.
48. Connect the water temperature sender wire.
49. Connect the heater hoses.
50. Install the two upper transmission-to-engine attaching bolts. Torque the bolts to 65 ft. lbs.
51. Connect the fuel return hose at the left rear of the engine.
52. Connect the main wiring harness connector at the right side of the engine and the ground strap from the rear of the engine.
53. Connect the transmission kickdown rod at the injection pump, if so equipped.
54. Connect the accelerator cable and the speed control cable, if so equipped, at the injection pump.
55. Install the cable bracket with the cables attached, to the intake manifold.
56. Install the oil pressure sending unit.
57. Connect the oil pressure sending unit wire at the sending unit.
58. Connect the fuel supply line heater and alternator wires at the alternator.
59. Install the power steering pump.
60. Install the radiator.
61. Install the condenser.
62. Connect the radiator hoses and the transmission cooler lines, if so equipped.
63. Install the fan and clutch assembly as described under water pump removal in this Section.

64. Install the radiator fan shroud halves.
65. On vehicles equipped with air conditioning, charge the system. See Section 1.
66. Install the grille and bumper.
67. Install the upper grille support bracket and upper air conditioning condenser mounting bracket.
68. Install the air cleaner and intake duct assembly.
69. Fill the cooling system.
70. Install the hood and engine cover.

Rocker Covers
REMOVAL AND INSTALLATION

6-4.9L Engine

1. Disconnect the inlet hose at the crankcase filler cap.
2. Remove the throttle body inlet tubes.
3. Disconnect the accelerator cable at the throttle body. Remove the cable retracting spring. Remove the accelerator cable bracket from the upper intake manifold and position the cable and bracket out of the way.
4. Remove the fuel line from the fuel rail. Be careful not to kink the line.
5. Remove the upper intake manifold and throttle body assembly. See Section 5.
6. Remove the ignition coil and wires.
7. Remove the rocker arm cover.
8. Remove and discard the gasket.

To install:
9. Clean the mating surfaces for the cover and head thoroughly.
10. Coat both mating surfaces with gasket sealer and place the new gasket on the head with the locating tabs downward.
11. Place the cover on the head making sure the gasket is evenly seated. Torque the bolts to 48-84 inch lbs.
12. The remainder of installation is the reverse of removal.

8-5.0L Engine
8.5-8L Engine

1. Disconnect the battery ground cable.
2. Remove the air cleaner and inlet duct.
3. Remove the coil.
4. For the right cover, remove the lifting eye and Thermactor tube; for the left cover, remove the oil filler pipe attaching bolt.
5. Mark and remove the spark plug wires.
6. Remove any vacuum lines, wires or pipes in the way. Make sure that you tag them for identification.
7. Remove the cover bolts and lift off the cover. It may be necessary to break the cover loose by rapping on it with a rubber mallet. NEVER pry the cover off!

To install:
8. Thoroughly clean the mating surfaces of both the cover and head.
9. Coat both mating surfaces with gasket sealer and place the new gasket(s) in the cover(s) with the locating tabs engaging the slots.
10. Place the cover on the head making sure the gasket is evenly seated. Torque the bolts to 10-13 ft. lbs. After 2 minutes, retighten the bolts.
11. The remainder of installation is the reverse of removal.

8-7.5L Engine

1. Disconnect the battery ground cable(s).
2. Remove the air cleaner and inlet duct.
3. Remove the Thermactor air supply control valve and bracket.
4. Remove the coil.
5. Disconnect the MTA hose at the Thermactor valve. Dis-

connect the Thermactor air control valve-to-air pump hose and tube.

6. Mark and remove the spark plug wires.

7. Remove any vacuum lines, wires or pipes in the way. Make sure that you tag them for identification.

8. Remove the cover bolts and lift off the cover. It may be necessary to break the cover loose by rapping on it with a rubber mallet. NEVER pry the cover off!

To install:

9. Thoroughly clean the mating surfaces of both the cover and head.

10. Place the new cover seal(s) in the cover(s) with the locating tab engaging the slot.

11. Place the cover on the head. Torque the bolts to 6-9 ft. lbs. from right to left.

12. The remainder of installation is the reverse of removal.

Diesel Engine

1. Disconnect the battery ground cables.

2. Remove the cover bolts and lift off the covers. It may be necessary to break the covers loose by rapping on them with a rubber mallet. NEVER pry a cover off!

3. Clean the mating surfaces of the covers and heads thoroughly, coat the mating surfaces with gasket sealer, place new gaskets in the covers, position the covers on the heads and torque the bolts to 72 inch lbs.

Rocker Arms

REMOVAL AND INSTALLATION

6-4.9L Engine

1. Disconnect the inlet hose at the crankcase filler cap.

2. Remove the throttle body inlet tubes.

3. Disconnect the accelerator cable at the throttle body. Remove the cable retracting spring. Remove the accelerator cable bracket from the upper intake manifold and position the cable and bracket out of the way.

4. Remove the fuel line from the fuel rail. Be careful not to kink the line.

5. Remove the upper intake manifold and throttle body assembly. See Section 5.

6. Remove the ignition coil and wires.

7. Remove the rocker arm cover.

8. Remove the spark plug wires.

9. Remove the distributor cap.

10. Remove the pushrod cover (engine side cover).

11. Loosen the rocker arm bolts until the pushrods can be removed. KEEP THE PUSHRODS IN ORDER, FOR INSTALLATION!

12. Using a magnetic lifter removal tool, remove the lifters. Wipe clean the exterior of each lifter as it's removed and mark it with an indelible marker, so that it can be installed in its original bore.

To install:

13. Coat the bottom surface of each lifter with multi-purpose grease, and coat the rest of the lifter with clean engine oil.

14. Install each lifter in it original bore using the magnetic tool.

15. Coat each end of each pushrod with multi-purpose grease and install each in its original position. Make sure that each pushrod is properly seated in the lifter socket.

16. Engage the rocker arms with the pushrods and tighten the rocker arm bolts enough to hold the pushrods in place.

17. Adjust the valve clearance as described below.

18. The remainder of installation is the reverse of removal.

8-5.0L Engine
8-5.8L Engine

1. Remove the intake manifold.

2. Disconnect the Thermactor air supply hose at the pump.

3. Remove the rocker arm covers.

4. Loosen the rocker arm fulcrum bolts, fulcrum seats and rocker arms. KEEP ALL PARTS IN ORDER FOR INSTALLATION!

To install:

5. Apply multi-purpose grease to the valve stem tips, the fulcrum seats and sockets.

6. Install the fulcrum guides, rocker arms, seats and bolts. Torque the bolts to 18–25 ft. lbs.

7. The remainder of installation is the reverse of removal.

8-7.5L Engine

1. Remove the intake manifold.

2. Remove the rocker arm covers.

3. Loosen the rocker arm fulcrum bolts, fulcrum, oil deflector, seat and rocker arms. KEEP EVERYTHING IN ORDER FOR INSTALLATION!

To install:

8. Coat each end of each pushrod with multi-purpose grease.

9. Coat the top of the valve stems, the rocker arms and the fulcrum seats with multi-purpose grease.

10. Rotate the crankshaft by hand until No.1 piston is at TDC of compression. The firing order marks on the damper will be aligned at TDC with the timing pointer.

11. Install the rocker arms, seats, deflectors and bolts on the following valves:

- No.1 intake and exhaust
- No.3 intake
- No.8 exhaust
- No.7 intake
- No.5 exhaust
- No.8 intake
- No.4 exhaust

Engage the rocker arms with the pushrods and tighten the rocker arm fulcrum bolts to 18–25 ft. lbs.

12. Rotate the crankshaft on full turn — 360° — and re-align the TDC mark and pointer. Install the parts and tighten the bolts on the following valves:

- No.2 intake and exhaust
- No.4 intake
- No.3 exhaust
- No.5 intake
- No.6 exhaust
- No.6 intake
- No.7 exhaust

13. The remainder of installation is the reverse of removal.

14. Check the valve clearance as described under Hydraulic Valve Clearance, below.

Diesel Engines

1. Disconnect the ground cables from both batteries.

2. Remove the valve cover attaching screws and remove both valve cover.

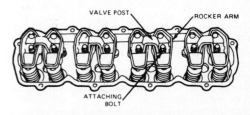

Diesel V8 rocker arm assembly

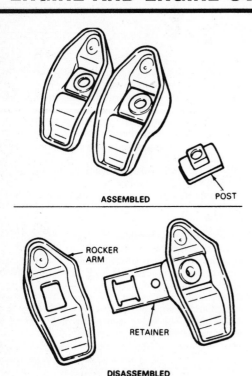

ASSEMBLED

POST

ROCKER ARM

RETAINER

DISASSEMBLED

Diesel rocker arms

3. Remove the valve rocker arm post mounting bolts. Remove the rocker arms and posts in order and mark them with tape so they can be installed in their original positions.

4. If the cylinder heads are to be removed, then the pushrods can now be removed. Make a holder for the pushrods out of a piece of wood or cardboard, and remove the pushrods in order. It is very important that the pushrods be re-installed in their original order. The pushrods can remain in position if no further disassembly is required.

5. If the pushrods were removed, install them in their original locations. make sure they are fully seated in the tappet seats.

NOTE: The copper colored end of the pushrod goes toward the rocker arm.

6. Apply a polyethylene grease to the valve stem tips. Install the rocker arms and posts in their original positions.

7. Turn the engine over by hand until the valve timing mark is at the 11:00 o'clock position, as viewed from the front of the engine. Install all of the rocker arm post attaching bolts and torque to 20 ft.lbs.

8. Install new valve cover gaskets and install the valve cover. Install the battery cables, start the engine and check for leaks.

Hydraulic Lash Adjuster
8-7.5L Engine

REMOVAL AND INSTALLATION

1. Remove the lower intake manifold.
2. Remove the rocker arm assemblies.
3. Remove the pushrods.
4. Lift out the hydraulic lash adjuster.
5. Installation is the reverse of removal.

Rocker Studs

REMOVAL AND INSTALLATION

6–4.9L
8–5.0L

Rocker arm studs which are broken or have damaged threads may be replaced with standard studs. Studs which are loose in the cylinder head must be replaced with oversize studs which are available for service. The amount of oversize and diameter of the studs are as follows:

- 0.006 in. (0.152mm) oversize: 0.3774–0.3781 in. (9.586–9.604mm)
- 0.010 in. (0.254mm) oversize: 0.3814–0.3821 in. (9.688–9.705mm)
- 0.015 in. (0.381mm) oversize: 0.3864–0.3871 in. (9.815–9.832mm)

A tool kit for replacing the rocker studs is available and contains a stud remover and two oversize reamers: one for 0.006 in. (0.152mm) and one for 0.015 in. (0.381mm) oversize studs. For 0.010 in. (0.254mm) oversize studs, use reamer tool T66P-6A527-B. To press the replacement studs into the cylinder head, use the stud replacer tool T69P-6049-D. Use the smaller reamer tool first when boring the hole for oversize studs.

1. Remove the valve rocker cover(s) by moving all hoses aside and unbolting the cover(s). Position the sleeve of the rocker arm stud remover over the stud with the bearing end down. When working on a 5.0L V8, cut the threaded part of the stud off with a hacksaw. Thread the puller into the sleeve and over the stud until it is fully bottomed. Hold the sleeve with a wrench and rotate the puller clockwise to remove the stud.

An alternate method of removing the rocker studs without the special tool is to put spacers over the stud until just enough threads are left showing at the top so a nut can be screwed onto the top of the rocker arm stud and get a full bite. Turn the nut clockwise until the stud is removed, adding spacers under the nut as necessary.

NOTE: If the rocker stud was broken off flush with the stud boss, use an easy-out tool to remove the broken off part of the stud from the cylinder head.

Use a silicone sealant when installing valve covers

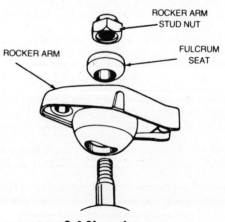

ROCKER ARM STUD NUT

ROCKER ARM

FULCRUM SEAT

6-4.9L rocker arm

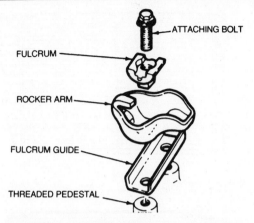

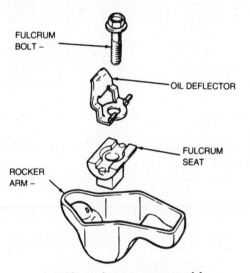

8-5.0L and 8-5.8L rocker arm assembly

8-7.5L rocker arm assembly

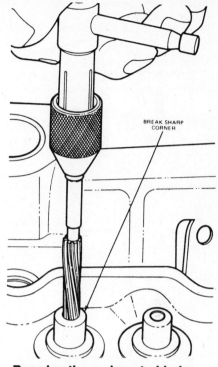

Reaming the rocker stud holes

2. If a loose rocker arm stud is being replaced, ream the stud bore for the selected oversize stud.

NOTE: Keep all metal particles away from the valves.

3. Coat the end of the stud with Lubriplate®. Align the stud and installer with the stud bore and top the sliding driver until it bottoms. When the installer contacts the stud boss, the stud is installed to its correct height.

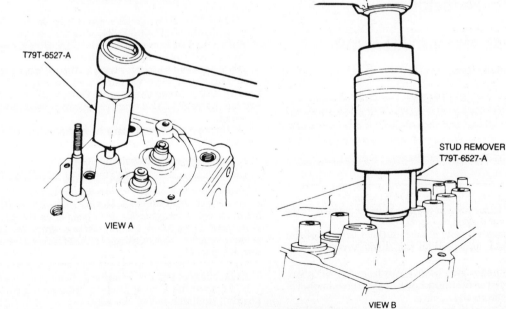

VIEW A

STUD REMOVER
T79T-6527-A

VIEW B

Removing the 6-4.9L rocker arm stud

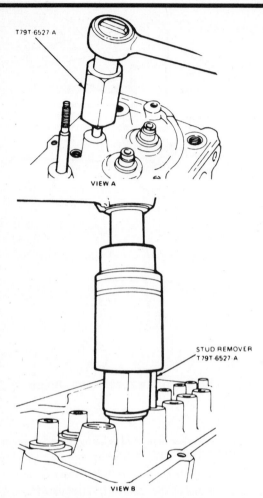

VIEW A

VIEW B

Installing a new rocker stud

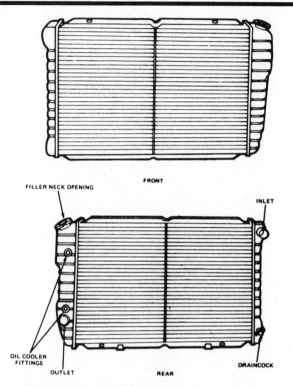

Crossflow radiator. Diesels have a vertical flow radiator

Radiator

REMOVAL AND INSTALLATION

1. Drain the cooling system.

———————— CAUTION ————————

When draining the coolant, keep in mind that cats and dogs are attracted by the ethylene glycol antifreeze, and are quite likely to drink any that is left in an uncovered container or in puddles on the ground. This will prove fatal in sufficient quantity. Always drain the coolant into a sealable container. Coolant should be reused unless it is contaminated or several years old.

2. Disconnect the transmission cooling lines from the bottom of the radiator, if so equipped.
3. Remove the retaining bolts at each of the 4 corners of the shroud, if so equipped, and position the shroud over the fan, clear of the radiator.
4. Disconnect the upper and lower hoses from the radiator.
5. Remove the radiator retaining bolts or the upper supports and lift the radiator from the vehicle.
6. Install the radiator in the reverse order of removal. Fill the cooling system and check for leaks.

Air Conditioning Condenser

REMOVAL AND INSTALLATION

1. Discharge the refrigerant system. See Section 1.
2. Disconnect the refrigerant lines from the condenser using the proper spring lock tool shown in the accompanying illustration. Cap all opening immediately!

NOTE: The fittings are spring-lock couplings and a special tool, T81P-19623-G, should be used. The larger opening end of the tool is for ½ in. discharge lines; the smaller end for ⅜ in. liquid lines.

To operate the tool, close the tool and push the tool into the open side of the cage to expand the garter spring and release the female fitting. If the tool is not inserted straight, the garter spring will cock and not release.

After the garter spring is released, pull the fittings apart.

3. Drain the cooling system.

———————— CAUTION ————————

When draining the coolant, keep in mind that cats and dogs are attracted by the ethylene glycol antifreeze, and are quite likely to drink any that is left in an uncovered container or in puddles on the ground. This will prove fatal in sufficient quantity. Always drain the coolant into a sealable container. Coolant should be reused unless it is contaminated or several years old.

4. Disconnect the upper radiator hose.
5. Remove the 2 hood latch-to-radiator support screws and position the latch out of the way.
6. Remove the 9 screws retaining the top edge of the grille to the radiator support.

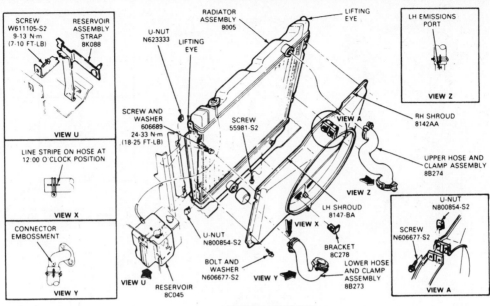

4-ROW 585 SQ. IN. MANUAL STANDARD AND A/C AUTO-STANDARD

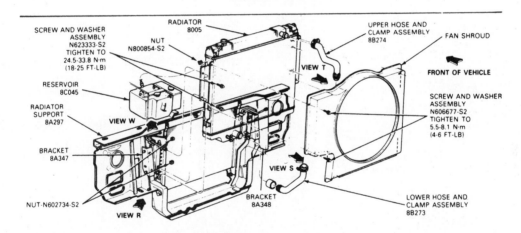

3-AND 4-ROW 735 SQ. IN. AUTO-A/C AUTO MANUAL SUPER COOL WITH/WITHOUT A/C

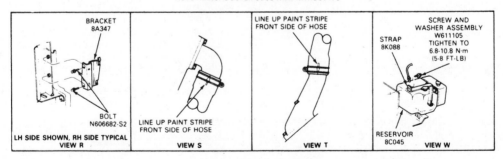

Diesel radiators

7. Remove the screw retaining the center of the grille support to the radiator support.

8. Remove the lower splash shield and remove the 2 lower condenser retaining nuts.

9. Remove the 2 upper condenser retaining bolts.

10. Remove the 4 bolts retaining the ends of the radiator upper supports to the side supports.

11. Carefully pull the top edge of the grille forward and remove the upper support.

12. Lift out the condenser.

13. If a new condenser is being installed, add 1 fl.oz. of new refrigerant oil to the new condenser. Installation is the reverse of removal. Always use new O-rings coated with clean refrigerant oil on the line fittings. Evacuate, charge and leak test the system.

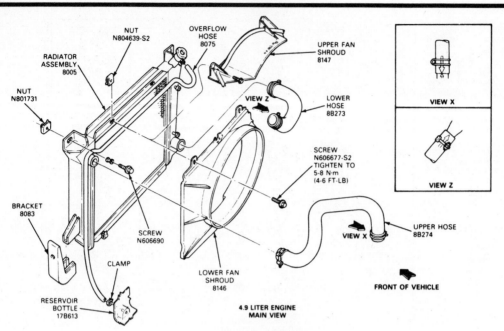

6-4.9L radiator

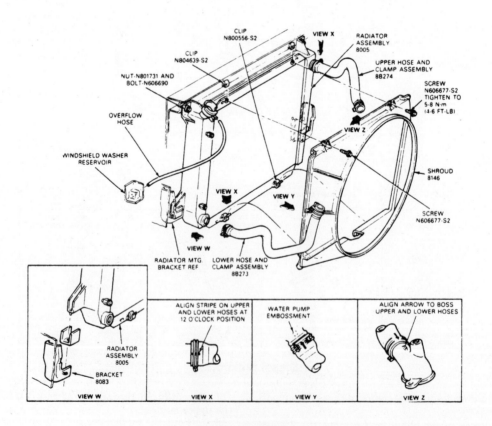

8-7.5L radiator

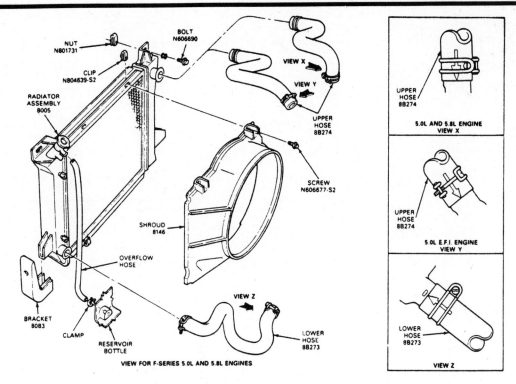

8-5.0L and 8-5.8L radiator

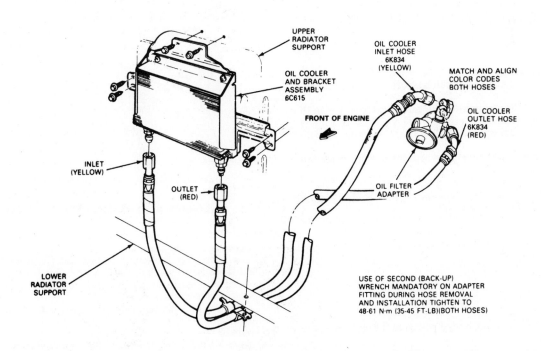

8-7.5L oil cooler

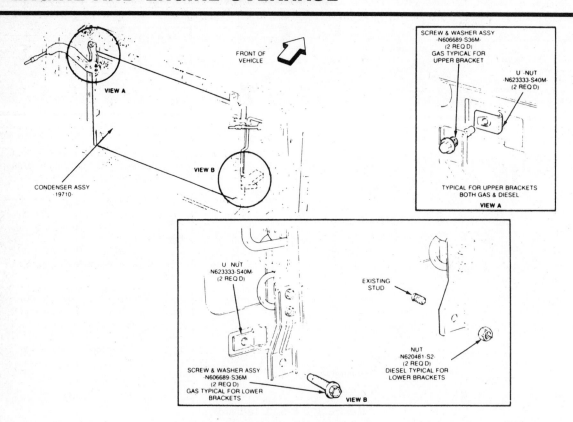

Condenser removal

Engine Fan and Fan Clutch

REMOVAL AND INSTALLATION

6-4.9L Engine

1. Remove the fan shroud.
2. Remove one of the fan-to-clutch bolts, to access the clutch-to-hub nut.
3. Turn the large fan clutch-to-hub nut counterclockwise to remove the fan and clutch from the hub. There are 2 tools made for this purpose, holding tool T84T-6312-C and nut wrench T84T-6312-D.
4. If the fan and clutch have to be separated, remove the remaining fan-to-clutch bolts.
To install:
5. Attach the fan to the clutch using all but one of the bolts. The bolts are tightened to 18 ft. lbs.
6. Install the assembly on the hub and tighten the hub nut to a maximum of 100 ft. lbs., or a minimum of 30 ft. lbs.
7. Install and torque the last fan-to-clutch bolt.
8. Install the shroud.

8-5.0L Engine
8-5.8L Engine
8-7.5L Engine

1. Remove the fan shroud, and, if you need the clearance, the radiator.
2. Remove the 4 fan clutch-to-water pump hub bolts and lift off the fan/clutch assembly.
3. Remove the 4 fan-to-clutch bolts and separate the fan from the clutch.
4. Installation is the reverse of removal. Torque the all the bolts to 18 ft. lbs.

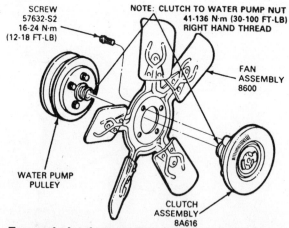

Fan and clutch assembly for the 6-4.9L engine

Diesel Engine

1. Remove the fan shroud.
2. Turn the large fan clutch-to-hub nut CLOCKWISE (left-handed threads) to remove the fan and clutch from the hub. There are 2 tools made for this purpose, holding tool T84T-6312-A and nut wrench T84T-6312-B.
3. If the fan and clutch have to be separated, remove the fan-to-clutch bolts.
To install:
4. Attach the fan to the clutch. The bolts are tightened to 18 ft. lbs.
5. Install the assembly on the hub and tighten the hub nut to a maximum of 120 ft. lbs., or a minimum of 40 ft. lbs. Remember, the nut is left-handed. Tighten it by turning it COUNTERCLOCKWISE.
6. Install the shroud.

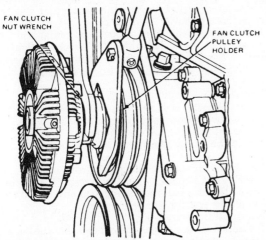

FAN CLUTCH
NUT WRENCH

FAN CLUTCH
PULLEY
HOLDER

Loosening the fan clutch on the 6-4.9L engine

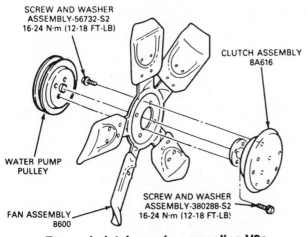

SCREW AND WASHER
ASSEMBLY-56732-S2
16-24 N·m (12-18 FT-LB)

CLUTCH ASSEMBLY
8A616

WATER PUMP
PULLEY

FAN ASSEMBLY
8600

SCREW AND WASHER
ASSEMBLY-380288-S2
16-24 N·m (12-18 FT-LB)

Fan and clutch used on gasoline V8s

Water Pump

REMOVAL AND INSTALLATION

6–4.9L

1. Drain the cooling system.

━━━━━━━━━ **CAUTION** ━━━━━━━━━

When draining the coolant, keep in mind that cats and dogs are attracted by the ethylene glycol antifreeze, and are quite likely to drink any that is left in an uncovered container or in puddles on the ground. This will prove fatal in sufficient quantity. Always drain the coolant into a sealable container. Coolant should be reused unless it is contaminated or several years old.

2. Disconnect the lower radiator hose from the water pump.
3. Remove the drive belt, fan, fan spacer, fan shroud, if so equipped, and water pump pulley.
4. Remove the alternator pivot arm from the pump.
5. Disconnect the heater hose at the water pump.
6. Remove the water pump.
7. Before installing the old water pump, clean the gasket mounting surfaces on the pump and on the cylinder block. If a new water pump is being installed, remove the heater hose fitting from the old pump and install it on the new one. Coat the new gaskets with sealer on both sides and install the water pump in the reverse order of removal. Torque the mounting bolts to 18 ft. lbs.

8–5.0L
8–5.8L
8–7.5L

1. Drain the cooling system.

━━━━━━━━━ **CAUTION** ━━━━━━━━━

When draining the coolant, keep in mind that cats and dogs are attracted by the ethylene glycol antifreeze, and are quite likely to drink any that is left in an uncovered container or in puddles on the ground. This will prove fatal in sufficient quantity. Always drain the coolant into a sealable container. Coolant should be reused unless it is contaminated or several years old.

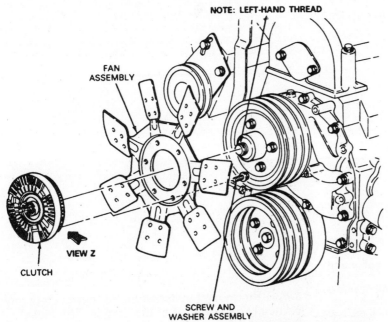

NOTE: LEFT-HAND THREAD

FAN
ASSEMBLY

VIEW Z

CLUTCH

SCREW AND
WASHER ASSEMBLY

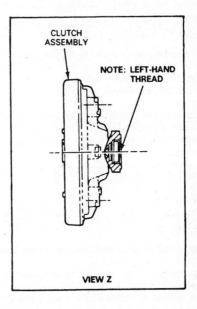

CLUTCH
ASSEMBLY

NOTE: LEFT-HAND
THREAD

VIEW Z

Diesel fan and clutch

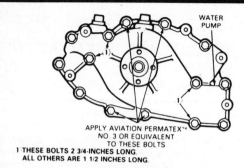

APPLY AVIATION PERMATEX™
NO. 3 OR EQUIVALENT
TO THESE BOLTS

1 THESE BOLTS 2 3/4-INCHES LONG.
ALL OTHERS ARE 1 1/2 INCHES LONG.

Diesel water pump

2. Remove the bolts securing the fan shroud to the radiator, if so equipped, and position the shroud over the fan.

3. Disconnect the lower radiator hose, heater hose and by-pass hose at the water pump. Remove the drive belts, fan, fan spacer and pulley. Remove the fan shroud, if so equipped.

4. Loosen the alternator pivot bolt and the bolt attaching the alternator adjusting arm to the water pump. Remove the power steering pump bracket from the water pump and position it out of the way.

5. Remove the bolts securing the water pump to the timing chain cover and remove the water pump.

6. Install the water pump in the reverse order of removal, using a new gasket. Torque the bolts to 18 ft. lbs.

8-7.3L Diesel

1. Disconnect both battery ground cables.
2. Drain the cooling system.

--- **CAUTION** ---

When draining the coolant, keep in mind that cats and dogs are attracted by the ethylene glycol antifreeze, and are quite likely to drink any that is left in an uncovered container or in puddles on the ground. This will prove fatal in sufficient quantity. Always drain the coolant into a sealable container. Coolant should be reused unless it is contaminated or several years old.

3. Remove the radiator shroud halves.
4. Remove the fan clutch and fan.

NOTE: The fan clutch bolts are left hand thread. Remove them by turning them clockwise.

5. Remove the power steering pump belt.
6. Remove the air conditioning compressor belt.
7. Remove the vacuum pump drive belt.
8. Remove the alternator drive belt.
9. Remove the water pump pulley.
10. Disconnect the heater hose at the water pump.
11. If you're installing a new pump, remove the heater hose fitting from the old pump at this time.
12. Remove the alternator adjusting arm and bracket.
13. Unbolt the air conditioning compressor and position it out of the way. DO NOT DISCONNECT THE REFRIGERANT LINES!
14. Remove the air conditioning compressor brackets.
15. Unbolt the power steering pump and bracket and position it out of the way. DO NOT DISCONNECT THE POWER STEERING FLUID LINES!
16. Remove the bolts attaching the water pump to the front cover and lift off the pump.
17. Thoroughly clean the mating surfaces of the pump and front cover.
18. Get a hold of two dowel pins - anything that will fit into 2 mounting bolt holes in the front cover. You'll need these to ensure proper bolt hole alignment when you're installing the water pump.

19. Using a new gasket, position the water pump over the dowel pins and into place on the front cover.
20. Install the attaching bolts. The 2 top center and 2 bottom center bolts must be coated with RTV silicone sealant prior to installation. See the illustration. Also, the 4 bolts marked No.1 in the illustration are a different length than the other bolts. Torque the bolts to 14 ft. lbs.
21. Install the water pump pulley.
22. Wrap the heater hose fitting threads with Teflon® tape and screw it into the water pump. Torque it to 18 ft. lbs.
23. Connect the heater hose to the pump.
24. Install the power steering pump and bracket. Install the belt.
25. Install the air conditioning compressor bracket.
26. Install the air conditioning compressor. Install the belt.
27. Install the alternator adjusting arm and install the belt.
28. Install the vacuum pump drive belt.
29. Adjust all the drive belts.
30. Install the fan and clutch. Remember that the bolts are left hand thread. Turn them counterclockwise to tighten them. Torque them to 45 ft. lbs.
31. Install the fan shroud halves.
32. Fill and bleed the cooling system.
33. Connect the battery ground cables.
34. Start the engine and check for leaks.

Thermostat

NOTE: It is a good practice to check the operation of a new thermostat before it is installed in an engine. Place the thermostat in a pan of boiling water. If it does not open more than ¼ in. (6mm), do not install it in the engine.

REMOVAL AND INSTALLATION

6–4.9L

1. Drain the cooling system below the level of the coolant outlet housing. Use the petcock valve at the bottom of the radiator to drain the system. It is not necessary to remove any of the hoses.

--- **CAUTION** ---

When draining the coolant, keep in mind that cats and dogs are attracted by the ethylene glycol antifreeze, and are quite likely to drink any that is left in an uncovered container or in puddles on the ground. This will prove fatal in sufficient quantity. Always drain the coolant into a sealable container. Coolant should be reused unless it is contaminated or several years old.

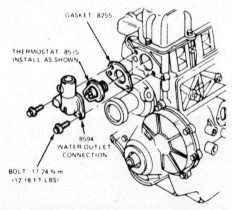

GASKET 8255

THERMOSTAT 8575
INSTALL AS SHOWN

8594
WATER OUTLET
CONNECTION

BOLT 17 24 N m
(12 18 FT LBS)

6-4.9L thermostat installation. V8 thermostats mount vertically on the front of the engine. The diesel thermostat is on the side/front of the intake manifold

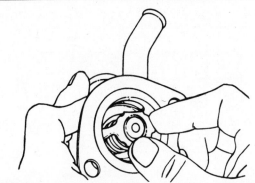

The thermostat spring faces down/in towards the engine

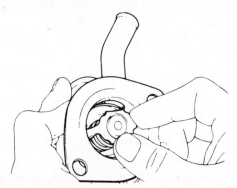

On gasoline engines, turn the thermostat clockwise to lock it into position

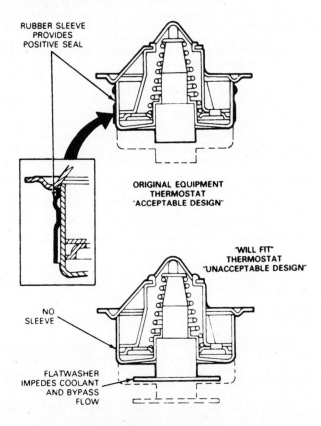

Thermostat positioning

2. Remove the coolant outlet housing retaining bolts and slide the housing with the hose attached to one side.

3. Remove the thermostat and gasket from the cylinder head and clean both mating surfaces.

4. To install the thermostat, coat a new gasket with water resistant sealer and position it on the outlet of the engine. The gasket must be in place before the thermostat is installed.

5. Install the thermostat with the bridge (opposite end of the spring) inside the elbow connection.

6. Position the elbow connection onto the mounting surface of the outlet, so that the thermostat flange is resting on the gasket and install the retaining bolts. Torque the bolts to 15 ft. lbs.

7. Fill the radiator and operate the engine until it reaches operating temperature. Check the coolant level and adjust if necessary.

8–5.0L
8–5.8L
8–7.5L

1. Drain the cooling system below the level of the coolant outlet housing. Use the petcock valve at the bottom of the radiator to drain the system. It is not necessary to remove any of the hoses.

———— CAUTION ————

When draining the coolant, keep in mind that cats and dogs are attracted by the ethylene glycol antifreeze, and are quite likely to drink any that is left in an uncovered container or in puddles on the ground. This will prove fatal in sufficient quantity. Always drain the coolant into a sealable container. Coolant should be reused unless it is contaminated or several years old.

2. Disconnect the bypass hoses at the water pump and intake manifold.

3. Remove the bypass tube.

4. Remove the coolant outlet housing retaining bolts, bend the hose and lift the housing with the hose attached to one side.

5. Remove the thermostat and gasket from the intake manifold and clean both mating surfaces.

6. To install the thermostat, coat a new gasket with water resistant sealer and position it on the outlet of the engine. The gasket must be in place before the thermostat is installed.

7. Install the thermostat with the bridge (opposite end of the spring) inside the elbow connection and the thermostat flange positioned in the recess in the manifold.

8. Position the elbow connection onto the mounting surface of the outlet. Torque the bolts to 18 ft. lbs. on the 8–5.0L and 5.8L; 28 ft. lbs. on the 8–7.5L.

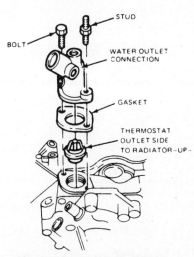

V8 thermostat installation

9. Install the bypass tube and hoses.

10. Fill the radiator and operate the engine until it reaches operating temperature. Check the coolant level and adjust if necessary.

8-7.3L Diesel

WARNING: The factory specified thermostat does not contain an internal bypass. On these engines, an internal bypass is located in the block. The use of any replacement thermostat other than that meeting the manufacturer's specifications will result in engine overheating! Use only thermostats meeting the specifications of Ford part number E5TZ–8575–C or Navistar International part number 1807945–C1.

1. Disconnect both battery ground cables.
2. Drain the coolant to a point below the thermostat housing.

CAUTION

When draining the coolant, keep in mind that cats and dogs are attracted by the ethylene glycol antifreeze, and are quite likely to drink any that is left in an uncovered container or in puddles on the ground. This will prove fatal in sufficient quantity. Always drain the coolant into a sealable container. Coolant should be reused unless it is contaminated or several years old.

---

3. Remove the alternator and vacuum pump belts
4. Remove the alternator.
5. Remove the vacuum pump and bracket.
6. Remove all but the lowest vacuum pump/alternator mounting casting bolt.
7. Loosen that lowest bolt and pivot the casting outboard of the engine.
8. Remove the thermostat housing attaching bolts, bend the hose and lift the housing up and to one side.
9. Remove the thermostat and gasket.
10. Clean the thermostat housing and block surfaces thoroughly.
11. Coat a new gasket with waterproof sealer and position the gasket on the manifold outlet opening.
12. Install the thermostat in the manifold opening with the spring element end downward and the flange positioned in the recess in the manifold.
13. Place the outlet housing into position and install the bolts. Torque the bolts to 20 ft. lbs.
14. Reposition the casting.
15. Install the vacuum pump and bracket.
16. Install the alternator.
17. Adjust the drive belts.
18. Fill and bleed the cooling system.
19. Connect both battery cables.
20. Run the engine and check for leaks.

Intake Manifold

REMOVAL AND INSTALLATION

6–4.9L

The intake and exhaust manifolds on these engines are known as combination manifolds and are serviced as a unit.
1. Remove the air inlet hose at the crankcase filter cap.
2. Remove the throttle body inlet hoses.
3. Disconnect the accelerator cable at the throttle body.
4. Remove the cable retracting spring.
5. Remove the cable bracket from the upper intake manifold.
6. Disconnect the fuel inlet line at the fuel rail. Don't kink the line!
7. Remove the upper intake and throttle body as an assembly. See Section 5.
8. Tag and disconnect all vacuum lines attached to the parts in question.

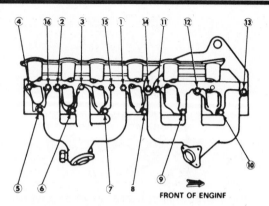

6-4.9L manifold bolt torque sequence

9. Disconnect the inlet pipe from the exhaust manifold.
10. Disconnect the power brake vacuum line, if so equipped.
11. Remove the bolts and nuts attaching the manifolds to the cylinder head. Lift the manifold assemblies from the engine. Remove and discard the gaskets.
12. To separate the manifold, remove the nuts joining the intake and exhaust manifolds.
To install:
13. Clean the mating surfaces of the cylinder head and the manifolds.
14. If the intake and exhaust manifolds have been separated, coat the mating surfaces lightly with graphite grease and place the exhaust manifold over the studs on the intake manifold. Install the lockwashers and nuts. Tighten them finger tight.
15. Install a new intake manifold gasket.
16. Coat the mating surfaces lightly with graphite grease. Place the manifold assemblies in position against the cylinder head. Make sure that the gaskets have not become dislodged. Install the attaching nuts and bolts in the proper sequence to 26 ft.lbs. If the intake and exhaust manifolds were separated, tighten the nuts joining them.
17. Position a new gasket on the muffler inlet pipe and connect the inlet pipe to the exhaust manifold.
18. Connect the crankcase vent hose to the intake manifold inlet tube and position the hose clamp.
19. Connect the power brake vacuum line, if so equipped.
20. Connect the inlet pipe at the exhaust manifold.
21. Connect all vacuum lines.
22. Install the upper intake and throttle body as an assembly. See Section 5.
23. Connect the fuel inlet line at the fuel rail.
24. Install the accelerator cable bracket at the upper intake manifold.
25. Install the cable retracting spring.
26. Connect the accelerator cable at the throttle body.
27. Install the throttle body inlet hoses.
28. Install the air inlet hose at the crankcase filter cap.

8-5.0L
8-5.8L
8-7.5L

NOTE: Discharge fuel system pressure before starting any work that involves disconnecting fuel system lines. See Fuel Supply Manifold removal and installation procedures in Section 5 (Gasoline Fuel System section).

1. To remove the upper manifold: Remove the air cleaner. Disconnect the electrical connectors at the air bypass valve, throttle position sensor and EGR position sensor.

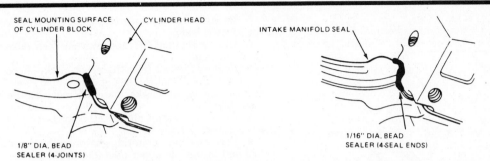

Sealer application for intake manifold installation on all V8 except the 8-7.5L

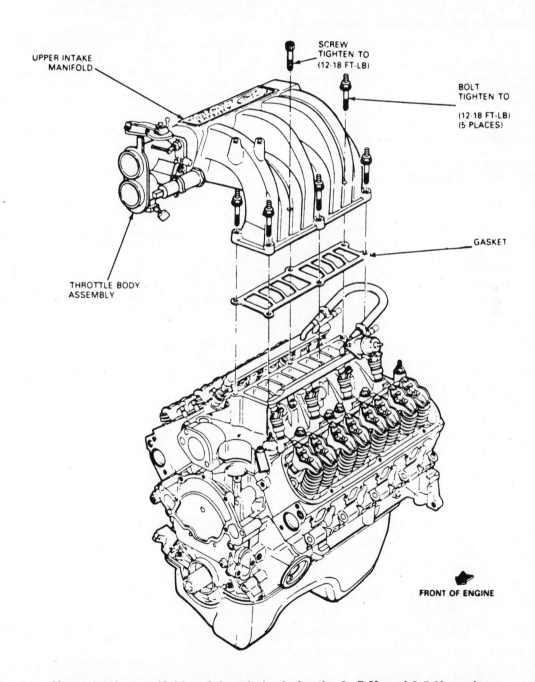

Upper intake manifold and throttle body for the 8- 5.0L and 8-5.8L engines

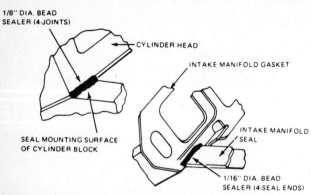

1/8" DIA. BEAD SEALER (4-JOINTS)

CYLINDER HEAD

INTAKE MANIFOLD GASKET

SEAL MOUNTING SURFACE OF CYLINDER BLOCK

INTAKE MANIFOLD SEAL

1/16" DIA. BEAD SEALER (4-SEAL ENDS)

Sealer application for intake manifold installation on the 8-7.5L

2. Disconnect the throttle linkage at the throttle ball and the AOD transmission linkage from the throttle body. Remove the bolts that secure the bracket to the intake and position the bracket and cables out of the way.

3. Disconnect the upper manifold vacuum fitting connections by removing all the vacuum lines at the vacuum tree (label lines for position identification). Remove the vacuum lines to the EGR valve and fuel pressure regulator.

4. Disconnect the PCV system by disconnecting the hose from the fitting at the rear of the upper manifold.

5. Remove the two canister purge lines from the fittings at the throttle body.

6. Disconnect the EGR tube from the EGR valve by loosening the flange nut.

7. Remove the bolt from the upper intake support bracket to upper manifold. Remove the upper manifold retaining bolts and remove the upper intake manifold and throttle body as an assembly.

8. Clean and inspect all mounting surfaces of the upper and lower intake manifolds.

9. Position a new mounting gasket on the lower intake manifold and install the upper manifold in the reverse order of removal. Mounting bolts are torqued to 12–18 ft. lbs.

10. To remove the lower intake manifold: Upper manifold and throttle body must be removed first.

11. Drain the cooling system.

CAUTION

When draining the coolant, keep in mind that cats and dogs are attracted by the ethylene glycol antifreeze, and are quite likely to drink any that is left in an uncovered container or in puddles on the ground. This will prove fatal in sufficient quantity. Always drain the coolant into a sealable container. Coolant should be reused unless it is contaminated or several years old.

12. Remove the distributor assembly, cap and wires.

13. Disconnect the electrical connectors at the engine, coolant temperature sensor and sending unit, at the air charge temperature sensor and at the knock sensor.

14. Disconnect the injector wiring harness from the main har-

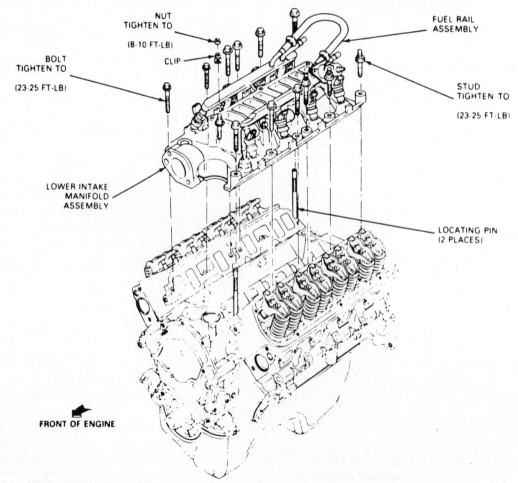

NUT TIGHTEN TO (8-10 FT-LB)

CLIP

BOLT TIGHTEN TO (23-25 FT-LB)

FUEL RAIL ASSEMBLY

STUD TIGHTEN TO (23-25 FT-LB)

LOWER INTAKE MANIFOLD ASSEMBLY

LOCATING PIN (2 PLACES)

FRONT OF ENGINE

Lower intake manifold and throttle body for the 8- 5.0L and 8-5.8L engines

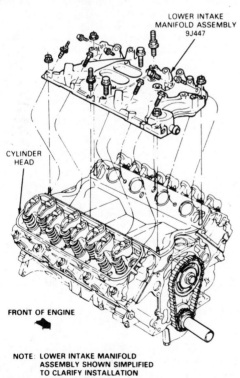

Lower intake manifold installation for the 8-7.5L engine

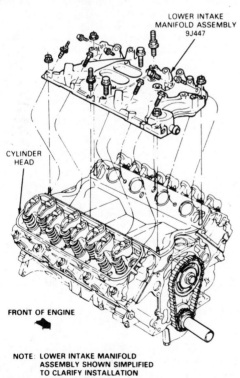

NOTE: LOWER INTAKE MANIFOLD
ASSEMBLY SHOWN SIMPLIFIED
TO CLARIFY INSTALLATION

Intake manifold installation torque sequence for the 8-7.5L

ness assembly. Remove the ground wire from the intake manifold stud. The ground wire must be installed at the same position it was removed from.

15. Disconnect the fuel supply and return lines from the fuel rails.

16. Remove the upper radiator hose from the thermostat housing. Remove the bypass hose. Remove the heater outlet hose at the intake manifold.

17. Remove the air cleaner mounting bracket. Remove the intake manifold mounting bolts and studs. Pay attention to the location of the bolts and studs for reinstallation. Remove the lower intake manifold assembly.

18. Clean and inspect the mounting surfaces of the heads and manifold.

19. Apply a $\frac{1}{16}$ in. (1.5mm) bead of RTV sealer to the ends of the manifold seal (the junction point of the seals and gaskets). Install the end seals and intake gaskets on the cylinder heads. The gaskets must interlock with the seal tabs.

20. Install locator bolts at opposite ends of each head and carefully lower the intake manifold into position. Install and tighten the mounting bolts and studs to 23–25 ft. lbs. Install the remaining components in the reverse order of removal.

8-7.3L Diesel

1. Open the hood and remove both battery ground cables.

2. Remove the air cleaner and install clean rags into the air intake of the intake manifold. It is important that no dirt or foreign objects get into the diesel intake.

3. Remove the injection pump as described in Section 5 under Diesel Fuel Systems.

4. Remove the fuel return hose from No. 7 and No. 8 rear nozzles and remove the return hose to the fuel tank.

5. Label the positions of the wires and remove the engine wiring harness from the engine.

NOTE: The engine harness ground cables must be removed from the back of the left cylinder head.

6. Remove the bolts attaching the intake manifold to the cylinder heads and remove the manifold.

7. Remove the CDR tube grommet from the valley pan.

8. Remove the bolts attaching the valley pan strap to the front of the engine block, and remove the strap.

9. Remove the valley pan drain plug and remove the valley pan.

10. Apply a $\frac{1}{8}$ in. (3mm) bead of RTV sealer to each end of the cylinder block as shown in the accompanying illustration.

NOTE: The RTV sealer should be applied immediately prior to the valley pan installation.

11. Install the valley pan drain plug, CDR tube and new grommet into the valley pan.

12. Install a new O-ring and new back-up ring on the CDR valve.

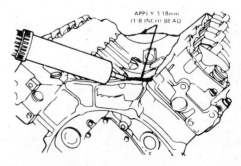

Apply sealer to the diesel cylinder block-to-intake manifold mating surfaces at each end

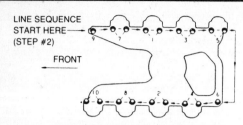

LINE SEQUENCE
START HERE
(STEP #2)

FRONT

STEP 1. TORQUE BOLTS TO 33 N·m (24 lbf-ft), IN NUM-
BERED SEQUENCE SHOWN ABOVE
STEP 2. TORQUE BOLTS TO 33 N·m (24 lbf-ft), IN LINE
SEQUENCE SHOWN ABOVE.

Diesel intake manifold bolt torque sequence

13. Install the valley pan strap on the front of the valley pan.
14. Install the intake manifold and torque the bolts to 24 ft. lbs. using the sequence shown in the illustration.
15. Reconnect the engine wiring harness and the engine ground wire located to the rear of the left cylinder head.
16. Install the injection pump using the procedure shown in Section 5 under Diesel fuel Systems.
17. Install the no. 7 and no. 8 fuel return hoses and the fuel tank return hose.
18. Remove the rag from the intake manifold and replace the air cleaner. Reconnect the battery ground cables to both batteries.
19. Run the engine and check for oil and fuel leaks.

NOTE: If necessary, purge the nozzle high pressure lines of air by loosening the connector one half to one turn and cranking the engine until solid stream of fuel, devoid of any bubbles, flows from the connection.

—————— CAUTION ——————

Keep eyes and hands away from the nozzle spray. Fuel spraying from the nozzle under high pressure can penetrate the skin.

20. Check and adjust the injection pump timing, as described in Section 5 under Diesel Fuel Systems.

Exhaust Manifold

REMOVAL AND INSTALLATION

6–4.9L

The intake and exhaust manifolds on these engines are known as combination manifolds and are serviced as a unit. See Intake Manifold Removal and Installation.

Gasoline V8

1. Remove the air cleaner.
2. On the 8–5.0L, remove the dipstick bracket.
3. Disconnect the exhaust pipe or catalytic converter from the exhaust manifold. Remove and discard the doughnut gasket.
4. Remove the exhaust manifold attaching screws and remove the manifold from the cylinder head.
5. Install the exhaust manifold in the reverse order of removal. Apply a light coat of graphite grease to the mating surface of the manifold. Install and tighten the attaching bolts, starting from the center and working to both ends alternately. Tighten to the proper specifications.

8-7.3L Diesel

1. Disconnect the ground cables from both batteries.
2. Jack up the van and safely support it with jackstands.
3. Disconnect the muffler inlet pipe from the exhaust manifolds.
4. Lower the van to remove the right manifold. When removing the left manifold, jack the tuck up. Bend the tabs on the manifold attaching bolts, then remove the bolts and manifold.
5. Before installing, clean all mounting surfaces on the cylinder heads and the manifold. Apply an anti-seize compound on the manifold both threads and install the left manifold, using a new gasket and new locking tabs.
6. Torque the bolts to specifications and bend the tabs over the flats on the bolt heads to prevent the bolts from loosening.
7. Jack up the van to install the right manifold. Install the right manifold following procedures 5 and 6 above.
8. Connect the inlet pipes to the manifold and tighten. Lower the van, connect the batteries and run the engine to check for exhaust leaks.

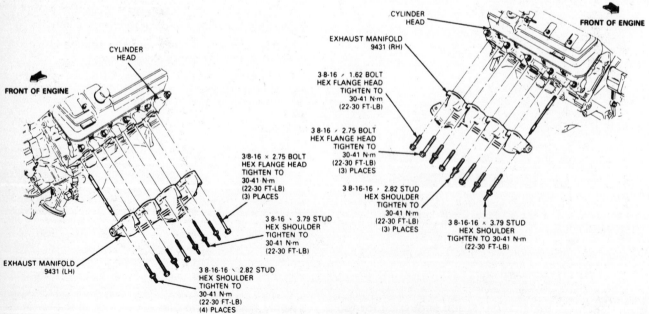

Exhaust manifold torque sequence for the 8-7.5L

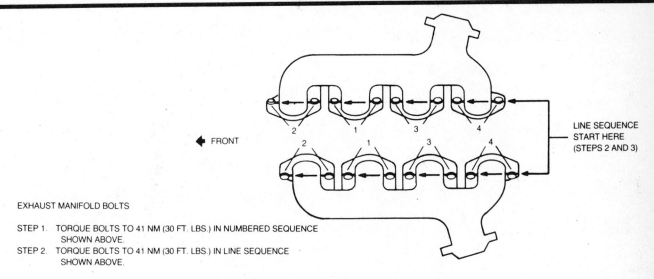

EXHAUST MANIFOLD BOLTS

STEP 1. TORQUE BOLTS TO 41 NM (30 FT. LBS.) IN NUMBERED SEQUENCE
SHOWN ABOVE.
STEP 2. TORQUE BOLTS TO 41 NM (30 FT. LBS.) IN LINE SEQUENCE
SHOWN ABOVE.

Diesel exhaust manifold torque sequence

Air Conditioning Compressor

REMOVAL AND INSTALLATION

6-4.9L Engines

1. Discharge the refrigerant system. See Section 1.
2. Disconnect the two refrigerant lines from the compressor. Cap the openings immediately!
3. Remove tension from the drive belt. Remove the belt.

4. Disconnect the clutch wire at the connector.
5. Remove the bolt attaching the adjusting arm to the mounting bracket.
6. Remove the 4 bolts attaching the front and rear support to the mounting bracket.
7. Remove the compressor along with the front and rear braces.
8. Installation is the reverse of removal. Use new O-rings coated with clean refrigerant oil at all fittings. If a new, replacement compressor is being installed, remove the shipping plates and add 120ml (4 fl. oz.) of clean refrigerant oil through the service ports. Assemble all parts loosely and adjust the belt tension. Tighten all mounting bolts to 50 ft. lbs. Tighten the compressor manifold bolts to 13–17 ft. lbs. Evacuate, charge and leak test the system. See Section 1.

V8 Gasoline Engines

1. Discharge the refrigerant system. See Section 1.
2. Disconnect the two refrigerant lines from the compressor. Cap the openings immediately!
3. Remove tension from the drive belt. Remove the belt.
4. Disconnect the clutch wire at the connector.
5. Remove the bolts attaching the compressor to the brackets.
6. Remove the compressor.
7. Installation is the reverse of removal. Use new O-rings coated with clean refrigerant oil at all fittings. If a new, replacement compressor is being installed, remove the shipping plates and add 120ml (4 fl. oz.) of clean refrigerant oil through the service ports. Assemble all parts loosely and adjust the belt tension. Tighten all mounting bolts to 32 ft. lbs. Tighten the compressor

manifold bolts to 13–17 ft. lbs. Evacuate, charge and leak test the system. See Section 1.

Diesel Engines

1. Discharge the refrigerant system. See Section 1.
2. Disconnect the two refrigerant lines from the compressor. Cap the openings immediately!
3. Loosen the pivot and adjusting bolts. Remove the belt.
4. Disconnect the clutch wire at the connector.
5. Remove the 5 bolts attaching the compressor to the mounting bracket.
6. Remove the compressor.
7. Installation is the reverse of removal. Use new O-rings coated with clean refrigerant oil at all fittings. If a new, replacement compressor is being installed, remove the shipping plates and add 120ml (4 fl. oz.) of clean refrigerant oil through the service ports. Assemble all parts loosely and adjust the belt tension. Tighten all mounting bolts to 32 ft. lbs. Tighten the compressor manifold bolts to 13–17 ft. lbs. Evacuate, charge and leak test the system. See Section 1.

Cylinder Head

REMOVAL AND INSTALLATION

6–4.9L

1. Drain the cooling system. Remove the hood.

————————————— CAUTION —————————————
When draining the coolant, keep in mind that cats and dogs are attracted by the ethylene glycol antifreeze, and are quite likely to drink any that is left in an uncovered container or in puddles on the ground. This will prove fatal in sufficient quantity. Always drain the coolant into a sealable container. Coolant should be reused unless it is contaminated or several years old.
————————————————————————————————————

2. Remove the throttle body inlet tubes.
3. Remove the air conditioning compressor.
4. Remove the condenser.
5. Disconnect the battery ground cable.
6. Disconnect the heater hoses from the water pump and coolant outlet housing.
7. Disconnect the fuel line at the fuel pump.

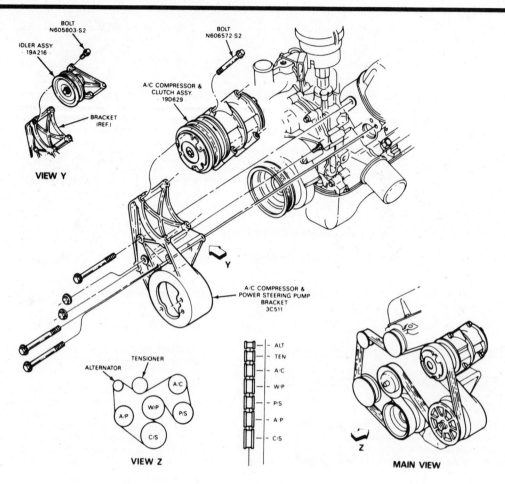

Compressor installation for the 8-5.0L and 8-5.8L engines

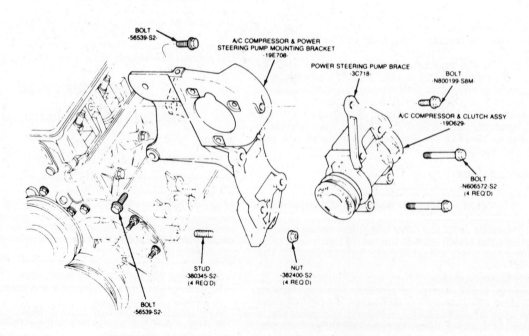

Compressor installation for the 6-4.9L engine

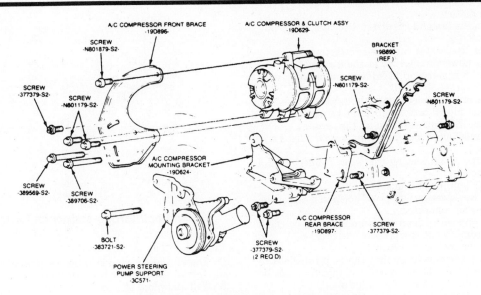

Compressor installation for the diesel

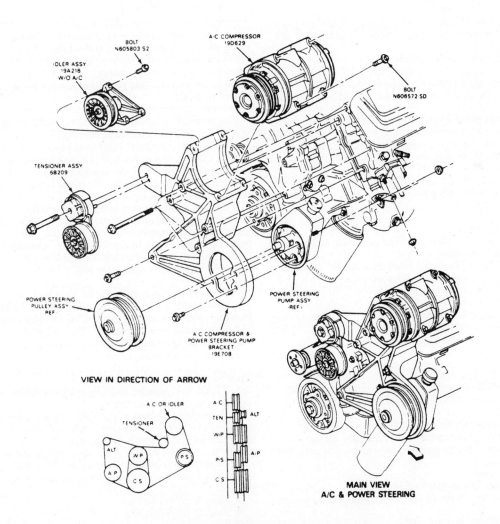

VIEW IN DIRECTION OF ARROW

MAIN VIEW
A/C & POWER STEERING

Compressor installation for the 8-7.5L

8. Remove the radiator.

9. Remove the engine fan and fan drive, the water pump pulley and the drive belt.

10. Disconnect the accelerator cable and retracting spring.

11. Disconnect the power brake hose at the manifold.

12. Disconnect the transmission kickdown rod on vans with automatic transmission.

13. Disconnect the muffler inlet pipe at the exhaust manifold. Pull the muffler inlet pipe down. Remove the gasket.

14. Disconnect the EEC harness from all the sensors.

15. Tag and disconnect all remaining wiring from the head and related components.

16. Remove the alternator, leaving the wires connected and position it out of the way.

17. Remove the air pump and bracket.

18. Remove the power steering pump and position it out of the way with the hoses still connected.

19. If the van is equipped with an air compressor, bleed the 2 pressure lines and remove the compressor and bracket.

20. Remove the valve rocker arm cover.

21. Loosen the rocker arm bolts so they can be pivoted out of the way. Remove the pushrods in sequence so that they can be identified and reinstalled in their original positions.

22. Disconnect the spark plug wires at the spark plugs.

12. Remove the cylinder head bolts and remove the cylinder head. Do not pry between the cylinder head and the block as the gasket surfaces maybe damaged.

To install the cylinder head:

1. Clean the head and block gasket surfaces. If the cylinder head was removed for a gasket change, check the flatness of the cylinder head and block.

2. Position the gasket on the cylinder block.

3. Install a new gasket on the flange of the muffler inlet pipe.

4. Lift the cylinder head above the cylinder block and lower it into position using two head bolts installed through the head as guides.

5. Coat the threads of the Nos. 1 and 6 bolts for the right side of the cylinder head with a small mount of water-resistant sealer. Oil the threads of the remaining bolts. Install, but do not tighten, two bolts at the opposite ends of the head to hold the head and gasket in position.

6. The cylinder head bolts are tightened in 3 progressive steps. Torque them (in the proper sequence):
- Step 1: 50–55 ft. lbs.
- Step 2: 60–65 ft. lbs.
- Step 3: 70–85 ft. lbs.

7. Apply Lubriplate® to both ends of the pushrods and install them in their original positions.

8. Apply Lubriplate® to both the fulcrum and seat and position the rocker arms on the valves and pushrods.

9. Adjust the valves, as outlined below.

10. Install the valve rocker arm cover.

11. Install the air compressor and bracket.

12. Install the power steering pump.

13. Install the air pump and bracket.

14. Install the alternator.

15. Connect all wiring at the head and related components.

16. Connect the EEC harness to all the sensors.

17. Connect the muffler inlet pipe at the exhaust manifold.

18. Connect the transmission kickdown rod on vans with automatic transmission.

19. Connect the power brake hose at the manifold.

20. Connect the accelerator cable and retracting spring.

21. Install the water pump pulley, the engine fan and fan drive, and the drive belt.

22. Install the radiator.

23. Connect the fuel line at the fuel pump.

24. Connect the heater hoses at the water pump and coolant outlet housing.

25. Connect the battery ground cable.

26. Install the condenser.

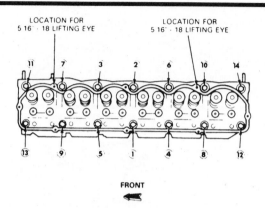

Head bolt torque sequence for the 6-4.9L

27. Install the air conditioning compressor.

28. Install the throttle body inlet tubes.

29. Fill and bleed the cooling system.

30. Install the hood.

8-5.0L and 8-5.8L

1. Drain the cooling system.

— **CAUTION** —

When draining the coolant, keep in mind that cats and dogs are attracted by the ethylene glycol antifreeze, and are quite likely to drink any that is left in an uncovered container or in puddles on the ground. This will prove fatal in sufficient quantity. Always drain the coolant into a sealable container. Coolant should be reused unless it is contaminated or several years old.

2. Remove the intake manifold and EFI throttle body.

3. Remove the rocker arm cover(s).

4. If the right cylinder head is to be removed, lift the tensioner and remove the drive belt. Loosen the alternator adjusting arm bolt and remove the alternator mounting bracket bolt and spacer. Swing the alternator down and out of the way. Remove the air cleaner inlet duct.

If the left cylinder head is being removed, remove the air conditioning compressor. See Section 1. Persons not familiar with air conditioning systems should exercise extreme caution, perhaps leaving this job to a professional. Remove the oil dipstick and tube. Remove the cruise control bracket.

5. Disconnect the exhaust manifold(s) from the muffler inlet pipe(s).

6. Loosen the rocker arm stud nuts so that the rocker arms can be rotated to the side. Remove the pushrods and identify them so that they can be reinstalled in their original positions.

7. Disconnect the Thermactor® air supply hoses at the check valves. Cover the check valve openings.

8. Remove the cylinder head bolts and lift the cylinder head from the block. Removce the discard the gasket.

To install the cylinder head(s):

1. Clean the cylinder head, intake manifold, the valve cover and the head gasket surfaces.

2. A specially treated composition head gasket is used. Do not apply sealer to a composition gasket. Position the new gasket over the locating dowels on the cylinder block. Then, position the cylinder head on the block and install the attaching bolts.

3. The cylinder head bolts are tightened in progressive steps. Tighten all the bolts in the proper sequence to:

8-5.0L
- Step 1: 55–65 ft. lbs.
- Step 2: 66–72 ft. lbs.

8-5.8L
- Step 1: 85 ft. lbs.

Gasoline V8 head bolt torque sequence

- Step 2: 95 ft. lbs.
- Step 3: 105–112 ft. lbs.

4. Clean the pushrods. Blow out the oil passage in the rods with compressed air. Check the pushrods for straightness by rolling them on a piece of glass. Never try to straighten a pushrod; always replace it.

5. Apply Lubriplate® to the ends of the pushrods and install them in their original positions.

6. Apply Lubriplate® to the rocker arms and their fulcrum seats and install the rocker arms. Adjust the valves.

7. Position a new gasket(s) on the muffler inlet pipe(s) as necessary. Connect the exhaust manifold(s) at the muffler inlet pipe(s).

8. If the right cylinder head was removed, install the alternator, and air cleaner duct. Install the drive belt.

If the left cylinder head was removed, install the compressor. See Section 1. Install the dipstick and cruise control bracket.

9. Clean the valve rocker arm cover and the cylinder head gasket surfaces. Place the new gaskets in the covers, making sure that the tabs of the gasket engage the notches provided in the cover. Evacuate, charge and leak test the air conditioning system. See Section 1.

10. Install the intake manifold and related parts. Install the Thermactor® hoses.

11. Fill and bleed the cooling system.

8–7.5L

1. Drain the cooling system.

---------------- **CAUTION** ----------------

When draining the coolant, keep in mind that cats and dogs are attracted by the ethylene glycol antifreeze, and are quite likely to drink any that is left in an uncovered container or in puddles on the ground. This will prove fatal in sufficient quantity. Always drain the coolant into a sealable container. Coolant should be reused unless it is contaminated or several years old.

---

2. Remove the upper and lower intake manifolds. See above and Section 5.

3. Disconnect the exhaust pipe from the exhaust manifold.

4. Loosen the air conditioning compressor drive belt, if so equipped.

5. Loosen the alternator attaching bolts and remove the bolt attaching the alternator bracket to the right cylinder head.

6. Disconnect the air conditioning compressor from the engine and move it aside, out of the way. Do not discharge the air conditioning system.

7. Remove the bolts securing the power steering reservoir bracket to the left cylinder head. Position the reservoir and bracket out of the way. On motor home chassis, remove the oil filler tube.

8. Remove the valve rocker arm covers. Remove the rocker arm bolts, rocker arms, oil deflectors, fulcrums and pushrods in sequence so that they can be reinstalled in their original positions.

9. Remove the cylinder head bolts and lift the head and exhaust manifold off the engine. If necessary, pry at the forward corners of the cylinder head against the casting bosses provided on the cylinder block. Do not damage the gasket mating surfaces of the cylinder head and block by prying against them.

10. Remove all gasket material from the cylinder head and block. Clean all gasket material from the mating surfaces of the intake manifold. If the exhaust manifold was removed, clean the mating surfaces of the cylinder head and exhaust manifold. Apply a thin coat of graphite grease to the cylinder head exhaust port areas and install the exhaust manifold.

11. Position two long cylinder head bolts in the two rear lower bolt holes of the left cylinder head. Place a long cylinder head bolt in the rear lower bolt hole of the right cylinder head. Use rubber bands to keep the bolts in position until the cylinder heads are installed on the cylinder block.

12. Position new cylinder head gaskets on the cylinder block dowels. Do not apply sealer to the gaskets, heads, or block.

13. Place the cylinder heads on the block, guiding the exhaust manifold studs into the exhaust pipe connections. Install the remaining cylinder head bolts. The longer bolts go in the lower row of holes.

14. Tighten all the cylinder head attaching bolts in the proper sequence in three stages: 80–90 ft. lbs., 100–110 ft.lbs., and finally to 130–140 ft. lbs. When this procedure is used, it is not necessary to retorque the heads after extended use.

15. Make sure that the oil holes in the pushrods are open and install the pushrods in their original positions. Make sure a dab of Lubriplate® to the ends of the pushrods before installing them.

16. Lubricate and install the valve rockers. Make sure that the pushrods remain seated in their lifters.

17. Connect the exhaust pipes to the exhaust manifolds.

18. Install the upper and lower intake manifolds.

19. Install the air conditioning compressor.

20. Install the power steering reservoir.

21. Apply oil-resistant sealer to one side of the new valve cover gaskets and lay the cemented side in place in the valve cover. Install the covers.

22. Install the alternator and adjust the drive belt.

23. Adjust the air conditioning compressor drive belt tension.

24. On motor home chassis, install the oil filler tube.

25. Fill and bleed the cooling system.

26. Start the engine and check for leaks.

8-7.3L Diesel

1. Open the hood and disconnect the negative cables from both batteries.

2. Drain the cooling system and remove the radiator fan shroud halves.

---------------- **CAUTION** ----------------

When draining the coolant, keep in mind that cats and dogs are attracted by the ethylene glycol antifreeze, and are quite likely to drink any that is left in an uncovered container or in puddles on the ground. This will prove fatal in sufficient quantity. Always drain the coolant into a sealable container. Coolant should be reused unless it is contaminated or several years old.

---

3. Remove the radiator fan and clutch assembly using special tool T83T-6312-A and B. This tool is available through the Owatonna Tool Co. whose address is listed in the front of this boot, or through Ford Dealers. It is also available through many tool rental shops.

NOTE: The fan clutch uses a left hand thread and must be removed by turning the nut clockwise.

4. Label and disconnect the wiring from the alternator.

5. Remove the adjusting bolts and pivot bolts from the alternator and the vacuum pump and remove both units.

6. Remove the fuel filter lines and cap to prevent fuel leakage.

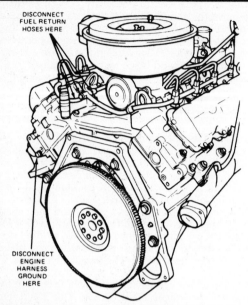

Diesel fuel hose and engine ground harness connections

7. Remove the alternator, vacuum pump, and fuel filter brackets with the fuel filter attached.

8. Remove the heater hose from the cylinder head.

9. Remove the fuel injection pump as described in Section 5 under Diesel Fuel Systems.

10. Remove the intake manifold and valley cover.

11. Jack up the van and safely support it with jackstands.

12. Disconnect the exhaust pipes from the exhaust manifolds.

13. Remove the clamp holding the engine oil dipstick tube in place and the bolt attaching the transmission oil dipstick to the cylinder head.

14. Lower the van.

15. Remove the engine oil dipstick tube.

16. Remove the valve covers, rocker arms and pushrods. Keep the pushrods in order so they can be returned to their original positions.

17. Remove the nozzles and glow plugs as described in Section 5 under Diesel Fuel Systems.

18. Remove the cylinder head bolts and attach lifting eyes, using special tool T70P–6000 or equivalent, to each end of the cylinder heads.

19. Carefully lift the cylinder heads out of the engine compartment and remove the head gaskets.

NOTE: The cylinder head prechambers may fall out of the heads upon removal.

To install:

20. Position the cylinder head gasket on the engine block and carefully lower the cylinder head in place.

NOTE: Use care in installing the cylinder heads to prevent the prechambers from falling out into the cylinder bores.

21. Install the cylinder head bolt and torque in 4 steps using the sequence shown in the illustration.

NOTE: Lubricate the threads and the mating surfaces of the bolt heads and washers with engine oil.

22. Dip the pushrod ends in clean engine oil and install the pushrods with the copper colored ends toward the rocker arms, making sure the pushrods are fully seated in the tappet pushrod seats.

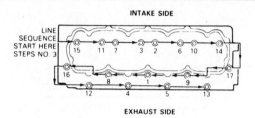

STEP 1. TIGHTEN BOLTS TO 88 N·m (65 FT-LB) IN NUMBERED SEQUENCE SHOWN ABOVE.
STEP 2. TIGHTEN BOLTS TO 115 N·m (85 FT-LB) IN NUMBERED SEQUENCE SHOWN ABOVE.
STEP 3. TIGHTEN BOLTS TO 136 N·m (100 FT-LB) IN LINE SEQUENCE SHOWN ABOVE.
STEP 4. REPEAT STEP NO. 3.

Head bolt torque sequence for the diesel

23. Install the rocker arms and posts in their original positions. Apply Lubriplate® grease to the valve stem tips. Turn the engine over by hand until the timing mark is at the 11 o'clock position as viewed from the front. Install the rocker arm posts, bolts, and torque to 27 ft. lbs. Install the valve covers.

24. Install the valley pan and the intake manifold.

25. Install the fuel injection pump as described in Section 5 under Diesel Fuel Systems.

26. Connect the heater hose to the cylinder head.

27. Install the fuel filter, alternator, vacuum pump, and their drive belts.

28. Install the engine oil and transmission dip stick.

29. Connect the exhaust pipe to the exhaust manifolds.

30. Reconnect the alternator wiring harness and replace the air cleaner. Connect both battery ground cables.

31. Refill and bleed the cooling system.

32. Run the engine and check for fuel, coolant and exhaust leaks.

NOTE: If necessary, purge the high pressure fuel lines of air by loosening the connector one half to one turn and cranking the engine until a solid stream of fuel, free from any bubbles, flows from the connections.

33. Check the injection pump timing. Refer to Section 5 for these procedures.

34. Install the radiator fan and clutch assembly using special tools T83T–6312A and B or equivalent.

NOTE: The fan clutch uses a left hand thread. Tighten by turning the nut counterclockwise. Install the radiator fan shroud halves.

CLEANING AND INSPECTION

1. With the valves installed to protect the valve seats, remove deposits from the combustion chambers and valve heads with a scraper and a wire brush. Be careful not to damage the cylinder head gasket surface. After the valves are removed, clean the

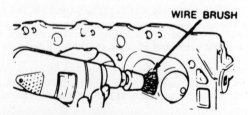

Remove combustion chamber carbon from the head with a drill-mounted wire brush. Make sure all carbon is removed and not just burnished

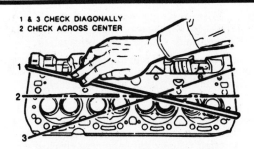

Checking the head for warpage

valve guide bores with a valve guide cleaning tool. Using cleaning solvent to remove dirt, grease and other deposits, clean all bolts holes; be sure the oil passage is clean (V8 engines).

2. Remove all deposits from the valves with a fine wire brush or buffing wheel.
3. Inspect the cylinder heads for cracks or excessively burned areas in the exhaust outlet ports.
4. Check the cylinder head for cracks and inspect the gasket surface for burrs and nicks. Replace the head if it is cracked.
5. On cylinder heads that incorporate valve seat inserts, check the inserts for excessive wear, cracks, or looseness.

RESURFACING

Cylinder Head Flatness

When the cylinder head is removed, check the flatness of the cylinder head gasket surfaces.
1. Place a straightedge across the gasket surface of the cylinder head. Using feeler gauges, determine the clearance at the center of the straightedge.
2. If warpage exceeds 0.003 in. (0.076mm) in a 6 in. (152mm) span, or 0.006 in. (0.152mm) over the total length, the cylinder head must be resurfaced.
3. If necessary to refinish the cylinder head gasket surface, do not plane or grind off more than 0.254mm (0.010 in.) from the original gasket surface.

NOTE: When milling the cylinder heads of V8 engines, the intake manifold mounting position is altered, and must be corrected by milling the manifold flange a proportionate amount. Consult an experienced machinist about this.

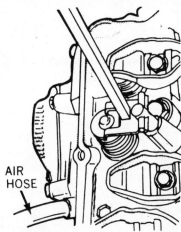

Compressing the gasoline engine valve springs. Note the spring compressor position and the air hose. The cylinder is at TDC

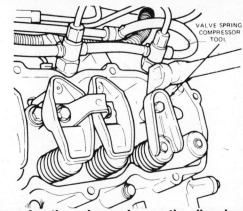

Compressing the valve spring on the diesel using a special tool

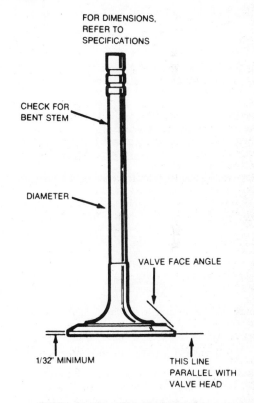

Critical valve dimensions

Valves and Springs

REMOVAL AND INSTALLATION

1. Block the head on its side, or install a pair of head-holding brackets made especially for valve removal.
2. Use a socket slightly larger than the valve stem and keepers, place the socket over the valve stem and gently hit the socket with a plastic hammer to break loose any varnish buildup.
3. Remove the valve keepers, retainer, spring shield and valve spring using a valve spring compressor (the locking C-clamp type is the easiest kind to use).
4. Put the parts in a separate container numbered for the cylinder being worked on; do not mix them with other parts removed.

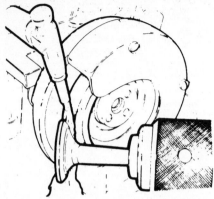

Well equipped machine shops can handle refacing jobs

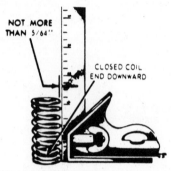

Check the valve spring for length and squareness

Checking the valve spring test pressure

5. Remove and discard the valve stem oil seals. A new seal will be used at assembly time.

6. Remove the valves from the cylinder head and place them, in order, through numbered holes punched in a stiff piece of cardboard or wood valve holding stick.

NOTE: The exhaust valve stems, on some engines, are equipped with small metal caps. Take care not to lose the caps. Make sure to reinstall them at assembly time. Replace any caps that are worn.

7. Use an electric drill and rotary wire brush to clean the intake and exhaust valve ports, combustion chamber and valve seats. In some cases, the carbon will need to be chipped away. Use a blunt pointed drift for carbon chipping. Be careful around the valve seat areas.

8. Use a wire valve guide cleaning brush and safe solvent to clean the valve guides.

9. Clean the valves with a revolving wires brush. Heavy carbon deposits may be removed with the blunt drift.

NOTE: When using a wire brush to clean carbon on the valve ports, valves etc., be sure that the deposits are actually removed, rather than burnished.

10. Wash and clean all valve springs, keepers, retaining caps etc., in safe solvent.

11. Clean the head with a brush and some safe solvent and wipe dry.

12. Check the head for cracks. Cracks in the cylinder head usually start around an exhaust valve seat because it is the hottest part of the combustion chamber. If a crack is suspected but cannot be detected visually have the area checked with dye penetrant or other method by the machine shop.

13. After all cylinder head parts are reasonably clean, check the valve stem-to-guide clearance. If a dial indicator is not on hand, a visual inspection can give you a fairly good idea if the guide, valve stem or both are worn.

14. Insert the valve into the guide until slight away from the valve seat. Wiggle the valve sideways. A small amount of wobble is normal, excessive wobble means a worn guide or valve stem. If a dial indicator is on hand, mount the indicator so that the stem of the valve is at 90° to the valve stem, as close to the valve guide as possible. Move the valve off the seat, and measure the valve guide-to-stem clearance by rocking the stem back and forth to actuate the dial indicator. Measure the valve stem using a micrometer and compare to specifications to determine whether stem or guide wear is causing excessive clearance.

15. The valve guide, if worn, must be repaired before the valve seats can be resurfaced. Ford supplies valves with oversize stems to fit valve guides that are reamed to oversize for repair. The machine shop will be able to handle the guide reaming for you. In some cases, if the guide is not too badly worn, knurling may be all that is required.

16. Reface, or have the valves and valve seats refaced. The valve seats should be a true 45° angle. Remove only enough material to clean up any pits or grooves. Be sure the valve seat is not too wide or narrow. Use a 60° grinding wheel to remove material from the bottom of the seat for raising and a 30° grinding

Reaming the valve seat with a hand reamer

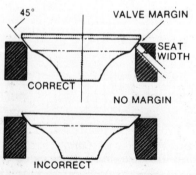

Valve seat width and centering after reaming

Checking seat concentricity

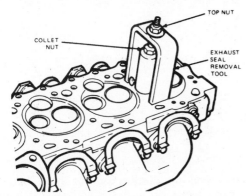

Diesel valve insert removal using a special tool

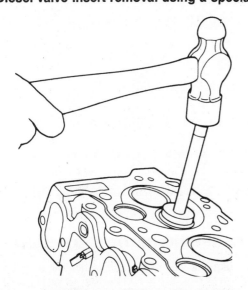

Installing the diesel valve seats

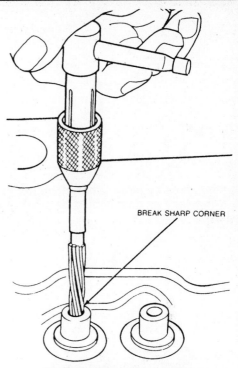

Reaming the valve guides

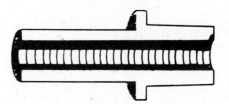

Cross-section of a knurled valve guide

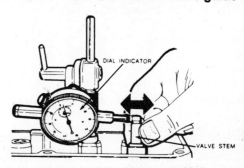

Measuring stem-to-guide clearance. Make sure that the indicator is mounted at 90 degrees to the valve stem and as close to the guide as possible

wheel to remove material from the top of the seat to narrow.

17. After the valves are refaced by machine, hand lap them to the valve seat. Clean the grinding compound off and check the position of face-to-seat contact. Contact should be close to the center of the valve face. If contact is close to the top edge of the valve, narrow the seat; if too close to the bottom edge, raise the seat.

18. Valves should be refaced to a true angle of 44°. Remove only enough metal to clean up the valve face or to correct run-out. If the edge of a valve head, after machining, is $\frac{1}{32}$ in. (0.8mm) or less replace the valve. The tip of the valve stem should also be dressed on the valve grinding machine, however, do not remove more than 0.010 in. (0.254mm).

19. After all valve and valve seats have been machined, check the remaining valve train parts (springs, retainers, keepers, etc.) for wear. Check the valve springs for straightness and tension.

20. Install the valves in the cylinder head and metal caps.

Lapping the valves by hand. When done the finish on both the valve face an seat should be smooth and evenly shiny

Installing the nylon oil shield

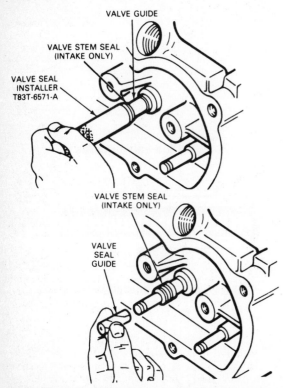

Installing the valve stem seals on the diesel

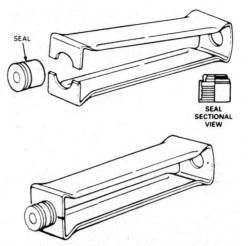

Valve seal installation tool for the 8-7.5L

21. Install new valve stem oil seals.
22. Install the valve keepers, retainer, spring shield and valve spring using a valve spring compressor (the locking C-clamp type is the easiest kind to use).
23. Check the valve spring installed height, shim or replace as necessary.

CHECKING VALVE SPRINGS

Place the valve spring on a flat surface next to a carpenter's square. Measure the height of the spring, and rotate the spring against the edge of the square to measure distortion. If the spring height varies (by comparison) by more than $1/16$ in. (1.5mm) or if the distortion exceeds $1/16$ in. (1.5mm), replace the spring.

Have the valve springs tested for spring pressure at the installed and compressed (installed height minus valve lift) height using a valve spring tester. Springs should be within one pound, plus or minus each other. Replace springs as necessary.

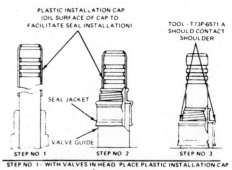

STEP NO 1 – WITH VALVES IN HEAD, PLACE PLASTIC INSTALLATION CAP OVER END OF VALVE STEM
STEP NO 2 – START VALVE STEM SEAL CAREFULLY OVER CAP. PUSH SEAL DOWN UNTIL JACKET TOUCHES TOP OF GUIDE
STEP NO 3 – REMOVE PLASTIC INSTALLATION CAP. USE INSTALLATION TOOL - T73P-6571 A OR SCREWDRIVERS TO BOTTOM SEAL ON VALVE GUIDE

Valve stem seal installation

VALVE SPRING INSTALLED HEIGHT

After installing the valve spring, measure the distance between the spring mounting pad and the lower edge of the spring retainer. Compare the measurement to specifications. If the installed height is incorrect, add shim washers between the spring mounting pad and the spring. Use only washers designed for valve springs, available at most parts houses.

VALVE STEM OIL SEALS

When installing valve stem oil seals, ensure that a small amount of oil is able to pass the seal to lubricate the valve stems and guide walls, otherwise, excessive wear will occur.

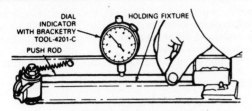

Checking pushrod runout

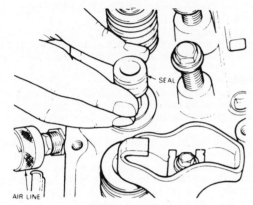

Removing or installing the valve stem seal on the 6-4.9L

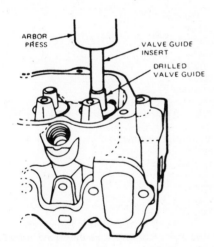

Installing the valve guide inserts on the diesel

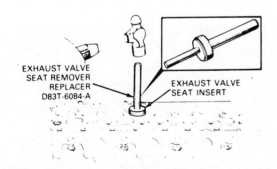

Installing the exhaust seat inserts on the diesel

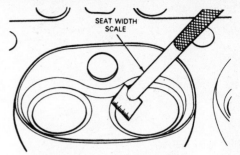

Checking valve seat width

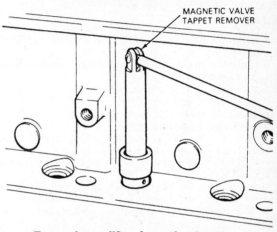

Removing a lifter from the 6-4.9L

VALVE SEATS

If the valve seat is damaged or burnt and cannot be serviced by refacing, it may be possible to have the seat machined and an insert installed. Consult an automotive machine shop for their advice.

VALVE GUIDES

Worn valve guides can, in most cases, be reamed to accept a valve with an oversized stem. Valve guides that are not excessively worn or distorted may, in some cases, be knurled rather than reamed. However, if the valve stem is worn reaming for an oversized valve stem is the answer since a new valve would be required.

Knurling is a process in which metal is displaced and raised, thereby reducing clearance. Knurling also produces excellent oil control. The possibility of knurling instead of reaming the valve guides should be discussed with a machinist.

Valve Lifters

REMOVAL AND INSTALLATION

6-4.9L Engine

1. Disconnect the inlet hose at the crankcase filler cap.
2. Remove the throttle body inlet tubes.
3. Disconnect the accelerator cable at the throttle body. Remove the cable retracting spring. Remove the accelerator cable bracket from the upper intake manifold and position the cable and bracket out of the way.

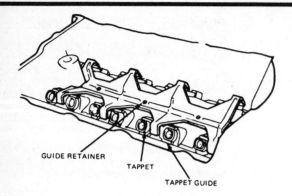

Diesel engine lifter removal

4. Remove the fuel line from the fuel rail. Be careful not to kink the line.

5. Remove the upper intake manifold and throttle body assembly. See Section 5.

6. Remove the ignition coil and wires.

7. Remove the rocker arm cover.

8. Remove the spark plug wires.

9. Remove the distributor cap.

10. Remove the pushrod cover (engine side cover).

11. Loosen the rocker arm bolts until the pushrods can be removed. KEEP THE PUSHRODS IN ORDER, FOR INSTALLATION!

12. Using a magnetic lifter removal tool, remove the lifters. Wipe clean the exterior of each lifter as it's removed and mark it with an indelible marker, so that it can be installed in its original bore.

To install:

13. Coat the bottom surface of each lifter with multi-purpose grease, and coat the rest of the lifter with clean engine oil.

14. Install each lifter in it original bore using the magnetic tool.

15. Coat each end of each pushrod with multi-purpose grease and install each in its original position. Make sure that each pushrod is properly seated in the lifter socket.

16. Engage the rocker arms with the pushrods and tighten the rocker arm bolts enough to hold the pushrods in place.

17. Adjust the valve clearance as described below.

18. The remainder of installation is the reverse of removal.

8-5.0L Engine
8-5.8L Engine

1. Remove the intake manifold.

2. Disconnect the Thermactor air supply hose at the pump.

3. Remove the rocker arm covers.

4. Loosen the rocker arm fulcrum bolts until the rocker arms can be rotated off the pushrods.

5. Remove the pushrods. KEEP THE PUSHRODS IN ORDER, FOR INSTALLATION!

6. Using a magnetic lifter removal tool, remove the lifters. Wipe clean the exterior of each lifter as it's removed and mark it with an indelible marker, so that it can be installed in its original bore.

To install:

7. Coat the bottom surface of each lifter with multi-purpose grease, and coat the rest of the lifter with clean engine oil.

8. Install each lifter in it original bore using the magnetic tool.

9. Coat each end of each pushrod with multi-purpose grease and install each in its original position. Make sure that each pushrod is properly seated in the lifter socket.

10. Engage the rocker arms with the pushrods and tighten the

rocker arm fulcrum bolts to 18–25 ft. lbs. No valve adjustment should be necessary, however, if there is any question as to post-assembly collapsed lifter clearance, see the Hydraulic Lifter Clearance procedure below.

11. The remainder of installation is the reverse of removal.

8-7.5L Engine

1. Remove the intake manifold.

2. Remove the rocker arm covers.

3. Loosen the rocker arm fulcrum bolts until the rocker arms can be rotated off the pushrods.

4. Remove the pushrods. KEEP THE PUSHRODS IN ORDER, FOR INSTALLATION!

5. Using a magnetic lifter removal tool, remove the lifters. Wipe clean the exterior of each lifter as it's removed and mark it with an indelible marker, so that it can be installed in its original bore.

To install:

6. Coat the bottom surface of each lifter with multi-purpose grease, and coat the rest of the lifter with clean engine oil.

7. Install each lifter in it original bore using the magnetic tool.

8. Coat each end of each pushrod with multi-purpose grease and install each in its original position. Make sure that each pushrod is properly seated in the lifter socket.

9. Rotate the crankshaft by hand until No.1 piston is at TDC of compression. The firing order marks on the damper will be aligned at TDC with the timing pointer.

10. Engage the rocker arms with the pushrods and tighten the rocker arm fulcrum bolts to 18–25 ft. lbs. in the following sequence:

- No.1 intake and exhaust
- No.3 intake
- No.8 exhaust
- No.7 intake
- No.5 exhaust
- No.8 intake
- No.4 exhaust

11. Rotate the crankshaft on full turn — 360° — and re-align the TDC mark and pointer. Tighten the fulcrum bolt on the following valves:

- No.2 intake and exhaust
- No.4 intake
- No.3 exhaust
- No.5 intake
- No.6 exhaust
- No.6 intake
- No.7 exhaust

12. The remainder of installation is the reverse of removal.

13. Check the valve clearance as described under Hydraulic Valve Clearance, below.

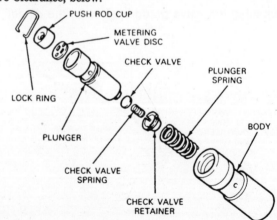

Explode view of the lifter used in all gasoline engines

Diesel Engine

1. Remove the intake manifold.
2. Remove the CDR tube and grommet from the valley pan.
3. Remove the valley pan strap from the front of the block.
4. Remove the valley pan drain plug and lift out the valley pan.
5. Remove the rocker arm covers.
6. Remove the rocker arms. KEEP THEM IN ORDER FOR INSTALLATION!
7. Remove the pushrods. KEEP THEM IN ORDER FOR INSTALLATION!
8. Remove the lifter guide retainer.
9. Using a magnetic lifter removal tool, remove the lifters. Wipe clean the exterior of each lifter as it's removed and mark it with an indelible marker, so that it can be installed in its original bore.

To install:

10. Coat the bottom surface of each lifter with multi-purpose grease, and coat the rest of the lifter with clean engine oil.
11. Install each lifter in it original bore using the magnetic tool.
12. Install the lifter guide retainer.
13. Install the pushrods, copper colored end up, into their original locations, making sure that they are firmly seated in the lifters.
14. Coat the valve stem tips with multi-purpose grease and install the rocker arms and posts in their original positions.
15. Turn the crankshaft by hand, until the timing mark is at the 11 o'clock position — viewed from the front.
16. Install all the rocker arm post bolts and torque them to 20 ft. lbs.
17. Install the rocker arm covers.
18. Clean all old RTV gasket material from the block and run a 1/8 in. (3mm) bead of new RTV gasket material at each end of the block. Within 15 minutes, install the valley pan. Install the pan drain plug.
19. Install the CDR tube, new grommet and new O-ring.
20. Install the intake manifold and related parts.

DISASSEMBLY AND ASSEMBLY

NOTE: Each lifter is an assembly of matched parts. When disassembling more than one lifter, keep the parts segregated. Mixing of parts between or among different lifters will result in improper operation of the lifter(s).

Always mark the lifters so that you won't forget which bore from which they originally came. Lifters must be returned to their original bore.

Always work on a clean work surface.

1. Using needle-nosed pliers, remove the plunger lockring from the lifter. It may be necessary to depress the plunger.
2. Remove the pushrod cup, metering valve, plunger and spring from the lifter body.
3. Invert the plunger and remove the check valve retainer by prying up on it carefully. Remove the check valve (either a disc or ball) and the spring.
4. Clean all parts thoroughly and replace any damaged or worn parts.

To install:

5. Place the plunger upside down on the clean work surface.
6. Place the check valve in position over the oil hole on the

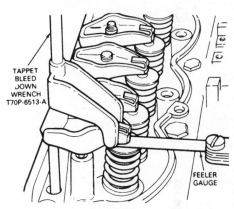

Valve clearance check

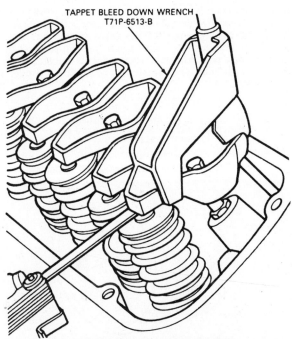

Special lifter bleed-down tool

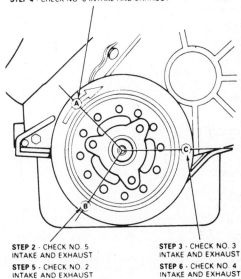

6-4.9L valve timing

bottom of the plunger. Place the check valve spring on top of the check valve.

7. Place the check valve retainer over the check valve and spring. Push the retainer down, into place on the plunger.

8. Place the plunger spring and plunger, with the open end up, into the lifter body.

9. Place the metering valve in the plunger, followed by the pushrod cup.

10. Depress the plunger and install the lockring. Release the plunger and make sure the lockring stays in place with the spring pressure against it.

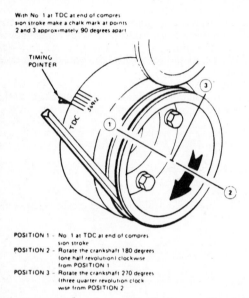

POSITION 1 - No. 1 at TDC at end of compression stroke
POSITION 2 - Rotate the crankshaft 180 degrees (one half revolution) clockwise from POSITION 1
POSITION 3 - Rotate the crankshaft 270 degrees (three quarter revolution) clockwise from POSITION 2

Crankshaft positions for valve timing on the 8-5.0L

STEP 1 - SET NO. 1 PISTON ON T.D.C. AT END OF COMPRESSION STROKE ADJUST NO. 1 INTAKE AND EXHAUST
STEP 4 - CHECK NO. 6 INTAKE AND EXHAUST

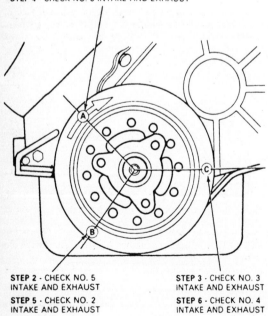

STEP 2 - CHECK NO. 5 INTAKE AND EXHAUST
STEP 5 - CHECK NO. 2 INTAKE AND EXHAUST

STEP 3 - CHECK NO. 3 INTAKE AND EXHAUST
STEP 6 - CHECK NO. 4 INTAKE AND EXHAUST

6-4.9L engine valve adjustment positions

DIESEL HYDRAULIC VALVE LIFTER INSPECTION

NOTE: The lifters used on diesel engines require a special test fluid, kerosene is not satisfactory.

Remove the lifters from their bores and remove any gum and varnish with safe solvent. Check the lifters for concave wear. If the bottom of the lifter is worn concave or flat, replace the lifter. Lifters are built with a convex bottom, flatness indicates wear. If a worn lifter is detected, carefully check the camshaft for wear.

To test lifter leak down, submerge the lifter in a container of kerosene. Chuck a used pushrod or its equivalent into a drill press. Position the container of kerosene so the pushrod acts on the lifter plunger. Pump the lifter with the drill press until resistance increases. Pump several more times to bleed any air from the lifter. Apply very firm, constant pressure to the lifter and observe the rate which fluid bleeds out of the lifter. If the lifter bleeds down very quickly (less than 15 seconds), the lifter should be replaced. If the time exceeds 60 seconds, the lifter is sticking and should be cleaned or replaced. If the lifter is operating properly (leak down time 15–60 seconds) and not worn, lubricate and reinstall in engine.

NOTE: Always inspect the valve pushrods for wear, straightness and oil blockage. Damaged pushrods will cause erratic valve operation.

GASOLINE ENGINE HYDRAULIC VALVE CLEARANCE ADJUSTMENT

When a valve in the engine is in the closed position, the valve lifter is resting on the base circle of the camshaft lobe and the pushrod is in its lowest position. To remove this additional clearance from the valve train, the valve lifter expands to maintain zero clearance in the valve system. When a rocker arm is loosened or removed from the engine, the lifter expands to it fullest travel. When the rocker arm is reinstalled on the engine, the proper valve setting is obtained by tightening the rocker arm to a specified limit. But with the lifter fully expanded, if the camshaft lobe is on a high point it will require excessive torque to compress the lifter and obtain the proper setting. Because of this, when any component of the valve system has been removed, a preliminary valve adjustment procedure must be followed to ensure that when the rocker arm is reinstalled on the engine and tightened, the camshaft lobe for that cylinder is in the low position.

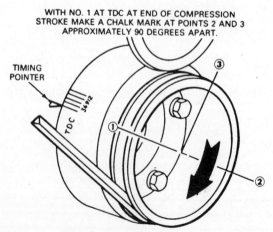

Marking the damper on the 8-5.0L and 8-5.8L engines

To determine whether a shorter or longer pushrod is necessary, make the following check:

6-4.9L Engine

1. Rotate the crankshaft by hand so that No.1 piston is at TDC of the compression stroke. Make a chalk mark on the damper at that point, then, make 2 more chalk marks about 120° apart, dividing the damper into 3 equal parts. See the accompanying illustration.

2. With No.1 at TDC, tighten the rocker arm bolts on No.1 cylinder intake and exhaust to 17–23 ft. lbs. Then, slowly apply pressure, using Lifter Bleed-down wrench T70P-6513-A, or equivalent, to completely bottom the lifter. Take care to avoid excessive pressure that might bend the pushrod. Hold the lifter in this position and check the clearance between the rocker arm and the valve stem tip. Allowable clearance is 2.5–5.0mm (0.10–0.20 in.) with a desired clearance of 3.0–4.5mm (0.125–0.175 in.)

3. If the clearance is less than specified, install a shorter pushrod. If the clearance is greater than specified, install a longer pushrod.

4. Rotate the crankshaft clockwise — viewed from the front — until the next chalk mark is aligned with the timing pointer. Repeat the procedure for No.5 intake and exhaust.

5. Rotate the crankshaft to the next chalk mark and repeat the procedure for No.3 intake and exhaust.

6. Repeat the rotation/checking procedure for the remaining valves in firing order, that is: 6–2–4.

8-5.0L Engine

1. Rotate the crankshaft by hand so that No.1 piston is at TDC of the compression stroke. Make a chalk mark on the damper at that point, then, make 2 more chalk marks about 90° apart in a clockwise direction. See the accompanying illustration.

2. With No.1 at TDC, slowly apply pressure, using Lifter Bleed-down wrench T70P-6513-A, or equivalent, to completely bottom the lifter, on the following valves:
- No.1 intake and exhaust
- No.7 intake
- No.5 exhaust
- No.8 intake
- No.4 exhaust

Take care to avoid excessive pressure that might bend the pushrod. Hold the lifter in this position and check the clearance between the rocker arm and the valve stem tip. Allowable clearance is 1.8–4.9mm (0.071–0.193 in.) with a desired clearance of 2.4–4.2mm (0.096–0.165 in.).

3. If the clearance is less than specified, install a shorter pushrod. If the clearance is greater than specified, install a longer pushrod.

4. Rotate the crankshaft clockwise — viewed from the front — 180°, until the next chalk mark is aligned with the timing pointer. Repeat the procedure for:
- No.5 intake
- No.2 exhaust
- No.4 intake
- No.6 exhaust

5. Rotate the crankshaft to the next chalk mark — 90° — and repeat the procedure for:
- No.2 intake
- No.7 exhaust
- No.3 intake and exhaust
- No.6 intake
- No.8 exhaust

8-5.8L Engine

1. Rotate the crankshaft by hand so that No.1 piston is at TDC of the compression stroke. Make a chalk mark on the damper at that point, then, make 2 more chalk marks about 90° apart in a clockwise direction. See the accompanying illustration.

2. With No.1 at TDC, slowly apply pressure, using Lifter Bleed-down wrench T70P-6513-A, or equivalent, to completely bottom the lifter, on the following valves:
- No.1 intake and exhaust
- No.4 intake
- No.3 exhaust
- No.8 intake
- No.7 exhaust

Take care to avoid excessive pressure that might bend the pushrod. Hold the lifter in this position and check the clearance between the rocker arm and the valve stem tip. Allowable clearance is 2.5–5.0mm (0.098–0.198 in.) with a desired clearance of 3.1–4.4mm (0.123–0.173 in.).

3. If the clearance is less than specified, install a shorter pushrod. If the clearance is greater than specified, install a longer pushrod.

4. Rotate the crankshaft clockwise — viewed from the front — 180°, until the next chalk mark is aligned with the timing pointer. Repeat the procedure for:
- No.3 intake
- No.2 exhaust
- No.7 intake
- No.6 exhaust

5. Rotate the crankshaft to the next chalk mark — 90° — and repeat the procedure for:
- No.2 intake
- No.4 exhaust
- No.5 intake and exhaust
- No.6 intake
- No.8 exhaust

8-7.5L Engine

1. Rotate the crankshaft by hand so that No.1 piston is at TDC of the compression stroke. Make a chalk mark on the damper at that point. See the accompanying illustration.

2. With No.1 at TDC, slowly apply pressure, using Lifter Bleed-down wrench T70P-6513-A, or equivalent, to completely bottom the lifter, on the following valves:
- No.1 intake and exhaust
- No.3 intake
- No.4 exhaust
- No.7 intake
- No.5 exhaust
- No.8 intake and exhaust

Take care to avoid excessive pressure that might bend the pushrod. Hold the lifter in this position and check the clearance between the rocker arm and the valve stem tip. Allowable clearance is 1.9–4.4mm (0.075–0.175 in.) with a desired clearance of 2.5–3.8mm (0.100-0.150 in.).

3. If the clearance is less than specified, install a shorter pushrod. If the clearance is greater than specified, install a longer pushrod.

4. Rotate the crankshaft clockwise — viewed from the front — 360°, until the chalk mark is once again aligned with the timing pointer. Repeat the procedure for:
- No.2 intake and exhaust
- No.4 intake
- No.3 exhaust
- No.5 intake
- No.7 exhaust
- No.6 intake and exhaust

Valve Seats

REMOVAL AND INSTALLATION

8-7.3L Diesel

NOTE: The diesel is the only engine covered in this guide which has removable valve seats.

1. Using Ford Rotunda tool 14–0309 the exhaust valve seats may be removed. Position the remover collet into the insert and rotate the collet nut clockwise to expand the collet jaws under the lip of the seat insert.
2. Rotate the top nut clockwise to remove the insert.

NOTE: If an oversize seat insert is required, the cylinder head should be sent out to a qualified machine shop.

3. To install a new exhaust valve seat, drive the seat in place using Rotunda tool 14–0309 and a hammer.

Valve seat inserts are supplied for service in standard size, 0.015 in. (0.381mm) oversize and 0.030 in. (0.762mm) oversize.

Valve Guides

REAMING VALVE GUIDES

If it becomes necessary to ream a valve guide to install with an oversize stem, a reaming kit is available which contains a oversize reamers and pilot tools.

When replacing a standard size valve with an oversize valve always use the reamer in sequence (smallest oversize first, then next smallest, etc.) so as not to overload the reamers. Always reface the valve seat after the valve guide has been reamed, and use a suitable scraper to brake the sharp corner at the top of the valve guide.

KNURLING

Valve guides which are not excessively worn or distorted may, in some cases, be knurled rather than reamed. Knurling is a process in which metal inside the valve guide bore is displaced and raised (forming a very fine cross-hatch pattern), thereby reducing clearance. Knurling also provides for excellent oil control. The possibility of knurling rather than reaming the guides should be discussed with a machinist.

STEM-TO-GUIDE CLEARANCE

Valve stem-to-guide clearance should be checked upon assembling the cylinder head, and is especially necessary if the valve guides have been reamed or knurled, or if oversize valve have been installed. Excessive oil consumption often is a result of too much clearance between the valve guide and valve stem.

1. Clean the valve stem with lacquer thinner or a similar solvent to remove all gum and varnish. Clean the valve guides using solvent and an expanding wire-type valve guide cleaner (a rifle cleaning brush works well here).
2. Mount a dial indicator so that the stem is 90° to the valve stem and as close to the valve guide as possible.
3. Move the valve off its seat, and measure the valve guide-to-stem clearance by rocking the stem back and forth to actuate the dial indicator. Measure the valve stems using a micrometer and compare to specifications, to determine whether stem or guide wear is responsible for excessive clearance.

VALVE LAPPING

The valve must be lapped into their seats after resurfacing, to ensure proper sealing. Even if the valve have not been refaced, they should be lapped into the head before reassembly.

Set the cylinder head on the workbench, combustion chamber side up. Rest the head on wooden blocks on either end, so there are 2–3 in. (51–76mm) between the tops of the valve guides and the bench.

1. Lightly lube the valve stem with clean engine oil. Coat the valve seat completely with valve grinding compound. Use just enough compound so that the full width and circumference of the seat are covered.
2. Install the valve in its proper location in the head. Attach the suction cup end of the valve lapping tool to the valve head. It usually helps to put a small amount of saliva into the suction cup to aid it sticking to the valve.
3. Rotate the tool between the palms, changing position and lifting the tool often to prevent grooving. Lap the valve in until a smooth, evenly polished seat and valve face are evident.
4. Remove the valve from the head. Wipe away all traces of grinding compound from the valve face and seat. Wipe out the port with a solvent soaked rag, and swab out the valve guide with a piece of solvent soaked rag to make sure there are no traces of compound grit inside the guide. This cleaning is very important, as the engine will ingest any grit remaining when started.
5. Proceed through the remaining valves, one at a time. Make sure the valve faces, sets, cylinder ports and valve guides are clean before reassembling the valve train.

Crankshaft Pulley (Vibration Damper)

REMOVAL AND INSTALLATION

1. Remove the fan shroud, as required. If necessary, drain the cooling system and remove the radiator. Remove drive belts from pulley.

--- **CAUTION** ---

When draining the coolant, keep in mind that cats and dogs are attracted by the ethylene glycol antifreeze, and are quite likely to drink any that is left in an uncovered container or in puddles on the ground. This will prove fatal in sufficient quantity. Always drain the coolant into a sealable container. Coolant should be reused unless it is contaminated or several years old.

2. On those engines with a separate pulley, remove the retaining bolts and separate the pulley from the vibration damper.
3. Remove the vibration damper/pulley retaining bolt from the crankshaft end.
4. Using a puller, remove the damper/pulley from the crankshaft.
5. Upon installation, align the key slot of the pulley hub to the crankshaft key. Complete the assembly in the reverse order of removal. Torque the retaining bolts to the specifications found in the Torque Specifications Chart.

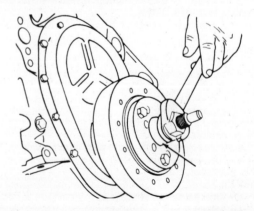

Vibration damper installation on gasoline V8s

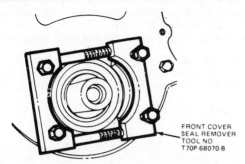

Removing the front crankshaft seal on gasoline V8s

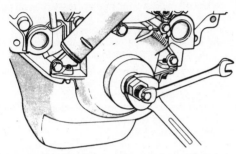

Installing the front crankshaft seal on gasoline V8s

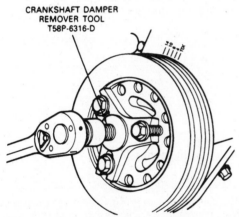

Removing the damper on 6-4.9L engines

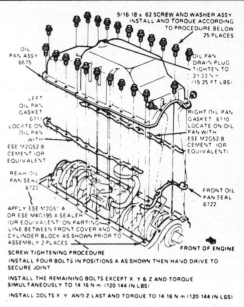

6-4.9L oil pan installation

CAUTION

When draining the coolant, keep in mind that cats and dogs are attracted by the ethylene glycol antifreeze, and are quite likely to drink any that is left in an uncovered container or in puddles on the ground. This will prove fatal in sufficient quantity. Always drain the coolant into a sealable container. Coolant should be reused unless it is contaminated or several years old.

---

3. Remove the upper intake manifold and throttle body. See Section 5.

4. Remove the starter.

5. Remove the engine front support insulator to support bracket nuts and washers on both supports. Raise the front of the engine with a transmission jack and wood block and place 1 in. (25mm) thick wood blocks between the front support insulators and support brackets. Lower the engine and remove the transmission jack.

6. Remove the oil pan attaching bolts and lower the pan to the crossmember. Remove the 2 oil pump inlet tube and screw assembly bolts and drop the assembly in the pan. Remove the oil pan. Remove the oil pump inlet tube attaching bolts. Remove the inlet tube and screen assembly from the oil pump and leave it in the bottom of the oil pan. Remove the oil pan gaskets. Remove the inlet tube and screen from the oil pan.

To install:

7. Clean the gasket surfaces of the oil pump, oil pan and cylinder block. Remove the rear main bearing cap to oil pan seal and cylinder front cover to oil pan seal. Clean the seal grooves.

8. Apply oil-resistant sealer in the cavities between the bearing cap and cylinder block. Install a new seal in the rear main bearing cap and apply a bead of oil-resistant sealer to the tapered ends of the seal.

9. Install new side gaskets on the oil pan with oil-resistant sealer. Position a new oil pan to cylinder front cover seal on the oil pan.

10. Clean the inlet tube and screen assembly and place it in the oil pan.

11. Position the oil pan under the engine. Install the inlet tube and screen assembly on the oil pump with a new gasket. Tighten the screws to 5–7 ft. lbs. Position the oil pan against the cylinder block and install the attaching bolts. Tighten the bolts in sequence to 10–12 ft. lbs.

12. Raise the engine with a transmission jack and remove the wood blocks from the engine front supports. Lower the engine

Oil Pan

REMOVAL AND INSTALLATION

6–4.9L

1. Drain the crankcase.

CAUTION

The EPA warns that prolonged contact with used engine oil may cause a number of skin disorders, including cancer! You should make every effort to minimize your exposure to used engine oil. Protective gloves should be worn when changing the oil. Wash your hands and any other exposed skin areas as soon as possible after exposure to used engine oil. Soap and water, or waterless hand cleaner should be used.

---

2. Drain the cooling system.

until the front support insulators are positioned on the support brackets. Install the washers and nuts on the insulator studs and tighten the nuts.

13. Install the starter and connect the starter cable.
14. Install the manifold and throttle body.
15. Fill the crankcase and cooling system.
16. Start the engine and check for coolant and oil leaks.

8-5.0L, 8-5.8L

1. Drain the cooling system.

— CAUTION —

When draining the coolant, keep in mind that cats and dogs are attracted by the ethylene glycol antifreeze, and are quite likely to drink any that is left in an uncovered container or in puddles on the ground. This will prove fatal in sufficient quantity. Always drain the coolant into a sealable container. Coolant should be reused unless it is contaminated or several years old.

2. Remove the bolts attaching the fan shroud to the radiator and position the shroud over the fan.
3. Remove the upper intake manifold and throttle body. See Section 5.
4. Remove the nuts and lockwashers attaching the engine support insulators to the chassis bracket.
5. If equipped with an automatic transmission, disconnect the oil cooler line at the left side of the radiator.
6. Remove the exhaust system.
7. Raise the engine and place wood blocks under the engine supports.
8. Drain the crankcase.

— CAUTION —

The EPA warns that prolonged contact with used engine oil may cause a number of skin disorders, including cancer! You should make every effort to minimize your exposure to used engine oil. Protective gloves should be worn when changing the oil. Wash your hands and any other exposed skin areas as soon as possible after exposure to used engine oil. Soap and water, or waterless hand cleaner should be used.

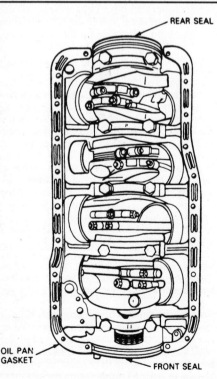

8＝5.0L/8-5.8L engine oil pan and gaskets

9. Support the transmission with a floor jack and remove the transmission crossmember.
10. Remove the oil pan attaching bolts and lower the oil pan onto the crossmember.
11. Remove the two bolts attaching the oil pump pickup tube to the oil pump. Remove nut attaching oil pump pickup tube to the number 3 main bearing cap stud. Lower the pickup tube and screen into the oil pan.
12. Remove the oil pan from the vehicle.

To install:

13. Clean the oil pan, inlet tube and gasket surfaces. Inspect the gasket sealing surface for damages and distortion due to overtightening of the bolts. Repair and straighten as required.
14. Position a new oil pan gasket and seal to the cylinder block.
15. Position the oil pickup tube and screen to the oil pump, and install the lower attaching bolt and gasket loosely. Install nut attaching to number 3 main bearing cap stud.
16. Place the oil pan on the crossmember. Install the upper pickup tube bolt. Tighten the pickup tube bolts.
17. Position the oil pan to the cylinder block and install the attaching bolts. Tighten to 10–12 ft. lbs.
18. Install the transmission crossmember.
19. Raise the engine and remove the blocks under the engine supports. Bolt the engine to the supports.
20. Install the exhaust system.
21. If equipped with an automatic transmission, connect the oil cooler line at the left side of the radiator.
22. Install the nuts and lockwashers attaching the engine support insulators to the chassis bracket.
23. Install the upper intake manifold and throttle body. See Section 5.
24. Install the fan shroud.
25. Fill the crankcase.
26. Fill and bleed the cooling system.

8–7.5L

1. Remove the hood.
2. Disconnect the battery ground cable.
3. Drain the cooling system.

— CAUTION —

When draining the coolant, keep in mind that cats and dogs are attracted by the ethylene glycol antifreeze, and are quite likely to drink any that is left in an uncovered container or in puddles on the ground. This will prove fatal in sufficient quantity. Always drain the coolant into a sealable container. Coolant should be reused unless it is contaminated or several years old.

4. Remove the air intake tube and air cleaner assembly.
5. Disconnect the throttle linkage at the throttle body.
6. Disconnect the power brake vacuum line at the manifold.
7. Disconnect the fuel lines at the fuel rail.
8. Disconnect the air tubes at the throttle body.
9. Remove the radiator.
10. Remove the power steering pump and position it out of the way without disconnecting the lines.
11. Remove the oil dipstick tube. On motor home chassis, remove the oil filler tube.
12. Remove the front engine mount through-bolts.
13. Position the air conditioner refrigerant hoses so that they are clear of the firewall. If necessary, discharge the system and remove the compressor. See Section 1.
14. Remove the upper intake manifold and throttle body. See Section 5.
15. Drain the crankcase. Remove the oil filter.

16. Disconnect the exhaust pipe at the manifolds.
17. Disconnect the transmission linkage at the transmission.
18. Remove the driveshaft(s).
19. Remove the transmission fill tube.
20. Raise the engine with a jack placed under the crankshaft damper and a block of wood to act as a cushion. Raise the engine until the transmission contacts the underside of the floor. Place wood blocks under the engine supports. The engine *must* remain centralized at a point at least 4 in. (102mm) above the mounts, to remove the oil pan!
21. Remove the oil pan attaching screws and lower the oil pan onto the crossmember. Remove the two bolts attaching the oil pump pickup tube to the oil pump. Lower the assembly from the oil pump. Leave it on the bottom of the oil pan. Remove the oil pan and gaskets. Remove the inlet tube and screen from the oil pan.

To install:
22. Clean the gasket surfaces of the oil pan and cylinder block.
23. Apply a coating of gasket adhesive on the block mating surface and stick the 1-piece silicone gasket on the block.
24. Clean the inlet tube and screen assembly and place on the pump.
25. Position the oil pan against the cylinder block and install the retaining bolts. Torque all bolts to 10 ft. lbs.
26. Lower the engine and bolt it in place.
27. Install the transmission fill tube.
28. Install the driveshaft(s).
29. Connect the transmission linkage at the transmission.
30. Connect the exhaust pipe at the manifolds.
31. Install the oil filter.
32. Install the upper intake manifold and throttle body. See Section 5.
33. Install the compressor or reposition the hoses.
34. Install the oil dipstick tube. On motor home chassis, install the oil filler tube.
35. Install the power steering pump.
36. Install the radiator.
37. Connect the air tubes at the throttle body.
38. Connect the fuel lines at the fuel rail.
39. Connect the power brake vacuum line at the manifold.
40. Connect the throttle linkage at the throttle body.
41. Install the air intake tube and air cleaner assembly.
42. Fill and bleed the cooling system.
43. Fill the crankcase.
44. Connect the battery ground cable.
45. Install the hood.

8-7.3L Diesel

1. Disconnect both battery ground cables.
2. Remove the engine oil dipstick.
3. Remove the transmission oil dipstick.
4. Remove the air cleaner and cover the intake opening.
5. Remove the fan and fan clutch.

NOTE: The fan uses left hand threads. Remove them by turning them clockwise.

6. Drain the cooling system.
7. Disconnect the lower radiator hose.
8. Disconnect the power steering return hose and plug the line and pump.
9. Disconnect the alternator wiring harness.

10. Disconnect the fuel line heater connector from the alternator.
11. Raise and support the front end on jackstands.
12. On vans with automatic transmission, disconnect the transmission cooler lines at the radiator and plug them.
13. Disconnect and plug the fuel pump inlet line.
14. Drain the crankcase and remove the oil filter.

15. Remove the engine oil filler tube.
16. Disconnect the exhaust pipes at the manifolds.
17. Disconnect the muffler inlet pipe from the muffler and remove the pipe.
18. Remove the upper inlet mounting stud from the right exhaust manifold.
19. Unbolt the engine from the No.1 crossmember.
20. Lower the vehicle.
21. Install lifting brackets on the front of the engine.
22. Raise the engine until the transmission contact the body.
23. Install wood blocks — 2¾ in. (70mm) on the left side; 2 in. (50mm) on the right side — between the engine insulators and crossmember.
24. Lower the engine onto the blocks.
25. Raise and support the front end on jackstands.
26. Remove the flywheel inspection plate.
27. Position fuel pump inlet line No.1 rearward of the crossmember and position the oil cooler lines out of the way.
28. Remove the oil pan bolts.
29. Lower the oil pan.

NOTE: The oil pan is sealed to the crankcase with RTV silicone sealant in place of a gasket. It may be necessary to separate the pan from the crankcase with a utility knife.

CHILTON TIP: The crankshaft may have to be turned to allow the pan to clear the crankshaft throws.

30. Clean the pan and crankcase mating surfaces thoroughly.
To install:
31. Apply a ⅛ in. (3mm) bead of RTV silicone sealant to the pan mating surfaces, and a ¼ in. (6mm) bead on the front and rear covers and in the corners. You have 15 minutes within which to install the pan!
32. Install locating dowels (which you supply) into position as shown.
33. Position the pan on the engine and install the pan bolts loosely.
34. Remove the dowels.
35. Torque the pan bolts to 7 ft. lbs. for ¼ in.-20 bolts; 14 ft. lbs. for ⁵⁄₁₆ in.-18 bolts; 24 ft.lb for ⅜ in.-16 bolts.
36. Install the flywheel inspection cover.
37. Lower the van.
38. Raise the engine and remove the wood blocks.
39. Lower the engine onto the crossmember and remove the lifting brackets.
40. Raise and support the front end on jackstands.
41. Torque the engine-to-crossmember nuts to 70 ft. lbs.
42. Install the upper inlet pipe mounting stud.
43. Install the inlet pipe, using a new gasket.
44. Install the transmission oil filler tube, using a new gasket.
45. Install the oil pan drain plug.
46. Install a new oil filter.

47. Connect the fuel pump inlet line. Make sure that the clip is installed on the crossmember.
48. Connect the transmission cooler lines.
49. Lower the van.
50. Connect all wiring.
51. Connect the power steering return line.
52. Connect the lower radiator hose.
53. Install the fan and fan clutch.

NOTE: The fan uses left hand threads. Install them by turning them counterclockwise.

54. Remove the cover and install the air cleaner.
55. Install the dipsticks.
56. Fill the crankcase.
57. Fill and bleed the cooling system.
58. Fill the power steering reservoir.
59. Connect the batteries.
60. Run the engine and check for leaks.

Oil Pump

REMOVAL AND INSTALLATION

Gasoline Engines

1. Remove the oil pan.
2. Remove the oil pump inlet tube and screen assembly.

3. Remove the oil pump attaching bolts and remove the oil pump gasket and intermediate driveshaft.
4. Before installing the oil pump, prime it by filling the inlet and outlet port with engine oil and rotating the shaft of the pump to distribute it.
5. Position the intermediate driveshaft into the distributor socket.

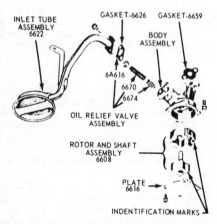

Exploded view of a gasoline V8 oil pump

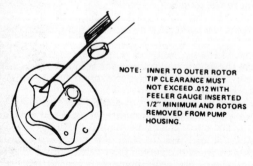

NOTE: INNER TO OUTER ROTOR TIP CLEARANCE MUST NOT EXCEED .012 WITH FEELER GAUGE INSERTED 1/2" MINIMUM AND ROTORS REMOVED FROM PUMP HOUSING.

Checking inner rotor tip clearance

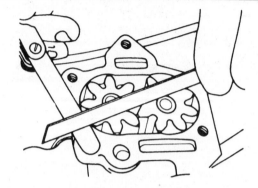

Checking rotor endplay

6. Position the new gasket on the pump body and insert the intermediate driveshaft into the pump body.
7. Install the pump and intermediate driveshaft as an assembly. Do not force the pump if it does not seal readily. The driveshaft may be misaligned with the distributor shaft. To align it, rotate the intermediate driveshaft into a new position.
8. Install the oil pump attaching bolts and torque them to 12–15 ft. lbs. on the inline sixes and to 20–25 ft. lbs. on the V8s.

Diesel Engines

1. Remove the oil pan.

2. Remove the oil pickup tube from the pump.
3. Unbolt and remove the oil pump.
4. Assemble the pickup tube and pump. Use a new gasket.
5. Install the oil pump and torque the bolts to 14 ft. lbs.

OVERHAUL

1. Wash all parts in solvent and dry them thoroughly with compressed air. Use a brush to clean the inside of the pump housing and the pressure relief valve chamber. Be sure all dirt and metal particles are removed.
2. Check the inside of the pump housing and the outer race and rotor for damage or excessive wear or scoring.
3. Check the mating surface of the pump cover for wear. If the cover mating surface is worn, scored, or grooved, replace the pump.
4. Measure the inner rotor tip clearance.
5. With the rotor assembly installed in the housing, place a straight edge over the rotor assembly and the housing. Measure the clearance (rotor end play) between the straight edge and the rotor and the outer race.

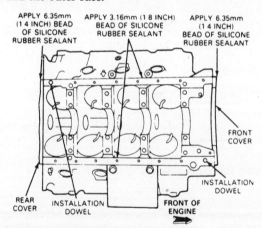

RTV sealant and dowel location for the diesel oil pan

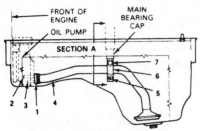

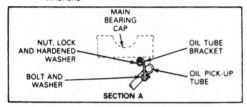

1. OIL PICK-UP TUBE MOUNTING GASKET
2. 5 16"-18 × 2" BOLT AND 5 16" HARDENED WASHER
3. 5 16"-18 × 1-1 2" BOLT AND 5-16" HARDENED WASHER
4. OIL PICK-UP TUBE ASSEMBLY
5. 5 16"-18 × 0.930 BOLT W WASHER
6. OIL TUBE BRACKET
7. 5 16"-18 NUT AND 5 16" LOCK AND HARDENED WASHERS

Diesel oil pickup tube installation

6. Check the drive shaft to housing bearing clearance by measuring the OD of the shaft and the ID of the housing bearing.

7. Components of the oil pump are not serviced. If any part of the pump requires replacement, replace the complete pump assembly.

8. Inspect the relief valve spring to see if it is collapsed or worn.

9. Check the relief valve piston for scores and free operation in the bore.

Oil Cooler

REMOVAL AND INSTALLATION

8-7.3L Diesel

The diesel oil cooler should be disassembled if the cooler O-rings begin to leak.

1. Gently rap the front and oil cooler headers to loosen the O-rings. Carefully twist the oil cooler apart.

2. Using a suitable solvent, thoroughly clean the oil cooler and the front and filter headers.

3. Always use new O-rings when reassembling. Lubricate the new rings and all O-ring mating surfaces with clean engine oil. Install the two narrow O-rings into their respective grooves inside the front and filter headers.

4. Place the large O-ring over the oil cooler shell.

5. Press the assembly together, making sure the locating clips align with the slots.

Front Cover and Oil Seal

REMOVAL AND INSTALLATION

6–4.9L

1. Drain the cooling system and disconnect the radiator upper hose at the coolant outlet elbow and remove the two upper radiator retaining bolts.

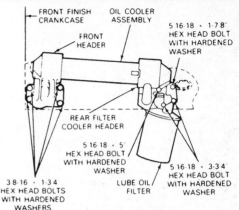

Diesel oil cooler

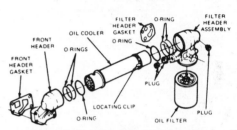

Diesel oil cooler explode view

──────────── CAUTION ────────────

When draining the coolant, keep in mind that cats and dogs are attracted by the ethylene glycol antifreeze, and are quite likely to drink any that is left in an uncovered container or in puddles on the ground. This will prove fatal in sufficient quantity. Always drain the coolant into a sealable container. Coolant should be reused unless it is contaminated or several years old.

2. Raise the vehicle and drain the crankcase.

──────────── CAUTION ────────────

The EPA warns that prolonged contact with used engine oil may cause a number of skin disorders, including cancer! You should make every effort to minimize your exposure to used engine oil. Protective gloves should be worn when changing the oil. Wash your hands and any other exposed skin areas as soon as possible after exposure to used engine oil. Soap and water, or waterless hand cleaner should be used.

3. Remove the splash shield and the automatic transmission oil cooling lines, if so equipped, then remove the radiator.

4. Loosen and remove the fan belt, fan and pulley.

5. Use a gear puller to remove the crankshaft pulley damper.

6. Remove the cylinder front cover retaining bolts and gently pry the cover away from the block. Remove the gasket.

7. Drive out the old seal with a pin punch from the rear of the cover. Clean out the recess in the cover.

8. Coat the new seal with grease and drive it into the cover until it is fully seated. Check the seal to make sure that the spring around the seal is in the proper position.

9. Clean the cylinder front cover and the gasket surface of the cylinder block. Apply an oil-resistant sealer to the new front cover gasket and install the gasket onto the cover.

10. Position the front cover assembly over the end of the crankshaft and against the cylinder block. Start, but do not tighten, the cover and pan attaching screws. Slide a front cover alignment tool (Ford part no. T68P–6019–A or equivalent) over the crank stub and into the seal bore of the cover. Tighten all front cover and oil pan attaching screws to 12–18 ft. lbs. front cover; 10–15 ft. lbs. oil pan, tightening the oil pan screws first.

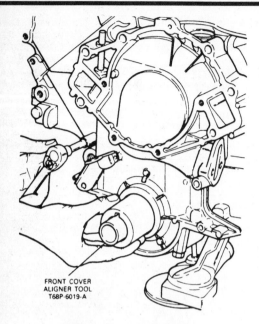

FRONT COVER
ALIGNER TOOL
T68P-6019-A

Alining the timing cover

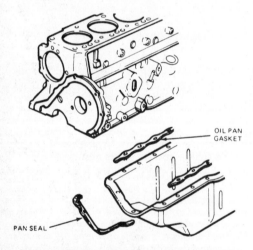

OIL PAN
GASKET

PAN SEAL

Front pan/cover seal on the 6-4.9L

NOTE: Trim away the exposed portion of the old oil pan gasket flush with the front of the engine block. Cut and position the required portion of a new gasket to the oil pan and apply sealer to both sides.

11. Lubricate the hub of the crankshaft damper pulley with Lubriplate® to prevent damage to the seal during installation or on initial starting of the engine.

12. Install and assemble the remaining components in the reverse order of removal, starting from Step 4. Start the engine and check for leaks.

Gasoline V8 Except 8–7.5L

1. Drain the cooling system and the crankcase.

CAUTION

When draining the coolant, keep in mind that cats and dogs are attracted by the ethylene glycol antifreeze, and are quite likely to drink any that is left in an uncovered container or in puddles on the ground. This will prove fatal in sufficient quantity. Always drain the coolant into a sealable container. Coolant should be reused unless it is contaminated or several years old.

The EPA warns that prolonged contact with used engine oil may cause a number of skin disorders, including cancer! You should make every effort to minimize your exposure to used engine oil. Protective gloves should be worn when changing the oil. Wash your hands and any other exposed skin areas as soon as possible after exposure to used engine oil. Soap and water, or waterless hand cleaner should be used.

2. Disconnect the upper and lower radiator hoses from the water pump, transmission oil cooler lines from the radiator, and remove the radiator.

3. Disconnect the heater hose from the water pump. Slide the water pump by-pass hose clamp toward the water pump.

4. Loosen the alternator pivot bolt and the bolt which secures the alternator adjusting arm to the water pump. Position the alternator out of the way.

5. Remove the power steering pump and air conditioning compressor from their mounting brackets, if so equipped.

6. Remove the bolts holding the fan shroud to the radiator, if so equipped. Remove the fan, spacer, pulley and drive belts.

7. Remove the crankshaft pulley from the crankshaft damper. Remove the damper attaching bolt and washer and remove the damper with a puller.

8. Disconnect the fuel pump outlet line at the fuel pump. Disconnect the vacuum inlet and outlet lines from the fuel pump. Remove the fuel pump attaching bolts and lay the pump to one side with the fuel inlet line still attached.

9. Remove the oil level dipstick and the bolt holding the dipstick tube to the exhaust manifold on the 8–5.0L.

10. Remove the oil pan-to-cylinder front cover attaching bolts. Use a sharp, thin cutting blade to cut the oil pan gasket flush with the cylinder block. Remove the front cover and water pump as an assembly.

11. Discard the front cover gasket.

12. Place the front seal removing tool (Ford part no. T70P–6B070–A or equivalent) into the front cover plate and over the front of the seal as shown in the illustration. Tighten the two through bolts to force the seal puller under the seal flange, then alternately tighten the four puller bolts a half turn at a time to pull the oil seal from the cover.

13. Coat a new front cover oil seal with Lubriplate® or equivalent and place it onto the front oil seal alignment and installation tool (Ford part no. T70P–6B070–A or equivalent) as shown in the illustration. Place the tool and the seal onto the end of the crankshaft and push it toward the engine until the seal starts into the front cover.

14. Place the installation screw, washer, and nut onto the end of the crankshaft, then thread the screw into the crankshaft. Tighten the nut against the washer and tool to force the seal into the front cover plate. Remove the tool.

15. Apply Lubriplate® or equivalent to the oil seal rubbing surface of the vibration damper inner hub to prevent damage to the seal. Coat the front of the crankshaft with engine oil for damper installation.

16. To install the damper, line up the damper keyway with the key on the crankshaft, then install the damper onto the crankshaft. Install the cap screw and washer, and tighten the screw to 80 ft. lbs. Install the crankshaft pulley.

17. Assemble the rest of the engine in the reverse order of disassembly.

8–7.5L

1. Drain the cooling system and crankcase.

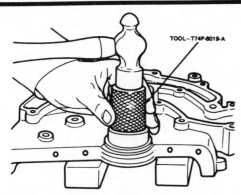

Installing the oil seal into the 8-7.5L front cover. The tool makes it easier to drive the seal evenly

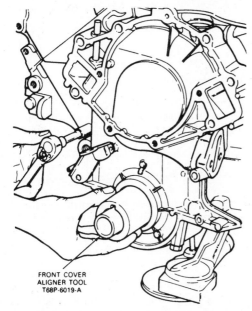

Aligning the front cover on the 8-7.5L

CAUTION

When draining the coolant, keep in mind that cats and dogs are attracted by the ethylene glycol antifreeze, and are quite likely to drink any that is left in an uncovered container or in puddles on the ground. This will prove fatal in sufficient quantity. Always drain the coolant into a sealable container. Coolant should be reused unless it is contaminated or several years old.

The EPA warns that prolonged contact with used engine oil may cause a number of skin disorders, including cancer! You should make every effort to minimize your exposure to used engine oil. Protective gloves should be worn when changing the oil. Wash your hands and any other exposed skin areas as soon as possible after exposure to used engine oil. Soap and water, or waterless hand cleaner should be used.

---

2. Remove the radiator shroud and fan.
3. Disconnect the upper and lower radiator hoses, and the automatic transmission oil cooler lines from the radiator.
4. Remove the radiator upper support and remove the radiator.
5. Loosen the alternator attaching bolts and air conditioning compressor idler pulley and remove the drive belts with the water pump pulley. Remove the bolts attaching the compressor support to the water pump and remove the bracket (support), if so equipped.

6. Remove the crankshaft pulley from the vibration damper. Remove the bolt and washer attaching the crankshaft damper and remove the damper with a puller. Remove the woodruff key from the crankshaft.
7. Loosen the by-pass hose at the water pump, and disconnect the heater return tube at the water pump.
8. Disconnect and plug the fuel inlet and outlet lines at the fuel pump, and remove the fuel pump.
9. Remove the bolts attaching the front cover to the cylinder block. Cut the oil pan seal flush with the cylinder block face with a thin knife blade prior to separating the cover from the cylinder block. Remove the cover and water pump as an assembly. Discard the front cover gasket and oil pan seal.
10. Transfer the water pump if a new cover is going to be installed. Clean all of the gasket sealing surfaces on both the front cover and the cylinder block.
11. Coat the gasket surface of the oil pan with sealer. Cut and position the required sections of a new seal on the oil pan. Apply sealer to the corners.
12. Drive out the old front cover oil seal with a pin punch. Clean out the seal recess in the cover. coat a new seal with Lubriplate® or equivalent grease. Install the seal, making sure the seal spring remains in the proper position. A front cover seal tool, Ford part no. T72J–117 or equivalent, makes installation easier.
13. Coat the gasket surfaces of the cylinder block and cover with sealer and position the new gasket on the block.
14. Position the front cover on the cylinder block. Use care not to damage the seal and gasket or misplace them.
15. Coat the front cover attaching screws with sealer and install them.

NOTE: It may be necessary to force the front cover downward to compress the oil pan seal in order to install the front cover attaching bolts. Use a screwdriver or drift to engage the cover screw holes through the cover and pry downward.

16. Assemble and install the remaining components in the reverse order of removal. Tighten the front cover bolts to 15–20 ft. lbs., the water pump attaching screws to 12–15 ft. lbs., the crankshaft damper to 70–90 ft. lbs., the crankshaft pulley to 35–50 ft. lbs., fuel pump to 19–27 ft. lbs., the oil pan bolts to 9–11 ft. lbs. for the $^5/_{16}$ in. screws and to 7–9 ft. lbs. for the ¼ in. screws, and the alternator pivot bolt to 45–57 ft. lbs.

8-7.3L Diesel

1. Disconnect both battery ground cables. Drain the cooling system.

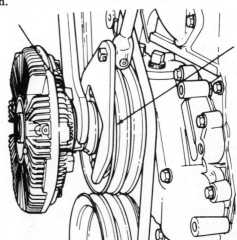

Removing the diesel fan clutch using a puller (arrows)

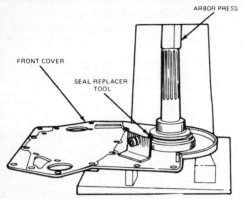

Diesel font oil seal removal and installation using an arbor press

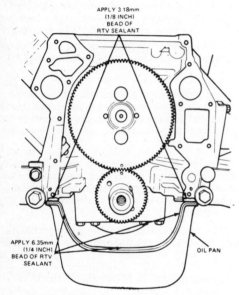

Diesel front cover sealer location

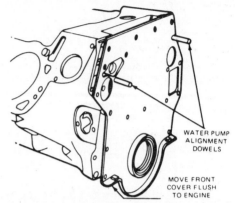

Front cover installation on the diesel, showing alignment dowels

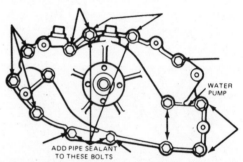

Water pump-to-front cover installation on the diesel. The 2 top pump bolts must be no more than 31.75mm long

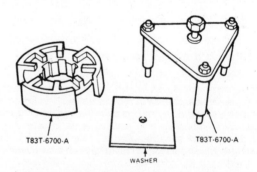

Tools for replacing the diesel front seal

—— CAUTION ——

When draining the coolant, keep in mind that cats and dogs are attracted by the ethylene glycol antifreeze, and are quite likely to drink any that is left in an uncovered container or in puddles on the ground. This will prove fatal in sufficient quantity. Always drain the coolant into a sealable container. Coolant should be reused unless it is contaminated or several years old.

2. Remove the air cleaner and cover the air intake on the manifold with clean rags. Do not allow any foreign material to enter the intake.

3. Remove the radiator fan shroud halves.

4. Remove the fan and fan clutch assembly. You will need a puller or ford tool No. T83T–6312–A for this.

NOTE: The nut is a left hand thread; remove by turning the nut clockwise.

5. Remove the injection pump as described in Section 5 under Diesel Fuel Systems.

6. Remove the water pump.

7. Jack up the van and safely support it with jackstands.

8. Remove the crankshaft pulley and vibration damper as described in this Section.

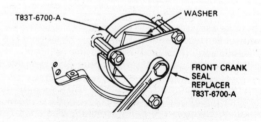

Diesel front seal installation

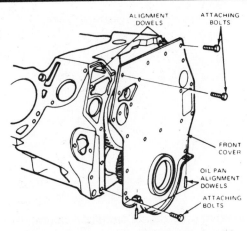

Diesel front cover alignment dowels

9. Remove the engine ground cables at the front of the engine.
10. Remove the five bolts attaching the engine front cover to the engine block and oil pan.
11. Lower the van.
12. Remove the front cover.

NOTE: The front cover oil seal on the diesel must be driven out with an arbor press and a 3¼ in. (82.5mm) spacer. Take the cover to a qualified machinist or engine specialist for this procedure. See also steps 14 and 15.

13. Remove all old gasket material from the front cover, engine block, oil pan sealing surfaces and water pump surfaces.
14. Coat the new front oil seal with Lubriplate® or equivalent grease.
15. The new seal must be installed using a seal installation tool, Ford part no. T83T–6700–A or an arbor press. A qualified machinist or engine specialist can handle seal installation as well as removal. When the seal bottoms out on the front cover surface, it is installed at the proper depth.
16. Install alignment dowels into the engine block to align the front cover and gaskets. These can be made out of round stock. Apply a gasket sealer to the engine block sealing surfaces, then install the gaskets on the block.
17. Apply a ⅛ in. (3mm) bead of RTV sealer on the front of the engine block as shown in the illustration. Apply a ¼ in. (6mm) bead of RTV sealer on the oil pan as shown.
18. Install the front cover immediately after applying RTV sealer. The sealer will begin to cure and lose its effectiveness unless the cover is installed quickly.
19. Install the water pump gasket on the engine front cover. Apply RTV sealer to the four water pump bolts illustrated. Install the water pump and hand tighten all bolts.

WARNING: The two top water pump bolts must be no more than 1¼ in. (31.75mm) long bolts any longer will interfere with (hit) the engine drive gears.

20. Torque the water pump bolts to 19 ft. lbs. Torque the front cover bolts to specifications according to bolt size (see Torque Specifications chart).
21. Install the injection pump adaptor and injection pump as described in Section 5 under Diesel Fuel System.
22. Install the heater hose fitting in the pump using pipe sealant, and connect the heater hose to the water pump.
23. Jack up the van and safely support it with jackstands.
24. Lubricate the front of the crankshaft with clean engine oil. Apply RTV sealant to the engine side of the retaining bolt washer to prevent oil seepage past the keyway. Install the crankshaft vibration damper using Ford Special tools T83T–6316B. Torque

the damper-to-crankshaft bolt to 90 ft. lbs.
25. Install the remaining engine components in the reverse order of removal.

CRANKSHAFT DRIVE GEAR

1. Complete the front cover removal procedures.
2. Install the crankshaft drive gear remover Tool T83T–6316–A, and using a breaker bar to prevent crankshaft rotation, or flywheel holding Tool T74R–6375–A, remove the crankshaft gear.
3. Install the crankshaft gear using Tool T83T–6316–B aligning the crankshaft drive gear timing mark with the camshaft drive gear timing mark.

NOTE: The gear may be heated to 300–350°F (149–260°C) for ease of installation. Heat it in an oven. Do not use a torch.

4. Complete the front cover installation procedures.

INJECTION PUMP DRIVE GEAR AND ADAPTER

1. Disconnect the battery ground cables from both batteries. Remove the air cleaner and install an intake opening cover.
2. Remove the injection pump. Remove the bolts attaching the injection pump adapter to the engine block, and remove the adapter.
3. Remove the engine front cover. Remove the drive gear.
4. Clean all gasket and sealant surfaces of the components removed with a suitable solvent and dry them thoroughly.
5. Install the drive gear in position, aligning all the drive gear timing marks.

NOTE: To determine that the No. 1 piston is at TDC of the compression stroke, position the injection pump drive gear dowel at the 4 o'clock position. The scribe line on the vibration damper should be at TDC.

Use extreme care to avoid disturbing the injection pump drive gear, once it is in position.

6. Install the engine front cover. Apply a ⅛ in. (3mm) bead of RTV Sealant along the bottom surface of the injection pump adapter.

NOTE: RTV should be applied immediately prior to adapter installation.

7. Install the injection pump adaptor. Apply sealer to the bolt threads before assembly.

NOTE: With the injection pump adapter installed, the injection pump drive gear cannot jump timing.

8. Install all removed components. Run the engine and check for leaks.

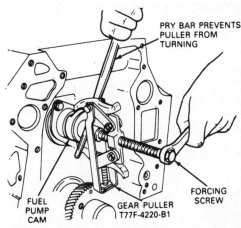

Removing the diesel fuel pump cam

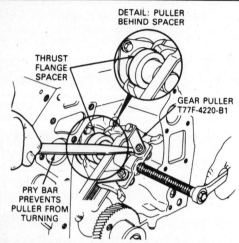

Removing the thrust flange spacer on the diesel

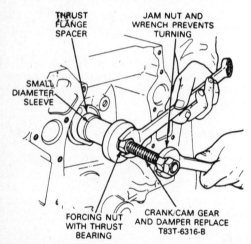

Installing the thrust flange spacer on th diesel

NOTE: If necessary, purge the high pressure fuel lines of air by loosening the connector one half to one turn and crank the engine until a solid flow of fuel, free of air bubbles, flows from the connection.

CAMSHAFT DRIVE GEAR, FUEL PUMP CAM, SPACER AND THRUST PLATE

1. Complete the front cover removal procedures.

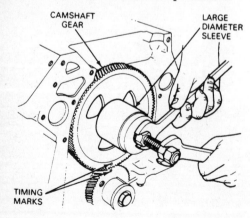

Installing the diesel camshaft gear

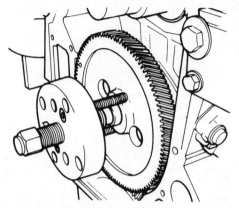

Removing he diesel camshaft timing gear

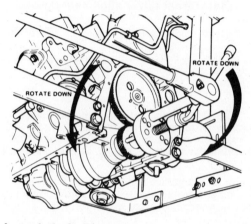

Diesel crankshaft drive gear removal; engine out of van

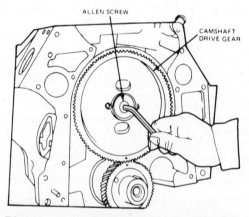

Diesel camshaft timing gear installation

2. Remove the camshaft allen screw.

3. Install a gear puller, Tool T83T–6316–A and remove the gear. Remove the fuel supply pump, if necessary.

4. Install a gear puller, Tool T77E–4220–B and shaft protector T83T–6316–A and remove the fuel pump cam and spacer, if necessary.

5. Remove the bolts attaching the thrust plate, and remove the thrust plate, if necessary.

6. Install a new thrust plate, if removed.

7. Install the spacer and fuel pump cam against the camshaft thrust flange, using installation sleeve and replacer Tool T83T–6316–B, if removed.

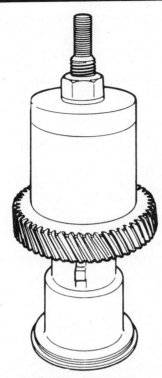

Special installation tool installed on the diesel crankshaft drive gear

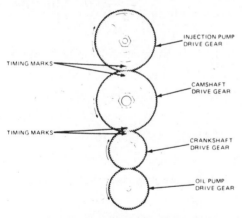

Diesel timing gear alignment

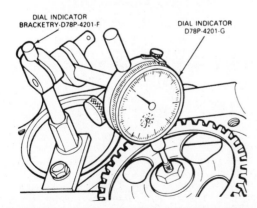

Checking camshaft endplay on the diesel

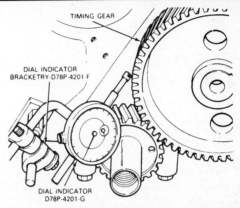

Checking drive gear backlash on the diesel

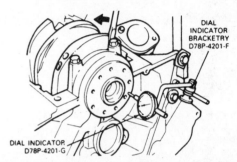

Checking crankshaft endplay on the diesel

8. Install the camshaft drive gear against the fuel pump cam, aligning the timing mark with the timing mark on the crankshaft drive gear, using installation sleeve and replacer Tool T83T–6316–B.
9. Install the camshaft allen screw and tighten to 18 ft. lbs.
10. Install the fuel pump, if removed.
11. Install the front cover, following the previous procedure.

CHECKING TIMING CHAIN DEFLECTION

To measure timing chain deflection, rotate the crankshaft clockwise to take up slack on the left side of chain. Choose a reference point and measure the distance from this point and the chain. Rotate the crankshaft in the opposite direction to take up slack on the right side of the chain. Force the left (slack) side of the chain out and measure the distance to the reference point chosen earlier. The difference between the two measurements is the deflection.

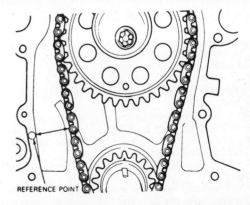

Checking V8 timing chain deflection

3 ENGINE AND ENGINE OVERHAUL

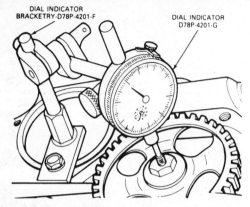

Checking gasoline V8 camshaft endplay

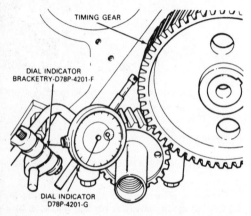

Checking timing gear backlash on the diesel

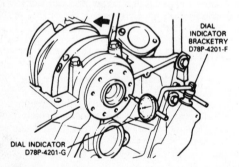

Checking crankshaft endplay on the diesel

The timing chain should be replaced if the deflection measurement exceeded the specified limit. The deflection measurement should not exceed ½ in. (13mm).

CAMSHAFT ENDPLAY MEASUREMENT

The camshaft gears used on some engines are easily damaged if pried upon while the valve train load is on the camshaft. Loosen the rocker arm nuts or rocker arm shaft support bolts before checking the camshaft endplay.

Push the camshaft toward the rear of engine, install and zero a dial indicator, then pry between the camshaft gear and the block to pull the camshaft forward. If the endplay is excessive,

check for correct installation of the spacer. If the spacer is installed correctly, replace the thrust plate.

MEASURING TIMING GEAR BACKLASH

Use a dial indicator installed on block to measure timing gear backlash. Hold the gear firmly against the block while making the measurement. If excessive backlash exists, replace both gears.

Timing Chain

REMOVAL AND INSTALLATION

V8 Gasoline Engines

1. Remove the front cover.
2. Rotate the crankshaft counterclockwise to take up the slack on the left side of the chain.
3. Establish a reference point on the cylinder block and measure from this point to the chain.
4. Rotate the crankshaft in the opposite direction to take up the slack on the right side of the chain.

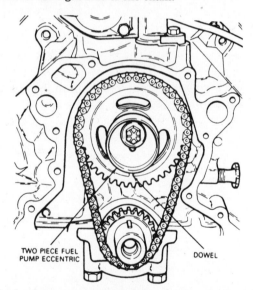

Fuel pump eccentric on the 8-5.0L and 8-5.8L

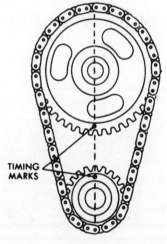

V8 timing chain installation

3-72

5. Force the left side of the chain out with your fingers and measure the distance between the reference point and the chain. The timing chain deflection is the difference between the two measurements. If the deflection exceeds ½ in. (13mm), replace the timing chain and sprockets.

To replace the timing chain and sprockets:

6. Turn the crankshaft until the timing marks on the sprockets are aligned vertically.

7. Remove the camshaft sprocket retaining screw and remove the fuel pump eccentric and washers.

8. Alternately slide both of the sprockets and timing chain off the crankshaft and camshaft until free of the engine.

9. Position the timing chain on the sprockets so that the timing marks on the sprockets are aligned vertically. Alternately slide the sprockets and chain onto the crankshaft and camshaft sprockets.

10. Install the fuel pump eccentric washers and attaching bolt on the camshaft sprocket. Tighten to 40–45 ft. lbs.

11. Install the front cover.

Timing Gears

REMOVAL AND INSTALLATION

6–4.9L

1. Drain the cooling system and remove the front cover.

CAUTION

When draining the coolant, keep in mind that cats and dogs are attracted by the ethylene glycol antifreeze, and are quite likely to drink any that is left in an uncovered container or in puddles on the ground. This will prove fatal in sufficient quantity. Always drain the coolant into a sealable container. Coolant should be reused unless it is contaminated or several years old.

---

2. Crank the engine until the timing marks on the camshaft and crankshaft gears are aligned.

3. Use a gear puller to removal both of the timing gears.

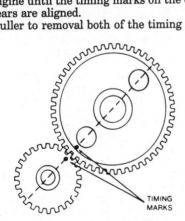

6-4.9L timing gear mark alignment

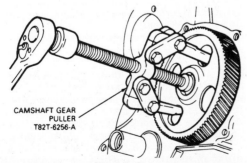

Removing the camshaft gear from the 6-4.9L

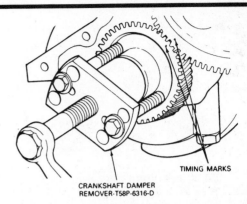

Removing the crankshaft gear from the 6-4.9L

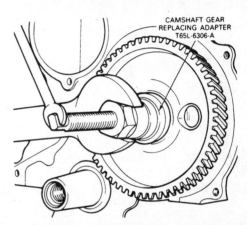

Installing the camshaft gear on the 6-4.9L

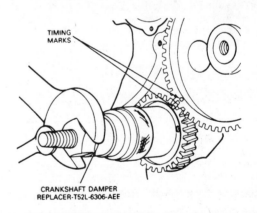

Installing the crankshaft gear on the 6-4.9L

4. Before installing the timing gears, be sure that the key and spacer are properly installed. Align the gear key way with the key and install the gear on the camshaft. Be sure that the timing marks line up on the camshaft and the crankshaft gears and install the crankshaft gear.

5. Install the front cover, and assemble the rest of the engine in the reverse order of disassembly. Fill the cooling system.

8-7.3L Diesel

1. Follow the procedures for timing gear cover removal and installation, and remove the front cover.

2. To remove the crankshaft gear, install gear puller (Ford part) no. T83T–6316–A or equivalent, and using a breaker bar

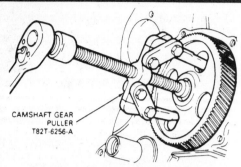

6-4.9L camshaft gear removal

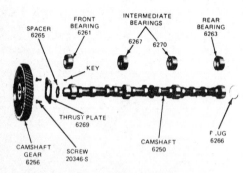

6-4.9L camshaft components

to prevent the crankshaft from rotating, remove the crankshaft gear. To install the crankshaft gear use tool (Ford part) no. T83T-6316-B or equivalent while aligning the timing marks as shown in the illustration, and press the gear into place.

3. The camshaft gear may be removed by taking out the Allen screw and installing a gear puller, Ford part no. T83T-6316-A or equivalent and removing the gear. The gear may be replaced by using tool (Ford part) no. T83T-6316-B or equivalent. Torque the Allen screw to 12-18 ft. lbs.

Camshaft

REMOVAL AND INSTALLATION

6-4.9L

1. Remove the grille, radiator, air conditioner condenser, and timing cover.
2. Remove the distributor, fuel pump, oil pan and oil pump.
3. Align the timing marks. Unbolt the camshaft thrust plate, working through the holes in the camshaft gear.
4. Loosen the rocker arms, remove the pushrods, take off the side cover and remove the valve lifter with a magnet.
5. Remove the camshaft very carefully to prevent nicking the bearings.
6. Oil the camshaft bearing journals and use Lubriplate® or something similar on the lobes. Install the camshaft, gear, and thrust plate, aligning the gear marks. Tighten down the thrust plate. Make sure that the camshaft end-play is not excessive.
7. The last item to be replaced is the distributor. The rotor should be at the firing position for no. 1 cylinder, with the timing gear marks aligned.

V8 Including Diesel

NOTE: Ford recommends removing the diesel engine for camshaft removal.

1. Remove the intake manifold and valley pan, if so equipped.

2. Remove the rocker covers, and either remove the rocker arm shafts or loosen the rockers on their pivots and remove the pushrods. The pushrods must be reinstalled in their original positions.
3. Remove the valve lifters in sequence with a magnet. They must be replaced in their original positions.
4. Remove the timing gear cover and timing chain (timing gear on V8 diesel) and sprockets.
5. In addition to the radiator and air conditioning condenser, if so equipped, it may be necessary to remove the front grille assembly and the hook lock assembly to gain the necessary clearance to code the camshaft out of the front of the engine.

NOTE: A camshaft removal tool, Ford part no. T65L-6250-A and adaptor 14-0314 are needed to remove the diesel camshaft.

6. Coat the camshaft with engine oil liberally before installing it. Slide the camshaft into the engine very carefully so as not to scratch the bearing bores with the camshaft lobes. Install the camshaft thrust plate and tighten the attaching screws to 9-12 ft. lbs. Measure the camshaft end-play. If the end-play is more than 0.009 in. (0.228mm), replace the thrust plate. Assemble the remaining components in the reverse order of removal.

CHECKING CAMSHAFT

Camshaft Lobe Lift

Check the lift of each lobe in consecutive order and make a note of the reading.

1. Remove the fresh air inlet tube and the air cleaner. Remove the heater hose and crankcase ventilation hoses. Remove valve rocker arm cover(s).
2. Remove the rocker arm stud nut or fulcrum bolts, fulcrum seat and rocker arm.
3. Make sure the pushrod is in the valve tappet socket. Install a dial indicator D78P-4201-B or equivalent. so that the actuating point of the indicator is in the push rod socket (or the indicator ball socket adaptor tool 6565-AB is on the end of the push rod) and in the same plane as the push rod movement.
4. Disconnect the I terminal and the S terminal at the starter relay. Install an auxiliary starter switch between the battery and S terminals of the start relay. Crank the engine with the ignition switch off. Turn the crankshaft over until the tappet is on the base circle of the camshaft lobe. At this position, the push rod will be in its lowest position.
5. Zero the dial indicator. Continue to rotate the crankshaft slowly until the push rod is in the fully raised position.
6. Compare the total lift recorded on the dial indicator with the specification shown on the Camshaft Specification chart.

To check the accuracy of the original indicator reading, continue to rotate the crankshaft until the indicator reads zero. If the left on any lobe is below specified wear limits listed, the camshaft and the valve tappet operating on the worn lobe(s) must be replaced.

7. Install the dial indicator and auxiliary starter switch.
8. Install the rocker arm, fulcrum seat and stud nut or fulcrum bolts. Check the valve clearance. Adjust if required (refer to procedure in this Section).
9. Install the valve rocker arm cover(s) and the air cleaner.

Camshaft End Play

NOTE: On all gasoline V8 engines, prying against the aluminum-nylon camshaft sprocket, with the valve train load on the camshaft, can break or damage the sprocket. Therefore, the rocker arm adjusting nuts must be backed off, or the rocker arm and shaft assembly must be loosened sufficiently to free the camshaft. After checking the camshaft end play, check the valve clearance. Adjust if required (refer to procedure in this Section).

1. Push the camshaft toward the rear of the engine. Install a dial indicator (Tool D78P–4201–F, –G or equivalent so that the indicator point is on the camshaft sprocket attaching screw.

2. Zero the dial indicator. Position a prybar between the camshaft gear and the block. Pull the camshaft forward and release it. Compare the dial indicator reading with the specifications.

3. If the end play is excessive, check the spacer for correct installation before it is removed. If the spacer is correctly installed, replace the thrust plate.

4. Remove the dial indicator.

CAMSHAFT BEARING REPLACEMENT

1. Remove the engine following the procedures in this Section and install it on a work stand.

2. Remove the camshaft, flywheel and crankshaft, following the appropriate procedures. Push the pistons to the top of the cylinder.

3. Remove the camshaft rear bearing bore plug. Remove the camshaft bearings with Tool T65L–6250–A or equivalent.

4. Select the proper size expanding collet and back-up nut and assemble on the mandrel. With the expanding collet collapsed, install the collet assembly in the camshaft bearing and tighten the back-up nut on the expanding mandrel until the collet fits the camshaft bearing.

5. Assemble the puller screw and extension (if necessary) and install on the expanding mandrel. Wrap a cloth around the threads of the puller screw to protect the front bearing or journal. Tighten the pulling nut against the thrust bearing and pulling plate to remove the camshaft bearing. Be sure to hold a wrench on the end of the puller screw to prevent it from turning.

6. To remove the front bearing, install the puller from the rear of the cylinder block.

7. Position the new bearings at the bearing bores, and press them in place with tool T65L–6250–A or equivalent. Be sure to center the pulling plate and puller screw to avoid damage to the bearing. Failure to use the correct expanding collet can cause severe bearing damage. Align the oil holes in the bearings with the oil holes in the cylinder block before pressing bearings into place.

NOTE: Be sure the front bearing is installed 0.020–0.035 in. (0.508–0.889mm) for the inline six cylinder engines, 0.005–0.020 in. (0.127–0.508mm) for the gasoline V8, 0.040–0.060 in. (1.016–1.524mm) for the diesel V8, below the front face of the cylinder block.

8. Install the camshaft rear bearing bore plug.

9. Install the camshaft, crankshaft, flywheel and related parts, following the appropriate procedures.

10. Install the engine in the van, following procedures described earlier in this Section.

Core (Freeze) Plugs

REPLACEMENT

Core plugs need replacement only if they are found to be leaking, are excessively rusty, have popped due to freezing or, if the engine is being overhauled.

If the plugs are accessible with the engine in the van, they can be removed as-is. If not, the engine will have to be removed.

1. If necessary, remove the engine and mount it on a work stand. If the engine is being left in the van, drain the engine coolant and engine oil

--- **CAUTION** ---

When draining the coolant, keep in mind that cats and dogs are attracted by the ethylene glycol antifreeze, and are quite likely to drink any that is left in an uncovered container or in puddles on the ground. This will prove fatal in sufficient quantity. Always drain the coolant into a sealable container. Coolant should be reused unless it is contaminated or several years old.

2. Remove anything blocking access to the plug or plugs to be replaced.

3. Drill or center-punch a hole in the plug. For large plugs, drill a ½ in. hole; for small plugs, drill a ¼ in. hole.

4. For large plugs, using a slide-hammer, thread a machine screw adapter or insert 2-jawed puller adapter into the hole in the plug. Pull the plug from the block; for small plugs, pry the plug out with a pin punch.

5. Thoroughly clean the opening in the block, using steel wool or emery paper to polish the hole rim.

6. Coat the outer diameter of the new plug with sealer and place it in the hole.

For cup-type core plugs: These plugs are installed with the flanged end outward. The maximum diameter of this type of plug is located at the outer edge of the flange. Carefully and evenly, drive the new plug into place.

For expansion-type plugs: These plugs are installed with the flanged end inward. The maximum diameter of this type of plug is located at the base of the flange. It is imperative that the correct type of installation tool is used with this type of plug. Under no circumstances is this type of plug to be driven in using a tool that contacts the crowned portion of the plug. Driving in this plug incorrectly will cause the plug to expand prior to installation. When installed, the trailing (maximum) diameter of the plug MUST be below the chamfered edge of the bore to create an effective seal. If the core plug replacing tool has a depth seating

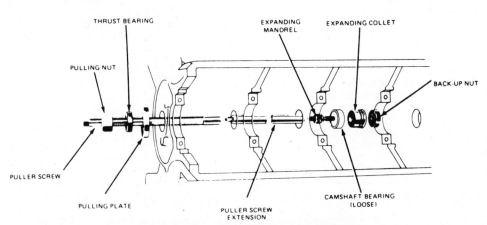

Camshaft bearing replacement

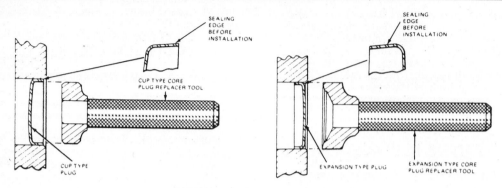

Core plugs and installation tools

surface, do not seat the tool against a non-machined (casting) surface.

7. Install any removed parts and, if necessary, install the engine in the van.

8. Refill the cooling system and crankcase.

9. Start the engine and check for leaks.

Pistons and Connecting Rods

REMOVAL AND INSTALLATION

6–4.9L

1. Drain the cooling system and the crankcase.

------------------------------ **CAUTION** ------------------------------

When draining the coolant, keep in mind that cats and dogs are attracted by the ethylene glycol antifreeze, and are quite likely to drink any that is left in an uncovered container or in puddles on the ground. This will prove fatal in sufficient quantity. Always drain the coolant into a sealable container. Coolant should be reused unless it is contaminated or several years old.

The EPA warns that prolonged contact with used engine oil may cause a number of skin disorders, including cancer! You should make every effort to minimize your exposure to used engine oil. Protective gloves should be worn when changing the oil. Wash your hands and any other exposed skin areas as soon as possible after exposure to used engine oil. Soap and water, or waterless hand cleaner should be used.

----

2. Remove the cylinder head.

3. Remove the oil pan, the oil pump inlet tube and the oil pump.

4. Turn the crankshaft until the piston to be removed is at the bottom of its travel and place a cloth on the piston head to collect filings. Using a ridge reaming tool, remove any ridge of carbon or any other deposit from the upper cylinder walls where piston travel ends. Do not cut into the piston ring travel area more than $^1/_{32}$ in. (0.8mm) while removing the ridge.

5. Mark all of the connecting rod caps so that they can be reinstalled in the original positions from which they are removed and remove the connecting rod bearing cap. Also identify the piston assemblies as they, too, must be reinstalled in the same cylinder from which removed.

6. With the bearing caps removed, the connecting rod bearing bolts are potentially damaging to the cylinder walls during removal. To guard against cylinder wall damage, install 4 in. (101.6mm) or 5 in. (127mm) lengths of ⅜ in. (9.5mm) rubber tubing onto the connecting rod bolts. These will also protect the crankshaft journal from scratches when the connecting rod is installed, and will serve as a guide for the rod.

7. Squirt some clean engine oil into each cylinder before removing the pistons. Using a wooden hammer handle, push the connecting rod and piston assembly out of the top of the cylinder (pushing from the bottom of the rod). Be careful to avoid damaging both the crank journal and the cylinder wall when removing the rod and piston assembly.

8. Before installing the piston/connecting rod assembly, be sure to clean all gasket mating surfaces, oil the pistons, piston rings and the cylinder walls with light engine oil.

9. Be sure to install the pistons in the cylinders from which they were removed. The connecting rod and bearing caps are numbered from 1 to 6 beginning at the front of the engine. The numbers on the connecting rod and bearing cap must be on the same side when installed in the cylinder bore. If a connecting rod is ever transposed from one engine or cylinder to another, new bearings should be fitted and the connecting rod should be numbered to correspond with the new cylinder number. The notch on the piston head goes toward the front of the engine.

10. Make sure the ring gaps are properly spaced around the circumference of the piston. Make sure rubber hose lengths are fitted to the rod bolts. Fit a piston ring compressor around the piston and slide the piston and connecting rod assembly down into the cylinder bore, pushing it in with the wooden hammer handle. Push the piston down until it is only slightly below the top of the cylinder bore. Guide the connecting rods onto the crankshaft bearing journals carefully, using the rubber hose lengths, to avoid damaging the crankshaft.

11. Check the bearing clearance of all the rod bearings, fitting them to the crankshaft bearing journals.

12. After the bearings have been fitted, apply a light coating of engine oil to the journals and bearings.

13. Turn the crankshaft until the appropriate bearing journal is at the bottom of its stroke, then push the piston assembly all the way down until the connecting rod bearing seats on the crankshaft journal. Be careful not to allow the bearing cap screws to strike the crankshaft bearing journals and damage them.

14. After the piston and connecting rod assemblies have been installed, check the connecting rod side clearance on each crankshaft journal.

15. Prime and install the oil pump and the oil pump intake tube, then install the oil pan.

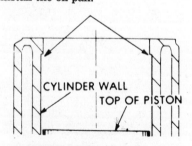

Ridge caused by wear

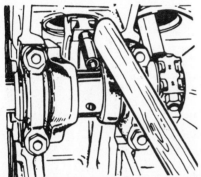

Make connecting rod bolt guide from pieces of hose. These protect journals and cylinder walls

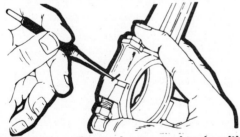

Push the piston and rod assembly out with a hammer handle

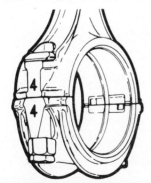

Match the connecting rod caps and rods with a scribe mark

Number each rod and cap with its cylinder number

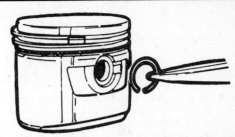

Use needle-nose pliers to remove the piston pin clips

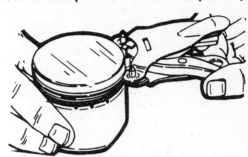

Removing/Installing the piston rings

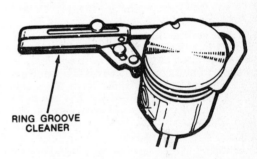

RING GROOVE CLEANER

Clean the ring grooves with this tool

16. Reassemble the rest of the engine in the reverse order of disassembly.

V8 Engines Including Diesel

1. Drain the cooling system and the crankcase.

CAUTION

When draining the coolant, keep in mind that cats and dogs are attracted by the ethylene glycol antifreeze, and are quite likely to drink any that is left in an uncovered container or in puddles on the ground. This will prove fatal in sufficient quantity. Always drain the coolant into a sealable container. Coolant should be reused unless it is contaminated or several years old.

The EPA warns that prolonged contact with used engine oil may cause a number of skin disorders, including cancer! You should make every effort to minimize your exposure to used engine oil. Protective gloves should be worn when changing the oil. Wash your hands and any other exposed skin areas as soon as possible after exposure to used engine oil. Soap and water, or waterless hand cleaner should be used.

---

2. Remove the intake manifold.
3. Remove the cylinder heads.
4. Remove the oil pan.
5. Remove the oil pump.
6. Turn the crankshaft until the piston to be removed is at the bottom of its travel, then place a cloth on the piston head to collect filings.

7. Remove any ridge of deposits at the end of the piston travel from the upper cylinder bore, using a ridge reaming tool. Do not cut into the piston ring travel area more than $\frac{1}{32}$ in. (0.8mm) when removing the ridge.

8. Make sure that all of the connecting rod bearing caps can be identified, so they will be reinstalled in their original positions.

9. Turn the crankshaft until the connecting rod that is to be removed is at the bottom of its stroke and remove the connecting rod nuts and bearing cap.

10. With the bearing caps removed, the connecting rod bearing bolts are potentially damaging to the cylinder walls during removal. To guard against cylinder wall damage, install four or five inch lengths of ⅜ in. (0.8mm) rubber tubing onto the connecting rod bolts. These will also protect the crankshaft journal from scratches when the connecting rod is installed, and will serve as a guide for the rod.

11. Squirt some clean engine oil into each cylinder before removing the piston assemblies. Using a wooden hammer handle, push the connecting rod and piston assembly out of the top of the cylinder (pushing from the bottom of the rod). Be careful to avoid damaging both the crank journal and the cylinder wall when removing the rod and piston assembly.

12. Remove the bearing inserts from the connecting rod and cap if the bearings are to be replace, and place the cap onto the piston/rod assembly from which it was removed.

13. Install the piston/rod assemblies in the same manner as that for the 6-cylinder engines. See the procedure given for 6-cylinder engines.

NOTE: The connecting rod and bearing caps are numbered from 1 to 4 in the right bank and from 5 to 8 in the left bank, beginning at the front of the engine. The numbers on the rod and cap must be on the same side when they are installed in the cylinder bore. Also, the largest chamfer at the bearing end of the rod should be positioned toward the crank pin thrust face of the crankshaft and the notch in the head of the piston faces toward the front of the engine.

14. See the appropriate component procedures to assemble the engine.

Piston Ring and Wrist Pin
REMOVAL

All of the Ford gasoline engines covered in this guide utilize pressed-in wrist pins, which can only be removed by an arbor press. The diesel pistons are removed in the same way, only the pistons are heated before the wrist pins are pressed out. On both gasoline and diesel engines, the piston/connecting rod assemblies should be taken to an engine specialist or qualified machinist for piston removal and installation.

A piston ring expander is necessary for removing the piston rings without damaging them; any other method (screwdriver blades, pliers, etc.) usually results in the rings being bent, scratched or distorted, or the piston itself being damaged. When the rings are removed, clean the ring grooves using an appropriate ring groove cleaning tool, using care not to cut too deeply. Thoroughly clean all carbon and varnish from the piston with solvent.

WARNING: Do not use a wire brush or caustic solvent (acids, etc.) on pistons.

Inspect the pistons for scuffing, scoring, cracks, pitting, or excessive ring groove wear. If these are evident, the piston must be replaced.

The piston should also be checked in relation to the cylinder diameter. Using a telescoping gauge and micrometer, or a dial gauge, measure the cylinder bore diameter perpendicular (90%) to the piston pin, 2½ in. (64mm) below the cylinder block deck (surface where the block mates with the heads). Then, with the micrometer, measure the piston, perpendicular to its wrist pin on the skirt. the difference between the two measurements is the piston clearance. If the clearance is within specifications or slightly below (after the cylinders have been bored or hones), finish honing is all that is necessary. If the clearance is excessive, try to obtain a slightly larger piston to bring clearance to within specifications. If this is not possible, obtain the first oversize piston and hone (or if necessary, bore) the cylinder to size. Generally, if the cylinder bore is tapered 0.005 in. (0.127mm) or

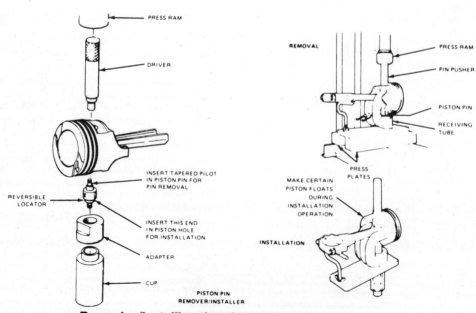

Removing/Installing the piston pins with a press

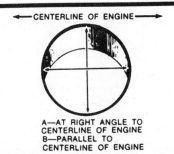

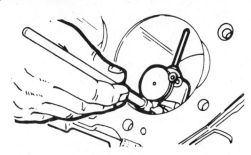

Cylinder measurement points. Take a top measurement 13mm blow the top of the block deck; bottom measurements are at 13mm above he top of the piston at BDC

Measuring cylinder bore with a dial gauge

more or is out-of-round 0.003 in. (0.076mm) or more, it is advisable to rebore for the smallest possible oversize piston and rings.

After measuring, mark pistons with a felt tip pen for reference and for assembly.

NOTE: Cylinder honing and/or boring should be performed by a reputable, professional mechanic with the proper equipment. In some cases, clean-up honing can be done with the cylinder block in the car, but most excessive honing and all cylinder boring must be done with the block stripped and removed from the car.

Before honing the diesel cylinders, the piston oil cooling jets must be removed. this procedure should be handled by a diesel specialist, as special tools are needed. Jets cannot be reused; new jets should be fitted.

MEASURING THE OLD PISTONS

Check used piston-to-cylinder bore clearance as follows:
1. Measure the cylinder bore diameter with a telescope gauge.

2. Measure the piston diameter. When measuring the pistons for size or taper, measurements must be made with the piston pin removed.
3. Subtract the piston diameter from the cylinder bore diameter to determine piston-to-bore clearance.
4. Compare the piston-to-bore clearances obtained with those clearances recommended. Determine if the piston-to-bore clearance is in the acceptable range.
5. When measuring taper, the largest reading must be at the bottom of the skirt.

SELECTING NEW PISTONS

1. If the used piston is not acceptable, check the service piston size and determine if a new piston can be selected. (Service pistons are available in standard, high limit and standard oversize.
2. If the cylinder bore must be reconditioned, measure the

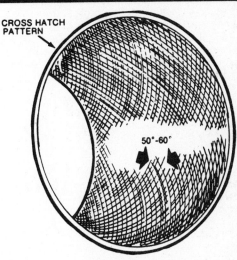

Proper bore cross-hatching after honing

new piston diameter, then hone the cylinder bore to obtain the preferred clearance.
3. Select a new piston and mark the piston to identify the cylinder for which it was fitted. (On some vehicles, oversize pistons may be found. These pistons will be 0.254mm [0.010 in.] oversize).

CYLINDER HONING

1. When cylinders are being honed, follow the manufacturer's recommendations for the use of the hone.
2. Occasionally, during the honing operation, the cylinder bore should be thoroughly cleaned and the selected piston checked for correct fit.
3. When finish-honing a cylinder bore, the hone should be moved up and down at a sufficient speed to obtain a very fine uniform surface finish in a cross-hatch pattern of approximately 45–65° included angle. The finish marks should be clean but not sharp, free from embedded particles and torn or folded metal.
4. Permanently mark the piston for the cylinder to which it has been fitted and proceed to hone the remaining cylinders.

WARNING: Handle the pistons with care. Do not attempt to force the pistons through the cylinders until the cylinders have been honed to the correct size. Pistons can be distorted through careless handling.

5. Thoroughly clean the bores with hot water and detergent. Scrub well with a stiff bristle brush and rinse thoroughly with hot water. It is extremely essential that a good cleaning operation be performed. If any of the abrasive material is allowed to remain in the cylinder bores, it will rapidly wear the new rings and cylinder bores. The bores should be swabbed several times with light engine oil and a clean cloth and then wiped with a clean dry cloth. CYLINDERS SHOULD NOT BE CLEANED WITH KEROSENE OR GASOLINE! Clean the remainder of the cylinder block to remove the excess material spread during the honing operation.

PISTON RING END GAP

Piston ring end gap should be checked while the rings are removed from the pistons. Incorrect end gap indicates that the wrong size rings are being used; ring breakage could occur.

Compress the piston rings to be used in a cylinder, one at a time, into that cylinder. Squirt clean oil into the cylinder, so that the rings and the top 2 in. (51mm) of cylinder wall are coated. Using an inverted piston, press the rings approximately 1 in.

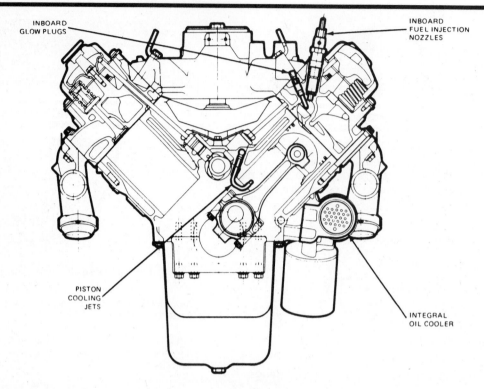

Diesel V8 cross-section

(25mm) below the deck of the block (on diesels, measure ring gap clearance with the ring positioned at the bottom of ring travel in the bore). Measure the ring end gap with the feeler gauge, and compare to the Ring Gap chart in this Section. Carefully pull the ring out of the cylinder and file the ends squarely with a fine file to obtain the proper clearance.

PISTON RING SIDE CLEARANCE CHECK AND INSTALLATION

Check the pistons to see that the ring grooves and oil return holes have been properly cleaned. Slide a piston ring into its groove, and check the side clearance with a feeler gauge. On gasoline engines, make sure you insert the gauge between the ring and its lower land (lower edge of the groove), because any wear that occurs forms a step at the inner portion of the lower land. On diesels, insert the gauge between the ring and the upper land. If the piston grooves have worn to the extend that relatively high steps exist on the lower land, the piston grooves have worn to the extent that relatively high steps exist on the lower land, the piston should be replaced, because these will interfere with the operation of the new rings and ring clearance will be excessive. Piston rings are not furnished in oversize widths to compensate for ring groove wear.

Install the rings on the piston, lowest ring first, using a piston ring expander. There is a high risk of breaking or distorting the rings, or scratching the piston, if the rings are installed by hand or other means.

Position the rings on the piston as illustrated; spacing of the various piston ring gaps is crucial to proper oil retention and even cylinder wear. When installing new rings, refer to the installation diagram furnished with the new parts.

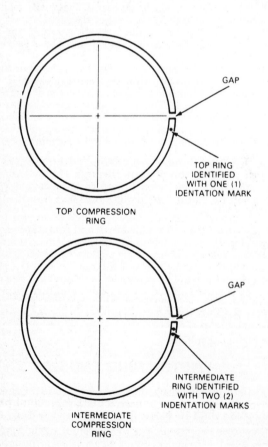

Diesel piston ring identification

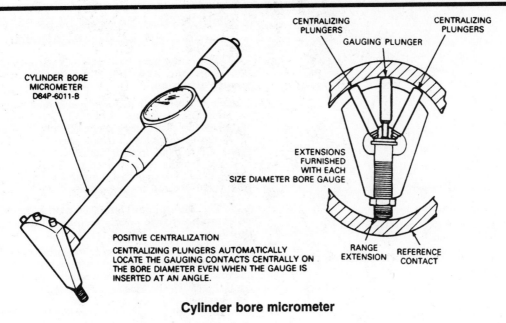

Cylinder bore micrometer

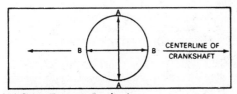

A - At Right angle to center line of engine
B - Parallel to center line of engine

Top Measurement: Make 12.70mm (1/2 inch) below top of block deck

Bottom Measurement: Make within 12.70mm (1/2 inch) above top of piston - when piston is at its lowest travel (B.D.C)

Bore Service Limit: Equals the average of "A" and "B" when measured at the center of the piston travel.

Taper: Equals difference between "A" top and "A" bottom.

Out-of-Round: Equals difference between "A" and "B" when measured at the center of piston travel.

Cylinder bore measurement

Check piston diameter at these points

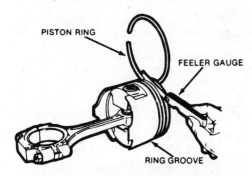

Checking ring side clearance

Check piston ring end gap with a feeler gauge, with the ring positioned squarely in the bore 1 inch below the block deck

Connecting Rod Bearings

INSPECTION

Connecting rod bearings for the engines covered in this guide consist of two halves or shells which are interchangeable in the rod and cap. when the shells are placed in position, the ends extend slightly beyond the rod and cap surfaces so that when the rod bolts are torqued the shells will be clamped tightly in place to insure positive seating and to prevent turning. A tang holds the shells in place.

NOTE: The ends of the bearing shells must never be filed flush with the mating surfaces of the rod and cap.

If a rod bearing becomes noisy or is worn so that its clearance on the crank journal is sloppy, a new bearing of the correct undersize must be selected and installed since there is a provision for adjustment.

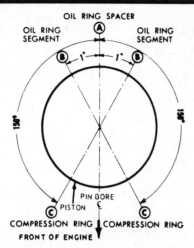

Proper spacing the the ring gaps around the piston on gasoline engines

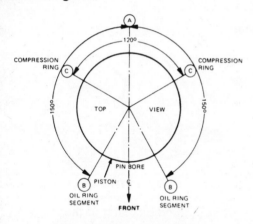

Diesel piston ring spacing

WARNING: Under no circumstances should the rod end or cap be filed to adjust the bearing clearance, nor should shims of any kind be used.

Inspect the rod bearings while the rod assemblies are out of the engine. If the shells are scored or show flaking, they should be replaced. If they are in good shape, check for proper clearance on the crank journal (see below). Any scoring or ridges on the crank journal means the crankshaft must be reground and fitted with undersized bearings, or replaced.

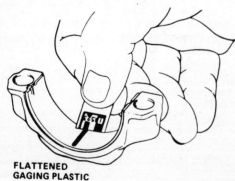

FLATTENED GAGING PLASTIC

Checking rod bearing clearance with a Plastigage®

CHECKING BEARING CLEARANCE AND REPLACING BEARINGS

NOTE: Make sure connecting rods and their caps are kept together, and that the caps are installed in the proper direction.

Replacement bearings are available in standard size, and in undersizes for reground crankshaft. Connecting rod-to-crankshaft bearing clearance is checked using Plastigage® at either the top or bottom of each crank journal. the Plastigage® has a range of 0 to 0.003 in. (0.076mm).

1. Remove the rod cap with the bearing shell. Completely clean the bearing shell and the crank journal, and blow any oil from the oil hole in the crankshaft.

NOTE: The journal surfaces and bearing shells must be completely free of oil, because Plastigage® is soluble in oil.

2. Place a strip of Plastigage® lengthwise along the bottom center of the lower bearing shell, then install the cap with shell and torque the bolt or nuts to specification. DO NOT TURN the crankshaft with the Plastigage® installed in the bearing.

3. Remove the bearing cap with the shell. The flattened Plastigage® will be found sticking to either the bearing shell or crank journal. Do not remove it yet.

4. Use the printed scale on the Plastigage® envelope to measure the flattened material at its widest point. The number within the scale which most closely corresponds to the width of the Plastigage® indicated bearing clearance in thousandths of an inch.

5. Check the specifications chart in this Section for the desired clearance. It is advisable to install a new bearing if clearance exceeds 0.003 in. (0.076mm); however, if the bearing is in good condition and is not being checked because of bearing noise, bearing replacement is not necessary.

6. If you are installing new bearings, try a standard size, then each undersize in order until one is found that is within the specified limits when checked for clearance with Plastigage®. Each under size has its size stamped on it.

7. When the proper size shell is found, clean off the Plastigage® material from the shell, oil the bearing thoroughly, reinstall the cap with its shell and torque the rod bolt nuts to specification.

NOTE: With the proper bearing selected and the nuts torqued, it should be possible to move the connecting rod back and forth freely on the crank journal as allowed by the specified connecting rod end clearance. If the rod cannot be moved, either the rod bearing is too far undersize or the rod is misaligned.

Piston and Connecting Rod

ASSEMBLY AND INSTALLATION

Install the connecting rod to the piston making sure piston installation notches and any marks on the rod are in proper relation to one another. Lubricate the wrist pin with clean engine oil and install the pin into the rod and piston assembly by using an arbor press as required. Install the wrist pin snaprings if equipped, and rotate them in their grooves to make sure they are seated. To install the piston and rod assemblies:

1. Make sure the connecting rod big bearings (including end cap) are of the correct size and properly installed.

2. Fit rubber hoses over the connecting rod bolt to protect the crankshaft journals, as in the Piston Removal procedure. Coat the rod bearings with clean oil.

3. Using the proper ring compressor, insert the piston assembly into the cylinder so that the notch in the top of the piston

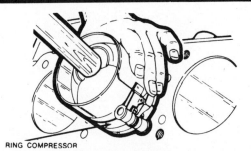

Tap the piston into the bore with a ring compressor and hammer handle. The notches on the piston crown face the front of the engine

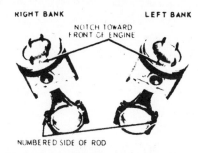

8-5.0L/8-5.8L piston and rod assemblies

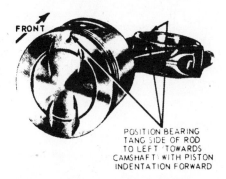

6-4.9L piston and rod assembly

8-7.5L piston and rod assemblies

faces the front of the engine (this assumes that the dimple(s) or other markings on the connecting rods are in correct relation to the piston notch(s).

4. From beneath the engine, coat each crank journal with clean oil. Pull the connecting rod, with the bearing shell in place, into position against the crank journal.

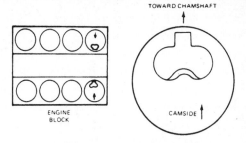

Diesel piston positioning

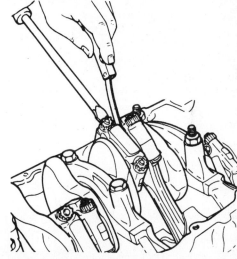

Checking rod side clearance with a feeler gauge. Use a small prybar to spread the rods

5. Remove the rubber hoses. Install the bearing cap and cap nuts and torque to specification.

NOTE: When more than one rod and piston assembly is being installed, the connecting rod cap attaching nuts should only be tightened enough to keep each rod in position until all have been installed. This will ease the installation of the remaining piston assemblies.

6. Check the clearance between the sides of the connecting rods and the crankshaft using a feeler gauge. Spread the rods slightly with a screwdriver to insert the gauge. If clearance is below the minimum tolerance, the rod may be machined to provide adequate clearance. If clearance is excessive, substitute an unworn rod, and recheck. If clearance is still outside specifications, the crankshaft must be welded and reground, or replaced.

7. Replace the oil pump if removed, and the oil pan.
8. Install the cylinder head(s) and intake manifold.

Crankshaft and Main Bearings

REMOVAL AND INSTALLATION

Engine Removed

1. With the engine removed from the vehicle and placed in a work stand, disconnect the spark plug wires from the spark plugs and remove the wires and bracket assembly from the attaching stud on the valve rocker arm cover(s) if so equipped. Disconnect the coil to distributor high tension lead at the coil. Remove the distributor cap and spark plug wires as an assembly. Remove the spark plugs to allow easy rotation of the crankshaft.

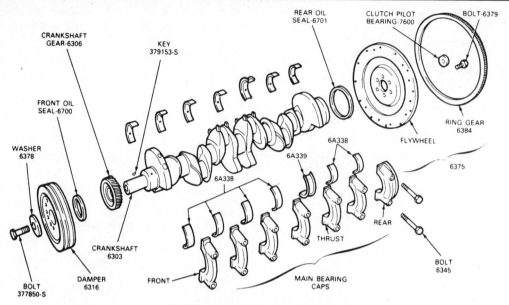

6-4.9L crankshaft and bearings

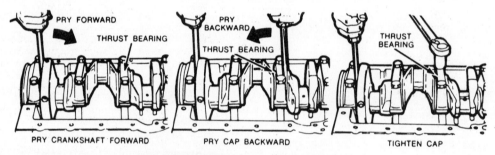

Crankshaft thrust bearing alignment

2. Remove the fuel pump and oil filter. Slide the water pump by-pass hose clamp (if so equipped) toward the water pump. Remove the alternator and mounting brackets.

3. Remove the crankshaft pulley from the crankshaft vibration damper. Remove the capscrew and washer from the end of the crankshaft. Install a universal puller, Tool T58P-6316-D or equivalent on the crankshaft vibration damper and remove the damper.

4. Remove the cylinder front cover and crankshaft gear, refer to Cylinder Front Cover and Timing Chain in this Section.

5. Invert the engine on the work stand. Remove the clutch pressure plate and disc (manual shift transmission). Remove the flywheel and engine rear cover plate. Remove the oil pan and gasket. Remove the oil pump.

6. Make sure all bearing caps (main and connecting rod) are marked so that they can be installed in their original locations. Turn the crankshaft until the connecting rod from which the cap is being removed is down, and remove the bearing cap. Push the connecting rod and piston assembly up into the cylinder. Repeat this procedure until all the connecting rod bearing caps are removed.

7. Remove the main bearings caps.

8. Carefully lift the crankshaft out of the block so that the thrust bearing surfaces are not damaged. Handle the crankshaft with care to avoid possible fracture to the finished surfaces.

9. Remove the rear journal seal from the block and rear main bearing cap.

10. Remove the main bearing inserts from the block and bearing caps.

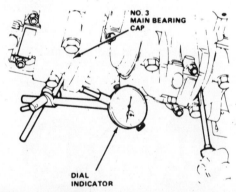

Checking crankshaft endplay with a dial indicator

11. Remove the connecting rod bearing inserts from the connecting rods and caps.

12. If the crankshaft main bearing journals have been refinished to a definite undersize, install the correct undersize bearings. Be sure the bearing inserts and bearing bores are clean. Foreign material under the inserts will distort the bearing and cause a failure.

13. Place the upper main bearing inserts in position in the bores with the tang fitting in the slot. Be sure the oil holes in the bearing inserts are aligned with the oil holes in the cylinder block.

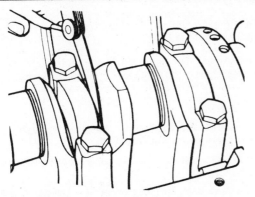

Crankshaft endplay can be checked with a feeler gauge

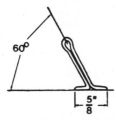

Make a bearing roll-out pin from a cotter pin

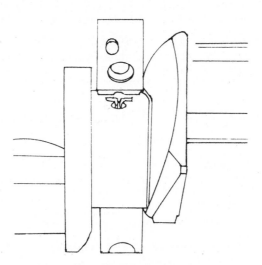

Bearing roll-out pin in place

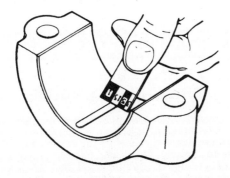

Checking main bearing clearance with a Plastigage®

14. Install the lower main bearing inserts in the bearing caps.

15. Clean the rear journal oil seal groove and the mating surfaces of the block and rear main bearing cap.

16. Dip the lip-type seal halves in clean engine oil. Install the seals in the bearing cap and block with the undercut side of the seal toward the front of the engine.

NOTE: This procedure applies only to engines with two piece rear main bearing oil seals. those having one piece seals (6–4.9L engines) will be installed after the crankshaft is in place.

17. Carefully lower the crankshaft into place. Be careful not to damage the bearing surfaces.

CHECKING MAIN BEARING CLEARANCES

18. Check the clearance of each main bearing by using the following procedure:

a. Place a piece of Plastigage® or its equivalent, on bearing surface across full width of bearing cap and about ¼ in. (6mm) off center.

b. Install cap and tighten bolts to specifications. Do not turn crankshaft while Plastigage® is in place.

c. Remove the cap. Using Plastigage® scale, check width of Plastigage® at widest point to get the minimum clearance. Check at narrowest point to get maximum clearance. Difference between readings is taper of journal.

d. If clearance exceeds specified limits, try a 0.001 in. (0.0254mm) or 0.002 in. (0.051mm) undersize bearing in combination with the standard bearing. Bearing clearance must be within specified limits. If standard and 0.002 in. (0.051mm) undersize bearing does not bring clearance within desired limits, refinish crankshaft journal, then install undersize bearings.

NOTE: Refer to Rear Main Oil Seal removal and installation, for special instructions in applying RTV sealer to rear main bearing cup.

19. Install all the bearing caps except the thrust bearing cap (no. 3 bearing on all except the 6–4.9L which use the no. 5 as the thrust bearing). BE sure the main bearing caps are installed in their original locations. Tighten the bearing cap bolts to specifications.

21. install the thrust bearing cap with the bolts finger tight.

22. Pry the crankshaft forward against the thrust surface of the upper half of the bearing.

23. hold the crankshaft forward and pry the thrust bearing cap to the rear. This will align the thrust surfaces of both halves of the bearing.

24. Retain the forward pressure on the crankshaft. Tighten the cap bolts to specifications.

25. Check the crankshaft end play using the following procedures:

a. Force the crankshaft toward the rear of the engine.

b. Install a dial indicator (tools D78P–4201–F, –G or equivalent) so that the contact point rests against the crankshaft flange and the indicator axis is parallel to the crankshaft axis.

c. Zero the dial indicator. Push the crankshaft forward and note the reading on the dial.

d. If the end play exceeds the wear limit listed in the Crankshaft and Connecting Rod Specifications chart, replace the thrust bearing. If the end play is less than the minimum limit, inspect the thrust bearing faces for scratches, burrs, nicks, or dirt. If the thrust faces are not damaged or dirty, then they probably were not aligned properly. Lubricate and install the new thrust bearing and align the faces following procedures 21 through 24.

26. On 6–4.9L engines with one piece rear main bearing oil seal, coat a new crankshaft rear oil seal with oil and install using Tool T65P–6701–A or equivalent. Inspect the seal to be sure it was not damaged during installation.

27. Install new bearing inserts in the connecting rods and caps. Check the clearance of each bearing, following the procedure (18a through 18d).

28. After the connecting rod bearings have been fitted, apply a light coat of engine oil to the journals and bearings.

29. Turn the crankshaft throw to the bottom of its stroke. Push the piston all the way down until the rod bearing seats on the crankshaft journal.

30. Install the connecting rod cap. Tighten the nuts to specification.

31. After the piston and connecting rod assemblies have been installed, check the side clearance with a feeler gauge between the connecting rods on each connecting rod crankshaft journal. Refer to Crankshaft and Connecting Rod specifications chart in this Section.

32. Install the timing chain and sprockets or gears, cylinder front cover and crankshaft pulley and adapter, following steps under Cylinder Front Cover and Timing Chain Installation in this Section.

Engine in the Van

1. With the oil pan, oil pump and spark plugs removed, remove the cap from the main bearing needing replacement and remove the bearing from the cap.

2. Make a bearing roll-out pin, using a bent cotter pin as shown in the illustration. Install the end of the pin in the oil hole in the crankshaft journal.

3. Rotate the crankshaft clockwise as viewed from the front of the engine. This will roll the upper bearing out of the block.

4. Lube the new upper bearing with clean engine oil and insert the plain (un-notched) end between the crankshaft and the indented or notched side of the block. Roll the bearing into place, making sure that the oil holes are aligned. Remove the roll pin from the oil hole.

5. Lube the new lower bearing and install it in the main bearing cap. Install the main bearing cap onto the block, making sure it is positioned in proper direction with the matchmarks in alignment.

6. Torque the main bearing cap to specification.

NOTE: See Crankshaft Installation for thrust bearing alignment.

CRANKSHAFT CLEANING AND INSPECTION

NOTE: handle the crankshaft carefully to avoid damage to the finish surfaces.

1. Clean the crankshaft with solvent, and blow out all oil passages with compressed air. On the 6–4.9L engine, clean the oil seal contact surface at the rear of the crankshaft with solvent to remove any corrosion, sludge or varnish deposits.

2. Use crocus cloth to remove any sharp edges, burrs or other imperfections which might damage the oil seal during installation or cause premature seal wear.

NOTE: Do not use crocus cloth to polish the seal surfaces. A finely polished surface may produce poor sealing or cause premature seal wear.

3. Inspect the main and connecting rod journals for cracks, scratches, grooves or scores.

4. Measure the diameter of each journal at least four places to determine out-of-round, taper or undersize condition.

5. On an engine with a manual transmission, check the fit of the clutch pilot bearing in the bore of the crankshaft. A needle roller bearing and adapter assembly is used as a clutch pilot bearing. It is inserted directly into the engine crank shaft. The bearing and adapter assembly cannot be serviced separately. A new bearing must be installed whenever a bearing is removed.

6. Inspect the pilot bearing, when used, for roughness, evidence of overheating or loss of lubricant. Replace if any of these conditions are found.

7. On the 6–4.9L engine, inspect the rear oil seal surface of the crankshaft for deep grooves, nicks, burrs, porosity, or scratches which could damage the oil seal lip during installation. Remove all nicks and burrs with crocus cloth.

Main Bearings

1. Clean the bearing inserts and caps thoroughly in solvent, and dry them with compressed air.

NOTE: Do not scrape varnish or gum deposits from the bearing shells.

2. Inspect each bearing carefully. Bearings that have a scored, chipped, or worn surface should be replaced.

3. The copper-lead bearing base may be visible through the bearing overlay in small localized areas. This may not mean that the bearing is excessively worn. It is not necessary to replace the bearing if the bearing clearance is within recommended specifications.

4. Check the clearance of bearings that appear to be satisfactory with Plastigage® or its equivalent. Fit the new bearings following the procedure Crankshaft and Main Bearings removal and installation, they should be reground to size for the next undersize bearing.

5. Regrind the journals to give the proper clearance with the next undersize bearing. If the journal will not clean up to maximum undersize bearing available, replace the crankshaft.

6. Always reproduce the same journal shoulder radius that existed originally. Too small a radius will result in fatigue failure of the crankshaft. Too large a radius will result in bearing failure due to radius ride of the bearing.

7. After regrinding the journals, chamfer the oil holes, then polish the journals with a #320 grit polishing cloth and engine oil. Crocus cloth may also be used as a polishing agent.

COMPLETING THE REBUILDING PROCESS

Fill the oil pump with oil, to prevent cavitating (sucking air) on initial engine start up. Install the oil pump and the pickup tube on the engine. Coat the oil pan gasket as necessary, and install the gasket and the oil pan. Mount the flywheel and the crankshaft vibration damper or pulley on the crankshaft.

NOTE: Always use new bolts when installing the flywheel. Inspect the clutch shaft pilot bushing in the crankshaft. If the bushing is excessively worn, remove it with an expanding puller and a slide hammer, and tap a new bushing into place.

Position the engine, cylinder head side up. Lubricate the lifters, and install them into their bores. Install the cylinder head, and torque it as specified. Insert the pushrods (where applicable), and install the rocker shaft(s) (if so equipped) or position the rocker.

Install the intake and exhaust manifolds, the distributor and spark plugs. Mount all accessories and install the engine in the car. Fill the radiator with coolant, and the crankcase with high quality engine oil.

BREAK-IN PROCEDURE

Start the engine, and allow it to run at low speed for a few minutes, while checking for leaks. Stop the engine, check the oil level, and fill as necessary. Restart the engine, and fill the cooling system to capacity. Check and adjust the ignition timing. Run the engine at low to medium speed (800–2,500 rpm) for approximately ½ hour, and retorque the cylinder head bolts. Road test the car, and check again for leaks.

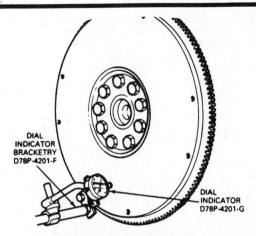

Checking flywheel runout

NOTE: Some gasket manufacturers recommend not retorquing the cylinder head(s) due to the composition of the head gasket. Follow the directions in the gasket set.

Flywheel/Flex Plate and Ring Gear

NOTE: Flex plate is the term for a flywheel mated with an automatic transmission.

REMOVAL AND INSTALLATION

All Engines

NOTE: The ring gear is replaceable only on engines mated with a manual transmission. Engines with automatic transmissions have ring gears which are welded to the flex plate.

1. Remove the transmission.
2. Remove the clutch, if equipped, or torque converter from the flywheel. The flywheel bolts should be loosened a little at a time in a cross pattern to avoid warping the flywheel. On vans with manual transmissions, replace the pilot bearing in the end of the crankshaft if removing the flywheel.
3. The flywheel should be checked for cracks and glazing. It can be resurfaced by a machine shop.
4. If the ring gear is to be replaced, drill a hole in the gear between two teeth, being careful not to contact the flywheel surface. Using a cold chisel at this point, crack the ring gear and remove it.

5. Polish the inner surface of the new ring gear and heat it in an oven to about 600°F (316°C). Quickly place the ring gear on the flywheel and tap it into place, making sure that it is fully seated.

WARNING: Never heat the ring gear past 800°F (426°C), or the tempering will be destroyed.

6. Position the flywheel on the end of the crankshaft. Torque the bolts a little at a time, in a cross pattern, to the torque figure shown in the Torque Specifications Chart.
7. Install the clutch or torque converter.
8. Install the transmission.

Rear Main Oil Seal

REPLACEMENT — TWO PIECE SEAL

Gasoline V8

1. Remove the oil pan and the oil pump (if required).
2. Loosen all the main bearing cap bolts, thereby lowering the crankshaft slightly but not to exceed $\frac{1}{32}$ in. (0.8mm).

3. Remove the rear main bearing cap, and remove the oil seal from the bearing cap and cylinder block. On the block half of the seal use a seal removal tool, or install a small metal screw in one end of the seal, and pull on the screw to remove the seal. Exercise caution to prevent scratching or damaging the crankshaft seal surfaces.
4. Remove the oil seal retaining pin from the bearing cap if so equipped. The pin is not used with the split-lip seal.
5. Carefully clean the seal groove in the cap and block with a brush and solvent such as lacquer thinner, spot remover, or equivalent, or trichlorethylene. Also, clean the area thoroughly, so that no solvent touches the seal.
6. Dip the split lip-type seal halves in clean engine oil.
7. Carefully install the upper seal (cylinder block) into its groove with undercut side of the seal toward the FRONT of the engine, by rotating it on the seal journal of the crankshaft until approximately ⅜ in. (9.5mm) protrudes below the parting surface.

Be sure no rubber has been shaved from the outside diameter of the seal by the bottom edge of the groove. Do not allow oil to get on the sealer area.

8. Tighten the remaining bearing cap bolts to the specifications listed in the Torque chart at the beginning of this Section.
9. Install the lower seal in the rear main bearing cap under undercut side of seal toward the FRONT of the engine, allow the seal to protrude approximately ⅜ in. (9.5mm) above the parting surface to mate with the upper seal when the cap is installed.

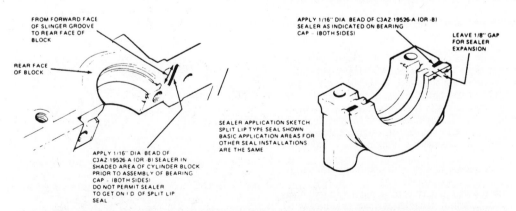

RTV sealant application on the main bearing cap of all V8 gasoline engines

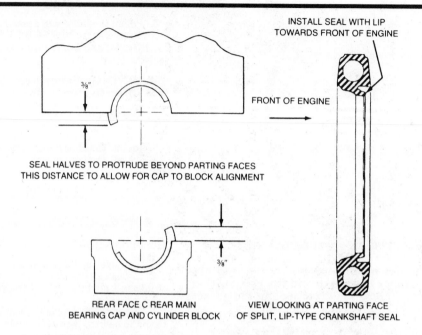

INSTALL SEAL WITH LIP
TOWARDS FRONT OF ENGINE

FRONT OF ENGINE

SEAL HALVES TO PROTRUDE BEYOND PARTING FACES
THIS DISTANCE TO ALLOW FOR CAP TO BLOCK ALIGNMENT

REAR FACE C REAR MAIN
BEARING CAP AND CYLINDER BLOCK

VIEW LOOKING AT PARTING FACE
OF SPLIT, LIP-TYPE CRANKSHAFT SEAL

2-piece rear main seal used on gasoline V8s

10. Apply an even $\frac{1}{16}$ in. (1.6mm) bead of RTV silicone rubber sealer, to the areas shown, following the procedure given in the illustration.

NOTE: This sealer sets up in 15 minutes.

11. Install the rear main bearing cap. Tighten the cap bolts to specifications.
12. Install the oil pump and oil pan. Fill the crankcase with the proper amount and type of oil.
13. Operate the engine and check for oil leaks.

6–4.9L

If the crankshaft rear oil seal replacement is the only operation being performed, it can be done in the vehicle as detailed in the following procedure. If the oil seal is being replaced in conjunction with a rear main bearing replacement, the engine must be removed from the vehicle and install on a work stand.

1. Remove the starter.
2. Remove the transmission from the vehicle, following procedures in Section 6.
3. On manual shift transmission, remove the pressure plate and cover assembly and the clutch disc following the procedure in Section 7.
4. Remove the flywheel attaching bolts and remove the flywheel and engine rear cover plate.
5. Use an awl to punch two holes in the crankshaft rear oil seal. Punch the holes on opposite sides of the crankshaft and just above the bearing cap to cylinder block split line. Install a sheet metal screw in each hole. Use two large screwdrivers or small pry bars and pry against both screws at the same time to remove the crankshaft rear oil seal. It may be necessary to place small blocks of wood against the cylinder block to provide a fulcrum point for the pry bars. Use caution throughout this procedure to avoid scratching or otherwise damaging the crankshaft oil seal surface.
6. Clean the oil seal recess in the cylinder block and main bearing cap.
7. Clean, inspect and polish the rear oil seal rubbing surface on the crankshaft. Coat the new oil seal and the crankshaft with a light film of engine oil. Start the seal in the recess with the seal

lip facing forward and install it with a seal driver. Keep the tool straight with the centerline of the crankshaft and install the seal until the tool contacts the cylinder block surface. Remove the tool and inspect the seal to be sure it was not damaged during installation.

8. Install the engine rear cover plate. Position the flywheel on the crankshaft flange. Coat the threads of the flywheel attaching bolts with oil-resistant sealer and install the bolts. Tighten the bolts in sequence across from each other to the specifications listed in the Torque chart at the beginning of this Section.

9. On a manual shift transmission, install the clutch disc and the pressure plate assembly following the procedure in Section 7.

10. Install the transmission, following the procedure in Section 7.

8–7.3L Diesel

1. Remove the transmission, clutch and flywheel assemblies.
2. Remove the engine rear cover.

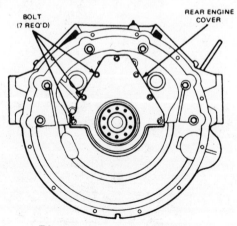

BOLT
(7 REQ'D)

REAR ENGINE
COVER

Diesel rear cover removal

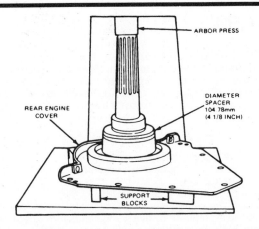

1-piece diesel rear main seal removal/installation

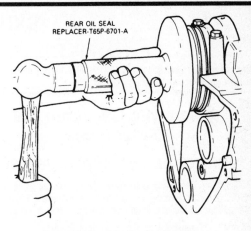

Installing the 1-piece seal

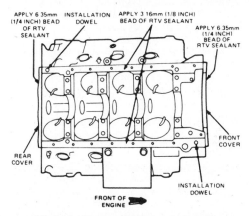

Diesel oil pan sealer application

3. Using an arbor press and a 4⅛ in. (104.775mm) diameter spacer, press out the rear oil seal from the cover.

4. To install, clean the rear cover and engine block surfaces. Remove all traces of old RTV sealant from the oil pan and rear cover sealing surface by cleaning with a suitable solvent and drying thoroughly.

5. Coat the new rear oil seal with Lubriplate® or equivalent. Using an arbor press and spacer, install the new seal into the cover.

NOTE: The seal must be installed from the engine block side of the rear cover, flush with the seal bore inner surface.

6. Install a seal pilot, Ford part no. T83T–6701B or equivalent onto the crankshaft.

7. Apply gasket sealant to the engine block gasket surfaces, and install the rear cover gasket to the engine.

8. Apply a ¼ in. (6mm) bead of RTV sealant onto the oil pan sealing surface, immediately after rear cover installation.

9. Push the rear cover into position on the engine and install the cover bolts. Torque to specification.

10. Position the flywheel on the crankshaft flange. Coat the threads of the flywheel attaching bolts with sealant and install the bolts and flexplate, if equipped. Torque the bolts to specification, alternating across from each bolt.

11. Install the clutch and transmission. Run the engine and check for oil leaks.

REPLACEMENT — ONE PIECE SEAL

1. Remove the transmission, clutch assembly or converter and flywheel.

2. (See Step 7 for diesel engines). Lower the oil pan if necessary for working room.

3. On gasoline engines, use an awl to punch two small holes on opposite sides of the seal just above the split between the main bearing cap and engine block. Install a sheet metal screw in each hole. Use two small pry bars and pry evenly on both screws using two small blocks of wood as a fulcrum point for the pry bars. Use caution throughout to avoid scratching or damage to the oil seal mounting surfaces.

4. When the seal has been removed, clean the mounting recess.

5. Coat the seal and block mounting surfaces with oil. Apply white lube to the contact surface of the seal and crankshaft. Start the seal into the mounting recess and install with seal mounting tool Ford number T82L–6701–A or equivalent.

6. Install the remaining components in the reverse.

7. On the diesel engines, the oil seal is one piece but mounted on a retaining plate. Remove the mounting plate from the rear of the engine and replace the seal. Reinstall in reverse order of removal.

EXHAUST SYSTEM

CAUTION
---

*When working on exhaust systems, ALWAYS wear protective goggles!
Avoid working on a hot exhaust system!*

Muffler, Catalytic Converter, Inlet and Outlet Pipes

REMOVAL AND INSTALLATION

NOTE: The following applies to exhaust systems using clamped joints. Some models, use welded joints at the muffler. These joints will, of course, have to be cut.

1. Raise and support the van on jackstands.
2. Remove the U-clamps securing the muffler and outlet pipe.
3. Disconnect the muffler and outlet pipe bracket and insulator assemblies.
4. Remove the muffler and outlet pipe assembly. It may be necessary to heat the joints to get the parts to come off. Special tools are available to aid in breaking loose the joints.
5. Remove the extension pipe.
6. Disconnect the catalytic converter bracket and insulator assembly.

NOTE: For rod and insulator type hangers, apply a soap solution to the insulator surface and rod ends to allow easier removal of the insulator from the rod end. Don't use oil-based or silicone-based solutions since they will allow the insulator to slip back off once it's installed.

7. Remove the catalytic converter.
8. On models with Managed Thermactor Air, disconnect the MTA tube assembly.
9. Remove the inlet pipe assembly.
10. Install the components making sure that all the components in the system are properly aligned before tightening any fasteners. Make sure all tabs are indexed and all parts are clear of surrounding body panels. See the accompanying illustrations for proper clearances and alignment.
   Observe the following torque specifications:
* Inlet pipe-to-manifold: 35 ft. lbs.
* MTA U-bolt: 60–96 inch lbs.
* Inlet pipe or converter-to-muffler or extension: 45 ft. lbs.
* Hanger bracket and insulator-to-frame: 24 ft. lbs.
* Bracket and insulator-to-exhaust: 15 ft. lbs.
* Flat flange bolts (8–7.5L and diesel) 30 ft. lbs.

Emission Controls

4

QUICK REFERENCE INDEX

GENERAL INDEX

EMISSION CONTROLS APPLICATIONS

6–4.9L:
Positive Crankcase Ventilation system (PCV)
Evaporative Emission system (canister)
Three-way Catalyst (TWC)
Conventional Oxidation Catalyst (COC)
Electronic Fuel Injection Fuel System (EFI)
Electronic Engine Control IV system (EEC-IV)
Electronic (Sonic) Exhaust Gas Recirculation (EEGR)
Managed Thermactor Air system (MTA)
Air Management 1 system (AM1)
Air Management 2 system (AM2)
Thick Film Ignition system (TFI-IV)
Bypass Air idle speed control (BPA)

8–5.0L
8–5.8L
Positive Crankcase Ventilation system (PCV)
Evaporative Emission system (canister)
Three-way Catalyst (TWC)
Conventional Oxidation Catalyst (COC)
Electronic Fuel Injection Fuel System (EFI)
Electronic Engine Control IV system (EEC-IV)
Electronic (Sonic) Exhaust Gas Recirculation (EEGR)
Managed Thermactor Air system (MTA)
Air Management 1 system (AM1)
Air Management 2 system (AM2)
Thick Film Ignition system (TFI-IV)
Bypass Air idle speed control (BPA)

8–7.5L
Positive Crankcase Ventilation system (PCV)
Evaporative Emission system (canister)
4 Reduction-Oxidation Catalysts (REDOX)
Electronic Fuel Injection fuel system (EFI)
Electronic Engine Control IV system (EEC-IV)
Electronic (Sonic) Exhaust Gas Recirculation (EEGR)
Managed Thermactor Air System (MTA)
Thick Film Ignition ignition system (TFI-IV)
Bypass Air idle speed control (BPA)

Positive Crankcase Ventilation System

The crankcase emission control equipment consists of a positive crankcase ventilation (PCV) valve, a closed oil filler cap and the hoses that connect this equipment.

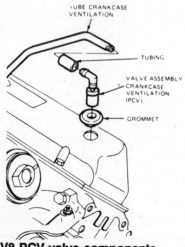

V8 PCV valve components

FROM CRANKCASE
AND/OR ROCKER
ARM COVER

TO INTAKE MANIFOLD

LOW SPEED OPERATION—HIGH MANIFOLD VACUUM

HIGH SPEED OPERATION—LOW MANIFOLD VACUUM

TO INTAKE MANIFOLD

FROM CRANKCASE
AND/OR ROCKER
ARM COVER

Cutaway of a PCV valve

When the engine is running, a small portion of the gases which are formed in the combustion chamber leak by the piston rings and enter the crankcase. Since these gases are under pressure they tend to escape from the crankcase and enter into the atmosphere. If these gases are allowed to remain in the crankcase for any length of time, they would contaminate the engine oil and cause sludge to build up. If the gases are allowed to escape into the atmosphere, they would pollute the air, as they contain unburned hydrocarbons. The crankcase emission control equipment recycles these gases back into the engine combustion chamber, where they are burned.

Crankcase gases are recycled in the following manner. While the engine is running, clean filtered air is drawn into the crankcase through the intake air filter and then through a hose leading to the oil filler cap. As the air passes through the crankcase it picks up the combustion gases and carries them out of the crankcase, up through the PCV valve and into the intake manifold. After they enter the intake manifold they are drawn into the combustion chamber and are burned.

The most critical component of the system is the PCV valve. This vacuum-controlled valve regulates the amount of gases which are recycled into the combustion chamber. At low engine speeds the valve is partially closed, limiting the flow of gases into the intake manifold. As engine speed increases, the valve opens to admit greater quantities of the gases into the intake manifold. If the valve should become blocked or plugged, the gases will be prevented from escaping the crankcase by the normal route. Since these gases are under pressure, they will find their own way out of the crankcase. This alternate route is usually a weak oil seal or gasket in the engine. As the gas escapes by the gasket, it also creates an oil leak. Besides causing oil leaks, a clogged PCV valve also allows these gases to remain in the crankcase for an extended period of time, promoting the formation of sludge in the engine.

The above explanation and the troubleshooting procedure which follows applies to all of the gasoline engines installed in Ford vans, since all are equipped with PCV systems.

TROUBLESHOOTING

With the engine running, pull the PCV valve and hose from the valve rocker cover rubber grommet.

A hissing noise should be heard as air passes through the valve and a strong vacuum should be felt when you place a finger over the valve inlet if the valve is working properly. While

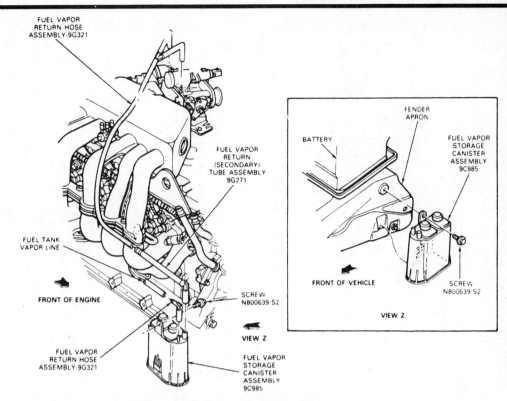

FUEL VAPOR RETURN HOSE ASSEMBLY-9G321

FUEL VAPOR RETURN (SECONDARY) TUBE ASSEMBLY 9G271

FUEL TANK VAPOR LINE

FRONT OF ENGINE

SCREW N800639-S2

VIEW Z

FUEL VAPOR RETURN HOSE ASSEMBLY-9G321

FUEL VAPOR STORAGE CANISTER ASSEMBLY 9C985

FENDER APRON

BATTERY

FUEL VAPOR STORAGE CANISTER ASSEMBLY 9C985

FRONT OF VEHICLE

SCREW N800639 S2

VIEW Z

6-4.9L evaporative emission system

you have your finger over the PCV valve inlet, check for vacuum leaks in the hose and at the connections.

When the PCV valve is removed from the engine, a metallic licking noise should be heard when it is shaken. This indicates that the metal check ball inside the valve is still free and is not gummed up.

REPLACEMENT

1. Pull the PCV valve and hose from the rubber grommet in the rocker cover.
2. Remove the PCV valve from the hose. Inspect the inside of the PCV valve. If it is dirty, disconnect it from the intake mani-

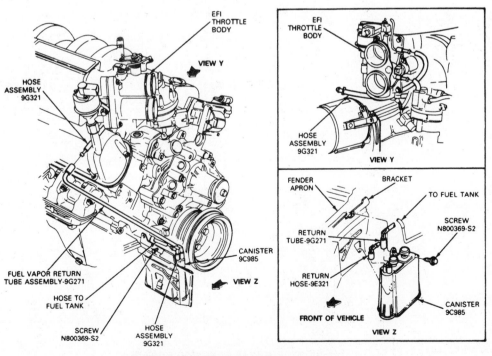

EFI THROTTLE BODY

VIEW Y

HOSE ASSEMBLY 9G321

CANISTER 9C985

VIEW Z

FUEL VAPOR RETURN TUBE ASSEMBLY-9G271

HOSE TO FUEL TANK

SCREW N800369-S2

HOSE ASSEMBLY 9G321

EFI THROTTLE BODY

HOSE ASSEMBLY 9G321

VIEW Y

FENDER APRON

BRACKET

TO FUEL TANK

SCREW N800369-S2

RETURN TUBE-9G271

RETURN HOSE-9E321

CANISTER 9C985

FRONT OF VEHICLE

VIEW Z

8-5.0L evaporative emission system

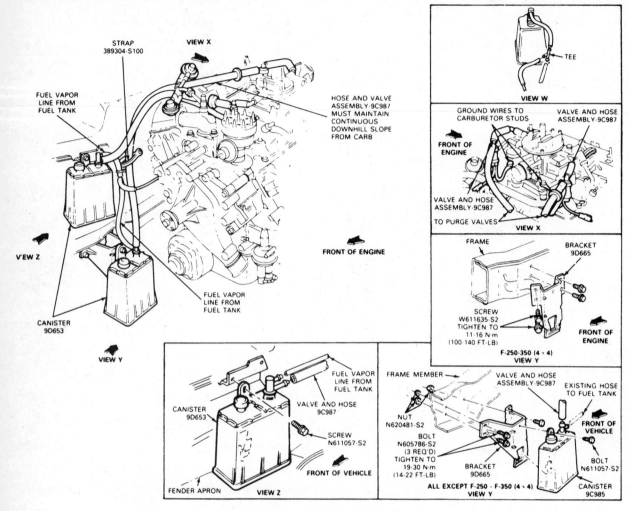

8-7.5L California emission system

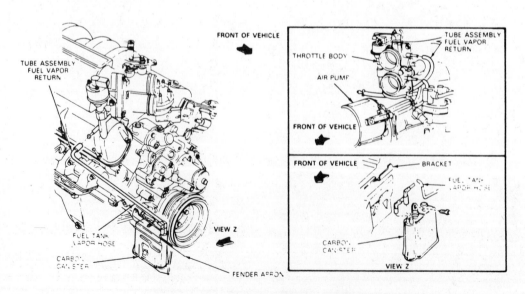

8-5.0L evaporative emission system

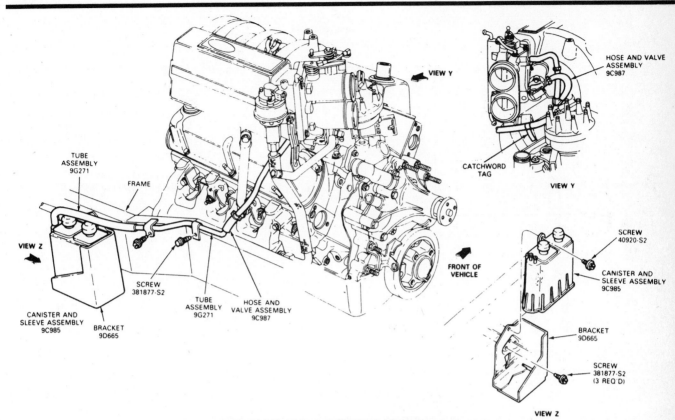

1988-91 8-5.8L evaporative emission system

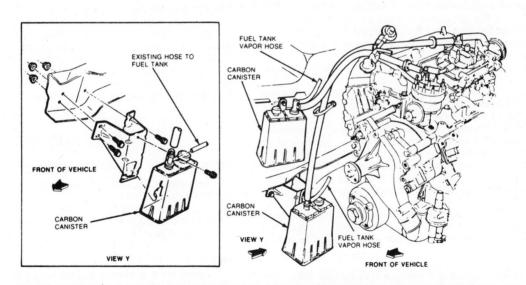

8-7.5L California and Canada Heavy Duty Truck evaporative emission system

fold and clean it in a suitable, safe solvent.
To install, proceed as follows:
 1. If the PCV valve hose was removed, connect it to the intake manifold.
 2. Connect the PCV valve to its hose.
 3. Install the PCV valve into the rubber grommet in the valve rocker cover.

Evaporative Emission Controls

Changes in atmospheric temperature cause fuel tanks to breathe; that is, the air within the tank expands and contracts with outside temperature changes. As the temperature rises, air escapes through the tank vent tube or the vent in the tank cap. The air which escapes contains gasoline vapors.

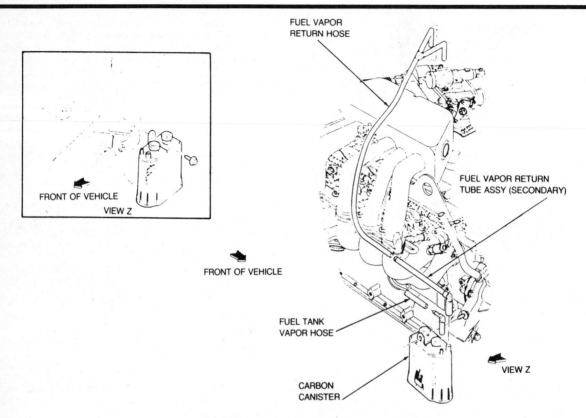

6-4.9L EFI evaporative emission system

The Evaporative Emission Control System provides a sealed fuel system with the capability to store and condense fuel vapors. The system has three parts: a fill control vent system; a vapor vent and storage system; and a pressure and vacuum relief system (special fill cap).

The fill control vent system is a modification to the fuel tank. It uses a dome air space within the tank which is 10–12% of the tank's volume. The air space is is sufficient to provide for the thermal expansion of the fuel. The space also serves as part of the in-tank vapor vent system.

The in-tank vent system consists of the domed air space previously described and a vapor separator assembly. The separator assembly is mounted to the top of the fuel tank and is secured by a cam-lockring, similar to the one which secures the fuel sending unit. Foam material fills the vapor separator assembly. The foam material separates raw fuel and vapors, thus retarding the entrance of fuel into the vapor line.

The vapor separator is an orifice valve located in the dome of the tank. The restricted size of the orifice, 0.050 in. (1.27mm) tends to allow only vapor to pass out of the tank. The orifice valve is connected to the vent line which runs forward to the carbon filled canister in the engine compartment.

The sealed filler cap has a pressure-vacuum relief valve. Under normal operating conditions, the filler cap operates as a check valve, allowing air to enter the tank to replace the fuel consumed. At the same time, it prevents vapors from escaping through the cap. In case of excessive pressure within the tank, the filler cap valve opens to relieve the pressure.

Because the filler cap is sealed, fuel vapors have only one place through which they may escape: the vapor separator assembly at the top of the fuel tank. The vapors pass through the foam material and continue through a single vapor line which leads to a canister in the engine compartment. The canister is filled with activated charcoal.

Another vapor line runs from the intake manifold, or the throttle body, to the charcoal canister.

As the fuel vapors (hydrocarbons), enter the charcoal canister, they are absorbed by the charcoal. The air is dispelled through the open bottom of the charcoal canister, leaving the hydrocarbons trapped within the charcoal. When the engine is started, vacuum causes fresh air to be drawn into the canister from its open bottom. The fresh air passes through the charcoal picking up the hydrocarbons which are trapped there and feeding them into the engine for burning with the fuel mixture.

DIAGNOSIS AND TESTING

Canister Purge Regulator Valve

1. Disconnect the hoses at the purge regulator valve. Disconnect the electrical lead.
2. Connect a vacuum pump to the vacuum source port.
3. Apply 5 in.Hg to the port. The valve should hold the vacuum. If not, replace it.

Canister Purge Valve

1. Apply vacuum to port **A**. The valve should hold vacuum. If not, replace it.
2. Apply vacuum to port **B**. Valves E5VE–AA, E4VE–AA and E77E–AA should show a slight vacuum leak-down. All other valves should hold vacuum. If the valve doesn't operate properly, replace it.
3. Apply 16 in.Hg to port **A** and apply vacuum to port **B**. Air should pass. On valves E5VE–AA, E4VE–AA and E77E–AA, the flow should be greater than that noted in Step 2.

NOTE: Never apply vacuum to port C. Doing so will damage the valve.

4. If the valve fails to perform properly in any of these tests, replace it.

Catalytic Converters

The catalytic converter, mounted in the vans exhaust system is a muffler-shaped device containing a ceramic honeycomb shaped material coated with alumina and impregnated with catalytically active precious metals such as platinum, palladium and rhodium.

The catalyst's job is to reduce air pollutants by oxidizing hydrocarbons (HC) and carbon monoxide (CO). Catalysts containing palladium and rhodium also oxidize nitrous oxides (NOx).

On some vans, the catalyst is also fed by the secondary air system, via a small supply tube in the side of the catalyst.

No maintenamce is possible on the converter, other than keeping the heat shield clear of flammable debris, such as leaves and twigs.

Other than external damage, the only significant damage possible to a converter is through the use of leaded gasoline, or by way of a too rich fuel/air mixture. Both of these problems will ruin the converter through contamination of the catalyst and will eventually plug the converter causing loss of power and engine performance.

When this occurs, the catalyst must be replaced. For catalyst replacement, see the Exhaust System section in Section 3.

Electronic Fuel Injection

For a description of and maintenance to the EFI systems, see Section 5.

Electronic Engine Controls

The Universal Distributor (EEC-IV) has a diecast base which incorporates an externally mounted TFI-IV ignition module, and contains a Hall Effect vane switch stator assembly and provision for fixed octane adjustment. No distributor calibration is required and initial timing adjustment is normally not required. The primary function of the EEC-IV Universal Distributor system is to direct high secondary voltage to the spark plugs. In ad-

dition, the distributor supplies crankshaft position and frequency information to a computer using a profile Ignition Pickup. The Hall Effect switch in the distributor consists of a Hall Effect device on one side and a magnet on the other side. A rotary cup which has windows and tabs rotates and passes through the space between the device and the magnet. When a window is between the sides of the switch the magnetic path is not completed and the switch is Off, sending no signal. When a tab passes between the switch the magnetic path is completed and the Hall Effect Device is turned On and a signal is sent. The voltage pulse (signal) is used by is EEC-IV system for sensing crankshaft position and computing the desired spark advance based on engine demand and calibration.

The heart of the EEC-IV system is a microprocessor called the Electronic Control Assembly (ECA). The ECA receives data from a number of sensors, switches and relays. The ECA contains a specific calibration for peak fuel economy, driveability and emissions control. Based on information stored in its memory, the ECA generates signals to control the various engine functions.

The ECA calibration module is located inside the ECA assembly. On all vans, the ECA is located inside the van on the left of the firewall, behind the kick panel.

Exhaust Gas Recirculation

EEGR

The Electronic EGR system (EEGR) is found in all systems in which EGR flow is controlled according to computer commands by means of an EGR valve position sensor (EVP) attached to the valve.

The EEGR valve is operated by a vacuum signal from the dual EGR Solenoid Valves, or the electronic vacuum regulator which actuates the valve diaphragm.

As supply vacuum overcomes the spring load, the diaphragm is actuated lifting the pintle off of its seat allowing the exhaust gas to flow. The amount of flow is directly proportional to the

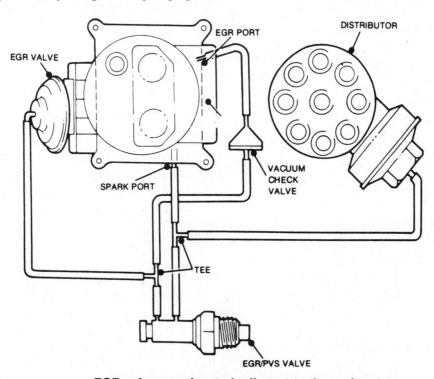

EGR valves are located adjacent to the carburetor

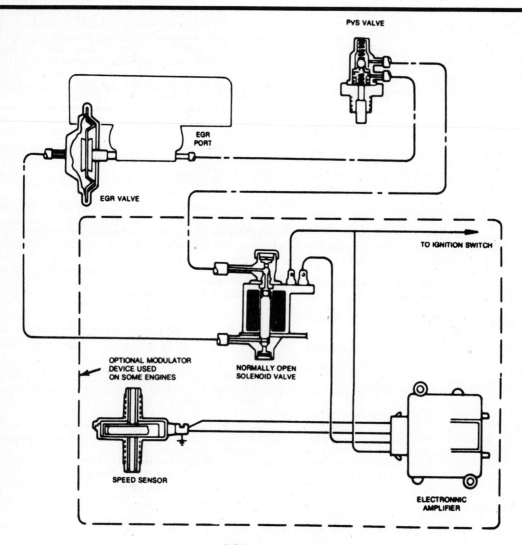

EGR system schematic

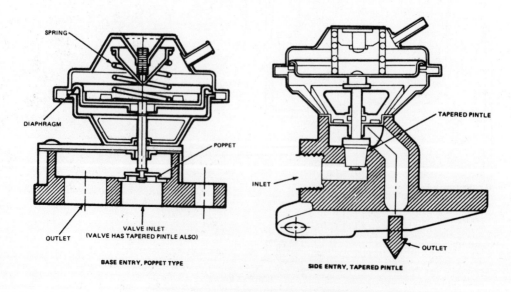

Vacuum-type EGR valve cutaways

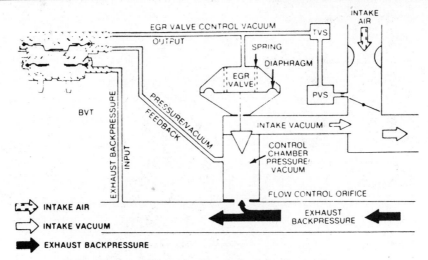

Backpressure Variable Transducer schematic

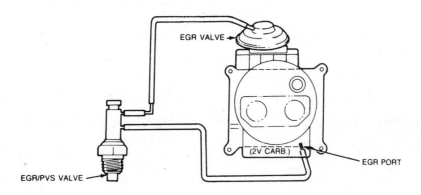

Vacuum operated EGR schematic

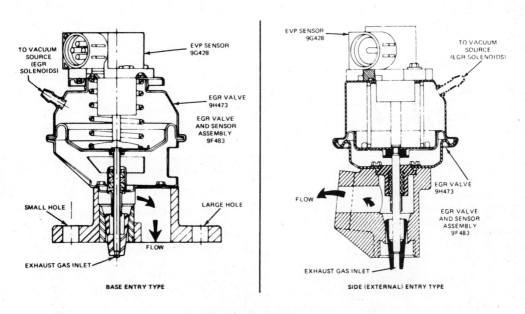

Electronic EGR valve

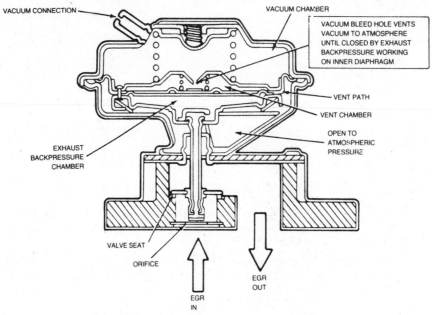

Integral backpressure transducer EGR valve

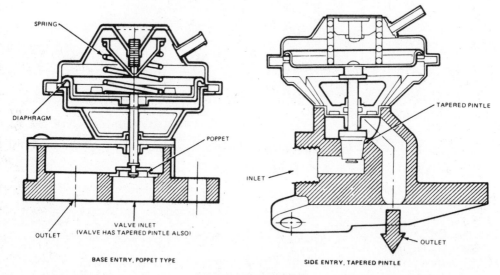

Ported EGR valve

pintle position. The EVP sensor sends an electrical signal notify the EEC of its position.

The EEGR valve is not serviceable. The EVP sensor must be serviced separately.

IBP EGR

The Integral Backpressure (IBP) EGR system combines inputs of EGR port vacuum and backpressure into one unit. The valve won't operate on vacuum alone.

There are two types of backpressure valves: the poppet type and the tapered pintle type.

Managed Thermactor Air System

The MTA system is used to inject fresh air into the exhaust manifolds or catalytic converters via an air control valve. Under some operating conditions, the air can be dumped back into the atmosphere via an air bypass valve. On some applications the two valves are combined into one unit. The air bypass valve can be either the normally closed type, when the valves are separate, or the normally open type, when the valves are combined.

Normally Closed Air Bypass Valve Functional Test

1. Disconnect the air supply hose at the valve.
2. Run the engine to normal operating temperature.
3. Disconnect the vacuum line and make sure vacuum is present. If no vacuum is present, remove or bypass any restrictors or delay valves in the vacuum line.
4. Run the engine at 1,500 rpm with the vacuum line connected. Air pump supply air should be heard and felt at the valve outlet.
5. With the engine still at 1,500 rpm, disconnect the vacuum line. Air at the outlet should shut off or dramatically decrease.

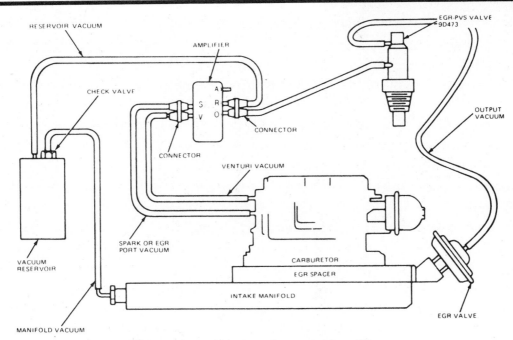

EGR system with ventrui vacuum amplifier

Air pump supply air should now be felt or heard at the silencer ports.

6. If the valve doesn't pass each of these tests, replace it.

Normally Open Air Bypass Valve Functional Test

1. Disconnect the air supply hose at the valve.
2. Run the engine to normal operating temperature.
3. Disconnect the vacuum lines from the valve.
4. Run the engine at 1,500 rpm with the vacuum lines disconnected. Air pump supply air should be heard and felt at the valve outlet.
5. Shut off the engine. Using a spare length of vacuum hose, connect the vacuum nipple of the valve to direct manifold vacuum.
6. Run the engine at 1,500 rpm. Air at the outlet should shut off or dramatically decrease. Air pump supply air should now be felt or heard at the silencer ports.
7. With the engine still in this mode, cap the vacuum vent. Accelerate the engine to 2,000 rpm and suddenly release the throttle. A momentary interruption of air pump supply air should be felt at the valve outlet.
8. If the valve doesn't pass each of these tests, replace it. Reconnect all lines.

Air Control Valve Functional Test

1. Run the engine to normal operating temperature, then increase the speed to 1,500 rpm.
2. Disconnect the air supply hose at the valve inlet and verify that there is airflow present.
3. Reconnect the air supply hose.
4. Disconnect both air supply hoses.
5. Disconnect the vacuum hose from the valve.
6. With the engine running at 1,500 rpm, airflow should be felt and heard at the outlet on the side of the valve, with no airflow heard or felt at the outlet opposite the vacuum nipple.
7. Shut off the engine.
8. Using a spare piece of vacuum hose, connect direct manifold vacuum to the valve's vacuum fitting. Airflow should be heard and felt at the outlet opposite the vacuum nipple, and no airflow should be present at the other outlet.
9. If the valve is not functioning properly, replace it.

Air Supply Pump Functional Check

1. Check and, if necessary, adjust the belt tension. Press at the mid-point of the belt's longest straight run. You should be able to depress the belt about ½ in. (13mm) at most.
2. Run the engine to normal operating temperature and let it idle.
3. Disconnect the air supply hose from the bypass control valve. If the pump is operating properly, airflow should be felt at the pump outlet. The flow should increase as you increase the engine speed. The pump is not serviceable and should be replaced if it is not functioning properly.

Thick Film Ignition System

For complete testing and operation of the TFI-IV system, see Section 2.

Bypass Air Idle Speed Control

The air bypass solenoid is used to control the engine idle speed and is operated by the EEC module.
The valve allows air to pass around the throttle plates to control:

- Cold engine fast idle
- Cold starting
- Dashpot operation
- Over-temperature idle boost
- Engine load correction

The valve is not serviceable and correction is by replacement only.

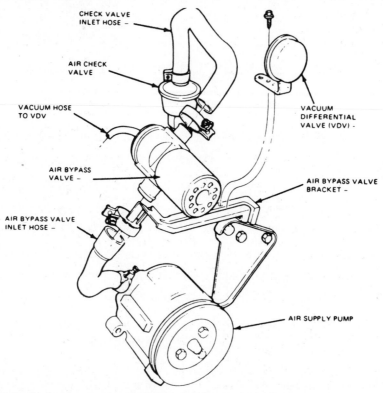

CHECK VALVE
INLET HOSE –

AIR CHECK
VALVE

VACUUM HOSE
TO VDV

VACUUM
DIFFERENTIAL
VALVE (VDV) –

AIR BYPASS
VALVE –

AIR BYPASS VALVE
BRACKET –

AIR BYPASS VALVE
INLET HOSE –

AIR SUPPLY PUMP

Thermactor® air pump components. Locations vary slightly among engines

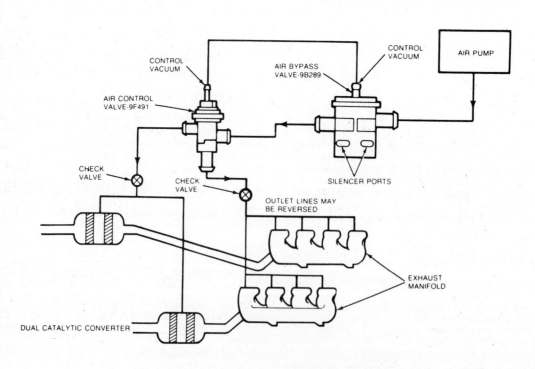

CONTROL
VACUUM

CONTROL
VACUUM

AIR PUMP

AIR BYPASS
VALVE-9B289

AIR CONTROL
VALVE-9F491

SILENCER PORTS

CHECK
VALVE

CHECK
VALVE

OUTLET LINES MAY
BE REVERSED

EXHAUST
MANIFOLD

DUAL CATALYTIC CONVERTER

Managed Air Thermactor® System schematic

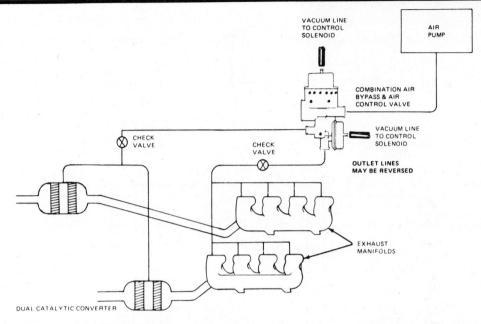

VACUUM LINE
TO CONTROL
SOLENOID

AIR
PUMP

COMBINATION AIR
BYPASS & AIR
CONTROL VALVE

VACUUM LINE
TO CONTROL
SOLENOID

OUTLET LINES
MAY BE REVERSED

CHECK
VALVE

CHECK
VALVE

EXHAUST
MANIFOLDS

DUAL CATALYTIC CONVERTER

Managed Air Thermactor® System schematic with Electronically controlled bypass/control valve

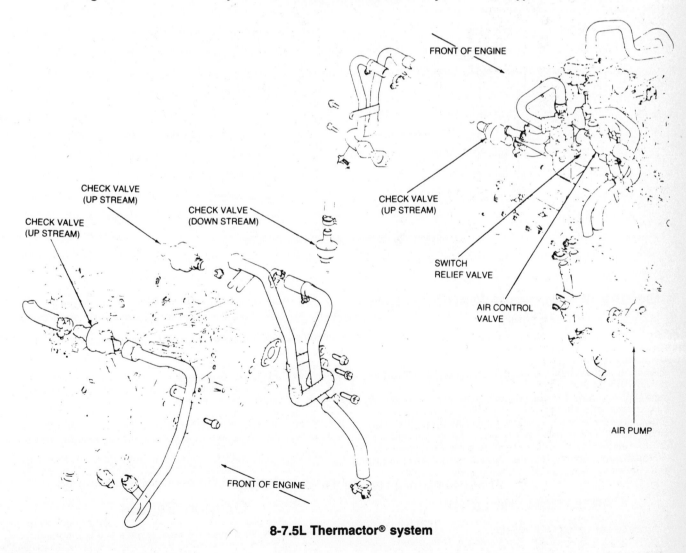

FRONT OF ENGINE

CHECK VALVE
(UP STREAM)

CHECK VALVE
(DOWN STREAM)

CHECK VALVE
(UP STREAM)

CHECK VALVE
(UP STREAM)

SWITCH
RELIEF VALVE

AIR CONTROL
VALVE

AIR PUMP

FRONT OF ENGINE

8-7.5L Thermactor® system

4 EMISSION CONTROLS

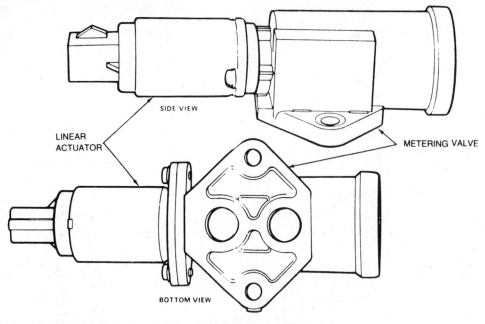

Air Bypass Valve

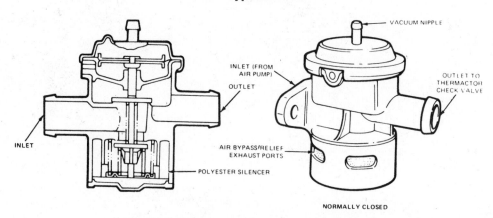

Normally closed Air Bypass Valve

Emissions Maintenance Warning Light (EMW)

DESCRIPTION

All gasoline engined light vans built for sale outside of California employ this device.

The EMW consists of an instrument panel mounted amber light imprinted with the word EGR, EMISS, or EMISSIONS. The light is connected to a sensor module located under the instrument panel. The purpose is the warn the driver that the 60,000 mile emission system maintenance is required on the vehicle. Specific emission system maintenance requirements are listed in the van's owner's manual maintenance schedule.

RESETTING THE LIGHT

1. Turn the key to the OFF position.

2. Lightly push a phillips screwdriver through the 0.2 in. (5mm) diameter hole labeled RESET, and lightly press down and hold it.

3. While maintaining pressure with the screwdriver, turn the key to the RUN position. The EMW lamp will light and stay lit as long as you keep pressure on the screwdriver. Hold the screwdriver down for about 5 seconds.

4. Remove the screwdriver. The lamp should go out with 2–5 seconds. If not, repeat Steps 1–3.

5. Turn the key OFF.

6. Turn the key to the RUN position. The lamp will light for 2–5 seconds and then go out. If not, repeat the rest procedure.

NOTE: If the light comes on between 15,000 and 45,000 miles or between 75,000 and 105,000 miles, you'll have to replace the 1,000 hour pre-timed module.

Oxygen Sensor

An oxygen sensor is used on most models and is mounted in

4-14

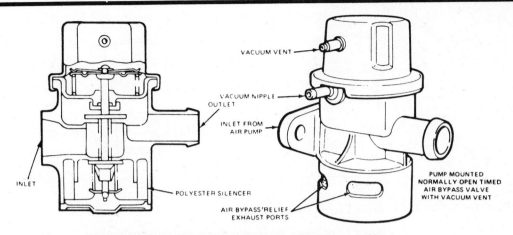

Normally open Air Bypass Valves with Vacuum Vent

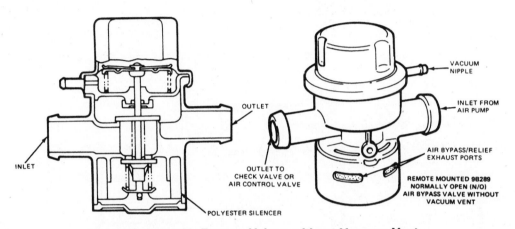

Normally open Air Bypass Valves without Vacuum Vent

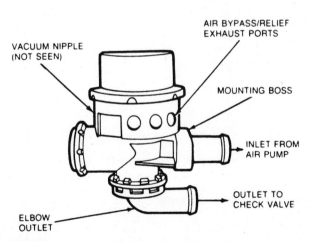

Normally open Air Bypass Valves without Vacuum Vent

the exhaust manifold. The sensor protrudes into the exhaust stream and monitors the oxygen content of the exhaust hoses. The difference between the oxygen content of the exhaust gases and that of the outside air generates a voltage signal to the ECM. The ECM monitors this voltage and, depending upon the value of the signal received, issues a command to adjust for a rich or a lean condition.

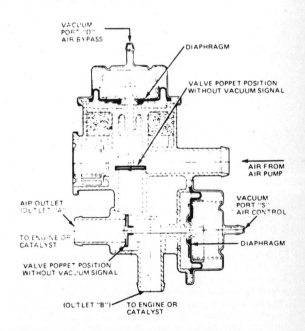

Normally closed exhaust air supply control valve wo/bleed

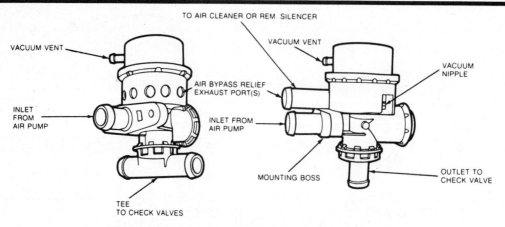

Heavy Duty truck Normally open Air Bypass Valves

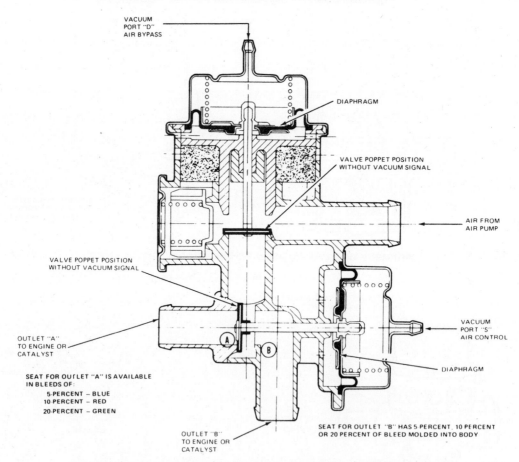

Normally closed exhaust air supply control valve w/bleed

No attempt should ever be made to measure the voltage output of the sensor. The current drain of any conventional voltmeter would be such that it would permanently damage the sensor. No jumpers, test leads or any other electrical connections should ever be made to the sensor. Use these tools ONLY on the ECM side of the wiring harness connector AFTER disconnecting it from the sensor.

REMOVAL AND INSTALLATION

The oxygen sensor must be replaced every 48,000 km (30,000 miles). The sensor may be difficult to remove when the engine temperature is blow 120°F (48°C). Excessive removal force may damage the threads in the exhaust manifold or pipe; follow the removal procedure carefully.

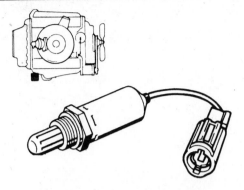

Exhaust Gas Oxygen Sensor

1. Locate the oxygen sensor. It protrudes from the center of the exhaust manifold and looks somewhat like a spark plug.

2. Disconnect the electrical connector from the oxygen sensor.

3. Spray a commercial solvent onto the sensor threads and allow it to soak in for at least five minutes.

4. Carefully unscrew and remove the sensor.

5. To install, first coat the new sensor's threads with anti-seize compound made for oxygen sensors. This is NOT a conventional anti-seize paste. The use of a regular compound may electrically insulate the sensor, rendering it inoperative. You must coat the threads with an electrically conductive anti-seize compound.

6. Installation torque is 30 ft. lbs. (42 Nm.). Do not overtighten.

7. Reconnect the electrical connector. Be careful not to damage the connector.

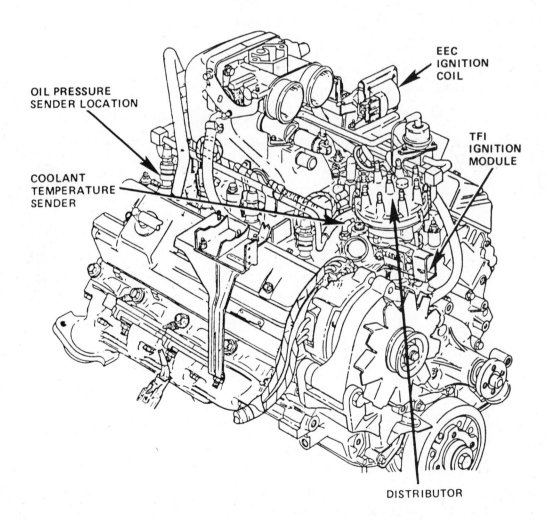

Sensors and components—E-Series with 5.0L and 5.8L engines (7.5L engine is similar)

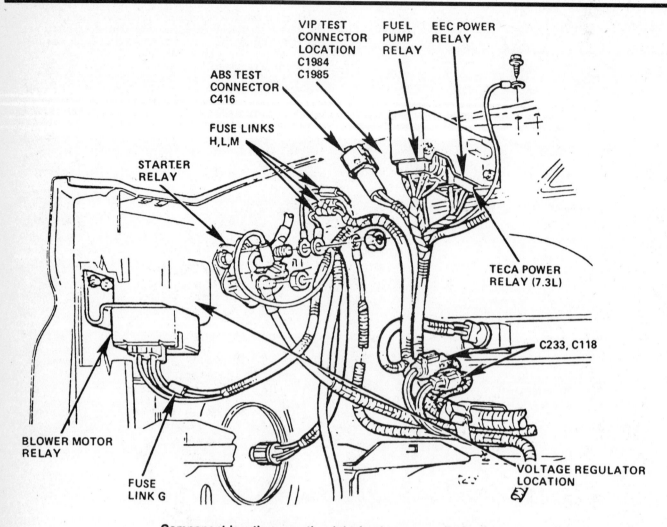

Component locations, on the right fender apron — E- Series

Fuel System

QUICK REFERENCE INDEX

GENERAL INDEX

GENERAL FUEL SYSTEM COMPONENTS

Electric Fuel Pump

Two electric pumps are used: a low pressure boost pump mounted in the fuel tank and a high pressure pump mounted on the vehicle frame.

The low pressure pump is used to provide pressurized fuel to the inlet of the high pressure pump and helps prevent noise and heating problems. The externally mounted high pressure pump is capable of supplying 15.9 gallons of fuel an hour. System pressure is controlled by a pressure regulator mounted on the engine.

REMOVAL AND INSTALLATION

In-Tank Pump

1. Remove the fuel tank as described below.
2. On steel tanks:
   a. Disconnect the wiring at the connector.
   b. Remove all dirt from the area of the sender.
   c. Disconnect the fuel lines.
   d. Turn the locking ring counterclockwise to remove it. There is a wrench designed for this purpose. If the wrench is not available, you can loosen the locking ring by placing a WOOD dowel against on the the tabs on the locking ring and hammering it loose. NEVER USE A METAL DRIFT! Use of metal will result in sparks which could cause an explosion! Lift out the fuel pump and sending unit. Discard the gasket.
3. On plastic tanks:
   a. Disconnect the wiring at the connector.
   b. Remove all dirt from the area of the sender.
   c. Disconnect the fuel lines.
   d. Turn the locking ring counterclockwise to remove it. A band-type oil filter wrench is ideal for this purpose. Lift out the fuel pump and sending unit. Discard the gasket.

To install:

4. Place a new gasket in position in the groove in the tank.
5. Place the sending unit/fuel pump assembly in the tank, in-dexing the tabs with the slots in the tank. Make sure the gasket stays in place.
6. Hold the assembly in place and position the locking ring.
   • On steel tanks, turn the locking ring clockwise until the stop is against the retainer ring tab.
   • On plastic tanks, turn the retaining ring clockwise until hand-tight. There is a special too available to set the tightening torque for the locking ring. If you have this tool, torque the ring to 40–55 ft. lbs. If you don't have the tool, just tighten the ring securely with the oil filter wrench.
7. Make sure the gasket is still in place.
8. Connect the fuel lines and wiring.
9. Install the tank.

External Pump

1. Disconnect the negative battery cable.

―――――――――― CAUTION ――――――――――
Never smoke when working around gasoline! Avoid all sources of sparks or ignition. Gasoline vapors are EXTREMELY volatile!
――――――――――――――――――――――――――

2. Depressurize the fuel system.

3. Raise and support the rear of the vehicle on jackstands.
4. Disconnect the inlet and outlet fuel lines.
5. Remove the pump from the mounting bracket.
6. Install in reverse order, make sure the pump is indexed correctly in the mounting bracket Insulator.
7. Disconnect the fuel inlet line at the fuel filter. Use care to prevent fire, due to fuel spillage. Place an absorbent cloth under the connection before removing the line to catch any fuel that might flow out of the line.
8. Connect a pressure gauge, a restrictor and flexible hose in the fuel line.
9. Position the flexible hose and the restrictor so that the fuel can be discharged into a suitable, graduated container.
10. Before taking a pressure reading, operate the Engine at the specified idle rpm and vent the system into the container by opening the hose restrictor momentarily.

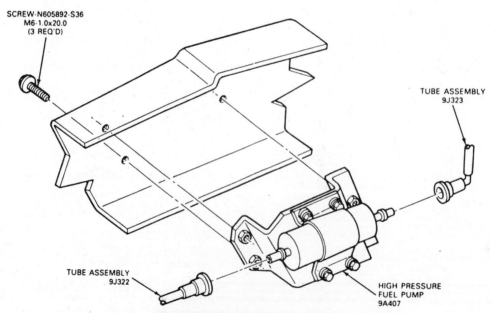

SCREW-N605892-S36
M6-1.0x20.0
(3 REQ'D)

TUBE ASSEMBLY
9J323

TUBE ASSEMBLY
9J322

HIGH PRESSURE
FUEL PUMP
9A407

High pressure EFI fuel pump

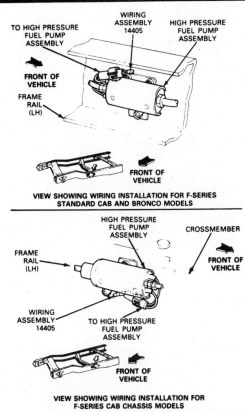

VIEW SHOWING WIRING INSTALLATION FOR F-SERIES
STANDARD CAB AND BRONCO MODELS

VIEW SHOWING WIRING INSTALLATION FOR
F-SERIES CAB CHASSIS MODELS

8-7.5L EFI fuel pump installation

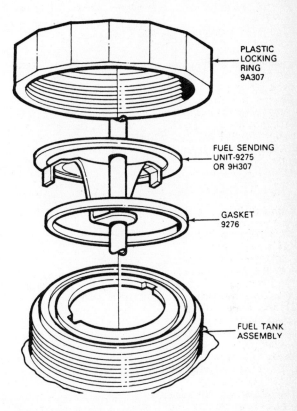

Plastic type fuel sending unit/pump locking ring

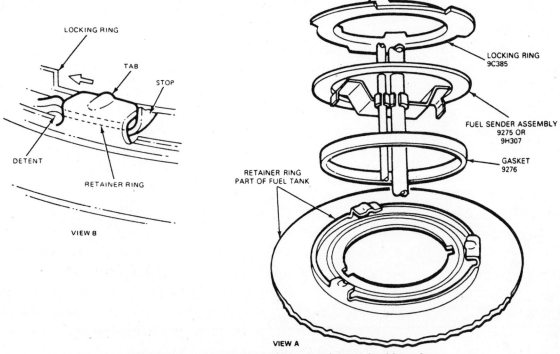

VIEW B

VIEW A

Steel tank type fuel sending unit/pump locking ring

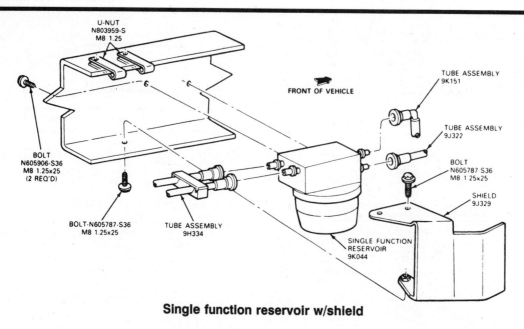

Single function reservoir w/shield

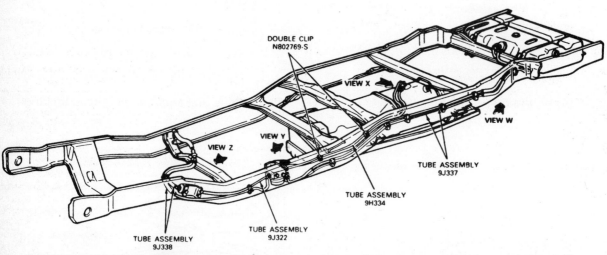

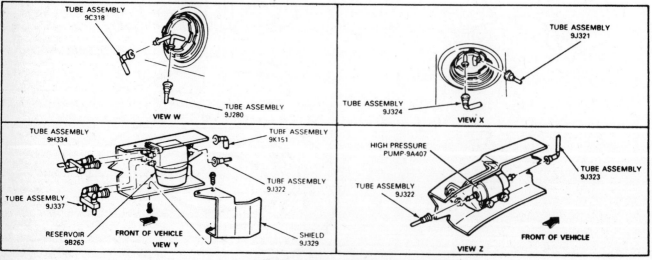

8-5.0L EFI dual fuel tanks

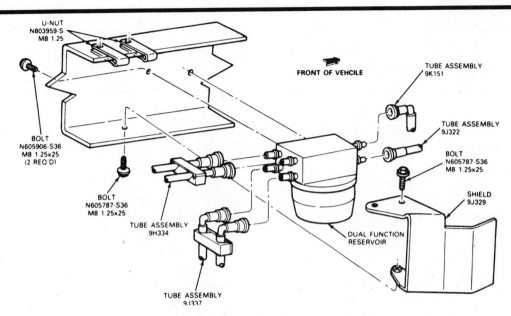

Dual function reservoir w/shield

11. Close the hose restrictor, allow the pressure to stabilize and note the reading. The pressure should be 5 psi. If the pump pressure is not within 4–6 psi and the fuel lines and filter are in satisfactory condition, the pump is defective and should be replaced. If the pump pressure is within the proper range, perform the test for fuel volume.

VOLUME TEST

1. Operate the engine at the specified idle rpm.

─── **CAUTION** ───

Never smoke when working around gasoline! Avoid all sources of sparks or ignition. Gasoline vapors are EXTREMELY volatile!

2. Open the hose restrictor and catch the fuel in the container while observing the time it takes to pump 1 pint. 1 pint should be pumped in 20 seconds. If the pump does not pump to specifications, check for proper fuel tank venting or a restriction in the fuel line leading from the fuel tank before replacing the fuel pump.

Quick-Connect Line Fittings

REMOVAL AND INSTALLATION

NOTE: Quick-Connect (push) type fittings must be disconnected using proper procedures or the fitting may be damaged. Two types of retainers are used on the push connect fittings. Line sizes of ⅜ in. and 5/16 in. use a hairpin clip retainer. ¼ in. line connectors use a Duck bill clip retainer.

Hairpin Clip

1. Clean all dirt and/or grease from the fittings. Spread the two clip legs about an ⅛ in. each to disengage from the fitting and pull the clip outward from the fitting. Use finger pressure only, do not use any tools.

─── **CAUTION** ───

Never smoke when working around gasoline! Avoid all sources of sparks or ignition. Gasoline vapors are EXTREMELY volatile!

2. Grasp the fittings and hose assembly and pull away from the steel line. Twist the fitting and hose assembly slightly while pulling, if necessary, when a sticking condition exists.
3. Inspect the hairpin clip for damage, replace the clip if necessary. Reinstall the clip in position on the fitting.
4. Inspect the fitting and inside of the connector to insure freedom Of dirt or obstruction. Install fitting into the connector and push together. A click will be heard when the hairpin snaps into proper connection. Pull on the line to insure full engagement.

Duck Bill Clip

1. A special tool is available for Ford for removing the retaining clip (Ford Tool No. T82L–9500–AH). If the tool is not on hand see Step 2. Align the slot on the push connector disconnect tool with either tab on the retaining clip. Pull the line from the connector.

─── **CAUTION** ───

Never smoke when working around gasoline! Avoid all sources of sparks or ignition. Gasoline vapors are EXTREMELY volatile!

2. If the special clip tool is not available, use a pair of narrow 6 in. (152mm) locking pliers with a jaw width of 0.2 in. (5mm) or less. Align the jaws of the pliers with the openings of the fitting case and compress the part of the retaining clip that engages the case. Compressing the retaining clip will release the fitting which may be pulled from the connector. Both sides of the clip must be compressed at the same time to disengage.
3. Inspect the retaining clip, fitting end and connector. Replace the clip if any damage is apparent.
4. Push the line into the steel connector until a click is heard, indicating the clip is in place. Pull on the line to check engagement.

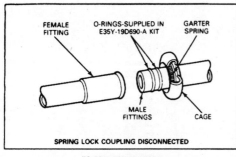

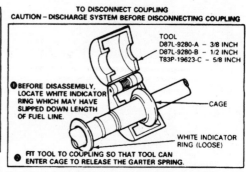

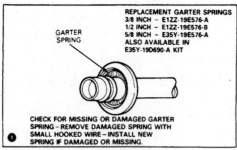

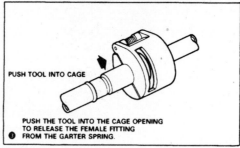

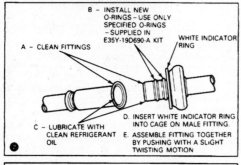

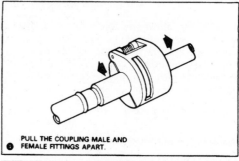

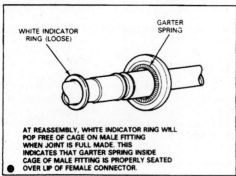

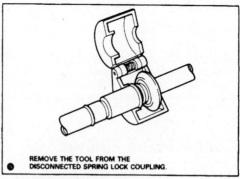

EFI Fuel line connectors

Fuel Tank
REMOVAL AND INSTALLATION
Steel Mid-Ships Fuel Tank(s)

— CAUTION —

Never smoke when working around gasoline! Avoid all sources of sparks or ignition. Gasoline vapors are EXTREMELY volatile!
Depressurize the fuel system. Refer to the Fuel Injection System procedures, below.

1. On vehicles with a single fuel tank, disconnect the battery ground cable, then, drain the fuel from the tank into a suitable container by either removing the drain plug, if so equipped, or siphoning through the filler cap opening.
2. On vehicles with dual tanks, drain the fuel tanks by disconnecting the connector hoses, then disconnect the battery ground cable.
3. Disconnect the fuel gauge sending unit wire and fuel outlet line.
4. Disconnect the air relief tube from the filler neck and fuel tank.

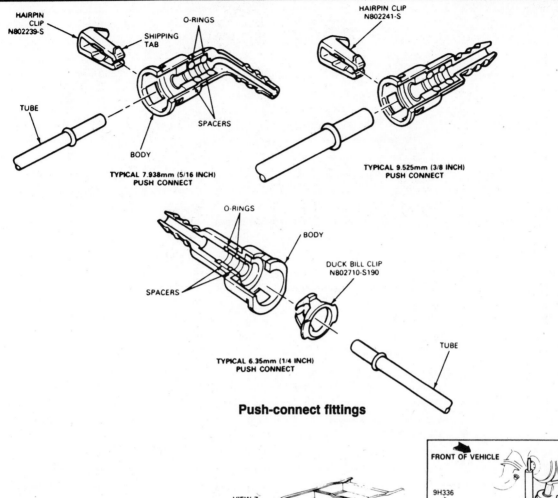

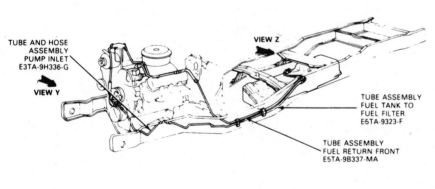

Push-connect fittings

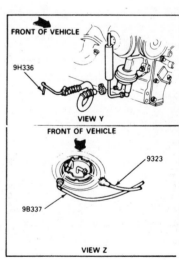

Diesel fuel lines w/midship tank

5. Loosen the filler neck hose clamp at the fuel tank and pull the filler neck away from the tank.

6. Remove the retaining strap mounting nuts and/or bolts and lower the tank(s) to the floor.

7. If a new tank is being installed, change over the fuel gauge sending unit to the new tank.

8. Install the fuel tank(s) in the reverse order of removal. Torque the strap nuts to 30 ft. lbs.

Plastic Mid-Ships Fuel Tank

--------- CAUTION ---------

Never smoke when working around gasoline! Avoid all sources of sparks or ignition. Gasoline vapors are EXTREMELY volatile!

Depressurize the fuel system. Refer to the Fuel Injection System procedures, below.

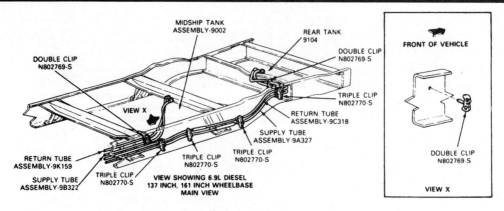

Diesel fuel lines w/dual tanks

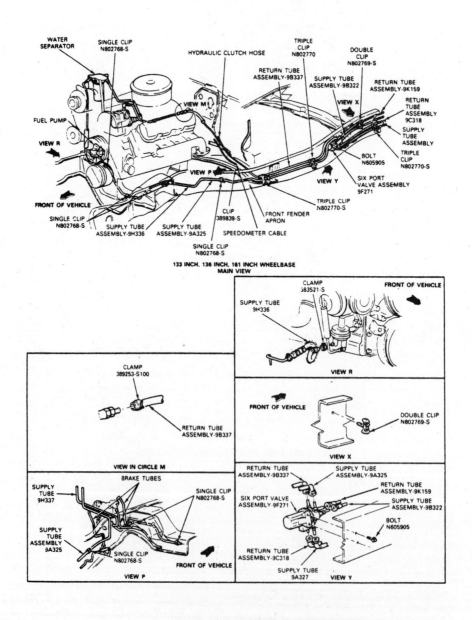

Diesel fuel line installation w/aft fuel tank and 133 in. (337.8cm) wheel base

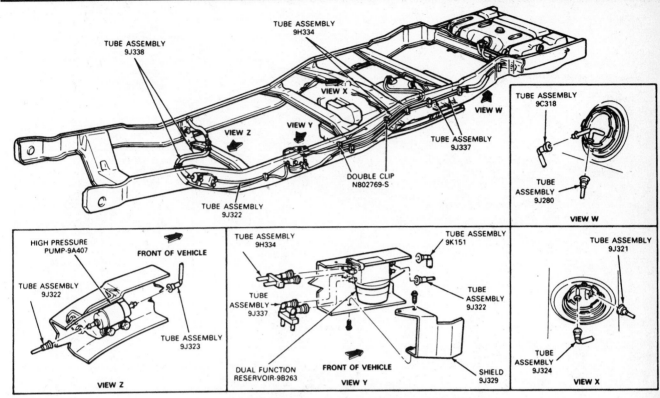

8-5.0L EFI dual tanks w/139 in. (353cm) wheel base

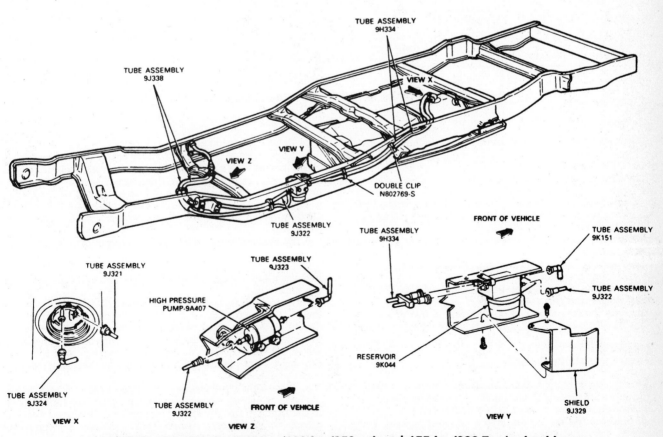

8-5.0L EFI midships fuel tank w/139 in. (353cm) and 155 in. (393.7cm) wheel base

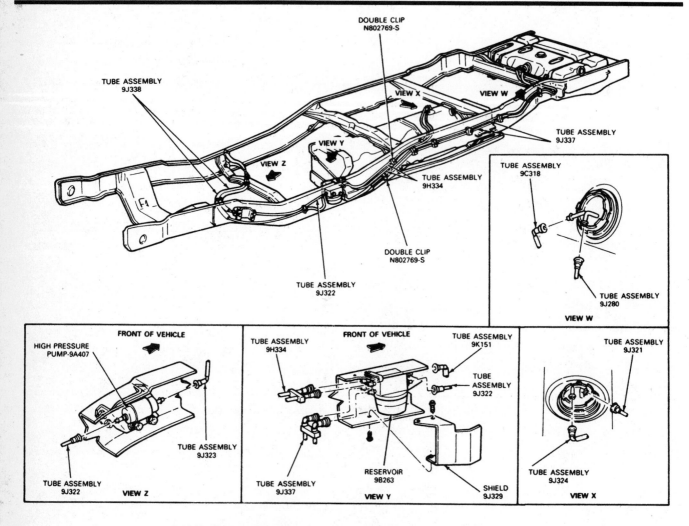

8-5.0L EFI dual tanks w/133 in. (337.8cm) wheel base

1. Drain the fuel from the tank into a suitable container by either removing the drain plug, if so equipped, or siphoning through the filler cap opening.

2. Disconnect the battery ground cable(s).

3. Remove the skid plate and heat shields.

4. Disconnect the fuel gauge sending unit wire at the tank.

5. Loosen the filler neck hose clamp at the fuel tank and pull the filler neck away from the tank.

6. Disconnect the fuel line push-connect fittings at the fuel gauge sending unit.

7. Support the tank. Remove the retaining strap mounting bolts and lower the tank to the floor.

8. If a new tank is being installed, change over the fuel gauge sending unit to the new tank.

9. Install the fuel tank(s) in the reverse order of removal. Torque the strap bolts to 12–18 ft. lbs.

Plastic or Steel
Behind-The-Axle Fuel Tank

──── **CAUTION** ────

Never smoke when working around gasoline! Avoid all sources of sparks or ignition. Gasoline vapors are EXTREMELY volatile!

Depressurize the fuel system. Refer to the Fuel Injection System procedures, below.

1. Raise the rear of the van.

2. Disconnect the negative battery cable.

3. On vans with a single tank, disconnect the fuel gauge sending unit wire at the fuel tank, then, remove the fuel drain plug or siphon the fuel from the tank into a suitable container.

4. On vehicles with dual tanks, drain the fuel tanks by disconnecting the connector hoses, then disconnect the battery ground cable.

5. Disconnect the fuel line push-connect fittings at the fuel gauge sending unit.

6. Loosen the clamps on the fuel filler pipe and vent hose as necessary and disconnect the filler pipe hose and vent hose from the tank.

7. If the tank is the metal type, support the tank and remove the bolts attaching the tank support or skid plate to the frame. Carefully lower the tank or tank/skid plate assembly and disconnect the vent tube from the vapor emission control valve in the top of the tank. Finish removing the filler pipe and filler pipe vent hose if not possible previously. Remove the tank from under the vehicle.

8. If the tank is the plastic type, support the tank and remove the bolts attaching the combination skid plate and tank support to the frame. Carefully lower the tank and disconnect the vent tube from the vapor emission control valve in the top of the tank. Finish removing the filler pipe and filler pipe vent hose if

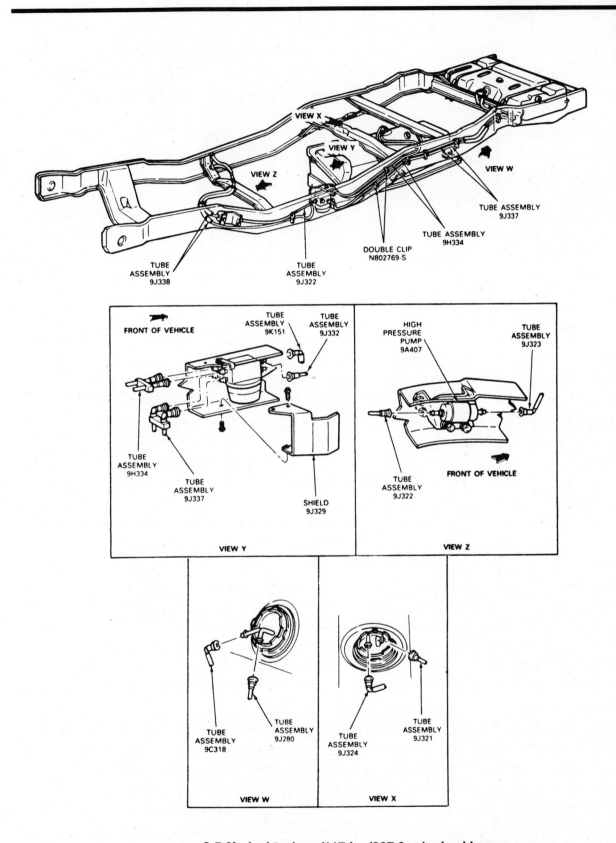

8-5.0L dual tanks w/117 in. (297.2cm) wheel base

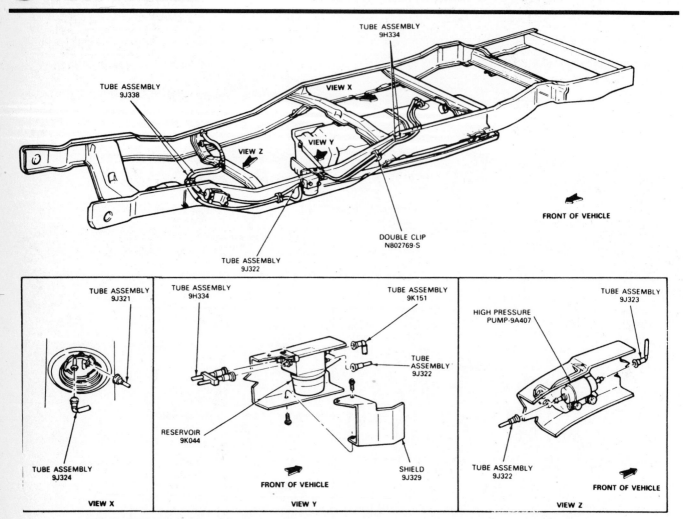

8-5.0L EFI mmidships fuel tank w/117 in (297.2cm) and 133 in. (337.8cm) wheel base

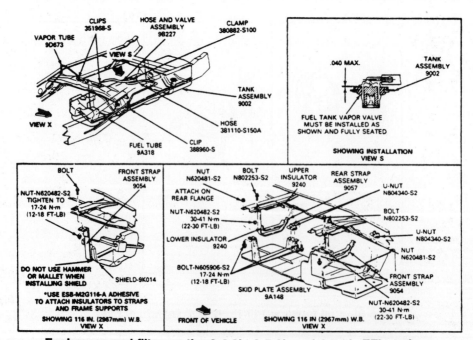

Fuel pump and filter on the 6-4.9L, 8-5.0L and 8-7.5L EFI engines

it was not possible previously. Remove the skid plate and tank from under the vehicle. Remove the skid plate from the tank.

9. If the sending unit is to be removed, turn the unit retaining ring counterclockwise and remove the sending unit, retaining ring and gasket. Discard the gasket.

10. Install the tank in the reverse order of removal.

With metal tanks, use thread adhesive such as Locktite® on the bolt threads. Torque these bolts to 27–37 ft. lbs.

With plastic tanks, DO NOT use thread adhesive. Torque the bolts to 25–35 ft. lbs.

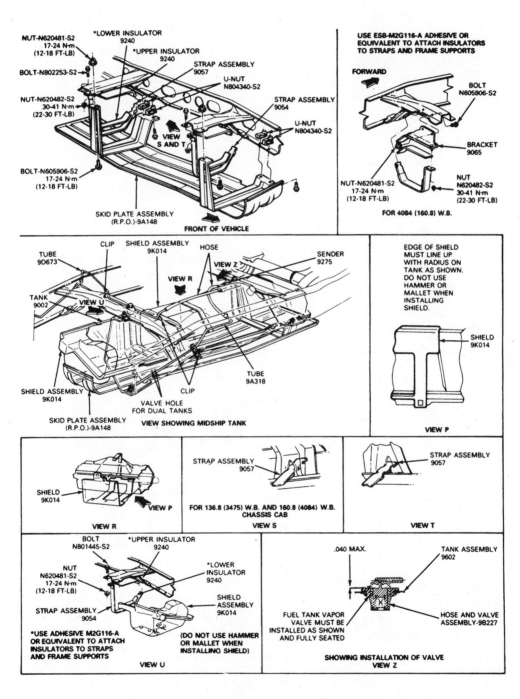

19 gallon midships fuel tank

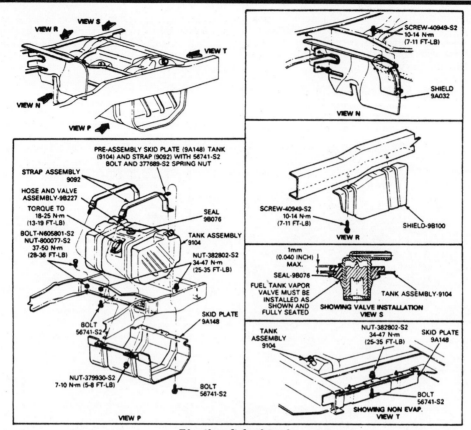

Plastic aft fuel tank

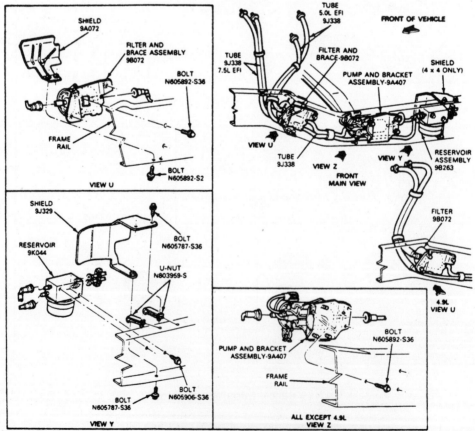

Fuel pump and filter on the 6-4.9L, 8-5.0L and 8-7.5L EFI engines

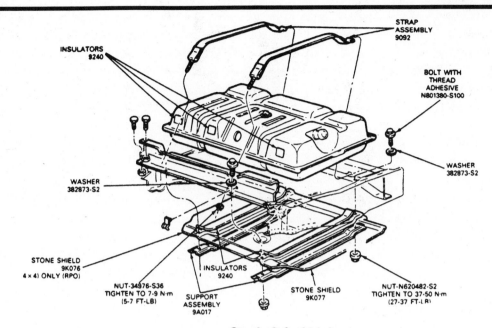

Steel aft fuel tank

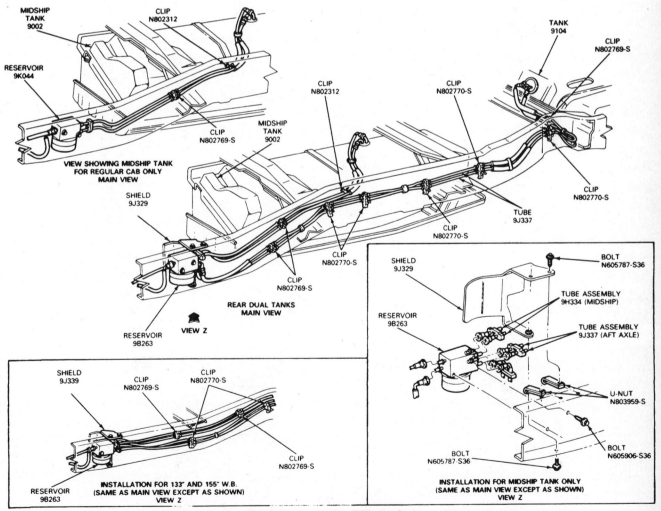

Fuel lines on the EFI engines

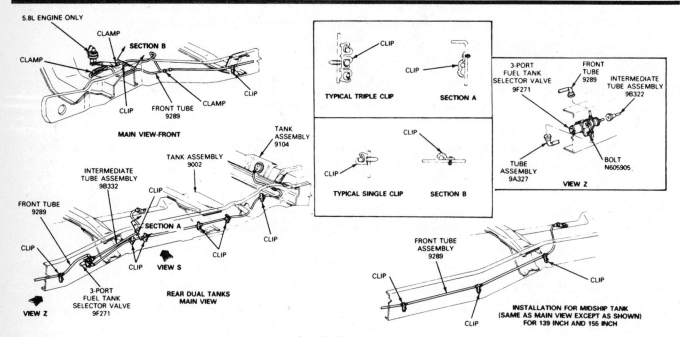

8-5.8L fuel lines

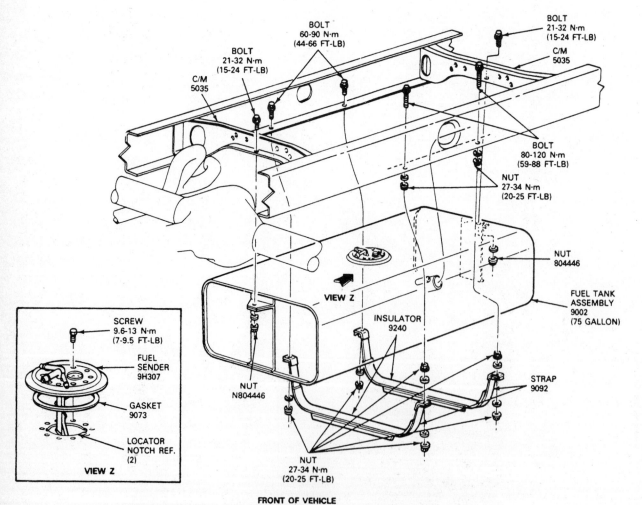

75 gallon aft-of-axle fuel tank used on the motor home chassis

GASOLINE FUEL INJECTION
6–4.9L ENGINE

Relieving Fuel System Pressure

NOTE: A special tool is necessary for this procedure.

1. Make sure the ignition switch is in the OFF position.

──────── **CAUTION** ────────
Never smoke when working around gasoline! Avoid all sources of sparks or ignition. Gasoline vapors are EXTREMELY volatile!

2. Disconnect the battery ground.
3. Remove the fuel filler cap.
4. Using EFI Pressure Gauge T80L–9974–A, or equivalent, at the fuel pressure relief valve (located in the fuel line in the upper right corner of the engine compartment) relieve the fuel system pressure. A valve cap must first be removed to gain access to the pressure relief valve.

Fuel Charging Assembly

REMOVAL AND INSTALLATION

1. Relieve the fuel system pressure.

──────── **CAUTION** ────────
Never smoke when working around gasoline! Avoid all sources of sparks or ignition. Gasoline vapors are EXTREMELY volatile!

2. Disconnect the battery ground cable and drain the cooling system.

──────── **CAUTION** ────────
When draining the coolant, keep in mind that cats and dogs are attracted by the ethylene glycol antifreeze, and are quite likely to drink any that is left in an uncovered container or in puddles on the ground. This will prove fatal in sufficient quantity. Always drain the coolant into a sealable container. Coolant should be reused unless it is contaminated or several years old.

3. Label and disconnect the wiring at the:
● Throttle position sensor
● Air bypass valve
● EVP sensor at the EGR valve
● Injection wiring harness
● Engine coolant temperature sensor
4. Label and disconnect the following vacuum connectors:

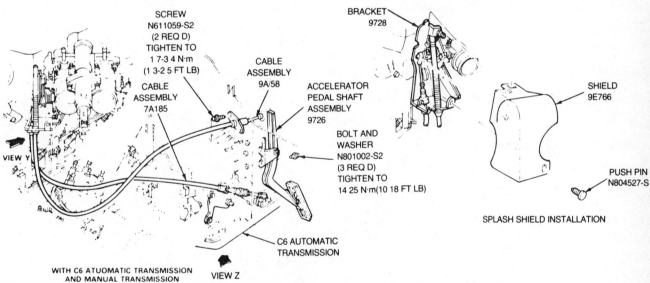

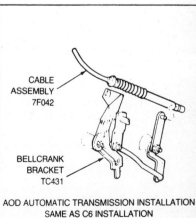

SPLASH SHIELD INSTALLATION

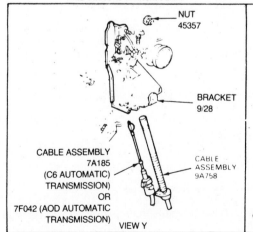

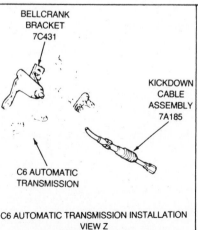

6-4.9L EFI throttle linkage

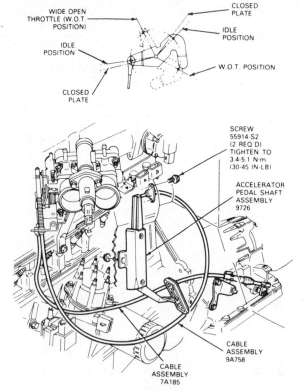

C6 AUTOMATIC TRANSMISSION KICKDOWN CABLE INSTALLATION AND ADJUSTMENT

1. SELECT KICKDOWN CABLE. INSERT CONDUIT FITTING INTO ENGINE BRACKET AND SLIDE CABLE END FITTING ONTO NAILHEAD STUD ON THROTTLE LEVER. ENSURE THAT THROW-AWAY RED SPACER IS SECURED ON CABLE END FITTING. IF SPACER IS MISSING, REUSE A DISCARDED ONE.
2. ROUTE CABLE DOWN TO TRANSMISSION AND INSERT CONDUIT FITTING INTO BRACKET, THEN SNAP CABLE END ONTO BALL STUD ON TRANSMISSION LEVER.
3. RATCHET CABLE ADJUSTING MECHANISM TO CORRECT SETTING BY ROTATING TO WIDE OPEN THROTTLE POSITION, WITH TOOL NO. 52F-23415 OR BY HAND. REMOVE RED SPACER.

AOD AUTOMATIC TRANSMISSION TV CABLE INSTALLATION AND ADJUSTMENT

1. SELECT TV CABLE. INSERT CONDUIT FITTING INTO ENGINE BRACKET. SLIDE CABLE END FITTING OVER NAILHEAD STUD ON THROTTLE LEVER.
2. ROUTE CABLE DOWN TO TRANSMISSION. INSERT CONDUIT FITTING INTO BRACKET ON TRANSMISSION. SNAP CABLE END OVER BALL STUD ON TRANSMISSION LEVER. ENSURE SPRING IS ON TRANSMISSION TO HOLD TV LEVER IN FULL CLOCKWISE POSITION.
3. PUSH DOWN LOCKING TAB AT ENGINE END OF CONDUIT FITTING TO LOCK CONDUIT AT CORRECT LENGTH. TAB TO BE FLUSH WITH CIRCULAR PROFILE OF FITTING.
4. REMOVE SPRING.

6-4.9L EFI throttle linkage, cont.

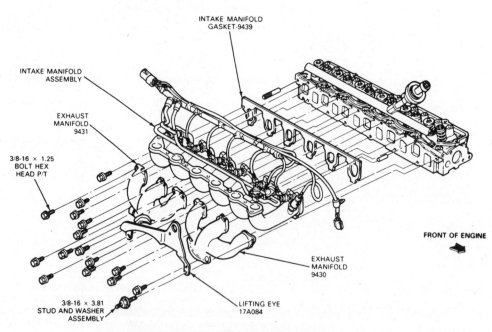

6-4.9L EFI lower intake manifold removal

- EGR valve
- Thermactor air bypass valve
- Throttle body
- Fuel pressure regulator
- Upper intake manifold vacuum tree
5. Disconnect the PCV hose at the upper intake manifold.

6. Remove the throttle linkage shield.
7. Disconnect the throttle linkage and speed control cables.
8. Unbolt the accelerator cable from its bracket and position it out of the way.
9. Disconnect the air inlet hoses from the throttle body.
10. Remove the EGR tube.

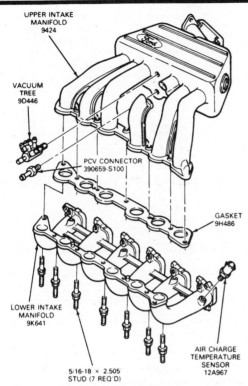

6-4.9L upper intake manifold removal

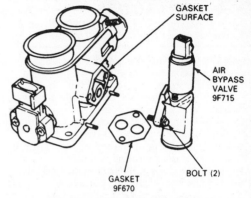

6-4.9L EFI air bypass valve

18. Remove the injector cooling manifold from the lifting eye attachment.

19. Disconnect the fuel supply and return lines at the quick disconnect couplings using tools T81P–19623–G or T81P–19623–G1.

20. Remove the 16 attaching bolts that the lower intake manifold and exhaust manifolds have in common. DON'T REMOVE THE BOLTS THAT ATTACH ONLY THE EXHAUST MANIFOLDS!

21. Remove the lower intake manifold from the head.

22. Clean and inspect all mating surfaces. All surfaces MUST be flat and free from debris or damage!

23. Clean and oil all fastener threads.

24. Position the lower manifold on the head using a new gasket. Tighten the bolts to 30 ft. lbs.

25. Reconnect the vacuum lines at the fuel pressure regulator.

26. Position the upper manifold and new gasket on the lower manifold. Install the fasteners finger tight.

27. Install the upper intake manifold support on the manifold and tighten the retaining screw to 30 ft. lbs.

28. Torque the upper-to-lower manifold fasteners to 18 ft. lbs.

29. Install the injector heat shield.

30. Install the EGR tube. The tube should be routed between the no. 4 and 5 lower intake runners. Torque the fittings to 35 ft. lbs.

31. Install the injector cooling manifold and torque the fasteners to 12 ft. lbs.

32. Connect the PCV hose.

33. Install the Thermactor tube and tighten the nuts to 12 ft. lbs.

34. Install the accelerator cable and throttle linkages.

35. Connect the air inlet hoses to the throttle body.

36. Connect the vacuum hoses.

37. Connect the electrical wiring.

38. Connect the air intake hose, air bypass hose and crankcase vent hose.

39. Connect the battery ground.

40. Refill the cooling system.

41. Install the fuel pressure relief cap. Turn the ignition switch from **OFF** to **ON** at least half a dozen times, **WITHOUT STARTING THE ENGINE**, leaving it in the ON position for about 5 seconds each time. This will build up fuel pressure in the system.

42. Start the engine and allow it to run at idle until normal operating temperature is reached. Check for leaks.

Fuel Injector

REMOVAL AND INSTALLATION

1. Relieve the fuel system pressure.

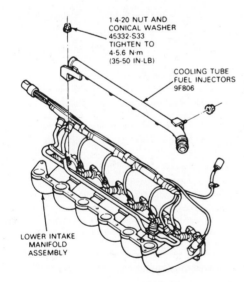

6-4.9L injector cooling manifold removal

11. Remove the Thermactor tube from the lower intake manifold.

12. Remove the nut attaching the Thermactor bypass valve bracket to the lower intake manifold.

13. Remove the injector heat shield (2 clips).

14. Remove the 7 studs which retain the upper intake manifold.

15. Remove the screw and washer which retains the upper intake manifold support bracket to the upper intake manifold.

16. Remove the upper intake manifold assembly from the lower intake manifold.

17. Move the vacuum harness away from the lower intake manifold.

───────── CAUTION ─────────
Never smoke when working around gasoline! Avoid all sources of sparks or ignition. Gasoline vapors are EXTREMELY volatile!

2. Remove the upper intake manifold assembly.
3. Remove the fuel supply manifold.
4. Disconnect the wiring at each injector.
5. Pull upward on the injector body while gently rocking it from side-to-side.
6. Inspect the O-rings on the injector for any sign of leakage or damage. Replace any suspected O-rings.
7. Inspect the plastic cap at the top of each injector and replace it if any sign of deterioration is noticed.
8. Lubricate the O-rings with clean engine oil ONLY!
9. Install the injectors by pushing them in with a gentle rocking motion.
10. Install the fuel supply manifold.
11. Connect the electrical wiring.
12. Install the upper intake manifold.

Fuel Pressure Regulator

REMOVAL AND INSTALLATION

1. Relieve the fuel system pressure.

───────── CAUTION ─────────
Never smoke when working around gasoline! Avoid all sources of sparks or ignition. Gasoline vapors are EXTREMELY volatile!

2. Disconnect the vacuum line at the regulator.
3. Remove the 3 allen screws from the regulator housing.
4. Remove the regulator.
5. Inspect the regulator O-ring for signs of deterioration or damage. Discard the gasket.
6. Lubricate the O-ring with clean engine oil ONLY!
7. Make sure that the mounting surfaces are clean.
8. Using a new gasket, install the regulator. Tighten the retaining screws to 40 inch lbs.
9. Connect the vacuum line.

Pressure Relief Valve

REMOVAL AND INSTALLATION

1. Relieve the fuel system pressure.

───────── CAUTION ─────────
Never smoke when working around gasoline! Avoid all sources of sparks or ignition. Gasoline vapors are EXTREMELY volatile!

2. Unscrew the valve from the fuel line.
3. When installing the valve, tighten it to 80 inch lbs.
4. Tighten the cap to 5 inch lbs.

Throttle Position Sensor

REMOVAL AND INSTALLATION

1. Disconnect the wiring harness from the TPS.
2. Matchmark the sensor and throttle body for installation reference.

───────── CAUTION ─────────
Never smoke when working around gasoline! Avoid all sources of sparks or ignition. Gasoline vapors are EXTREMELY volatile!

3. Remove the 2 retaining screws and remove the TPS.
4. Install the TPS so that the wiring harness is parallel with the venturi bores, then, rotate the TPS clockwise to align the scribe marks.

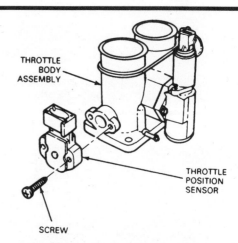

6-4.9L EFI throttle position sensor

───────── CAUTION ─────────
Slide the rotary tanks into position over the throttle shaft blade, then rotate the TPS CLOCKWISE ONLY to the installed position. FAILURE TO INSTALL THE TPS IN THIS MANNER WILL RESULT IN EXCESSIVE IDLE SPEEDS!

5. Tighten the retaining screws to 16 inch lbs.

NOTE: When correctly installed, the TPS wiring harness should be pointing directly at the air bypass valve.

6. Connect the wiring.

Upper Intake Manifold

REMOVAL AND INSTALLATION

1. Relieve the fuel system pressure.

───────── CAUTION ─────────
Never smoke when working around gasoline! Avoid all sources of sparks or ignition. Gasoline vapors are EXTREMELY volatile!

2. Disconnect the battery ground cable and drain the cooling system.

───────── CAUTION ─────────
When draining the coolant, keep in mind that cats and dogs are attracted by the ethylene glycol antifreeze, and are quite likely to drink any that is left in an uncovered container or in puddles on the ground. This will prove fatal in sufficient quantity. Always drain the coolant into a sealable container. Coolant should be reused unless it is contaminated or several years old.

3. Label and disconnect the wiring at the:
- Throttle position sensor
- Air bypass valve
- EVP sensor at the EGR valve
- Injection wiring harness
- Engine coolant temperature sensor
4. Label and disconnect the following vacuum connectors:
- EGR valve
- Thermactor air bypass valve
- Throttle body
- Fuel pressure regulator
- Upper intake manifold vacuum tree
5. Disconnect the PCV hose at the upper intake manifold.
6. Remove the throttle linkage shield.
7. Disconnect the throttle linkage and speed control cables.
8. Unbolt the accelerator cable from its bracket and position it out of the way.

9. Disconnect the air inlet hoses from the throttle body.

10. Remove the EGR tube.

11. Remove the Thermactor tube from the lower intake manifold.

12. Remove the nut attaching the Thermactor bypass valve bracket to the lower intake manifold.

13. Remove the injector heat shield (2 clips).

14. Remove the 7 studs which retain the upper intake manifold.

15. Remove the screw and washer which retains the upper intake manifold support bracket to the upper intake manifold.

16. Remove the upper intake manifold assembly from the lower intake manifold.

17. Clean and inspect all mating surfaces. All surfaces MUST be flat and free from debris or damage!

18. Clean and oil all fastener threads.

19. Position the upper manifold and new gasket on the lower manifold. Install the fasteners finger tight.

20. Install the upper intake manifold support on the manifold and tighten the retaining screw to 30 ft. lbs.

21. Torque the upper-to-lower manifold fasteners to 18 ft. lbs.

22. Install the injector heat shield.

23. Install the EGR tube. The tube should be routed between the no. 4 and 5 lower intake runners. Torque the fittings to 35 ft. lbs.

24. Install the injector cooling manifold and torque the fasteners to 12 ft. lbs.

25. Connect the PCV hose.

26. Install the Thermactor tube and tighten the nuts to 12 ft. lbs.

27. Install the accelerator cable and throttle linkages.

28. Connect the air inlet hoses to the throttle body.

29. Connect the vacuum hoses.

30. Connect the electrical wiring.

31. Connect the air intake hose, air bypass hose and crankcase vent hose.

32. Connect the battery ground.

33. Refill the cooling system.

34. Install the fuel pressure relief cap. Turn the ignition switch from **OFF** to **ON** at least half a dozen times, **WITHOUT STARTING THE ENGINE,** leaving it in the ON position for about 5 seconds each time. This will build up fuel pressure in the system.

35. Start the engine and allow it to run at idle until normal operating temperature is reached. Check for leaks.

Air Intake Throttle Body

REMOVAL AND INSTALLATION

1. Disconnect the air intake hose.

——————————— CAUTION ———————————

Never smoke when working around gasoline! Avoid all sources of sparks or ignition. Gasoline vapors are EXTREMELY volatile!

2. Disconnect the throttle position sensor and air by-pass valve connectors.

3. Remove the four throttle body mounting nuts and carefully separate the air throttle body from the upper intake manifold.

4. Remove and discard the mounting gasket. Clean all mounting surfaces using care not to damage the gasket surfaces

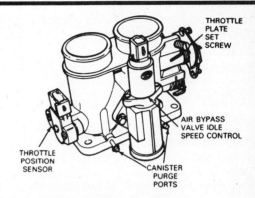

6-4.9L EFI throttle body

of the throttle body and manifold. Do not allow any material to drop into the intake manifold.

5. Install the throttle body in the reverse order of removal. The mounting nuts are tightened to 12–15 ft. lbs.

Fuel Supply Manifold

REMOVAL AND INSTALLATION

——————————— CAUTION ———————————

Never smoke when working around gasoline! Avoid all sources of sparks or ignition. Gasoline vapors are EXTREMELY volatile!

1. Remove the fuel tank fill cap. Relieve fuel system pressure by locating and disconnecting the electrical connection to either the fuel pump relay, the inertia switch or the in line high pressure fuel pump. Crank the engine for about ten seconds. If the engine starts, crank for an additional five seconds after the engine stalls. Reconnect the connector. Disconnect the negative battery cable. Remove the upper intake manifold assembly.

NOTE: Special tool T81P–19623–G or equivalent is necessary to release the garter springs that secure the fuel line/hose connections.

2. Disconnect the fuel crossover hose from the fuel supply manifold. Disconnect the fuel supply and return line connections at the fuel supply manifold.

3. Remove the two fuel supply manifold retaining bolts. Carefully disengage the manifold from the fuel injectors and remove the manifold.

4. When installing: make sure the injector caps are clean and free of contamination. Place the fuel supply manifold over each injector and seat the injectors into the manifold. Make sure the caps are seated firmly.

5. Torque the fuel supply manifold retaining bolts to 15–22 ft.lbs. Install the remaining components in the reverse order of removal.

NOTE: Fuel injectors may be serviced after the fuel supply manifold is removed. Grasp the injector and pull up on it while gently rocking injector from side to side. Inspect the mounting O-rings and replace any that show deterioration.

5 FUEL SYSTEM

GASOLINE FUEL INJECTION
8–5.0L ENGINE
8–5.8L ENGINE

Relieving Fuel System Pressure

NOTE: A special tool is necessary for this procedure.

1. Make sure the ignition switch is in the OFF position.

--- CAUTION ---

Never smoke when working around gasoline! Avoid all sources of sparks or ignition. Gasoline vapors are EXTREMELY volatile!

2. Disconnect the battery ground.
3. Remove the fuel filler cap.
4. Using EFI Pressure Gauge T80L–9974–A, or equivalent, at the fuel pressure relief valve (located in the fuel line in the upper right corner of the engine compartment) relieve the fuel system pressure. A valve cap must first be removed to gain access to the pressure relief valve.

Air Bypass Valve

REMOVAL AND INSTALLATION

1. Disconnect the wiring at the valve.

--- CAUTION ---

Never smoke when working around gasoline! Avoid all sources of sparks or ignition. Gasoline vapors are EXTREMELY volatile!

2. Remove the 2 retaining screws and lift off the valve.
3. Discard the gasket and clean and inspect the mating surfaces.
4. Install the valve with a new gasket, tightening the screws to 102 inch lbs.
5. Connect the wiring.

Air Intake Throttle Body

REMOVAL AND INSTALLATION

1. Disconnect the air intake hose.

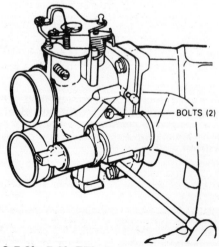

8-5.0L, 5.8L EFI air bypass valve

--- CAUTION ---

Never smoke when working around gasoline! Avoid all sources of sparks or ignition. Gasoline vapors are EXTREMELY volatile!

2. Disconnect the throttle position sensor and air by-pass valve connectors.
3. Remove the four throttle body mounting nuts and carefully separate the air throttle body from the upper intake manifold.
4. Remove and discard the mounting gasket. Clean all mounting surfaces using care not to damage the gasket surfaces of the throttle body and manifold. Do not allow any material to drop into the intake manifold.
5. Install the throttle body in the reverse order of removal. The mounting nuts are tightened to 12–18 ft. lbs.

Fuel Charging Assembly

REMOVAL AND INSTALLATION

1. Relieve the fuel system pressure.

--- CAUTION ---

Never smoke when working around gasoline! Avoid all sources of sparks or ignition. Gasoline vapors are EXTREMELY volatile!

2. Disconnect the battery ground cable and drain the cooling system.

--- CAUTION ---

When draining the coolant, keep in mind that cats and dogs are attracted by the ethylene glycol antifreeze, and are quite likely to drink any that is left in an uncovered container or in puddles on the ground. This will prove fatal in sufficient quantity. Always drain the coolant into a sealable container. Coolant should be reused unless it is contaminated or several years old.

3. Label and disconnect the wiring at the:
- Throttle position sensor
- Air bypass valve
- EGR sensor
4. Label and disconnect the following vacuum connectors:
- EGR valve
- Fuel pressure regulator
- Upper intake manifold vacuum tree
5. Disconnect the PCV hose at the upper intake manifold.
6. Remove the throttle linkage at the throttle ball and AOD transmission linkage at the throttle body.

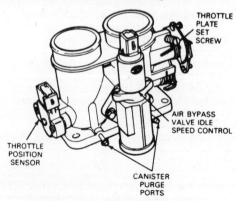

8-5.0L, 5.8L air throttle body

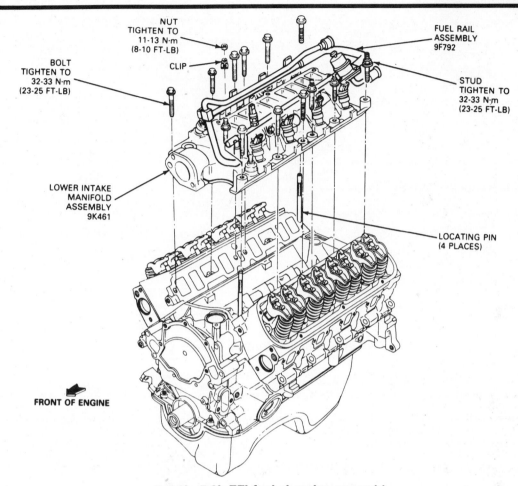

NUT
TIGHTEN TO
11-13 N·m
(8-10 FT-LB)

CLIP

BOLT
TIGHTEN TO
32-33 N·m
(23-25 FT-LB)

FUEL RAIL
ASSEMBLY
9F792

STUD
TIGHTEN TO
32-33 N·m
(23-25 FT-LB)

LOWER INTAKE
MANIFOLD
ASSEMBLY
9K461

LOCATING PIN
(4 PLACES)

FRONT OF ENGINE

8-5.0L, 5.8L EFI fuel charging assembly

7. Unbolt the cable bracket from the manifold and position the cables and bracket away from the engine.

8. Disconnect the 2 canister purge lines at the throttle body.

9. Disconnect the water heater lines from the throttle body.

10. Remove the EGR tube.

11. Remove the screw and washer which retains the upper intake manifold support bracket to the upper intake manifold.

12. Remove the 6 bolts which retain the upper intake manifold.

13. Remove the upper intake manifold assembly from the lower intake manifold.

14. Remove the distributor. (See Section 3).

15. Disconnect the wiring at the:
- Engine coolant temperature sensor.
- Engine temperature sending unit.
- Air charge temperature sensor.
- Knock sensor.
- Electrical vacuum regulator.
- Thermactor solenoids.

16. Disconnect the injector wiring harness at the main harness.

17. Remove the EGO ground wire at its intake manifold stud. Note the position of the stud and ground wire for installation.

18. Disconnect the fuel supply and return lines from the fuel rails using tool T81P–19623–G or G1.

19. Remove the upper radiator hose.

20. Remove the coolant bypass hose.

21. Disconnect the heater outlet hose at the manifold.

22. Remove the air cleaner bracket.

23. Remove the coil.

24. Noting the location of each bolt, remove the intake manifold retaining bolts.

25. Remove the lower intake manifold from the head.

26. Clean and inspect all mating surfaces. All surfaces MUST be flat and free from debris or damage!

27. Clean and oil all fastener threads.

28. Place a 1/16 in. (1.5mm) bead of RTV silicone sealant to the end seals' junctions.

29. Position the end seals on the block.

30. Install 2 locator pins at opposite corners of the block.

31. Position the lower manifold on the head using new gaskets. Install the bolts and remove the locating pins.

32. Tighten the bolts to 25 ft. lbs. in sequence. Wait ten minutes and retorque the bolts in sequence.

33. Install the coil.

34. Connect the cooling system hoses.

35. Connect the fuel supply and return lines.

36. Connect the wiring at the:
- Engine coolant temperature sensor.
- Engine temperature sending unit.
- Air charge temperature sensor.
- Knock sensor.
- Electrical vacuum regulator.
- Thermactor solenoids.

37. Install the distributor.

38. Position the upper manifold and new gasket on the lower manifold. Install the fasteners finger tight.

39. Install the upper intake manifold support on the manifold and tighten the retaining screw to 30 ft. lbs.

40. Torque the upper-to-lower manifold fasteners to 18 ft. lbs.

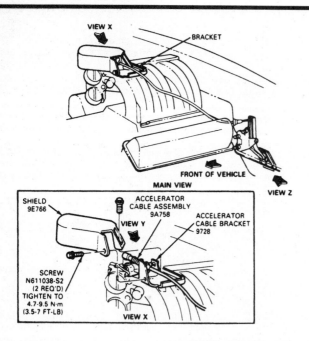

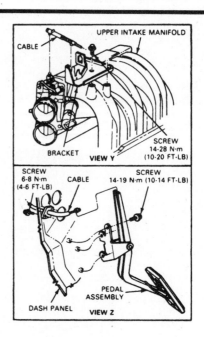

8-5.0L, 8-5.8L EFI throttle linkage

41. Install the EGR tube. Torque the fittings to 35 ft. lbs.
42. Install the canister purge lines at the throttle body.
43. Connect the water heater lines at the throttle body.
44. Connect the PCV hose.
45. Install the accelerator cable and throttle linkages.
46. Connect the vacuum hoses.
47. Connect the electrical wiring.
48. Connect the air intake hose, air bypass hose and crankcase vent hose.
49. Connect the battery ground.
50. Refill the cooling system.
51. Install the fuel pressure relief cap. Turn the ignition switch from **OFF** to **ON** at least half a dozen times, **WITHOUT STARTING THE ENGINE**, leaving it in the ON position for about 5 seconds each time. This will build up fuel pressure in the system.
52. Start the engine and allow it to run at idle until normal operating temperature is reached. Check for leaks.

Fuel Injectors

REMOVAL AND INSTALLATION

1. Relieve the fuel system pressure.

—————————— **CAUTION** ——————————
Never smoke when working around gasoline! Avoid all sources of sparks or ignition. Gasoline vapors are EXTREMELY volatile!
———————————————————————————————————

2. Disconnect the battery ground.
3. Remove the upper intake manifold.
4. Disconnect the wiring at the injectors.
5. Pull upward on the injector body while gently rocking it from side-to-side.
6. Inspect the O-rings on the injector for any sign of leakage or damage. Replace any suspected O-rings.
7. Inspect the plastic cap at the top of each injector and replace it if any sign of deterioration is noticed.
8. Lubricate the O-rings with clean engine oil ONLY!
9. Install the injectors by pushing them in with a gentle rocking motion.

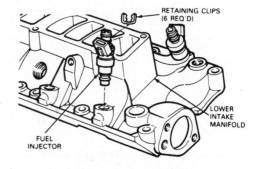

8-5.0L, 5.8L EFI fuel injector

10. Install the fuel supply manifold.
11. Connect the electrical wiring.
12. Install the upper intake manifold.

Fuel Pressure Regulator

REMOVAL AND INSTALLATION

1. Relieve the fuel system pressure.

—————————— **CAUTION** ——————————
Never smoke when working around gasoline! Avoid all sources of sparks or ignition. Gasoline vapors are EXTREMELY volatile!
———————————————————————————————————

2. Disconnect the vacuum line at the regulator.
3. Remove the 3 allen screws from the regulator housing.
4. Remove the regulator.
5. Inspect the regulator O-ring for signs of deterioration or damage. Discard the gasket.
6. Lubricate the O-ring with clean engine oil ONLY!
7. Make sure that the mounting surfaces are clean.
8. Using a new gasket, install the regulator. Tighten the retaining screws to 40 inch lbs.
9. Connect the vacuum line.

Fuel Supply Manifold

REMOVAL AND INSTALLATION

1. Relieve the fuel system pressure.

---------------- CAUTION ----------------

Never smoke when working around gasoline! Avoid all sources of sparks or ignition. Gasoline vapors are EXTREMELY volatile!

---

2. Remove the upper manifold.
3. Disconnect the chassis fuel inlet and outlet lines at the fuel supply manifold using tool T81P–19623–G or G1.
4. Disconnect the fuel supply and return lines at the fuel supply manifold.
5. Remove the 4 fuel supply manifold retaining bolts.
6. Carefully disengage the manifold from the injectors and lift it off.
7. Inspect all components for signs of damage. Make sure that the injector caps are clean.
8. Place the fuel supply manifold over the injectors and seat the injectors carefully in the manifold.
9. Install the 4 bolts and torque them to 20 ft. lbs.
10. Connect the fuel lines.
11. Install the upper manifold.

Lower Intake Manifold

REMOVAL AND INSTALLATION

1. Relieve the fuel system pressure.

---------------- CAUTION ----------------

Never smoke when working around gasoline! Avoid all sources of sparks or ignition. Gasoline vapors are EXTREMELY volatile!

---

2. Disconnect the battery ground cable and drain the cooling system.

---------------- CAUTION ----------------

When draining the coolant, keep in mind that cats and dogs are attracted by the ethylene glycol antifreeze, and are quite likely to drink any that is left in an uncovered container or in puddles on the ground. This will prove fatal in sufficient quantity. Always drain the coolant into a sealable container. Coolant should be reused unless it is contaminated or several years old.

---

3. Label and disconnect the wiring at the:
- Throttle position sensor
- Air bypass valve
- EGR sensor
4. Label and disconnect the following vacuum connectors:
- EGR valve

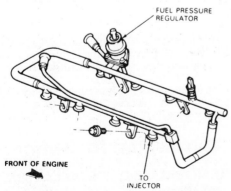

8-5.0L, 5.8L fuel pressure regulator

FUEL PRESSURE REGULATOR

FRONT OF ENGINE

TO INJECTOR

- Fuel pressure regulator
- Upper intake manifold vacuum tree
5. Disconnect the PCV hose at the upper intake manifold.
6. Remove the throttle linkage at the throttle ball and AOD transmission linkage at the throttle body.
7. Unbolt the cable bracket from the manifold and position the cables and bracket away from the engine.
8. Disconnect the 2 canister purge lines at the throttle body.
9. Disconnect the water heater lines from the throttle body.
10. Remove the EGR tube.
11. Remove the screw and washer which retains the upper intake manifold support bracket to the upper intake manifold.
12. Remove the 6 bolts which retain the upper intake manifold.
13. Remove the upper intake manifold assembly from the lower intake manifold.
14. Remove the distributor. (See Section 3).
15. Disconnect the wiring at the:
- Engine coolant temperature sensor.
- Engine temperature sending unit.
- Air charge temperature sensor.
- Knock sensor.
- Electrical vacuum regulator.
- Thermactor solenoids.
16. Disconnect the injector wiring harness at the main harness.
17. Remove the EGO ground wire at its intake manifold stud. Note the position of the stud and ground wire for installation.
18. Disconnect the fuel supply and return lines from the fuel rails using tool T81P–19623–G or G1.
19. Remove the upper radiator hose.
20. Remove the coolant bypass hose.
21. Disconnect the heater outlet hose at the manifold.
22. Remove the air cleaner bracket.
23. Remove the coil.
24. Noting the location of each bolt, remove the intake manifold retaining bolts.
25. Remove the lower intake manifold from the head.
26. Clean and inspect all mating surfaces. All surfaces MUST be flat and free from debris or damage!
27. Clean and oil all fastener threads.
28. Place a $\frac{1}{16}$ in. (1.5mm) bead of RTV silicone sealant to the end seals' junctions.
29. Position the end seals on the block.
30. Install 2 locator pins at opposite corners of the block.
31. Position the lower manifold on the head using new gaskets. Install the bolts and remove the locating pins.
32. Tighten the bolts to 25 ft. lbs. in sequence. Wait ten minutes and retorque the bolts in sequence.
33. Install the coil.
34. Connect the cooling system hoses.
35. Connect the fuel supply and return lines.
36. Connect the wiring at the:
- Engine coolant temperature sensor.
- Engine temperature sending unit.
- Air charge temperature sensor.
- Knock sensor.
- Electrical vacuum regulator.
- Thermactor solenoids.
37. Install the distributor.
38. Position the upper manifold and new gasket on the lower manifold. Install the fasteners finger tight.
39. Install the upper intake manifold support on the manifold and tighten the retaining screw to 30 ft. lbs.
40. Torque the upper-to-lower manifold fasteners to 18 ft. lbs.
41. Install the EGR tube. Torque the fittings to 35 ft. lbs.
42. Install the canister purge lines at the throttle body.
43. Connect the water heater lines at the throttle body.
44. Connect the PCV hose.
45. Install the accelerator cable and throttle linkages.

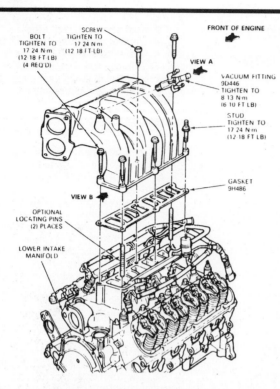

8-5.0L, 5.8L EFI upper intake manifold

1. Screw and washer assembly—M4 × 22
2. Throttle position sensor
3. Bolt—5 16-18 × 1.25
4. Gasket—air intake charge throttle
5. Manifold—intake upper
6. Plug—throttle plate set screw locking
7. Spring—throttle plate set screw
8. Screw—10.32 × 1/50 hex head slotted
9. Cap—throttle plate set screw
10. Bolt—M6 × 20
11. Air bypass valve assembly
12. Gasket—air bypass

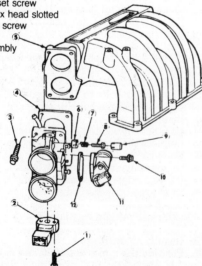

8-5.0L, 5.8L throttle body removal

46. Connect the vacuum hoses.
47. Connect the electrical wiring.
48. Connect the air intake hose, air bypass hose and crankcase vent hose.
49. Connect the battery ground.

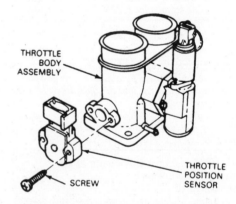

8-5.0L, 5.8L throttle position sensor

50. Refill the cooling system.
51. Install the fuel pressure relief cap. Turn the ignition switch from **OFF** to **ON** at least half a dozen times, **WITHOUT STARTING THE ENGINE**, leaving it in the ON position for about 5 seconds each time. This will build up fuel pressure in the system.
52. Start the engine and allow it to run at idle until normal operating temperature is reached. Check for leaks.

Throttle Position Sensor

REMOVAL AND INSTALLATION

1. Disconnect the wiring harness from the TPS.

2. Matchmark the sensor and throttle body for installation reference.
3. Remove the 2 retaining screws and remove the TPS.
4. Install the TPS so that the wiring harness is parallel with the venturi bores, then, rotate the TPS clockwise to align the scribe marks.

5. Tighten the retaining screws to 16 inch lbs.

NOTE: When correctly installed, the TPS wiring harness should be pointing directly at the air bypass valve.

6. Connect the wiring.

GASOLINE FUEL INJECTION
8–7.5L ENGINE

Relieving Fuel System Pressure

NOTE: A special tool is necessary for this procedure.

1. Make sure the ignition switch is in the OFF position.

2. Disconnect the battery ground.
3. Remove the fuel filler cap.
4. Using EFI Pressure Gauge T80L–9974–A, or equivalent, at the fuel pressure relief valve (located in the fuel line in the upper right corner of the engine compartment) relieve the fuel system pressure. A valve cap must first be removed to gain access to the pressure relief valve.

Upper Intake Manifold

REMOVAL AND INSTALLATION

1. Disconnect the throttle and transmission linkages at the throttle body.

2. Remove the two canister purge lines from the throttle body.
3. Tag and disconnect the:
- throttle bypass valve wire
- throttle position sensor wire

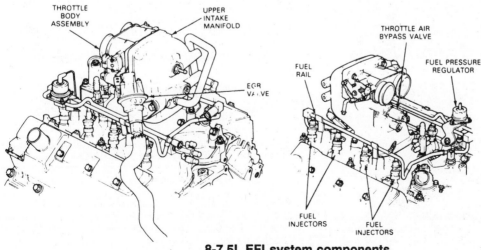

8-7.5L EFI system components

5–27

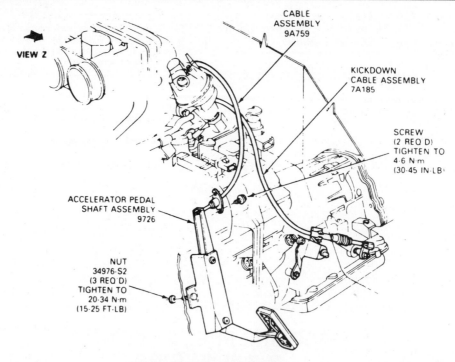

8-7.5L EFI throttle linkage

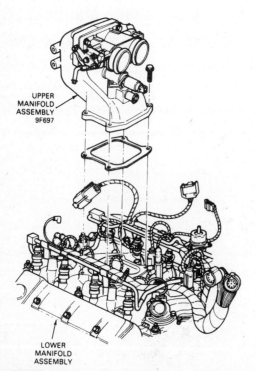

8-7.5L upper intake manifold removal

- EGR position sensor wire
- MAP sensor vacuum line
- EGR vacuum line
- fuel pressure regulator vacuum line
- EGR valve flange nut
- PCV hose
4. Disconnect the water lines at the throttle body.

5. Remove the 4 upper intake manifold bolts and lift off the manifold.

6. Installation is the reverse of removal. Always use new gaskets. Torque the manifold bolts to 18 ft. lbs.

Throttle Body

REMOVAL AND INSTALLATION

1. Relieve the fuel system pressure.

—————— CAUTION ——————
Never smoke when working around gasoline! Avoid all sources of sparks or ignition. Gasoline vapors are EXTREMELY volatile!
—————————————————————

2. Disconnect the throttle position sensor wire.
3. Disconnect the water lines at the throttle body.
4. Remove the 4 throttle body bolts and carefully lift off the throttle body. Discard the gasket.
5. Installation is the reverse of removal. Torque the bolts to 18 ft. lbs.

Throttle Position Sensor

REMOVAL AND INSTALLATION

1. Disconnect the wiring harness from the TPS.

—————— CAUTION ——————
Never smoke when working around gasoline! Avoid all sources of sparks or ignition. Gasoline vapors are EXTREMELY volatile!
—————————————————————

2. Matchmark the sensor and throttle body for installation reference.
3. Remove the 2 retaining screws and remove the TPS.
4. Install the TPS so that the wiring harness is parallel with the venturi bores, then, rotate the TPS clockwise to align the scribe marks.
5. Tighten the retaining screws to 16 inch lbs.

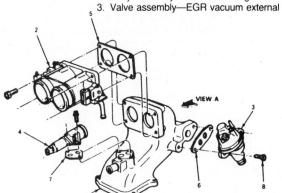
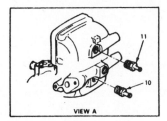

1. Manifold assembly—intake
2. Body assembly—air intake charge throttle
3. Valve assembly—EGR vacuum external
4. Valve assembly—throttle air bypass
5. Gasket—air charge control intake manifold
6. Gasket—EGR valve
7. Gasket—air bypass valve
8. Bolt ⁵⁄₁₆ × 1.5 hex head UBS (6 reqd)
9. Bolt M6 × 25mm hex head UBS (2 reqd)
10. Connector ⅜″ hose × ⅜″ external pipe
11. Connector ⅜″ hose × ⅜″ external pipe
12. Connector ¼″ hose × ⅜″ external pipe

8-7.5L throttle body and upper intake manifold

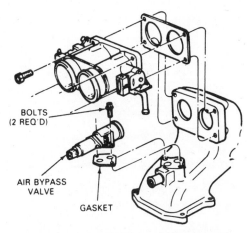

8-7.5L air bypass valve removal

NOTE: When correctly installed, the TPS wiring harness should be pointing directly at the air bypass valve.

6. Connect the wiring.

Air Bypass Valve

REMOVAL AND INSTALLATION

1. Disconnect the wiring at the valve.

─── CAUTION ───
Never smoke when working around gasoline! Avoid all sources of sparks or ignition. Gasoline vapors are EXTREMELY volatile!

2. Remove the 2 retaining screws and lift off the valve.
3. Discard the gasket and clean and inspect the mating surfaces.
4. Install the valve with a new gasket, tightening the screws to 102 inch lbs.
5. Connect the wiring.

Fuel Supply Manifold

REMOVAL AND INSTALLATION

1. Relieve the fuel system pressure.

─── CAUTION ───
Never smoke when working around gasoline! Avoid all sources of sparks or ignition. Gasoline vapors are EXTREMELY volatile!

2. Remove the upper manifold.
3. Disconnect the chassis fuel inlet and outlet lines at the fuel supply manifold using tool T81P–19623–G or G1.
4. Disconnect the fuel supply and return lines at the fuel supply manifold.
5. Remove the 4 fuel supply manifold retaining bolts.
6. Carefully disengage the manifold from the injectors and lift it off.
7. Inspect all components for signs of damage. Make sure that the injector caps are clean.
8. Place the fuel supply manifold over the injectors and seat the injectors carefully in the manifold.
9. Install the 4 bolts and torque them to 20 ft. lbs.
10. Connect the fuel lines.
11. Install the upper manifold.

Fuel Pressure Regulator

REMOVAL AND INSTALLATION

1. Relieve the fuel system pressure.

─── CAUTION ───
Never smoke when working around gasoline! Avoid all sources of sparks or ignition. Gasoline vapors are EXTREMELY volatile!

2. Disconnect the vacuum line at the regulator.
3. Remove the 3 allen screws from the regulator housing.
4. Remove the regulator.
5. Inspect the regulator O-ring for signs of deterioration or damage. Discard the gasket.
6. Lubricate the O-ring with clean engine oil ONLY!
7. Make sure that the mounting surfaces are clean.
8. Using a new gasket, install the regulator. Tighten the retaining screws to 40 inch lbs.
9. Connect the vacuum line.

Fuel Injectors

REMOVAL AND INSTALLATION

1. Relieve the fuel system pressure.

5 FUEL SYSTEM

2. Disconnect the battery ground.
3. Remove the fuel supply manifold.
4. Disconnect the wiring at the injectors.
5. Pull upward on the injector body while gently rocking it from side-to-side.

6. Inspect the O-rings (2 per injector) on the injector for any sign of leakage or damage. Replace any suspected O-rings.
7. Inspect the plastic cap at the top of each injector and replace it if any sign of deterioration is noticed.
8. Lubricate the O-rings with clean engine oil ONLY!
9. Install the injectors by pushing them in with a gentle rocking motion.
10. Install the fuel supply manifold.
11. Connect the electrical wiring.

DIESEL ENGINE FUEL SYSTEM

Fuel Pump

REMOVAL

1. Loosen the threaded connections with the proper size wrench (a flare nut wrench is preferred) and retighten snugly. Do not remove the lines at this time.
2. Loosen the mounting bolts, one to two turns. Apply force with your hand to loosen the fuel pump if the gasket is stuck. Rotate the engine by nudging the starter, until the fuel pump cam lobe is at the low position. At this position, spring tension against the fuel pump bolts will be greatly reduced.
3. Disconnect the fuel supply pump inlet, outlet and fuel return line.

4. Remove the fuel pump attaching bolts and remove the pump and gasket. Discard the old gasket.

INSTALLATION

1. Remove the remaining fuel pump gasket material from the engine and from the fuel pump if you are reinstalling the old pump. Make sure both mounting surfaces are clean.
2. Install the attaching bolts into the fuel supply pump and install a new gasket on the bolts. Position the fuel pump onto the mounting pad. Turn the attaching bolts alternately and evenly and tighten the bolts to the specifications according to the size bolts used on the pump. See the accompanying standard torque chart for reference.

NOTE: The cam must be at its low position before attempting to install the fuel supply pump. If it is difficult to start the mounting bolts, remove the pump and reinstall with a lever on the bottom side of the cam.

3. Install the fuel outlet line. Start the fitting by hand to avoid crossthreading.
4. Install the inlet line and the fuel return line.
5. Start the engine and observe all connections for fuel leaks for two minutes.
6. Stop the engine and check all fuel supply pump fuel line connections. Check for oil leaks at the pump mounting pad.

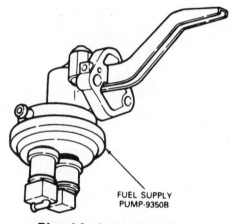

FUEL SUPPLY
PUMP-9350B

Diesel fuel supply pump

Glow Plug System

The diesel engine utilizes an electric glow plug system to aid in the start of the engine. The function of this stem is to preheat the combustion chamber to aid ignition of the fuel.

The system consists of eight glow plugs (one for each cylinder), control switch, power relay, after glow relay, wait lamp latching relay, wait lamp and the eight fusible links located between the harness and the glow plug terminal.

On initial start with cold engine, the glow plug system operates as follows: The glow plug control switch energizes the power relay (which is a magnetic switch) and the power relay contacts close. Battery current energizes the glow plugs. Current to the glow plugs and a wait lamp will be shut off when the glow plugs are hot enough. This takes from 2 to 10 second after the key is first turned on. When the wait lamp goes off, the engine is ready to start. After the engine is started the glow plugs begin an on-off cycle for about 40 to 90 seconds. This cycle helps to clear start-up smoke. The control switch (the brain of the operation) is threaded into the left cylinder head coolant jacket. the control unit senses engine coolant temperature. Since the con-

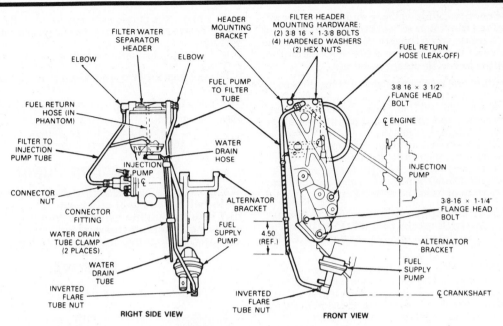

Diesel fuel supply lines

trol unit senses temperature and glow plug operation the glow plug system will not be activated unless needed. On a restart (warm engine) the glow plug system will not be activated unless the coolant temperature drops before 165°F (91°C).

Since the fast start system utilizes 6 volt glow plugs in a 12 volt system to achieve rapid heating of the glow plug, a cycling device is required in the circuit.

CAUTION

Never bypass the power relay of the glow plug system. Constant battery current (12 volts) to glow plugs will cause them to overheat and fail.

Injection Nozzles

REMOVAL

NOTE: Before removing the nozzle assemblies, clean

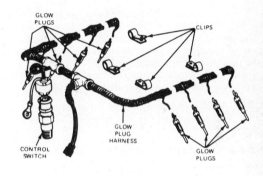

Diesel glow plug system

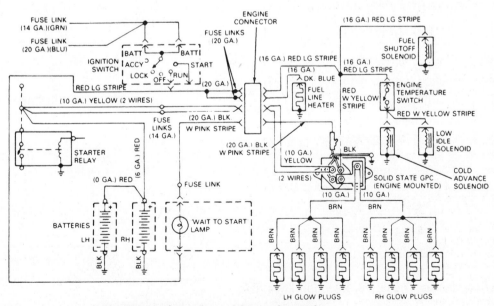

7.3L diesel glow plug wiring schematic

the exterior of each nozzle assembly and the surrounding area with clean fuel oil or solvent to prevent entry of dirt into the engine when nozzle assemblies are removed. Also, clean the fuel inlet and fuel leak-off piping connections. Blow dry with compressed air.

1. Remove the fuel line retaining clamp(s) from the nozzle lines that are to be removed.

2. Disconnect the nozzle fuel inlet (high pressure) and fuel leak-off tees from each nozzle assembly and position out of the way. Cover the open ends of the fuel inlet and outlet or nozzles with protective caps, to prevent dirt from entering.

3. Remove the injection nozzles by turning them counter-clockwise. Pull the nozzle assembly with the copper washer attached from the engine. Cover the nozzle fuel opening and spray tip, with plastic caps, to prevent the entry of dirt.

NOTE: Remove the copper injector nozzle gasket from the nozzle bore with special tool, T71P-19703-C, or equivalent, whenever the gasket does not come out with the nozzle.

4. Place the nozzle assemblies in a fabricated holder as they are removed from the heads. The holder should be marked with numbers corresponding to the cylinder numbering of the engine. This will allow for reinstallation of the nozzle in the same ports from which they were removed.

INSTALLATION

1. Thoroughly clean the nozzle bore in cylinder head before reinserting the nozzle assembly with nozzle seat cleaner, special tool T83T-9527-A or equivalent. Make certain that no small particles of metal or carbon remain on the seating surface. Blow out the particles with compressed air.

2. Remove the protective cap and install a new copper gasket on the nozzle assembly, with a small dab of grease.

NOTE: Anti-seize compound or equivalent should be used on nozzle threads to aid in installation and future removal.

3. Install the nozzle assembly into the cylinder head nozzle bore.

4. Tighten the nozzle assembly to 33 ft. lbs.

5. Remove the protective caps from nozzle assemblies and fuel lines.

6. Install the leak-off tees to the nozzle assemblies.

NOTE: Install two new O-ring seals for each fuel return tee.

7. Connect the high pressure fuel line and tighten, using a flare nut wrench.

8. Install the fuel line retainer clamps.

9. Start the engine and check for leaks.

Injection Pump

WARNING: Before removing the fuel lines, clean the exterior with clean fuel oil or solvent to prevent entry of dirt into the engine when the fuel lines are removed.

Do not wash or steam clean engine while engine is running. Serious damage to injection pump could occur.

REMOVAL

1. Disconnect battery ground cables from both batteries.

2. Remove the engine oil filler neck.

3. Remove the bolts attaching injection pump to drive gear.

4. Disconnect the electrical connectors to injection pump.

5. Disconnect the accelerator cable and speed control cable from throttle lever, if so equipped.

6. Remove the air cleaner and install clean rags to prevent dirt from entering the intake manifold.

7. Remove the accelerator cable bracket, with cables attached, from the intake manifold and position out of the way.

NOTE: All fuel lines and fittings must be capped using Fuel System Protective Cap Set T83T-9395-A or equivalent, to prevent fuel contamination.

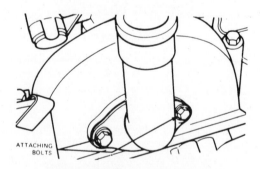

Diesel oil filter neck removal

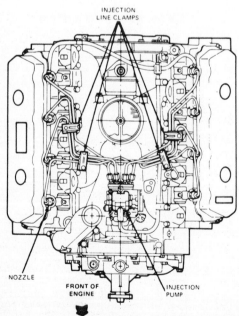

Injection line clamps, Diesel V8. Injection lines also shown

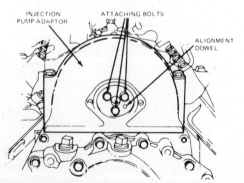

Diesel injection pump drive gear attaching bolts

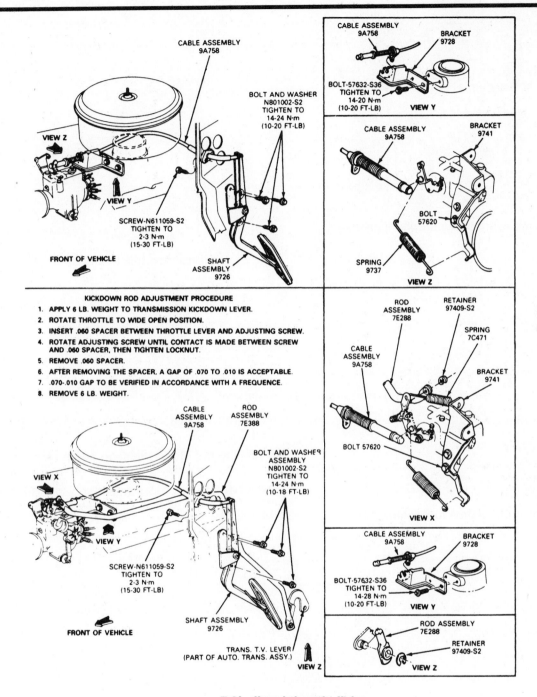

KICKDOWN ROD ADJUSTMENT PROCEDURE

1. APPLY 6 LB. WEIGHT TO TRANSMISSION KICKDOWN LEVER.
2. ROTATE THROTTLE TO WIDE OPEN POSITION.
3. INSERT .060 SPACER BETWEEN THROTTLE LEVER AND ADJUSTING SCREW.
4. ROTATE ADJUSTING SCREW UNTIL CONTACT IS MADE BETWEEN SCREW AND .060 SPACER, THEN TIGHTEN LOCKNUT.
5. REMOVE .060 SPACER.
6. AFTER REMOVING THE SPACER, A GAP OF .070 TO .010 IS ACCEPTABLE.
7. .070-.010 GAP TO BE VERIFIED IN ACCORDANCE WITH A FREQUENCE.
8. REMOVE 6 LB. WEIGHT.

7.3L diesel throttle linkage

8. Remove the fuel filter-to-injection pump fuel line and cap fittings.

9. Remove and cap the injection pump inlet elbow and the injection pump fitting adapter.

10. Remove the fuel return line on injection pump, rotate out of the way, And cap all fittings.

NOTE: It is not necessary to remove injection lines from injection pump. If lines are to be removed, loosen injection line fittings at injection pump before removing it from engine.

11. Remove the fuel injection lines from the nozzles and cap lines and nozzles.

12. Remove the three nuts attaching the Injection pump to injection pump adapter using Tool T83T–9000–B.

13. If the injection pump is to be replaced, loosen the injection line retaining clips and the injection nozzle fuel lines with Tool T83T–9396–A and cap all fittings at this time with protective cap set T83T–9395–A or equivalent. Do not install the injection nozzle fuel lines until the new pump is installed in the engine.

14. Lift the Injection pump, with the nozzle lines attached, up and out of the engine compartment.

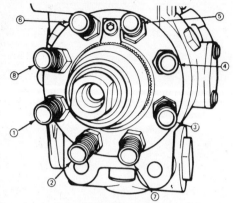

Injection pump cylinder numbering sequence

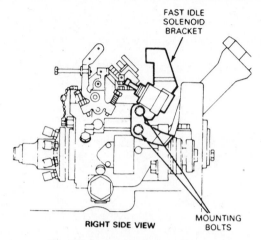

FAST IDLE
SOLENOID
BRACKET

RIGHT SIDE VIEW

MOUNTING
BOLTS

Diesel fast idle solenoid bracket

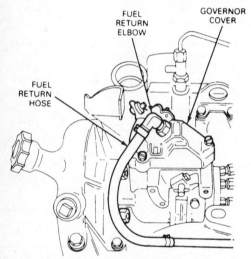

FUEL
RETURN
ELBOW

GOVERNOR
COVER

FUEL
RETURN
HOSE

Removing the diesel fuel return line

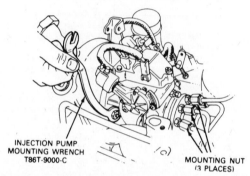

INJECTION PUMP
MOUNTING WRENCH
T86T-9000-C

MOUNTING NUT
(3 PLACES)

Removing the diesel injection pump mounting nuts

WARNING: Do not carry injection pump by Injection nozzle fuel lines as this could cause lines to bend or crimp.

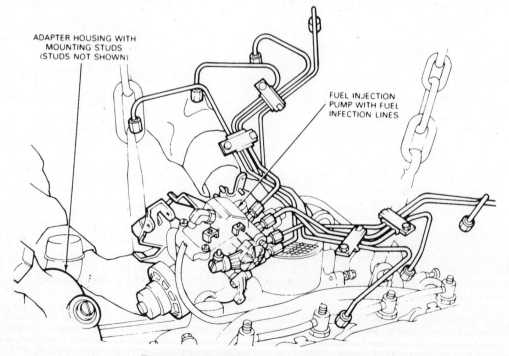

ADAPTER HOUSING WITH
MOUNTING STUDS
(STUDS NOT SHOWN)

FUEL INJECTION
PUMP WITH FUEL
INFECTION LINES

Removing the diesel injection pump

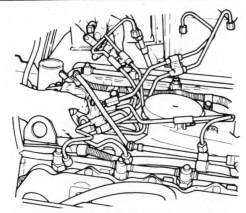

Diesel injection pump removal. Be careful not to crimp or bend the fuel lines

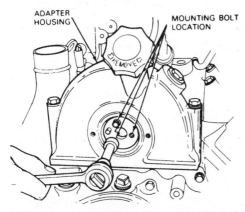

Diesel injection pump drive gear attaching bolts

INSTALLATION

1. Install a new O-ring on the drive gear end of the injection pump.
2. Move the injection pump down and into position.
3. Position the alignment dowel on injection pump into the alignment hole on Drive gear.
4. Install the bolts attaching the injection pump to drive gear and tighten.
5. Install the nuts attaching injection pump to adapter. Align scribe lines on the injection pump flange and the injection pump

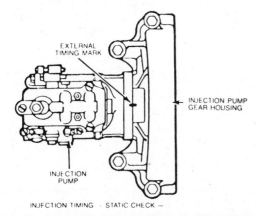

Diesel injection pump static timing marks

adapter and tighten to 14 ft.lbs.
6. If the injection nozzle fuel lines were removed from the injection pump install at this time, refer to Fuel Lines — Installation, in this Section.
7. Remove the caps from nozzles and the fuel lines and install the fuel line nuts on the nozzles and tighten to 22 ft. lbs.
8. Connect the fuel return line to injection pump and tighten the nuts.
9. Install the injection pump fitting adapter with a new O-ring.
10. Clean the old sealant from the injection pump elbow threads, using clean solvent, and dry thoroughly. Apply a light coating of pipe sealant to the elbow threads.
11. Install the elbow in the injection pump adapter and tighten to a minimum of 6 ft. lbs. Then tighten further, if necessary, to align the elbow with the injection pump fuel inlet line, but do not exceed 360 degrees of rotation or 10 ft. lbs.
12. Remove the caps and connect the fuel filter-to-Injection pump fuel line.
13. Install the accelerator cable bracket to the intake manifold.
14. Remove the rags from the intake manifold and install the air cleaner.
15. Connect the accelerator and speed control cable, if so equipped, to throttle lever.
16. Install the electrical connectors on injection pump.
17. Clean the injection pump adapter and oil filler neck sealing surfaces.
18. Apply a ⅛ in. (3mm) bead of RTV sealant on the adapter housing.
19. Install the oil filler neck and tighten the bolts.
20. Connect the battery ground cables to both batteries.
21. Run the engine and check for fuel leaks.
22. If necessary, purge high pressure fuel lines of air by loosening connector one half to one turn and cranking engine until solid fuel, free from bubbles flows from connection.

---- **CAUTION** ----

Keep eyes and hands away from nozzle spray. Fuel spraying from the nozzle under high pressure can penetrate the skin.

---

23. Check and adjust injection pump timing as described in this Section.

Fuel Lines

REMOVAL

NOTE: Before removing any fuel lines, clean the exterior with clean fuel oil, or solvent to prevent entry of dirt into fuel system when the fuel lines are removed. Blow dry with compressed air.

1. Disconnect the battery ground cables from both batteries.
2. Remove the air cleaner and cap intake manifold opening with clean rags.
3. Disconnect the accelerator cable and speed control cable, if so equipped, from the injection pump.
4. remove the accelerator cable bracket from the intake manifold and position out of the way with cable(s) attached.

WARNING: To prevent fuel system contamination, cap all fuel lines and fittings.

5. Disconnect the fuel line from the fuel filter to injection pump and cap all fittings.
6. Disconnect and cap the nozzle fuel lines at nozzles.
7. Remove the fuel line clamps from the fuel lines to be removed.
8. Remove and cap the injection pump inlet elbow.
9. Remove and cap the inlet fitting adapter.
10. Remove the injection nozzle lines, one at a time, from injection pump using Tool T83T–9396–A.

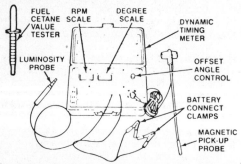

Rotunda dynamic timing meter used for diesel injection timing. Cetane tester, magnetic pick-up probe and luminosity probe also shown

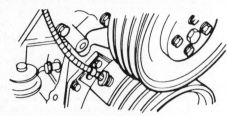

MAGNETIC PICK-UP

V8 diesel magnetic pick-up probe hole location

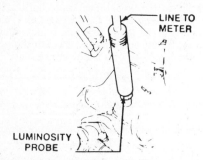

Luminosity probe used for diesel injection timing

NOTE: Fuel lines must be removed following this sequence: 5-6-4-8-3-1-7-2. Install caps on each end of each fuel line and pump fittings as it is removed and identify each fuel line accordingly.

INSTALLATION

1. Install fuel lines on injection pump, one at a time, and Tighten to 22 ft.lbs.

NOTE: Fuel lines must be installed in the sequence: 2-7-1-3-8-4-6-5.

2. Clean the old sealant from the injection pump elbow, using clean solvent, and dry thoroughly.
3. Apply a light coating of pipe sealant on the elbow threads.

Diesel Injection Timing

STATIC TIMING

1. Break the torque of the injection pump mounting nuts (keeping the nuts snug).
2. Rotate the injection pump using Tool T83–9000–C or

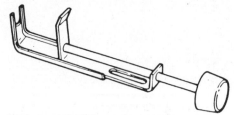

Rotunda diesel throttle control tool

Fuel Cetane Value	Altitude	
	0-3000 Ft ①	Above 3000 Ft ①
38–42	6° ATDC	7° ATDC
43–46	5° ATDC	6° ATDC
47–50	4° ATDC	5° ATDC

① Installation of resetting tolerance for dynamic timing is ± 1°. Service limit is ± 2°.

Dynamic Timing Specifications

equivalent to bring the mark on the pump into alignment with the mark on pump mounting adapter.
3. Visually recheck the alignment of the timing marks and tighten injection pump mounting nuts.

DYNAMIC TIMING

1. Bring the engine up to normal operating temperature.
2. Stop the engine and install a dynamic timing meter, Rotunda 78–0100 or equivalent, by placing the magnetic probe pickup into the probe hole.
3. Remove the no. 1 glow plug wire and remove the glow plug, install the luminosity probe and tighten to 12 ft.lbs. Install the photocell over the probe.
4. Connect the dynamic timing meter to the battery and adjust the offset of the meter.
5. Set the transmission in neutral and raise the rear wheels off the ground. Using Rotunda 14–0302, throttle control, set the engine speed to 1,400 rpm with no accessory load. Observe the injection timing on the dynamic timing meter.

NOTE: Obtain the fuel sample from the vehicle and check the cetane value using the tester supplied with the Ford special tools 78–0100 or equivalent. Refer to the dynamic timing chart to find the correct timing in degrees.

6. If the dynamic timing is not within plug or minus 2 degrees of specification, then the injection pump timing will require adjustment.
7. Turn the engine off. Note the timing mark alignment. Loosen the injection pump-to-adapter nuts.
8. Rotate the injection pump clockwise (when viewed from the front of the engine) to retard and counterclockwise to advance timing. Two degrees of dynamic timing is approximately 0.030 in. (0.76mm) of timing mark movement.
9. Start the engine and recheck the timing. If the timing is not within plus or minus 1 degree of specification, repeat steps 7 through 9.
10. Turn off the engine. Remove the dynamic timing equipment. Lightly coat the glow plug thread with anti-seize compound, install the glow plugs and tighten to 12 ft. lbs. Connect the glow plug wires.

Chassis Electrical

QUICK REFERENCE INDEX

GENERAL INDEX

UNDERSTANDING AND TROUBLESHOOTING ELECTRICAL SYSTEMS

With the rate at which both import and domestic manufacturers are incorporating electronic control systems into their production lines, it won't be long before every new vehicle is equipped with one or more on-board computer, like the unit installed on the truck. These electronic components (with no moving parts) should theoretically last the life of the vehicle, provided nothing external happens to damage the circuits or memory chips.

While it is true that electronic components should never wear out, in the real world malfunctions do occur. It is also true that any computer-based system is extremely sensitive to electrical voltages and cannot tolerate careless or haphazard testing or service procedures. An inexperienced individual can literally do major damage looking for a minor problem by using the wrong kind of test equipment or connecting test leads or connectors with the ignition switch ON. When selecting test equipment, make sure the manufacturers instructions state that the tester is compatible with whatever type of electronic control system is being serviced. Read all instructions carefully and double check all test points before installing probes or making any test connections.

The following section outlines basic diagnosis techniques for dealing with computerized automotive control systems. Along with a general explanation of the various types of test equipment available to aid in servicing modern electronic automotive systems, basic repair techniques for wiring harnesses and connectors is given. Read the basic information before attempting any repairs or testing on any computerized system, to provide the background of information necessary to avoid the most common and obvious mistakes that can cost both time and money. Although the replacement and testing procedures are simple in themselves, the systems are not, and unless one has a thorough understanding of all components and their function within a particular computerized control system, the logical test sequence these systems demand cannot be followed. Minor malfunctions can make a big difference, so it is important to know how each component affects the operation of the overall electronic system to find the ultimate cause of a problem without replacing good components unnecessarily. It is not enough to use the correct test equipment; the test equipment must be used correctly.

Safety Precautions

—— CAUTION ——
Whenever working on or around any computer based microprocessor control system, always observe these general precautions to prevent the possibility of personal injury or damage to electronic components.

• Never install or remove battery cables with the key ON or the engine running. Jumper cables should be connected with the key OFF to avoid power surges that can damage electronic control units. Engines equipped with computer controlled systems should avoid both giving and getting jump starts due to the possibility of serious damage to components from arcing in the engine compartment when connections are made with the ignition ON.

• Always remove the battery cables before charging the battery. Never use a high output charger on an installed battery or attempt to use any type of "hot shot" (24 volt) starting aid.

• Exercise care when inserting test probes into connectors to insure good connections without damaging the connector or spreading the pins. Always probe connectors from the rear (wire) side, NOT the pin side, to avoid accidental shorting of terminals during test procedures.

• Never remove or attach wiring harness connectors with the ignition switch ON, especially to an electronic control unit.

• Do not drop any components during service procedures and never apply 12 volts directly to any component (like a solenoid or relay) unless instructed specifically to do so. Some component electrical windings are designed to safely handle only 4 or 5 volts and can be destroyed in seconds if 12 volts are applied directly to the connector.

• Remove the electronic control unit if the vehicle is to be placed in an environment where temperatures exceed approximately 176°F (80°C), such as a paint spray booth or when arc or gas welding near the control unit location in the car.

ORGANIZED TROUBLESHOOTING

When diagnosing a specific problem, organized troubleshooting is a must. The complexity of a modern automobile demands that you approach any problem in a logical, organized manner. There are certain troubleshooting techniques that are standard:

1. Establish when the problem occurs. Does the problem appear only under certain conditions? Were there any noises, odors, or other unusual symptoms?

2. Isolate the problem area. To do this, make some simple tests and observations; then eliminate the systems that are working properly. Check for obvious problems such as broken wires, dirty connections or split or disconnected vacuum hoses. Always check the obvious before assuming something complicated is the cause.

3. Test for problems systematically to determine the cause once the problem area is isolated. Are all the components functioning properly? Is there power going to electrical switches and motors? Is there vacuum at vacuum switches and/or actuators? Is there a mechanical problem such as bent linkage or loose mounting screws? Doing careful, systematic checks will often turn up most causes on the first inspection without wasting time checking components that have little or no relationship to the problem.

4. Test all repairs after the work is done to make sure that the problem is fixed. Some causes can be traced to more than one component, so a careful verification of repair work is important to pick up additional malfunctions that may cause a problem to reappear or a different problem to arise. A blown fuse, for example, is a simple problem that may require more than another fuse to repair. If you don't look for a problem that caused a fuse to blow, for example, a shorted wire may go undetected.

Experience has shown that most problems tend to be the result of a fairly simple and obvious cause, such as loose or corroded connectors or air leaks in the intake system; making careful inspection of components during testing essential to quick and accurate troubleshooting. Special, hand held computerized testers designed specifically for diagnosing the EEC-IV system are available from a variety of aftermarket sources, as well as from the vehicle manufacturer, but care should be taken that any test equipment being used is designed to diagnose that particular computer controlled system accurately without damaging the control unit (ECU) or components being tested.

NOTE: Pinpointing the exact cause of trouble in an electrical system can sometimes only be accomplished by the use of special test equipment. The following describes commonly used test equipment and explains how to put it to best use in diagnosis. In addition to the information covered below, the manufacturer's instructions booklet provided with the tester should be read and clearly understood before attempting any test procedures.

TEST EQUIPMENT

Jumper Wires

Jumper wires are simple, yet extremely valuable, pieces of test equipment. Jumper wires are merely wires that are used to bypass sections of a circuit. The simplest type of jumper wire is merely a length of multistrand wire with an alligator clip at each end. Jumper wires are usually fabricated from lengths of standard automotive wire and whatever type of connector (alligator clip, spade connector or pin connector) that is required for the particular vehicle being tested. The well equipped tool box will have several different styles of jumper wires in several different lengths. Some jumper wires are made with three or more terminals coming from a common splice for special purpose testing. In cramped, hard-to-reach areas it is advisable to have insulated boots over the jumper wire terminals in order to prevent accidental grounding, sparks, and possible fire, especially when testing fuel system components.

Jumper wires are used primarily to locate open electrical circuits, on either the ground (-) side of the circuit or on the hot (+) side. If an electrical component fails to operate, connect the jumper wire between the component and a good ground. If the component operates only with the jumper installed, the ground circuit is open. If the ground circuit is good, but the component does not operate, the circuit between the power feed and component is open. You can sometimes connect the jumper wire directly from the battery to the hot terminal of the component, but first make sure the component uses 12 volts in operation. Some electrical components, such as fuel injectors, are designed to operate on about 4 volts and running 12 volts directly to the injector terminals can burn out the wiring. By inserting an inline fuseholder between a set of test leads, a fused jumper wire can be used for bypassing open circuits. Use a 5 amp fuse to provide protection against voltage spikes. When in doubt, use a voltmeter to check the voltage input to the component and measure how much voltage is being applied normally. By moving the jumper wire successively back from the lamp toward the power source, you can isolate the area of the circuit where the open is located. When the component stops functioning, or the power is cut off, the open is in the segment of wire between the jumper and the point previously tested.

CAUTION

Never use jumpers made from wire that is of lighter gauge than used in the circuit under test. If the jumper wire is of too small gauge, it may overheat and possibly melt. Never use jumpers to bypass high resistance loads (such as motors) in a circuit. Bypassing resistances, in effect, creates a short circuit which may, in turn, cause damage and fire. Never use a jumper for anything other than temporary bypassing of components in a circuit.

---

12 Volt Test Light

The 12 volt test light is used to check circuits and components while electrical current is flowing through them. It is used for voltage and ground tests. Twelve volt test lights come in different styles but all have three main parts; a ground clip, a probe, and a light. The most commonly used 12 volt test lights have pick-type probes. To use a 12 volt test light, connect the ground clip to a good ground and probe wherever necessary with the pick. The pick should be sharp so that it can penetrate wire insulation to make contact with the wire, without making a large hole in the insulation. The wrap-around light is handy in hard to reach areas or where it is difficult to support a wire to push a probe pick into it. To use the wrap around light, hook the wire to probed with the hook and pull the trigger. A small pick will be forced through the wire insulation into the wire core.

CAUTION

Do not use a test light to probe electronic ignition spark plug or coil wires. Never use a pick-type test light to probe wiring on computer controlled systems unless specifically instructed to do so. Any wire insulation that is pierced by the test light probe should be taped and sealed with silicone after testing.

Like the jumper wire, the 12 volt test light is used to isolate opens in circuits. But, whereas the jumper wire is used to bypass the open to operate the load, the 12 volt test light is used to locate the presence of voltage in a circuit. If the test light glows, you know that there is power up to that point; if the 12 volt test light does not glow when its probe is inserted into the wire or connector, you know that there is an open circuit (no power). Move the test light in successive steps back toward the power source until the light in the handle does glow. When it does glow, the open is between the probe and point previously probed.

NOTE: The test light does not detect that 12 volts (or any particular amount of voltage) is present; it only detects that some voltage is present. It is advisable before using the test light to touch its terminals across the battery posts to make sure the light is operating properly.

Self-Powered Test Light

The self-powered test light usually contains a 1.5 volt penlight battery. One type of self-powered test light is similar in design to the 12 volt test light. This type has both the battery and the light in the handle and pick-type probe tip. The second type has the light toward the open tip, so that the light illuminates the contact point. The self-powered test light is dual purpose piece of test equipment. It can be used to test for either open or short circuits when power is isolated from the circuit (continuity test). A powered test light should not be used on any computer controlled system or component unless specifically instructed to do so. Many engine sensors can be destroyed by even this small amount of voltage applied directly to the terminals.

Open Circuit Testing

To use the self-powered test light to check for open circuits, first isolate the circuit from the vehicle's 12 volt power source by disconnecting the battery or wiring harness connector. Connect the test light ground clip to a good ground and probe sections of the circuit sequentially with the test light. (start from either end of the circuit) If the light is out, the open is between the probe and the circuit ground. If the light is on, the open is between the probe and end of the circuit toward the power source.

Short Circuit Testing

By isolating the circuit both from power and from ground, and using a self-powered test light, you can check for shorts to ground in the circuit. Isolate the circuit from power and ground. Connect the test light ground clip to a good ground and probe any easy-to-reach test point in the circuit. If the light comes on, there is a short somewhere in the circuit. To isolate the short, probe a test point at either end of the isolated circuit (the light should be on). Leave the test light probe connected and open connectors, switches, remove parts, etc., sequentially, until the light goes out. When the light goes out, the short is between the last circuit component opened and the previous circuit opened.

NOTE: The 1.5 volt battery in the test light does not provide much current. A weak battery may not provide enough power to illuminate the test light even when a complete circuit is made (especially if there are high resistances in the circuit). Always make sure that the test battery is strong. To check the battery, briefly touch the

ground clip to the probe; if the light glows brightly the battery is strong enough for testing. **Never use a self-powered test light to perform checks for opens or shorts when power is applied to the electrical system under test. The 12 volt vehicle power will quickly burn out the 1.5 volt light bulb in the test light.**

Voltmeter

A voltmeter is used to measure voltage at any point in a circuit, or to measure the voltage drop across any part of a circuit. It can also be used to check continuity in a wire or circuit by indicating current flow from one end to the other. Voltmeters usually have various scales on the meter dial and a selector switch to allow the selection of different voltages. The voltmeter has a positive and a negative lead. To avoid damage to the meter, always connect the negative lead to the negative (-) side of circuit (to ground or nearest the ground side of the circuit) and connect the positive lead to the positive (+) side of the circuit (to the power source or the nearest power source). Note that the negative voltmeter lead will always be black and that the positive voltmeter will always be some color other than black (usually red). Depending on how the voltmeter is connected into the circuit, it has several uses.

A voltmeter can be connected either in parallel or in series with a circuit and it has a very high resistance to current flow. When connected in parallel, only a small amount of current will flow through the voltmeter current path; the rest will flow through the normal circuit current path and the circuit will work normally. When the voltmeter is connected in series with a circuit, only a small amount of current can flow through the circuit. The circuit will not work properly, but the voltmeter reading will show if the circuit is complete or not.

Available Voltage Measurement

Set the voltmeter selector switch to the 20V position and connect the meter negative lead to the negative post of the battery. Connect the positive meter lead to the positive post of the battery and turn the ignition switch ON to provide a load. Read the voltage on the meter or digital display. A well charged battery should register over 12 volts. If the meter reads below 11.5 volts, the battery power may be insufficient to operate the electrical system properly. This test determines voltage available from the battery and should be the first step in any electrical trouble diagnosis procedure. Many electrical problems, especially on computer controlled systems, can be caused by a low state of charge in the battery. Excessive corrosion at the battery cable terminals can cause a poor contact that will prevent proper charging and full battery current flow.

Normal battery voltage is 12 volts when fully charged. When the battery is supplying current to one or more circuits it is said to be "under load". When everything is off the electrical system is under a "no-load" condition. A fully charged battery may show about 12.5 volts at no load; will drop to 12 volts under medium load; and will drop even lower under heavy load. If the battery is partially discharged the voltage decrease under heavy load may be excessive, even though the battery shows 12 volts or more at no load. When allowed to discharge further, the battery's available voltage under load will decrease more severely. For this reason, it is important that the battery be fully charged during all testing procedures to avoid errors in diagnosis and incorrect test results.

Voltage Drop

When current flows through a resistance, the voltage beyond the resistance is reduced (the larger the current, the greater the reduction in voltage). When no current is flowing, there is no voltage drop because there is no current flow. All points in the circuit which are connected to the power source are at the same voltage as the power source. The total voltage drop always equals the total source voltage. In a long circuit with many con-

nectors, a series of small, unwanted voltage drops due to corrosion at the connectors can add up to a total loss of voltage which impairs the operation of the normal loads in the circuit.

INDIRECT COMPUTATION OF VOLTAGE DROPS

1. Set the voltmeter selector switch to the 20 volt position.
2. Connect the meter negative lead to a good ground.
3. Probe all resistances in the circuit with the positive meter lead.
4. Operate the circuit in all modes and observe the voltage readings.

DIRECT MEASUREMENT OF VOLTAGE DROPS

1. Set the voltmeter switch to the 20 volt position.
2. Connect the voltmeter negative lead to the ground side of the resistance load to be measured.
3. Connect the positive lead to the positive side of the resistance or load to be measured.
4. Read the voltage drop directly on the 20 volt scale.

Too high a voltage indicates too high a resistance. If, for example, a blower motor runs too slowly, you can determine if there is too high a resistance in the resistor pack. By taking voltage drop readings in all parts of the circuit, you can isolate the problem. Too low a voltage drop indicates too low a resistance. If, for example, a blower motor runs too fast in the MED and/or LOW position, the problem can be isolated in the resistor pack by taking voltage drop readings in all parts of the circuit to locate a possibly shorted resistor. The maximum allowable voltage drop under load is critical, especially if there is more than one high resistance problem in a circuit because all voltage drops are cumulative. A small drop is normal due to the resistance of the conductors.

HIGH RESISTANCE TESTING

1. Set the voltmeter selector switch to the 4 volt position.
2. Connect the voltmeter positive lead to the positive post of the battery.
3. Turn on the headlights and heater blower to provide a load.
4. Probe various points in the circuit with the negative voltmeter lead.
5. Read the voltage drop on the 4 volt scale. Some average maximum allowable voltage drops are:

FUSE PANEL — 7 volts
IGNITION SWITCH — 5 volts
HEADLIGHT SWITCH — 7 volts
IGNITION COIL (+) — 5 volts
ANY OTHER LOAD — 1.3 volts

NOTE: Voltage drops are all measured while a load is operating; without current flow, there will be no voltage drop.

Ohmmeter

The ohmmeter is designed to read resistance (ohms) in a circuit or component. Although there are several different styles of ohmmeters, all will usually have a selector switch which permits the measurement of different ranges of resistance (usually the selector switch allows the multiplication of the meter reading by 10, 100, 1000, and 10,000). A calibration knob allows the meter to be set at zero for accurate measurement. Since all ohmmeters are powered by an internal battery (usually 9 volts), the ohmmeter can be used as a self-powered test light. When the ohmmeter is connected, current from the ohmmeter flows through the circuit or component being tested. Since the ohmmeter's internal resistance and voltage are known values, the amount of current flow through the meter depends on the resistance of the circuit or component being tested.

The ohmmeter can be used to perform continuity test for opens or shorts (either by observation of the meter needle or as a self-powered test light), and to read actual resistance in a circuit. It should be noted that the ohmmeter is used to check the resistance of a component or wire while there is no voltage applied to the circuit. Current flow from an outside voltage source (such as the vehicle battery) can damage the ohmmeter, so the circuit or component should be isolated from the vehicle electrical system before any testing is done. Since the ohmmeter uses its own voltage source, either lead can be connected to any test point.

NOTE: When checking diodes or other solid state components, the ohmmeter leads can only be connected one way in order to measure current flow in a single direction. Make sure the positive (+) and negative (-) terminal connections are as described in the test procedures to verify the one-way diode operation.

In using the meter for making continuity checks, do not be concerned with the actual resistance readings. Zero resistance, or any resistance readings, indicate continuity in the circuit. Infinite resistance indicates an open in the circuit. A high resistance reading where there should be none indicates a problem in the circuit. Checks for short circuits are made in the same manner as checks for open circuits except that the circuit must be isolated from both power and normal ground. Infinite resistance indicates no continuity to ground, while zero resistance indicates a dead short to ground.

RESISTANCE MEASUREMENT

The batteries in an ohmmeter will weaken with age and temperature, so the ohmmeter must be calibrated or "zeroed" before taking measurements. To zero the meter, place the selector switch in its lowest range and touch the two ohmmeter leads together. Turn the calibration knob until the meter needle is exactly on zero.

NOTE: All analog (needle) type ohmmeters must be zeroed before use, but some digital ohmmeter models are automatically calibrated when the switch is turned on. Self-calibrating digital ohmmeters do not have an adjusting knob, but its a good idea to check for a zero readout before use by touching the leads together. All computer controlled systems require the use of a digital ohmmeter with at least 10 megohms impedance for testing. Before any test procedures are attempted, make sure the ohmmeter used is compatible with the electrical system or damage to the on-board computer could result.

To measure resistance, first isolate the circuit from the vehicle power source by disconnecting the battery cables or the harness connector. Make sure the key is OFF when disconnecting any components or the battery. Where necessary, also isolate at least one side of the circuit to be checked to avoid reading parallel resistances. Parallel circuit resistances will always give a lower reading than the actual resistance of either of the branches. When measuring the resistance of parallel circuits, the total resistance will always be lower than the smallest resistance in the circuit. Connect the meter leads to both sides of the circuit (wire or component) and read the actual measured ohms on the meter scale. Make sure the selector switch is set to the proper ohm scale for the circuit being tested to avoid misreading the ohmmeter test value.

CAUTION

Never use an ohmmeter with power applied to the circuit. Like the self-powered test light, the ohmmeter is designed to operate on its own power supply. The normal 12 volt automotive electrical system current could damage the meter.

Ammeters

An ammeter measures the amount of current flowing through a circuit in units called amperes or amps. Amperes are units of electron flow which indicate how fast the electrons are flowing through the circuit. Since Ohms Law dictates that current flow in a circuit is equal to the circuit voltage divided by the total circuit resistance, increasing voltage also increases the current level (amps). Likewise, any decrease in resistance will increase the amount of amps in a circuit. At normal operating voltage, most circuits have a characteristic amount of amperes, called "current draw" which can be measured using an ammeter. By referring to a specified current draw rating, measuring the amperes, and comparing the two values, one can determine what is happening within the circuit to aid in diagnosis. An open circuit, for example, will not allow any current to flow so the ammeter reading will be zero. More current flows through a heavily loaded circuit or when the charging system is operating.

An ammeter is always connected in series with the circuit being tested. All of the current that normally flows through the circuit must also flow through the ammeter; if there is any other path for the current to follow, the ammeter reading will not be accurate. The ammeter itself has very little resistance to current flow and therefore will not affect the circuit, but it will measure current draw only when the circuit is closed and electricity is flowing. Excessive current draw can blow fuses and drain the battery, while a reduced current draw can cause motors to run slowly, lights to dim and other components to not operate properly. The ammeter can help diagnose these conditions by locating the cause of the high or low reading.

Multimeters

Different combinations of test meters can be built into a single unit designed for specific tests. Some of the more common combination test devices are known as Volt/Amp testers, Tach/Dwell meters, or Digital Multimeters. The Volt/Amp tester is used for charging system, starting system or battery tests and consists of a voltmeter, an ammeter and a variable resistance carbon pile. The voltmeter will usually have at least two ranges for use with 6, 12 and 24 volt systems. The ammeter also has more than one range for testing various levels of battery loads and starter current draw and the carbon pile can be adjusted to offer different amounts of resistance. The Volt/Amp tester has heavy leads to carry large amounts of current and many later models have an inductive ammeter pickup that clamps around the wire to simplify test connections. On some models, the ammeter also has a zero-center scale to allow testing of charging and starting systems without switching leads or polarity. A digital multimeter is a voltmeter, ammeter and ohmmeter combined in an instrument which gives a digital readout. These are often used when testing solid state circuits because of their high input impedance (usually 10 megohms or more).

The tach/dwell meter combines a tachometer and a dwell (cam angle) meter and is a specialized kind of voltmeter. The tachometer scale is marked to show engine speed in rpm and the dwell scale is marked to show degrees of distributor shaft rotation. In most electronic ignition systems, dwell is determined by the control unit, but the dwell meter can also be used to check the duty cycle (operation) of some electronic engine control systems. Some tach/dwell meters are powered by an internal battery, while others take their power from the car battery in use. The battery powered testers usually require calibration much like an ohmmeter before testing.

Special Test Equipment

A variety of diagnostic tools are available to help troubleshoot and repair computerized engine control systems. The most sophisticated of these devices are the console type engine analyzers that usually occupy a garage service bay, but there are several types of aftermarket electronic testers available that will allow quick circuit tests of the engine control system by plugging directly into a special connector located in the engine compartment or under the dashboard. Several tool and equipment manufacturers offer simple, hand held testers that measure various

6 CHASSIS ELECTRICAL

circuit voltage levels on command to check all system components for proper operation. Although these testers usually cost about $300-$500, consider that the average computer control unit (or ECM) can cost just as much and the money saved by not replacing perfectly good sensors or components in an attempt to correct a problem could justify the purchase price of a special diagnostic tester the first time it's used.

These computerized testers can allow quick and easy test measurements while the engine is operating or while the car is being driven. In addition, the on-board computer memory can be read to access any stored trouble codes; in effect allowing the computer to tell you where it hurts and aid trouble diagnosis by pinpointing exactly which circuit or component is malfunctioning. In the same manner, repairs can be tested to make sure the problem has been corrected. The biggest advantage these special testers have is their relatively easy hookups that minimize or eliminate the chances of making the wrong connections and getting false voltage readings or damaging the computer accidentally.

NOTE: It should be remembered that these testers check voltage levels in circuits; they don't detect mechanical problems or failed components if the circuit voltage falls within the preprogrammed limits stored in the tester PROM unit. Also, most of the hand held testes are designed to work only on one or two systems made by a specific manufacturer.

A variety of aftermarket testers are available to help diagnose different computerized control systems. Owatonna Tool Company (OTC), for example, markets a device called the OTC Monitor which plugs directly into the assembly line diagnostic link (ALDL). The OTC tester makes diagnosis a simple matter of pressing the correct buttons and, by changing the internal PROM or inserting a different diagnosis cartridge, it will work on any model from full size to subcompact, over a wide range of years. An adapter is supplied with the tester to allow connection to all types of ALDL links, regardless of the number of pin terminals used. By inserting an updated PROM into the OTC tester, it can be easily updated to diagnose any new modifications of computerized control systems.

Wiring Harnesses

The average automobile contains about ½ mile of wiring, with hundreds of individual connections. To protect the many wires from damage and to keep them from becoming a confusing tangle, they are organized into bundles, enclosed in plastic or taped together and called wire harnesses. Different wiring harnesses serve different parts of the vehicle. Individual wires are color coded to help trace them through a harness where sections are hidden from view.

A loose or corroded connection or a replacement wire that is too small for the circuit will add extra resistance and an additional voltage drop to the circuit. A ten percent voltage drop can result in slow or erratic motor operation, for example, even though the circuit is complete. Automotive wiring or circuit conductors can be in any one of three forms:
1. Single strand wire
2. Multistrand wire
3. Printed circuitry

Single strand wire has a solid metal core and is usually used inside such components as alternators, motors, relays and other devices. Multistrand wire has a core made of many small strands of wire twisted together into a single conductor. Most of the wiring in an automotive electrical system is made up of multistrand wire, either as a single conductor or grouped together in a harness. All wiring is color coded on the insulator, either as a solid color or as a colored wire with an identification stripe. A printed circuit is a thin film of copper or other conductor that is printed on an insulator backing. Occasionally, a printed circuit is sandwiched between two sheets of plastic for more protection and flexibility. A complete printed circuit, consisting of conductors, insulating material and connectors for lamps or other components is called a printed circuit board. Printed circuitry is used in place of individual wires or harnesses in places where space is limited, such as behind instrument panels.

Wire Gauge

Since computer controlled automotive electrical systems are very sensitive to changes in resistance, the selection of properly sized wires is critical when systems are repaired. The wire gauge number is an expression of the cross section area of the conductor. The most common system for expressing wire size is the American Wire Gauge (AWG) system.

Wire cross section area is measured in circular mils. A mil is $1/1000$ in. (0.001 in.); a circular mil is the area of a circle one mil in diameter. For example, a conductor ¼ in. in diameter is 0.250 in. or 250 mils. The circular mil cross section area of the wire is 250 squared (250^2) or 62,500 circular mils. Imported car models usually use metric wire gauge designations, which is simply the cross section area of the conductor in square millimeters (mm^2).

Gauge numbers are assigned to conductors of various cross section areas. As gauge number increases, area decreases and the conductor becomes smaller. A 5 gauge conductor is smaller than a 1 gauge conductor and a 10 gauge is smaller than a 5 gauge. As the cross section area of a conductor decreases, resistance increases and so does the gauge number. A conductor with a higher gauge number will carry less current than a conductor with a lower gauge number.

NOTE: Gauge wire size refers to the size of the conductor, not the size of the complete wire. It is possible to have two wires of the same gauge with different diameters because one may have thicker insulation than the other.

12 volt automotive electrical systems generally use 10, 12, 14, 16 and 18 gauge wire. Main power distribution circuits and larger accessories usually use 10 and 12 gauge wire. Battery cables are usually 4 or 6 gauge, although 1 and 2 gauge wires are occasionally used. Wire length must also be considered when making repairs to a circuit. As conductor length increases, so does resistance. An 18 gauge wire, for example, can carry a 10 amp load for 10 feet without excessive voltage drop; however if a 15 foot wire is required for the same 10 amp load, it must be a 16 gauge wire.

An electrical schematic shows the electrical current paths when a circuit is operating properly. It is essential to understand how a circuit works before trying to figure out why it doesn't. Schematics break the entire electrical system down into individual circuits and show only one particular circuit. In a schematic, no attempt is made to represent wiring and components as they physically appear on the vehicle; switches and other components are shown as simply as possible. Face views of harness connectors show the cavity or terminal locations in all multi-pin connectors to help locate test points.

If you need to backprobe a connector while it is on the component, the order of the terminals must be mentally reversed. The wire color code can help in this situation, as well as a keyway, lock tab or other reference mark.

NOTE: Wiring diagrams are not included in this book. As trucks have become more complex and available with longer option lists, wiring diagrams have grown in size and complexity. It has become almost impossible to provide a readable reproduction of a wiring diagram in a book this size. Information on ordering wiring diagrams from the vehicle manufacturer can be found in the owner's manual.

WIRING REPAIR

Soldering is a quick, efficient method of joining metals permanently. Everyone who has the occasion to make wiring repairs should know how to solder. Electrical connections that are soldered are far less likely to come apart and will conduct electricity much better than connections that are only "pig-tailed" together. The most popular (and preferred) method of soldering is with an electrical soldering gun. Soldering irons are available in many sizes and wattage ratings. Irons with higher wattage ratings deliver higher temperatures and recover lost heat faster. A small soldering iron rated for no more than 50 watts is recommended, especially on electrical systems where excess heat can damage the components being soldered.

There are three ingredients necessary for successful soldering; proper flux, good solder and sufficient heat. A soldering flux is necessary to clean the metal of tarnish, prepare it for soldering and to enable the solder to spread into tiny crevices. When soldering, always use a resin flux or resin core solder which is non-corrosive and will not attract moisture once the job is finished. Other types of flux (acid core) will leave a residue that will attract moisture and cause the wires to corrode. Tin is a unique metal with a low melting point. In a molten state, it dissolves and alloys easily with many metals. Solder is made by mixing tin with lead. The most common proportions are 40/60, 50/50 and 60/40, with the percentage of tin listed first. Low priced solders usually contain less tin, making them very difficult for a beginner to use because more heat is required to melt the solder. A common solder is 40/60 which is well suited for all-around general use, but 60/40 melts easier, has more tin for a better joint and is preferred for electrical work.

Soldering Techniques

Successful soldering requires that the metals to be joined be heated to a temperature that will melt the solder—usually 360-460°F (182-238°C). Contrary to popular belief, the purpose of the soldering iron is not to melt the solder itself, but to heat the parts being soldered to a temperature high enough to melt the solder when it is touched to the work. Melting flux-cored solder on the soldering iron will usually destroy the effectiveness of the flux.

NOTE: **Soldering tips are made of copper for good heat conductivity, but must be "tinned" regularly for quick transference of heat to the project and to prevent the solder from sticking to the iron. To "tin" the iron, simply heat it and touch the flux-cored solder to the tip; the solder will flow over the hot tip. Wipe the excess off with a clean rag, but be careful as the iron will be hot.**

After some use, the tip may become pitted. If so, simply dress the tip smooth with a smooth file and "tin" the tip again. An old saying holds that "metals well cleaned are half soldered." Flux-cored solder will remove oxides but rust, bits of insulation and oil or grease must be removed with a wire brush or emery cloth. For maximum strength in soldered parts, the joint must start off clean and tight. Weak joints will result in gaps too wide for the solder to bridge.

If a separate soldering flux is used, it should be brushed or swabbed on only those areas that are to be soldered. Most solders contain a core of flux and separate fluxing is unnecessary. Hold the work to be soldered firmly. It is best to solder on a wooden board, because a metal vise will only rob the piece to be soldered of heat and make it difficult to melt the solder. Hold the soldering tip with the broadest face against the work to be soldered. Apply solder under the tip close to the work, using enough solder to give a heavy film between the iron and the piece being soldered, while moving slowly and making sure the solder melts properly. Keep the work level or the solder will run to the lowest part and favor the thicker parts, because these require more heat to melt the solder. If the soldering tip overheats

(the solder coating on the face of the tip burns up), it should be retinned. Once the soldering is completed, let the soldered joint stand until cool. Tape and seal all soldered wire splices after the repair has cooled.

Wire Harness and Connectors

The on-board computer (ECM) wire harness electrically connects the control unit to the various solenoids, switches and sensors used by the control system. Most connectors in the engine compartment or otherwise exposed to the elements are protected against moisture and dirt which could create oxidation and deposits on the terminals. This protection is important because of the very low voltage and current levels used by the computer and sensors. All connectors have a lock which secures the male and female terminals together, with a secondary lock holding the seal and terminal into the connector. Both terminal locks must be released when disconnecting ECM connectors.

These special connectors are weather-proof and all repairs require the use of a special terminal and the tool required to service it. This tool is used to remove the pin and sleeve terminals. If removal is attempted with an ordinary pick, there is a good chance that the terminal will be bent or deformed. Unlike standard blade type terminals, these terminals cannot be straightened once they are bent. Make certain that the connectors are properly seated and all of the sealing rings in place when connecting leads. On some models, a hinge-type flap provides a backup or secondary locking feature for the terminals. Most secondary locks are used to improve the connector reliability by retaining the terminals if the small terminal lock tangs are not positioned properly.

Molded-on connectors require complete replacement of the connection. This means splicing a new connector assembly into the harness. All splices in on-board computer systems should be soldered to insure proper contact. Use care when probing the connections or replacing terminals in them as it is possible to short between opposite terminals. If this happens to the wrong terminal pair, it is possible to damage certain components. Always use jumper wires between connectors for circuit checking and never probe through weatherproof seals.

Open circuits are often difficult to locate by sight because corrosion or terminal misalignment are hidden by the connectors. Merely wiggling a connector on a sensor or in the wiring harness may correct the open circuit condition. This should always be considered when an open circuit or a failed sensor is indicated. Intermittent problems may also be caused by oxidized or loose connections. When using a circuit tester for diagnosis, always probe connections from the wire side. Be careful not to damage sealed connectors with test probes.

All wiring harnesses should be replaced with identical parts, using the same gauge wire and connectors. When signal wires are spliced into a harness, use wire with high temperature insulation only. With the low voltage and current levels found in the system, it is important that the best possible connection at all wire splices be made by soldering the splices together. It is seldom necessary to replace a complete harness. If replacement is necessary, pay close attention to insure proper harness routing. Secure the harness with suitable plastic wire clamps to prevent vibrations from causing the harness to wear in spots or contact any hot components.

NOTE: **Weatherproof connectors cannot be replaced with standard connectors. Instructions are provided with replacement connector and terminal packages. Some wire harnesses have mounting indicators (usually pieces of colored tape) to mark where the harness is to be secured.**

In making wiring repairs, it's important that you always replace damaged wires with wires that are the same gauge as the wire being replaced. The heavier the wire, the smaller the gauge number. Wires are color-coded to aid in identification and whenever possible the same color coded wire should be used for replacement. A wire stripping and crimping tool is necessary to install solderless terminal connectors. Test all crimps by pulling on the wires; it should not be possible to pull the wires out of a good crimp.

Wires which are open, exposed or otherwise damaged are repaired by simple splicing. Where possible, if the wiring harness is accessible and the damaged place in the wire can be located, it is best to open the harness and check for all possible damage. In an inaccessible harness, the wire must be bypassed with a new insert, usually taped to the outside of the old harness.

When replacing fusible links, be sure to use fusible link wire, NOT ordinary automotive wire. Make sure the fusible segment is of the same gauge and construction as the one being replaced and double the stripped end when crimping the terminal connector for a good contact. The melted (open) fusible link segment of the wiring harness should be cut off as close to the harness as possible, then a new segment spliced in as described. In the case of a damaged fusible link that feeds two harness wires, the harness connections should be replaced with two fusible link wires so that each circuit will have its own separate protection.

NOTE: Most of the problems caused in the wiring harness are due to bad ground connections. Always check all vehicle ground connections for corrosion or looseness before performing any power feed checks to eliminate the chance of a bad ground affecting the circuit.

Repairing Hard Shell Connectors

Unlike molded connectors, the terminal contacts in hard shell connectors can be replaced. Weatherproof hard-shell connectors with the leads molded into the shell have non-replaceable terminal ends. Replacement usually involves the use of a special terminal removal tool that depress the locking tangs (barbs) on the connector terminal and allow the connector to be removed from the rear of the shell. The connector shell should be replaced if it shows any evidence of burning, melting, cracks, or breaks. Replace individual terminals that are burnt, corroded, distorted or loose.

NOTE: The insulation crimp must be tight to prevent the insulation from sliding back on the wire when the wire is pulled. The insulation must be visibly compressed under the crimp tabs, and the ends of the crimp should be turned in for a firm grip on the insulation.

The wire crimp must be made with all wire strands inside the crimp. The terminal must be fully compressed on the wire strands with the ends of the crimp tabs turned in to make a firm grip on the wire. Check all connections with an ohmmeter to insure a good contact. There should be no measurable resistance between the wire and the terminal when connected.

Mechanical Test Equipment

Vacuum Gauge

Most gauges are graduated in inches of mercury (in.Hg), although a device called a manometer reads vacuum in inches of water (in. H_2O). The normal vacuum reading usually varies between 18 and 22 in.Hg at sea level. To test engine vacuum, the vacuum gauge must be connected to a source of manifold vacuum. Many engines have a plug in the intake manifold which can be removed and replaced with an adapter fitting. Connect the vacuum gauge to the fitting with a suitable rubber hose or, if no manifold plug is available, connect the vacuum gauge to any device using manifold vacuum, such as EGR valves, etc. The vacuum gauge can be used to determine if enough vacuum is reaching a component to allow its actuation.

Hand Vacuum Pump

Small, hand-held vacuum pumps come in a variety of designs. Most have a built-in vacuum gauge and allow the component to be tested without removing it from the vehicle. Operate the pump lever or plunger to apply the correct amount of vacuum required for the test specified in the diagnosis routines. The level of vacuum in inches of Mercury (in.Hg) is indicated on the pump gauge. For some testing, an additional vacuum gauge may be necessary.

Intake manifold vacuum is used to operate various systems and devices on late model vehicles. To correctly diagnose and solve problems in vacuum control systems, a vacuum source is necessary for testing. In some cases, vacuum can be taken from the intake manifold when the engine is running, but vacuum is normally provided by a hand vacuum pump. These hand vacuum pumps have a built-in vacuum gauge that allow testing while the device is still attached to the component. For some tests, an additional vacuum gauge may be necessary.

HEATING AND AIR CONDITIONING

Blower Motor and/or Heater Core

REMOVAL AND INSTALLATION

Heater Core

1. Drain the cooling system.

—————————— CAUTION ——————————

When draining the coolant, keep in mind that cats and dogs are attracted by the ethylene glycol antifreeze, and are quite likely to drink any that is left in an uncovered container or in puddles on the ground. This will prove fatal in sufficient quantity. Always drain the coolant into a sealable container. Coolant should be reused unless it is contaminated or several years old.

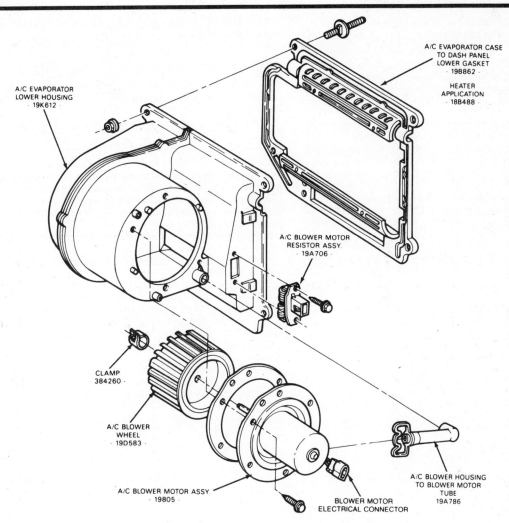

Blower motor and wheel

2. Disconnect the heater hoses at the core tubes in the engine compartment.

3. Remove the instrument panel lower trim panel.

4. Remove the heater core cover from the left side of the heater case (4 screws).

5. Remove the core retaining screw and bracket from the case.

6. Lift out the heater core and seal.

7. Installation is the reverse of removal. If the seal was damaged, replace it.

Blower Motor

1. Disconnect the wiring at the motor.

2. Remove the 4 mounting screws and lift the blower from the case.

3. Installation is the reverse of removal.

Auxiliary Hot Water Heater

REMOVAL AND INSTALLATION

Auxiliary Heater Case (With or Without Air Conditioning)

1. Remove the first bench seat (if so equipped).

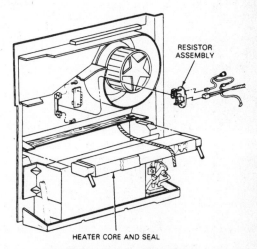

Auxiliary core and resistor

2. Discharge the air conditioning system, if so equipped. See Section 1.

3. Remove the auxiliary heater and/or air conditioning cover assembly attaching screws and remove the cover.

4. Drain the cooling system.

─────── CAUTION ───────

When draining the coolant, keep in mind that cats and dogs are attracted by the ethylene glycol antifreeze, and are quite likely to drink any that is left in an uncovered container or in puddles on the ground. This will prove fatal in sufficient quantity. Always drain the coolant into a sealable container. Coolant should be reused unless it is contaminated or several years old.

5. Disconnect the heater hoses from the core tubes.
6. On air conditioning systems, disconnect the liquid line from the expansion valve and the suction line from the evaporator core, using a back-up wrench on the fittings. Cap the lines immediately.
7. From under the van, disconnect the blower motor wiring.
8. Remove the case retaining screws. Lift the case, disengaging the wiring harness grommet from the floor seal, and remove the case.
9. Make sure that all seals and grommets are in good condition and in place. Route the wiring harness through the floor seal.
10. Position the case assembly on the floor and install the retaining screws.
11. Connect the heater hoses. Tighten the hose clamps to 12-18 in. lbs.
12. If equipped with air conditioning, connect the refrigerant lines, using new O-rings coated with clean refrigerant oil. Tighten the fitting using a back-up wrench.
13. Fill the cooling system.
14. Evacuate, charge and leak test the refrigerant system. See Section 1.
15. Run the engine and check for leaks in both the cooling and refrigerant systems.

16. Install the bench seat (if removed) and tighten the retaining bolts 25-45 ft. lbs.

Auxiliary Heater Core and Seal Assembly

1. Remove the first bench seat (if so equipped).
2. Remove auxiliary heater and/or air conditioning cover attaching screws and remove the cover.
3. Partially drain the engine coolant from the cooling system.

─────── CAUTION ───────

When draining the coolant, keep in mind that cats and dogs are attracted by the ethylene glycol antifreeze, and are quite likely to drink any that is left in an uncovered container or in puddles on the ground. This will prove fatal in sufficient quantity. Always drain the coolant into a sealable container. Coolant should be reused unless it is contaminated or several years old.

4. Remove the heater hoses from the auxiliary heater core assembly (2 clamps).
5. Pull the wiring assembly away from the heater core seal.
6. Remove and discard the strap retaining the heater core. Slide the heater core and seal assembly out of the housing slot.
7. Slide the heater core and seal assembly into the housing slot (position the wiring to one side).
8. Install the heater hoses to the heater core assembly (2 clamps).
9. Fill the cooling system to specification.
10. Position the cover assembly to the body side panel and install the attaching screws (15).
11. Install the bench seat (if removed) and tighten the retaining bolts 25-45 ft. lbs.

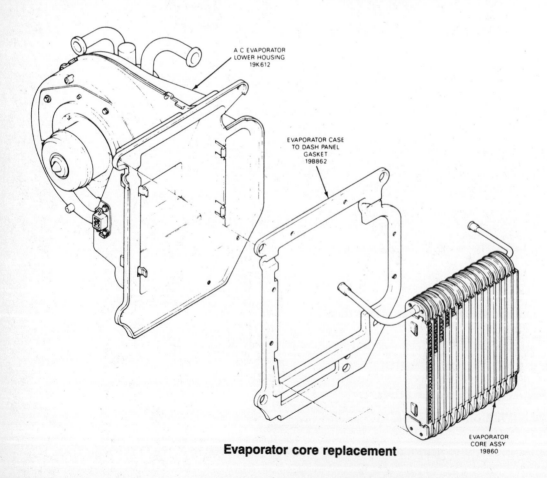

Evaporator core replacement

Evaporator Core

REMOVAL AND INSTALLATION

1. Disconnect all wiring and vacuum connections at the case.
2. Remove the battery(ies).
3. Disconnect the EEC-IV harness.
4. Drain the cooling system.

CAUTION

When draining the coolant, keep in mind that cats and dogs are attracted by the ethylene glycol antifreeze, and are quite likely to drink any that is left in an uncovered container or in puddles on the ground. This will prove fatal in sufficient quantity. Always drain the coolant into a sealable container. Coolant should be reused unless it is contaminated or several years old.

---

5. Discharge the refrigerant system. See Section 1.
6. Disconnect the suction and liquid lines at the receiver/drier and core. Use a back-up wrench on the fittings. Plug all openings immediately.
7. Disconnect the heater hoses at the core.

8. Unbolt and remove the evaporator case from under the instrument panel (5 bolts).
9. Remove the receiver/drier from the case.
10. Remove the accumulator from the case.
11. Pull back the retaining tab and lift the core from the case.
12. Installation is the reverse of removal. Use new O-rings coated with clean refrigerant oil and use a back-up wrench on the fittings. Evacuate, charge and leak test the system. See Section 1.

Auxiliary Evaporator Core

REMOVAL AND INSTALLATION

1. Remove the first bench seat.
2. Remove the cover assembly retaining screws and lift off the cover.
3. Discharge the refrigerant system. See Section 1.
4. Disconnect the liquid and suction lines from the receiver/drier and core. Use a back-up wrench on the fittings. Cap all openings at once.

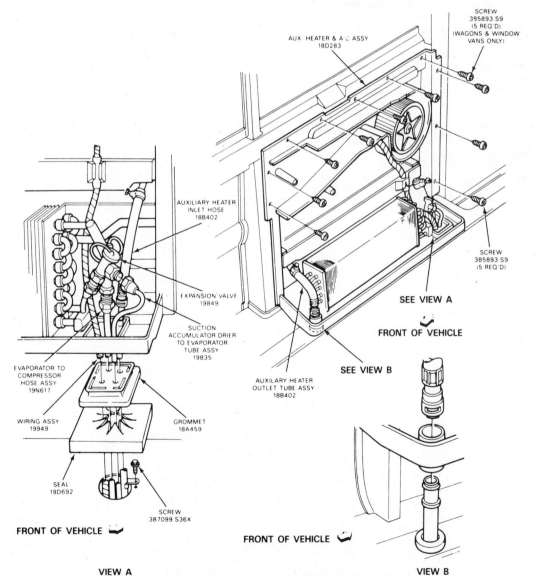

Side mounted auxiliary air conditioner/heater

5. Drain the cooling system.

───── CAUTION ─────

When draining the coolant, keep in mind that cats and dogs are attracted by the ethylene glycol antifreeze, and are quite likely to drink any that is left in an uncovered container or in puddles on the ground. This will prove fatal in sufficient quantity. Always drain the coolant into a sealable container. Coolant should be reused unless it is contaminated or several years old.

6. Disconnect the hoses from the heater core.
7. Remove the 4 core and bracket retaining bolts and lift the core and expansion valve from the case.

NOTE: Any time that the core is replaced, a new suction accumulator drier must be installed.

8. When installing the expansion valve on the core, use new O-rings coated with clean refrigerant oil on the line fittings. Tighten the expansion valve fittings, using a back-up wrench, to 15-20 ft. lbs.
9. Clamp the expansion valve capillary bulb to the core outlet tube making sure that the bulb makes good contact with the outlet tube. Make sure that both components are clean. Wrap the bulb and tube with insulating tape such as Motorcraft YZ-1.
10. Wrap the ends of the core with insulating tape.
11. Attach the mounting plate to the expansion valve end of the core.
12. Carefully position the core in the case.
13. Connect the refrigerant lines, using new O-rings coated with clean refrigerant oil. Torque the fittings to 30-35 ft. lbs. for the suction line and 10-15 ft.lb for the liquid line. Use a back-up wrench on the fittings.
14. Install the core-to-case screws.
15. Connect the heater hoses. Tighten the clamps to 12-18 inch lbs. DO NOT OVERTIGHTEN THE CLAMPS!
16. Fill the cooling system.
17. Evacuate, charge and leak test the system.
18. Install the cover.
19. Install the bench seat. Torque the bolts to 25-45 ft. lbs.

Control Unit
REMOVAL AND INSTALLATION

Heater and/or Air Conditioner

1. Remove the trim applique.

2. Remove the 4 control unit retaining screws.
3. Slowly pull the control unit from the instrument panel.
4. Disconnect the electrical connectors, vacuum lines and light bulb. The control cable can be disconnected using needlenosed pliers to depress the tabs. The cable S-bend is removed by rotating the cable wire 90° to the lever.
5. Installation is the reverse of removal. Adjust the cable, if necessary.

Blower Switch
REMOVAL AND INSTALLATION

1. Remove the control unit, but don't disconnect the cables.
2. Remove the knobs by depressing the spring retainer and pull the knobs off.
3. Unplug the blower switch wiring.
4. Remove the blower switch attaching screw.
5. Installation is the reverse of removal.

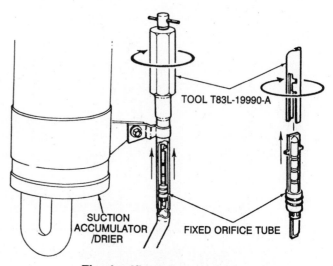

Fixed orifice tube removal

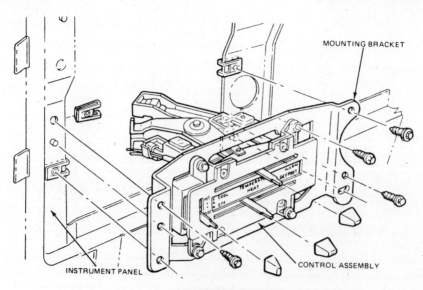

Control unit

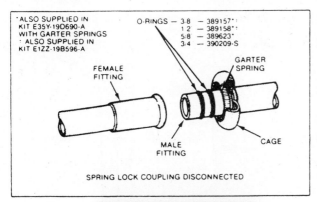

*ALSO SUPPLIED IN KIT E35Y-19D690-A WITH GARTER SPRINGS
* ALSO SUPPLIED IN KIT E1ZZ-19B596-A

O-RINGS — 3.8 — 389157*
          1 2 — 389158*
          5 8 — 389623*
          3 4 — 390209-S

FEMALE FITTING

GARTER SPRING

MALE FITTING

CAGE

SPRING LOCK COUPLING DISCONNECTED

TO DISCONNECT COUPLING

CAUTION — DISCHARGE SYSTEM BEFORE DISCONNECTING COUPLING

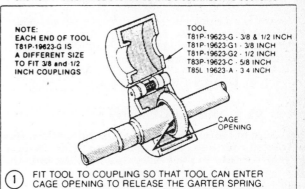

NOTE:
EACH END OF TOOL T81P-19623-G IS A DIFFERENT SIZE TO FIT 3/8 and 1/2 INCH COUPLINGS

TOOL
T81P-19623-G · 3/8 & 1/2 INCH
T81P-19623-G1 · 3/8 INCH
T81P-19623-G2 · 1/2 INCH
T83P-19623-C · 5/8 INCH
T85L 19623-A · 3 4 INCH

CAGE OPENING

(1) FIT TOOL TO COUPLING SO THAT TOOL CAN ENTER CAGE OPENING TO RELEASE THE GARTER SPRING.

TO CONNECT COUPLING

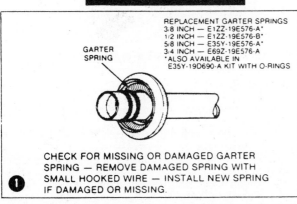

GARTER SPRING

REPLACEMENT GARTER SPRINGS
3.8 INCH — E1ZZ-19E576-A*
1/2 INCH — E1ZZ-19E576-B*
5/8 INCH — E35Y-19E576-A*
3/4 INCH — E69Z-19E576-A
*ALSO AVAILABLE IN E35Y-19D690-A KIT WITH O-RINGS

(1) CHECK FOR MISSING OR DAMAGED GARTER SPRING — REMOVE DAMAGED SPRING WITH SMALL HOOKED WIRE — INSTALL NEW SPRING IF DAMAGED OR MISSING.

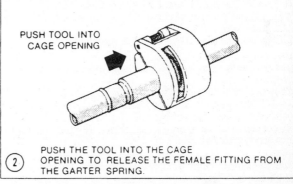

PUSH TOOL INTO CAGE OPENING

(2) PUSH THE TOOL INTO THE CAGE OPENING TO RELEASE THE FEMALE FITTING FROM THE GARTER SPRING.

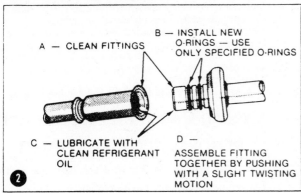

A — CLEAN FITTINGS

B — INSTALL NEW O-RINGS — USE ONLY SPECIFIED O-RINGS

C — LUBRICATE WITH CLEAN REFRIGERANT OIL

D — ASSEMBLE FITTING TOGETHER BY PUSHING WITH A SLIGHT TWISTING MOTION

(2)

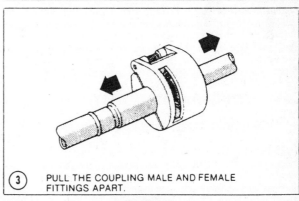

(3) PULL THE COUPLING MALE AND FEMALE FITTINGS APART.

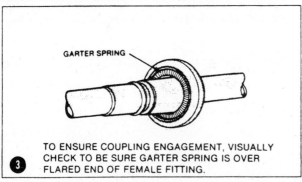

GARTER SPRING

(3) TO ENSURE COUPLING ENGAGEMENT, VISUALLY CHECK TO BE SURE GARTER SPRING IS OVER FLARED END OF FEMALE FITTING.

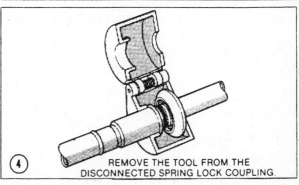

(4) REMOVE THE TOOL FROM THE DISCONNECTED SPRING LOCK COUPLING.

Quick-disconnect couplings and tools

Vacuum Selector Valve

REMOVAL AND INSTALLATION

With or Without Air Conditioning

1. Remove the control unit, but don't disconnect the cables.
2. Remove the selector valve attaching screws.
3. Remove the attaching nuts and disconnect the harness.
4. Installation is the reverse of removal.

Fixed Orifice Tube

REPLACEMENT

NOTE: Do not attempt to remove the tube with pliers or to twist or rotate the tube in the evaporator. To do so will break the tube in the evaporator core. Use only the tools recommended in the procedure.

1. Discharge the system. See Section 1.
2. Using back-up wrenches or a quick-disconnect coupling tool, disconnect the liquid line. Cap all openings at once!
3. Pour a small amount of clean refrigerant oil into the core inlet tube to ease removal.
4. Using remover tool T83L-19990-A, engage the 2 tangs on the orifice tube. DON NOT TWIST OR ROTATE THE TUBE!
5. Tighten the nut on the tool until the orifice tube is withdrawn from the core.
6. If the orifice tube breaks in the core, it must be extracted using tool T-83L-1990-B. Thread the end of the tool into the brass tube end of the orifice tube. Pull the orifice tube from the core. If only the brass tube comes out, thread the tool back into the orifice body and pull that out.

To install:

7. Coat the new O-rings with clean refrigerant oil. Place the O-rings on the new orifice tube.
8. Place the new orifice tube onto tool T83L-1990-A and insert it into the core until it is seated at its stop. Remove the tool.
9. Using a new O-ring coated with clean refrigerant oil, connect the liquid line. Push the coupling firmly together until is snaps securely. Test the coupling by trying to pull it apart.
10. Evacuate, charge and leak test the system. See Section 1.

Accumulator/Drier

REMOVAL AND INSTALLATION

1. Discharge the refrigerant system. See Section 1.
2. Disconnect the wiring from the pressure switch.
3. Unscrew the pressure switch from the accumulator.
4. Using a back-up wrench, disconnect the suction hose from the accumulator. Cap all openings at once!
5. Using a back-up wrench, loosen the accumulator-to-evaporator fitting.
6. Remove the 2 accumulator attaching strap screws, remove the inlet tube clip and remove the accumulator. Cap all openings at once!

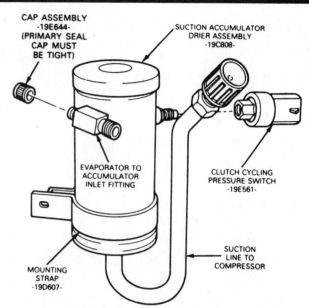

Accumulator/drier assembly

To install:

7. Using a new O-ring coated with clean refrigerant oil, connect the accumulator-to-evaporator fitting. Turn the fitting nut hand tight.
8. Install the retaining strap tube clip and tighten the strap screws hand tight.
9. Loosen the fitting and make sure everything is correctly aligned, then tighten the strap screws. After the strap screws are tightened, and you're satisfied that the accumulator is properly aligned, tighten the fitting, using a back-up wrench.
10. Using a new O-ring coated with clean refrigerant oil, connect the suction hose. Use a back-up wrench.
11. Using a new O-ring coated with clean refrigerant oil, install the pressure switch. Torque the switch to 10 ft. lbs. if the switch has a metal base. If the switch has a plastic base, handtighten it only!
12. Connect the wiring.
13. Evacuate, charge and lean test the system. See Section 1.

Cycling Clutch Pressure Switch

REMOVAL AND INSTALLATION

NOTE: It is not necessary to discharge the system.

1. Disconnect the wiring at the switch.
2. Unscrew the switch from the accumulator.
3. When installing the switch, always use a new O-ring coated with clean refrigerant oil. Torque the switch to 10 ft. lbs. if the switch has a metal base. If the switch has a plastic base, handtighten it only!
4. Connect the wiring.

RADIO

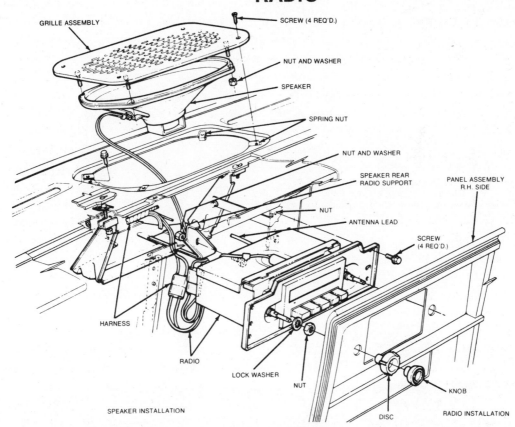

GRILLE ASSEMBLY

SCREW (4 REQ'D.)

NUT AND WASHER

SPEAKER

SPRING NUT

NUT AND WASHER

SPEAKER REAR RADIO SUPPORT

NUT

ANTENNA LEAD

PANEL ASSEMBLY R.H. SIDE

SCREW (4 REQ'D.)

HARNESS

RADIO

LOCK WASHER

NUT

KNOB

DISC

SPEAKER INSTALLATION

RADIO INSTALLATION

Radio installation

REMOVAL AND INSTALLATION

1. Detach the battery ground cable.
2. Remove the heater and air conditioning control knobs. Remove the lighter.
3. Remove the radio knobs and discs.
4. If the van has a lighter, snap out the name plate at the right side to remove the panel attaching screw.
5. Remove the five finish panel screws.
6. Very carefully pry out the cluster panel in two places.
7. Detach the antenna lead and speaker wires.
8. Remove the two nuts and washers and the mounting plate.
9. Remove the four front radio attaching screws. Remove the rear support nut and washer and remove the radio.
10. Reverse the procedure for installation.

WINDSHIELD WIPERS

Wiper Motor

REMOVAL AND INSTALLATION

1. Disconnect the battery ground.

2. Remove the fuse panel and bracket.
3. Disconnect the motor wiring.
4. Remove the wiper arms.
5. Remove the outer air intake cowl.
6. Remove the motor linkage clip.

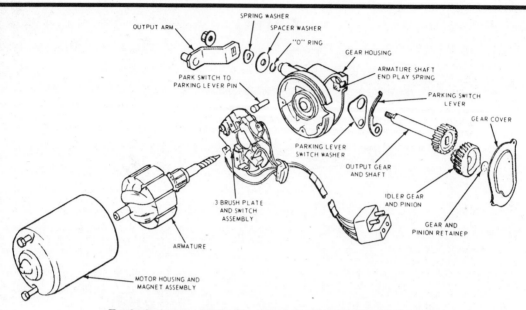

Exploded view of the two-speed windshield wiper motor

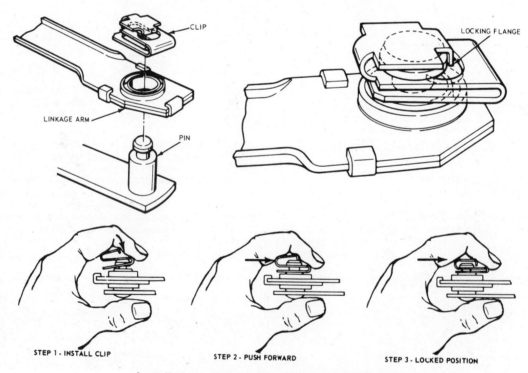

Installation of the wiper arm connecting clip

7. Remove the motor mounting bolts and lift out the motor.
8. Transfer the motor drive arm if a new motor is being installed.
9. Make sure the motor is in PARK and install it.
10. Connect the linkage.
11. Connect the wiring.
12. Install the cowl panel.
13. Install the wiper arms.
14. Install the fuse panel and bracket.
15. Check the motor operation.

Linkage
REMOVAL AND INSTALLATION

1. Diconnect the battery ground.
2. Remove the wiper arms.
3. Detach the washer hoses.
4. Remove the cowl.
5. Remove the linkage clips.
6. Remove the pivot-to-cowl screws and remove the linkage.
7. Installation is the reverse of removal.

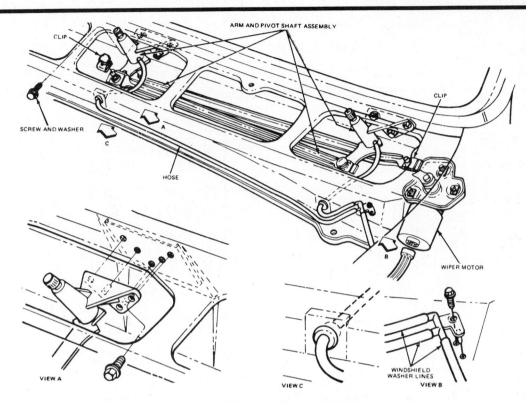

Wiper motor and linkage

SPEED CONTROL SYSTEM

Control Switches

See Section 8, under Steering Wheel Removal and Installation.

Speed Sensor

REMOVAL AND INSTALLATION

1. Unplug the wiring at the sensor on the transmission.
2. Disconnect the speedometer cable from the speed sensor.
3. Remove the retaining bolt and remove the sensor. Remove the drive gear.
4. Installation is the reverse of removal.

Amplifier

REMOVAL AND INSTALLATION

1. Disconnect the wiring at the amplifier, located behind the instrument panel.

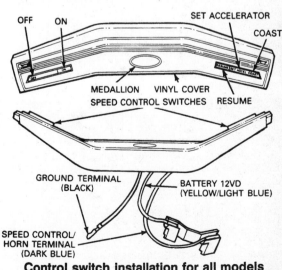

Control switch installation for all models

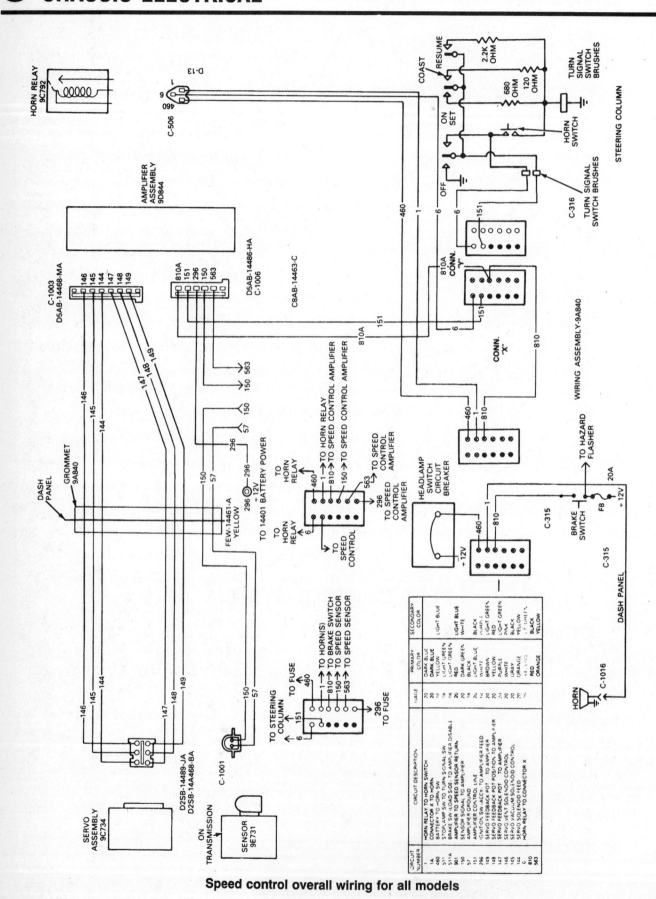

Speed control overall wiring for all models

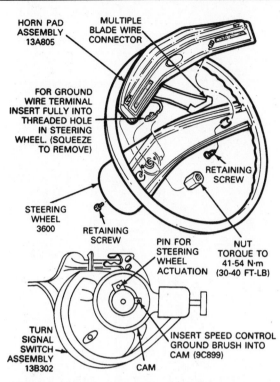

Wiring routing for the speed control switch

2. Remove the amplifier mounting bracket attaching screws or nuts and remove the amplifier and bracket.
3. Remove the amplifier from the bracket.
4. Installation is the reverse of removal.

Servo Assembly

The servo is the throttle actuator and is located under the hood.

REMOVAL AND INSTALLATION

1. Disconnect the wiring at the servo.
2. Disconnect the adjuster from the accelerator cable.
3. Disconnect the vacuum line at the servo.
4. Remove the actuator cable-to-bracket screw.
5. Remove the pins and nuts retaining the servo to its mounting bracket and lift it out.
6. Installation is the reverse of removal.

LINKAGE ADJUSTMENT

1. Snap the molded cable retainer over the accelerator cable end fitting attached, to the throttle ball stud.
2. Remove the adjuster retainer clip, if installed, from the adjuster mounting tab.
3. Insert the speed control actuator cable adjuster mounting tab in the slot provided in the accelerator cable support bracket.
4. Pull the cable through the adjuster until a slight tension is felt **without** opening the throttle plate.
5. Insert the adjuster cable retainer clip slowly, until engagement is felt, then, push it downwards until it locks in position.

Vacuum Dump Valve

REMOVAL AND INSTALLATION

1. Remove the vacuum hose at the valve.
2. Remove the valve and bracket. Separate the valve from the bracket.
3. Installation is the reverse of removal.

ADJUSTMENT

The dump valve disconnects the speed control whenever the brake pedal is depressed.
1. Make sure that the brake pedal is fully released and the valve's plunger is in contact with the brake pedal adapter.
2. Move the valve forward in its retaining clip until 3mm (1/8 in.) of the valve plunger is exposed.
3. Make sure that the brake pedal is still in the fully released position — against its stop.

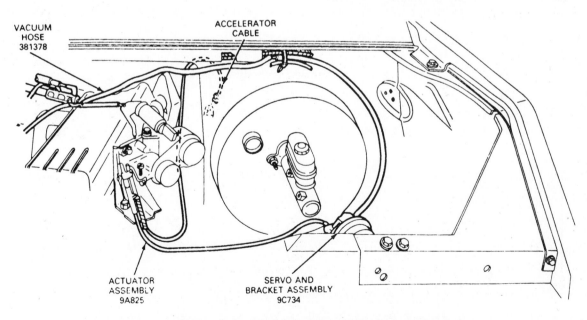

Servo and cable for all models with the 6-4.9L

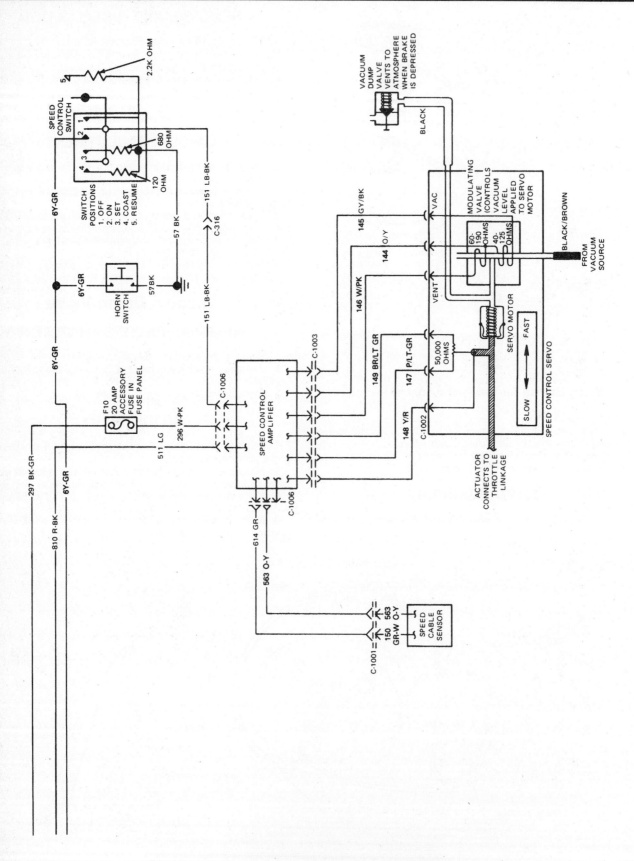

Speed control main wiring diagram for all models

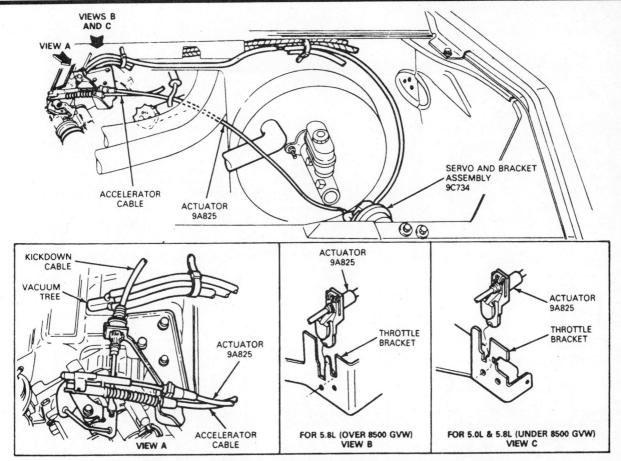

Servo and cable for all models with the 8-5.0L and 8- 5.8L

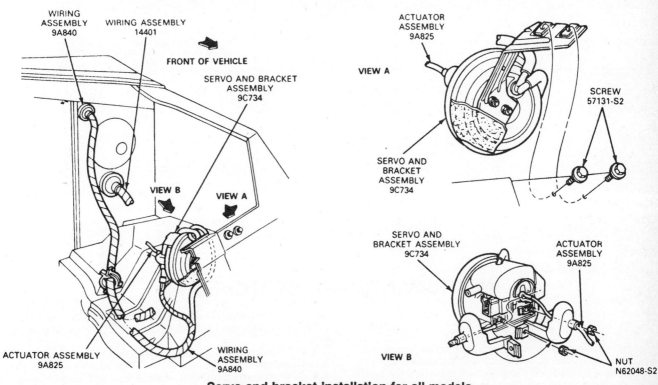

Servo and bracket installation for all models

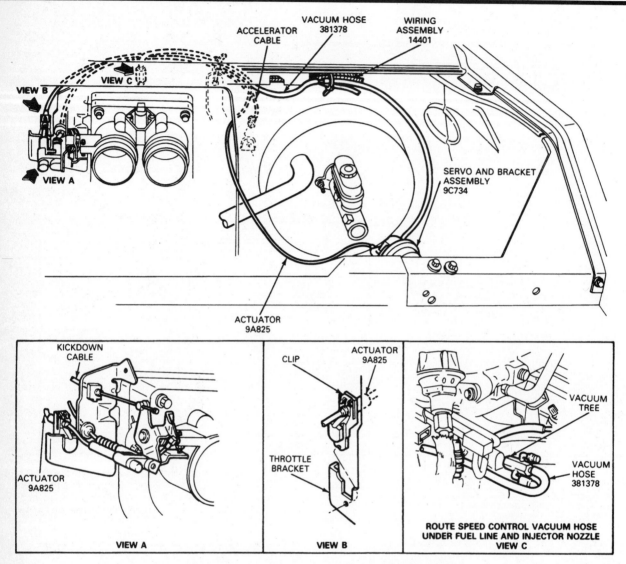

Servo and cable for all models with the 8-7.5L

INSTRUMENTS AND SWITCHES

Precautions

Electronic modules, such as instrument clusters, powertrain controls and sound systems are sensitive to static electricity and can be damaged by static discharges which are below the levels that you can hear "snap" or detect on your skin. A detectable snap or shock of static electricity is in the 3,000 volt range. Some of these modules can be damaged by a charge of as little as 100 volts.

The following are some basic safeguards to avoid static electrical damage:
• Leave the replacement module in its original packing until you are ready to install it.

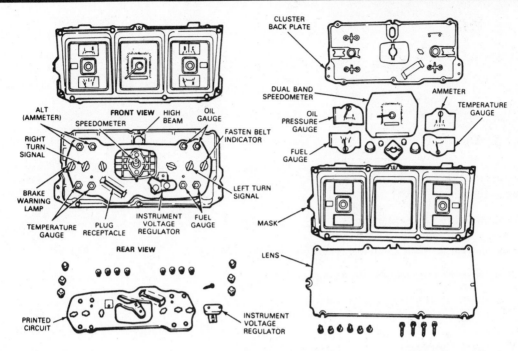

Instrument Cluster

- Avoid touching the module connector pins
- Avoid placing the module on a non-conductive surface
- Use a commercially available static protection kit. These kits contain such things as grounding cords and conductive mats.

Instrument Cluster

REMOVAL AND INSTALLATION

1. Disconnect the battery ground cable.
2. Remove the two steering column shroud to panel retaining screws and remove the shroud.
3. Loosen the bolts which attach the column to the B and C support to provide sufficient clearance for cluster removal. (Required for tilt steering column vehicles only).
4. Remove the seven instrument cluster to panel retaining screws.
5. Position the cluster slightly away from the panel for access to the back of the cluster to disconnect the speedometer.

   If there is not sufficient access to disengage the speedometer cable form the speedometer, it may be necessary to remove the speedometer cable at the transmission and pull the cable through the cowl, to allow room to reach the speedometer quick disconnect.
6. Disconnect the harness connector plug from the printed circuit board and remove the cluster assembly from the instrument panel.
7. Apply an approximately $\frac{1}{16}$ in. diameter ball of silicone lubricant or equivalent in the drive hole of the speedometer head.
8. Position the cluster near its opening in the instrument panel.
9. Connect the harness connector plug to the printed circuit board.
10. Connect the speedometer cable (quick disconnect) to the speedometer head.
11. Connect the speedometer cable and housing assembly to the transmission (if removed).
12. Install the seven instrument cluster-to-panel retaining screws and connect the battery ground cable.

13. Check the operation of all gauges, lights, and signals.
14. Install the steering column.
15. Position the steering column shroud on the instrument panel and install the two screws.

Speedometer Cable

NOTE: These vans have a speed sensor attached to the transmission. This device sends information on vehicle speed to the Engine Management System and Speed Control System. For replacement of this unit, see the procedures below.

REMOVAL AND INSTALLATION

1. Reach up behind the cluster and disconnect the cable by depressing the quick disconnect tab and pulling the cable away.
2. Remove the cable from the casing. If the cable is broken, raise the vehicle on a hoist and disconnect the cable from the transmission.
3. Remove the cable from the casing.

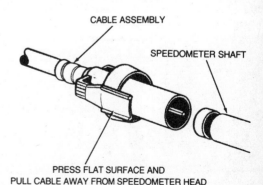

Speedometer cable quick-disconnect

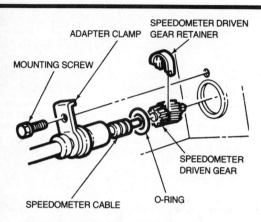

Speedometer cable drive gear end

4. To remove the casing from the vehicle pull it through the floor pan.

5. To replace the cable, slide the new cable into the casing and connect it at the transmission.

6. Route the cable through the floor pan and position the grommet in its groove in the floor.

7. Push the cable onto the speedometer head.

Speed Sensor

REMOVAL AND INSTALLATION

1. Unplug the wiring at the sensor on the transmission.

2. Disconnect the speedometer cable from the speed sensor.

3. Remove the retaining bolt and remove the sensor. Remove the drive gear.

4. Installation is the reverse of removal.

Speedometer Head

REMOVAL AND INSTALLATION

1. Remove the instrument cluster.

2. Disconnect the cable from the head.

3. Remove the lens and any surrounding trim.

4. Remove the 2 attaching screws.

5. Installation is the reverse of removal. Place a glob of silicone grease on the end of the cable core prior to connection.

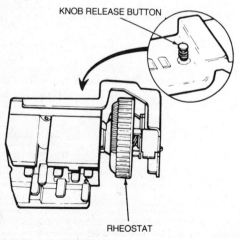

Headlight switch

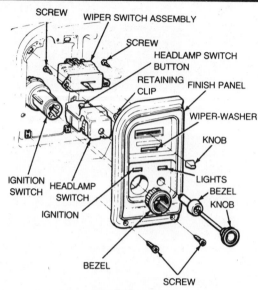

Wiper switch

Windshield Wiper Switch

REPLACEMENT

1. Disconnect the negative battery cable.

2. Remove the windshield wiper switch knob.

3. Remove the ignition switch bezel.

4. Remove the headlamp switch knob and shaft by pulling the switch to the headlamp **ON** position then depress the button on top of the switch and pull the knob and shaft out of the headlamp switch.

5. Remove the two screws at the bottom of the finish panel. Then, carefully pry the two upper retainers away from the instrument panel assembly.

6. Disconnect the connector from the wiper switch.

7. Remove the wiper switch attaching screws and remove the switch.

8. Reverse the procedure for installation.

Headlight Switch

REPLACEMENT

1. Remove the headlamp control knob and shaft by pressing the knob release button on the switch housing, with the knob in the full ON position.

2. Pull the knob and shaft assembly out of the switch.

3. Remove the switch, then remove the wiring connector from the switch.

4. To install the switch, connect the wiring connector to the headlamp switch, position the switch in the instrument panel, and install the bezel and mounting nut.

5. Install the knob and shaft assembly by inserting it all the way into the switch until a distinct click is heard. In some instances it may be necessary to rotate the shaft slightly until it engages the switch contact carrier.

6. Connect the battery ground cable.

Ignition Switch and Lock Cylinder

REMOVAL AND INSTALLATION

These are steering column mounted units. For service procedures, see Section 8.

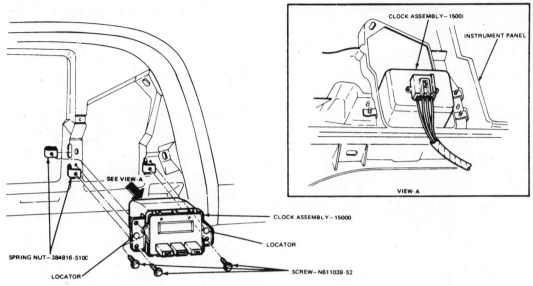

Electronic clock replacement

Clock
REMOVAL AND INSTALLATION

1. Disconnect the battery ground.

2. Remove the instrument finish panel covering the clock.
3. Remove the three clock retaining screws.
4. Pull the clock out and disconnect the wiring.
5. Installation is the reverse of removal.

LIGHTING

Headlights

REMOVAL AND INSTALLATION

1. Loosen or remove the headlight retaining ring by rotating it counterclockwise. Do not disturb the adjusting screw settings.
2. Pull the headlight bulb forward and disconnect the wiring assembly plug from the bulb.
3. Connect the wiring assembly plug to the new bulb. Place the bulb in position, making sure that the locating tabs of the bulb are fitted in the positioning slots.
4. Install the headlight retaining ring.
5. Place the headlight trim ring or door into position, and install the retaining screws.

HEADLIGHT ADJUSTMENT

NOTE: Before making any headlight adjustments, preform the following steps for preparation:

1. Make sure all tires are properly inflated.

2. Take into consideration any faulty wheel alignment or improper rear axle tracking.
3. Make sure there is no load in the truck other than the driver.
4. Make sure all lenses are clean.

Each headlight is adjusted by means of two screws located at the 12 o'clock and 9 o'clock positions on the headlight underneath the trim ring. Always bring each beam into final position by turning the adjusting screws clockwise so that the headlight will be held against the tension springs when the operation is completed.

Front Side Marker Lamps
Rear Lamps
Rear Marker Lamps

REMOVAL AND INSTALLATION

Remove the 2 lamp body screws and remove the bulb from the lamp body by turning it counterclockwise. Installation is the reverse of removal.

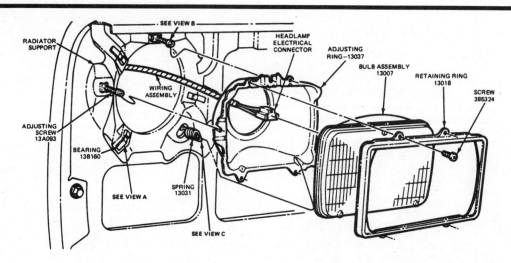

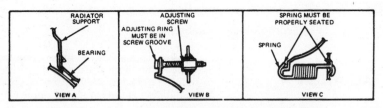

Square headlamp replacement

Parking Lamps

REMOVAL AND INSTALLATION

1. Remove the headlamp trim ring and rim.

2. Remove the parking lamp by removing the 2 mounting screws.

3. Pull the lamp body out and turn the bulb socket counterclockwise to remove it.

4. Installation is the reverse of removal.

CIRCUIT PROTECTION

Fuses

The fuse panel is located on the firewall above the driver's left foot.

Circuit Breakers

Two circuit are protected by circuit breakers located in the fuse panel: the power windows (20 amp) and the power door locks (30 amp). The breakers are self-resetting.

Turn Signal and Hazard Flasher Locations

Both the turn signal flasher and the hazard warning flasher

Circuit	Location	Protective Device
Air Conditioner, Clutch, Blower Relay	Fuse Panel	30 Amp
Air Conditioner	Starter Motor Relay	16 Gauge Fuse Link
Alternator	Starter Motor Relay	16 Gauge* Fuse Link
Alternator	Electric Choke	20 Gauge Fuse Link
Dual Batteries	Starter Motor Relay	14 Gauge Fuse Link

*14 gauge for 70 and 100 amp alternators

Fuse Link Location Chart — All Models

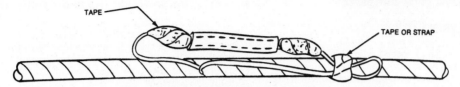

REMOVE EXISTING VINYL TUBE SHIELDING
REINSTALL OVER FUSE LINK BEFORE CRIMPING
FUSE LINK TO WIRE ENDS

TAPE

TAPE OR STRAP

TYPICAL REPAIR USING THE SPECIAL #17 GA. (9.00" LONG-YELLOW) FUSE LINK REQUIRED FOR THE AIR/COND.
CIRCUITS (2) #687E and #261A LOCATED IN THE ENGINE COMPARTMENT

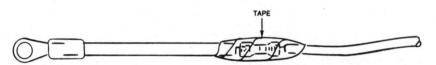

FUSE LINK

TAPE OR STRAP

TYPICAL REPAIR FOR ANY IN-LINE FUSE LINK USING THE SPECIFIED GAUGE FUSE LINK FOR THE SPECIFIC CIRCUIT

TAPE

TYPICAL REPAIR USING THE EYELET TERMINAL FUSE LINK OF THE SPECIFIED GAUGE FOR ATTACHMENT TO A CIRCUIT WIRE END

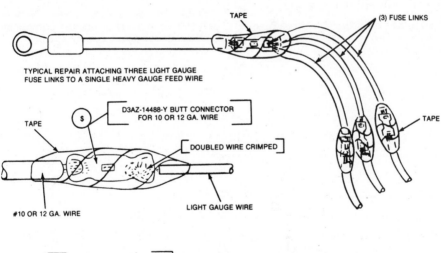

TAPE

(3) FUSE LINKS

TYPICAL REPAIR ATTACHING THREE LIGHT GAUGE
FUSE LINKS TO A SINGLE HEAVY GAUGE FEED WIRE

TAPE

$ | D3AZ-14488-Y BUTT CONNECTOR
FOR 10 OR 12 GA. WIRE

DOUBLED WIRE CRIMPED

TAPE

#10 OR 12 GA. WIRE

LIGHT GAUGE WIRE

$ | D3AZ-14488-Z BUTT CONNECTOR
FOR #14 OR 16 WIRE

$

FUSIBLE LINK REPAIR PROCEDURE

General fuse link repair procedure

are mounted on the fuse panel. The turn signal flasher is mounted on the front of the fuse panel, and the hazard warning flasher is mounted on the rear of the fuse panel.

Fuse Link

The fuse link is a short length of special, Hypalon (high temperature) insulated wire, integral with the engine compartment wiring harness and should not be confused with standard wire. It is several wire gauges smaller than the circuit which it protects. Under no circumstances should a fuse link replacement repair be made using a length of standard wire cut from bulk stock or from another wiring harness.

To repair any blown fuse link use the following procedure:

1. Determine which circuit is damaged, its location and the cause of the open fuse link. If the damaged fuse link is one of three fed by a common No. 10 or 12 gauge feed wire, determine the specific affected circuit.

2. Disconnect the negative battery cable.

3. Cut the damaged fuse link from the wiring harness and discard it. If the fuse link is one of three circuits fed by a single feed wire, cut it out of the harness at each splice end and discard it.

4. Identify and procure the proper fuse link and butt connectors for attaching the fuse link to the harness.

5. To repair any fuse link in a 3-link group with one feed:

a. After cutting the open link out of the harness, cut each of the remaining undamaged fuse links close to the feed wire weld.

b. Strip approximately ½ in. of insulation from the detached ends of the two good fuse links. Then insert two wire ends into one end of a butt connector and carefully push one stripped end of the replacement fuse link into the same end of the butt connector and crimp all three firmly together.

NOTE: Care must be taken when fitting the three fuse links into the butt connector as the internal diameter is a snug it for three wires. Make sure to use a proper crimping tool. Pliers, side cutters, etc. will not apply the proper crimp to retain the wires and withstand a pull test.

c. After crimping the butt connector to the three fuse links, cut the weld portion from the feed wire and strip approximately ½ in. of insulation from the cut end. Insert the stripped end into the open end of the butt connector and crimp very firmly.

d. To attach the remaining end of the replacement fuse link, strip approximately ½ in. of insulation from the wire end of the circuit from which the blown fuse link was removed, and firmly crimp a butt connector or equivalent to the stripped wire. Then, insert the end of the replacement link into the other end of the butt connector and crimp firmly.

e. Using rosin core solder with a consistency of 60 percent tin and 40 percent lead, solder the connectors and the wires at the repairs and insulate with electrical tape.

6. To replace any fuse link on a single circuit in a harness, cut out the damaged portion, strip approximately ½ in. of insulation from the two wire ends and attach the appropriate replacement fuse link to the stripped wire ends with two proper size butt connectors. Solder the connectors and wires and insulate the tape.

7. To repair any fuse link which has an eyelet terminal on one end such as the charging circuit, cut off the open fuse link behind the weld, strip approximately ½ in. of insulation from the cut end and attach the appropriate new eyelet fuse link to the cut stripped wire with an appropriate size butt connector. Solder the connectors and wires at the repair and insulate with tape.

8. Connect the negative battery cable to the battery and test the system for proper operation.

NOTE: Do not mistake a resistor wire for a fuse link. The resistor wire is generally longer and has print stating, "Resistor: don't cut or splice."

TRAILER WIRING

Wiring the truck for towing is fairly easy. There are a number of good wiring kits available and these should be used, rather than trying to design your own. All trailers will need brake lights and turn signals as well as tail lights and side marker lights. Most states require extra marker lights for overly wide trailers. Also, most states have recently required back-up lights for trailers, and most trailer manufacturers have been building trailers with back-up lights for several years.

Additionally, some Class I, most Class II and just about all Class III trailers will have electric brakes.

Add to this number an accessories wire, to operate trailer internal equipment or to charge the trailer's battery, and you can have as many as seven wires in the harness.

Determine the equipment on your trailer and buy the wiring kit necessary. The kit will contain all the wires needed, plus a plug adapter set which included the female plug, mounted on the bumper or hitch, and the male plug, wired into, or plugged into the trailer harness.

When installing the kit, follow the manufacturer's instructions. The color coding of the wires is standard throughout the industry.

One point to note, some domestic vehicles, and most imported vehicles, have separate turn signals. On most domestic vehicles, the brake lights and rear turn signals operate with the same bulb. For those vehicles with separate turn signals, you can purchase an isolation unit so that the brake lights won't blink whenever the turn signals are operated, or, you can go to your local electronics supply house and buy four diodes to wire in series with the brake and turn signal bulbs. Diodes will isolate the brake and turn signals. The choice is yours. The isolation units are simple and quick to install, but far more expensive than the diodes. The diodes, however, require more work to install properly, since they require the cutting of each bulb's wire and soldering in place of the diode.

One final point, the best kits are those with a spring loaded cover on the vehicle mounted socket. This cover prevents dirt and moisture from corroding the terminals. Never let the vehicle socket hang loosely. Always mount it securely to the bumper or hitch.

Troubleshooting Basic Turn Signal and Flasher Problems

Most problems in the turn signals or flasher system can be reduced to defective flashers or bulbs, which are easily replaced. Occasionally, problems in the turn signals are traced to the switch in the steering column, which will require professional service.

F = Front   R = Rear   ● = Lights off   o = Lights on

Problem		Solution
Turn signals light, but do not flash		• Replace the flasher
No turn signals light on either side		• Check the fuse. Replace if defective. • Check the flasher by substitution • Check for open circuit, short circuit or poor ground
Both turn signals on one side don't work		• Check for bad bulbs • Check for bad ground in both housings
One turn signal light on one side doesn't work		• Check and/or replace bulb • Check for corrosion in socket. Clean contacts. • Check for poor ground at socket
Turn signal flashes too fast or too slow		• Check any bulb on the side flashing too fast. A heavy-duty bulb is probably installed in place of a regular bulb. • Check the bulb flashing too slow. A standard bulb was probably installed in place of a heavy-duty bulb. • Check for loose connections or corrosion at the bulb socket

Troubleshooting Basic Turn Signal and Flasher Problems

Most problems in the turn signals or flasher system can be reduced to defective flashers or bulbs, which are easily replaced. Occasionally, problems in the turn signals are traced to the switch in the steering column, which will require professional service.

F = Front   R = Rear   • = Lights off   o = Lights on

Problem		Solution
Indicator lights don't work in either direction		· Check if the turn signals are working · Check the dash indicator lights · Check the flasher by substitution

One indicator light doesn't light		· On systems with 1 dash indicator:
		  See if the lights work on the same side. Often the filaments have been reversed in systems combining stoplights with taillights and turn signals.
		  Check the flasher by substitution
		· On systems with 2 indicators:
		  Check the bulbs on the same side
		  Check the indicator light bulb
		  Check the flasher by substitution

Troubleshooting Basic Lighting Problems

Problem	Cause	Solution
Lights		
One or more lights don't work, but others do	· Defective bulb(s) · Blown fuse(s) · Dirty fuse clips or light sockets · Poor ground circuit	· Replace bulb(s) · Replace fuse(s) · Clean connections · Run ground wire from light socket housing to car frame
Lights burn out quickly	· Incorrect voltage regulator setting or defective regulator · Poor battery/alternator connections	· Replace voltage regulator · Check battery/alternator connections
Lights go dim	· Low/discharged battery · Alternator not charging · Corroded sockets or connections · Low voltage output	· Check battery · Check drive belt tension; repair or replace alternator · Clean bulb and socket contacts and connections · Replace voltage regulator

Troubleshooting Basic Lighting Problems

Problem	Cause	Solution
Lights flicker	• Loose connection • Poor ground • Circuit breaker operating (short circuit)	• Tighten all connections • Run ground wire from light housing to car frame • Check connections and look for bare wires
Lights "flare"—Some flare is normal on acceleration—if excessive, see "Lights Burn Out Quickly"	• High voltage setting	• Replace voltage regulator
Lights glare—approaching drivers are blinded	• Lights adjusted too high • Rear springs or shocks sagging • Rear tires soft	• Have headlights aimed • Check rear springs/shocks • Check/correct rear tire pressure

Turn Signals

Problem	Cause	Solution
Turn signals don't work in either direction	• Blown fuse • Defective flasher • Loose connection	• Replace fuse • Replace flasher • Check/tighten all connections
Right (or left) turn signal only won't work	• Bulb burned out • Right (or left) indicator bulb burned out • Short circuit	• Replace bulb • Check/replace indicator bulb • Check/repair wiring
Flasher rate too slow or too fast	• Incorrect wattage bulb • Incorrect flasher	• Flasher bulb • Replace flasher (use a variable load flasher if you pull a trailer)
Indicator lights do not flash (burn steadily)	• Burned out bulb • Defective flasher	• Replace bulb • Replace flasher
Indicator lights do not light at all	• Burned out indicator bulb • Defective flasher	• Replace indicator bulb • Replace flasher

Troubleshooting Basic Dash Gauge Problems

Problem	Cause	Solution
Coolant Temperature Gauge		
Gauge reads erratically or not at all	• Loose or dirty connections • Defective sending unit • Defective gauge	• Clean/tighten connections • Bi-metal gauge: remove the wire from the sending unit. Ground the wire for an instant. If the gauge registers, replace the sending unit. • Magnetic gauge: disconnect the wire at the sending unit. With ignition ON gauge should register COLD. Ground the wire; gauge should register HOT.

Troubleshooting Basic Dash Gauge Problems

Problem	Cause	Solution
Ammeter Gauge—Turn Headlights ON (do not start engine). Note reaction		
Ammeter shows charge Ammeter shows discharge Ammeter does not move	• Connections reversed on gauge • Ammeter is OK • Loose connections or faulty wiring • Defective gauge	• Reinstall connections • Nothing • Check/correct wiring • Replace gauge
Oil Pressure Gauge		
Gauge does not register or is inaccurate	• On mechanical gauge, Bourdon tube may be bent or kinked	• Check tube for kinks or bends preventing oil from reaching the gauge
	• Low oil pressure	• Remove sending unit. Idle the engine briefly. If no oil flows from sending unit hole, problem is in engine.
	• Defective gauge	• Remove the wire from the sending unit and ground it for an instant with the ignition ON. A good gauge will go to the top of the scale.
	• Defective wiring	• Check the wiring to the gauge. If it's OK and the gauge doesn't register when grounded, replace the gauge.
	• Defective sending unit	• If the wiring is OK and the gauge functions when grounded, replace the sending unit
All Gauges		
All gauges do not operate	• Blown fuse • Defective instrument regulator	• Replace fuse • Replace instrument voltage regulator
All gauges read low or erratically	• Defective or dirty instrument voltage regulator	• Clean contacts or replace
All gauges pegged	• Loss of ground between instrument voltage regulator and car • Defective instrument regulator	• Check ground • Replace regulator
Warning Lights		
Light(s) do not come on when ignition is ON, but engine is not started	• Defective bulb • Defective wire	• Replace bulb • Check wire from light to sending unit
	• Defective sending unit	• Disconnect the wire from the sending unit and ground it. Replace the sending unit if the light comes on with the ignition ON.
Light comes on with engine running	• Problem in individual system • Defective sending unit	• Check system • Check sending unit (see above)

Troubleshooting the Heater

Problem	Cause	Solution
Blower motor will not turn at any speed	• Blown fuse • Loose connection • Defective ground • Faulty switch • Faulty motor • Faulty resistor	• Replace fuse • Inspect and tighten • Clean and tighten • Replace switch • Replace motor • Replace resistor
Blower motor turns at one speed only	• Faulty switch • Faulty resistor	• Replace switch • Replace resistor
Blower motor turns but does not circulate air	• Intake blocked • Fan not secured to the motor shaft	• Clean intake • Tighten security
Heater will not heat	• Coolant does not reach proper temperature • Heater core blocked internally • Heater core air-bound • Blend-air door not in proper position	• Check and replace thermostat if necessary • Flush or replace core if necessary • Purge air from core • Adjust cable
Heater will not defrost	• Control cable adjustment incorrect • Defroster hose damaged	• Adjust control cable • Replace defroster hose

COMPONENT INDEX

SUBTITLED CIRCUITS RELATE TO THE NEW TRANSMISSION USAGE

STANDARD CIRCUIT CHART (BY NUMBER)

CIRCUIT	DESCRIPTION *	COLOR
1	HORN SWITCH CONTROL	DK BLUE
2	RH FRONT TURN SIGNAL LAMP	WHITE-LT BLUE
3	LH FRONT TURN SIGNAL LAMP	LT GREEN-WHITE
4	ALTERNATOR REG. "S" TERM. TO ALTERNATOR "S" TERM.	WHITE-BLACK
5	RH REAR TURN SIGNAL LAMP	ORANGE-LT BLUE
6	HORN RELAY TO HORN	YELLOW-LT GREEN
7	SEAT SWITCH ARM TERM. TO RELAY FIELD TERM.	LT GREEN-YELLOW
8	TURN SIGNAL FLASHER FEED	ORANGE-YELLOW
9	LH REAR TURN SIGNAL LAMP	LT GREEN-ORANGE
10	STOPLAMP SWITCH FEED	LT GREEN-RED
11	ELECTRONIC SWITCH TO IGNITION COIL NEG. TERMINAL	DK GREEN-YELLOW
12	HEADLAMP DIMMER SWITCH TO HIGH BEAMS	LT GREEN-BLACK
13	HEADLAMP DIMMER SWITCH TO LOW BEAMS	RED-BLACK
14	HEADLAMP SWITCH TO TAIL LAMPS AND SIDE MARKER LAMPS	BROWN
15	HEADLAMP SWITCH FEED	RED-YELLOW
16	IGNITION SWITCH TO IGNITION COIL "BATT." TERMINAL	RED-LT GREEN
17	ASH RECEPTACLE LAMP FEED	WHITE
18	SEAT SWITCH TO RELAY FIELD TERMINAL	ORANGE-YELLOW
19	INSTRUMENT PANEL LAMPS FEED	LT BLUE-RED
20	DISTRIBUTOR ELECTRONIC CONTROL FEED	WHITE-LT BLUE
21	EMA CONTROL TO SPARK RETARD SWITCH	DK GREEN-LT GREEN
22	BRAKE FEED	LT BLUE-BLACK
23	ANTI-THEFT SYSTEM SWITCH FEED	TAN-LT GREEN
24	ANTI-THEFT SWITCH ARM	DK BLUE-ORANGE
25	ANTI-THEFT SWITCH DISARM	DK GREEN-PURPLE
26	DECK LID SWITCH TO ANTI-THEFT MODULE	WHITE-PURPLE
27	EMA CONTROL TO EGR SWITCH	ORANGE-LT GREEN
28	WINDSHIELD WIPER SW. TO WINDSHIELD WIPER MOTOR	BLACK-PINK
29	FUEL GAUGE TO FUEL GAUGE SENDER	YELLOW-WHITE
30	CONSTANT VOLTAGE UNIT AND INDICATOR LAMPS FEED	BLACK-LT GREEN
31	OIL PRESSURE INDICATOR TO OIL PRESSURE SENDING UNIT	WHITE-RED
32	STARTER CONTROL	RED-LT BLUE
33	STARTER CONTROL TO INTERLOCK MODULE	WHITE-PINK
34	HORN CONTROL MODULE TO OVERRIDE SWITCH	LT BLUE-ORANGE
35	ALTERNATOR REGULATOR "F" TERMINAL TO ALTERNATOR	ORANGE-LT BLUE
36	ALTERNATOR OUTPUT	YELLOW-WHITE
37	BATTERY TO LOAD	YELLOW
38	POWER SUPPLY TO BATTERY	BLACK-ORANGE
39	TEMP. GAUGE TO TEMP. SENDING UNIT	RED-WHITE
40	CIGAR LIGHTER FEED	LT BLUE-WHITE
41	WARNING LAMP PROVE OUT	BLACK-LT BLUE
42	SWITCH TO WARNING LAMP	RED-WHITE
43	TRAILER STOP LAMPS	DK BLUE
44	TURN SIGNAL FLASHER TO TURN SIGNAL SWITCH	LT BLUE
45	HOT WATER TEMP. RELAY TO HOT WATER TEMP. SENDING UNIT	YELLOW-RED
46	ELECTRONIC CONTROL UNIT TO ACCELERATION SOLENOID	YELLOW-BLACK
47	ELECTRONIC CONTROL UNIT TO DECELERATION SOLENOID	GRAY-ORANGE
48	BLIND CIRCUIT TERM. IN HARNESS CANNOT BE CHECKED FOR CONT.	(COLOR OPT)
49	TRAILER GROUND	WHITE
50	TRAILER BRAKES	RED
51	SEAT REG. CONTROL SWITCH FEED	BLACK-WHITE
52	TRAILER LH TURN SIGNAL	YELLOW
53	COURTESY LAMP SWITCH TO COURTESY LAMP	BLACK-LT BLUE
54	INTERIOR LAMP SWITCH FEED	LT GREEN-YELLOW
55	CARGO LAMP SW. TO CARGO LAMP	BLACK-PINK
56	WINDSHIELD WIPER SW. TO WINDSHIELD WIPER MOTOR	DK BLUE-ORANGE
57	GROUND CIRCUIT	BLACK
58	WINDSHIELD WIPER SW. TO WINDSHIELD WIPER MOTOR	WHITE
59	HEATED EXTERIOR MIRROR FEED	DK GREEN-PURPLE
60	CONSTANT VOLTAGE UNIT TO GAUGE	BLACK-LT GREEN
61	WINDSHIELD WIPER SW. TO WINDSHIELD WIPER MOTOR	YELLOW-RED
62	BATTERY TO HI-BEAM	BROWN-YELLOW
63	WINDSHIELD WIPER SW. TO WINDSHIELD WIPER MOTOR	RED
64	TRAILER RH TURN SIGNAL	DK GREEN
65	WINDSHIELD WIPER SW. TO WINDSHIELD WIPER MOTOR	DK GREEN
66	KEYLESS DOOR LOCK SWITCH ILLUMINATION FEED	LT BLUE
67	CHOKE RELAY TO CHOKE	GRAY-WHITE
68	ELECTRIC CHOKE FEED	ORANGE-BLACK
69	MODULE TO THROTTLE ACTUATOR	RED-LT GREEN
70	SUPPLEMENTAL ALTERNATOR STATOR A TERM. TO WINDSHIELD	RED
71	SUPPLEMENTAL ALTERNATOR STATOR B TERM. TO WINDSHIELD	WHITE
72	SUPPLEMENTAL ALTERNATOR STATOR C TERM. TO WINDSHIELD	DK GREEN
73	ELECTRONIC CONTROL UNIT TO WIDE OPEN THROTTLE ACTUATOR	ORANGE-LT BLUE
74	ELECTRONIC CONTROL UNIT TO EXHAUST GAS OXYGEN SENSOR	DK GREEN-YELLOW
75	ELECTRONIC CONTROL UNIT TO ENGINE VACUUM SWITCH	DK GREEN-LT GREEN
76	KEYLESS DOOR LOCK ILLUMINATION GROUND TO MODULE	BLACK-LT GREEN
77	ELECTRONIC CONTROL UNIT TO SOLENOID ACTUATOR	DK BLUE-YELLOW
78	KEYLESS DOOR LOCK SWITCH DATA BIT 1 TO MODULE	LT BLUE-YELLOW
79	KEYLESS DOOR LOCK SWITCH DATA BIT 2 TO MODULE	LT GREEN-RED
80	ENGINE COMPARTMENT LAMP FEED	BLACK-ORANGE
81	EMISSION CONTROL VALVE TO SWITCH	BROWN-YELLOW
82	WASHER FLUID LEVEL INDICATOR	PINK-YELLOW
83	INTERLOCK MODULE TO CENTER BUCKLE SWITCH	WHITE-ORANGE
84	DECK LID SOLENOID FEED	PURPLE-YELLOW
85	SEAT BELT WARNING TIMER TO L.F. RETRACTOR SWITCH	BROWN-LT BLUE
86	SEAT BELT WARNING TIMER TO R.F. SEAT SENSOR	DK BLUE-WHITE
87	INTERLOCK MODULE TO CENTER SEAT SENSOR SWITCH	TAN-WHITE
88	INSTRUMENT PANEL LAMP SWITCH FEED	BLACK-WHITE
89	FUEL SENSOR GROUND TO E.C.U.	ORANGE
90	THERMOCOUPLE POS TO EXHAUST SYST. OVERTEMP PROTECT MODULE	DK BLUE-LT GREEN
91	THERMOCOUPLE 1 NEG. TO EXHAUST SYS. OVERTEMP PROTECT MODULE	GRAY-RED
92	THERMOCOUPLE 2 NEG. TO EXHAUST SYS. OVERTEMP PROTECT MODULE	WHITE-BLACK
93	AIR DUMP VALVE NEG. TO EXHAUST SYS. OVERTEMP MODULE	ORANGE-WHITE
94	AIR FUEL SENSOR TO E.C.U.	DK GREEN-PURPLE
95	FEED BACK CARB. COIL 1	TAN-RED
96	FEED BACK CARB. COIL 2	TAN-ORANGE
97	FEED BACK CARB. COIL 3	TAN-LT GREEN
98	FEED BACK CARB. COIL 4	TAN-LT BLUE
99	AIR PORT SOLENOID SIGNAL	LT GREEN-BLACK
100	AIR PUMP SOLENOID SIGNAL	WHITE-RED
101	ELECTRONIC CONTROL UNIT TO CANISTER PURGE SOLENOID	GRAY-YELLOW
102	LH REAR TAIL LAMP BULB OUTAGE	WHITE BASE
103	RH REAR TAIL LAMP BULB OUTAGE	WHITE-RED
104	LH REAR STOP & TURN BULB OUTAGE	LT BLUE-ORANGE
105	RH REAR STOP & TURN BULB OUTAGE	RED-WHITE
106	LOW FUEL INDICATOR	LT BLUE
107	BUCKLE SW. TO CENTER OCCUPANT SEAT SENSOR	LT BLUE-PINK
108	LH HEADLAMP BULB OUTAGE	BROWN-LT BLUE
109	RH HEADLAMP BULB OUTAGE	PINK-LT BLUE
110	R AND LH REAR RUNNING LAMP BULB OUTAGE	WHITE-LT GREEN
111	WARNING LAMP TO LIGHTS ON RELAY	BLACK-YELLOW
112	WARNING LAMP RELAY FEED	BLACK-YELLOW
113	STARTING MOTOR TO STARTING MOTOR RELAY	YELLOW-LT BLUE
114	FEED TO VACUUM DOOR LOCK SWITCH	TAN-YELLOW HASH
115	VACUUM DOOR LOCK SWITCH TO SOLENOID (LOCK)	LT GREEN
116	VACUUM DOOR LOCK SWITCH TO SOLENOID (UNLOCK)	BROWN-ORANGE
117	DOOR LOCK MOTOR (LOCK)	PINK-BLACK
118	DOOR LOCK MOTOR (UNLOCK)	PINK-ORANGE
119	DOOR LOCK SWITCH (LOCK)	PINK-YELLOW
120	DOOR LOCK SWITCH (UNLOCK)	PINK-LT GREEN
121	KEYLESS DOOR LOCK SWITCH DATA BIT 3 TO MODULE	YELLOW-BLACK
122	KEYLESS DOOR LOCK SWITCH DATA BIT 4 TO MODULE	YELLOW
123	KEYLESS DOOR LOCK SWITCH DATA BIT 5 TO MODULE	RED
124	KEYLESS DOOR LOCK SWITCH ENABLE FROM MODULE	BROWN
125	MAP LAMP SWITCH TO RH MAP LAMP	BROWN-YELLOW
126	COURTESY LAMP SW. TO INSTR. PANEL COURTESY LAMP	BLACK-ORANGE
127	COURTESY LAMP SW. TO "C" PILLAR LAMPS	BLACK-LT BLUE
128	BRAKE FLUID LEVEL UNIT TO MESSAGE CENTER	PURPLE-YELLOW
129	KEYLESS DOOR LOCK OUTPUT FROM MODULE	LT GREEN
130	HEADLAMP BULB OUTAGE TO MESSAGE CENTER	RED-LT GREEN
131	CIGAR LIGHTER LAMP FEED	PURPLE-ORANGE
132	TAIL LAMP BULB OUTAGE TO MESSAGE CENTER	ORANGE-BLACK
133	RELAY TO MAP LAMP SWITCH	TAN-RED
134	KEYLESS DOOR LOCK OUTPUT (ALL) FROM MODULE	WHITE
135	STOP AND TURN BULB OUTAGE TO MESSAGE CENTER	YELLOW-RED
136	SPEED INPUT TO MESSAGE CENTER	YELLOW-LT BLUE
137	RADIO ANTENNA SWITCH FEED	YELLOW-BLACK
138	DOOR JAMP SWITCH TO LIGHTS ON RELAY	BROWN-LT BLUE
139	FUEL PULSE TO MESSAGE CENTER	LT GREEN-PURPLE
140	BACK UP LAMP	BLACK-PINK
141	CLOCK ADVANCE SWITCH TO MESSAGE CENTER	DK GREEN-LT GREEN
142	CLOCK SELECT SWITCH TO MESSAGE CENTER	LT BLUE-RED
143	CHECKOUT SWITCH TO MESSAGE CENTER	LT BLUE-YELLOW
144	AMPLIFIER TO SERVO TRANSDUCER FEED	ORANGE-YELLOW
145	SERVO SOURCE VACUUM SOLENOID TO CONTROL TRANSISTOR	GRAY-BLACK
146	SERVO VENT SOLENOID TO CONTROL TRANSISTOR	WHITE-PINK
147	AMPLIFIER FEEDBACK POTENTIOMETER FEED	PURPLE-LT BLUE
148	SERVO FEEDBACK POTENTIOMETER SIGNAL TO AMPLIFIER	YELLOW-RED
149	SERVO FEEDBACK POTENTIOMETER BASE TO AMPLIFIER	BROWN-LT GREEN
150	SENSOR SIGNAL TO AMPLIFIER	DK GREEN-WHITE
151	SPEED CONTROL ON-OFF SWITCH TO AMPLIFIER	LT BLUE-BLACK
152	ARRIVAL SWITCH TO MESSAGE CENTER	LT BLUE-WHITE
153	ECONOMY SWITCH TO MESSAGE CENTER	PURPLE-YELLOW
154	DESTINATION SWITCH TO MESSAGE CENTER	PURPLE-LT GREEN
155	DISTANCE TO EMPTY SWITCH TO MESSAGE CENTER	GRAY-RED
156	AVERAGE SPEED SWITCH TO MESSAGE CENTER	GRAY-ORANGE
157	WINDOW REGULATOR MOTOR TO GROUND	GRAY-BLACK
158	KEY WARNING SWITCH TO BUZZER	BLACK-PINK
159	DOOR JAMB SWITCH TO BUZZER	RED-PINK
160	BUZZER TO WARNING INDICATOR RELAY	WHITE-PINK
161	MILES/KILOMETERS SWITCH TO MESSAGE CENTER	GRAY-LT BLUE
162	EMERG. BRAKE WARNING LAMP TO EMERG. BRAKE SWITCH	LT GREEN-RED
163	KEYLESS DOOR LOCK OUTPUT (DRIVER) FROM MODULE	RED-ORANGE
164	DISTANCE SWITCH TO MESSAGE CENTER	GRAY-WHITE
165	ELAPSED TIME SWITCH TO MESSAGE CENTER	WHITE-BLACK
166	RESET SWITCH TO MESSAGE CENTER	WHITE-ORANGE
167	MESSAGE CENTER OUTPUT CLOCK TO DISPLAY	WHITE-YELLOW
168	5V DO-MESSAGE CENTER TO DISPLAY	WHITE-BLACK
169	TRANSFORMER POWER-MESSAGE CENTER TO DISPLAY	LT BLUE-PINK
170	WINDOW REGULATOR SWITCH FEED	RED-LT BLUE
171	CIRCUIT BREAKER TO SEAT LATCH RELAY	BLACK-WHITE
172	RELAY TO SEAT LATCH SOLENOID	ORANGE
173	DOOR SWITCH TO SEAT LATCH RELAY (COIL TERM.)	PINK-WHITE
174	DATA-MESSAGE CENTER TO DISPLAY	DK GREEN-PURPLE
175	RELAY FEED	BLACK-YELLOW

* IN SOME CASES, THERE MAY BE ADDITIONAL CIRCUIT
FUNCTIONS INCLUDED IN THE CIRCUIT DESCRIPTION LISTED.

STANDARD CIRCUIT CHART (BY NUMBER)

CIRCUIT	DESCRIPTION *	COLOR
176	REAR WINDOW REGULATOR SWITCH FEED	WHITE
177	KEYLESS DOOR LOCK SEAT SWITCH SENSOR TO MODULE	WHITE
178	PARITY BIT-DISPLAY TO MESSAGE CENTER	DK GREEN-ORANGE
179	HORIZONTAL SEAT REG. MOTOR TO RELAY	YELLOW
180	HORIZONTAL SEAT REG. MOTOR TO RELAY	RED
181	BLOWER MOTOR FEED	BROWN-ORANGE
182	THERMOSTAT SWITCH FEED	BROWN-WHITE
183	TONE GENERATOR	TAN-YELLOW
184	AIR COND. SW. (LO) TO AIR COND. BLOWER MOTOR	TAN-ORANGE
185	INSIDE DOOR HANDLE SWITCH TO RETRACTOR INHIBITOR MODULE	GRAY-BLACK
186	DEFOGGER SW. TO DEFOGGER MOTOR	BROWN-LT BLUE
187	INHIBITOR MODULE TO RETRACTOR OVERRIDE SOLENOID	GRAY-RED
188	HEADLAMP SWITCH TO AUXILIARY LAMPS	WHITE-BLACK
189	IDLE TRACKING SWITCH FEED	LT BLUE-PINK
190	THERMACTOR DUMP VALVE FEED	WHITE-RED
191	DEFOGGER SW. TO DEFOGGER MOTOR	DK BLUE-YELLOW
192	HEADLAMP SWITCH TO ELECTRONIC CLUSTER DIMMING	BROWN-WHITE
193	WINDOW REGULATOR RELAY FEED	YELLOW-LT GREEN
194	WINDOW REGULATOR RELAY ACCY FEED	PINK
195	TAILLAMP SWITCH FEED	TAN-WHITE
196	HEADLAMP FLASH TO PASS SWITCH FEED	DK BLUE-ORANGE
197	COOLANT TEMPERATURE SWITCH TO CONTROL RELAY	TAN-ORANGE
198	A/C PRESSURE SWITCH TO CONTROL RELAY	TAN-YELLOW
199	MODULE TO NEUTRAL SENSOR SWITCH	LT BLUE-YELLOW
200	THERMACTOR DIVERTER VALVE FEED	WHITE-BLACK
201	MCV MODULE TO VIP FUNCTION TESTER	TAN-RED
202	SPEED CONTROL AMPLIFIER TO CRUISE LAMP INTERFACE MODULE	RED-PINK
203	CRUISE INDICATING LAMP TO CRUISE LAMP INTERFACE MODULE	ORANGE-LT BLUE
204	TANK SELECT CIRCUIT ELECTRONIC FUEL GAUGE	ORANGE-LT GREEN
205	BUFFER FUEL LEVEL OUTPUT TO TRIPMINDER	DK BLUE-LT GREEN
206	GROUND RETURN TO TOWING VEHICLE	WHITE
207	MARKER LAMP SWITCH TO MARKER LAMPS	BLACK
208	LOW OIL LEVEL RELAY TO WARNING LAMP	GRAY
209	ELECT. ENG. CONTL. MOD. TO TEST CONN #1	WHITE-RED
210	INDICATOR LAMP TO SWITCH (4x4)	LT BLUE
211	ECU TO VACUUM SWITCH 4	BLACK-PINK
213	ECU TO VACUUM SWITCH 2	WHITE-PINK
214	ECU TO VACUUM SWITCH 3	RED-BLACK
215	SIGNAL UNIT LAMP TO FUEL SIGNAL RELAY	YELLOW-BLACK
216	AUTOLAMP AMPLIFIER TO RHEOSTAT	TAN-LT BLUE
217	AUTOLAMP AMPLIFIER TO RHEOSTAT	DK BLUE-ORANGE
218	AUTOLAMP AMPLIFIER TO SENSOR	WHITE-PURPLE
219	HEADLAMP SWITCH TO AUTOLAMP AMPLIFIER	DK GREEN-YELLOW
220	AUTOLAMP AMPLIFIER TO CONTROL SWITCH	PURPLE-ORANGE
221	HEADLAMP SWITCH TO SENSOR AND AUTOLAMP AMPLIFIER	ORANGE-WHITE
222	AUTOLAMP AMPLIFIER TO SENSOR	BROWN-LT GREEN
223	ODOMETER SENSOR TO EEC MODULE	TAN-LT GREEN
224	TRANSMISSION OVERDRIVE SWITCH TO EEC MODULE	TAN-LT BLUE
225	INJECTION PUMP FUEL TEMPERATURE SENSOR	BLACK-YELLOW
226	LF WINDOW REG. SW. TO LF WINDOW REG. MOTOR	WHITE-BLACK
227	LF WINDOW REG. SW. TO LF WINDOW REG. MOTOR	YELLOW
228	ELECTRIC DRIVE COOLING FAN	BROWN-YELLOW
229	EFE CARBURETOR SPACE FEED	BLACK-YELLOW
230	COLD START INJECTOR	BLACK-LT GREEN
231	ACCESSORY FEED TO MESSAGE CENTER	BLACK-YELLOW
232	FUEL METERING CONTROL LEVER ACTUATOR 1 MINUS	BROWN-LT BLUE
233	THERMOMETER SENSOR FEED	DK BLUE-YELLOW
234	THERMOMETER AMBIENT SENSOR RETURN	DK BLUE-WHITE
235	LAMP RETURN TO PULSE WITH DIMMER	RED-BLACK
236	FUEL PRESSURE BOOST SOLENOID	RED-YELLOW
237	TRANSMISSION THROTTLE VALVE SOLENOID 1	ORANGE-YELLOW
238	FUEL SUPPLY PUMP RELAY	ORANGE-LT BLUE
239	FUEL INJECTION PUMP POSITION SENSOR	PURPLE-YELLOW
240	COLD START TIMING RETARD SOLENOID	WHITE-RED
241	DE-ICE SOLENOID CONTROL	LT BLUE-YELLOW
243	POWER SERVO TO CLIMATE CONTROL UNIT (MODE)	LT GREEN-ORANGE
244	THERMAL SW. TO CLIMATE CONTROL UNIT	YELLOW-WHITE
245	POWER SERVO TO CLIMATE CONTROL UNIT (AMP)	BROWN-LT GREEN
246	POWER SERVO TO CLIMATE CONTROL UNIT (AMP)	PURPLE
247	POWER SERVO TO CLIMATE CONTROL UNIT (AMP)	WHITE-YELLOW
248	HEATER & A/C CONTROL SW. (DE-ICE) TO CLIMATE CONTROL UNIT	YELLOW-LT BLUE
249	HEATER & A/C CONTROL SW. (LO-NORM) TO CLIMATE CONTROL UNIT	DK BLUE-LT GREEN
250	HEATER & A/C CONTROL SW. (LO-NORM) TO POWER SERVO	ORANGE
251	IGNITION SWITCH TO THERMACTOR TIMER	BROWN-ORANGE
252	THERMACTOR TIMER TO RELAY	TAN-RED
253	START CIRCUIT TO THERMACTOR RELAY	ORANGE-YELLOW
254	OIL PRESSURE SWITCH TO TIMER	DK GREEN-WHITE
255	THERMACTOR DUMP VALVE FEED	LT. BLUE-RED
256	TEMPERATURE COMPENSATED PUMP TO PROCESSOR	ORANGE-WHITE
257	H L SW. TO CHIMES	WHITE-RED
258	LOW OIL LEVEL RELAY TO SENSOR	WHITE-PINK
259	ELECT. ENG. CONTROL MOD. TO THICK FILM IGN. MOD.	BLACK-ORANGE
260	BLOWER MOTOR TO SWITCH — LO	RED-ORANGE
261	BLOWER MOTOR TO SWITCH — HI	ORANGE-BLACK
262	STARTING MOTOR RELAY TO IGNITION COIL "I" TERM.	BROWN-PINK
263	CLICKER RELAY TERM. NO. 4 TO AIR VALVE ASSY.	PURPLE-LT BLUE
264	ELECT. ENG. CONTL. MOD. TO IDLE SPD. CONTL. MOTOR #1	WHITE-LT BLUE
265	ELECT. ENG. CONTL. MOD. TO IDLE SPD. CONTL. MOTOR #2	LT GREEN-WHITE
266	MEMORY SEAT SWITCH ENABLE	PURPLE-WHITE
267	MEMORY SEAT SWITCH POSITION #1	BROWN-LT GREEN
268	MEMORY SEAT SWITCH POSITION #2	BLACK-ORANGE
269	HEATER BLOWER MOTOR TO SWITCH (MEDIUM)	LT BLUE-ORANGE
270	MEMORY SEAT SWITCH SET	BROWN-ORANGE
271	MEMORY SEAT SWITCH LAMP ENABLE	LT GREEN-WHITE
272	MEMORY SEAT SWITCH LAMP DRIVE	WHITE-ORANGE
273	TO ELECTRONIC CLUSTER FROM ENGLISH/METRIC SWITCH IN KEYBOARD	BROWN
274	SWITCH OFF TO RELAY	ORANGE
275	SWITCH ON TO RELAY	YELLOW
276	SWITCH FEED	BROWN
277	AMPLIFIER SPEAKER SWITCH TO LEFT REAR SPEAKER	LT BLUE-BLACK
278	AMPLIFIER SPEAKER SWITCH FEED TO RIGHT REAR SPEAKER	PURPLE-WHITE
279	SPEAKER VOICE COIL FEED FRONT (R. CHANNEL) AMP INPUT	WHITE-RED
280	SPEAKER VOICE COIL FEED FRONT (LEFT CHANNEL) AMP INPUT	LT GREEN
281	SPEAKER VOICE COIL RETURN AMP INPUT	WHITE
285	TO ELECTRONIC CLUSTER FROM EXPANDED FUEL IN KEYBOARD	ORANGE
286	TO ELECTRONIC CLUSTER FROM TRIP RESET SWITCH IN KEYBOARD	YELLOW
287	SPEAKER VOICE COIL RETURN	BLACK-WHITE
288	TO ELECTRONIC CLUSTER FROM TRIP RECALL SWITCH IN KEYBOARD	PURPLE
289	TO ELECTRONIC CLUSTER FROM GAUGE SELECT SWITCH IN KEYBOARD	WHITE
290	12 GA FUSE LINK	GRAY
291	16 GA FUSE LINK	BLACK
292	18 GA FUSE LINK	BROWN
293	INSTRUMENT PANEL ILLUMINATION CONTROL MODULE FEED	ORANGE-RED
294	FUSED ACCY FEED #3	WHITE-LT BLUE
295	ELECTRONIC CLUSTER ACCESSORY FEED	LT. BLUE-PINK
296	FUSED ACCY FEED #1	WHITE-PURPLE
297	ACCY FEED FROM IGNITION SWITCH	BLACK-LT GREEN
298	FUSED ACCY FEED #2	PURPLE-ORANGE
299	14 GA FUSE LINK	DK GREEN
300	16 GA FUSE LINK	ORANGE
301	18 GA FUSE LINK	RED
302	20 GA FUSE LINK	DK BLUE
303	12 GA FUSE LINK	YELLOW
304	FEEDBACK CARBURETOR COIL "A"	BROWN
305	EEC MODULE TO TIME METER	LT BLUE-PINK
306	SEAT REG. SW. TO HORIZ. SOLENOID BATT. TERM	LT BLUE
307	SEAT REG. SW. TO VERT. SOLENOID BATT. TERM	WHITE
308	HI-TEMP SWITCH TO MCU MODULE	LT BLUE-ORANGE
309	LO-TEMP SWITCH TO MCU MODULE	ORANGE-RED
310	MCU MODULE TO KNOCK SENSOR	YELLOW-RED
311	MCU MODULE TO KNOCK SENSOR	DK GREEN-ORANGE
312	FUEL METERING CONTROL LEVER ACTUATOR 2 PLUS	WHITE-PURPLE
313	LEFT FRONT WINDOW REGULATOR SWITCH TO RIGHT FRONT WINDOW REGULATOR MOTOR	YELLOW-BLACK
314	LEFT FRONT WINDOW REGULATOR SWITCH TO RIGHT FRONT WINDOW REGULATOR MOTOR	RED-BLACK
315	TRANSMISSION THROTTLE VALVE SOLENOID 2	DK GREEN-PURPLE
316	LEFT FRONT WINDOW REGULATOR SWITCH TO LEFT REAR WINDOW REGULATOR MOTOR	YELLOW-LT BLUE
317	LEFT FRONT WINDOW REGULATOR SWITCH TO LEFT REAR WINDOW REGULATOR MOTOR	RED-LT BLUE
318	EXHAUST BACK PRESSURE VALVE ACTUATOR	GRAY-RED
319	LEFT FRONT WINDOW REGULATOR SWITCH TO RIGHT REAR WINDOW REGULATOR MOTOR	YELLOW-BLACK
320	LEFT FRONT WINDOW REGULATOR SWITCH TO RIGHT REAR WINDOW REGULATOR MOTOR	RED-BLACK
321	AIR CONDITIONER CLUTCH RELAY	GRAY-WHITE
322	IDLE SPEED CONTROL TO EGR VENT SOLENOID	RED-ORANGE
323	IDLE SPEED CONTROL TO EGR VACUUM SOLENOID	ORANGE-BLACK
324	TRANSMISSION OVERDRIVE SWITCH TO HEAT MODULE	YELLOW-LT GREEN
325	CRANK ENABLE TO IGNITION MODULE	DK BLUE-ORANGE
326	FUSE PANEL FEED TO RELAY	WHITE-PURPLE
327	DIESEL WATER IN FUEL SENDER TO WARNING LAMP GROUND	BLACK-ORANGE
328	WINDOW REG. MASTER CONT. SW. TO WINDOW REG. SW. FEED	RED-YELLOW
329	CRANK ENABLE RELAY	PINK
330	POWER STEERING PRESSURE SWITCH	YELLOW-LT GREEN
331	WIDE OPEN THROTTLE A/C CUTOUT SWITCH	RED
332	TIME DELAY RELAY	WHITE
333	WINDOW REG. SW. TO WINDOW REG. MOTOR	YELLOW-RED
334	WINDOW REG. SW. TO WINDOW REG. MOTOR	RED-YELLOW
335	AFTER GLOW RELAY TO DIESEL CONTROL SWITCH	ORANGE-LT BLUE
336	POWER RELAY TO GLOW PLUGS (RIGHT BANK)	BLACK-LT GREEN
337	POWER RELAY TO GLOW PLUGS (LEFT BANK)	ORANGE-WHITE
338	DIESEL CONTROL SWITCH TO LAMP CONTROL RELAY	BROWN-PINK
339	DIESEL CONTROL SWITCH TO POWER RELAY & LAMP CONTROL RELAY	GRAY
340	ANTI-THEFT MODULE TO ALARM RELAY	RED-LT BLUE
341	DOOR OPENING WARNING TO ANTI-THEFT MODULE	ORANGE-WHITE
342	START INTERRUPT RELAY TO ANTI-THEFT MODULE	LT GREEN-PURPLE
343	WARNING LAMP TO ANTI-THEFT MODULE	DK BLUE-LT GREEN
344	DOOR AJAR SWITCH TO INDICATOR LAMP LEFT FRONT GROUND	BLACK-YELLOW

* IN SOME CASES, THERE MAY BE ADDITIONAL CIRCUIT
FUNCTIONS INCLUDED IN THE CIRCUIT DESCRIPTION LISTED.

STANDARD CIRCUIT CHART (BY NUMBER)

CIRCUIT	DESCRIPTION *	COLOR	CIRCUIT	DESCRIPTION *	COLOR
345	DOOR AJAR SWITCH TO INDICATOR LAMP RIGHT FRONT GROUND	BLACK-PINK	434	RELAY TO DAY/NIGHT ILLUMINATION LAMPS	LT BLUE-BLACK
346	DOOR AJAR SWITCH TO INDICATOR LAMP RIGHT REAR GROUND	BLACK-WHITE	435	POSITION SENSE RETURN	YELLOW-LT BLUE
347	COMPRESSOR CLUTCH FEED	BLACK-YELLOW	436	REAR TILT POSITION SENSE	RED-LT GREEN
348	THERMOSTATIC SW. TO AIR COND. SW. SELECTOR TERM.	LT GREEN-PURPLE	437	POSITION SENSE ENABLE	YELLOW-LT GREEN
349	CRANKSHAFT POSITION SENSOR FEED	DK BLUE	438	HORIZONTAL POSITION SENSE	RED-WHITE
350	CRANKSHAFT SENSOR SIGNAL RETURN	GRAY	439	SEAT PROCESSOR TO RECLINER MOTOR "UP"	YELLOW-WHITE
351	SENSOR SIGNAL FEED	ORANGE-WHITE	440	SEAT PROCESSOR TO RECLINER MOTOR "DOWN"	RED-LT BLUE
352	EGR VALVE POSITION FEED	BROWN-LT GREEN	441	FRONT TILT POSITION SENSE	GRAY-BLACK
353	VEHICLE SPEED SENSOR FEED	LT BLUE	442	SEQUENTIAL LH REAR INBOARD TURN SIGNAL LAMP	LT GREEN-ORANGE
354	ENGINE COOLANT TEMPERATURE SENSOR FEED	LT GREEN-YELLOW	443	SEQUENTIAL LH REAR CENTER TURN SIGNAL LAMP	LT GREEN-RED
355	THROTTLE ANGLE POSITION SENSOR FEED	DK GREEN-LT GREEN	444	SEQUENTIAL LH REAR OUTBOARD TURN SIGNAL LAMP	LT GREEN-BLACK
356	BAROMETRIC PRESSURE SENSOR FEED	DK BLUE-LT GREEN	445	SEQUENTIAL RH REAR INBOARD TURN SIGNAL LAMP	ORANGE-LT BLUE
357	CARBURETOR AIR TEMPERATURE SENSOR FEED	LT GREEN-PURPLE	446	SEQUENTIAL RH REAR CENTER TURN SIGNAL LAMP	ORANGE-WHITE
358	MANIFOLD ABSOLUTE PRESSURE SENSOR FEED	LT GREEN-BLACK	447	SEQUENTIAL RH REAR OUTBOARD TURN SIGNAL LAMP	ORANGE-RED
359	SENSOR SIGNAL RETURN	BLACK-WHITE	448	ANTENNA SWITCH TO ANTENNA RELAY	ORANGE-YELLOW
360	EGR VALVE TO EEC MODULE	DK GREEN	449	RADIO SWITCH TO ANTENNA RELAY	BROWN-ORANGE
361	POWER RELAY TO EEC MODULE	RED	450	SEAT BELT WARNING INDICATOR LAMP FEED	DK GREEN-LT GREEN
362	EGR VALVE TO EEC MODULE FEED	YELLOW	451	BATTERY TO AUTOMATIC ANTENNA SWITCH	LT BLUE-YELLOW
363	DOOR AJAR SWITCH TO INDICATOR LAMP LEFT REAR GROUND	BLACK-LT BLUE	452	SEAT PROCESSOR ASSY TO FRONT MOTOR LH	GRAY-RED
364	BLOWER MOTOR RELAY FEED	BLACK-LT GREEN	453	TRANSMISSION DIAGNOSTIC	PURPLE
365	FUEL LEVEL WARNING RELAY FEED	LT BLUE-RED	454	IGN. SW. COIL TERM. TO CIRCUIT BREAKER	RED-LT GREEN
366	FUEL WARNING RELAY CONTROL	RED-BLACK	455	SWITCH TO VALVE	GRAY-RED
367	FUEL LEVEL RECEIVER TO FUEL LEVEL WARNING RELAY (REG. TERM.)	DK GREEN-WHITE	456	AUX WATER VALVE FEED	WHITE-LT GREEN
368	RADIO "SEEK UP"	RED-BLACK	457	BRAKE WEAR SENSOR	TAN-BLACK
369	VACUUM SOLENOID TO TEMP. SW.	BROWN-ORANGE	458	TURN SIGNAL SWITCH TO INDICATOR RELAY	ORANGE-BLACK
370	RADIO SEEK "DOWN"	ORANGE-BLACK	459	INDICATOR RELAY TO FLASHER	ORANGE-LT GREEN
371	BLOWER MOTOR RELAY TO MOTOR	PINK-WHITE	460	HORN SWITCH FEED	YELLOW-LT BLUE
372	RADIO MEMORY SEEK	BROWN-ORANGE	461	MODULE TO RELAY	ORANGE
373	TO ELECTRONIC CLUSTER FROM GROUND IN KEYBOARD	BLACK	462	MODULE TO RELAY	PURPLE
374	DOOR AJAR RELAY TO DOOR SWITCH	BROWN	463	ELECTRIC SHIFT MODULE TO NEUTRAL START SWITCH	RED-WHITE
375	MOVABLE STEERING COLUMN SOLENOID FEED	YELLOW-LT GREEN	464	MODULE TO LIGHT	BLACK-PINK
376	ELECT. ENG. CONTL. MOD. TO IDLE SPD. CONTL. MOTOR #3	BROWN-WHITE	465	MODULE TO SWITCH	WHITE-LT BLUE
377	ELECT. ENG. CONTL. MOD. TO EXHAUST HEAT CONTRL SOC.	WHITE	466	DIESEL CONTROL MODULE FEED	PINK-ORANGE
378	ELECT. ENG. CONTL. MOD. TO WIDE OPEN THROTTLE KICKER SOC.	RED-BLACK	467	PRESSURE SWITCH TO INERTIA SWITCH	GRAY-YELLOW
379	TURN SIGNAL SWITCH TO RH CORNERING LAMP	BROWN-WHITE	468	EATC LH SUNLOAD SENSOR POSITIVE	BROWN
380	TURN SIGNAL SWITCH TO LH CORNERING LAMP	PURPLE-YELLOW	469	SEAT BELT WARNING SWITCH FEED	LT GREEN
381	MOVABLE STEERING COLUMN SOLENOID TO COURTESY LAMP SWITCH	ORANGE-WHITE	470	THERMO SWITCH TO CONTROL MODULE	PINK-BLACK
382	ELECT. ENG. CONTL. MOD. TO TEST CONN #2	YELLOW-BLACK	471	DROPPING RESISTOR TO RELAY #2	ORANGE-LT GREEN
383	EMERGENCY WARNING FLASHER FEED	RED-WHITE	472	GLOW PLUG TO CONTROL MODULE	YELLOW-BLACK
384	ELECT. ENG. CONTL. MOD. TO IDLE SPD CONTL. MOTOR #3	PINK-ORANGE	473	CONTROL MODULE TO OIL PRESSURE SWITCH	LT GREEN-BLACK
385	FLASHER TO EMERGENCY WARNING SWITCH	WHITE-RED	474	STOPLAMP RELAY FEED	PINK-BLACK
386	ELECT. ENG. CONTL. MOD. TO ELECTRO DRIVE FAN	LT BLUE	475	STOPLAMP SW. TO STOPLAMP RELAY (COIL TERM.)	DK GREEN-WHITE
387	READING LAMP SWITCH TO READING LAMP (LH)	LT GREEN	476	EATC LH SUNLOAD SENSOR NEGATIVE	BROWN-YELLOW
388	REAR VIEW OUTSIDE MIRROR FEED	RED	477	FOG LAMP SWITCH TO FOG LAMP RELAY	LT BLUE-BLACK
389	R.F. DOOR LOCK SWITCH TO L.F. DOOR LOCK SWITCH	DK. GREEN-LT GREEN	478	FOG LAMP SW. TO FOG LAMP	TAN-ORANGE
390	R.F. DOOR UNLOCK SWITCH TO L.F. DOOR UNLOCK SWITCH	DK BLUE-WHITE	479	EATC RH SUNLOAD SENSOR POSITIVE	PURPLE BASE
391	CHOKE RELAY TO MCU MODULE	WHITE-YELLOW	480	CLUTCH SWITCH TO EFI MODULE	PURPLE-YELLOW
392	ELECTRIC PVS TO MCU MODULE	WHITE-ORANGE	481	EFI MODULE TO CLUTCH SWITCH	GRAY-YELLOW
393	THROTTLE KICKER RELAY TO MCU MODULE	WHITE-BLACK	482	FUEL FILLER DOOR RELEASE SWITCH TO FUEL FILLER DOOR RELEASE SOLENOID	WHITE-PINK
394	ANEROID SWITCH TO MCU MODULE	GRAY-LT BLUE	483	EATC RH SUNLOAD SENSOR NEGATIVE	GRAY
395	SPARK MODULE TO MCU MODULE	GRAY-ORANGE	484	LIQUID CRYSTAL DISPLAY	ORANGE-BLACK
396	FUEL 1 GROUND TO TACH/GAUGE MODULE	BLACK-ORANGE	485	IGNITION SWITCH ACCY TERM. TO DECK LID OPEN WARNING LAMP	BROWN-PINK
397	SIGNAL GROUND TO TACH/GAUGE MODULE	BLACK-WHITE	486	DECK LID OPEN WARNING LAMP TO DECK LID OPEN SWITCH	BROWN-WHITE
398	TACHOMETER GROUND TO TACH/GAUGE MODULE	BLACK-YELLOW	487	READING LAMP SWITCH TO READING LAMP	PINK-ORANGE
399	HEATER BLOWER SWITCH FEED	BROWN-YELLOW	488	DIESEL CONTROL MODULE GROUND RETURN	BLACK-LT BLUE
400	SAFETY RELAY LOAD TERM. TO WIND. REG. SW. FEED	LT BLUE-BLACK	489	ELECTRONIC CLUSTER IGNITION RUN FEED	PINK-BLACK
401	LIMIT SW. TO BACK WINDOW REG. MOTOR	GRAY-BLACK	490	POWER LUMBAR FEED	RED
402	WINDOW REG. SW. TO BACK WINDOW REG. MOTOR	GRAY-RED	491	POWER "THIGH" BOLSTER UP	YELLOW
403	WINDOW REG. SW. TO WINDOW REG. MOTOR	GRAY-WHITE	492	POWER "THIGH" BOLSTER DOWN	BROWN
404	WINDOW REG. SW. TO BACK WINDOW SW.	PURPLE-LT GREEN	493	HCU (MAIN) TO MODULE	BLACK-PINK
405	WINDOW REG. SW. TO BACK WINDOW SW.	PURPLE-LT BLUE	494	TURN SIGNAL RELAY TO TURN SIGNAL FLASHER	TAN-LT GREEN
406	WINDOW REG. SW. TO WINDOW AUX. SW.	TAN	495	VALVE #1 TO MODULE	TAN
407	WINDOW REG. SW. REAR TO LIMIT SW.	TAN-BLACK	496	VALVE #2 TO MODULE	ORANGE
408	WINDOW REG. SW. FRONT TO LIMIT SW.	TAN-RED	497	VALVE #3 TO MODULE	WHITE
409	PRESSURE SWITCH TO KEY SWITCH	TAN-BLACK	498	VALVE #4 TO MODULE	PINK
410	REARVIEW OUTSIDE MIRROR UP	YELLOW	499	VALVE #5 TO MODULE	GRAY-BLACK
411	REARVIEW OUTSIDE MIRROR DOWN	DK GREEN	500	HEADLAMP DIMMER SWITCH TO HEADLAMP DIMMER RELAY	PURPLE
412	REARVIEW OUTSIDE MIRROR COUNTER CLOCKWISE	WHITE	501	ELECTRONIC FUEL GAGE TO MESSAGE CENTER	LT BLUE
413	REARVIEW OUTSIDE MIRROR CLOCKWISE	LT BLUE	502	HEADLAMP DIMMER RELAY TO HEADLAMP DIMMER SWITCH	GRAY
414	AIR SOLENOID CONTROL R.F.	ORANGE-RED	503	HEADLAMP DIMMER RELAY TO FUSE HOLDER	LT BLUE
415	AIR SOLENOID CONTROL L.F.	LT GREEN-ORANGE	504	FUSE HOLDER TO HEADLAMP DIMMER AMPLIFIER	DK BLUE-WHITE
416	AIR SOLENOID CONTROL-REAR	LT BLUE-BLACK	505	HEADLAMP DIMMER SWITCH TO HEADLAMP DIMMER AMPLIFIER	GRAY-YELLOW
417	AIR SUSPENSION SWITCH FEED	PURPLE-ORANGE	506	MPH/KPH SWITCH TO MESSAGE CENTER	RED
418	AIR SUSPENSION CONTROL MODULE FEED	DK GREEN-YELLOW	507	AMPLIFIER TO RHEOSTAT	YELLOW
419	AIR SUSPENSION MANFUNCTION WARNING LAMP	DK GREEN-LT GREEN	508	RHEOSTAT TO SENSOR	WHITE
420	AIR COMPRESSOR POWER RELAY CONTROL	DK BLUE-YELLOW	509	AIR COND. CONDENSER THERMAL SWITCH FEED	TAN-YELLOW
421	AIR COMPRESSOR VENT SOLENOID	PINK	510	VALVE #6 TO MODULE	TAN-RED
422	AIR SUSPENSION HEIGHT SENSOR HI-L.F.	PINK-BLACK	511	STOPLAMP SWITCH TO TURN SIGNAL SWITCH	LT GREEN
423	AIR SUSPENSION HEIGHT SENSOR LO-L.F.	PURPLE-LT GREEN	512	BRAKE FLUID RES. SWITCH TO MODULE	TAN-LT GREEN
424	AIR SUSPENSION HEIGHT SENSOR HI-R.F.	TAN	513	POWER RELAY COIL TO MODULE	BROWN-PINK
425	AIR SUSPENSION HEIGHT SENSOR LO-R.F.	BROWN-PINK	514	RH FRONT SENSOR (HIGH) TO MODULE	YELLOW-RED
426	FRONT AIR SUSPENSION HEIGHT SENSOR FEED	RED-BLACK	515	RESISTOR TO BLOWER MOTOR (HI)	ORANGE-RED
427	AIR SUSPENSION HEIGHT SENSOR HI-REAR	PINK-BLACK	516	RH FRONT SENSOR (LOW) TO MODULE	YELLOW-BLACK
428	AIR SUSPENSION HEIGHT SENSOR LO-REAR	ORANGE-BLACK	517	CIRCUIT BREAKER (LOAD TERM) TO CONTROL SWITCH (BATT. TERM)	BLACK-WHITE
429	REAR AIR SUSPENSION HEIGHT SENSOR FEED	PURPLE-LT GREEN	518	REAR SENSOR (HIGH) TO MODULE	LT GREEN-RED
430	AIR SUSPENSION SYSTEM GROUND	GRAY	519	LH REAR SENSOR (LOW) TO MODULE	LT GREEN-BLACK
431	AIR SUSP. MOD. TO L.F. HEIGHT SENSOR	PINK-WHITE	520	SEAT BELT WARNING LAMP TO WARNING LAMP SWITCH	PURPLE-WHITE
432	AIR SUSPENSION ELECTRONICS GROUND	BLACK-PINK	521	LH FRONT SENSOR (HIGH) TO MODULE	TAN-ORANGE
433	FUEL PUMP BYPASS	LT BLUE-RED	522	LH FRONT SENSOR (LOW) TO MODULE	TAN-BLACK
			523	LH REAR SENSOR (HIGH) TO MODULE	RED-PINK
			524	RH REAR SENSOR (LOW) TO MODULE	PINK-BLACK

*** IN SOME CASES, THERE MAY BE ADDITIONAL CIRCUIT
FUNCTIONS INCLUDED IN THE CIRCUIT DESCRIPTION LISTED.**

STANDARD CIRCUIT CHART (BY NUMBER)

CIRCUIT	DESCRIPTION *	COLOR	CIRCUIT	DESCRIPTION *	COLOR
525	SPLICE TO MODULE	ORANGE-YELLOW	616	AIR BAG DIAGNOSTIC MODULE TO PASSENGER INFLATOR	PINK-BLACK
526	CORNERING LAMP SWITCH FEED	BLACK-WHITE	617	AIR BAG DIAGNOSTIC MODULE (DEPLOY) TO RH SENSOR	PINK-ORANGE
527	HEADLAMP DIMMER SWITCH OVERRIDE TO RHEOSTAT	RED	618	AIR BAG DIAGNOSTIC MODULE (MONITOR) TO RH SENSOR	PURPLE-LT GREEN
528	POWER RELAY TO MODULE GROUND	ORANGE-YELLOW	619	AIR BAG DIAGNOSTIC MODULE (DEPLOY) TO CENTER SENSOR	PINK-WHITE
529	SPLICE #2 TO MODULE	YELLOW-LT GREEN	620	AIR BAG DIAGNOSTIC MODULE (MONITOR) TO CENTER SENSOR	PURPLE-LT BLUE
530	SPLICE #3 TO POWER RELAY	LT GREEN-YELLOW	621	AIR BAG DIAGNOSTIC MODULE (DEPLOY) TO LH SENSOR	WHITE-YELLOW
531	SPLICE TO DIODE	ORANGE-YELLOW	622	AIR BAG DIAGNOSTIC MODULE (MONITOR) TO LH SENSOR	TAN-BLACK
532	SPLICE TO POWER RELAY	ORANGE-YELLOW	623	AIR BAG DIAGNOSTIC MODULE (MONITOR) TO SAFING SENSOR	PURPLE-WHITE
533	POWER RELAY TO FUSE LINK	TAN-RED	624	DCP MODULE TO HEATED BACKLITE RELAY	LT BLUE-ORANGE
534	SPLICE #3 TO PRESSURE SWITCH	YELLOW-LT GREEN	625	DCP MODULE TO PARKLAMP RELAY	LT BLUE-WHITE
535	PRESSURE SWITCH TO MODULE	LT BLUE-RED	626	OPEN DOOR WARNING LAMP FEED	PINK-YELLOW
536	BLOWER MOTOR RELAY (LOAD TERM) TO BLOWER MOTOR	BLACK-LT GREEN	627	OPEN DOOR WARNING LAMP TO OPEN DOOR WARNING SWITCH	BLACK-ORANGE
537	FUSE LINK TO MOTOR RELAY	TAN-YELLOW	628	DOOR WIRE	WHITE
538	MOTOR TO MOTOR RELAY	GRAY-RED	629	DOOR WIRE	BLACK
539	PRESSURE SWITCH TO MOTOR RELAY	PINK-LT BLUE	630	DOOR WIRE	RED
540	L.H. REMOTE MIRROR MOTOR FEED -- C.W.	RED	631	DOOR WIRE	YELLOW
541	L.H. REMOTE MIRROR MOTOR FEED — C.C.W.	DK BLUE	632	DCP MODULE TO HEADLAMP RELAY	PINK-YELLOW
542	L.H. REMOTE MIRROR MOTOR SOLENOID CONTROL	YELLOW	633	STEERING RATE SENSOR TERMINAL A CONTROL MODULE	RED
543	R.H. REMOTE MIRROR MOTOR FEED — C.W.	DK GREEN	634	STEERING RATE SENSOR TERMINAL B CONTROL MODULE	BROWN
544	R.H. REMOTE MIRROR MOTOR FEED — C.C.W.	PURPLE	635	AIR SUSPENSION DIODE SWITCH TO CONTROL MODULE	YELLOW
545	R.H. REMOTE MIRROR MOTOR SOLENOID CONTROL	WHITE	636	BRAKE PRESSURE SWITCH TO CONTROL MODULE	ORANGE
546	SPLICE #3 TO POWER RELAY	DK GREEN-YELLOW	637	AIR SUSPENSION CONTROL SIGNAL	LT GREEN
547	PRESSURE SWITCH TO FLUID RES. SWITCH	LT GREEN-YELLOW	638	RIGHT FRONT SHOCK DAMPENING RELAY TO CONTROL MODULE	PURPLE
548	GROUND STUD TO SPLICE #2	YELLOW-LT GREEN	639	HIGH ELECTRO DRIVE FAN	PINK
549	FLUID WARNING SWITCH TO PRESSURE SWITCH	BROWN-WHITE	640	WARNING LAMPS FEED	RED-YELLOW
550	FLUID SWITCH TO GROUND STUD	YELLOW-LT GREEN	641	LEFT FRONT SHOCK DAMPENING RELAY TO CONTROL MODULE	LT BLUE
551	SPLICE #2 TO SPLICE #3	YELLOW-LT GREEN	642	WATER TEMP. WARNING LAMP TO WATER TEMP. SW. (COLD)	WHITE-LT GREEN
552	SPLICE #2 TO COUP GROUND "B"	YELLOW-LT GREEN	643	DIESEL WATER IN FUEL SENDER TO WARNING LAMP	RED
554	POWER RELAY BATTERY FEED	YELLOW-BLACK	644	DIESEL TACH GROUND TO TACH GAGE MODULE	BLACK-YELLOW
555	FUEL INJECTOR #1 CYLINDER	TAN	645	SPEAKER VOICE COIL FEED RIGHT REAR CHANNEL AMP INPUT	PINK-BLACK
556	FUEL INJECTOR #2 CYLINDER	WHITE	646	SPEAKER VOICE COIL FEED LEFT REAR CHANNEL AMP INPUT	PINK-YELLOW
557	FUEL INJECTOR #3 CYLINDER	BROWN-YELLOW	647	WATER TEMP. WARNING LAMP TO WATER TEMP. SW. (HOT)	RED-BLACK
558	FUEL INJECTOR #4 CYLINDER	BROWN-LT BLUE	648	TACHOMETER FEED	RED-LT BLUE
559	FUEL INJECTOR #5 CYLINDER	TAN-LT BLUE	649	SPEAKER VOICE COIL FEED LEFT FRONT CHANNEL AMP INPUT	ORANGE
560	FUEL INJECTOR #6 CYLINDER	LT GREEN	650	RIGHT REAR SHOCK DAMPENING RELAY TO CONTROL MODULE	WHITE
561	FUEL INJECTOR #7 CYLINDER	TAN-ORANGE	651	LEFT REAR SHOCK DAMPENING RELAY TO CONTROL MODULE	DK GREEN
562	FUEL INJECTOR #8 CYLINDER	LT BLUE	652	SHOCK DAMPENING RELAY HARD TO SHOCK DAMPENING CONTROL	PINK-BLACK
563	SPEED SENSOR LO V REF TO SPEEDO TACH MODULE	ORANGE-YELLOW	653	SHOCK DAMPENING RELAY SOFT TO SHOCK DAMPENING CONTROL	DK BLUE
564	FUEL SIGNAL TACH MODULE TO FUEL COMPUTER	BROWN	654	ALT. SHUNT TO AMMETER	YELLOW-LT GREEN
565	SPEED SIGNAL SPEEDO TACH MODULE TO FUEL COMPUTER	BLACK-WHITE	655	STARTING MOTOR RELAY SHUNT TO AMMETER	RED-ORANGE
566	PROCESSOR TO THERMACTOR CLUTCH RELAY	WHITE-RED	656	REDUNDANT MODULE TO ENGINE WARNING LAMP	PURPLE
567	THERMACTOR CLUTCH RELAY TO CLUTCH	WHITE-BLACK	657	EEC MODULE TO MALFUNCTION INDICATOR LITE	TAN
568	ALTERNATOR RELAY TO ALTERNATOR REGULATOR	LT GREEN	658	EEC MODULE TO CHECK ENGINE INDICATOR LAMP	PINK-LT GREEN
569	STOPLAMP SWITCH TO HI MOUNT STOPLAMP	DK GREEN	659	MODULE TO DOWN SWITCH	WHITE-LT BLUE
570	DEDICATED GROUND	BLACK-WHITE	660	AIR COND. CONTROL SW. TO FRESH-AIR RECIRC. DOOR SOLENOID	YELLOW-LT GREEN
571	REMOTE CONVENIENCE SELF DIAGNOSTIC GROUND	BLACK-ORANGE	661	MODULE TO OVERRIDE SWITCH	LT GREEN-WHITE
572	ENGLISH METRIC SIGNAL TO MULTIGAGE	ORANGE-BLACK	662	MODULE TO MOTOR FEED	WHITE-BLACK
573	CENTER REAR TAILLAMP BULB OUTAGE	BLACK-ORANGE	663	MODULE TO MOTOR FEED	LT GREEN-YELLOW
574	EXTENDED USEFUL LIFE SENSOR TO WARNING LAMP	BROWN-WHITE	664	MODULE TO RELEASE SOLENOID	YELLOW-LT GREEN
575	RELAY TO ATC CONTROL	YELLOW-BLACK	665	OVERRIDE SWITCH TO LATCH	ORANGE-YELLOW
576	REAR LAMP TO TRAILER RELAY FEED	DK GREEN	666	BATTERY FEED CAMPER	RED
577	AIR SUSPENSION SYSTEM GROUND	LT GREEN-RED	667	LAMP RELAY TO MARKER LAMPS	WHITE-RED
578	AIR COMPRESSOR VENT SOLENOID	LT BLUE-PINK	668	I TERMINAL STARTER MOTOR RELAY TO INERTIA SWITCH	ORANGE-LT BLUE
579	HEATED WINDSHIELD CONTROL TO ELECT ALTERNATOR REGULATOR	BLACK-ORANGE	669	OIL PRESSURE SWITCH TO CUTOUT RELAY	YELLOW
580	HEATED WINDSHIELD CONTROL TO ALT POWER RELAY	BROWN	670	INERTIA SWITCH TO FUEL TANK SELECTOR SWITCH	RED
581	HEATED WINDSHIELD CONTROL TO ALT STATOR TERM	RED	671	FUEL TANK SELECTOR SWITCH TO AFT FUEL PUMP	LT BLUE-YELLOW
582	HEATED WINDSHIELD SWITCH TO HEATED WINDSHIELD CONTROL	ORANGE	672	FUEL TANK SELECTOR SWITCH TO MIDSHIP FUEL PUMP	LT GREEN-YELLOW
583	ALT POWER RELAY TO CONTROL MODULE	YELLOW	673	SELECTOR SWITCH TO MIDSHIP TANK	DK BLUE-YELLOW
584	POWER FEED DECEL TIMER TO THROTTLE KICKER	DK GREEN-PURPLE	674	SELECTOR SWITCH TO AUX. FUEL SOLENOID	BROWN-WHITE
585	HEATED WINDSHIELD CONTROL TO EEC AIR COND TERM	PURPLE	675	SELECTOR SWITCH TO AFT AXLE TANK	YELLOW-LT BLUE
586	CONVERTIBLE TOP RELAY TO SWITCH	YELLOW	676	EEC MODULE TO SPEED CONTROL GROUND	RED
587	WINDSHIELD WIPER INTERMITTENT GOVERNOR FEED	BLACK-WHITE	677	ANTI-SKID MODULE TO ANTI-SKID CONTROL VALVE	LT BLUE
588	CONVERTIBLE TOP RELAY TO SWITCH	PURPLE	678	ANTI-LOCK MODULE TO ANTI-LOCK CONTROL VALVE	YELLOW
589	WINDSHIELD WIPER SWITCH TO INTERMITTENT GOVERNOR GROUND	ORANGE	679	SPEED CONTROL SENSE EEC MODULE TO SENSOR	GRAY-BLACK
590	INTERMITTENT GOVERNOR TO W/S WIPER SWITCH	DK BLUE-WHITE	681	HEATED WINDSHIELD TRIGGER CIRCUIT SW. TO MODULE	TAN-RED
591	DCP MODULE TO WASHER RELAY	BROWN-YELLOW	682	TEMP WARNING LAMP TO SENDING UNIT	GRAY-RED
592	DCP MODULE TO WIPER PARK OVER-RIDE RELAY	BROWN-LT GREEN	683	SPEED CONTROL SENSE EEC MODULE TO CLUSTER	PURPLE-LT BLUE
593	DCP MODULE TO WIPER GOVERNOR RELAY	RED-ORANGE	684	COMPASS SENSOR FEED	PINK-BLACK
594	DCP MODULE TO WIPER HI-LO RELAY	ORANGE-LT GREEN	685	ANTI-LOCK MODULE TO ANTI-LOCK CONTROL VALVE	BLACK-WHITE
595	DCP MODULE CONTROL INTERFACE TO RADIO	LT BLUE-RED	686	HEAD LP TIME DELAY CONTROL RELAY TO CIR. BREAKER	GRAY-ORANGE
596	DCP MODULE SIGNAL GROUND TO RADIO	BLACK	687	ACC FEED	GRAY-YELLOW
597	DCP MODULE TRIP SCAN HIGH TO TRIPMINDER	LT GREEN-BLACK	688	HTD BACKLITE SW. TO TIME DELAY RELAY	GRAY-LT BLUE
598	DCP MODULE TRIP SCAN LOW TO TRIPMINDER	LT GREEN-PURPLE	689	LOGIC MODE	DK BLUE
599	MODULE TO SOLENOID	PINK-LT GREEN	690	RIGHT CHANNEL SIGNAL	GRAY
600	FEED TO FAILURE SWITCH	DK GREEN	691	MOONROOF RELAY TO MICRO SWITCH OPEN	DK BLUE
601	BRAKE SKID CONTROL MODULE FEED	LT BLUE-PINK	692	MOONROOF RELAY TO MICRO SWITCH CLOSED	RED
602	COIL TERM. OF IGN. SW. TO BRAKE SKID CONTROL MODULE	RED-LT GREEN	693	MODULE DIAGNOSTIC	ORANGE
603	FAILURE WARNING LIGHT	DK GREEN	694	AMPLIFIER POWER RETURN	RED
604	SKID CONTROL MODULE TO RH WHEEL SENSOR HI	ORANGE-RED	695	MULTIPLEX WINDSHIELD WIPER OFF	BLACK-ORANGE
605	SOLENOID	RED	696	MULTIPLEX FARRING LAMPS	ORANGE-BLACK
606	SURE TRACK DIAGNOSTIC	WHITE-LT BLUE			
607	DIESEL COLD ADVANTAGE	GRAY-RED			
608	AIR BAG DIAGNOSTIC MODULE TO RELAY INDICATOR LAMP	BLACK-YELLOW			
609	AIR BAG READY INDICATOR LAMP TO AIR BAG FLASHER	ORANGE-YELLOW			
610	AIR BAG DIAGNOSTIC MODULE TO AIR BAG FLASHER	ORANGE-LT GREEN			
611	AIR BAG READY INDICATOR L (DEPLOY) TO SAFING SENSOR	WHITE-ORANGE			
612	AIR BAG READY INDICATOR L (MONITOR) TO SAFING SENSOR	PURPLE-ORANGE			
613	AIR BAG DIAGNOSTIC MODULE TO SAFING SENSOR (GROUND)	DK BLUE-WHITE			
614	AIR BAG SAFING SENSORS TO INFLATORS	GRAY-ORANGE			
615	AIR BAG DIAGNOSTIC MODULE TO DRIVER INFLATOR	GRAY-WHITE			

* IN SOME CASES, THERE MAY BE ADDITIONAL CIRCUIT
FUNCTIONS INCLUDED IN THE CIRCUIT DESCRIPTION LISTED.

STANDARD CIRCUIT CHART (BY NUMBER)

CIRCUIT	DESCRIPTION *	COLOR
697	MULTIPLEX HEADLAMPS	BROWN
698	MULTIPLEX WINDSHIELD WIPER OFF	RED
699	MULTIPLEX RELAY COIL FEED	ORANGE
700	MULTIPLEX WIPER RATE	YELLOW
701	C.B. SQUELCH POT	WHITE-PURPLE
702	C.B. PUSH TO TALK	WHITE-BLACK
703	C.B. DOWN SWITCH	WHITE-ORANGE
704	C.B. C-DIGIT	ORANGE
705	C.B. NOISE BLANKER	LT GREEN-ORANGE
706	C.B. SCAN L.E.D.	GRAY
707	C.B. UP SWITCH	WHITE-YELLOW
708	C.B. D-DIGIT	BROWN
709	C.B. VOLUME CONTROL	WHITE-LT BLUE
710	C.B. SCAN SWITCH	WHITE-LT GREEN
711	C.B. REGULATED 5V	LT GREEN-BLACK
712	C.B. A + DIGIT	PURPLE
713	C.B. MIC-AUDIO	WHITE
714	RELAY COIL FEED #2	PURPLE
715	C.B. A-DIGIT	LT GREEN
716	C.B. B-DIGIT	YELLOW
717	C.B. SPEAKER TO TRANSCEIVER	LT BLUE-RED
718	C.B. ON/OFF	RED-WHITE
719	WINDSHIELD WIPER HIGH	GRAY
720	C.B. B + DIGIT	LT BLUE
721	C.B. SPEAKER VOICE COIL RETURN	DK BLUE-LT GREEN
722	C.B. RELAY DRIVE	LT GREEN-RED
723	C.B. SPEAKER RELAY TO MIC	LT BLUE-ORANGE
724	C.B. C + DIGIT	LT GREEN-WHITE
725	RELAY COIL FEED #3	WHITE
726	WINDSHIELD WASHER	LT GREEN
727	REMOTE DEFROST	YELLOW-BLACK
728	RADIO SEEK	WHITE-ORANGE
729	RADIO MEMORY	RED-WHITE
730	CRT SCAN	LT BLUE-YELLOW
731	MULTIPLEX REVERSE DIMMING	WHITE-BLACK
732	MULTIPLEX LCD ILLUMINATION	BROWN-WHITE
733	MULTIPLEX SERVICE REMINDER RESET	PURPLE-WHITE
734	MULTIPLEX SERVICE REMINDER	TAN
735	MULTIPLEX MESSAGE O	DK BLUE-WHITE
736	MULTIPLEX MESSAGE I	PINK
737	TEMP SWITCH TO WARNING DEVICE	WHITE-LT BLUE
738	HEATED WINDSHIELD CONTROL TO HEATED WINDSHIELD SWITCH	YELLOW-WHITE
739	HEATED WINDSHIELD GROUND TEST LEAD	BLACK
740	VAC SWITCH TO VAC PUMP	ORANGE-LT BLUE
741	TIMER CONTROL VALVE TO CONTROL UNIT	LT BLUE-WHITE
742	RADIATOR COOLANT TEMP SWITCH TO CONTROL UNIT	LT BLUE-YELLOW
743	AIR TEMP SENSOR TO CONTROL UNIT	BLACK-LT BLUE
744	IDLE RPM SOLENOID TO CONTROL UNIT	TAN-WHITE
745	ANTENNA SWITCH TO POWER ANTENNA (UP)	RED-PINK
746	ANTENNA SWITCH TO POWER ANTENNA (DOWN)	DK GREEN-YELLOW
747	RADIO RECEIVER ASSY. TO FOOT CONTROL SWITCH	ORANGE-LT BLUE
748	BOOST SENSOR TO CONTROL UNIT	TAN
749	SENSOR AMPLIFY UNIT TO CONTROL UNIT #1	PINK-BLACK
750	SENSOR AMPLIFY UNIT TO CONTROL UNIT #2	GRAY-LT BLUE
751	BLOWER MOTOR SPEED CONTROLLER TO RESISTOR #3 (MED.)	DK BLUE-WHITE
752	BLOWER MOTOR SPEED CONTROLLER TO RESISTOR #2 (MED.)	YELLOW-RED
753	HEATER & A/C CONTROL SW. TO BLOWER RELAY SW.	YELLOW-RED
754	BLOWER MOTOR SPEED CONTROLLER TO RESISTOR #1 (MED.)	LT GREEN-WHITE
755	BLOWER MOTOR SWITCH RELAY TO RESISTOR (LOW SPEED)	BROWN-WHITE
756	HEATER & A/C CONTROL SW. (HI-NORM) TO RESISTOR (LOW RANGE)	RED-PINK
757	HEATER & A/C CONTROL SW. (HI-NORM) TO BLOWER MOTOR SW. RELAY	RED-WHITE
758	HEATER & A/C CONTROL SW (LO-HI-NORM) TO RESISTOR (LOW RANGE)	PURPLE-WHITE
759	SENSOR AMPLIFY UNIT TO CONTROL UNIT #3	DK GREEN-WHITE
760	SENSOR AMPLIFY UNIT TO CONTROL UNIT #4	WHITE-PURPLE
761	BLOWER MOTOR RELAY TO ENG. WATER TEMP. SWITCH (COLD)	WHITE-LT GREEN
762	ELECT SHIFT 4x4 MODULE TO MOTOR POSITION #1	YELLOW-WHITE
763	ELECT SHIFT 4x4 MODULE TO MOTOR POSITION #2	ORANGE-WHITE
764	ELECT SHIFT 4x4 MODULE TO MOTOR POSITION #3	BROWN-WHITE
765	HEATER & A/C CONTROL SW. TO REHEAT & A/C FEED	LT GREEN-YELLOW
766	HEATER & A/C CONTROL SW. (DE-FOG) TO INLET AIR CONTROL SOLENOID	RED-LT GREEN
767	AMBIENT SENSOR TO INST. PANEL THERMISTOR	LT BLUE-ORANGE
768	REFERENCE SENSOR TO HEAT DUCT THERMISTOR	LT GREEN-YELLOW
769	HATER & A/C CONTROL SW. (HI & LO NORM) TO BLOWER MOTOR SW. RELAY	LT BLUE-YELLOW
770	ELECT SHIFT 4x4 MODULE TO MOTOR POSITION #4	WHITE
771	ELECT SHIFT 4x4 MODULE TO MOTOR POSITION #5	PURPLE-YELLOW
772	ELECT SHIFT 4x4 MODULE TO SPEED SENSOR COIL	LT BLUE
773	HEATER & A/C CONTROL SW. (TEMP. SELECTOR) TO REHEAT AMPL.	DK GREEN-ORANGE
774	ELECT SHIFT 4x4 MODULE TO SPEED SENSOR RETURN	LT GREEN
775	HEATER & A/C CONTROL SW. (DEFOG) TO DEFROST CONT. SOLENOID	WHITE-PINK
776	CLIMATE CONTROL BOX TO HIGH BLOWER RELAY	ORANGE-BLACK
777	ELECT SHIFT 4x4 MODLUE TO MOTOR CONTROL COUNTER CLOCK WISE	YELLOW
778	ELECT SHIFT 4x4 MODULE TO MOTOR CONTROL	ORANGE
779	ELECT SHIFT 4x4 MODULE TO ELECT CLUTCH	BROWN
780	ELECT SHIFT MODULE TO 2H 4H SWITCH	DK BLUE
781	ELECT SHIFT TO 4L SWITCH	ORANGE-LT BLUE
782	ELECT SHIFT MODULE TO LOW RANGE INDICATOR LAMP ROOF CONSOLE	BROWN-WHITE
783	ELECT SHIFT MODULE TO GRAPHIC DISPLAY ROOF CONSOLE	GRAY
784	INDICATOR LAMP TO LOW RANGE SWITCH 4x4	LT BLUE-BLACK
785	BATTERY TO MULTIPLEX MODULE	BLACK-LT GREEN
786	FUEL TANK SELECTOR TO FUEL PUMP FRONT	RED
787	FUEL PUMP SAFETY SWITCH TO FUEL PUMP MOTOR	PINK-BLACK
789	FUEL TANK SELECTOR TO FUEL PUMP REAR	BROWN-WHITE
790	HEATER & A/C CONTROL SW. TO INST. PANEL THERMISTOR	WHITE-ORANGE
791	BATTERY TO MULTIPLEX SYSTEM	BLACK-WHITE
792	MULTIPLEX COMPUTER FEED	TAN-RED
793	LOW WASHER LEVEL TO SENSOR	YELLOW-BLACK
794	LOW COOLANT LEVEL RELAY TO SENSOR	LT BLUE
795	CAM SENSOR TO EEC MODULE	DK GREEN
796	CAM SENDER SIGNAL RETURN	LT BLUE
797	BATTERY FEED TO STEREO	LT GREEN-PURPLE
798	LEFT CHANNEL SIGNAL OUT	LT GREEN-RED
799	RIGHT CHANNEL SIGNAL OUT	ORANGE-BLACK
800	AMPLIFIER/SPEAKER SWITCH FEED TO LEFT REAR SPEAKER	GRAY-LT BLUE
801	AMPLIFIER/SPEAKER SWITCH GROUND TO LEFT REAR SPEAKER	PINK-LT BLUE
802	AMPLIFIER/SPEAKER SWITCH FEED TO RIGHT REAR SPEAKER	ORANGE-RED
803	AMPLIFIER/SPEAKER SWITCH GROUND TO RIGHT REAR SPEAKER	DK GREEN-ORANGE
804	SPEAKER VOICE COIL FEED — FRONT (LEFT CHANNEL)	ORANGE-LT GREEN
805	SPEAKER VOICE COIL FEED — FRONT (RIGHT CHANNEL)	WHITE-LT GREEN
806	SPEAKER VOICE COIL FEED — REAR (RIGHT CHANNEL)	PINK-LT BLUE
807	SPEAKER VOICE COIL FEED — REAR (LEFT CHANNEL)	PINK-LT GREEN
810	STOPLAMP SW. TO STOPLAMPS	RED-LT GREEN
811	SPEAKER SWITCH GROUND TO RIGHT FRONT SPEAKER	DK GREEN-ORANGE
812	SPEAKER SWITCH FEED TO RIGHT FRONT SPEAKER	PINK-ORANGE
813	SPEAKER SWITCH GROUND TO LEFT FRONT SPEAKER	LT BLUE-WHITE
814	SPEAKER SWITCH FEED TO LEFT FRONT SPEAKER	PINK-WHITE
815	AMPLIFIER SWITCH GROUND TO RIGHT FRONT SPEAKER	LT GREEN-ORANGE
816	AMPLIFIER SWITCH FEED TO RIGHT FRONT SPEAKER	LT GREEN-PURPLE
817	INDICATOR RELAY TO RH TURN LAMP	TAN-LT BLUE
818	INDICATOR RELAY TO LH TURN LAMP	TAN-WHITE
819	AMPLIFIER SWITCH GROUND TO LEFT FRONT SPEAKER	LT GREEN-WHITE
820	AMPLIFIER SWITCH FEED TO LEFT FRONT SPEAKER	DK BLUE-YELLOW
822	SPEAKER VOICE COIL FEED	BLACK-LT GREEN
823	RADIO TO FADER CONTROL	LT GREEN
824	AMPLIFIER SWITCH GROUND TO RIGHT REAR SPEAKER	WHITE-PURPLE
825	AMPLIFIER SWITCH FEED TO RIGHT REAR SPEAKER	TAN-LT GREEN
826	AMPLIFIER SWITCH GROUND TO LEFT REAR SPEAKER	DK BLUE-ORANGE
827	AMPLIFIER SWITCH FEED TO LEFT REAR SPEAKER	TAN-WHITE
828	POWER FEED-SWITCH TO REAR AMPLIFIER	PURPLE-LT BLUE
829	POWER FEED-SWITCH TO FRONT AMPLIFIER	WHITE-PURPLE
830	SWITCH TO FADER RIGHT CHANNEL FEED	PINK-YELLOW
831	SWITCH TO FADER LEFT CHANNEL FEED	TAN
832	MODE SELECT SWITCH FEED	BROWN-LT GREEN
833	MODE SELECT SWITCH LAMP	RED-BLACK
834	ELECTRONIC SHOCK SENSOR A	RED-YELLOW
835	ELECTRONIC SHOCK SENSOR B	RED-WHITE
836	ACCELERATE DECELERATE SENSOR	ORANGE-WHITE
837	ACCELERATE DECELERATE SENSOR RETURN	YELLOW-BLACK
838	ELECTRONIC SHOCK HARD CONTROL	LT GREEN-PURPLE
839	ELECTRONIC SHOCK SOFT CONTROL	LT GREEN-WHITE
840	ACTUATOR POSITION SENSOR LEFT FRONT	WHITE-BLACK
841	ACTUATOR POSITION SENSOR RIGHT FRONT	WHITE-RED
842	ACTUATOR POSITION SENSOR LEFT REAR	WHITE-ORANGE
843	ACTUATOR POSITION SENSOR RIGHT REAR	WHITE
844	ELECTRONIC SHOCK DIAGNOSTIC	GRAY-RED
845	ELECTRONIC SHOCK FEEDBACK ACTUATOR TO RELAY	TAN-BLACK
846	ELECTRONIC SHOCK METAL OXIDE VERISTOR	TAN-RED
847	DECELERATION SENSOR	ORANGE-LT GREEN
848	PROCESSOR LOOP SIGNAL RETURN	DK GREEN-ORANGE
849	DIGITAL AUDIO DISC LOGIC SENSOR	TAN-BLACK
850	COIL "A" TO DISTRIBUTORLESS IGNITION MODULE	YELLOW-BLACK
851	COIL "B" TO DISTRIBUTORLESS IGNITION MODULE	YELLOW-RED
852	COIL "C" TO DISTRIBUTORLESS IGNITION MODULE	YELLOW-WHITE
853	HEATED WINDSHIELD FUSE RESISTOR	BROWN
854	THIRD LOCKOUT SOLENOID	GRAY-WHITE
855	RIGHT REAR AIR INPUT RETURN	LT BLUE
856	LEFT CHANNEL SIGNAL	PURPLE
857	LEFT FRONT AIR INPUT RETURN	WHITE-ORANGE
858	RIGHT FRONT AIR INPUT RETURN	BROWN
859	LEFT REAR AIR INPUT RETURN	YELLOW
860	LEFT MOTOR-DRIVER — F	PURPLE-YELLOW
861	LEFT MOTOR-DRIVER — R	BLACK-WHITE
862	LEFT LIMIT-A — DRIVER	BROWN-YELLOW
863	RIGHT DOOR OPEN — PASSENGER	RED
864	RIGHT MOTOR-PASSENGER — F	ORANGE
865	RIGHT MOTOR-PASSENGER — R	PURPLE-WHITE
866	INERTIA SWITCH TO MODULE	WHITE
867	LEFT DOOR OPEN — DRIVER	DK BLUE
868	EMERGENCY RELEASE LEVERS	GRAY-RED
869	RETARD VALVE TO CONTROL RELAY TERM. #1	LT GREEN-YELLOW
871	SEAT BELT INDICATOR LAMP TO MODULE	YELLOW

* IN SOME CASES, THERE MAY BE ADDITIONAL CIRCUIT FUNCTIONS INCLUDED IN THE CIRCUIT DESCRIPTION LISTED.

STANDARD CIRCUIT CHART (BY NUMBER)

CIRCUIT	DESCRIPTION *	COLOR	CIRCUIT	DESCRIPTION *	COLOR
872	LEFT LIMIT-B — DRIVER	LT GREEN	916	SPEED CONTROL VACUUM TO EEC MODULE	LT GREEN
873	RIGHT LIMIT-B — PASSENGER	TAN	917	VENT SWITCH TO BLOWER MOTOR — LO	PINK-LT GREEN
874	RIGHT LIMIT-A — PASSENGER	GRAY	918	SEAT REG. SW. TO RECLINER MOTOR — UP	GRAY
875	GROUND LOGIC MODULE	BLACK-LT BLUE	919	SEAT REG. SW. TO RECLINER MOTOR — DOWN	GRAY-BLACK
876	VENT SWITCH TO RIGHT FRONT VENT — CONSOLE	BLACK-ORANGE	920	HEATED WINDSHIELD LH TO SENSE RESISTOR	BROWN-WHITE
877	RELEASE LEVER WARN INDICATOR LAMP — CONSOLE	WHITE-ORANGE	921	FEED TO FUEL SHUTOFF LAMP	GRAY-ORANGE
878	VENT SWITCH TO RIGHT FRONT VENT MOTOR	BLACK-LT BLUE	922	FUEL PUMP RESISTOR TO RELAY	WHITE-RED
879	VENT CROSSOVER FEED	RED-BLACK	923	TRANSMISSION OIL TEMP	ORANGE-BLACK
880	VENT CROSSOVER FEED	RED-LT BLUE	924	COAST CLUTCH SOLENOID	BROWN
881	WINDOW SWITCH TO RIGHT REAR MOTOR	BROWN	925	ELECTRONIC THROTTLE VALVE POWER	YELLOW-WHITE
882	WINDOW SWITCH TO RIGHT REAR MOTOR	BROWN-YELLOW	926	EEC MODULE CONTROL OF HIGH SPEED FUEL PUMP	LT BLUE-ORANGE
883	AIR COND. CONTROL RELAY FEED	PINK-LT BLUE	927	EVO MODULE TO TEST CONNECTOR	ORANGE-BLACK
884	WINDOW SWITCH TO LEFT REAR MOTOR	YELLOW-BLACK	928	POWER FEED FROM AMPLIFIER	PURPLE
885	WINDOW SWITCH TO LEFT REAR MOTOR	YELLOW-LT BLUE	929	EEC MODULE TO SPARK ADVANCE	PINK
886	VENT SWITCH TO LEFT FRONT VENT MOTOR	ORANGE-WHITE	930	PROGRAMMABLE RIDE CONTROL MODULE TO STAR TEST CONNECTOR	DK BLUE
887	VENT SWITCH TO LEFT FRONT VENT MOTOR	YELLOW	931	BATTERY FEED TO RELAY CONTROLLER	ORANGE
888	MEMORY MIRROR MODULE TO RH HORIZONTAL DRIVER	LT BLUE	932	DAYTIME RUNNING LAMP	GRAY-WHITE
889	MEMORY MIRROR MODULE MOTOR DIRECTION	BLACK-ORANGE	933	ESC SWITCH TO ESC VALVE CONTROL	LT GREEN-BLACK
890	MEMORY MIRROR MODULE TO RH VERTICAL DRIVE	BROWN-WHITE	934	EMISSION SPEED SENSOR TO MODULATOR CONTROL	TAN-WHITE
891	MEMORY MIRROR MODULE POSITION +	RED-BLACK	935	HEATED WINDSHIELD TO FUSE	DK BLUE-YELLOW
892	MEMORY MIRROR MODULE RH HORIZONTAL POSITION	ORANGE	936	KEY CYLINDER SENSOR TO ANTI-THEFT MODULE	DK GREEN-WHITE
893	MEMORY MIRROR MODULE RH VERTICAL POSITION	LT BLUE-BLACK	939	MODULATOR TO THERMO. SWITCH	TAN-BLACK
894	MEMORY MIRROR MODULE POSITION —	GRAY	941	WASHER PUMP MOTOR FEED	BLACK-WHITE
895	MEMORY MIRROR MODULE	WHITE-PURPLE	946	REAR WASHER PUMP FEED	PURPLE-LT GREEN
896	MEMORY MIRROR MODULE LH HORIZONTAL POSITION	PINK-ORANGE	950	WASHER CONTROL SWITCH FEED	WHITE-BLACK
897	MEMORY MIRROR MODULE TO LH VERTICAL DRIVE	TAN-BLACK	955	W/S WIPER MOTOR ARM RH TO W/S WIPER SWITCH	RED-ORANGE
898	MEMORY MIRROR MODULE TO LH HORIZONTAL DRIVER	TAN-RED	956	W/W WIPER SWITCH TO W/S WIPER MOTOR FIELD RH	LT GREEN-ORANGE
899	MEMORY SEAT TO NEUTRAL SENSOR SWITCH	RED-WHITE	965	SUPERCHARGER SOLENOID #1	LT GREEN-PURPLE
900	STARTER INTERRUPT RELAY TO NEUTRAL START SWITCH	WHITE-LT BLUE	966	SUPERCHARGER SOLENOID #2	RED-YELLOW
901	AMPLIFIER TO SPEED SENSOR RETURN	RED-LT BLUE	967	MASS AIR FLOW	DK BLUE-ORANGE
902	TOP CONTROL RELAY TO MOTOR — UP	YELLOW	968	MASS AIR FLOW RETURN	TAN-LT BLUE
903	TOP CONTROL RELAY TO MOTOR — DOWN	RED	969	MASS AIR FLOW GROUND	BLACK
904	(COIL) OR (ACCY) TERM OF IGNITION SWITCH TO ALTERNATOR REGULATOR (IGN. TERM)	LT GREEN-RED	973	BATTERY FEED TO AUX. FUEL SELECTOR SWITCH	RED
905	VEHICLE MAINTENANCE MONITOR MODULE TO OIL TEMP INPUT	LT BLUE	974	FUEL CONTROL SWITCH TO FUEL CONTROL VALVE	ORANGE
906	VEHICLE MAINTENANCE MONITOR MODULE TO OIL TEMP OUTPUT	WHITE-LT BLUE	977	BRAKE WARNING SWITCH TO INDICATOR LAMP	PURPLE-WHITE
907	VEHICLE MAINTENANCE MONITOR MODULE TO ELEC. INSTR. CLUST. SENSE	PURPLE-LT GREEN	978	SEAT REGULATOR SWITCH TO FRONT MOTOR (LH)	YELLOW-LT BLUE
908	VEHICLE MAINTENANCE MONITOR MODULE TO ENGINE STRAP	TAN-BLACK	979	SEAT REGULATOR SWITCH TO FRONT MOTOR (LH)	RED-LT BLUE
909	VEHICLE MAINTENANCE MONITOR MODULE TO SPEED SENSOR	LT BLUE-WHITE	980	SEAT REGULATOR SWITCH TO HORZ. MOTOR (LH)	YELLOW-WHITE
910	FUSED ACCY FEED — TRIPMINDER	BLACK-WHITE	981	SEAT REGULATOR SWITCH TO HORZ. MOTOR (LH)	RED-WHITE
911	OVERDRIVE CANCEL INDICATOR LAMP	LT GREEN-WHITE	982	SEAT REGULATOR SWITCH TO REAR MOTOR (LH)	YELLOW-LT GREEN
912	EEC MODULE TO TRANSMISSION	LT BLUE-WHITE	983	SEAT REGULATOR SWITCH TO REAR MOTOR (LH)	RED-LT GREEN
913	LIFTGATE SW. TO LIFTGATE RELAY	GRAY-RED	984	SEAT REGULATOR SWITCH TO FRONT MOTOR (RH)	YELLOW-LT BLUE
914	EEC MODULE — DATA PLUS	TAN-ORANGE	985	SEAT REGULATOR SWITCH TO FRONT MOTOR (RH)	RED-LT BLUE
915	EEC MODULE — DATA MINUS	PINK-LT BLUE	986	SEAT REGULATOR SWITCH TO HORZ. MOTOR (RH)	YELLOW-WHITE
			987	SEAT REGULATOR SWITCH TO HORZ. MOTOR (RH)	RED-WHITE
			988	SEAT REGULATOR SWITCH TO REAR MOTOR (RH)	YELLOW-LT GREEN
			989	SEAT REGULATOR SWITCH TO REAR MOTOR (RH)	RED-LT GREEN
			990	SEAT REGULATOR SWITCH TO FRONT MOTOR (LH)	YELLOW-LT BLUE
			993	INTERMITTENT GOVERNOR TO WINDSHIELD WIPER SWITCH	BROWN-WHITE

* IN SOME CASES, THERE MAY BE ADDITIONAL CIRCUIT
FUNCTIONS INCLUDED IN THE CIRCUIT DESCRIPTION LISTED.

STANDARD CIRCUIT CHART (BY COLOR)

COLOR	DESCRIPTION *	CIRCUIT
(COLOR OPT.)	BLIND CIRCUIT TERM. IN HARNESS CANNOT BE CHECKED FOR CONT.	48
BLACK	GROUND CIRCUIT	57
BLACK	MARKER LAMP SWITCH TO MARKER LAMPS	207
BLACK	16 GA FUSE LINK	291
BLACK	HEATED WINDSHIELD GROUND TEST LEAD	739
BLACK	DOOR WIRE	629
BLACK	DCP MODULE SIGNAL GROUND TO RADIO	596
BLACK	MASS AIR FLOW GROUND	969
BLACK	ELECTRONIC CLUSTER FROM GROUND IN KEYBOARD	373
BLACK-LT BLUE	DOOR AJAR SWITCH TO INDICATOR LAMP LEFT REAR GROUND	363
BLACK-LT BLUE	DIESEL CONTROL MODULE GROUND RETURN	488
BLACK-LT BLUE	AIR TEMP SENSOR TO CONTROL UNIT	743
BLACK-LT BLUE	VENT SWITCH TO RIGHT FRONT VENT MOTOR	878
BLACK-LT BLUE	GROUND LOGIC MODULE	875
BLACK-LT BLUE	COURTESY LAMP SWITCH TO COURTESY LAMP	53
BLACK-LT BLUE	WARNING LAMP PROVE OUT	41
BLACK-LT BLUE	COURTESY LAMP SW. TO "C" PILLAR LAMPS	127
BLACK-LT GREEN	KEYLESS DOOR LOCK ILLUMINATION GROUND TO MODULE	76
BLACK-LT GREEN	CONSTANT VOLTAGE UNIT TO GAUGE	60
BLACK-LT GREEN	CONSTANT VOLTAGE UNIT AND INDICATOR LAMPS FEED	30
BLACK-LT GREEN	ACCY FEED FROM IGNITION SWITCH	297
BLACK-LT GREEN	COLD START INJECTOR	230
BLACK-LT GREEN	BATTERY TO MULTIPLEX MODULE	785
BLACK-LT GREEN	BLOWER MOTOR RELAY (LOAD TERM) TO BLOWER MOTOR	536
BLACK-LT GREEN	SPEAKER VOICE COIL FEED	822
BLACK-LT GREEN	BLOWER MOTOR FEED	364
BLACK-LT GREEN	POWER RELAY TO GLOW PLUGS (RIGHT BANK)	336
BLACK-ORANGE	FUEL 1 GROUND TO TACH/GAUGE MODULE	396
BLACK-ORANGE	REMOTE CONVENIENCE SELF DIAGNOSTIC GROUND	571
BLACK-ORANGE	HEATED WINDSHIELD CONTROL TO ELECT ALTERNATOR REGULATOR	579
BLACK-ORANGE	CENTER REAR TAILLAMP BULB OUTAGE	573
BLACK-ORANGE	OPEN DOOR WARNING LAMP TO OPEN DOOR WARNING SWITCH	627
BLACK-ORANGE	MULTIPLEX WINDSHIELD WIPER OFF	695
BLACK-ORANGE	VENT SWITCH TO RIGHT FRONT VENT—CONSOLE	876
BLACK-ORANGE	MEMORY MIRROR MODULE MOTOR DIRECTION	889
BLACK-ORANGE	ELEC. ENG. CONTROL MOD. TO THICK FILM IGN. MOD.	259
BLACK-ORANGE	MEMORY SEAT SWITCH POSITION #2	268
BLACK-ORANGE	DIESEL WATER IN FUEL SENDER TO WARNING LAMP GROUND	327
BLACK-ORANGE	POWER SUPPLY TO BATTERY	38
BLACK-ORANGE	ENGINE COMPARTMENT LAMP FEED	80
BLACK-ORANGE	COURTESY LAMP SW. TO INSTR. PANEL COURTESY LAMP	126
BLACK-PINK	KEY WARNING SWITCH TO BUZZER	158
BLACK-PINK	BACKUP LAMP	140
BLACK-PINK	CARGO LAMP SW. TO CARGO LAMP	55
BLACK-PINK	WINDSHIELD WIPER SW. TO WINDSHIELD WIPER MOTOR	28
BLACK-PINK	ECU TO VACUUM SWITCH 4	211
BLACK-PINK	AIR SUSPENSION ELECTRONICS GROUND	432
BLACK-PINK	HCU (MAIN) TO MODULE	493
BLACK-PINK	MODULE TO SWITCH	464
BLACK-PINK	DOOR AJAR SWITCH TO INDICATOR LAMP RIGHT FRONT GROUND	345
BLACK-PINK	DOOR AJAR SWITCH TO INDICATOR LAMP RIGHT REAR GROUND	346
BLACK-WHITE	SENSOR SIGNAL RETURN	359
BLACK-WHITE	SIGNAL GROUND TO TACH/GAUGE MODULE	397
BLACK-WHITE	LEFT MOTOR-DRIVER - R	861
BLACK-WHITE	ANTI-LOCK MODULE TO ANTI-LOCK CONTROL VALVE	685
BLACK-WHITE	BATTERY TO MULTIPLEX SYSTEM	791
BLACK-WHITE	WINDSHIELD WIPER INTERMITTENT GOVERNOR FEED	587
BLACK-WHITE	DEDICATED GROUND	570
BLACK-WHITE	SPEED SIGNAL SPEEDO TACH MODULE TO FUEL COMPUTER	565
BLACK-WHITE	CIRCUIT BREAKER (LOAD TERM) TO CONTROL SWITCH (BATT. TERM)	517
BLACK-WHITE	CORNERING LAMP SWITCH FEED	526
BLACK-WHITE	WASHER PUMP MOTOR FEED	941
BLACK-WHITE	FUSED ACCY FEED — TRIPMINDER	910
BLACK-WHITE	CIRCUIT BREAKER TO SEAT LATCH RELAY	171
BLACK-WHITE	SPEAKER VOICE COIL RETURN	287
BLACK-WHITE	SEAT REG. CONTROL SWITCH FEED	51
BLACK-WHITE	INSTRUMENT PANEL LAMP SWITCH FEED	88
BLACK-YELLOW	WARNING LAMP TO LIGHTS ON RELAY	111
BLACK-YELLOW	WARNING LAMP RELAY FEED	112
BLACK-YELLOW	ACCESSORY FEED TO MESSAGE CENTER	231
BLACK-YELLOW	EFE CARBURETOR SPACE FEED	229
BLACK-YELLOW	RELAY FEED	175
BLACK-YELLOW	INJECTION PUMP FUEL TEMPERATURE SENSOR	225
BLACK-YELLOW	AIR BAG DIAGNOSTIC MODULE TO RELAY INDICATOR LAMP	608
BLACK-YELLOW	DIESEL TACH GROUND TO TACH GAGE MODULE	644
BLACK-YELLOW	TACHOMETER GROUND TO TACH/GAUGE MODULE	398
BLACK-YELLOW	DOOR AJAR SWITCH TO INDICATOR LAMP LEFT FRONT GROUND	344
BLACK-YELLOW	COMPRESSOR CLUTCH FEED	347
BROWN	DOOR AJAR RELAY TO DOOR SWITCH	374
BROWN	POWER "THIGH" BOLSTER DOWN	492
BROWN	STEERING RATE SENSOR TERMINAL B CONTROL MODULE	634
BROWN	FUEL SIGNAL TACH MODULE TO FUEL COMPUTER	564
BROWN	HEATED WINDSHIELD CONTROL TO ALT POWER RELAY	580
BROWN	ELECT SHIFT 4 × 4 MODULE TO ELECT CLUTCH	779
BROWN	MULTIPLEX HEADLAMPS	697
BROWN	C.B. D-DIGIT	708
BROWN	COAST CLUTCH SOLENOID	924
BROWN	EATC LH SUNLOAD SENSOR POSITIVE	468
BROWN	WINDOW SWITCH TO RIGHT REAR MOTOR	881
BROWN	HEATED WINDSHIELD FUSE RESISTOR	853
BROWN	RIGHT FRONT AIR INPUT RETURN	858
BROWN	TO ELECTRONIC CLUSTER FROM ENGLISH/METRIC SWITCH IN KEYBOARD	273
BROWN	FEEDBACK CARBURETOR COIL "A"	304
BROWN	SWITCH FEED	276
BROWN	18 GA FUSE LINK	292
BROWN	KEYLESS DOOR LOCK SWITCH ENABLE FROM MODULE	124
BROWN	HEADLAMP SWITCH TO TAIL LAMPS & SIDE MARKER LAMPS	14
BROWN-LT BLUE	DOOR JAMB SWITCH TO LIGHTS ON RELAY	138
BROWN-LT BLUE	LH HEADLAMP BULB OUTAGE	108
BROWN-LT BLUE	SEAT BELT WARNING TIMER TO L.F. RETRACTOR SWITCH	85
BROWN-LT BLUE	FUEL METERING CONTROL LEVER ACTUATOR 1 MINUS	232
BROWN-LT BLUE	DEFOGGER SW. TO DEFOGGER MOTOR	186
BROWN-LT BLUE	FUEL INJECTOR #4 CYLINDER	558
BROWN-LT GREEN	DCP MODULE TO WIPER PARK OVER-RIDE RELAY	592
BROWN-LT GREEN	MODE SELECT SWITCH FEED	832
BROWN-LT GREEN	EGR VALVE POSITION FEED	352
BROWN-LT GREEN	AUTOLAMP AMPLIFIER TO SENSOR	222
BROWN-LT GREEN	POWER SERVO TO CLIMATE CONTROL UNIT (AMP)	245
BROWN-LT GREEN	MEMORY SEAT SWITCH POSITION #1	267
BROWN-LT GREEN	SERVO FEEDBACK POTENTIOMETER BASE TO AMPLIFIER	149
BROWN-ORANGE	VACUUM DOOR LOCK SWITCH TO SOLENOID (UNLOCK)	116
BROWN-ORANGE	MEMORY SEAT SWITCH SET	270
BROWN-ORANGE	IGNITION SWITCH TO THERMACTOR TIMER	251
BROWN-ORANGE	BLOWER MOTOR FEED	181
BROWN-ORANGE	VACUUM SOLENOID TO TEMP. SW.	369
BROWN-ORANGE	RADIO MEMORY SEEK	372
BROWN-ORANGE	RADIO SWITCH TO ANTENNA RELAY	449
BROWN-PINK	AIR SUSPENSION HEIGHT SENSOR LO — R.F.	425
BROWN-PINK	DIESEL CONTROL SWITCH TO LAMP CONTROL RELAY	338
BROWN-PINK	IGNITION SWITCH ACCY TERM. TO DECK LID OPEN WARNING LAMP	485
BROWN-PINK	POWER RELAY COIL TO MODULE	513
BROWN-PINK	STARTING MOTOR RELAY TO IGNITION COIL "I" TERM.	262
BROWN-WHITE	THERMOSTAT SWITCH FEED	182
BROWN-WHITE	HEADLAMP SWITCH TO ELECTRONIC CLUSTER DIMMING	192
BROWN-WHITE	FLUID WARNING SWITCH TO PRESSURE SWITCH	549
BROWN-WHITE	EXTENDED USEFUL LIFE SENSOR TO WARNING LAMP	574
BROWN-WHITE	SELECTOR SWITCH TO AUX. FUEL SOLENOID	674
BROWN-WHITE	ELECT SHIFT 4 × 4 MODULE TO MOTOR POSITION #3	764
BROWN-WHITE	ELECT SHIFT MODULE TO LOW RANGE INDICATOR LAMP ROOF CONSOLE	782
BROWN-WHITE	MULTIPLEX LCD ILLUMINATION	732
BROWN-WHITE	BLOWER MOTOR SWITCH RELAY TO RESISTOR (LOW SPEED)	755
BROWN-WHITE	FUEL TANK SELECTOR TO FUEL PUMP REAR	789
BROWN-WHITE	INTERMITTENT GOVERNOR TO WINDSHIELD WIPER SWITCH	993
BROWN-WHITE	HEATED WINDSHIELD LH TO SENSE RESISTOR	920
BROWN-WHITE	DECK LID OPEN WARNING LAMP TO DECK LID OPEN SWITCH	486
BROWN-WHITE	MEMORY MIRROR MODULE TO RH VERTICAL DRIVE	890
BROWN-WHITE	TURN SIGNAL SWITCH TO RH CORNERING LAMP	379
BROWN-WHITE	ELECT. ENG. CONTL. MOD. TO IDLE SPD. CONTL. MOTOR #3	376
BROWN-YELLOW	HEATER BLOWER SWITCH FEED	399
BROWN-YELLOW	LEFT LIMIT-A — DRIVER	862
BROWN-YELLOW	WINDOW SWITCH TO RIGHT REAR MOTOR	882
BROWN-YELLOW	EATC LH SUNLOAD SENSOR NEGATIVE	476
BROWN-YELLOW	DCP MODULE TO WASHER RELAY	591
BROWN-YELLOW	FUEL INJECTOR #3 CYLINDER	557
BROWN-YELLOW	ELECTRIC DRIVE COOLING FAN	228
BROWN-YELLOW	MAP LAMP SWITCH TO RH MAP LAMP	125
BROWN-YELLOW	EMISSION CONTROL VALVE TO SWITCH	81
BROWN-YELLOW	BATTERY TO HI-BEAM	62
DK BLUE	HORN SWITCH CONTROL	1
DK BLUE	20 GA FUSE LINK	302
DK BLUE	L.H. REMOTE MIRROR MOTOR FEED — C.C.W.	541
DK BLUE	FEED TO FAILURE SWITCH	600
DK BLUE	ELECT SHIFT MODULE TO 2H 4H SWITCH	780
DK BLUE	MOONROOF RELAY TO MICRO SWITCH OPEN	691
DK BLUE	SHOCK DAMPENING RELAY SOFT TO SHOCK DAMPENING CONTROL	653
DK BLUE	LOGIC MODE	689
DK BLUE	PROGRAMMABLE RIDE CONTROL MODULE TO STAR TEST CONNECTOR	930
DK BLUE	LEFT DOOR OPEN — DRIVER	867
DK BLUE	CRANKSHAFT POSITION SENSOR FEED	349
DK BLUE-LT GREEN	WARNING LAMP TO ANTI-THEFT MODULE	343
DK BLUE-LT GREEN	BAROMETRIC PRESSURE SENSOR FEED	356
DK BLUE-LT GREEN	C.B. SPEAKER VOICE COIL RETURN	721
DK BLUE-LT GREEN	HEATER & A/C CONTROL SW. (LO-NORM) TO CLIMATE CONTROL UNIT	249
DK BLUE-LT GREEN	BUFFER FUEL LEVEL OUTPUT TO TRIPMINDER	205
DK BLUE-LT GREEN	THERMOCOUPLE POS TO EXHAUST SYST. OVERTEMP PROTECT MODULE	90
DK BLUE-ORANGE	ANTI-THEFT SWITCH ARM	24
DK BLUE-ORANGE	WINDSHIELD WIPER SW. TO WINDSHIELD WIPER MOTOR	56
DK BLUE-ORANGE	AUTOLAMP AMPLIFIER TO RHEOSTAT	217
DK BLUE-ORANGE	HEADLAMP FLASH TO PASS SWITCH FEED	196
DK BLUE-ORANGE	AMPLIFIER SWITCH GROUND TO LEFT REAR SPEAKER	826
DK BLUE-ORANGE	MASS AIR FLOW	967
DK BLUE-ORANGE	CRANK ENABLE TO IGNITION MODULE	325
DK BLUE-WHITE	R.F. DOOR UNLOCK SWITCH TO L.F. DOOR UNLOCK SWITCH	390
DK BLUE-WHITE	BLOWER MOTOR SPEED CONTROLLER TO RESISTOR #3 (MED.)	751
DK BLUE-WHITE	MULTIPLEX MESSAGE O	735
DK BLUE-WHITE	INTERMITTENT GOVERNOR TO W/S WIPER SWITCH	590
DK BLUE-WHITE	AIR BAG DIAGNOSTIC MODULE SAFING SENSOR (GROUND)	613
DK BLUE-WHITE	FUSE HOLDER TO HEADLAMP DIMMER AMPLIFIER	504
DK BLUE-WHITE	THERMOMETER AMBIENT SENSOR RETURN	234
DK BLUE-WHITE	SEAT BELT WARNING TIMER TO R.F. SEAT SENSOR	86
DK BLUE-YELLOW	ELECTRONIC CONTROL UNIT TO SOLENOID ACTUATOR	77
DK BLUE-YELLOW	DEFOGGER SW. TO DEFOGGER MOTOR	191
DK BLUE-YELLOW	THERMOMETER SENSOR FEED	233
DK BLUE-YELLOW	SELECTOR SWITCH TO MIDSHIP TANK	673
DK BLUE-YELLOW	AMPLIFIER SWITCH FEED TO LEFT FRONT SPEAKER	820
DK BLUE-YELLOW	HEATED WINDSHIELD TO FUSE	935
DK BLUE-YELLOW	AIR COMPRESSOR POWER RELAY CONTROL	420
DK GREEN	REARVIEW OUTSIDE MIRROR DOWN	411
DK GREEN	EGR VALVE TO EEC MODULE	360
DK GREEN	CAM SENSOR TO EEC MODULE	795

* IN SOME CASES, THERE MAY BE ADDITIONAL CIRCUIT
FUNCTIONS INCLUDED IN THE CIRCUIT DESCRIPTION LISTED.

STANDARD CIRCUIT CHART (BY COLOR)

COLOR	DESCRIPTION *	CIRCUIT
DK GREEN	STOPLAMP SWITCH TO HI MOUNT STOPLAMP	569
DK GREEN	REAR LAMP TO TRAILER RELAY FEED	576
DK GREEN	R.H. REMOTE MIRROR MOTOR FEED — C.W.	543
DK GREEN	LEFT REAR SHOCK DAMPENING RELAY TO CONTROL MODULE	651
DK GREEN	FAILURE WARNING LIGHT	603
DK GREEN	14 GA FUSE LINK	299
DK GREEN	TRAILER RH TURN SIGNAL	64
DK GREEN	WINDSHIELD WIPER SW. TO WINDSHIELD WIPER MOTOR	65
DK GREEN	SUPPLEMENTAL ALTERNATOR STATOR C TERM. TO WINDSHIELD	72
DK GREEN-LT GREEN	CLOCK ADVANCE SWITCH TO MESSAGE CENTER	141
DK GREEN-LT GREEN	ELECTRONIC CONTROL UNIT TO ENGINE VACUUM SWITCH	75
DK GREEN-LT GREEN	EMA CONTROL TO SPARK RETARD SWITCH	21
DK GREEN-LT GREEN	THROTTLE ANGLE POSITION SENSOR FEED	355
DK GREEN-LT GREEN	AIR SUSPENSION MALFUNCTION WARNING LAMP	419
DK GREEN-LT GREEN	R.F. DOOR LOCK SWITCH TO L.F. DOOR LOCK SWITCH	389
DK GREEN-LT GREEN	SEAT BELT WARNING INDICATOR LAMP FEED	450
DK GREEN-ORANGE	HEATER & A/C CONTROL SW. (TEMP. SELECTOR) TO REHEAT AMPL.	773
DK GREEN-ORANGE	SPEAKER SWITCH GROUND TO RIGHT FRONT SPEAKER	811
DK GREEN-ORANGE	AMPLIFIER/SPEAKER SWITCH GROUND TO RIGHT REAR SPEAKER	803
DK GREEN-ORANGE	PROCESSOR LOOP SIGNAL RETURN	848
DK GREEN-ORANGE	MCU MODULE TO KNOCK SENSOR	311
DK GREEN-ORANGE	PARITY BIT-DISPLAY TO MESSAGE CENTER	178
DK GREEN-PURPLE	TRANSMISSION THROTTLE VALVE SOLENOID 2	315
DK GREEN-PURPLE	ANTI-THEFT SWITCH DISARM	25
DK GREEN-PURPLE	HEATED EXTERIOR MIRROR FEED	59
DK GREEN-PURPLE	DATA-MESSAGE CENTER TO DISPLAY	174
DK GREEN-PURPLE	AIR FUEL SENSOR TO E.C.U.	94
DK GREEN-PURPLE	POWER FEED DECEL TIMER TO THROTTLE KICKER	584
DK GREEN-WHITE	SENSOR AMPLIFY UNIT TO CONTROL UNIT #3	759
DK GREEN-WHITE	KEY CYLINDER SENSOR TO ANTI-THEFT MODULE	936
DK GREEN-WHITE	STOPLAMP SW. TO STOPLAMP RELAY (COIL TERM.)	475
DK GREEN-WHITE	FUEL LEVEL RECEIVER TO FUEL LEVEL WARNING RELAY (REG. TERM.)	367
DK GREEN-WHITE	SENSOR SIGNAL TO AMPLIFIER	150
DK GREEN-WHITE	OIL PRESSURE SWITCH TO TIMER	254
DK GREEN-YELLOW	HEADLAMP SWITCH TO AUTOLAMP AMPLIFIER	219
DK GREEN-YELLOW	ELECTRONIC CONTROL UNIT TO EXHAUST GAS OXYGEN SENSOR	74
DK GREEN-YELLOW	ELECTRONIC SWITCH TO IGNITION COIL NEG. TERMINAL	11
DK GREEN-YELLOW	AIR SUSPENSION CONTROL MODULE FEED	418
DK GREEN-YELLOW	ANTENNA SWITCH TO POWER ANTENNA (DOWN)	746
DK GREEN-YELLOW	SPLICE #3 TO POWER RELAY	546
DL BLUE	TRAILER STOP LAMPS	43
GRAY	LOW OIL LEVEL RELAY TO WARNING LAMP	208
GRAY	12 GA FUSE LINK	290
GRAY	HEADLAMP DIMMER RELAY TO HEADLAMP DIMMER SWITCH	502
GRAY	ELECT SHIFT MODULE TO GRAPHIC DISPLAY ROOF CONSOLE	783
GRAY	C.B. SCAN L.E.D.	706
GRAY	WINDSHIELD WIPER HIGH	719
GRAY	RIGHT CHANNEL SIGNAL	690
GRAY	SEAT REG. SW. TO RECLINER MOTOR — UP	918
GRAY	RIGHT LIMIT-A — PASSENGER	874
GRAY	MEMORY MIRROR MODULE POSITION	894
GRAY	AIR SUSPENSION SYSTEM GROUND	430
GRAY	EATC RH SUNLOAD SENSOR NEGATIVE	483
GRAY	CRANKSHAFT SENSOR SIGNAL RETURN	350
GRAY	DIESEL CONTROL SWITCH TO POWER RELAY & LAMP CONTROL RELAY	339
GRAY-BLACK	LIMIT SW. TO BACK WINDOW REG. MOTOR	401
GRAY-BLACK	FRONT TILT POSITION SENSE	441
GRAY-BLACK	SEAT REG. SW. TO RECLINER MOTOR — DOWN	919
GRAY-BLACK	VALVE #5 TO MODULE	499
GRAY-BLACK	SPEED CONTROL SENSE EEC MODULE TO SENSOR	679
GRAY-BLACK	WINDOW REGULATOR MOTOR TO GROUND	157
GRAY-BLACK	INSIDE DOOR HANDLE SWITCH TO RETRACTOR INHIBITOR MODULE	185
GRAY-BLACK	SERVO SOURCE VACUUM SOLENOID TO CONTROL TRANSISTOR	145
GRAY-LT BLUE	MILES/KILOMETERS SWITCH TO MESSAGE CENTER	161
GRAY-LT BLUE	HTD BACKLITE SW. TO TIME DELAY RELAY	688
GRAY-LT BLUE	SENSOR AMPLIFY UNIT TO CONTROL UNIT #2	750
GRAY-LT BLUE	AMPLIFIER/SPEAKER SWITCH FEED TO LEFT REAR SPEAKER	800
GRAY-LT BLUE	ANEROID SWITCH TO MCU MODULE	394
GRAY-ORANGE	SPARK MODULE TO MCU MODULE	395
GRAY-ORANGE	HEAD LP TIME DELAY CONTROL RELAY TO CIR. BREAKER	686
GRAY-ORANGE	AIR BAG SAFING SENSORS TO INFLATORS	614
GRAY-ORANGE	FEED TO FUEL SHUTOFF LAMP	921
GRAY-ORANGE	AVERAGE SPEED SWITCH TO MESSAGE CENTER	156
GRAY-ORANGE	ELECTRONIC CONTROL UNIT TO DECELERATION SOLENOID	47
GRAY-RED	DISTANCE TO EMPTY SWITCH TO MESSAGE CENTER	155
GRAY-RED	THERMOCOUPLE 1 NEG. TO EXHAUST SYST. OVERTEMP PROTECT MODULE	91
GRAY-RED	INHIBITOR MODULE TO RETRACTOR OVERRIDE SOLENOID	187
GRAY-RED	EXHAUST BACK PRESSURE VALVE ACTUATOR	318
GRAY-RED	LIFTGATE SW. TO LIFTGATE RELAY	913
GRAY-RED	DIESEL COLD ADVANTAGE	607
GRAY-RED	MOTOR TO MOTOR FEED	538
GRAY-RED	TEMP WARNING LAMP TO SENDING UNIT	682
GRAY-RED	ELECTRONIC SHOCK DIAGNOSTIC	844
GRAY-RED	EMERGENCY RELEASE LEVERS	868
GRAY-RED	SWITCH TO VALVE	455
GRAY-RED	SEAT PROCESSOR ASSY TO FRONT MOTOR LH	452
GRAY-RED	WINDOW REG. SW. TO BACK WINDOW REG. MOTOR	402
GRAY-WHITE	WINDOW REG. SW. TO WINDOW REG. MOTOR	403
GRAY-WHITE	THIRD LOCKOUT SOLENOID	854
GRAY-WHITE	AIR BAG DIAGNOSTIC MODULE TO DRIVER INFLATOR	615
GRAY-WHITE	DAYTIME RUNNING LAMP	932
GRAY-WHITE	AIR CONDITIONER CLUTCH RELAY	321
GRAY-WHITE	DISTANCE TO MESSAGE CENTER	164
GRAY-WHITE	CHOKE RELAY TO CHOKE	67
GRAY-YELLOW	ELECTRONIC CONTROL UNIT TO CANISTER PURGE SOLENOID	101
GRAY-YELLOW	HEADLAMP DIMMER SWITCH TO HEADLAMP DIMMER AMPLIFIER	505

COLOR	DESCRIPTION *	CIRCUIT
GRAY-YELLOW	ACC FEED	687
GRAY-YELLOW	EFI MODULE TO CLUTCH SWITCH	481
GRAY-YELLOW	PRESSURE SWITCH TO INERTIA SWITCH	467
LT BLUE	REARVIEW OUTSIDE MIRROR CLOCKWISE	413
LT BLUE	ELECT. ENG. CONTL. MOD. TO ELECTRO DRIVE FAN	386
LT BLUE	VEHICLE SPEED SENSOR FEED	353
LT BLUE	ANTI-SKID MODULE TO ANTI-SKID CONTROL VALVE	677
LT BLUE	C.B. B+ DIGIT	720
LT BLUE	CAM SENDER SIGNAL RETURN	796
LT BLUE	ELECT SHIFT 4 × 4 MODULE TO SPEED SENSOR COIL	772
LT BLUE	LOW COOLANT LEVEL RELAY TO SENSOR	794
LT BLUE	HEADLAMP DIMMER RELAY TO FUSE HOLDER	503
LT BLUE	ELECTRONIC FUEL GAGE TO MESSAGE CENTER	501
LT BLUE	FUEL INJECTOR #8 CYLINDER	562
LT BLUE	LEFT FRONT SHOCK DAMPENING RELAY TO CONTROL MODULE	641
LT BLUE	RIGHT REAR AIR INPUT RETURN	855
LT BLUE	MEMORY MIRROR MODULE TO RH HORIZONTAL DRIVER	888
LT BLUE	VEHICLE MAINTENANCE MONITOR MODULE TO OIL TEMP INPUT	905
LT BLUE	LOW FUEL INDICATOR	106
LT BLUE	KEYLESS DOOR LOCK SWITCH ILLUMINATION FEED	66
LT BLUE	TURN SIGNAL FLASHER TO TURN SIGNAL SWITCH	44
LT BLUE	SEAT REG. SW. TO HORIZ. SOLENOID BATT. TERM	306
LT BLUE	INDICATOR LAMP TO SWITCH (4 × 4)	210
LT BLUE-BLACK	AMPLIFIER SPEAKER SWITCH TO LEFT REAR SPEAKER	277
LT BLUE-BLACK	BRAKE FEED	22
LT BLUE-BLACK	SPEED CONTROL ON-OFF SWITCH TO AMPLIFIER	151
LT BLUE-BLACK	MEMORY MIRROR MODULE RH VERTICAL POSITION	893
LT BLUE-BLACK	FOG LAMP SWITCH TO FOG LAMP RELAY	477
LT BLUE-BLACK	INDICATOR LAMP TO LOW RANGE SWITCH 4 × 4	784
LT BLUE-BLACK	SAFETY RELAY LOAD TERM. TO WIND. REG. SW. FEED	400
LT BLUE-BLACK	AIR SOLENOID CONTROL — REAR	416
LT BLUE-BLACK	RELAY TO DAY/NIGHT ILLUMINATION LAMPS	434
LT BLUE-ORANGE	AMBIENT SENSOR TO INST. PANEL THERMISTOR	767
LT BLUE-ORANGE	C.B. SPEAKER RELAY TO MIC	723
LT BLUE-ORANGE	DCP MODULE TO HEATED BACKLITE RELAY	624
LT BLUE-ORANGE	EEC MODULE CONTROL OF HIGH SPEED FUEL PUMP	926
LT BLUE-ORANGE	LH REAR STOP & TURN BULB OUTAGE	104
LT BLUE-ORANGE	HORN CONTROL MODULE TO OVERRIDE SWITCH	34
LT BLUE-ORANGE	HI-TEMP SWITCH TO MCU MODULE	308
LT BLUE-ORANGE	HEATER BLOWER MOTOR TO SWITCH (MEDIUM)	269
LT BLUE-PINK	EEC MODULE TO TIME METER	305
LT BLUE-PINK	ELECTRONIC CLUSTER ACCESSORY FEED	295
LT BLUE-PINK	TRANSFORMER POWER — MESSAGE CENTER TO DISPLAY	169
LT BLUE-PINK	IDLE TRACKING SWITCH FEED	189
LT BLUE-PINK	BUCKLE SW. TO CENTER OCCUPANT SEAT SENSOR	107
LT BLUE-PINK	AIR COMPRESSOR VENT SOLENOID	578
LT BLUE-PINK	BRAKE SKID CONTROL MODULE FEED	601
LT BLUE-RED	DCP MODULE CONTROL INTERFACE TO RADIO	595
LT BLUE-RED	PRESSURE SWITCH TO MODULE	535
LT BLUE-RED	C.B. SPEAKER TO TRANSCEIVER	717
LT BLUE-RED	FUEL PUMP BYPASS	433
LT BLUE-RED	FUEL LEVEL WARNING RELAY FEED	365
LT BLUE-RED	CLOCK SELECT SWITCH TO MESSAGE CENTER	142
LT BLUE-RED	INSTRUMENT PANEL LAMPS FEED	19
LT BLUE-RED	THERMACTOR DUMP VALVE FEED	255
LT BLUE-WHITE	CIGAR LIGHTER FEED	40
LT BLUE-WHITE	ARRIVAL SWITCH TO MESSAGE CENTER	152
LT BLUE-WHITE	TIMER CONTROL VALVE TO CONTROL UNIT	741
LT BLUE-WHITE	SPEAKER SWITCH GROUND TO LEFT FRONT SPEAKER	813
LT BLUE-WHITE	DCP MODULE TO PARKLAMP RELAY	625
LT BLUE-WHITE	VEHICLE MAINTENANCE MONITOR MODULE TO SPEED SENSOR	909
LT BLUE-WHITE	EEC MODULE TO TRANSMISSION	912
LT BLUE-YELLOW	HEATER & A/C CONTROL SW. (HI & LO NORM) TO BLOWER MOTOR SW. RELAY	769
LT BLUE-YELLOW	RADIATOR COOLANT TEMP SWITCH TO CONTROL UNIT	742
LT BLUE-YELLOW	CRT SCAN	730
LT BLUE-YELLOW	FUEL TANK SELECTOR SWITCH TO AFT FUEL PUMP	671
LT BLUE-YELLOW	BATTERY TO AUTOMATIC ANTENNA SWITCH	451
LT BLUE-YELLOW	CHECKOUT SWITCH TO MESSAGE CENTER	143
LT BLUE-YELLOW	KEYLESS DOOR LOCK SWITCH DATA BIT 1 TO MODULE	78
LT BLUE-YELLOW	DE-ICE SOLENOID CONTROL	241
LT BLUE-YELLOW	MODULE TO NEUTRAL SENSOR SWITCH	199
LT GREEN	SPEAKER VOICE COIL FEED FRONT (LEFT CHANNEL) AMP INPUT	280
LT GREEN	VACUUM DOOR LOCK SWITCH TO SOLENOID (LOCK)	115
LT GREEN	KEYLESS DOOR LOCK OUTPUT FROM MODULE	129
LT GREEN	READING LAMP SWITCH TO READING LAMP (LH)	387
LT GREEN	C.B. A-DIGIT	715
LT GREEN	WINDSHIELD WASHER	726
LT GREEN	ELECT SHIFT 4 × 4 MODULE TO SPEED SENSOR RETURN	774
LT GREEN	AIR SUSPENSION CONTROL SIGNAL	637
LT GREEN	ALTERNATOR RELAY TO ALTERNATOR REGULATOR	568
LT GREEN	FUEL INJECTOR #6 CYLINDER	560
LT GREEN	STOPLAMP SWITCH TO TURN SIGNAL SWITCH	511
LT GREEN	RADIO TO FADER CONTROL	823
LT GREEN	SPEED CONTROL VACUUM TO EEC MODULE	916
LT GREEN	SEAT BELT WARNING SWITCH FEED	469
LT GREEN	LEFT LIMIT-B — DRIVER	872
LT GREEN-BLACK	ESC SWITCH TO ESC VOICE CONTROL	933
LT GREEN-BLACK	LH REAR SENSOR (LOW) TO MODULE	519
LT GREEN-BLACK	DCP MODULE TRIP SCAN HIGH TO TRIPMINDER	597
LT GREEN-BLACK	C.B. REGULATED 5V	711
LT GREEN-BLACK	MANIFOLD ABSOLUTE PRESSURE SENSOR FEED	358
LT GREEN-BLACK	CONTROL MODULE TO OIL PRESSURE SWITCH	473
LT GREEN-BLACK	SEQUENTIAL LH REAR OUTBOARD TURN SIGNAL LAMP	444
LT GREEN-BLACK	AIR PORT SOLENOID SIGNAL	99
LT GREEN-BLACK	HEADLAMP DIMMER SWITCH TO HIGH BEAMS	12
LT GREEN-ORANGE	LH REAR TURN SIGNAL LAMP	9
LT GREEN-ORANGE	POWER SERVO TO CLIMATE CONTROL UNIT (MODE)	243
LT GREEN-ORANGE	AIR SOLENOID CONTROL L.F.	415
LT GREEN-ORANGE	SEQUENTIAL LH REAR INBOARD TURN SIGNAL LAMP	442
LT GREEN-ORANGE	C.B. NOISE BLANKER	705

* IN SOME CASES, THERE MAY BE ADDITIONAL CIRCUIT FUNCTIONS INCLUDED IN THE CIRCUIT DESCRIPTION LISTED.

STANDARD CIRCUIT CHART (BY COLOR)

COLOR	DESCRIPTION *	CIRCUIT
LT GREEN-ORANGE	AMPLIFIER SWITCH GROUND TO RIGHT FRONT SPEAKER	815
LT GREEN-ORANGE	W/W WIPER SWITCH TO W/S WIPER MOTOR FIELD RH	956
LT GREEN-PURPLE	SUPERCHARGER SOLENOID #1	965
LT GREEN-PURPLE	AMPLIFIER SWITCH FEED TO RIGHT FRONT SPEAKER	816
LT GREEN-PURPLE	BATTERY FEED TO STEREO	797
LT GREEN-PURPLE	DCP MODULE TRIP SCAN LOW TO TRIPMINDER	598
LT GREEN-PURPLE	ELECTRONIC SHOCK HARD CONTROL	838
LT GREEN-PURPLE	THERMOSTATIC SW. TO AIR COND. SW. SELECTOR TERM.	348
LT GREEN-PURPLE	START INTERRUPT RELAY TO ANTI-THEFT MODULE	342
LT GREEN-PURPLE	CARBURETOR AIR TEMPERATURE SENSOR FEED	357
LT GREEN-PURPLE	FUEL PULSE TO MESSAGE CENTER	139
LT GREEN-RED	KEYLESS DOOR LOCK SWITCH DATA BIT 2 TO MODULE	79
LT GREEN-RED	STOPLAMP SWITCH FEED	10
LT GREEN-RED	EMERG. BRAKE WARNING LAMP TO EMERG. BRAKE SWITCH	162
LT GREEN-RED	SEQUENTIAL LH REAR CENTER TURN SIGNAL LAMP	443
LT GREEN-RED	(COIL) OR (ACCY) TERM OF IGNITION SWITCH TO ALTERNATOR REGULATOR (IGN. TERM)	904
LT GREEN-RED	REAR SENSOR (HIGH) TO MODULE	518
LT GREEN-RED	AIR SUSPENSION SYSTEM GROUND	577
LT GREEN-RED	LEFT CHANNEL SIGNAL OUT	798
LT GREEN-RED	C.B. RELAY DRIVE	722
LT GREEN-WHITE	BLOWER MOTOR SPEED CONTROLLER TO RESISTOR #1 (MED.)	754
LT GREEN-WHITE	AMPLIFIER SWITCH GROUND TO LEFT FRONT SPEAKER	819
LT GREEN-WHITE	C.B. C+ DIGIT	724
LT GREEN-WHITE	MODULE TO OVERRIDE SWITCH	661
LT GREEN-WHITE	OVERDRIVE CANCEL INDICATOR LAMP	911
LT GREEN-WHITE	ELECTRONIC SHOCK SOFT CONTROL	839
LT GREEN-WHITE	ELECT. ENG. CONTL. MOD. TO IDLE SPD. CONTL. MOTOR #2	265
LT GREEN-WHITE	MEMORY SEAT SWITCH LAMP ENABLE	271
LT GREEN-WHITE	LH FRONT TURN SIGNAL LAMP	3
LT GREEN-YELLOW	SEAT SWITCH ARM TERM. TO RELAY FIELD TERM	7
LT GREEN-YELLOW	INTERIOR LAMP SWITCH FEED	54
LT GREEN-YELLOW	RETARD VALVE TO CONTROL RELAY TERM. #1	869
LT GREEN-YELLOW	FUEL TANK SELECTOR SWITCH TO MIDSHIP FUEL PUMP	672
LT GREEN-YELLOW	MODULE TO MOTOR FEED	663
LT GREEN-YELLOW	HEATER & A/C CONTROL SW. TO REHEAT & A/C FEED	765
LT GREEN-YELLOW	REFERENCE SENSOR TO HEAT DUCT THERMISTOR	768
LT GREEN-YELLOW	PRESSURE SWITCH TO FLUID RES. SWITCH	547
LT GREEN-YELLOW	SPLICE #3 TO POWER RELAY	530
LT GREEN-YELLOW	ENGINE COOLANT TEMPERATURE SENSOR FEED	354
ORANGE	MODULE TO RELAY	461
ORANGE	WINDSHIELD WIPER SWITCH TO INTERMITTENT GOVERNOR GROUND	589
ORANGE	HEATED WINDSHIELD SWITCH TO HEATED WINDSHIELD CONTROL	582
ORANGE	BRAKE PRESSURE SWITCH TO CONTROL MODULE	636
ORANGE	ELECT SHIFT 4 × 4 MODULE TO MOTOR CONTROL	778
ORANGE	BRAKE PRESSURE SWITCH TO CONTROL MODULE	636
ORANGE	SPEAKER VOICE COIL FEED LEFT FRONT CHANNEL AMP INPUT	649
ORANGE	MODULE DIAGNOSTIC	693
ORANGE	C.B. C-DIGIT	704
ORANGE	MULTIPLEX RELAY COIL FEED	699
ORANGE	FUEL CONTROL MODULE TO FUEL CONTROL VALVE	974
ORANGE	BATTERY FEED TO RELAY CONTROLLER	931
ORANGE	RIGHT MOTOR-PASSENGER — F	864
ORANGE	VALVE #2 TO MODULE	496
ORANGE	MEMORY MIRROR MODULE RH HORIZONTAL POSITION	892
ORANGE	FUEL SENSOR GROUND TO E.C.U.	89
ORANGE	SWITCH OFF TO RELAY	274
ORANGE	HEATER & A/C CONTROL SW. (LO-NORM) TO POWER SERVO	250
ORANGE	ELECTRONIC CLUSTER FROM EXPANDED FUEL IN KEYBOARD	285
ORANGE	16 GA FUSE LINK	300
ORANGE	RELAY TO SEAT LATCH SOLENOID	172
ORANGE-BLACK	BLOWER MOTOR TO SWITCH — HI	261
ORANGE-BLACK	TAIL LAMP BULB OUTAGE TO MESSAGE CENTER	132
ORANGE-BLACK	ELECTRIC CHOKE FEED	68
ORANGE-BLACK	EVO MODULE TO TEST CONNECTOR	927
ORANGE-BLACK	TRANSMISSION OIL TEMP	923
ORANGE-BLACK	MULTIPLEX FARRING LAMPS	696
ORANGE-BLACK	CLIMATE CONTROL BOX TO HIGH BLOWER RELAY	776
ORANGE-BLACK	RIGHT CHANNEL SIGNAL OUT	799
ORANGE-BLACK	ENGLISH METRIC SIGNAL TO MULTIGAGE	572
ORANGE-BLACK	LIQUID CRYSTAL DISPLAY	484
ORANGE-BLACK	TURN SIGNAL SWITCH TO INDICATOR RELAY	458
ORANGE-BLACK	AIR SUSPENSION HEIGHT SENSOR LO — REAR	428
ORANGE-BLACK	IDLE SPEED CONTROL TO EGR VACUUM SOLENOID	323
ORANGE-BLACK	RADIO SEEK "DOWN"	370
ORANGE-LT BLUE	AFTER GLOW RELAY TO DIESEL CONTROL SWITCH	335
ORANGE-LT BLUE	SEQUENTIAL RH REAR INBOARD TURN SIGNAL LAMP	445
ORANGE-LT BLUE	I TERMINAL STARTER MOTOR RELAY TO INERTIA SWITCH	668
ORANGE-LT BLUE	ELECT SHIFT TO 4L SWITCH	781
ORANGE-LT BLUE	RADIO RECEIVER ASSY. TO FOOT CONTROL SWITCH	747
ORANGE-LT BLUE	VAC SWITCH TO VAC PUMP	740
ORANGE-LT BLUE	RH REAR TURN SIGNAL LAMP	5
ORANGE-LT BLUE	ALTERNATOR REGULATOR "F" TERMINAL TO ALTERNATOR	35
ORANGE-LT BLUE	ELECTRONIC CONTROL UNIT TO WIDE OPEN THROTTLE ACTUATOR	73
ORANGE-LT BLUE	FUEL SUPPLY PUMP RELAY	238
ORANGE-LT BLUE	CRUISE INDICATING LAMP TO CRUISE LAMP INTERFACE MODULE	203
ORANGE-LT GREEN	TANK SELECT CIRCUIT ELECTRONIC FUEL GAUGE	204
ORANGE-LT GREEN	EMA CONTROL TO EGR SWITCH	27
ORANGE-LT GREEN	AIR BAG DIAGNOSTIC MODULE TO AIR BAG FLASHER	610
ORANGE-LT GREEN	DCP MODULE TO WIPER HI-LO RELAY	594
ORANGE-LT GREEN	SPEAKER VOICE COIL FEED — FRONT (LEFT CHANNEL)	804
ORANGE-LT GREEN	DECELERATION SENSOR	847
ORANGE-LT GREEN	INDICATOR RELAY TO FLASHER	459
ORANGE-LT GREEN	DROPPING RESISTOR TO RELAY #2	471
ORANGE-RED	SEQUENTIAL RH REAR OUTBOARD TURN SIGNAL LAMP	447
ORANGE-RED	AIR SOLENOID CONTROL R.F.	414
ORANGE-RED	RESISTOR TO BLOWER MOTOR (HI)	515
ORANGE-RED	SKID CONTROL MODULE RH WHEEL SENSOR (HI)	604

COLOR	DESCRIPTION *	CIRCUIT
ORANGE-RED	AMPLIFIER/SPEAKER SWITCH FEED TO RIGHT REAR SPEAKER	802
ORANGE-RED	LO-TEMP SWITCH TO MCU MODULE	309
ORANGE-RED	INSTRUMENT PANEL ILLUMINATION CONTROL MODULE FEED	293
ORANGE-WHITE	TEMPERATURE COMPENSATED PUMP TO PROCESSOR	256
ORANGE-WHITE	HEADLAMP SWITCH TO SENSOR AND AUTOLAMP AMPLIFIER	221
ORANGE-WHITE	AIR DUMP VALVE NEG. TO EXHAUST SYS. OVERTEMP MODULE	93
ORANGE-WHITE	ELECT SHIFT 4 × 4 MODULE TO MOTOR POSITION #2	763
ORANGE-WHITE	ACCELERATE DECELERATE SENSOR	836
ORANGE-WHITE	VENT SWITCH TO LEFT FRONT VENT MOTOR	886
ORANGE-WHITE	SEQUENTIAL RH REAR CENTER TURN SIGNAL LAMP	446
ORANGE-WHITE	POWER RELAY TO GLOW PLUGS (LEFT BANK)	337
ORANGE-WHITE	SENSOR SIGNAL FEED	351
ORANGE-WHITE	DOOR OPENING WARNING TO ANTI-THEFT MODULE	341
ORANGE-WHITE	MOVABLE STEERING COLUMN SOLENOID TO COURTESY LAMP SWITCH	381
ORANGE-YELLOW	ANTENNA SWITCH TO ANTENNA RELAY	448
ORANGE-YELLOW	OVERRIDE SWITCH TO LATCH	665
ORANGE-YELLOW	AIR BAG READY INDICATOR LAMP TO AIR BAG FLASHER	609
ORANGE-YELLOW	SPLICE TO DIODE	531
ORANGE-YELLOW	SPLICE TO POWER RELAY	532
ORANGE-YELLOW	SPLICE TO MODULE	525
ORANGE-YELLOW	POWER RELAY TO MODULE GROUND	528
ORANGE-YELLOW	SPEED SENSOR LO V REF TO SPEEDO TACH MODULE	563
ORANGE-YELLOW	AMPLIFIER TO SERVO TRANSDUCER FEED	144
ORANGE-YELLOW	TURN SIGNAL FLASHER FEED	8
ORANGE-YELLOW	SEAT SWITCH TO RELAY FIELD TERMINAL	18
ORANGE-YELLOW	TRANSMISSION THROTTLE VALVE SOLENOID 1	237
ORANGE-YELLOW	START CIRCUIT TO THERMACTOR RELAY	253
PINK	WINDOW REGULATOR RELAY ACCY FEED	194
PINK	HIGH ELECTRO DRIVE FAN	639
PINK	MULTIPLEX MESSAGE I	736
PINK	EEC MODULE TO SPARK ADVANCE	929
PINK	AIR COMPRESSOR VENT SOLENOID	421
PINK	VALVE #4 TO MODULE	498
PINK	CRANK ENABLE RELAY	329
PINK-BLACK	ELECTRONIC CLUSTER IGNITION RUN FEED	489
PINK-BLACK	STOPLAMP RELAY FEED	474
PINK-BLACK	AIR SUSPENSION HEIGHT SENSOR HI — L.F.	422
PINK-BLACK	AIR SUSPENSION HEIGHT SENSOR HI — REAR	427
PINK-BLACK	COMPASS SENSOR FEED	684
PINK-BLACK	FUEL PUMP SAFETY SWITCH TO FUEL PUMP MOTOR	787
PINK-BLACK	SENSOR AMPLIFY UNIT TO CONTROL UNIT #1	749
PINK-BLACK	RH REAR SENSOR (LOW) TO MODULE	524
PINK-BLACK	AIR BAG DIAGNOSTIC MODULE TO PASSENGER INFLATOR	616
PINK-BLACK	SHOCK DAMPENING RELAY HARD TO SHOCK DAMPENING CONTROL	652
PINK-BLACK	SPEAKER VOICE COIL FEED RIGHT REAR CHANNEL AMP INPUT	645
PINK-BLACK	THERMO SWITCH TO CONTROL MODULE	470
PINK-BLACK	DOOR LOCK MOTOR (LOCK)	117
PINK-LT BLUE	RH HEADLAMP BULB OUTAGE	109
PINK-LT BLUE	AIR COND. CONTROL RELAY FEED	883
PINK-LT BLUE	PRESSURE SWITCH TO MOTOR RELAY	539
PINK-LT BLUE	SPEAKER VOICE COIL FEED—REAR (RIGHT CHANNEL)	806
PINK-LT BLUE	AMPLIFIER/SPEAKER SWITCH GROUND TO LEFT REAR SPEAKER	801
PINK-LT BLUE	EEC MODULE—DATA MINUS	915
PINK-LT GREEN	VENT SWITCH TO BLOWER MOTOR—LO	917
PINK-LT GREEN	SPEAKER VOICE COIL FEED—REAR (LEFT CHANNEL)	807
PINK-LT GREEN	EEC MODULE TO CHECK ENGINE INDICATOR LAMP	658
PINK-LT GREEN	MODULE TO SOLENOID	599
PINK-LT GREEN	DOOR LOCK SWITCH (UNLOCK)	120
PINK-ORANGE	DOOR LOCK MOTOR (UNLOCK)	118
PINK-ORANGE	AIR BAG DIAGNOSTIC MODULE (DEPLOY) TO RH SENSOR	617
PINK-ORANGE	SPEAKER SWITCH FEED TO RIGHT FRONT SPEAKER	812
PINK-ORANGE	READING LAMP SWITCH TO READING LAMP	487
PINK-ORANGE	MEMORY MIRROR MODULE LH HORIZONTAL POSITION	896
PINK-ORANGE	DIESEL CONTROL MODULE FEED	466
PINK-ORANGE	ELECT. ENG. CONTL. MOD. TO IDLE SPD CONTL. MOTOR #3	384
PINK-WHITE	BLOWER MOTOR RELAY TO MOTOR	371
PINK-WHITE	AIR SUSP. MOD. TO L.F. HEIGHT SENSOR	431
PINK-WHITE	AIR BAG DIAGNOSTIC MODULE (DEPLOY) TO CENTER SENSOR	619
PINK-WHITE	SPEAKER SWITCH FEED TO LEFT FRONT SPEAKER	814
PINK-WHITE	DOOR SWITCH TO SEAT LATCH RELAY (COIL TERM.)	173
PINK-YELLOW	DOOR LOCK SWITCH (LOCK)	119
PINK-YELLOW	WASHER FLUID LEVEL INDICATOR	82
PINK-YELLOW	DPC MODULE TO HEADLAMP RELAY	632
PINK-YELLOW	SPEAKER VOICE COIL FEED LEFT REAR CHANNEL AMP INPUT	646
PINK-YELLOW	OPEN DOOR WARNING LAMP FEED	626
PINK-YELLOW	SWITCH TO FADER RIGHT CHANNEL FEED	830
PURPLE	RIGHT FRONT SHOCK DAMPENING RELAY TO CONTROL MODULE	638
PURPLE	HEATED WINDSHIELD CONTROL TO EEC AIR COND TERM	585
PURPLE	CONVERTIBLE TOP RELAY TO SWITCH	588
PURPLE	R.H. REMOTE MIRROR MOTOR FEED—C.C.W.	544
PURPLE	HEADLAMP DIMMER SWITCH TO HEADLAMP DIMMER RELAY	500
PURPLE	C.B. A+ DIGIT	712
PURPLE	RELAY COIL FEED #2	714
PURPLE	REDUNDANT MODULE TO ENGINE WARNING LAMP	656
PURPLE	POWER FEED FROM AMPLIFIER	928
PURPLE	LEFT CHANNEL SIGNAL	856
PURPLE	MODULE TO RELAY	462
PURPLE	TRANSMISSION DIAGNOSTIC	453
PURPLE	POWER SERVO TO CLIMATE CONTROL UNIT (AMP)	246
PURPLE	ELECTRONIC CLUSTER FROM TRIP RECALL SWITCH IN KEYBOARD	288
PURPLE BASE	EATC RH SUNLOAD SENSOR POSITIVE	479
PURPLE-LT BLUE	WINDOW REG. SW. TO BACK WINDOW SW.	405
PURPLE-LT BLUE	SPEED CONTROL SENSE EEC MODULE TO CLUSTER	683
PURPLE-LT BLUE	AIR BAG DIAGNOSTIC MODULE (MONITOR) TO CENTER SENSOR	620
PURPLE-LT BLUE	POWER FEED-SWITCH TO REAR AMPLIFIER	828
PURPLE-LT BLUE	CLICKER RELAY TERM. NO. 4 TO AIR VALVE ASSY.	263
PURPLE-LT BLUE	AMPLIFIER FEEDBACK POTENTIOMETER FEED	147
PURPLE-LT GREEN	DESTINATION SWITCH TO MESSAGE CENTER	154

* IN SOME CASES, THERE MAY BE ADDITIONAL CIRCUIT
FUNCTIONS INCLUDED IN THE CIRCUIT DESCRIPTION LISTED.

STANDARD CIRCUIT CHART (BY COLOR)

COLOR	DESCRIPTION *	CIRCUIT
PURPLE-LT GREEN	AIR BAG DIAGNOSTIC MODULE (MONITOR) TO RH SENSOR	618
PURPLE-LT GREEN	REAR WASHER PUMP FEED	946
PURPLE-LT GREEN	VEHICLE MAINTENANCE MONITOR MODULE TO ELEC. INSTR CLUST. SENSE	907
PURPLE-LT GREEN	WINDOW REG. SW. TO BACK WINDOW SW.	404
PURPLE-LT GREEN	AIR SUSPENSION HEIGHT SENSOR LO — L.F.	423
PURPLE-LT GREEN	REAR AIR SUSPENSION HEIGHT SENSOR FEED	429
PURPLE-ORANGE	AIR SUSPENSION SWITCH FEED	417
PURPLE-ORANGE	AIR BAG READY INDICATOR L (MONITOR) TO SAFING SENSOR	612
PURPLE-ORANGE	CIGAR LIGHTER LAMP FEED	131
PURPLE-ORANGE	FUSED ACCY FEED #2	298
PURPLE-ORANGE	AUTOLAMP AMPLIFIER TO CONTROL SWITCH	220
PURPLE-WHITE	AMPLIFIER SPEAKER SWITCH FEED TO RIGHT REAR SPEAKER	278
PURPLE-WHITE	MEMORY SEAT SWITCH ENABLE	266
PURPLE-WHITE	AIR BAG DIAGNOSTIC MODULE (MONITOR) TO SAFING SENSOR	623
PURPLE-WHITE	SEAT BELT WARNING LAMP TO WARNING LAMP SWITCH	520
PURPLE-WHITE	HEATER & A/C CONTROL SW (LO-HI-NORM) TO RESISTOR (LOW RANGE)	758
PURPLE-WHITE	MULTIPLEX SERVICE REMINDER RESET	733
PURPLE-WHITE	BRAKE WARNING SWITCH TO INDICATOR LAMP	977
PURPLE-WHITE	RIGHT MOTOR — PASSENGER — R	865
PURPLE-YELLOW	LEFT MOTOR — DRIVER—F	860
PURPLE-YELLOW	ELECT SHIFT 4 x 4 MODULE TO MOTOR POSITION #5	771
PURPLE-YELLOW	CLUTCH SWITCH TO EFI MODULE	480
PURPLE-YELLOW	TURN SIGNAL SWITCH TO LH CORNERING LAMP	380
PURPLE-YELLOW	FUEL INJECTION PUMP POSITION SENSOR	239
PURPLE-YELLOW	BRAKE FLUID LEVEL UNIT TO MESSAGE CENTER	128
PURPLE-YELLOW	ECONOMY SWITCH TO MESSAGE CENTER	153
PURPLE-YELLOW	DECK LID SOLENOID FEED	84
RED	KEYLESS DOOR LOCK SWITCH DATA BIT 5 TO MODULE	123
RED	TRAILER BRAKES	50
RED	SUPPLEMENTAL ALTERNATOR STATOR A TERM. TO WINDSHIELD	70
RED	WINDSHIELD WIPER SW. TO WINDSHIELD WIPER MOTOR	63
RED	18 GA FUSE LINK	301
RED	HORIZONTAL SEAT REG. MOTOR TO RELAY	180
RED	POWER RELAY TO EEC MODULE	361
RED	REAR VIEW OUTSIDE MIRROR FEED	388
RED	WIDE OPEN THROTTLE A/C CUTOUT SWITCH	331
RED	POWER LUMBAR FEED	490
RED	FUEL TANK SELECTOR TO FUEL PUMP FRONT	786
RED	DIESEL WATER IN FUEL SENDER TO WARNING LAMP	643
RED	BATTERY FEED CAMPER	666
RED	AMPLIFIER POWER RETURN	694
RED	INERTIA SWITCH TO FUEL TANK SELECTOR SWITCH	670
RED	EED MODULE TO SPEED CONTROL GROUND	676
RED	MOONROOF RELAY TO MICRO SWITCH CLOSED	692
RED	HEADLAMP DIMMER SWITCH OVERRIDE TO RHEOSTAT	527
RED	MPH/KPH SWITCH TO MESSAGE CENTER	506
RED	L.H. REMOTE MIRROR MOTOR FEED — C.W.	540
RED	HEATED WINDSHIELD CONTROL TO ALT STATOR TERM SOLENOID	581 605
RED	STEERING RATE SENSOR TERMINAL A CONTROL MODULE DOOR WIRE	633 630
RED	STEERING RATE SENSOR TERMINAL A CONTROL MODULE	633
RED	BATTERY FEED TO AUX. FUEL SELECTOR SWITCH	973
RED	TOP CONTROL RELAY TO MOTOR—DOWN	903
RED	RIGHT DOOR OPEN — PASSENGER	863
RED-BLACK	MEMORY MIRROR MODULE POSITION +	891
RED-BLACK	VENT CROSSOVER FEED	879
RED-BLACK	MODE SELECT SWITCH LAMP	833
RED-BLACK	WATER TEMP. WARNING LAMP TO WATER TEMP. SW. (HOT)	647
RED-BLACK	FRONT AIR SUSPENSION HEIGHT SENSOR FEED	426
RED-BLACK	ELECT. ENG. CONTL. MOD. TO WIDE OPEN THROTTLE KICKER SOC.	378
RED-BLACK	FUEL WARNING RELAY CONTROL	366
RED-BLACK	RADIO "SEEK UP"	368
RED-BLACK	ECU TO VACUUM SWITCH 3	214
RED-BLACK	LAMP RETURN TO PULSE WITH DIMMER	235
RED-BLACK	LEFT FRONT WINDOW REGULATOR SWITCH TO RIGHT FRONT WINDOW REGULATOR MOTOR	314
RED-BLACK	LEFT FRONT WINDOW REGULATOR SWITCH TO RIGHT REAR WINDOW REGULATOR MOTOR	320
RED-BLACK	HEADLAMP DIMMER SWITCH TO LOW BEAMS	13
RED-LT BLUE	STARTER CONTROL	32
RED-LT BLUE	WINDOW REGULATOR SWITCH FEED	170
RED-LT BLUE	ANTI-THEFT MODULE TO ALARM RELAY	340
RED-LT BLUE	LEFT FRONT WINDOW REGULATOR SWITCH TO LEFT REAR WINDOW REGULATOR MOTOR	317
RED-LT BLUE	SEAT PROCESSOR TO RECLINER MOTOR "DOWN"	440
RED-LT BLUE	TACHOMETER FEED	648
RED-LT BLUE	SEAT REGULATOR SWITCH TO FRONT MOTOR (LH)	979
RED-LT BLUE	SEAT REGULATOR SWITCH TO FRONT MOTOR (RH)	985
RED-LT BLUE	VENT CROSSOVER FEED	880
RED-LT BLUE	AMPLIFIER TO SPEED SENSOR RETURN	901
RED-LT GREEN	COIL TERM. OF IGN. SW. TO BRAKE SKID CONTROL MODULE	602
RED-LT GREEN	STOPLAMP SW. TO STOPLAMPS	810
RED-LT GREEN	HEATER & A/C CONTROL SW. (DE-FOG) TO INLET AIR CONTROL SOLENOID	766
RED-LT GREEN	SEAT REGULATOR SWITCH TO REAR MOTOR (LH)	983
RED-LT GREEN	SEAT REGULATOR SWITCH TO REAR MOTOR (RH)	989
RED-LT GREEN	REAR TILT POSITION SENSE	436
RED-LT GREEN	IGN. SW. COIL TERM. TO CIRCUIT BREAKER	454
RED-LT GREEN	IGNITION SWITCH TO IGNITION COIL "BATT." TERMINAL	16
RED-LT GREEN	MODULE TO THROTTLE ACTUATOR	69
RED-LT GREEN	HEADLAMP BULB OUTAGE TO MESSAGE CENTER	130
RED-ORANGE	KEYLESS DOOR LOCK OUTPUT (DRIVER) FROM MODULE	163
RED-ORANGE	IDLE SPEED CONTROL TO EGR VENT SOLENOID	322
RED-ORANGE	BLOWER MOTOR TO SWITCH — LO	260
RED-ORANGE	W/S WIPER MOTOR ARM RH TO W/S WIPER SWITCH	955
RED-ORANGE	DCP MODULE TO WIPER GOVERNOR RELAY	593
RED-ORANGE	STARTING MOTOR RELAY SHUNT TO AMMETER	655

COLOR	DESCRIPTION *	CIRCUIT
RED-PINK	RH REAR SENSOR (HIGH) TO MODULE	523
RED-PINK	HEATER & A/C CONTROL SW. (HI-NORM) TO RESISTOR (LOW RANGE)	756
RED-PINK	ANTENNA SWITCH TO POWER ANTENNA (UP)	745
RED-PINK	SPEED CONTROL AMPLIFIER TO CRUISE LAMP INTERFACE MODULE	202
RED-WHITE	DOOR JAMB SWITCH TO BUZZER	159
RED-WHITE	RH REAR STOP & TURN BULB OUTAGE	105
RED-WHITE	TEMP. GAUGE TO TEMP. SENDING UNIT	39
RED-WHITE	SWITCH TO WARNING LAMP	42
RED-WHITE	HEATER & A/C CONTROL SW. (HI-NORM) TO BLOWER MOTOR SW. RELAY	757
RED-WHITE	C.B. ON/OFF	718
RED-WHITE	RADIO MEMORY	729
RED-WHITE	SEAT REGULATOR SWITCH TO HORZ. MOTOR (RH)	987
RED-WHITE	SEAT REGULATOR SWITCH TO HORZ. MOTOR (LH)	981
RED-WHITE	MEMORY SEAT TO NEUTRAL SENSOR SWITCH	899
RED-WHITE	ELECTRONIC SHOCK SENSOR B	835
RED-WHITE	ELECTRIC SHIFT MODULE TO NEUTRAL START SWITCH	463
RED-WHITE	HORIZONTAL POSITION SENSE	438
RED-YELLOW	EMERGENCY WARNING FLASHER FEED	383
RED-YELLOW	WINDOW REG. SW. TO WINDOW REG. MOTOR	334
RED-YELLOW	ELECTRONIC SHOCK SENSOR A	834
RED-YELLOW	WARNING LAMPS FEED	640
RED-YELLOW	SUPERCHARGER SOLENOID #2	966
RED-YELLOW	HEADLAMP DIMMER SWITCH FEED	15
RED-YELLOW	FUEL PRESSURE BOOST SOLENOID	236
RED-YELLOW	WINDOW REG. MASTER CONT. SW. TO WINDOW REG. SW. FEED	328
TAN	EEC MODULE TO MALFUNCTION INDICATOR LITE	657
TAN	MULTIPLEX SERVICE REMINDER	734
TAN	BOOST SENSOR TO CONTROL UNIT	748
TAN	FUEL INJECTOR #1 CYLINDER	555
TAN	SWITCH TO FADER LEFT CHANNEL FEED	831
TAN	VALVE #1 TO MODULE	495
TAN	RIGHT LIMIT-B — PASSENGER	873
TAN	WINDOW REG. SW. TO BACK WINDOW AUX. SW.	406
TAN	AIR SUSPENSION HEIGHT SENSOR HI — R.F.	424
TAN-BLACK	PRESSURE SWITCH TO KEY SWITCH	409
TAN-BLACK	BRAKE WEAR SENSOR	457
TAN-BLACK	WINDOW REG. SW. REAR TO LIMIT SW.	407
TAN-BLACK	ELECTRONIC SHOCK FEEDBACK ACTUATOR TO RELAY	845
TAN-BLACK	DIGITAL AUDIO DISC LOGIC SENSOR	849
TAN-BLACK	MEMORY MIRROR MODULE TO LH VERTICAL DRIVE	897
TAN-BLACK	LH FRONT SENSOR (LOW) TO MODULE	522
TAN-BLACK	AIR BAG DIAGNOSTIC MODULE (MONITOR) TO LH SENSOR	622
TAN-BLACK	VEHICLE MAINTENANCE MONITOR MODULE TO ENGINE STRAP	908
TAN-BLACK	MODULATOR TO THERMO. SWITCH	939
TAN-LT BLUE	MASS AIR FLOW RETURN	968
TAN-LT BLUE	FUEL INJECTOR #5 CYLINDER	559
TAN-LT BLUE	INDICATOR RELAY TO RH TURN LAMP	817
TAN-LT BLUE	TRANSMISSION OVERDRIVE SWITCH TO EEC MODULE	224
TAN-LT BLUE	AUTOLAMP AMPLIFIER TO RHEOSTAT	216
TAN-LT BLUE	FEEDBACK CARB. COIL 4	98
TAN-LT GREEN	FEEDBACK CARB. COIL 3	97
TAN-LT GREEN	ANTI-THEFT SYSTEM SWITCH FEED	23
TAN-LT GREEN	ODOMETER SENSOR TO EEC MODULE	223
TAN-LT GREEN	AMPLIFIER SWITCH FEED TO RIGHT REAR SPEAKER	825
TAN-LT GREEN	BRAKE FLUID RES. SWITCH TO MODULE	512
TAN-LT GREEN	TURN SIGNAL RELAY TO TURN SIGNAL FLASHER	494
TAN-ORANGE	LH FRONT SENSOR (HIGH) TO MODULE	521
TAN-ORANGE	FUEL INJECTOR #7 CYLINDER	561
TAN-ORANGE	EEC MODULE—DATA PLUS	914
TAN-ORANGE	FOG LAMP SW. TO FOG LAMP	478
TAN-ORANGE	COOLANT TEMPERATURE SWITCH TO CONTROL RELAY	197
TAN-ORANGE	AIR COND. SW. (LO) TO AIR COND. BLOWER MOTOR	184
TAN-ORANGE	FEEDBACK CARB. COIL 2	96
TAN-RED	FEEDBACK CARB. COIL 1	95
TAN-RED	RELAY TO MAP LAMP SWITCH	133
TAN-RED	MCV MODULE TO VIP FUNCTION TESTER	201
TAN-RED	THERMACTOR TIMER TO RELAY	252
TAN-RED	ELECTRONIC SHOCK METAL OXIDE VERISTOR	846
TAN-RED	MEMORY MIRROR MODULE TO LH HORIZONTAL DRIVE	898
TAN-RED	POWER RELAY TO FUSE LINK	533
TAN-RED	VALVE #6 TO MODULE	510
TAN-RED	MULTIPLEX COMPUTER FEED	792
TAN-RED	HEATED WINDSHIELD TRIGGER CIRCUIT SW. TO MODULE	681
TAN-RED	WINDOW REG. SW. FRONT TO LIMIT SW.	408
TAN-WHITE	AMPLIFIER SWITCH FEED TO LEFT REAR SPEAKER	827
TAN-WHITE	IDLE RPM SOLENOID TO CONTROL UNIT	744
TAN-WHITE	INDICATOR RELAY TO LH TURN LAMP	818
TAN-WHITE	EMISSION SPEED SENSOR TO MODULATOR CONTROL	934
TAN-WHITE	TAILLAMP SWITCH FEED	195
TAN-WHITE	INTERLOCK MODULE TO CENTER SEAT SENSOR SWITCH	87
TAN-YELLOW	A/C PRESSURE SWITCH TO CONTROL RELAY	198
TAN-YELLOW	TONE GENERATOR	183
TAN-YELLOW	AIR COND. CONDENSOR THERMAL SWITCH FEED	509
TAN-YELLOW	FUSE LINK TO MOTOR RELAY	537
TAN-YELLOW HASH	FEED TO VACUUM DOOR LOCK SWITCH	114
WHITE	KEYLESS DOOR LOCK OUTPUT (ALL) FROM MODULE	134
WHITE	ASH RECEPTACLE LAMP FEED	17
WHITE	TRAILER GROUND	49
WHITE	WINDSHIELD WIPER SW. TO WINDSHIELD WIPER MOTOR	58
WHITE	SUPPLEMENTAL ALTERNATOR STATOR B TERM. TO WINDSHIELD	71
WHITE	REAR WINDOW REGULATOR SWITCH FEED	176
WHITE	KEYLESS DOOR LOCK SEAT SWITCH SENSOR TO MODULE	177
WHITE	GROUND RETURN TO TOWING VEHICLE	206
WHITE	ELECTRONIC CLUSTER FROM GAUGE SELECT SWITCH IN KEYBOARD	289
WHITE	SPEAKER VOICE COIL RETURN AMP INPUT	281
WHITE	SEAT REG. SW. TO VERT. SOLENOID BATT. TERM.	307
WHITE	R.H. REMOTE MIRROR SOLENOID CONTROL	545

* IN SOME CASES, THERE MAY BE ADDITIONAL CIRCUIT
FUNCTIONS INCLUDED IN THE CIRCUIT DESCRIPTION LISTED.

STANDARD CIRCUIT CHART (BY COLOR)

COLOR	DESCRIPTION *	CIRCUIT
WHITE	FUEL INJECTOR #2 CYLINDER	556
WHITE	RHEOSTAT TO SENSOR	508
WHITE	DOOR WIRE	628
WHITE	ELECT SHIFT 4 X 4 MODULE TO MOTOR POSITION #4	770
WHITE	C.B. MIC-AUDIO	713
WHITE	RELAY COIL FEED #3	725
WHITE	RIGHT REAR SHOCK DAMPENING RELAY TO CONTROL MODULE	650
WHITE	ACTUATOR POSITION SENSOR RIGHT REAR	843
WHITE	VALVE #3 TO MODULE	497
WHITE	INERTIA SWITCH TO MODULE	866
WHITE	ELECT. ENG. CONTL. MOD. TO EXHAUST HEAT CONTRL SOC.	377
WHITE	TIME DELAY RELAY	332
WHITE	REARVIEW OUTSIDE MIRROR COUNTERCLOCKWISE	412
WHITE BASE	LH REAR TAIL LAMP BULB OUTAGE	102
WHITE-BLACK	THERMOCOUPLE 2 NEG. TO EXHAUST SYST. OVERTEMP PROTECT MODULE	92
WHITE-BLACK	ELAPSED TIME SWITCH TO MESSAGE CENTER	165
WHITE-BLACK	ALTERNATOR REG. "S" TERM. TO ALTERNATOR "S" TERM.	4
WHITE-BLACK	LF WINDOW REG. SW. TO LF WINDOW REG. MOTOR	226
WHITE-BLACK	5V TO-MESSAGE CENTER TO DISPLAY	168
WHITE-BLACK	HEADLAMP SWITCH TO AUXILIARY LAMPS	188
WHITE-BLACK	THERMACTOR DIVERTER VALVE FEED	200
WHITE-BLACK	THROTTLE KICKER RELAY TO MCU MODULE	393
WHITE-BLACK	ACTUATOR POSITION SENSOR LEFT FRONT	840
WHITE-BLACK	MODULE TO MOTOR FEED	662
WHITE-BLACK	C.B. PUSH TO TALK	702
WHITE-BLACK	MULTIPLEX REVERSE DIMMING	731
WHITE-BLACK	THERMACTOR CLUTCH RELAY TO CLUTCH	567
WHITE-BLACK	WASHER CONTROL SWITCH FEED	950
WHITE-LT BLUE	MODULE TO DOWN SWITCH	659
WHITE-LT BLUE	SURE TRACK DIAGNOSTIC	606
WHITE-LT BLUE	C.B. VOLUME CONTROL	709
WHITE-LT BLUE	TEMP SWITCH TO WARNING DEVICE	737
WHITE-LT BLUE	STARTER INTERRUPT RELAY TO NEUTRAL START SWITCH	900
WHITE-LT BLUE	VEHICLE MAINTENANCE MONITOR MODULE TO OIL TEMP OUTPUT	906
WHITE-LT BLUE	MODULE TO SWITCH	465
WHITE-LT BLUE	FUSED ACCY FEED #3	294
WHITE-LT BLUE	ELECT. ENG. CONTL. MOD. TO IDLE SPD. CONTL. MOTOR #1	264
WHITE-LT BLUE	RH FRONT TURN SIGNAL LAMP	2
WHITE-LT BLUE	DISTRIBUTOR ELECTRONIC CONTROL FEED	20
WHITE-LT GREEN	RH AND LH REAR RUNNING LAMP BULB OUTAGE	110
WHITE-LT GREEN	AUX WATER VALVE FEED	456
WHITE-LT GREEN	C.B. SCAN SWITCH	710
WHITE-LT GREEN	BLOWER MOTOR RELAY TO ENG. WATER TEMP. SWITCH (COLD)	761
WHITE-LT GREEN	WATER TEMP. WARNING LAMP TO WATER TEMP. SW. (COLD)	642
WHITE-LT GREEN	SPEAKER VOICE COIL FEED — FRONT (RIGHT CHANNEL)	805
WHITE-ORANGE	HEATER & A/C CONTROL SW. TO INST. PANEL THERMISTOR	790
WHITE-ORANGE	AIR BAG READY INDICATOR L (DEPLOY) TO SAFING SENSOR	611
WHITE-ORANGE	C.B. DOWN SWITCH	703
WHITE-ORANGE	RADIO SEEK	728
WHITE-ORANGE	RELEASE LEVER WARN INDICATOR LAMP — CONSOLE	877
WHITE-ORANGE	ACTUATOR POSITION SENSOR LEFT REAR	842
WHITE-ORANGE	LEFT FRONT AIR INPUT RETURN	857
WHITE-ORANGE	ELECTRIC PVS TO MCU MODULE	392
WHITE-ORANGE	INTERLOCK MODULE TO CENTER BUCKLE SWITCH	83
WHITE-ORANGE	RESET SWITCH TO MESSAGE CENTER	166
WHITE-ORANGE	MEMORY SEAT SWITCH LAMP DRIVE	272
WHITE-PINK	LOW OIL LEVEL RELAY TO SENSOR	258
WHITE-PINK	ECU TO VACUUM SWITCH 2	213
WHITE-PINK	SERVO VENT SOLENOID TO CONTROL TRANSISTOR	146
WHITE-PINK	BUZZER TO WARNING INDICATOR RELAY	160
WHITE-PINK	STARTER CONTROL TO INTERLOCK MODULE	33
WHITE-PINK	FUEL FILLER DOOR RELEASE SWITCH TO FUEL FILLER DOOR RELEASE SOLENOID	482
WHITE-PINK	HEATER & A/C CONTROL SW. (DEFOG) TO DEFROST CONT. SOLENOID	775
WHITE-PURPLE	SENSOR AMPLIFY UNIT TO CONTROL UNIT #4	760
WHITE-PURPLE	C.B. SQUELCH POT	701
WHITE-PURPLE	AMPLIFIER SWITCH GROUND TO RIGHT REAR SPEAKER	824
WHITE-PURPLE	POWER FEED-SWITCH TO FRONT AMPLIFIER	829
WHITE-PURPLE	MEMORY MIRROR MODULE	895
WHITE-PURPLE	FUSE PANEL FEED TO RELAY	326
WHITE-PURPLE	DECK LID SWITCH TO ANTI-THEFT MODULE	26
WHITE-PURPLE	AUTOLAMP AMPLIFIER TO SENSOR	218
WHITE-PURPLE	FUSED ACCY FEED #1	296
WHITE-PURPLE	FUEL METERING CONTROL LEVER ACTUATOR 2 PLUS	312
WHITE-RED	SPEAKER VOICE COIL FEED FRONT (R. CHANNEL) AMP INPUT	279
WHITE-RED	COLD START TIMING RETARD SOLENOID	240
WHITE-RED	H L SW. TO CHIMES	257
WHITE-RED	ELECT. ENG. CONTRL. MOD. TO TEST CONN #1	209
WHITE-RED	THERMACTOR DUMP VALVE FEED	190
WHITE-RED	OIL PRESSURE INDICATOR TO OIL PRESSURE SENDING UNIT	31
WHITE-RED	RH REAR TAIL LAMP BULB OUTAGE	103
WHITE-RED	AIR PUMP SOLENOID SIGNAL	100
WHITE-RED	FLASHER TO EMERGENCY WARNING SWITCH	385
WHITE-RED	ACTUATOR POSITION SENSOR RIGHT FRONT	841
WHITE-RED	LAMP RELAY TO MARKER LAMPS	667
WHITE-RED	PROCESSOR TO THERMACTOR CLUTCH RELAY	566
WHITE-RED	FUEL PUMP RESISTOR TO RELAY	922
WHITE-YELLOW	AIR BAG DIAGNOSTIC MODULE (DEPLOY) TO LH SENSOR	621
WHITE-YELLOW	C.B. UP SWITCH	707
WHITE-YELLOW	CHOKE RELAY TO MCU MODULE	391
WHITE-YELLOW	MESSAGE CENTER OUTPUT CLOCK TO DISPLAY	167
WHITE-YELLOW	POWER SERVO TO CLIMATE CONTROL UNIT (AMP)	247
YELLOW	SWITCH ON TO RELAY	275

COLOR	DESCRIPTION *	CIRCUIT
YELLOW	ELECTRONIC CLUSTER FROM TRIP RESET SWITCH IN KEYBOARD	286
YELLOW	12 GA FUSE LINK	303
YELLOW	HORIZONTAL SEAT REG. MOTOR TO RELAY	179
YELLOW	LF WINDOW REG. SW. TO LF WINDOW REG. MOTOR	227
YELLOW	KEYLESS DOOR LOCK SWITCH DATA BIT 4 TO MODULE	122
YELLOW	TRAILER LH TURN SIGNAL	52
YELLOW	BATTERY TO LOAD	37
YELLOW	REARVIEW OUTSIDE MIRROR UP	410
YELLOW	POWER "THIGH" BOLSTER UP	491
YELLOW	EGR VALVE TO EEC MODULE FEED	362
YELLOW	C.B. B-DIGIT	716
YELLOW	MULTIPLEX WIPER RATE	700
YELLOW	ANTI-LOCK MODULE TO ANTI-LOCK CONTROL VALVE	678
YELLOW	ELECT SHIFT 4 × 4 MODULE TO MOTOR CONTROL COUNTER CLOCKWISE	777
YELLOW	AIR SUSPENSION DIODE SWITCH TO CONTROL MODULE	635
YELLOW	ALT POWER RELAY TO CONTROL MODULE	583
YELLOW	CONVERTIBLE TOP RELAY TO SWITCH	586
YELLOW	AIR SUSPENSION DIODE SWITCH TO CONTROL MODULE	635
YELLOW	DOOR WIRE	631
YELLOW	OIL PRESSURE SWITCH TO CUTOUT RELAY	669
YELLOW	AMPLIFIER TO RHEOSTAT	507
YELLOW	L.H. REMOTE MIRROR SOLENOID CONTROL	542
YELLOW	LEFT REAR AIR INPUT RETURN	859
YELLOW	SEAT BELT INDICATOR LAMP TO MODULE	871
YELLOW	VENT SWITCH TO LEFT FRONT VENT MOTOR	887
YELLOW	TOP CONTROL RELAY TO MOTOR — UP	902
YELLOW-BLACK	COIL "A" TO DISTRIBUTORLESS IGNITION MODULE	850
YELLOW-BLACK	WINDOW SWITCH TO LEFT REAR	884
YELLOW-BLACK	ACCELERATE DECELERATE SENSOR RETURN	837
YELLOW-BLACK	POWER RELAY BATTERY FEED	554
YELLOW-BLACK	RH FRONT SENSOR (LOW) TO MODULE	516
YELLOW-BLACK	RELAY TO ATC CONTROL	575
YELLOW-BLACK	LOW WASHER LEVEL TO SENSOR	793
YELLOW-BLACK	REMOTE DEFROST	727
YELLOW-BLACK	ELECT. ENG. CONTL. MOD. TO TEST CONN #2	382
YELLOW-BLACK	GLOW PLUG TO CONTROL MODULE	472
YELLOW-BLACK	ELECTRONIC CONTROL UNIT TO ACCELERATION SOLENOID	46
YELLOW-BLACK	RADIO ANTENNA SWITCH FEED	137
YELLOW-BLACK	KEYLESS DOOR LOCK SWITCH DATA BIT 3 TO MODULE	121
YELLOW-BLACK	SIGNAL UNIT LAMP TO FUEL SIGNAL RELAY	215
YELLOW-BLACK	LEFT FRONT WINDOW REGULATOR SWITCH TO RIGHT FRONT WINDOW REGULATOR MOTOR	313
YELLOW-BLACK	LEFT FRONT WINDOW REGULATOR SWITCH TO RIGHT REAR WINDOW REGULATOR MOTOR	319
YELLOW-LT BLUE	LEFT FRONT WINDOW REGULATOR SWITCH TO LEFT REAR WINDOW REGULATOR MOTOR	316
YELLOW-LT BLUE	HEATER & A/C CONTROL SW. (DE-ICE) TO CLIMATE CONTROL UNIT	248
YELLOW-LT BLUE	SPEED INPUT TO MESSAGE CENTER	136
YELLOW-LT BLUE	STARTING MOTOR TO STARTING MOTOR RELAY	113
YELLOW-LT BLUE	POSITION SENSE RETURN	435
YELLOW-LT BLUE	HORN SWITCH FEED	460
YELLOW-LT BLUE	SELECTOR SWITCH TO AFT AXLE TANK	675
YELLOW-LT BLUE	SEAT REGULATOR SWITCH TO FRONT MOTOR (RH)	984
YELLOW-LT BLUE	SEAT REGULATOR SWITCH TO FRONT MOTOR (LH)	990
YELLOW-LT BLUE	SEAT REGULATOR SWITCH TO FRONT MOTOR (LH)	978
YELLOW-LT BLUE	WINDOW SWITCH TO LEFT REAR MOTOR	885
YELLOW-LT GREEN	SEAT REGULATOR SWITCH TO REAR MOTOR (LH)	982
YELLOW-LT GREEN	AIR COND. CONTROL SW. TO FRESH-AIR RECIRC. DOOR SOLENOID	660
YELLOW-LT GREEN	SPLICE #2 TO MODULE	529
YELLOW-LT GREEN	SPLICE #3 TO PRESSURE SWITCH	534
YELLOW-LT GREEN	FLUID SWITCH TO GROUND STUD	550
YELLOW-LT GREEN	SPLICE #2 TO SPLICE #3	551
YELLOW-LT GREEN	SPLICE #2 TO COUP GROUND "B"	552
YELLOW-LT GREEN	ALT. SHUNT TO AMMETER	654
YELLOW-LT GREEN	MODULE TO RELEASE SOLENOID	664
YELLOW-LT GREEN	SEAT REGULATOR SWITCH TO REAR MOTOR (RH)	988
YELLOW-LT GREEN	POSITION SENSE ENABLE	437
YELLOW-LT GREEN	MOVABLE STEERING COLUMN SOLENOID FEED	375
YELLOW-LT GREEN	POWER STEERING PRESSURE SWITCH	330
YELLOW-LT GREEN	TRANSMISSION OVERDRIVE SWITCH TO HEAT MODULE	324
YELLOW-LT GREEN	HORN RELAY TO HORN	6
YELLOW-LT GREEN	WINDOW REGULATOR RELAY FEED	193
YELLOW-LT. GREEN	GROUND STUD TO SPLICE #2	548
YELLOW-RED	RH FRONT SENSOR (HIGH) TO MODULE	514
YELLOW-RED	BLOWER MOTOR SPEED CONTROLLER TO RESISTOR #2 (MED.)	752
YELLOW-RED	HEATER & A/C CONTROL SW. TO BLOWER RELAY SW.	753
YELLOW-RED	COIL "B" TO DISTRIBUTORLESS IGNITION MODULE	851
YELLOW-RED	WINDOW REG. SW. TO WINDOW REG. MOTOR	333
YELLOW-RED	MCU MODULE TO KNOCK SENSOR	310
YELLOW-RED	HOT WATER TEMP. RELAY TO HOT WATER TEMP. SENDING UNIT	45
YELLOW-RED	WINDSHIELD WIPER SW. TO WINDSHIELD WIPER MOTOR	61
YELLOW-RED	SERVO FEEDBACK POTENTIOMETER SIGNAL TO AMPLIFIER	148
YELLOW-RED	STOP AND TURN BULB OUTAGE TO MESSAGE CENTER	135
YELLOW-WHITE	ALTERNATOR OUTPUT	36
YELLOW-WHITE	FUEL GAUGE TO FUEL GAUGE SENDER	29
YELLOW-WHITE	THERMAL SW. TO CLIMATE CONTROL UNIT	244
YELLOW-WHITE	SEAT PROCESSOR TO RECLINER MOTOR "UP"	439
YELLOW-WHITE	COIL "C" TO DISTRIBUTORLESS IGNITION MODULE	852
YELLOW-WHITE	ELECT SHIFT 4 X 4 MODULE TO MOTOR POSITION #1	762
YELLOW-WHITE	HEATED WINDSHIELD CONTROL TO HEATED WINDSHIELD SWITCH	738
YELLOW-WHITE	SEAT REGULATOR SWITCH TO HORZ. MOTOR (LH)	980
YELLOW-WHITE	SEAT REGULATOR SWITCH TO FRONT MOTOR (RH)	986
YELLOW-WHITE	ELECTRONIC THROTTLE VALVE POWER	925

* IN SOME CASES, THERE MAY BE ADDITIONAL CIRCUIT
FUNCTIONS INCLUDED IN THE CIRCUIT DESCRIPTION LISTED.

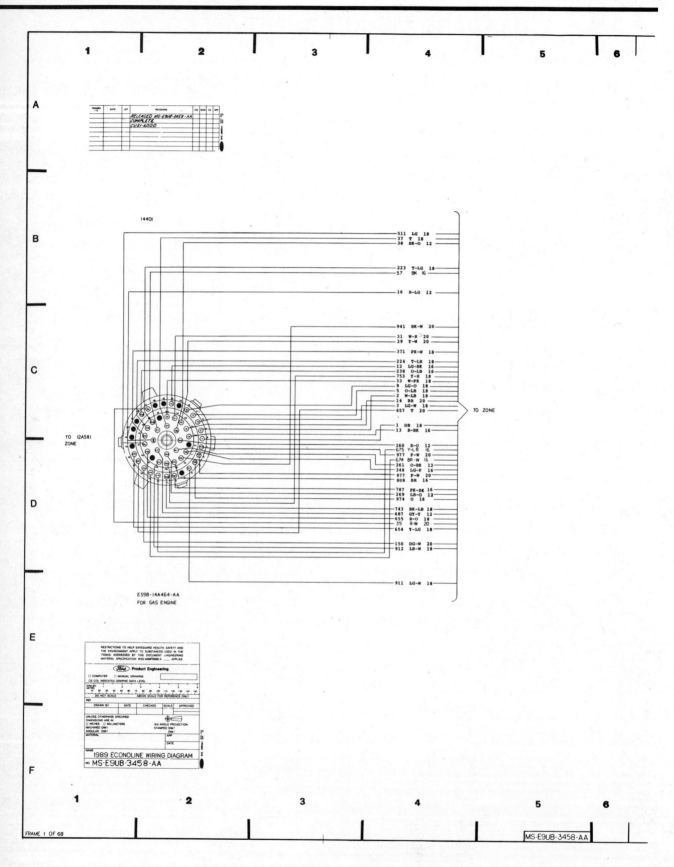

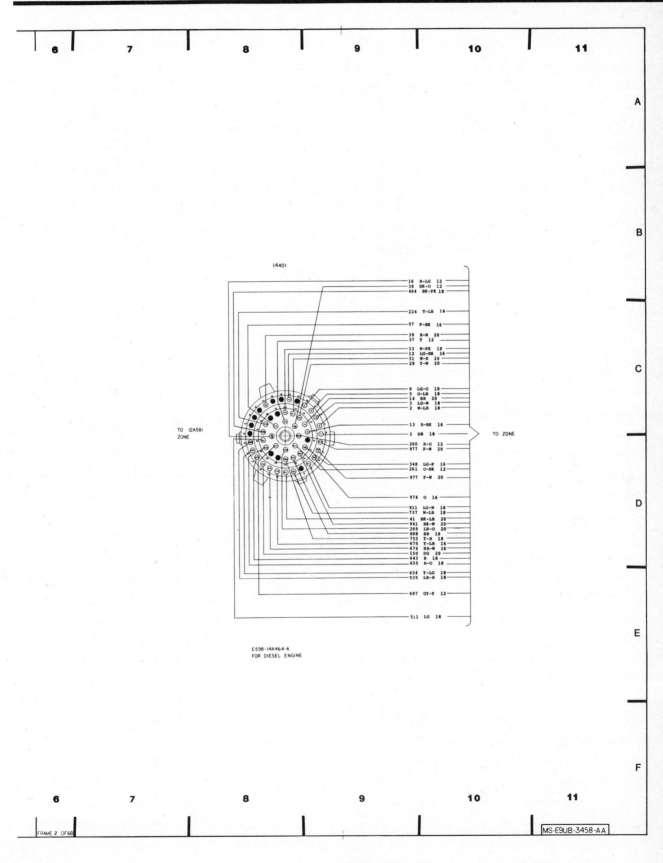

14401

16 R-LG 12
38 BK-O 12
464 BK-PK 18

224 T-LB 18

57 P-BK 16

39 R-W 20
37 Y 12

33 W-PK 18
12 LG-BK 16
31 W-R 20
29 Y-W 20

9 LG-O 18
5 O-LB 18
14 BR 20
3 LG-W 18
2 W-LB 18

13 R-BK 16

1 DB 18

260 R-O 12
977 P-W 20

348 LG-P 16
261 O-BK 12

977 P-W 20

974 O 16

911 LG-W 18
737 W-LB 18
41 BK-LB 20
941 BK-W 20
269 LB-O 20
808 BR 16
753 Y-R 18
675 Y-LB 16
674 BR-W 16
150 DG 20
643 R 18
655 R-O 18

654 Y-LG 18
535 LB-R 18

687 GY-Y 12

511 LG 18

TO I2A581
ZONE

TO ZONE

E59B-14A464-A
FOR DIESEL ENGINE

MS-E9UB-3458-AA

1989

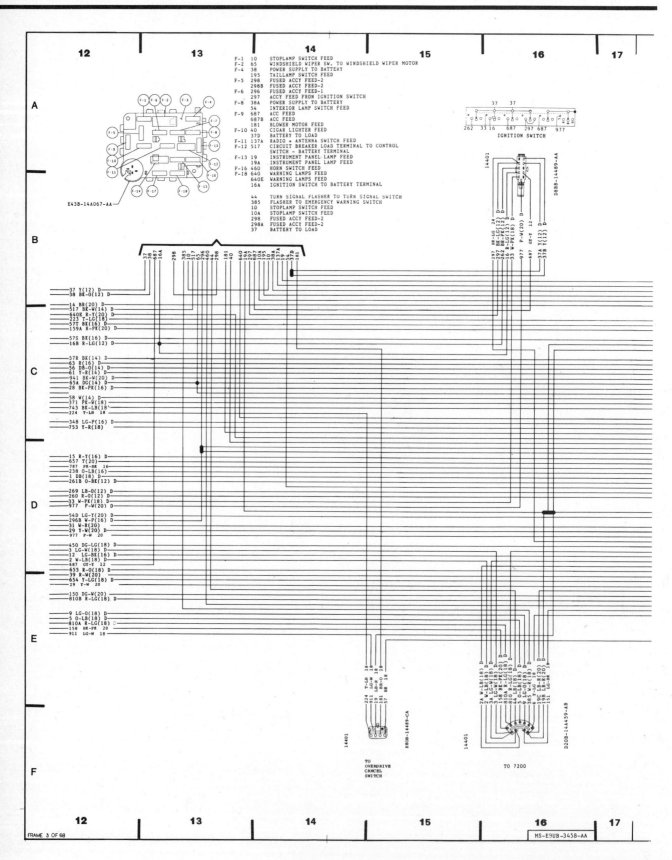

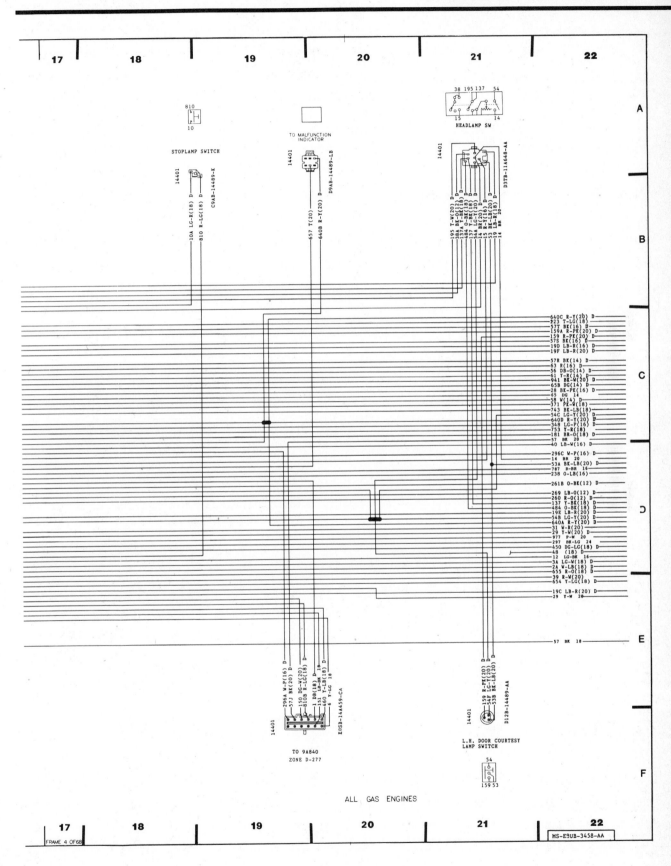

1989

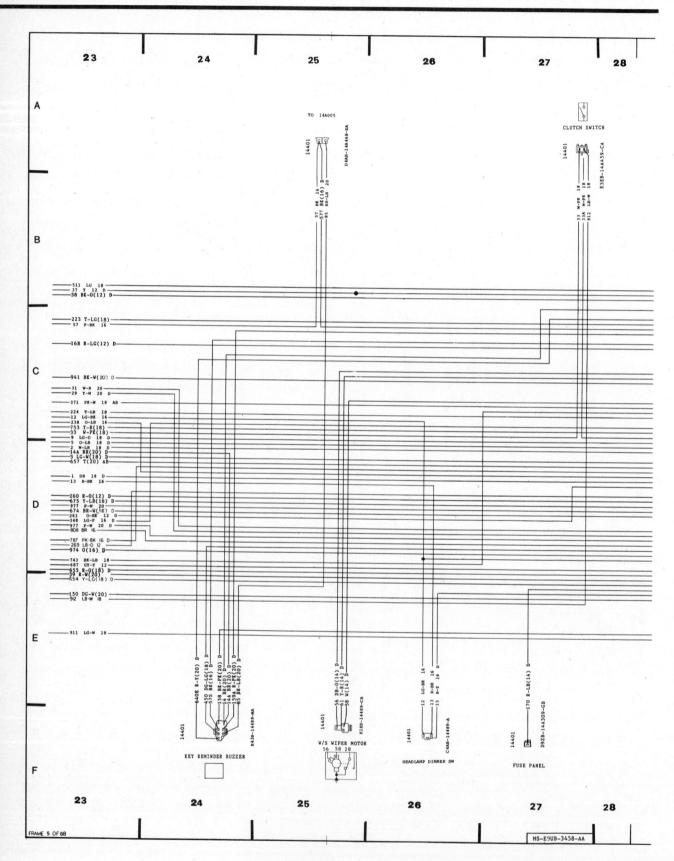

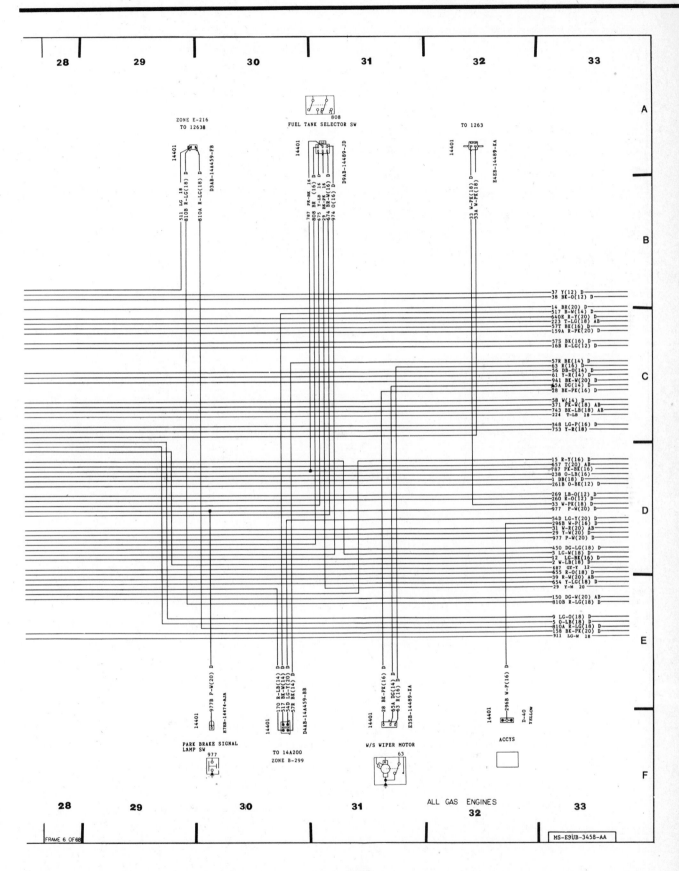

FUEL TANK SELECTOR SW

PARK BRAKE SIGNAL
LAMP SW

TO 14A200
ZONE B-299

W/S WIPER MOTOR

ACCYS

ALL GAS ENGINES

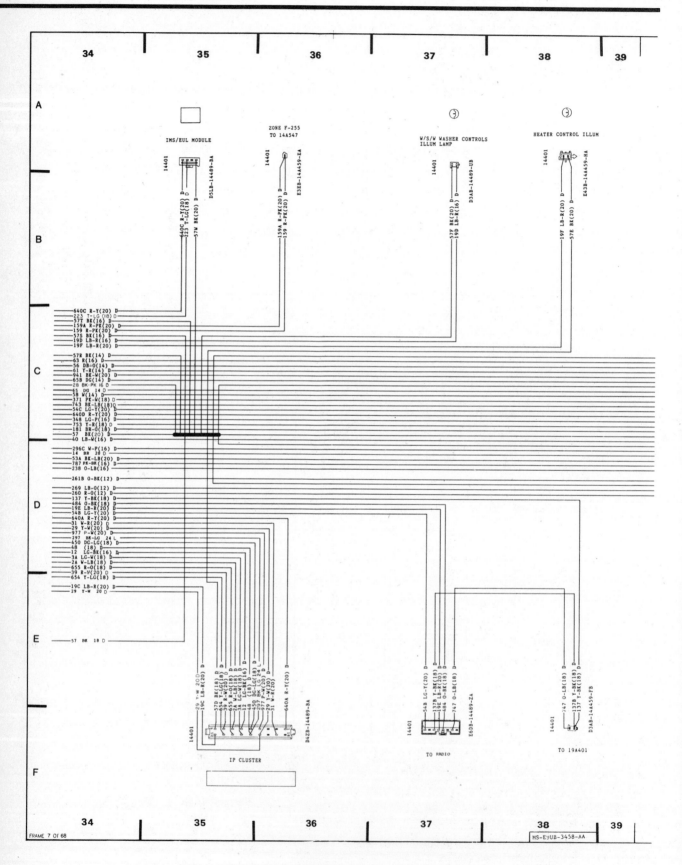

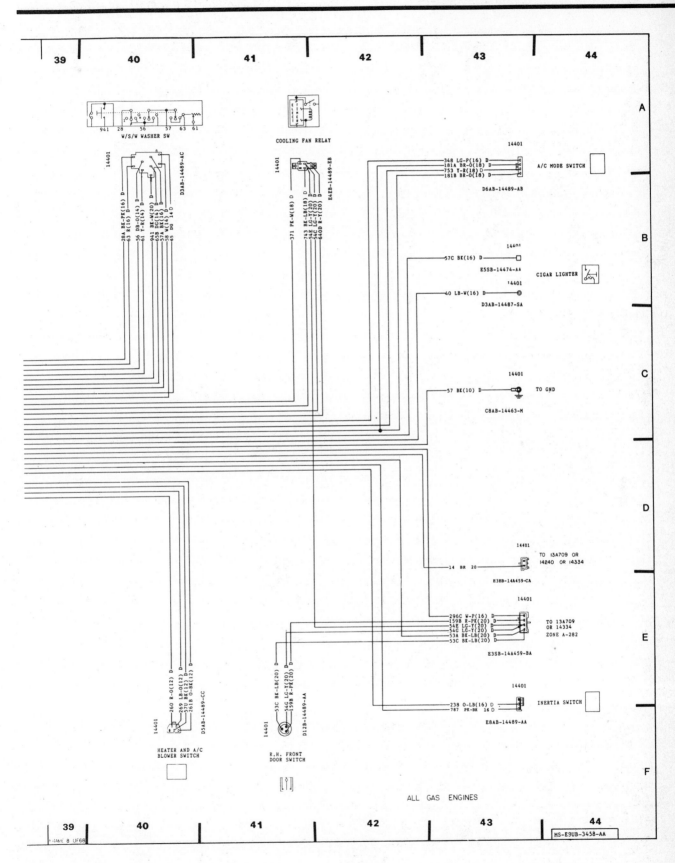

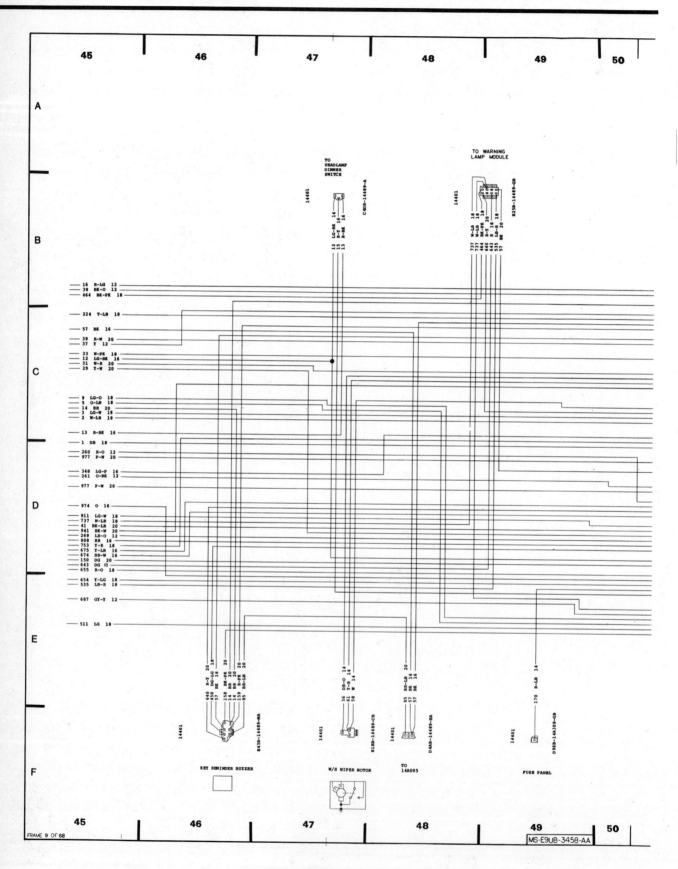

1989

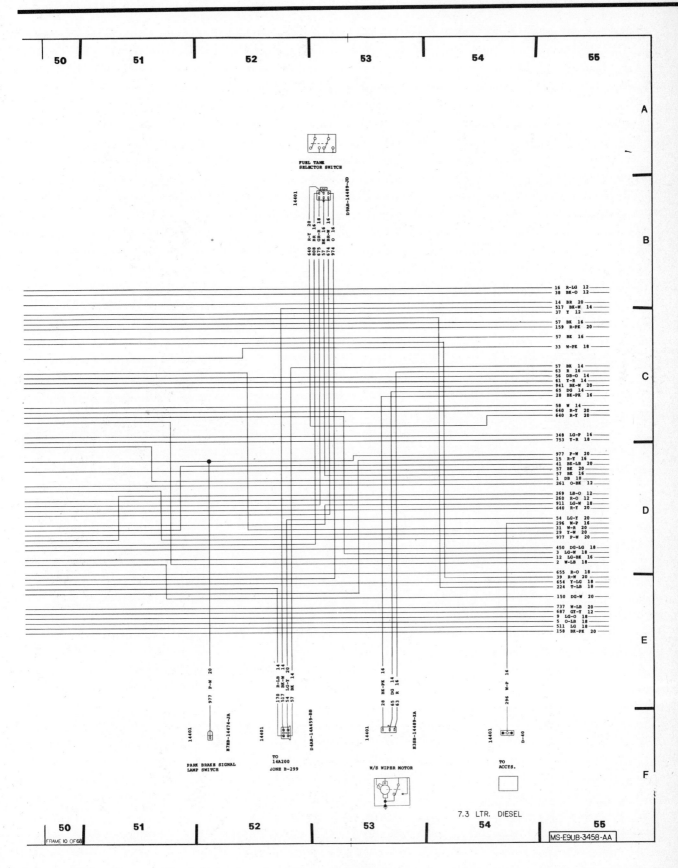

FUEL TANK
SELECTOR SWITCH

PARK BRAKE SIGNAL
LAMP SWITCH

TO
14A200
ZONE B-299

W/S WIPER MOTOR

TO
ACCYS.

7.3 LTR. DIESEL

6 CHASSIS ELECTRICAL

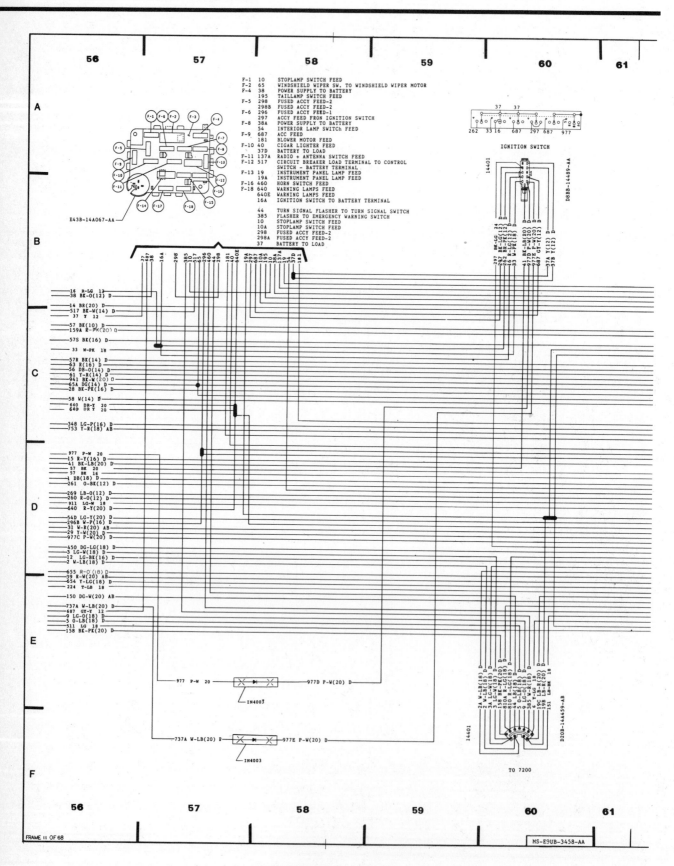

1989

6–56

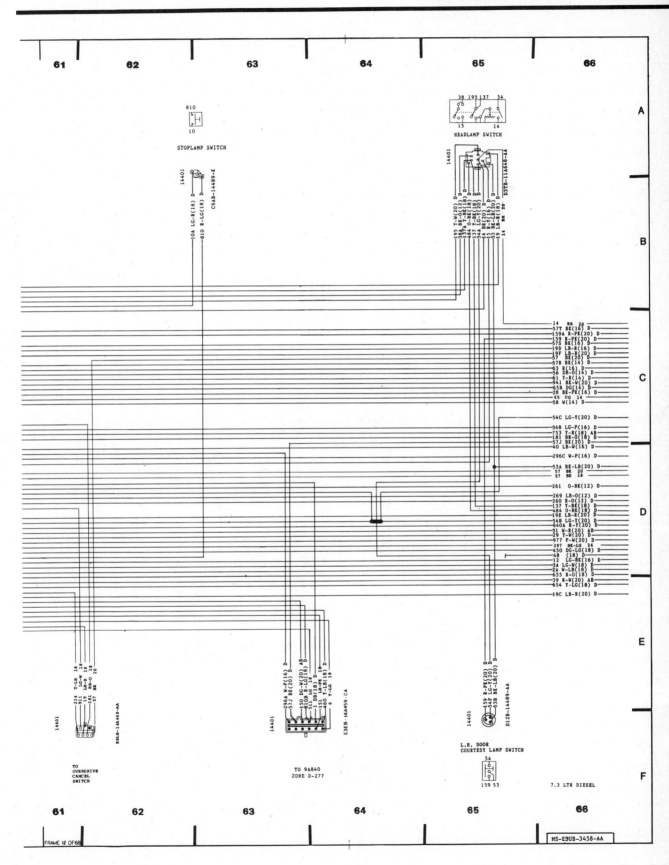

STOPLAMP SWITCH

HEADLAMP SWITCH

L.H. DOOR
COURTESY LAMP SWITCH

7.3 LTR DIESEL

TO
OVERDRIVE
CANCEL
SWITCH

TO 9A840
ZONE D-277

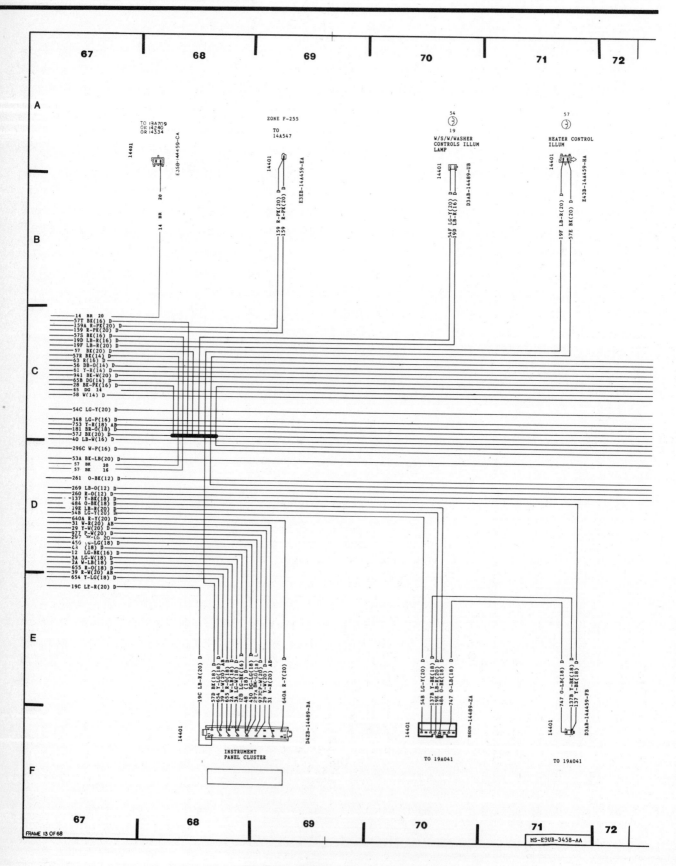

1989

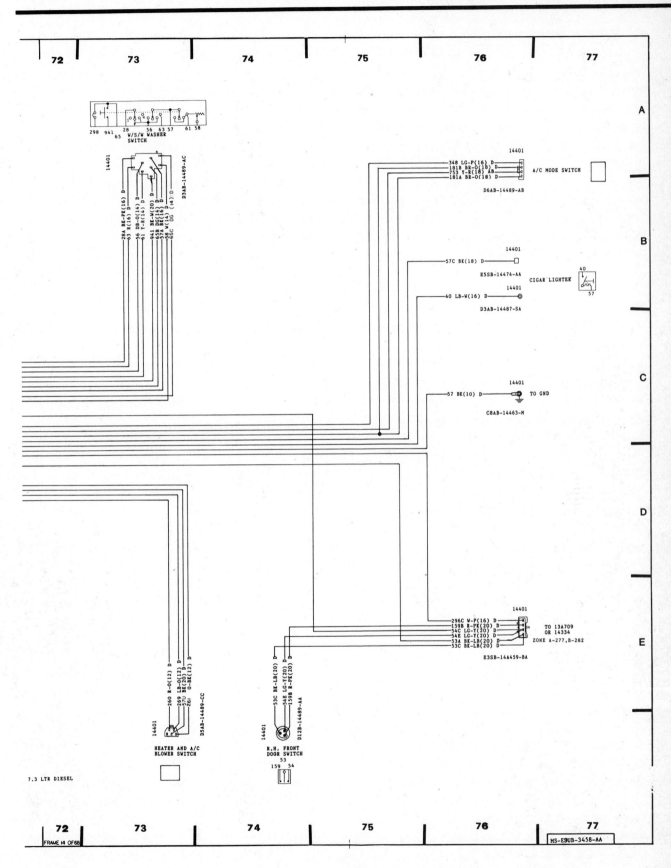

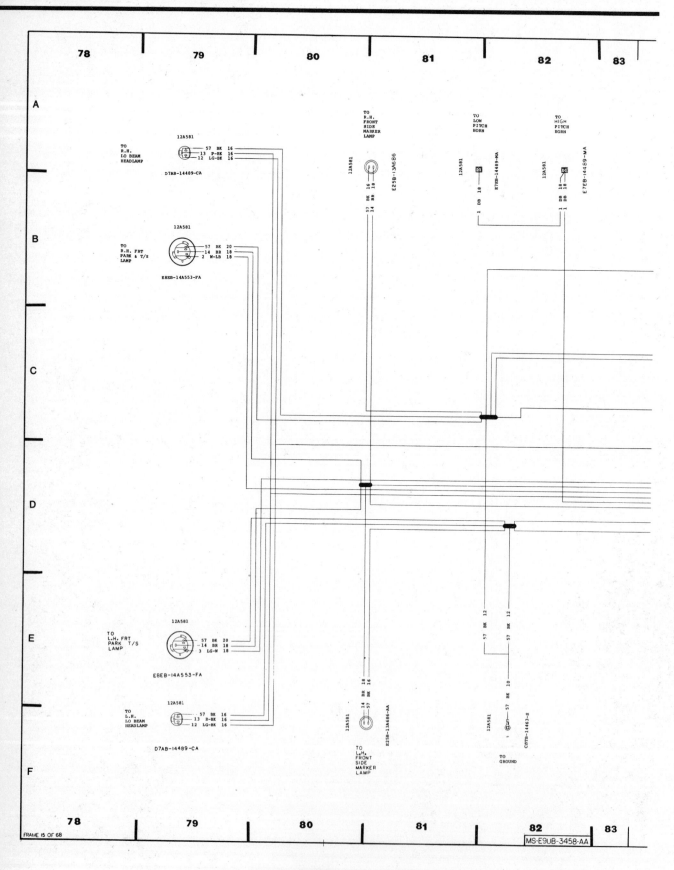

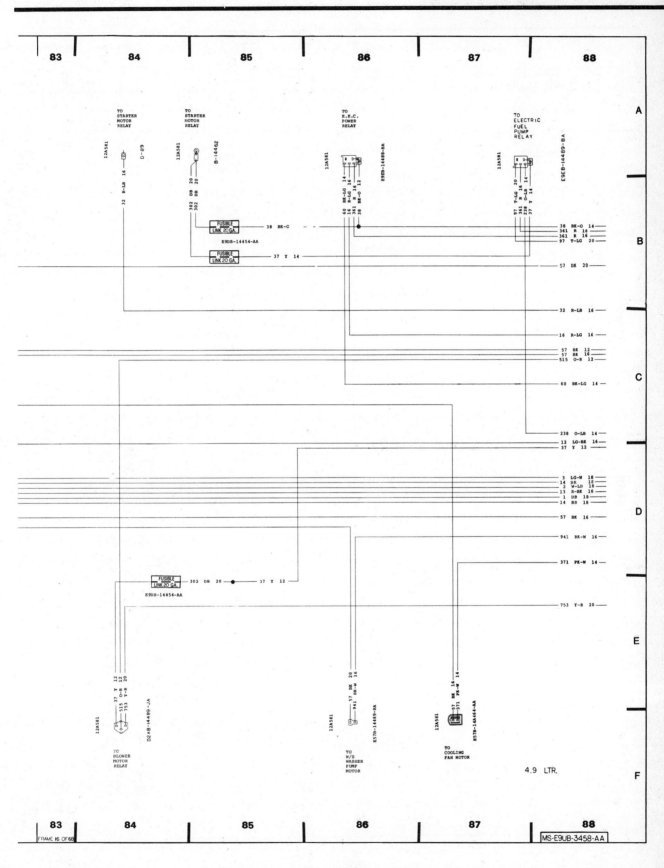

MS-E9UB-3458-AA

1989

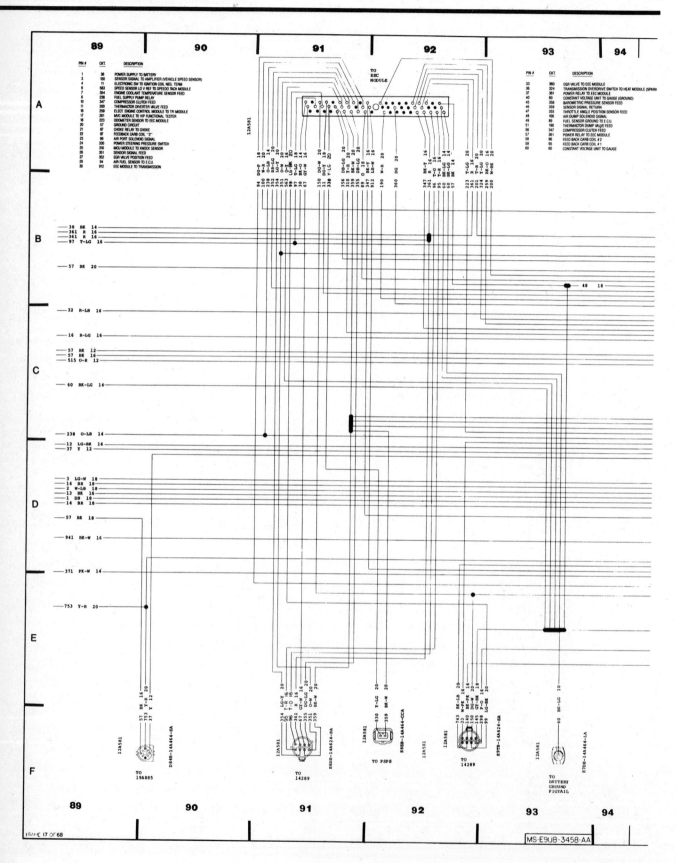

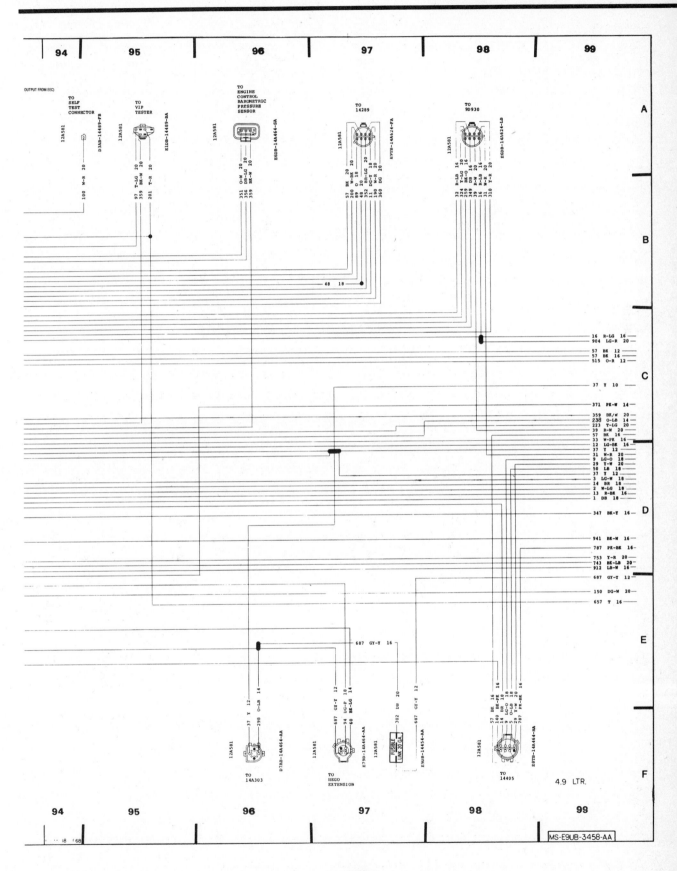

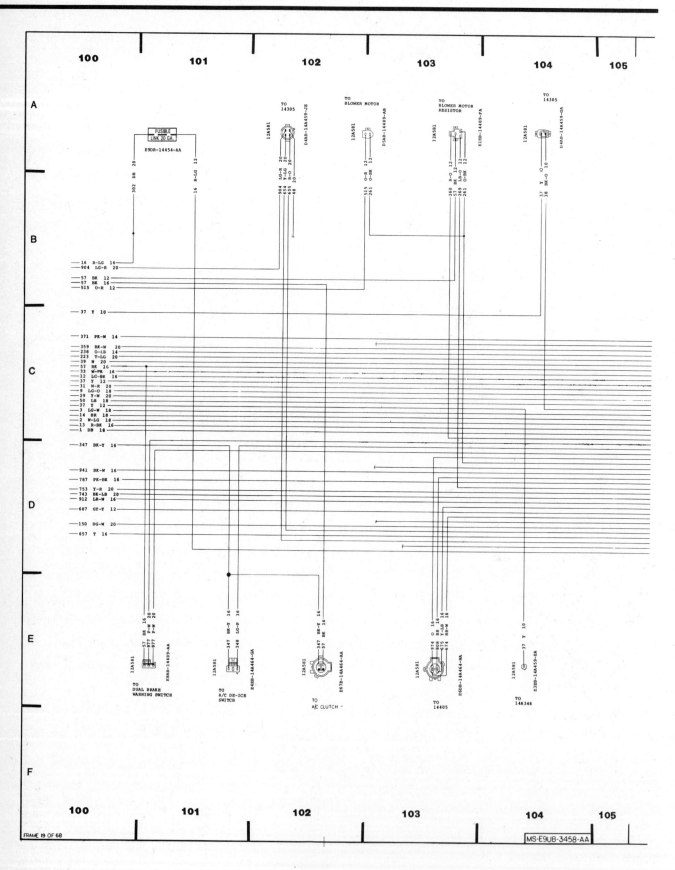

105 106 107 108 109 110

A

B

C

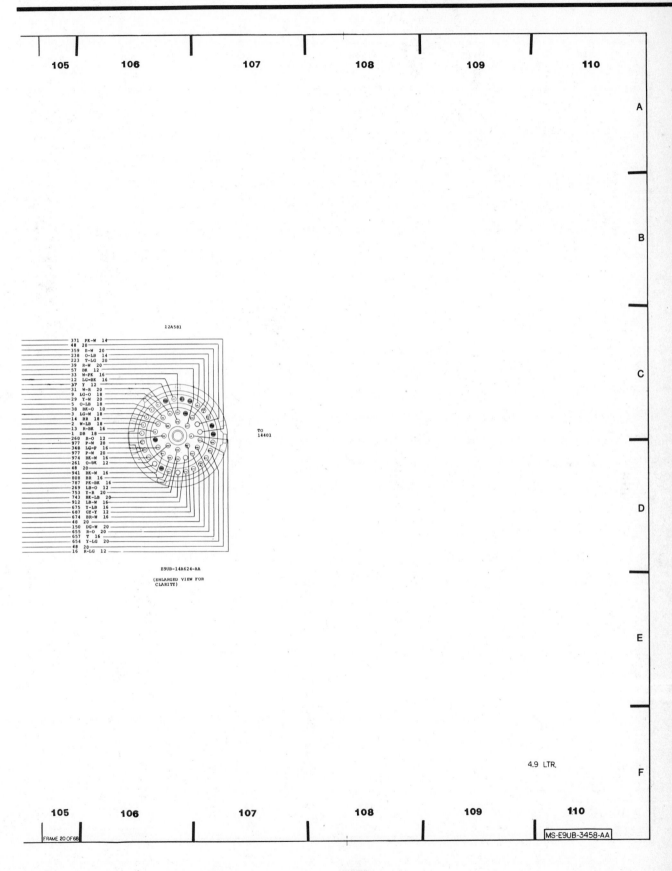

12A581

371 PK-W 14
48 20
359 B-W 20
238 O-LB 14
223 T-LG 20
39 R-W 20
57 BK 12
33 W-PK 16
12 LG-BK 16
37 Y 12
31 W-R 20
9 LG-O 18
29 Y-W 20
5 O-LB 18
38 BK-O 10
3 LG-W 18
14 BR 18
2 W-LB 18
13 R-BK 16
1 DB 18
260 R-O 12
977 P-W 20
348 LG-P 16
977 P-W 20
974 BK-W 16
261 O-BK 12
48 20
941 BK-W 16
808 BR 16
707 PK-BK 16
269 LB-O 12
753 Y-R 20
743 BK-LB 20
912 LB-W 16
675 Y-LB 16
687 GY-Y 12
674 BR-W 16
48 20
150 DG-W 20
655 R-O 20
657 T 16
654 Y-LG 20
48 20
16 R-LG 12

TO
14401

E9UB-14A624-AA

(ENLARGED VIEW FOR
CLARITY)

D

E

4.9 LTR.

F

105 106 107 108 109 110

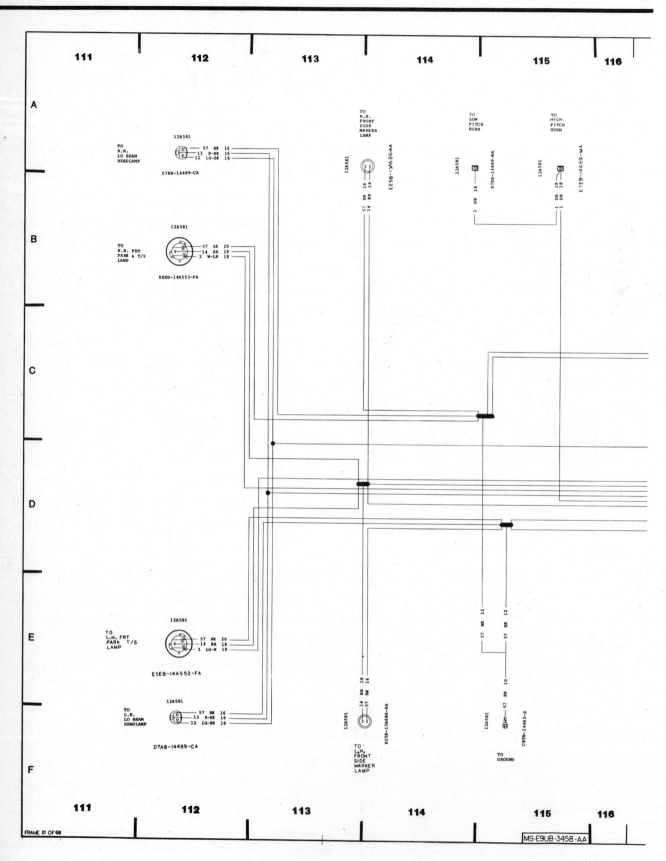

MS-E9UB-3458-AA

1989

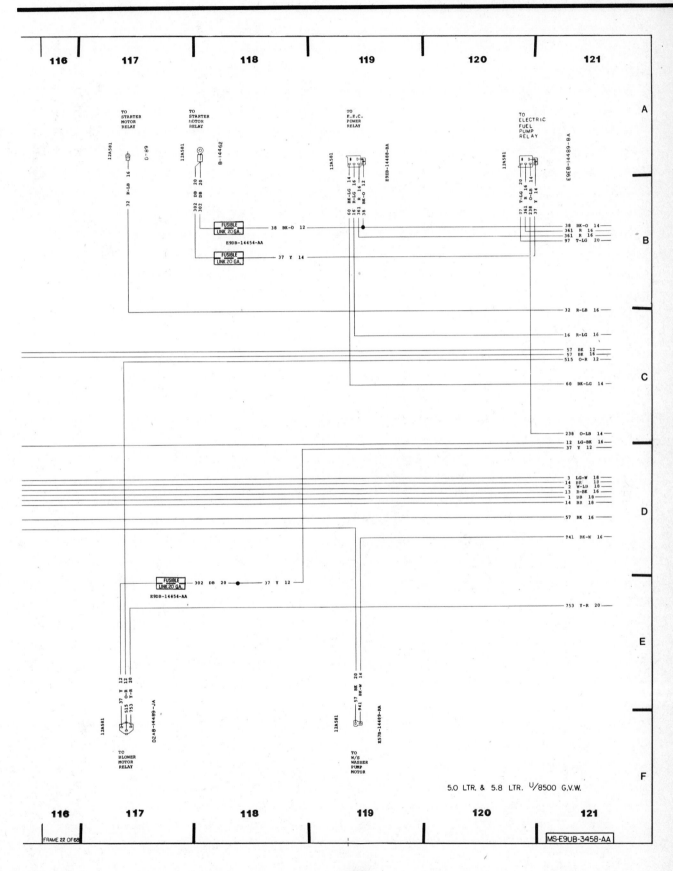

116   117   118   119   120   121

116   117   118   119   120   121

5.0 LTR. & 5.8 LTR. U/8500 G.V.W.

FRAME 22 OF 68

MS-E9UB-3458-AA

1989

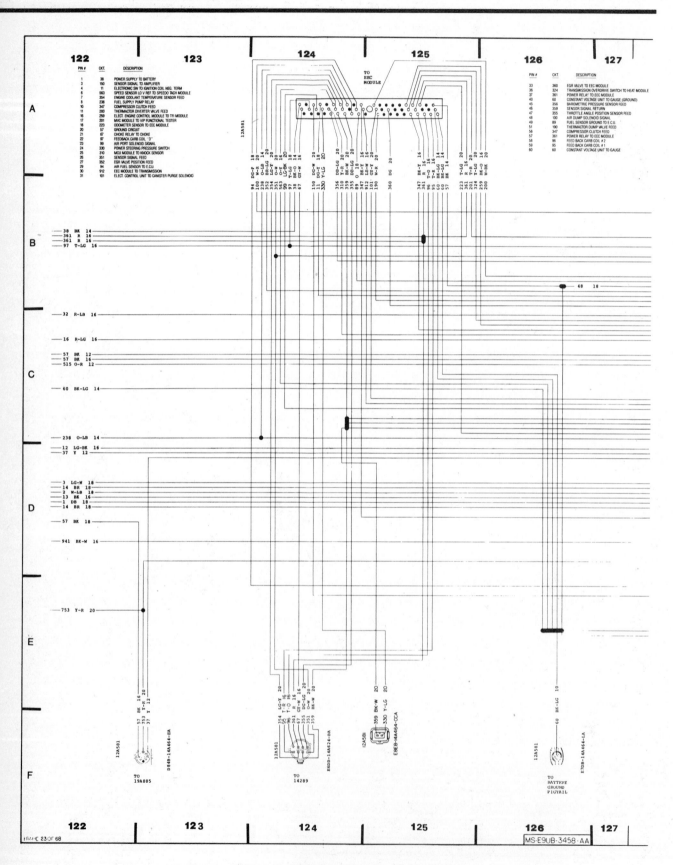

MS-E9UB-3458-AA

1989

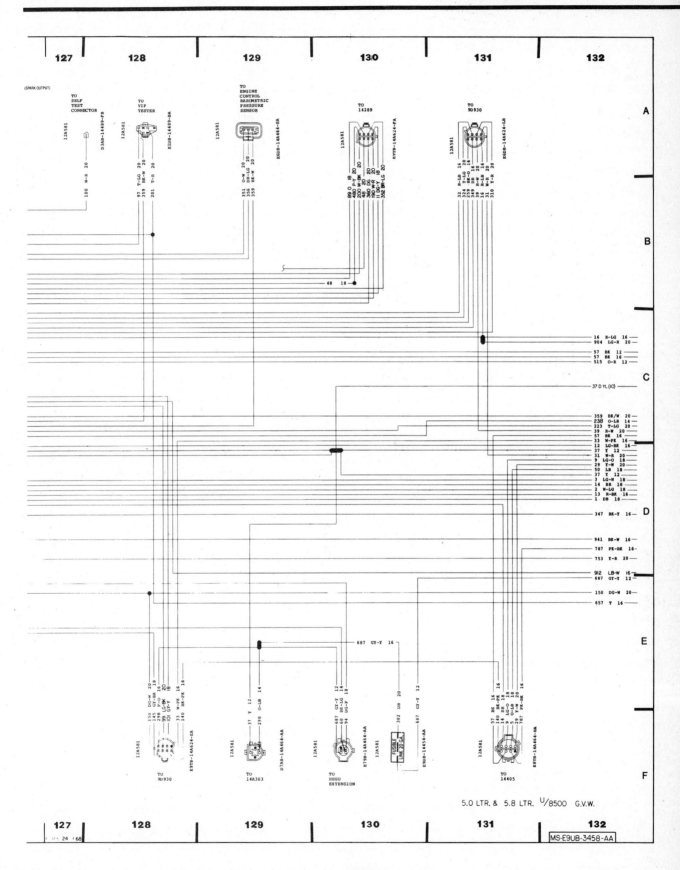

5.0 LTR. & 5.8 LTR. ^{U}/8500 G.V.W.

MS-E9UB-3458-AA

1989

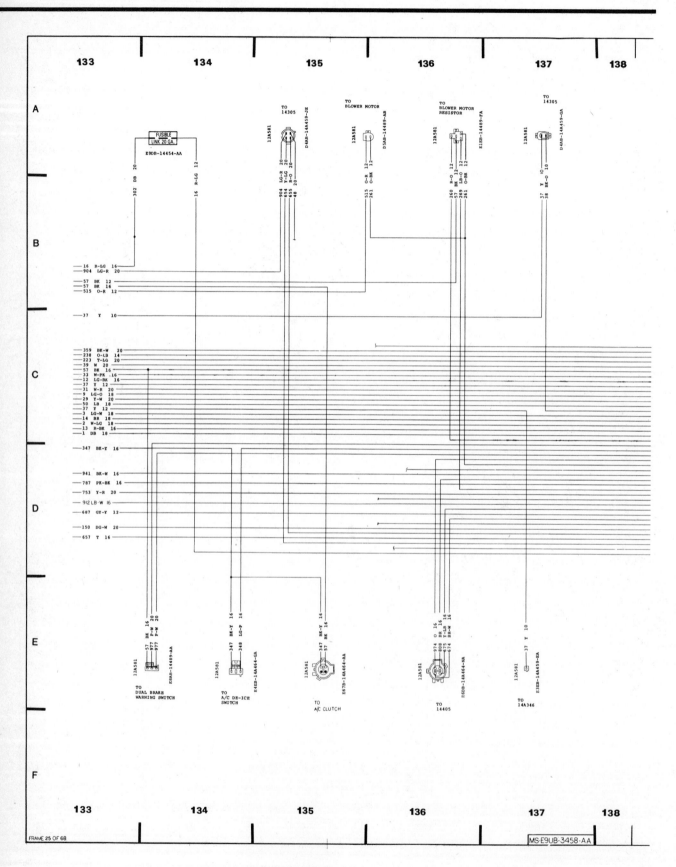

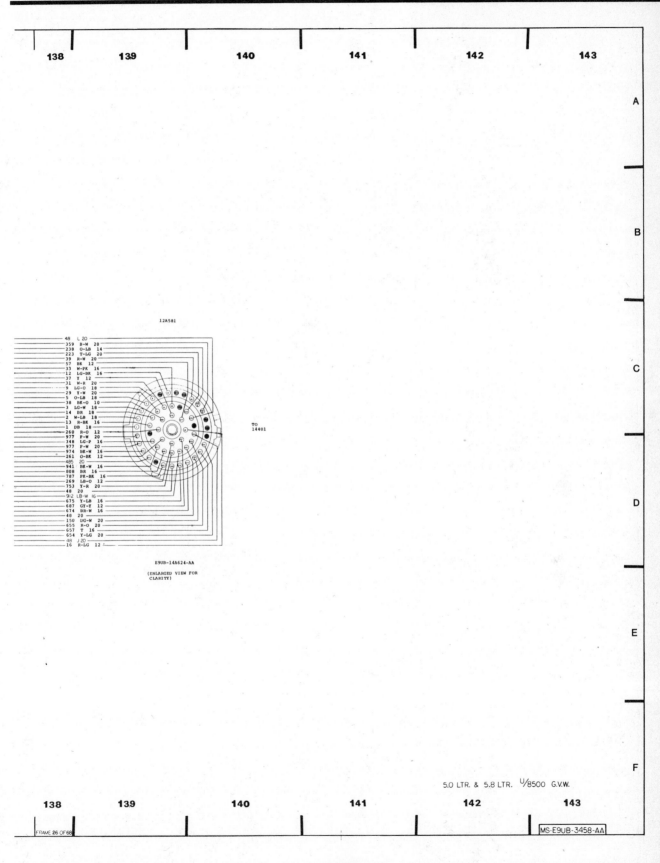

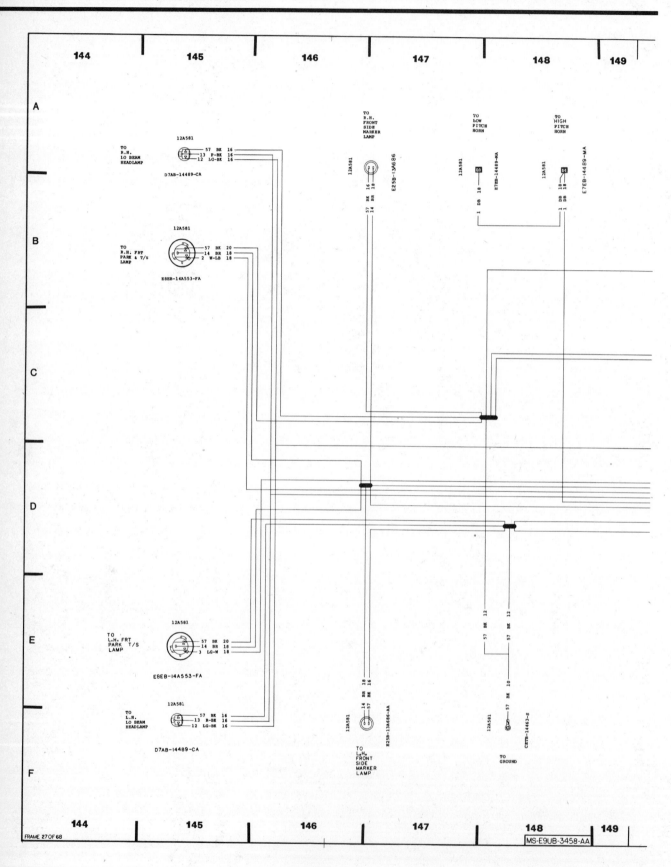

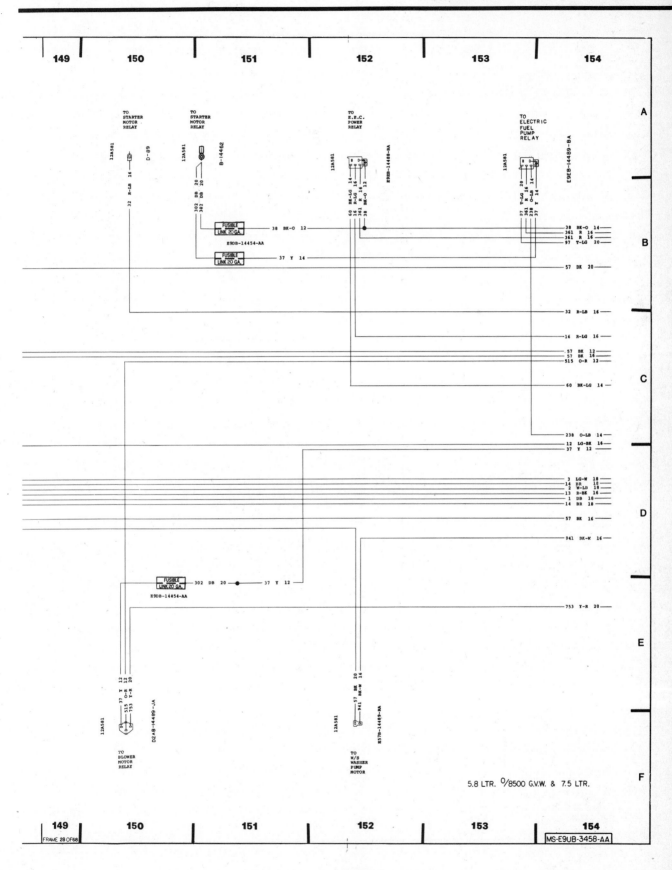

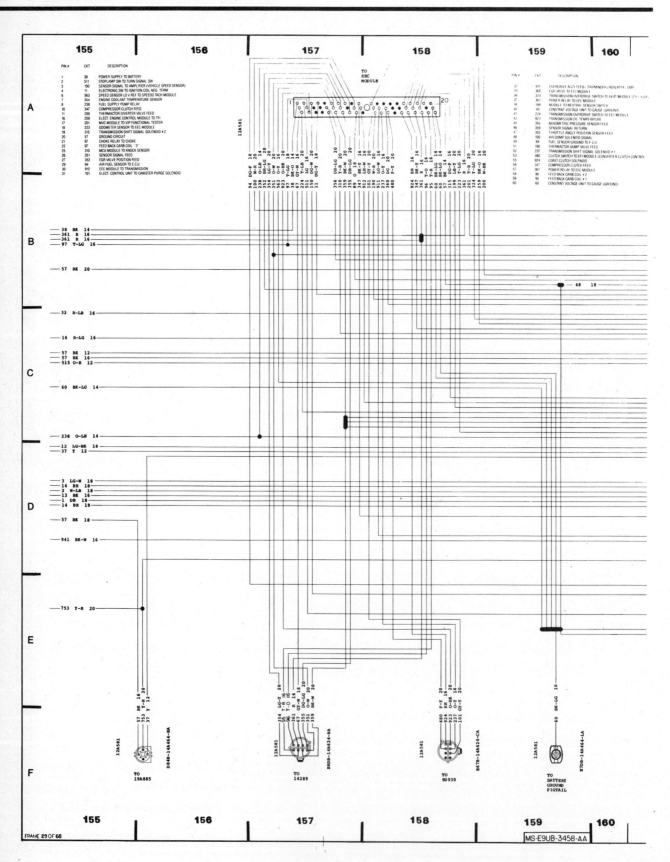

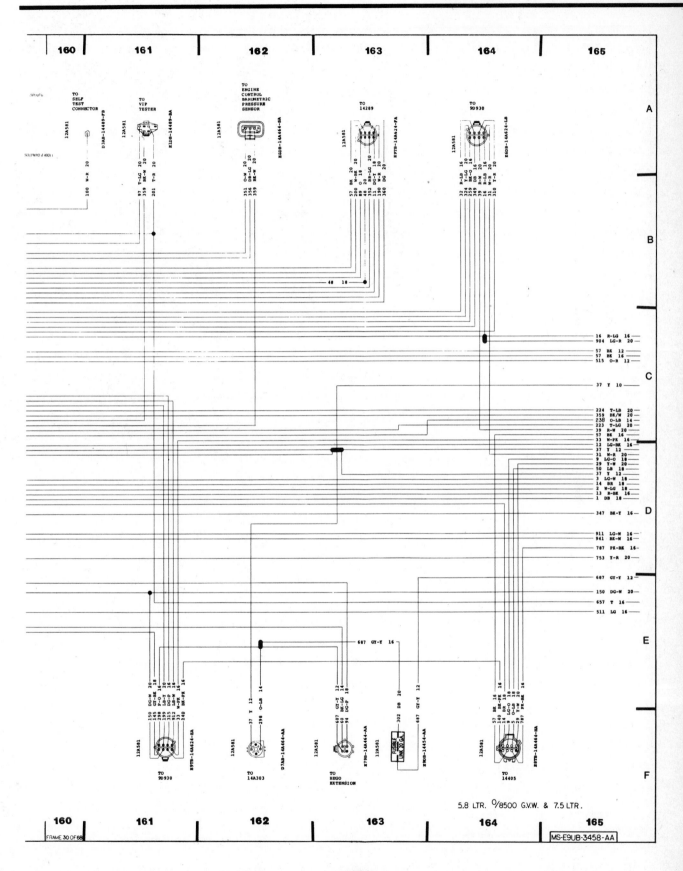

5.8 LTR. ^{0}/8500 G.V.W. & 7.5 LTR.

1989

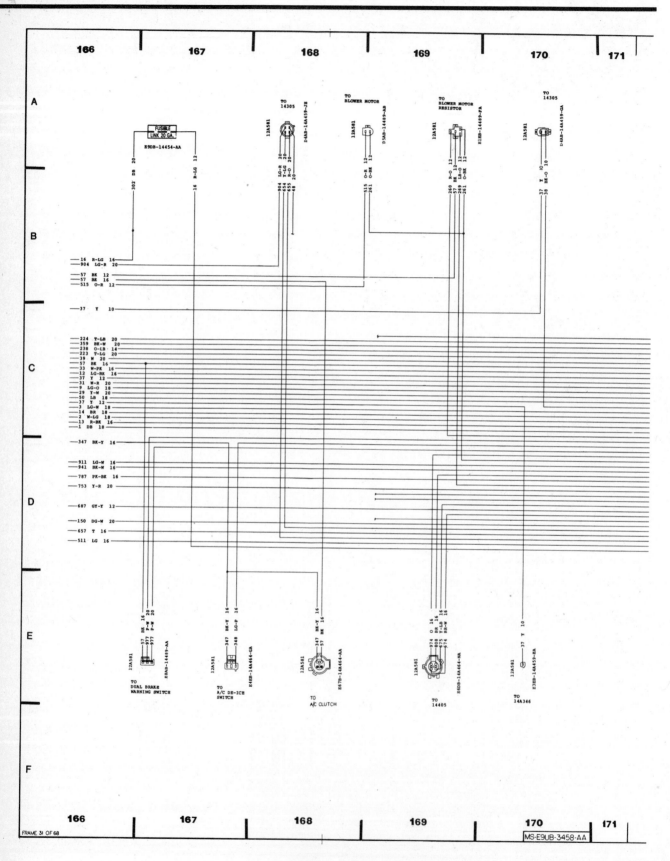

171 172 173 174 175 176

A

B

C

D

E

F

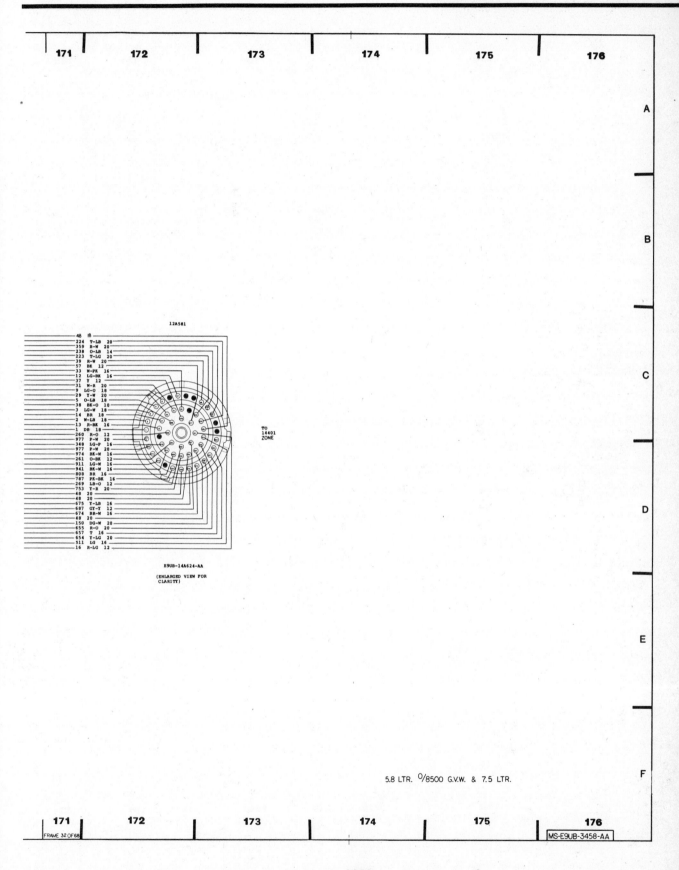

12A581

```
48  18
224  T-LB  20
359  B-W  20
238  O-LB  14
223  T-LG  20
39  R-W  20
57  BK  12
33  W-PK  16
12  LG-BK  16
37  Y  12
31  W-R  20
9  LG-O  18
29  Y-W  20
5  O-LB  18
38  BK-O  10
3  LG-W  18
14  BR  18
2  W-LB  18
13  R-BK  16
1  DB  18
260  R-O  12
977  P-W  20
348  LG-P  16
977  P-W  20
974  BK-W  16
261  O-BK  12
911  LG-W  16
941  BK-W  16
808  BR  16
787  PK-BK  16
269  LB-O  12
753  Y-R  20
48  20
48  20
675  Y-LB  16
687  GY-Y  12
674  BR-W  16
48  20
150  DG-W  20
655  R-O  20
657  T  16
654  Y-LG  20
511  LG  16
16  R-LG  12
```

TO 14401 ZONE

E9UB-14A624-AA

(ENLARGED VIEW FOR CLARITY)

5.8 LTR. O/8500 G.V.W. & 7.5 LTR.

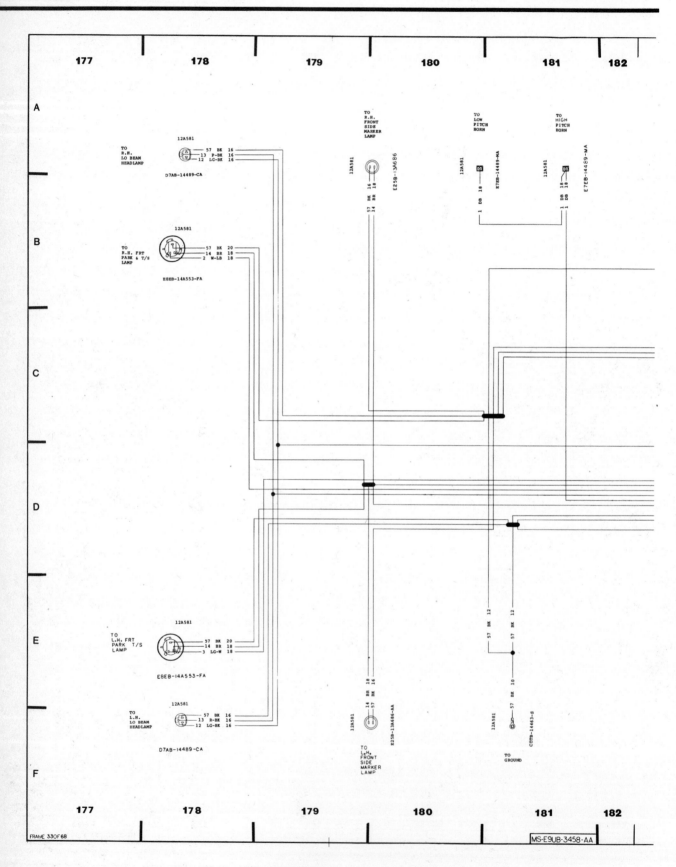

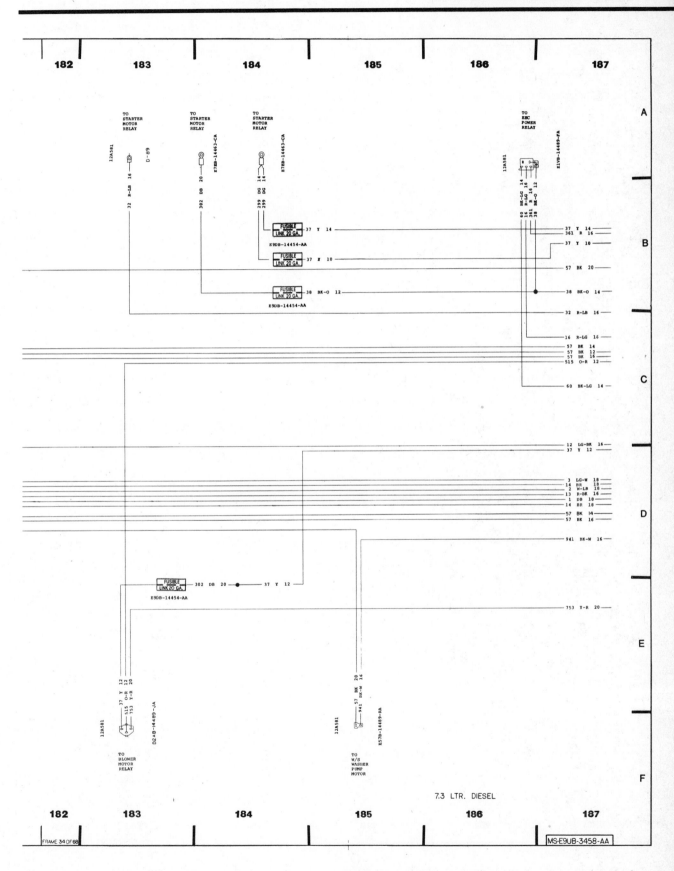

182   183   184   185   186   187

TO STARTER MOTOR RELAY

TO STARTER MOTOR RELAY

TO STARTER MOTOR RELAY

TO EEC POWER RELAY

12A581   D-89

E7BB-14463-CA

E7BB-14463-CA

12A581   E1VB-14489-FA

32 R-LB 16

302 DB 20

299 DG 14
299 DG 14

60 BK-LG 14
16 R-LG 16
361 R 16
38 BK-O 12

FUSIBLE LINK 20 GA.   37 Y 14
E9DB-14454-AA

37 Y 14
361 R 16

FUSIBLE LINK 20 GA.   37 Y 10

37 Y 10

57 BK 20

FUSIBLE LINK 20 GA.   38 BK-O 12
E9DB-14454-AA

38 BK-O 14

32 R-LB 16

16 R-LG 16

57 BK 14
57 BK 12
57 BK 16
515 O-R 12

60 BK-LG 14

12 LG-BK 16
37 Y 12

3 LG-W 18
14 BR 18
2 W-LB 18
13 R-BK 16
1 DB 18
14 BR 18
57 BK 14
57 BK 16

941 BK-W 16

FUSIBLE LINK 20 GA.   302 DB 20   37 Y 12
E9DB-14454-AA

753 Y-R 20

37 Y 12
515 O-R 12
753 Y-R 20

57 BK 20
941 BK-W 16

12A581   D2AB-14489-JA

E57B-14489-RA

TO BLOWER MOTOR RELAY

TO W/S WASHER PUMP MOTOR

7.3 LTR. DIESEL

182   183   184   185   186   187

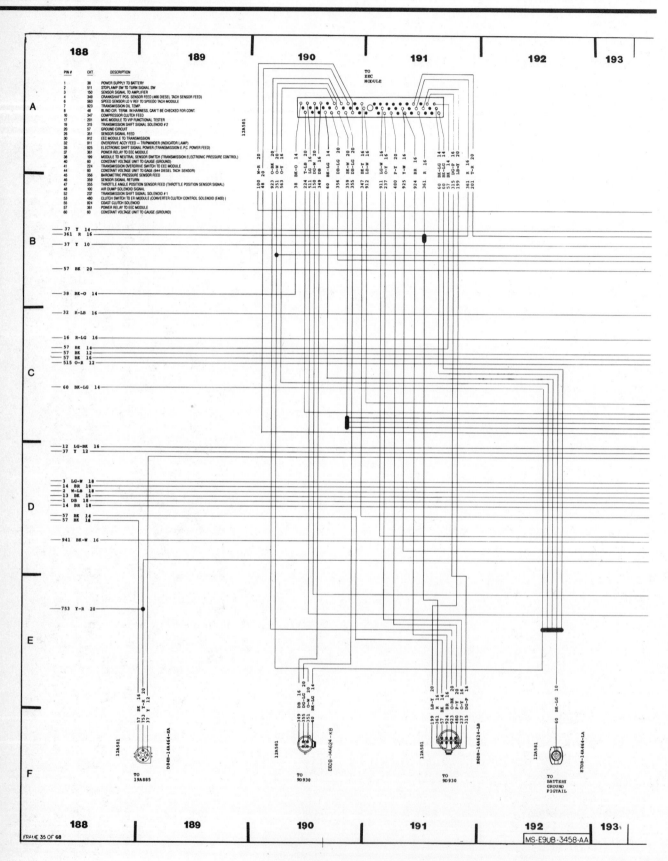

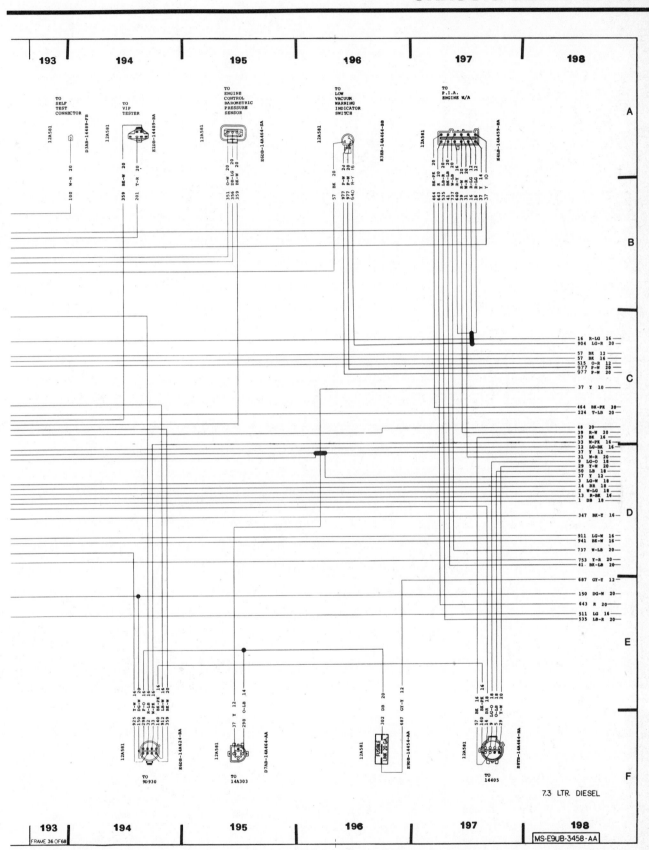

7.3 LTR. DIESEL

MS-E9UB-3458-AA

1989

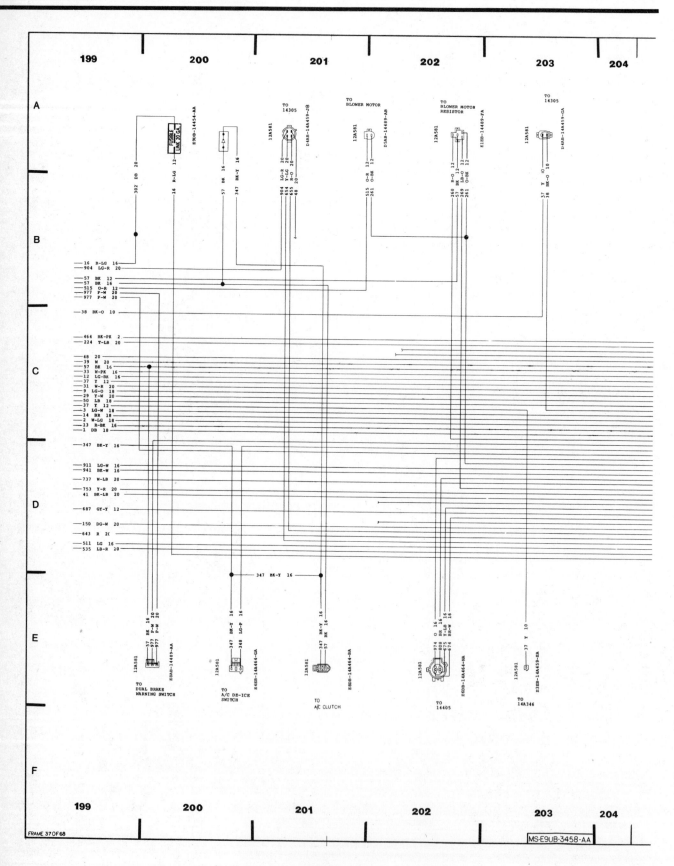

204   205   206   207   208   209

A

B

C

D

E

F

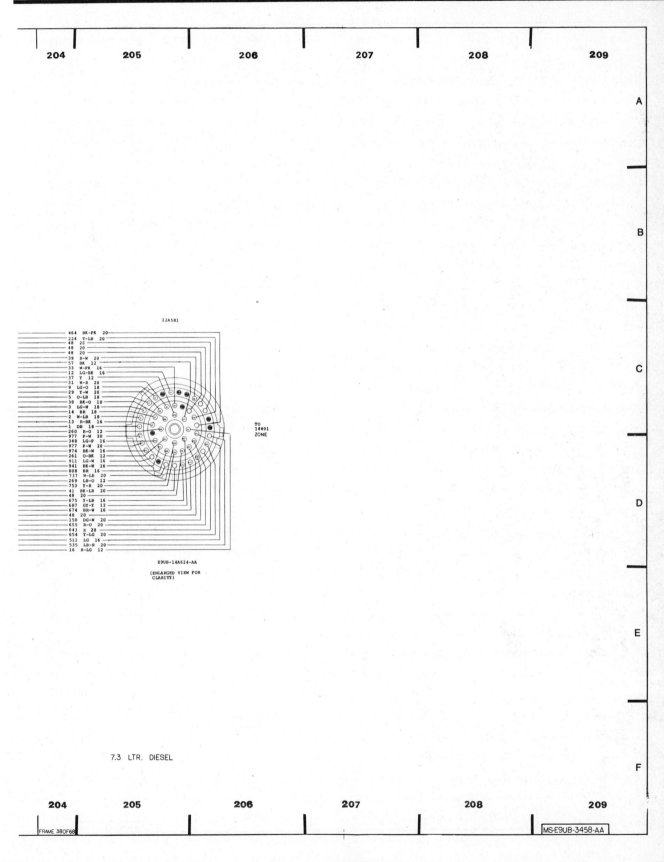

12A581

464 BK-PK 20
224 T-LB   20
48   2C
48   20
48   20
39   R-W   20
57   DK   12
33   W-PK 16
12   LG-BK 16
37   Y   12
31   W-R   20
9   LG-O 18
29   Y-W   20
5   O-LB 18
38   BK-O 10
3   LG-W 18
14   BR   18
2   W-LB 18
13   R-BK 16
1   DB   18
260 R-O   12
977 P-W   20
348 LG-P 16
977 P-W   20
974 BK-W 16
261 O-BK 12
911 LG-W 16
941 BK-W 16
808 BR   16
737 W-LB 20
269 LB-O 12
753 Y-R   20
41   BK-LB 20
48   20
675 Y-LB 16
687 GY-Y 12
674 BR-W 16
48   20
150 DG-W 20
655 R-O   20
643 R   20
654 Y-LG 20
511 LG   16
535 LB-R 20
16   R-LG 12

TO
14401
ZONE

E9UB-14A624-AA

(ENLARGED VIEW FOR
CLARITY)

7.3 LTR. DIESEL

204   205   206   207   208   209

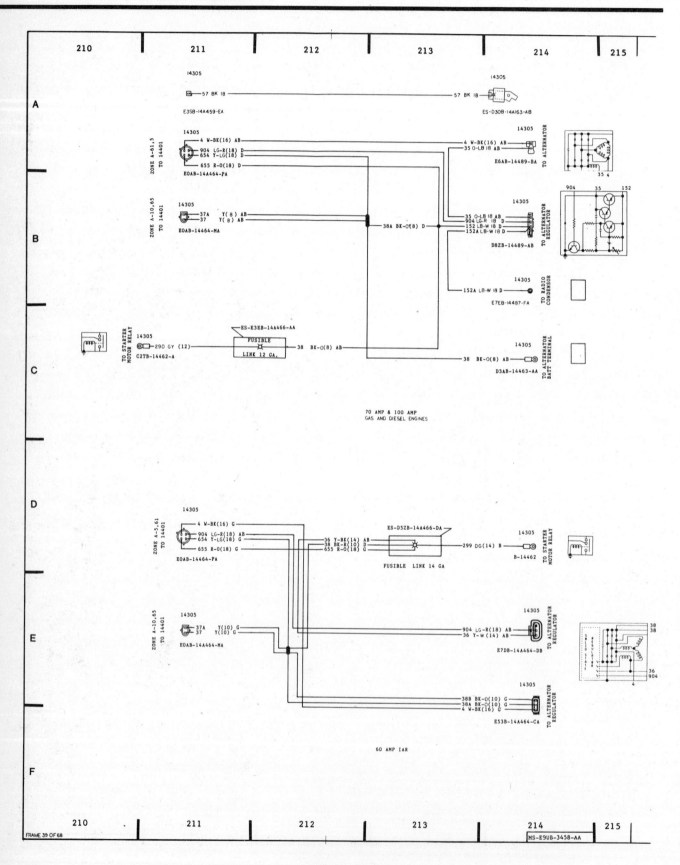

| 215 | 216 | 217 | 218 | 219 | 220 |

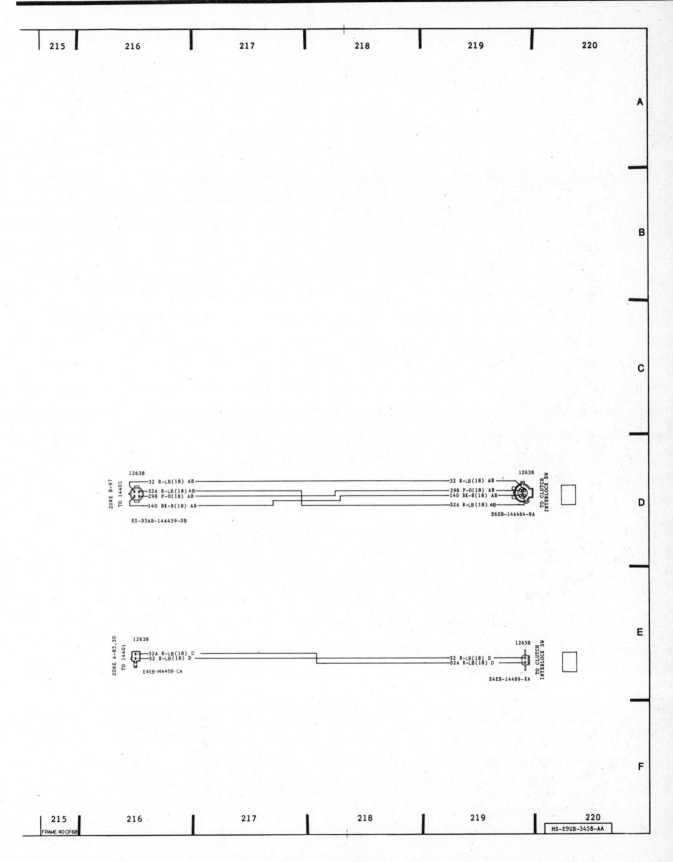

A

B

C

D

12638

ZONE B-97
TO 14401

32 R-LB(18) AB
32A R-LB(18) AB
298 P-O(18) AB
140 BK-R(18) AB

32 R-LB(18) AB
298 P-O(18) AB
140 BK-R(18) AB
32A R-LB(18) AB

12638

TO CLUTCH
INTERLOCK SW

ES-D3AB-14A459-DB

E6DB-14A464-NA

E

12638

ZONE A-85,30
TO 14401

32A R-LB(18) D
32 R-LB(18) D

32 R-LB(18) D
32A R-LB(18) D

12638

TO CLUTCH
INTERLOCK SW

E4EB-14A459-CA

E4EB-14489-KA

F

| 215 | 216 | 217 | 218 | 219 | 220 |

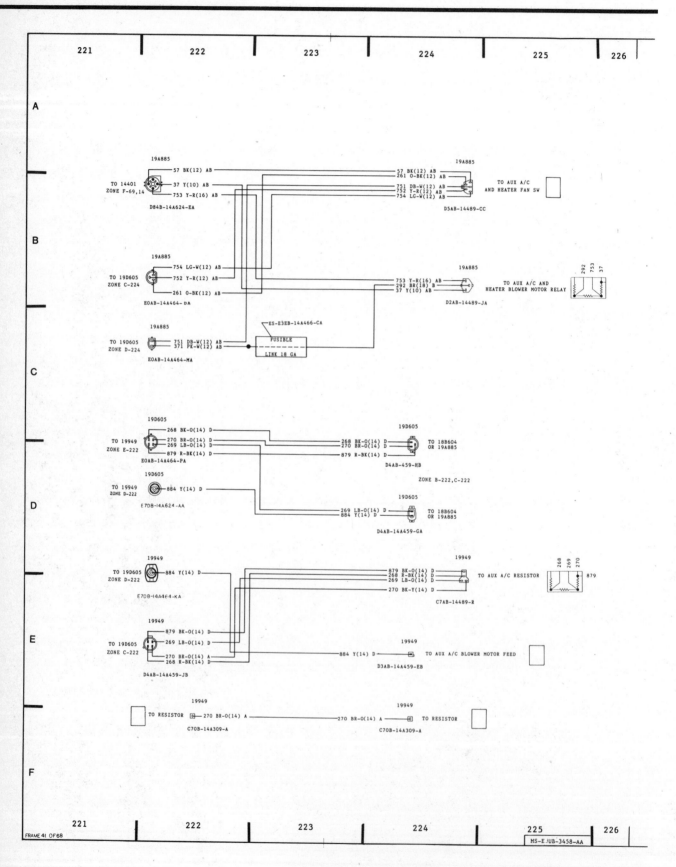

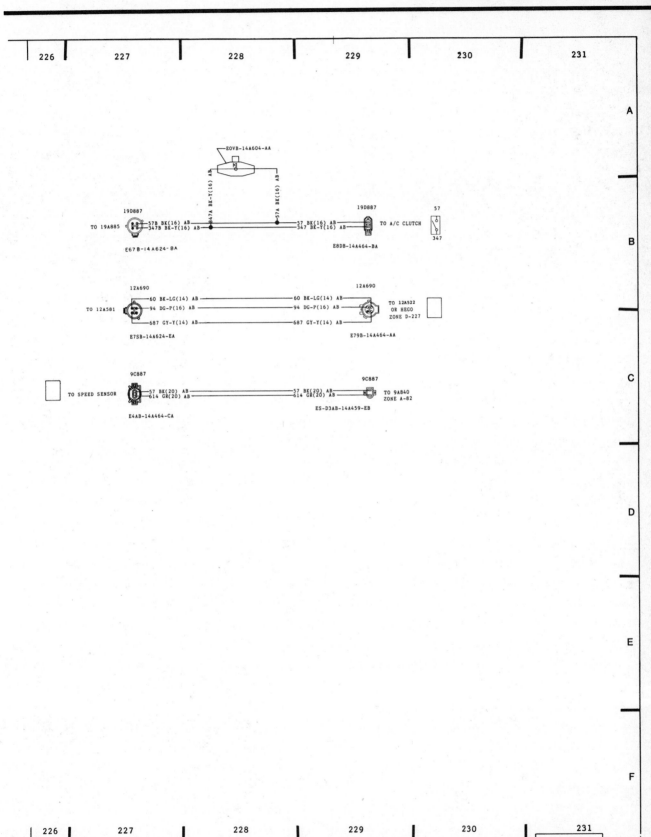

| 226 | 227 | 228 | 229 | 230 | 231 |

EOVB-14A604-AA

19D887

TO 19A885
—57B BK(16) AB—
—347B BK-Y(16) AB—

347A BK-Y(16) AB

57A BK(16) AB

19D887

—57 BK(16) AB—
—347 BK-Y(16) AB—
TO A/C CLUTCH

57

347

E67B-14A624-BA

E8DB-14A464-BA

12A690

TO 12A581
—60 BK-LG(14) AB—
—94 DG-P(16) AB—
—687 GY-Y(14) AB—

12A690

—60 BK-LG(14) AB—
—94 DG-P(16) AB—
—687 GY-Y(14) AB—
TO 12A522
OR HEGO
ZONE D-227

E7SB-14A624-EA

E79B-14A464-AA

9C887

TO SPEED SENSOR
—57 BK(20) AB—
—614 GR(20) AB—

9C887

—57 BK(20) AB—
—614 GR(20) AB—
TO 9A840
ZONE A-82

E4AB-14A464-CA

ES-D3AB-14A459-EB

| 226 | 227 | 228 | 229 | 230 | 231 |

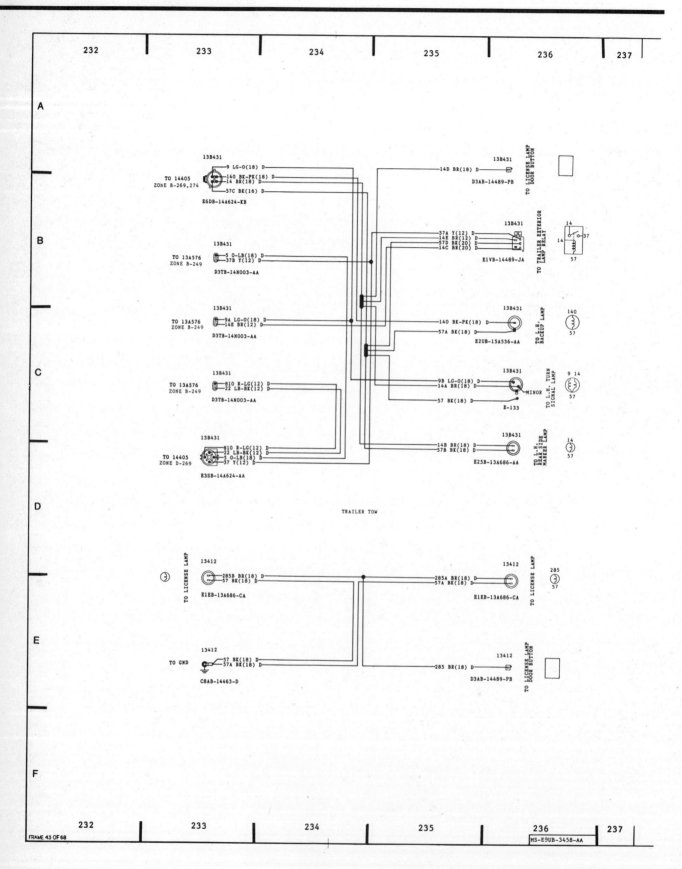

TRAILER TOW

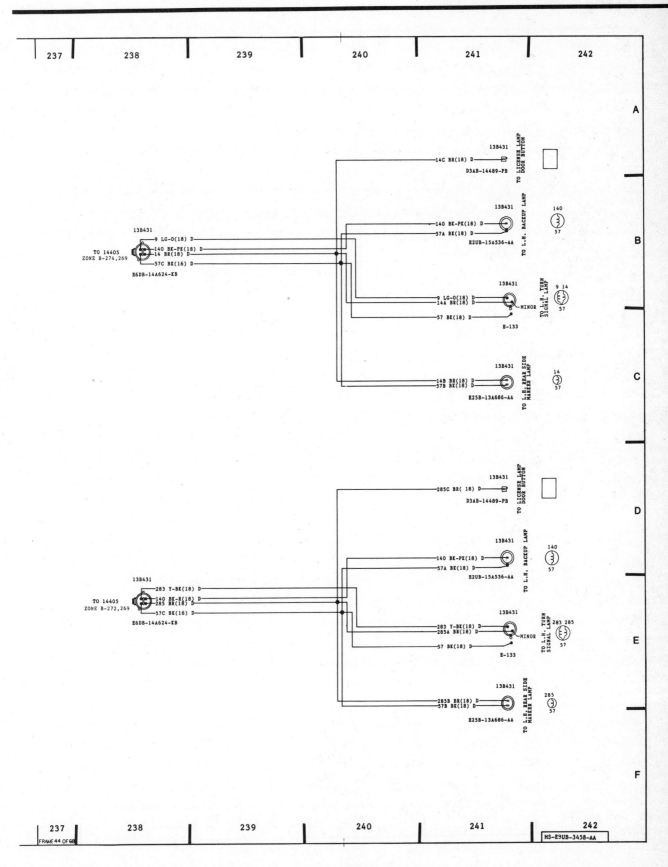

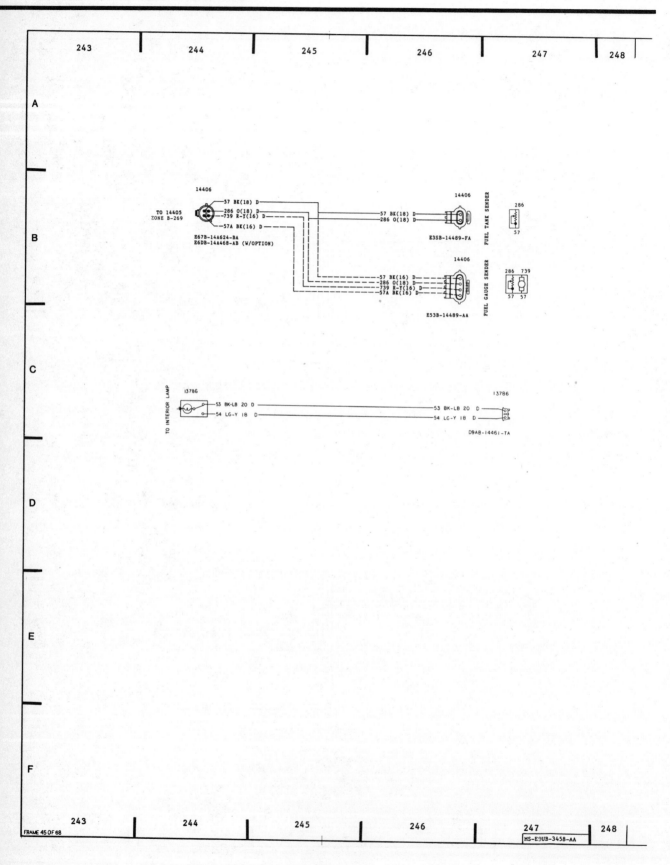

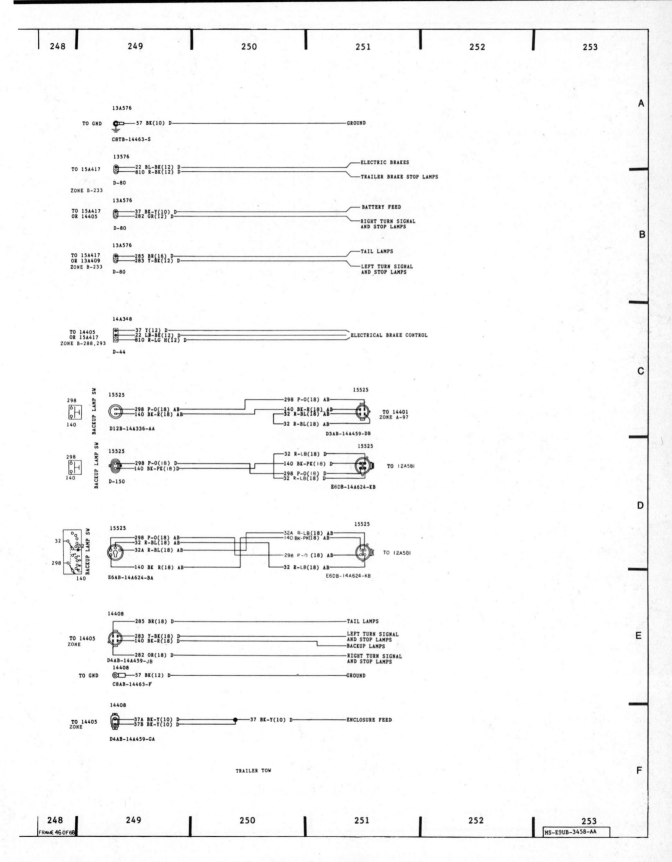

A

13A576

TO GND ——— 57 BK(10) D ——————————— GROUND

C8TB-14463-S

13576

TO 15A417 ——— 22 BL-BK(12) D ——————————— ELECTRIC BRAKES
——— 810 R-BK(12) D ——————————— TRAILER BRAKE STOP LAMPS

ZONE B-233   D-80

13A576

TO 15A417 ——— 37 BK-Y(10) D ——————————— BATTERY FEED
OR 14405 ——— 282 GR(12) D ——————————— RIGHT TURN SIGNAL
D-80   AND STOP LAMPS

B

13A576

TO 15A417 ——— 285 BR(16) D ——————————— TAIL LAMPS
OR 13A409 ——— 283 Y-BK(12) D ——————————— LEFT TURN SIGNAL
ZONE B-233   D-80   AND STOP LAMPS

14A348

TO 14405 ——— 37 Y(12) D ———————————————
OR 15A417 ——— 22 LB-BK(12) D ——————————— ELECTRICAL BRAKE CONTROL
ZONE B-288,293 ——— 810 R-LG H(12) D —————
D-44

C

298 ╷BACKUP LAMP SW╷ 15525

298 ——— 298 P-O(18) AB ——————— 298 P-O(18) AB ——— 15525
140 ——— 140 BK-R(18) AB ——————— 140 BK-R(18) AB ——— TO 14401
D12B-14A336-AA ——— 32 R-BL(18) AB —— 32 R-BL(18) AB   ZONE A-97
            ——— 32 R-BL(18) AB ——————
                                    D3AB-14A459-DB

298 ╷BACKUP LAMP SW╷ 15525

298 ——— 298 P-O(18) D ——————— 32 R-LB(18) D ——— 15525
140 ——— 140 BK-PK(18) D ——————— 140 BK-PK(18) D ——— TO 12A581
D-150   ——— 298 P-O(18) D ——————
                ——— 32 R-LB(18) D ——————
                                    E6DB-14A624-KB

D

32 ╷BACKUP LAMP SW╷ 15525

    ——— 298 P-O(18) AB ——————— 32A R-LB(18) AB ——— 15525
    ——— 32 R-BL(18) AB ——————— 140 BK-PK(18) AB ——— TO 12A581
32 ——— 32A R-BL(18) AB ——————
298   ——— 298 P-O (18) AB ——————
    ——— 140 BK R(18) AB ——————— 32 R-LB(18) AB ——————
140 E6AB-14A624-BA   E6DB-14A624-KB

E

14408

    ——— 285 BR(18) D ——————————— TAIL LAMPS
TO 14405 ——— 283 Y-BK(18) D ——————————— LEFT TURN SIGNAL
ZONE ——— 140 BK-R(18) D ——————————— AND STOP LAMPS
                                        BACKUP LAMPS
    ——— 282 OR(18) D ——————————— RIGHT TURN SIGNAL
D4AB-14A459-JB   AND STOP LAMPS

14408

TO GND ——— 57 BK(12) D ——————————— GROUND

C8AB-14463-F

14408

TO 14405 ——— 37A BK-Y(10) D ———————
ZONE ——— 37B BK-Y(10) D ——————— 37 BK-Y(10) D ——— ENCLOSURE FEED

D4AB-14A459-GA

F

TRAILER TOW

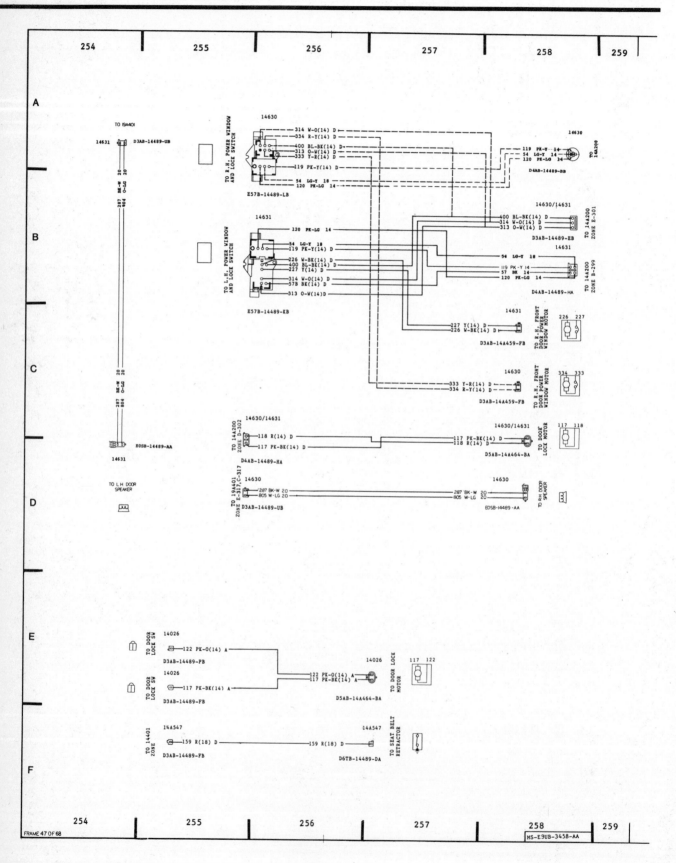

MS-E9UB-3458-AA

1989

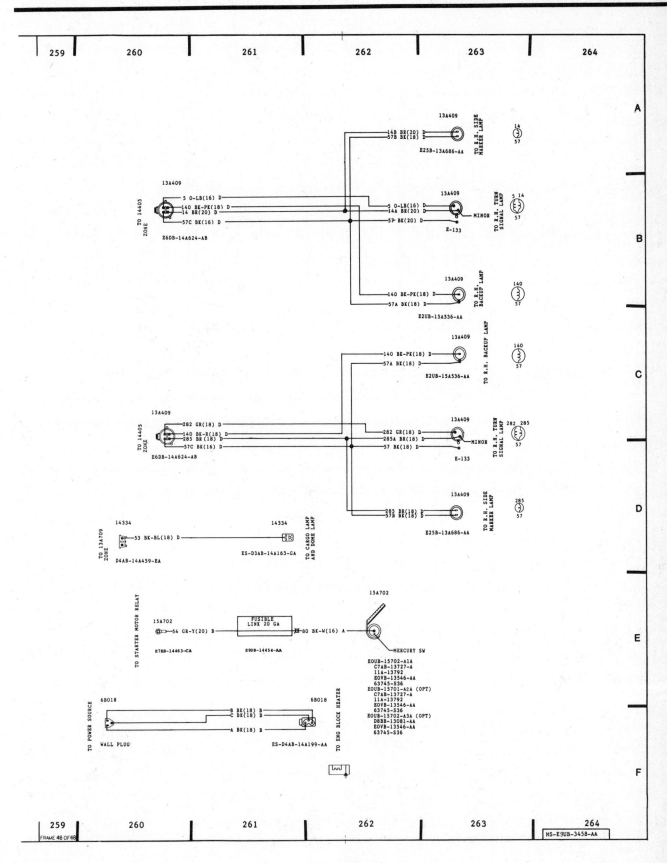

259   260   261   262   263   264

A

13A409
14B BR(20) D
57B BK(18) D
TO R.H. SIDE
MARKER LAMP
14
57
E25B-13A686-AA

13A409
TO 14405
5 O-LB(16) D
140 BK-PK(18) D
14 BR(20) D
57C BK(16) D
TO 14405
ZONE
E6DB-14A624-AB

13A409
5 O-LB(16) D
14A BR(20) D
57 BK(20) D
MINOR
TO R.H. TURN
SIGNAL LAMP
E-133
5 14
57

B

13A409
140 BK-PK(18) D
57A BK(18) D
TO R.H.
BACKUP LAMP
140
57
E2UB-15A536-AA

C

13A409
140 BK-PK(18) D
57A BK(18) D
TO R.H. BACKUP LAMP
140
57
E2UB-15A536-AA

13A409
TO 14405
282 GR(18) D
140 BK-R(18) D
285 BR(18) D
57C BK(16) D
TO 14405
ZONE
E6DB-14A624-AB

13A409
282 GR(18) D
285A BR(18) D
57 BK(18) D
MINOR
TO R.H. TURN
SIGNAL LAMP
E-133
282 285
57

D

13A409
285 BR(18) D
57B BK(18) D
TO R.H. SIDE
MARKER LAMP
285
57
E25B-13A686-AA

14334
53 BK-BL(18) D
TO 13A709
ZONE
D4AB-14A459-EA

14334
ES-D3AB-14A163-GA
TO CARGO LAMP
AND DOME LAMP

E

TO STARTER MOTOR RELAY
15A702
54 GR-Y(20) B
E7EB-14463-CA

FUSIBLE
LINK 20 GA
E9DB-14454-AA

80 BK-W(16) A

15A702

MERCURY SW
EOUB-15702-A1A
C7AB-13727-A
11A-13792
EOVB-13546-AA
63745-S36
EOUB-15701-A2A (OPT)
C7AB-13727-A
11A-13792
EOVB-13546-AA
63745-S36
EOUB-15702-A3A (OPT)
D8BB-13081-AA
EOVB-13546-AA
63745-S36

6B018
TO POWER SOURCE
WALL PLUG
B BK(18) B
C BK(18) B
A BK(18) B
6B018
ES-D4AB-14A199-AA
TO ENG BLOCK HEATER

F

259   260   261   262   263   264
FRAME 48 OF 68

MS-E9UB-3458-AA

1989

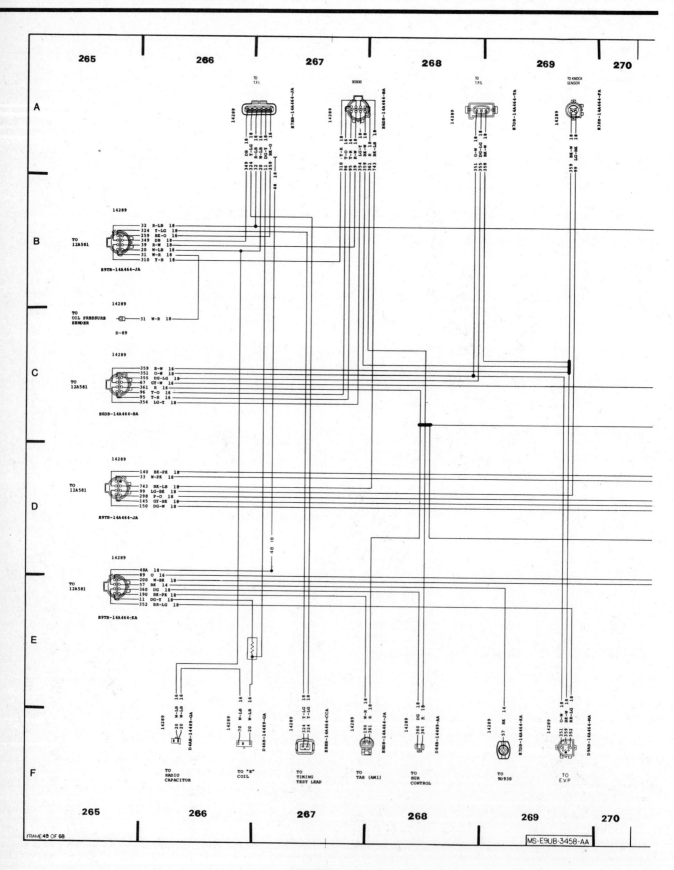

1989

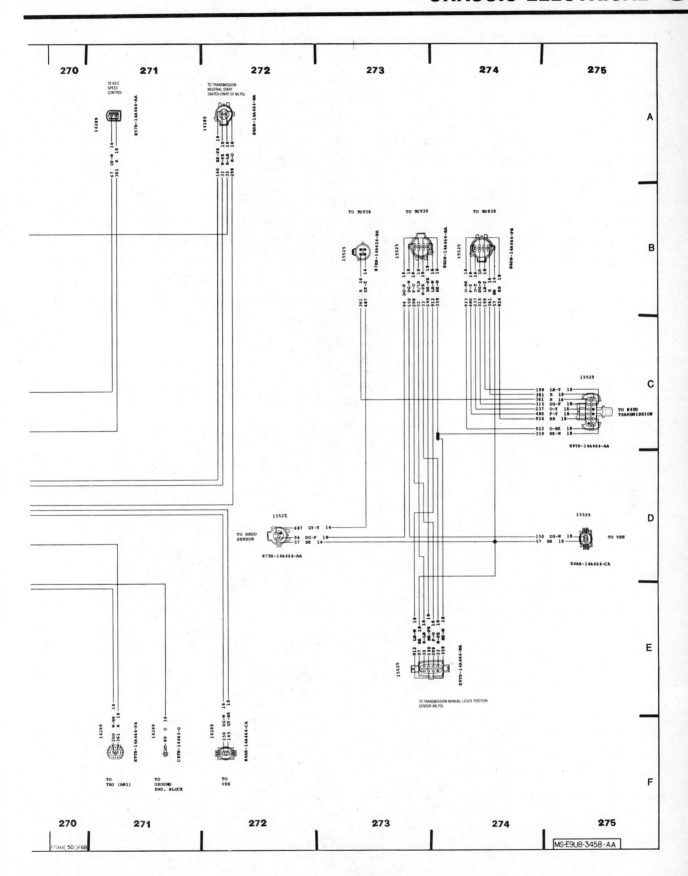

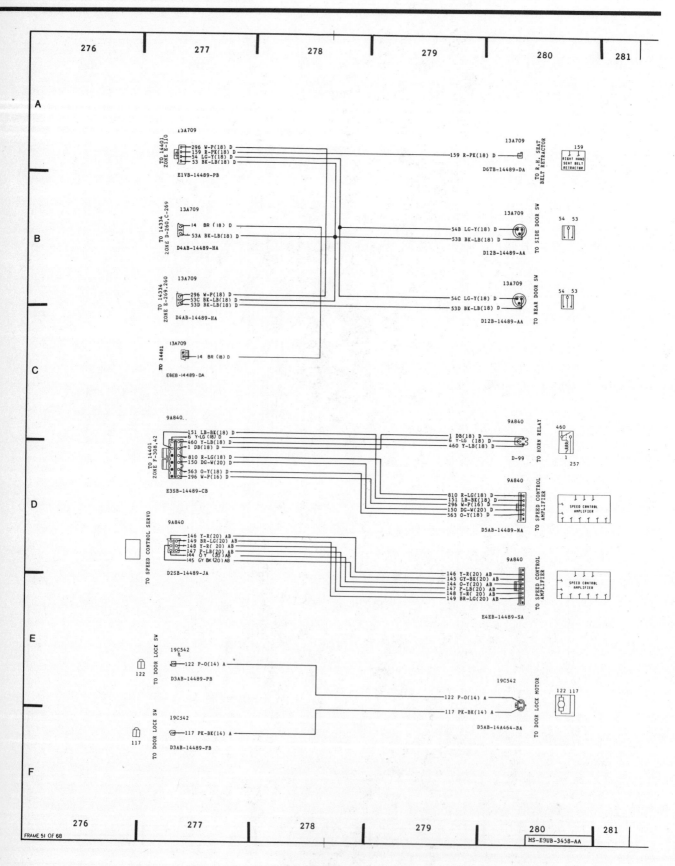

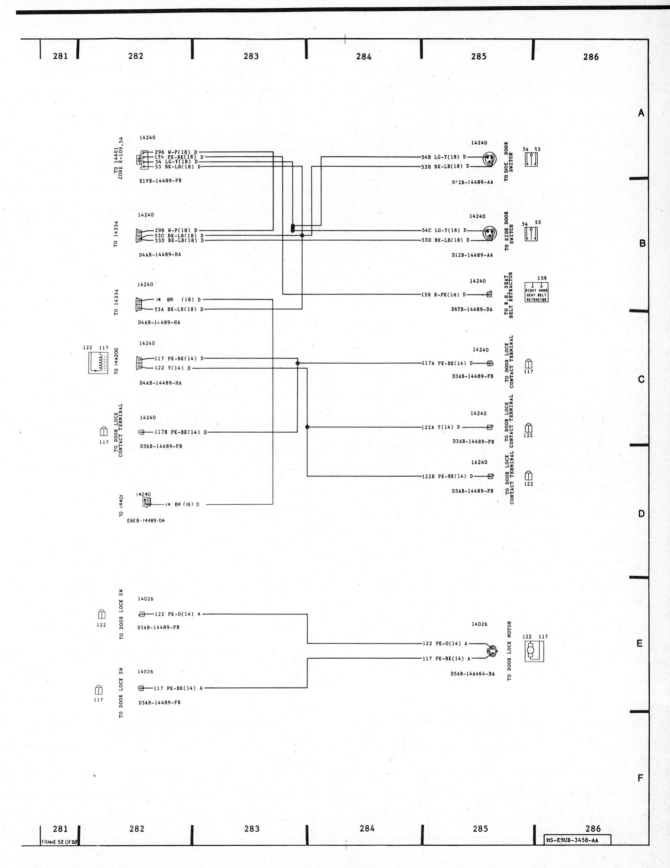

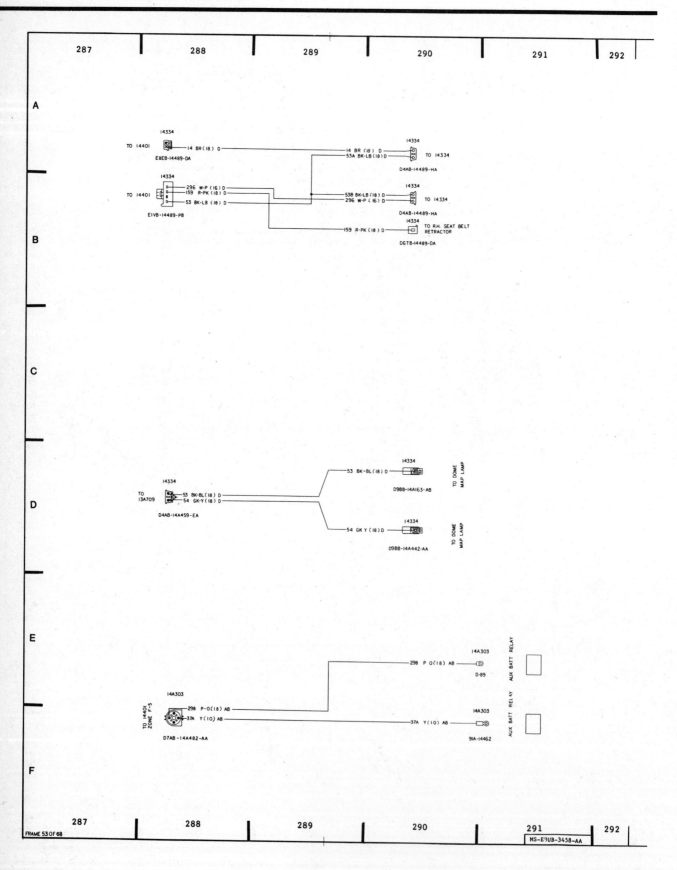

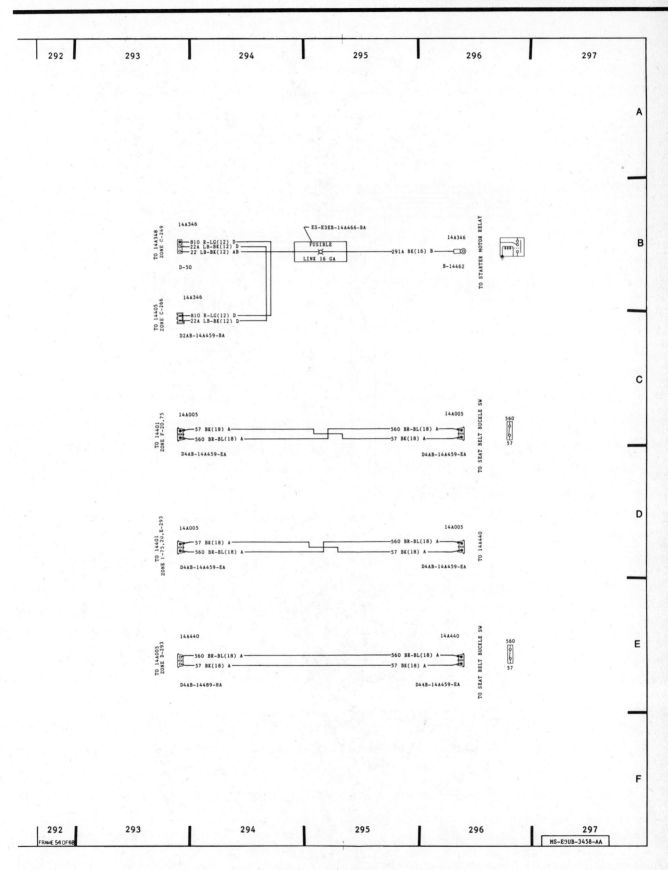

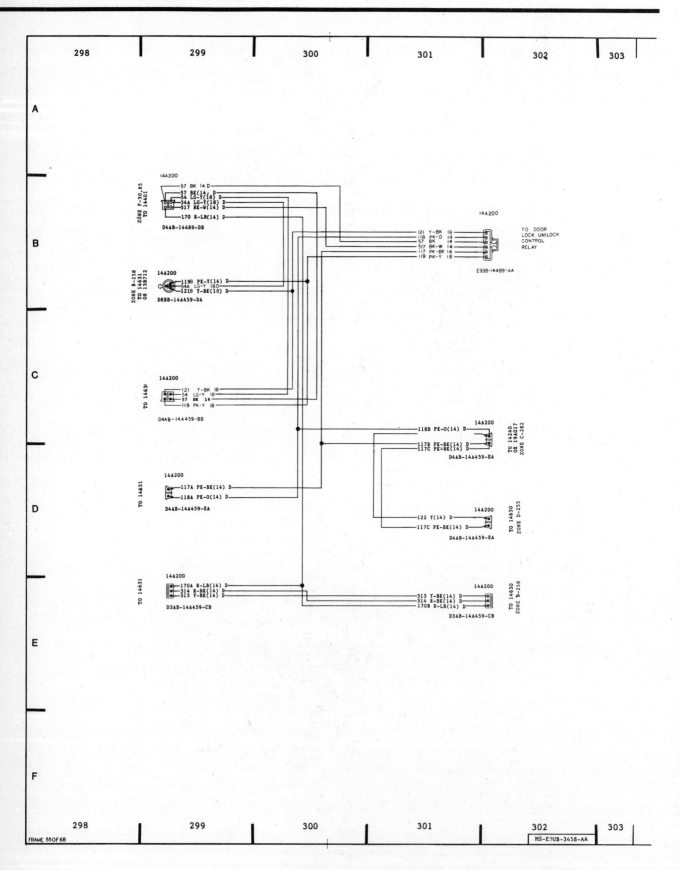

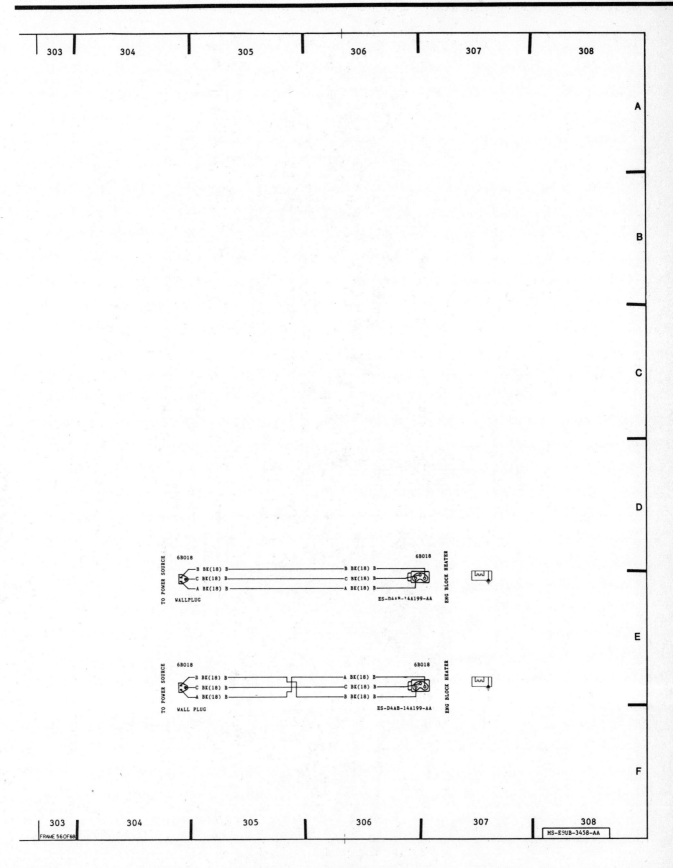

303   304   305   306   307   308

				A

6B018   6B018
B BK(18) B ———————————— B BK(18) B
TO POWER SOURCE C BK(18) B ———————————— C BK(18) B   ENG BLOCK HEATER
A BK(18) B ———————————— A BK(18) B

WALLPLUG   ES-D4AR-14A199-AA

6B018   6B018
B BK(18) B ———————————— A BK(18) B
TO POWER SOURCE C BK(18) B ———————————— C BK(18) B   ENG BLOCK HEATER
A BK(18) B ———————————— B BK(18) B

WALL PLUG   ES-D4AB-14A199-AA

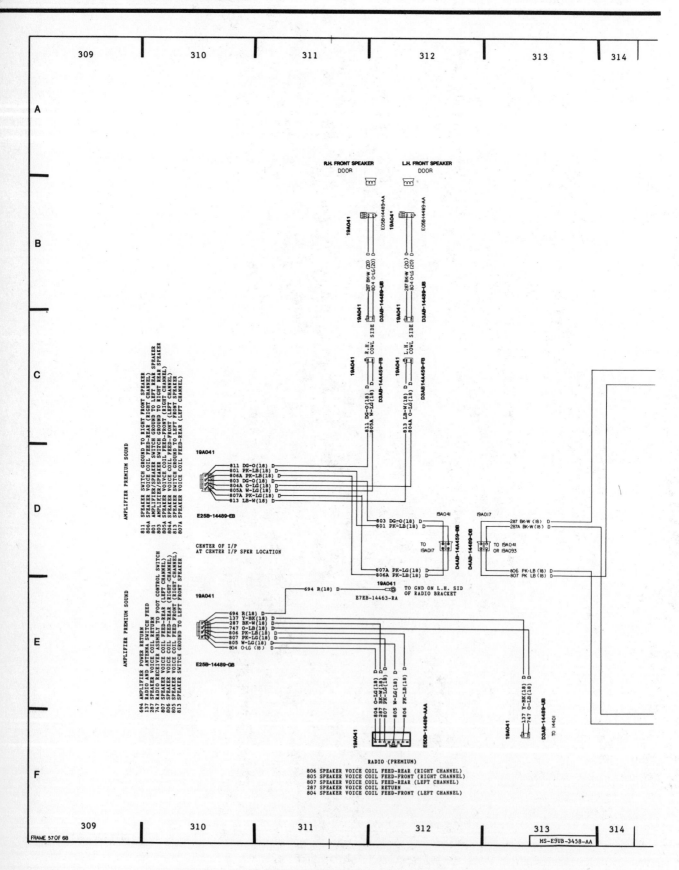

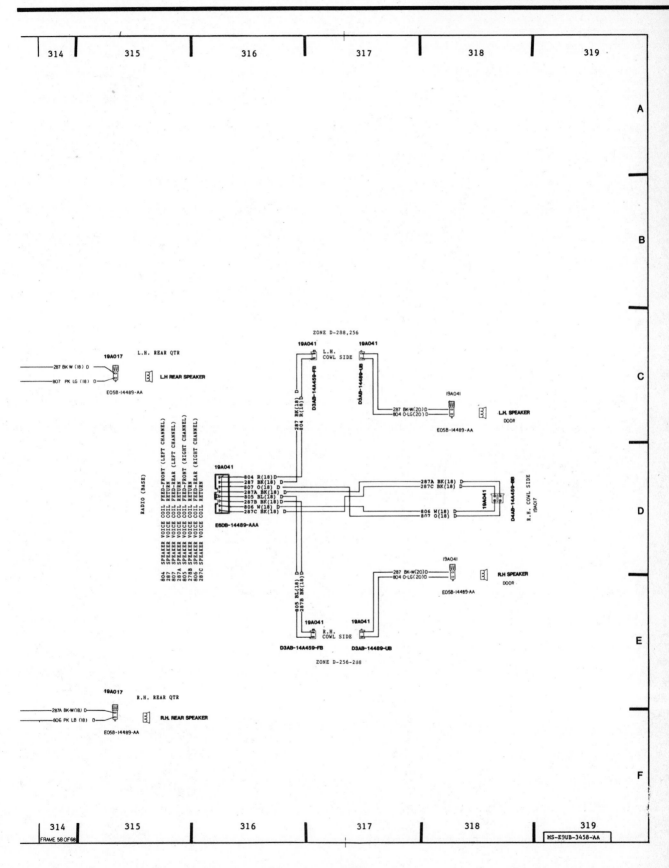

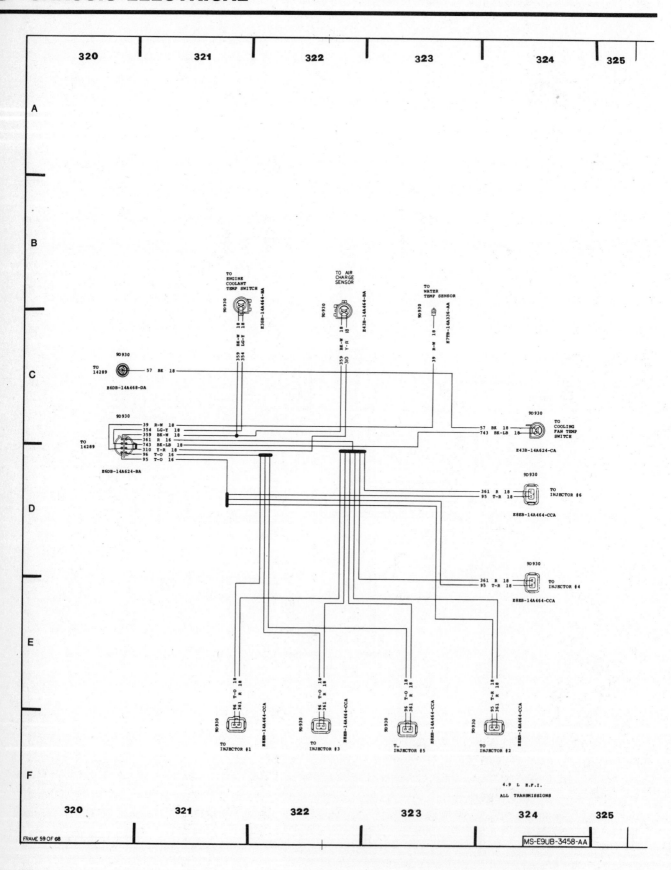

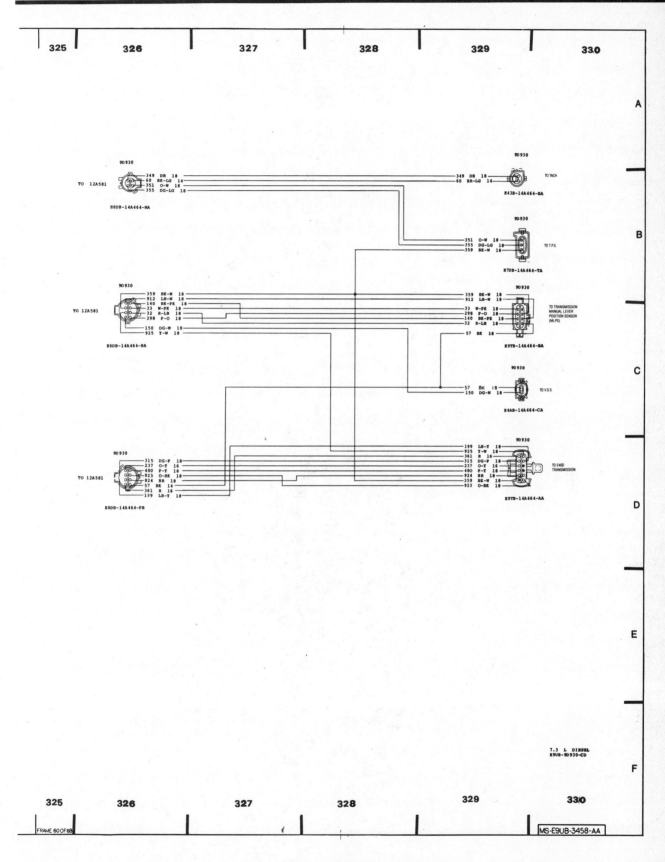

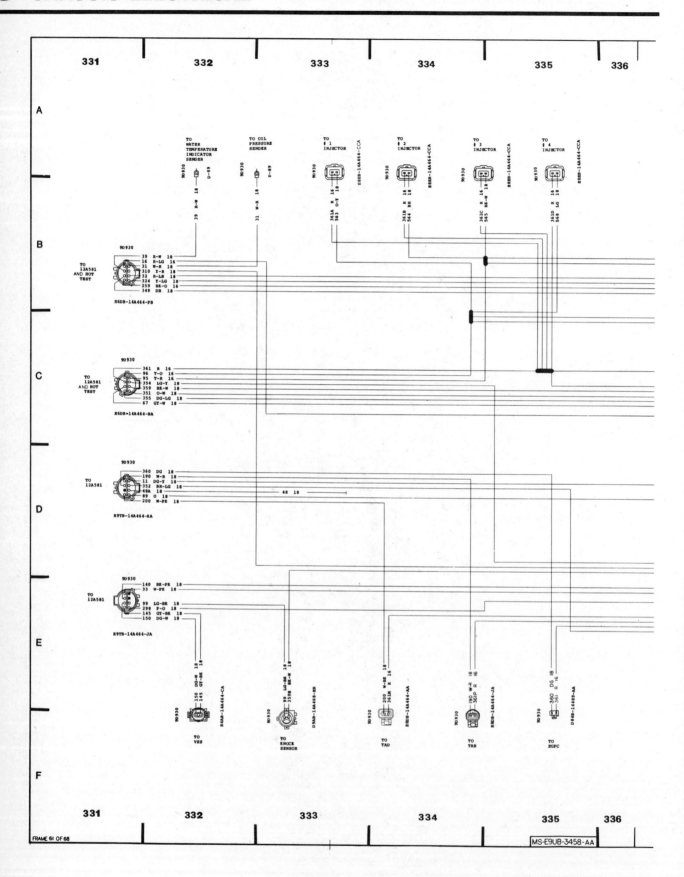

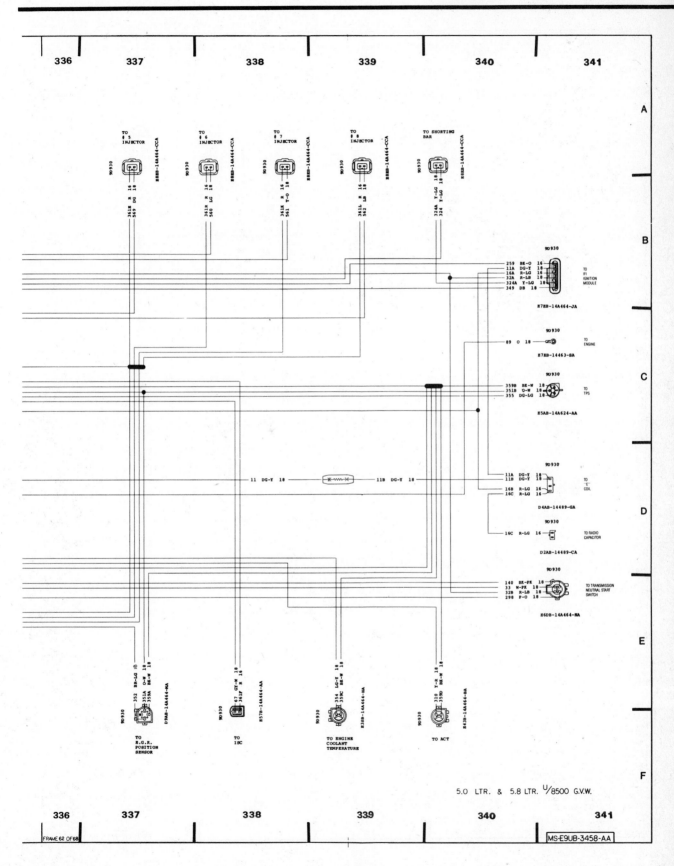

336 337 338 339 340 341

A

TO
5
INJECTOR   E8BB-14A464-CCA

TO
6
INJECTOR   E8BB-14A464-CCA

TO
7
INJECTOR   E8BB-14A464-CCA

TO
8
INJECTOR   E8BB-14A464-CCA

TO SHORTING
BAR   E8BB-14A464-CCA

90930   90930   90930   90930   90930

B

361M R 16
569 DG 18

361R R 16
560 LG 18

361X R 16
561 T-O 18

361L R 16
562 LB 18

32A Y-LG 18
324 T-LG 18

259 BK-O 16
11A DG-Y 18
16A R-LG 18
32A R-LB 18
324A Y-LG 18
349 DB 18

90930

TO
IFI
IGNITION
MODULE

E7EB-14A464-JA

89 O 18   TO
ENGINE

90930

E7EB-14463-BA

359B BK-W 18
351B O-W 18
355 DG-LG 18

90930

TO
TPS

C

E5AB-14A624-AA

11 DG-Y 18   11B DG-Y 18

11A DG-Y 18
11B DG-Y 18

16B R-LG 16
16C R-LG 16

90930

TO
"E"
COIL

D4AB-14489-GA

D

16C R-LG 16   90930

TO RADIO
CAPACITOR

D2AB-14489-CA

140 BK-PK 18
33 W-PK 18
32B R-LB 18
298 P-O 18

90930

TO TRANSMISSION
NEUTRAL START
SWITCH

E6DB-14A464-NA

E

352 BK-LG 18
351A O-W 18
359A BK-W 18

67 GT-W 18
361F R 16

354 LG-Y 18
359C BK-W 18

310 Y-R 18
359D BK-W 18

90930   90930   90930   90930

D7AB-14A464-NA

E57B-14A464-AA

E38B-14A464-NA

E43B-14A464-NA

TO
E.G.R.
POSITION
SENSOR

TO
ISC

TO ENGINE
COOLANT
TEMPERATURE

TO ACT

F

5.0 LTR. & 5.8 LTR. ᵁ/8500 G.V.W.

336 337 338 339 340 341

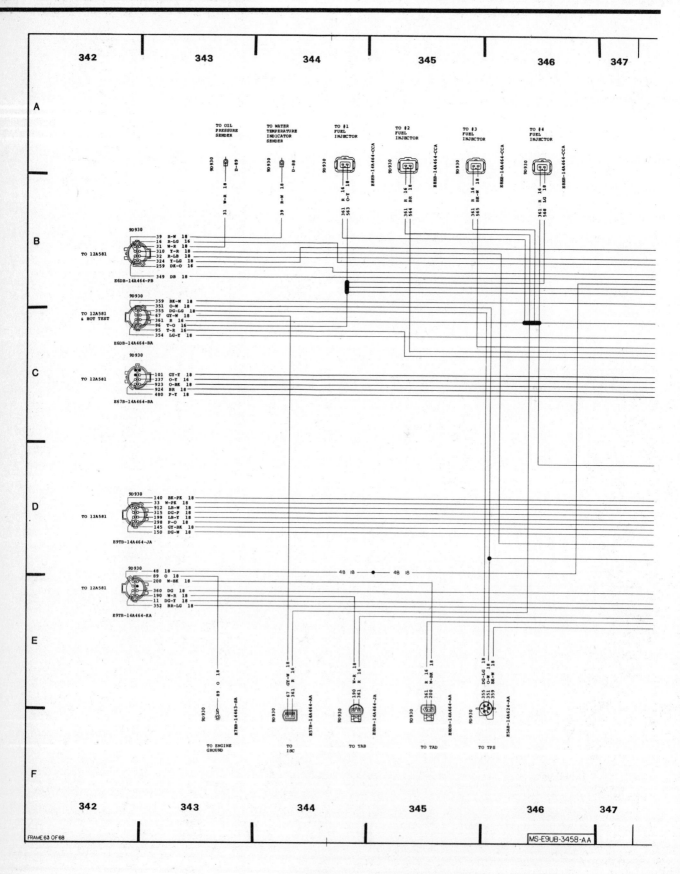

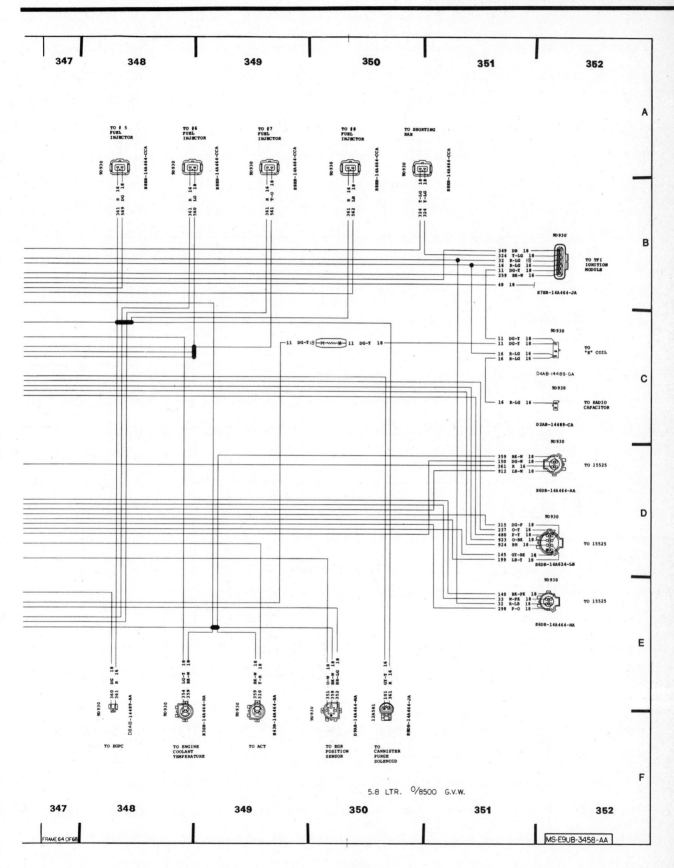

5.8 LTR. 0/8500 G.V.W.

FRAME 64 OF 68

MS-E9UB-3458-AA

1989

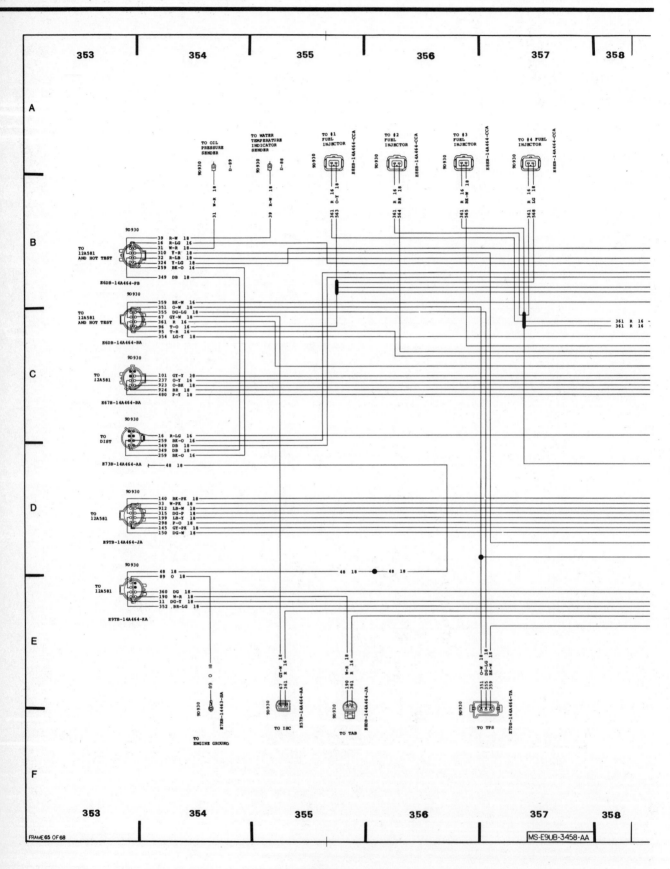

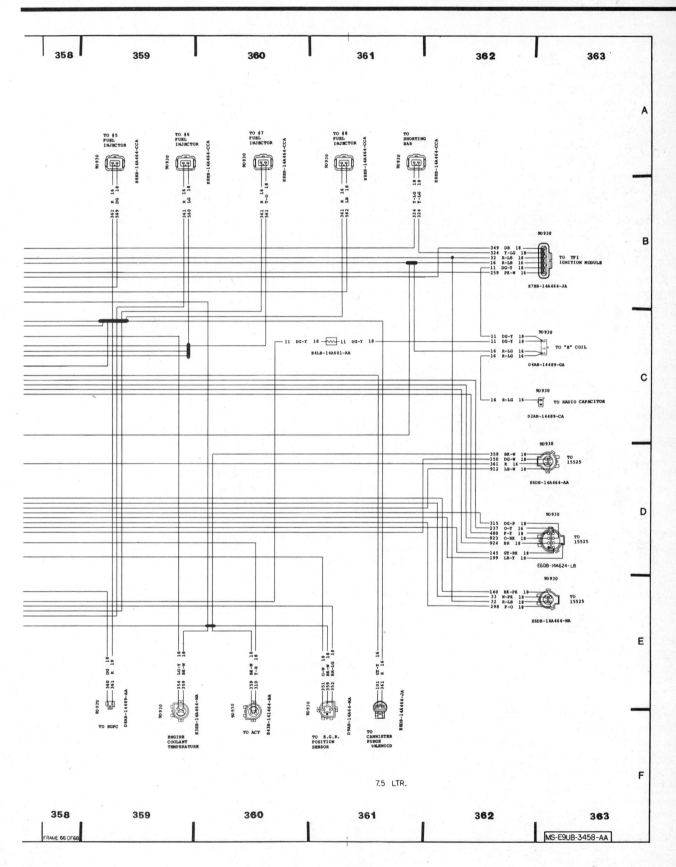

7.5 LTR.

1989

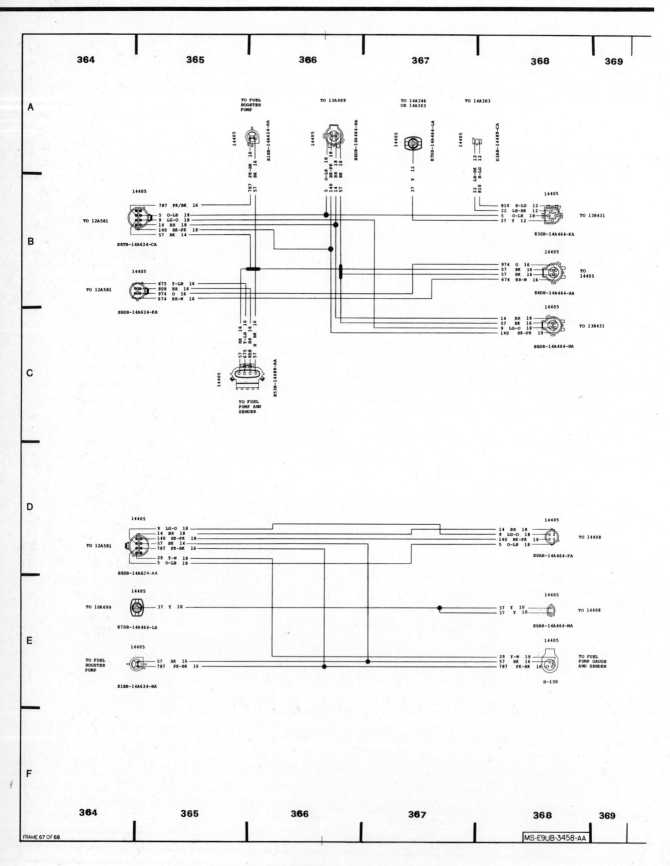

MS-E9UB-3458-AA

1989

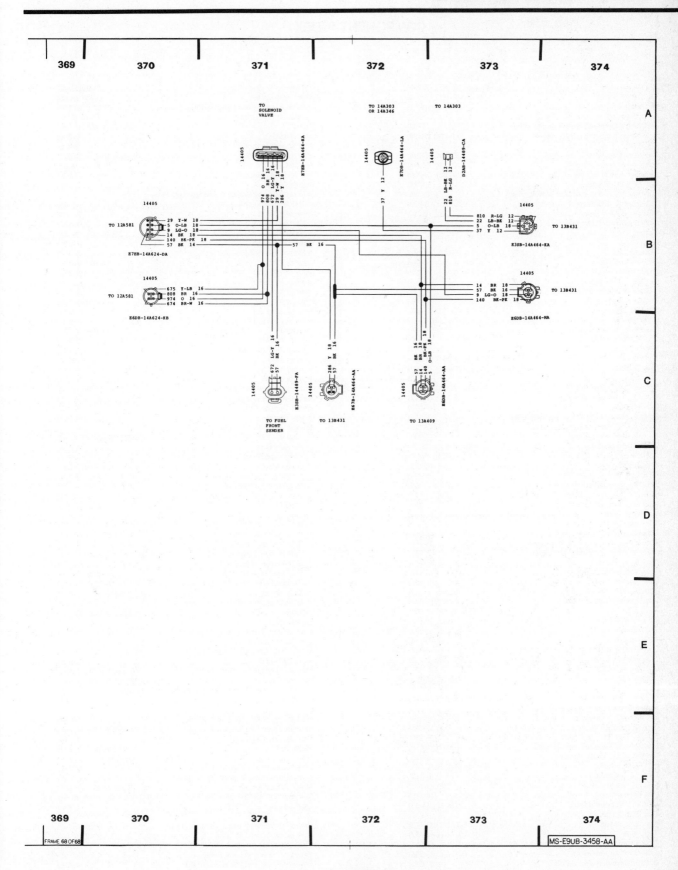

COMPONENT INDEX

STANDARD CIRCUIT CHART (BY NUMBER)

CIRCUIT	DESCRIPTION *	COLOR	CIRCUIT	DESCRIPTION *	COLOR
1	HORN SWITCH CONTROL	DK BLUE	90	THERMOCOUPLE POS. TO EXHAUST SYST. OVERTEMP PROTECT MODULE	DK BLUE-LT GREEN
2	R.H. FRONT TURN SIGNAL LAMP	WHITE-LT BLUE	91	THERMOCOUPLE 1 NEG. TO EXHAUST SYST. OVERTEMP PROTECT MODULE	GRAY-RED
3	L.H. FRONT TURN SIGNAL LAMP	LT GREEN-WHITE	92	THERMOCOUPLE 2 NEG. TO EXHAUST SYST. OVERTEMP PROTECT MODULE	WHITE-BLACK
4	ALTERNATOR REG. "S" TERM. TO ALTERNATOR "S" TERM.	WHITE-BLACK	93	AIR DUMP VALVE NEG. TO EXHAUST SYST. OVERTEMP MODULE	ORANGE-WHITE
5	R.H. REAR TURN SIGNAL LAMP	ORANGE-LT BLUE	94	AIR FUEL SENSOR TO ECU	DK GREEN-PURPLE
6	HORN RELAY TO HORN	YELLOW-LT GREEN	**94	EEC TO EXHAUST GAS OXYGEN SENSOR (#2 IN DUAL SYSTEM)	RED-BLACK
7	SEAT SWITCH ARM TERM. TO REPLAY FIELD TERM.	LT GREEN-YELLOW	95	FEEDBACK CARB. COIL 1	TAN-RED
8	TURN SIGNAL FLASHER FEED	ORANGE-YELLOW	96	FEEDBACK CARB. COIL 2	TAN-ORANGE
9	L.H. REAR TURN SIGNAL LAMP	LT GREEN-ORANGE	97	FEEDBACK CARB. COIL 3	TAN-LT GREEN
10	STOPLAMP SWITCH FEED	LT GREEN-RED	98	FEEDBACK CARB. COIL 4	TAN-LT BLUE
11	ELECTRONIC SWITCH TO IGNITION COIL NEG. TERMINAL	DK GREEN-YELLOW	99	AIR PORT SOLENOID SIGNAL	LT GREEN-BLACK
**11	IGNITION COIL NEGATIVE TERMINAL	TAN-YELLOW	100	AIR PUMP SOLENOID SIGNAL	WHITE-RED
12	HEADLAMP DIMMER SWITCH TO HIGH BEAMS	LT GREEN-BLACK	101	ELECTRONIC CONTROL UNIT TO CANISTER PURGE SOLENOID	GRAY-YELLOW
13	HEADLAMP DIMMER SWITCH TO LOW BEAMS	RED-BLACK	102	L.H. REAR TAILLAMP BULB OUTAGE	WHITE
14	HEADLAMP SWITCH TO TAIL LAMPS & SIDE MARKER LAMPS	BROWN	103	R.H. REAR TAILLAMP BULB OUTAGE	WHITE-RED
15	HEADLAMP DIMMER SWITCH FEED	RED-YELLOW	104	L.H. REAR STOP & TURN BULB OUTAGE	LT BLUE-ORANGE
16	IGNITION SWITCH TO IGNITION COIL "BATT." TERMINAL	RED-LT GREEN	105	R.H. REAR STOP & TURN BULB OUTAGE	RED-WHITE
17	ASH RECEPTACLE LAMP FEED	WHITE	106	LOW FUEL INDICATOR	LT BLUE
18	SEAT SWITCH TO RELAY FIELD TERMINAL	ORANGE-YELLOW	107	BUCKLE SW. TO CENTER OCCUPANT SEAT SENSOR	LT BLUE-PINK
19	INSTRUMENT PANEL LAMPS FEED	LT BLUE-RED	108	L.H. HEADLAMP BULB OUTAGE	BROWN-LT BLUE
20	DISTRIBUTOR ELECTRONIC CONTROL FEED	WHITE-LT BLUE	109	R.H. HEADLAMP BULB OUTAGE	PINK-LT BLUE
21	EMA CONTROL TO SPARK RETARD SWITCH	DK GREEN-LT GREEN	110	R. AND L.H. REAR RUNNING LAMP BULB OUTAGE	WHITE-LT GREEN
22	BRAKE FEED	LT BLUE-BLACK	111	WARNING LAMP TO LIGHTS ON RELAY	BLACK-YELLOW
23	ANTI-THEFT SYSTEM SWITCH FEED	TAN-LT GREEN	112	WARNING LAMP RELAY FEED	BLACK-YELLOW
24	ANTI-THEFT SWITCH ARM	DK BLUE-ORANGE	113	STARTING MOTOR TO STARTING MOTOR RELAY	YELLOW-LT BLUE
25	ANTI-THEFT SWITCH DISARM	DK GREEN-PURPLE	114	FEED TO VACUUM DOOR LOCK SWITCH	TAN-YELLOW
26	DECK LID SWITCH TO ANTI-THEFT MODULE	WHITE-PURPLE	115	VACUUM DOOR LOCK SWITCH TO SOLENOID (LOCK)	LT GREEN
27	EMA CONTROL TO EGR SWITCH	ORANGE-LT GREEN	116	VACUUM DOOR LOCK SWITCH TO SOLENOID (UNLOCK)	BROWN-ORANGE
28	WINDSHIELD WIPER SW. TO WINDSHIELD WIPER MOTOR	BLACK-PINK	117	DOOR LOCK MOTOR (LOCK)	PINK-BLACK
29	FUEL GAGE TO FUEL GAGE SENDER	YELLOW-WHITE	118	DOOR LOCK MOTOR (UNLOCK)	PINK-ORANGE
30	CONSTANT VOLTAGE UNIT & INDICATOR LAMPS FEED	BLACK-LT GREEN	119	DOOR LOCK SWITCH (LOCK)	PINK-YELLOW
31	OIL PRESSURE INDICATOR TO OIL PRESSURE SENDING UNIT	WHITE-RED	120	DOOR LOCK SWITCH (UNLOCK)	PINK-LT GREEN
32	STARTER CONTROL	RED-LT BLUE	121	KEYLESS DOOR LOCK SWITCH DATA BIT 3 TO MODULE	YELLOW-BLACK
33	STARTER CONTROL TO INTERLOCK MODULE	WHITE-PINK	122	KEYLESS DOOR LOCK SWITCH DATA BIT 4 TO MODULE	YELLOW
34	HORN CONTROL MODULE TO OVERRIDE SWITCH	LT BLUE-ORANGE	123	KEYLESS DOOR LOCK SWITCH DATA BIT 5 TO MODULE	RED
35	ALTERNATOR REGULATOR "F" TERMINAL TO ALTERNATOR	ORANGE-LT BLUE	124	KEYLESS DOOR LOCK SWITCH ENABLE FROM MODULE	BROWN
36	ALTERNATOR OUTPUT	YELLOW-WHITE	125	MAP LAMP SWITCH TO RH MAP LAMP	BROWN-YELLOW
37	BATTERY TO LOAD	YELLOW	126	COURTESY LAMP SW. TO INSTR. PANEL COURTESY LAMP	BLACK-ORANGE
38	POWER SUPPLY TO BATTERY	BLACK-ORANGE	127	COURTESY LAMP SW. TO "C" PILLAR LAMPS	BLACK-LT BLUE
39	TEMP. GAGE TO TEMP. SENDING UNIT	RED-WHITE	128	BRAKE FLUID LEVEL UNIT TO MESSAGE CENTER	PURPLE-YELLOW
40	CIGAR LIGHTER FEED	LT BLUE-WHITE	129	KEYLESS DOOR LOCK OUTPUT FROM MODULE	LT GREEN
41	WARNING LAMP PROVE OUT	BLACK-LT BLUE	130	HEADLAMP BULB OUTAGE TO MESSAGE CENTER	RED-LT GREEN
42	SWITCH TO WARNING LAMP	RED-WHITE	131	CIGAR LIGHTER LAMP FEED	PURPLE-ORANGE
43	TRAILER STOPLAMPS	DK BLUE	132	TAILLAMP BULB OUTAGE TO MESSAGE CENTER	ORANGE-BLACK
**43	TRAILER BRAKES	DK BLUE	133	RELAY TO ROAD MAP LAMP SWITCH	TAN-RED
44	TURN SIGNAL FLASHER TO TURN SIGNAL SWITCH	LT BLUE	134	KEYLESS DOOR LOCK OUTPUT (ALL) FROM MODULE	WHITE
45	HOT WATER TEMP. RELAY TO HOT WATER TEMP. SENDING UNIT	YELLOW-RED	135	STOP AND TURN BULB OUTAGE TO MESSAGE CENTER	YELLOW-RED
46	ELECTRONIC CONTROL UNIT TO SOLENOID	YELLOW-BLACK	136	SPEED INPUT TO MESSAGE CENTER	YELLOW-LT BLUE
47	ELECTRONIC CONTROL UNIT TO SOLENOID	GRAY-ORANGE	137	RADIO ANTENNA SWITCH FEED	YELLOW-BLACK
48	BLIND CIRCUIT TERM. IN HARNESS CANNOT BE CHECKED FOR CONT.	(COLOR OPT.)	138	DOOR JAMB SWITCH TO LIGHTS ON RELAY	BROWN-LT BLUE
49	TRAILER GROUND	WHITE	139	FUEL PULSE TO MESSAGE CENTER	LT GREEN-PURPLE
**49	TRAILER BATTERY CHARGE	ORANGE	140	BACKUP PUMP	BLACK-PINK
50	TRAILER BRAKES	RED	141	CLOCK ADVANCE SWITCH TO MESSAGE CENTER	DK GREEN-LT GREEN
**50	TRAILER CONTROLLER FEED	RED	142	CLOCK SELECT SWITCH TO MESSAGE CENTER	LT BLUE-RED
51	SEAT REG. CONTROL SWITCH FEED	BLACK-WHITE	143	CHECKOUT SWITCH TO MESSAGE CENTER	LT BLUE-YELLOW
52	TRAILER L.H. TURN SIGNAL	YELLOW	144	AMPLIFIER TO SERVO TRANSDUCER FEED	ORANGE-YELLOW
53	COURTESY LAMP SWITCH TO COURTESY LAMP	BLACK-LT BLUE	145	SERVO SOURCE VACUUM SOLENOID TO CONTROL TRANSISTOR	GRAY-BLACK
54	INTERIOR LAMP SWITCH FEED	LT GREEN-YELLOW	146	SERVO VENT SOLENOID TO CONTROL TRANSISTOR	WHITE-PINK
55	CARGO LAMP SW. TO CARGO LAMP	BLACK-PINK	147	AMPLIFIER FEEDBACK POTENTIOMETER FEED	PURPLE-LT BLUE
56	WINDSHIELD WIPER SW. TO WINDSHIELD WIPER MOTOR	DK BLUE-ORANGE	148	SERVO FEEDBACK POTENTIOMETER SIGNAL TO AMPLIFIER	YELLOW-RED
57	GROUND CIRCUIT	BLACK	149	SERVO FEEDBACK POTENTIOMETER BASE TO AMPLIFIER	BROWN-LT GREEN
58	WINDSHIELD WIPER SW. TO WINDSHIELD WIPER MOTOR	WHITE	150	SENSOR SIGNAL TO AMPLIFIER	DK GREEN-WHITE
59	HEATED EXTERIOR MIRROR FEED	DK GREEN-PURPLE	151	SPEED CONTROL ON-OFF SWITCH TO AMPLIFIER	LT BLUE-BLACK
60	CONSTANT VOLTAGE UNIT TO GAGE	BLACK-LT GREEN	152	ARRIVAL SWITCH TO MESSAGE CENTER	LT BLUE-WHITE
61	WINDSHIELD WIPER SW. TO WINDSHIELD WIPER MOTOR	YELLOW-RED	153	ECONOMY SWITCH TO MESSAGE CENTER	PURPLE-YELLOW
62	BATTERY TO HI-BEAM	BROWN-YELLOW	154	DESTINATION SWITCH TO MESSAGE CENTER	PURPLE-LT GREEN
63	WINDSHIELD WIPER SW. TO WINDSHIELD WIPER MOTOR	RED	155	DISTANCE TO EMPTY SWITCH TO MESSAGE CENTER	GRAY-RED
64	TRAILER R.H. TURN SIGNAL	DK GREEN	156	AVERAGE SPEED SWITCH TO MESSAGE CENTER	GRAY-ORANGE
65	WINDSHIELD WIPER SW. TO WINDSHIELD WIPER MOTOR	DK GREEN	157	WINDOW REGULATOR MOTOR TO GROUND	GRAY-BLACK
66	KEYLESS DOOR LOCK SWITCH ILLUMINATION FEED	LT BLUE	158	KEY WARNING SWITCH TO BUZZER	BLACK-PINK
67	CHOKE RELAY TO CHOKE	GRAY-WHITE	159	DOOR JAMB SWITCH TO BUZZER	RED-PINK
68	ELECTRIC CHOKE FEED	ORANGE-BLACK	160	BUZZER TO WARNING INDICATOR RELAY	WHITE-PINK
69	MODULE TO ACTUATOR	RED-LT GREEN	161	MILES/KILOMETERS SWITCH TO MESSAGE CENTER	GRAY-LT BLUE
70	SUPPLEMENTAL ALTERNATOR STATOR A TERM. TO WINDSHIELD	RED	162	BRAKE WARNING LAMP TO BRAKE SWITCH	LT GREEN-RED
71	SUPPLEMENTAL ALTERNATOR STATOR B TERM. TO WINDSHIELD	WHITE	163	KEYLESS DOOR LOCK OUTPUT (DRIVER) FROM MODULE	RED-ORANGE
72	SUPPLEMENTAL ALTERNATOR STATOR C TERM. TO WINDSHIELD	DK GREEN	164	DISTANCE TO MESSAGE CENTER	GRAY-WHITE
73	ELECTRONIC CONTROL UNIT TO ACTUATOR	ORANGE-LT BLUE	165	ELAPSED TIME SWITCH TO MESSAGE CENTER	WHITE-BLACK
74	ELECTRONIC CONTROL UNIT TO EXHAUST GAS OXYGEN SENSOR	DK GREEN-YELLOW	166	RESET SWITCH TO MESSAGE CENTER	WHITE-ORANGE
**74	ELECTRONIC CONTROL UNIT TO EXHAUST GAS OXYGEN SENSOR (#1 IN DUAL SYSTEM)	GRAY-LT BLUE	167	MESSAGE CENTER OUTPUT CLOCK TO DISPLAY	WHITE-YELLOW
75	ELECTRONIC CONTROL UNIT TO ENGINE VACUUM SWITCH	DK GREEN-LT GREEN	168	5V DO-MESSAGE CENTER TO DISPLAY	WHITE-BLACK
76	KEYLESS DOOR LOCK ILLUMINATION GROUND TO MODULE	BLACK-LT GREEN	169	TRANSFORMER POWER-MESSAGE CENTER TO DISPLAY	LT BLUE-PINK
77	ELECTRONIC CONTROL UNIT TO SOLENOID ACTUATOR	DK BLUE-YELLOW	170	WINDOW REGULATOR SWITCH FEED	RED-LT BLUE
78	KEYLESS DOOR LOCK SWITCH DATA BIT 1 TO MODULE	LT BLUE-YELLOW	171	CIRCUIT BREAKER TO SEAT LATCH RELAY	BLACK-WHITE
79	KEYLESS DOOR LOCK SWITCH DATA BIT 2 TO MODULE	LT GREEN-RED	172	RELAY TO SEAT LATCH SOLENOID	ORANGE
80	ENGINE COMPARTMENT LAMP FEED	BLACK-ORANGE	173	DOOR SWITCH TO SEAT LATCH RELAY (COIL TERM.)	PINK-WHITE
81	EMISSION CONTROL VALVE TO SWITCH	BROWN-YELLOW	174	DATA-MESSAGE CENTER TO DISPLAY	DK GREEN-PURPLE
82	WASHER FLUID LEVEL INDICATOR	PINK-YELLOW	175	RELAY FEED	BLACK-YELLOW
83	INTERLOCK MODULE TO CENTER BUCKLE SWITCH	WHITE-ORANGE	176	REAR WINDOW REGULATOR SWITCH FEED	WHITE
84	DECK LID SOLENOID FEED	PURPLE-YELLOW	177	KEYLESS DOOR LOCK SEAT SWITCH SENSOR TO MODULE	WHITE
85	SEAT BELT WARNING TIMER TO L.F. RETRACTOR SWITCH	BROWN-LT BLUE	178	PARITY BIT-DISPLAY TO MESSAGE CENTER	DK GREEN-ORANGE
86	SEAT BELT WARNING TIMER TO R.F. SEAT SENSOR	DK BLUE-WHITE	179	HORIZONTAL SEAT REG. MOTOR TO RELAY	YELLOW
87	INTERLOCK MODULE TO CENTER SEAT SENSOR SWITCH	TAN-WHITE	180	HORIZONTAL SEAT REG. MOTOR TO RELAY	RED
88	INSTRUMENT PANEL LAMP SWITCH FEED	BLACK-WHITE			
89	FUEL SENSOR GROUND TO ECU	ORANGE			
**89	EXHAUST GAS OXYGEN SENSOR RETURN TO EEC MODULE	ORANGE			

* IN SOME CASES, THERE MAY BE ADDITIONAL CIRCUIT FUNCTIONS INCLUDED IN THE CIRCUIT DESCRIPTION LISTED.

** DENOTES A NEW OR STANDARDIZED CIRCUIT.

STANDARD CIRCUIT CHART (BY NUMBER)

CIRCUIT	DESCRIPTION*	COLOR
181	BLOWER MOTOR FEED	BROWN-ORANGE
182	THERMOSTAT SWITCH FEED	BROWN-WHITE
183	TONE GENERATOR	TAN-YELLOW
184	AIR COND. SW. (LO) TO AIR COND. BLOWER MOTOR	TAN-ORANGE
185	INSIDE DOOR HANDLE SWITCH TO RETRACTOR INHIBITOR MODULE	GRAY-BLACK
186	DEFOGGER SW. TO DEFOGGER MOTOR	BROWN-LT BLUE
187	INHIBITOR MODULE TO RETRACTOR OVERRIDE SOLENOID	GRAY-RED
188	HEADLAMP SWITCH TO AUXILIARY LAMPS	WHITE-BLACK
189	IDLE TRACKING SWITCH FEED	LT BLUE-PINK
190	THERMACTOR DUMP VALVE FEED	WHITE-RED
**190	THERMACTOR AIR BYPASS (TAB)	WHITE-ORANGE
191	DEFOGGER SW. TO DEFOGGER MOTOR	DK BLUE-YELLOW
192	HEADLAMP SWITCH TO ELECTRONIC CLUSTER DIMMING	BROWN-WHITE
193	WINDOW REGULATOR RELAY FEED	YELLOW-LT GREEN
194	WINDOW REGULATOR REPLAY ACCY. FEED	PINK
195	TAILLAMP SWITCH FEED	TAN-WHITE
196	HEADLAMP FLASH TO PASS SWITCH FEED	DK BLUE-ORANGE
197	COOLANT TEMPERATURE SWITCH TO CONTROL RELAY	TAN-ORANGE
198	A/C PRESSURE SWITCH TO CONTROL RELAY	TAN-YELLOW
199	MODULE TO NEUTRAL SENSOR SWITCH	LT BLUE-YELLOW
**199	MANUAL LEVER POSITION OR CLUTCH	LT BLUE-YELLOW
200	THERMACTOR DIVERTER VALVE FEED	WHITE-BLACK
*200	THERMACTOR AIR DIVERTER (TAD)	BROWN
201	MCV MODULE TO VIP FUNCTION TESTER	TAN-RED
202	SPEED CONTROL AMPLIFIER TO CRUISE LAMP INTERFACE MODULE	RED-PINK
203	CRUISE INDICATING LAMP TO CRUISE LAMP INTERFACE MODULE	ORANGE-LT BLUE
204	TANK SELECT CIRCUIT ELECTRONIC FUEL GAGE	ORANGE-LT GREEN
205	BUFFER FUEL LEVEL OUTPUT TO TRIPMINDER	DK BLUE-LT GREEN
206	GROUND RETURN TO TOWING VEHICLE	WHITE
*206	TRAILER BROWN	WHITE
207	MARKER LAMP SWITCH TO MARKER LAMPS	BLACK
208	LOW OIL LEVEL RELAY TO WARNING LAMP	GRAY
209	ELECT. ENG. CONTL. MOD. TO TEST CONN #1	WHITE-RED
**209	TO TEST CONNECTOR	WHITE-PURPLE
210	INDICATOR LAMP TO SWITCH (4×4)	LT BLUE
211	ECU TO VACUUM SWITCH 4	BLACK-PINK
**212	AUXILIARY CIRCUIT FEED TO TRACTOR TRAILER PLUG	DK BLUE
213	ECU TO VACUUM SWITCH 2	WHITE-PINK
214	ECU TO VACUUM SWITCH 3	RED-BLACK
215	SIGNAL UNIT LAMP TO FUEL SIGNAL RELAY	YELLOW-BLACK
216	AUTOLAMP AMPLIFIER TO RHEOSTAT	TAN-LT BLUE
217	AUTOLAMP AMPLIFIER TO RHEOSTAT	DK BLUE-ORANGE
218	AUTOLAMP AMPLIFIER TO SENSOR	WHITE-PURPLE
219	HEADLAMP SWITCH TO AUTOLAMP AMPLIFIER	DK GREEN-YELLOW
220	AUTOLAMP AMPLIFIER TO CONTROL SWITCH	PURPLE-ORANGE
221	HEADLAMP SWITCH TO SENSOR AND AUTOLAMP AMPLIFIER	ORANGE-WHITE
222	AUTOLAMP AMPLIFIER TO SENSOR	BROWN-LT GREEN
223	ODOMETER SENSOR TO EEC MODULE	TAN-LT GREEN
**223	MILEAGE SENSOR TO EEC MODULE	TAN-LT GREEN
224	TRANSMISSION OVERDRIVE SWITCH TO EEC MODULE	TAN-LT BLUE
**224	TRANSMISSION OVERDRIVE SWITCH TO EEC MODULE	TAN-WHITE
225	INJECTION PUMP FUEL TEMPERATURE SENSOR	BLACK-YELLOW
226	L.F. WINDOW REG. SW. TO LF WINDOW REG. MOTOR	WHITE-BLACK
227	L.F. WINDOW REG. SW. TO LF WINDOW REG. MOTOR	YELLOW
228	ELECTRIC DRIVE COOLING FAN	BROWN-YELLOW
**228	ELECTRIC DRIVE COOLING FAN (SINGLE OR LOW)	DK BLUE
229	EFE CARBURETOR SPACE FEED	BLACK-YELLOW
230	COLD START INJECTOR	BLACK-LT GREEN
231	ACCESSORY FEED TO MESSAGE CENTER	BLACK-YELLOW
232	FUEL METERING CONTROL LEVER ACTUATOR 1 MINUS	BROWN-LT BLUE
233	THERMOMETER SENSOR FEED	DK BLUE-YELLOW
234	THERMOMETER AMBIENT SENSOR RETURN	DK BLUE-WHITE
235	LAMP RETURN TO PULSE WITH DIMMER	RED-BLACK
236	FUEL PRESSURE BOOST SOLENOID	RED-YELLOW
237	TRANSMISSION THROTTLE VALVE SOLENOID 1	ORANGE-YELLOW
**237	SHIFT SOLENOID 1	ORANGE-YELLOW
238	FUEL SUPPLY PUMP RELAY	ORANGE-LT BLUE
**238	FUEL PUMP RELAY TO SAFETY SWITCH	DK GREEN-YELLOW
239	FUEL INJECTION POSITION SENSOR	PURPLE-YELLOW
240	COLD START TIMING RETARD SOLENOID	WHITE-RED
241	DE-ICE SOLENOID CONTROL	LT BLUE-YELLOW
243	POWER SERVO TO CLIMATE CONTROL UNIT (MODE)	LT GREEN-ORANGE
244	THERMAL SW. TO CLIMATE CONTROL UNIT	YELLOW-WHITE
245	POWER SERVO TO CLIMATE CONTROL UNIT (AMP)	BROWN-LT GREEN
246	POWER SERVO TO CLIMATE CONTROL UNIT (AMP)	PURPLE
247	POWER SERVO TO CLIMATE CONTROL UNIT (AMP)	WHITE-YELLOW
248	HEATER & A/C CONTROL SW. (DE-ICE) TO CLIMATE CONTROL UNIT	YELLOW-LT BLUE
249	HEATER & A/C CONTROL SW. (LO-NORM) TO CLIMATE CONTROL UNIT	DK BLUE-LT GREEN
250	HEATER & A/C CONTROL SW. (LO-NORM) TO POWER SERVO	ORANGE
251	IGNITION SWITCH TO THERMACTOR TIMER	BROWN-ORANGE
252	THERMACTOR TIMER TO RELAY	TAN-RED
253	START CIRCUIT TO THERMACTOR RELAY	ORANGE-YELLOW
254	OIL PRESSURE SWITCH TO TIMER	DK GREEN-WHITE
255	THERMACTOR DUMP VALVE FEED	LT BLUE-RED
256	TEMPERATURE COMPENSATED PUMP TO PROCESSOR	ORANGE-WHITE
257	H L SW. TO CHIMES	WHITE-RED
258	LOW OIL LEVEL RELAY TO SENSOR	WHITE-PINK
259	ELECT. ENG. CONTROL MOD. TO THICK FILM IGN. MOD.	BLACK-ORANGE
**259	DEDICATED GROUND TO TFI MODULE	ORANGE
260	BLOWER MOTOR TO SWITCH — LO	RED-ORANGE
261	BLOWER MOTOR TO SWITCH — HI	ORANGE-BLACK
262	STARTING MOTOR RELAY TO IGNITION COIL "I" TERM.	BROWN-PINK
263	CLICKER RELAY TERM. NO. 4 TO AIR VALVE ASSY.	PURPLE-LT BLUE
264	ELECT. ENG. CONTL. MOD. TO IDLE SPD. CONTL. MOTOR #1	WHITE-LT BLUE
265	ELECT. ENG. CONTL. MOD. TO IDLE SPD. CONTL. MOTOR #2	LT GREEN-WHITE
266	MEMORY SEAT SWITCH ENABLE	PURPLE-WHITE
267	MEMORY SEAT SWITCH POSITION #1	BROWN-LT GREEN
268	MEMORY SEAT SWITCH POSITION #2	BLACK-ORANGE
269	HEATER BLOWER MOTOR TO SWITCH (MEDIUM)	LT BLUE-ORANGE
270	MEMORY SEAT SWITCH SET	BROWN-ORANGE
271	MEMORY SEAT SWITCH LAMP ENABLE	LT GREEN-WHITE
272	MEMORY SEAT SWITCH LAMP DRIVE	WHITE-ORANGE
273	TO ELECTRONIC CLUSTER FROM ENGLISH/METRIC SWITCH IN KEYBOARD	BROWN
274	SWITCH OFF TO RELAY	ORANGE
275	SWITCH ON TO RELAY	YELLOW
276	SWITCH TO FEED	BROWN
277	AMPLIFIER SPEAKER SWITCH TO LEFT REAR SPEAKER	LT BLUE-BLACK
278	AMPLIFIER SPEAKER SWITCH FEED TO RIGHT REAR SPEAKER	PURPLE-WHITE
279	SPEAKER VOICE COIL FEED FRONT (R. CHANNEL) AMP INPUT	WHITE-RED
280	SPEAKER VOICE COIL FEED FRONT (LEFT CHANNEL) AMP INPUT	LT GREEN
281	SPEAKER VOICE COIL RETURN AMP INPUT	WHITE
285	ELECTRONIC CLUSTER FROM EXPANDED FUEL IN KEYBOARD	ORANGE
286	ELECTRONIC CLUSTER FROM TRIP RESET SWITCH IN KEYBOARD	YELLOW
287	SPEAKER VOICE COIL RETURN	BLACK-WHITE
288	TO ELECTRONIC CLUSTER FROM TRIP RECALL SWITCH IN KEYBOARD	PURPLE
289	TO ELECTRONIC CLUSTER FROM GAGE SELECT SWITCH IN KEYBOARD	WHITE
290	12 GA FUSE LINK	GRAY
291	16 GA FUSE LINK	BLACK
292	18 GA FUSE LINK	BROWN
293	INSTRUMENT PANEL ILLUMINATION CONTROL MODULE FEED	ORANGE-RED
294	FUSED ACCY. FEED #3	WHITE-LT BLUE
295	ELECTRONIC CLUSTER ACCESSORY FEED	LT BLUE-PINK
296	FUSED ACCY. FEED #1	WHITE-PURPLE
297	ACCY. FEED FROM IGNITION SWITCH	BLACK-LT GREEN
298	FUSED ACCY. FEED #2	PURPLE-ORANGE
299	14 GA FUSE LINK	DK GREEN
300	16 GA FUSE LINK	ORANGE
301	18 GA FUSE LINK	RED
302	20 GA FUSE LINK	DK BLUE
303	12 GA FUSE LINK	YELLOW
304	FEEDBACK CARBURETOR COIL "A"	BROWN
305	EEC MODULE TO TIME METER	LT BLUE-PINK
306	SEAT REG. SW. TO HORIZ. SOLENOID BATT. TERM.	LT BLUE
307	SEAT REG. SW. TO VERT. SOLENOID BATT. TERM.	WHITE
308	HI-TEMP SWITCH TO MCU MODULE	LT BLUE-ORANGE
309	LO-TEMP SWITCH TO MCU MODULE	ORANGE-RED
310	MCU MODULE TO KNOCK SENSOR	YELLOW-RED
**310	ELECT. ENG. CONTL. MOD. TO KNOCK SENSOR	YELLOW-RED
311	MCU MODULE TO KNOCK SENSOR	DK GREEN-ORANGE
312	FUEL METERING CONTROL LEVER ACTUATOR 2 PLUS	WHITE-ORANGE
313	LEFT FRONT WINDOW REGULATOR SWITCH TO RIGHT FRONT WINDOW REGULATOR MOTOR	YELLOW-BLACK
314	LEFT FRONT WINDOW REGULATOR SWITCH TO RIGHT FRONT WINDOW REGULATOR MOTOR	RED-BLACK
315	TRANSMISSION THROTTLE VALVE SOLENOID 2	DK GREEN-PURPLE
**315	SHIFT SOLENOID 2	PURPLE ORANGE
316	LEFT FRONT WINDOW REGULATOR SWITCH TO LEFT REAR WINDOW REGULATOR MOTOR	YELLOW-LT BLUE
317	LEFT FRONT WINDOW REGULATOR SWITCH TO LEFT REAR WINDOW REGULATOR MOTOR	RED-LT BLUE
318	EXHAUST BACK PRESSURE VALVE ACTUATOR	GRAY-RED
319	LEFT FRONT WINDOW REGULATOR SWITCH TO RIGHT REAR WINDOW REGULATOR MOTOR	YELLOW-BLACK
320	LEFT FRONT WINDOW REGULATOR SWITCH TO RIGHT REAR WINDOW REGULATOR MOTOR	RED-BLACK
321	AIR CONDITIONER CLUTCH RELAY	GRAY-WHITE
322	IDLE SPEED CONTROL TO EGR VENT SOLENOID	RED-ORANGE
323	IDLE SPEED CONTROL TO EGR VACUUM SOLENOID	ORANGE-BLACK
324	TRANSMISSION OVERDRIVE SWITCH TO HEAT MODULE	YELLOW-LT GREEN
325	CRANK ENABLE TO IGNITION MODULE	DK BLUE-ORANGE
326	FUSE PANEL FEED TO RELAY	WHITE-PURPLE
327	DIESEL WATER IN FUEL SENDER TO WARNING LAMP GROUND	BLACK-ORANGE
328	WINDOW REG. MASTER CONT. SW. TO WINDOW REG. SW. FEED	RED-YELLOW
329	CRANK ENABLE RELAY	PINK
330	POWER STEERING PRESSURE SWITCH	YELLOW-LT GREEN
331	WIDE OPEN THROTTLE A/C CUTOUT SWITCH	RED
**331	WIDE OPEN THROTTLE A/C CUTOUT SWITCH	PINK-YELLOW
332	TIME DELAY RELAY	WHITE
333	WINDOW REG. SW. TO WINDOW REG. MOTOR	YELLOW-RED
334	WINDOW REG. SW. TO WINDOW REG. MOTOR	RED-YELLOW
335	AFTER GLOW RELAY TO DIESEL CONTROL SWITCH	ORANGE-LT BLUE
336	POWER RELAY TO GLOW PLUGS (RIGHT BANK)	BLACK-LT GREEN
337	POWER RELAY TO GLOW PLUGS (LEFT BANK)	ORANGE-WHITE
338	DIESEL CONTROL SWITCH TO LAMP CONTROL RELAY	BROWN-PINK
339	DIESEL CONTROL SWITCH TO POWER RELAY & LAMP CONTROL RELAY	GRAY
340	ANTI-THEFT MODULE TO ALARM RELAY	RED-LT BLUE
341	DOOR OPENING WARNING TO ANTI-THEFT MODULE	ORANGE-WHITE
342	START INTERRUPT RELAY TO ANTI-THEFT MODULE	LT GREEN-PURPLE
343	WARNING LAMP TO ANTI-THEFT MODULE	DK BLUE-LT GREEN
344	DOOR AJAR SWITCH TO INDICATOR LAMP LEFT FRONT GROUND	BLACK-YELLOW
345	DOOR AJAR SWITCH TO INDICATOR LAMP RIGHT FRONT GROUND	BLACK-PINK
346	DOOR AJAR SWITCH TO INDICATOR LAMP REAR GROUND	BLACK-WHITE
347	A/C COMPRESSOR CLUTCH FEED	BLACK-YELLOW
348	THERMOSTATIC SW. TO AIR COND. SW. SELECTOR TERM.	LT GREEN-PURPLE
**348	A/C DEMAND SIGNAL	PURPLE
349	CRANKSHAFT POSITION SENSOR FEED	DK BLUE
350	CRANKSHAFT SENSOR SIGNAL RETURN	GRAY

* IN SOME CASES, THERE MAY BE ADDITIONAL CIRCUIT
FUNCTIONS INCLUDED IN THE CIRCUIT DESCRIPTION LISTED.

** DENOTES A NEW OR STANDARDIZED CIRCUIT.

STANDARD CIRCUIT CHART (BY NUMBER)

CIRCUIT	DESCRIPTION *	COLOR
351	SENSOR SIGNAL FEED	ORANGE-WHITE
**351	POWER TO ENGINE SENSORS	BROWN-WHITE
352	EGR VALVE POSITION FEED	BROWN-LT GREEN
'352	EGR FEEDBACK	BROWN-LT GREEN
353	VEHICLE SPEED SENSOR FEED	LT BLUE
354	ENGINE COOLANT TEMPERATURE SENSOR FEED	LT GREEN-YELLOW
**354	ENGINE COOLANT TEMPERATURE SENSOR FEED	LT GREEN-RED
355	THROTTLE ANGLE POSITION SENSOR FEED	DK GREEN-LT GREEN
**355	THROTTLE ANGLE POSITION SENSOR TO EEC MODULE	GRAY-WHITE
356	BAROMETRIC PRESSURE SENSOR FEED	DK BLUE-LT GREEN
357	CARBURETOR AIR TEMPERATURE SENSOR FEED	LT GREEN-PURPLE
358	MANIFOLD ABSOLUTE PRESSURE SENSOR FEED	LT GREEN-BLACK
**358	MANIFOLD ABSOLUTE PRESSURE TO EEC MODULE	LT GREEN-BLACK
359	SENSOR SIGNAL RETURN	BLACK-WHITE
**359	SENSOR SIGNAL RETURN	GRAY-RED
360	EGR VALVE TO EEC MODULE	DK GREEN
**360	EGR VALVE REGULATOR SOLENOID TO EEC MODULE	BROWN-PINK
361	POWER RELAY TO EEC MODULE	RED
**361	POWER OUTPUT FROM EEC RELAY	RED
362	EGR VALVE TO EEC MODULE FEED	YELLOW
363	DOOR AJAR SWITCH TO INDICATOR LAMP LEFT REAR GROUND	BLACK-LT BLUE
364	BLOWER MOTOR RELAY FEED	BLACK-LT GREEN
365	FUEL LEVEL WARNING RELAY FEED	LT BLUE-RED
366	FUEL WARNING RELAY CONTROL	RED-BLACK
367	FUEL LEVEL RECEIVER TO FUEL LEVEL WARNING RELAY (REC. TERM.)	DK GREEN-WHITE
368	RADIO SEEK "UP"	RED-BLACK
369	VACUUM SOLENOID TO TEMP. SW.	BROWN-ORANGE
370	RADIO SEEK "DOWN"	ORANGE-BLACK
371	BLOWER MOTOR RELAY TO MOTOR	PINK-WHITE
372	RADIO MEMORY SEEK	BROWN-ORANGE
373	TO ELECTRONIC CLUSTER FROM GROUND IN KEYBOARD	BLACK
374	DOOR AJAR RELAY TO DOOR SWITCH	BROWN
375	MOVABLE STEERING COLUMN SOLENOID FEED	YELLOW-LT GREEN
376	ELECT. ENG. CONTL. MOD. TO IDLE SPD. CONTL. MOTOR #3	BROWN-WHITE
377	ELECT. ENG. CONTL. MOD. TO EXHAUST HEAT CONTL SOLENOID	WHITE
378	ELECT. ENG. CONTL. MOD. TO THROTTLE LEVER SOLENOID	RED-BLACK
379	TURN SIGNAL SWITCH TO RH CORNERING LAMP	BROWN-WHITE
380	TURN SIGNAL SWITCH TO LH CORNERING LAMP	PURPLE-YELLOW
381	MOVABLE STEERING COLUMN SOLENOID TO COURTESY LAMP SWITCH	ORANGE-WHITE
382	ELECT. ENG. CONTL. MOD. TO TEST CONNECTOR #2	YELLOW-BLACK
383	EMERGENCY WARNING FLASHER FEED	RED-WHITE
384	ELECT. ENG. CONTL. MOD. TO IDLE SPD. CONTL. MOTOR #3	PINK-ORANGE
385	FLASHER TO EMERGENCY WARNING SWITCH	WHITE-RED
386	ELECT. ENG. CONTL. MOD. TO ELECTRO DRIVE FAN	LT BLUE
387	READING LAMP SWITCH TO READING LAMP (LH)	LT GREEN
388	REARVIEW OUTSIDE MIRROR FEED	RED
389	R.F. DOOR LOCK SWITCH TO L.F. DOOR LOCK SWITCH	DK GREEN-LT GREEN
390	R.F. DOOR UNLOCK SWITCH TO L.F. DOOR UNLOCK SWITCH	DK BLUE-WHITE
391	CHOKE RELAY TO MCU MODULE	WHITE-YELLOW
392	ELECTRIC PVS TO MCU MODULE	WHITE-ORANGE
393	THROTTLE LEVER SOLENOID RELAY TO MCU MODULE	WHITE-BLACK
394	ANEROID SWITCH TO MCU MODULE	GRAY-LT BLUE
395	SPARK MODULE TO MCU MODULE	GRAY-ORANGE
**395	PROFILE IGNITION PICKUP FROM TFI MODULE	GRAY-ORANGE
396	FUEL 1 GROUND TO TACH/GAGE MODULE	BLACK-ORANGE
397	SIGNAL GROUND TO TACH/GAGE MODULE	BLACK-WHITE
398	TACHOMETER GROUND TO TACH/GAGE MODULE	BLACK-YELLOW
399	HEATER BLOWER SWITCH FEED	BROWN-YELLOW
400	SAFETY RELAY LOAD TERM. TO WIND. REG. SW. FEED	LT BLUE-BLACK
401	LIMIT SW. TO BACK WINDOW REG. MOTOR	GRAY-BLACK
402	WINDOW REG. SW. TO BACK WINDOW REG. MOTOR	GRAY-RED
403	WINDOW REG. SW. TO WINDOW REG. MOTOR	GRAY-WHITE
404	WINDOW REG. SW. TO BACK WINDOW SW.	PURPLE-LT GREEN
405	WINDOW REG. SW. TO BACK WINDOW AUX. SW.	PURPLE-LT BLUE
406	WINDOW REG. SW. TO BACK WINDOW AUX. SW.	TAN
407	WINDOW REG. SW. REAR TO LIMIT SW.	TAN-BLACK
408	WINDOW REG. SW. FRONT TO LIMIT SW.	TAN-RED
409	PRESSURE SWITCH TO KEY SWITCH	TAN-BLACK
410	REARVIEW OUTSIDE MIRROR UP	YELLOW
411	REARVIEW OUTSIDE MIRROR DOWN	DK GREEN
412	REARVIEW OUTSIDE MIRROR COUNTERCLOCKWISE	WHITE
413	REARVIEW OUTSIDE MIRROR CLOCKWISE	LT BLUE
414	AIR SOLENOID CONTROL R.F.	ORANGE-RED
415	AIR SOLENOID CONTROL L.F.	LT GREEN-ORANGE
416	AIR SOLENOID CONTROL — REAR	LT BLUE-BLACK
417	AIR SUSPENSION SWITCH FEED	PURPLE-ORANGE
418	AIR SUSPENSION CONTROL MODULE FEED	DK GREEN-YELLOW
419	AIR SUSPENSION MALFUNCTION WARNING LAMP	DK GREEN-LT GREEN
420	AIR COMPRESSOR POWER RELAY CONTROL	DK BLUE-YELLOW
421	AIR COMPRESSOR VENT SOLENOID	PINK
422	AIR SUSPENSION HEIGHT SENSOR HI — L.F.	PINK-BLACK
423	AIR SUSPENSION HEIGHT SENSOR LO — L.F.	PURPLE-LT GREEN
424	AIR SUSPENSION HEIGHT SENSOR HI — R.F.	TAN
425	AIR SUSPENSION HEIGHT SENSOR LO — R.F.	BROWN-PINK
426	FRONT AIR SUSPENSION HEIGHT SENSOR FEED	RED-BLACK
427	AIR SUSPENSION HEIGHT SENSOR HI — REAR	PINK-BLACK
428	AIR SUSPENSION HEIGHT SENSOR LO — REAR	ORANGE-BLACK
429	REAR AIR SUSPENSION HEIGHT SENSOR FEED	PURPLE-LT GREEN
430	AIR SUSPENSION SYSTEM GROUND	GRAY
431	AIR SUSP. MOD. TO L.F. HEIGHT SENSOR	PINK-WHITE
432	AIR SUSPENSION ELECTRONIC GROUND	BLACK-PINK
433	FUEL PUMP BYPASS	LT BLUE-RED
434	RELAY TO DAY/NIGHT ILLUMINATION LAMPS	LT BLUE-BLACK
435	POSITION SENSE RETURN	YELLOW-LT BLUE
436	REAR TILT POSITION SENSE	RED-LT GREEN
437	POSITION SENSE ENABLE	YELLOW-LT GREEN
438	HORIZONTAL POSITION SENSE	RED-WHITE
439	SEAT PROCESSOR TO RECLINER MOTOR "UP"	YELLOW-WHITE
440	SEAT PROCESSOR TO RECLINER MOTOR "DOWN"	RED-LT BLUE
441	FRONT TILT POSITION SENSE	GRAY-BLACK
442	SEQUENTIAL L.H. REAR INBOARD TURN SIGNAL LAMP	LT GREEN-ORANGE
443	SEQUENTIAL L.H. REAR CENTER TURN SIGNAL LAMP	LT GREEN-RED
444	SEQUENTIAL L.H. REAR OUTBOARD TURN SIGNAL LAMP	LT GREEN-BLACK
445	SEQUENTIAL R.H. REAR INBOARD TURN SIGNAL LAMP	ORANGE-LT BLUE
446	SEQUENTIAL R.H. REAR CENTER TURN SIGNAL LAMP	ORANGE-WHITE
447	SEQUENTIAL R.H. REAR OUTBOARD TURN SIGNAL LAMP	ORANGE-RED
448	ANTENNA SWITCH TO ANTENNA RELAY	ORANGE-YELLOW
449	RADIO SWITCH TO ANTENNA RELAY	BROWN-ORANGE
450	SEAT BELT WARNING INDICATOR LAMP FEED	DK GREEN-LT GREEN
451	BATTERY TO AUTOMATIC ANTENNA SWITCH	LT BLUE-YELLOW
452	SEAT PROCESSOR ASSY. TO FRONT MOTOR L.H.	GRAY-RED
453	TRANSMISSION DIAGNOSTIC	PURPLE
454	IGN. SW. COIL TERM. TO CIRCUIT BREAKER	RED-LT GREEN
455	SWITCH TO VALVE	GRAY-RED
456	AUX. WATER VALVE FEED	WHITE-LT GREEN
457	BRAKE WEAR SENSOR	TAN-BLACK
458	TURN SIGNAL SWITCH TO INDICATOR RELAY	ORANGE-BLACK
459	INDICATOR RELAY TO FLASHER	ORANGE-LT GREEN
460	HORN SWITCH FEED	YELLOW-LT BLUE
461	MODULE TO RELAY	ORANGE
462	MODULE TO RELAY	PURPLE
463	ELECTRIC SHIFT MODULE TO NEUTRAL START SWITCH	RED-WHITE
464	MODULE TO LIGHT	BLACK-PINK
465	MODULE TO SWITCH	WHITE-LT BLUE
466	DIESEL CONTROL MODULE FEED	PINK-ORANGE
467	PRESSURE SWITCH TO INERTIA SWITCH	GRAY-YELLOW
468	EATC L.H. SUNLOAD SENSOR POSITIVE	BROWN
469	SEAT BELT WARNING SWITCH FEED	LT GREEN
470	THERMO SWITCH TO CONTROL MODULE	PINK-BLACK
471	DROPPING RESISTOR TO RELAY #2	ORANGE-LT GREEN
472	GLOW PLUG TO CONTROL MODULE	YELLOW-BLACK
473	CONTROL MODULE TO OIL PRESSURE SWITCH	LT GREEN-BLACK
474	STOPLAMP RELAY FEED	PINK-BLACK
475	STOPLAMP SW. TO STOPLAMP RELAY (COIL TERM.)	DK GREEN-WHITE
476	EATC L.H. SUNLOAD SENSOR NEGATIVE	BROWN-YELLOW
477	FOG LAMP SWITCH TO FOG LAMP RELAY	LT BLUE-BLACK
478	FOG LAMP SW. TO FOG LAMP	TAN-ORANGE
479	EATC R.H. SUNLOAD SENSOR POSITIVE	PURPLE
480	CLUTCH SWITCH TO EFI MODULE	PURPLE-YELLOW
**480	TRANSMISSION CLUTCH CONTROL TO EEC MODULE	PURPLE-YELLOW
481	EFI MODULE TO CLUTCH SWITCH	GRAY-YELLOW
482	FUEL FILLER DOOR RELEASE SWITCH TO FUEL FILLER DOOR RELEASE SOLENOID	WHITE-PINK
483	EATC R.H. SUNLOAD SENSOR NEGATIVE	GRAY
484	LIQUID CRYSTAL DISPLAY	ORANGE-BLACK
485	IGNITION SWITCH ACCY. TERM. TO DECK LID OPEN WARNING LAMP	BROWN-PINK
486	DECK LID OPEN WARNING LAMP TO DECK LID OPEN SWITCH	BROWN-WHITE
487	READING LAMP SWITCH TO READING LAMP	PINK-ORANGE
488	DIESEL CONTROL MODULE GROUND RETURN	BLACK-LT BLUE
489	ELECTRONIC CLUSTER IGNITION RUN FEED	PINK-BLACK
490	POWER LUMBAR FEED	RED
491	POWER "THIGH" BOLSTER UP	YELLOW
492	POWER "THIGH" BOLSTER DOWN	BROWN
493	HCU (MAIN) TO MODULE	BLACK-PINK
494	TURN SIGNAL RELAY TO TURN SIGNAL FLASHER	TAN-LT GREEN
495	VALVE #1 TO MODULE	TAN
496	VALVE #2 TO MODULE	ORANGE
497	VALVE #3 TO MODULE	WHITE
498	VALVE #4 TO MODULE	PINK
499	VALVE #5 TO MODULE	GRAY-BLACK
500	HEADLAMP DIMMER SWITCH TO HEADLAMP DIMMER RELAY	PURPLE
501	ELECTRONIC FUEL GAGE TO MESSAGE CENTER	LT BLUE
502	HEADLAMP DIMMER RELAY TO HEADLAMP DIMMER SWITCH	GRAY
503	HEADLAMP DIMMER RELAY TO FUSE HOLDER	LT BLUE
504	FUSE HOLDER TO HEADLAMP DIMMER AMPLIFIER	DK BLUE-WHITE
505	HEADLAMP DIMMER SWITCH TO HEADLAMP DIMMER AMPLIFIER	GRAY-YELLOW
506	MPH/KPH SWITCH TO MESSAGE CENTER	RED
507	AMPLIFIER TO RHEOSTAT	YELLOW
508	RHEOSTAT TO SENSOR	WHITE
509	AIR COND. CONDENSOR THERMAL SWITCH FEED	TAN-YELLOW
510	VALVE #6 TO MODULE	TAN-RED
511	STOPLAMP SWITCH TO TURN SIGNAL SWITCH	LT GREEN
**511	STOPLAMP SWITCH TO STOPLAMPS	LT GREEN
512	BRAKE FLUID RES. SWITCH TO MODULE	TAN-LT GREEN
513	POWER RELAY COIL TO MODULE	BROWN-PINK
514	RH FRONT SENSOR (HIGH) TO MODULE	YELLOW-RED
515	RESISTOR TO BLOWER MOTOR (HI)	ORANGE-RED
516	R.H. FRONT SENSOR (LOW) TO MODULE	YELLOW-BLACK
517	CIRCUIT BREAKER (LOAD TERM.) TO CONTROL SWITCH (BATT. TERM.)	BLACK-WHITE
518	REAR SENSOR (HIGH) TO MODULE	LT GREEN-RED
519	L.H. REAR SENSOR (LOW) TO MODULE	LT GREEN-BLACK
520	SEAT BELT WARNING LAMP TO WARNING LAMP SWITCH	PURPLE-WHITE
521	L.H. FRONT SENSOR (HIGH) TO MODULE	TAN-ORANGE
522	L.H. FRONT SENSOR (LOW) TO MODULE	TAN-BLACK
523	R.H. REAR SENSOR (HIGH) TO MODULE	RED-PINK
524	R.H. REAR SENSOR (LOW) TO MODULE	PINK-BLACK
525	SPLICE TO MODULE	ORANGE-YELLOW
526	CORNERING LAMP SWITCH FEED	BLACK-WHITE
527	HEADLAMP DIMMER SWITCH OVERRIDE TO RHEOSTAT	RED
528	POWER RELAY TO MODULE GROUND	ORANGE-YELLOW
529	SPLICE #2 TO MODULE	YELLOW-LT GREEN

* IN SOME CASES, THERE MAY BE ADDITIONAL CIRCUIT
FUNCTIONS INCLUDED IN THE CIRCUIT DESCRIPTION LISTED.

** DENOTES A NEW OR STANDARDIZED CIRCUIT.

STANDARD CIRCUIT CHART (BY NUMBER)

CIRCUIT	DESCRIPTION*	COLOR	CIRCUIT	DESCRIPTION*	COLOR
530	SPLICE #3 TO POWER RELAY	LT GREEN-YELLOW	623	AIR BAG DIAGNOSTIC MODULE (MONITOR) TO SAFING SENSOR	PURPLE-WHITE
531	SPLICE TO DIODE	ORANGE-YELLOW	624	DCP MODULE TO HEATED BACKLITE RELAY	LT BLUE-ORANGE
532	SPLICE TO POWER RELAY	ORANGE-YELLOW	625	DCP MODULE TO PARKLAMP RELAY	LT BLUE-WHITE
533	POWER RELAY TO FUSE LINK	TAN-RED	626	OPEN DOOR WARNING LAMP FEED	PINK-YELLOW
534	SPLICE #3 TO PRESSURE SWITCH	YELLOW-LT GREEN	627	OPEN DOOR WARNING LAMP TO OPEN DOOR WARNING SWITCH	BLACK-ORANGE
535	PRESSURE SWITCH TO MODULE	LT BLUE-RED	628	DOOR WIRE	WHITE
536	BLOWER MOTOR RELAY (LOAD TERM.) TO BLOWER MOTOR	BLACK-LT GREEN	629	DOOR WIRE	BLACK
537	FUSE LINK TO MOTOR RELAY	TAN-YELLOW	630	DOOR WIRE	RED
538	MOTOR TO MOTOR RELAY	GRAY-RED	631	DOOR WIRE	YELLOW
539	PRESSURE SWITCH TO MOTOR RELAY	PINK-LT BLUE	632	DCP MODULE TO HEADLAMP RELAY	PINK-YELLOW
540	L.H. REMOTE MIRROR MOTOR FEED—C.W.	RED	633	STEERING RATE SENSOR TERM. A TO CONTROL MODULE	RED
541	L.H. REMOTE MIRROR MOTOR FEED—C.C.W.	DK BLUE	634	STEERING RATE SENSOR TERM. B TO CONTROL MODULE	BROWN
542	L.H. REMOTE MIRROR SOLENOID CONTROL	YELLOW	635	AIR SUSPENSION MODE SWITCH TO CONTROL MODULE	YELLOW
543	R.H. REMOTE MIRROR MOTOR FEED—C.W.	DK GREEN	635	AIR SUSPENSION DIODE SWITCH TO CONTROL MODULE	YELLOW
544	R.H. REMOTE MIRROR MOTOR FEED—C.C.W.	PURPLE	636	BRAKE PRESSURE SWITCH TO CONTROL MODULE	ORANGE
545	R.H. REMOTE MIRROR SOLENOID CONTROL	WHITE	637	AIR SUSPENSION CONTROL SIGNAL	LT GREEN
546	SPLICE #3 TO POWER RELAY	DK GREEN-YELLOW	638	RIGHT FRONT SHOCK DAMPENING RELAY TO CONTROL MODULE	PURPLE
547	PRESSURE SWITCH TO FLUID RES. SWITCH	LT GREEN-YELLOW	639	HIGH ELECTRO DRIVE FAN	PINK
548	GROUND STUD TO SPLICE #2	YELLOW-LT GREEN	**639	HIGH ELECTRIC DRIVE COOLING FAN	LT GREEN-PURPLE
549	FLUID WARNING SWITCH TO PRESSURE SWITCH	BROWN-WHITE	640	WARNING LAMPS FEED	RED-YELLOW
550	FLUID SWITCH TO GROUND STUD	YELLOW-LT GREEN	641	LEFT FRONT SHOCK DAMPENING RELAY TO CONTROL MODULE	LT BLUE
551	SPLICE #2 TO SPLICE #3	YELLOW-LT GREEN	642	WATER TEMP. WARNING LAMP TO WATER TEMP. SW. (COLD)	WHITE-LT GREEN
552	SPLICE #2 TO COUP GROUND "B"	YELLOW-LT GREEN	643	DIESEL WATER IN FUEL SENDER TO WARNING LAMP	RED
554	POWER RELAY BATTERY FEED	YELLOW-BLACK	644	DIESEL TACH GROUND TO TACH GAGE MODULE	BLACK-YELLOW
555	FUEL INJECTOR #1 CYLINDER	TAN	**644	TACHOMETER SIGNAL RETURN	DK GREEN
**555	FUEL INJECTOR #1 CYLINDER OR BANK #1	TAN	645	SPEAKER VOICE COIL FEED RIGHT REAR CHANNEL AMP INPUT	PINK-BLACK
556	FUEL INJECTOR #2 CYLINDER	WHITE	646	SPEAKER VOICE COIL FEED LEFT REAR CHANNEL AMP INPUT	PINK-YELLOW
**556	FUEL INJECTOR #2 CYLINDER OR BANK #2	WHITE	647	WATER TEMP. WARNING LAMP TO WATER TEMP. SW. (HOT)	RED-BLACK
557	FUEL INJECTOR #3 CYLINDER	BROWN-YELLOW	648	TACHOMETER FEED	RED-LT BLUE
558	FUEL INJECTOR #4 CYLINDER	BROWN-LT BLUE	**648	TACHOMETER FEED	WHITE-PINK
559	FUEL INJECTOR #5 CYLINDER	TAN-LT BLUE	649	SPEAKER VOICE COIL FEED LEFT FRONT CHANNEL AMP INPUT	ORANGE
**559	HIGH ELECTRIC DRIVE COOLING FAN	TAN-BLACK	650	RIGHT REAR SHOCK DAMPENING RELAY TO CONTROL MODULE	WHITE
560	FUEL INJECTOR #6 CYLINDER	LT GREEN	651	LEFT REAR SHOCK DAMPENING RELAY TO CONTROL MODULE	DK GREEN
**560	FUEL INJECTOR #6 CYLINDER	LT GREEN-ORANGE	652	SHOCK DAMPENING RELAY HARD TO SHOCK DAMPENING CONTROL	PINK-BLACK
561	FUEL INJECTOR #7 CYLINDER	TAN-ORANGE	653	SHOCK DAMPENING RELAY SOFT TO SHOCK DAMPENING CONTROL	DK BLUE
**561	FUEL INJECTOR #7 CYLINDER	TAN-RED	654	ALT. SHUNT TO AMMETER	YELLOW-LT GREEN
562	FUEL INJECTOR #8 CYLINDER	LT BLUE	655	STARTING MOTOR RELAY SHUNT TO AMMETER	RED-ORANGE
563	SPEED SENSOR LO V REF TO SPEEDO TACH MODULE	ORANGE-YELLOW	656	REDUNDANT MODULE TO ENGINE WARNING LAMP	PURPLE
564	FUEL SIGNAL TACH MODULE TO FUEL COMPUTER	BROWN	657	EEC MODULE TO MALFUNCTION INDICATOR LITE	TAN
565	SPEED SIGNAL SPEEDO TACH MODULE TO FUEL COMPUTER	BLACK-WHITE	658	EEC MODULE TO CHECK ENGINE INDICATOR LAMP	PINK-LT GREEN
566	PROCESSOR TO THERMACTOR CLUTCH RELAY	WHITE-RED	659	MODULE TO DOWN SWITCH	WHITE-LT BLUE
567	THERMACTOR CLUTCH RELAY TO CLUTCH	WHITE-BLACK	660	AIR COND. CONTROL SW. TO FRESH-AIR RECIRC. DOOR SOLENOID	YELLOW-LT GREEN
568	ALTERNATOR RELAY TO ALTERNATOR REGULATOR	LT GREEN	661	MODULE TO OVERRIDE SWITCH	LT GREEN-WHITE
569	STOPLAMP SWITCH TO HI MOUNT STOPLAMP	DK GREEN	662	MODULE TO MOTOR FEED	WHITE-BLACK
570	DEDICATED GROUND	BLACK-WHITE	663	MODULE TO MOTOR FEED	LT GREEN-YELLOW
571	REMOTE CONVENIENCE SELF-DIAGNOSTIC GROUND	BLACK-ORANGE	**663	MODULE TO MOTOR RETURN	LT GREEN-YELLOW
572	ENGLISH METRIC SIGNAL TO MULTIGAGE	ORANGE-BLACK	664	MODULE TO RELEASE SOLENOID	YELLOW-LT GREEN
573	CENTER REAR TAILLAMP BULB OUTAGE	BLACK-ORANGE	665	OVERRIDE SWITCH TO LATCH	ORANGE-YELLOW
574	EXTENDED USEFUL LIFE SENSOR TO WARNING LAMP	BROWN-WHITE	666	BATTERY FEED CAMPER	RED
575	RELAY TO ATC CONTROL	YELLOW-BLACK	667	LAMP RELAY TO MARKER LAMPS	WHITE-RED
576	REAR LAMP TO TRAILER RELAY FEED	DK GREEN	668	I TERMINAL STARTER MOTOR RELAY TO INERTIA SWITCH	ORANGE-LT BLUE
577	AIR SUSPENSION SYSTEM GROUND	LT GREEN-RED	669	OIL PRESSURE SWITCH TO CUTOUT RELAY	YELLOW
578	AIR COMPRESSOR VENT SOLENOID	LT BLUE-PINK	670	INERTIA SWITCH TO FUEL TANK SELECTOR SWITCH	RED
579	HEATED WINDSHIELD CONTROL TO ELECT. ALTERNATOR REGULATOR	BLACK-ORANGE	**670	INERTIA SWITCH TO FUEL TANK SELECTOR SWITCH	RED-YELLOW
580	HEATED WINDSHIELD CONTROL TO ALT. POWER RELAY	BROWN	671	FUEL TANK SELECTOR SWITCH TO AFT FUEL PUMP	LT BLUE-YELLOW
581	HEATED WINDSHIELD CONTROL TO ALT. STATOR TERM.	RED	672	FUEL TANK SELECTOR SWITCH TO MIDSHIP FUEL PUMP	LT GREEN-YELLOW
582	HEATED WINDSHIELD SWITCH TO HEATED WINDSHIELD CONTROL	ORANGE	673	SELECTOR SWITCH TO MIDSHIP TANK	DK BLUE-YELLOW
583	ALT. POWER RELAY TO CONTROL MODULE	YELLOW	674	SELECTOR SWITCH TO AUX. FUEL SOLENOID	BROWN-WHITE
584	POWER FEED DECAY TIMER TO THROTTLE LEVER SOLENOID	DK GREEN-PURPLE	675	SELECTOR SWITCH TO AFT AXLE TANK	YELLOW-LT BLUE
585	HEATED WINDSHIELD CONTROL TO AIR COND. TERM.	PURPLE	676	EEC MODULE TO SPEED CONTROL GROUND	RED
586	CONVERTIBLE TOP RELAY TO SWITCH	YELLOW	**676	VEHICLE SPEED SENSOR RETURN	PINK-ORANGE
587	WINDSHIELD WIPER INTERMITTENT GOVERNOR FEED	BLACK-WHITE	677	ANTI-LOCK MODULE TO ANTI-LOCK CONTROL VALVE	LT BLUE
588	CONVERTIBLE TOP RELAY TO SWITCH	PURPLE	678	ANTI-LOCK MODULE TO ANTI-LOCK CONTROL VALVE	YELLOW
589	WINDSHIELD WIPER SWITCH TO INTERMITTENT GOVERNOR GROUND	ORANGE	679	SPEED CONTROL SENSE EEC MODULE TO SENSOR	GRAY-BLACK
590	INTERMITTENT GOVERNOR TO W/S WIPER SWITCH	DK BLUE-WHITE	**679	VEHICLE SPEED SIGNAL	GRAY-BLACK
591	DCP MODULE TO WASHER RELAY	BROWN-YELLOW	681	HEATED WINDSHIELD TRIGGER CIRCUIT SW. TO MODULE	TAN-RED
592	DCP MODULE TO WIPER PARK OVERRIDE RELAY	BROWN-LT GREEN	682	TEMP. WARNING LAMP TO SENDING UNIT	GRAY-RED
593	DCP MODULE TO WIPER GOVERNOR RELAY	RED-ORANGE	683	SPEED CONTROL SENSE TO EEC MODULE TO CLUSTER	PURPLE-LT BLUE
594	DCP MODULE TO WIPER HI-LO RELAY	ORANGE-LT GREEN	684	COMPASS SENSOR FEED	PINK-BLACK
595	DCP MODULE CONTROL INTERFACE TO RADIO	LT BLUE-RED	685	ANTI-LOCK MODULE TO ANTI-LOCK CONTROL VALVE	BLACK-WHITE
596	DCP MODULE SIGNAL GROUND TO RADIO	BLACK	686	HEAD LP TIME DELAY CONTROL RELAY TO CIR. BREAKER	GRAY-ORANGE
597	DCP MODULE TRIP SCAN HIGH TO TRIPMINDER	LT GREEN-BLACK	687	ACC FEED	GRAY-YELLOW
598	DCP MODULE TRIP SCAN LOW TO TRIPMINDER	LT GREEN-PURPLE	688	HTD BACKLITE SW. TO TIME DELAY RELAY	GRAY-LT BLUE
599	MODULE TO SOLENOID	PINK-LT GREEN	689	LOGIC MODE	DK BLUE
600	FEED TO FAILURE SWITCH	DK BLUE	690	RIGHT CHANNEL SIGNAL IN	GRAY
601	BRAKE ANTI-LOCK CONTROL MODULE FEED	LT BLUE-PINK	691	MOONROOF RELAY TO MICRO SWITCH OPEN	DK BLUE
602	COIL TERM. OF IGN. SW. TO BRAKE ANTI-LOCK CONTROL MODULE	RED-LT GREEN	692	MOONROOF RELAY TO MICRO SWITCH CLOSED	RED
603	FAILURE WARNING LIGHT	DK GREEN	693	MODULE DIAGNOSTIC	ORANGE
604	ANTI-LOCK CONTROL MODULE R.H. WHEEL SENSOR HI	ORANGE-RED	694	AMPLIFIER POWER RETURN	RED
605	SOLENOID	RED	695	MULTIPLEX WINDSHIELD WIPER OFF	BLACK-ORANGE
606	ANTI-LOCK DIAGNOSTIC	WHITE-LT BLUE	696	MULTIPLEX PARKING LAMPS	ORANGE-BLACK
607	DIESEL COLD ADVANCE	GRAY-RED	697	MULTIPLEX HEADLAMPS	BROWN
608	AIR BAG DIAGNOSTIC MODULE TO RELAY INDICATOR LAMP	BLACK-YELLOW	698	MULTIPLEX WINDSHIELD WIPER OFF	RED
609	AIR BAG READY INDICATOR LAMP TO AIR BAG FLASHER	ORANGE-YELLOW	**698	MULTIPLEX WINDSHIELD WIPER MAIN	RED
610	AIR BAG DIAGNOSTIC MODULE TO AIR BAG FLASHER	ORANGE-LT GREEN	699	MULTIPLEX RELAY COIL FEED	ORANGE
611	AIR BAG READY INDICATOR L (DEPLOY) TO SAFING SENSOR	WHITE-ORANGE	**699	MULTIPLEX RELAY COIL FEED #1	ORANGE
612	AIR BAG READY INDICATOR L (MONITOR) TO SAFING SENSOR	PURPLE-ORANGE	700	MULTIPLEX WIPER RATE	YELLOW
613	AIR BAG DIAGNOSTIC MODULE SAFING SENSOR (GROUND)	DK BLUE-WHITE	701	C.B. SQUELCH POT	WHITE-PURPLE
614	AIR BAG SAFING SENSORS TO INFLATORS	GRAY-ORANGE	702	C.B. PUSH TO TALK	WHITE-BLACK
615	AIR BAG DIAGNOSTIC MODULE TO DRIVER INFLATOR	GRAY-WHITE	703	C.B. DOWN SWITCH	WHITE-ORANGE
616	AIR BAG DIAGNOSTIC MODULE TO PASSENGER INFLATOR	PINK-BLACK	704	C.B. C-DIGIT	ORANGE
617	AIR BAG DIAGNOSTIC MODULE (DEPLOY) TO R.H. SENSOR	PINK-ORANGE	705	C.B. NOISE BLANKER	LT GREEN-ORANGE
618	AIR BAG DIAGNOSTIC MODULE (MONITOR) TO R.H. SENSOR	PURPLE-LT GREEN	706	C.B. SCAN L.E.D.	GRAY
619	AIR BAG DIAGNOSTIC MODULE (DEPLOY) TO CENTER SENSOR	PINK-WHITE	707	C.B. UP SWITCH	WHITE-YELLOW
620	AIR BAG DIAGNOSTIC MODULE (MONITOR) TO CENTER SENSOR	PURPLE-LT BLUE	708	C.B. D-DIGIT	BROWN
621	AIR BAG DIAGNOSTIC MODULE (MONITOR) TO L.H. SENSOR	WHITE-YELLOW	709	C.B. VOLUME CONTROL	WHITE-LT BLUE
622	AIR BAG DIAGNOSTIC MODULE (MONITOR) TO L.H. SENSOR	TAN-BLACK	710	C.B. SCAN SWITCH	WHITE-LT GREEN

* IN SOME CASES, THERE MAY BE ADDITIONAL CIRCUIT
FUNCTIONS INCLUDED IN THE CIRCUIT DESCRIPTION LISTED.

** DENOTES A NEW OR STANDARDIZED CIRCUIT.

STANDARD CIRCUIT CHART (BY NUMBER)

CIRCUIT	DESCRIPTION*	COLOR
711	C.B. REGULATED 5V	LT GREEN-BLACK
712	C.B. A & – DIGIT	PURPLE
713	C.B. MIC-AUDIO	WHITE
714	RELAY COIL FEED #2	PURPLE
715	C.B. A– DIGIT	LT GREEN
716	C.B. B– DIGIT	YELLOW
717	C.B. SPEAKER TO TRANSCEIVER	LT BLUE-RED
718	C.B. ON/OFF	RED-WHITE
719	WINDSHIELD WIPER HIGH	GRAY
720	C.B. B & – DIGIT	LT BLUE
721	C.B. SPEAKER VOICE COIL RETURN	DK BLUE-LT GREEN
722	C.B. RELAY DRIVE	LT GREEN-RED
723	C.B. SPEAKER RELAY TO MIC	LT BLUE-ORANGE
724	C.B. C & – DIGIT	LT GREEN-WHITE
725	RELAY COIL FEED #3	WHITE
726	WINDSHIELD WASHER	LT GREEN
727	REMOTE DEFROST	YELLOW-BLACK
728	RADIO SEEK	WHITE-ORANGE
729	RADIO MEMORY	RED-WHITE
730	CRT SCAN	LT BLUE-YELLOW
731	MULTIPLEX REVERSE DIMMING	WHITE-BLACK
732	MULTIPLEX LCD ILLUMINATION	BROWN-WHITE
733	MULTIPLEX SERVICE REMINDER RESET	PURPLE-WHITE
734	MULTIPLEX SERVICE REMINDER	TAN
735	MULTIPLEX MESSAGE O	DK BLUE-WHITE
736	MULTIPLEX MESSAGE I	PINK
737	TEMP. SWITCH TO WARNING DEVICE	WHITE-LT BLUE
738	HEATED WINDSHIELD CONTROL TO HEATED WINDSHIELD SWITCH	YELLOW-WHITE
739	HEATED WINDSHIELD GROUND TEST LEAD	BLACK
740	VAC SWITCH TO VAC PUMP	ORANGE-LT BLUE
741	TIMER CONTROL VALVE TO CONTROL UNIT	LT BLUE-WHITE
742	RADIATOR COOLANT TEMP. SWITCH TO CONTROL UNIT	LT BLUE-YELLOW
743	AIR TEMP. SENSOR TO CONTROL UNIT	BLACK-LT BLUE
**743	AIR CHARGE TEMPERATURE	GRAY
744	IDLE RPM SOLENOID TO CONTROL UNIT	TAN-WHITE
745	ANTENNA SWITCH TO POWER ANTENNA (UP)	RED-PINK
746	ANTENNA SWITCH TO POWER ANTENNA (DOWN)	DK GREEN-YELLOW
747	RADIO RECEIVER ASSY. TO FOOT CONTROL SWITCH	ORANGE-LT BLUE
748	BOOST SENSOR TO CONTROL UNIT	TAN
749	SENSOR AMPLIFY UNIT TO CONTROL UNIT #1	PINK-BLACK
750	SENSOR AMPLIFY UNIT TO CONTROL UNIT #2	GRAY-LT BLUE
751	BLOWER MOTOR SPEED CONTROLLER TO RESISTOR 73 (MED.)	DK BLUE-WHITE
752	BLOWER MOTOR SPEED CONTROLLER TO RESISTOR 72 (MED.)	YELLOW-RED
753	HEATER & A/C CONTROL SW. TO BLOWER RELAY SW.	YELLOW-RED
754	BLOWER MOTOR SPEED CONTROLLER TO RESISTOR 71 (MED.)	LT GREEN-WHITE
755	BLOWER MOTOR SWITCH RELAY TO RESISTOR (LOW SPEED)	BROWN-WHITE
756	HEATER & A/C CONTROL SW. (HI-NORM) TO RESISTOR (LOW RANGE)	RED-PINK
757	HEATER & A/C CONTROL SW. (HI-NORM) TO BLOWER MOTOR SW. RELAY	RED-WHITE
758	HEATER & A/C CONTROL SW. (HI-NORM) TO RESISTOR (LOW RANGE)	PURPLE-WHITE
759	SENSOR AMPLIFY UNIT TO CONTROL UNIT #3	DK GREEN-WHITE
760	SENSOR AMPLIFY UNIT TO CONTROL UNIT #4	WHITE-PURPLE
761	BLOWER MOTOR RELAY TO ENG. WATER TEMP. SWITCH (COLD)	WHITE-LT GREEN
762	ELECT. SHIFT 4×4 MODULE TO MOTOR POSITION #1	YELLOW-WHITE
763	ELECT. SHIFT 4×4 MODULE TO MOTOR POSITION #2	ORANGE-WHITE
764	ELECT. SHIFT 4×4 MODULE TO MOTOR POSITION #3	BROWN-WHITE
765	HEATER & A/C CONTROL SW. TO REHEAT & A/C FEED	LT GREEN-YELLOW
766	HEATER & A/C CONTROL SW. (DEFOG) TO INLET AIR CONTROL SOLENOID	RED-LT GREEN
767	AMBIENT SENSOR TO INST. PANEL THERMISTOR	LT BLUE-ORANGE
768	REFERENCE SENSOR TO HEAT DUCT THERMISTOR	LT GREEN-WHITE
769	HEATER & A/C CONTROL SW. (HI-LO-NORM) TO BLOWER MOTOR SW. RELAY	LT BLUE-YELLOW
770	ELECT. SHIFT 4×4 MODULE TO MOTOR POSITION #4	WHITE
771	ELECT. SHIFT 4×4 MODULE TO MOTOR POSITION #5	PURPLE-YELLOW
772	ELECT. SHIFT 4×4 MODULE TO SPEED SENSOR COIL	LT BLUE
773	HEATER & A/C CONTROL SW. (TEMP. SELECTOR) TO REHEAT AMPL.	DK GREEN-ORANGE
774	ELECT. SHIFT 4×4 MODULE TO SENSOR RETURN	LT GREEN
775	HEATER & A/C CONTROL SW. (DEFOG) TO DEFROST CONT. SOLENOID	WHITE-PINK
776	CLIMATE CONTROL BOX TO HIGH BLOWER RELAY	ORANGE-BLACK
777	ELECT. SHIFT 4×4 MODULE TO MOTOR CONTROL COUNTERCLOCKWISE	YELLOW
778	ELECT. SHIFT 4×4 MODULE TO MOTOR CONTROL	ORANGE
779	ELECT. SHIFT 4×4 MODULE TO ELECT. CLUTCH	BROWN
780	ELECT. SHIFT MODULE TO 2H 4H SWITCH	DK BLUE
781	ELECT. SHIFT TO 4L SWITCH	ORANGE-LT BLUE
782	ELECT. SHIFT MODULE TO LOW RANGE INDICATOR LAMP ROOF CONSOLE	BROWN-WHITE
783	ELECT. SHIFT MODULE TO GRAPHIC DISPLAY ROOF CONSOLE	GRAY
784	INDICATOR LAMP TO LOW RANGE SWITCH 4×4	LT BLUE-BLACK
785	BATTERY TO MULTIPLEX MODULE	BLACK-LT GREEN
786	FUEL TANK SELECTOR TO FUEL PUMP FRONT	RED
787	FUEL PUMP SAFETY SWITCH TO FUEL PUMP MOTOR	PINK-BLACK
**787	FUEL PUMP POWER	PINK-BLACK
**788	REHEAT AMPLIFIER TO HEAT DUCT THERMISTOR	RED-ORANGE
789	FUEL TANK SELECTOR TO FUEL PUMP REAR	BROWN-WHITE
790	HEATER & A/C CONTROL SW. TO INST. PANEL THERMISTOR	WHITE-ORANGE
791	BATTERY TO MULTIPLEX SYSTEM	BLACK-WHITE
792	MULTIPLEX COMPUTER FEED	TAN-RED
793	LOW WASHER LEVEL TO SENSOR	YELLOW-BLACK
794	LOW COOLANT LEVEL RELAY TO SENSOR	LT BLUE
795	CAM SENSOR TO EEC MODULE	DK GREEN
796	CAM SENDER SIGNAL RETURN	LT BLUE
797	BATTERY FEED TO STEREO	LT GREEN-PURPLE
798	LEFT CHANNEL SIGNAL OUT	LT GREEN-RED
799	RIGHT CHANNEL SIGNAL OUT	ORANGE-BLACK
800	AMPLIFIER/SPEAKER SWITCH FEED TO LEFT REAR SPEAKER	GRAY-LT BLUE
801	AMPLIFIER/SPEAKER SWITCH GROUND TO LEFT REAR SPEAKER	PINK-LT BLUE
802	AMPLIFIER/SPEAKER SWITCH FEED TO RIGHT REAR SPEAKER	ORANGE-RED

CIRCUIT	DESCRIPTION*	COLOR
803	AMPLIFIER/SPEAKER SWITCH GROUND TO RIGHT REAR SPEAKER	DK GREEN-ORANGE
804	SPEAKER VOICE COIL FEED—FRONT (LEFT CHANNEL)	ORANGE-LT GREEN
805	SPEAKER VOICE COIL FEED—FRONT (RIGHT CHANNEL)	WHITE-LT GREEN
806	SPEAKER VOICE COIL FEED—REAR (RIGHT CHANNEL)	PINK-LT BLUE
807	SPEAKER VOICE COIL FEED—REAR (LEFT CHANNEL)	PINK-LT GREEN
810	STOPLAMP SW. TO STOPLAMPS	RED-LT GREEN
811	SPEAKER SWITCH GROUND TO RIGHT FRONT SPEAKER	DK GREEN-ORANGE
812	SPEAKER SWITCH FEED TO RIGHT FRONT SPEAKER	PINK-ORANGE
813	SPEAKER SWITCH GROUND TO LEFT FRONT SPEAKER	LT BLUE-WHITE
814	SPEAKER SWITCH FEED TO LEFT FRONT SPEAKER	PINK-WHITE
815	AMPLIFIER SWITCH GROUND TO RIGHT FRONT SPEAKER	LT GREEN-ORANGE
816	AMPLIFIER SWITCH FEED TO RIGHT FRONT SPEAKER	LT GREEN-PURPLE
817	INDICATOR RELAY TO R.H. TURN LAMP	TAN-LT BLUE
818	INDICATOR RELAY TO L.H. TURN LAMP	TAN-WHITE
819	AMPLIFIER SWITCH GROUND TO LEFT FRONT SPEAKER	LT GREEN-WHITE
820	AMPLIFIER SWITCH FEED TO LEFT FRONT SPEAKER	DK BLUE-YELLOW
822	SPEAKER VOICE COIL FEED	BLACK-LT GREEN
823	RADIO TO FADER CONTROL	LT GREEN
824	AMPLIFIER SWITCH GROUND TO RIGHT REAR SPEAKER	WHITE-PURPLE
825	AMPLIFIER SWITCH FEED TO RIGHT REAR SPEAKER	TAN-LT GREEN
826	AMPLIFIER SWITCH GROUND TO LEFT REAR SPEAKER	DK BLUE-ORANGE
827	AMPLIFIER SWITCH FEED TO LEFT REAR SPEAKER	TAN-WHITE
828	POWER FEED-SWITCH TO REAR AMPLIFIER	PURPLE-LT BLUE
829	POWER FEED-SWITCH TO FRONT AMPLIFIER	WHITE-PURPLE
830	SWITCH TO FADER RIGHT CHANNEL FEED	PINK-YELLOW
831	SWITCH TO FADER LEFT CHANNEL FEED	TAN
832	MODE SELECT SWITCH FEED	BROWN-LT GREEN
833	MODE SELECT SWITCH LAMP	RED-BLACK
834	ELECTRONIC RIDE CONTROL DAMPENING SENSOR A	RED-YELLOW
835	ELECTRONIC RIDE CONTROL DAMPENING SENSOR B	RED-WHITE
836	SENSOR	ORANGE-WHITE
837	SENSOR RETURN	YELLOW-BLACK
838	ELECTRONIC RIDE CONTROL DAMPENING HARD CONTROL	LT GREEN-PURPLE
839	ELECTRONIC SHOCK SOFT CONTROL	LT GREEN-WHITE
840	ACTUATOR POSITION SENSOR LEFT FRONT	WHITE-BLACK
841	ACTUATOR POSITION SENSOR RIGHT FRONT	WHITE-RED
842	ACTUATOR POSITION SENSOR LEFT REAR	WHITE-ORANGE
843	ACTUATOR POSITION SENSOR RIGHT REAR	WHITE
844	ELECTRONIC SHOCK DIAGNOSTIC	GRAY-RED
845	ELECTRONIC SHOCK FEEDBACK ACTUATOR TO RELAY	TAN-BLACK
846	ELECTRONIC SHOCK METAL OXIDE VARISTOR	TAN-RED
847	DECELERATION SENSOR	ORANGE-LT GREEN
848	PROCESSOR LOOP SIGNAL RETURN	DK GREEN-ORANGE
849	DIGITAL AUDIO DISCRIMINATOR DISC LOGIC SENSE	TAN-BLACK
850	COIL "A" TO DISTRIBUTORLESS IGNITION MODULE	YELLOW-BLACK
851	COIL "B" TO DISTRIBUTORLESS IGNITION MODULE	YELLOW-RED
852	COIL "C" TO DISTRIBUTORLESS IGNITION MODULE	YELLOW-WHITE
853	HEATED WINDSHIELD SENSE TO RESISTOR	BROWN
854	THIRD GEAR LOCKOUT SOLENOID	GRAY-WHITE
855	RIGHT REAR AMP INPUT RETURN	LT BLUE
856	LEFT CHANNEL SIGNAL IN	PURPLE
857	LEFT FRONT AMP INPUT RETURN	WHITE-ORANGE
858	RIGHT FRONT AMP INPUT RETURN	BROWN
859	LEFT REAR AMP INPUT RETURN	YELLOW
860	LEFT MOTOR-DRIVER—F	PURPLE-YELLOW
**860	LEFT MOTOR-DRIVER—A	PURPLE—YELLOW
861	LEFT MOTOR-DRIVER—R	BLACK-WHITE
**861	LEFT MOTOR-DRIVER—B	BLACK-WHITE
862	LEFT LIMIT-A—DRIVER	BROWN-YELLOW
863	RIGHT DOOR OPEN—PASSENGER	RED
864	RIGHT MOTOR-PASSENGER—F	ORANGE
**864	RIGHT MOTOR-PASSENGER — A	ORANGE
865	RIGHT MOTOR-PASSENGER—R	PURPLE-WHITE
**865	RIGHT MOTOR-PASSENGER — B	PURPLE-WHITE
866	INERTIA SWITCH TO WINDOW	WHITE
867	LEFT DOOR OPEN — DRIVER	DK BLUE
868	EMERGENCY RELEASE LEVERS	GRAY-RED
869	RETARD VALVE TO CONTROL RELAY TERM. #1	LT GREEN-YELLOW
871	SEAT BELT INDICATOR LAMP TO MODULE	YELLOW
872	LEFT LIMIT-B — DRIVER	LT GREEN
873	RIGHT LIMIT-B — PASSENGER	TAN
874	RIGHT LIMIT-A — PASSENGER	GRAY
875	GROUND LOGIC MODULE	BLACK-LT BLUE
876	VENT SWITCH TO RIGHT FRONT VENT — CONSOLE	BLACK-ORANGE
*876	VENT SWITCH TO RIGHT FRONT VENT MOTOR	BLACK-ORANGE
877	RELEASE LEVER WARN INDICATOR LAMP — CONSOLE	WHITE-ORANGE
878	VENT SWITCH TO RIGHT FRONT VENT MOTOR	BLACK-LT BLUE
879	VENT CROSSOVER FEED	RED-BLACK
880	VENT CROSSOVER FEED	RED-LT BLUE
881	WINDOW SWITCH TO RIGHT REAR MOTOR	BROWN
882	WINDOW SWITCH TO RIGHT REAR MOTOR	BROWN-YELLOW
883	AIR COND. CONTROL RELAY FEED	PINK-LT BLUE
884	WINDOW SWITCH TO LEFT REAR MOTOR	YELLOW-BLACK
885	WINDOW SWITCH TO LEFT REAR MOTOR	YELLOW-LT BLUE
886	VENT SWITCH TO LEFT FRONT VENT MOTOR	ORANGE-WHITE
887	VENT SWITCH TO LEFT FRONT VENT MOTOR	YELLOW
888	MEMORY MIRROR MODULE TO R.H. HORIZONTAL DRIVER	LT BLUE
889	MEMORY MIRROR MODULE MOTOR DIRECTION	BLACK-ORANGE
890	MEMORY MIRROR MODULE TO R.H. VERTICAL DRIVE	BROWN-WHITE
891	MEMORY MIRROR MODULE POSITION +	RED-BLACK
892	MEMORY MIRROR MODULE R.H. HORIZONTAL POSITION	ORANGE
893	MEMORY MIRROR MODULE R.H. VERTICAL POSITION–	LT BLUE-BLACK
894	MEMORY MIRROR MODULE VERTICAL POSITION	GRAY
895	MEMORY MIRROR MODULE	WHITE-PURPLE
**895	MEMORY MIRROR MODULE L.H. VERTICAL POSITION	WHITE-PURPLE
896	MEMORY MIRROR MODULE L.H. HORIZONTAL POSITION	PINK-ORANGE
897	MEMORY MIRROR MODULE TO L.H. VERTICAL DRIVE	TAN-BLACK

* IN SOME CASES, THERE MAY BE ADDITIONAL CIRCUIT FUNCTIONS INCLUDED IN THE CIRCUIT DESCRIPTION LISTED.

** DENOTES A NEW OR STANDARDIZED CIRCUIT.

STANDARD CIRCUIT CHART (BY NUMBER)

CIRCUIT	DESCRIPTION *	COLOR	CIRCUIT	DESCRIPTION *	COLOR
898	MEMORY MIRROR MODULE TO L.H. HORIZONTAL DRIVE	TAN-RED	**945	MIRROR SWITCH COMMON	YELLOW-BLACK
899	MEMORY SEAT TO NEUTRAL SENSOR SWITCH	RED-WHITE	946	REAR WASHER PUMP FEED	PURPLE-LT GREEN
**899	MEMORY SEAT TO NEUTRAL SENSE MODULE	RED-WHITE	**947	L.H. MIRROR LEFT/RIGHT MOTOR COMMON	YELLOW-RED
900	STARTER INTERRUPT RELAY TO NEUTRAL START SWITCH	WHITE-LT BLUE	**948	L.H. UP/DOWN MOTOR COMMON	YELLOW-LT BLUE
901	AMPLIFIER TO SPEED SENSOR RETURN	RED-LT BLUE	**949	L.H. MIRROR LEFT/RIGHT POSITION SENSOR	RED-WHITE
902	TOP CONTROL RELAY TO MOTOR — UP	YELLOW	950	WASHER CONTROL SWITCH FEED	WHITE-BLACK
903	TOP CONTROL RELAY TO MOTOR — DOWN	RED	**951	L.H. MIRROR UP/DOWN POSITION SENSOR	DK BLUE-WHITE
904	(COIL) OR (ACCY.) TERM. OF IGNITION SWITCH TO ALTERNATOR REGULATOR (IGN. TERM.)	LT GREEN-RED	**952	R.H. MIRROR LEFT/RIGHT MOTOR COMMON	WHITE-LT GREEN
905	VEHICLE MAINTENANCE MONITOR MODULE TO OIL TEMP. INPUT	LT BLUE	**953	R.H. MIRROR UP/DOWN MOTOR COMMON	WHITE-PURPLE
906	VEHICLE MAINTENANCE MONITOR MODULE TO OIL TEMP. OUTPUT	WHITE-LT BLUE	**954	R.H. MIRROR LEFT/RIGHT POSITION SENSOR	DK GREEN-WHITE
907	VEHICLE MAINTENANCE MONITOR MODULE TO ELEC. INSTR. CLUST. SENSE	PURPLE-LT GREEN	955	W/S WIPER MOTOR ARM RH TO W/S WIPER SWITCH	RED-ORANGE
908	VEHICLE MAINTENANCE MONITOR MODULE TO ENGINE STRAP	TAN-BLACK	956	W/S WIPER SWITCH TO W/S WIPER MOTOR FIELD R.H.	LT GREEN-ORANGE
909	VEHICLE MAINTENANCE MONITOR MODULE TO SPEED SENSOR	LT BLUE-WHITE	**957	R.H. MIRROR UP/DOWN POSITION SENSOR	PURPLE-WHITE
910	FUSED ACCY. FEED — TRIPMINDER	BLACK-WHITE	**958	MIRROR POSITION SENSOR FEED	GRAY-RED
911	OVERDRIVE CANCEL INDICATOR LAMP	LT GREEN-WHITE	**959	MIRROR POSITION SENSOR COMMON	GRAY
**911	OVERDRIVE CANCEL INDICATOR LAMP	WHITE-LT GREEN	**960	CLUSTER GAGE ROUND	BLACK-LT BLUE
912	EEC MODULE TO TRANSMISSION |	LT BLUE-WHITE	**961	TRACTION CONTROL MALFUNCTION WARNING LAMP	RED-LT GREEN
**912	EEC MODULE TO TRANSMISSION	WHITE-RED	**962	TRAILER RUNNING LAMPS	BROWN-WHITE
913	LIFTGATE SW. TO LIFTGATE RELAY	GRAY-RED	**963	TRAILER BACKUP LAMPS	RED-YELLOW
914	EEC MODULE — DATA PLUS	TAN-ORANGE	**964	FUSED ACCESSORY #4	DK BLUE-LT GREEN
915	EEC MODULE — DATA MINUS	PINK-LT BLUE	965	SUPERCHARGER SOLENOID #1	LT GREEN-PURPLE
**915	DATA LINK RETURN	PINK-LT BLUE	966	SUPERCHARGER SOLENOID #2	RED-YELLOW
916	SPEED CONTROL VACUUM TO EEC MODULE	LT GREEN	967	MASS AIR FLOW	DK BLUE-ORANGE
917	VENT SWITCH TO BLOWER MOTOR — LO	PINK-LT GREEN	**967	MASS AIR FLOW SIGNAL	LT BLUE-RED
918	SEAT REG. SW. TO RECLINER MOTOR — UP	GRAY	968	MASS AIR FLOW RETURN	TAN-LT BLUE
919	SEAT REG. SW. TO RECLINER MOTOR — DOWN	GRAY-BLACK	969	MASS AIR FLOW GROUND	BLACK
920	HEATED WINDSHIELD LH TO SENSE RESISTOR	BROWN-WHITE	970	TRANSMISSION TURBINE SPEED SENSOR	PURPLE
921	FEED TO FUEL SHUTOFF LAMP	GRAY-ORANGE	**971	TRANSMISSION SHIFT SOLENOID #3	BROWN
922	FUEL PUMP RESISTOR TO RELAY	WHITE-RED	**972	AWD MODULE POWER FEED	BLACK-WHITE
923	TRANSMISSION OIL TEMP.	ORANGE-BLACK	973	BATTERY FEED TO AUX. FUEL SELECTOR SWITCH	RED
924	COAST CLUTCH SOLENOID	BROWN	974	FUEL CONTROL SWITCH TO FUEL CONTROL VALVE	ORANGE
**924	COAST CLUTCH SOLENOID	BROWN-ORANGE	**975	AWD MODULE TO TRANSFER CASE CLUTCH RELAY	BROWN-YELLOW
925	ELECTRONIC THROTTLE VALVE POWER	YELLOW-WHITE	**976	AWD MODULE TO TRANSFER CASE CLUTCH RELAY COIL	ORANGE
**925	ELECTRONIC PRESSURE CONTROL	WHITE-YELLOW	977	BRAKE WARNING SWITCH TO INDICATOR LAMP	PURPLE-WHITE
926	EEC MODULE CONTROL OF HIGH SPEED FUEL PUMP	LT BLUE-ORANGE	978	SEAT REGULATOR SWITCH TO FRONT MOTOR (LH)	YELLOW-LT BLUE
**926	FUEL PUMP RELAY CONTROL	LT BLUE-ORANGE	979	SEAT REGULATOR SWITCH TO FRONT MOTOR (LH)	RED-LT BLUE
927	EVO MODULE TO TEST CONNECTOR	ORANGE-BLACK	980	SEAT REGULATOR SWITCH TO HORZ. MOTOR (LH)	YELLOW-WHITE
928	POWER FEED FROM AMPLIFIER	PURPLE	981	SEAT REGULATOR SWITCH TO HORZ. MOTOR (LH)	RED-WHITE
929	EEC MODULE TO SPARK ADVANCE	PINK	982	SEAT REGULATOR SWITCH TO REAR MOTOR (LH)	YELLOW-LT GREEN
**929	SPARK OUTPUT SIGNAL FROM TFI MODULE	PINK	983	SEAT REGULATOR SWITCH TO REAR MOTOR (LH)	RED-LT GREEN
930	PROGRAMMABLE RIDE CONTROL MODULE TO STAR TEST CONNECTOR	DK BLUE	984	SEAT REGULATOR SWITCH TO FRONT MOTOR (RH)	YELLOW-LT BLUE
931	BATTERY FEED TO RELAY CONTROLLER	ORANGE	985	SEAT REGULATOR SWITCH TO FRONT MOTOR (RH)	RED-LT BLUE
932	DAYTIME RUNNING LAMP	GRAY-WHITE	986	SEAT REGULATOR SWITCH TO FRONT MOTOR (RH)	YELLOW-WHITE
933	ESC SWITCH TO ESC VALVE CONTROL	LT GREEN-BLACK	987	SEAT REGULATOR SWITCH TO HORZ. MOTOR (RH)	RED-WHITE
934	EMISSION SPEED SENSOR TO MODULATOR CONTROL	TAN-WHITE	988	SEAT REGULATOR SWITCH TO REAR MOTOR (RH)	YELLOW-LT GREEN
935	HEATED WINDSHIELD TO FUSE	DK BLUE-YELLOW	989	SEAT REGULATOR SWITCH TO REAR MOTOR (RH)	RED-LT GREEN
936	KEY CYLINDER SENSOR TO ANTI-THEFT MODULE	DK GREEN-WHITE	990	SEAT REGULATOR SWITCH TO FRONT MOTOR (LH)	YELLOW-LT BLUE
**937	FUSED BATTERY FEED TO AIR BAG DIAGNOSTIC MODULE	RED-WHITE	**991	AWD SAFETY LAMP RELAY COIL	ORANGE-BLACK
**938	LOGIC GROUND	BLACK-LT GREEN	**992	AWD MODULE TO TRANSFER CASE CLUTCH	YELLOW-BLACK
939	MODULATOR TO THERMO. SWITCH	TAN-BLACK	993	INTERMITTENT GOVERNOR TO WINDSHIELD WIPER SWITCH	BROWN-WHITE
**940	MIRROR SWITCH VERTICAL LEFT	DK BLUE-ORANGE	**994	AWD MODULE TO AWD FUNCTION LAMP	WHITE
941	WASHER PUMP MOTOR FEED	BLACK-WHITE	**995	ABS MODULE DIFFERENTIAL SHIFT LOCK #1 OUTPUT	DK BLUE-WHITE
**942	MIRROR SWITCH HORIZONTAL LEFT	RED-ORANGE	**996	ABS MODULE REAR LEFT WHEEL SPEED OUTPUT	GRAY-BLACK
**943	MIRROR SWITCH VERTICAL RIGHT	PURPLE-ORANGE	**997	ABS MODULE FRONT RIGHT WHEEL SPEED OUTPUT	PINK
**944	MIRROR SWITCH HORIZONTAL RIGHT	DK GREEN-ORANGE	**998	ABS MODULE FRONT LEFT WHEEL SPEED OUTPUT	TAN
			**999	ABS MODULE REAR RIGHT WHEEL SPEED OUTPUT	TAN-BLACK
			**1000	TRANSFER CASE CLUTCH RELAY TO TRANSFER CASE CLUTCH	LT GREEN

* IN SOME CASES, THERE MAY BE ADDITIONAL CIRCUIT
FUNCTIONS INCLUDED IN THE CIRCUIT DESCRIPTION LISTED.

** DENOTES A NEW OR STANDARDIZED CIRCUIT.

STANDARD CIRCUIT CHART (BY COLOR)

COLOR	DESCRIPTION*	CIRCUIT
(COLOR OPT.)	BLIND CIRCUIT TERM. IN HARNESS CANNOT BE CHECKED FOR CONT.	48
BLACK	GROUND CIRCUIT	57
BLACK	MARKER LAMP SWITCH TO MARKER LAMPS	207
BLACK	16 GA FUSE LINK	291
BLACK	HEATED WINDSHIELD GROUND TEST LEAD	739
BLACK	DOOR WIRE	629
BLACK	DCP MODULE SIGNAL GROUND TO RADIO	596
BLACK	MASS AIR FLOW GROUND	969
BLACK	ELECTRONIC CLUSTER FROM GROUND IN KEYBOARD	373
BLACK-LT BLUE	DOOR AJAR SWITCH TO INDICATOR LAMP LEFT REAR GROUND	363
BLACK-LT BLUE	DIESEL CONTROL MODULE GROUND RETURN	488
BLACK-LT BLUE	AIR TEMP SENSOR TO CONTROL UNIT	743
BLACK-LT BLUE	VENT SWITCH TO RIGHT FRONT VENT MOTOR	878
BLACK-LT BLUE	GROUND LOGIC MODULE	875
** BLACK-LT BLUE	CLUSTER GAUGE GROUND	960
BLACK-LT BLUE	COURTESY LAMP SWITCH TO COURTESY LAMP	53
BLACK-LT BLUE	WARNING LAMP PROVE OUT	41
BLACK-LT BLUE	COURTESY LAMP SW. TO "C" PILLAR LAMPS	127
BLACK-LT GREEN	KEYLESS DOOR LOCK ILLUMINATION GROUND TO MODULE	76
BLACK-LT GREEN	CONSTANT VOLTAGE UNIT TO GAUGE	60
BLACK-LT GREEN	CONSTANT VOLTAGE UNIT AND INDICATOR LAMPS FEED	30
BLACK-LT GREEN	ACCY FEED FROM IGNITION SWITCH	297
BLACK-LT GREEN	COLD START INJECTOR	230
** BLACK-LT GREEN	LOGIC GROUND	938
BLACK-LT GREEN	BATTERY TO MULTIPLEX MODULE	785
BLACK-LT GREEN	BLOWER MOTOR RELAY (LOAD TERM) TO BLOWER MOTOR	536
BLACK-LT GREEN	SPEAKER VOICE COIL FEED	822
BLACK-LT GREEN	BLOWER MOTOR RELAY FEED	364
BLACK-LT GREEN	POWER RELAY TO GLOW PLUGS (RIGHT BANK)	336
BLACK-ORANGE	FUEL 1 GROUND TO TACH/GAUGE MODULE	396
BLACK-ORANGE	REMOTE CONVENIENCE SELF DIAGNOSTIC GROUND	571
BLACK-ORANGE	HEATED WINDSHIELD CONTROL TO ELECT ALTERNATOR REGULATOR	579
BLACK-ORANGE	CENTER REAR TAILLAMP BULB OUTAGE	573
BLACK-ORANGE	OPEN DOOR WARNING LAMP TO OPEN DOOR WARNING SWITCH	627
BLACK-ORANGE	MULTIPLEX WINDSHIELD WIPER OFF	695
BLACK-ORANGE	VENT SWITCH TO RIGHT FRONT VENT—CONSOLE	876
BLACK-ORANGE	MEMORY MIRROR MODULE MOTOR DIRECTION	889
** BLACK-ORANGE	VENT SWITCH TO RIGHT FRONT VENT MOTOR	876
BLACK-ORANGE	ELEC. ENG. CONTROL MOD. TO THIN FILM IGN. MOD.	259
BLACK-ORANGE	MEMORY SEAT SWITCH POSITION #2	268
BLACK-ORANGE	DIESEL WATER IN FUEL SENDER TO WARNING LAMP GROUND	327
BLACK-ORANGE	POWER SUPPLY TO BATTERY	38
BLACK-ORANGE	ENGINE COMPARTMENT LAMP FEED	80
BLACK-ORANGE	COURTESY LAMP SW. TO INSTR. PANEL COURTESY LAMP	126
BLACK-PINK	KEY WARNING SWITCH TO BUZZER	158
BLACK-PINK	BACKUP LAMP	140
BLACK-PINK	CARGO LAMP SW. TO CARGO LAMP	55
BLACK-PINK	WINDSHIELD WIPER SW. TO WINDSHIELD WIPER MOTOR	28
BLACK-PINK	ECU TO VACUUM SWITCH 4	211
BLACK-PINK	AIR SUSPENSION ELECTRONICS GROUND	432
BLACK-PINK	HCU (MAIN) TO MODULE	493
BLACK-PINK	MODULE TO LIGHT	464
BLACK-PINK	DOOR AJAR SWITCH TO INDICATOR LAMP RIGHT FRONT GROUND	345
BLACK-PINK	DOOR AJAR SWITCH TO INDICATOR LAMP RIGHT REAR GROUND	346
BLACK-WHITE	SENSOR SIGNAL RETURN	359
BLACK-WHITE	SIGNAL GROUND TO TACH/GAUGE MODULE	397
BLACK-WHITE	LEFT MOTOR—DRIVER—R	861
BLACK-WHITE	ANTI-LOCK MODULE TO ANTI-LOCK CONTROL VALVE	685
BLACK-WHITE	BATTERY TO MULTIPLEX SYSTEM	791
** BLACK-WHITE	AWD MODULE POWER FEED	972
BLACK-WHITE	WINDSHIELD WIPER INTERMITTENT GOVERNOR FEED	587
BLACK-WHITE	DEDICATED GROUND	570
BLACK-WHITE	SPEED SIGNAL SPEEDO TACH MODULE TO FUEL COMPUTER	565
BLACK-WHITE	CIRCUIT BREAKER (LOAD TERM) TO CONTROL SWITCH (BATT. TERM)	517
BLACK-WHITE	CORNERING LAMP SWITCH FEED	526
BLACK-WHITE	WASHER PUMP MOTOR FEED	941
BLACK-WHITE	FUSED ACCY FEED—TRIPMINDER	910
** BLACK-WHITE	LEFT MOTOR—DRIVER—B	861
BLACK-WHITE	CIRCUIT BREAKER TO SEAT LATCH RELAY	171
BLACK-WHITE	SPEAKER VOICE COIL RETURN	287
BLACK-WHITE	SEAT REG. CONTROL SWITCH FEED	51
BLACK-WHITE	INSTRUMENT PANEL LAMP SWITCH FEED	88
BLACK-YELLOW	WARNING LAMP TO LIGHTS ON RELAY	111
BLACK-YELLOW	WARNING LAMP FEED	112
BLACK-YELLOW	ACCESSORY FEED TO MESSAGE CENTER	231
BLACK-YELLOW	EFE CARBURETOR SPACE FEED	229
BLACK-YELLOW	RELAY FEED	175
BLACK-YELLOW	INJECTION PUMP FUEL TEMPERATURE SENSOR	225
BLACK-YELLOW	AIR BAG DIAGNOSTIC MODULE TO RELAY INDICATOR LAMP	608
BLACK-YELLOW	DIESEL TACH GROUND TO TACH GAGE MODULE	644
BLACK-YELLOW	TACHOMETER GROUND TO TACH/GAUGE MODULE	398
BLACK-YELLOW	DOOR AJAR SWITCH TO INDICATOR LAMP LEFT FRONT GROUND	344
BLACK-YELLOW	COMPRESSOR CLUTCH FEED	347
BROWN	DOOR AJAR RELAY TO DOOR SWITCH	374
BROWN	POWER "THIGH" BOLSTER DOWN	492
BROWN	STEERING RATE SENSOR TERMINAL B CONTROL MODULE	634
BROWN	FUEL SIGNAL TACH MODULE TO FUEL COMPUTER	564
BROWN	HEATED WINDSHIELD CONTROL TO ALT POWER RELAY	580
BROWN	ELECT SHIFT 4 × 4 MODULE TO ELECT CLUTCH	779
BROWN	MULTIPLEX HEADLAMPS	697
** BROWN	TRANSMISSION SHIFT SOLENOID #3	971
BROWN	C.B. D-DIGIT	708
BROWN	COAST CLUTCH SOLENOID	924
BROWN	EATC LH SUNLOAD SENSOR POSITIVE	468
BROWN	WINDOW SWITCH TO RIGHT REAR MOTOR	881
BROWN	HEATED WINDSHIELD FUSE RESISTOR	853
BROWN	RIGHT FRONT AIR INPUT RETURN	858
BROWN	TO ELECTRONIC CLUSTER FROM ENGLISH/METRIC SWITCH IN KEYBOARD	273
BROWN	FEEDBACK CARBURETOR COIL "A"	304
BROWN	SWITCH FEED	276
BROWN	18 GA FUSE LINK	292
BROWN	KEYLESS DOOR LOCK SWITCH ENABLE FROM MODULE	124
BROWN	HEADLAMP SWITCH TO TAIL LAMPS & SIDE MARKER LAMPS	14
** BROWN	THERMACTOR AIR DIVERTER (TAD)	200
BROWN-LT BLUE	DOOR JAMB SWITCH TO LIGHTS ON RELAY	138
BROWN-LT BLUE	LH HEADLAMP BULB OUTAGE	108
BROWN-LT BLUE	SEAT BELT WARNING TIMER TO L.F. RETRACTOR SWITCH	85
BROWN-LT BLUE	FUEL METERING CONTROL LEVER ACTUATOR 1 MINUS	232
BROWN-LT BLUE	DEFOGGER SW. TO DEFOGGER MOTOR	186
BROWN-LT BLUE	FUEL INJECTOR #4 CYLINDER	558
BROWN-LT GREEN	DCP MODULE TO WIPER PARK OVER-RIDE RELAY	592
BROWN-LT GREEN	MODE SELECT SWITCH FEED	832
BROWN-LT GREEN	EGR VALVE POSITION FEED	352
BROWN-LT GREEN	AUTOLAMP AMPLIFIER TO SENSOR	222
BROWN-LT GREEN	POWER SERVO TO CLIMATE CONTROL UNIT (AMP)	245
BROWN-LT GREEN	MEMORY SEAT SWITCH POSITION #1	267
BROWN-LT GREEN	SERVO FEEDBACK POTENTIOMETER BASE TO AMPLIFIER	149
** BROWN-LT GREEN	EGR FEEDBACK	352
BROWN-ORANGE	VACUUM DOOR LOCK SWITCH TO SOLENOID (UNLOCK)	116
BROWN-ORANGE	MEMORY SEAT SWITCH SET	270
BROWN-ORANGE	IGNITION SWITCH TO THERMACTOR TIMER	251
BROWN-ORANGE	BLOWER MOTOR FEED	181
BROWN-ORANGE	VACUUM SOLENOID TO TEMP. SW.	369
** BROWN-ORANGE	COAST CLUTCH SOLENOID	924
BROWN-ORANGE	RADIO MEMORY SEEK	372
BROWN-ORANGE	RADIO SWITCH TO ANTENNA RELAY	449
BROWN-PINK	AIR SUSPENSION HEIGHT SENSOR LO—R.F.	425
BROWN-PINK	DIESEL CONTROL SWITCH TO LAMP CONTROL RELAY	338
BROWN-PINK	IGNITION SWITCH ACCY TERM. TO DECK LID OPEN WARNING LAMP	485
BROWN-PINK	POWER RELAY COIL TO MODULE	513
BROWN-PINK	STARTING MOTOR RELAY TO IGNITION COIL "I" TERM.	262
** BROWN-PINK	EGR VALVE REGULATOR SOLENOID TO EEC MODULE	360
BROWN-WHITE	THERMOSTAT SWITCH FEED	182
BROWN-WHITE	HEADLAMP SWITCH TO ELECTRONIC CLUSTER DIMMING	192
BROWN-WHITE	FLUID WARNING SWITCH TO PRESSURE SWITCH	549
BROWN-WHITE	EXTENDED USEFUL LIFE SENSOR TO WARNING LAMP	574
BROWN-WHITE	SELECTOR SWITCH TO AUX. FUEL SOLENOID	674
BROWN-WHITE	ELECT SHIFT 4 × 4 MODULE TO MOTOR POSITION #3	764
BROWN-WHITE	ELECT SHIFT MODULE TO LOW RANGE INDICATOR LAMP ROOF CONSOLE	782
BROWN-WHITE	MULTIPLEX LCD ILLUMINATION	732
BROWN-WHITE	BLOWER MOTOR SWITCH RELAY TO RESISTOR (LOW SPEED)	755
** BROWN-WHITE	TRAILER RUNNING LAMPS	962
BROWN-WHITE	FUEL TANK SELECTOR TO FUEL PUMP REAR	789
BROWN-WHITE	INTERMITTENT GOVERNOR TO WINDSHIELD WIPER SWITCH	993
BROWN-WHITE	HEATED WINDSHIELD LH TO SENSE RESISTOR	920
BROWN-WHITE	DECK LID OPEN WARNING LAMP TO DECK LID OPEN SWITCH	486
BROWN-WHITE	MEMORY MIRROR MODULE TO RH VERTICAL DRIVE	890
BROWN-WHITE	TURN SIGNAL SWITCH TO RH CORNERING LAMP	379
BROWN-WHITE	ELECT. ENG. CONTL. MOD. TO IDLE SPD. CONTL. MOTOR #3	376
** BROWN-WHITE	POWER TO ENGINE SENSORS	351
BROWN-YELLOW	HEATER BLOWER SWITCH FEED	399
BROWN-YELLOW	LEFT LIMIT-A—DRIVER	862
BROWN-YELLOW	WINDOW SWITCH TO RIGHT REAR MOTOR	882
** BROWN-YELLOW	AWD MODULE TO TRANSFER CASE CLUTCH RELAY	975
BROWN-YELLOW	EATC LH SUNLOAD SENSOR NEGATIVE	476
BROWN-YELLOW	DCP MODULE TO WASHER RELAY	591
BROWN-YELLOW	FUEL INJECTOR #3 CYLINDER	557
BROWN-YELLOW	ELECTRIC DRIVE COOLING FAN	228
BROWN-YELLOW	MAP LAMP SWITCH TO RH MAP LAMP	125
BROWN-YELLOW	EMISSION CONTROL VALVE TO SWITCH	81
BROWN-YELLOW	BATTERY TO HI-BEAM	62
DK BLUE	HORN SWITCH CONTROL	1
DK BLUE	20 GA FUSE LINK	302
** DK BLUE	AUXILIARY CIRCUIT FEED TO TRACTOR TRAILER PLUG	212
DK BLUE	L.H. REMOTE MIRROR MOTOR FEED—C.C.W.	541
DK BLUE	FEED TO FAILURE SWITCH	600
DK BLUE	ELECT SHIFT MODULE TO 2H 4H SWITCH	780
** DK BLUE	ELECTRIC DRIVE COOLING FAN (SINGLE OR LOW)	228
DK BLUE	MOONROOF RELAY TO MICRO SWITCH OPEN	691
DK BLUE	SHOCK DAMPENING RELAY SOFT TO SHOCK DAMPENING CONTROL	653
DK BLUE	LOGIC MODE	689
DK BLUE	PROGRAMMABLE RIDE CONTROL MODULE TO STAR TEST CONNECTOR	930
DK BLUE	LEFT DOOR OPEN—DRIVER	867
DK BLUE	CRANKSHAFT POSITION SENSOR FEED	349
** DK BLUE	TRAILER BRAKES	43
DK BLUE-LT GREEN	WARNING LAMP TO ANTI-THEFT MODULE	343
DK BLUE-LT GREEN	BAROMETRIC PRESSURE SENSOR FEED	356
** DK BLUE-LT GREEN	FUSED ACCESSORY #4	964
DK BLUE-LT GREEN	C.B. SPEAKER VOICE COIL RETURN	721
DK BLUE-LT GREEN	HEATER & A/C CONTROL SW. (LO-NORM) TO CLIMATE CONTROL UNIT	249
DK BLUE-LT GREEN	BUFFER FUEL LEVEL OUTPUT TO TRIPMINDER	205
DK BLUE-LT GREEN	THERMOCOUPLE POS TO EXHAUST SYST. OVERTEMP PROTECT MODULE	90
DK BLUE-ORANGE	ANTI-THEFT SWITCH ARM	24
DK BLUE-ORANGE	WINDSHIELD WIPER SW. TO WINDSHIELD WIPER MOTOR	56
DK BLUE-ORANGE	AUTOLAMP AMPLIFIER TO RHEOSTAT	217
DK BLUE-ORANGE	HEADLAMP FLASH TO PASS SWITCH FEED	196
** DK BLUE-ORANGE	MIRROR SWITCH VERTICAL LEFT	940
DK BLUE-ORANGE	AMPLIFIER SWITCH GROUND TO LEFT REAR SPEAKER	826
DK BLUE-ORANGE	MASS AIR FLOW	967
DK BLUE-ORANGE	CRANK ENABLE TO IGNITION MODULE	325
DK BLUE-WHITE	R.F. DOOR UNLOCK SWITCH TO L.F. DOOR UNLOCK SWITCH	390

* IN SOME CASES, THERE MAY BE ADDITIONAL CIRCUIT FUNCTIONS INCLUDED IN THE CIRCUIT DESCRIPTION LISTED.

** DENOTES A NEW OR STANDARDIZED CIRCUIT.

STANDARD CIRCUIT CHART (BY COLOR)

COLOR	DESCRIPTION*	CIRCUIT
DK BLUE-WHITE	BLOWER MOTOR SPEED CONTROLLER TO RESISTOR #3 (MED.)	751
DK BLUE-WHITE	MULTIPLEX MESSAGE O	735
** DK BLUE-WHITE	ABS MODULE DIFFERENTIAL SHIFT LOCK #1 OUTPUT	995
DK BLUE-WHITE	INTERMITTENT GOVERNOR TO W/S WIPER SWITCH	590
DK BLUE-WHITE	AIR BAG DIAGNOSTIC MODULE SAFING SENSOR (GROUND)	613
DK BLUE-WHITE	FUSE HOLDER TO HEADLAMP DIMMER AMPLIFIER	504
** DK BLUE-WHITE	LH MIRROR UP/DOWN POSITION SENSOR	951
DK BLUE-WHITE	THERMOMETER AMBIENT SENSOR RETURN	234
DK BLUE-WHITE	SEAT BELT WARNING TIMER TO R.F. SEAT SENSOR	86
DK BLUE-YELLOW	ELECTRONIC CONTROL UNIT TO SOLENOID ACTUATOR	77
DK BLUE-YELLOW	DEFOGGER SW. TO DEFOGGER MOTOR	191
DK BLUE-YELLOW	THERMOMETER SENSOR FEED	233
DK BLUE-YELLOW	SELECTOR SWITCH TO MIDSHIP TANK	673
DK BLUE-YELLOW	AMPLIFIER SWITCH FEED TO LEFT FRONT SPEAKER	820
DK BLUE-YELLOW	HEATED WINDSHIELD TO FUSE	935
DK BLUE-YELLOW	AIR COMPRESSOR POWER RELAY CONTROL	420
DK GREEN	REARVIEW OUTSIDE MIRROR DOWN	411
DK GREEN	EGR VALVE TO EEC MODULE	360
DK GREEN	CAM SENSOR TO EEC MODULE	795
DK GREEN	STOPLAMP SWITCH TO HI MOUNT STOPLAMP	569
DK GREEN	REAR LAMP TO TRAILER RELAY FEED	576
DK GREEN	R.H. REMOTE MIRROR MOTOR FEED — C.W.	543
** DK GREEN	TACHOMETER SIGNAL RETURN	644
DK GREEN	LEFT REAR SHOCK DAMPENING RELAY TO CONTROL MODULE	651
DK GREEN	FAILURE WARNING LIGHT	603
DK GREEN	14 GA FUSE LINK	299
DK GREEN	TRAILER RH TURN SIGNAL	64
DK GREEN	WINDSHIELD WIPER SW. TO WINDSHIELD WIPER MOTOR	65
DK GREEN	SUPPLEMENTAL ALTERNATOR STATOR C TERM. TO WINDSHIELD	72
DK GREEN-LT GREEN	CLOCK ADVANCE SWITCH TO MESSAGE CENTER	141
DK GREEN-LT GREEN	ELECTRONIC CONTROL UNIT TO ENGINE VACUUM SWITCH	75
DK GREEN-LT GREEN	EMA CONTROL TO SPARK RETARD SWITCH	21
DK GREEN-LT GREEN	THROTTLE ANGLE POSITION SENSOR FEED	355
DK GREEN-LT GREEN	AIR SUSPENSION MALFUNCTION WARNING LAMP	419
DK GREEN-LT GREEN	R.F. DOOR LOCK SWITCH TO L.F. DOOR LOCK SWITCH	389
DK GREEN-LT GREEN	SEAT BELT WARNING INDICATOR LAMP FEED	450
DK GREEN-ORANGE	HEATER & A/C CONTROL SW. (TEMP. SELECTOR) TO REHEAT AMPL.	773
DK GREEN-ORANGE	SPEAKER SWITCH GROUND TO RIGHT FRONT SPEAKER	811
DK GREEN-ORANGE	AMPLIFIER/SPEAKER SWITCH GROUND TO RIGHT REAR SPEAKER	803
** DK GREEN-ORANGE	MIRROR SWITCH HORIZONTAL RIGHT	944
DK GREEN-ORANGE	PROCESSOR LOOP SIGNAL RETURN	848
DK GREEN-ORANGE	MCU MODULE TO KNOCK SENSOR	311
DK GREEN-ORANGE	PARITY BIT-DISPLAY TO MESSAGE CENTER	178
DK GREEN-PURPLE	TRANSMISSION THROTTLE VALVE SOLENOID 2	315
DK GREEN-PURPLE	ANTI-THEFT SWITCH DISARM	25
DK GREEN-PURPLE	HEATED EXTERIOR MIRROR FEED	59
DK GREEN-PURPLE	DATA-MESSAGE CENTER TO DISPLAY	174
DK GREEN-PURPLE	AIR FUEL SENSOR TO E.C.U.	94
DK GREEN-PURPLE	POWER FEED DECEL TIMER TO THROTTLE KICKER	584
DK GREEN-WHITE	SENSOR AMPLIFY UNIT TO CONTROL UNIT #3	759
DK GREEN-WHITE	KEY CYLINDER SENSOR TO ANTI-THEFT MODULE	936
** DK GREEN-WHITE	RH MIRROR LEFT/RIGHT POSITION SENSOR	954
DK GREEN-WHITE	STOPLAMP SW. TO STOPLAMP RELAY (COIL TERM.)	475
DK GREEN-WHITE	FUEL LEVEL RECEIVER TO FUEL LEVEL WARNING RELAY (REG. TERM.)	367
DK GREEN-WHITE	SENSOR SIGNAL TO AMPLIFIER	150
DK GREEN-WHITE	OIL PRESSURE SWITCH TO TIMER	254
DK GREEN-YELLOW	HEADLAMP SWITCH TO AUTOLAMP AMPLIFIER	219
DK GREEN-YELLOW	ELECTRONIC CONTROL UNIT TO EXHAUST GAS OXYGEN SENSOR	74
DK GREEN-YELLOW	ELECTRONIC SWITCH TO IGNITION COIL NEG. TERMINAL	11
DK GREEN-YELLOW	AIR SUSPENSION CONTROL MODULE FEED	418
DK GREEN-YELLOW	ANTENNA SWITCH TO POWER ANTENNA (DOWN)	746
DK GREEN-YELLOW	SPLICE #3 TO POWER RELAY	546
** DK GREEN-YELLOW	FUEL PUMP RELAY TO SAFETY SWITCH	238
DL BLUE	TRAILER STOP LAMPS	43
GRAY	LOW OIL LEVEL RELAY TO WARNING LAMP	208
GRAY	12 GA FUSE LINK	290
GRAY	HEADLAMP DIMMER RELAY TO HEADLAMP DIMMER SWITCH	502
GRAY	ELECT SHIFT MODULE TO GRAPHIC DISPLAY ROOF CONSOLE	783
GRAY	C.B. SCAN L.E.D.	706
GRAY	WINDSHIELD WIPER HIGH	719
GRAY	RIGHT CHANNEL SIGNAL	690
GRAY	SEAT REG. SW. TO RECLINER MOTOR — UP	918
** GRAY	AIR CHARGE TEMPERATURE	743
GRAY	RIGHT LIMIT-A — PASSENGER	874
GRAY	MEMORY MIRROR MODULE POSITION	894
** GRAY	MIRROR POSITION SENSOR COMMON	959
GRAY	AIR SUSPENSION SYSTEM GROUND	430
GRAY	EATC RH SUNLOAD SENSOR NEGATIVE	483
GRAY	CRANKSHAFT SENSOR SIGNAL RETURN	350
GRAY	DIESEL CONTROL SWITCH TO POWER RELAY & LAMP CONTROL RELAY	339
GRAY-BLACK	LIMIT SW. TO BACK WINDOW REG. MOTOR	401
** GRAY-BLACK	ABS MODULE REAR LEFT WHEEL SPEED OUTPUT	996
GRAY-BLACK	FRONT TILT POSITION SENSE	441
GRAY-BLACK	SEAT REG. SW. TO RECLINER MOTOR — DOWN	919
GRAY-BLACK	VALVE #5 TO MODULE	499
** GRAY-BLACK	VEHICLE SPEED SIGNAL	679
GRAY-BLACK	SPEED CONTROL SENSE EEC MODULE TO SENSOR	679
GRAY-BLACK	WINDOW REGULATOR MOTOR TO GROUND	157
GRAY-BLACK	INSIDE DOOR HANDLE SWITCH TO RETRACTOR INHIBITOR MODULE	185
GRAY-BLACK	SERVO SOURCE VACUUM SOLENOID TO CONTROL TRANSISTOR	145
GRAY-LT BLUE	MILES/KILOMETERS SW. TO MESSAGE CENTER	161
GRAY-LT BLUE	HTD BACKLITE SW. TO TIME DELAY RELAY	688
GRAY-LT BLUE	SENSOR AMPLIFY UNIT TO CONTROL UNIT #2	750
GRAY-LT BLUE	AMPLIFIER/SPEAKER FEED TO LEFT REAR SPEAKER	800
GRAY-LT BLUE	ANEROID SWITCH TO MCU MODULE	394
** GRAY-LT BLUE	ELECTRONIC CONTROL UNIT TO EXHAUST GAS OXYGEN SENSOR (#1 IN DUAL SYSTEM)	74
GRAY-ORANGE	SPARK MODULE TO MCU MODULE	395
GRAY-ORANGE	HEAD LP TIME DELAY CONTROL RELAY TO CIR. BREAKER	686
GRAY-ORANGE	AIR BAG SAFING SENSORS TO INFLATORS	614
GRAY-ORANGE	FEED TO FUEL SHUTOFF LAMP	921
GRAY-ORANGE	AVERAGE SPEED SWITCH TO MESSAGE CENTER	156
GRAY-ORANGE	ELECTRONIC CONTROL UNIT TO DECELERATION SOLENOID	47
** GRAY-ORANGE	PROFILE IGNITION PICKUP FROM TFI MODULE	395
GRAY-RED	DISTANCE TO EMPTY SWITCH TO MESSAGE CENTER	155
GRAY-RED	THERMOCOUPLE 1 NEG. TO EXHAUST SYST. OVERTEMP PROTECT MODULE	91
GRAY-RED	INHIBITOR MODULE TO RETRACTOR OVERRIDE SOLENOID	187
GRAY-RED	EXHAUST BACK PRESSURE VALVE ACTUATOR	318
GRAY-RED	LIFTGATE SW. TO LIFTGATE RELAY	913
GRAY-RED	DIESEL COLD ADVANTAGE	607
GRAY-RED	MOTOR TO MOTOR RELAY	538
** GRAY-RED	MIRROR POSITION SENSOR FEED	958
GRAY-RED	TEMP WARNING LAMP TO SENDING UNIT	682
GRAY-RED	ELECTRONIC SHOCK DIAGNOSTIC	844
GRAY-RED	EMERGENCY RELEASE LEVERS	868
GRAY-RED	SWITCH TO VALVE	455
GRAY-RED	SEAT PROCESSOR ASSY TO FRONT MOTOR LH	452
GRAY-RED	WINDOW REG. SW. TO BACK WINDOW REG. MOTOR	402
** GRAY-RED	SENSOR SIGNAL RETURN	359
GRAY-WHITE	WINDOW REG. SW. TO WINDOW REG. MOTOR	403
GRAY-WHITE	THIRD LOCKOUT SOLENOID	854
GRAY-WHITE	AIR BAG DIAGNOSTIC MODULE TO DRIVER INFLATOR	615
GRAY-WHITE	DAYTIME RUNNING LAMP	932
** GRAY-WHITE	THROTTLE ANGLE POSITION SENSOR TO EEC MODULE	355
GRAY-WHITE	AIR CONDITIONER CLUTCH RELAY	321
GRAY-WHITE	DISTANCE SWITCH TO MESSAGE CENTER	164
GRAY-WHITE	CHOKE RELAY TO CHOKE	67
GRAY-YELLOW	ELECTRONIC CONTROL UNIT TO CANISTER PURGE SOLENOID	101
GRAY-YELLOW	HEADLAMP DIMMER SWITCH TO HEADLAMP DIMMER AMPLIFIER	505
GRAY-YELLOW	ACC FEED	687
GRAY-YELLOW	EFI MODULE TO CLUTCH SWITCH	481
GRAY-YELLOW	PRESSURE SWITCH TO INERTIA SWITCH	467
LT BLUE	REARVIEW OUTSIDE MIRROR CLOCKWISE	413
LT BLUE	ELECT. ENG. CONTL. MOD. TO ELECTRO DRIVE FAN	386
LT BLUE	VEHICLE SPEED SENSOR FEED	353
LT BLUE	ANTI-SKID MODULE TO ANTI-SKID CONTROL VALVE	677
LT BLUE	C.B. B+ DIGIT	720
LT BLUE	CAM SENDER SIGNAL RETURN	796
LT BLUE	ELECT SHIFT 4 × 4 MODULE TO SPEED SENSOR COIL	772
LT BLUE	LOW COOLANT LEVEL RELAY TO SENSOR	794
LT BLUE	HEADLAMP DIMMER RELAY TO FUSE HOLDER	503
LT BLUE	ELECTRONIC FUEL GAGE TO MESSAGE CENTER	501
LT BLUE	FUEL INJECTOR #8 CYLINDER	562
LT BLUE	LEFT FRONT SHOCK DAMPENING RELAY TO CONTROL MODULE	641
LT BLUE	RIGHT REAR AIR INPUT RETURN	855
LT BLUE	MEMORY MIRROR MODULE TO RH HORIZONTAL DRIVER	888
LT BLUE	VEHICLE MAINTENANCE MONITOR MODULE TO OIL TEMP INPUT	905
LT BLUE	LOW FUEL INDICATOR	106
LT BLUE	KEYLESS DOOR LOCK SWITCH ILLUMINATION FEED	66
LT BLUE	TURN SIGNAL FLASHER TO TURN SIGNAL SWITCH	44
LT BLUE	SEAT REG. SW. TO HORIZ. SOLENOID BATT. TERM.	306
LT BLUE	INDICATOR LAMP TO SWITCH (4 × 4)	210
LT BLUE-BLACK	AMPLIFIER SPEAKER SWITCH TO LEFT REAR SPEAKER	277
LT BLUE-BLACK	BRAKE FEED	22
LT BLUE-BLACK	SPEED CONTROL ON-OFF SWITCH TO AMPLIFIER	151
LT BLUE-BLACK	MEMORY MIRROR MODULE RH VERTICAL POSITION	893
LT BLUE-BLACK	FOG LAMP SWITCH TO FOG LAMP RELAY	477
LT BLUE-BLACK	INDICATOR LAMP TO LOW RANGE SWITCH 4 × 4	784
LT BLUE-BLACK	SAFETY RELAY LOAD TERM. TO WIND. REG. SW. FEED	400
LT BLUE-BLACK	AIR SOLENOID CONTROL — REAR	416
LT BLUE-BLACK	RELAY TO DAY/NIGHT ILLUMINATION LAMPS	434
LT BLUE-ORANGE	AMBIENT SENSOR TO INST. PANEL THERMISTOR	767
LT BLUE-ORANGE	C.B. SPEAKER RELAY TO MIC	723
LT BLUE-ORANGE	DCP MODULE TO HEATED BACKLITE RELAY	624
LT BLUE-ORANGE	EEC MODULE CONTROL OF HIGH SPEED FUEL PUMP	926
** LT BLUE-ORANGE	FUEL PUMP RELAY CONTROL	926
LT BLUE-ORANGE	LH REAR STOP & TURN BULB OUTAGE	104
LT BLUE-ORANGE	HORN CONTROL MODULE TO OVERRIDE SWITCH	34
LT BLUE-ORANGE	HI-TEMP SWITCH TO MCU MODULE	308
LT BLUE-ORANGE	HEATER BLOWER MOTOR TO SWITCH (MEDIUM)	269
LT BLUE-PINK	EEC MODULE TO TIME METER	305
LT BLUE-PINK	ELECTRONIC CLUSTER ACCESSORY FEED	295
LT BLUE-PINK	TRANSFORMER POWER — MESSAGE CENTER TO DISPLAY	169
LT BLUE-PINK	IDLE TRACKING SWITCH FEED	189
LT BLUE-PINK	BUCKLE SW. TO CENTER OCCUPANT SEAT SENSOR	107
LT BLUE-PINK	AIR COMPRESSOR VENT SOLENOID	578
LT BLUE-PINK	BRAKE SKID CONTROL MODULE FEED	601
LT BLUE-RED	DCP MODULE CONTROL INTERFACE TO RADIO	595
LT BLUE-RED	PRESSURE SWITCH TO MODULE	535
** LT BLUE-RED	MASS AIRFLOW SIGNAL	967
LT BLUE-RED	C.B. SPEAKER TO TRANSCEIVER	717
LT BLUE-RED	FUEL PUMP BYPASS	433
LT BLUE-RED	FUEL LEVEL WARNING RELAY FEED	365
LT BLUE-RED	CLOCK SELECT SWITCH TO MESSAGE CENTER	142
LT BLUE-RED	INSTRUMENT PANEL LAMPS FEED	19
LT BLUE-RED	THERMACTOR DUMP VALVE FEED	255
LT BLUE-WHITE	CIGAR LIGHTER FEED	40
LT BLUE-WHITE	ARRIVAL SWITCH TO MESSAGE CENTER	152
LT BLUE-WHITE	TIMER CONTROL VALVE TO CONTROL UNIT	741
LT BLUE-WHITE	SPEAKER SWITCH GROUND TO LEFT FRONT SPEAKER	813
LT BLUE-WHITE	DCP MODULE TO PARKLAMP RELAY	625
LT BLUE-WHITE	VEHICLE MAINTENANCE MONITOR MODULE TO SPEED SENSOR	909
LT BLUE-WHITE	EEC MODULE TO TRANSMISSION	912

* IN SOME CASES, THERE MAY BE ADDITIONAL CIRCUIT
FUNCTIONS INCLUDED IN THE CIRCUIT DESCRIPTION LISTED.

** DENOTES A NEW OR STANDARDIZED CIRCUIT.

STANDARD CIRCUIT CHART (BY COLOR)

COLOR	DESCRIPTION*	CIRCUIT
LT BLUE-YELLOW	HEATER & A/C CONTROL SW. (HI & LO NORM) TO BLOWER MOTOR SW. RELAY	769
LT BLUE-YELLOW	RADIATOR COOLANT TEMP SWITCH TO CONTROL UNIT	742
LT BLUE-YELLOW	CRT SCAN	730
LT BLUE-YELLOW	FUEL TANK SELECTOR SWITCH TO AFT FUEL PUMP	671
LT BLUE-YELLOW	BATTERY TO AUTOMATIC ANTENNA SWITCH	451
LT BLUE-YELLOW	CHECKOUT SWITCH TO MESSAGE CENTER	143
LT BLUE-YELLOW	KEYLESS DOOR LOCK SWITCH DATA BIT 1 TO MODULE	78
LT BLUE-YELLOW	DE-ICE SOLENOID CONTROL	241
LT BLUE-YELLOW	MODULE TO NEUTRAL SENSOR SWITCH	199
** LT BLUE-YELLOW	MANUAL LEVER POSITION OR CLUTCH	199
LT GREEN	SPEAKER VOICE COIL FEED FRONT (LEFT CHANNEL) AMP INPUT	280
LT GREEN	VACUUM DOOR LOCK SWITCH TO SOLENOID (LOCK)	115
LT GREEN	KEYLESS DOOR LOCK OUTPUT FROM MODULE	129
LT GREEN	READING LAMP SWITCH TO READING LAMP (LH)	387
LT GREEN	C.B. A-DIGIT	715
LT GREEN	WINDSHIELD WASHER	726
LT GREEN	ELECT SHIFT 4 × 4 MODULE TO SPEED SENSOR RETURN	774
LT GREEN	AIR SUSPENSION CONTROL SIGNAL	637
LT GREEN	ALTERNATOR RELAY TO ALTERNATOR REGULATOR	568
** LT GREEN	TRANSFER CASE CLUTCH RELAY TO TRANSFER CASE CLUTCH	1000
LT GREEN	FUEL INJECTOR #6 CYLINDER	560
LT GREEN	STOPLAMP SWITCH TO TURN SIGNAL SWITCH	511
LT GREEN	RADIO TO FADER CONTROL	823
LT GREEN	SPEED CONTROL VACUUM TO EEC MODULE	916
LT GREEN	SEAT BELT WARNING SWITCH FEED	469
LT GREEN	LEFT LIMIT-B—DRIVER	872
** LT GREEN	STOPLAMP SWITCH TO STOPLAMPS	511
LT GREEN-BLACK	ESC SWITCH TO ESC VALVE CONTROL	933
LT GREEN-BLACK	LH REAR SENSOR (LOW) TO MODULE	519
LT GREEN-BLACK	DCP MODULE TRIP SCAN HIGH TO TRIPMINDER	597
LT GREEN-BLACK	C.B. REGULATED 5V	711
LT GREEN-BLACK	MANIFOLD ABSOLUTE PRESSURE SENSOR FEED	358
LT GREEN-BLACK	CONTROL MODULE TO OIL PRESSURE SWITCH	473
LT GREEN-BLACK	SEQUENTIAL LH REAR OUTBOARD TURN SIGNAL LAMP	444
LT GREEN-BLACK	AIR PORT SOLENOID SIGNAL	99
LT GREEN-BLACK	HEADLAMP DIMMER SWITCH TO HIGH BEAMS	12
** LT GREEN-BLACK	MANIFOLD ABSOLUTE PRESSURE TO EEC MODULE	358
LT GREEN-ORANGE	LH REAR TURN SIGNAL LAMP	9
LT GREEN-ORANGE	POWER SERVO TO CLIMATE CONTROL UNIT (MODE)	243
LT GREEN-ORANGE	AIR SOLENOID CONTROL L.F.	415
LT GREEN-ORANGE	SEQUENTIAL LH REAR INBOARD TURN SIGNAL LAMP	442
LT GREEN-ORANGE	C.B. NOISE BLANKER	705
LT GREEN-ORANGE	AMPLIFIER SWITCH GROUND TO RIGHT FRONT SPEAKER	815
** LT GREEN-ORANGE	FUEL INJECTOR #6 CYLINDER	560
LT GREEN-ORANGE	W/W WIPER SWITCH TO W/S WIPER MOTOR FIELD RH	956
LT GREEN-PURPLE	SUPERCHARGER SOLENOID #1	965
LT GREEN-PURPLE	AMPLIFIER SWITCH FEED TO RIGHT FRONT SPEAKER	816
LT GREEN-PURPLE	BATTERY FEED TO STEREO	797
LT GREEN-PURPLE	DCP MODULE TRIP SCAN LOW TO TRIPMINDER	598
LT GREEN-PURPLE	ELECTRONIC SHOCK HARD CONTROL	838
LT GREEN-PURPLE	THERMOSTATIC SW. TO AIR COND. SW. SELECTOR TERM.	348
** LT GREEN-PURPLE	HIGH ELECTRIC DRIVE COOLING FAN	639
LT GREEN-PURPLE	START INTERRUPT RELAY TO ANTI-THEFT MODULE	342
LT GREEN-PURPLE	CARBURETOR AIR TEMPERATURE SENSOR FEED	357
LT GREEN-PURPLE	FUEL PULSE TO MESSAGE CENTER	139
LT GREEN-RED	KEYLESS DOOR LOCK SWITCH DATA BIT 2 TO MODULE	79
LT GREEN-RED	STOPLAMP SWITCH	10
LT GREEN-RED	EMERG. BRAKE WARNING LAMP TO EMERG. BRAKE SWITCH	162
LT GREEN-RED	SEQUENTIAL LH REAR CENTER TURN SIGNAL LAMP	443
LT GREEN-RED	(COIL) OR (ACCY) TERM OF IGNITION SWITCH TO ALTERNATOR REGULATOR (IGN. TERM)	904
LT GREEN-RED	REAR SENSOR (HIGH) TO MODULE	518
LT GREEN-RED	AIR SUSPENSION SYSTEM GROUND	577
LT GREEN-RED	LEFT CHANNEL SIGNAL OUT	798
LT GREEN-RED	C.B. RELAY DRIVE	722
** LT GREEN-RED	ENGINE COOLANT TEMPERATURE FEED	354
LT GREEN-WHITE	BLOWER MOTOR SPEED CONTROLLER TO RESISTOR #1 (MED.)	754
LT GREEN-WHITE	AMPLIFIER SWITCH GROUND TO LEFT FRONT SPEAKER	819
LT GREEN-WHITE	C.B. C+ DIGIT	724
LT GREEN-WHITE	MODULE TO OVERRIDE SWITCH	661
LT GREEN-WHITE	OVERDRIVE CANCEL INDICATOR LAMP	911
LT GREEN-WHITE	ELECTRONIC SHOCK SOFT CONTROL	839
LT GREEN-WHITE	ELECT. ENG. CONTL. MOD. TO IDLE SPD. CONTL. MOTOR #2	265
LT GREEN-WHITE	MEMORY SEAT SWITCH LAMP ENABLE	271
LT GREEN-WHITE	LH FRONT TURN SIGNAL LAMP	3
LT GREEN-YELLOW	SEAT SWITCH ARM TERM. TO RELAY FIELD TERM	7
LT GREEN-YELLOW	INTERIOR LAMP SWITCH FEED	54
LT GREEN-YELLOW	RETARD VALVE TO CONTROL RELAY TERM. #1	869
LT GREEN-YELLOW	FUEL TANK SELECTOR SWITCH TO MIDSHIP FUEL PUMP	672
LT GREEN-YELLOW	MODULE TO MOTOR FEED	663
LT GREEN-YELLOW	HEATER & A/C CONTROL SW. TO REHEAT & A/C FEED	765
** LT GREEN-YELLOW	MODULE TO MOTOR RETURN	663
LT GREEN-YELLOW	REFERENCE SENSOR TO HEAT DUCT THERMISTOR	768
LT GREEN-YELLOW	PRESSURE SWITCH TO FLUID RES. SWITCH	547
LT GREEN-YELLOW	SPLICE #3 TO POWER RELAY	530
LT GREEN-YELLOW	ENGINE COOLANT TEMPERATURE SENSOR FEED	354
ORANGE	MODULE TO RELAY	461
ORANGE	WINDSHIELD WIPER SWITCH TO INTERMITTENT GOVERNOR GROUND	589
ORANGE	HEATED WINDSHIELD SWITCH TO HEATED WINDSHIELD CONTROL	582
ORANGE	BRAKE PRESSURE SWITCH TO CONTROL MODULE	636
** ORANGE	AWD MODULE TO TRANSFER CASE CLUTCH RELAY COIL	976
ORANGE	ELECT SHIFT 4 × 4 MODULE TO MOTOR CONTROL	778
ORANGE	BRAKE PRESSURE SWITCH TO CONTROL MODULE	636
ORANGE	SPEAKER VOICE COIL FEED LEFT FRONT CHANNEL AMP INPUT	649
* ORANGE	MODULE DIAGNOSTIC	693
** ORANGE	RIGHT MOTOR — PASSENGER — A	864
ORANGE	C.B. C-DIGIT	704
ORANGE	MULTIPLEX RELAY COIL FEED	699
ORANGE	FUEL CONTROL SWITCH TO FUEL CONTROL VALVE	974
** ORANGE	MULTIPLEX RELAY COIL FEED #1	699
ORANGE	BATTERY FEED TO RELAY CONTROLLER	931
ORANGE	RIGHT MOTOR — PASSENGER — F	864
ORANGE	VALVE #2 TO MODULE	496
ORANGE	MEMORY MIRROR MODULE RH HORIZONTAL POSITION	892
ORANGE	FUEL SENSOR GROUND TO E.C.U.	89
** ORANGE	EXHAUST GAS OXYGEN SENSOR RETURN TO EEC MODULE	89
ORANGE	SWITCH OFF TO RELAY	274
ORANGE	HEATER & A/C CONTROL SW. (LO-NORM) TO POWER SERVO	250
ORANGE	ELECTRONIC CLUSTER FROM EXPANDED FUEL IN KEYBOARD	285
** ORANGE	DEDICATED GROUND TO TFI MODULE	259
ORANGE	16 GA FUSE LINK	300
ORANGE	RELAY TO SEAT LATCH SOLENOID	172
** ORANGE	TRAILER BATTERY CHARGE	49
ORANGE-BLACK	BLOWER MOTOR TO SWITCH — HI	261
ORANGE-BLACK	TAIL LAMP BULB OUTAGE TO MESSAGE CENTER	132
ORANGE-BLACK	ELECTRIC CHOKE FEED	68
ORANGE-BLACK	EVO MODULE TO TEST CONNECTOR	927
ORANGE-BLACK	TRANSMISSION OIL TEMP	923
ORANGE-BLACK	MULTIPLEX FARRING LAMPS	696
ORANGE-BLACK	CLIMATE CONTROL BOX TO HIGH BLOWER RELAY	776
** ORANGE-BLACK	AWD SAFETY LAMP RELAY COIL	991
ORANGE-BLACK	RIGHT CHANNEL SIGNAL OUT	799
ORANGE-BLACK	ENGLISH METRIC SIGNAL TO MULTIGAGE	572
ORANGE-BLACK	LIQUID CRYSTAL DISPLAY	484
ORANGE-BLACK	TURN SIGNAL SWITCH TO INDICATOR RELAY	458
ORANGE-BLACK	AIR SUSPENSION HEIGHT SENSOR LO — REAR	428
ORANGE-BLACK	IDLE SPEED CONTROL TO EGR VACUUM SOLENOID	323
ORANGE-BLACK	RADIO SEEK "DOWN"	370
ORANGE-LT BLUE	AFTER GLOW RELAY TO DIESEL CONTROL SWITCH	335
ORANGE-LT BLUE	SEQUENTIAL RH REAR INBOARD TURN SIGNAL LAMP	445
ORANGE-LT BLUE	I TERMINAL STARTER MOTOR RELAY TO INERTIA SWITCH	668
ORANGE-LT BLUE	ELECT SHIFT TO 4L SWITCH	781
ORANGE-LT BLUE	RADIO RECEIVER ASSY. TO FOOT CONTROL SWITCH	747
ORANGE-LT BLUE	VAC SWITCH TO VAC PUMP	740
ORANGE-LT BLUE	RH REAR TURN SIGNAL LAMP	5
ORANGE-LT BLUE	ALTERNATOR REGULATOR "F" TERMINAL TO ALTERNATOR	35
ORANGE-LT BLUE	ELECTRONIC CONTROL UNIT TO WIDE OPEN THROTTLE ACTUATOR	73
ORANGE-LT BLUE	FUEL SUPPLY PUMP RELAY	238
ORANGE-LT BLUE	CRUISE INDICATING LAMP TO CRUISE LAMP INTERFACE MODULE	203
ORANGE-LT GREEN	TANK SELECT CIRCUIT ELECTRONIC FUEL GAUGE	204
ORANGE-LT GREEN	EMA CONTROL TO EGR SWITCH	27
ORANGE-LT GREEN	AIR BAG DIAGNOSTIC MODULE TO AIR BAG FLASHER	610
ORANGE-LT GREEN	DCP MODULE TO WIPER HI-LO RELAY	594
ORANGE-LT GREEN	SPEAKER VOICE COIL FEED — FRONT (LEFT CHANNEL)	804
ORANGE-LT GREEN	DECELERATION SENSOR	847
ORANGE-LT GREEN	INDICATOR RELAY TO FLASHER	459
ORANGE-LT GREEN	DROPPING RESISTOR TO RELAY #2	471
ORANGE-RED	SEQUENTIAL RH REAR OUTBOARD TURN SIGNAL LAMP	447
ORANGE-RED	AIR SOLENOID CONTROL R.F.	414
ORANGE-RED	RESISTOR TO BLOWER MOTOR (HI)	515
ORANGE-RED	SKID CONTROL MODULE RH WHEEL SENSOR (HI)	604
ORANGE-RED	AMPLIFIER/SPEAKER SWITCH FEED TO RIGHT REAR SPEAKER	802
ORANGE-RED	LO-TEMP SWITCH TO MCU MODULE	309
ORANGE-RED	INSTRUMENT PANEL ILLUMINATION CONTROL MODULE FEED	293
ORANGE-WHITE	TEMPERATURE COMPENSATED PUMP TO PROCESSOR	256
ORANGE-WHITE	HEADLAMP SWITCH TO SENSOR AND AUTOLAMP AMPLIFIER	221
ORANGE-WHITE	AIR DUMP VALVE NEG. TO EXHAUST SYS. OVERTEMP MODULE	93
ORANGE-WHITE	ELECT SHIFT 4 × 4 MODULE TO MOTOR POSITION #2	763
ORANGE-WHITE	ACCELERATE DECELERATE SENSOR	836
ORANGE-WHITE	VENT SWITCH TO LEFT FRONT VENT MOTOR	886
ORANGE-WHITE	SEQUENTIAL RH REAR CENTER TURN SIGNAL LAMP	446
ORANGE-WHITE	POWER RELAY TO GLOW PLUGS (LEFT BANK)	337
ORANGE-WHITE	SENSOR SIGNAL FEED	351
ORANGE-WHITE	DOOR OPENING WARNING TO ANTI-THEFT MODULE	341
ORANGE-WHITE	MOVABLE STEERING COLUMN SOLENOID TO COURTESY LAMP SWITCH	381
ORANGE-YELLOW	ANTENNA SWITCH TO ANTENNA RELAY	448
ORANGE-YELLOW	OVERRIDE SWITCH TO LATCH	665
ORANGE-YELLOW	AIR BAG READY INDICATOR LAMP TO AIR BAG FLASHER	609
ORANGE-YELLOW	SPLICE TO DIODE	531
ORANGE-YELLOW	SPLICE TO POWER RELAY	532
ORANGE-YELLOW	SPLICE TO MODULE	525
ORANGE-YELLOW	POWER RELAY TO MODULE GROUND	528
ORANGE-YELLOW	SPEED SENSOR LO V REF TO SPEEDO TACH MODULE	563
ORANGE-YELLOW	AMPLIFIER TO SERVO TRANSDUCER FEED	144
ORANGE-YELLOW	TURN SIGNAL FLASHER FEED	8
ORANGE-YELLOW	SEAT SWITCH TO RELAY FIELD TERMINAL	18
ORANGE-YELLOW	TRANSMISSION THROTTLE VALVE SOLENOID 1	237
** ORANGE-YELLOW	SHIFT SOLENOID 1	237
ORANGE-YELLOW	START CIRCUIT TO THERMACTOR RELAY	253
PINK	WINDOW REGULATOR RELAY ACCY FEED	194
PINK	HIGH ELECTRO DRIVE FAN	639
** PINK	ABS MODULE FRONT RIGHT WHEEL SPEED OUTPUT	997
PINK	MULTIPLEX MESSAGE I	736
PINK	EEC MODULE TO SPARK ADVANCE	929
** PINK	SPARK OUTPUT SIGNAL FROM TFI MODULE	929
PINK	AIR COMPRESSOR VENT SOLENOID	421
PINK	VALVE #4 TO MODULE	498
PINK	CRANK ENABLE RELAY	329
PINK-BLACK	ELECTRONIC CLUSTER IGNITION RUN FEED	489
PINK-BLACK	STOPLAMP RELAY FEED	474
PINK-BLACK	AIR SUSPENSION HEIGHT SENSOR HI — L.F.	422
PINK-BLACK	AIR SUSPENSION HEIGHT SENSOR HI — REAR	427
** PINK-BLACK	FUEL PUMP POWER	787

* IN SOME CASES, THERE MAY BE ADDITIONAL CIRCUIT FUNCTIONS INCLUDED IN THE CIRCUIT DESCRIPTION LISTED.

** DENOTES A NEW OR STANDARDIZED CIRCUIT.

STANDARD CIRCUIT CHART (BY COLOR)

COLOR	DESCRIPTION*	CIRCUIT
PINK-BLACK	COMPASS SENSOR FEED	684
PINK-BLACK	FUEL PUMP SAFETY SWITCH TO FUEL PUMP MOTOR	787
PINK-BLACK	SENSOR AMPLIFY UNIT TO CONTROL UNIT #1	749
PINK-BLACK	RH REAR SENSOR (LOW) TO MODULE	524
PINK-BLACK	AIR BAG DIAGNOSTIC MODULE TO PASSENGER INFLATOR	616
PINK-BLACK	SHOCK DAMPENING RELAY HARD TO SHOCK DAMPENING CONTROL	652
PINK-BLACK	SPEAKER VOICE COIL FEED RIGHT REAR CHANNEL AMP INPUT	645
PINK-BLACK	THERMO SWITCH TO CONTROL MODULE	470
PINK-BLACK	DOOR LOCK MOTOR (LOCK)	117
PINK-LT BLUE	RH HEADLAMP BULB OUTAGE	109
PINK-LT BLUE	AIR COND. CONTROL RELAY FEED	883
PINK-LT BLUE	PRESSURE SWITCH TO MOTOR RELAY	539
** PINK-LT BLUE	DATA LINK RETURN	915
PINK-LT BLUE	SPEAKER VOICE COIL FEED—REAR (RIGHT CHANNEL)	806
PINK-LT BLUE	AMPLIFIER/SPEAKER SWITCH GROUND TO LEFT REAR SPEAKER	801
PINK-LT BLUE	EEC MODULE—DATA MINUS	915
PINK-LT GREEN	VENT SWITCH TO BLOWER MOTOR—LO	917
PINK-LT GREEN	SPEAKER VOICE COIL FEED—REAR (LEFT CHANNEL)	807
PINK-LT GREEN	EEC MODULE TO CHECK ENGINE INDICATOR LAMP	658
PINK-LT GREEN	MODULE TO SOLENOID	599
PINK-LT GREEN	DOOR LOCK SWITCH (UNLOCK)	120
PINK-ORANGE	DOOR LOCK MOTOR (UNLOCK)	118
PINK-ORANGE	AIR BAG DIAGNOSTIC MODULE (DEPLOY) TO RH SENSOR	617
PINK-ORANGE	SPEAKER SWITCH FEED TO RIGHT FRONT SPEAKER	812
** PINK-ORANGE	VEHICLE SPEED SENSOR RETURN	676
PINK-ORANGE	READING LAMP SWITCH TO READING LAMP	487
PINK-ORANGE	MEMORY MIRROR MODULE LH HORIZONTAL POSITION	896
PINK-ORANGE	DIESEL CONTROL MODULE FEED	466
PINK-ORANGE	ELECT. ENG. CONTL. MOD. TO IDLE SPD CONTL. MOTOR #3	384
PINK-WHITE	BLOWER MOTOR RELAY TO MOTOR	371
PINK-WHITE	AIR SUSP. MOD. TO L.F. HEIGHT SENSOR	431
PINK-WHITE	AIR BAG DIAGNOSTIC MODULE (DEPLOY) TO CENTER SENSOR	619
PINK-WHITE	SPEAKER SWITCH FEED TO LEFT FRONT SPEAKER	814
PINK-WHITE	DOOR SWITCH TO SEAT LATCH RELAY (COIL TERM.)	173
PINK-YELLOW	DOOR LOCK SWITCH (LOCK)	119
PINK-YELLOW	WASHER FLUID LEVEL INDICATOR	82
PINK-YELLOW	DPC MODULE TO HEADLAMP RELAY	632
PINK-YELLOW	SPEAKER VOICE COIL FEED LEFT REAR CHANNEL AMP INPUT	646
PINK-YELLOW	OPEN DOOR WARNING LAMP FEED	626
PINK-YELLOW	SWITCH TO FADER RIGHT CHANNEL FEED	830
** PINK-YELLOW	WIDE OPEN THROTTLE A/C CUTOUT SWITCH	331
PURPLE	RIGHT FRONT SHOCK DAMPENING RELAY TO CONTROL MODULE	638
PURPLE	HEATED WINDSHIELD CONTROL TO EEC AIR COND TERM	585
PURPLE	CONVERTIBLE TOP RELAY TO SWITCH	588
PURPLE	R.H. REMOTE MIRROR MOTOR FEED—C.C.W.	544
PURPLE	HEADLAMP DIMMER SWITCH TO HEADLAMP DIMMER RELAY	500
** PURPLE	TRANSMISSION TURBINE SPEED SENSOR	970
PURPLE	C.B. A+ DIGIT	712
PURPLE	RELAY COIL FEED #2	714
PURPLE	REDUNDANT MODULE TO ENGINE WARNING LAMP	656
PURPLE	POWER FEED FROM AMPLIFIER	928
** PURPLE	A/C DEMAND SIGNAL	348
PURPLE	LEFT CHANNEL SIGNAL	856
PURPLE	MODULE TO RELAY	462
PURPLE	TRANSMISSION DIAGNOSTIC	453
PURPLE	POWER SERVO TO CLIMATE CONTROL UNIT (AMP)	246
PURPLE	ELECTRONIC CLUSTER FROM TRIP RECALL SWITCH IN KEYBOARD	288
PURPLE BASE	EATC RH SUNLOAD SENSOR POSITIVE	479
PURPLE-LT BLUE	WINDOW REG. SW. TO BACK WINDOW SW.	405
PURPLE-LT BLUE	SPEED CONTROL SENSE EEC MODULE TO CLUSTER	683
PURPLE-LT BLUE	AIR BAG DIAGNOSTIC MODULE (MONITOR) TO CENTER SENSOR	620
PURPLE-LT BLUE	POWER FEED SWITCH TO REAR AMPLIFIER	828
PURPLE-LT BLUE	CLICKER RELAY TERM. NO. 4 TO AIR VALVE ASSY.	263
PURPLE-LT BLUE	AMPLIFIER FEEDBACK POTENTIOMETER FEED	147
PURPLE-LT GREEN	DESTINATION SWITCH TO MESSAGE CENTER	154
PURPLE-LT GREEN	AIR BAG DIAGNOSTIC MODULE (MONITOR) TO RH SENSOR	618
PURPLE-LT GREEN	REAR WASHER PUMP FEED	946
PURPLE-LT GREEN	VEHICLE MAINTENANCE MONITOR MODULE TO ELEC. INSTR CLUST. SENSE	907
PURPLE-LT GREEN	WINDOW REG. SW. TO BACK WINDOW SW.	404
PURPLE-LT GREEN	AIR SUSPENSION HEIGHT SENSOR LO—L.F.	423
PURPLE-LT GREEN	REAR AIR SUSPENSION HEIGHT SENSOR FEED	429
PURPLE-ORANGE	AIR SUSPENSION SWITCH FEED	417
PURPLE-ORANGE	AIR BAG READY INDICATOR L (MONITOR) TO SAFING SENSOR	612
** PURPLE-ORANGE	MIRROR SWITCH VERTICAL RIGHT	943
PURPLE-ORANGE	CIGAR LIGHTER LAMP FEED	131
PURPLE-ORANGE	FUSED ACCY FEED #2	298
PURPLE-ORANGE	AUTOLAMP AMPLIFIER TO CONTROL SWITCH	220
** PURPLE-ORANGE	SHIFT SOLENOID 2	315
PURPLE-WHITE	AMPLIFIER SPEAKER SWITCH FEED TO RIGHT REAR SPEAKER	278
PURPLE-WHITE	MEMORY SEAT SWITCH ENABLE	266
PURPLE-WHITE	AIR BAG DIAGNOSTIC MODULE (MONITOR) TO SAFING SENSOR	623
** PURPLE-WHITE	RH MIRROR UP/DOWN POSITION SENSOR	957
PURPLE-WHITE	SEAT BELT WARNING LAMP TO WARNING LAMP SWITCH	520
PURPLE-WHITE	HEATER & A/C CONTROL SW (LO-HI-NORM) TO RESISTOR (LOW RANGE)	758
PURPLE-WHITE	MULTIPLEX SERVICE REMINDER RESET	733
PURPLE-WHITE	BRAKE WARNING SWITCH TO INDICATOR LAMP	977
PURPLE-WHITE	RIGHT MOTOR — PASSENGER — R	865
** PURPLE-WHITE	RIGHT MOTOR—PASSENGER—B	865
PURPLE-YELLOW	LEFT MOTOR — DRIVER—F	860
PURPLE-YELLOW	ELECT SHIFT 4 x 4 MODULE TO MOTOR POSITION #5	771
PURPLE-YELLOW	CLUTCH SWITCH TO EFI MODULE	480
PURPLE-YELLOW	TURN SIGNAL SWITCH TO LH CORNERING LAMP	380
** PURPLE-YELLOW	LEFT MOTOR — DRIVER — A	860
PURPLE-YELLOW	FUEL INJECTION PUMP POSITION SENSOR	239

COLOR	DESCRIPTION*	CIRCUIT
PURPLE-YELLOW	BRAKE FLUID LEVEL UNIT TO MESSAGE CENTER	128
PURPLE-YELLOW	ECONOMY SWITCH TO MESSAGE CENTER	153
PURPLE-YELLOW	DECK LID SOLENOID FEED	84
** PURPLE-YELLOW	TRANSMISSION CLUTCH CONTROL TO EEC MODULE	480
RED	KEYLESS DOOR LOCK SWITCH DATA BIT 5 TO MODULE	123
RED	TRAILER BRAKES	50
** RED	TRAILER CONTROLLER FEED	50
RED	SUPPLEMENTAL ALTERNATOR STATOR A TERM. TO WINDSHIELD	70
RED	WINDSHIELD WIPER SW. TO WINDSHIELD WIPER MOTOR	63
RED	18 GA FUSE LINK	301
RED	HORIZONTAL SEAT REG. MOTOR TO RELAY	180
RED	POWER RELAY TO EEC MODULE	361
RED	REAR VIEW OUTSIDE MIRROR FEED	388
RED	WIDE OPEN THROTTLE A/C CUTOUT SWITCH	331
RED	POWER LUMBAR FEED	490
RED	FUEL TANK SELECTOR TO FUEL PUMP FRONT	786
RED	DIESEL WATER IN FUEL SENDER TO WARNING LAMP	643
RED	BATTERY FEED CAMPER	666
RED	AMPLIFIER POWER RETURN	694
RED	INERTIA SWITCH TO FUEL TANK SELECTOR SWITCH	670
RED	EED MODULE TO SPEED CONTROL GROUND	676
RED	MOONROOF RELAY TO MICRO SWITCH CLOSED	692
RED	HEADLAMP DIMMER SWITCH OVERRIDE TO RHEOSTAT	527
RED	MPH/KPH SWITCH TO MESSAGE CENTER	506
** RED	MULTIPLEX WINDSHIELD WIPER MAIN	698
RED	L.H. REMOTE MIRROR MOTOR FEED—C.W.	540
RED	HEATED WINDSHIELD CONTROL TO ALT STATOR TERM	581
RED	SOLENOID	605
RED	STEERING RATE SENSOR TERMINAL A CONTROL MODULE	633
RED	DOOR WIRE	630
RED	STEERING RATE SENSOR TERMINAL A CONTROL MODULE	633
RED	BATTERY FEED TO AUX. FUEL SELECTOR SWITCH	973
RED	TOP CONTROL RELAY TO MOTOR—DOWN	903
RED	RIGHT DOOR OPEN — PASSENGER	863
** RED	POWER OUTPUT FROM EEC RELAY	361
RED-BLACK	MEMORY MIRROR MODULE POSITION +	891
RED-BLACK	VENT CROSSOVER FEED	879
RED-BLACK	MODE SELECT SWITCH LAMP	833
RED-BLACK	WATER TEMP. WARNING LAMP TO WATER TEMP. SW. (HOT)	647
RED-BLACK	FRONT AIR SUSPENSION HEIGHT SENSOR FEED	426
RED-BLACK	ELECT. ENG. CONTL. MOD. TO WIDE OPEN THROTTLE KICKER SOC.	378
RED-BLACK	FUEL WARNING RELAY CONTROL	366
RED-BLACK	RADIO "SEEK UP"	368
RED-BLACK	ECU TO VACUUM SWITCH 3	214
RED-BLACK	LAMP RETURN TO PULSE WITH DIMMER	235
RED-BLACK	LEFT FRONT WINDOW REGULATOR SWITCH TO RIGHT FRONT WINDOW REGULATOR MOTOR	314
RED-BLACK	LEFT FRONT WINDOW REGULATOR SWITCH TO RIGHT REAR WINDOW REGULATOR MOTOR	320
RED-BLACK	HEADLAMP DIMMER SWITCH TO LOW BEAMS	13
** RED-BLACK	EEC TO EXHAUST GAS OXYGEN SENSOR (#2 IN DUAL SYSTEM)	94
RED-LT BLUE	STARTER CONTROL	32
RED-LT BLUE	WINDOW REGULATOR SWITCH FEED	170
RED-LT BLUE	ANTI-THEFT MODULE TO ALARM RELAY	340
RED-LT BLUE	LEFT FRONT WINDOW REGULATOR SWITCH TO LEFT REAR WINDOW REGULATOR MOTOR	317
RED-LT BLUE	SEAT PROCESSOR TO RECLINER MOTOR "DOWN"	440
RED-LT BLUE	TACHOMETER FEED	648
RED-LT BLUE	SEAT REGULATOR SWITCH TO FRONT MOTOR (LH)	979
RED-LT BLUE	SEAT REGULATOR SWITCH TO FRONT MOTOR (RH)	985
RED-LT BLUE	VENT CROSSOVER FEED	880
RED-LT BLUE	AMPLIFIER TO SPEED SENSOR RETURN	901
RED-LT GREEN	COIL TERM. OF IGN. SW. TO BRAKE SKID CONTROL MODULE	602
RED-LT GREEN	STOPLAMP SW. TO STOPLAMPS	810
RED-LT GREEN	HEATER & A/C CONTROL SW. (DE-FOG) TO INLET AIR CONTROL SOLENOID	766
RED-LT GREEN	SEAT REGULATOR SWITCH TO REAR MOTOR (LH)	983
** RED-LT GREEN	TRACTION CONTROL MALFUNCTION WARNING LAMP	961
RED-LT GREEN	SEAT REGULATOR SWITCH TO REAR MOTOR (RH)	989
RED-LT GREEN	REAR TILT POSITION SENSE	436
RED-LT GREEN	IGN. SW. COIL TERM. TO CIRCUIT BREAKER	454
RED-LT GREEN	IGNITION SWITCH TO IGNITION COIL "BATT." TERMINAL	16
RED-LT GREEN	MODULE TO THROTTLE ACTUATOR	69
RED-LT GREEN	HEADLAMP BULB OUTAGE TO MESSAGE CENTER	130
RED-ORANGE	KEYLESS DOOR LOCK OUTPUT (DRIVER) FROM MODULE	163
RED-ORANGE	IDLE SPEED CONTROL TO EGR VENT SOLENOID	322
RED-ORANGE	BLOWER MOTOR TO SWITCH — LO	260
** RED-ORANGE	REHEAT AMPLIFIER TO HEAT DUCT THERMISTOR	788
RED-ORANGE	W/S WIPER MOTOR ARM RH TO W/S WIPER SWITCH	955
RED-ORANGE	DCP MODULE TO WIPER GOVERNOR RELAY	593
** RED-ORANGE	MIRROR SWITCH HORIZONTAL LEFT	942
RED-ORANGE	STARTING MOTOR RELAY SHUNT TO AMMETER	655
RED-PINK	RH REAR SENSOR (HIGH) TO MODULE	523
RED-PINK	HEATER & A/C CONTROL SW. (HI-NORM) TO RESISTOR (LOW RANGE)	756
RED-PINK	ANTENNA SWITCH TO POWER ANTENNA (UP)	745
RED-PINK	SPEED CONTROL AMPLIFIER TO CRUISE LAMP INTERFACE MODULE	202
RED-PINK	DOOR JAMB SWITCH TO BUZZER	159
RED-WHITE	RH REAR STOP & TURN BULB OUTAGE	105
RED-WHITE	TEMP. GAUGE TO TEMP. SENDING UNIT	39
RED-WHITE	SWITCH TO WARNING LAMP	42
RED-WHITE	HEATER & A/C CONTROL SW. (HI-NORM) TO BLOWER MOTOR SW. RELAY	757
RED-WHITE	C.B. ON/OFF	718
RED-WHITE	RADIO MEMORY	729
** RED-WHITE	FUSED BATTERY FEED TO AIR BAG DIAGNOSTIC MODULE	937
RED-WHITE	SEAT REGULATOR SWITCH TO HORZ. MOTOR (RH)	987

* IN SOME CASES, THERE MAY BE ADDITIONAL CIRCUIT
FUNCTIONS INCLUDED IN THE CIRCUIT DESCRIPTION LISTED.

** DENOTES A NEW OR STANDARDIZED CIRCUIT.

STANDARD CIRCUIT CHART (BY COLOR)

COLOR	DESCRIPTION*	CIRCUIT
RED-WHITE	SEAT REGULATOR SWITCH TO HORZ. MOTOR (LH)	981
RED-WHITE	MEMORY SEAT TO NEUTRAL SENSOR SWITCH	899
RED-WHITE	ELECTRONIC SHOCK SENSOR B	835
** RED-WHITE	MEMORY SEAT TO NEUTRAL SENSE MODULE	899
RED-WHITE	ELECTRIC SHIFT MODULE TO NEUTRAL START SWITCH	463
RED-WHITE	HORIZONTAL POSITION SENSE	438
RED-WHITE	EMERGENCY WARNING FLASHER FEED	383
** RED-WHITE	LH MIRROR LEFT/RIGHT POSITION SENSOR	949
RED-YELLOW	WINDOW REG. SW. TO WINDOW REG. MOTOR	334
RED-YELLOW	ELECTRONIC SHOCK SENSOR A	834
RED-YELLOW	WARNING LAMPS FEED	640
RED-YELLOW	SUPERCHARGER SOLENOID #2	966
** RED-YELLOW	INERTIA SWITCH TO FUEL TANK SELECTOR SWITCH	670
RED-YELLOW	HEADLAMP DIMMER SWITCH FEED	15
RED-YELLOW	FUEL PRESSURE BOOST SOLENOID	236
** RED-YELLOW	TRAILER BACKUP LAMPS	963
RED-YELLOW	WINDOW REG. MASTER CONT. SW. TO WINDOW REG. SW. FEED	328
TAN	EEC MODULE TO MALFUNCTION INDICATOR LITE	657
TAN	MULTIPLEX SERVICE REMINDER	734
TAN	BOOST SENSOR TO CONTROL UNIT	748
** TAN	ABS MODULE FRONT LEFT WHEEL SPEED OUTPUT	998
TAN	FUEL INJECTOR #1 CYLINDER	555
TAN	SWITCH TO FADER LEFT CHANNEL FEED	831
TAN	VALVE #1 TO MODULE	495
TAN	RIGHT LIMIT — B — PASSENGER	873
TAN	WINDOW REG. SW. TO BACK WINDOW AUX. SW.	406
TAN	AIR SUSPENSION HEIGHT SENSOR HI—R.F.	424
** TAN	FUEL INJECTOR #1 CYLINDER OR BANK #1	555
TAN-BLACK	PRESSURE SWITCH TO KEY SWITCH	409
TAN-BLACK	BRAKE WEAR SENSOR	457
TAN-BLACK	WINDOW REG. SW. REAR TO LIMIT SW.	407
** TAN-BLACK	ABS MODULE REAR RIGHT WHEEL SPEED OUTPUT	999
TAN-BLACK	ELECTRONIC SHOCK FEEDBACK ACTUATOR TO RELAY	845
TAN-BLACK	DIGITAL AUDIO DISC LOGIC SENSOR	849
TAN-BLACK	MEMORY MIRROR MODULE TO LH VERTICAL DRIVE	897
** TAN-BLACK	HIGH ELECTRIC DRIVE COOLING FAN	559
TAN-BLACK	LH FRONT SENSOR (LOW) TO MODULE	522
TAN-BLACK	AIR BAG DIAGNOSTIC MODULE (MONITOR) TO LH SENSOR	622
TAN-BLACK	VEHICLE MAINTENANCE MONITOR MODULE TO ENGINE STRAP	908
TAN-BLACK	MODULATOR TO THERMO. SWITCH	939
TAN-LT BLUE	MASS AIR FLOW RETURN	968
TAN-LT BLUE	FUEL INJECTOR #5 CYLINDER	559
TAN-LT BLUE	INDICATOR RELAY TO RH TURN LAMP	817
TAN-LT BLUE	TRANSMISSION OVERDRIVE SWITCH TO EEC MODULE	224
TAN-LT BLUE	AUTOLAMP AMPLIFIER TO RHEOSTAT	216
TAN-LT BLUE	FEEDBACK CARB. COIL 4	98
TAN-LT GREEN	FEEDBACK CARB. COIL 3	97
TAN-LT GREEN	ANTI-THEFT SYSTEM SWITCH FEED	23
TAN-LT GREEN	ODOMETER SENSOR TO EEC MODULE	223
** TAN-LT GREEN	MILEAGE SENSOR TO EEC MODULE	223
TAN-LT GREEN	AMPLIFIER SWITCH FEED TO RIGHT REAR SPEAKER	825
TAN-LT GREEN	BRAKE FLUID RES. SWITCH TO MODULE	512
TAN-LT GREEN	TURN SIGNAL RELAY TO TURN FLASHER	494
TAN-ORANGE	LH FRONT SENSOR (HIGH) TO MODULE	521
TAN-ORANGE	FUEL INJECTOR #7 CYLINDER	561
TAN-ORANGE	EEC MODULE—DATA PLUS	914
TAN-ORANGE	FOG LAMP SW. TO FOG LAMP	478
TAN-ORANGE	COOLANT TEMPERATURE SWITCH TO CONTROL RELAY	197
TAN-ORANGE	AIR COND. SW. (LO) TO AIR COND. BLOWER MOTOR	184
TAN-ORANGE	FEEDBACK CARB. COIL 2	96
TAN-RED	FEEDBACK CARB. COIL 1	95
TAN-RED	RELAY TO MAP LAMP SWITCH	133
TAN-RED	MCV MODULE TO VIP FUNCTION TESTER	201
TAN-RED	THERMACTOR TIMER TO RELAY	252
TAN-RED	ELECTRONIC SHOCK METAL OXIDE VERISTOR	846
TAN-RED	MEMORY MIRROR MODULE TO LH HORIZONTAL DRIVE	898
** TAN-RED	FUEL INJECTOR #7 CYLINDER	561
TAN-RED	POWER RELAY TO FUSE LINK	533
TAN-RED	VALVE #6 TO MODULE	510
TAN-RED	MULTIPLEX COMPUTER FEED	792
TAN-RED	HEATED WINDSHIELD TRIGGER CIRCUIT SW. TO MODULE	681
TAN-RED	WINDOW REG. SW. FRONT TO LIMIT SW.	408
TAN-WHITE	AMPLIFIER SWITCH FEED TO LEFT REAR SPEAKER	827
TAN-WHITE	IDLE RPM SOLENOID TO CONTROL UNIT	744
TAN-WHITE	INDICATOR RELAY TO LH TURN LAMP	818
TAN-WHITE	EMISSION SPEED SENSOR TO MODULATOR CONTROL	934
TAN-WHITE	TAILLAMP SWITCH FEED	195
TAN-WHITE	INTERLOCK MODULE TO CENTER SEAT SENSOR SWITCH	87
** TAN-WHITE	TRANSMISSION OVERDRIVE SWITCH TO EEC MODULE	224
TAN-YELLOW	A/C PRESSURE SWITCH TO CONTROL RELAY	198
TAN-YELLOW	TONE GENERATOR	183
TAN-YELLOW	AIR COND. CONDENSOR THERMAL SWITCH FEED	509
TAN-YELLOW	FUSE LINK TO MOTOR RELAY	537
** TAN-YELLOW	IGNITION COIL NEGATIVE TERMINAL	11
TAN-YELLOW HASH	FEED TO VACUUM DOOR LOCK SWITCH	114
WHITE	KEYLESS DOOR LOCK OUTPUT (ALL) FROM MODULE	134
WHITE	ASH RECEPTACLE LAMP FEED	17
WHITE	TRAILER GROUND	49
WHITE	WINDSHIELD WIPER SW. TO WINDSHIELD WIPER MOTOR	58
WHITE	SUPPLEMENTAL ALTERNATOR STATOR B TERM. TO WINDSHIELD	71
WHITE	REAR WINDOW REGULATOR SWITCH FEED	176
WHITE	KEYLESS DOOR LOCK SEAT SWITCH SENSOR TO MODULE	177
WHITE	GROUND RETURN TO TOWING VEHICLE	206
** WHITE	TRAILER BROWN	206
WHITE	ELECTRONIC CLUSTER FROM GAUGE SELECT SWITCH IN KEYBOARD	289
WHITE	SPEAKER VOICE COIL RETURN AMP INPUT	281

COLOR	DESCRIPTION*	CIRCUIT
WHITE	SEAT REG. SW. TO VERT. SOLENOID BATT. TERM.	307
WHITE	R.H. REMOTE MIRROR SOLENOID CONTROL	545
WHITE	FUEL INJECTOR #2 CYLINDER	556
WHITE	RHEOSTAT TO SENSOR	508
WHITE	DOOR WIRE	628
** WHITE	AWD MODULE TO AWD FUNCTION LAMP	994
WHITE	ELECT SHIFT 4 X 4 MODULE TO MOTOR POSITION #4	770
WHITE	C.B. MIC-AUDIO	713
WHITE	RELAY COIL FEED #3	725
WHITE	RIGHT REAR SHOCK DAMPENING RELAY TO CONTROL MODULE	650
WHITE	ACTUATOR POSITION SENSOR RIGHT REAR	843
WHITE	VALVE #3 TO MODULE	497
WHITE	INERTIA SWITCH TO MODULE	866
WHITE	ELECT. ENG. CONTL. MOD. TO EXHAUST HEAT CONTRL SOC.	377
** WHITE	FUEL INJECTOR #2 CYLINDER OR BANK #2	556
WHITE	TIME DELAY RELAY	332
WHITE	REARVIEW OUTSIDE MIRROR COUNTERCLOCKWISE	412
WHITE BASE	LH REAR TAIL LAMP BULB OUTAGE	102
WHITE-BLACK	THERMOCOUPLE 2 NEG. TO EXHAUST SYST. OVERTEMP PROTECT MODULE	92
WHITE-BLACK	ELAPSED TIME SWITCH TO MESSAGE CENTER	165
WHITE-BLACK	ALTERNATOR REG. "S" TERM. TO ALTERNATOR "S" TERM.	4
WHITE-BLACK	LF WINDOW REG. SW. TO LF WINDOW REG. MOTOR	226
WHITE-BLACK	5V TO-MESSAGE CENTER TO DISPLAY	168
WHITE-BLACK	HEADLAMP SWITCH TO AUXILIARY LAMPS	188
WHITE-BLACK	THERMACTOR DIVERTER VALVE FEED	200
WHITE-BLACK	THROTTLE KICKER RELAY TO MCU MODULE	393
WHITE-BLACK	ACTUATOR POSITION SENSOR LEFT FRONT	840
WHITE-BLACK	MODULE TO MOTOR FEED	662
WHITE-BLACK	C.B. PUSH TO TALK	702
WHITE-BLACK	MULTIPLEX REVERSE DIMMING	731
WHITE-BLACK	THERMACTOR CLUTCH RELAY TO CLUTCH	567
WHITE-BLACK	WASHER CONTROL SWITCH FEED	950
WHITE-LT BLUE	MODULE TO DOWN SWITCH	659
WHITE-LT BLUE	SURE TRACK DIAGNOSTIC	606
WHITE-LT BLUE	C.B. VOLUME CONTROL	709
WHITE-LT BLUE	TEMP SWITCH TO WARNING DEVICE	737
WHITE-LT BLUE	STARTER INTERRUPT RELAY TO NEUTRAL START SWITCH	900
WHITE-LT BLUE	VEHICLE MAINTENANCE MONITOR MODULE TO OIL TEMP OUTPUT	906
WHITE-LT BLUE	MODULE TO SWITCH	465
WHITE-LT BLUE	FUSED ACCY FEED #3	294
WHITE-LT BLUE	ELECT. ENG. CONTL. MOD. TO IDLE SPD. CONTL. MOTOR #1	264
WHITE-LT BLUE	RH FRONT TURN SIGNAL LAMP	2
WHITE-LT BLUE	DISTRIBUTOR ELECTRONIC CONTROL FEED	20
WHITE-LT GREEN	RH AND LH REAR RUNNING LAMP BULB OUTAGE	110
WHITE-LT GREEN	AUX WATER VALVE FEED	456
WHITE-LT GREEN	C.B. SCAN SWITCH	710
WHITE-LT GREEN	BLOWER MOTOR RELAY TO ENG. WATER TEMP. SWITCH (COLD)	761
** WHITE-LT GREEN	OVERDRIVE CANCEL INDICATOR LAMP	911
WHITE-LT GREEN	WATER TEMP. WARNING LAMP TO WATER TEMP. SW. (COLD)	642
WHITE-LT GREEN	RH MIRROR LEFT/RIGHT MOTOR COMMON	952
WHITE-LT GREEN	SPEAKER VOICE COIL FEED—FRONT (RIGHT CHANNEL)	805
WHITE-ORANGE	HEATER & A/C CONTROL SW. TO INST. PANEL THERMISTOR	790
WHITE-ORANGE	AIR BAG READY INDICATOR L (DEPLOY) TO SAFING SENSOR	611
WHITE-ORANGE	C.B. DOWN SWITCH	703
WHITE-ORANGE	RADIO SEEK	728
WHITE-ORANGE	RELEASE LEVER WARN INDICATOR LAMP — CONSOLE	877
WHITE-ORANGE	ACTUATOR POSITION SENSOR LEFT REAR	842
WHITE-ORANGE	LEFT FRONT AIR INPUT RETURN	857
WHITE-ORANGE	ELECTRIC PVS TO MCU MODULE	392
WHITE-ORANGE	INTERLOCK MODULE TO CENTER BUCKLE SWITCH	83
WHITE-ORANGE	RESET SWITCH TO MESSAGE CENTER	166
WHITE-ORANGE	MEMORY SEAT SWITCH LAMP DRIVE	272
** WHITE-ORANGE	THERMACTOR AIR BYPASS (TAB)	190
WHITE-PINK	LOW OIL LEVEL RELAY TO SENSOR	258
WHITE-PINK	ECU TO VACUUM SWITCH 2	213
WHITE-PINK	SERVO VENT SOLENOID TO CONTROL TRANSISTOR	146
** WHITE-PINK	TACHOMETER FEED	648
WHITE-PINK	BUZZER TO WARNING INDICATOR RELAY	160
WHITE-PINK	STARTER CONTROL TO INTERLOCK MODULE	33
WHITE-PINK	FUEL FILLER DOOR RELEASE SWITCH TO FUEL FILLER DOOR RELEASE SOLENOID	482
WHITE-PINK	HEATER & A/C CONTROL SW. (DEFOG) TO DEFROST CONT. SOLENOID	775
WHITE-PURPLE	SENSOR AMPLIFY UNIT TO CONTROL UNIT #4	760
WHITE-PURPLE	C.B. SQUELCH POT	701
** WHITE-PURPLE	RH MIRROR UP/DOWN MOTOR COMMON	953
WHITE-PURPLE	AMPLIFIER SWITCH GROUND TO RIGHT REAR SPEAKER	824
WHITE-PURPLE	POWER FEED-SWITCH TO FRONT AMPLIFIER	829
WHITE-PURPLE	MEMORY MIRROR MODULE	895
** WHITE-PURPLE	MEMORY MIRROR MODULE LH VERTICAL POSITION	895
WHITE-PURPLE	FUSE PANEL FEED TO RELAY	326
WHITE-PURPLE	DECK LID SWITCH TO ANTI-THEFT MODULE	26
WHITE-PURPLE	AUTOLAMP AMPLIFIER TO SENSOR	218
WHITE-PURPLE	FUSED ACCY FEED #1	296
WHITE-PURPLE	FUEL METERING CONTROL LEVER ACTUATOR 2 PLUS	312
** WHITE-PURPLE	TO TEST CONNECTOR	209
WHITE-RED	SPEAKER VOICE COIL FEED FRONT (R. CHANNEL) AMP INPUT	279
WHITE-RED	COLD START TIMING RETARD SOLENOID	240
** WHITE-RED	EEC MODULE TO TRANSMISSION	912
WHITE-RED	H L SW. TO CHIMES	257
WHITE-RED	ELECT. ENG. CONTRL. MOD. TO TEST CONN #1	209
WHITE-RED	THERMACTOR DUMP VALVE FEED	190
WHITE-RED	OIL PRESSURE INDICATOR TO OIL PRESSURE SENDING UNIT	31
WHITE-RED	RH REAR TAIL LAMP BULB OUTAGE	103
WHITE-RED	AIR PUMP SOLENOID SIGNAL	100
WHITE-RED	FLASHER TO EMERGENCY WARNING SWITCH	385

* IN SOME CASES, THERE MAY BE ADDITIONAL CIRCUIT FUNCTIONS INCLUDED IN THE CIRCUIT DESCRIPTION LISTED.

** DENOTES A NEW OR STANDARDIZED CIRCUIT.

STANDARD CIRCUIT CHART (BY COLOR)

COLOR	DESCRIPTION*	CIRCUIT	COLOR	DESCRIPTION*	CIRCUIT
WHITE-RED	ACTUATOR POSITION SENSOR RIGHT FRONT	841	YELLOW-BLACK	LEFT FRONT WINDOW REGULATOR SWITCH TO RIGHT REAR WINDOW REGULATOR MOTOR	319
WHITE-RED	LAMP RELAY TO MARKER LAMPS	667	YELLOW-LT BLUE	LEFT FRONT WINDOW REGULATOR SWITCH TO LEFT REAR WINDOW REGULATOR MOTOR	316
WHITE-RED	PROCESSOR TO THERMACTOR CLUTCH RELAY	566	YELLOW-LT BLUE	HEATER & A/C CONTROL SW. (DE-ICE) TO CLIMATE CONTROL UNIT	248
WHITE-RED	FUEL PUMP RESISTOR TO RELAY	922	YELLOW-LT BLUE	SPEED INPUT TO MESSAGE CENTER	136
WHITE-YELLOW	AIR BAG DIAGNOSTIC MODULE (DEPLOY) TO LH SENSOR	621	YELLOW-LT BLUE	STARTING MOTOR TO STARTING MOTOR RELAY	113
WHITE-YELLOW	C.B. UP SWITCH	707	YELLOW-LT BLUE	POSITION SENSE RETURN	435
WHITE-YELLOW	CHOKE RELAY TO MCU MODULE	391	YELLOW-LT BLUE	HORN SWITCH FEED	460
WHITE-YELLOW	MESSAGE CENTER OUTPUT CLOCK TO DISPLAY	167	YELLOW-LT BLUE	SELECTOR SWITCH TO AFT AXLE TANK	675
** WHITE-YELLOW	ELECTRONIC PRESSURE CONTROL	925	YELLOW-LT BLUE	SEAT REGULATOR SWITCH TO FRONT MOTOR (RH)	984
WHITE-YELLOW	POWER SERVO TO CLIMATE CONTROL UNIT (AMP)	247	** YELLOW-LT BLUE	LH UP/DOWN MOTOR COMMON	948
YELLOW	SWITCH ON TO RELAY	275	YELLOW-LT BLUE	SEAT REGULATOR SWITCH TO FRONT MOTOR (LH)	990
YELLOW	ELECTRONIC CLUSTER FROM TRIP RESET SWITCH IN KEYBOARD	286	YELLOW-LT BLUE	SEAT REGULATOR SWITCH TO FRONT MOTOR (LH)	978
YELLOW	12 GA FUSE LINK	303	YELLOW-LT BLUE	WINDOW SWITCH TO LEFT REAR MOTOR	885
YELLOW	HORIZONTAL SEAT REG. MOTOR TO RELAY	179	YELLOW-LT GREEN	SEAT REGULATOR SWITCH TO REAR MOTOR (LH)	982
YELLOW	LF WINDOW REG. SW. TO LF WINDOW REG. MOTOR	227	YELLOW-LT GREEN	AIR COND. CONTROL SW. TO FRESH-AIR RECIRC. DOOR SOLENOID	660
YELLOW	KEYLESS DOOR LOCK SWITCH DATA BIT 4 TO MODULE	122	YELLOW-LT GREEN	SPLICE #2 TO MODULE	529
YELLOW	TRAILER LH TURN SIGNAL	52	YELLOW-LT GREEN	SPLICE #3 TO PRESSURE SWITCH	534
YELLOW	BATTERY TO LOAD	37	YELLOW-LT GREEN	FLUID SWITCH TO GROUND STUD	550
YELLOW	REARVIEW OUTSIDE MIRROR UP	410	YELLOW-LT GREEN	SPLICE #2 TO SPLICE #3	551
YELLOW	POWER "THIGH" BOLSTER UP	491	YELLOW-LT GREEN	SPLICE #2 TO COUP GROUND "B"	552
YELLOW	EGR VALVE TO EEC MODULE FEED	362	YELLOW-LT GREEN	ALT. SHUNT TO AMMETER	654
YELLOW	C.B. B-DIGIT	716	YELLOW-LT GREEN	MODULE TO RELEASE SOLENOID	664
YELLOW	MULTIPLEX WIPER RATE	700	YELLOW-LT GREEN	SEAT REGULATOR SWITCH TO REAR MOTOR (RH)	988
YELLOW	ANTI-LOCK MODULE TO ANTI-LOCK CONTROL VALVE	678	YELLOW-LT GREEN	POSITION SENSE ENABLE	437
YELLOW	ELECT SHIFT 4 × 4 MODULE TO MOTOR CONTROL COUNTER CLOCKWISE	777	YELLOW-LT GREEN	MOVABLE STEERING COLUMN SOLENOID FEED	375
YELLOW	AIR SUSPENSION DIODE SWITCH TO CONTROL MODULE	635	YELLOW-LT GREEN	POWER STEERING PRESSURE SWITCH	330
YELLOW	ALT POWER RELAY TO CONTROL MODULE	583	YELLOW-LT GREEN	TRANSMISSION OVERDRIVE SWITCH TO HEAT MODULE	324
YELLOW	CONVERTIBLE TOP RELAY TO SWITCH	586	YELLOW-LT GREEN	HORN RELAY TO HORN	6
YELLOW	AIR SUSPENSION DIODE SWITCH TO CONTROL MODULE	635	YELLOW-LT GREEN	WINDOW REGULATOR RELAY FEED	193
YELLOW	DOOR WIRE	631	YELLOW-LT GREEN	GROUND STUD TO SPLICE #2	548
YELLOW	OIL PRESSURE SWITCH TO CUTOUT RELAY	669	YELLOW-RED	RH FRONT SENSOR (HIGH) TO MODULE	514
YELLOW	AMPLIFIER TO RHEOSTAT	507	YELLOW-RED	BLOWER MOTOR SPEED CONTROLLER TO RESISTOR #2 (MED.)	752
YELLOW	L.H. REMOTE MIRROR SOLENOID CONTROL	542	YELLOW-RED	HEATER & A/C CONTROL SW. TO BLOWER RELAY SW.	753
YELLOW	LEFT REAR AIR INPUT RETURN	859	YELLOW-RED	COIL "B" TO DISTRIBUTORLESS IGNITION MODULE	851
YELLOW	SEAT BELT INDICATOR LAMP TO MODULE	871	** YELLOW-RED	LH MIRROR LEFT/RIGHT MOTOR COMMON	947
YELLOW	VENT SWITCH TO LEFT FRONT VENT MOTOR	887	YELLOW-RED	WINDOW REG. SW. TO WINDOW REG. MOTOR	333
YELLOW	TOP CONTROL RELAY TO MOTOR — UP	902	YELLOW-RED	MCU MODULE TO KNOCK SENSOR	310
YELLOW-BLACK	COIL "A" TO DISTRIBUTORLESS IGNITION MODULE	850	YELLOW-RED	HOT WATER TEMP. RELAY TO HOT WATER TEMP. SENDING UNIT	45
YELLOW-BLACK	WINDOW SWITCH TO LEFT REAR MOTOR	884	YELLOW-RED	WINDSHIELD WIPER SW. TO WINDSHIELD WIPER MOTOR	61
YELLOW-BLACK	ACCELERATE DECELERATE SENSOR RETURN	837	YELLOW-RED	SERVO FEEDBACK POTENTIOMETER SIGNAL TO AMPLIFIER	148
YELLOW-BLACK	POWER RELAY BATTERY FEED	554	YELLOW-RED	STOP AND TURN BULB OUTAGE TO MESSAGE CENTER	135
YELLOW-BLACK	RH FRONT SENSOR (LOW) TO MODULE	516	** YELLOW-RED	ELECT. ENG. CONTRL. MOD. TO KNOCK SENSOR	310
** YELLOW-BLACK	MIRROR SWITCH COMMON	945	YELLOW-WHITE	ALTERNATOR OUTPUT	36
YELLOW-BLACK	RELAY TO ATC CONTROL	575	YELLOW-WHITE	FUEL GAUGE TO FUEL GAUGE SENDER	29
YELLOW-BLACK	LOW WASHER LEVEL TO SENSOR	793	YELLOW-WHITE	THERMAL SW. TO CLIMATE CONTROL UNIT	244
YELLOW-BLACK	REMOTE DEFROST	727	YELLOW-WHITE	SEAT PROCESSOR TO RECLINER MOTOR "UP"	439
YELLOW-BLACK	ELECT. ENG. CONTL. MOD. TO TEST CONN #2	382	YELLOW-WHITE	COIL "C" TO DISTRIBUTORLESS IGNITION MODULE	852
** YELLOW-BLACK	AWD MODULE TO TRANSFER CASE CLUTCH	992	YELLOW-WHITE	ELECT SHIFT 4 X 4 MODULE TO MOTOR POSITION #1	762
YELLOW-BLACK	GLOW PLUG TO CONTROL MODULE	472	YELLOW-WHITE	HEATED WINDSHIELD CONTROL TO HEATED WINDSHIELD SWITCH	738
YELLOW-BLACK	ELECTRONIC CONTROL UNIT TO ACCELERATION SOLENOID	46	YELLOW-WHITE	SEAT REGULATOR SWITCH TO HORZ. MOTOR (LH)	980
YELLOW-BLACK	RADIO ANTENNA SWITCH FEED	137	YELLOW-WHITE	SEAT REGULATOR SWITCH TO FRONT MOTOR (RH)	986
YELLOW-BLACK	KEYLESS DOOR LOCK SWITCH DATA BIT 3 TO MODULE	121	YELLOW-WHITE	ELECTRONIC THROTTLE VALVE POWER	925
YELLOW-BLACK	SIGNAL UNIT LAMP TO FUEL SIGNAL RELAY	215			
YELLOW-BLACK	LEFT FRONT WINDOW REGULATOR SWITCH TO RIGHT FRONT WINDOW REGULATOR MOTOR	313			

*IN SOME CASES, THERE MAY BE ADDITIONAL CIRCUIT
FUNCTIONS INCLUDED IN THE CIRCUIT DESCRIPTION LISTED.

** DENOTES A NEW OR STANDARDIZED CIRCUIT.

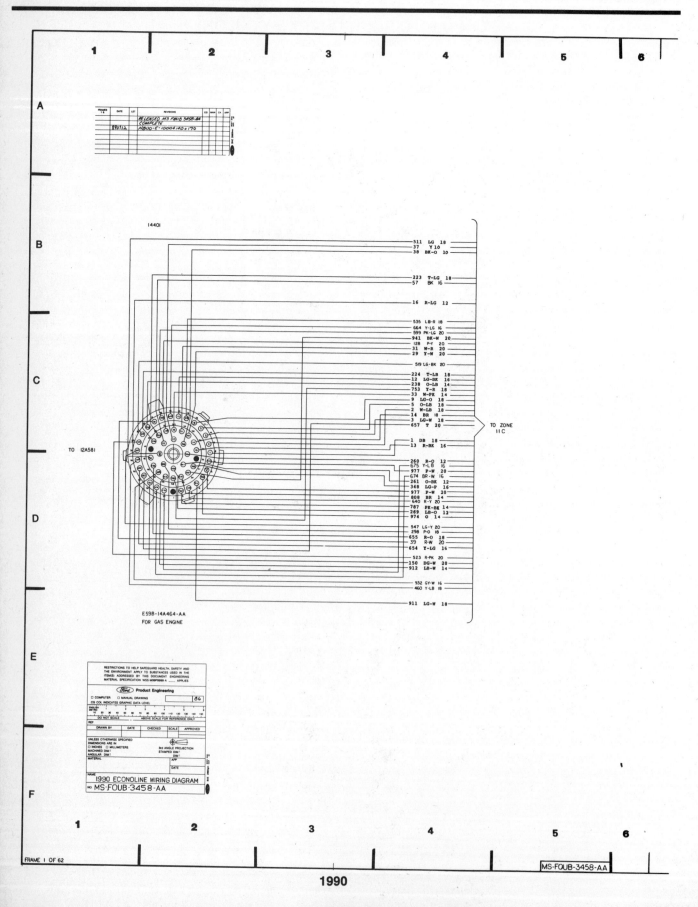

14401

511 LG 18
37 Y 10
38 BK-O 10

223 T-LG 18
57 BK 16

16 R-LG 12

535 LB-R 18
664 Y-LG 16
599 PK-LG 20
941 BK 20
128 P-Y 20
31 W-R 20
29 Y-W 20

519 LG-BK 20

224 T-LB 18
12 LG-DK 16
238 O-LB 14
753 Y-R 18
33 W-PK 14
9 LG-O 18
5 O-LB 18
2 W-LB 18
14 BR 18
3 LG-W 18
657 T 20

1 DB 18
13 R-BK 16

260 R-O 12
675 Y-LB 16
977 P-W 20
674 BR-W 16
261 O-BK 12
348 LG-P 16
977 P-W 20
808 BR 14
640 R-Y 20
787 PK-BK 14
269 LB-O 18
974 O 14

547 LG-Y 20
298 P-O 18
655 R-O 18
39 R-W 20
654 Y-LG 16

523 R-PK 20
150 DG-W 20
912 LB-W 14

932 GY-W 16
460 Y-LB 18

911 LG-W 18

TO ZONE
11C

TO 12A581

E59B-14A464-AA
FOR GAS ENGINE

RESTRICTIONS TO HELP SAFEGUARD HEALTH, SAFETY AND
THE ENVIRONMENT APPLY TO SUBSTANCES USED IN THE
ITEM(S) ADDRESSED BY THIS DOCUMENT ENGINEERING
MATERIAL SPECIFICATION WSS-M99P9999 A ____ APPLIES

Ford Product Engineering
□ COMPUTER   □ MANUAL DRAWING   86
CG COL INDICATES GRAPHIC DATA LEVEL
ENGLISH/
METRIC
10 20 30 40 50 60 70 80 90 100 110 120 130 140 150
DO NOT SCALE   ABOVE SCALE FOR REFERENCE ONLY
REF
DRAWN BY   DATE   CHECKED   SCALE   APPROVED

UNLESS OTHERWISE SPECIFIED
DIMENSIONS ARE IN
□ INCHES □ MILLIMETERS   3rd ANGLE PROJECTION
MACHINED DIM!   STAMPED DIM!
ANGULAR DIM!   DIM!
MATERIAL   APP!
                               DATE
NAME 1990 ECONOLINE WIRING DIAGRAM
NO. MS-FOUB-3458-AA

FRAME I OF 62

MS-FOUB-3458-AA

1990

6-128

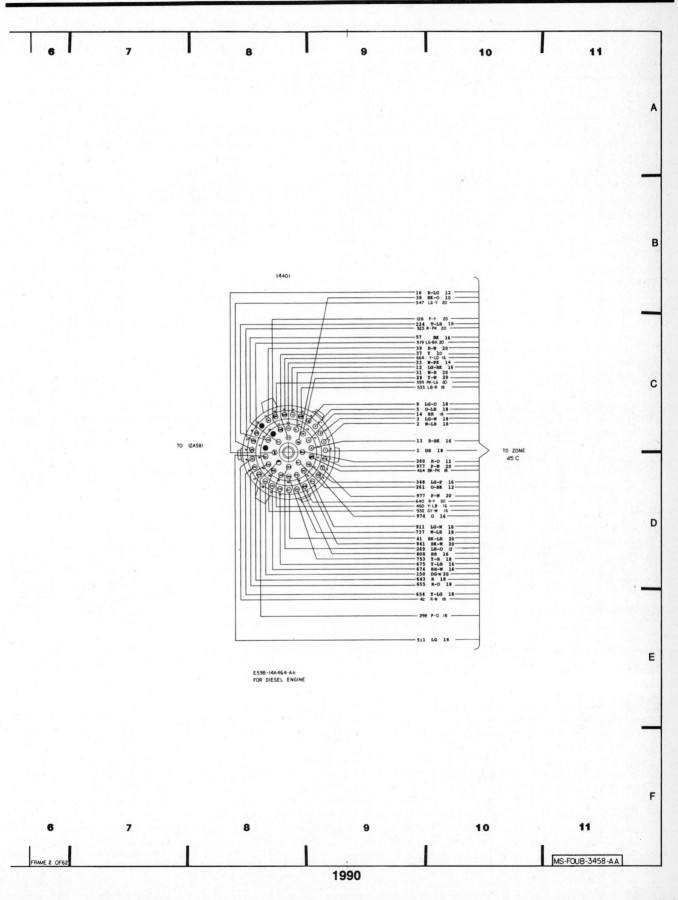

14401

TO 12A581

16   R-LG   12
38   BK-O   10
547 LG-Y   20

128 P-Y   20
224 T-LB   18
523 R-PK   20

57   BK   16
519 LG-BK 20
39   R-W   20
37   Y   10
664 Y-LG   16
33   W-PK   14
12   LG-BK 16
31   W-R   20
29   Y-W   20
599 PK-LG 20
535 LB-R   18

9   LG-O   18
5   O-LB   18
14   BR   18
3   LG-W   18
2   W-LB   18

13   R-BK   16

1   DB   18

260 R-O   12
977 P-W   20
464 BK-PK 18

348 LG-P   16
261 O-BK   12

977 P-W   20
640 R-Y   20
460 Y-LB   18
932 GY-W   16
974 O   16

911 LG-W   18
737 W-LB   18
41   BK-LB 20
941 BK-W   20
269 LB-O   12
808 BR   16
753 Y-R   18
675 Y-LB   16
674 BR-W   16
150 DG-W   20
643 R   18
655 R-O   18

654 Y-LG   18
42   R-W   18

298 P-O   18

511 LG   18

TO ZONE
45 C

E59B-14A464-AA
FOR DIESEL ENGINE

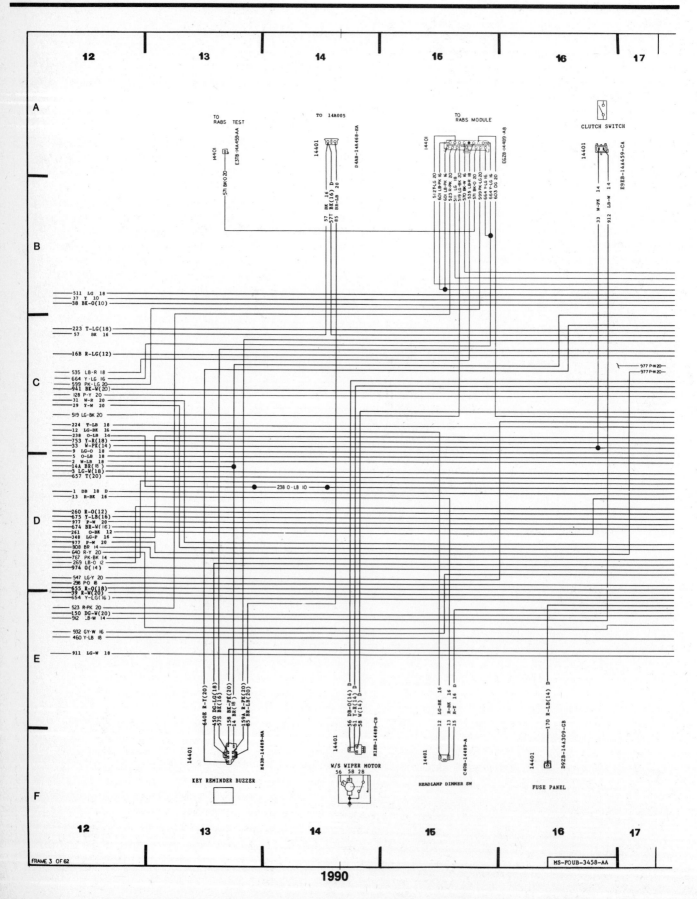

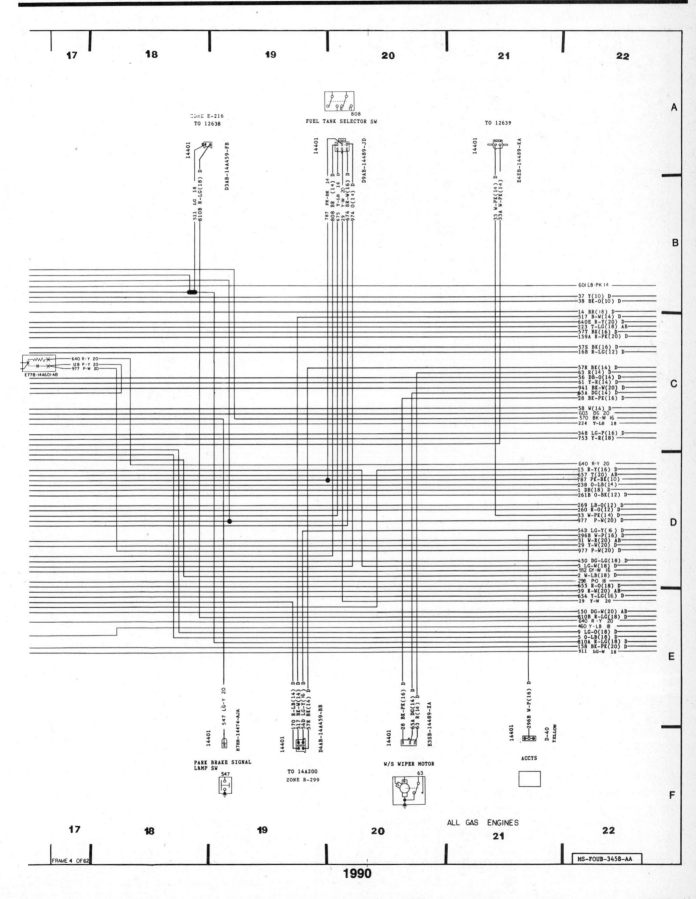

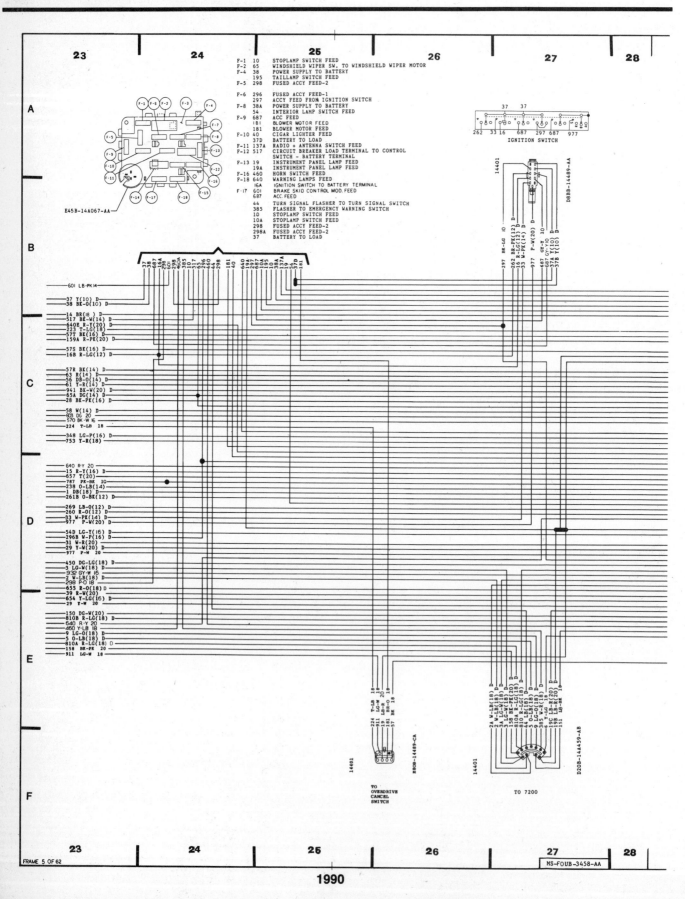

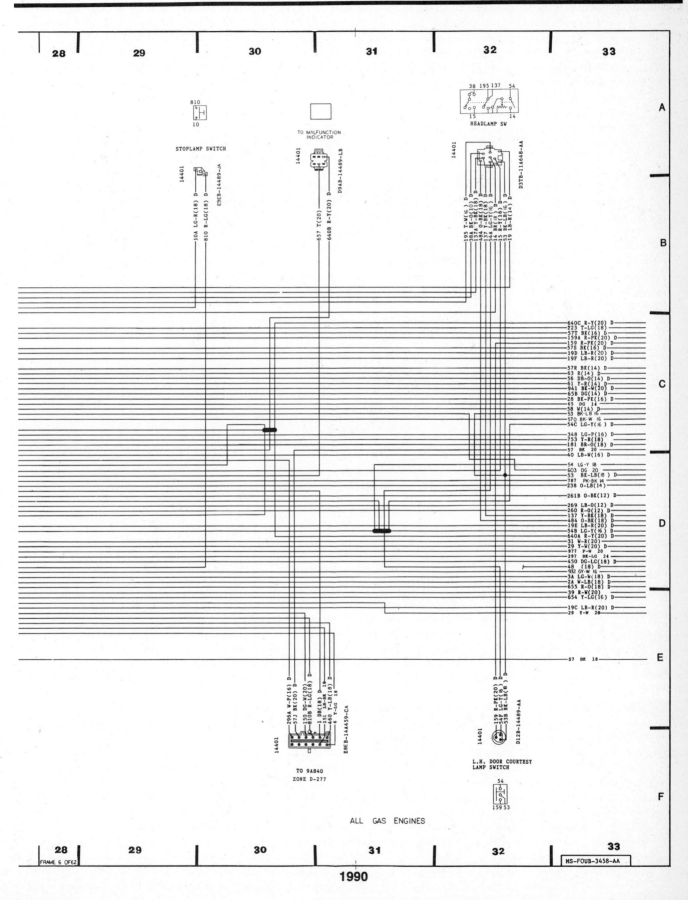

STOPLAMP SWITCH

TO MALFUNCTION
INDICATOR

HEADLAMP SW

L.H. DOOR COURTESY
LAMP SWITCH

ALL GAS ENGINES

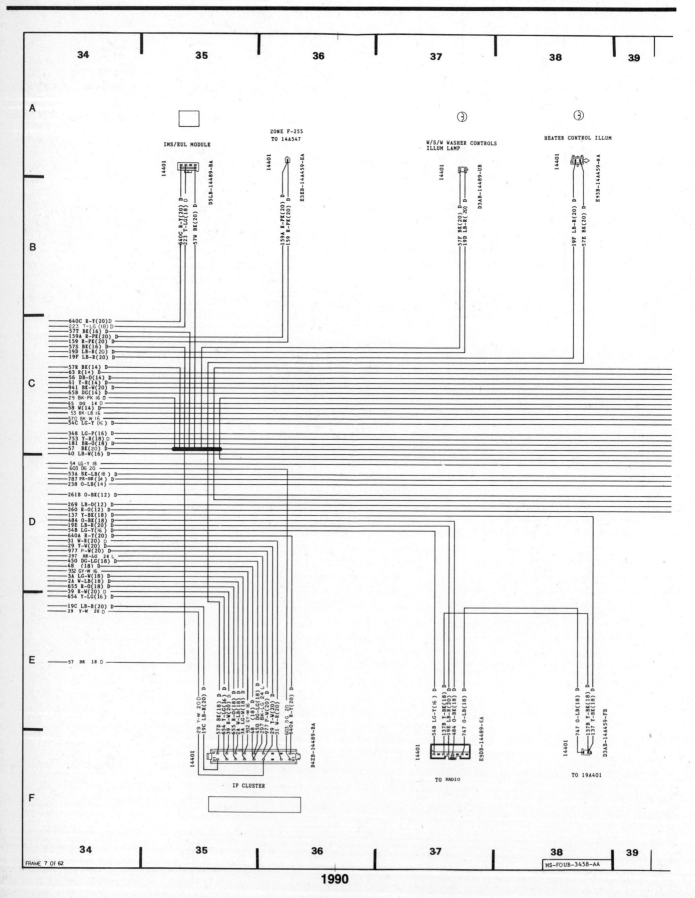

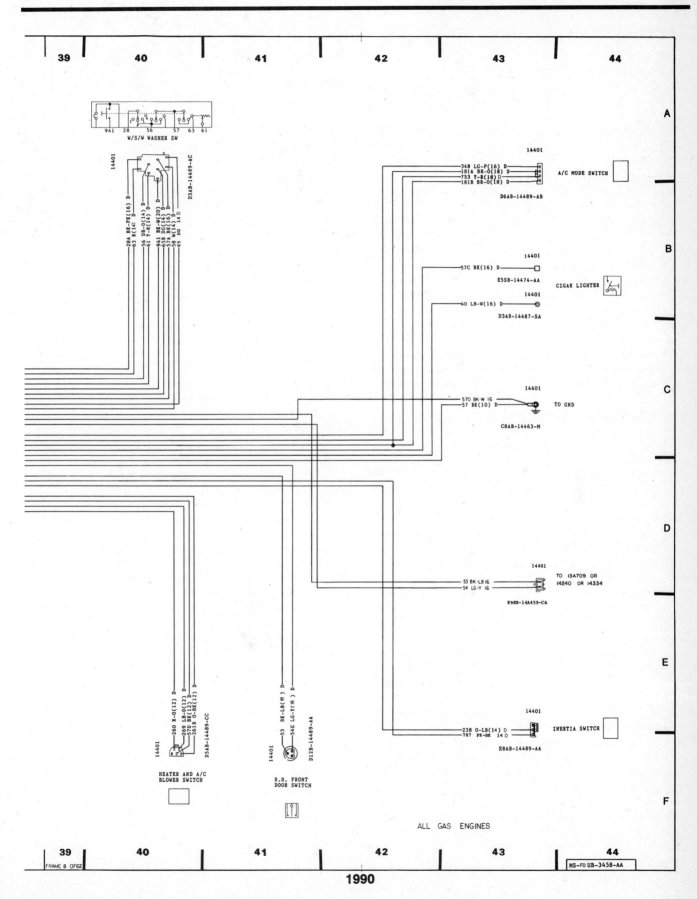

W/S/W WASHER SW

941 28 56 57 63 61

A/C MODE SWITCH

348 LG-P(16) D
181A BR-O(18) D
753 Y-R(18) D
181B BR-O(18) D

14401

D6AB-14489-AB

CIGAR LIGHTER

57C BK(16) D

14401

E5SB-14474-AA

40 LB-W(16) D

14401

D3AB-14487-SA

TO GND

570 BK-W 16
57 BK(10) D

14401

C8AB-14463-M

TO 13A709 OR
14240 OR 14334

53 BK-LB 16
54 LG-Y 16

14401

E9EB-14A459-CA

INERTIA SWITCH

238 O-LB(14) D
787 PK-BK 14 D

14401

E8AB-14489-AA

HEATER AND A/C
BLOWER SWITCH

260 R-O(12) D
269 LB-O(12) D
57U BK(12) D
261B O-BR(12) D
D5AB-14489-CC
14401

R.H. FRONT
DOOR SWITCH

53 BK-LB(18) D
54G LG-Y(18) D
D12B-14489-AA
14401

ALL GAS ENGINES

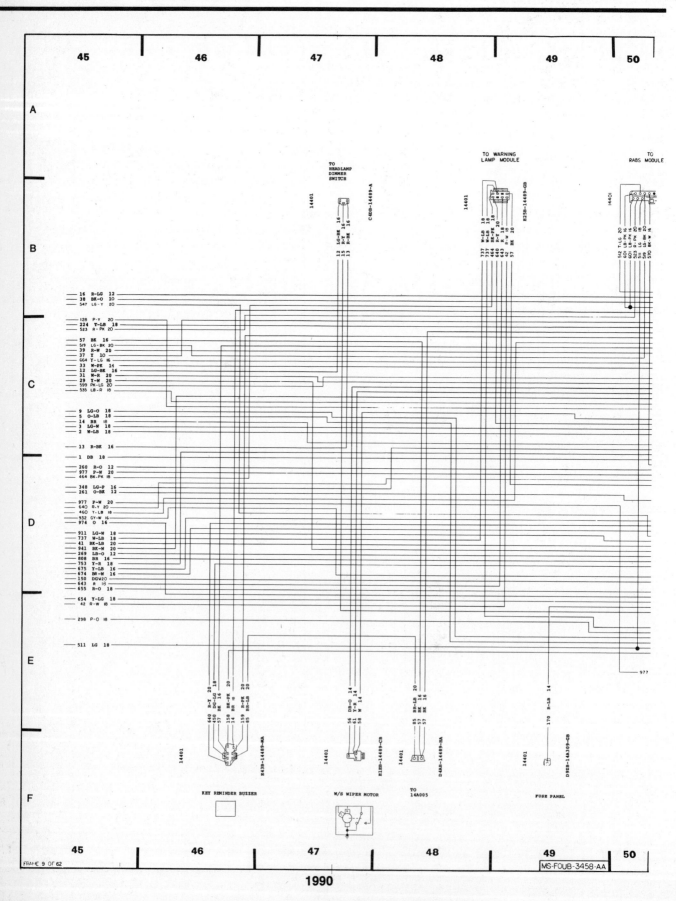

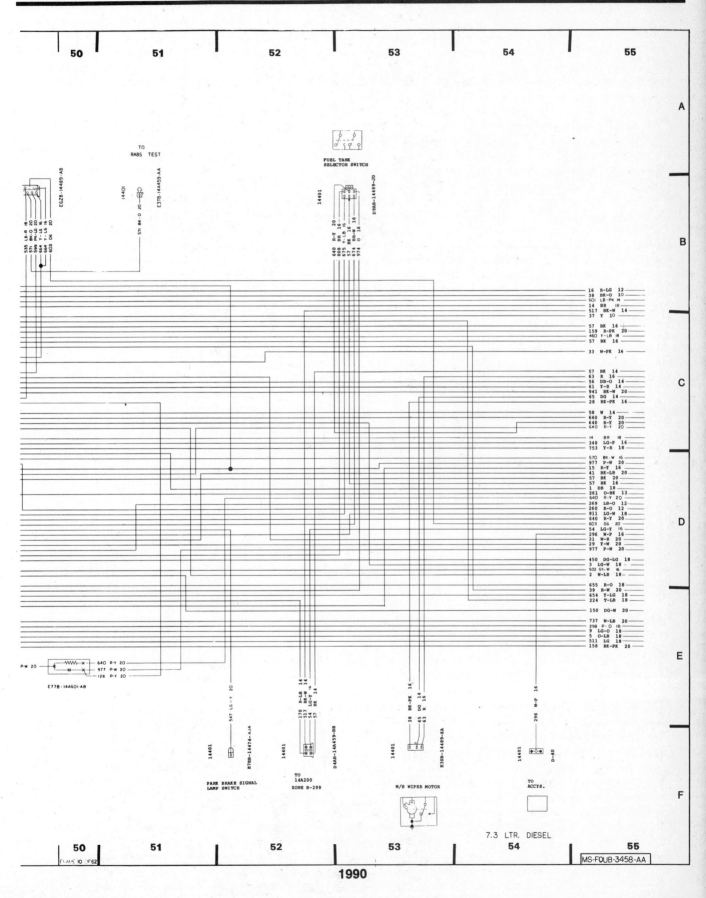

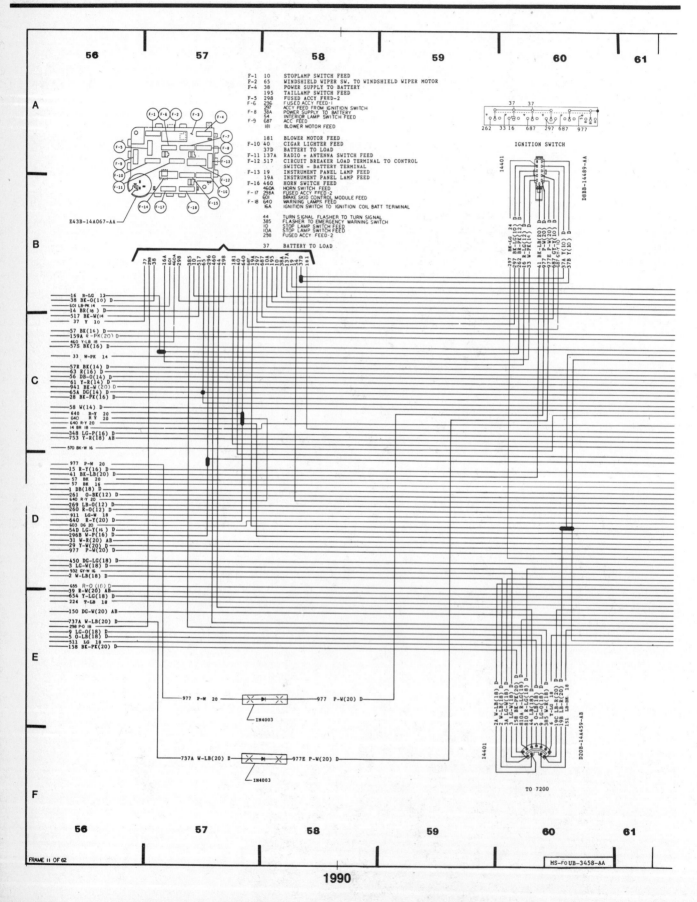

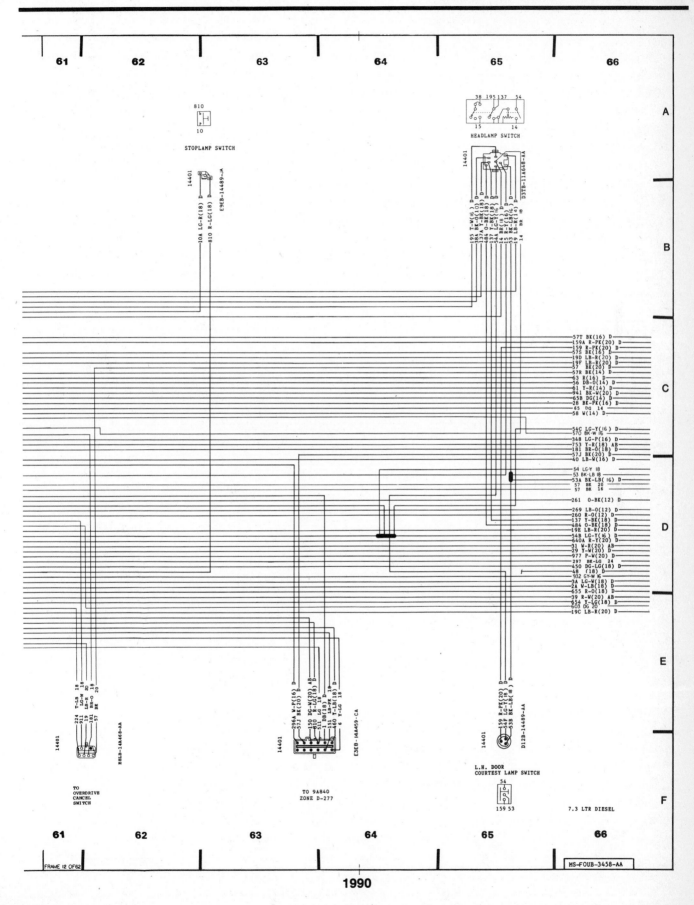

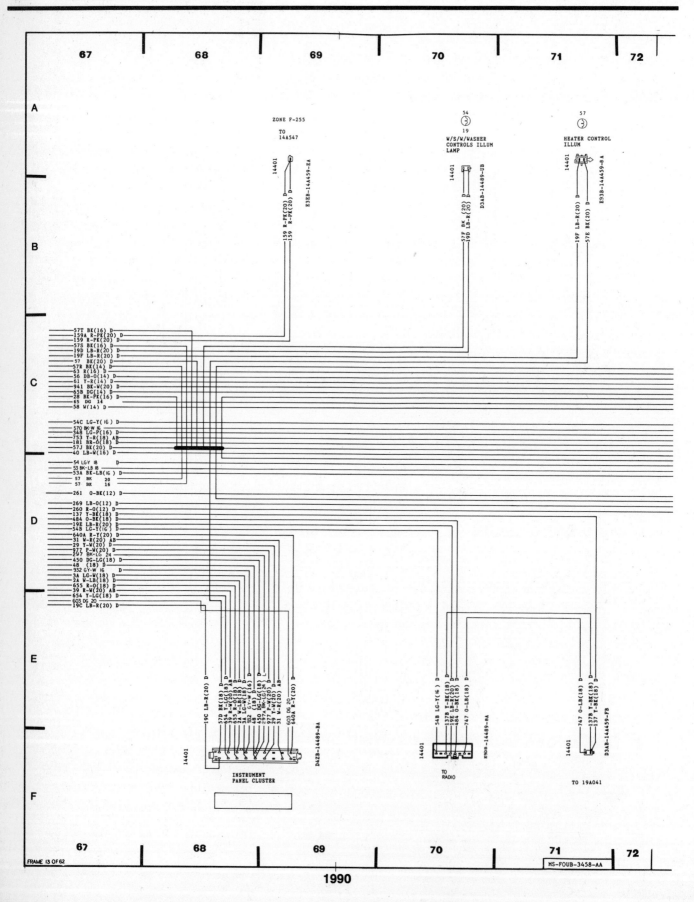

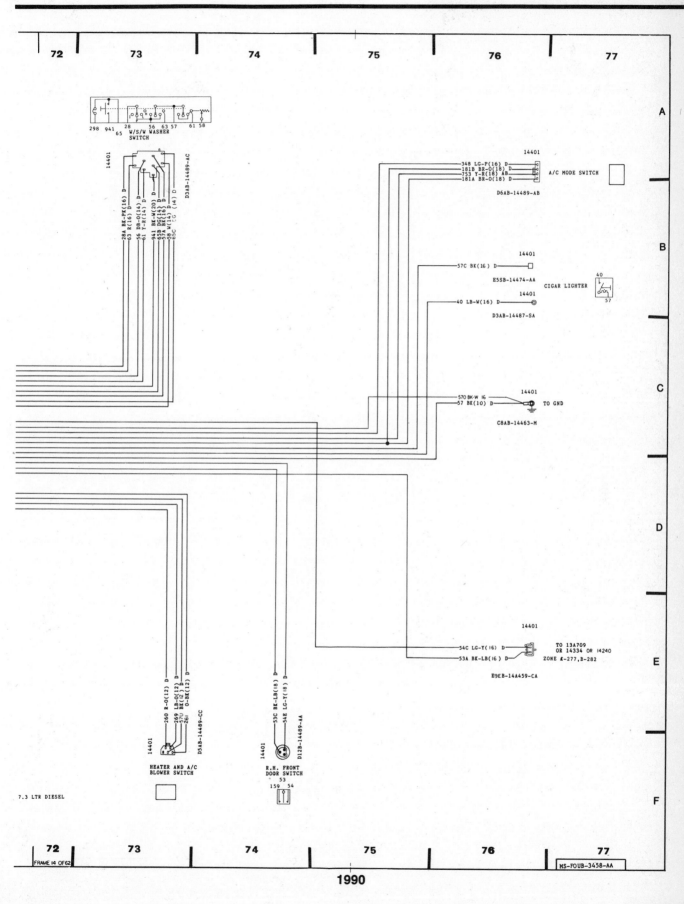

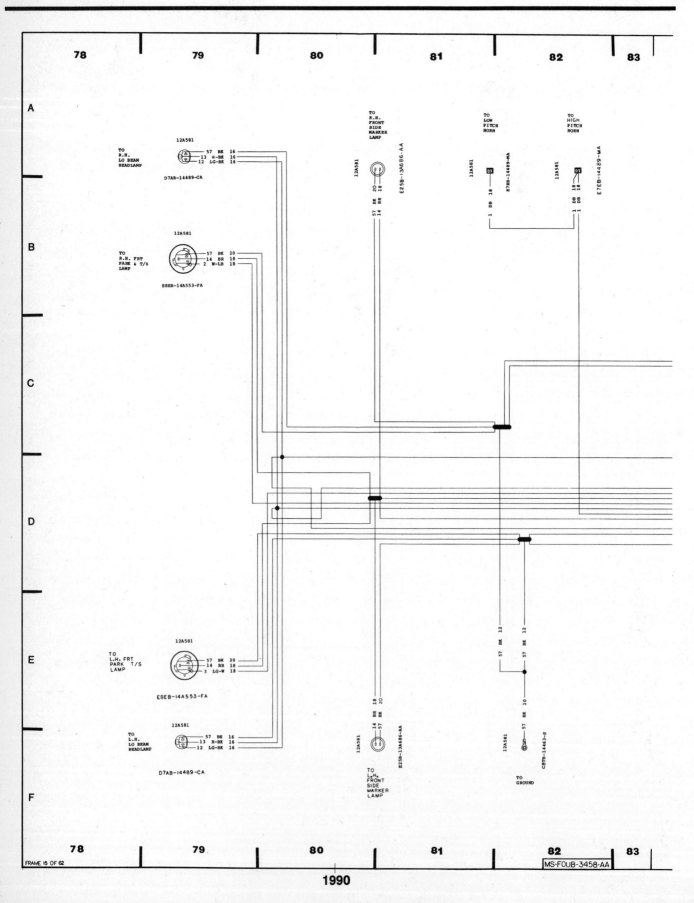

MS-F0UB-3458-AA

1990

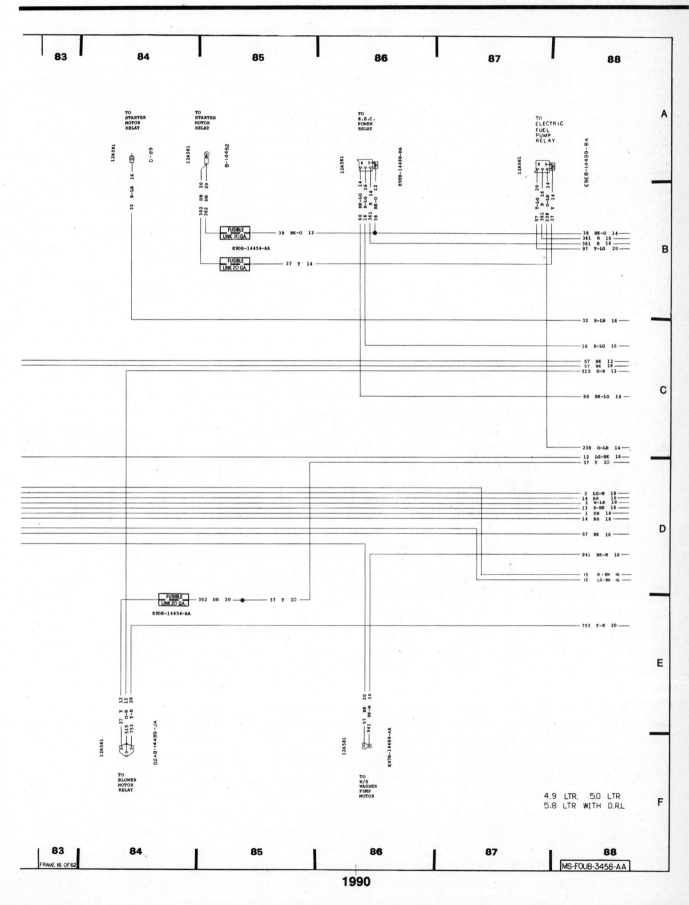

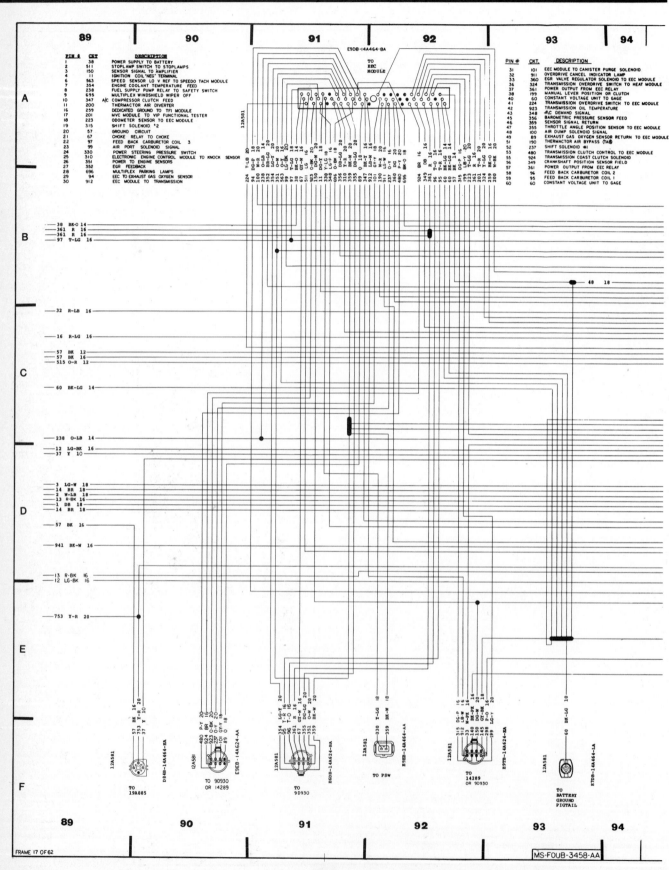

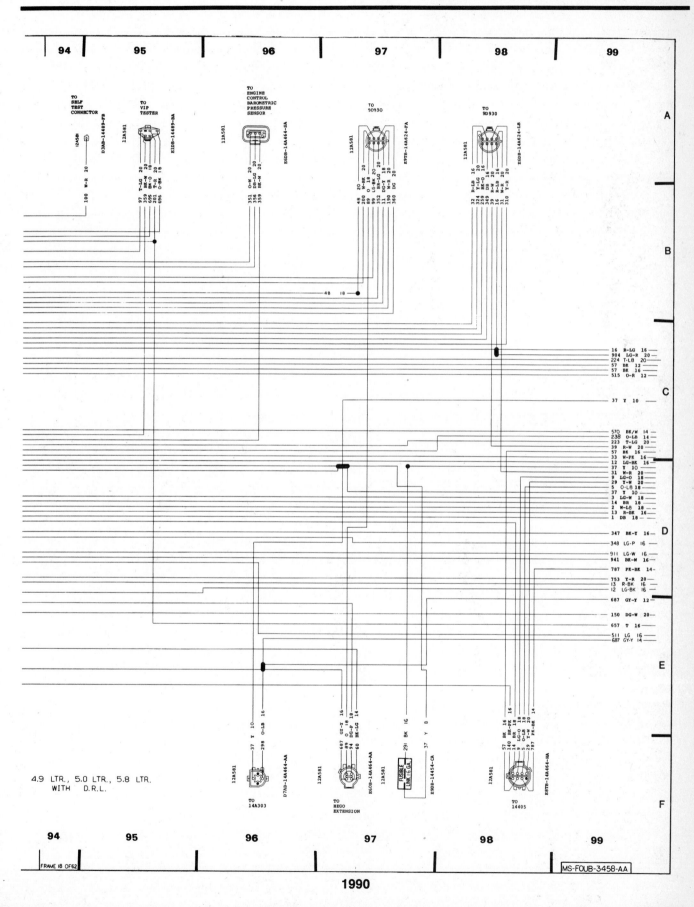

4.9 LTR., 5.0 LTR., 5.8 LTR.
WITH   D.R.L.

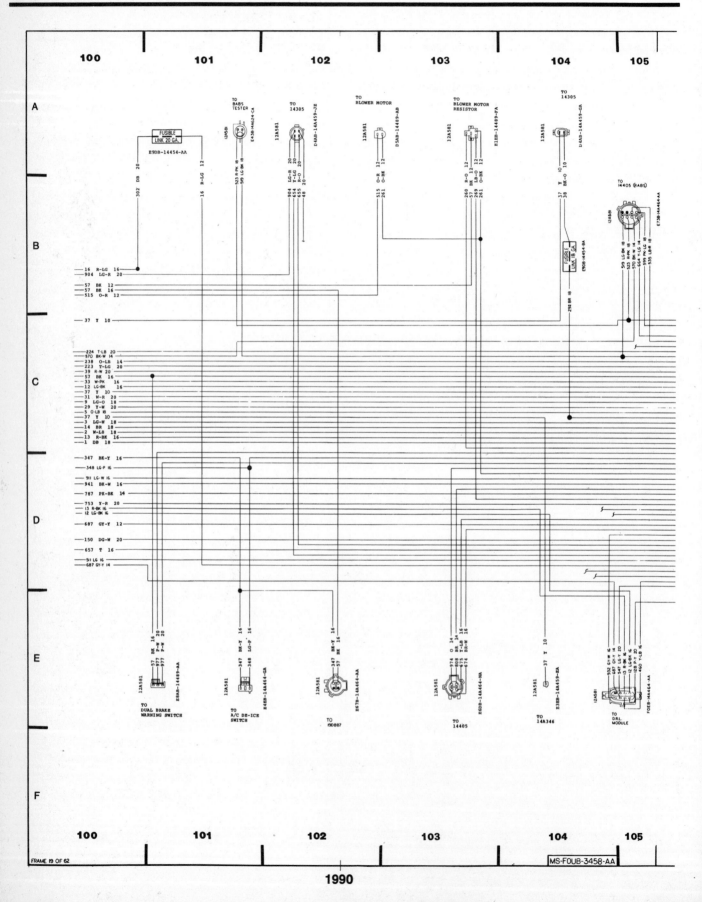

105   106   107   108   109   110

A

B

12A581

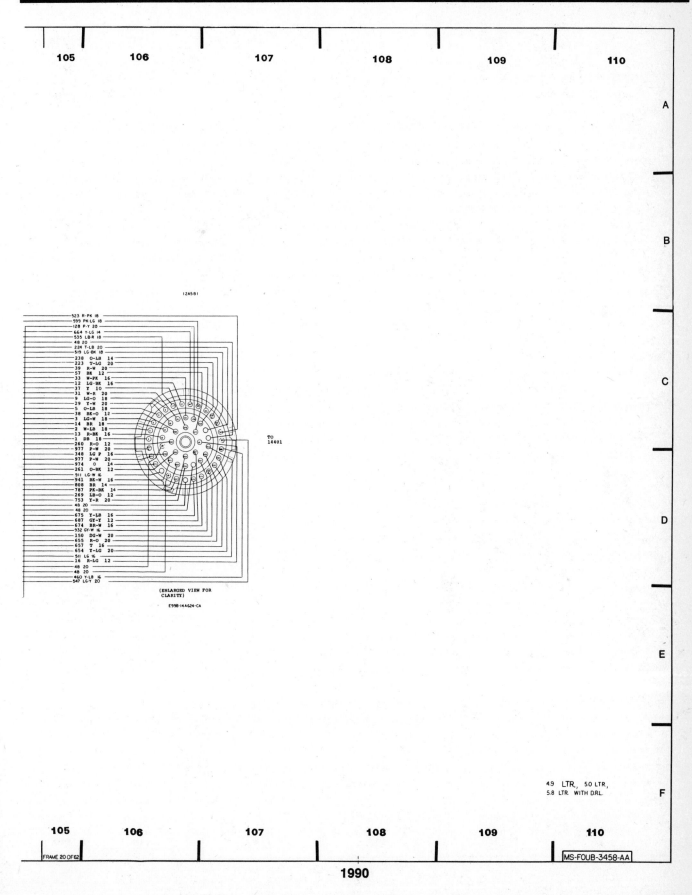

523 R-PK 18
599 PK-LG 18
128 P-Y 20
664 Y-LG 14
535 LB-R 18
48 20
224 T-LB 20
519 LG-BK 18
238 O-LB 14
223 T-LG 20
39 R-W 20
57 BK 12
33 W-PK 16
12 LG-BK 16
37 Y 10
31 W-R 20
9 LG-O 18
29 Y-W 20
5 O-LB 20
38 BK-O 12
3 LG-W 18
14 BR 18
2 W-LB 18
13 R-BK 16
1 DB 18
260 R-O 12
977 P-W 20
348 LG P 16
977 P-W 20
974 O 14
261 O-BK 12
911 LG-W 16
941 BK-W 16
808 BR 14
787 PK-BK 14
269 LB-O 12
753 Y-R 20
48 20
48 20
675 Y-LB 16
687 GY-Y 12
674 BR-W 16
932 GY-W 16
150 DG-W 20
655 R-O 20
657 T 16
654 Y-LG 20
511 LG 16
16 R-LG 12
48 20
48 20
460 Y-LB 16
547 LG-Y 20

TO
14401

(ENLARGED VIEW FOR
CLARITY)

E99B-14A624-CA

C

D

E

4.9 LTR., 5.0 LTR,
5.8 LTR. WITH D.R.L.

F

105   106   107   108   109   110

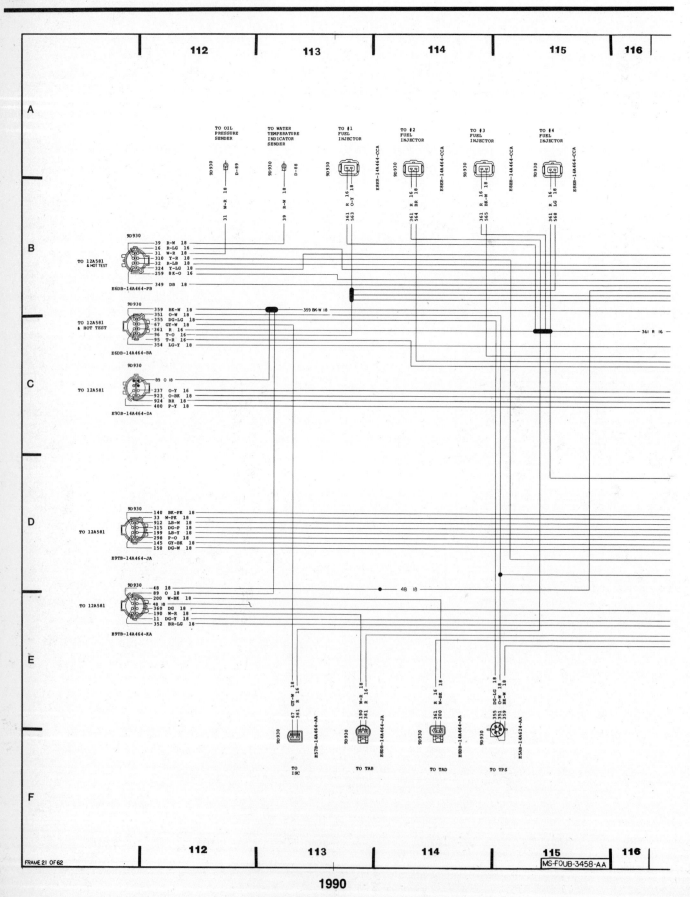

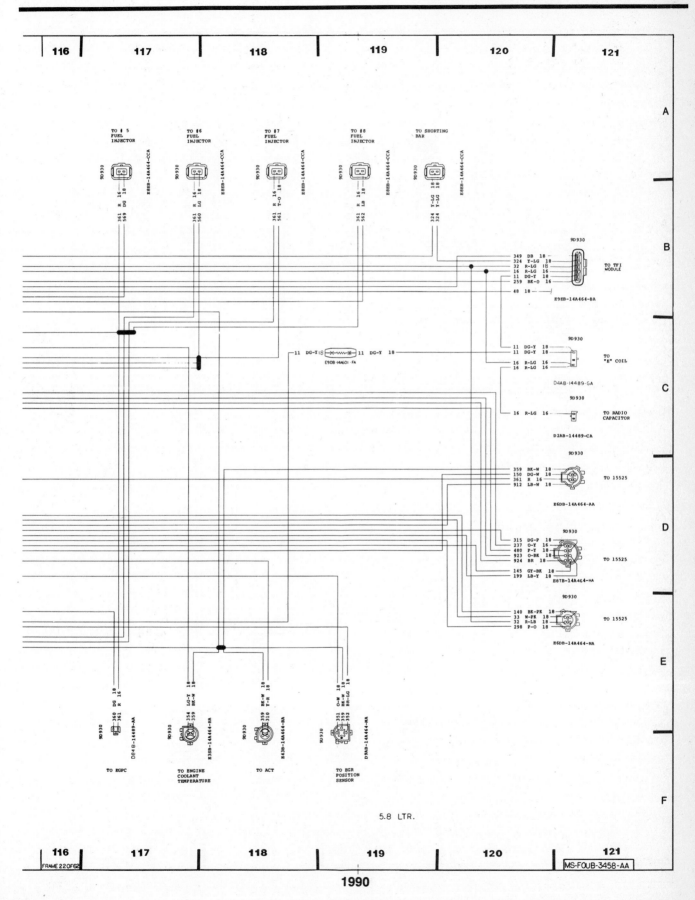

5.8 LTR.

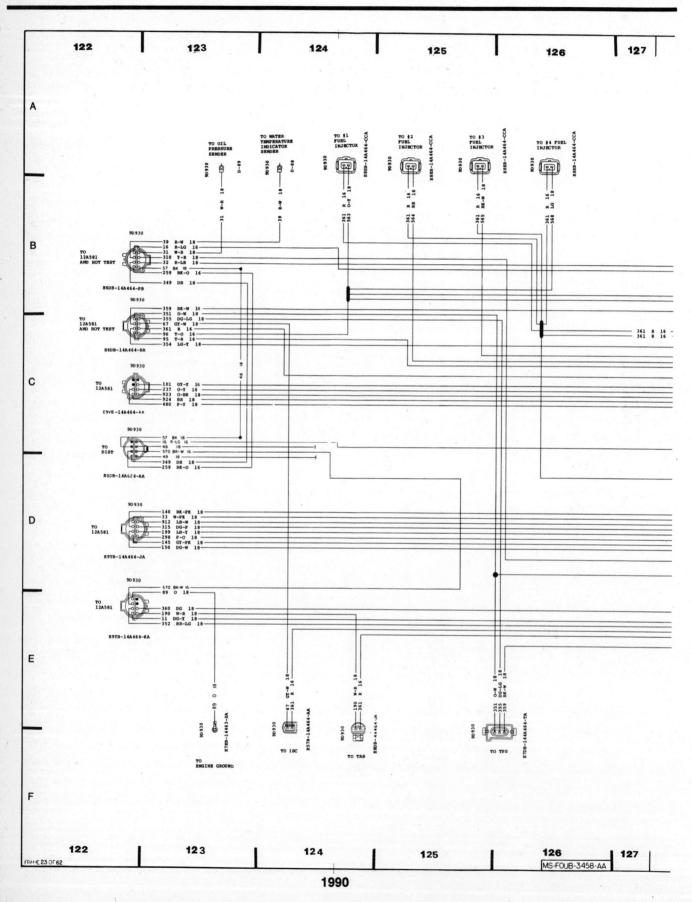

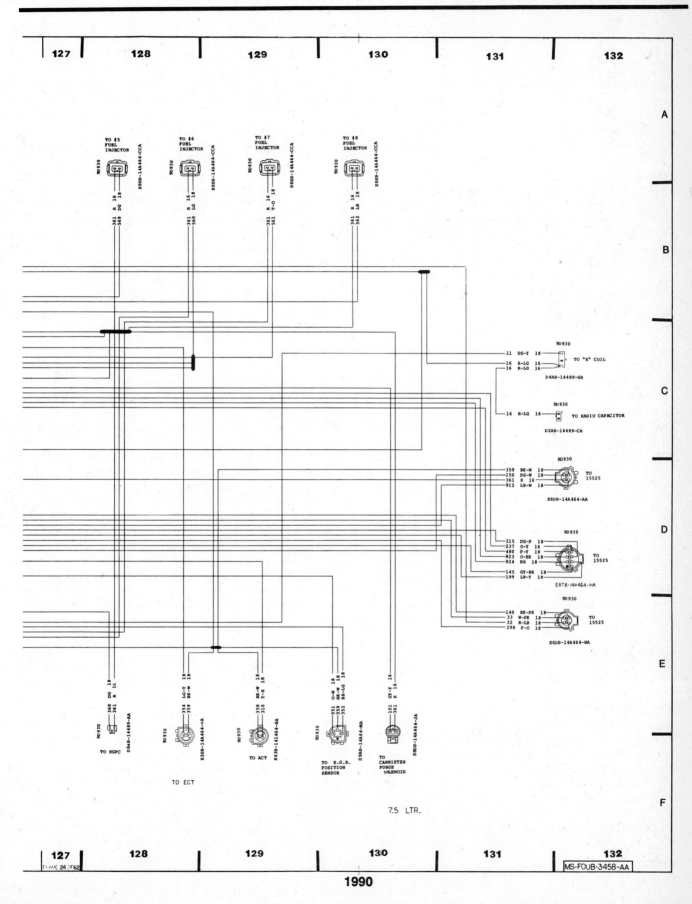

7.5 LTR.

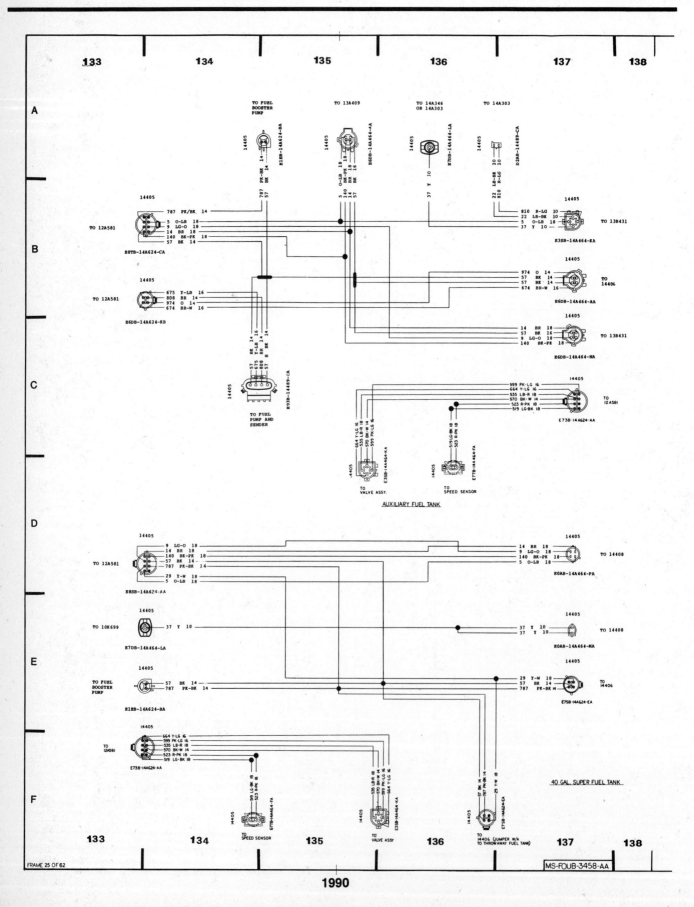

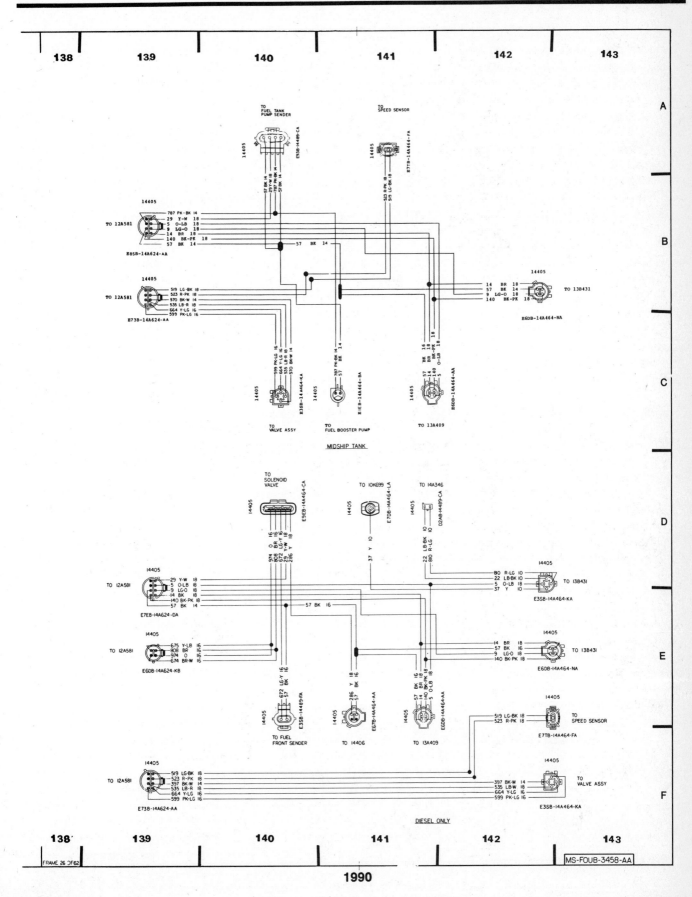

MIDSHIP TANK

DIESEL ONLY

1990

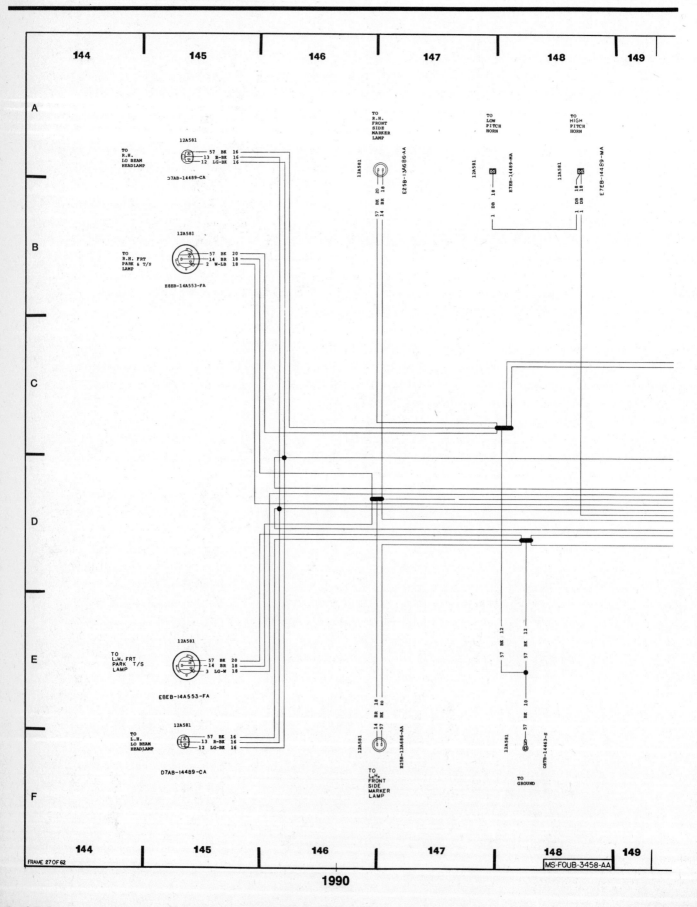

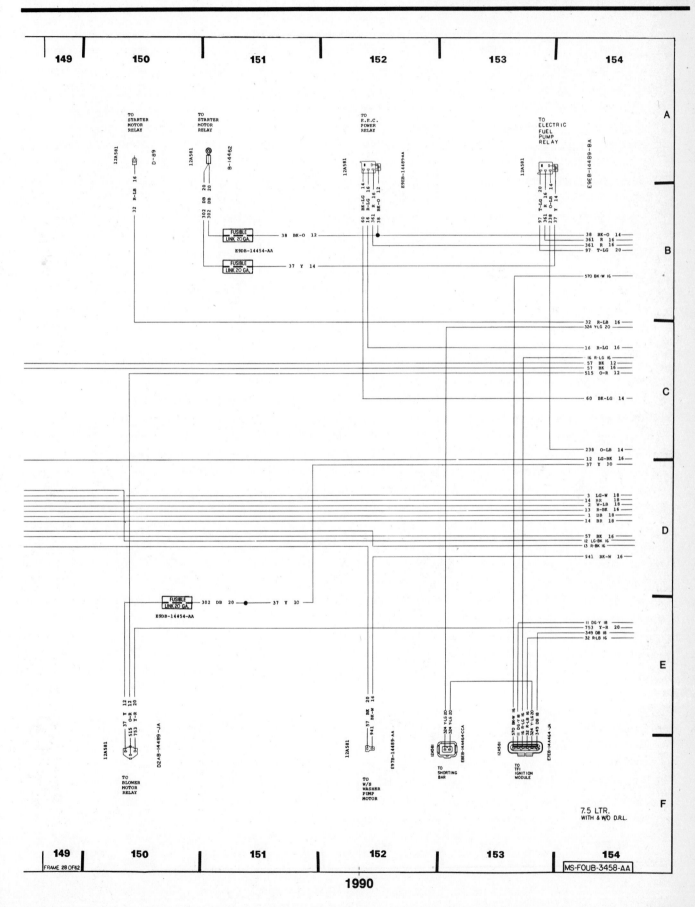

7.5 LTR.
WITH & W/O D.R.L.

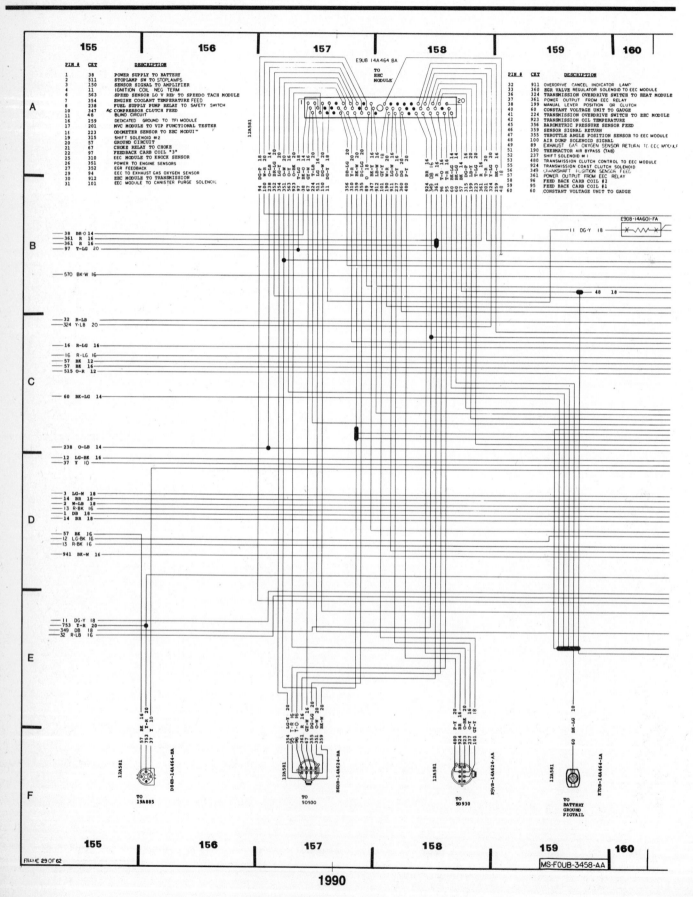

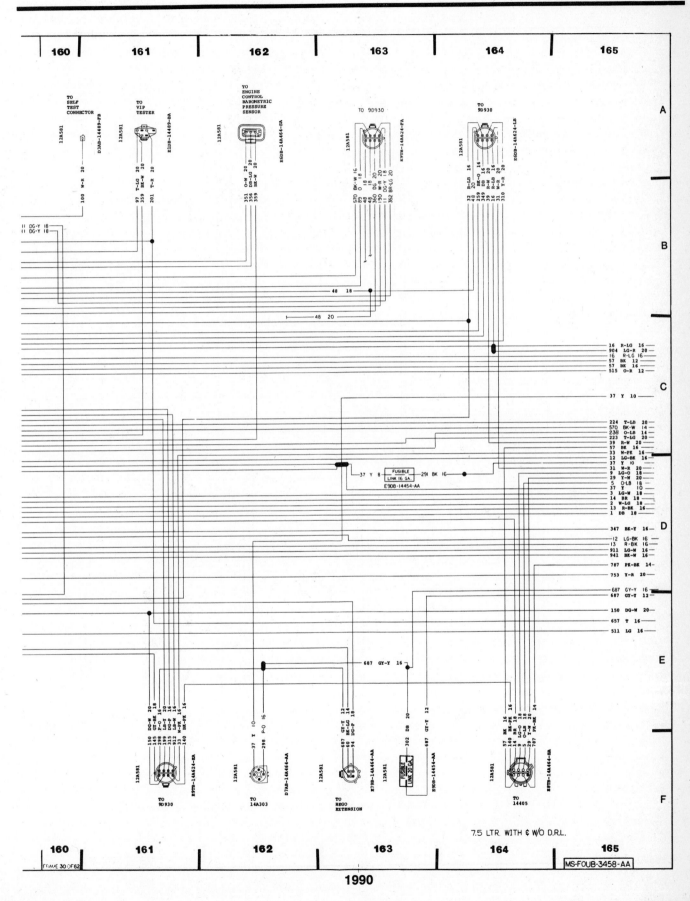

7.5 LTR. WITH & W/O D.R.L.

1990

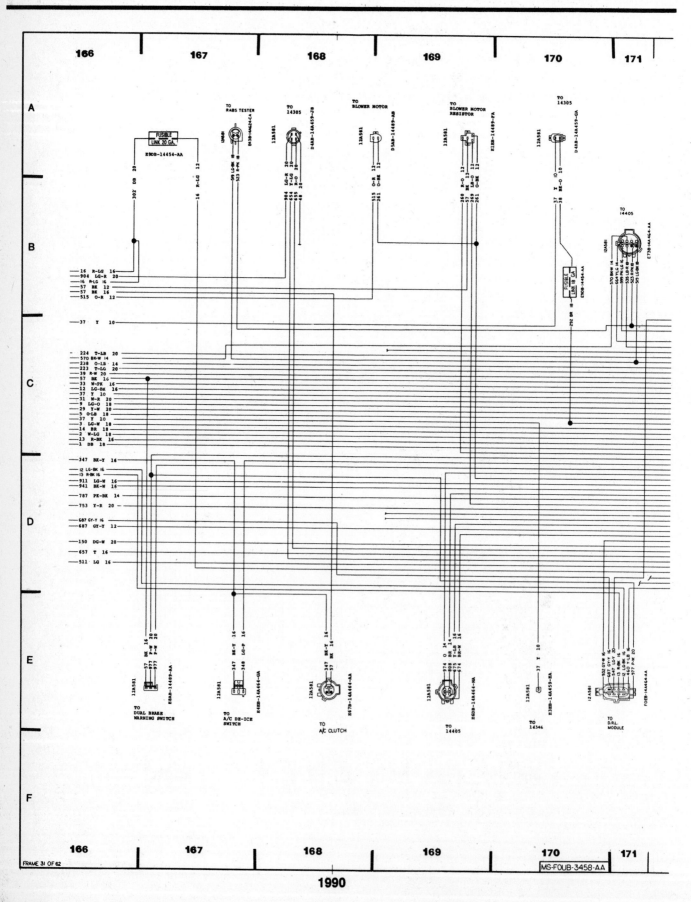

A

B

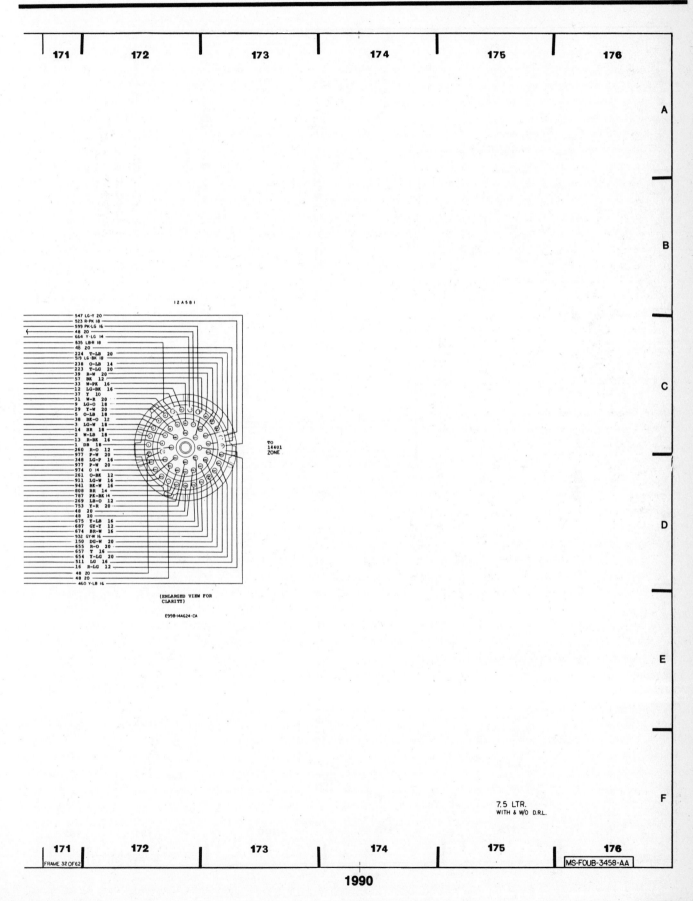

12A581

547 LG-Y 20
523 R-PK 18
599 PK-LG 16
48 20
664 Y-LG 14
535 LB-R 18
48 20
224 T-LB 20
519 LG-BK 18
238 O-LB 14
223 T-LG 20
39 R-W 20
57 BK 12
33 W-PK 16
12 LG-BK 16
37 Y 10
31 W-R 20
9 LG-O 18
29 Y-W 20
5 O-LB 18
38 BK-O 12
3 LG-W 18
14 BR 18
2 W-LB 18
13 R-BK 16
1 DB 18
260 R-O 12
977 P-W 20
348 LG-P 16
977 P-W 20
974 O 14
261 O-BK 12
911 LG-W 16
941 BK-W 16
808 BR 14
787 PK-BK 14
269 LB-O 12
753 Y-R 20
48 20
48 20
675 Y-LB 16
687 GY-Y 12
674 BR-W 16
932 GY-W 16
150 DG-W 20
655 R-O 20
657 T 16
654 T-LG 20
511 LG 16
16 R-LG 12
48 20
48 20
460 Y-LB 16

TO
14401
ZONE

C

(ENLARGED VIEW FOR
CLARITY)

E99B-14A624-CA

D

E

F

7.5 LTR.
WITH & W/O D.R.L.

1990

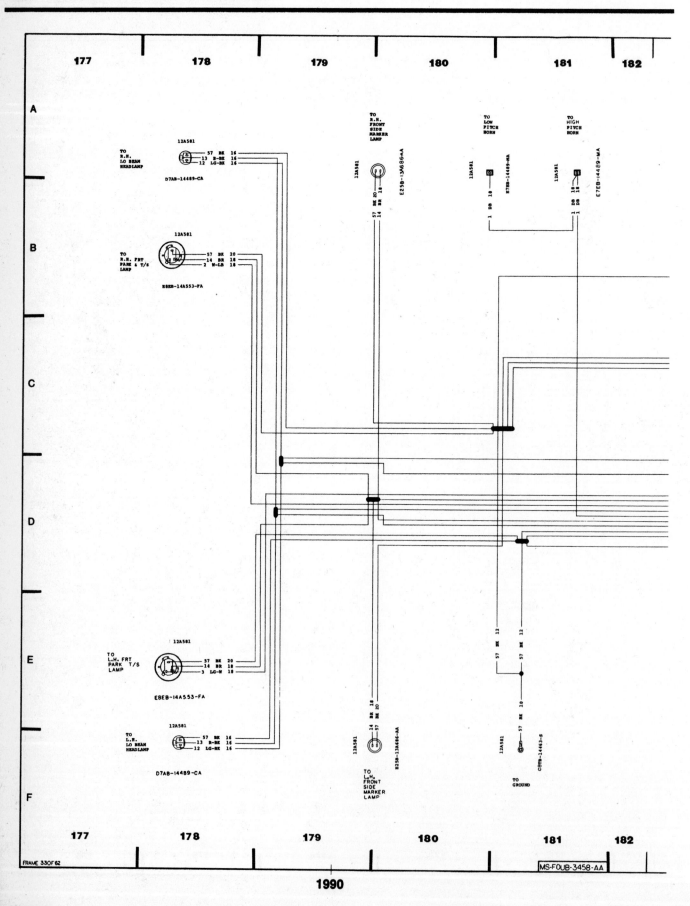

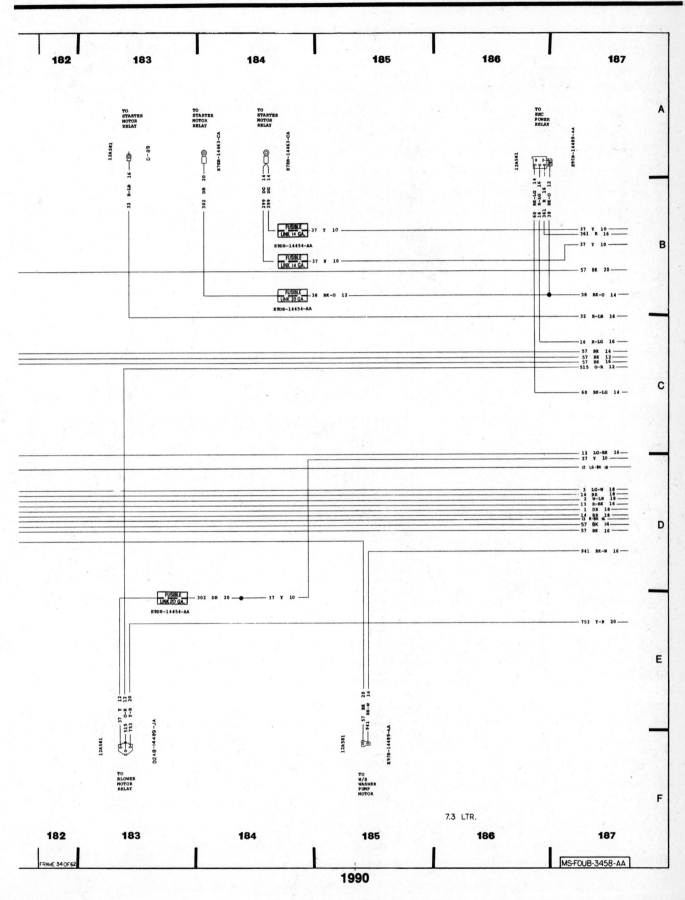

7.3 LTR.

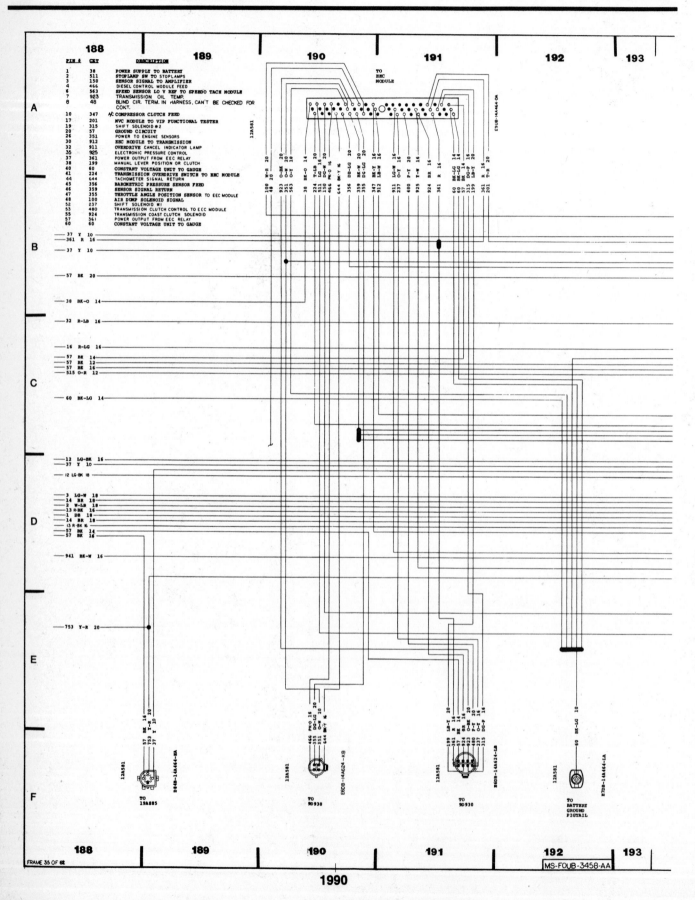

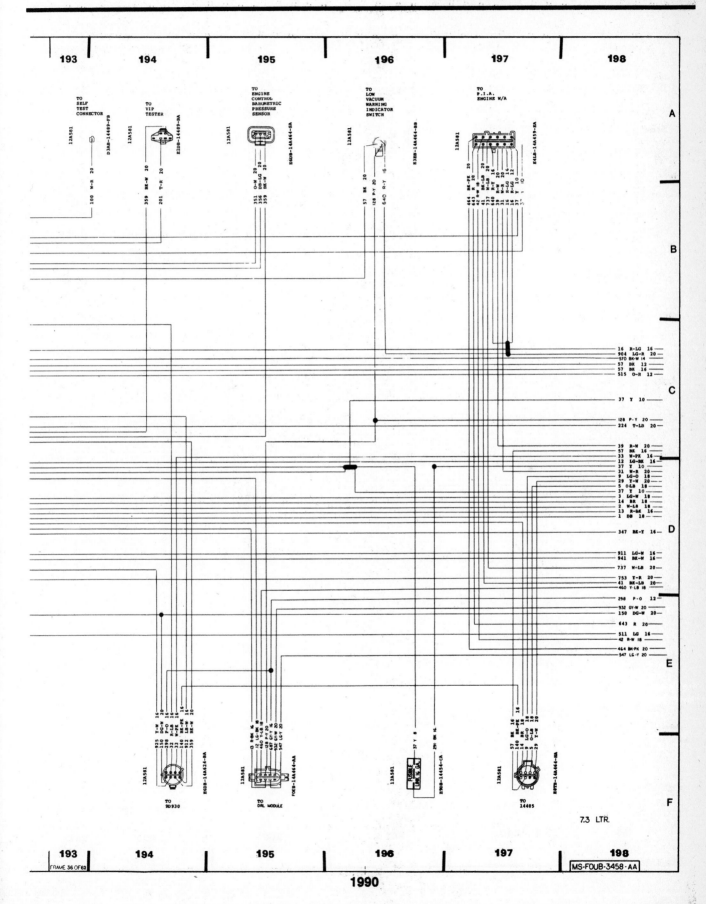

7.3 LTR.

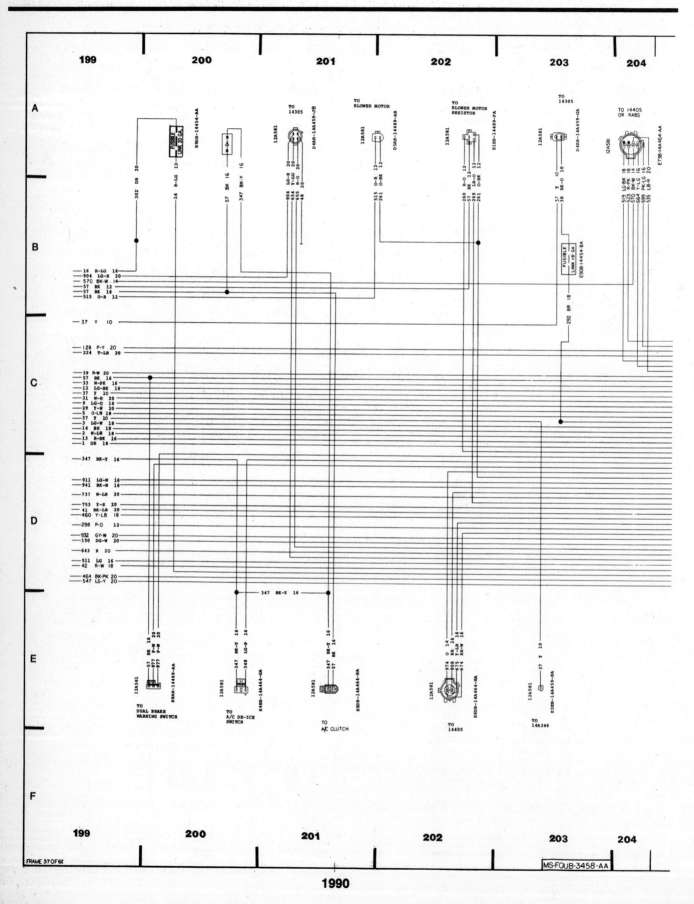

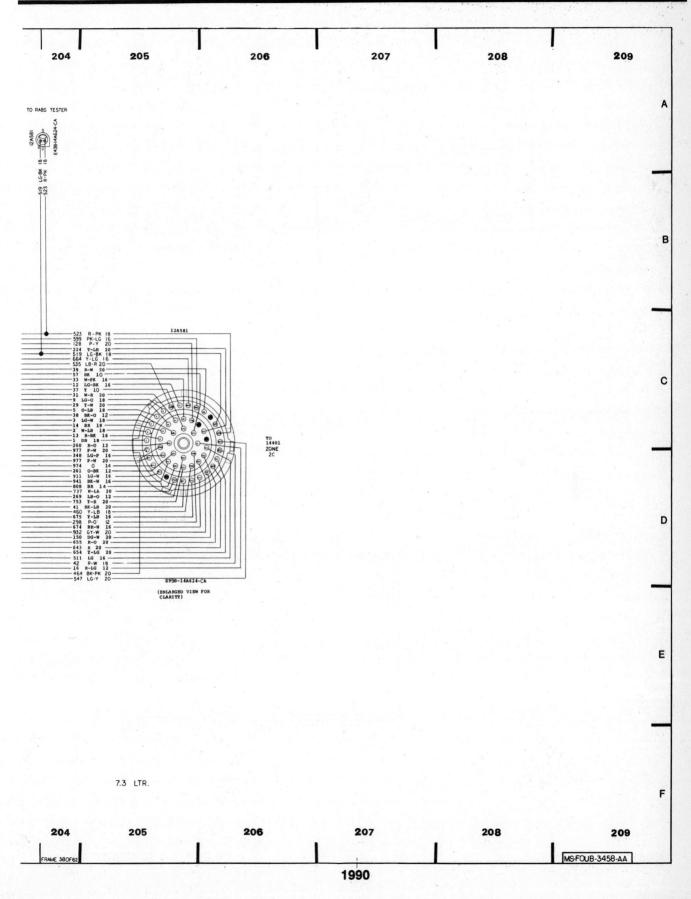

A

B

TO RABS TESTER

12A581

E43B-14A624-CA

519 LG-BK 18
523 R-PK 18

523 R-PK 18
599 PK-LG 16
128 P-Y 20
224 T-LB 20
519 LG-BK 18
664 Y-LG 16
535 LB-R 20
39   R-W 20
57   BK 10
33   W-PK 16
12   LG-BK 16
37   Y 10
31   W-R 20
9   LG-O 18
29   Y-W 20
5   O-LB 18
38   BK-O 12
3   LG-W 18
14   BR 18
2   W-LB 18
13   R-BK 16
1   DB 18
260 R-O 12
977 P-W 20
348 LG-P 16
977 P-W 20
974 O 14
261 O-BK 12
911 LG-W 16
941 BK-W 16
808 BR 14
737 W-LB 20
269 LB-O 12
753 Y-R 20
41   BK-LB 20
460 Y-LB 18
675 Y-LB 16
298 P-O 12
674 BR-W 16
932 GY-W 20
150 DG-W 20
655 R-O 20
643 R 20
654 Y-LG 20
511 LG 16
42   R-W 18
16   R-LG 12
464 BK-PK 20
547 LG-Y 20

12A581

TO
14401
ZONE
2C

E99B-14A624-CA

(ENLARGED VIEW FOR
CLARITY)

C

D

E

7.3 LTR.

F

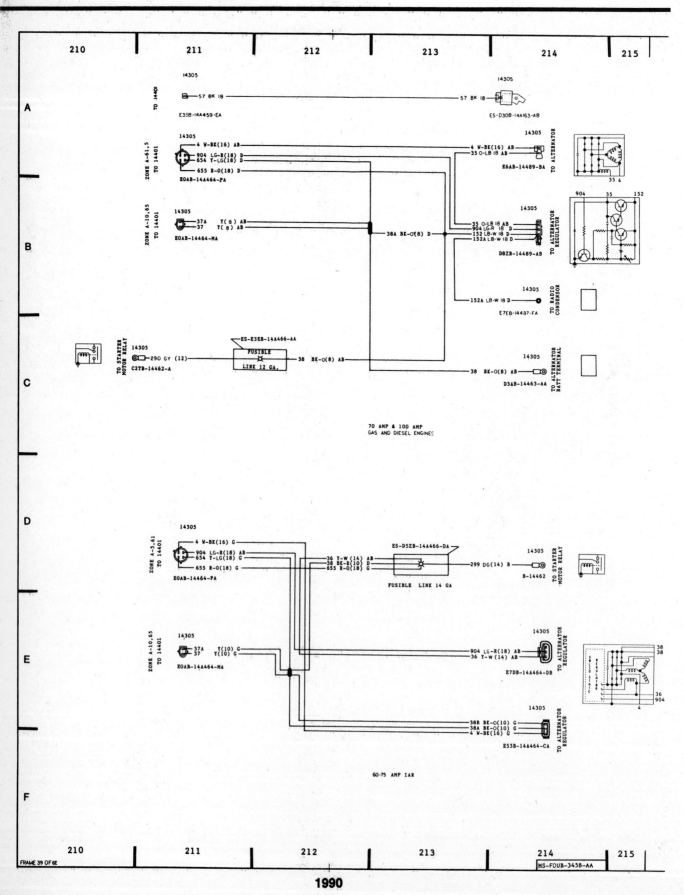

215 216 217 218 219 220

A

B

C

D

E

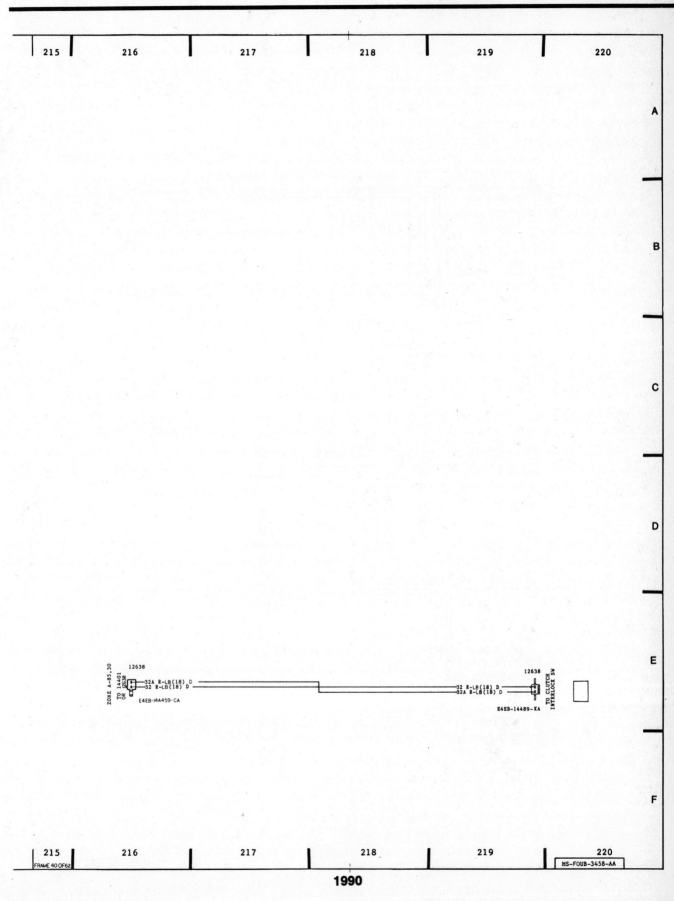

F

216 217 218 219

1990

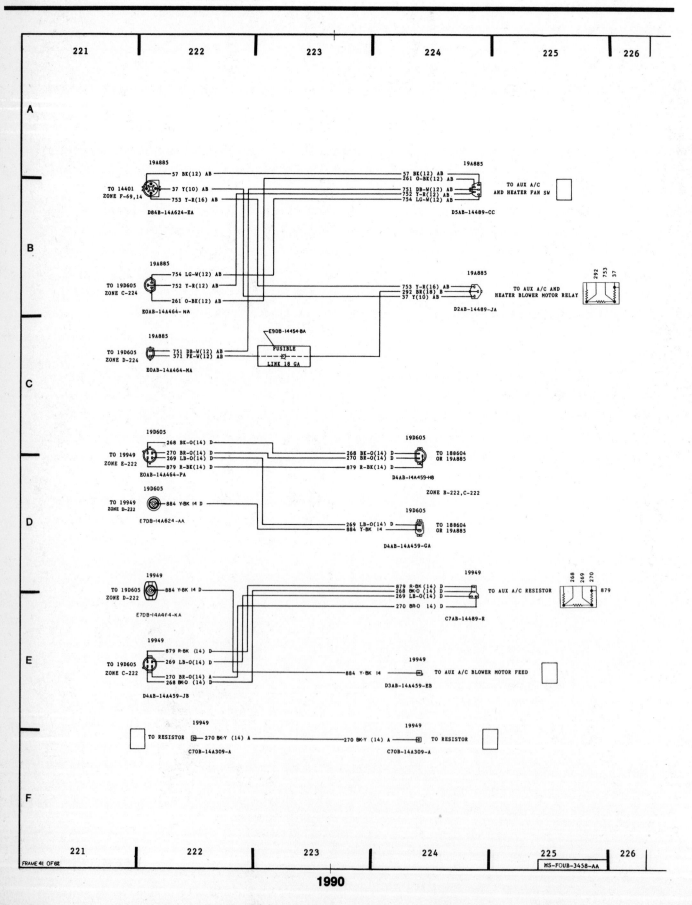

226	227	228	229	230	231

A

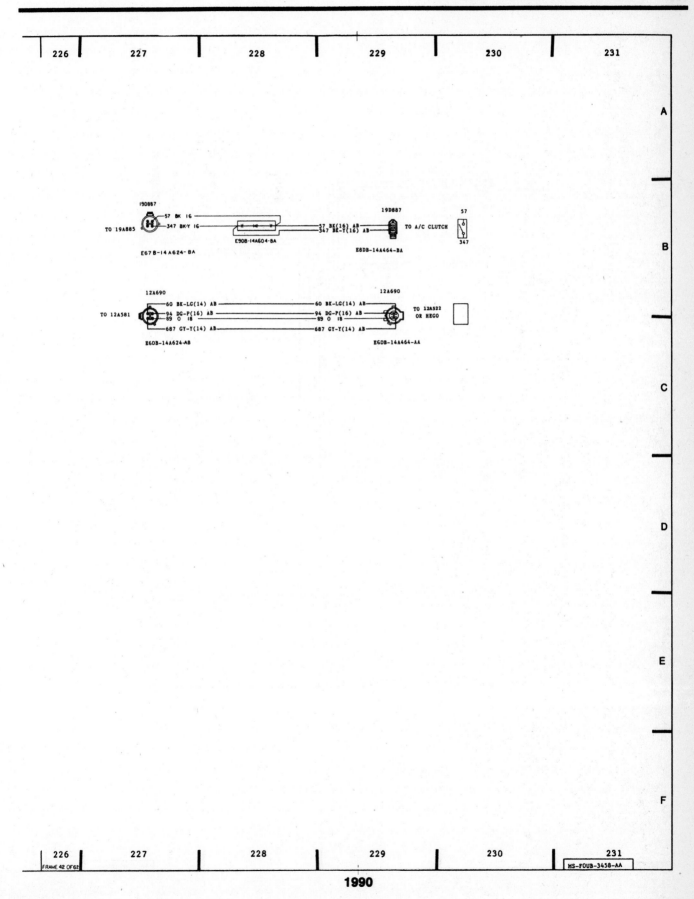

19D887

57 BK 16

347 BK-Y 16

TO 19A885

E90B-14A604-BA

E67B-14A624-BA

57 BK(16) AB

347 BK-Y(16) AB

19D887

TO A/C CLUTCH

E8DB-14A464-BA

57

347

B

12A690

60 BK-LG(14) AB

94 DG-P(16) AB

89 O 18

687 GY-Y(14) AB

TO 12A581

E6DB-14A624-AB

60 BK-LG(14) AB

94 DG-P(16) AB

89 O 18

687 GY-Y(14) AB

12A690

TO 12A522
OR HEGO

E6DB-14A464-AA

C

D

E

F

226	227	228	229	230	231

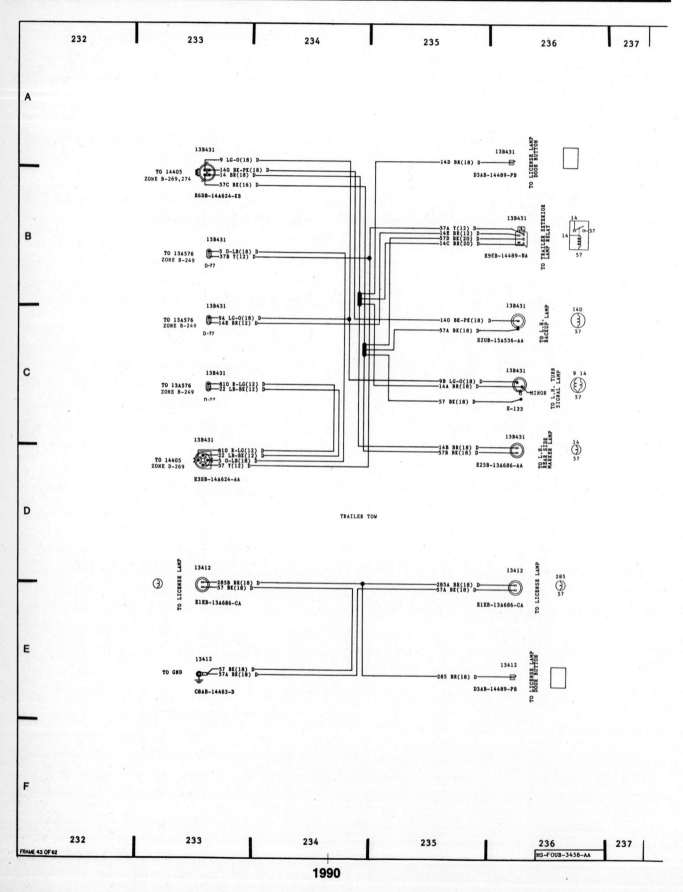

TRAILER TOW

1990

237   238   239   240   241   242

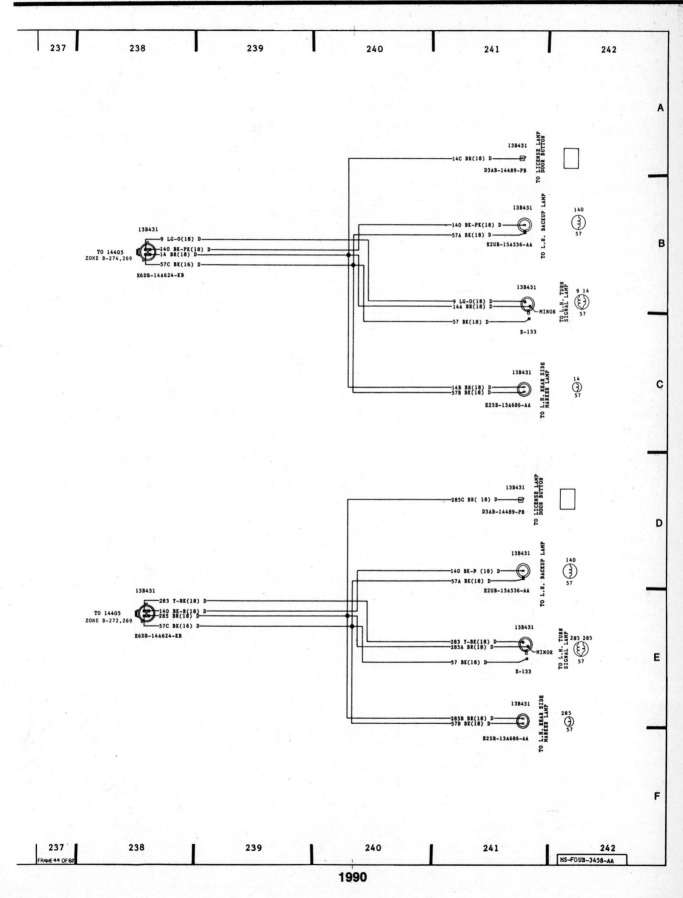

A

B

TO 14405
ZONE B-274,269

13B431
9 LG-O(18) D
140 BK-PK(18) D
14 BR(18) D
57C BK(16) D

E6DB-14A624-KB

13B431
14C BR(18) D
D3AB-14489-PB

TO LICENSE LAMP
DOOR BUTTON

13B431
140 BK-PK(18) D
57A BK(18) D
E2UB-15A536-AA

140
57

TO L.H. BACKUP LAMP

13B431
9 LG-O(18) D
14A BR(18) D
MINOR
57 BK(18) D
E-133

9 14
57

TO L.H. TURN
SIGNAL LAMP

13B431
14B BR(18) D
57B BK(18) D
E25B-13A686-AA

14
57

TO L.H. REAR SIDE
MARKER LAMP

C

D

TO 14405
ZONE B-272,269

13B431
283 Y-BK(18) D
140 BK-R(18) D
285 BR(18) D
57C BK(16) D

E6DB-14A624-KB

13B431
285C BR(18) D
D3AB-14489-PB

TO LICENSE LAMP
DOOR BUTTON

13B431
140 BK-R (18) D
57A BK(18) D
E2UB-15A536-AA

140
57

TO L.H. BACKUP LAMP

13B431
283 Y-BK(18) D
285A BR(18) D
MINOR
57 BK(18) D
E-133

283 285
57

TO L.H. TURN
SIGNAL LAMP

13B431
285B BR(18) D
57B BK(18) D
E25B-13A686-AA

285
57

TO L.H. REAR SIDE
MARKER LAMP

E

F

237   238   239   240   241   242

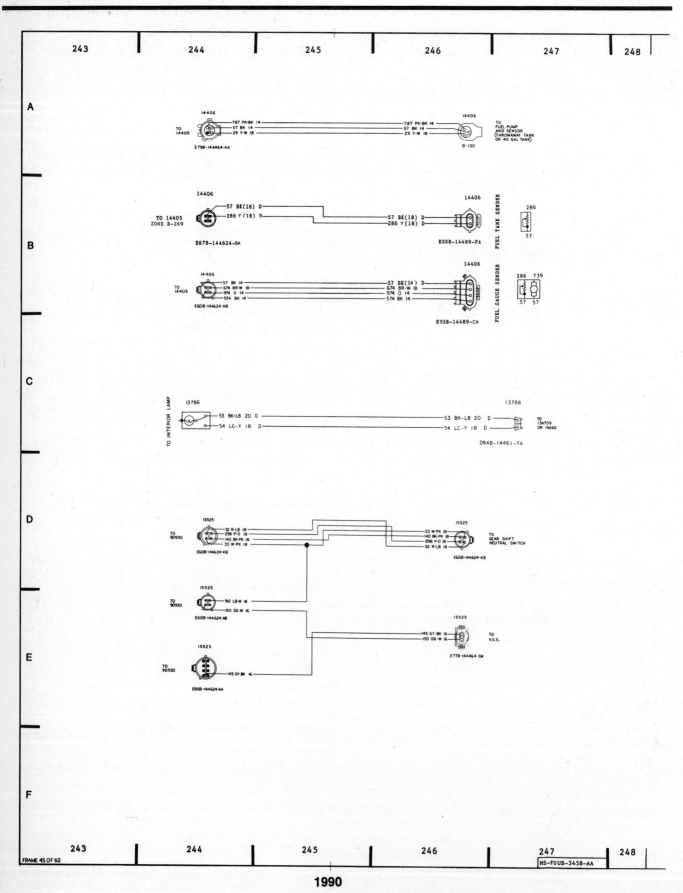

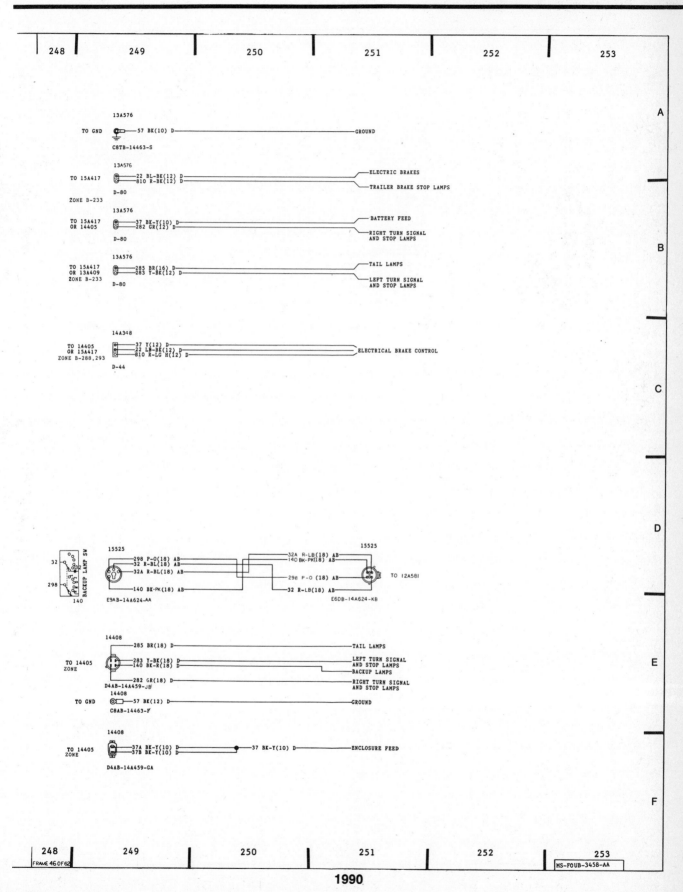

13A576

TO GND   —57 BK(10) D —————————————— GROUND

C8TB-14463-S

13A576

TO 15A417   —22 BL-BK(12) D ————————— ELECTRIC BRAKES
          —810 R-BK(12) D ————————— TRAILER BRAKE STOP LAMPS

ZONE B-233   D-80

13A576

TO 15A417   —37 BK-Y(10) D ————————— BATTERY FEED
OR 14405   —282 GR(12) D ————————— RIGHT TURN SIGNAL
                                       AND STOP LAMPS

D-80

13A576

TO 15A417   —285 BR(16) D ————————— TAIL LAMPS
OR 13A409   —283 Y-BK(12) D ————————— LEFT TURN SIGNAL
ZONE B-233   AND STOP LAMPS

D-80

14A348

TO 14405   —37 Y(12) D ——————————
OR 15A417   —22 LB-BK(12) D ——————
ZONE B-288,293   —810 R-LG H(12) D ————— ELECTRICAL BRAKE CONTROL

D-44

15525   15525

32   —298 P-O(18) AB ———— 32A R-LB(18) AB
         —32 R-BL(18) AB ———— 140 BK-PK(18) AB
         —32A R-BL(18) AB
298   —298 P-O (18) AB   TO 12A581
         —140 BK-PK(18) AB ——— 32 R-LB(18) AB

140   E9AB-14A624-AA   E6DB-14A624-KB

BACKUP LAMP SW

14408

TO 14405   —285 BR(18) D ————————— TAIL LAMPS
ZONE   —283 Y-BK(18) D ————————— LEFT TURN SIGNAL
       —140 BK-R(18) D   AND STOP LAMPS
                              —BACKUP LAMPS
       —282 GR(18) D ————————— RIGHT TURN SIGNAL
D4AB-14A459-JB   AND STOP LAMPS

14408

TO GND   —57 BK(12) D ————————— GROUND

C8AB-14463-F

14408

TO 14405   —37A BK-Y(10) D ——————
ZONE   —37B BK-Y(10) D ———— 37 BK-Y(10) D ——— ENCLOSURE FEED

D4AB-14A459-GA

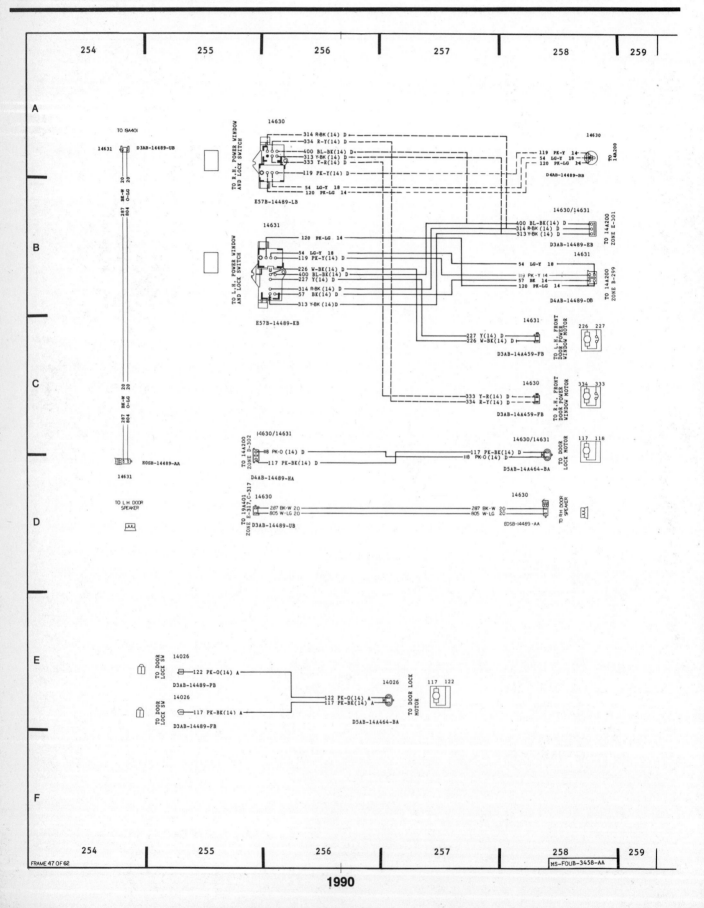

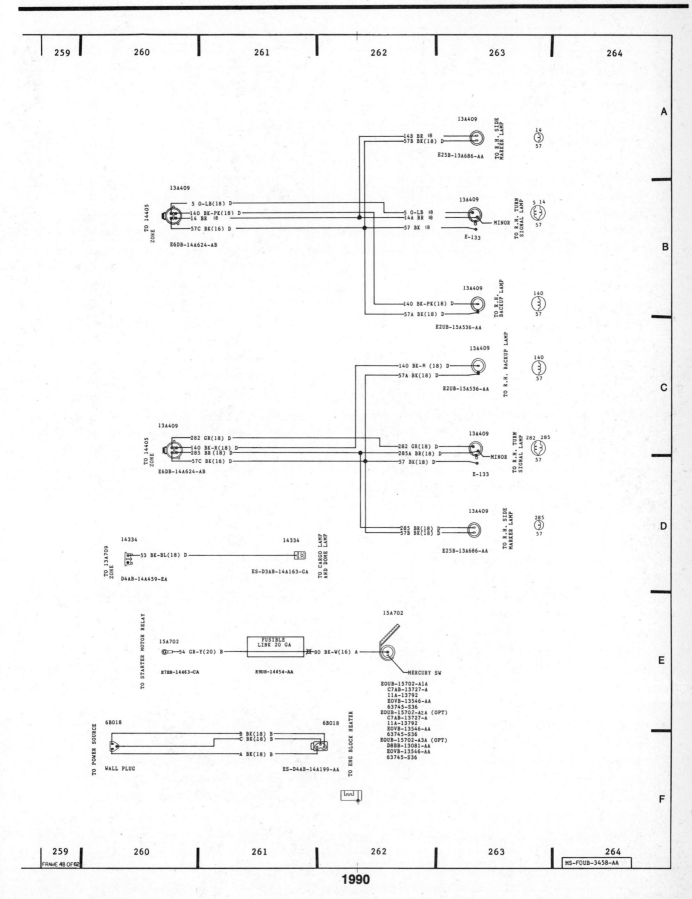

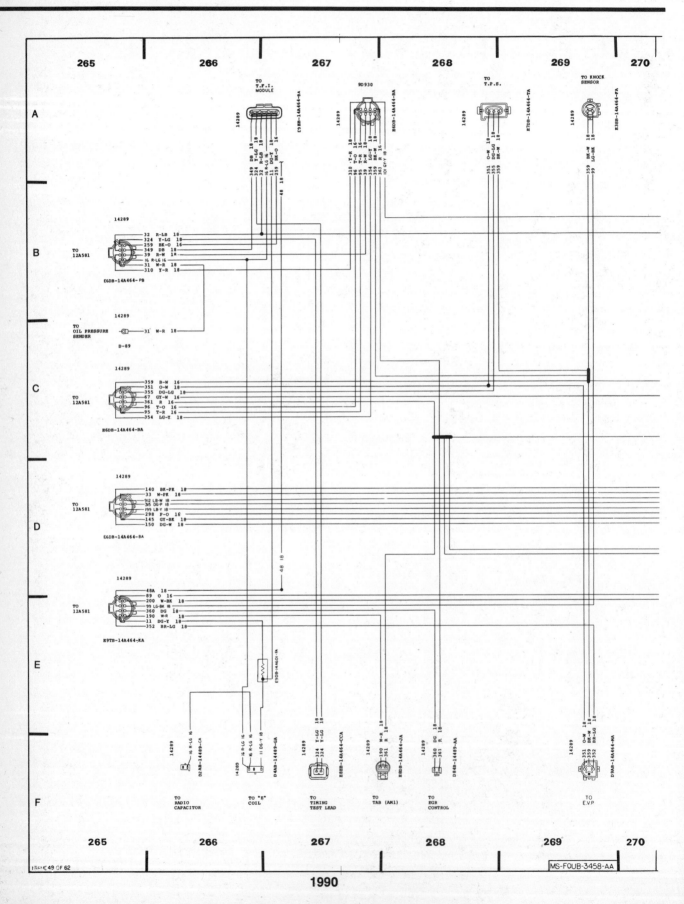

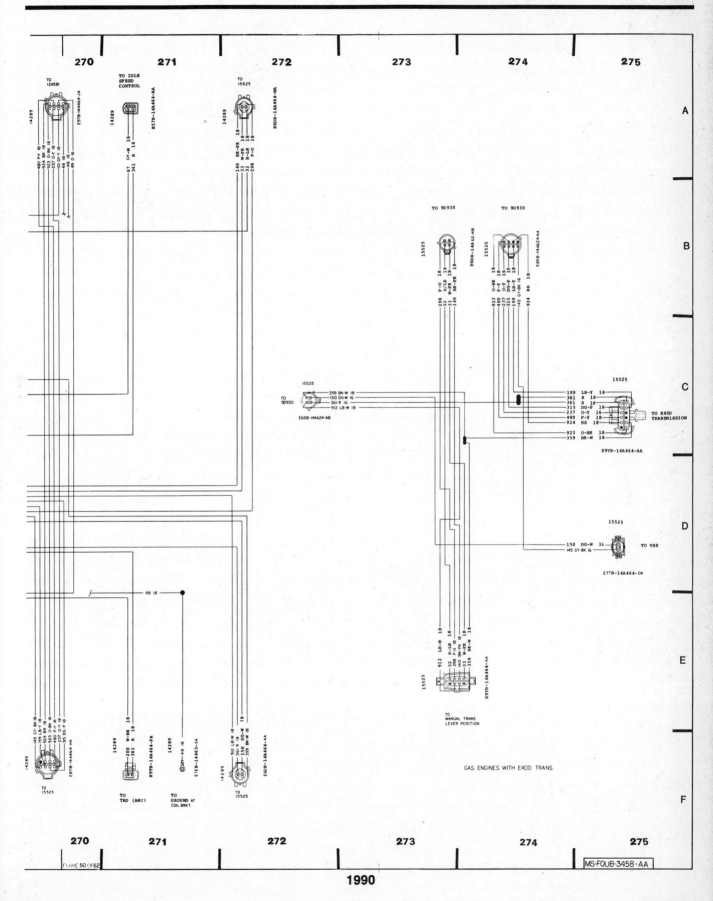

GAS ENGINES WITH E40D TRANS.

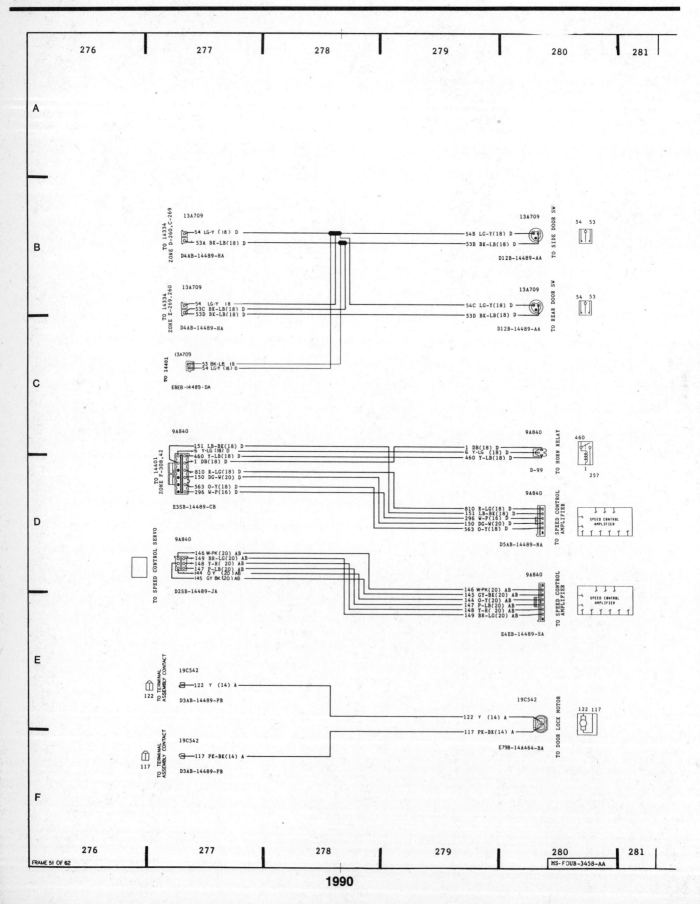

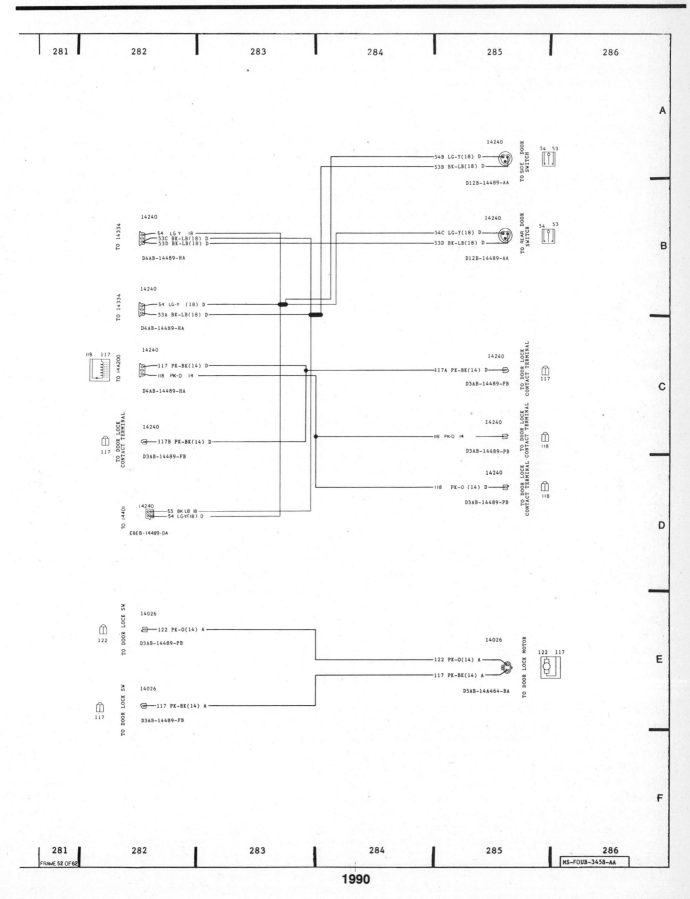

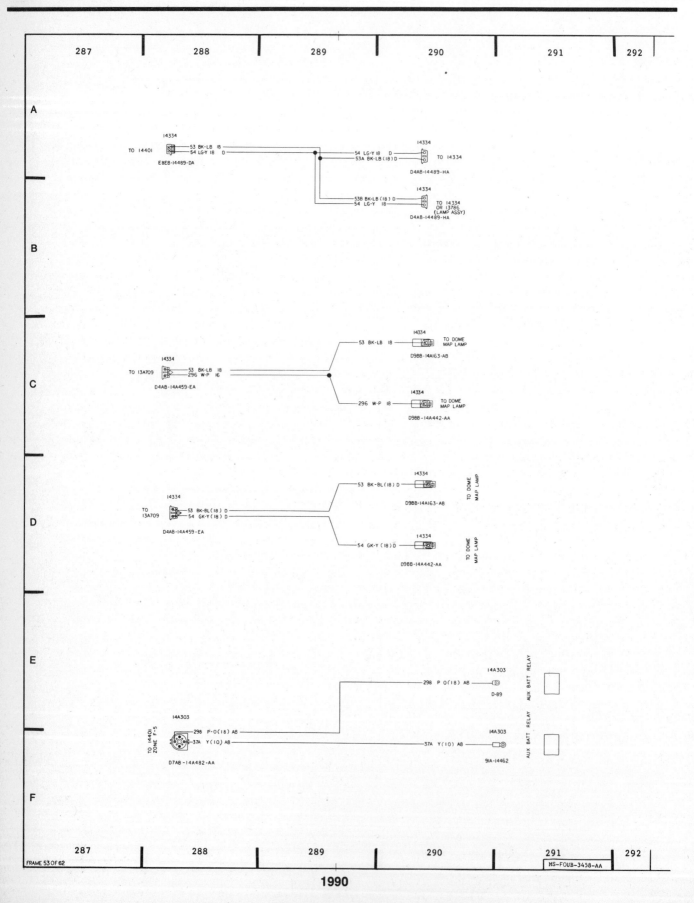

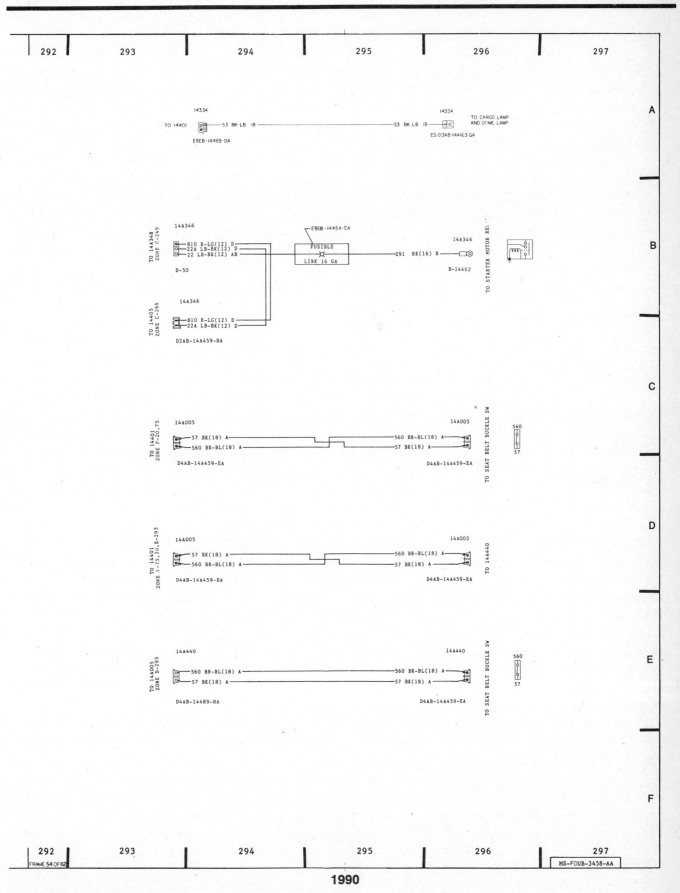

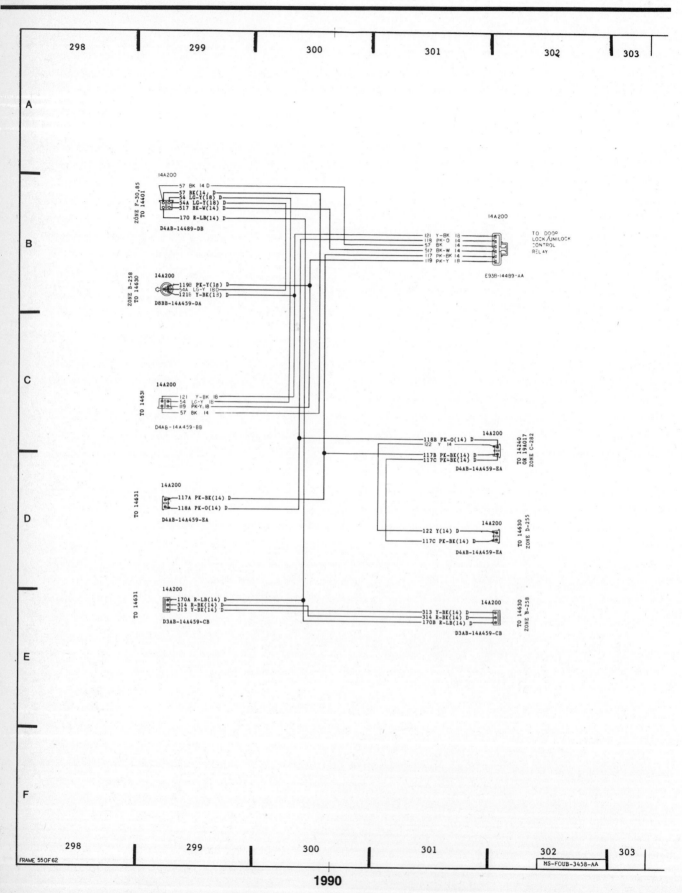

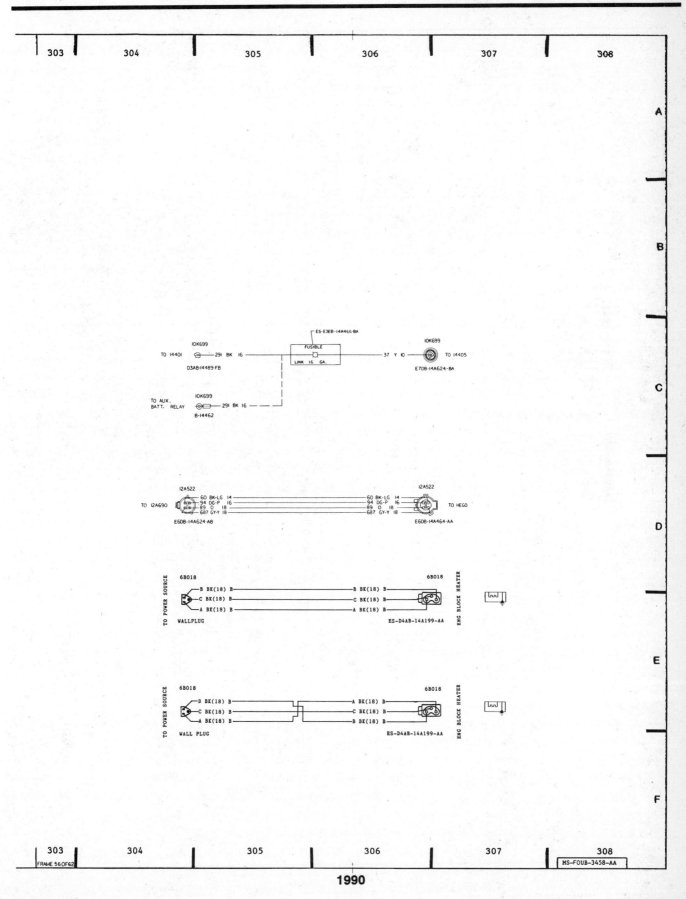

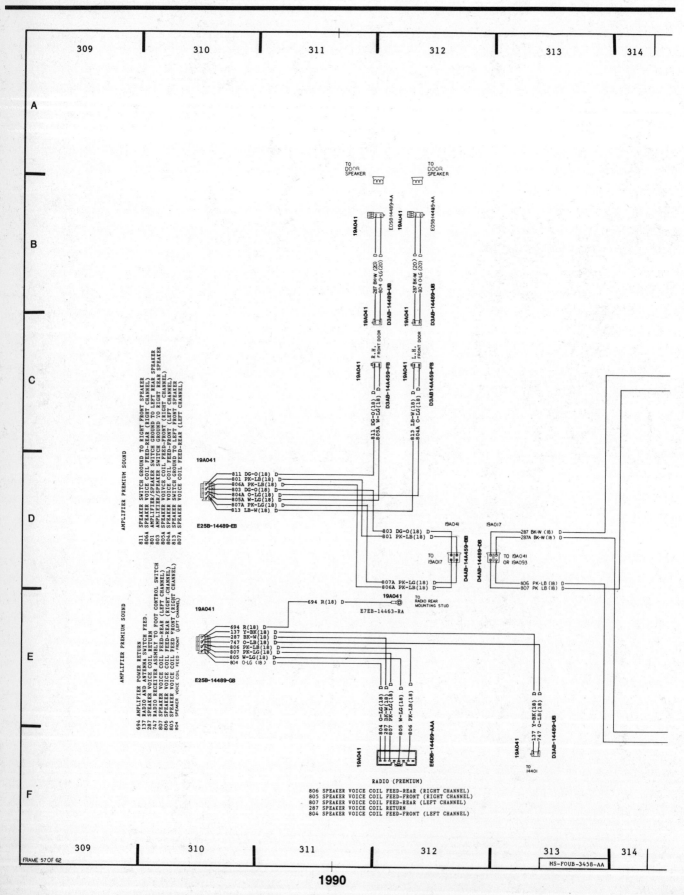

RADIO (PREMIUM)

806 SPEAKER VOICE COIL FEED-REAR (RIGHT CHANNEL)
805 SPEAKER VOICE COIL FEED-FRONT (RIGHT CHANNEL)
807 SPEAKER VOICE COIL FEED-REAR (LEFT CHANNEL)
287 SPEAKER VOICE COIL RETURN
804 SPEAKER VOICE COIL FEED-FRONT (LEFT CHANNEL)

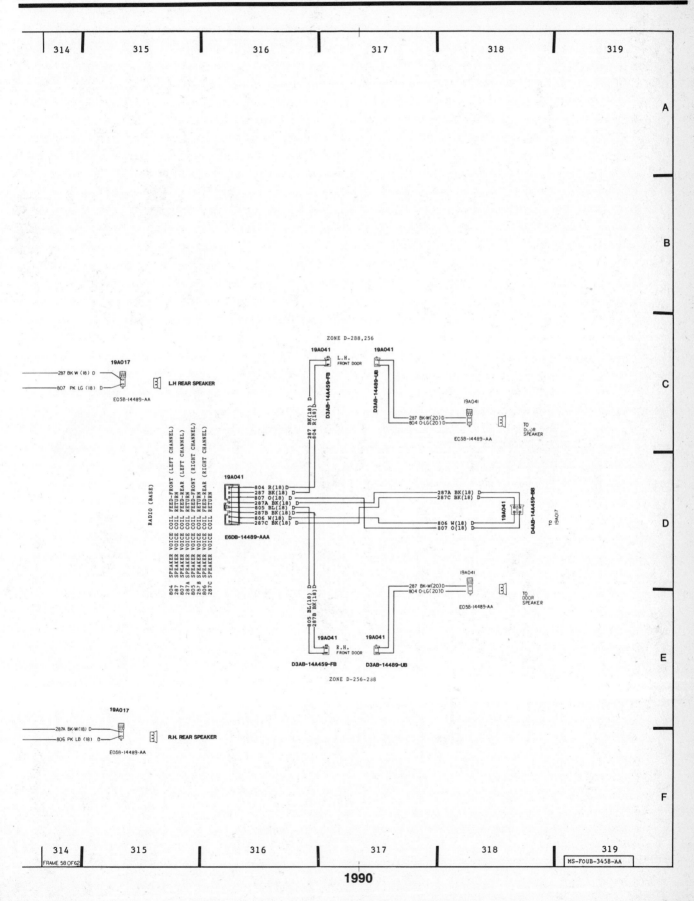

A

B

ZONE D-288,256

19A041   19A041

L.H.
FRONT DOOR

287 BK(18) D
804 R(18) D

D3AB-14A459-FB

D3AB-14489-UB

19A041

287 BK-W(20)D
804 O-LG(20)D

ECSB-14489-AA

TO
DOOR
SPEAKER

C

287 BK W (18) D   19A017

807 PK LG (18) D

LH REAR SPEAKER

E05B-14489-AA

RADIO (BASE)

804 SPEAKER VOICE COIL FEED-FRONT (LEFT CHANNEL)
287 SPEAKER VOICE COIL RETURN (LEFT CHANNEL)
807 SPEAKER VOICE COIL FEED-REAR (LEFT CHANNEL)
287A SPEAKER VOICE COIL RETURN
805 SPEAKER VOICE COIL FEED-FRONT (RIGHT CHANNEL)
287B SPEAKER VOICE COIL RETURN
806 SPEAKER VOICE COIL FEED-REAR (RIGHT CHANNEL)
287C SPEAKER VOICE COIL RETURN

19A041

804 R(18)D
287 BK(18)D
807 O(18) D
287A BK(18)
805 BL(18)
287B BK(18)D
806 W(18) D
287C BK(18) D

E6DB-14489-AAA

287A BK(18) D
287C BK(18) D

D4AB-14A459-BB

19A041

806 W(18) D
807 O(18) D

TO
19A017

D

287 BK(18) D
804 R(18) D

805 BL(18) D
287B BK(18) D

287 BK-W(20)D
804 O-LG(20)D

19A041

E05B-14489-AA

TO
DOOR
SPEAKER

19A041   19A041

R.H.
FRONT DOOR

D3AB-14A459-FB   D3AB-14489-UB

ZONE D-256-288

E

287A BK-W(18) D   19A017

806 PK LB (18) D

R.H. REAR SPEAKER

E05B-14489-AA

F

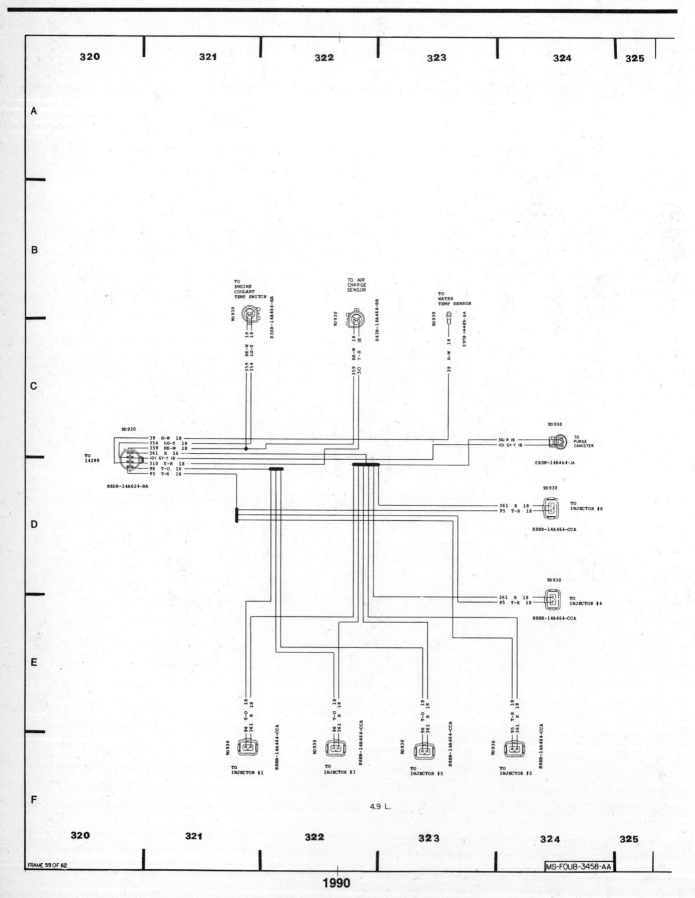

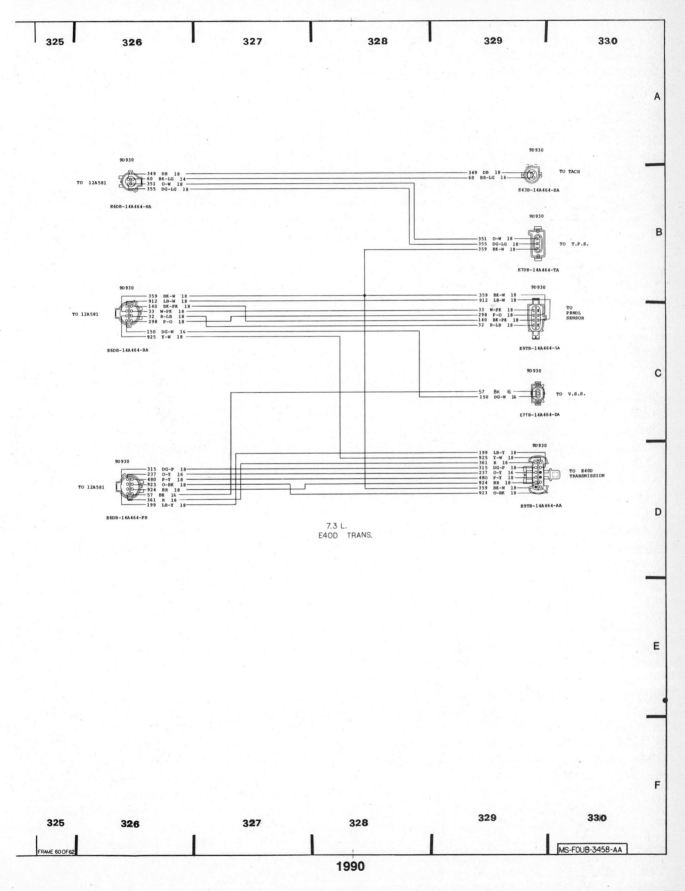

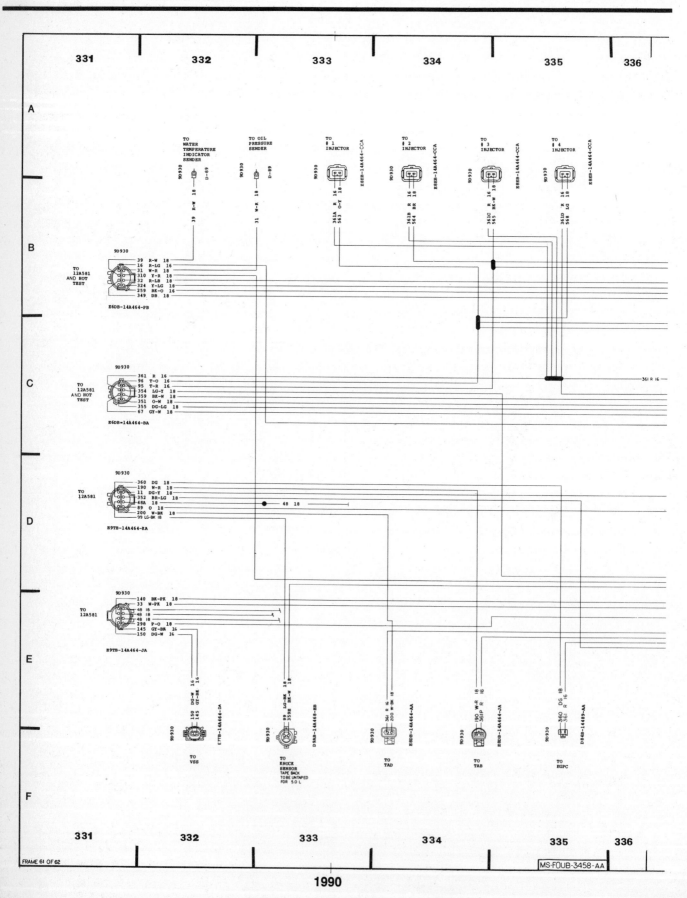

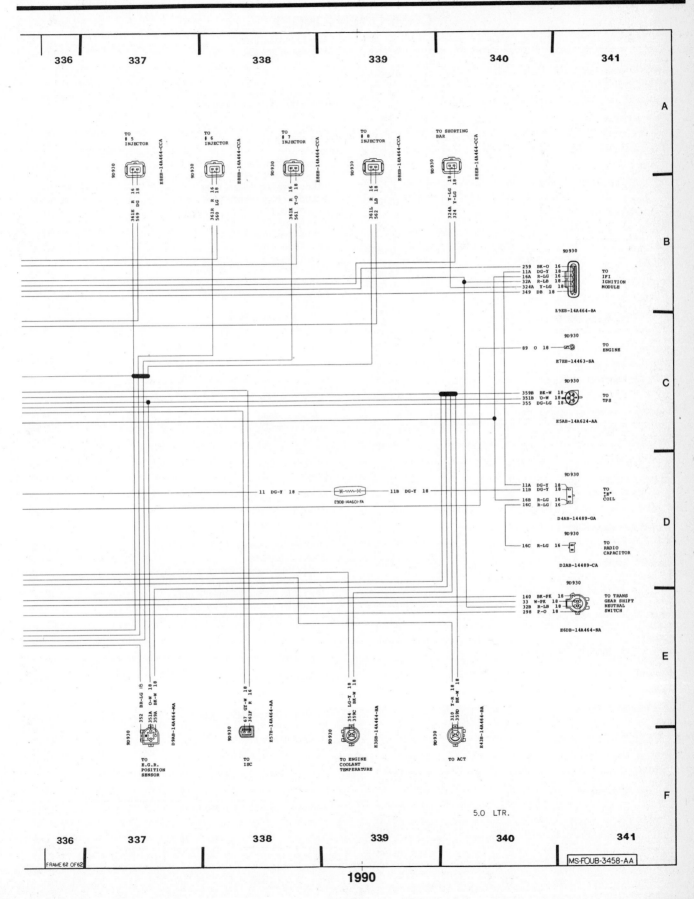

5.0 LTR.

1990

COMPONENT INDEX

COMPONENT INDEX

COMPONENT INDEX

STANDARD CIRCUIT CHART (BY NUMBER)

CIRCUIT	DESCRIPTION *	COLOR
1	HORN SWITCH CONTROL	DK BLUE
2	R.H. FRONT TURN SIGNAL LAMP	WHITE-LT BLUE
3	L.H. FRONT TURN SIGNAL LAMP	LT GREEN-WHITE
4	ALTERNATOR REG. "S" TERM. TO ALTERNATOR "S" TERM.	WHITE-BLACK
5	R.H. REAR TURN SIGNAL LAMP	ORANGE-LT BLUE
6	HORN RELAY TO HORN	YELLOW-LT GREEN
7	SEAT SWITCH ARM TERM. TO REPLAY FIELD TERM.	LT GREEN-YELLOW
8	TURN SIGNAL FLASHER FEED	ORANGE-YELLOW
9	L.H. REAR TURN SIGNAL LAMP	LT GREEN-ORANGE
10	STOPLAMP SWITCH FEED	LT GREEN-RED
11	IGNITION COIL NEGATIVE TERMINAL	TAN-YELLOW
12	HEADLAMP DIMMER SWITCH TO HIGH BEAMS	LT GREEN-BLACK
13	HEADLAMP DIMMER SWITCH TO LOW BEAMS	RED-BLACK
14	HEADLAMP SWITCH TO TAILLAMPS & SIDE MARKER LAMPS	BROWN
15	HEADLAMP DIMMER SWITCH FEED	RED-YELLOW
16	IGNITION SWITCH TO IGNITION COIL "BATT." TERMINAL	RED-LT GREEN
17	ASH RECEPTACLE LAMP FEED	WHITE
18	SEAT SWITCH TO RELAY FIELD TERMINAL	ORANGE-YELLOW
19	INSTRUMENT PANEL LAMPS FEED	LT BLUE-RED
20	DISTRIBUTOR ELECTRONIC CONTROL FEED	WHITE-LT BLUE
21	EMA CONTROL TO SPARK RETARD SWITCH	DK GREEN-LT GREEN
22	BRAKE FEED	LT BLUE-BLACK
23	ANTI-THEFT SYSTEM SWITCH FEED	TAN-LT GREEN
24	ANTI-THEFT SWITCH ARM	DK BLUE-ORANGE
25	ANTI-THEFT SWITCH DISARM	DK GREEN-PURPLE
26	DECK LID SWITCH TO ANTI-THEFT MODULE	WHITE-PURPLE
27	EMA CONTROL TO EGR SWITCH	ORANGE-LT GREEN
28	WINDSHIELD WIPER SW. TO WINDSHIELD WIPER MOTOR	BLACK-PINK
29	FUEL GAGE TO FUEL GAGE SENDER	YELLOW-WHITE
30	CONSTANT VOLTAGE UNIT & INDICATOR LAMPS FEED	BLACK-LT GREEN
31	OIL PRESSURE INDICATOR TO OIL PRESSURE SENDING UNIT	WHITE-RED
32	STARTER CONTROL	RED-LT BLUE
33	STARTER CONTROL TO INTERLOCK MODULE	WHITE-PINK
34	HORN CONTROL MODULE TO OVERRIDE SWITCH	LT BLUE-ORANGE
35	ALTERNATOR REGULATOR "F" TERMINAL TO ALTERNATOR	ORANGE-LT BLUE
36	ALTERNATOR OUTPUT	YELLOW-WHITE
37	BATTERY TO LOAD	YELLOW
38	POWER SUPPLY TO BATTERY	BLACK-ORANGE
39	TEMP. GAGE TO TEMP. SENDING UNIT	RED-WHITE
40	CIGAR LIGHTER FEED	LT BLUE-WHITE
41	WARNING LAMP PROVE OUT	BLACK-LT BLUE
42	SWITCH TO WARNING LAMP	RED-WHITE
43	TRAILER BRAKES	DK BLUE
44	TURN SIGNAL FLASHER TO TURN SIGNAL SWITCH	LT BLUE
45	HOT WATER TEMP. RELAY TO HOT WATER TEMP. SENDING UNIT	YELLOW-RED
46	ELECTRONIC CONTROL UNIT TO SOLENOID	YELLOW-BLACK
47	ELECTRONIC CONTROL UNIT TO SOLENOID	GRAY-ORANGE
48	BLIND CIRCUIT TERM. IN HARNESS CANNOT BE CHECKED FOR CONT.	(COLOR OPT.)
49	TRAILER BATTERY CHARGE	ORANGE
50	TRAILER CONTROLLER FEED	RED
51	SEAT REG. CONTROL SWITCH FEED	BLACK-WHITE
52	TRAILER L.H. TURN SIGNAL	YELLOW
53	COURTESY LAMP SWITCH TO COURTESY LAMP	BLACK-LT BLUE
54	INTERIOR LAMP SWITCH FEED	LT GREEN-YELLOW
55	CARGO LAMP SW. TO CARGO LAMP	BLACK-PINK
56	WINDSHIELD WIPER SW. TO WINDSHIELD WIPER MOTOR	DK BLUE-ORANGE
57	GROUND CIRCUIT	BLACK
58	WINDSHIELD WIPER SW. TO WINDSHIELD WIPER MOTOR	WHITE
59	HEATED EXTERIOR MIRROR FEED	DK GREEN-PURPLE
60	CONSTANT VOLTAGE UNIT TO GAGE	BLACK-LT GREEN
61	WINDSHIELD WIPER SW. TO WINDSHIELD WIPER MOTOR	YELLOW-RED
62	BATTERY TO HI-BEAM	BROWN-YELLOW
63	WINDSHIELD WIPER SW. TO WINDSHIELD WIPER MOTOR	RED
64	TRAILER R.H. TURN SIGNAL	DK GREEN
65	WINDSHIELD WIPER SW. TO WINDSHIELD WIPER MOTOR	DK GREEN
66	KEYLESS DOOR LOCK SWITCH ILLUMINATION FEED	LT BLUE
67	CHOKE RELAY TO CHOKE	GRAY-WHITE
68	ELECTRIC CHOKE FEED	ORANGE-BLACK
69	MODULE TO ACTUATOR	RED-LT GREEN
70	SUPPLEMENTAL ALTERNATOR STATOR A TERM. TO WINDSHIELD	RED
71	SUPPLEMENTAL ALTERNATOR STATOR B TERM. TO WINDSHIELD	WHITE
72	SUPPLEMENTAL ALTERNATOR STATOR C TERM. TO WINDSHIELD	DK GREEN
73	ELECTRONIC CONTROL UNIT TO ACTUATOR	ORANGE-LT BLUE
74	ELECTRONIC CONTROL UNIT TO EXHAUST GAS OXYGEN SENSOR (#1 IN DUAL SYSTEM)	GRAY-LT BLUE
75	ELECTRONIC CONTROL UNIT TO ENGINE VACUUM SWITCH	DK GREEN-LT GREEN
76	KEYLESS DOOR LOCK ILLUMINATION GROUND TO MODULE	BLACK-LT GREEN
77	ELECTRONIC CONTROL UNIT TO SOLENOID ACTUATOR	DK BLUE-YELLOW
78	KEYLESS DOOR LOCK SWITCH DATA BIT 1 TO MODULE	LT BLUE-YELLOW
79	KEYLESS DOOR LOCK SWITCH DATA BIT 2 TO MODULE	LT GREEN-RED
80	ENGINE COMPARTMENT LAMP FEED	BLACK-ORANGE
81	EMISSION CONTROL VALVE TO SWITCH	BROWN-YELLOW
82	WASHER FLUID LEVEL INDICATOR	PINK-YELLOW
83	INTERLOCK MODULE TO CENTER BUCKLE SWITCH	WHITE-ORANGE
84	DECK LID SOLENOID FEED	PURPLE-YELLOW
85	SEAT BELT WARNING TIMER TO L.F. RETRACTOR SWITCH	BROWN-LT BLUE
86	SEAT BELT WARNING TIMER TO R.F. SEAT SENSOR	DK BLUE-WHITE
87	INTERLOCK MODULE TO CENTER SEAT SENSOR SWITCH	TAN-WHITE
88	INSTRUMENT PANEL LAMP FEED	BLACK-WHITE
89	EXHAUST GAS OXYGEN SENSOR RETURN TO EEC MODULE	ORANGE
90	THERMOCOUPLE POS. TO EXHAUST SYST. OVERTEMP PROTECT MODULE	DK BLUE-LT GREEN
91	THERMOCOUPLE 1 NEG. TO EXHAUST SYST. OVERTEMP PROTECT MODULE	GRAY-RED
92	THERMOCOUPLE 2 NEG. TO EXHAUST SYST. OVERTEMP PROTECT MODULE	WHITE-BLACK
93	AIR DUMP VALVE NEG. TO EXHAUST SYST. OVERTEMP MODULE	ORANGE-WHITE
94	EEC TO EXHAUST GAS OXYGEN SENSOR (#2 IN DUAL SYSTEM)	RED-BLACK
95	FEEDBACK CARB. COIL 1	TAN-RED
96	FEEDBACK CARB. COIL 2	TAN-ORANGE
97	FEEDBACK CARB. COIL 3	TAN-LT GREEN
98	FEEDBACK CARB. COIL 4	TAN-LT BLUE
99	AIR PORT SOLENOID SIGNAL	LT GREEN-BLACK
100	AIR PUMP SOLENOID SIGNAL	WHITE-RED
101	ELECTRONIC CONTROL UNIT TO CANISTER PURGE SOLENOID	GRAY-YELLOW
102	L.H. REAR TAILLAMP BULB OUTAGE	WHITE
103	R.H. REAR TAILLAMP BULB OUTAGE	WHITE-RED
104	L.H. REAR STOP & TURN BULB OUTAGE	LT BLUE-ORANGE
105	R.H. REAR STOP & TURN BULB OUTAGE	RED-WHITE
106	LOW FUEL INDICATOR	LT BLUE
107	BUCKLE SW. TO CENTER OCCUPANT SEAT SENSOR	LT BLUE-PINK
108	L.H. HEADLAMP BULB OUTAGE	BROWN-LT BLUE
109	R.H. HEADLAMP BULB OUTAGE	PINK-LT BLUE
110	R. AND L.H. REAR RUNNING LAMP BULB OUTAGE	WHITE-LT GREEN
111	WARNING LAMP TO LIGHTS ON RELAY	BLACK-YELLOW
112	WARNING LAMP RELAY FEED	BLACK-YELLOW
113	STARTING MOTOR TO STARTING MOTOR RELAY	YELLOW-LT BLUE
114	FEED TO VACUUM DOOR LOCK SWITCH	TAN-YELLOW
115	VACUUM DOOR LOCK SWITCH TO SOLENOID (LOCK)	LT GREEN
116	VACUUM DOOR LOCK SWITCH TO SOLENOID (UNLOCK)	BROWN-ORANGE
117	DOOR LOCK MOTOR (LOCK)	PINK-BLACK
118	DOOR LOCK MOTOR (UNLOCK)	PINK-ORANGE
119	DOOR LOCK SWITCH (LOCK)	PINK-YELLOW
120	DOOR LOCK SWITCH (UNLOCK)	PINK-LT GREEN
121	KEYLESS DOOR LOCK SWITCH DATA BIT 3 TO MODULE	YELLOW-BLACK
122	KEYLESS DOOR LOCK SWITCH DATA BIT 4 TO MODULE	YELLOW
123	KEYLESS DOOR LOCK SWITCH DATA BIT 5 TO MODULE	RED
124	KEYLESS DOOR LOCK SWITCH ENABLE FROM MODULE	BROWN
125	MAP LAMP SWITCH TO RH MAP LAMP	BROWN-YELLOW
126	COURTESY LAMP SW. TO INSTR. PANEL COURTESY LAMP	BLACK-ORANGE
127	COURTESY LAMP SW. TO "C" PILLAR LAMPS	BLACK-LT BLUE
128	BRAKE FLUID LEVEL UNIT TO MESSAGE CENTER	PURPLE-YELLOW
129	KEYLESS DOOR LOCK OUTPUT FROM MODULE	LT GREEN
130	HEADLAMP BULB OUTAGE TO MESSAGE CENTER	RED-LT GREEN
131	CIGAR LIGHTER LAMP FEED	PURPLE-ORANGE
132	TAILLAMP BULB OUTAGE TO MESSAGE CENTER	ORANGE-BLACK
133	RELAY TO ROAD MAP LAMP SWITCH	TAN-RED
134	KEYLESS DOOR LOCK OUTPUT (ALL) FROM MODULE	WHITE
135	STOP AND TURN BULB OUTAGE TO MESSAGE CENTER	YELLOW-RED
136	SPEED INPUT TO MESSAGE CENTER	YELLOW-LT BLUE
137	RADIO ANTENNA SWITCH FEED	YELLOW-BLACK
138	DOOR JAMB SWITCH TO LIGHTS ON RELAY	BROWN-LT BLUE
139	FUEL PULSE TO MESSAGE CENTER	LT GREEN-PURPLE
140	BACKUP PUMP	BLACK-PINK
141	CLOCK ADVANCE SWITCH TO MESSAGE CENTER	DK GREEN-LT GREEN
142	CLOCK SELECT SWITCH TO MESSAGE CENTER	LT BLUE-RED
143	CHECKOUT SWITCH TO MESSAGE CENTER	LT BLUE-YELLOW
144	AMPLIFIER TO SERVO TRANSDUCER FEED	ORANGE-YELLOW
145	SERVO SOURCE VACUUM SOLENOID TO CONTROL TRANSISTOR	GRAY-BLACK
146	SERVO VENT SOLENOID TO CONTROL TRANSISTOR	WHITE-PINK
147	AMPLIFIER FEEDBACK POTENTIOMETER FEED	PURPLE-LT BLUE
148	SERVO FEEDBACK POTENTIOMETER SIGNAL TO AMPLIFIER	YELLOW-RED
149	SERVO FEEDBACK POTENTIOMETER BASE TO AMPLIFIER	BROWN-LT GREEN
150	SENSOR SIGNAL TO AMPLIFIER	DK GREEN-WHITE
151	SPEED CONTROL ON-OFF SWITCH TO AMPLIFIER	LT BLUE-BLACK
152	ARRIVAL SWITCH TO MESSAGE CENTER	LT BLUE-WHITE
153	ECONOMY SWITCH TO MESSAGE CENTER	PURPLE-YELLOW
154	DESTINATION SWITCH TO MESSAGE CENTER	PURPLE-LT GREEN
155	DISTANCE TO EMPTY SWITCH TO MESSAGE CENTER	GRAY-RED
156	AVERAGE SPEED SWITCH TO MESSAGE CENTER	GRAY-ORANGE
157	WINDOW REGULATOR MOTOR TO GROUND	GRAY-BLACK
158	KEY WARNING SWITCH TO BUZZER	BLACK-PINK
159	DOOR JAMB SWITCH TO BUZZER	RED-PINK
160	BUZZER TO WARNING INDICATOR RELAY	WHITE-PINK
161	MILES/KILOMETERS SWITCH TO MESSAGE CENTER	GRAY-LT BLUE
162	BRAKE WARNING LAMP TO BRAKE SWITCH	LT GREEN-RED
163	KEYLESS DOOR LOCK OUTPUT (DRIVER) FROM MODULE	RED-ORANGE
164	DISTANCE SWITCH TO MESSAGE CENTER	GRAY-WHITE
165	ELAPSED TIME SWITCH TO MESSAGE CENTER	WHITE-BLACK
166	RESET SWITCH TO MESSAGE CENTER	WHITE-ORANGE
167	MESSAGE CENTER OUTPUT CLOCK TO DISPLAY	WHITE-YELLOW
168	5V DO-MESSAGE CENTER TO DISPLAY	WHITE-BLACK
169	TRANSFORMER POWER-MESSAGE CENTER TO DISPLAY	LT BLUE-PINK
170	WINDOW REGULATOR SWITCH FEED	RED-LT BLUE
171	CIRCUIT BREAKER TO SEAT LATCH RELAY	BLACK-WHITE
172	RELAY TO SEAT LATCH SOLENOID	ORANGE
173	DOOR SWITCH TO SEAT LATCH RELAY (COIL TERM.)	PINK-WHITE
174	DATA-MESSAGE CENTER TO DISPLAY	DK GREEN-PURPLE
175	RELAY FEED	BLACK-YELLOW
176	REAR WINDOW REGULATOR SWITCH FEED	WHITE
177	KEYLESS DOOR LOCK SWITCH SENSOR TO MODULE	WHITE
178	PARITY BIT-DISPLAY TO MESSAGE CENTER	DK GREEN-ORANGE
179	HORIZONTAL SEAT REG. MOTOR TO RELAY	YELLOW
180	HORIZONTAL SEAT REG. MOTOR TO RELAY	RED
181	BLOWER MOTOR FEED	BROWN-ORANGE
182	THERMOSTAT SWITCH FEED	BROWN-WHITE
183	TONE GENERATOR	TAN-YELLOW

' IN SOME CASES, THERE MAY BE ADDITIONAL CIRCUIT FUNCTIONS INCLUDED IN THE CIRCUIT DESCRIPTION LISTED.

STANDARD CIRCUIT CHART (BY NUMBER)

CIRCUIT	DESCRIPTION*	COLOR
184	AIR COND. SW. (LO) TO AIR COND. BLOWER MOTOR	TAN-ORANGE
185	INSIDE DOOR HANDLE SWITCH TO RETRACTOR INHIBITOR MODULE	GRAY-BLACK
186	DEFOGGER SW. TO DEFOGGER MOTOR	BROWN-LT BLUE
187	INHIBITOR MODULE TO RETRACTOR OVERRIDE SOLENOID	GRAY-RED
188	HEADLAMP SWITCH TO AUXILIARY LAMPS	WHITE-BLACK
189	IDLE TRACKING SWITCH FEED	LT BLUE-PINK
190	THERMACTOR AIR BYPASS (TAB)	WHITE-ORANGE
191	DEFOGGER SW. TO DEFOGGER MOTOR	DK BLUE-YELLOW
192	HEADLAMP SWITCH TO ELECTRONIC CLUSTER DIMMING	BROWN-WHITE
193	WINDOW REGULATOR RELAY FEED	YELLOW-LT GREEN
194	WINDOW REGULATOR REPLAY ACCY. FEED	PINK
195	TAILLAMP SWITCH FEED	TAN-WHITE
196	HEADLAMP FLASH TO PASS SWITCH FEED	DK BLUE-ORANGE
197	COOLANT TEMPERATURE SWITCH TO CONTROL RELAY	TAN-ORANGE
198	A/C PRESSURE SWITCH TO CONTROL RELAY	TAN-YELLOW
199	AUTO TRANS MANUAL LEVER POSITION OR CLUTCH	LT BLUE-YELLOW
200	THERMACTOR AIR DIVERTER (TAD)	BROWN
201	MCV MODULE TO VIP FUNCTION TESTER	TAN-RED
202	SPEED CONTROL AMPLIFIER TO CRUISE LAMP INTERFACE MODULE	RED-PINK
203	CRUISE INDICATING LAMP TO CRUISE LAMP INTERFACE MODULE	ORANGE-LT BLUE
204	TANK SELECT CIRCUIT ELECTRONIC FUEL GAGE	ORANGE-LT GREEN
205	BUFFER FUEL LEVEL OUTPUT TO TRIPMINDER	DK BLUE-LT GREEN
206	TRAILER GROUND	WHITE
207	MARKER LAMP SWITCH TO MARKER LAMPS	BLACK
208	LOW OIL LEVEL RELAY TO WARNING LAMP	GRAY
209	TO TEST CONNECTOR	WHITE-PURPLE
210	INDICATOR LAMP TO SWITCH (4x4)	LT BLUE
211	ECU TO VACUUM SWITCH 4	BLACK-PINK
212	AUXILIARY CIRCUIT FEED TO TRACTOR TRAILER PLUG	DK BLUE
213	ECU TO VACUUM SWITCH 2	WHITE-PINK
214	ECU TO VACUUM SWITCH 3	RED-BLACK
215	SIGNAL UNIT LAMP TO FUEL SIGNAL RELAY	YELLOW-BLACK
216	AUTOLAMP AMPLIFIER TO RHEOSTAT	TAN-LT BLUE
217	AUTOLAMP AMPLIFIER TO RHEOSTAT	DK BLUE-ORANGE
218	AUTOLAMP AMPLIFIER TO SENSOR	WHITE-PURPLE
219	HEADLAMP SWITCH TO AUTOLAMP AMPLIFIER	DK GREEN-YELLOW
220	AUTOLAMP AMPLIFIER TO CONTROL SWITCH	PURPLE-ORANGE
221	HEADLAMP SWITCH TO SENSOR AND AUTOLAMP AMPLIFIER	ORANGE-WHITE
222	AUTOLAMP AMPLIFIER TO SENSOR	BROWN-LT GREEN
223	MILEAGE SENSOR TO EEC MODULE	TAN-LT GREEN
224	TRANSMISSION OVERDRIVE SWITCH TO EEC MODULE	TAN-WHITE
225	INJECTION PUMP FUEL TEMPERATURE SENSOR	BLACK-YELLOW
226	L.F. WINDOW REG. SW. TO LF WINDOW REG. MOTOR	WHITE-BLACK
227	L.F. WINDOW REG. SW. TO LF WINDOW REG. MOTOR	YELLOW
228	ELECTRIC DRIVE COOLING FAN (SINGLE OR LOW)	DK BLUE
229	EFE CARBURETOR SPACE FEED	BLACK-YELLOW
230	COLD START INJECTOR	BLACK-LT GREEN
231	ACCESSORY FEED TO MESSAGE CENTER	BLACK-YELLOW
232	FUEL METERING CONTROL LEVER ACTUATOR 1 MINUS	BROWN-LT BLUE
233	THERMOMETER SENSOR FEED	DK BLUE-YELLOW
234	THERMOMETER AMBIENT SENSOR RETURN	DK BLUE-WHITE
235	LAMP RETURN TO PULSE WITH DIMMER	RED-BLACK
236	FUEL PRESSURE BOOST SOLENOID	RED-YELLOW
237	SHIFT SOLENOID 1	ORANGE-YELLOW
238	FUEL PUMP RELAY TO SAFETY SWITCH	DK GREEN-YELLOW
239	FUEL INJECTION PUMP POSITION SENSOR	PURPLE-YELLOW
240	COLD START TIMING RETARD SOLENOID	WHITE-RED
241	DE-ICE SOLENOID CONTROL	LT BLUE-YELLOW
242	FUEL OCTANE ADJUST SIGNAL	DK GREEN
243	POWER SERVO TO CLIMATE CONTROL UNIT (MODE)	LT GREEN-ORANGE
244	THERMAL SW. TO CLIMATE CONTROL UNIT	YELLOW-WHITE
245	POWER SERVO TO CLIMATE CONTROL UNIT (AMP)	BROWN-LT GREEN
246	POWER SERVO TO CLIMATE CONTROL UNIT (AMP)	PURPLE
247	POWER SERVO TO CLIMATE CONTROL UNIT (AMP)	WHITE-YELLOW
248	HEATER & A/C CONTROL SW. (DE-ICE) TO CLIMATE CONTROL UNIT	YELLOW-LT BLUE
249	HEATER & A/C CONTROL SW. (LO-NORM) TO CLIMATE CONTROL UNIT	DK BLUE-LT GREEN
250	HEATER & A/C CONTROL SW. (LO-NORM) TO POWER SERVO	ORANGE
251	IGNITION SWITCH TO THERMACTOR TIMER	BROWN-ORANGE
252	THERMACTOR TIMER TO RELAY	TAN-RED
253	START CIRCUIT TO THERMACTOR RELAY	ORANGE-YELLOW
254	OIL PRESSURE SWITCH TO TIMER	DK GREEN-WHITE
255	THERMACTOR DUMP VALVE FEED	LT BLUE-RED
256	TEMPERATURE COMPENSATED PUMP TO PROCESSOR	ORANGE-WHITE
257	H L SW. TO CHIMES	WHITE-RED
258	LOW OIL LEVEL RELAY TO SENSOR	WHITE-PINK
259	DEDICATED GROUND TO TFI MODULE	ORANGE
260	BLOWER MOTOR TO SWITCH — LO	RED-ORANGE
261	BLOWER MOTOR TO SWITCH — HI	ORANGE-BLACK
262	STARTING MOTOR RELAY TO IGNITION COIL "I" TERM.	BROWN-PINK
263	CLICKER RELAY TERM. NO. 4 TO AIR VALVE ASSY.	PURPLE-LT BLUE
264	ELECT. ENG. CONTL. MOD. TO IDLE SPD. CONTL. MOTOR #1	WHITE-LT BLUE
265	ELECT. ENG. CONTL. MOD. TO IDLE SPD. CONTL. MOTOR #2	LT GREEN-WHITE
266	MEMORY SEAT SWITCH ENABLE	PURPLE-WHITE
267	MEMORY SEAT SWITCH POSITION #1	BROWN-LT GREEN
268	MEMORY SEAT SWITCH POSITION #2	BLACK-ORANGE
269	HEATER BLOWER MOTOR TO SWITCH (MEDIUM)	LT BLUE-ORANGE
270	MEMORY SEAT SWITCH SET	BROWN-ORANGE
271	MEMORY SEAT SWITCH LAMP ENABLE	LT GREEN-WHITE
272	MEMORY SEAT SWITCH LAMP DRIVE	WHITE-ORANGE
273	TO ELECTRONIC CLUSTER FROM ENGLISH/METRIC SWITCH IN KEYBOARD	BROWN
274	SWITCH OFF TO RELAY	ORANGE
275	SWITCH ON TO RELAY	YELLOW
276	SWITCH TO FEED	BROWN
277	AMPLIFIER SPEAKER SWITCH TO LEFT REAR SPEAKER	LT BLUE-BLACK
278	AMPLIFIER SPEAKER SWITCH FEED TO RIGHT REAR SPEAKER	PURPLE-WHITE
279	SPEAKER VOICE COIL FEED FRONT (R. CHANNEL) AMP INPUT	WHITE-RED
280	SPEAKER VOICE COIL FEED FRONT (LEFT CHANNEL) AMP INPUT	LT GREEN
281	SPEAKER VOICE COIL RETURN AMP INPUT	WHITE
282	CYLINDER IDENTIFICATION	DK BLUE-ORANGE
283	DUAL PLUG INHIBIT	DK BLUE-YELLOW
285	ELECTRONIC CLUSTER FROM EXPANDED FUEL IN KEYBOARD	ORANGE
286	ELECTRONIC CLUSTER FROM TRIP RESET SWITCH IN KEYBOARD	YELLOW
287	SPEAKER VOICE COIL RETURN	BLACK-WHITE
288	TO ELECTRONIC CLUSTER FROM TRIP RECALL SWITCH IN KEYBOARD	PURPLE
289	TO ELECTRONIC CLUSTER FROM GAGE SELECT SWITCH IN KEYBOARD	WHITE
290	12 GA FUSE LINK	GRAY
291	16 GA FUSE LINK	BLACK
292	18 GA FUSE LINK	BROWN
293	INSTRUMENT PANEL ILLUMINATION CONTROL MODULE FEED	ORANGE-RED
294	FUSED ACCY. FEED #3	WHITE-LT BLUE
295	ELECTRONIC CLUSTER ACCESSORY FEED	LT BLUE-PINK
296	FUSED ACCY. FEED #1	WHITE-PURPLE
297	ACCY. FEED FROM IGNITION SWITCH	BLACK-LT GREEN
298	FUSED ACCY. FEED #2	PURPLE-ORANGE
299	14 GA FUSE LINK	DK GREEN
300	16 GA FUSE LINK	ORANGE
301	18 GA FUSE LINK	RED
302	20 GA FUSE LINK	DK BLUE
303	12 GA FUSE LINK	YELLOW
304	FEEDBACK CARBURETOR COIL "A"	BROWN
305	EEC MODULE TO TIME METER	LT BLUE-PINK
306	SEAT REG. SW. TO HORIZ. SOLENOID BATT. TERM.	LT BLUE
307	SEAT REG. SW. TO VERT. SOLENOID BATT. TERM.	WHITE
308	HI-TEMP SWITCH TO MCU MODULE	LT BLUE-ORANGE
309	LO-TEMP SWITCH TO MCU MODULE	ORANGE-RED
310	ELECT. ENG. CONTL. MOD. TO KNOCK SENSOR	YELLOW-RED
311	MCU MODULE TO KNOCK SENSOR	DK GREEN-ORANGE
312	FUEL METERING CONTROL LEVER ACTUATOR 2 PLUS	WHITE-PURPLE
313	LEFT FRONT WINDOW REGULATOR SWITCH TO RIGHT FRONT WINDOW REGULATOR MOTOR	YELLOW-BLACK
314	LEFT FRONT WINDOW REGULATOR SWITCH TO RIGHT FRONT WINDOW REGULATOR MOTOR	RED-BLACK
315	SHIFT SOLENOID 2	PURPLE ORANGE
316	LEFT FRONT WINDOW REGULATOR SWITCH TO LEFT REAR WINDOW REGULATOR MOTOR	YELLOW-LT BLUE
317	LEFT FRONT WINDOW REGULATOR SWITCH TO LEFT REAR WINDOW REGULATOR MOTOR	RED-LT BLUE
318	EXHAUST BACK PRESSURE VALVE ACTUATOR	GRAY-RED
319	LEFT FRONT WINDOW REGULATOR SWITCH TO RIGHT REAR WINDOW REGULATOR MOTOR	YELLOW-BLACK
320	LEFT FRONT WINDOW REGULATOR SWITCH TO RIGHT REAR WINDOW REGULATOR MOTOR	RED-BLACK
321	AIR CONDITIONER CLUTCH RELAY	GRAY-WHITE
322	IDLE SPEED CONTROL TO EGR VENT SOLENOID	RED-ORANGE
323	IDLE SPEED CONTROL TO EGR VACUUM SOLENOID	ORANGE-BLACK
324	TRANSMISSION OVERDRIVE SWITCH TO HEAT MODULE	YELLOW-LT GREEN
325	CRANK ENABLE TO IGNITION MODULE	DK BLUE-ORANGE
326	FUSE PANEL FEED TO RELAY	WHITE-PURPLE
327	DIESEL WATER IN FUEL SENDER TO WARNING LAMP GROUND	BLACK-ORANGE
328	WINDOW REG. MASTER CONT. SW. TO WINDOW REG. SW. FEED	RED-YELLOW
329	CRANK ENABLE RELAY	PINK
330	POWER STEERING PRESSURE SWITCH	YELLOW-LT GREEN
331	WIDE OPEN THROTTLE A/C CUTOUT SWITCH	PINK-YELLOW
332	TIME DELAY RELAY	WHITE
333	WINDOW REG. SW. TO WINDOW REG. MOTOR	YELLOW-RED
334	WINDOW REG. SW. TO WINDOW REG. MOTOR	RED-YELLOW
335	AFTER GLOW RELAY TO DIESEL CONTROL SWITCH	ORANGE-LT BLUE
336	POWER RELAY TO GLOW PLUGS (RIGHT BANK)	BLACK-LT GREEN
337	POWER RELAY TO GLOW PLUGS (LEFT BANK)	ORANGE-WHITE
338	DIESEL CONTROL SWITCH TO LAMP CONTROL RELAY	BROWN-PINK
339	DIESEL CONTROL SWITCH TO POWER RELAY & LAMP CONTROL RELAY	GRAY
340	ANTI-THEFT MODULE TO ALARM RELAY	RED-LT BLUE
341	DOOR OPENING WARNING TO ANTI-THEFT MODULE	ORANGE-WHITE
342	START INTERRUPT RELAY TO ANTI-THEFT MODULE	LT GREEN-PURPLE
343	WARNING LAMP TO ANTI-THEFT MODULE	DK BLUE-LT GREEN
344	DOOR AJAR SWITCH TO INDICATOR LAMP LEFT FRONT GROUND	BLACK-YELLOW
345	DOOR AJAR SWITCH TO INDICATOR LAMP RIGHT FRONT GROUND	BLACK-PINK
346	DOOR AJAR SWITCH TO INDICATOR LAMP RIGHT REAR GROUND	BLACK-WHITE
347	A/C COMPRESSOR CLUTCH FEED	BLACK-YELLOW
348	A/C DEMAND SIGNAL	PURPLE
349	CRANKSHAFT POSITION SENSOR FEED	DK BLUE
350	CRANKSHAFT SENSOR SIGNAL RETURN	GRAY
351	POWER TO ENGINE SENSORS	BROWN-WHITE
352	EGR FEEDBACK	BROWN-LT GREEN
353	VEHICLE SPEED SENSOR FEED	LT BLUE
354	ENGINE COOLANT TEMPERATURE FEED	LT GREEN-RED
355	THROTTLE ANGLE POSITION SENSOR TO EEC MODULE	GRAY-WHITE
356	BAROMETRIC PRESSURE SENSOR FEED	DK BLUE-LT GREEN
357	CARBURETOR AIR TEMPERATURE SENSOR FEED	LT GREEN-PURPLE
358	MANIFOLD ABSOLUTE PRESSURE TO EEC MODULE	LT GREEN-BLACK
359	SENSOR SIGNAL RETURN	GRAY-RED
360	EGR VALVE REGULATOR SOLENOID TO EEC MODULE	BROWN-PINK
361	POWER OUTPUT FROM EEC RELAY	RED
362	EGR VALVE TO EEC MODULE FEED	YELLOW

* IN SOME CASES, THERE MAY BE ADDITIONAL CIRCUIT FUNCTIONS INCLUDED IN THE CIRCUIT DESCRIPTION LISTED.

STANDARD CIRCUIT CHART (BY NUMBER)

CIRCUIT	DESCRIPTION *	COLOR	CIRCUIT	DESCRIPTION *	COLOR
363	DOOR AJAR SWITCH TO INDICATOR LAMP LEFT REAR GROUND	BLACK-LT BLUE	456	AUX. WATER VALVE FEED	WHITE-LT GREEN
364	BLOWER MOTOR RELAY FEED	BLACK-LT GREEN	457	BRAKE WEAR SENSOR	TAN-BLACK
365	FUEL LEVEL WARNING RELAY FEED	LT BLUE-RED	458	TURN SIGNAL SWITCH TO INDICATOR RELAY	ORANGE-BLACK
366	FUEL WARNING RELAY CONTROL	RED-BLACK	459	INDICATOR RELAY TO FLASHER	ORANGE-LT GREEN
367	FUEL LEVEL RECEIVER TO FUEL LEVEL WARNING RELAY (REC. TERM.)	DK GREEN-WHITE	460	HORN SWITCH FEED	YELLOW-LT BLUE
368	RADIO SEEK "UP"	RED-BLACK	461	MODULE TO RELAY	ORANGE
369	VACUUM SOLENOID TO TEMP. SW.	BROWN-ORANGE	462	MODULE TO RELAY	PURPLE
370	RADIO SEEK "DOWN"	ORANGE-BLACK	463	ELECTRIC SHIFT MODULE TO NEUTRAL START SWITCH	RED-WHITE
371	BLOWER MOTOR RELAY TO MOTOR	PINK-WHITE	464	MODULE TO LIGHT	BLACK-PINK
372	RADIO MEMORY SEEK	BROWN-ORANGE	465	MODULE TO SWITCH	WHITE-LT BLUE
373	TO ELECTRONIC CLUSTER FROM GROUND IN KEYBOARD	BLACK	466	DIESEL CONTROL MODULE FEED	PINK-ORANGE
374	DOOR AJAR RELAY TO DOOR SWITCH	BROWN	467	PRESSURE SWITCH TO INERTIA SWITCH	GRAY-YELLOW
375	MOVABLE STEERING COLUMN SOLENOID FEED	YELLOW-LT GREEN	468	EATC L.H. SUNLOAD SENSOR POSITIVE	BROWN
376	ELECT. ENG. CONTL. MOD. TO IDLE SPD. CONTL. MOTOR #3	BROWN-WHITE	469	SEAT BELT WARNING SWITCH FEED	LT GREEN
377	ELECT. ENG. CONTL. MOD. TO EXHAUST HEAT CONTL SOLENOID	WHITE	470	THERMO SWITCH TO CONTROL MODULE	PINK-BLACK
378	ELECT. ENG. CONTL. MOD. TO THROTTLE LEVER SOLENOID	RED-BLACK	471	DROPPING RESISTOR TO RELAY #2	ORANGE-LT GREEN
379	TURN SIGNAL SWITCH TO RH CORNERING LAMP	BROWN-WHITE	472	GLOW PLUG TO CONTROL MODULE	YELLOW-BLACK
380	TURN SIGNAL SWITCH TO LH CORNERING LAMP	PURPLE-YELLOW	473	CONTROL MODULE TO OIL PRESSURE SWITCH	LT GREEN-BLACK
381	MOVABLE STEERING COLUMN SOLENOID TO COURTESY LAMP SWITCH	ORANGE-WHITE	474	STOPLAMP RELAY FEED	PINK-BLACK
			475	STOPLAMP SW. TO STOPLAMP RELAY (COIL TERM.)	DK GREEN-WHITE
382	ELECT. ENG. CONTL. MOD. TO TEST CONNECTOR #2	YELLOW-BLACK	476	EATC L.H. SUNLOAD SENSOR NEGATIVE	BROWN-YELLOW
383	EMERGENCY WARNING FLASHER FEED	RED-WHITE	477	FOG LAMP SWITCH TO FOG LAMP RELAY	LT BLUE-BLACK
384	ELECT. ENG. CONTL. MOD. TO IDLE SPD. CONTL. MOTOR #3	PINK-ORANGE	478	FOG LAMP SW. TO FOG LAMP	TAN-ORANGE
385	FLASHER TO EMERGENCY WARNING SWITCH	WHITE-RED	479	EATC R.H. SUNLOAD SENSOR POSITIVE	PURPLE
386	ELECT. ENG. CONTL. MOD. TO ELECTRO DRIVE FAN	LT BLUE	480	TRANSMISSION CLUTCH CONTROL TO EEC MODULE	PURPLE-YELLOW
387	READING LAMP SWITCH TO READING LAMP (LH)	LT GREEN	481	EFI MODULE TO CLUTCH SWITCH	GRAY-YELLOW
388	REARVIEW OUTSIDE MIRROR FEED	RED	482	FUEL FILLER DOOR RELEASE SWITCH TO FUEL FILLER DOOR RELEASE SOLENOID	WHITE-PINK
389	R.F. DOOR LOCK SWITCH TO L.F. DOOR LOCK SWITCH	DK GREEN-LT GREEN	483	EATC R.H. SUNLOAD SENSOR NEGATIVE	GRAY
390	R.F. DOOR UNLOCK SWITCH TO L.F. DOOR UNLOCK SWITCH	DK BLUE-WHITE	484	LIQUID CRYSTAL DISPLAY	ORANGE-BLACK
391	CHOKE RELAY TO MCU MODULE	WHITE-YELLOW	485	IGNITION SWITCH ACCY. TERM. TO DECK LID OPEN WARNING LAMP	BROWN-PINK
392	ELECTRIC PVS TO MCU MODULE	WHITE-ORANGE			
393	THROTTLE LEVER SOLENOID RELAY TO MCU MODULE	WHITE-BLACK	486	DECK LID OPEN WARNING LAMP TO DECK LID OPEN SWITCH	BROWN-WHITE
394	ANEROID SWITCH TO MCU MODULE	GRAY-LT BLUE	487	READING LAMP SWITCH TO READING LAMP	PINK-ORANGE
395	PROFILE IGNITION PICKUP FROM TFI MODULE	GRAY-ORANGE	488	DIESEL CONTROL MODULE GROUND RETURN	BLACK-LT BLUE
396	FUEL 1 GROUND TO TACH/GAGE MODULE	BLACK-ORANGE	489	ELECTRONIC CLUSTER IGNITION RUN FEED	PINK-BLACK
397	SIGNAL GROUND TO TACH/GAGE MODULE	BLACK-WHITE	490	POWER LUMBAR FEED	RED
398	TACHOMETER GROUND TO TACH/GAGE MODULE	BLACK-YELLOW	491	POWER "THIGH" BOLSTER UP	YELLOW
399	HEATER BLOWER SWITCH FEED	BROWN-YELLOW	492	POWER "THIGH" BOLSTER DOWN	BROWN
400	SAFETY RELAY LOAD TERM. TO WIND. REG. SW. FEED	LT BLUE-BLACK	493	HCU (MAIN) TO MODULE	BLACK-PINK
401	LIMIT SW. TO BACK WINDOW REG. MOTOR	GRAY-BLACK	494	TURN SIGNAL RELAY TO TURN SIGNAL FLASHER	TAN-LT GREEN
402	WINDOW REG. SW. TO BACK WINDOW REG. MOTOR	GRAY-RED	495	VALVE #1 TO MODULE	TAN
403	WINDOW REG. SW. TO WINDOW REG. MOTOR	GRAY-WHITE	496	VALVE #2 TO MODULE	ORANGE
404	WINDOW REG. SW. TO BACK WINDOW SW.	PURPLE-LT GREEN	497	VALVE #3 TO MODULE	WHITE
405	WINDOW REG. SW. TO BACK WINDOW SW.	PURPLE-LT BLUE	498	VALVE #4 TO MODULE	PINK
406	WINDOW REG. SW. TO BACK WINDOW AUX. SW.	TAN	499	VALVE #5 TO MODULE	GRAY-BLACK
407	WINDOW REG. SW. REAR TO LIMIT SW.	TAN-BLACK	500	HEADLAMP DIMMER SWITCH TO HEADLAMP DIMMER RELAY	PURPLE
408	WINDOW REG. SW. FRONT TO LIMIT SW.	TAN-RED	501	ELECTRONIC FUEL GAGE TO MESSAGE CENTER	LT BLUE
409	PRESSURE SWITCH TO KEY SWITCH	TAN-BLACK	502	HEADLAMP DIMMER RELAY TO HEADLAMP DIMMER SWITCH	GRAY
410	REARVIEW OUTSIDE MIRROR UP	YELLOW	503	HEADLAMP DIMMER RELAY TO FUSE HOLDER	LT BLUE
411	REARVIEW OUTSIDE MIRROR DOWN	DK GREEN	504	FUSE HOLDER TO HEADLAMP DIMMER AMPLIFIER	DK BLUE-WHITE
412	REARVIEW OUTSIDE MIRROR COUNTERCLOCKWISE	WHITE	505	HEADLAMP DIMMER SWITCH TO HEADLAMP DIMMER AMPLIFIER	GRAY-YELLOW
413	REARVIEW OUTSIDE MIRROR CLOCKWISE	LT BLUE	506	MPH/KPH SWITCH TO MESSAGE CENTER	RED
414	AIR SOLENOID CONTROL R.F.	ORANGE-RED	507	AMPLIFIER TO RHEOSTAT	YELLOW
415	AIR SOLENOID CONTROL L.F.	LT GREEN-ORANGE	508	RHEOSTAT TO SENSOR	WHITE
416	AIR SOLENOID CONTROL — REAR	LT BLUE-BLACK	509	AIR COND. CONDENSOR THERMAL SWITCH FEED	TAN-YELLOW
417	AIR SUSPENSION SWITCH FEED	PURPLE-ORANGE	510	VALVE #6 TO MODULE	TAN-RED
418	AIR SUSPENSION CONTROL MODULE FEED	DK GREEN-YELLOW	511	STOPLAMP SWITCH TO STOPLAMPS	LT GREEN
419	AIR SUSPENSION MALFUNCTION WARNING LAMP	DK GREEN-LT GREEN	512	BRAKE FLUID RES. SWITCH TO MODULE	TAN-LT GREEN
420	AIR COMPRESSOR POWER RELAY CONTROL	DK BLUE-YELLOW	513	POWER RELAY COIL TO MODULE	BROWN-PINK
421	AIR COMPRESSOR VENT SOLENOID	PINK	514	RH FRONT SENSOR (HIGH) TO MODULE	YELLOW-RED
422	AIR SUSPENSION HEIGHT SENSOR HI — L.F.	PINK-BLACK	515	RESISTOR TO BLOWER MOTOR (HI)	ORANGE-RED
423	AIR SUSPENSION HEIGHT SENSOR LO — L.F.	PURPLE-LT GREEN	516	R.H. FRONT SENSOR (LOW) TO MODULE	YELLOW-BLACK
424	AIR SUSPENSION HEIGHT SENSOR HI — R.F.	TAN	517	CIRCUIT BREAKER (LOAD TERM.) TO CONTROL SWITCH BATT. TERM.)	BLACK-WHITE
425	AIR SUSPENSION HEIGHT SENSOR LO — R.F.	BROWN-PINK			
426	FRONT AIR SUSPENSION HEIGHT SENSOR FEED	RED-BLACK	518	REAR SENSOR (HIGH) TO MODULE	LT GREEN-RED
427	AIR SUSPENSION HEIGHT SENSOR HI — REAR	PINK-BLACK	519	L.H. REAR SENSOR (LOW) TO MODULE	LT GREEN-BLACK
428	AIR SUSPENSION HEIGHT SENSOR LO — REAR	ORANGE-BLACK	520	SEAT BELT WARNING LAMP TO WARNING LAMP SWITCH	PURPLE-WHITE
429	REAR AIR SUSPENSION HEIGHT SENSOR FEED	PURPLE-LT GREEN	521	L.H. FRONT SENSOR (HIGH) TO MODULE	TAN-ORANGE
430	AIR SUSPENSION SYSTEM GROUND	GRAY	522	L.H. FRONT SENSOR (LOW) TO MODULE	TAN-BLACK
431	AIR SUSP. MOD. TO L.F. HEIGHT SENSOR	PINK-WHITE	523	R.H. REAR SENSOR (HIGH) TO MODULE	RED-PINK
432	AIR SUSPENSION ELECTRONIC GROUND	BLACK-PINK	524	R.H. REAR SENSOR (LOW) TO MODULE	PINK-BLACK
433	FUEL PUMP BYPASS	LT BLUE-RED	525	SPLICE TO MODULE	ORANGE-YELLOW
434	RELAY TO DAY/NIGHT ILLUMINATION LAMPS	LT BLUE-BLACK	526	CORNERING LAMP SWITCH FEED	BLACK-WHITE
435	POSITION SENSE RETURN	YELLOW-LT BLUE	527	HEADLAMP DIMMER SWITCH OVERRIDE TO RHEOSTAT	RED
436	REAR TILT POSITION SENSE	RED-LT GREEN	528	POWER RELAY TO MODULE GROUND	ORANGE-YELLOW
437	POSITION SENSE ENABLE	YELLOW-LT GREEN	529	SPLICE #2 TO MODULE	YELLOW-LT GREEN
438	HORIZONTAL POSITION SENSE	RED-WHITE	530	SPLICE #3 TO POWER RELAY	LT GREEN-YELLOW
439	SEAT PROCESSOR TO RECLINER MOTOR "UP"	YELLOW-WHITE	531	SPLICE TO DIODE	ORANGE-YELLOW
440	SEAT PROCESSOR TO RECLINER MOTOR "DOWN"	RED-LT BLUE	532	SPLICE TO POWER RELAY	ORANGE-YELLOW
441	FRONT TILT POSITION SENSE	GRAY-BLACK	533	POWER RELAY TO FUSE LINK	TAN-RED
442	SEQUENTIAL L.H. REAR INBOARD TURN SIGNAL LAMP	LT GREEN-ORANGE	534	SPLICE #3 TO PRESSURE SWITCH	YELLOW-LT GREEN
443	SEQUENTIAL L.H. REAR CENTER TURN SIGNAL LAMP	LT GREEN-RED	535	PRESSURE SWITCH TO MODULE	LT BLUE-RED
444	SEQUENTIAL L.H. REAR OUTBOARD TURN SIGNAL LAMP	LT GREEN-BLACK	536	BLOWER MOTOR RELAY (LOAD TERM.) TO BLOWER MOTOR	BLACK-LT GREEN
445	SEQUENTIAL R.H. REAR INBOARD TURN SIGNAL LAMP	ORANGE-LT BLUE	537	FUSE LINK TO MOTOR RELAY	TAN-YELLOW
446	SEQUENTIAL R.H. REAR CENTER TURN SIGNAL LAMP	ORANGE-WHITE	538	MOTOR TO MOTOR RELAY	GRAY-RED
447	SEQUENTIAL R.H. REAR OUTBOARD TURN SIGNAL LAMP	ORANGE-RED	539	PRESSURE SWITCH TO MOTOR RELAY	PINK-LT BLUE
448	ANTENNA SWITCH TO ANTENNA RELAY	ORANGE-YELLOW	540	L.H. REMOTE MIRROR MOTOR FEED—C.W.	RED
449	RADIO SWITCH TO ANTENNA RELAY	BROWN-ORANGE	541	L.H. REMOTE MIRROR MOTOR FEED—C.C.W.	DK BLUE
450	SEAT BELT WARNING INDICATOR LAMP FEED	DK GREEN-LT GREEN	542	L.H. REMOTE MIRROR SOLENOID CONTROL	YELLOW
451	BATTERY TO AUTOMATIC ANTENNA SWITCH	LT BLUE-YELLOW	543	R.H. REMOTE MIRROR MOTOR FEED—C.W.	DK GREEN
452	SEAT PROCESSOR ASSY. TO FRONT MOTOR L.H.	GRAY-RED	544	R.H. REMOTE MIRROR MOTOR FEED—C.C.W.	PURPLE
453	TRANSMISSION DIAGNOSTIC	PURPLE	545	R.H. REMOTE MIRROR SOLENOID CONTROL	WHITE
454	IGN. SW. COIL TERM. TO CIRCUIT BREAKER	RED-LT GREEN	546	SPLICE #3 TO POWER RELAY	DK GREEN-YELLOW
455	SWITCH TO VALVE	GRAY-RED			

* IN SOME CASES, THERE MAY BE ADDITIONAL CIRCUIT
FUNCTIONS INCLUDED IN THE CIRCUIT DESCRIPTION LISTED.

STANDARD CIRCUIT CHART (BY NUMBER)

CIRCUIT	DESCRIPTION*	COLOR	CIRCUIT	DESCRIPTION*	COLOR
547	PRESSURE SWITCH TO FLUID RES. SWITCH	LT GREEN-YELLOW	641	LEFT FRONT SHOCK DAMPENING RELAY TO CONTROL MODULE	LT BLUE
548	GROUND STUD TO SPLICE #2	YELLOW-LT GREEN	642	WATER TEMP. WARNING LAMP TO WATER TEMP. SW. (COLD)	WHITE-LT GREEN
549	FLUID WARNING SWITCH TO PRESSURE SWITCH	BROWN-WHITE	643	DIESEL WATER IN FUEL SENDER TO WARNING LAMP	RED
550	FLUID SWITCH TO GROUND STUD	YELLOW-LT GREEN	644	TACHOMETER SIGNAL RETURN	DK GREEN
551	SPLICE #2 TO SPLICE #3	YELLOW-LT GREEN	645	SPEAKER VOICE COIL FEED RIGHT REAR CHANNEL AMP INPUT	PINK-BLACK
552	SPLICE #2 TO COUP GROUND "B"	YELLOW-LT GREEN	646	SPEAKER VOICE COIL FEED LEFT REAR CHANNEL AMP INPUT	PINK-YELLOW
554	POWER RELAY BATTERY FEED	YELLOW-BLACK	647	WATER TEMP. WARNING LAMP TO WATER TEMP. SW. (HOT)	RED-BLACK
555	FUEL INJECTOR #1 CYLINDER OR BANK #1	TAN	648	TACHOMETER FEED	WHITE-PINK
556	FUEL INJECTOR #2 CYLINDER OR BANK #2	WHITE	649	SPEAKER VOICE COIL FEED LEFT FRONT CHANNEL AMP INPUT	ORANGE
557	FUEL INJECTOR #3 CYLINDER	BROWN-YELLOW	650	RIGHT REAR SHOCK DAMPENING RELAY TO CONTROL MODULE	WHITE
558	FUEL INJECTOR #4 CYLINDER	BROWN-LT BLUE	651	LEFT REAR SHOCK DAMPENING RELAY TO CONTROL MODULE	DK GREEN
559	HIGH ELECTRIC DRIVE COOLING FAN	TAN-BLACK	652	SHOCK DAMPENING RELAY HARD TO SHOCK DAMPENING CONTROL	PINK-BLACK
560	FUEL INJECTOR #6 CYLINDER	LT GREEN-ORANGE	653	SHOCK DAMPENING RELAY SOFT TO SHOCK DAMPENING CONTROL	DK BLUE
561	FUEL INJECTOR #7 CYLINDER	TAN-RED	654	ALT. SHUNT TO AMMETER	YELLOW-LT GREEN
562	FUEL INJECTOR #8 CYLINDER	LT BLUE	655	STARTING MOTOR RELAY SHUNT TO AMMETER	RED-ORANGE
563	SPEED SENSOR LO V REF TO SPEEDO TACH MODULE	ORANGE-YELLOW	656	REDUNDANT MODULE TO ENGINE WARNING LAMP	PURPLE
564	FUEL SIGNAL TACH MODULE TO FUEL COMPUTER	BROWN	657	EEC MODULE TO MALFUNCTION INDICATOR LITE	TAN
565	SPEED SIGNAL SPEEDO TACH MODULE TO FUEL COMPUTER	BLACK-WHITE	658	EEC MODULE TO CHECK ENGINE INDICATOR LAMP	PINK-LT GREEN
566	PROCESSOR TO THERMACTOR CLUTCH RELAY	WHITE-RED	659	MODULE TO DOWN SWITCH	WHITE-LT BLUE
567	THERMACTOR CLUTCH RELAY TO CLUTCH	WHITE-BLACK	660	AIR COND. CONTROL SW. TO FRESH-AIR RECIRC. DOOR SOLENOID	YELLOW-LT GREEN
568	ALTERNATOR RELAY TO ALTERNATOR REGULATOR	LT GREEN	661	MODULE TO OVERRIDE SWITCH	LT GREEN-WHITE
569	STOPLAMP SWITCH TO HI MOUNT STOPLAMP	DK GREEN	662	MODULE TO MOTOR FEED	WHITE-BLACK
570	DEDICATED GROUND	BLACK-WHITE	663	MODULE TO MOTOR RETURN	LT GREEN-YELLOW
571	REMOTE CONVENIENCE SELF-DIAGNOSTIC GROUND	BLACK-ORANGE	664	MODULE TO RELEASE SOLENOID	YELLOW-LT GREEN
572	ENGLISH METRIC SIGNAL TO MULTIGAGE	ORANGE-BLACK	665	OVERRIDE SWITCH TO LATCH	ORANGE-YELLOW
573	CENTER REAR TAILLAMP BULB OUTAGE	BLACK-ORANGE	666	BATTERY FEED CAMPER	RED
574	EXTENDED USEFUL LIFE SENSOR TO WARNING LAMP	BROWN-WHITE	667	LAMP RELAY TO MARKER LAMPS	WHITE-RED
575	RELAY TO ATC CONTROL	YELLOW-BLACK	668	I TERMINAL STARTER MOTOR RELAY TO INERTIA SWITCH	ORANGE-LT BLUE
576	REAR LAMP TO TRAILER RELAY FEED	DK GREEN	669	OIL PRESSURE SWITCH TO CUTOUT RELAY	YELLOW
577	AIR SUSPENSION SYSTEM GROUND	LT GREEN-RED	670	INERTIA SWITCH TO FUEL TANK SELECTOR SWITCH	RED-YELLOW
578	AIR COMPRESSOR VENT SOLENOID	LT BLUE-PINK	671	FUEL TANK SELECTOR SWITCH TO AFT FUEL PUMP	LT BLUE-YELLOW
579	HEATED WINDSHIELD CONTROL TO ELECT. ALTERNATOR REGULATOR	BLACK-ORANGE	672	FUEL TANK SELECTOR SWITCH TO MIDSHIP FUEL PUMP	LT GREEN-YELLOW
580	HEATED WINDSHIELD CONTROL TO ALT. POWER RELAY	BROWN	673	SELECTOR SWITCH TO MIDSHIP TANK	DK BLUE-YELLOW
581	HEATED WINDSHIELD CONTROL TO ALT. STATOR TERM.	RED	674	SELECTOR SWITCH TO AUX. FUEL SOLENOID	BROWN-WHITE
582	HEATED WINDSHIELD SWITCH TO HEATED WINDSHIELD CONTROL	ORANGE	675	SELECTOR SWITCH TO AFT AXLE TANK	YELLOW-LT BLUE
583	ALT. POWER RELAY TO CONTROL MODULE	YELLOW	676	VEHICLE SPEED SENSOR RETURN	PINK-ORANGE
584	POWER FEED DECAY TIMER TO THROTTLE LEVER SOLENOID	DK GREEN-PURPLE	677	ANTI-LOCK MODULE TO ANTI-LOCK CONTROL VALVE	LT BLUE
585	HEATED WINDSHIELD CONTROL TO AIR COND. TERM.	PURPLE	678	ANTI-LOCK MODULE TO ANTI-LOCK CONTROL VALVE	YELLOW
586	CONVERTIBLE TOP RELAY TO SWITCH	YELLOW	679	VEHICLE SPEED SIGNAL	GRAY-BLACK
587	WINDSHIELD WIPER INTERMITTENT GOVERNOR FEED	BLACK-WHITE	681	HEATED WINDSHIELD TRIGGER CIRCUIT SW. TO MODULE	TAN-RED
588	CONVERTIBLE TOP RELAY TO SWITCH	PURPLE	682	TEMP. WARNING LAMP TO SENDING UNIT	GRAY-RED
589	WINDSHIELD WIPER SWITCH TO INTERMITTENT GOVERNOR GROUND	ORANGE	683	SPEED CONTROL SENSE TO EEC MODULE TO CLUSTER	PURPLE-LT BLUE
590	INTERMITTENT GOVERNOR TO W/S WIPER SWITCH	DK BLUE-WHITE	684	COMPASS SENSOR FEED	PINK-BLACK
591	DCP MODULE TO WASHER RELAY	BROWN-YELLOW	685	ANTI-LOCK MODULE TO ANTI-LOCK CONTROL VALVE	BLACK-WHITE
592	DCP MODULE TO WIPER PARK OVERRIDE RELAY	BROWN-LT GREEN	686	HEAD LP TIME DELAY CONTROL RELAY TO CIR. BREAKER	GRAY-ORANGE
593	DCP MODULE TO WIPER GOVERNOR RELAY	RED-ORANGE	687	ACC FEED	GRAY-YELLOW
594	DCP MODULE TO WIPER HI-LO RELAY	ORANGE-LT GREEN	688	HTD BACKLITE SW. TO TIME DELAY RELAY	GRAY-LT BLUE
595	DCP MODULE CONTROL INTERFACE TO RADIO	LT BLUE-RED	689	LOGIC MODE	DK BLUE
596	DCP MODULE SIGNAL GROUND TO RADIO	BLACK	690	RIGHT CHANNEL SIGNAL IN	GRAY
597	DCP MODULE TRIP SCAN HIGH TO TRIPMINDER	LT GREEN-BLACK	691	MOONROOF RELAY TO MICRO SWITCH OPEN	DK BLUE
598	DCP MODULE TRIP SCAN LOW TO TRIPMINDER	LT GREEN-PURPLE	692	MOONROOF RELAY TO MICRO SWITCH CLOSED	RED
599	MODULE TO SOLENOID	PINK-LT GREEN	693	MODULE DIAGNOSTIC	ORANGE
600	FEED TO FAILURE SWITCH	DK BLUE	694	AMPLIFIER POWER RETURN	RED
601	BRAKE ANTI-LOCK CONTROL MODULE FEED	LT BLUE-PINK	695	MULTIPLEX WINDSHIELD WIPER OFF	BLACK-ORANGE
602	COIL TERM. OF IGN. SW. TO BRAKE ANTI-LOCK CONTROL MODULE	RED-LT GREEN	696	MULTIPLEX PARKING LAMPS	ORANGE-BLACK
603	FAILURE WARNING LIGHT	DK GREEN	697	MULTIPLEX HEADLAMPS	BROWN
604	ANTI-LOCK CONTROL MODULE R.H. WHEEL SENSOR HI	ORANGE-RED	698	MULTIPLEX WINDSHIELD WIPER MAIN	RED
605	SOLENOID	RED	699	MULTIPLEX RELAY COIL FEED #1	ORANGE
606	ANTI-LOCK DIAGNOSTIC	WHITE-LT BLUE	700	MULTIPLEX WIPER RATE	YELLOW
607	DIESEL COLD ADVANCE	GRAY-RED	701	C.B. SQUELCH POT	WHITE-PURPLE
608	AIR BAG DIAGNOSTIC MODULE TO RELAY INDICATOR LAMP	BLACK-YELLOW	702	C.B. PUSH TO TALK	WHITE-BLACK
609	AIR BAG READY INDICATOR LAMP TO AIR BAG FLASHER	ORANGE-YELLOW	703	C.B. DOWN SWITCH	WHITE-ORANGE
610	AIR BAG DIAGNOSTIC MODULE TO AIR BAG FLASHER	ORANGE-LT GREEN	704	C.B. C-DIGIT	ORANGE
611	AIR BAG READY INDICATOR L (DEPLOY) TO SAFING SENSOR	WHITE-ORANGE	705	C.B. NOISE BLANKER	LT GREEN-ORANGE
612	AIR BAG READY INDICATOR L (MONITOR) TO SAFING SENSOR	PURPLE-ORANGE	706	C.B. SCAN L.E.D.	GRAY
613	AIR BAG DIAGNOSTIC MODULE SAFING SENSOR (GROUND)	DK BLUE-WHITE	707	C.B. UP SWITCH	WHITE-YELLOW
614	AIR BAG SAFING SENSORS TO INFLATORS	GRAY-ORANGE	708	C.B. D-DIGIT	BROWN
615	AIR BAG DIAGNOSTIC MODULE TO DRIVER INFLATOR	GRAY-WHITE	709	C.B. VOLUME CONTROL	WHITE-LT BLUE
616	AIR BAG DIAGNOSTIC MODULE TO PASSENGER INFLATOR	PINK-BLACK	710	C.B. SCAN SWITCH	WHITE-LT GREEN
617	AIR BAG DIAGNOSTIC MODULE (DEPLOY) TO R.H. SENSOR	PINK-ORANGE	711	C.B. REGULATED 5V	LT GREEN-BLACK
618	AIR BAG DIAGNOSTIC MODULE (MONITOR) TO R.H. SENSOR	PURPLE-LT GREEN	712	C.B. A & – DIGIT	PURPLE
619	AIR BAG DIAGNOSTIC MODULE (DEPLOY) TO CENTER SENSOR	PINK-WHITE	713	C.B. MIC-AUDIO	WHITE
620	AIR BAG DIAGNOSTIC MODULE (MONITOR) TO CENTER SENSOR	PURPLE-LT BLUE	714	RELAY COIL FEED #2	PURPLE
621	AIR BAG DIAGNOSTIC MODULE (DEPLOY) TO L.H. SENSOR	WHITE-YELLOW	715	C.B. A– DIGIT	LT GREEN
622	AIR BAG DIAGNOSTIC MODULE (MONITOR) TO L.H. SENSOR	TAN-BLACK	716	C.B. B– DIGIT	YELLOW
623	AIR BAG DIAGNOSTIC MODULE (MONITOR) TO SAFING SENSOR	PURPLE-WHITE	717	C.B. SPEAKER TO TRANSCEIVER	LT BLUE-RED
624	DCP MODULE TO HEATED BACKLITE RELAY	LT BLUE-ORANGE	718	C.B. ON/OFF	RED-WHITE
625	DCP MODULE TO PARKLAMP RELAY	LT BLUE-PINK	719	WINDSHIELD WIPER HIGH	GRAY
626	OPEN DOOR WARNING LAMP FEED	PINK-YELLOW	720	C.B. B & – DIGIT	LT BLUE
627	OPEN DOOR WARNING LAMP TO OPEN DOOR WARNING SWITCH	BLACK-ORANGE	721	C.B. SPEAKER VOICE COIL RETURN	DK BLUE-LT GREEN
628	DOOR WIRE	WHITE	722	C.B. RELAY DRIVE	LT GREEN-RED
629	DOOR WIRE	BLACK	723	C.B. SPEAKER RELAY TO MIC	LT BLUE-ORANGE
630	DOOR WIRE	RED	724	C.B. C & – DIGIT	LT GREEN-WHITE
631	DOOR WIRE	YELLOW	725	RELAY COIL FEED #3	WHITE
632	DCP MODULE TO HEADLAMP RELAY	PINK-YELLOW	726	WINDSHIELD WASHER	LT GREEN
633	STEERING RATE SENSOR TERM. A TO CONTROL MODULE	RED	727	REMOTE DEFROST	YELLOW-BLACK
634	STEERING RATE SENSOR TERM. B TO CONTROL MODULE	BROWN	728	RADIO SEEK	WHITE-ORANGE
635	AIR SUSPENSION MODE SWITCH TO CONTROL MODULE	YELLOW	729	RADIO MEMORY	RED-WHITE
635	AIR SUSPENSION DIODE SWITCH TO CONTROL MODULE	YELLOW	730	CRT SCAN	LT BLUE-YELLOW
636	BRAKE PRESSURE SWITCH TO CONTROL MODULE	ORANGE	731	MULTIPLEX REVERSE DIMMING	WHITE-BLACK
637	AIR SUSPENSION CONTROL SIGNAL	LT GREEN	732	MULTIPLEX LCD ILLUMINATION	BROWN-WHITE
638	RIGHT FRONT SHOCK DAMPENING RELAY TO CONTROL MODULE	PURPLE	733	MULTIPLEX SERVICE REMINDER RESET	PURPLE-WHITE
639	HIGH ELECTRIC DRIVE COOLING FAN	LT GREEN-PURPLE	734	MULTIPLEX SERVICE REMINDER	TAN
640	WARNING LAMPS FEED	RED-YELLOW	735	MULTIPLEX MESSAGE O	DK BLUE-WHITE

* IN SOME CASES, THERE MAY BE ADDITIONAL CIRCUIT
FUNCTIONS INCLUDED IN THE CIRCUIT DESCRIPTION LISTED.

STANDARD CIRCUIT CHART (BY NUMBER)

CIRCUIT	DESCRIPTION*	COLOR	CIRCUIT	DESCRIPTION*	COLOR
736	MULTIPLEX MESSAGE I	PINK	830	SWITCH TO FADER RIGHT CHANNEL FEED	PINK-YELLOW
737	TEMP. SWITCH TO WARNING DEVICE	WHITE-LT BLUE	831	SWITCH TO FADER LEFT CHANNEL FEED	TAN
738	HEATED WINDSHIELD CONTROL TO HEATED WINDSHIELD SWITCH	YELLOW-WHITE	832	MODE SELECT SWITCH FEED	BROWN-LT GREEN
739	HEATED WINDSHIELD GROUND TEST LEAD	BLACK	833	MODE SELECT SWITCH LAMP	RED-BLACK
740	VAC SWITCH TO VAC PUMP	ORANGE-LT BLUE	834	ELECTRONIC RIDE CONTROL DAMPENING SENSOR A	RED-YELLOW
741	TIMER CONTROL VALVE TO CONTROL UNIT	LT BLUE-WHITE	835	ELECTRONIC RIDE CONTROL DAMPENING SENSOR B	RED-WHITE
742	RADIATOR COOLANT TEMP. SWITCH TO CONTROL UNIT	LT BLUE-YELLOW	836	SENSOR	ORANGE-WHITE
743	AIR CHARGE TEMPERATURE	GRAY	837	SENSOR RETURN	YELLOW-BLACK
744	IDLE RPM SOLENOID TO CONTROL UNIT	TAN-WHITE	838	ELECTRONIC RIDE CONTROL DAMPENING HARD CONTROL	LT GREEN-PURPLE
745	ANTENNA SWITCH TO POWER ANTENNA (UP)	RED-PINK	839	ELECTRONIC RIDE CONTROL DAMPENING SOFT CONTROL	LT GREEN-WHITE
746	ANTENNA SWITCH TO POWER ANTENNA (DOWN)	DK GREEN-YELLOW	840	ACTUATOR POSITION SENSOR LEFT FRONT	WHITE-BLACK
747	RADIO RECEIVER ASSY. TO FOOT CONTROL SWITCH	ORANGE-LT BLUE	841	ACTUATOR POSITION SENSOR RIGHT FRONT	WHITE-RED
748	BOOST SENSOR TO CONTROL UNIT	TAN	842	ACTUATOR POSITION SENSOR LEFT REAR	WHITE-ORANGE
749	SENSOR AMPLIFY UNIT TO CONTROL UNIT #1	PINK-BLACK	843	ACTUATOR POSITION SENSOR RIGHT REAR	WHITE
750	SENSOR AMPLIFY UNIT TO CONTROL UNIT #2	GRAY-LT BLUE	844	ELECTRONIC RIDE SHOCK DIAGNOSTIC	GRAY-RED
751	BLOWER MOTOR SPEED CONTROLLER TO RESISTOR 73 (MED.)	DK BLUE-WHITE	845	ELECTRONIC RIDE SHOCK FEEDBACK ACTUATOR TO RELAY	TAN-BLACK
752	BLOWER MOTOR SPEED CONTROLLER TO RESISTOR 72 (MED.)	YELLOW-RED	846	ELECTRONIC RIDE SHOCK METAL OXIDE VARISTOR	TAN-RED
753	HEATER & A/C CONTROL SW. TO BLOWER RELAY SW.	YELLOW-RED	847	DECELERATION SENSOR	ORANGE-LT GREEN
754	BLOWER MOTOR SPEED CONTROLLER TO RESISTOR 71 (MED.)	LT GREEN-WHITE	848	PROCESSOR LOOP SIGNAL RETURN	DK GREEN-ORANGE
755	BLOWER MOTOR SWITCH RELAY TO RESISTOR (LOW SPEED)	BROWN-WHITE	849	DIGITAL AUDIO DISCRIMINATOR DISC LOGIC SENSE	TAN-BLACK
756	HEATER & A/C CONTROL SW. (HI-NORM) TO RESISTOR (LOW RANGE)	RED-PINK	850	COIL "A" TO DISTRIBUTORLESS IGNITION MODULE	YELLOW-BLACK
757	HEATER & A/C CONTROL SW. (HI-NORM) TO BLOWER MOTOR SW. RELAY	RED-WHITE	851	COIL "B" TO DISTRIBUTORLESS IGNITION MODULE	YELLOW-RED
758	HEATER & A/C CONTROL SW. (HI-NORM) TO RESISTOR (LOW RANGE)	PURPLE-WHITE	852	COIL "C" TO DISTRIBUTORLESS IGNITION MODULE	YELLOW-WHITE
759	SENSOR AMPLIFY UNIT TO CONTROL UNIT #3	DK GREEN-WHITE	853	HEATED WINDSHIELD SENSE TO RESISTOR	BROWN
760	SENSOR AMPLIFY UNIT TO CONTROL UNIT #4	WHITE-PURPLE	854	THIRD GEAR LOCKOUT SOLENOID	GRAY-WHITE
761	BLOWER MOTOR RELAY TO ENG. WATER TEMP. SWITCH (COLD)	WHITE-LT GREEN	855	RIGHT REAR AMP INPUT RETURN	LT BLUE
762	ELECT. SHIFT 4×4 MODULE TO MOTOR POSITION #1	YELLOW-WHITE	856	LEFT CHANNEL SIGNAL IN	PURPLE
763	ELECT. SHIFT 4×4 MODULE TO MOTOR POSITION #2	ORANGE-WHITE	857	LEFT FRONT AMP INPUT RETURN	WHITE-ORANGE
764	ELECT. SHIFT 4×4 MODULE TO MOTOR POSITION #3	BROWN-WHITE	858	RIGHT FRONT AMP INPUT RETURN	BROWN
765	HEATER & A/C CONTROL SW. TO REHEAT & A/C FEED	LT GREEN-YELLOW	859	LEFT REAR AMP INPUT RETURN	YELLOW
766	HEATER & A/C CONTROL SW. (DEFOG) TO INLET AIR CONTROL SOLENOID	RED-LT GREEN	860	LEFT MOTOR-DRIVER—A	PURPLE—YELLOW
			861	LEFT MOTOR-DRIVER—B	BLACK-WHITE
767	AMBIENT SENSOR TO INST. PANEL THERMISTOR	LT BLUE-ORANGE	862	LEFT LIMIT-A—DRIVER	BROWN-YELLOW
768	REFERENCE SENSOR TO HEAT DUCT THERMISTOR	LT GREEN-YELLOW	863	RIGHT DOOR OPEN—PASSENGER	RED
769	HEATER & A/C CONTROL SW. (HI-LO-NORM) TO BLOWER MOTOR SW. RELAY	LT BLUE-YELLOW	864	RIGHT MOTOR-PASSENGER — A	ORANGE
			865	RIGHT MOTOR-PASSENGER — B	PURPLE-WHITE
770	ELECT. SHIFT 4×4 MODULE TO MOTOR POSITION #4	WHITE	866	INERTIA SWITCH TO MODULE	WHITE
771	ELECT. SHIFT 4×4 MODULE TO MOTOR POSITION #5	PURPLE-YELLOW	867	LEFT DOOR OPEN — DRIVER	DK BLUE
772	ELECT. SHIFT 4×4 MODULE TO SPEED SENSOR COIL	LT BLUE	868	EMERGENCY RELEASE LEVERS	GRAY-RED
773	HEATER & A/C CONTROL SW. (TEMP. SELECTOR) TO REHEAT AMPL.	DK GREEN-ORANGE	869	RETARD VALVE TO CONTROL RELAY TERM. #1	LT GREEN-YELLOW
774	ELECT. SHIFT 4×4 MODULE TO SPEED SENSOR RETURN	LT GREEN	871	SEAT BELT INDICATOR LAMP TO MODULE	YELLOW
775	HEATER & A/C CONTROL SW. (DEFOG) TO DEFROST CONT. SOLENOID	WHITE-PINK	872	LEFT LIMIT-B — DRIVER	LT GREEN
776	CLIMATE CONTROL BOX TO HIGH BLOWER RELAY	ORANGE-BLACK	873	RIGHT LIMIT-B — PASSENGER	TAN
777	ELECT. SHIFT 4×4 MODULE TO MOTOR CONTROL COUNTERCLOCKWISE	YELLOW	874	RIGHT LIMIT-A — PASSENGER	GRAY
778	ELECT. SHIFT 4×4 MODULE TO MOTOR CONTROL	ORANGE	875	GROUND LOGIC MODULE	BLACK-LT BLUE
779	ELECT. SHIFT 4×4 MODULE TO ELECT. CLUTCH	BROWN	876	VENT SWITCH TO RIGHT FRONT VENT — CONSOLE	BLACK-ORANGE
780	ELECT. SHIFT MODULE TO 2H 4H SWITCH	DK BLUE	876	VENT SWITCH TO RIGHT FRONT VENT MOTOR	BLACK-ORANGE
781	ELECT. SHIFT TO 4L SWITCH	ORANGE-LT BLUE	877	RELEASE LEVER WARN INDICATOR LAMP — CONSOLE	WHITE-ORANGE
782	ELECT. SHIFT MODULE TO LOW RANGE INDICATOR LAMP ROOF CONSOLE	BROWN-WHITE	878	VENT SWITCH TO RIGHT FRONT VENT MOTOR	BLACK-LT BLUE
			879	VENT CROSSOVER FEED	RED-BLACK
783	ELECT. SHIFT MODULE TO GRAPHIC DISPLAY ROOF CONSOLE	GRAY	880	VENT CROSSOVER FEED	RED-LT BLUE
784	INDICATOR LAMP TO LOW RANGE SWITCH 4×4	LT BLUE-BLACK	881	WINDOW SWITCH TO RIGHT REAR MOTOR	BROWN
785	BATTERY TO MULTIPLEX MODULE	BLACK-LT GREEN	882	WINDOW SWITCH TO RIGHT REAR MOTOR	BROWN-YELLOW
786	FUEL TANK SELECTOR TO FUEL PUMP FRONT	RED	883	AIR COND. CONTROL RELAY FEED	PINK-LT BLUE
787	FUEL PUMP POWER	PINK-BLACK	884	WINDOW SWITCH TO LEFT REAR MOTOR	YELLOW-BLACK
788	REHEAT AMPLIFIER TO HEAT DUCT THERMISTOR	RED-ORANGE	885	WINDOW SWITCH TO LEFT REAR MOTOR	YELLOW-LT BLUE
789	FUEL TANK SELECTOR TO FUEL PUMP REAR	BROWN-WHITE	886	VENT SWITCH TO LEFT FRONT VENT MOTOR	ORANGE-WHITE
790	HEATER & A/C CONTROL SW. TO INST. PANEL THERMISTOR	WHITE-ORANGE	887	VENT SWITCH TO LEFT FRONT VENT MOTOR	YELLOW
791	BATTERY TO MULTIPLEX SYSTEM	BLACK-WHITE	888	MEMORY MIRROR MODULE TO R.H. HORIZONTAL DRIVER	LT BLUE
792	MULTIPLEX COMPUTER FEED	TAN-RED	889	MEMORY MIRROR MODULE MOTOR DIRECTION	BLACK-ORANGE
793	LOW WASHER LEVEL TO SENSOR	YELLOW-BLACK	890	MEMORY MIRROR MODULE TO R.H. VERTICAL DRIVE	BROWN-WHITE
794	LOW COOLANT LEVEL RELAY TO SENSOR	LT BLUE	891	MEMORY MIRROR MODULE POSITION +	RED-BLACK
795	CAM SENSOR TO EEC MODULE	DK GREEN	892	MEMORY MIRROR MODULE R.H. HORIZONTAL POSITION	ORANGE
796	CAM SENDER SIGNAL RETURN	LT BLUE	893	MEMORY MIRROR MODULE R.H. VERTICAL POSITION-	LT BLUE-BLACK
797	BATTERY FEED TO STEREO	LT GREEN-PURPLE	894	MEMORY MIRROR MODULE POSITION	GRAY
798	LEFT CHANNEL SIGNAL OUT	LT GREEN-RED	895	MEMORY MIRROR MODULE L.H. VERTICAL POSITION	WHITE-PURPLE
799	RIGHT CHANNEL SIGNAL OUT	ORANGE-BLACK	896	MEMORY MIRROR MODULE L.H. HORIZONTAL POSITION	PINK-ORANGE
800	AMPLIFIER/SPEAKER SWITCH FEED TO LEFT REAR SPEAKER	GRAY-LT BLUE	897	MEMORY MIRROR MODULE TO L.H. VERTICAL DRIVE	TAN-BLACK
801	AMPLIFIER/SPEAKER SWITCH GROUND TO LEFT REAR SPEAKER	PINK-LT BLUE	898	MEMORY MIRROR MODULE TO L.H. HORIZONTAL DRIVE	TAN-RED
802	AMPLIFIER/SPEAKER SWITCH FEED TO RIGHT REAR SPEAKER	ORANGE-RED	899	MEMORY SEAT TO NEUTRAL SENSE MODULE	RED-WHITE
803	AMPLIFIER/SPEAKER SWITCH GROUND TO RIGHT REAR SPEAKER	DK GREEN-ORANGE	900	STARTER INTERRUPT RELAY TO NEUTRAL START SWITCH	WHITE-LT BLUE
804	SPEAKER VOICE COIL FEED—FRONT (LEFT CHANNEL)	ORANGE-LT GREEN	901	AMPLIFIER TO SPEED SENSOR RETURN	RED-LT BLUE
805	SPEAKER VOICE COIL FEED—FRONT (RIGHT CHANNEL)	WHITE-LT GREEN	902	TOP CONTROL RELAY TO MOTOR—UP	YELLOW
806	SPEAKER VOICE COIL FEED—REAR (RIGHT CHANNEL)	PINK-LT BLUE	903	TOP CONTROL RELAY TO MOTOR—DOWN	RED
807	SPEAKER VOICE COIL FEED—REAR (LEFT CHANNEL)	PINK-LT GREEN	904	(COIL) OR (ACCY.) TERM. OF IGNITION SWITCH TO ALTERNATOR REGULATOR (IGN. TERM.)	LT GREEN-RED
810	STOPLAMP SW. TO STOPLAMPS	RED-LT GREEN			
811	SPEAKER SWITCH GROUND TO RIGHT FRONT SPEAKER	DK GREEN-ORANGE	905	VEHICLE MAINTENANCE MONITOR MODULE TO OIL TEMP. INPUT	LT BLUE
812	SPEAKER SWITCH FEED TO RIGHT FRONT SPEAKER	PINK-ORANGE	906	VEHICLE MAINTENANCE MONITOR MODULE TO OIL TEMP. OUTPUT	WHITE-LT BLUE
813	SPEAKER SWITCH GROUND TO LEFT FRONT SPEAKER	LT BLUE-WHITE	907	VEHICLE MAINTENANCE MONITOR MODULE TO ELEC. INSTR. CLUST. SENSE	PURPLE-LT GREEN
814	SPEAKER SWITCH FEED TO LEFT FRONT SPEAKER	PINK-WHITE			
815	AMPLIFIER SWITCH GROUND TO RIGHT FRONT SPEAKER	LT GREEN-ORANGE	908	VEHICLE MAINTENANCE MONITOR MODULE TO ENGINE STRAP	TAN-BLACK
816	AMPLIFIER SWITCH FEED TO RIGHT FRONT SPEAKER	LT GREEN-PURPLE	909	VEHICLE MAINTENANCE MONITOR MODULE TO SPEED SENSOR	LT BLUE-WHITE
817	INDICATOR RELAY TO R.H. TURN LAMP	TAN-LT BLUE	910	FUSED ACCY. FEED — TRIPMINDER	BLACK-WHITE
818	INDICATOR RELAY TO L.H. TURN LAMP	TAN-WHITE	911	OVERDRIVE CANCEL INDICATOR LAMP	WHITE-LT GREEN
819	AMPLIFIER SWITCH GROUND TO LEFT FRONT SPEAKER	LT GREEN-WHITE	912	EEC MODULE TO TRANSMISSION	WHITE-RED
820	AMPLIFIER SWITCH FEED TO LEFT FRONT SPEAKER	DK BLUE-YELLOW	913	LIFTGATE SW. TO LIFTGATE RELAY	GRAY-RED
822	SPEAKER VOICE COIL FEED	BLACK-LT GREEN	914	EEC MODULE — DATA PLUS	TAN-ORANGE
823	RADIO TO FADER CONTROL	LT GREEN	915	DATA LINK RETURN	PINK-LT BLUE
824	AMPLIFIER SWITCH GROUND TO RIGHT REAR SPEAKER	WHITE-PURPLE	916	SPEED CONTROL VACUUM TO EEC MODULE	LT GREEN
825	AMPLIFIER SWITCH FEED TO RIGHT REAR SPEAKER	TAN-LT GREEN	917	VENT SWITCH TO BLOWER MOTOR — LO	PINK-LT GREEN
826	AMPLIFIER SWITCH GROUND TO LEFT REAR SPEAKER	DK BLUE-ORANGE	918	SEAT REG. SW. TO RECLINER MOTOR — UP	GRAY
827	AMPLIFIER SWITCH FEED TO LEFT REAR SPEAKER	TAN-WHITE	919	SEAT REG. SW. TO RECLINER MOTOR — DOWN	GRAY-BLACK
828	POWER FEED-SWITCH TO REAR AMPLIFIER	PURPLE-LT BLUE	920	HEATED WINDSHIELD LH TO SENSE RESISTOR	BROWN-WHITE
829	POWER FEED-SWITCH TO FRONT AMPLIFIER	WHITE-PURPLE	921	FEED TO FUEL SHUTOFF LAMP	GRAY-ORANGE

*** IN SOME CASES, THERE MAY BE ADDITIONAL CIRCUIT
FUNCTIONS INCLUDED IN THE CIRCUIT DESCRIPTION LISTED.**

6 CHASSIS ELECTRICAL

STANDARD CIRCUIT CHART (BY NUMBER)

CIRCUIT	DESCRIPTION*	COLOR
922	FUEL PUMP RESISTOR TO RELAY	WHITE-RED
923	TRANSMISSION OIL TEMP.	ORANGE-BLACK
924	COAST CLUTCH SOLENOID	BROWN-ORANGE
925	ELECTRONIC PRESSURE CONTROL	WHITE-YELLOW
926	FUEL PUMP RELAY CONTROL	LT BLUE-ORANGE
927	EVO MODULE TO TEST CONNECTOR	ORANGE-BLACK
928	POWER FEED FROM AMPLIFIER	PURPLE
929	SPARK OUTPUT SIGNAL FROM TFI MODULE	PINK
930	PROGRAMMABLE RIDE CONTROL MODULE TO STAR TEST CONNECTOR	DK BLUE
931	BATTERY FEED TO RELAY CONTROLLER	ORANGE
932	DAYTIME RUNNING LAMP	GRAY-WHITE
933	ESC SWITCH TO ESC VALVE CONTROL	LT GREEN-BLACK
934	EMISSION SPEED SENSOR TO MODULATOR CONTROL	TAN-WHITE
935	HEATED WINDSHIELD TO FUSE	DK BLUE-YELLOW
936	KEY CYLINDER SENSOR TO ANTI-THEFT MODULE	DK GREEN-WHITE
937	FUSED BATTERY FEED TO AIR BAG DIAGNOSTIC MODULE	RED-WHITE
938	LOGIC GROUND	BLACK-LT GREEN
939	MODULATOR TO THERMO. SWITCH	TAN-BLACK
940	MIRROR SWITCH VERTICAL LEFT	DK BLUE-ORANGE
941	WASHER PUMP MOTOR FEED	BLACK-WHITE
942	MIRROR SWITCH HORIZONTAL LEFT	RED-ORANGE
943	MIRROR SWITCH VERTICAL RIGHT	PURPLE-ORANGE
944	MIRROR SWITCH HORIZONTAL RIGHT	DK GREEN-ORANGE
945	MIRROR SWITCH COMMON	YELLOW-BLACK
946	REAR WASHER PUMP MOTOR	PURPLE-LT GREEN
947	L.H. MIRROR LEFT/RIGHT MOTOR COMMON	YELLOW-RED
948	L.H. UP/DOWN MOTOR COMMON	YELLOW-LT BLUE
949	L.H. MIRROR LEFT/RIGHT POSITION SENSOR	RED-WHITE
950	WASHER CONTROL SWITCH FEED	WHITE-BLACK
951	L.H. MIRROR UP/DOWN POSITION SENSOR	DK BLUE-WHITE
952	R.H. MIRROR LEFT/RIGHT MOTOR COMMON	WHITE-LT GREEN
953	R.H. MIRROR UP/DOWN MOTOR COMMON	WHITE-PURPLE
954	R.H. MIRROR LEFT/RIGHT POSITION SENSOR	DK GREEN-WHITE
955	W/S WIPER MOTOR ARM RH TO W/S WIPER SWITCH	RED-ORANGE
956	W/S WIPER SWITCH TO W/S WIPER MOTOR FIELD R.H.	LT GREEN-ORANGE
957	R.H. MIRROR UP/DOWN POSITION SENSOR	PURPLE-WHITE
958	MIRROR POSITION SENSOR FEED	GRAY-RED
959	MIRROR POSITION SENSOR COMMON	GRAY
960	CLUSTER GAGE GROUND	BLACK-LT BLUE

CIRCUIT	DESCRIPTION*	COLOR
961	TRACTION CONTROL MALFUNCTION WARNING LAMP	RED-LT GREEN
962	TRAILER RUNNING LAMPS	BROWN-WHITE
963	TRAILER BACKUP LAMPS	RED-YELLOW
964	FUSED ACCESSORY #4	DK BLUE-LT GREEN
965	SUPERCHARGER SOLENOID #1	LT GREEN-PURPLE
966	SUPERCHARGER SOLENOID #2	RED-YELLOW
967	MASS AIR FLOW SIGNAL	LT BLUE-RED
968	MASS AIR FLOW RETURN	TAN-LT BLUE
969	MASS AIR FLOW GROUND	BLACK
970	TRANSMISSION TURBINE SPEED SENSOR	PURPLE
971	TRANSMISSION SHIFT SOLENOID #3	BROWN
972	AWD MODULE POWER FEED	BLACK-WHITE
973	BATTERY FEED TO AUX. FUEL SELECTOR SWITCH	RED
974	FUEL CONTROL SWITCH TO FUEL CONTROL VALVE	ORANGE
975	AWD MODULE TO TRANSFER CASE CLUTCH RELAY	BROWN-YELLOW
976	AWD MODULE TO TRANSFER CASE CLUTCH RELAY COIL	ORANGE
977	BRAKE WARNING SWITCH TO INDICATOR LAMP	PURPLE-WHITE
978	SEAT REGULATOR SWITCH TO FRONT MOTOR (LH)	YELLOW-LT BLUE
979	SEAT REGULATOR SWITCH TO FRONT MOTOR (LH)	RED-LT BLUE
980	SEAT REGULATOR SWITCH TO HORZ. MOTOR (LH)	YELLOW-WHITE
981	SEAT REGULATOR SWITCH TO HORZ. MOTOR (LH)	RED-WHITE
982	SEAT REGULATOR SWITCH TO REAR MOTOR (LH)	YELLOW-LT GREEN
983	SEAT REGULATOR SWITCH TO REAR MOTOR (LH)	RED-LT GREEN
984	SEAT REGULATOR SWITCH TO FRONT MOTOR (RH)	YELLOW-LT BLUE
985	SEAT REGULATOR SWITCH TO FRONT MOTOR (RH)	RED-LT BLUE
986	SEAT REGULATOR SWITCH TO FRONT MOTOR (RH)	YELLOW-WHITE
987	SEAT REGULATOR SWITCH TO HORZ. MOTOR (RH)	RED-WHITE
988	SEAT REGULATOR SWITCH TO REAR MOTOR (RH)	YELLOW-LT GREEN
989	SEAT REGULATOR SWITCH TO REAR MOTOR (RH)	RED-LT GREEN
990	SEAT REGULATOR SWITCH TO FRONT MOTOR (LH)	YELLOW-LT BLUE
991	AWD SAFETY LAMP RELAY COIL	ORANGE-BLACK
992	AWD MODULE TO TRANSFER CASE CLUTCH	YELLOW-BLACK
993	INTERMITTENT GOVERNOR TO WINDSHIELD WIPER SWITCH	BROWN-WHITE
994	AWD MODULE TO AWD FUNCTION LAMP	WHITE
995	ABS MODULE DIFFERENTIAL SHIFT LOCK #1 OUTPUT	DK BLUE-WHITE
996	ABS MODULE REAR LEFT WHEEL SPEED OUTPUT	GRAY-BLACK
997	ABS MODULE FRONT RIGHT WHEEL SPEED OUTPUT	PINK
998	ABS MODULE FRONT LEFT WHEEL SPEED OUTPUT	TAN
999	ABS MODULE REAR RIGHT WHEEL SPEED OUTPUT	TAN-BLACK
1000	TRANSFER CASE CLUTCH RELAY TO TRANSFER CASE CLUTCH	LT GREEN

* IN SOME CASES, THERE MAY BE ADDITIONAL CIRCUIT FUNCTIONS INCLUDED IN THE CIRCUIT DESCRIPTION LISTED.

STANDARD CIRCUIT CHART (BY COLOR)

COLOR	DESCRIPTION*	CIRCUIT
(COLOR OPT.)	BLIND CIRCUIT TERM. IN HARNESS CANNOT BE CHECKED FOR CONT.	48
BLACK	GROUND CIRCUIT	57
BLACK	MARKER LAMP SWITCH TO MARKER LAMPS	207
BLACK	16 GA FUSE LINK	291
BLACK	HEATED WINDSHIELD GROUND TEST LEAD	739
BLACK	DOOR WIRE	629
BLACK	DCP MODULE SIGNAL GROUND TO RADIO	596
BLACK	MASS AIR FLOW GROUND	969
BLACK	ELECTRONIC CLUSTER FROM GROUND IN KEYBOARD	373
BLACK-LT BLUE	DOOR AJAR SWITCH TO INDICATOR LAMP LEFT REAR GROUND	363
BLACK-LT BLUE	DIESEL CONTROL MODULE GROUND RETURN	488
BLACK-LT BLUE	VENT SWITCH TO RIGHT FRONT VENT MOTOR	878
BLACK-LT BLUE	GROUND LOGIC MODULE	875
BLACK-LT BLUE	CLUSTER GAUGE GROUND	960
BLACK-LT BLUE	COURTESY LAMP SWITCH TO COURTESY LAMP	53
BLACK-LT BLUE	WARNING LAMP PROVE OUT	41
BLACK-LT BLUE	COURTESY LAMP SW. TO "C" PILLAR LAMPS	127
BLACK-LT GREEN	KEYLESS DOOR LOCK ILLUMINATION GROUND TO MODULE	76
BLACK-LT GREEN	CONSTANT VOLTAGE UNIT TO GAUGE	60
BLACK-LT GREEN	CONSTANT VOLTAGE UNIT AND INDICATOR LAMPS FEED	30
BLACK-LT GREEN	ACCY FEED FROM IGNITION SWITCH	297
BLACK-LT GREEN	COLD START INJECTOR	230
BLACK-LT GREEN	LOGIC GROUND	938
BLACK-LT GREEN	BATTERY TO MULTIPLEX MODULE	785
BLACK-LT GREEN	BLOWER MOTOR RELAY (LOAD TERM) TO BLOWER MOTOR	536
BLACK-LT GREEN	SPEAKER VOICE COIL FEED	822
BLACK-LT GREEN	BLOWER MOTOR RELAY FEED	364
BLACK-LT GREEN	POWER RELAY TO GLOW PLUGS (RIGHT BANK)	336
BLACK-ORANGE	FUEL 1 GROUND TO TACH/GAUGE MODULE	396
BLACK-ORANGE	REMOTE CONVENIENCE SELF DIAGNOSTIC GROUND	571
BLACK-ORANGE	HEATED WINDSHIELD CONTROL TO ELECT ALTERNATOR REGULATOR	579
BLACK-ORANGE	CENTER REAR TAILLAMP BULB OUTAGE	573
BLACK-ORANGE	OPEN DOOR WARNING LAMP TO OPEN DOOR WARNING SWITCH	627
BLACK-ORANGE	MULTIPLEX WINDSHIELD WIPER OFF	695
BLACK-ORANGE	VENT SWITCH TO RIGHT FRONT VENT—CONSOLE	876
BLACK-ORANGE	MEMORY MIRROR MODULE MOTOR DIRECTION	889
BLACK-ORANGE	VENT SWITCH TO RIGHT FRONT VENT MOTOR	876
BLACK-ORANGE	MEMORY SEAT SWITCH POSITION #2	268
BLACK-ORANGE	DIESEL WATER IN FUEL SENDER TO WARNING LAMP GROUND	327
BLACK-ORANGE	POWER SUPPLY TO BATTERY	38
BLACK-ORANGE	ENGINE COMPARTMENT LAMP FEED	80
BLACK-ORANGE	COURTESY LAMP SW. TO INSTR. PANEL COURTESY LAMP	126
BLACK-PINK	KEY WARNING SWITCH TO BUZZER	158

COLOR	DESCRIPTION*	CIRCUIT
BLACK-PINK	BACKUP LAMP	140
BLACK-PINK	CARGO LAMP SW. TO CARGO LAMP	55
BLACK-PINK	WINDSHIELD WIPER SW. TO WINDSHIELD WIPER MOTOR	28
BLACK-PINK	ECU TO VACUUM SWITCH 4	211
BLACK-PINK	AIR SUSPENSION ELECTRONICS GROUND	432
BLACK-PINK	HCU (MAIN) TO MODULE	493
BLACK-PINK	MODULE TO LIGHT	464
BLACK-PINK	DOOR AJAR SWITCH TO INDICATOR LAMP RIGHT FRONT GROUND	345
BLACK-WHITE	DOOR AJAR SWITCH TO INDICATOR LAMP RIGHT REAR GROUND	346
BLACK-WHITE	SIGNAL GROUND TO TACH/GAUGE MODULE	397
BLACK-WHITE	ANTI-LOCK MODULE TO ANTI-LOCK CONTROL VALVE	685
BLACK-WHITE	BATTERY TO MULTIPLEX SYSTEM	791
BLACK-WHITE	AWD MODULE POWER FEED	972
BLACK-WHITE	WINDSHIELD WIPER INTERMITTENT GOVERNOR FEED	587
BLACK-WHITE	DEDICATED GROUND	570
BLACK-WHITE	SPEED SIGNAL SPEEDO TACH MODULE TO FUEL COMPUTER	565
BLACK-WHITE	CIRCUIT BREAKER (LOAD TERM) TO CONTROL SWITCH (BATT. TERM)	517
BLACK-WHITE	CORNERING LAMP SWITCH FEED	526
BLACK-WHITE	WASHER PUMP MOTOR FEED	941
BLACK-WHITE	FUSED ACCY FEED — TRIPMINDER	910
BLACK-WHITE	LEFT MOTOR–DRIVER – B	861
BLACK-WHITE	CIRCUIT BREAKER TO SEAT LATCH RELAY	171
BLACK-WHITE	SPEAKER VOICE COIL RETURN	287
BLACK-WHITE	SEAT REG. CONTROL SWITCH FEED	51
BLACK-WHITE	INSTRUMENT PANEL LAMP SWITCH FEED	88
BLACK-YELLOW	WARNING LAMP TO LIGHTS ON RELAY	111
BLACK-YELLOW	WARNING LAMP RELAY FEED	112
BLACK-YELLOW	ACCESSORY FEED TO MESSAGE CENTER	231
BLACK-YELLOW	EFE CARBURETOR SPACE FEED	229
BLACK-YELLOW	RELAY FEED	175
BLACK-YELLOW	INJECTION PUMP FUEL TEMPERATURE SENSOR	225
BLACK-YELLOW	AIR BAG DIAGNOSTIC MODULE TO RELAY INDICATOR LAMP	608
BLACK-YELLOW	TACHOMETER GROUND TO TACH/GAUGE MODULE	398
BLACK-YELLOW	DOOR AJAR SWITCH TO INDICATOR LAMP LEFT FRONT GROUND	344
BLACK-YELLOW	COMPRESSOR CLUTCH FEED	347
BROWN	DOOR AJAR RELAY TO DOOR SWITCH	374
BROWN	POWER "THIGH" BOLSTER DOWN	492
BROWN	STEERING RATE SENSOR TERMINAL B CONTROL MODULE	634
BROWN	FUEL SIGNAL TACH MODULE TO FUEL COMPUTER	564
BROWN	HEATED WINDSHIELD CONTROL TO ALT POWER RELAY	580
BROWN	ELECT SHIFT 4 × 4 MODULE TO ELECT CLUTCH	779
BROWN	MULTIPLEX HEADLAMPS	697
BROWN	TRANSMISSION SHIFT SOLENOID #3	971

* IN SOME CASES, THERE MAY BE ADDITIONAL CIRCUIT FUNCTIONS INCLUDED IN THE CIRCUIT DESCRIPTION LISTED.

6–198

STANDARD CIRCUIT CHART (BY COLOR)

COLOR	DESCRIPTION*	CIRCUIT
BROWN	C.B. D-DIGIT	708
BROWN	EATC LH SUNLOAD SENSOR POSITIVE	468
BROWN	WINDOW SWITCH TO RIGHT REAR MOTOR	881
BROWN	HEATED WINDSHIELD FUSE RESISTOR	853
BROWN	RIGHT FRONT AIR INPUT RETURN	858
BROWN	TO ELECTRONIC CLUSTER FROM ENGLISH/METRIC SWITCH IN KEYBOARD	273
BROWN	FEEDBACK CARBURETOR COIL "A"	304
BROWN	SWITCH FEED	276
BROWN	18 GA FUSE LINK	292
BROWN	KEYLESS DOOR LOCK SWITCH ENABLE FROM MODULE	124
BROWN	HEADLAMP SWITCH TO TAIL LAMPS & SIDE MARKER LAMPS	14
BROWN	THERMACTOR AIR DIVERTER (TAD)	200
BROWN-LT BLUE	DOOR JAMB SWITCH TO LIGHTS ON RELAY	138
BROWN-LT BLUE	LH HEADLAMP BULB OUTAGE	108
BROWN-LT BLUE	SEAT BELT WARNING TIMER TO L.F. RETRACTOR SWITCH	85
BROWN-LT BLUE	FUEL METERING CONTROL LEVER ACTUATOR 1 MINUS	232
BROWN-LT BLUE	DEFOGGER SW. TO DEFOGGER MOTOR	186
BROWN-LT BLUE	FUEL INJECTOR #4 CYLINDER	558
BROWN-LT GREEN	DCP MODULE TO WIPER PARK OVER-RIDE RELAY	592
BROWN-LT GREEN	MODE SELECT SWITCH FEED	832
BROWN-LT GREEN	AUTOLAMP AMPLIFIER TO SENSOR	222
BROWN-LT GREEN	POWER SERVO TO CLIMATE CONTROL UNIT (AMP)	245
BROWN-LT GREEN	MEMORY SEAT SWITCH POSITION #1	267
BROWN-LT GREEN	SERVO FEEDBACK POTENTIOMETER BASE TO AMPLIFIER	149
BROWN-LT GREEN	EGR FEEDBACK	352
BROWN-ORANGE	VACUUM DOOR LOCK SWITCH TO SOLENOID (UNLOCK)	116
BROWN-ORANGE	MEMORY SEAT SWITCH SET	270
BROWN-ORANGE	IGNITION SWITCH TO THERMACTOR TIMER	251
BROWN-ORANGE	BLOWER MOTOR FEED	181
BROWN-ORANGE	VACUUM SOLENOID TO TEMP. SW.	369
BROWN-ORANGE	COAST CLUTCH SOLENOID	924
BROWN-ORANGE	RADIO MEMORY SEEK	372
BROWN-ORANGE	RADIO SWITCH TO ANTENNA RELAY	449
BROWN-PINK	AIR SUSPENSION HEIGHT SENSOR LO — R.F.	425
BROWN-PINK	DIESEL CONTROL SWITCH TO LAMP CONTROL RELAY	338
BROWN-PINK	IGNITION SWITCH ACCY TERM. TO DECK LID OPEN WARNING LAMP	485
BROWN-PINK	POWER RELAY COIL TO MODULE	513
BROWN-PINK	STARTING MOTOR RELAY TO IGNITION COIL "I" TERM.	262
BROWN-PINK	EGR VALVE REGULATOR SOLENOID TO EEC MODULE	360
BROWN-WHITE	THERMOSTAT SWITCH FEED	182
BROWN-WHITE	HEADLAMP SWITCH TO ELECTRONIC CLUSTER DIMMING	192
BROWN-WHITE	FLUID WARNING SWITCH TO PRESSURE SWITCH	549
BROWN-WHITE	EXTENDED USEFUL LIFE SENSOR TO WARNING LAMP	574
BROWN-WHITE	SELECTOR SWITCH TO AUX. FUEL SOLENOID	674
BROWN-WHITE	ELECT SHIFT 4 x 4 MODULE TO MOTOR POSITION #3	764
BROWN-WHITE	ELECT SHIFT MODULE TO LOW RANGE INDICATOR LAMP ROOF CONSOLE	782
BROWN-WHITE	MULTIPLEX LCD ILLUMINATION	732
BROWN-WHITE	BLOWER MOTOR SWITCH RELAY TO RESISTOR (LOW SPEED)	755
BROWN-WHITE	TRAILER RUNNING LAMPS	962
BROWN-WHITE	FUEL TANK SELECTOR TO FUEL PUMP REAR	789
BROWN-WHITE	INTERMITTENT GOVERNOR TO WINDSHIELD WIPER SWITCH	993
BROWN-WHITE	HEATED WINDSHIELD LH TO SENSE RESISTOR	920
BROWN-WHITE	DECK LID OPEN WARNING LAMP TO DECK LID OPEN SWITCH	486
BROWN-WHITE	MEMORY MIRROR MODULE TO RH VERTICAL DRIVE	890
BROWN-WHITE	TURN SIGNAL SWITCH TO RH CORNERING LAMP	379
BROWN-WHITE	ELECT. ENG. CONTL. MOD. TO IDLE SPD. CONTL. MOTOR #3	376
BROWN-WHITE	POWER TO ENGINE SENSORS	351
BROWN-YELLOW	HEATER BLOWER SWITCH FEED	399
BROWN-YELLOW	LEFT LIMIT-A — DRIVER	862
BROWN-YELLOW	WINDOW SWITCH TO RIGHT REAR MOTOR	882
BROWN-YELLOW	AWD MODULE TO TRANSFER CASE CLUTCH RELAY	975
BROWN-YELLOW	EATC LH SUNLOAD SENSOR NEGATIVE	476
BROWN-YELLOW	DCP MODULE TO WASHER RELAY	591
BROWN-YELLOW	FUEL INJECTOR #3 CYLINDER	557
BROWN-YELLOW	MAP LAMP SWITCH TO RH MAP LAMP	125
BROWN-YELLOW	EMISSION CONTROL VALVE TO SWITCH	81
BROWN-YELLOW	BATTERY TO HI-BEAM	62
DK BLUE	HORN SWITCH CONTROL	1
DK BLUE	20 GA FUSE LINK	302
DK BLUE	AUXILIARY CIRCUIT FEED TO TRACTOR TRAILER PLUG	212
DK BLUE	L.H. REMOTE MIRROR MOTOR FEED — C.C.W.	541
DK BLUE	FEED TO FAILURE SWITCH	600
DK BLUE	ELECT SHIFT MODULE TO 2H 4H SWITCH	780
DK BLUE	ELECTRIC DRIVE COOLING FAN (SINGLE OR LOW)	228
DK BLUE	MOONROOF RELAY TO MICRO SWITCH OPEN	691
DK BLUE	SHOCK DAMPENING RELAY SOFT TO SHOCK DAMPENING CONTROL	653
DK BLUE	LOGIC MODE	689
DK BLUE	PROGRAMMABLE RIDE CONTROL MODULE TO STAR TEST CONNECTOR	930
DK BLUE	LEFT DOOR OPEN — DRIVER	867
DK BLUE	CRANKSHAFT POSITION SENSOR FEED	349
DK BLUE	TRAILER BRAKES	43
DK BLUE-LT GREEN	WARNING LAMP TO ANTI-THEFT MODULE	343
DK BLUE-LT GREEN	BAROMETRIC PRESSURE SENSOR FEED	356
DK BLUE-LT GREEN	FUSED ACCESSORY #4	964
DK BLUE-LT GREEN	C.B. SPEAKER VOICE COIL RETURN	721
DK BLUE-LT GREEN	HEATER & A/C CONTROL SW. (LO-NORM) TO CLIMATE CONTROL UNIT	249
DK BLUE-LT GREEN	BUFFER FUEL LEVEL OUTPUT TO TRIPMINDER	205
DK BLUE-LT GREEN	THERMOCOUPLE POS TO EXHAUST SYST. OVERTEMP PROTECT MODULE	90
DK BLUE-ORANGE	ANTI-THEFT SWITCH ARM	24
DK BLUE-ORANGE	WINDSHIELD WIPER SW. TO WINDSHIELD WIPER MOTOR	56
DK BLUE-ORANGE	AUTOLAMP AMPLIFIER TO RHEOSTAT	217

COLOR	DESCRIPTION*	CIRCUIT
DK BLUE-ORANGE	HEADLAMP FLASH TO PASS SWITCH FEED	196
DK BLUE-ORANGE	MIRROR SWITCH VERTICAL LEFT	940
DK BLUE-ORANGE	AMPLIFIER SWITCH GROUND TO LEFT REAR SPEAKER	826
DK BLUE-ORANGE	CRANK ENABLE TO IGNITION MODULE	325
DK BLUE-ORANGE	CYLINDER IDENTIFICATION	282
DK BLUE-WHITE	R.F. DOOR UNLOCK SWITCH TO L.F. DOOR UNLOCK SWITCH	390
DK BLUE-WHITE	BLOWER MOTOR SPEED CONTROLLER TO RESISTOR #3 (MED.)	751
DK BLUE-WHITE	MULTIPLEX MESSAGE O	735
DK BLUE-WHITE	ABS MODULE DIFFERENTIAL SHIFT LOCK #1 OUTPUT	995
DK BLUE-WHITE	INTERMITTENT GOVERNOR TO W/S WIPER SWITCH	590
DK BLUE-WHITE	AIR BAG DIAGNOSTIC MODULE SAFING SENSOR (GROUND)	613
DK BLUE-WHITE	FUSE HOLDER TO HEADLAMP DIMMER AMPLIFIER	504
DK BLUE-WHITE	LH MIRROR UP/DOWN POSITION SENSOR	951
DK BLUE-WHITE	THERMOMETER AMBIENT SENSOR RETURN	234
DK BLUE-WHITE	SEAT BELT WARNING TIMER TO R.F. SEAT SENSOR	86
DK BLUE-YELLOW	ELECTRONIC CONTROL UNIT TO SOLENOID ACTUATOR	77
DK BLUE-YELLOW	DEFOGGER SW. TO DEFOGGER MOTOR	191
DK BLUE-YELLOW	THERMOMETER SENSOR FEED	233
DK BLUE-YELLOW	SELECTOR SWITCH TO MIDSHIP TANK	673
DK BLUE-YELLOW	AMPLIFIER SWITCH FEED TO LEFT FRONT SPEAKER	820
DK BLUE-YELLOW	HEATED WINDSHIELD TO FUSE	935
DK BLUE-YELLOW	AIR COMPRESSOR POWER RELAY CONTROL	420
DK BLUE-YELLOW	DUAL PLUG INHIBIT	283
DK GREEN	REARVIEW OUTSIDE MIRROR DOWN	411
DK GREEN	CAM SENSOR TO EEC MODULE	795
DK GREEN	STOPLAMP SWITCH TO HI MOUNT STOPLAMP	569
DK GREEN	REAR LAMP TO TRAILER RELAY FEED	576
DK GREEN	R.H. REMOTE MIRROR MOTOR FEED — C.W.	543
DK GREEN	TACHOMETER SIGNAL RETURN	644
DK GREEN	LEFT REAR SHOCK DAMPENING RELAY TO CONTROL MODULE	651
DK GREEN	FAILURE WARNING LIGHT	603
DK GREEN	14 GA FUSE LINK	299
DK GREEN	TRAILER RH TURN SIGNAL	64
DK GREEN	WINDSHIELD WIPER SW. TO WINDSHIELD WIPER MOTOR	65
DK GREEN	SUPPLEMENTAL ALTERNATOR STATOR C TERM. TO WINDSHIELD	72
DK GREEN	FUEL OCTANE ADJUST SIGNAL	242
DK GREEN-LT GREEN	CLOCK ADVANCE SWITCH TO MESSAGE CENTER	141
DK GREEN-LT GREEN	ELECTRONIC CONTROL UNIT TO ENGINE VACUUM SWITCH	75
DK GREEN-LT GREEN	EMA CONTROL TO SPARK RETARD SWITCH	21
DK GREEN-LT GREEN	AIR SUSPENSION MALFUNCTION WARNING LAMP	419
DK GREEN-LT GREEN	R.F. DOOR LOCK SWITCH TO L.F. DOOR LOCK SWITCH	389
DK GREEN-LT GREEN	SEAT BELT WARNING INDICATOR LAMP FEED	450
DK GREEN-ORANGE	HEATER & A/C CONTROL SW. (TEMP. SELECTOR) TO REHEAT AMPL.	773
DK GREEN-ORANGE	SPEAKER SWITCH GROUND TO RIGHT FRONT SPEAKER	811
DK GREEN-ORANGE	AMPLIFIER/SPEAKER SWITCH GROUND TO RIGHT REAR SPEAKER	803
DK GREEN-ORANGE	MIRROR SWITCH HORIZONTAL RIGHT	944
DK GREEN-ORANGE	PROCESSOR LOOP SIGNAL RETURN	848
DK GREEN-ORANGE	MCU MODULE TO KNOCK SENSOR	311
DK GREEN-ORANGE	PARITY BIT-DISPLAY TO MESSAGE CENTER	178
DK GREEN-PURPLE	ANTI-THEFT SWITCH DISARM	25
DK GREEN-PURPLE	HEATED EXTERIOR MIRROR FEED	59
DK GREEN-PURPLE	DATA-MESSAGE CENTER TO DISPLAY	174
DK GREEN-PURPLE	POWER FEED DECEL TIMER TO THROTTLE KICKER	584
DK GREEN-WHITE	SENSOR AMPLIFY UNIT TO CONTROL UNIT #3	759
DK GREEN-WHITE	KEY CYLINDER SENSOR TO ANTI-THEFT MODULE	936
DK GREEN-WHITE	RH MIRROR LEFT/RIGHT POSITION SENSOR	954
DK GREEN-WHITE	STOPLAMP SW. TO STOPLAMP RELAY (COIL TERM.)	475
DK GREEN-WHITE	FUEL LEVEL RECEIVER TO FUEL LEVEL WARNING RELAY (REG. TERM.)	367
DK GREEN-WHITE	SENSOR SIGNAL TO AMPLIFIER	150
DK GREEN-WHITE	OIL PRESSURE SWITCH TO TIMER	254
DK GREEN-YELLOW	HEADLAMP SWITCH TO AUTOLAMP AMPLIFIER	219
DK GREEN-YELLOW	AIR SUSPENSION CONTROL MODULE FEED	418
DK GREEN-YELLOW	ANTENNA SWITCH TO POWER ANTENNA (DOWN)	746
DK GREEN-YELLOW	SPLICE #3 TO POWER RELAY	546
DK GREEN-YELLOW	FUEL PUMP RELAY TO SAFETY SWITCH	238
DL BLUE	TRAILER STOP LAMPS	43
GRAY	LOW OIL LEVEL RELAY TO WARNING LAMP	208
GRAY	12 GA FUSE LINK	290
GRAY	HEADLAMP DIMMER RELAY TO HEADLAMP DIMMER SWITCH	502
GRAY	ELECT SHIFT MODULE TO GRAPHIC DISPLAY ROOF CONSOLE	783
GRAY	C.B. SCAN L.E.D.	706
GRAY	WINDSHIELD WIPER HIGH	719
GRAY	RIGHT CHANNEL SIGNAL	690
GRAY	SEAT REG. SW. TO RECLINER MOTOR — UP	918
GRAY	AIR CHARGE TEMPERATURE	743
GRAY	RIGHT LIMIT-A — PASSENGER	874
GRAY	MEMORY MIRROR MODULE POSITION	894
GRAY	MIRROR POSITION SENSOR COMMON	959
GRAY	AIR SUSPENSION SYSTEM GROUND	430
GRAY	EATC RH SUNLOAD SENSOR NEGATIVE	483
GRAY	CRANKSHAFT SENSOR SIGNAL RETURN	350
GRAY	DIESEL CONTROL SWITCH TO POWER RELAY & LAMP CONTROL RELAY	339
GRAY-BLACK	LIMIT SW. TO BACK WINDOW REG. MOTOR	401
GRAY-BLACK	ABS MODULE REAR LEFT WHEEL SPEED OUTPUT	996
GRAY-BLACK	FRONT TILT POSITION SENSE	441
GRAY-BLACK	SEAT REG. SW. TO RECLINER MOTOR — DOWN	919
GRAY-BLACK	VALVE #5 TO MODULE	499
GRAY-BLACK	VEHICLE SPEED SIGNAL	679
GRAY-BLACK	WINDOW REGULATOR MOTOR TO GROUND	157
GRAY-BLACK	INSIDE DOOR HANDLE SWITCH TO RETRACTOR INHIBITOR MODULE	185
GRAY-BLACK	SERVO SOURCE VACUUM SOLENOID TO CONTROL TRANSISTOR	145
GRAY-LT BLUE	MILES/KILOMETERS SWITCH TO MESSAGE CENTER	161
GRAY-LT BLUE	HTD BACKLITE SW. TO TIME DELAY RELAY	688
GRAY-LT BLUE	SENSOR AMPLIFY UNIT TO CONTROL UNIT #2	750

* IN SOME CASES, THERE MAY BE ADDITIONAL CIRCUIT
FUNCTIONS INCLUDED IN THE CIRCUIT DESCRIPTION LISTED.

STANDARD CIRCUIT CHART (BY COLOR)

COLOR	DESCRIPTION*	CIRCUIT
GRAY-LT BLUE	AMPLIFIER/SPEAKER SWITCH FEED TO LEFT REAR SPEAKER	800
GRAY-LT BLUE	ANEROID SWITCH TO MCU MODULE	394
GRAY-LT BLUE	ELECTRONIC CONTROL UNIT TO EXHAUST GAS OXYGEN SENSOR (#1 IN DUAL SYSTEM)	74
GRAY-ORANGE	HEAD LP TIME DELAY CONTROL RELAY TO CIR. BREAKER	686
GRAY-ORANGE	AIR BAG SAFING SENSORS TO INFLATORS	614
GRAY-ORANGE	FEED TO FUEL SHUTOFF LAMP	921
GRAY-ORANGE	AVERAGE SPEED SWITCH TO MESSAGE CENTER	156
GRAY-ORANGE	ELECTRONIC CONTROL UNIT TO DECELERATION SOLENOID	47
GRAY-ORANGE	PROFILE IGNITION PICKUP FROM TFI MODULE	395
GRAY-RED	DISTANCE TO EMPTY SWITCH TO MESSAGE CENTER	155
GRAY-RED	THERMOCOUPLE 1 NEG. TO EXHAUST SYST. OVERTEMP PROTECT MODULE	91
GRAY-RED	INHIBITOR MODULE TO RETRACTOR OVERRIDE SOLENOID	187
GRAY-RED	EXHAUST BACK PRESSURE VALVE ACTUATOR	318
GRAY-RED	LIFTGATE SW. TO LIFTGATE RELAY	913
GRAY-RED	DIESEL COLD ADVANTAGE	607
GRAY-RED	MOTOR TO MOTOR RELAY	538
GRAY-RED	MIRROR POSITION SENSOR FEED	958
GRAY-RED	TEMP WARNING LAMP TO SENDING UNIT	682
GRAY-RED	ELECTRONIC RIDE SHOCK DIAGNOSTIC	844
GRAY-RED	EMERGENCY RELEASE LEVERS	868
GRAY-RED	SWITCH TO VALVE	455
GRAY-RED	SEAT PROCESSOR ASSY TO FRONT MOTOR LH	452
GRAY-RED	WINDOW REG. SW. TO BACK WINDOW REG. MOTOR	402
GRAY-RED	SENSOR SIGNAL RETURN	359
GRAY-WHITE	WINDOW REG. SW. TO WINDOW REG. MOTOR	403
GRAY-WHITE	THIRD LOCKOUT SOLENOID	854
GRAY-WHITE	AIR BAG DIAGNOSTIC MODULE TO DRIVER INFLATOR	615
GRAY-WHITE	DAYTIME RUNNING LAMP	932
GRAY-WHITE	THROTTLE ANGLE POSITION SENSOR TO EEC MODULE	355
GRAY-WHITE	AIR CONDITIONER CLUTCH RELAY	321
GRAY-WHITE	DISTANCE SWITCH TO MESSAGE CENTER	164
GRAY-WHITE	CHOKE RELAY TO CHOKE	67
GRAY-YELLOW	ELECTRONIC CONTROL UNIT TO CANISTER PURGE SOLENOID	101
GRAY-YELLOW	HEADLAMP DIMMER SWITCH TO HEADLAMP DIMMER AMPLIFIER	505
GRAY-YELLOW	ACC FEED	687
GRAY-YELLOW	EFI MODULE TO CLUTCH SWITCH	481
GRAY-YELLOW	PRESSURE SWITCH TO INERTIA SWITCH	467
LT BLUE	REARVIEW OUTSIDE MIRROR CLOCKWISE	413
LT BLUE	ELECT. ENG. CONTL. MOD. TO ELECTRO DRIVE FAN	386
LT BLUE	VEHICLE SPEED SENSOR FEED	353
LT BLUE	ANTI-SKID MODULE TO ANTI-SKID CONTROL VALVE	677
LT BLUE	C.B. B+ DIGIT	720
LT BLUE	CAM SENDER SIGNAL RETURN	796
LT BLUE	ELECT SHIFT 4 x 4 MODULE TO SPEED SENSOR COIL	772
LT BLUE	LOW COOLANT LEVEL RELAY TO SENSOR	794
LT BLUE	HEADLAMP DIMMER RELAY TO FUSE HOLDER	503
LT BLUE	ELECTRONIC FUEL GAGE TO MESSAGE CENTER	501
LT BLUE	FUEL INJECTOR #8 CYLINDER	562
LT BLUE	LEFT FRONT SHOCK DAMPENING RELAY TO CONTROL MODULE	641
LT BLUE	RIGHT REAR AIR INPUT RETURN	855
LT BLUE	MEMORY MIRROR MODULE TO RH HORIZONTAL DRIVER	888
LT BLUE	VEHICLE MAINTENANCE MONITOR MODULE TO OIL TEMP INPUT	905
LT BLUE	LOW FUEL INDICATOR	106
LT BLUE	KEYLESS DOOR LOCK SWITCH ILLUMINATION FEED	66
LT BLUE	TURN SIGNAL FLASHER TO TURN SIGNAL SWITCH	44
LT BLUE	SEAT REG. SW. TO HORIZ. SOLENOID BATT. TERM	306
LT BLUE	INDICATOR LAMP TO SWITCH (4 x 4)	210
LT BLUE-BLACK	AMPLIFIER SPEAKER SWITCH TO LEFT REAR SPEAKER	277
LT BLUE-BLACK	BRAKE FEED	22
LT BLUE-BLACK	SPEED CONTROL ON-OFF SWITCH TO AMPLIFIER	151
LT BLUE-BLACK	MEMORY MIRROR MODULE RH VERTICAL POSITION	893
LT BLUE-BLACK	FOG LAMP SWITCH TO FOG LAMP RELAY	477
LT BLUE-BLACK	INDICATOR LAMP TO LOW RANGE SWITCH 4 x 4	784
LT BLUE-BLACK	SAFETY RELAY LOAD TERM. TO WIND. REG. SW. FEED	400
LT BLUE-BLACK	AIR SOLENOID CONTROL — REAR	416
LT BLUE-BLACK	RELAY TO DAY/NIGHT ILLUMINATION LAMPS	434
LT BLUE-ORANGE	AMBIENT SENSOR TO INST. PANEL THERMISTOR	767
LT BLUE-ORANGE	C.B. SPEAKER RELAY TO MIC	723
LT BLUE-ORANGE	DCP MODULE TO HEATED BACKLITE RELAY	624
LT BLUE-ORANGE	FUEL PUMP RELAY CONTROL	926
LT BLUE-ORANGE	LH REAR STOP & TURN BULB OUTAGE	104
LT BLUE-ORANGE	HORN CONTROL MODULE TO OVERRIDE SWITCH	34
LT BLUE-ORANGE	HI-TEMP SWITCH TO MCU MODULE	308
LT BLUE-ORANGE	HEATER BLOWER MOTOR TO SWITCH (MEDIUM)	269
LT BLUE-PINK	EEC MODULE TO TIME METER	305
LT BLUE-PINK	ELECTRONIC CLUSTER ACCESSORY FEED	295
LT BLUE-PINK	TRANSFORMER POWER — MESSAGE CENTER TO DISPLAY	169
LT BLUE-PINK	IDLE TRACKING SWITCH FEED	189
LT BLUE-PINK	BUCKLE SW. TO CENTER OCCUPANT SEAT SENSOR	107
LT BLUE-PINK	AIR COMPRESSOR VENT SOLENOID	578
LT BLUE-PINK	BRAKE SKID CONTROL MODULE FEED	601
LT BLUE-RED	DCP MODULE CONTROL INTERFACE TO RADIO	595
LT BLUE-RED	PRESSURE SWITCH TO MODULE	535
LT BLUE-RED	MASS AIRFLOW SIGNAL	967
LT BLUE-RED	C.B. SPEAKER TO TRANSCEIVER	717
LT BLUE-RED	FUEL PUMP BYPASS	433
LT BLUE-RED	FUEL LEVEL WARNING RELAY FEED	365
LT BLUE-RED	CLOCK SELECT SWITCH TO MESSAGE CENTER	142
LT BLUE-RED	INSTRUMENT PANEL LAMPS FEED	19
LT BLUE-RED	THERMACTOR DUMP VALVE FEED	255
LT BLUE-WHITE	CIGAR LIGHTER FEED	40
LT BLUE-WHITE	ARRIVAL SWITCH TO MESSAGE CENTER	152
LT BLUE-WHITE	TIMER CONTROL VALVE TO CONTROL UNIT	741

COLOR	DESCRIPTION*	CIRCUIT
LT BLUE-WHITE	SPEAKER SWITCH GROUND TO LEFT FRONT SPEAKER	813
LT BLUE-WHITE	DCP MODULE TO PARKLAMP RELAY	625
LT BLUE-WHITE	VEHICLE MAINTENANCE MONITOR MODULE TO SPEED SENSOR	909
LT BLUE-YELLOW	HEATER & A/C CONTROL SW. (HI & LO NORM) TO BLOWER MOTOR SW. RELAY	769
LT BLUE-YELLOW	RADIATOR COOLANT TEMP SWITCH TO CONTROL UNIT	742
LT BLUE-YELLOW	CRT SCAN	730
LT BLUE-YELLOW	FUEL TANK SELECTOR SWITCH TO AFT FUEL PUMP	671
LT BLUE-YELLOW	BATTERY TO AUTOMATIC ANTENNA SWITCH	451
LT BLUE-YELLOW	CHECKOUT SWITCH TO MESSAGE CENTER	143
LT BLUE-YELLOW	KEYLESS DOOR LOCK SWITCH DATA BIT 1 TO MODULE	78
LT BLUE-YELLOW	DE-ICE SOLENOID CONTROL	241
LT BLUE-YELLOW	AUTO TRANS MANUAL LEVER POSITION OR CLUTCH	199
LT GREEN	SPEAKER VOICE COIL FEED FRONT (LEFT CHANNEL) AMP INPUT	280
LT GREEN	VACUUM DOOR LOCK SWITCH TO SOLENOID (LOCK)	115
LT GREEN	KEYLESS DOOR LOCK OUTPUT FROM MODULE	129
LT GREEN	READING LAMP SWITCH TO READING LAMP (LH)	387
LT GREEN	C.B. A-DIGIT	715
LT GREEN	WINDSHIELD WASHER	726
LT GREEN	ELECT SHIFT 4 x 4 MODULE TO SPEED SENSOR RETURN	774
LT GREEN	AIR SUSPENSION CONTROL SIGNAL	637
LT GREEN	ALTERNATOR RELAY TO ALTERNATOR REGULATOR	568
LT GREEN	TRANSFER CASE CLUTCH RELAY TO TRANSFER CASE CLUTCH	1000
LT GREEN	RADIO TO FADER CONTROL	823
LT GREEN	SPEED CONTROL VACUUM TO EEC MODULE	916
LT GREEN	SEAT BELT WARNING SWITCH FEED	469
LT GREEN	LEFT LIMIT-B—DRIVER	872
LT GREEN	STOPLAMP SWITCH TO STOPLAMPS	511
LT GREEN-BLACK	ESC SWITCH TO ESC VALVE CONTROL	933
LT GREEN-BLACK	LH REAR SENSOR (LOW) TO MODULE	519
LT GREEN-BLACK	DCP MODULE TRIP SCAN HIGH TO TRIPMINDER	597
LT GREEN-BLACK	C.B. REGULATED 5V	711
LT GREEN-BLACK	CONTROL MODULE TO OIL PRESSURE SWITCH	473
LT GREEN-BLACK	SEQUENTIAL LH REAR OUTBOARD TURN SIGNAL LAMP	444
LT GREEN-BLACK	AIR PORT SOLENOID SIGNAL	99
LT GREEN-BLACK	HEADLAMP DIMMER SWITCH TO HIGH BEAMS	12
LT GREEN-BLACK	MANIFOLD ABSOLUTE PRESSURE TO EEC MODULE	358
LT GREEN-ORANGE	LH REAR TURN SIGNAL LAMP	9
LT GREEN-ORANGE	POWER SERVO TO CLIMATE CONTROL UNIT (MODE)	243
LT GREEN-ORANGE	AIR SOLENOID CONTROL L.F.	415
LT GREEN-ORANGE	SEQUENTIAL LH REAR INBOARD TURN SIGNAL LAMP	442
LT GREEN-ORANGE	C.B. NOISE BLANKER	705
LT GREEN-ORANGE	AMPLIFIER SWITCH GROUND TO RIGHT FRONT SPEAKER	815
LT GREEN-ORANGE	FUEL INJECTOR #6 CYLINDER	560
LT GREEN-ORANGE	W/W WIPER SWITCH TO W/S WIPER MOTOR FIELD RH	956
LT GREEN-PURPLE	SUPERCHARGER SOLENOID #1	965
LT GREEN-PURPLE	AMPLIFIER SWITCH FEED TO RIGHT FRONT SPEAKER	816
LT GREEN-PURPLE	BATTERY FEED TO STEREO	797
LT GREEN-PURPLE	DCP MODULE TRIP SCAN LOW TO TRIPMINDER	598
LT GREEN-PURPLE	ELECTRONIC SHOCK HARD CONTROL	838
LT GREEN-PURPLE	HIGH ELECTRIC DRIVE COOLING FAN	639
LT GREEN-PURPLE	START INTERRUPT RELAY TO ANTI-THEFT MODULE	342
LT GREEN-PURPLE	CARBURETOR AIR TEMPERATURE SENSOR FEED	357
LT GREEN-PURPLE	FUEL PULSE TO MESSAGE CENTER	139
LT GREEN-RED	KEYLESS DOOR LOCK SWITCH DATA BIT 2 TO MODULE	79
LT GREEN-RED	STOPLAMP SWITCH FEED	10
LT GREEN-RED	EMERG. BRAKE WARNING LAMP TO EMERG. BRAKE SWITCH	162
LT GREEN-RED	SEQUENTIAL LH REAR CENTER TURN SIGNAL LAMP	443
LT GREEN-RED	(COIL) OR (ACCY) TERM OF IGNITION SWITCH TO ALTERNATOR REGULATOR (IGN. TERM)	904
LT GREEN-RED	REAR SENSOR (HIGH) TO MODULE	518
LT GREEN-RED	AIR SUSPENSION SYSTEM GROUND	577
LT GREEN-RED	LEFT CHANNEL SIGNAL OUT	798
LT GREEN-RED	C.B. RELAY DRIVE	722
LT GREEN-RED	ENGINE COOLANT TEMPERATURE FEED	354
LT GREEN-WHITE	BLOWER MOTOR SPEED CONTROLLER TO RESISTOR #1 (MED.)	754
LT GREEN-WHITE	AMPLIFIER SWITCH GROUND TO LEFT FRONT SPEAKER	819
LT GREEN-WHITE	C.B. C+ DIGIT	724
LT GREEN-WHITE	MODULE TO OVERRIDE SWITCH	661
LT GREEN-WHITE	ELECTRONIC RIDE CONTROL DAMPENING SOFT CONTROL	839
LT GREEN-WHITE	ELECT. ENG. CONTL. MOD. TO IDLE SPD. CONTL. MOTOR #2	265
LT GREEN-WHITE	MEMORY SEAT SWITCH LAMP ENABLE	271
LT GREEN-WHITE	LH FRONT TURN SIGNAL LAMP	3
LT GREEN-YELLOW	SEAT SWITCH ARM TERM. TO RELAY FIELD TERM	7
LT GREEN-YELLOW	INTERIOR LAMP SWITCH FEED	54
LT GREEN-YELLOW	RETARD VALVE TO CONTROL RELAY TERM. #1	869
LT GREEN-YELLOW	FUEL TANK SELECTOR SWITCH TO MIDSHIP FUEL PUMP	672
LT GREEN-YELLOW	HEATER & A/C CONTROL SW. TO REHEAT & A/C FEED	765
LT GREEN-YELLOW	MODULE TO MOTOR RETURN	663
LT GREEN-YELLOW	REFERENCE SENSOR TO HEAT DUCT THERMISTOR	768
LT GREEN-YELLOW	PRESSURE SWITCH TO FLUID RES. SWITCH	547
LT GREEN-YELLOW	SPLICE #3 TO POWER RELAY	530
ORANGE	MODULE TO RELAY	461
ORANGE	WINDSHIELD WIPER SWITCH TO INTERMITTENT GOVERNOR GROUND	589
ORANGE	HEATED WINDSHIELD SWITCH TO HEATED WINDSHIELD CONTROL	582
ORANGE	BRAKE PRESSURE SWITCH TO CONTROL MODULE	636
ORANGE	AWD MODULE TO TRANSFER CASE CLUTCH RELAY COIL	976
ORANGE	ELECT SHIFT 4 x 4 MODULE TO MOTOR CONTROL	778
ORANGE	BRAKE PRESSURE SWITCH TO CONTROL MODULE	636
ORANGE	SPEAKER VOICE COIL FEED LEFT FRONT CHANNEL AMP INPUT	649
ORANGE	MODULE DIAGNOSTIC	693
ORANGE	RIGHT MOTOR — PASSENGER — A	864
ORANGE	C.B. C-DIGIT	704
ORANGE	FUEL CONTROL SWITCH TO FUEL CONTROL VALVE	974
ORANGE	MULTIPLEX RELAY COIL FEED #1	699

* IN SOME CASES, THERE MAY BE ADDITIONAL CIRCUIT FUNCTIONS INCLUDED IN THE CIRCUIT DESCRIPTION LISTED.

STANDARD CIRCUIT CHART (BY COLOR)

COLOR	DESCRIPTION*	CIRCUIT
ORANGE	BATTERY FEED TO RELAY CONTROLLER	931
ORANGE	VALVE #2 TO MODULE	496
ORANGE	MEMORY MIRROR MODULE RH HORIZONTAL POSITION	892
ORANGE	EXHAUST GAS OXYGEN SENSOR RETURN TO EEC MODULE	89
ORANGE	SWITCH OFF TO RELAY	274
ORANGE	HEATER & A/C CONTROL SW. (LO-NORM) TO POWER SERVO	250
ORANGE	ELECTRONIC CLUSTER FROM EXPANDED FUEL IN KEYBOARD	285
ORANGE	DEDICATED GROUND TO TFI MODULE	259
ORANGE	16 GA FUSE LINK	300
ORANGE	RELAY TO SEAT LATCH SOLENOID	172
ORANGE	TRAILER BATTERY CHARGE	49
ORANGE-BLACK	BLOWER MOTOR TO SWITCH — HI	261
ORANGE-BLACK	TAIL LAMP BULB OUTAGE TO MESSAGE CENTER	132
ORANGE-BLACK	ELECTRIC CHOKE FEED	68
ORANGE-BLACK	EVO MODULE TO TEST CONNECTOR	927
ORANGE-BLACK	TRANSMISSION OIL TEMP	923
ORANGE-BLACK	MULTIPLEX FARRING LAMPS	696
ORANGE-BLACK	CLIMATE CONTROL BOX TO HIGH BLOWER RELAY	776
ORANGE-BLACK	AWD SAFETY LAMP RELAY COIL	991
ORANGE-BLACK	RIGHT CHANNEL SIGNAL OUT	799
ORANGE-BLACK	ENGLISH METRIC SIGNAL TO MULTIGAGE	572
ORANGE-BLACK	LIQUID CRYSTAL DISPLAY	484
ORANGE-BLACK	TURN SIGNAL SWITCH TO INDICATOR RELAY	458
ORANGE-BLACK	AIR SUSPENSION HEIGHT SENSOR LO — REAR	428
ORANGE-BLACK	IDLE SPEED CONTROL TO EGR VACUUM SOLENOID	323
ORANGE-BLACK	RADIO SEEK "DOWN"	370
ORANGE-LT BLUE	AFTER GLOW RELAY TO DIESEL CONTROL SWITCH	335
ORANGE-LT BLUE	SEQUENTIAL RH REAR INBOARD TURN SIGNAL LAMP	445
ORANGE-LT BLUE	I TERMINAL STARTER MOTOR RELAY TO INERTIA SWITCH	668
ORANGE-LT BLUE	ELECT SHIFT TO 4L SWITCH	781
ORANGE-LT BLUE	RADIO RECEIVER ASSY. TO FOOT CONTROL SWITCH	747
ORANGE-LT BLUE	VAC SWITCH TO VAC PUMP	740
ORANGE-LT BLUE	RH REAR TURN SIGNAL LAMP	5
ORANGE-LT BLUE	ALTERNATOR REGULATOR "F" TERMINAL TO ALTERNATOR	35
ORANGE-LT BLUE	ELECTRONIC CONTROL UNIT TO WIDE OPEN THROTTLE ACTUATOR	73
ORANGE-LT BLUE	CRUISE INDICATING LAMP TO CRUISE INTERFACE MODULE	203
ORANGE-LT GREEN	TANK SELECT CIRCUIT ELECTRONIC FUEL GAUGE	204
ORANGE-LT GREEN	EMA CONTROL TO EGR SWITCH	27
ORANGE-LT GREEN	AIR BAG DIAGNOSTIC MODULE TO AIR BAG FLASHER	610
ORANGE-LT GREEN	DCP MODULE TO WIPER HI-LO RELAY	594
ORANGE-LT GREEN	SPEAKER VOICE COIL FEED — FRONT (LEFT CHANNEL)	804
ORANGE-LT GREEN	DECELERATION SENSOR	847
ORANGE-LT GREEN	INDICATOR RELAY TO FLASHER	459
ORANGE-LT GREEN	DROPPING RESISTOR TO RELAY #2	471
ORANGE-RED	SEQUENTIAL RH REAR OUTBOARD TURN SIGNAL LAMP	447
ORANGE-RED	AIR SOLENOID CONTROL R.F.	414
ORANGE-RED	RESISTOR TO BLOWER MOTOR (HI)	515
ORANGE-RED	SKID CONTROL MODULE RH WHEEL SENSOR (HI)	604
ORANGE-RED	AMPLIFIER/SPEAKER SWITCH FEED TO RIGHT REAR SPEAKER	802
ORANGE-RED	LO-TEMP SWITCH TO MCU MODULE	309
ORANGE-RED	INSTRUMENT PANEL ILLUMINATION CONTROL MODULE FEED	293
ORANGE-WHITE	TEMPERATURE COMPENSATED PUMP TO PROCESSOR	256
ORANGE-WHITE	HEADLAMP SWITCH TO SENSOR AND AUTOLAMP AMPLIFIER	221
ORANGE-WHITE	AIR DUMP VALVE NEG. TO EXHAUST SYS. OVERTEMP MODULE	93
ORANGE-WHITE	ELECT SHIFT 4 x 4 MODULE TO MOTOR POSITION #2	763
ORANGE-WHITE	ACCELERATE DECELERATE SENSOR	836
ORANGE-WHITE	VENT SWITCH TO LEFT FRONT VENT MOTOR	886
ORANGE-WHITE	SEQUENTIAL RH REAR CENTER TURN SIGNAL LAMP	446
ORANGE-WHITE	POWER RELAY TO GLOW PLUGS (LEFT BANK)	337
ORANGE-WHITE	DOOR OPENING WARNING TO ANTI-THEFT MODULE	341
ORANGE-WHITE	MOVABLE STEERING COLUMN SOLENOID TO COURTESY LAMP SWITCH	381
ORANGE-YELLOW	ANTENNA SWITCH TO ANTENNA RELAY	448
ORANGE-YELLOW	OVERRIDE SWITCH TO LATCH	665
ORANGE-YELLOW	AIR BAG READY INDICATOR LAMP TO AIR BAG FLASHER	609
ORANGE-YELLOW	SPLICE TO DIODE	531
ORANGE-YELLOW	SPLICE TO POWER RELAY	532
ORANGE-YELLOW	SPLICE TO MODULE	525
ORANGE-YELLOW	POWER RELAY TO MODULE GROUND	528
ORANGE-YELLOW	SPEED SENSOR LO V REF TO SPEEDO TACH MODULE	563
ORANGE-YELLOW	AMPLIFIER TO SERVO TRANSDUCER FEED	144
ORANGE-YELLOW	TURN SIGNAL FLASHER FEED	8
ORANGE-YELLOW	SEAT SWITCH TO RELAY FIELD TERMINAL	18
ORANGE-YELLOW	SHIFT SOLENOID 1	237
ORANGE-YELLOW	START CIRCUIT TO THERMACTOR RELAY	253
PINK	WINDOW REGULATOR RELAY ACCY FEED	194
PINK	ABS MODULE FRONT RIGHT WHEEL SPEED OUTPUT	997
PINK	MULTIPLEX MESSAGE I	736
PINK	SPARK OUTPUT SIGNAL FROM TFI MODULE	929
PINK	AIR COMPRESSOR VENT SOLENOID	421
PINK	VALVE #4 TO MODULE	498
PINK	CRANK ENABLE RELAY	329
PINK-BLACK	ELECTRONIC CLUSTER IGNITION RUN FEED	489
PINK-BLACK	STOPLAMP RELAY FEED	474
PINK-BLACK	AIR SUSPENSION HEIGHT SENSOR HI — L.F.	422
PINK-BLACK	AIR SUSPENSION HEIGHT SENSOR HI — REAR	427
PINK-BLACK	FUEL PUMP POWER	787
PINK-BLACK	COMPASS SENSOR FEED	684
PINK-BLACK	SENSOR AMPLIFY UNIT TO CONTROL UNIT #1	749
PINK-BLACK	RH REAR SENSOR (LOW) TO MODULE	524
PINK-BLACK	AIR BAG DIAGNOSTIC MODULE TO PASSENGER INFLATOR	616
PINK-BLACK	SHOCK DAMPENING RELAY HARD TO SHOCK DAMPENING CONTROL	652
PINK-BLACK	SPEAKER VOICE COIL FEED RIGHT REAR CHANNEL AMP INPUT	645
PINK-BLACK	THERMO SWITCH TO CONTROL MODULE	470
PINK-BLACK	DOOR LOCK MOTOR (LOCK)	117
PINK-LT BLUE	RH HEADLAMP BULB OUTAGE	109
PINK-LT BLUE	AIR COND. CONTROL RELAY FEED	883
PINK-LT BLUE	PRESSURE SWITCH TO MOTOR RELAY	539
PINK-LT BLUE	DATA LINK RETURN	915
PINK-LT BLUE	SPEAKER VOICE COIL FEED—REAR (RIGHT CHANNEL)	806
PINK-LT BLUE	AMPLIFIER/SPEAKER SWITCH GROUND TO LEFT REAR SPEAKER	801
PINK-LT GREEN	VENT SWITCH TO BLOWER MOTOR—LO	917
PINK-LT GREEN	SPEAKER VOICE COIL FEED—REAR (LEFT CHANNEL)	807
PINK-LT GREEN	EEC MODULE TO CHECK ENGINE INDICATOR LAMP	658
PINK-LT GREEN	MODULE TO SOLENOID	599
PINK-LT GREEN	DOOR LOCK SWITCH (UNLOCK)	120
PINK-ORANGE	DOOR LOCK MOTOR (UNLOCK)	118
PINK-ORANGE	AIR BAG DIAGNOSTIC MODULE (DEPLOY) TO RH SENSOR	617
PINK-ORANGE	SPEAKER SWITCH FEED TO RIGHT FRONT SPEAKER	812
PINK-ORANGE	VEHICLE SPEED SENSOR RETURN	676
PINK-ORANGE	READING LAMP SWITCH TO READING LAMP	487
PINK-ORANGE	MEMORY MIRROR MODULE LH HORIZONTAL POSITION	896
PINK-ORANGE	DIESEL CONTROL MODULE FEED	466
PINK-ORANGE	ELECT. ENG. CONTL. MOD. TO IDLE SPD CONTL. MOTOR #3	384
PINK-WHITE	BLOWER MOTOR RELAY TO MOTOR	371
PINK-WHITE	AIR SUSP. MOD. TO L.F. HEIGHT SENSOR	431
PINK-WHITE	AIR BAG DIAGNOSTIC MODULE (DEPLOY) TO CENTER SENSOR	619
PINK-WHITE	SPEAKER SWITCH FEED TO LEFT FRONT SPEAKER	814
PINK-WHITE	DOOR SWITCH TO SEAT LATCH RELAY (COIL TERM.)	173
PINK-YELLOW	DOOR LOCK SWITCH (LOCK)	119
PINK-YELLOW	WASHER FLUID LEVEL INDICATOR	82
PINK-YELLOW	DPC MODULE TO HEADLAMP RELAY	632
PINK-YELLOW	SPEAKER VOICE COIL FEED LEFT REAR CHANNEL AMP INPUT	646
PINK-YELLOW	OPEN DOOR WARNING LAMP	626
PINK-YELLOW	SWITCH TO FADER RIGHT CHANNEL FEED	830
PINK-YELLOW	WIDE OPEN THROTTLE A/C CUTOUT SWITCH	331
PURPLE	RIGHT FRONT SHOCK DAMPENING RELAY TO CONTROL MODULE	638
PURPLE	HEATED WINDSHIELD CONTROL TO EEC AIR COND TERM	585
PURPLE	CONVERTIBLE TOP RELAY TO SWITCH	588
PURPLE	R.H. REMOTE MIRROR MOTOR FEED—C.C.W.	544
PURPLE	HEADLAMP DIMMER SWITCH TO HEADLAMP DIMMER RELAY	500
PURPLE	TRANSMISSION TURBINE SPEED SENSOR	970
PURPLE	C.B. A+ DIGIT	712
PURPLE	RELAY COIL FEED #2	714
PURPLE	REDUNDANT MODULE TO ENGINE WARNING LAMP	656
PURPLE	POWER FEED FROM AMPLIFIER	928
PURPLE	A/C DEMAND SIGNAL	348
PURPLE	LEFT CHANNEL SIGNAL	856
PURPLE	MODULE TO RELAY	462
PURPLE	TRANSMISSION DIAGNOSTIC	453
PURPLE	POWER SERVO TO CLIMATE CONTROL UNIT (AMP)	246
PURPLE	ELECTRONIC CLUSTER FROM TRIP RECALL SWITCH IN KEYBOARD	288
PURPLE BASE	EATC RH SUNLOAD SENSOR POSITIVE	479
PURPLE-LT BLUE	WINDOW REG. SW. TO BACK WINDOW SW.	405
PURPLE-LT BLUE	SPEED CONTROL SENSE EEC MODULE TO CLUSTER	683
PURPLE-LT BLUE	AIR BAG DIAGNOSTIC MODULE (MONITOR) TO CENTER SENSOR	620
PURPLE-LT BLUE	POWER FEED-SWITCH TO REAR AMPLIFIER	828
PURPLE-LT BLUE	CLICKER RELAY TERM. NO. 4 TO AIR VALVE ASSY.	263
PURPLE-LT BLUE	AMPLIFIER FEEDBACK POTENTIOMETER FEED	147
PURPLE-LT GREEN	DESTINATION SWITCH TO MESSAGE CENTER	154
PURPLE-LT GREEN	AIR BAG DIAGNOSTIC MODULE (MONITOR) TO RH SENSOR	618
PURPLE-LT GREEN	REAR WASHER PUMP FEED	946
PURPLE-LT GREEN	VEHICLE MAINTENANCE MONITOR MODULE TO ELEC. INSTR. CLUST. SENSE	907
PURPLE-LT GREEN	WINDOW REG. SW. TO BACK WINDOW SW.	404
PURPLE-LT GREEN	AIR SUSPENSION HEIGHT SENSOR LO — L.F.	423
PURPLE-LT GREEN	REAR AIR SUSPENSION HEIGHT SENSOR FEED	429
PURPLE-ORANGE	AIR SUSPENSION SWITCH FEED	417
PURPLE-ORANGE	AIR BAG READY INDICATOR L (MONITOR) TO SAFING SENSOR	612
PURPLE-ORANGE	MIRROR SWITCH VERTICAL RIGHT	943
PURPLE-ORANGE	CIGAR LIGHTER LAMP FEED	131
PURPLE-ORANGE	FUSED ACCY FEED #2	298
PURPLE-ORANGE	AUTOLAMP AMPLIFIER TO CONTROL SWITCH	220
PURPLE-ORANGE	SHIFT SOLENOID 2	315
PURPLE-WHITE	AMPLIFIER SPEAKER SWITCH FEED TO RIGHT REAR SPEAKER	278
PURPLE-WHITE	MEMORY SEAT SWITCH ENABLE	266
PURPLE-WHITE	AIR BAG DIAGNOSTIC MODULE (MONITOR) TO SAFING SENSOR	623
PURPLE-WHITE	RH MIRROR UP/DOWN POSITION SENSOR	957
PURPLE-WHITE	SEAT BELT WARNING LAMP TO WARNING LAMP SWITCH	520
PURPLE-WHITE	HEATER & A/C CONTROL SW (LO-HI-NORM) TO RESISTOR (LOW RANGE)	758
PURPLE-WHITE	MULTIPLEX SERVICE REMINDER RESET	733
PURPLE-WHITE	BRAKE WARNING SWITCH TO INDICATOR LAMP	977
PURPLE-WHITE	RIGHT MOTOR — PASSENGER — B	865
PURPLE-YELLOW	ELECT SHIFT 4 x 4 MODULE TO MOTOR POSITION #5	771
PURPLE-YELLOW	TURN SIGNAL SWITCH TO LH CORNERING LAMP	380
PURPLE-YELLOW	LEFT MOTOR — DRIVER — A	860
PURPLE-YELLOW	FUEL INJECTION PUMP POSITION SENSOR	239
PURPLE-YELLOW	BRAKE FLUID LEVEL UNIT TO MESSAGE CENTER	128
PURPLE-YELLOW	ECONOMY SWITCH TO MESSAGE CENTER	153
PURPLE-YELLOW	DECK LID SOLENOID FEED	84
PURPLE-YELLOW	TRANSMISSION CLUTCH CONTROL TO EEC MODULE	480
RED	KEYLESS DOOR LOCK SWITCH DATA BIT 5 TO MODULE	123
RED	TRAILER CONTROLLER FEED	50
RED	SUPPLEMENTAL ALTERNATOR STATOR A TERM. TO WINDSHIELD	70
RED	WINDSHIELD WIPER SW. TO WINDSHIELD WIPER MOTOR	63
RED	18 GA FUSE LINK	301
RED	HORIZONTAL SEAT REG. MOTOR TO RELAY	180
RED	REAR VIEW OUTSIDE MIRROR FEED	388
RED	POWER LUMBAR FEED	490
RED	FUEL TANK SELECTOR TO FUEL PUMP FRONT	786

* IN SOME CASES, THERE MAY BE ADDITIONAL CIRCUIT
FUNCTIONS INCLUDED IN THE CIRCUIT DESCRIPTION LISTED.

STANDARD CIRCUIT CHART (BY COLOR)

COLOR	DESCRIPTION*	CIRCUIT
RED	DIESEL WATER IN FUEL SENDER TO WARNING LAMP	643
RED	BATTERY FEED CAMPER	666
RED	AMPLIFIER POWER RETURN	694
RED	MOONROOF RELAY TO MICRO SWITCH CLOSED	692
RED	HEADLAMP DIMMER SWITCH OVERRIDE TO RHEOSTAT	527
RED	MPH/KPH SWITCH TO MESSAGE CENTER	506
RED	MULTIPLEX WINDSHIELD WIPER MAIN	698
RED	L.H. REMOTE MIRROR MOTOR FEED—C.W.	540
RED	HEATED WINDSHIELD CONTROL TO ALT STATOR TERM	581
RED	SOLENOID	605
RED	STEERING RATE SENSOR TERMINAL A CONTROL MODULE	633
RED	DOOR WIRE	630
RED	STEERING RATE SENSOR TERMINAL A CONTROL MODULE	633
RED	BATTERY FEED TO AUX. FUEL SELECTOR SWITCH	973
RED	TOP CONTROL RELAY TO MOTOR—DOWN	903
RED	RIGHT DOOR OPEN — PASSENGER	863
RED	POWER OUTPUT FROM EEC RELAY	361
RED-BLACK	MEMORY MIRROR MODULE POSITION +	891
RED-BLACK	VENT CROSSOVER FEED	879
RED-BLACK	MODE SELECT SWITCH LAMP	833
RED-BLACK	WATER TEMP. WARNING LAMP TO WATER TEMP. SW. (HOT)	647
RED-BLACK	FRONT AIR SUSPENSION HEIGHT SENSOR FEED	426
RED-BLACK	ELECT. ENG. CONTL. MOD. TO WIDE OPEN THROTTLE KICKER SOC.	378
RED-BLACK	FUEL WARNING RELAY CONTROL	366
RED-BLACK	RADIO "SEEK UP"	368
RED-BLACK	ECU TO VACUUM SWITCH 3	214
RED-BLACK	LAMP RETURN TO PULSE WITH DIMMER	235
RED-BLACK	LEFT FRONT WINDOW REGULATOR SWITCH TO RIGHT FRONT WINDOW REGULATOR MOTOR	314
RED-BLACK	LEFT FRONT WINDOW REGULATOR SWITCH TO RIGHT REAR WINDOW REGULATOR MOTOR	320
RED-BLACK	HEADLAMP DIMMER SWITCH TO LOW BEAMS	13
RED-BLACK	EEC TO EXHAUST GAS OXYGEN SENSOR (#2 IN DUAL SYSTEM)	94
RED-LT BLUE	STARTER CONTROL	32
RED-LT BLUE	WINDOW REGULATOR SWITCH FEED	170
RED-LT BLUE	ANTI-THEFT MODULE TO ALARM RELAY	340
RED-LT BLUE	LEFT FRONT WINDOW REGULATOR SWITCH TO LEFT REAR WINDOW REGULATOR MOTOR	317
RED-LT BLUE	SEAT PROCESSOR TO RECLINER MOTOR "DOWN"	440
RED-LT BLUE	SEAT REGULATOR SWITCH TO FRONT MOTOR (LH)	979
RED-LT BLUE	SEAT REGULATOR SWITCH TO FRONT MOTOR (RH)	985
RED-LT BLUE	VENT CROSSOVER FEED	880
RED-LT BLUE	AMPLIFIER TO SPEED SENSOR RETURN	901
RED-LT GREEN	COIL TERM. OF IGN. SW. TO BRAKE SKID CONTROL MODULE	602
RED-LT GREEN	STOPLAMP SW. TO STOPLAMPS	810
RED-LT GREEN	HEATER & A/C CONTROL SW. (DE-FOG) TO INLET AIR CONTROL SOLENOID	766
RED-LT GREEN	SEAT REGULATOR SWITCH TO REAR MOTOR (LH)	983
RED-LT GREEN	TRACTION CONTROL MALFUNCTION WARNING LAMP	961
RED-LT GREEN	SEAT REGULATOR SWITCH TO REAR MOTOR (RH)	989
RED-LT GREEN	REAR TILT POSITION SENSE	436
RED-LT GREEN	IGN. SW. COIL TERM. TO CIRCUIT BREAKER	454
RED-LT GREEN	IGNITION SWITCH TO IGNITION COIL "BATT." TERMINAL	16
RED-LT GREEN	MODULE TO THROTTLE ACTUATOR	69
RED-LT GREEN	HEADLAMP BULB OUTAGE TO MESSAGE CENTER	130
RED-ORANGE	KEYLESS DOOR LOCK OUTPUT (DRIVER) FROM MODULE	163
RED-ORANGE	IDLE SPEED CONTROL TO EGR VENT SOLENOID	322
RED-ORANGE	BLOWER MOTOR TO SWITCH — LO	260
RED-ORANGE	REHEAT AMPLIFIER TO HEAT DUCT THERMISTOR	788
RED-ORANGE	W/S WIPER ARM RH TO W/S WIPER SWITCH	955
RED-ORANGE	DCP MODULE TO WIPER GOVERNOR RELAY	593
RED-ORANGE	MIRROR SWITCH HORIZONTAL LEFT	942
RED-ORANGE	STARTING MOTOR RELAY SHUNT TO AMMETER	655
RED-PINK	RH REAR SENSOR (HIGH) TO MODULE	523
RED-PINK	HEATER & A/C CONTROL SW. (HI-NORM) TO RESISTOR (LOW RANGE)	756
RED-PINK	ANTENNA SWITCH TO POWER ANTENNA (UP)	745
RED-PINK	SPEED CONTROL AMPLIFIER TO CRUISE LAMP INTERFACE MODULE	202
RED-PINK	DOOR JAMB SWITCH TO BUZZER	159
RED-WHITE	RH REAR STOP & TURN BULB OUTAGE	105
RED-WHITE	TEMP. GAUGE TO TEMP. SENDING UNIT	39
RED-WHITE	SWITCH TO WARNING LAMP	42
RED-WHITE	HEATER & A/C CONTROL SW. (HI-NORM) TO BLOWER MOTOR SW. RELAY	757
RED-WHITE	C.B. ON/OFF	718
RED-WHITE	RADIO MEMORY	729
RED-WHITE	FUSED BATTERY FEED TO AIR BAG DIAGNOSTIC MODULE	937
RED-WHITE	SEAT REGULATOR SWITCH TO HORZ. MOTOR (RH)	987
RED-WHITE	SEAT REGULATOR SWITCH TO HORZ. MOTOR (LH)	981
RED-WHITE	ELECTRONIC SHOCK SENSOR B	835
RED-WHITE	MEMORY SEAT TO NEUTRAL SENSE MODULE	899
RED-WHITE	ELECTRIC SHIFT MODULE TO NEUTRAL START SWITCH	463
RED-WHITE	HORIZONTAL POSITION SENSE	438
RED-WHITE	EMERGENCY WARNING FLASHER FEED	383
RED-WHITE	LH MIRROR LEFT/RIGHT POSITION SENSOR	949
RED-YELLOW	WINDOW REG. SW. TO WINDOW REG. MOTOR	334
RED-YELLOW	ELECTRONIC SHOCK SENSOR A	834
RED-YELLOW	WARNING LAMPS FEED	640
RED-YELLOW	SUPERCHARGER SOLENOID #2	966
RED-YELLOW	INERTIA SWITCH TO FUEL TANK SELECTOR SWITCH	670
RED-YELLOW	HEADLAMP DIMMER SWITCH FEED	15
RED-YELLOW	FUEL PRESSURE BOOST SOLENOID	236
RED-YELLOW	TRAILER BACKUP LAMPS	963
RED-YELLOW	WINDOW REG. MASTER CONT. SW. TO WINDOW REG. SW. FEED	328
TAN	EEC MODULE TO MALFUNCTION INDICATOR LITE	657

COLOR	DESCRIPTION*	CIRCUIT
TAN	MULTIPLEX SERVICE REMINDER	734
TAN	BOOST SENSOR TO CONTROL UNIT	748
TAN	ABS MODULE FRONT LEFT WHEEL SPEED OUTPUT	998
TAN	SWITCH TO FADER LEFT CHANNEL FEED	831
TAN	VALVE #1 TO MODULE	495
TAN	RIGHT LIMIT — B — PASSENGER	873
TAN	WINDOW REG. SW. TO BACK WINDOW AUX. SW.	406
TAN	AIR SUSPENSION HEIGHT SENSOR HI — R.F.	424
TAN	FUEL INJECTOR #1 CYLINDER OR BANK #1	555
TAN-BLACK	PRESSURE SWITCH TO KEY SWITCH	409
TAN-BLACK	BRAKE WEAR SENSOR	457
TAN-BLACK	WINDOW REG. SW. REAR TO LIMIT SW.	407
TAN-BLACK	ABS MODULE REAR RIGHT WHEEL SPEED OUTPUT	999
TAN-BLACK	ELECTRONIC RIDE SHOCK FEEDBACK ACTUATOR TO RELAY	845
TAN-BLACK	DIGITAL AUDIO DISC LOGIC SENSOR	849
TAN-BLACK	MEMORY MIRROR MODULE TO LH VERTICAL DRIVE	897
TAN-BLACK	HIGH ELECTRIC DRIVE COOLING FAN	559
TAN-BLACK	LH FRONT SENSOR (LOW) TO MODULE	522
TAN-BLACK	AIR BAG DIAGNOSTIC MODULE (MONITOR) TO LH SENSOR	622
TAN-BLACK	VEHICLE MAINTENANCE MONITOR MODULE TO ENGINE STRAP	908
TAN-BLACK	MODULATOR TO THERMO. SWITCH	939
TAN-LT BLUE	MASS AIR FLOW RETURN	968
TAN-LT BLUE	INDICATOR RELAY TO RH TURN LAMP	817
TAN-LT BLUE	AUTOLAMP AMPLIFIER TO RHEOSTAT	216
TAN-LT BLUE	FEEDBACK CARB. COIL 4	98
TAN-LT GREEN	FEEDBACK CARB. COIL 3	97
TAN-LT GREEN	ANTI-THEFT SYSTEM SWITCH FEED	23
TAN-LT GREEN	MILEAGE SENSOR TO EEC MODULE	223
TAN-LT GREEN	AMPLIFIER SWITCH FEED TO RIGHT REAR SPEAKER	825
TAN-LT GREEN	BRAKE FLUID RES. SWITCH TO MODULE	512
TAN-LT GREEN	TURN SIGNAL RELAY TO TURN SIGNAL FLASHER	494
TAN-ORANGE	LH FRONT SENSOR (HIGH) TO MODULE	521
TAN-ORANGE	EEC MODULE—DATA PLUS	914
TAN-ORANGE	FOG LAMP SW. TO FOG LAMP	478
TAN-ORANGE	COOLANT TEMPERATURE SWITCH TO CONTROL RELAY	197
TAN-ORANGE	AIR COND. SW. (LO) TO AIR COND. BLOWER MOTOR	184
TAN-ORANGE	FEEDBACK CARB. COIL 2	96
TAN-RED	FEEDBACK CARB. COIL 1	95
TAN-RED	RELAY TO MAP LAMP SWITCH	133
TAN-RED	MCV MODULE TO VIP FUNCTION TESTER	201
TAN-RED	THERMACTOR TIMER TO RELAY	252
TAN-RED	ELECTRONIC RIDE SHOCK METAL OXIDE VERISTOR	846
TAN-RED	MEMORY MIRROR MODULE TO LH HORIZONTAL DRIVE	898
TAN-RED	FUEL INJECTOR #7 CYLINDER	561
TAN-RED	POWER RELAY TO FUSE LINK	533
TAN-RED	VALVE #6 TO MODULE	510
TAN-RED	MULTIPLEX COMPUTER FEED	792
TAN-RED	HEATED WINDSHIELD TRIGGER CIRCUIT SW. TO MODULE	681
TAN-RED	WINDOW REG. SW. FRONT TO LIMIT SW.	408
TAN-WHITE	AMPLIFIER SWITCH FEED TO LEFT REAR SPEAKER	827
TAN-WHITE	IDLE RPM SOLENOID TO CONTROL UNIT	744
TAN-WHITE	INDICATOR RELAY TO LH TURN LAMP	818
TAN-WHITE	EMISSION SPEED SENSOR TO MODULATOR CONTROL	934
TAN-WHITE	TAILLAMP SWITCH FEED	195
TAN-WHITE	INTERLOCK MODULE TO CENTER SEAT SENSOR SWITCH	87
TAN-WHITE	TRANSMISSION OVERDRIVE SWITCH TO EEC MODULE	224
TAN-YELLOW	A/C PRESSURE SWITCH TO CONTROL RELAY	198
TAN-YELLOW	TONE GENERATOR	183
TAN-YELLOW	AIR COND. CONDENSOR THERMAL SWITCH FEED	509
TAN-YELLOW	FUSE LINK TO MOTOR RELAY	537
TAN-YELLOW	IGNITION COIL NEGATIVE TERMINAL	11
TAN-YELLOW HASH	FEED TO VACUUM DOOR LOCK SWITCH	114
WHITE	KEYLESS DOOR LOCK OUTPUT (ALL) FROM MODULE	134
WHITE	ASH RECEPTACLE LAMP FEED	17
WHITE	WINDSHIELD WIPER SW. TO WINDSHIELD WIPER MOTOR	58
WHITE	SUPPLEMENTAL ALTERNATOR STATOR B TERM. TO WINDSHIELD	71
WHITE	REAR WINDOW REGULATOR SWITCH FEED	176
WHITE	KEYLESS DOOR LOCK SEAT SWITCH SENSOR TO MODULE	177
WHITE	TRAILER GROUND	206
WHITE	ELECTRONIC CLUSTER FROM GAUGE SELECT SWITCH IN KEYBOARD	289
WHITE	SPEAKER VOICE COIL RETURN AMP INPUT	281
WHITE	SEAT REG. SW. TO VERT. SOLENOID BATT. TERM.	307
WHITE	R.H. REMOTE MIRROR SOLENOID CONTROL	545
WHITE	RHEOSTAT TO SENSOR	508
WHITE	DOOR WIRE	628
WHITE	AWD MODULE TO AWD FUNCTION LAMP	994
WHITE	ELECT SHIFT 4 X 4 MODULE TO MOTOR POSITION #4	770
WHITE	C.B. MIC-AUDIO	713
WHITE	RELAY COIL FEED #3	725
WHITE	RIGHT REAR SHOCK DAMPENING RELAY TO CONTROL MODULE	650
WHITE	ACTUATOR POSITION SENSOR RIGHT REAR	843
WHITE	VALVE #3 TO MODULE	497
WHITE	INERTIA SWITCH TO MODULE	866
WHITE	ELECT. ENG. CONTL. MOD. TO EXHAUST HEAT CONTRL SOC.	377
WHITE	FUEL INJECTOR #2 CYLINDER OR BANK #2	556
WHITE	TIME DELAY RELAY	332
WHITE	REARVIEW OUTSIDE MIRROR COUNTERCLOCKWISE	412
WHITE BASE	LH REAR TAIL LAMP BULB OUTAGE	102
WHITE-BLACK	THERMOCOUPLE 2 NEG. TO EXHAUST SYST. OVERTEMP PROTECT MODULE	92
WHITE-BLACK	ELAPSED TIME SWITCH TO MESSAGE CENTER	165
WHITE-BLACK	ALTERNATOR REG. "S" TERM. TO ALTERNATOR "S" TERM.	4
WHITE-BLACK	LF WINDOW REG. SW. TO LF WINDOW REG. MOTOR	226

* IN SOME CASES, THERE MAY BE ADDITIONAL CIRCUIT FUNCTIONS INCLUDED IN THE CIRCUIT DESCRIPTION LISTED.

STANDARD CIRCUIT CHART (BY COLOR)

COLOR	DESCRIPTION*	CIRCUIT	COLOR	DESCRIPTION*	CIRCUIT
WHITE-BLACK	5V TO-MESSAGE CENTER TO DISPLAY	168	YELLOW	POWER "THIGH" BOLSTER UP	491
WHITE-BLACK	HEADLAMP SWITCH TO AUXILIARY LAMPS	188	YELLOW	EGR VALVE TO EEC MODULE FEED	362
WHITE-BLACK	THROTTLE KICKER RELAY TO MCU MODULE	393	YELLOW	C.B. B-DIGIT	716
WHITE-BLACK	ACTUATOR POSITION SENSOR LEFT FRONT	840	YELLOW	MULTIPLEX WIPER RATE	700
WHITE-BLACK	MODULE TO MOTOR FEED	662	YELLOW	ANTI-LOCK MODULE TO ANTI-LOCK CONTROL VALVE	678
WHITE-BLACK	C.B. PUSH TO TALK	702	YELLOW	ELECT SHIFT 4 × 4 MODULE TO MOTOR CONTROL COUNTER CLOCKWISE	777
WHITE-BLACK	MULTIPLEX REVERSE DIMMING	731	YELLOW	AIR SUSPENSION DIODE SWITCH TO CONTROL MODULE	635
WHITE-BLACK	THERMACTOR CLUTCH RELAY TO CLUTCH	567	YELLOW	ALT POWER RELAY TO CONTROL MODULE	583
WHITE-BLACK	WASHER CONTROL SWITCH FEED	950	YELLOW	CONVERTIBLE TOP RELAY TO SWITCH	586
WHITE-LT BLUE	MODULE TO DOWN SWITCH	659	YELLOW	AIR SUSPENSION DIODE SWITCH TO CONTROL MODULE	635
WHITE-LT BLUE	SURE TRACK DIAGNOSTIC	606	YELLOW	DOOR WIRE	631
WHITE-LT BLUE	C.B. VOLUME CONTROL	709	YELLOW	OIL PRESSURE SWITCH TO CUTOUT RELAY	669
WHITE-LT BLUE	TEMP SWITCH TO WARNING DEVICE	737	YELLOW	AMPLIFIER TO RHEOSTAT	507
WHITE-LT BLUE	STARTER INTERRUPT RELAY TO NEUTRAL START SWITCH	900	YELLOW	L.H. REMOTE MIRROR SOLENOID CONTROL	542
WHITE-LT BLUE	VEHICLE MAINTENANCE MONITOR MODULE TO OIL TEMP OUTPUT	906	YELLOW	LEFT REAR AIR INPUT RETURN	859
WHITE-LT BLUE	MODULE TO SWITCH	465	YELLOW	SEAT BELT INDICATOR LAMP TO MODULE	871
WHITE-LT BLUE	FUSED ACCY FEED #3	294	YELLOW	VENT SWITCH TO LEFT FRONT VENT MOTOR	887
WHITE-LT BLUE	ELECT. ENG. CONTL. MOD. TO IDLE SPD. CONTL. MOTOR #1	264	YELLOW	TOP CONTROL RELAY TO MOTOR — UP	902
WHITE-LT BLUE	RH FRONT TURN SIGNAL LAMP	2	YELLOW-BLACK	COIL "A" TO DISTRIBUTORLESS IGNITION MODULE	850
WHITE-LT BLUE	DISTRIBUTOR ELECTRONIC CONTROL FEED	20	YELLOW-BLACK	WINDOW SWITCH TO LEFT REAR MOTOR	884
WHITE-LT GREEN	RH AND LH REAR RUNNING LAMP BULB OUTAGE	110	YELLOW-BLACK	ACCELERATE DECELERATE SENSOR RETURN	837
WHITE-LT GREEN	AUX WATER VALVE FEED	456	YELLOW-BLACK	POWER RELAY BATTERY FEED	554
WHITE-LT GREEN	C.B. SCAN SWITCH	710	YELLOW-BLACK	RH FRONT SENSOR (LOW) TO MODULE	516
WHITE-LT GREEN	BLOWER MOTOR RELAY TO ENG. WATER TEMP. SWITCH (COLD)	761	YELLOW-BLACK	MIRROR SWITCH COMMON	945
WHITE-LT GREEN	OVERDRIVE CANCEL INDICATOR LAMP	911	YELLOW-BLACK	RELAY TO ATC CONTROL	575
WHITE-LT GREEN	WATER TEMP. WARNING LAMP TO WATER TEMP. SW. (COLD)	642	YELLOW-BLACK	LOW WASHER LEVEL TO SENSOR	793
WHITE-LT GREEN	RH MIRROR LEFT/RIGHT MOTOR COMMON	952	YELLOW-BLACK	REMOTE DEFROST	727
WHITE-LT GREEN	SPEAKER VOICE COIL FEED — FRONT (RIGHT CHANNEL)	805	YELLOW-BLACK	ELECT. ENG. CONTL. MOD. TO TEST CONN #2	382
WHITE-ORANGE	HEATER & A/C CONTROL SW. TO INST. PANEL THERMISTOR	790	YELLOW-BLACK	AWD MODULE TO TRANSFER CASE CLUTCH	992
WHITE-ORANGE	AIR BAG READY INDICATOR L (DEPLOY) TO SAFING SENSOR	611	YELLOW-BLACK	GLOW PLUG TO CONTROL MODULE	472
WHITE-ORANGE	C.B. DOWN SWITCH	703	YELLOW-BLACK	ELECTRONIC CONTROL UNIT TO ACCELERATION SOLENOID	46
WHITE-ORANGE	RADIO SEEK	728	YELLOW-BLACK	RADIO ANTENNA SWITCH FEED	137
WHITE-ORANGE	RELEASE LEVER WARN INDICATOR LAMP — CONSOLE	877	YELLOW-BLACK	KEYLESS DOOR LOCK SWITCH DATA BIT 3 TO MODULE	121
WHITE-ORANGE	ACTUATOR POSITION SENSOR LEFT REAR	842	YELLOW-BLACK	SIGNAL UNIT LAMP TO FUEL SIGNAL RELAY	215
WHITE-ORANGE	LEFT FRONT AIR INPUT RETURN	857	YELLOW-BLACK	LEFT FRONT WINDOW REGULATOR SWITCH TO RIGHT FRONT WINDOW REGULATOR MOTOR	313
WHITE-ORANGE	ELECTRIC PVS TO MCU MODULE	392	YELLOW-BLACK	LEFT FRONT WINDOW REGULATOR SWITCH TO RIGHT REAR WINDOW REGULATOR MOTOR	319
WHITE-ORANGE	INTERLOCK MODULE TO CENTER BUCKLE SWITCH	83	YELLOW-LT BLUE	LEFT FRONT WINDOW REGULATOR SWITCH TO LEFT REAR WINDOW REGULATOR MOTOR	316
WHITE-ORANGE	RESET SWITCH TO MESSAGE CENTER	166	YELLOW-LT BLUE	HEATER & A/C CONTROL SW. (DE-ICE) TO CLIMATE CONTROL UNIT	248
WHITE-ORANGE	MEMORY SEAT SWITCH LAMP DRIVE	272	YELLOW-LT BLUE	SPEED INPUT TO MESSAGE CENTER	136
WHITE-ORANGE	THERMACTOR AIR BYPASS (TAB)	190	YELLOW-LT BLUE	STARTING MOTOR TO STARTING MOTOR RELAY	113
WHITE-PINK	LOW OIL LEVEL RELAY TO SENSOR	258	YELLOW-LT BLUE	POSITION SENSE RETURN	435
WHITE-PINK	ECU TO VACUUM SWITCH 2	213	YELLOW-LT BLUE	HORN SWITCH FEED	460
WHITE-PINK	SERVO VENT SOLENOID TO CONTROL TRANSISTOR	146	YELLOW-LT BLUE	SELECTOR SWITCH TO AFT AXLE TANK	675
WHITE-PINK	TACHOMETER FEED	648	YELLOW-LT BLUE	SEAT REGULATOR SWITCH TO FRONT MOTOR (RH)	984
WHITE-PINK	BUZZER TO WARNING INDICATOR RELAY	160	YELLOW-LT BLUE	LH UP/DOWN MOTOR COMMON	948
WHITE-PINK	STARTER CONTROL TO INTERLOCK MODULE	33	YELLOW-LT BLUE	SEAT REGULATOR SWITCH TO FRONT MOTOR (LH)	990
WHITE-PINK	FUEL FILLER DOOR RELEASE SWITCH TO FUEL FILLER DOOR RELEASE SOLENOID	482	YELLOW-LT BLUE	SEAT REGULATOR SWITCH TO FRONT MOTOR (LH)	978
WHITE-PINK	HEATER & A/C CONTROL SW. (DEFOG) TO DEFROST CONT. SOLENOID	775	YELLOW-LT BLUE	WINDOW SWITCH TO LEFT REAR MOTOR	885
WHITE-PURPLE	SENSOR AMPLIFY UNIT TO CONTROL UNIT #4	760	YELLOW-LT GREEN	SEAT REGULATOR SWITCH TO REAR MOTOR (LH)	982
WHITE-PURPLE	C.B. SQUELCH POT	701	YELLOW-LT GREEN	AIR COND. CONTROL SW. TO FRESH-AIR RECIRC. DOOR SOLENOID	660
WHITE-PURPLE	RH MIRROR UP/DOWN MOTOR COMMON	953	YELLOW-LT GREEN	SPLICE #2 TO MODULE	529
WHITE-PURPLE	AMPLIFIER SWITCH GROUND TO RIGHT REAR SPEAKER	824	YELLOW-LT GREEN	SPLICE #3 TO PRESSURE SWITCH	534
WHITE-PURPLE	POWER FEED-SWITCH TO FRONT AMPLIFIER	829	YELLOW-LT GREEN	FLUID SWITCH TO GROUND STUD	550
WHITE-PURPLE	MEMORY MIRROR MODULE LH VERTICAL POSITION	895	YELLOW-LT GREEN	SPLICE #2 TO SPLICE #3	551
WHITE-PURPLE	FUSE PANEL FEED TO RELAY	326	YELLOW-LT GREEN	SPLICE #2 TO COUP GROUND "B"	552
WHITE-PURPLE	DECK LID SWITCH TO ANTI-THEFT MODULE	26	YELLOW-LT GREEN	ALT. SHUNT TO AMMETER	654
WHITE-PURPLE	AUTOLAMP AMPLIFIER TO SENSOR	218	YELLOW-LT GREEN	MODULE TO RELEASE SOLENOID	664
WHITE-PURPLE	FUSED ACCY FEED #1	296	YELLOW-LT GREEN	SEAT REGULATOR SWITCH TO REAR MOTOR (RH)	988
WHITE-PURPLE	FUEL METERING CONTROL LEVER ACTUATOR 2 PLUS	312	YELLOW-LT GREEN	POSITION SENSE ENABLE	437
WHITE-PURPLE	TO TEST CONNECTOR	209	YELLOW-LT GREEN	MOVABLE STEERING COLUMN SOLENOID FEED	375
WHITE-RED	SPEAKER VOICE COIL FEED FRONT (R. CHANNEL) AMP INPUT	279	YELLOW-LT GREEN	POWER STEERING PRESSURE SWITCH	330
WHITE-RED	COLD START TIMING RETARD SOLENOID	240	YELLOW-LT GREEN	TRANSMISSION OVERDRIVE SWITCH TO HEAT MODULE	324
WHITE-RED	EEC MODULE TO TRANSMISSION	912	YELLOW-LT GREEN	HORN RELAY TO HORN	6
WHITE-RED	H L SW. TO CHIMES	257	YELLOW-LT GREEN	WINDOW REGULATOR RELAY FEED	193
WHITE-RED	OIL PRESSURE INDICATOR TO OIL PRESSURE SENDING UNIT	31	YELLOW-LT. GREEN	GROUND STUD TO SPLICE #2	548
WHITE-RED	RH REAR TAIL LAMP BULB OUTAGE	103	YELLOW-RED	RH FRONT SENSOR (HIGH) TO MODULE	514
WHITE-RED	AIR PUMP SOLENOID SIGNAL	100	YELLOW-RED	BLOWER MOTOR SPEED CONTROLLER TO RESISTOR #2 (MED.)	752
WHITE-RED	FLASHER TO EMERGENCY WARNING SWITCH	385	YELLOW-RED	HEATER & A/C CONTROL SW. TO BLOWER RELAY SW.	753
WHITE-RED	ACTUATOR POSITION SENSOR RIGHT FRONT	841	YELLOW-RED	COIL "B" TO DISTRIBUTORLESS IGNITION MODULE	851
WHITE-RED	LAMP RELAY TO MARKER LAMPS	667	YELLOW-RED	LH MIRROR LEFT/RIGHT MOTOR COMMON	947
WHITE-RED	PROCESSOR TO THERMACTOR CLUTCH RELAY	566	YELLOW-RED	WINDOW REG. SW. TO WINDOW REG. MOTOR	333
WHITE-RED	FUEL PUMP RESISTOR TO RELAY	922	YELLOW-RED	HOT WATER TEMP. RELAY TO HOT WATER TEMP. SENDING UNIT	45
WHITE-YELLOW	AIR BAG DIAGNOSTIC MODULE (DEPLOY) TO LH SENSOR	621	YELLOW-RED	WINDSHIELD WIPER SW. TO WINDSHIELD WIPER MOTOR	61
WHITE-YELLOW	C.B. UP SWITCH	707	YELLOW-RED	SERVO FEEDBACK POTENTIOMETER SIGNAL TO AMPLIFIER	148
WHITE-YELLOW	CHOKE RELAY TO MCU MODULE	391	YELLOW-RED	STOP AND TURN BULB OUTAGE TO MESSAGE CENTER	135
WHITE-YELLOW	MESSAGE CENTER OUTPUT CLOCK TO DISPLAY	167	YELLOW-RED	ELECT. ENG. CONTRL. MOD. TO KNOCK SENSOR	310
WHITE-YELLOW	ELECTRONIC PRESSURE CONTROL	925	YELLOW-WHITE	ALTERNATOR OUTPUT	36
WHITE-YELLOW	POWER SERVO TO CLIMATE CONTROL UNIT (AMP)	247	YELLOW-WHITE	FUEL GAUGE TO FUEL GAUGE SENDER	29
YELLOW	SWITCH ON TO RELAY	275	YELLOW-WHITE	THERMAL SW. TO CLIMATE CONTROL UNIT	244
YELLOW	ELECTRONIC CLUSTER FROM TRIP RESET SWITCH IN KEYBOARD	286	YELLOW-WHITE	SEAT PROCESSOR TO RECLINER MOTOR "UP"	439
YELLOW	12 GA FUSE LINK	303	YELLOW-WHITE	COIL "C" TO DISTRIBUTORLESS IGNITION MODULE	852
YELLOW	HORIZONTAL SEAT REG. MOTOR TO RELAY	179	YELLOW-WHITE	ELECT SHIFT 4 X 4 MODULE TO MOTOR POSITION #1	762
YELLOW	LF WINDOW REG. SW. TO LF WINDOW REG. MOTOR	227	YELLOW-WHITE	HEATED WINDSHIELD CONTROL TO HEATED WINDSHIELD SWITCH	738
YELLOW	KEYLESS DOOR LOCK SWITCH DATA BIT 4 TO MODULE	122	YELLOW-WHITE	SEAT REGULATOR SWITCH TO HORZ. MOTOR (LH)	980
YELLOW	TRAILER LH TURN SIGNAL	52	YELLOW-WHITE	SEAT REGULATOR SWITCH TO FRONT MOTOR (RH)	986
YELLOW	BATTERY TO LOAD	37			
YELLOW	REARVIEW OUTSIDE MIRROR UP	410			

*IN SOME CASES, THERE MAY BE ADDITIONAL CIRCUIT
FUNCTIONS INCLUDED IN THE CIRCUIT DESCRIPTION LISTED.

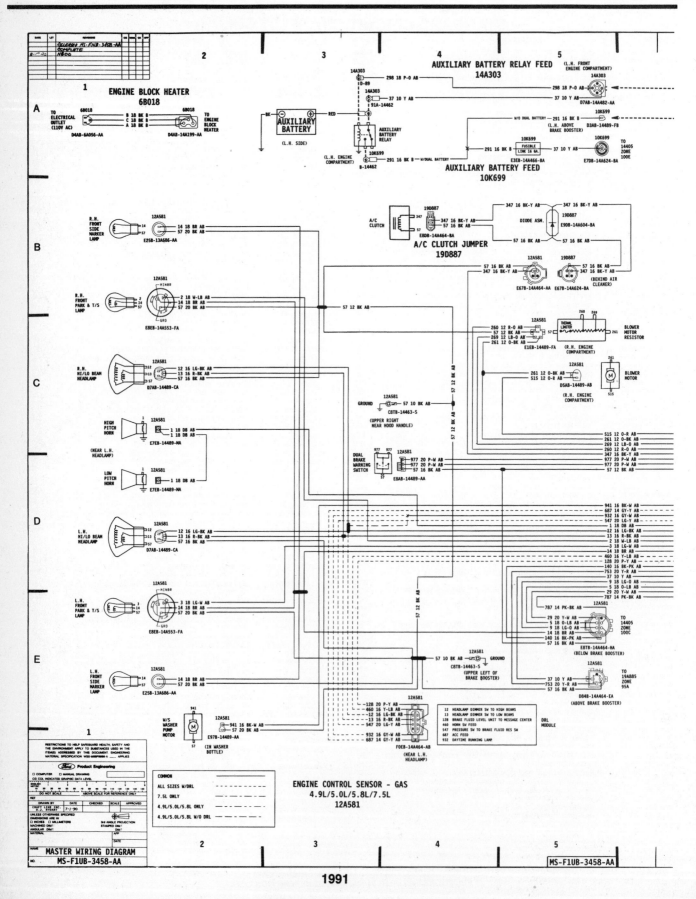

ENGINE CONTROL SENSOR - GAS
4.9L/5.0L/5.8L/7.5L
12A581

MASTER WIRING DIAGRAM
NO. MS-F1UB-3458-AA

1991

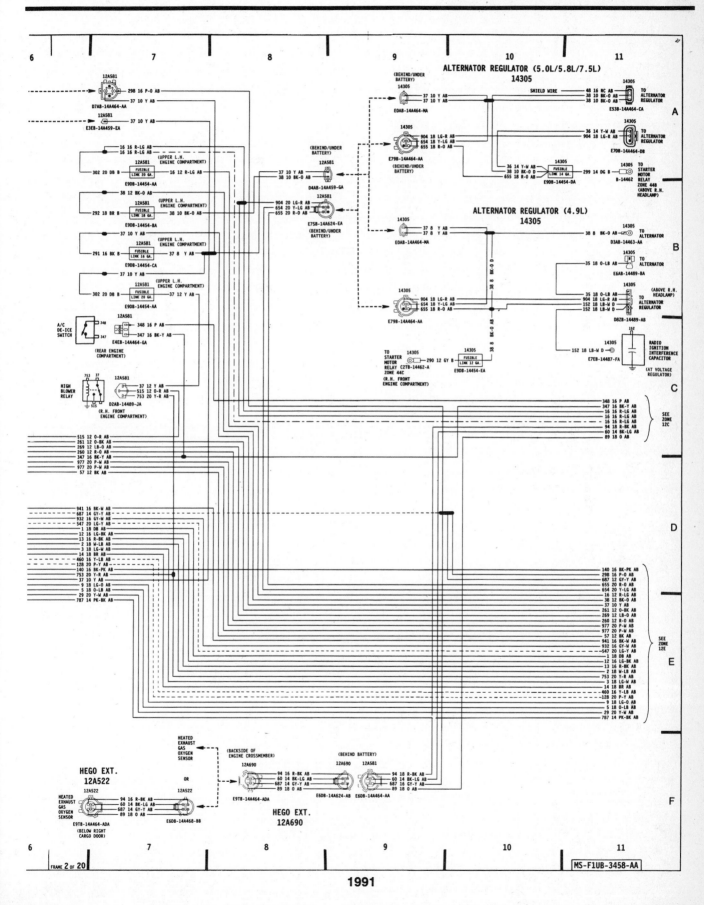

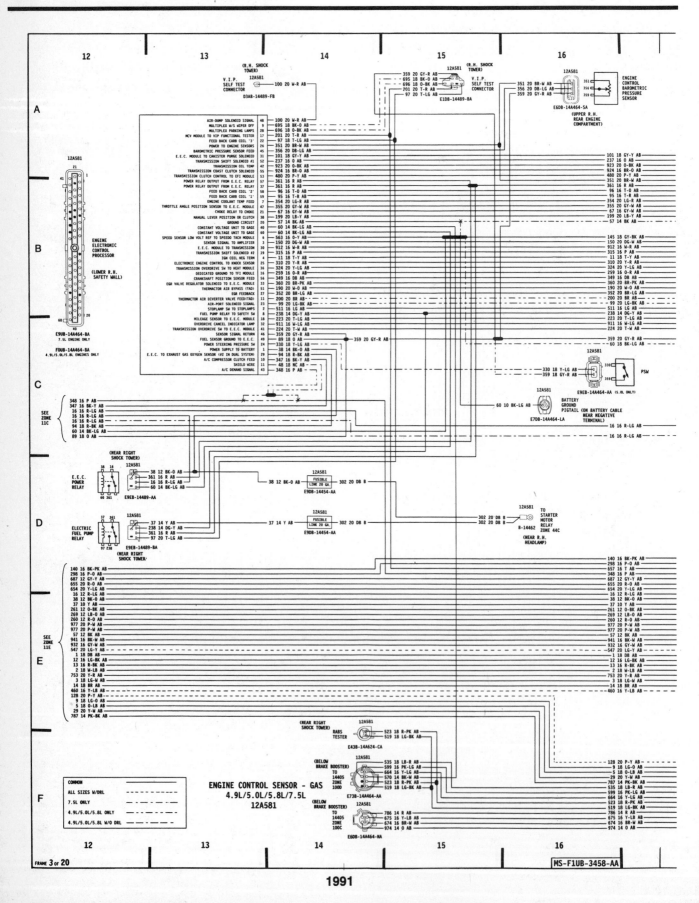

ENGINE CONTROL SENSOR - GAS
4.9L/5.0L/5.8L/7.5L
12A581

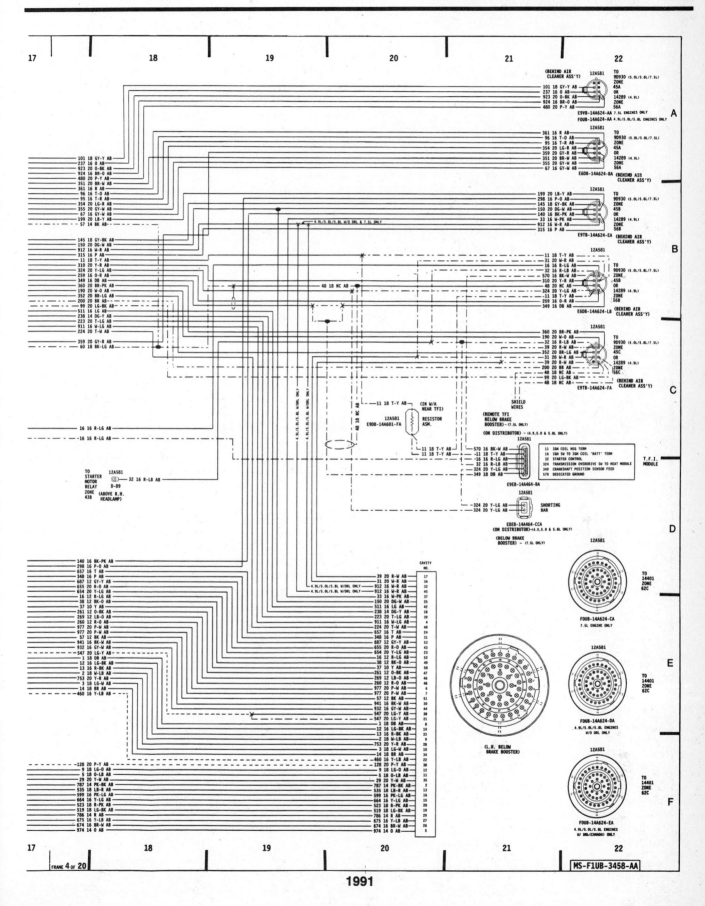

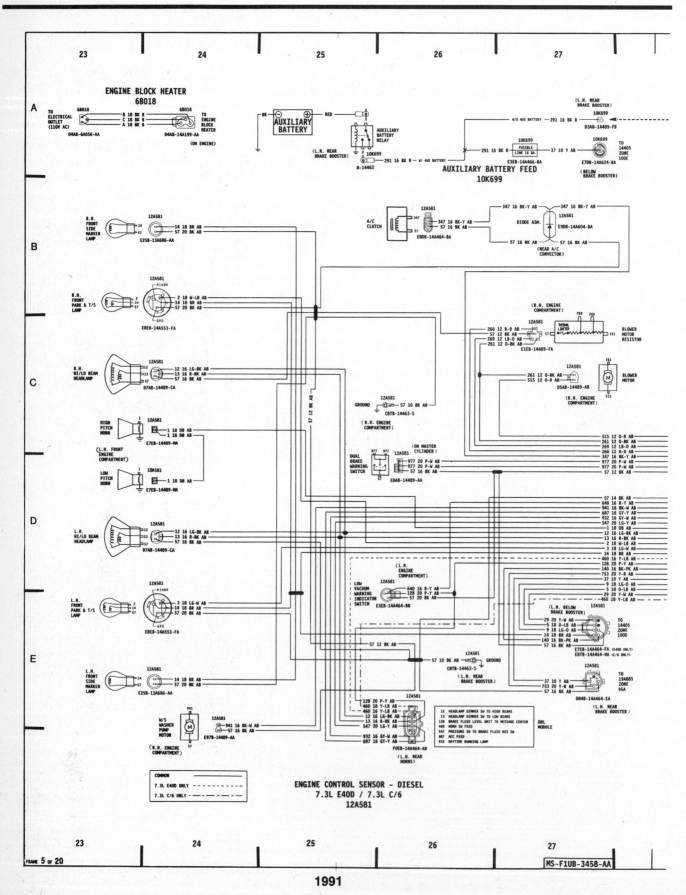

ENGINE CONTROL SENSOR - DIESEL
7.3L E40D / 7.3L C/6
12A581

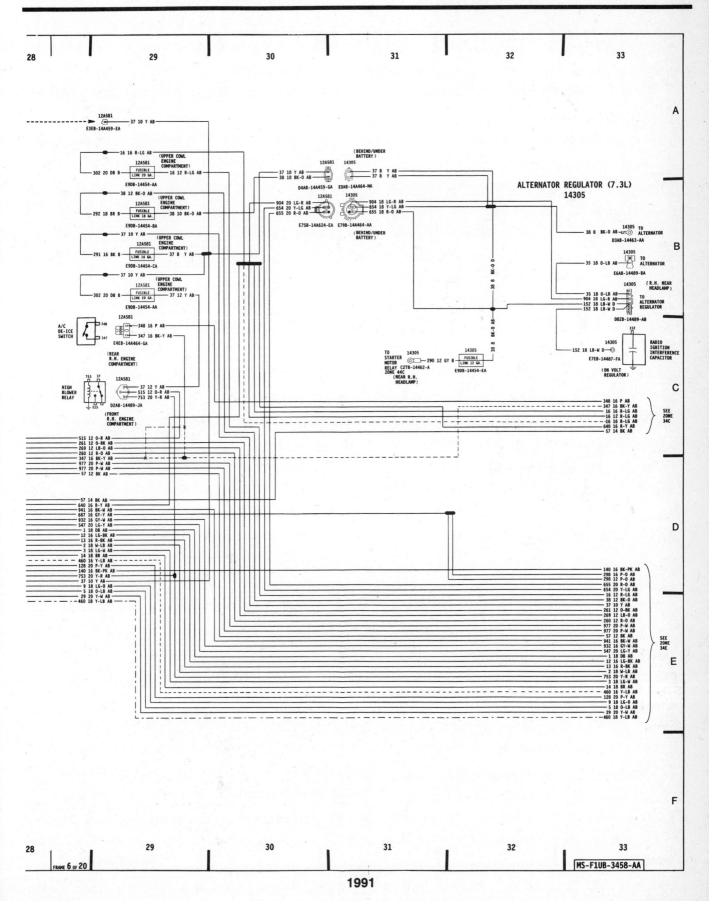

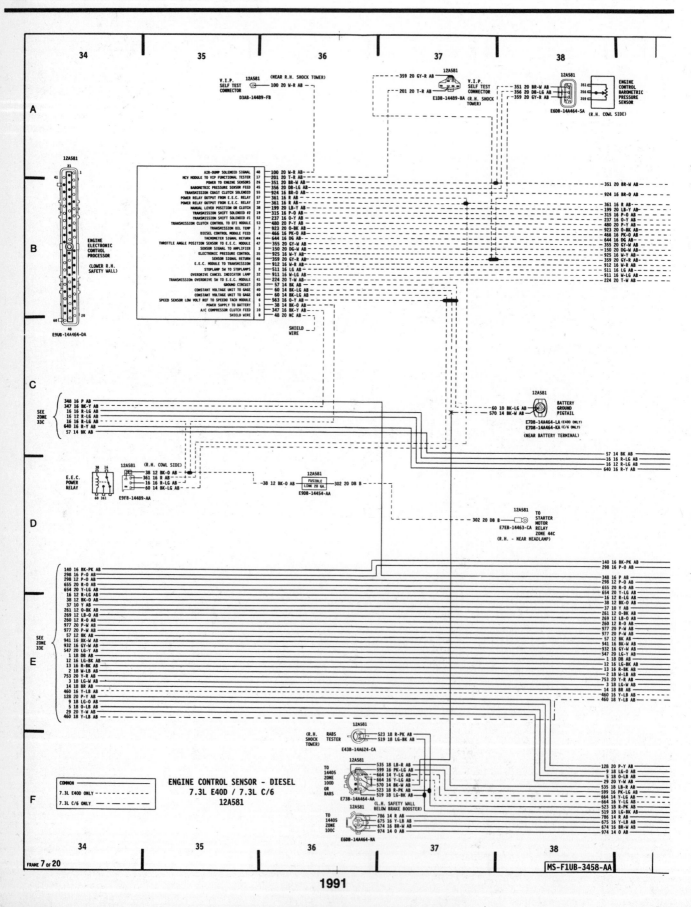

ENGINE CONTROL SENSOR - DIESEL
7.3L E40D / 7.3L C/6
12A581

COMMON
7.3L E40D ONLY ------
7.3L C/6 ONLY — — —

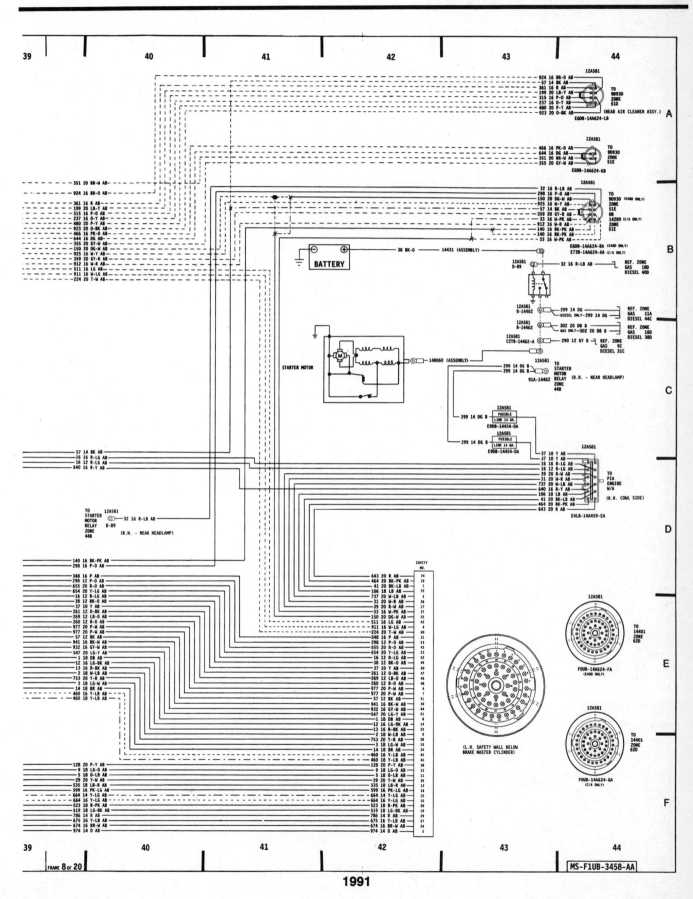

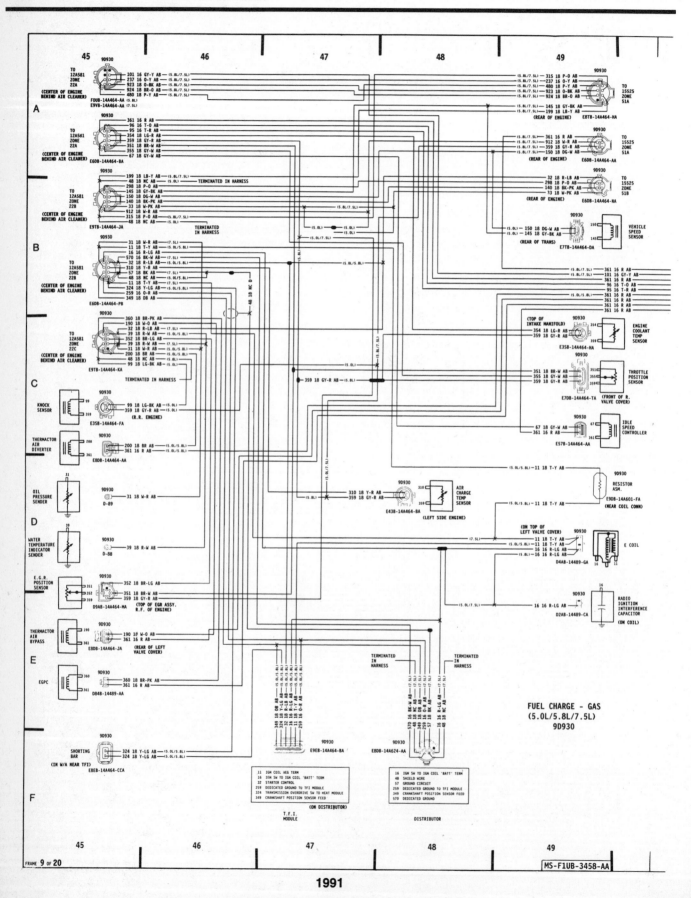

FUEL CHARGE - GAS
(5.0L/5.8L/7.5L)
9D930

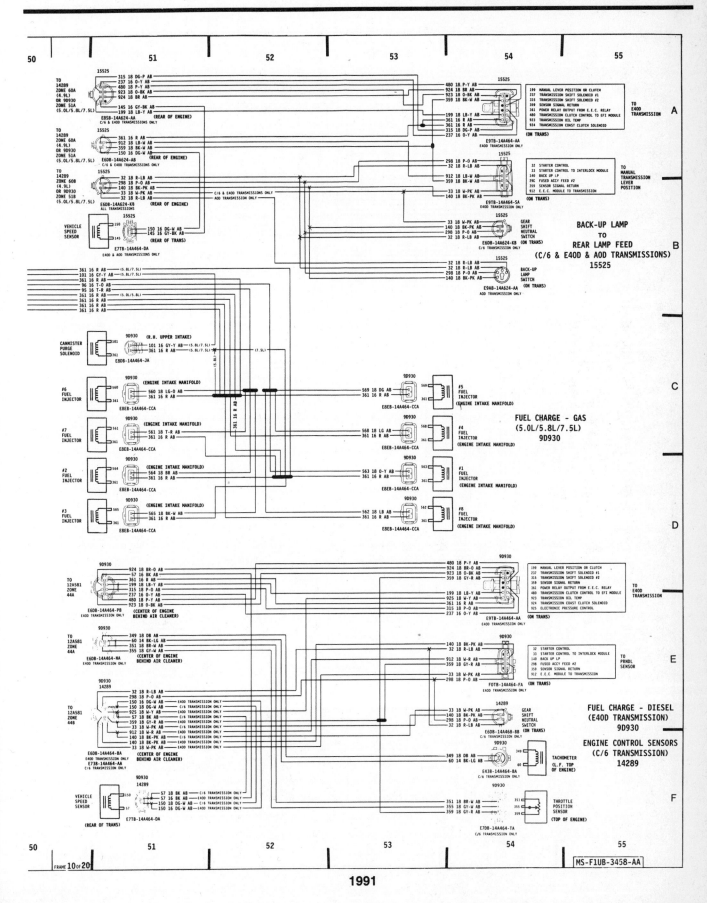

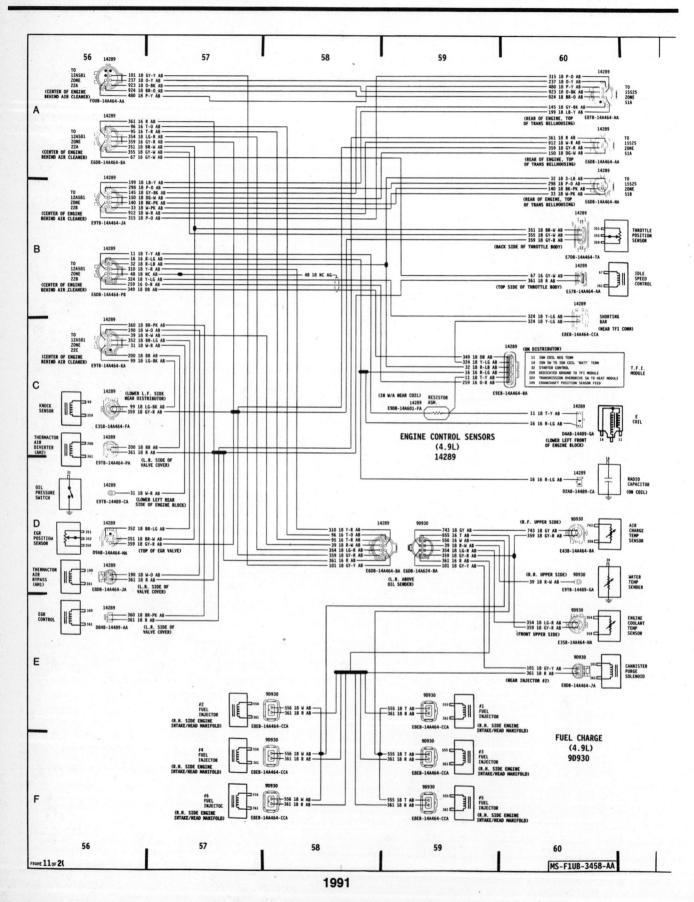

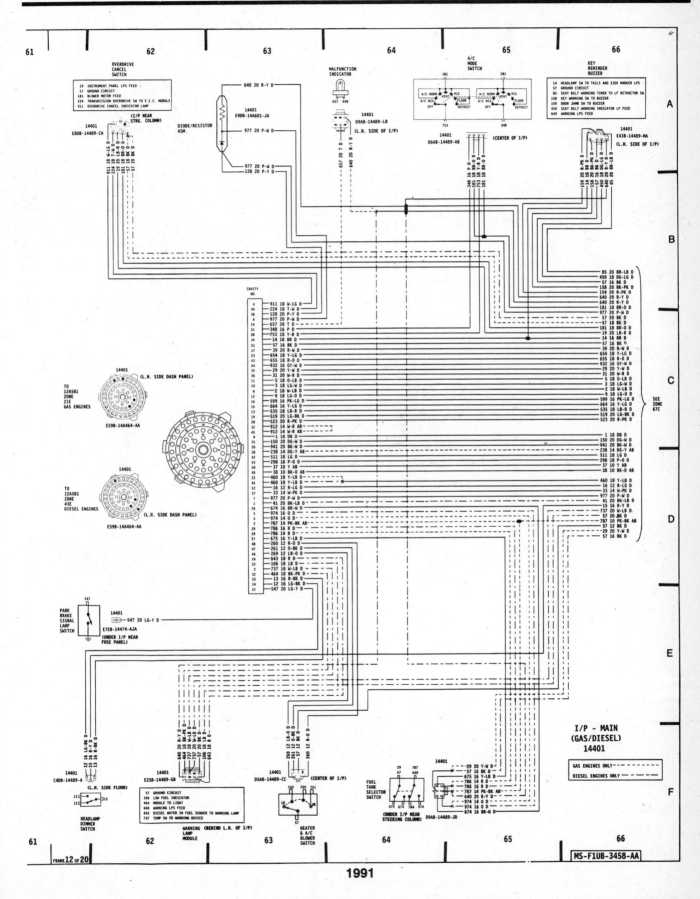

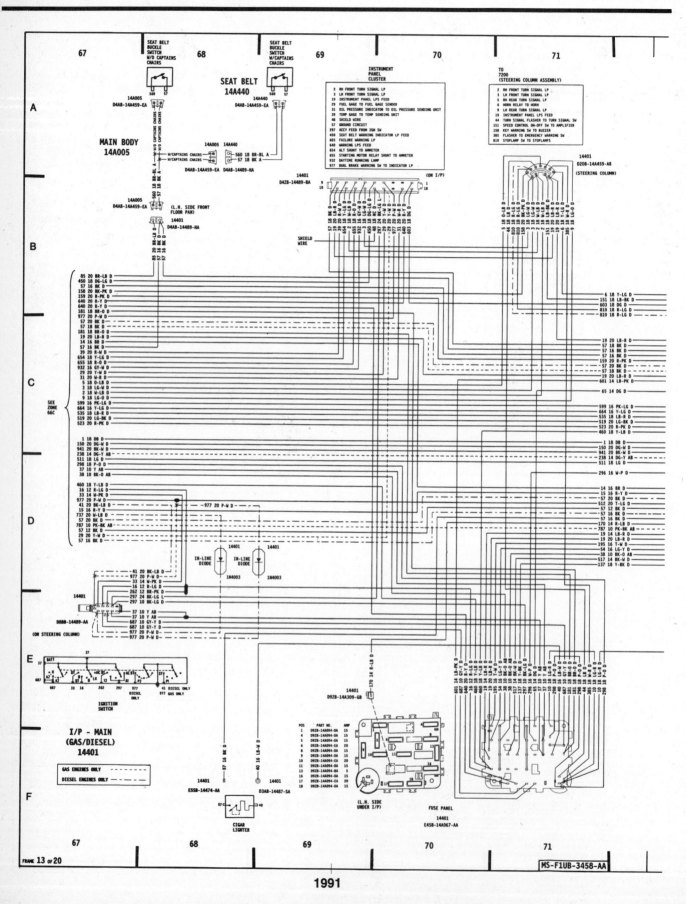

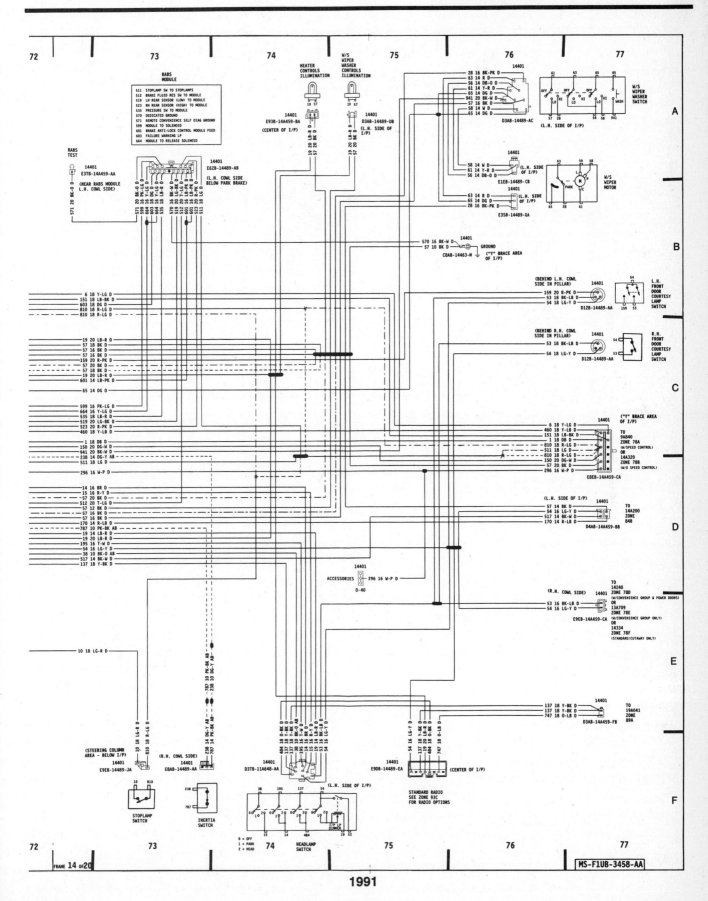

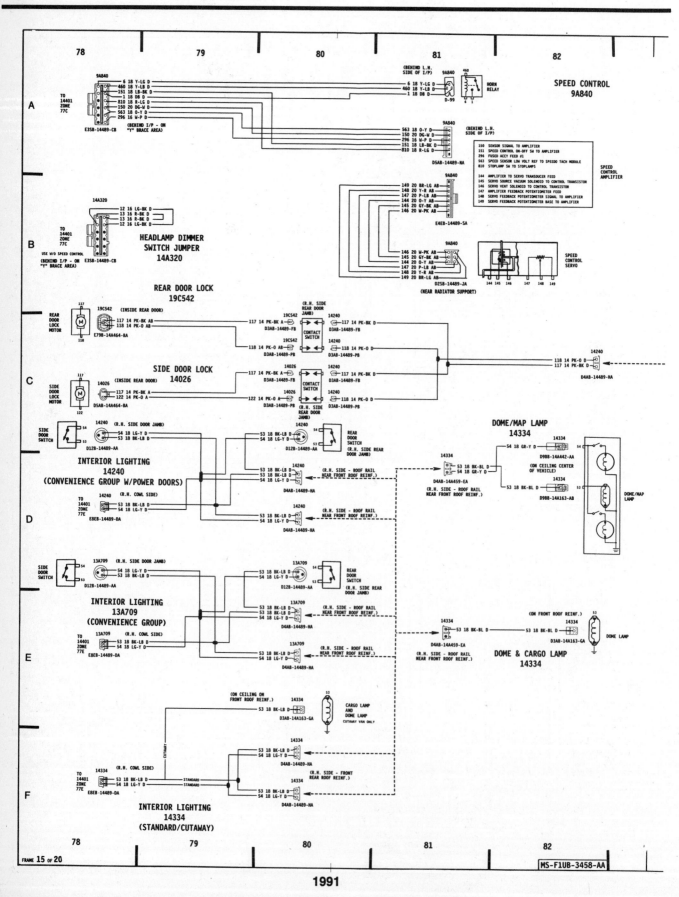

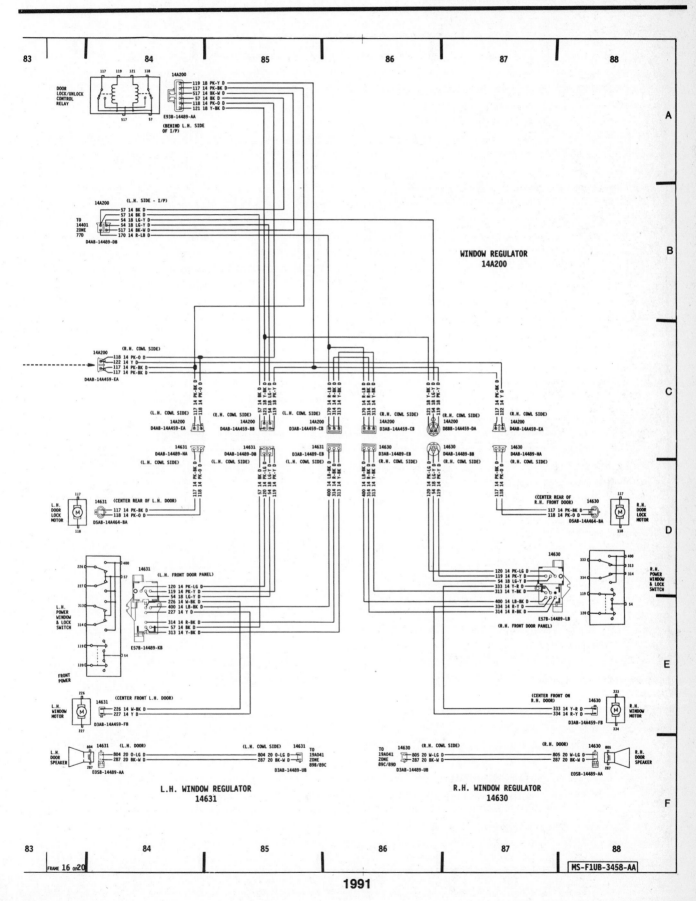

L.H. WINDOW REGULATOR
14631

R.H. WINDOW REGULATOR
14630

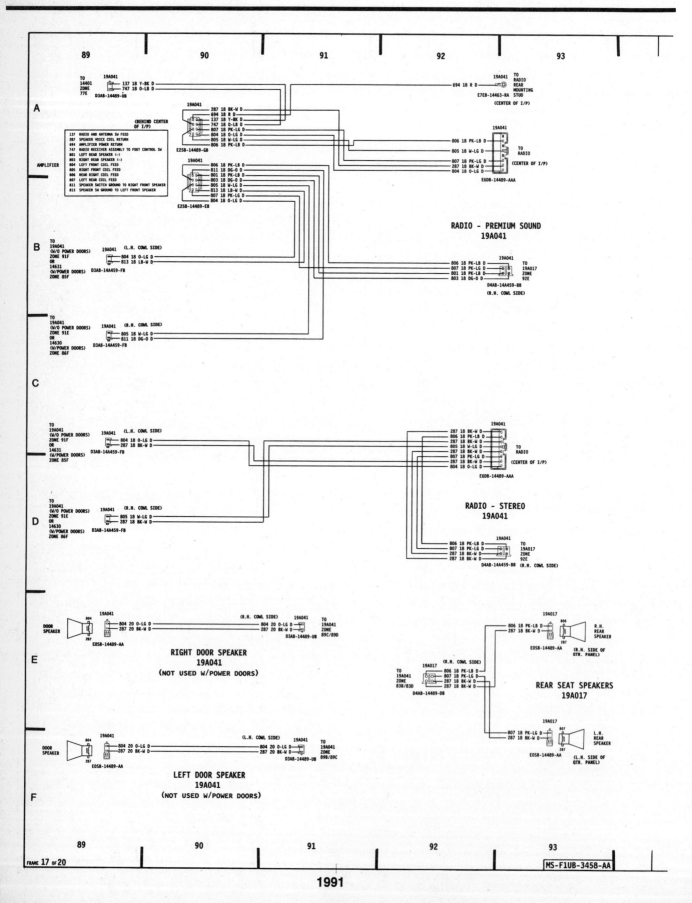

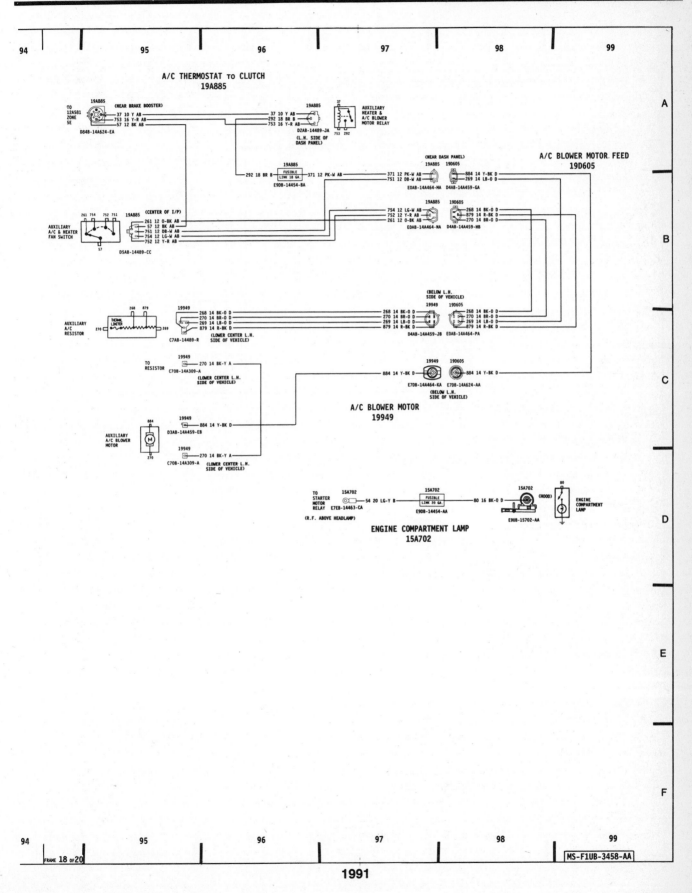

A/C THERMOSTAT TO CLUTCH
19A885

A/C BLOWER MOTOR FEED
19D605

A/C BLOWER MOTOR
19949

ENGINE COMPARTMENT LAMP
15A702

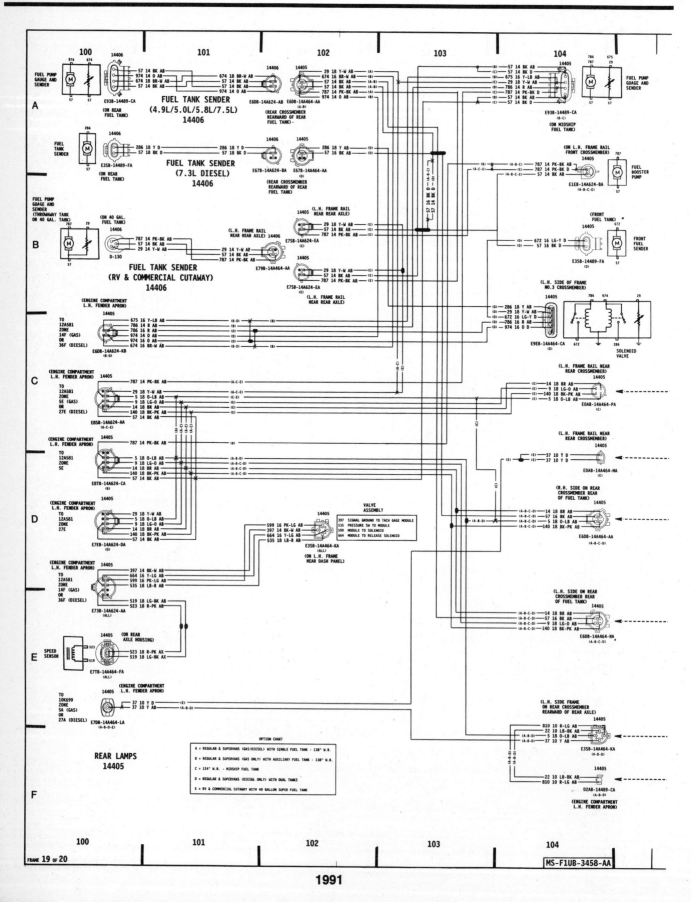

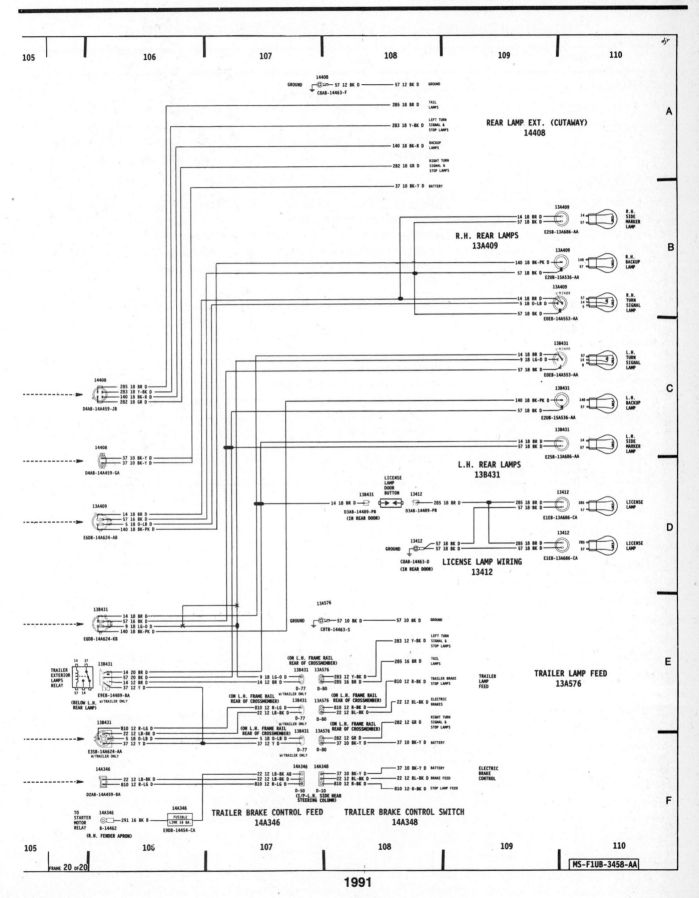

Troubleshooting Basic Windshield Wiper Problems

Problem	Cause	Solution
Electric Wipers		
Wipers do not operate— Wiper motor heats up or hums	• Internal motor defect • Bent or damaged linkage • Arms improperly installed on linking pivots	• Replace motor • Repair or replace linkage • Position linkage in park and reinstall wiper arms
Electric Wipers		
Wipers do not operate— No current to motor	• Fuse or circuit breaker blown • Loose, open or broken wiring • Defective switch • Defective or corroded terminals • No ground circuit for motor or switch	• Replace fuse or circuit breaker • Repair wiring and connections • Replace switch • Replace or clean terminals • Repair ground circuits
Wipers do not operate— Motor runs	• Linkage disconnected or broken	• Connect wiper linkage or replace broken linkage
Vacuum Wipers		
Wipers do not operate	• Control switch or cable inoperative • Loss of engine vacuum to wiper motor (broken hoses, low engine vacuum, defective vacuum/fuel pump) • Linkage broken or disconnected • Defective wiper motor	• Repair or replace switch or cable • Check vacuum lines, engine vacuum and fuel pump • Repair linkage • Replace wiper motor

7

Drive Train

QUICK REFERENCE INDEX

GENERAL INDEX

7 DRIVE TRAIN

Troubleshooting the Manual Transmission

Problem	Cause	Solution
Transmission shifts hard	• Clutch adjustment incorrect • Clutch linkage or cable binding • Shift rail binding	• Adjust clutch • Lubricate or repair as necessary • Check for mispositioned selector arm roll pin, loose cover bolts, worn shift rail bores, worn shift rail, distorted oil seal, or extension housing not aligned with case. Repair as necessary.
	• Internal bind in transmission caused by shift forks, selector plates, or synchronizer assemblies • Clutch housing misalignment • Incorrect lubricant • Block rings and/or cone seats worn	• Remove, dissemble and inspect transmission. Replace worn or damaged components as necessary. • Check runout at rear face of clutch housing • Drain and refill transmission • Blocking ring to gear clutch tooth face clearance must be 0.030 inch or greater. If clearance is correct it may still be necessary to inspect blocking rings and cone seats for excessive wear. Repair as necessary.
Gear clash when shifting from one gear to another	• Clutch adjustment incorrect • Clutch linkage or cable binding • Clutch housing misalignment • Lubricant level low or incorrect lubricant • Gearshift components, or synchronizer assemblies worn or damaged	• Adjust clutch • Lubricate or repair as necessary • Check runout at rear of clutch housing • Drain and refill transmission and check for lubricant leaks if level was low. Repair as necessary. • Remove, disassemble and inspect transmission. Replace worn or damaged components as necessary.
Transmission noisy	• Lubricant level low or incorrect lubricant • Clutch housing-to-engine, or transmission-to-clutch housing bolts loose • Dirt, chips, foreign material in transmission • Gearshift mechanism, transmission gears, or bearing components worn or damaged • Clutch housing misalignment	• Drain and refill transmission. If lubricant level was low, check for leaks and repair as necessary. • Check and correct bolt torque as necessary • Drain, flush, and refill transmission • Remove, disassemble and inspect transmission. Replace worn or damaged components as necessary. • Check runout at rear face of clutch housing

Troubleshooting the Manual Transmission   (cont.)

Problem	Cause	Solution
Jumps out of gear	• Clutch housing misalignment	• Check runout at rear face of clutch housing
	• Gearshift lever loose	• Check lever for worn fork. Tighten loose attaching bolts.
	• Offset lever nylon insert worn or lever attaching nut loose	• Remove gearshift lever and check for loose offset lever nut or worn insert. Repair or replace as necessary.
	• Gearshift mechanism, shift forks, selector plates, interlock plate, selector arm, shift rail, detent plugs, springs or shift cover worn or damaged	• Remove, disassemble and inspect transmission cover assembly. Replace worn or damaged components as necessary.
	• Clutch shaft or roller bearings worn or damaged	• Replace clutch shaft or roller bearings as necessary
Jumps out of gear (cont.)	• Gear teeth worn or tapered, synchronizer assemblies worn or damaged, excessive end play caused by worn thrust washers or output shaft gears	• Remove, disassemble, and inspect transmission. Replace worn or damaged components as necessary.
	• Pilot bushing worn	• Replace pilot bushing
Will not shift into one gear	• Gearshift selector plates, interlock plate, or selector arm, worn, damaged, or incorrectly assembled	• Remove, disassemble, and inspect transmission cover assembly. Repair or replace components as necessary.
	• Shift rail detent plunger worn, spring broken, or plug loose	• Tighten plug or replace worn or damaged components as necessary
	• Gearshift lever worn or damaged	• Replace gearshift lever
	• Synchronizer sleeves or hubs, damaged or worn	• Remove, disassemble and inspect transmission. Replace worn or damaged components.
Locked in one gear—cannot be shifted out	• Shift rail(s) worn or broken, shifter fork bent, setscrew loose, center detent plug missing or worn	• Inspect and replace worn or damaged parts
	• Broken gear teeth on countershaft gear, clutch shaft, or reverse idler gear	• Inspect and replace damaged part
	Gearshift lever broken or worn, shift mechanism in cover incorrectly assembled or broken, worn damaged gear train components	• Disassemble transmission. Replace damaged parts or assemble correctly.

Troubleshooting the Manual Transmission   (cont.)

Problem	Cause	Solution
Transfer case difficult to shift or will not shift into desired range	• Vehicle speed too great to permit shifting	• Stop vehicle and shift into desired range. Or reduce speed to 3–4 km/h (2–3 mph) before attempting to shift.
	• If vehicle was operated for extended period in 4H mode on dry paved surface, driveline torque load may cause difficult shifting	• Stop vehicle, shift transmission to neutral, shift transfer case to 2H mode and operate vehicle in 2H on dry paved surfaces
	• Transfer case external shift linkage binding	• Lubricate or repair or replace linkage, or tighten loose components as necessary
	• Insufficient or incorrect lubricant	• Drain and refill to edge of fill hole
	• Internal components binding, worn, or damaged	• Disassemble unit and replace worn or damaged components as necessary
Transfer case noisy in all drive modes	• Insufficient or incorrect lubricant	• Drain and refill to edge of fill hole Check for leaks and repair if necessary. Note: If unit is still noisy after drain and refill, disassembly and inspection may be required to locate source of noise.
Noisy in—or jumps out of four wheel drive low range	• Transfer case not completely engaged in 4L position	• Stop vehicle, shift transfer case in Neutral, then shift back into 4L position
	• Shift linkage loose or binding	• Tighten, lubricate, or repair linkage as necessary
	• Shift fork cracked, inserts worn, or fork is binding on shift rail	• Disassemble unit and repair as necessary
Lubricant leaking from output shaft seals or from vent	• Transfer case overfilled	• Drain to correct level
	• Vent closed or restricted	• Clear or replace vent if necessary
Lubricant leaking from output shaft seals or from vent (cont.)	• Output shaft seals damaged or installed incorrectly	• Replace seals. Be sure seal lip faces interior of case when installed. Also be sure yoke seal surfaces are not scored or nicked. Remove scores, nicks with fine sandpaper or replace yoke(s) if necessary.
Abnormal tire wear	• Extended operation on dry hard surface (paved) roads in 4H range	• Operate in 2H on hard surface (paved) roads

UNDERSTANDING THE MANUAL TRANSMISSION

Because of the way an internal combustion engine breathes, it can produce torque, or twisting force, only within a narrow speed range. Most modern, overhead valve engines must turn at about 2,500 rpm to produce their peak torque. By 4,500 rpm they are producing so little torque that continued increases in engine speed produce no power increases.

The torque peak on overhead camshaft engines is, generally, much higher, but much narrower.

The manual transmission and clutch are employed to vary the relationship between engine speed and the speed of the wheels so that adequate engine power can be produced under all circumstances. The clutch allows engine torque to be applied to the transmission input shaft gradually, due to mechanical slippage. The van can, consequently, be started smoothly from a full stop.

The transmission changes the ratio between the rotating speeds of the engine and the wheels by the use of gears. 4-speed or 5-speed transmissions are most common. The lower gears al-

low full engine power to be applied to the rear wheels during acceleration at low speeds.

The transmission contains a mainshaft which passes all the way through the transmission, from the clutch to the driveshaft. This shaft is separated at one point, so that front and rear portions can turn at different speeds.

Power is transmitted by a countershaft in the lower gears and reverse. The gears of the countershaft mesh with gears on the mainshaft, allowing power to be carried from one to the other. All the countershaft gears are integral with that shaft, while several of the mainshaft gears can either rotate independently of the shaft or be locked to it. Shifting from one gear to the next causes one of the gears to be freed from rotating with the shaft and locks another to it. Gears are locked and unlocked by internal dog clutches which slide between the center of the gear and the shaft. The forward gears usually employ synchronizers; friction members which smoothly bring gear and shaft to the same speed before the toothed dog clutches are engaged.

MANUAL TRANSMISSION

Back-Up Light Switch

REMOVAL AND INSTALLATION

The back-up light switch is mounted on the transmission extension housing. this switch is not adjustable. To remove, place the transmission shift lever in any gear but neutral, and disconnect the electrical connector from the switch. Remove the switch assembly from the transmission and install a new switch in the reverse order of removal.

Transmission

REMOVAL AND INSTALLATION

———————— CAUTION ————————

The clutch driven disc contains asbestos, which has been determined to be a cancer causing agent. Never clean clutch surfaces with compressed air! Avoid inhaling any dust from any clutch surface! When cleaning clutch surfaces, use a commercially available brake cleaning fluid.

Mazda M5OD 5-Speed

1. Raise and support the van on jackstands. Prop the clutch pedal in the full up position with a block of wood.
2. Matchmark the driveshaft-to-flange relation.
3. Disconnect the driveshaft at the axle and slide it off of the transmission output shaft. Lubricant will leak out of the transmission so be prepared to catch it, or plug the opening with rags or a seal installation tool.
4. Disconnect the speedometer cable at the transmission.

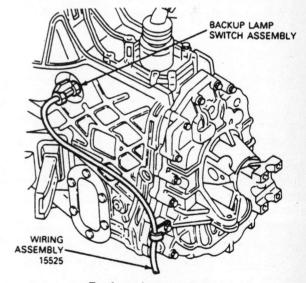

Back-up lamp switch

5. Disconnect the shift rods from the shift levers.
6. Remove the shift control from the extension housing and transmission case.
7. Remove the extension housing-to-rear support bolts.
8. Take up the weight of the transmission with a transmission jack. Chain the transmission to the jack.

9. Raise the transmission just enough to take the weight off of the No.3 crossmember.

10. Unbolt the crossmember from the frame rails and remove it.

11. Place a jackstand under the rear of the engine at the bellhousing.

12. Lower the jack and allow the jackstand to take the weight of the engine. The engine should be angled slightly downward to allow the transmission to roll backward.

13. Remove the transmission-to bellhousing bolts.

14. Roll the jack rearward until the input shaft clears the bellhousing. Lower the jack and remove the transmission.

WARNING: Do not depress the clutch pedal with the transmission removed.

To install:

15. Clean all machined mating surfaces thoroughly.

16. Install a guide pin in each lower bolt hole. Position the spacer plate on the guide pins.

17. Raise the transmission and start the input shaft through the clutch release bearing.

18. Align the input shaft splines with the clutch disc splines. Roll the transmission forward so that the input shaft will enter the clutch disc. If the shaft binds in the release bearing, work the release arm back and forth.

19. Once the transmission is all the way in, install the 2 upper retaining bolts and washers and remove the lower guide pins. Install the lower bolts. Torque the bolts to 50 ft. lbs.

20. Raise the transmission just enough to allow installation of the No.3 crossmember.

21. Install the crossmember on the frame rails. Torque the bolts to 80 ft. lbs.

22. Lower the transmission onto the crossmember and install the nuts. Torque the nuts to 70 ft. lbs.

23. Remove the transmission jack.

24. Install the shift control on the extension housing and transmission case.

25. Connect the shift rods at the shift levers.

26. Connect the speedometer cable at the transmission.

27. Slide the driveshaft onto the output shaft and connect the driveshaft at the axle, aligning the matchmarks.

ZF S5-42 5-Speed

1. Place the transmission in neutral.

2. Remove the carpet or floor mat.

3. Remove the ball from the shift lever.

4. Remove the boot and bezel assembly from the floor.

5. Remove the 2 bolts and disengage the upper shift lever from the lower shift lever.

6. Raise and support the tuck on jackstands.

7. Disconnect the speedometer cable.

8. Disconnect the back-up switch wire.

9. Place a drain pan under the case and drain the case through the drain plug.

10. Position a transmission jack under the case and safety-chain the case to the jack.

11. Remove the driveshaft.

12. Disconnect the clutch linkage.

13. Remove the transmission rear insulator and lower retainer.

14. Unbolt and remove the crossmember.

15. Remove the transmission-to-engine block bolts.

16. Roll the transmission rearward until the input shaft clears, lower the jack and remove the transmission.

17. Install 2 guide studs into the lower bolt holes.

18. Raise the transmission until the input shaft splines are aligned with the clutch disc splines. The clutch release bearing and hub must be properly positioned in the release lever fork.

19. Roll the transmission forward and into position.

20. Install the bolts and torque them to 50 ft. lbs. Remove the guide studs and install and tighten the 2 remaining bolts.

21. Install the crossmember and torque the bolts to 55 ft. lbs.

22. Install the transmission rear insulator and lower retainer. Torque the bolts to 60 ft. lbs.

23. Connect the clutch linkage.

24. Install the driveshaft.

25. Remove the transmission jack.

26. Fill the transmission.

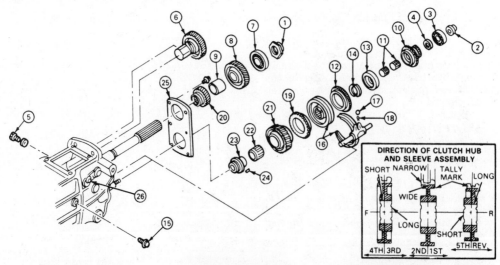

1. Locknut—output shaft	9. Sleeve—output shaft	17. Lock ball (steel) shift rail
2. Locknut—countershaft	10. Countershaft reverse gear	18. Spring—shift rail
3. Countershaft rear bearing	11. Needle bearings	19. Synchronizer ring—5th gear
4. Thrust washer	12. Synchronizer ring—reverse	20. 5th gear—output shaft
5. Fixing bolt—reverse idler gear	13. Thrust washer	21. 5th gear—countershaft
6. Reverse idle gear assembly	14. Split washer (2 pcs)	22. Needle bearing—5th gear
7. Bearing—output shaft rear	15. Fixing bolt—shift rod	
8. Reverse gear—output shaft	16. Shift rail/fork/hub/sleeve assembly	

M5OD rear housing components, exploded view

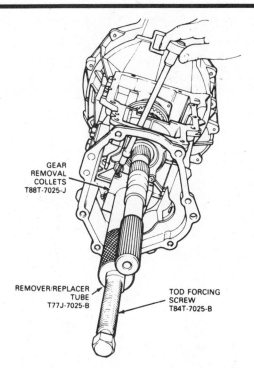

Removing 5th gear sleeve on the M5OD

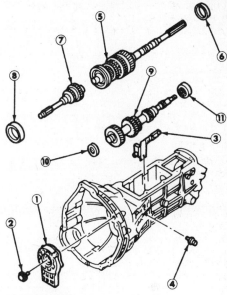

1. Front bearing cover
2. Front cover retaining bolt
3. Oil trough
4. Retaining bolt—oil trough
5. Output shaft assembly
6. Output shaft center bearing outer race
7. Input shaft assembly
8. Input shaft bearing outer race
9. Counter shaft assembly
10. Countershaft front bearing outer race
11. Countershaft rear bearing outer race

M5OD main case exploded view

27. Connect the back-up switch wire.
28. Connect the speedometer cable.
29. Lower the van.
30. Install the boot and bezel assembly.
31. Connect the upper shift to from the lower shift lever. Tighten the bolts to 20 ft. lbs.
32. Install the carpet or floor mat.
33. Install the ball from the shift lever.

OVERHAUL

Mazda M5OD 5-Speed
CASE DISASSEMBLY

1. Remove the drain plug.
2. Remove the shift lever from the top cover.
3. Remove the 10 top cover bolts and lift off the cover. Discard the gasket.
4. Remove the 9 extension housing bolts. Pry gently at the indentations provided and separate the extension housing from the case.

NOTE: If you would like to remove the extension housing seal, remove it with a puller BEFORE separating the extension housing from the case.

5. Remove the rear oil passage from the extension housing using a 10mm socket.
6. Remove and discard the anti-spill seal from the output shaft.
7. Remove the speedometer drive gear and ball. If you're going to replace the gear, replace it with one of the same color.
8. Lock the transmission into 1st and 3rd gears.
9. Using a hammer and chisel, release the staked areas securing the output shaft and countershaft locknuts.
10. Using a 32mm socket, remove and discard the countershaft rear bearing locknut.
11. Remove the counteshaft bearing and thrust washer.

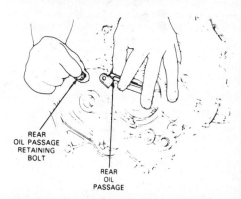

Rear oil passage removal from the M5OD 5-speed

12. Using Mainshaft Locknut Wrench T88T–7025–A and Remover Tube T75L–7025–B, or equivalents, remove and discard the output shaft locknut.
13. Using a 17mm wrench, remove the reverse idler shaft bolt.
14. Remove the reverse idler gear assembly by pulling it rearward.
15. Remove the output shaft rear bearing from the output shaft using Remover/Replacer Tube T75L–7025–B, TOD Forcing Screw T84T–7025–B, Bearing Puller T77J–7025–H and Puller Ring T77J–7025–J, or equivalents.
16. Using a brass drift, drive the reverse gear from the output shaft.
17. Remove the sleeve from the output shaft.
18. Remove the counter/reverse gear with two needle bearings and the reverse synchronizer ring.

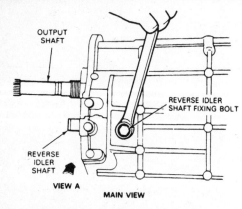

Removing the reverse idler gear shaft bolt

19. Remove the thrust washer and split washer from the countershaft.
20. Using a 12mm wrench, remove the 5th/reverse shift rod fixing bolt.
21. Remove the 5th/reverse hub and sleeve assembly.
22. Remove the 5th/reverse shift fork and rod.

NOTE: Do not separate the steel ball and spring unless necessary.

23. Remove the 5th gear synchronizer ring.
24. Remove the 5th/reverse counter lever lockplate retaining bolt and inner circlip.
25. Remove the counter lever assembly from the case.

NOTE: Do not remove the Torx® nut retaining the counter lever pin at this time.

26. Remove the 5th gear counter with the needle bearing.
27. Remove the 5th gear from the output shaft using the Bearing Collet Sleeve for the 3½ in. (89mm). Bearing Collets T75L-7025-G, Remover/Replacer Tube T85T-7025-A, TOD Forcing Screw T84T-7025-B and Gear Remover Collet T88T-7061-A, or equivalents.

NOTE: For reference during assembly, observe that the longer of the 2 collars on the 5th gear faces forward.

28. Remove the 5th gear sleeve and Woodruff key using TOD Forcing Screw T84T-7025-B, Countershaft 5th Gear Sleeve Puller T88T-7025-J, Gear Removal Collets T88T-7025-J1 and Remover/Replacer Tube T77J-7025-B, or equivalents.
29. Remove the 6 center bearing cover retaining bolts and lift off the cover.

NOTE: There is a reference arrow on the cover which points upward.

30. Remove the 6 front bearing cover bolts.

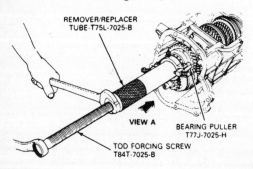

Removing the output shaft rear bearing on the M5OD

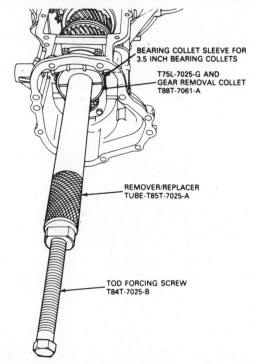

Removing 5th gear from the output shaft on the M5OD

31. Remove the front bearing cover by threading 2 of the retaining bolts back into the cover at the service bolt locations (9 and 3 o'clock). Alternately tighten the bolts until the cover pops off. Discard the front bearing oil baffle.

NOTE: Don't remove the plastic scoop ring from the input shaft at this time.

32. Remove the oil trough retaining bolt and lift out the oil trough from the upper case.
33. Pull the input shaft forward and remove the input bearing outer race. Pull the output shaft rearward.
34. Pull the input shaft forward and separate it from the output shaft.
35. Incline the output shaft upward and lift it from the case.
36. Remove the input shaft from the case.
37. Remove the countershaft bearing outer races (front and center) by moving the countershaft forward and rearward.
38. Pull the countershaft rearward far enough to permit tool clearance behind the front countershaft bearing. Using Bearing Race Puller T88T-7120-A and Slide Hammer T50T-100-A, or equivalents, remove the front countershaft bearing.

WARNING: Tap gently during bearing removal. A forceful blow can cause damage to the bearing and/or case.

39. Remove the countershaft through the upper opening of the case.
40. Input Shaft Disassembly and Assembly:
   a. Remove and discard the plastic scoop ring.
   b. Press the tapered roller bearing from the input shaft using Bearing Cone Remover T71P-4621–b, or equivalent, and an arbor press.
   c. Install the input shaft tapered roller bearing onto the input shaft using a press and Bearing Cone Replacer T88T-7025–B, or equivalent.
   d. Install the plastic scoop ring onto the input shaft. Manually rotate the ring clockwise to ensure that the input shaft oil holes properly engage the scoop ring. A click should be

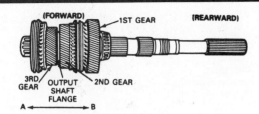

M5OD output shaft

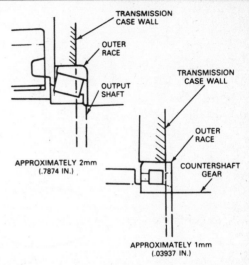

Installing the output shaft center bearing on the M5OD

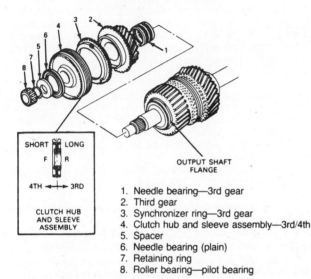

1. Needle bearing—3rd gear
2. Third gear
3. Synchronizer ring—3rd gear
4. Clutch hub and sleeve assembly—3rd/4th
5. Spacer
6. Needle bearing (plain)
7. Retaining ring
8. Roller bearing—pilot bearing

M5OD output shaft exploded view

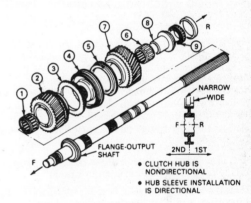

1. Needle bearing—2nd gear
2. 2nd gear
3. Synchronizer ring—2nd gear
4. Clutch hub and sleeve assembly—1st and 2nd
5. Synchronizer ring—1st gear
6. Needle bearing—1st gear
7. 1st gear
8. Sleeve—1st gear
9. Center bearing—inner

M5OD output shaft component assembly

heard as the scoop ring notches align with the input shaft holes.

41. Output Shaft Disassembly and Assembly:

   a. Remove the pilot bearing needle roller, snapring, needle bearing and spacer from the front (short side) of the output shaft.

   b. Position the front (short side) of the shaft upward and lift off the 3rd/4th clutch hub and sleeve assembly, 3rd gear synchronizing ring, 3rd gear, and needle bearing.

   c. Turn the shaft so that the long end faces upward.

   d. Place the output shaft into a press with the press cradle contacting the lower part of the 2nd gear.

NOTE: Make sure that the output shaft flange doesn't contact or ride up on the press cradle.

   e. Press off the following as a unit:
- center bearing,
- 1st gear sleeve,
- 1st gear,
- needle bearing,
- 1st/2nd clutch hub and sleeve,
- 1st/2nd synchronizer rings,
- 2nd gear, and
- needle bearing

using Bearing Replacer T53T–4621–B and Bearing Cone Replacer T88T–7025–B, or equivalents. Use T53T–4621–B as a press plate, and Bearing Cone Replacer T88T–7025–B to protect the inner race rollers.

   f. Position the output shaft so the rear (long end) faces upward and press on the following parts, in the order listed, using T53T–4621–B and T75L–1165–B, or equivalents:

- 2nd gear needle bearing
- 2nd gear
- 2nd gear synchronizer ring
- 1st/2nd clutch hub and sleeve
- 1st gear synchronizer ring
- 1st gear needle bearing
- 1st gear
- 1st gear sleeve
- center bearing

NOTE: Make sure that the center bearing race ins installed in the case. When installing the 1st/2nd clutch hub and sleeve make sure that the smaller width sleeve faces the 2nd gear side. Make sure that the reference marks face the rear of the transmission.

   g. Install the center bearing on the output shaft.

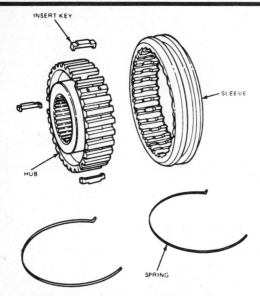

M5OD synchronizer exploded view

h. Position the output shaft so that the front of the shaft flange faces upward. Install the 3rd gear needle bearing, 3rd gear and 3rd gear synchronizer ring.

i. Install the 3rd/4th clutch hub and sleeve:
• Mate the clutch hub synchronizer key groove with the reference mark on the clutch hub sleeve. The mark should face rearward.
• Install the longer flange on the clutch hub sleeve towards the 3rd gear side.

NOTE: The front and rear sides of the clutch hub are identical, except for the reference mark.

j. Install the spacer, needle bearing (with rollers upward), retaining ring, and pilot bearing roller.

k. Install the original retaining ring. Using a feeler gauge, check the clutch hub endplay. Endplay should be 0–0.05mm (0–0.0019 in.). If necessary, adjust the endplay by using a new retaining ring. Retaining ring are available in 0.05mm increments in sizes ranging from 1.5mm to 1.95mm.

42. Countershaft Disassembly and Assembly:
a. Place the countershaft in a press with Bearing Cone Remover T71P–4621–B, or equivalent, and remove the countershaft bearing inner race.

b. Using a press and bearing splitter D84L–1123–A, pr equivalent, remove the countershaft front bearing inner race.

c. Assemble the shaft in the press in the reverse order of disassembly.

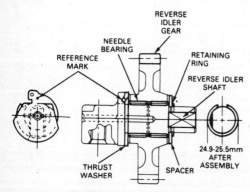

M5OD reverse gear shaft

43. Reverse Idler Gear Shaft Disassembly and Assembly:
a. Remove the following parts:
• Retaining ring
• Spacer
• Idler gear
• Needle bearings
• Thrust washer
b. Install the thrust washer making sure that the tab mates with the groove in the shaft.
c. Install the needle bearings, idler gear and spacer.
d. Install the original retaining ring onto the shaft.
e. Insert a flat feeler gauge between the retaining ring and the reverse idler gear to measure the reverse idler gear endplay. Endplay should be 0.1–0.2mm. If not, use a new retaining ring. Retaining rings are available in 0.5mm increments in thicknesses ranging from 1.5 to 1.9mm.

44. Top Cover Disassembly and Assembly:

a. Remove the dust cover (3 allen screws). Note that the grooves in the bushing align with the slots in the lower shift lever ball and the notch in the lower shift lever faces forward.
b. Remove the back-up lamp switch from the cover.
c. Drive out the spring pins retaining the shift forks to the shift rails. Discard the pins.
d. Place the 5th/reverse shift rail in the fully forward position. Remove the spring pin from the end of the 5th/reverse rail.
e. Remove the 3 rubber plugs from the shift rod service bores.

─── **CAUTION** ───
Wear safety goggles when performing the shift rail removal procedure! Cover the lock ball bores and friction device and spring seats with a heavy cloth held firmly in place. The ball/friction device and spring can fly out during removal, causing possible personal injury!

f. Remove the 5th/reverse shift rail from the top cover through the service bore. It may be necessary to rock the shift rail from side-to-side with a 5/16 in. (8mm) punch while maintaining rearward pressure.
g. Remove the 1st/2nd shift rail from the cover through the service bore. It may be necessary to rock the shift rail from side-to-side with a 5/16 in. (8mm) punch while maintaining rearward pressure.
h. Remove the 3rd/4th shift rail from the cover through the service bore. It may be necessary to rock the shift rail from side-to-side with a 5/16 in. (8mm) punch while maintaining rearward pressure.
i. Remove the 5th/reverse cam lockout plate retaining bolts using a 10mm socket. Remove the plate.
j. Install the 5th/reverse cam lockout plate. Torque the bolts to 72–84 inch lbs.
k. Position the 3rd/4th shift rail into the cover through the service bore. It may be necessary to rock the shift rail from side-to-side with a 5/16 in. (8mm) punch, while maintaining forward pressure.
l. Engage the 3rd/4th shift fork with the shift rail.
m. Position the detent ball and spring into the cover spring seats. Compress the detent ball and spring and push the shift rail into position over the detent ball.
n. Position the friction device and spring into the cover spring seats. Compress the friction device and spring and push the shift rail into position over the friction device.
o. Install the spring pins retaining the shift rail to the cover.
p. Install the spring retaining the 3rd/4th shift fork to the shift rail.
q. Position the 1st/2nd shift rail in the cover through the service bore. It may be necessary to rock the shift rail from side-to-side with a 5/16 in. (8mm) punch, while maintaining forward pressure.

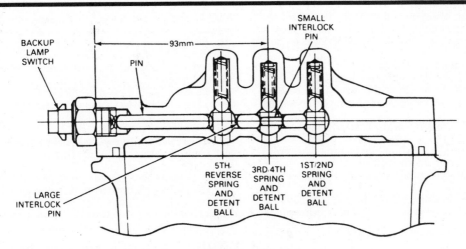

M5OD shift rails

r. Engage the 1st/2nd shift fork with the shift rail.

s. Position the detent ball and spring into the cover seats.

t. Compress the detent ball and spring and push the shift rail into position over the detent ball.

u. Position the friction device and spring into the cover seats. Compress the friction device and spring and push the shift rail into position over the friction device.

v. Install the spring pins retaining the shift rail to the cover. Install the spring pin retaining the 1st/2nd shift fork to the shift rail.

w. Position the 5th/reverse shift rail in the top cover through the service bore. It may be necessary to rock the shift rail from side-to-side with a ⁵⁄₁₆ in. (8mm) punch, while maintaining forward pressure. Engage the 5th/reverse shift fork with the shift rail. Position the detent ball and spring into the cover seats. Compress the detent ball and spring and push the shift rail into position over the detent ball.

x. Install the spring pins retaining the shift rail to the cover. Install the spring pin retaining the 5th/reverse shift fork to the shift rail.

y. Install the rubber plugs.

z. Install the interlock pins into the 1st/2nd and 3rd/4th shift rails. Note that the pins are different sizes.

WARNING: Use of the wrong size pins will affect neutral start and/or back-up light switch operation.

Apply non-hardening sealer to the threads of the back-up light switch and install it. Torque the switch to 18–26 ft. lbs. Install the dust cover.

GENERAL INSPECTION

Inspect all parts for wear or damage. Replace any part that seems suspect. Output shaft runout must not exceed 0.05mm. Replace the shaft is it does. Synchronizer-to-gear clearance must not exceed 0.8mm. Replace the synchronizer ring or gear if necessary. Shift fork-to-clutch hub clearance must not exceed 0.8mm.

GENERAL CASE ASSEMBLY

1. Place the countershaft assembly into the case.

2. Place the input shaft in the case. Make sure that the needle roller bearing is on the shaft.

3. Place the output shaft assembly in the case. Mate the input and out shafts. Make sure that the 4th gear synchronizer is installed.

4. Drive the output shaft center bearing into place with a brass drift.

5. Install the countershaft center bearing. Make sure that the center bearing outer races are squarely seated in their bores.

6. Position the center bearing cover on the case with the arrow upwards. Torque the cover bolts to 14–19 ft. lbs. Use only bolts marked with a grade **8** on the bolt head.

Part Number	Thickness (t)
E8TZ-7029-FA	1.4mm (0.0551 in.)
E8TZ-7029-GA	1.5mm (0.0590 in.)
E8TZ-7029-Ha	1.6mm (0.0629 in.)
E8TZ-7029-Ja	1.7mm (0.0669 in.)
E8TZ-7029-S	1.8mm (0.0708 in.)
E8TZ-7029-T	1.9mm (0.0748 in.)
E8TZ-7029-U	2.0mm (0.0787 in.)
E8TZ-7029-V	2.1mm (0.0826 in.)
E8TZ-7029-W	2.2mm (0.0866 in.)
E8TZ-7029-X	2.3mm (0.0905 in.)
E8TZ-7029-Y	2.4mm (0.0944 in.)
E8TZ-7029-Z	2.5mm (0.0984 in.)
E8TZ-7029-AA	2.6mm (0.1023 in.)
E8TZ-7029-BA	2.7mm (0.1062 in.)
E8TZ-7029-CA	2.8mm (0.1102 in.)
E8TZ-7029-DA	2.9mm (0.1141 in.)
E8TZ-7029-EA	3.0mm (0.1181 in.)

76mm (2.99 in.)

89.7mm (3.531 in.)

INSTALL SHIM THIS SIDE OUT

SHIM

M5OD shim selection chart

7. Position the transmission on end with the input end up. Make sure that the input shaft front bearing outer race is squarely positioned in its bore. Install the front cover oil seal with a seal driver.

8. Install the countershaft front bearing.

9. Check and record the following dimensions:

   a. Check and record the height of the input shaft bearing outer race above the transmission front bearing cover mating surface.

   b. Check and record the depth of the front cover outer race bore at the input shaft.

   c. Check and record the depth of the countershaft front bearing race (case-to-cover mating surface).

   d. Check and record the depth of the front cover outer race bore at the output shaft.

10. Select the proper shims using the following formulae:
   - Dimension b − (dimension a + the shim thickness) = 0.05–0.15mm
   - Dimension c + (dimension d − the shim thickness) = 0.15–0.25mm

   Shims are available in 0.1mm increments ranging from 1.4mm to 3.0mm thick.

11. Clean the mating surfaces of the transmission and front cover.

12. Wrap the input shaft splines with masking tape.

13. Apply a light coat of oil to the front cover oil seal lip. Position the bearing shim and baffle into the cover. The shim groove should be visible.

14. Install the spacer in the case countershaft front bearing bore. You may want to apply a coating of chassis grease to parts to hold them in place during assembly.

15. Apply a ⅛ in. (3mm) wide bead of silicone RTV sealant to the front cover mating surface and the bolt threads. Install the cover and torque the bolts to 9–12 ft. lbs. Always us bolts marked grade 6 on the bolt head.

16. Lay the transmission down and install the woodruff key and 5th gear sleeve.

NOTE: Install the 5th gear sleeve using the nut, Shaft Adapter T75L-7025-L, Adapter T88T-7025-J2 and Remover/Replacer Tube T75L-7025-B, or equivalents.

17. Install the 5th gear needle bearing onto the countershaft 5th gear.

18. Install the 5th gear onto the output shaft using Gear Installation Spacers T88T-7025-F, and –G, Shaft Adapter T75L-7025-P, Shaft Adapter Screw T75L-7025-K, Remover/Replacer Tube T75L-7025-B, nut and washer, or equivalents. Make sure that the long flange on the 5th gear faces forward.

19. Install T88T-7025-F. When the tool bottoms, add T88T-

7025-G and press the 5th gear assembly all the way into position.

20. Position counterlever assembly in the transmission and install the thrust washer and retaining ring. Apply sealant on the counterlever fixing bolt threads. Install the counterlever fixing bolt and torque it to 72–84 inch lbs.

21. Position the 5th/reverse shift fork and shift rail in the top cover. Insert the 5th/reverse shift rail through the top cover bore and the 5th/reverse shift fork. Install the spring and detent ball on the lower part of the rod.

22. Assemble the 5th/reverse synchronizer hub, sleeve and 5th gear synchronizer ring on the 5th/reverse shift fork and rod. The longer flange faces front. The reference mark on the synchronizer sleeve faces the reverse gear side.

23. Install the 5th/reverse shift fork and rail assembly on the countershaft. Mate the shift fork gate to the 5th/reverse counterlever end. Install the 5th/reverse fork and shift rail with the threaded fixing bolt bores aligned.

NOTE: It's easier if you place the 5th/reverse shift fork into the rearmost of the three detent positions. Return the shift fork to the neutral position after assembly.

24. Apply sealant to the 5th/reverse shift rail fixing bolt threads. Install the 5th/reverse shift rail fixing bolt in the case. Torque the 5th/reverse shift rail bolt to 16–22 ft. lbs.

25. Apply sealant to the oil passage retaining bolt. Position the oil passage in the case and torque the bolt to 72–84 inch lbs.

26. Install the split washer and thrust washer onto the countershaft. If the clutch hub and/or counter reverse gear have been replaced, new split washers must be selected to maintain endplay within specifications. Check the endplay with a flat feeler gauge. Endplay should be 0.2–0.3mm. Split washers are provided in 0.1mm increments ranging from 3.0–3.5mm.

27. Install the reverse synchronizer ring and needle bearings into the counter reverse gear. Install the counter reverse gear and needle bearings onto the countershaft. Install the thrust washer.

28. Push the thrust washer forward by hand against the shoulder on the countershaft. Maintain forward pressure and insert a flat feeler gauge between the thrust washer and the counter reverse gear. Counter reverse endplay should be 0.2–0.3mm. Thrust washers are available in 0.2mm increments ranging from 7.4–7.8mm thicknesses.

29. Temporarily install a spacer, with an inner bore larger than 21mm and an outer diameter smaller than 36mm, 15–20mm overall length, in place of the countershaft bearing. Loosely install the locknut.

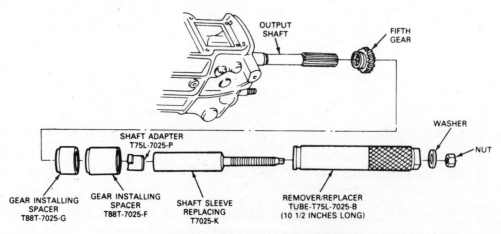

Installing 5th gear on the M5OD

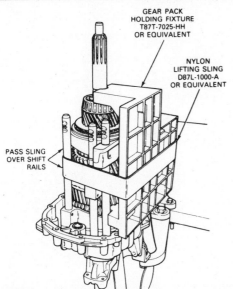

Lifting sling and holding fixture in place on the ZF

30. Install the reverse idler gear assembly. Apply sealant to the threads of the reverse idler gear fixing bolt. Torque the bolt to 58–86 ft. lbs.

31. Drive the sleeve and reverse gear assembly into place on the output shaft using Gear Installation Spacer T88T-7025-G, Shaft Adapter T75L-7025-P, Shaft Adapter Screw T75L-7025-P, Shaft Adapter Screw T75L-7025-K, Remover/Replacer Tube T75L-7025-B, nut and washer, or equivalents. Install the reverse gear with the longer flange facing forward.

32. Install the output shaft rear bearing using Gear Installation Spacer T88T-7025-G, Shaft Adapter T75L-7025-P, Shaft Adapter Screw T75L-7025-K, Remover/Replacer Tube T75L-7025-B, nut and washer, or equivalents.

33. Remove the temporary spacer.

34. Install the countershaft rear bearing.

35. Lock the transmission in 1st and 3rd. Install new output shaft and countershaft locknuts. Torque the output shaft locknut to 160–200 ft. lbs.; torque the countershaft locknut to 94–144 ft. lbs.

WARNING: Always use new locknuts. Make sure that the bearings are fully seated before torquing the locknuts.

36. Using a centerpunch, stake the locknuts.

37. Install the speedometer drive gear and steel ball on the output shaft. The ball can be installed in any of the three detents. Make sure, if you are installing a new speedometer gear, make sure that it is the same color code as the old one.

38. Clean the mating surfaces of the extension housing and case. Apply a ⅛ in. (3mm) wide bead of silicone RTV sealant to the case.

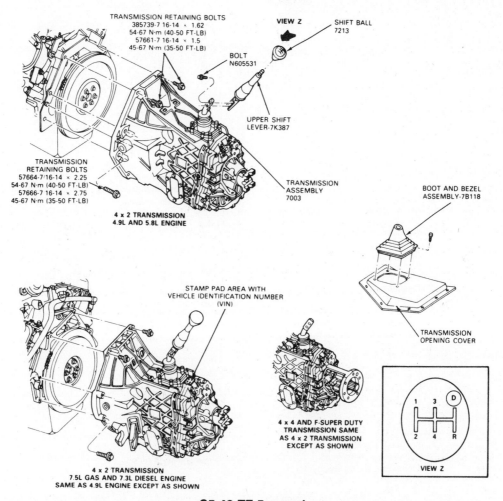

S5-42 ZF 5-speed

* SERVICED AS A COMPLETE
SUB ASSEMBLY

1. Shift lever boot
2. Snap ring
3. Capscrew
4. Shift tower cover
5. Gasket
6. Lower shift lever
7. Guide piece
8. Guide piece
9. Hex bolts
10. Shift housing
11. Shift detent
12. Gasket
13. 5th-reverse interlock
14. Interlock spring
15. Interlock roll pin
16. Interlock roll pin
17. Sealing cap
18. Spring
19. Shift rail detent
20. Front case
21. Sealing cap
22. Plug—drain
23. Bolt
24. Gasket
25. PTO cover
26. Bolt
27. Backup lamp switch
28. Sealing ring
29. Plug—filler
30. ID plate
31. Central shift rail bearing
32. O-ring
33. Quill
34. Oil seal
35. Shim
36. Baffle
37. Input shaft bearing
38. Input shaft

39. Mainshaft bearing
40. Snap ring
41. 4th gear synchronizer ring
42. Ball
43. Pressure piece
44. Spring
45. 3rd-4th synchronizer body
46. 3rd gear synchronizer ring
47. 3rd-4th sliding sleeve
48. 3rd gear
49. Caged needle rollers
50. Bearing race
51. Thrust washer
52. 2nd gear
53. Caged needle rollers
54. Snap ring
55. 2nd gear synchronizer ring
56. Ball
57. Pressure piece
58. Spring
59. 1st-2nd synchronizer body
60. 1st gear synchronizer ring
61. 1st-2nd sliding sleeve
62. 1st gear
63. Needle rollers
64. Mainshaft
65. Caged needle rollers
66. Reverse gear
67. Reverse gear synchronizer ring
68. Ball
69. Pressure piece
70. Spring
71. 5th-reverse synchronizer body
72. 5th gear syncrhonizer ring
73. 5th-reverse sliding sleeve

74. Snap ring
75. Caged needle rollers
76. 5th gear
77. Mainshaft bearing
78. Speedometer drive gear (4 × 2 only)
79. Central shift rail bearing
80. Magnet
81. Dowel
82. Bolt
83. Rear case (4 × 2)
84. Rear oil seal (4 × 2)
85. Output yoke (4 × 2)
86. Locknut (4 × 2)
87. Rear case (4 × 4)
88. Snap ring (4 × 4)
89. Oil seal (4 × 4)
90. Shim
91. Front countershaft bearing
92. Snap ring
93. Countershaft drive gear
94. Countershaft 3rd gear
95. Countershaft
96. Countershaft 5th gear
97. Snap ring
98. Countershaft rear bearing
99. Reverse idler shaft
100. Caged needle rollers
101. Reverse idler gear
102. Screw and sealing ring

103. Screw and sealing ring
104. Plug
105. Central shift rail
106. Shift finger
107. Plug
108. Roll pin
109. Roll pin
110. Shift fork
111. Shift rail
112. Shift rail
113. Shift fork
114. Roll pin
115. Bolt
116. Interlock plate
117. Roll pin
118. Shift rail
119. Shift fork

S5-42 ZF 5-speed exploded view

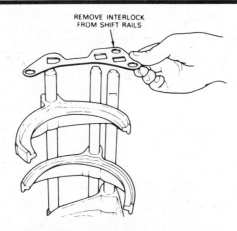

Removing the ZF shift interlock

NOTE: If the extension housing bushing is defective, the entire extension housing must be replaced.

39. Position the extension housing on the case and torque the bolts to 24–34 ft. lbs.
40. Place the synchronizers in the neutral position. Make sure that the shift forks in the cover are also in neutral.
41. Using a new gasket, without sealant, place the cover on the case and carefully engage the shift forks in the synchronizers. Apply sealant to the two rearmost cover bolts and install them. Install the remaining bolts without sealant. Torque the bolts to 12–16 ft. lbs.
42. Install the drain plug. Torque it to 40 ft. lbs.
43. Install the rear oil seal into the extension housing. Make sure that the drain hole faces downward.
44. Fill the case with Dexron®II fluid.

ZF S5-42 5-Speed Overdrive
MAIN COMPONENT DISASSEMBLY

1. Place the transmission face downward on a clean work surface.
2. Using a hammer and chisel, bend back the tab on the output shaft flange locknut.
3. Install a holding tool on the flange and loosen, but don't remove, the output shaft locknut.
4. Remove 15 of the 17 bolts holding the rear case cover to the case. Leave 2 bolts at opposite corners.
5. Remove any power take-off (pto) equipment.
6. Remove the shift tower assembly from the case.
7. Remove the interlock plate and compression spring which serves as a reverse gear interlock.

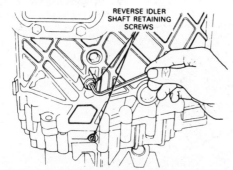

Removing the reverse idler shaft cap screws on the ZF

NOTE: Be careful...these parts tend to fall into the case.

8. Place a punch against the detent bolt cap, at an angle and slightly off center. Drive the cap inward until spring pressure against its underside forces the cap out of its hole. Repeat this procedure for the other two detent bolt sealing caps in the front case.

——— CAUTION ———
Always wear goggles! The cap is under spring pressure.

9. Remove the springs from the sealing cap holes.
10. Drive out the sealing caps from the two reverse idler shaft cap screws. Remove the screws.
11. Remove the back-up light switch and switch sealing ring.
12. Using a punch remove the two dowel pins from the two upper corners of the rear case mating surface. Drive them out towards the rear.
13. Remove the two remaining hex bolts from the rear case.
14. Carefully separate the front and rear cases. It may be necessary to push the central shift rail inwards to prevent it from hanging up on the front case. Be careful to ensure that the central shift rail is not lifted off with the front case.

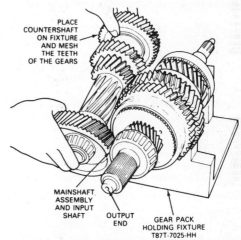

Using the gear pack holding fixture on the ZF

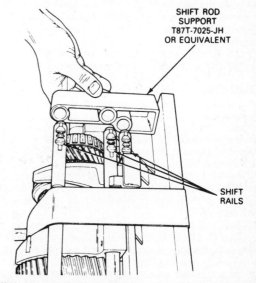

Installing the shift rod support on the ZF shift rails

WARNING: The case mating surfaces are sealed with RTV sealant in place of a gasket. If you experience difficulty in separating the case sections DON'T PRY THEM APART! Tap around the rear case section to break it loose with a rubber or plastic mallet.

15. Remove the central shift rail and shift finger assembly.

16. Lift the shaft out of the reverse idler gear and remove the gear and two caged roller bearings from the rear case.

17. Remove the three capscrews that retain the shift interlock to the rear case.

18. With the transmission on end, front up, install the Gear Pack Holding Fixture T87T-7025-HH using sling D87L-1000-A on the mainshaft and output shaft assemblies. Pass the sling over the shift rails.

19. Place Shift Rod Support T87T-7025-JH over the ends of the shift rails.

20. Turn the transmission to the horizontal position with the holding fixture under the gear pack.

21. Remove the output shaft flange retaining nut.

22. Remove the flange. If it's hard to get off, tap it off with a hammer.

23. Carefully pull the gearpack and shift rails, along with their holding fixtures, forward to dislodge them from the rear case.

24. Remove the speedometer drive gear from the mainshaft.

25. Remove the sling from around the shift rails, gearpack and fixture.

26. Turn the shift rails 45° to release them from the shift hubs.

27. Lift the shift rails, forks and interlock, together with the Support Tool from the mainshaft.

28. Using the shift rod support tool as a base, set the shift rail assembly on a work bench with the shift rails in a vertical position. Remove the interlock.

29. Make identifying marks on each shift fork and shift rail and position them in the holding fixture. Lift the shift rails from the support tool.

30. Lift the countershaft off of the workbench stand. Separate the input shaft from the mainshaft. Lift the mainshaft and output shaft from the stand.

31. Remove the rear cover from the holding fixture.

SUBASSEMBLIES

1. **Shift Tower:**
   a. Remove the lever cover from the shift housing.
   b. Lift the lever, boot, cover and attached parts off the housing.
   c. Slide the two pieces off the cardan joint.
   d. Slide the boot and cover off the top of the gearshift lever.
   e. Invert the cover and remove the boot snapring.
   f. Assemble the parts in reverse order of disassembly.

2. **Shift Rails:**
   a. Install each shift rail in a soft-jawed vise and drive the roll pins out of the shift forks with a punch.
   b. Assembly is the reverse of disassembly.

3. **Rear Case:**
   a. Drive the two dowel pins out of the rear case.
   b. Using a slide hammer and internal puller, remove the mainshaft rear bearing outer race from the rear case.
   c. Using a drift, drive the mainshaft rear seal out of the rear cover. Discard the seal.
   d. Using a slide hammer and bearing cup puller, remove the countershaft rear bearing outer race from the rear case.
   e. Remove the central shift rail bearing from the rear cover using Blind Hole Puller D80L-100-Q and Slide Hammer T50T-100-A.
   f. To install the central shift rail bearing, heat the rear case bore area to 320°F (160°C) with a heat gun. Insert the ball sleeve and drive the bearing in until it seats against its stop using Needle Bearing Replacer T87T-7025-DH.
   g. Heat the rear case in the area around the countershaft rear bearing outer race to 320°F (160°C) with a heat gun. In-

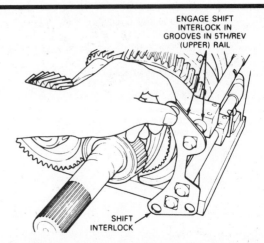

Installing the interlock on the ZF shift rails

stall the countershaft bearing outer race with a driver until it seats against its stop.

   h. Heat the case in the area of the mainshaft outer race to 320°F (160°C) with a heat gun. Drive the bearing cup into its bore with a driver and cup tool, until it seats against its stop.

4. **Front Case:**
   a. Using a slide hammer and cup puller, remove the input shaft bearing outer race from the front case.
   b. Remove the baffle and shims. Discard the baffle.
   c. Using a punch, drive out the input shaft oil seal from the base of the quill.
   d. Remove the O-ring from the quill. Remove the oil seal.
   e. Remove the countershaft front bearing outer race using a slide hammer and internal puller.
   f. Remove the fluid drain and fill plugs.
   g. Remove the sealing caps and three shift rail detents from the case.
   h. Remove the roll pins that hold the 5th/reverse interlock plate from their bores in the case, just below the shift housing.
   i. Remove the central shift rail needle bearings from the front case with a slide hammer and blind hole puller.
   j. Install the 5th/reverse roll pins into their bores until the bigger one bottoms out. It should stick out about 8mm. The small one sticks out about 4–5mm. Don't allow the small one to bottom out.

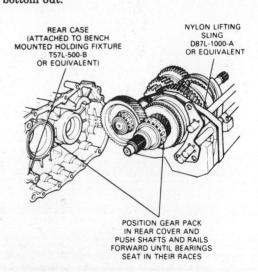

Assembling the ZF rear case to the main case

k. Heat the front case in the area of the central shift rail bearing bore to 320°F (160°C) with a heat gun. Drive the bearing sleeve in with a driver until it is flush with the surface of the bore.

l. Install the drain and fill plugs. Torque them to 44 ft. lbs.

m. Insert the three shift rail detent bolts into their bores. They must seat in the detents and must move freely when installed.

n. Place a new O-ring on the input shaft quill.

o. Position the seal in the front case. Drive it in with a seal driver until it seats against its stop in the quill.

NOTE: If the countershaft, input shaft, mainshaft or any tapered roller bearing is replaced, it will be necessary to adjust the tapered roller bearings to obtain a preload of 0.02–0.11mm. See the ADJUSTMENTS section below.

p. Heat the mounting bore in the front case for the tapered roller bearing outer race of the countershaft to 320°F (160°C) with a heat gun. Position the proper thickness shim in the bore. Using a bearing driver, drive the race in until it seats against the stop in the case.

q. Heat the front case in the area of the input shaft tapered roller bearing outer race to 320°F (160°C) with a heat gun.

r. Using the ADJUSTMENT procedures below, position the correct shim pack in the bore for the input shaft bearing outer race. Using a driver, drive the bearing cup into place until it seats against its stop in the bore.

5. Mainshaft:

a. Clamp the output end of the mainshaft in a soft-jawed vise.

b. Remove the 4th gear synchronizer ring from the 3rd/4th synchronizer assembly.

c. Place the bearing collets T87T–7025–FH on either side of the mainshaft front bearing. Position Puller Tube T77J–7025–B in the collets. Pass the Collet Retaining Ring T75L–7025–G over the puller and into the collets so they clamp firmly on the bearing. Pull the bearing from the mainshaft.

d. Remove the 3rd/4th gear sliding sleeve from the mainshaft. Place a cloth around the synchronizer to catch the compression springs, pressure pieces and balls that will be released when the sliding sleeves are removed.

e. Remove the cap ring that retains the 3rd/4th synchronizer body to the mainshaft.

f. Place the Collet Retaining ring T87T–7025–OH over the mainshaft and let it rest on the mainshaft 1st gear.

g. Position the two collet halves T87T–7025–NH on the 3rd/4th synchronizer body and slide the collet retaining ring over the collet halves to hold them in place on the synchronizer body.

h. Place the Shaft Protector D80L–625–4 on the end of the mainshaft. Place a 3-jawed puller on the collet halves and retaining ring, and pull the synchronizer body from the mainshaft.

i. Remove the synchronizer ring from the mainshaft 3rd gear.

j. Remove the 3rd gear from the mainshaft.

k. Remove the 3rd gear caged needle rollers from the mainshaft.

l. Lift the 1st/2nd gear sliding sleeve up as far as it will go. Position Collet Retaining Ring T87T–7025–OH over the mainshaft and let it rest on the 1st gear.

m. Position the two Collet Halves T87T–7025–MH so they seat in the groove in the 1st/2nd sliding sleeve. Pass the retaining ring from below over the two halves and secure them to the sliding sleeve.

n. Position the shaft protector D80L–625–4 on the end of the mainshaft. Position a 3-jawed puller on the collet retaining ring and pull off the 1st/2nd sliding sleeve, 2nd gear, thrust washer, and 3rd gear bearing inner race from the mainshaft.

CAUTION

Wrap a heavy cloth around the 1st/2nd synchronizer body to catch the springs, pressure pieces and balls.

o. Remove the snapring retaining the 1st/2nd synchronizer to the mainshaft.

p. Reposition the mainshaft in the vise so that the output end is facing upward.

q. Place a bearing gripper on the mainshaft rear tapered roller bearing. The gripper must be used to back the bearing during removal. Place a 3-jawed puller over the mainshaft and onto the gripper. Pull the bearing from the mainshaft.

r. Remove 5th gear from the mainshaft along with its caged needle rollers.

s. Remove the synchronizer ring from the 5th/reverse synchronizer.

t. Remove the snapring from the 5th/reverse synchronizer body. Remove the 5th/reverse sliding sleeve.

CAUTION

Wrap a heavy cloth around the 1st/2nd synchronizer body to catch the springs, pressure pieces and balls.

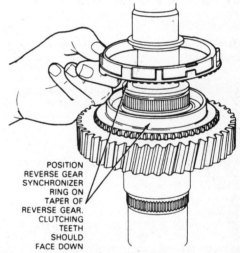

POSITION REVERSE GEAR SYNCHRONIZER RING ON TAPER OF REVERSE GEAR. CLUTCHING TEETH SHOULD FACE DOWN

Installing the reverse gear synchronizer ring on the ZF

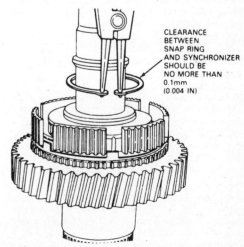

CLEARANCE BETWEEN SNAP RING AND SYNCHRONIZER SHOULD BE NO MORE THAN 0.1mm (0.004 IN)

5th/reverse synchronizer snapring on the ZF

u. Position Collet Retaining Ring T87T–7025–OH over the mainshaft and let it rest on the 1st gear. Position the two Collet Halves T87T–7025–NH so the ridge rests between the synchronizer body and the synchronizer ring. Slide the retaining ring upwards around the collets to secure them in position.

v. Position a 3-jawed puller on the collet retaining ring and pull the 5th/reverse synchronizer body from the mainshaft. Remove the synchronizer ring from the reverse gear. Remove the reverse gear from the mainshaft along with the caged needle bearings.

w. Remove the mainshaft from the vise. Position the mainshaft in a press and press off the 1st gear and 1st/2nd synchronizer body.

x. Remove the 1st gear caged needle rollers.

To assemble the mainshaft:

a. Clamp the input end of the mainshaft in a soft-jawed vise.

b. Place the reverse gear caged needle roller on the mainshaft.

c. Place the reverse gear on the mainshaft over the needle rollers. The clutch teeth must face upwards.

NOTE: Before installing the original synchronizer ring and body, check them for excessive wear.

d. Position the reverse gear synchronizer ring on the taper of the first gear.

e. Using a heat gun, heat the 5th/reverse synchronizer body to 320°F (160°C).

WARNING: Don't heat the synchronizer body for more than 15 minutes.

f. Position the synchronizer body on the mainshaft splines so that the side with the deeper hub faces downwards and the short lugs on the synchronizer ring engage the gaps in the synchronizer body. Push or lightly tap the synchronizer body down until it stops.

g. Install the snapring on the mainshaft next to the 5th/reverse synchronizer body. The clearance between the snapring and the synchronizer body should be 0–0.1mm, with 0 preferable.

h. Check the reverse gear endplay. Endplay should be 0.15–0.35mm.

i. Position the 5th/reverse sliding sleeve over the synchronizer body with the 2 grooves facing upwards. Align the tooth gaps and lugs. Slide the sleeve down until it rests against the reverse gear clutching teeth.

j. Insert the 3 compression springs and pressure pieces in the recesses of the synchronizer body. If the original springs are being reused, inspect them carefully and replace them if they appear worn or damaged.

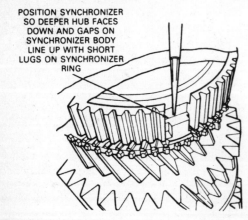

POSITION SYNCHRONIZER SO DEEPER HUB FACES DOWN AND GAPS ON SYNCHRONIZER BODY LINE UP WITH SHORT LUGS ON SYNCHRONIZER RING

Installing the synchronizer body on the ZF mainshaft

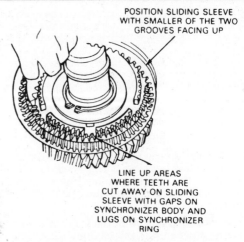

POSITION SLIDING SLEEVE WITH SMALLER OF THE TWO GROOVES FACING UP

LINE UP AREAS WHERE TEETH ARE CUT AWAY ON SLIDING SLEEVE WITH GAPS ON SYNCHRONIZER BODY AND LUGS ON SYNCHRONIZER RING

5th/reverse installation on the ZF

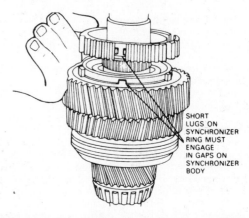

SHORT LUGS ON SYNCHRONIZER RING MUST ENGAGE IN GAPS ON SYNCHRONIZER BODY

Synchronizer ring installation showing engaging lugs, on the ZF

k. Push the pressure pieces back with a screwdriver. Push the balls in with a screwdriver and slide the pressure piece against the ball.

l. Place the 5th gear synchronizer ring on the synchronizer body. The short lugs on the synchronizer ring should be located over the gaps in the 5th/reverse synchronizer body.

m. Push the 5th gear synchronizer ring downwards while pulling the sliding sleeve into the center position.

n. Pace the 5th gear caged needle rollers on the mainshaft. Install the 5th gear on the mainshaft over the caged needle rollers.

o. Heat the inner race of the mainshaft rear tapered roller bearing to 320°F (160°C) with a heat gun. Place it on the mainshaft and drive it until it seats against its stop.

WARNING: Don't heat the bearing for more than 15 minutes.

p. Check the 5th gear endplay. Endplay should be 0.15–0.35mm.

q. Turn the mainshaft over and clamp it on the input end. Place the 1st gear caged needle rollers on the shaft. Place 1st gear over the rollers with the taper facing upward.

r. Place the 1st gear synchronizer ring on the 1st gear taper. Heat the 1st/2nd synchronizer body with a heat gun to 320°F (160°C). Position the synchronizer body on the mainshaft splines so that the short lugs on the synchronizer ring engage the gaps in the synchronizer body. Push the synchronizer body down until it stops against the ring. If the in-

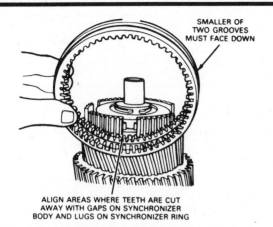

SMALLER OF
TWO GROOVES
MUST FACE DOWN

ALIGN AREAS WHERE TEETH ARE CUT
AWAY WITH GAPS ON SYNCHRONIZER
BODY AND LUGS ON SYNCHRONIZER RING

3rd gear sliding sleeve installation on the ZF

stallation was correct, the word ENGINE will appear on the synchronizer body.

WARNING: Don't heat the bearing for more than 15 minutes.

s. Install a snapring on the mainshaft next to the 1st/2nd synchronizer body. Clearance between the snapring and synchronizer body should be 0–0.1mm. 1st gear endplay should be 0.15–0.35mm.

t. Position the sliding sleeve over the synchronizer body with its tapered collar facing downward. Align the lugs and tooth gaps, and push the sleeve down until it rests against 1st gear.

u. Insert the three compression springs and pressure pieces in the recesses of the synchronizer body. Push the pressure pieces back with a screwdriver. Push the balls in with a screwdriver and slide the pressure piece against the ball.

v. Place the 2nd gear synchronizer ring on the synchronizer body. The short lugs on the synchronizer ring should be located over the gaps in the 1st/2nd synchronizer body.

w. Push the 2nd gear synchronizer ring downwards while pulling the sliding sleeve into the center position. Pace the 2nd gear caged needle rollers on the mainshaft. Install the 2nd gear on the mainshaft over the caged needle rollers.

x. Heat the thrust washer to 320°F (160°C) with a heat gun. Place it on the mainshaft and drive it until it seats against its stop.

WARNING: Don't heat the washer for more than 15 minutes.

y. Heat the 3rd gear bearing inner race to 320°F (160°C) with a heat gun. Place the race on the mainshaft and push it down until it seats against its stop. Check the 2nd gear endplay. Endplay should be 0.15–0.45mm. After the 3rd gear has cooled, place the 3rd gear caged needle rollers over it. Place the 3rd gear over the needle rollers with the taper upwards. Place the 3rd gear synchronizer ring on the 3rd gear taper. Heat the 3rd/4th synchronizer body with a heat gun to 320°F (160°C). Position the body on the mainshaft splines so that the short lugs on the synchronizer ring engage the gaps in the body. Push the body down until it stops against the ring. The recess in the body must face upwards.

z. Install a snapring on the mainshaft next to the 1st/2nd synchronizer body. Clearance between the snapring and synchronizer body should be 0–0.1mm. 1st gear endplay should be 0.15–0.35mm. Position the sliding sleeve over the synchronizer body with its tapered collar facing downward. Align the lugs and tooth gaps, and push the sleeve down until it rests against 1st gear. Insert the three compression springs and

pressure pieces in the recesses of the synchronizer body. Push the pressure pieces back with a screwdriver. Push the balls in with a screwdriver and slide the pressure piece against the ball. Place the 2nd gear synchronizer ring on the synchronizer body. The short lugs on the synchronizer ring should be located over the gaps in the 1st/2nd synchronizer body. Push the 2nd gear synchronizer ring downwards while pulling the sliding sleeve into the center position. Pace the 2nd gear caged needle rollers on the mainshaft. Install the 2nd gear on the mainshaft over the caged needle rollers. Heat the thrust washer to 320°F (160°C) with a heat gun. Place it on the mainshaft and drive it until it seats against its stop.

WARNING: Don't heat the washer for more than 15 minutes.

6. Input Shaft Disassembly and Assembly:
a. Position the two Collet Halves (44803 and 44797) of Universal Bearing Remover Set D81L-4220-A around the input shaft bearing cone. Install the pulling tube and pull the bearing from the shaft.

b. Inspect the bearing and shaft thoroughly. Replace any worn or damaged parts.

c. Place the bearing on the shaft.

d. Place the Bearing Cone Replacer T85T-4621-AH over the bearing.

e. Position the shaft, bearing and tool in Press Plate T75L-1165-B.

f. Press the bearing on until it seats against its stop.

INPUT SHAFT AND MAINSHAFT TAPERED ROLLER BEARING PRELOAD MEASUREMENT

This adjustment is necessary whenever a major, related component is replaced.

1. Place the transmission on a holding fixture with the output shaft facing upward.

2. Attach a dial indicator with a magnetic base so that the measurement bar rests on the output end of the mainshaft.

3. Zero the indicator and pry up on the input shaft and mainshaft with a prybar. Note the indicator reading. The shim and shaft seal must have a combined thickness equal to the indicator reading plus 0.02–0.11mm.

COUNTERSHAFT TAPERED ROLLER BEARING PRELOAD MEASUREMENT

1. Using two 10mm hex screws, attach the magnetic mount dial indicator near the pto opening on the front case. Position the dial indicator gauge on the support in such a way that the measurement bar rests against the flat face of the 5th speed helical gear on the countershaft. Zero the gauge.

2. Insert prybars through each of the two pto openings and position them beneath the 5th speed helical gear on the countershaft. Pry upward gently. Preload should be 0.0–0.11mm. Use shims to correct the preload.

MAINSHAFT AND INPUT SHAFT TAPERED ROLLER BEARING PRELOAD ADJUSTMENT

1. Position the transmission with the input shaft facing upwards.

2. Drive the two dowel pins out of their holes in the front and rear cases, and lift the front case off of the rear case.

3. Using a slide hammer and internal puller, remove the countershaft and mainshaft tapered roller bearing outer races from the front case.

4. Fit each race with a shim, or shim and shaft seal, to obtain the required preload determined above. The countershaft preload is set with shims alone. The input shaft and mainshaft preload is set using shims and a baffle. In both cases, parts are installed under the outer race of the tapered roller bearing which seats in the front case.

5. Apply Loctite 574® to the mating surfaces of the front and rear cases.

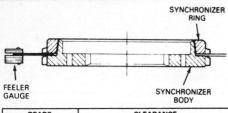

GEARS	CLEARANCE
1	0.6 mm (0.024 inch)
2	0.6 mm (0.024 inch)
3	0.6 mm (0.024 inch)
4	0.6 mm (0.024 inch)
5	0.6 mm (0.024 inch)
Reverse	0.2 mm (0.008 inch)

ZF synchronizer ring-to-body wear check

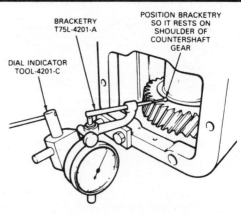

Measuring the ZF countershaft tapered roller bearing preload

WARNING: Do not use silicone type sealer.

6. Join the case sections and torque the bolts to 16 ft. lbs.

SYNCHRONIZER RING AND SYNCHRONIZER BODY WEAR CHECK

1. Install the ring on the body.
2. Insert a feeler gauge and measure the clearance at two opposite positions. If clearance is less than 0.6mm for the forward speed synchronizers and 0.2mm for the reverse synchronizer, replace the ring and/or synchronizer body as required.

SYNCHRONIZER COMPRESSION SPRING TENSION CHECK

The length of all springs should be 14.8mm; the outer diameter should be 5.96mm and the wire diameter should be 0.95mm. Replace any spring that is not to specifications.

MAIN COMPONENT ASSEMBLY

1. Place the input shaft and synchronizer ring assembly over the tapered roller bearing on the input end of the mainshaft.
2. Place the mainshaft and input shaft on Gear Pack Holding Fixture T87T–7025–HH. Place the countershaft on the fixture and mesh the gears of the two shafts.
3. Place the three shift rails and fork assemblies into Shift Rod Support Tool T87T–7025–JH in the same position from which they were removed during disassembly.
4. Position the three shift rail together with the shift rod support tool and interlock, so that the shift forks engage in the correct mainshaft sliding sleeves.
5. Place the shift interlock on the three gearshift rails and engage it in the interlock grooves in the 5th/reverse upper rail.
6. Slide the speedometer worm gear onto the mainshaft until it seats against its stop.
7. Secure the rear cover on the holding fixture T57L–500–B.
8. Position nylon lifting sling D87L–1000–A around the shift rails, holding fixture and mainshaft and countershaft.

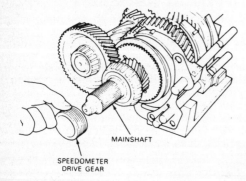

Installing the speedometer gear on the ZF mainshaft

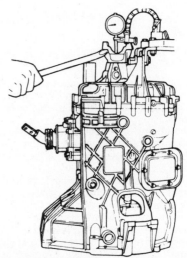

Measuring the preload on the ZF input shaft and mainshaft roller bearings

9. Position the gear pack into the rear cover and push the shafts and rails forward until the bearings seat in their races and the gearshift rails slide into their retaining holes.
10. Rotate the gear pack and rear case upwards so that the input shaft faces up.
11. Slide the output shaft flange onto the output end of the mainshaft so that it seats against its stop. Screw the hex nut onto the shaft finger-tightly.

NOTE: Make sure that the mainshaft bearing is not pushed off its race when the flange is installed.

12. Remove the shift rod support tool from the ends of the shift rails.
13. Remove the strap and gear pack holding fixture.
14. Attach the three capscrews that secure the shift interlock to the rear housing. Torque them to 84 inch lbs. Make sure that the interlock still moves freely.
15. Mesh the reverse idler gear and reverse gear. Slide the reverse idler shaft downward through the bearings and into the rear case. Tighten the bolt finger-tightly.
16. Insert the central shift rail and finger assembly into its bore in the rear case.
17. If the tapered roller bearings on the mainshaft or countershaft do not need adjustment, place a thin coating of Loctite 574® on the rear case mating surface. If the bearings need adjustment, do it at this time, then, apply sealer.

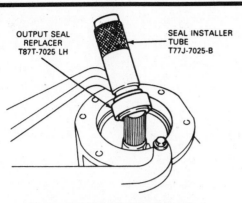

Replacing output shaft seal

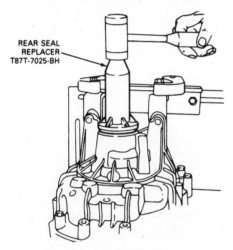

ZF rear oil seal installation

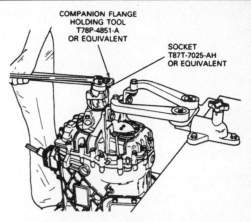

Installing the output flange on the ZF

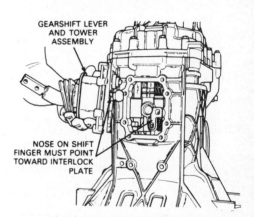

Installing the ZF shift tower assembly

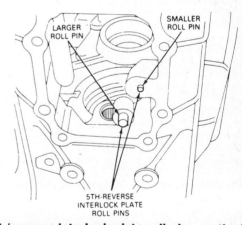

5th/reverse interlock plate roll pins on the ZF

NOTE: Do not use silicone type sealers.

18. Push the three shift rail detents back into their holes in the front case.

19. Carefully place the front case half over the shafts and gearshift rails until it rests on the mating surface of the rear case. It may be necessary to push the central shift rail inward to clear the inner surfaces of the front case.

20. Drive in the two dowels that align the rear case and front case. Insert the two hex screws and tighten them finger-tightly.

21. Screw to additional hex screws into the rear case and make them finger tight.

22. If shaft preload adjustment is not necessary, install all the hex screws and torque all of them to 18 ft. lbs. If adjustment is necessary, do it at this time, then install and tighten all the hex screws.

23. Insert the reverse idler shaft screws and torque them to 16 ft. lbs. Push the sealing cover into the screw heads.

24. Turn the transmission so that the input shaft is facing down.

25. Install the speedometer drive gear on the mainshaft.

26. Remove the hex nut that secures the output shaft flange to the mainshaft. Position the output shaft seal on the Output Shaft Seal Replacer Tool T87T-7025–BH. Position the seal and tool in the opening in the rear case. using a plastic or rubber mallet tap the seal in until it seats in the opening.

27. Install the output shaft flange on the shaft. Hold the flange with a holding fixture and torque the shaft nut to 184 ft. lbs.

28. Lock the nut by bending the locktabs.

29. Using new gaskets, install the pto covers and torque the bolts 28 ft. lbs.

30. Place the 5th/reverse gear interlock plate into position. Place the gasket over the shift tower mating surface on the front case. Make sure that the stop plate moves freely. Make sure that the plate and spring do not drop into the case.

31. Place the spring above the nose on the interlock plate and move both parts into their proper positions.

WARNING: Follow this sequence exactly to ensure proper interlock function!

32. Install the shift tower. The nose on the gearshift finger

must point towards the interlock plate. Install the spring washers and torque the screws to 18 ft. lbs.

33. Check the interlock operation.
34. Install the compression springs over each detent bolt.
35. Drive the sealing caps over the springs and detent bolts.

Each cap should seat ³⁄₆₄ in. (1.2mm) below the case surface. If you install them any deeper it will cause increased shift effort.

36. Install the back-up lamp switch and new sealing ring. Torque the switch to 15 ft. lbs.

CLUTCH

Understanding the Clutch

The purpose of the clutch is to disconnect and connect engine power from the transmission. A van at rest requires a lot of engine torque to get all that weight moving. An internal combustion engine does not develop a high starting torque (unlike steam engines), so it must be allowed to operate without any load until it builds up enough torque to move the van. Torque increases with engine rpm. The clutch allows the engine to build up torque by physically disconnecting the engine from the transmission, relieving the engine of any load or resistance. The transfer of engine power to the transmission (the load) must be smooth and gradual; if it weren't, drive line components would wear out or break quickly. This gradual power transfer is made possible by gradually releasing the clutch pedal. The clutch disc and pressure plate are the connecting link between the engine and transmission. When the clutch pedal is released, the disc and plate contact each other (clutch engagement), physically joining the engine and transmission. When the pedal is pushed in, the disc and plate separate (the clutch is disengaged), disconnecting the engine from the transmission.

The clutch assembly consists of the flywheel, the clutch disc, the clutch pressure plate, the throwout bearing and fork, the hydraulic system and the pedal. The flywheel and clutch pressure plate (driving members) are connected to the engine crankshaft and rotate with it. The clutch disc is located between the

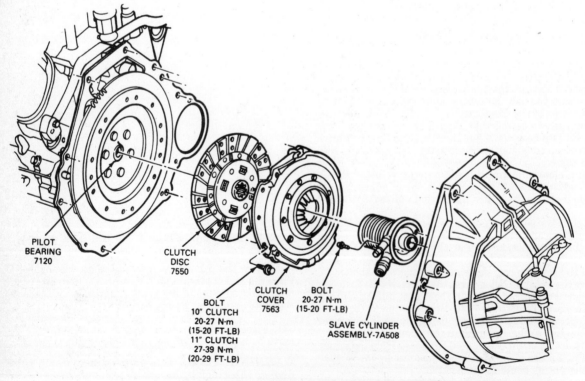

PILOT
BEARING
7120

CLUTCH
DISC
7550

BOLT
10" CLUTCH
20-27 N·m
(15-20 FT-LB)
11" CLUTCH
27-39 N·m
(20-29 FT-LB)

CLUTCH
COVER
7563

BOLT
20-27 N·m
(15-20 FT-LB)

SLAVE CYLINDER
ASSEMBLY-7A508

Clutch assembly for 1988 E-150 and E-250 with the 6- 4.9L, 8-5.0L and 8-5.8L engines

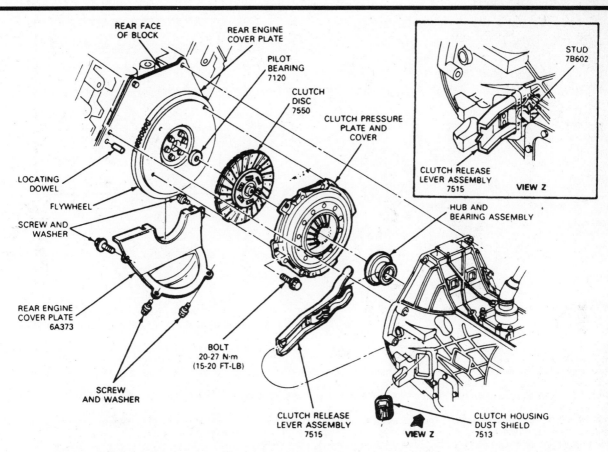

Clutch assembly for 1988 E-250 HD and E-350 with the 8-7.3L diesel and 8-7.5L engines

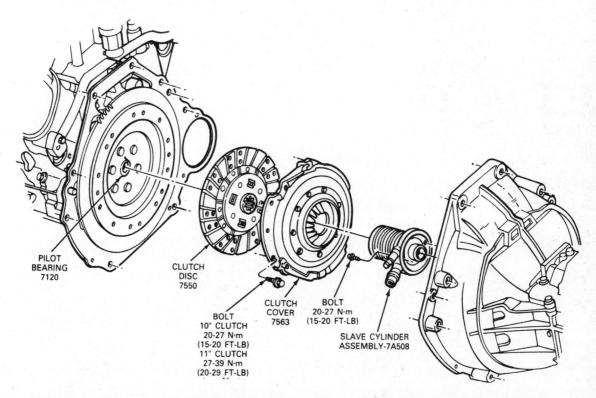

Clutch assembly for 1989 E-150 and E-250 with the 6- 4.9L, 8-5.0L and 8-5.8L engines

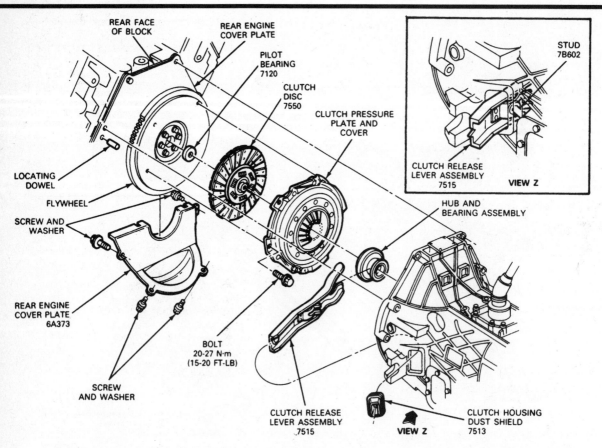

Clutch assembly for 1989 E-250 HD and E-350 with the 8-7.3L diesel and 8-7.5L engines

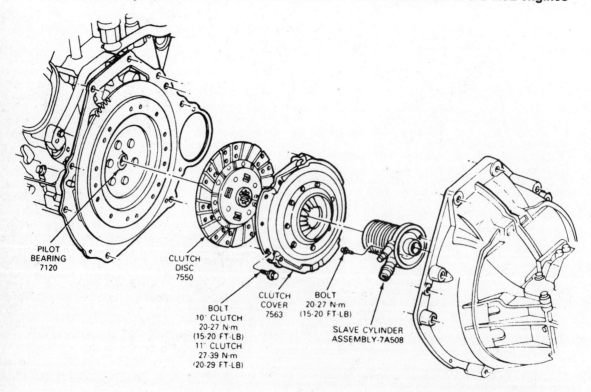

Clutch assembly for 1990-91 E-150 and E-250 with the 6-4.9L, 8-5.0L and 8-5.8L engines

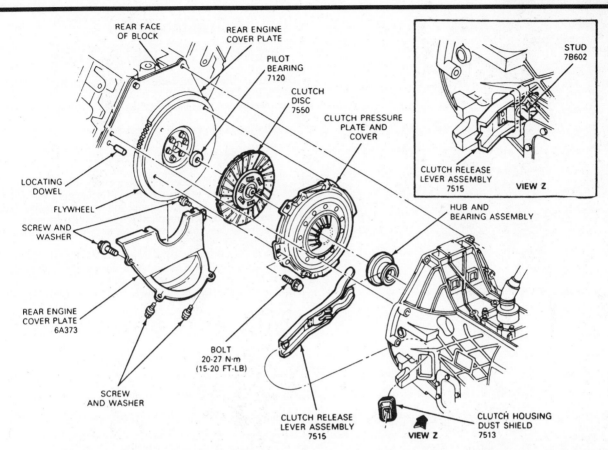

Clutch assembly for 1990-91 E-250 HD and E-350 with the 8-7.3L diesel and 8-7.5L engines

flywheel and pressure plate, and splined to the transmission shaft. A driving member is one that is attached to the engine and transfers engine power to a driven member (clutch disc) on the transmission shaft. A driving member (pressure plate) rotates (drives) a driven member (clutch disc) on contact and, in so doing, turns the transmission shaft. There is a circular diaphragm spring within the pressure plate cover (transmission side). In a relaxed state (when the clutch pedal is fully released), this spring is convex; that it, it is dished outward toward the transmission. Pushing in the clutch pedal actuates the hydraulic system. This system is comprised of a master cylinder, tubing and slave cylinder. The slave cylinder contacts the throwout bearing. The throwout bearing is attached to the fork. When the clutch pedal is depressed, the clutch slave cylinder pushes the fork and bearing forward to contact the diaphragm spring of the pressure plate. The outer edges of the spring are secured to the pressure plate and are pivoted on rings so that when the center of the spring is compressed by the throwout bearing, the outer edges bow outward and, by so doing, pull the pressure plate in the same direction — away from the clutch disc. This action separates the disc from the plate, disengaging the clutch and allowing the transmission to be shifted into another gear. A coil type clutch return spring attached to the clutch pedal arm permits full release of the pedal. Releasing the pedal pulls the throwout bearing away from the diaphragm spring resulting in a reversal of spring position. As bearing pressure is gradually released from the spring center, the outer edges of the spring bow outward, pushing the pressure plate into closer contact with the clutch disc. As the disc and plate move closer together, friction between the two increases and slippage is reduced until, when full spring pressure is applied (by fully releasing the pedal), The

speed of the disc and plate are the same. This stops all slipping, creating a direct connection between the plate and disc which results in the transfer of power from the engine to the transmission. The clutch disc is now rotating with the pressure plate at engine speed and, because it is splined to the transmission shaft, the shaft now turns at the same engine speed. Understanding clutch operation can be rather difficult at first; if you're still confused after reading this, consider the following analogy. The action of the diaphragm spring can be compared to that of an oil can bottom. The bottom of an oil can is shaped very much like the clutch diaphragm spring and pushing in on the can bottom and then releasing it produces a similar effect. As mentioned earlier, the clutch pedal return spring permits full release of the pedal.

The diaphragm spring type clutches used are available in two different designs: flat diaphragm springs or bent spring. The bent fingers are bent back to create a centrifugal boost ensuring quick re-engagement at higher engine speeds. This design enables pressure plate load to increase as the clutch disc wears and makes low pedal effort possible even with a heavy-duty clutch. The throwout bearing used with the bent finger design is 1¼ in. (31.75mm) long and is shorter than the bearing used with the flat finger design. These bearings are not interchangeable. If the longer bearing is used with the bent finger clutch, free-pedal travel will not exist. This results in clutch slippage and rapid wear.

The transmission varies the gear ratio between the engine and rear wheels. It can be shifted to change engine speed as driving conditions and loads change. The transmission allows disengaging and reversing power from the engine to the wheels.

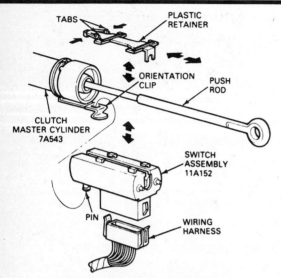

Clutch/starter interlock switch

Clutch Pedal

REMOVAL AND INSTALLATION

1. Disconnect the barbed retainer bushing on the inetrlock switch rod, from the pedal.
2. Remove the nut that secures the pedal to the shaft and remove the pedal.
3. Installation is the reverse of removal.

Hydraulic System

The hydraulic clutch system operates much like a hydraulic brake system. When you push down (disengage) the clutch pedal, the mechanical clutch pedal movement is converted into hydraulic fluid movement, which is then converted back into mechanical movement by the slave cylinder to actuate the clutch release lever.

The system consists of a combination clutch fluid reservoir/master cylinder assembly, a slave cylinder mounted on the bellhousing, and connecting tubing.

Fluid level is checked at the master cylinder reservoir. The

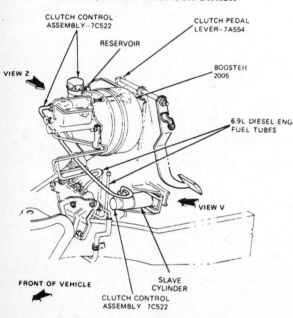

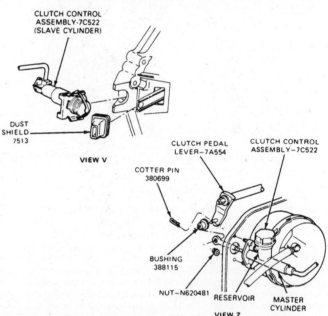

Clutch hydraulic system used on 1988-89 trucks with the Diesel and 8-7.5L gasoline engines

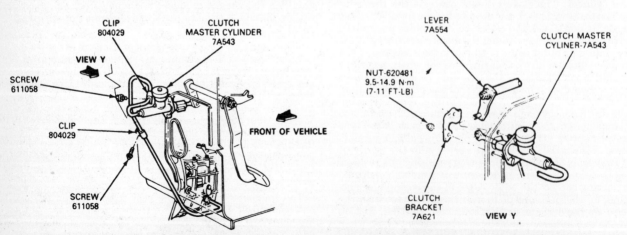

Clutch hydraulic system used on 1990-91 trucks equipped with the 6-4.9L, 8-5.0L and 8-5.8L engines

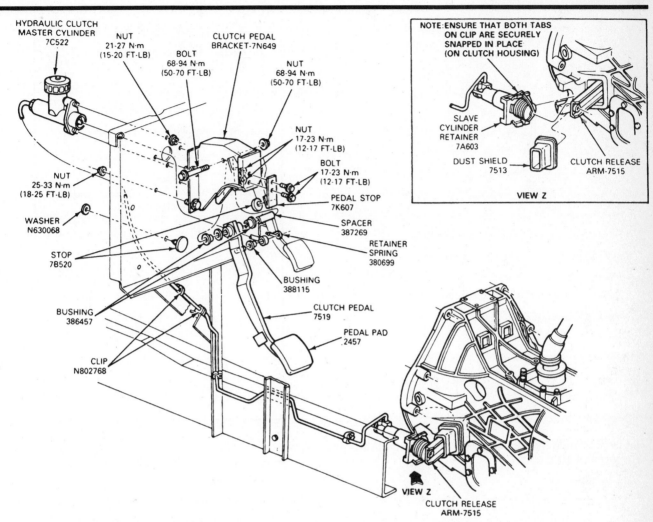

Clutch hydraulic system used on 1990-91 Stripped Chassis with the 8-7.3L diesel

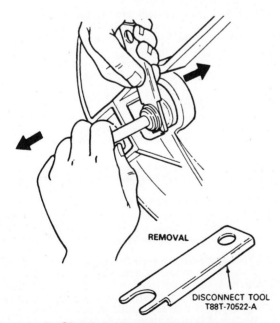

REMOVAL

DISCONNECT TOOL T88T-70522-A

Clutch hydraulic line removal

hydraulic clutch system continually remains in adjustment, like a hydraulic disc brake system, so not clutch linkage or pedal adjustment is necessary.

REMOVAL

There are 2 types of slave cylinders used: an internally mounted (in the bell housing) and an externally mounted type.

● 1989 — Diesel engines and the 8-7.5L gasoline engine use the externally mounted type; all others use the internally mounted type

● 1990–91 — Diesel engines, 8-7.5L gasoline engines, and V8 gasoline engines equipped with the M50DHD transmission use the externally mounted type; all others use the internally mounted type.

WARNING: Prior to any service on models with the externally mounted slave cylinder, that requires removal of the slave cylinder, such as transmission and/or clutch housing removal, the clutch master cylinder pushrod must be disconnected from the clutch pedal. Failure to do this may damage the slave cylinder if the clutch pedal is depressed while the slave cylinder is disconnected.

1. From inside the van, remove the cotter pin retaining the clutch master cylinder pushrod to the clutch pedal lever. Disconnect the pushrod and remove the bushing.

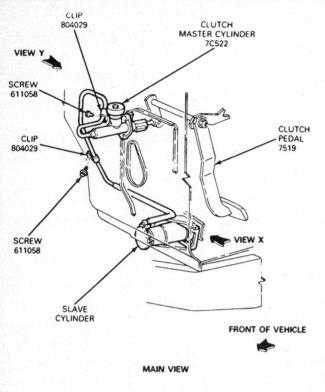
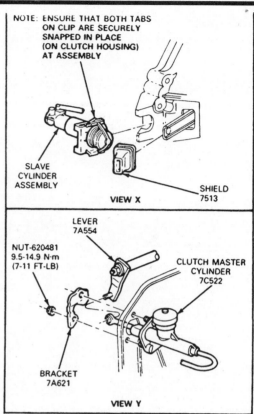

Clutch hydraulic system used on 1990-91 trucks equipped with the 6-4.9L, 8-5.0L, 8-7.3L diesel and 8- 7.5L engines and M5ODHD

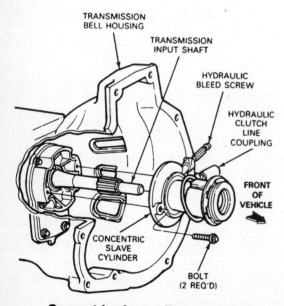

Concentric slave cylinder removal

2. Remove the two nuts retaining the clutch reservoir and master cylinder assembly to the firewall.

3. From the engine compartment, remove the clutch reservoir and master cylinder assembly from the firewall. Note here how the clutch tubing routes to the slave cylinder.

4. Push the release lever forward to compress the slave cylinder.

5. On all models with the internally mounted slave cylinder, remove the plastic clip that retains the slave cylinder to the bracket. Remove the slave cylinder.

6. On models with the externally mounted slave cylinder, the steel retaining clip is permanently attached to the slave cylinder. Remove the slave cylinder by prying on the clip to free the tangs while pulling the cylinder clear.

7. Remove the release lever by pulling it outward.

8. Remove the clutch hydraulic system from the van.

INSTALLATION

1. Position the clutch pedal reservoir and master cylinder assembly into the firewall from inside the cab, and install the two nuts and tighten.

2. Route the clutch tubing and slave cylinder to the bell housing, taking care that the nylon lines are kept away from any hot exhaust system components.

3. Install the slave cylinder by pushing the slave cylinder pushrod into the cylinder. Engage the pushrod into the release lever and slide the slave cylinder into the bell housing lugs. Seat the cylinder into the recess in the lugs.

NOTE: When installing a new hydraulic system, you'll notice that the slave cylinder contains a shipping strap that propositions the pushrod for installation, and also provides a bearing insert. Following installation of the new slave cylinder, the first actuation of the clutch pedal will break the shipping strap and give normal clutch action.

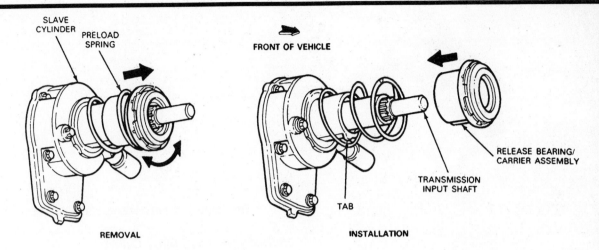

SLAVE CYLINDER
PRELOAD SPRING

FRONT OF VEHICLE

RELEASE BEARING/ CARRIER ASSEMBLY

TRANSMISSION INPUT SHAFT

TAB

REMOVAL

INSTALLATION

Clutch release bearing removal with the concentric slave cylinder

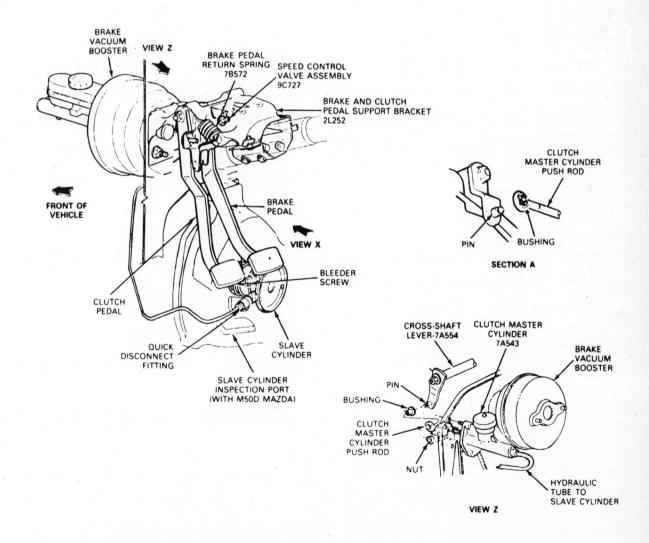

BRAKE VACUUM BOOSTER

VIEW Z

BRAKE PEDAL RETURN SPRING 7B572

SPEED CONTROL VALVE ASSEMBLY 9C727

BRAKE AND CLUTCH PEDAL SUPPORT BRACKET 2L252

CLUTCH MASTER CYLINDER PUSH ROD

FRONT OF VEHICLE

BRAKE PEDAL

VIEW X

PIN

BUSHING

SECTION A

CLUTCH PEDAL

BLEEDER SCREW

QUICK DISCONNECT FITTING

SLAVE CYLINDER

SLAVE CYLINDER INSPECTION PORT (WITH M50D MAZDA)

CROSS-SHAFT LEVER-7A554

CLUTCH MASTER CYLINDER 7A543

BRAKE VACUUM BOOSTER

PIN

BUSHING

CLUTCH MASTER CYLINDER PUSH ROD

NUT

HYDRAULIC TUBE TO SLAVE CYLINDER

VIEW Z

1988-89 clutch hydraulic system on trucks with the 6- 4.9L, 8-5.0L and 8-5.8L engines

Bleeding the external slave cylinder

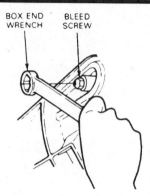

Bleeding the concentric slave cylinder

4. Clean the master cylinder pushrod bearing and apply a light film of SAE 30 engine oil.

5. From inside the cab, install the bushing on the clutch pedal lever. Connect the clutch master cylinder pushrod to the clutch pedal lever and install the cotter pin.

6. Check the clutch reservoir and add fluid if required. Depress the clutch pedal at least ten times to verify smooth operation and proper clutch release.

HYDRAULIC SYSTEM BLEEDING

Externally Mounted Slave Cylinder

1. Clean the reservoir cap and the slave cylinder connection.
2. Remove the slave cylinder from the housing.
3. Using a ³/₃₂ in. punch, drive out the pin that holds the tube in place.
4. Remove the tube from the slave cylinder and place the end of the tube in a container.
5. Hold the slave cylinder so that the connector port is at the highest point, by tipping it about 30° from horizontal. Fill the cylinder with DOT 3 brake fluid through the port. It may be necessary to rock the cylinder or slightly depress the pushrod to expel all the air.

WARNING: Pushing too hard on the pushrod will spurt fluid from the port!

6. When all air is expelled — no more bubble are seen — install the slave cylinder.

NOTE: Some fluid will be expelled during installation as the pushrod is depressed.

7. Remove the reservoir cap. Some fluid will run out of the tube end into the container. Pour fluid into the reservoir until a steady stream of fluid runs out of the tube and the reservoir is filled. Quickly install the diaphragm and cap. The flow should stop.

8. Connect the tube and install the pin. Check the fluid level.
9. Check the clutch operation.

Internally Mounted Slave Cylinder

NOTE: With the quick-disconnect coupling, no air should enter the system when the coupling is disconnected. However, if air should somehow enter the system, it must be bled.

1. Remove the reservoir cap and diaphragm. Fill the reservoir with DOT 3 brake fluid.
2. Connect a piece of rubber tubing to the slave cylinder bleed screw. Place the other end in a container.
3. Loosen the bleed screw. Gravity will force fluid from the master cylinder to flow down to the slave cylinder, forcing air out of the bleed screw. When a steady stream — no bubbles — flows out, the system is bled. Close the bleed screw.

NOTE: Check periodically to make sure the master cylinder reservoir doesn't run dry.

4. Add fluid to fill the master cylinder reservoir.
5. Fully depress the clutch pedal. Release it as quickly as possible. Pause for 2 seconds. Repeat this procedure 10 times.
6. Check the fluid level. Refill it if necessary. It should be kept full.
7. Repeat Steps 5 and 6 five more times.
8. Install the diaphragm and cap.
9. Have an assistant hold the pedal to the floor while you crack the bleed screw — not too far — just far enough to expel any trapped air. Close the bleed screw, then, release the pedal.
10. Check, and if necessary, fill the reservoir.

Clutch Disc and Pressure Plate
REMOVAL AND INSTALLATION

——————— CAUTION ———————
The clutch driven disc contains asbestos, which has been determined to be a cancer causing agent. Never clean clutch surfaces with compressed air! Avoid inhaling any dust from any clutch surface! When cleaning clutch surfaces, use a commercially available brake cleaning fluid.

1989

1. Raise and support the van on jackstands.
2. On vans with the externally mounted slave cylinder, remove the clutch slave cylinder.

On vans with an internally mounted slave cylinder, disconnect the quick-disconnect coupling with a spring coupling tool such as T88T-70522-A.

3. Remove the transmission.
4. On gasoline engine models, except the 8-7.5L engine, remove the starter. Remove the flywheel housing attaching bolts and remove the housing.

On diesel engine models and the 8-7.5L gasoline engine, remove the cover and then remove the release lever and bearing from the clutch housing. To remove the release lever:

a. Remove the dust boot.

b. Push the release lever forward to compress the slave cylinder.

c. Remove the slave cylinder by prying on the steel clip to free the tangs while pulling the cylinder clear.

d. Remove the release lever by pulling it outward.

5. Mark the pressure plate and cover assembly and the flywheel so that they can be reinstalled in the same relative position.

6. Loosen the pressure plate and cover attaching bolts evenly in a staggered sequence a turn at at time until the pressure plate springs are relieved of their tension. Remove the attaching bolts.

7. Remove the pressure plate and cover assembly and the clutch disc from the flywheel.

8. Position the clutch disc on the flywheel so that an aligning tool or spare transmission mainshaft can enter the clutch pilot bearing and align the disc.

9. When reinstalling the original pressure plate and cover assembly, align the assembly and flywheel according to the marks made during removal. Position the pressure plate and cover assembly on the flywheel, align the pressure plate and disc, and install the retaining bolts. Tighten the bolts in an alternating sequence a few turns at a time until the proper torque is reached:

- 10 in. and 12 in. clutch: 15–20 ft. lbs.
- 11 in. clutch: 20–29 ft. lbs.

10. Remove the tool used to align the clutch disc.

11. With the clutch fully released, apply a light coat of grease on the sides of the driving lugs.

12. Position the clutch release bearing and the bearing hub on the release lever. Install the release lever on the fulcrum in the flywheel housing. Apply a light coating of grease to the release lever fingers and the fulcrum. Fill the groove of the release bearing hub with grease.

13. If the flywheel housing has been removed, position it against the rear engine cover plate and install the attaching bolts and tighten them to 40–50 ft. lbs.

14. Install the starter motor, if removed.

15. Install the transmission.

16. Install the salve cylinder and bleed the system.

1990–91

1. Raise and support the van on jackstands.

2. On vans with the externally mounted slave cylinder, remove the clutch slave cylinder.

On vans with an internally mounted slave cylinder, disconnect the quick-disconnect coupling with a spring coupling tool such as T88T-70522-A.

3. Remove the transmission.

4. On models with the internally mounted slave cylinder, re-

move the starter. Remove the flywheel housing attaching bolts and remove the housing.

On models with the externally mounted slave cylinder, remove the cover and then remove the release lever and bearing from the clutch housing. To remove the release lever:

a. Remove the dust boot.

b. Push the release lever forward to compress the slave cylinder.

c. Remove the slave cylinder by prying on the steel clip to free the tangs while pulling the cylinder clear.

d. Remove the release lever by pulling it outward.

5. Mark the pressure plate and cover assembly and the flywheel so that they can be reinstalled in the same relative position.

6. Loosen the pressure plate and cover attaching bolts evenly in a staggered sequence a turn at at time until the pressure plate springs are relieved of their tension. Remove the attaching bolts.

7. Remove the pressure plate and cover assembly and the clutch disc from the flywheel.

8. Position the clutch disc on the flywheel so that an aligning tool or spare transmission mainshaft can enter the clutch pilot bearing and align the disc.

WARNING: New pressure plate/cover bolts have been issued for use on the diesel and the 8-7.5L gasoline engine. The bolts for the diesel are $5/16$ in. × 18 × $3/4$ in. The bolts for the 8-7.5L are $5/16$ in. × 18 × $59/64$ in. The $59/64$ in. bolts cannot be used with the dual mass flywheel used on the diesel, since they would interfere with the operation of the primary flywheel.

9. When reinstalling the original pressure plate and cover assembly, align the assembly and flywheel according to the marks made during removal. Position the pressure plate and cover assembly on the flywheel, align the pressure plate and disc, and install the retaining bolts. Tighten the bolts in an alternating sequence a few turns at a time until the proper torque is reached:

- 10 in. and 12 in. clutch: 15–20 ft. lbs.
- 11 in. clutch: 20–29 ft. lbs.

10. Remove the tool used to align the clutch disc.

11. With the clutch fully released, apply a light coat of grease on the sides of the driving lugs.

12. Position the clutch release bearing and the bearing hub on the release lever. On the diesel and the 8-7.5L engine, clean and lubricate the transmission bearing retainer. Install the release lever on the fulcrum in the flywheel housing. Apply a light coating of grease to the release lever fingers and the fulcrum. Fill the groove of the release bearing hub with grease.

13. If the flywheel housing has been removed, position it against the rear engine cover plate and install the attaching bolts and tighten them to 40–50 ft. lbs.

14. Install the starter motor, if removed.

15. Install the transmission.

16. Install the salve cylinder and bleed the system.

AUTOMATIC TRANSMISSION

Understanding Automatic Transmissions

The automatic transmission allows engine torque and power to be transmitted to the rear wheels within a narrow range of engine operating speeds. The transmission will allow the engine to turn fast enough to produce plenty of power and torque at very low speeds, while keeping it at a sensible rpm at high vehicle speeds. The transmission performs this job entirely without driver assistance. The transmission uses a light fluid as the medium for the transmission of power. This fluid also works in the operation of various hydraulic control circuits and as a lubricant. Because the transmission fluid performs all of these three functions, trouble within the unit can easily travel from one part to another. For this reason, and because of the complexity and unusual operating principles of the transmission, a very sound understanding of the basic principles of operation will simplify troubleshooting.

THE TORQUE CONVERTER

The torque converter replaces the conventional clutch. It has three functions:

1. It allows the engine to idle with the vehicle at a standstill, even with the transmission in gear.

2. It allows the transmission to shift from range to range smoothly, without requiring that the driver close the throttle during the shift.

3. It multiplies engine torque to an increasing extent as vehicle speed drops and throttle opening is increased. This has the effect of making the transmission more responsive and reduces the amount of shifting required.

The torque converter is a metal case which is shaped like a sphere that has been flattened on opposite sides. It is bolted to the rear end of the engine's crankshaft. Generally, the entire metal case rotates at engine speed and serves as the engine's flywheel.

The case contains three sets of blades. One set is attached directly to the case. This set forms the torus or pump. Another set is directly connected to the output shaft, and forms the turbine. The third set is mounted on a hub which, in turn, is mounted on a stationary shaft through a one-way clutch. This third set is known as the stator.

A pump, which is driven by the converter hub at engine speed, keeps the torque converter full of transmission fluid at all times. Fluid flows continuously through the unit to provide cooling.

Under low speed acceleration, the torque converter functions as follows:

The torus is turning faster than the turbine. It picks up fluid at the center of the converter and, through centrifugal force, slings it outward. Since the outer edge of the converter moves faster than the portions at the center, the fluid picks up speed.

The fluid then enters the outer edge of the turbine blades. It then travels back toward the center of the converter case along the turbine blades. In impinging upon the turbine blades, the fluid loses the energy picked up in the torus.

If the fluid were now to immediately be returned directly into the torus, both halves of the converter would have to turn at approximately the same speed at all times, and torque input and output would both be the same.

In flowing through the torus and turbine, the fluid picks up two types of flow, or flow in two separate directions. It flows through the turbine blades, and it spins with the engine. The stator, whose blades are stationary when the vehicle is being accelerated at low speeds, converts one type of flow into another. Instead of allowing the fluid to flow straight back into the torus,

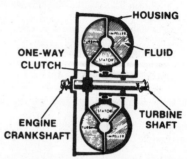

The torque converter housing is rotated by the engine's crankshaft, and turns the impeller. The impeller spins the turbine, which gives motion to the turbine shaft, driving the gears

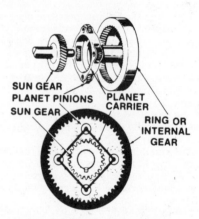

Planetary gears are similar to manual transmission gears but are composed of three parts

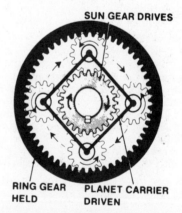

Planetary gears in the maximum reduction (low) range. The ring gear is held and a lower ration is obtained

the stator's curved blades turn the fluid almost 90° toward the direction of rotation of the engine. Thus the fluid does not flow as fast toward the torus, but is already spinning when the torus picks it up. This has the effect of allowing the torus to turn much faster than the turbine. This difference in speed may be compared to the difference in speed between the smaller and larger gears in any gear train. The result is that engine power output is higher, and engine torque is multiplied.

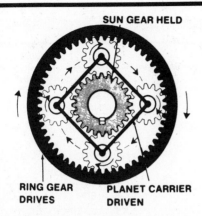

Planetary gears in the minimum reduction (drive) range. The ring gear is allowed to revolve, providing a higher gear ratio

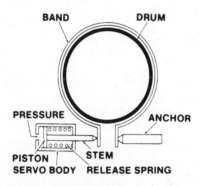

Servos, operated by pressure, are used to apply or release the bands, to either hold the ring gear or allow it to rotate

As the speed of the turbine increases, the fluid spins faster and faster in the direction of engine rotation. As a result, the ability of the stator to redirect the fluid flow is reduced. Under cruising conditions, the stator is eventually forced to rotate on its one-way clutch in the direction of engine rotation. Under these conditions, the torque converter begins to behave almost like a solid shaft, with the torus and turbine speeds being almost equal.

THE PLANETARY GEARBOX

The ability of the torque converter to multiply engine torque is limited. Also, the unit tends to be more efficient when the turbine is rotating at relatively high speeds. Therefore, a planetary gearbox is used to carry the power output of the turbine to the driveshaft.

Planetary gears function very similarly to conventional transmission gears. However, their construction is different in that three elements make up one gear system, and, in that all three elements are different from one another. The three elements are: an outer gear that is shaped like a hoop, with teeth cut into

the inner surface; a sun gear, mounted on a shaft and located at the very center of the outer gear; and a set of three planet gears, held by pins in a ring-like planet carrier, meshing with both the sun gear and the outer gear. Either the outer gear or the sun gear may be held stationary, providing more than one possible torque multiplication factor for each set of gears. Also, if all three gears are forced to rotate at the same speed, the gearset forms, in effect, a solid shaft.

Most modern automatics use the planetary gears to provide either a single reduction ratio of about 1.8:1, or two reduction gears: a low of about 2.5:1, and an intermediate of about 1.5:1. Bands and clutches are used to hold various portions of the gearsets to the transmission case or to the shaft on which they are mounted. Shifting is accomplished, then, by changing the portion of each planetary gearset which is held to the transmission case or to the shaft.

THE SERVOS AND ACCUMULATORS

The servos are hydraulic pistons and cylinders. They resemble the hydraulic actuators used on many familiar machines, such as bulldozers. Hydraulic fluid enters the cylinder, under pressure, and forces the piston to move to engage the band or clutches.

The accumulators are used to cushion the engagement of the servos. The transmission fluid must pass through the accumulator on the way to the servo. The accumulator housing contains a thin piston which is sprung away from the discharge passage of the accumulator. When fluid passes through the accumulator on the way to the servo, it must move the piston against spring pressure, and this action smooths out the action of the servo.

THE HYDRAULIC CONTROL SYSTEM

The hydraulic pressure used to operate the servos comes from the main transmission oil pump. This fluid is channeled to the various servos through the shift valves. There is generally a manual shift valve which is operated by the transmission selector lever and an automatic shift valve for each automatic upshift the transmission provides: i.e., 2-speed automatics have a low/high shift valve, while 3-speeds have a 1–2 valve, and a 2–3 valve.

There are two pressures which effect the operation of these valves. One is the governor pressure which is affected by vehicle speed. The other is the modulator pressure which is affected by intake manifold vacuum or throttle position. Governor pressure rises with an increase in vehicle speed, and modulator pressure rises as the throttle is opened wider. By responding to these two pressures, the shift valves cause the upshift points to be delayed with increased throttle opening to make the best use of the engine's power output.

Most transmissions also make use of an auxiliary circuit for downshifting. This circuit may be actuated by the throttle linkage or the vacuum line which actuates the modulator, or by a cable or solenoid. It applies pressure to a special downshift surface on the shift valve or valves.

The transmission modulator also governs the line pressure, used to actuate the servos. In this way, the clutches and bands will be actuated with a force matching the torque output of the engine.

Troubleshooting Basic Automatic Transmission Problems

Problem	Cause	Solution
Fluid leakage	• Defective pan gasket	• Replace gasket or tighten pan bolts
	• Loose filler tube	• Tighten tube nut
	• Loose extension housing to transmission case	• Tighten bolts
	• Converter housing area leakage	• Have transmission checked professionally
Fluid flows out the oil filler tube	• High fluid level	• Check and correct fluid level
	• Breather vent clogged	• Open breather vent
	• Clogged oil filter or screen	• Replace filter or clean screen (change fluid also)
	• Internal fluid leakage	• Have transmission checked professionally
Transmission overheats (this is usually accompanied by a strong burned odor to the fluid)	• Low fluid level	• Check and correct fluid level
	• Fluid cooler lines clogged	• Drain and refill transmission. If this doesn't cure the problem, have cooler lines cleared or replaced.
	• Heavy pulling or hauling with insufficient cooling	• Install a transmission oil cooler
	• Faulty oil pump, internal slippage	• Have transmission checked professionally
Buzzing or whining noise	• Low fluid level	• Check and correct fluid level
	• Defective torque converter, scored gears	• Have transmission checked professionally
No forward or reverse gears or slippage in one or more gears	• Low fluid level	• Check and correct fluid level
	• Defective vacuum or linkage controls, internal clutch or band failure	• Have unit checked professionally
Delayed or erratic shift	• Low fluid level	• Check and correct fluid level
	• Broken vacuum lines	• Repair or replace lines
	• Internal malfunction	• Have transmission checked professionally

Lockup Torque Converter Service Diagnosis

Problem	Cause	Solution
No lockup	• Faulty oil pump	• Replace oil pump
	• Sticking governor valve	• Repair or replace as necessary
	• Valve body malfunction	• Repair or replace valve body or its internal components as necessary
	(a) Stuck switch valve	
	(b) Stuck lockup valve	
	(c) Stuck fail-safe valve	
	• Failed locking clutch	• Replace torque converter
	• Leaking turbine hub seal	• Replace torque converter
	• Faulty input shaft or seal ring	• Repair or replace as necessary

Lockup Torque Converter Service Diagnosis

Problem	Cause	Solution
Will not unlock	• Sticking governor valve • Valve body malfunction (a) Stuck switch valve (b) Stuck lockup valve (c) Stuck fail-safe valve	• Repair or replace as necessary • Repair or replace valve body or its internal components as necessary
Stays locked up at too low a speed in direct	• Sticking governor valve • Valve body malfunction (a) Stuck switch valve (b) Stuck lockup valve (c) Stuck fail-safe valve	• Repair or replace as necessary • Repair or replace valve body or its internal components as necessary
Locks up or drags in low or second	• Faulty oil pump • Valve body malfunction (a) Stuck switch valve (b) Stuck fail-safe valve	• Replace oil pump • Repair or replace valve body or its internal components as necessary
Sluggish or stalls in reverse	• Faulty oil pump • Plugged cooler, cooler lines or fittings • Valve body malfunction (a) Stuck switch valve (b) Faulty input shaft or seal ring	• Replace oil pump as necessary • Flush or replace cooler and flush lines and fittings • Repair or replace valve body or its internal components as necessary
Loud chatter during lockup engagement (cold)	• Faulty torque converter • Failed locking clutch • Leaking turbine hub seal	• Replace torque converter • Replace torque converter • Replace torque converter
Vibration or shudder during lockup engagement	• Faulty oil pump • Valve body malfunction • Faulty torque converter • Engine needs tune-up	• Repair or replace oil pump as necessary • Repair or replace valve body or its internal components as necessary • Replace torque converter • Tune engine
Vibration after lockup engagement	• Faulty torque converter • Exhaust system strikes underbody • Engine needs tune-up • Throttle linkage misadjusted	• Replace torque converter • Align exhaust system • Tune engine • Adjust throttle linkage
Vibration when revved in neutral Overheating: oil blows out of dip stick tube or pump seal	• Torque converter out of balance • Plugged cooler, cooler lines or fittings • Stuck switch valve	• Replace torque converter • Flush or replace cooler and flush lines and fittings • Repair switch valve in valve body or replace valve body

Lockup Torque Converter Service Diagnosis

Problem	Cause	Solution
Shudder after lockup engagement	• Faulty oil pump • Plugged cooler, cooler lines or fittings • Valve body malfunction	• Replace oil pump • Flush or replace cooler and flush lines and fittings • Repair or replace valve body or its internal components as necessary
	• Faulty torque converter • Fail locking clutch • Exhaust system strikes underbody • Engine needs tune-up • Throttle linkage misadjusted	• Replace torque converter • Replace torque converter • Align exhaust system • Tune engine • Adjust throttle linkage

Transmission Fluid Indications

The appearance and odor of the transmission fluid can give valuable clues to the overall condition of the transmission. Always note the appearance of the fluid when you check the fluid level or change the fluid. Rub a small amount of fluid between your fingers to feel for grit and smell the fluid on the dipstick.

If the fluid appears:	It indicates:
Clear and red colored	• Normal operation
Discolored (extremely dark red or brownish) or smells burned	• Band or clutch pack failure, usually caused by an overheated transmission. Hauling very heavy loads with insufficient power or failure to change the fluid, often result in overheating. Do not confuse this appearance with newer fluids that have a darker red color and a strong odor (though not a burned odor).
Foamy or aerated (light in color and full of bubbles)	• The level is too high (gear train is churning oil) • An internal air leak (air is mixing with the fluid). Have the transmission checked professionally.
Solid residue in the fluid	• Defective bands, clutch pack or bearings. Bits of band material or metal abrasives are clinging to the dipstick. Have the transmission checked professionally.
Varnish coating on the dipstick	• The transmission fluid is overheating

Transmission

REMOVAL AND INSTALLATION

C6

1. From in the engine compartment, remove the two upper converter housing-to-engine bolts.
2. Disconnect the neutral switch wire at the inline connector.
3. Remove the bolt securing the fluid filler tube to the engine cylinder head.
4. Raise and support the van on jackstands.

5. Place the drain pan under the transmission fluid pan. Starting at the rear of the pan and working toward the front, loosen the attaching bolts and allow the fluid to drain. Finally remove all of the pan attaching bolts except two at the front, to allow the fluid to further drain. With fluid drained, install two bolts on the rear side of the pan to temporarily hold it in place.
6. Remove the converter drain plug access cover from the lower end of the converter housing.
7. Remove the converter-to-flywheel attaching nuts. Place a wrench on the crankshaft pulley attaching bolt to turn the converter to gain access to the nuts.
8. With the wrench on the crankshaft pulley attaching bolt,

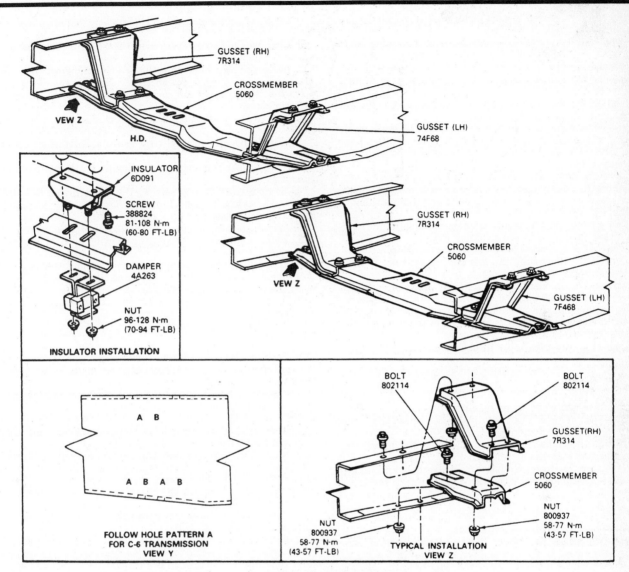

C6 mounting points

turn the converter to gain access to the converter drain plug. Place a drain pan under the converter to catch the fluid and remove the plug. After the fluid has been drained, reinstall the plug.

9. Disconnect the driveshaft from the axle and slide shaft rearward from the transmission. Install a seal installation tool in the extension housing to prevent fluid leakage.

10. Disconnect the speedometer cable from the extension housing.

11. Disconnect the downshift and manual linkage rods from the levers at the transmission.

12. Disconnect the oil cooler lines from the transmission.

13. Remove the vacuum hose from the vacuum diaphragm unit. Remove the vacuum line retaining clip.

14. Disconnect the cable from the terminal on the starter motor. Remove the three attaching bolts and remove the starter motor.

15. Remove the two engine rear support and insulator assembly-to-attaching bolts.

16. Remove the two engine rear support and insulator assembly-to-extension housing attaching bolts.

17. Remove the six bolts securing the No. 2 crossmember to the frame side rails.

18. Raise the transmission with a transmission jack and remove both crossmembers.

19. Secure the transmission to the jack with the safety chain.

20. Remove the remaining converter housing-to-engine attaching bolts.

21. Move the transmission away from the engine. Lower the jack and remove the converter and transmission assembly from under the vehicle.

To install:

22. Tighten the converter drain plug.

23. Position the converter on the transmission making sure the converter drive flats are fully engaged in the pump gear.

24. With the converter properly installed, place the transmission on the jack. Secure the transmission on the jack with the chain.

25. Rotate the converter until the studs and drain plug are in alignment with their holes in the flywheel.

26. Move the converter and transmission assembly forward into position, using care not to damage the flywheel and the converter pilot. The converter must rest squarely against the fly-

wheel. This indicates that the converter pilot is not binding in the engine crankshaft.

27. Install the converter housing-to-engine attaching bolts and torque them to 65 ft. lbs. for the diesel; 50 ft. lbs. for gasoline engines.

28. Remove the transmission jack safety chain from around the transmission.

29. Position the No. 2 crossmember to the frame side rails. Install and tighten the attaching bolts.

30. Position the engine rear support and insulator assembly above the crossmember. Install the rear support and insulator assembly-to-extension housing mounting bolts and tighten the bolts to 45 ft. lbs.

31. Lower the transmission and remove the jack.

32. Secure the engine rear support and insulator assembly to the crossmember with the attaching bolts and tighten them to 80 ft. lbs.

33. Connect the vacuum line to the vacuum diaphragm making sure that the line is in the retaining clip.

34. Connect the oil cooler lines to the transmission.

35. Connect the downshift and manual linkage rods to their respective levers on the transmission.

36. Connect the speedometer cable to the extension housing.

37. Secure the starter motor in place with the attaching bolts. Connect the cable to the terminal on the starter.

38. Install a new O-ring on the lower end of the transmission filler tube and insert the tube in the case.

39. Secure the converter-to-flywheel attaching nuts and tighten them to 30 ft. lbs.

40. Install the converter housing access cover and secure it with the attaching bolts.

41. Connect the driveshaft.

42. Adjust the shift linkage as required.

43. Lower the vehicle. Then install the two upper converter housing-to-engine bolts and tighten them.

44. Position the transmission fluid filler tube to the cylinder head and secure with the attaching bolts.

45. Make sure the drain pan is securely attached, and fill the transmission to the correct level with the Dexron®II fluid.

AOD

1. Raise the vehicle on hoist or stands.

2. Place the drain pan under the transmission fluid pan. Starting at the rear of the pan and working toward the front, loosen the attaching bolts and allow the fluid to drain. Finally remove all of the pan attaching bolts except two at the front, to allow the fluid to further drain. With fluid drained, install two bolts on the rear side of the pan to temporarily hold it in place.

3. Remove the converter drain plug access cover from the lower end of the converter.

4. Remove the converter-to-flywheel attaching nuts. Place a wrench on the crankshaft pulley attaching bolt to turn the converter to gain access to the nuts.

5. Place a drain pan under the converter to catch the fluid. With the wrench on the crankshaft pulley attaching bolt, turn the converter to gain access to the converter drain plug and remove the plug. After the fluid has been drained, reinstall the plug.

6. Matchmark and disconnect the driveshaft from the axle and slide shaft rearward from the transmission. Install a seal installation tool in the extension housing to prevent fluid leakage.

7. Disconnect the cable from the terminal on the starter motor. Remove the three attaching bolts and remove the starter motor. Disconnect the neutral start switch wires at the plug connector.

8. Remove the rear mount-to-crossmember attaching bolts and the two crossmember-to-frame attaching bolts.

9. Remove the two engine rear support-to-extension housing attaching bolts.

10. Disconnect the TV linkage rod from the transmission TV

lever. Disconnect the manual rod from the transmission manual lever at the transmission.

11. Remove the two bolts securing the bellcrank bracket to the converter housing.

12. Raise the transmission with a transmission jack to provide clearance to remove the crossmember. Remove the rear mount from the crossmember and remove the crossmember from the side supports.

13. Lower the transmission to gain access to the oil cooler lines.

14. Disconnect each oil line from the fittings on the transmission.

15. Disconnect the speedometer cable from the extension housing.

16. Remove the bolt that secures the transmission fluid filler tube to the cylinder block. Lift the filler tube and the dipstick from the transmission.

17. Secure the transmission to the jack with the chain.

18. Remove the converter housing-to-cylinder block attaching bolts.

19. Carefully move the transmission and converter assembly away from the engine and, at the same time, lower the jack to clear the underside of the vehicle.

20. Remove the converter and mount the transmission in a holding fixture.

21. Tighten the converter drain plug.

To install:

22. Position the converter on the transmission, making sure the converter drive flats are fully engaged in the pump gear by rotating the converter.

23. With the converter properly installed, place the transmission on the jack. Secure the transmission to the jack with a chain.

24. Rotate the converter until the studs and drain plug are in alignment with the holes in the flywheel.

25. Move the converter and transmission assembly forward into position, using care not to damage the flywheel and the converter pilot. The converter must rest squarely against the flywheel. This indicates that the converter pilot is not binding in the engine crankshaft.

26. Install and tighten the converter housing-to-engine attaching bolts to 40–50 ft. lbs.

27. Remove the safety chain from around the transmission.

28. Install a new O-ring on the lower end of the transmission filler tube. Insert the tube in the transmission case and secure the tube to the engine with the attaching bolt.

29. Connect the speedometer cable to the extension housing.

30. Connect the oil cooler lines to the right side of transmission case.

31. Position the crossmember on the side supports. Torque the bolts to 55 ft. lbs. Position the rear mount on the crossmember and install the attaching nuts to 90 ft. lbs.

32. Secure the rear support to the extension housing and tighten the bolts to 80 ft. lbs.

33. Lower the transmission and remove the jack.

E4OD

1. Raise and support the van on jackstands.

2. Place the drain pan under the transmission fluid pan. Starting at the rear of the pan and working toward the front, loosen the attaching bolts and allow the fluid to drain. Finally remove all of the pan attaching bolts except two at the front, to allow the fluid to further drain. With fluid drained, install two bolts on the rear side of the pan to temporarily hold it in place.

3. Remove the dipstick from the transmission.

4. Matchmark and remove the driveshaft. Install a seal installation tool in the extension housing to prevent fluid leakage.

5. Disconnect the linkage from the transmission.

6. Remove the heat shield and remove the manual lever position sensor connector by squeezing the tabs and pulling on the

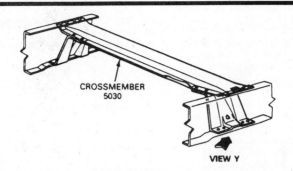

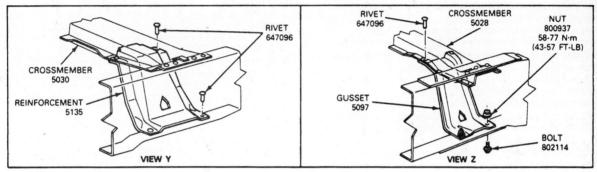

E4OD mounting points

connector. NEVER ATTEMPT TO PRY THE CONNECTOR APART!

7. Remove the solenoid body heat shield.

8. Remove the solenoid body connector by pushing on the center tab and pulling on the wiring harness. NEVER ATTEMPT TO PRY APART THE CONNECTOR!

9. Pry the harness connector from the extension housing wire bracket.

10. Disconnect the speedometer cable.

11. Remove the converter cover bolts.

12. Remove the rear engine cover plate bolts.

13. Disconnect the cable from the terminal on the starter motor. Remove the three attaching bolts and remove the starter motor. Disconnect the neutral start switch wires at the plug connector.

14. Remove the converter-to-flywheel attaching nuts. Place a

wrench on the crankshaft pulley attaching bolt to turn the converter to gain access to the nuts.

15. Secure the transmission to a transmission jack. Use a safety chain.

16. Remove the rear mount-to-crossmember attaching nuts and the two crossmember-to-frame attaching bolts.

17. Disconnect each oil line from the fittings on the transmission. Cap the lines.

18. Remove the 6 converter housing-to-cylinder block attaching bolts.

19. Carefully move the transmission and converter assembly away from the engine and, at the same time, lower the jack to clear the underside of the vehicle.

20. Remove the transmission filler tube.

21. Install Torque Converter Handles T81P-7902-C, or equivalent, at the 12 o'clock and 6 o'clock positions.

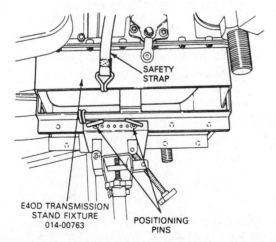

Placement of transmission holding fixture for the E4OD

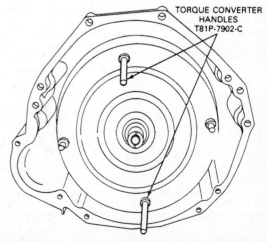

Installation of the torque converter handles on the E4OD

To install:

22. Install the converter with the handles at the 12 o'clock and 6 o'clock positions. Push and rotate the converter until it bottoms out. Check the seating of the converter by placing a straightedge across the converter and bellhousing. There must be a gap between the converter and straightedge. Remove the handles.

23. Install the transmission filler tube.

24. Rotate the converter to align the studs with the flywheel mounting holes.

25. Carefully raise the transmission into position at the engine. The converter must rest squarely against the flywheel.

26. Install the 6 converter housing-to-cylinder block attaching bolts. Snug them alternately and evenly, then, tighten them alternately and evenly to 40-50 ft. lbs.

27. Install the converter drain plug cover.

28. Connect each oil line at the fittings on the transmission.

29. Install the rear mount-to-crossmember attaching nuts and the two crossmember-to-frame attaching bolts. Torque the nuts and bolts to 50 ft. lbs.

30. Remove the transmission jack.

31. Install the converter-to-flywheel attaching nuts. Place a wrench on the crankshaft pulley attaching bolt to turn the converter to gain access to the nuts. Torque the nuts to 20–30 ft. lbs.

32. Install the starter motor. Connect the cable at the terminal on the starter motor. Connect the neutral start switch wires at the plug connector.

33. Install the rear engine cover plate bolts.

34. Install the converter cover bolts.

35. Connect the speedometer cable.

36. Connect the harness connector at the extension housing wire bracket.

37. Install the solenoid body connector. An audible click indicates connection.

38. Install the solenoid body heat shield.

39. Install the manual lever position sensor connector and the heat shield.

40. Connect the linkage at the transmission.

41. Install the driveshaft.

42. Install the dipstick.

43. Install the drain pan using a new gasket and sealer.

44. Lower the van.

45. Refill the transmission and check for leaks.

Fluid Pan

REMOVAL AND INSTALLATION

1. Raise the van on a hoist or jackstands.

2. Place a drain pan under the transmission.

3. Loosen the pan attaching bolts and drain the fluid from the transmission.

4. When the fluid has drained to the level of the pan flange, remove the remaining pan bolts working from the rear and both sides of the pan to allow it to drop and drain slowly.

5. When all of the fluid has drained, remove the pan and clean it thoroughly, Discard the pan gasket.

6. Place the new gasket on the pan, and install the pan on the transmission. Tighten the attaching bolts to 12–16 ft. lbs.

7. Add three quarts of fluid to the transmission through the filler tube.

FILTER SERVICE

1. Remove the transmission oil pan and gasket.

2. Remove the screws holding the fine mesh screen to the lower valve body.

3. Install the new filter screen and transmission oil pan gasket in the reverse order of removal.

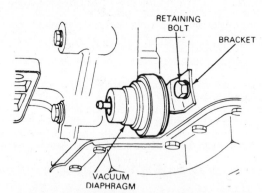

Vacuum modulator installed on the C6

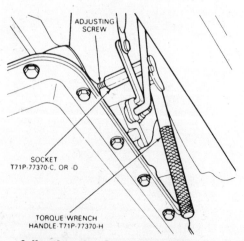

Adjusting the C6 intermediate band

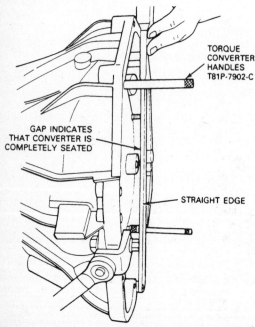

Check torque converter installation with a straightedge

Vacuum Modulator

REMOVAL AND INSTALLATION

C6

1. Disconnect the vacuum hose at the unit.
2. Remove the bracket bolt and bracket.
3. Pull the vacuum unit from the transmission.
4. Installation is the reverse of removal. Torque the bolt to 12–16 ft. lbs. Connect the vacuum hose.

Adjustments

INTERMEDIATE BAND ADJUSTMENT

C6 Only

1. Raise the van on a hoist or jackstands.
2. Clean all dirt away from the band adjusting screw. Remove and discard the locknut.
3. Install a new locknut and tighten the adjusting screw to 10 ft. lbs.
4. Back off the adjusting screw exactly 1½ turns.
5. Hold the adjusting screw from turning and tighten the locknut to 35–40 ft. lbs.
6. Remove the jackstands and lower the vehicle.

SHIFT LINKAGE ADJUSTMENT

1. With the engine stopped, place the transmission selector lever at the steering column in the D position for the C6 or the D overdrive position for the AOD and E4OD, and hold the lever against the stop by hanging an 8 lb. weight from the lever handle.
2. Loosen the shift rod adjusting nut at the transmission lever.

3. Shift the manual lever at the transmission to the **D** position, two detents from the rear.
4. With the selector lever and transmission manual lever in the D or D overdrive position, tighten the adjusting nut to 12–18 ft. lbs. Do not allow the rod or shift lever to move while tightening the nut. Remove the weight.
5. Check the operation of the shift linkage.

THROTTLE VALVE CABLE ADJUSTMENT

AOD Transmission

ADJUSTMENT WITH ENGINE OFF

1. Set the parking brake and put the selector lever in **N**.
2. Remove the protective cover from the cable.
3. Make sure that the throttle lever is at the idle stop. If it isn't, check for binding or interference. NEVER ATTEMPT TO ADJUST THE IDLE STOP!
4. Make sure that the cable is free of sharp bends or is not rubbing on anything throughout its entire length.
5. Lubricate the TV lever ball stud with chassis lube.
6. Unlock the locking tab at the throttle body by prying with a small screwdriver.
7. Install a spring on the TV control lever, to hold it in the rearmost travel position. The spring must exert at least 10 lbs. of force on the lever.
8. Rotate the transmission outer TV lever 10-30° and slowly allow it to return.

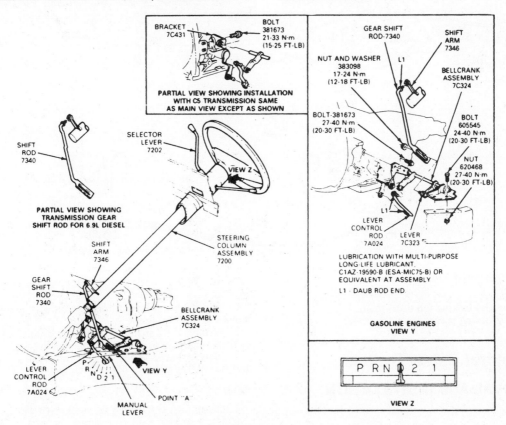

C6 shift linkage adjustment points

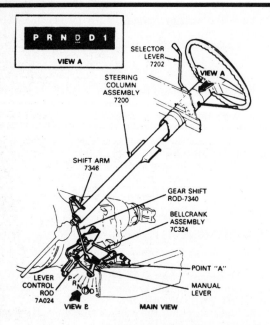

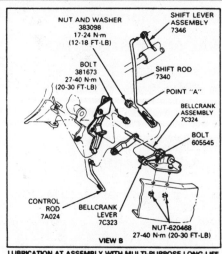

AOD shift linkage adjustment

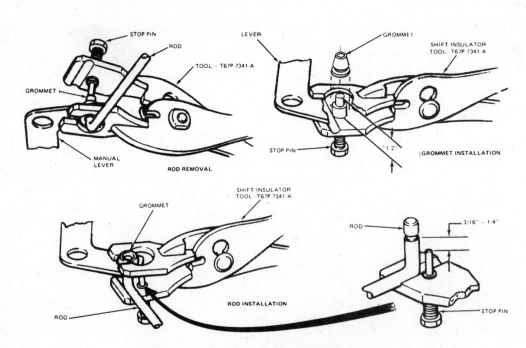

Removing or installing shift linkage grommets

9. Push down on the locking tab until flush.
10. Remove the retaining spring from the lever.

Neutral Safety Switch

REMOVAL AND INSTALLATION

C6

1. Remove the downshift linkage rod return spring at the low-reverse servo cover.

2. Coat the outer lever attaching nut with penetrating oil. Remove the nut and lever.
3. Remove the 2 switch attaching bolts, disconnect the wiring at the connectors and remove the switch.
4. Installation is the reverse of removal. Adjust the switch and torque the bolts to 55–75 inch lbs.

AOD

1. Disconnect the wiring from the switch.
2. Using a deep socket, unscrew the switch.
3. Installation is the reverse of removal. Torque the switch to 10 ft. lbs.

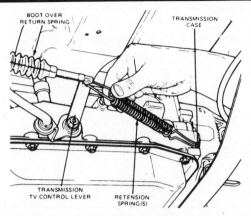

Throttle valve lever retention spring on the 6-300 EFI and 8-302 EFI

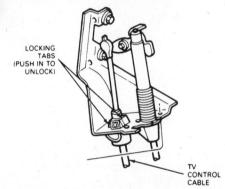

AOD throttle valve control cable locking tab installation

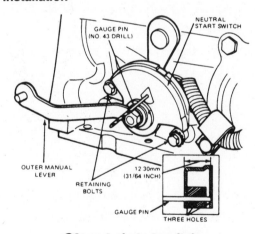

C6 neutral start switch

ADJUSTMENT

1. Hold the steering column transmission selector lever against the Neutral stop.

2. Move the sliding block assembly on the neutral switch to the neutral position and insert a 0.091 in. (2.3mm) gauge pin in the alignment hole on the terminal side of the switch.

3. Move the switch assembly housing so that the sliding block contacts the actuating pin lever. Secure the switch to the outer tube of the steering column and remove the gauge pin.

4. Check the operation of the switch. The engine should only start in Neutral and Park.

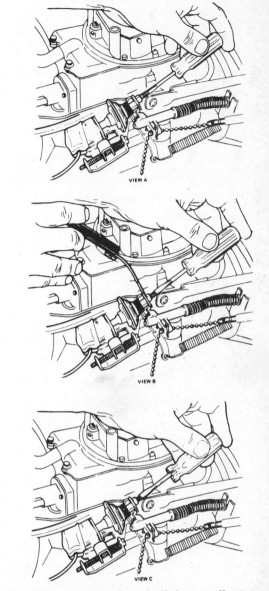

Automatic overdrive throttle linkage adjustment

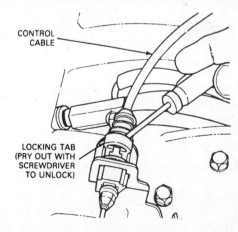

Unlocking the tab at the throttle body on the 5.0L EFI engine

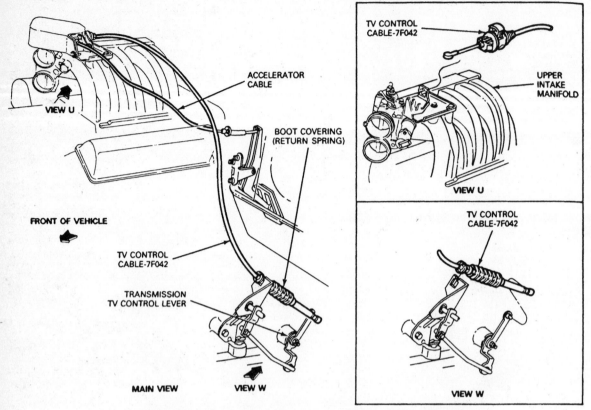

Throttle valve control cable adjustment — EFI engines

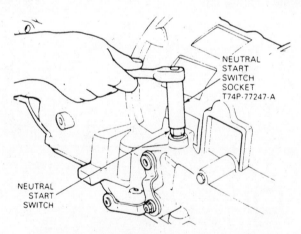

Removing the AOD neutral start switch

DRIVELINE
Troubleshooting Basic Driveshaft and Rear Axle Problems

When abnormal vibrations or noises are detected in the driveshaft area, this chart can be used to help diagnose possible causes. Remember that other components such as wheels, tires, rear axle and suspension can also produce similar conditions.

BASIC DRIVESHAFT PROBLEMS

Problem	Cause	Solution
Shudder as car accelerates from stop or low speed	• Loose U-joint • Defective center bearing	• Replace U-joint • Replace center bearing
Loud clunk in driveshaft when shifting gears	• Worn U-joints	• Replace U-joints
Roughness or vibration at any speed	• Out-of-balance, bent or dented driveshaft • Worn U-joints • U-joint clamp bolts loose	• Balance or replace driveshaft • Replace U-joints • Tighten U-joint clamp bolts
Squeaking noise at low speeds	• Lack of U-joint lubrication	• Lubricate U-joint; if problem persists, replace U-joint
Knock or clicking noise	• U-joint or driveshaft hitting frame tunnel • Worn CV joint	• Correct overloaded condition • Replace CV joint

BASIC REAR AXLE PROBLEMS

First, determine when the noise is most noticeable.

Drive Noise — Produced under vehicle acceleration.

Coast Noise — Produced while the car coast with a closed throttle.

Float Noise — Occurs while maintaining constant car speed (just enough to keep speed constant) on a level road.

Road Noise

Brick or rough surfaced concrete roads produce noises that seem to come from the rear axle. Road noise is usually identical in Drive or Coast and driving on a different type of road will tell whether the road is the problem.

Tire Noise

Tire noises are often mistaken for rear axle problems. Snow treads or unevenly worn tires produce vibrations seeming to originate elsewhere. Temporarily inflating the tire to 40 lbs will significantly alter tire noise, but will have no effect on rear axle noises (which normally cease below about 30 mph).

Engine/Transmission Noise

Determine at what speed the noise is more pronounced, then stop the car in a quiet place. With the transmission in Neutral, run the engine through speeds corresponding to road speeds where the noise was noticed. Noises produced with the car standing still are coming from the engine or transmission.

Front Wheel Bearings

While holding the car speed steady, lightly apply the foot brake; this will often decease bearing noise, as some of the load is taken from the bearing.

Rear Axle Noises

Eliminating other possible sources can narrow the cause to the rear axle, which normally produces noise from worn gears or bearings. Gear noises tend to peak in a narrow speed range, while bearing noises will usually vary in pitch with engine speeds.

DRIVELINE

Driveshaft

REMOVAL AND INSTALLATION

Single Type U-Joint

ONE PIECE DRIVESHAFT

1. Matchmark the driveshaft yoke and axle pinion flange.
2. Remove the U-bolt nuts and U-bolts attaching the yoke to the axle flange.
3. Separate the yoke from the flange. It may be necessary to pry it free with a small prybar. Immediately after separation, wrap tape around the U-joint caps to keep them from falling off.
4. Slip the driveshaft off the transmission splines.
5. Installation is the reverse of removal. Align the yoke-to-flange matchmarks. Torque the U-bolt nuts to 15 ft. lbs.

TWO PIECE DRIVESHAFT/COUPLING SHAFT

1. Matchmark the driveshaft yoke and axle pinion flange.
2. Remove the U-bolt nuts and U-bolts attaching the yoke to the axle flange.
3. Separate the yoke from the flange. It may be necessary to pry it free with a small prybar. Immediately after separation, wrap tape around the U-joint caps to keep them from falling off.
4. Slip the driveshaft off the coupling shaft splines.
5. Remove the center bearing.
6. Slide the coupling shaft from the transmission shaft splines.
7. Clean all parts and check for damage. Do not remove the blue plastic coating from the male splines.

8. Installation is the reverse of removal. Coat the splines with chassis lube. Torque the center bearing support bolts to 50 ft. lbs. Align the yoke-to-flange matchmarks. Torque the U-bolt nuts to:
- $5/16$ in.-18: 15 ft. lbs.
- $3/8$ in.-18: 17–26 ft. lbs.
- $7/16$ in.-20: 30–40 ft. lbs.

Double Cardan Type U-Joint

1. Matchmark the yoke and axle flange.
2. Matchmark the cardan joint and the yoke.
3. Remove the U-bolt nuts and U-bolts attaching the yoke to the axle flange.
4. Separate the yoke from the flange. It may be necessary to pry it free with a small prybar. Immediately after separation, wrap tape around the U-joint caps to keep them from falling off.
5. Remove the cardan joint-to-yoke bolts and separate the cardan joint from the yoke.
6. Installation is the reverse of removal. Align the matchmarks. Torque the U-bolt nuts to 15 ft. lbs.; the cardan joint bolts to 25 ft. lbs.

DRIVESHAFT BALANCING

Driveline vibration or shudder, felt mainly on acceleration, coasting or under engine braking, can be caused, among other things, by improper driveshaft installation or imbalance.

If the condition follows driveshaft replacement or installation after disconnection, try disconnecting the driveshaft at the axle

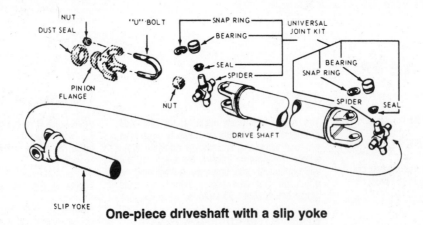

One-piece driveshaft with a slip yoke

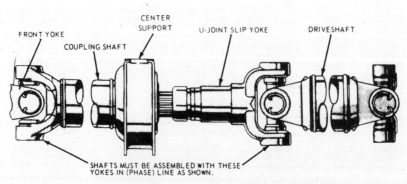

Two-piece driveshaft with a slip yoke at the transmission end

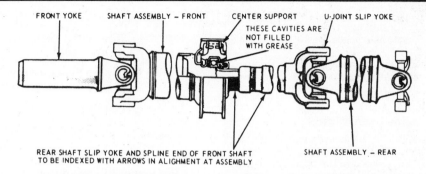

FRONT YOKE   SHAFT ASSEMBLY – FRONT   CENTER SUPPORT   U-JOINT SLIP YOKE

THESE CAVITIES ARE NOT FILLED WITH GREASE

REAR SHAFT SLIP YOKE AND SPLINE END OF FRONT SHAFT TO BE INDEXED WITH ARROWS IN ALIGHMENT AT ASSEMBLY

SHAFT ASSEMBLY – REAR

Two-piece driveshaft with a fixed yoke at the transmission end

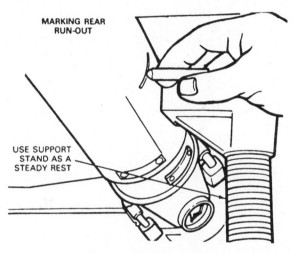

MARKING REAR RUN-OUT

USE SUPPORT STAND AS A STEADY REST

Marking the driveshaft

and rotating it 180°. Then, reconnect it. If that doesn't work, try the following procedure:

1. Raise and support the van on jackstands so that all wheels are off the ground and free to rotate. The van must be as level as possible.

2. Remove the wheels. Install the lug nuts to retain the brake drums or rotors.

3. Start the engine, place the transmission in gear and increase engine speed to the point at which the vibration is most severe. Record this speedometer speed as a reference point.

4. Shift into neutral and shut off the engine.

5. Check all driveshaft attachment fasteners, U-joint bearing caps, U-joint cap retaining rings or cap locating lugs. Tighten any loose fasteners, replace any missing, damaged or shaved retaining rings or lugs. If worn U-joints are suspected, replace them. If everything is normal, or if any corrections made do not solve the problem, continue.

6. Start the engine, place the transmission in gear and increase engine speed to an indicated road speed of 40–50 mph (64–80 kmh). Maintain this speed with some sort of accelerator control, such as a weight on the pedal, or have an assistant hold the pedal.

—————— CAUTION ——————

The following procedure can be dangerous! Be careful when approaching the spinning driveline parts!

7. Carefully raise a piece of chalk until it *just barely* touches the driveshaft at the front, middle and rear. At either end, try touching the shaft about an inch or so from the yokes. Don't touch any existing driveshaft balancing weights. The chalk

marks will indicate the heavy points of the driveshaft. Shut off the engine.

NOTE: It helps greatly to steady your hand on some sort of support.

8. Check the driveshaft end of the shaft first. If the chalk mark is continuous around the shaft proceed to the opposite

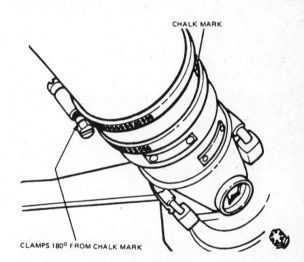

CHALK MARK

CLAMPS 180° FROM CHALK MARK

Installing the hose clamps on the driveshaft

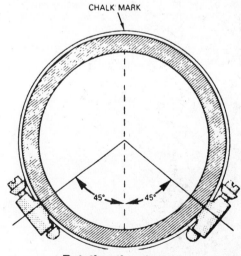

CHALK MARK

45° 45°

Rotating the clamps

end, then the middle.

If the chalk mark is not continuous, install 2 screw-type hose clamps on the shaft so that their heads are 180° from the center of the chalk mark.

9. Start the engine and run it to the speed recorded previously. If the vibration persists, stop the engine and move the screw portions of the clamps 45° from each other. Try the run test again.

WARNING: Check the engine temperature!

10. If the vibration persists, move the screw portions of the clamps apart in small increments until the vibration disappears. If this doesn't cure the problem, proceed to the other end, then the middle, performing the operation all over again. If the problem persists, investigate other driveline components.

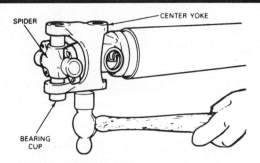

Removing the bearing from the center yoke

U-JOINT OVERHAUL

Except Double Cardan Universal

1. Remove the driveshaft from the vehicle and place it in a vise, being careful not to damage it.
2. Remove the snaprings which retain the bearings in the flange and in the driveshaft.
3. Remove the driveshaft tube from the vise and position the U-joint in the vise with a socket smaller than the bearing cap on one side and a socket larger than the bearing cap on the other side.
4. Slowly tighten the jaws of the vise so that the smaller socket forces the U-joint spider and the opposite bearing into the larger socket.
5. Remove the other side of the spider in the same manner (if applicable) and remove the spider assembly from the driveshaft. Discard the spider assemblies.
6. Clean all foreign matter from the yoke areas at the end of the driveshaft(s).
7. Start the new spider and one of the bearing cap assemblies into a yoke by positioning the yoke in a vise with the spider positioned in place with one of the bearing cap assemblies positioned over one of the holes in the yoke. Slowly close the vise, pressing the bearing cap assembly in the yoke. Press the cap in far enough so that the retaining snapring can be installed. Use the smaller socket to recess the bearing cap.
8. Open the vise and position the opposite bearing cap assembly over the proper hole in the yoke with the socket that is smaller than the diameter of the bearing cap located on the cap. Slowly close the vise, pressing the bearing cap into the hole in the yoke with the socket. Make sure that the spider assembly is in line with the bearing cap as it is pressed in. Press the bearing cap in far enough so that the retaining snapring can be installed.
9. Install all remaining U-joints in the same manner.
10. Install the driveshaft and grease the new U-joints.

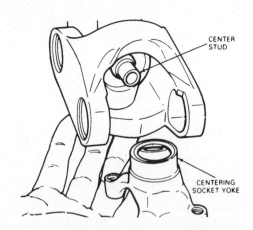

Removing the bearing cup from the center yoke socket

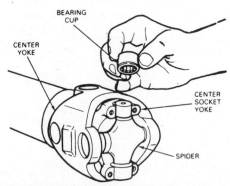

Removing the center socket yoke

Double Cardan Joint

1. Working at the axle end of the shaft, mark the position of

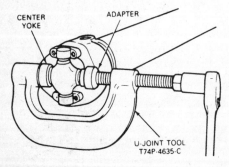

Partially pressing the bearing from the center yoke

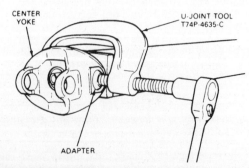

Removing the bearing from the rear of the center yoke

the spiders, the center yoke, and the centering socket yoke as related to the companion flange. The spiders must be assembled with the bosses in their original position to provide proper clearances.

2. Using a large vise or an arbor press and a socket smaller than the bearing cap on one side and a socket larger than the bearing cap on the other side, drive one of the bearings in toward the center of the universal joint, which will force the opposite bearing out.

3. Remove the driveshaft from the vise.

4. Tighten the bearing in the vise and tap on the yoke to free the bearing from the center yoke. Do not tap on the driveshaft tube.

5. Reposition the sockets on the yoke and force the opposite bearing outward and remove it.

6. Position the sockets on one of the remaining bearings and force it outward approximately ⅜ in. (9.5mm).

7. Grip the bearing in the vise and tap on the weld yoke to free the bearing from the center yoke. Do not tap on the driveshaft tube.

8. Reposition the sockets on the yoke to press out the remaining bearing.

9. Remove the spider from the center yoke.

10. Remove the bearings from the driveshaft yoke as outlined above and remove the spider from the yoke.

11. Insert a suitable tool into the centering ball socket located in the companion flange and pry out the rubber seal. Remove the retainer, three piece ball seat, washer and spring from the ball socket.

12. Inspect the centering ball socket assembly for worn or damaged parts. If any damage is evident replace the entire assembly.

13. Insert the spring, washer, three piece ball seat and retainer into the ball socket.

14. Using a suitable tool, install the centering ball socket seal.

15. Position the spider in the driveshaft yoke. Make sure the spider bosses are in the same position as originally installed. Press in the bearing cups with the sockets and vise. Install the internal snaprings provided in the repair kit.

16. Position the center yoke over the spider ends and press in the bearing cups. Install the snaprings.

17. Install the spider in the companion flange yoke. Make sure the spider bosses are in the position as originally installed. Press on the bearing cups and install the snaprings.

18. Position the center yoke over the spider ends and press on the bearing cups. Install the snaprings.

Center Bearing

REMOVAL AND INSTALLATION

1. Remove the driveshafts.

2. Remove the two center support bearing attaching bolts and remove the assembly from the vehicle.

3. Do not immerse the sealed bearing in any type of cleaning fluid. Wipe the bearing and cushion clean with a cloth dampened with cleaning fluid.

4. Check the bearing for wear or rough action by rotating the inner race while holding the outer race. If wear or roughness is evident, replace the bearing. Examine the rubber cushion for evidence of hardening, cracking, or deterioration. Replace it if it is damaged in any way.

5. Place the bearing in the rubber support and the rubber support in the U-shaped support and install the bearing in the reverse order of removal. Torque the bearing to support bracket fasteners to 50 ft. lbs.

REAR AXLE

Understanding Drive Axles

The drive axle is a special type of transmission that reduces the speed of the drive from the engine and transmission and divides the power to the wheels. Power enters the axle from the driveshaft via the companion flange. The flange is mounted on the drive pinion shaft. The drive pinion shaft and gear which carry the power into the differential turn at engine speed. The gear on the end of the pinion shaft drives a large ring gear the axis of rotation of which is 90° away from the of the pinion. The pinion and gear reduce the gear ratio of the axle, and change the direction of rotation to turn the axle shafts which drive both wheels. The axle gear ratio is found by dividing the number of pinion gear teeth into the number of ring gear teeth.

The ring gear drives the differential case. The case provides the two mounting points for the ends of a pinion shaft on which are mounted two pinion gears. The pinion gears drive the two side gears, one of which is located on the inner end of each axle shaft.

By driving the axle shafts through the arrangement, the differential allows the outer drive wheel to turn faster than the inner drive wheel in a turn.

The main drive pinion and the side bearings, which bear the weight of the differential case, are shimmed to provide proper bearing preload, and to position the pinion and ring gears properly.

WARNING: The proper adjustment of the relationship of the ring and pinion gears is critical. It should be attempted only by those with extensive equipment and/or experience.

Limited-slip differentials include clutches which tend to link each axle shaft to the differential case. Clutches may be engaged either by spring action or by pressure produced by the torque on the axles during a turn. During turning on a dry pavement, the effects of the clutches are overcome, and each wheel turns at the required speed. When slippage occurs at either wheel, however, the clutches will transmit some of the power to the wheel which has the greater amount of traction. Because of the presence of clutches, limited-slip units require a special lubricant.

Determining Axle Ratio

The drive axle is said to have a certain axle ratio. This number (usually a whole number and a decimal fraction) is actually a comparison of the number of gear teeth on the ring gear and the pinion gear. For example, a 4.11 rear means that theoretically, there are 4.11 teeth on the ring gear and one tooth on the pinion gear or, put another way, the driveshaft must turn 4.11 times to turn the wheels once. Actually, on a 4.11 rear, there might be 37 teeth on the ring gear and 9 teeth on the pinion gear. By dividing the number of teeth on the pinion gear into the number of teeth on the ring gear, the numerical axle ratio (4.11) is obtained. This also provides a good method of ascertaining exactly what axle ratio one is dealing with.

Another method of determining gear ratio is to jack up and support the car so that both rear wheels are off the ground. Make a chalk mark on the rear wheel and the driveshaft. Put the transmission in neutral. Turn the rear wheel one complete turn and count the number of turns that the driveshaft makes. The number of turns that the driveshaft makes in one complete revolution of the rear wheel is an approximation of the rear axle ratio.

Differential Overhaul

A differential overhaul is a complex, highly technical, and time-consuming operation, which requires a great many tools, extensive knowledge of the unit and the way it works, and a high degree of mechanical experience and ability. While complete overhaul procedures are provided here, it is highly advisable that the amateur mechanic not attempt any work on the differential unit.

Improved Traction Differentials

In this assembly, a multiple-disc clutch is employed to control differential action.

Identification

On a full floating rear axle, the weight of the vehicle is supported by the axle housing. The axle shafts can be removed without disturbing the wheel bearings.

On a semi-floating axle, the outboard end of the axle shaft is supported by the bearing which is mounted in a recess in the end of the axle housing.

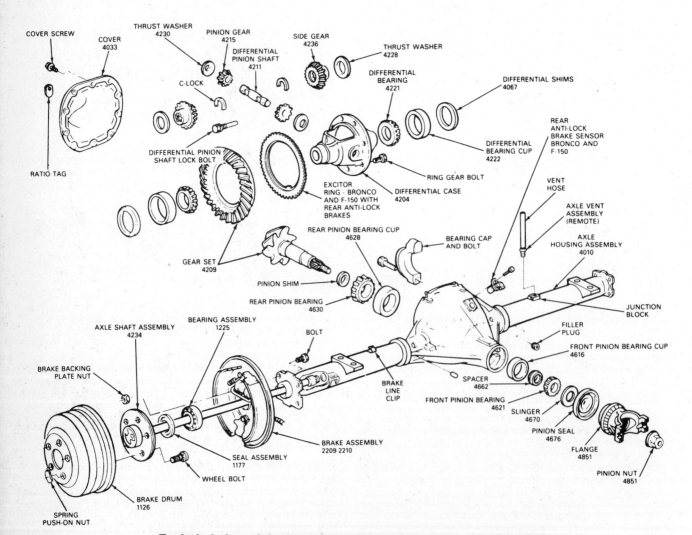

Exploded view of the Ford 8.8 inch integral carrier rear drive axle

The axle shaft on a full-floating rear axle is held in place by a flange and bolts attaching it to the hub on the outboard side. The hub is held to the rear spindle by nuts which are also used to adjust the preload of the rear axle bearings.

The axle shaft on the semi-floating rear axle is held in position by C-locks in the differential housing.

Axle Identification and Ratio are found on an I.D. tag located under one of the bolts on the differential housing. Also refer to the Drive Axle Section of the Capacities Chart in Section 1 for complete model application.

Axle Shaft, Bearing and Seal

REMOVAL AND INSTALLATION

Ford 8.8 in. (223.5mm) Ring Gear Integral Carrier

1. Raise and safely support the vehicle on jackstands.
2. Remove the wheels from the brake drums.
3. Place a drain pan under the housing and drain the lubricant by loosening the housing cover.
4. Remove the locks securing the brake drums to the axle shaft flanges and remove the drums.
5. Remove the housing cover and gasket.
6. Remove the side gear pinion shaft lockbolt and the side gear pinion shaft.
7. Push the axle shafts inward and remove the C-locks from the inner end of the axle shafts. Temporarily replace the shaft and lockbolt to retain the differential gears in position.
8. Remove the axle shafts with a slide hammer. Be sure the seal is not damaged by the splines on the axle shaft.

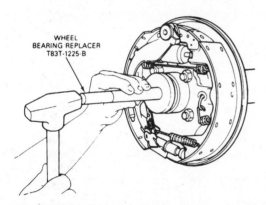

Ford 8.8 inch rear axle bearing installation

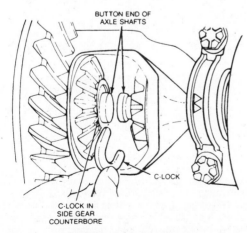

Installing the C-locks

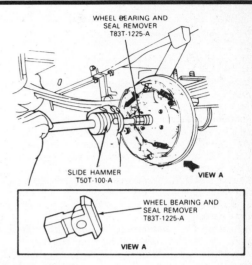

Rear axle bearing and seal removal for the Ford 8.8 inch axle

9. Remove the bearing and oil seal from the housing. Both the seal and bearing can be removed with a slide hammer
10. Two types of bearings are used on some axles, one requiring a press fit and the other a loose fit. A loose fitting bearing does not necessarily indicate excessive wear.
11. Inspect the axle shaft housing and axle shafts for burrs or other irregularities. Replace any work or damaged parts. A light yellow color on the bearing journal of the axle shaft is normal, and does not require replacement of the axle shaft. Slight pitting and wear is also normal.
12. Lightly coat the wheel bearing rollers with axle lubricant. Install the bearings in the axle housing until the bearing seats firmly against the shoulder.
13. Wipe all lubricant from the oil seal bore, before installing the seal.
14. Inspect the original seals for wear. If necessary, these may be replaced with new seals, which are prepacked with lubricant and do not require soaking.
15. Install the oil seal.
16. Remove the lockbolt and pinion shaft. Carefully slide the axle shafts into place. Be careful that you do not damage the seal with the splined end of the axle shaft. Engage the splined end of the shaft with the differential side gears.
17. Install the axle shaft C-locks on the inner end of the axle shafts and seat the C-locks in the counterbore of the differential side gears.
18. Rotate the differential pinion gears until the differential pinion shaft can be installed. Install the differential pinion shaft lockbolt. Tighten to 15–22 ft. lbs.
19. Install the brake drum on the axle shaft flange.
20. Install the wheel and tire on the brake drum and tighten the attaching nuts.
21. Clean the gasket surface of the rear housing and install a new cover gasket and the housing cover. Some covers do not use a gasket. On these models, apply a bead of silicone sealer on the gasket surface. The bead should run inside of the bolt holes.
22. Raise the rear axle so that it is in the running position. Add the amount of specified lubricant to bring the lubricant level to ½ in. (12.7mm) below the filler hole.

Dana Axles

— **CAUTION** —

New Dual Rear Wheel models have flat-faced lug nut replacing the old cone-shaped lug nuts. NEVER replace these new nuts with the older design! Never replace the newer designed wheels with older design wheels! The newer wheels have lug holes with special shoulders to accommodate the newly designed lug nuts.

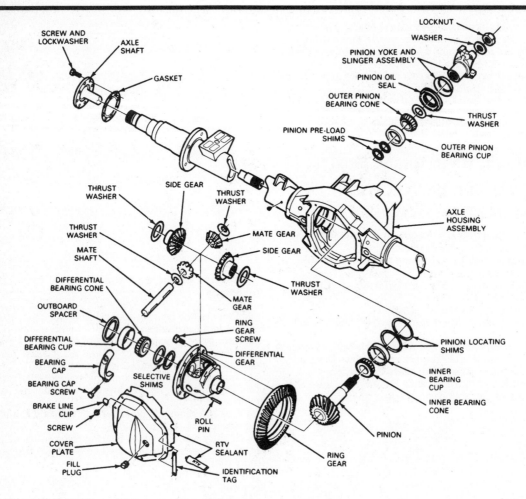

SCREW AND LOCKWASHER

AXLE SHAFT

GASKET

LOCKNUT

WASHER

PINION YOKE AND SLINGER ASSEMBLY

PINION OIL SEAL

OUTER PINION BEARING CONE

THRUST WASHER

PINION PRE-LOAD SHIMS

OUTER PINION BEARING CUP

THRUST WASHER

SIDE GEAR

THRUST WASHER

THRUST WASHER

MATE GEAR

SIDE GEAR

MATE SHAFT

THRUST WASHER

DIFFERENTIAL BEARING CONE

MATE GEAR

OUTBOARD SPACER

RING GEAR SCREW

DIFFERENTIAL BEARING CUP

DIFFERENTIAL GEAR

BEARING CAP

BEARING CAP SCREW

SELECTIVE SHIMS

BRAKE LINE CLIP

SCREW

ROLL PIN

COVER PLATE

RTV SEALANT

FILL PLUG

IDENTIFICATION TAG

RING GEAR

PINION

AXLE HOUSING ASSEMBLY

PINION LOCATING SHIMS

INNER BEARING CUP

INNER BEARING CONE

Dana 70 exploded view

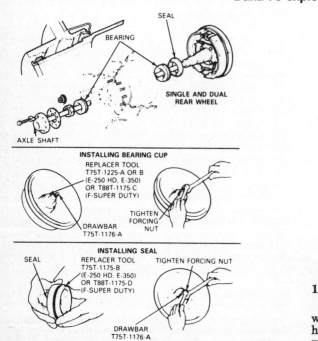

SEAL

BEARING

SINGLE AND DUAL REAR WHEEL

AXLE SHAFT

INSTALLING BEARING CUP

REPLACER TOOL
T75T-1225-A OR B
(E-250 HD, E-350)
OR T88T-1175-C
(F-SUPER DUTY)

TIGHTEN FORCING NUT

DRAWBAR
T75T-1176-A

INSTALLING SEAL

SEAL

REPLACER TOOL
T75T-1175-B
(E-250 HD, E-350)
OR T88T-1175-D
(F-SUPER DUTY)

TIGHTEN FORCING NUT

DRAWBAR
T75T-1176-A

Installation of the rear wheel bearings and seal on the Dana 70 rear axle

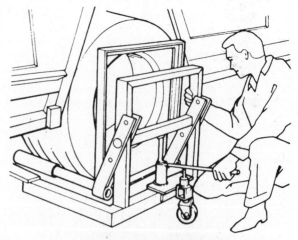

Heavy duty wheel dolly

1989

The wheel bearings on full floating rear axles are packed with wheel bearing grease. Axle lubricant can also flow into the wheel hubs and bearings, however, wheel bearing grease is the primary lubricant. The wheel bearing grease provides lubrication until the axle lubricant reaches the bearings during normal operation.

1. Set the parking brake and loosen — do not remove — the axle shaft bolts.

2. Raise the rear wheels off the floor and place jackstands under the rear axle housing so that the axle is parallel with the floor. Release the parking brake.

3. Remove the axle shaft bolts and lockwashers. They should not be re-used.

4. Place a heavy duty wheel dolly under the wheels and raise them so that all weight is off the wheel bearings.

5. Remove the axle shaft and gasket(s).

6. Remove the caliper. See Section 9.

7. Using a special hub nut wrench, remove the hub nut.

NOTE: The hub nut on the right spindle is right hand thread; the one on the left spindle is left hand thread. They are marked RH and LH. NEVER use an impact wrench on the hub nut!

8. Remove the outer bearing cone and pull the wheel straight off the axle.

9. With a piece of hardwood or a brass drift which will just clear the outer bearing cup, drive the inner bearing cone and inner seal out of the wheel hub.

10. Wash all the old grease or axle lubricant out of the wheel hub, using a suitable solvent.

11. Wash the bearing cups and rollers and inspect them for pitting, galling, and uneven wear patterns. Inspect the roller for end wear.

12. If the bearing cups are to be replaced, drive them out with a brass drift. Install the new cups with a block of wood and hammer or press them in.

13. If the bearing cups are properly seated, a 0.0015 in. (0.038mm) feeler gauge will not fit between the cup and the wheel hub. The gauge should not fit beneath the cup. Check several places to make sure the cups are squarely seated.

14. Pack each bearing cone and roller with a bearing packer or in the manner outlined for the front wheel bearings in Section 1. Use a multi-purpose wheel bearing grease.

15. Place the inner bearing cone and roller assembly in the wheel hub. Install a new inner seal in the hub with a seal installation tool.

16. Wrap the threads of the spindle with tape and carefully slide the hub straight on the spindle. Take care to avoid damaging the seal! Remove the tape.

17. Install the outer bearing. Start the hub nut, making sure that the hub tab is engaged with the keyway prior to threading.

18. Tighten the nut to 65–75 ft.lbs. while rotating the wheel.

NOTE: The hub will ratchet at torque is applied. This ratcheting can be avoided by using Ford tool No. T88T-4252-A. Avoiding ratcheting will give more even bearing preloads.

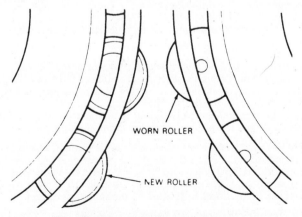

Roller bearing end wheel

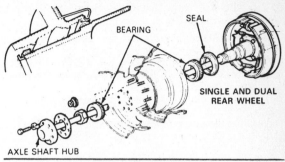

Installing the rear wheel bearings and seal

19. Back off (loosen) the adjusting nut 90° (¼ turn). Then, tighten it to 15–20 ft. lbs.

20. Using a dial indicator, check endplay of the hub. No endplay is permitted.

21. Clean the hub bolt holes thoroughly. Replace the hub if any cracks are found around the holes or if the threads in the holes are in any way damaged.

22. Install the axle shaft, new flange gasket, lock washers and *new* shaft retaining bolts. Coat the bolt threads with thread adhesive. Tighten them snugly, but not completely.

23. Install the caliper.

24. Install the wheels.

25. Lower the van to the ground.

26. Tighten the wheel lug nuts.

27. Tighten the axle shaft bolts to 70–85 ft. lbs.

1990–91

The wheel bearings on full floating rear axles are packed with wheel bearing grease. Axle lubricant can also flow into the wheel hubs and bearings, however, wheel bearing grease is the primary lubricant. The wheel bearing grease provides lubrication until the axle lubricant reaches the bearings during normal operation.

1. Set the parking brake and loosen — do not remove — the axle shaft bolts.

2. Raise the rear wheels off the floor and place jackstands under the rear axle housing so that the axle is parallel with the floor. The axle shafts must turn freely, so release the parking brake.

3. Remove the axle shaft bolts and lockwashers. They should not be re-used.

4. Place a heavy duty wheel dolly under the wheels and raise them so that all weight is off the wheel bearings.

5. Remove the axle shaft and gasket(s).

6. Remove the brake caliper. See Section 9.

7. Using a special hub nut wrench, remove the hub nut.

NOTE: The hub nuts for both sides are right hand thread and marked RH.

8. Remove the outer bearing cone and pull the wheel straight off the axle.

9. With a piece of hardwood or a brass drift which will just clear the outer bearing cup, drive the inner bearing cone and inner seal out of the wheel hub.

10. Wash all the old grease or axle lubricant out of the wheel hub, using a suitable solvent.

11. Wash the bearing cups and rollers and inspect them for pitting, galling, and uneven wear patterns. Inspect the roller for end wear.

12. If the bearing cups are to be replaced, drive them out with a brass drift. Install the new cups with a block of wood and hammer or press them in.

13. If the bearing cups are properly seated, a 0.0015 in. (0.038mm) feeler gauge will not fit between the cup and the wheel hub. The gauge should not fit beneath the cup. Check several places to make sure the cups are squarely seated.

14. Pack each bearing cone and roller with a bearing packer or in the manner outlined for the front wheel bearings in Section 1. Use a multi-purpose wheel bearing grease.

15. Place the inner bearing cone and roller assembly in the wheel hub. Install a new inner seal in the hub with a seal installation tool.

16. Wrap the threads of the spindle with tape and carefully slide the hub straight on the spindle. Take care to avoid damaging the seal! Remove the tape.

17. Install the outer bearing. Start the hub nut, making sure that the hub tab is engaged with the keyway prior to threading.

18. Tighten the nut to 65–75 ft.lbs. while rotating the wheel.

NOTE: The hub will ratchet at torque is applied. This ratcheting can be avoided by using Ford tool No. T88T-4252-A. Avoiding ratcheting will give more even bearing preloads.

19. Back off (loosen) the adjusting nut 90° (¼ turn). Then, tighten it to 15–20 ft. lbs.

20. Using a dial indicator, check endplay of the hub. No endplay is permitted.

21. Clean the hub bolt holes thoroughly. Replace the hub if any cracks are found around the holes or if the threads in the holes are in any way damaged.

22. Install the axle shaft, new flange gasket, lock washers and *new* shaft retaining bolts. Coat the bolt threads with thread adhesive. Tighten them snugly, but not completely.

23. Install the caliper.

24. Install the wheels.

25. Lower the van to the ground.

26. Tighten the wheel lug nuts.

27. Tighten the axle shaft bolts to 40–55 ft. lbs.

Pinion Seal

REMOVAL AND INSTALLATION

Ford 8.8 in. (223.5mm) Ring Gear Integral Carrier Axle

NOTE: A torque wrench capable of at least 225 ft. lbs. is required for pinion seal installation.

1. Raise and safely support the vehicle with jackstands under the frame rails. Allow the axle to drop to rebound position for working clearance.

2. Remove the rear wheels and brake drums. No drag must be present on the axle.

3. Mark the companion flanges and U-joints for correct reinstallation position.

4. Remove the driveshaft.

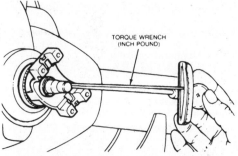

Measuring pinion bearing preload

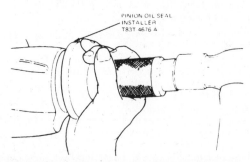

Pinion seal installation for the Ford 8.8 inch rear axle

5. Using an inch pound torque wrench and socket on the pinion yoke nut measure the amount of torque needed to maintain differential rotation through several clockwise revolutions. Record the measurement.

6. Use a suitable tool to hold the companion flange. Remove the pinion nut.

7. Place a drain pan under the differential, clean the area around the seal, and mark the yoke-to-pinion relation.

8. Use a 2-jawed puller to remove the pinion.

9. Remove the seal with a small prybar.

10. Thoroughly clean the oil seal bore.

NOTE: If you are not absolutely certain of the proper seal installation depth, the proper seal driver must be used. If the seal is misaligned or damaged during installation, it must be removed and a new seal installed.

11. Drive the new seal into place with a seal driver such as T83T–4676–A. Coat the seal lip with clean, waterproof wheel bearing grease.

12. Coat the splines with a small amount of wheel bearing grease and install the yoke, aligning the matchmarks. Never hammer the yoke onto the pinion!

13. Install a NEW nut on the pinion.

14. Hold the yoke with a holding tool. Tighten the pinion nut to at least 160 ft. lbs., taking frequent turning torque readings until the original preload reading is attained.

If the original preload reading, that you noted before disassembly, is lower than the specified reading of 8–14 inch lbs. for used bearings; 16–29 inch lbs. for new bearings, keep tightening the pinion nut until the specified reading is reached.

If the original preload reading is higher than the specified values, torque the nut just until the original reading is reached.

WARNING: Under no circumstances should the nut be backed off to reduce the preload reading! If the preload is exceeded, the yoke and bearing must be removed and a new collapsible spacer must be installed. The entire process of preload adjustment must be repeated.

15. Install the driveshaft using the matchmarks. Torque the nuts to 15 ft. lbs.

Dana 60

NOTE: A torque wrench capable of at least 300 ft. lbs. is required for pinion seal installation.

1. Raise and support the van on jackstands.
2. Allow the axle to hang freely.
3. Matchmark and disconnect the driveshaft from the axle.
4. Using a tool such as T75T–4851–B, or equivalent, hold the pinion flange while removing the pinion nut.
5. Using a puller, remove the pinion flange.
6. Use a puller to remove the seal, or punch the seal out using a pin punch.
7. Thoroughly clean the seal bore and make sure that it is not damaged in any way. Coat the sealing edge of the new seal with a small amount of 80W/90 oil and drive the seal into the housing using a seal driver.
8. Coat the inside of the pinion flange with clean 80W/90 oil and install the flange onto the pinion shaft.
9. Install the nut on the pinion shaft and tighten it to 250–300 ft. lbs.
10. Connect the driveshaft.

Dana 70

NOTE: A torque wrench capable of at least 500 ft. lbs. is required for pinion seal installation.

1. Raise and safely support the vehicle with jackstands under the frame rails. Allow the axle to drop to the rebound position for working clearance.
2. Remove the rear wheels and brake drums. No drag must be present on the axle.
3. Mark the companion flanges and U-joints for correct reinstallation position.
4. Remove the driveshaft.
5. Use a suitable tool to hold the companion flange. Remove the pinion nut.
6. Place a drain pan under the differential, clean the area around the seal, and mark the yoke-to-pinion relation.
7. Use a 2-jawed puller to remove the pinion.
8. Remove the seal with a small prybar.
9. Thoroughly clean the oil seal bore.

NOTE: If you are not absolutely certain of the proper seal installation depth, the proper seal driver must be used. If the seal is misaligned or damaged during installation, it must be removed and a new seal installed.

10. Coat the new oil seal with wheel bearing grease. Install the seal using oil seal driver T56T–4676–B. After the seal is installed, make sure that the seal garter spring has not become dislodged. If it has, remove and replace the seal.
11. Install the yoke, using flange replacer tool D81T–4858–A if necessary to draw the yoke into place.
12. Install a new pinion nut and washer. Torque the nut to 440–500 ft. lbs.
13. Connect the driveshaft. Torque the fasteners to 15–20 ft. lbs.

Axle Damper

REMOVAL AND INSTALLATION

This device is a large, heavy weight attached to a mounting flange on the differential carrier. Its purpose is to suppress driveline vibrations.

To remove/install the damper, simply support it and remove/install the bolts. Bolt torque is 40–60 ft. lbs.

Axle Housing

REMOVAL AND INSTALLATION

Ford 8.8 in. (223.5mm) Ring Gear Integral Carrier

1. Raise and support the rear end on jackstands under the rear frame members, and support the housing with a floor jack.
2. Matchmark and disconnect the driveshaft at the axle.
3. Remove the wheels and brake drums.
4. Disengage the brake line from the clips that retain the line to the housing.
5. Disconnect the vent tube from the housing.
6. Remove the axle shafts.
7. Remove the brake backing plate from the housing, and support them with wire. Do not disconnect the brake line.
8. Disconnect each rear shock absorber from the mounting bracket stud on the housing.
9. Lower the axle slightly to reduce some of the spring tension. At each rear spring, remove the spring clip (U-bolt) nuts, spring clips, and spring seat caps.
10. Remove the housing from under the vehicle.

To Install:
1. Position the axle housing under the rear springs. Install the spring clips (U-bolts), spring seat clamps and nuts. Tighten the spring clamps evenly to 115 ft. lbs.
2. If a new axle housing is being installed, remove the bolts that attach the brake backing plate and bearing retainer from the old housing flanges. Position the bolts in the new housing flanges to hold the brake backing plates in position. Torque the bolts to 40 ft. lbs.
3. Install the axle shafts.
4. Connect the vent tube to the housing.
5. Position the brake line to the housing, and secure it with the retaining clips.
6. Raise the axle housing and springs enough to allow connecting the rear shock absorbers to the mounting bracket studs on the housing. Torque the nuts to 60 ft. lbs.
7. Connect the driveshaft to the axle. Torque the nuts to 8-15 ft. lbs.
8. Install the brake drums and wheels.

Dana Axles

1. Disconnect the shock absorbers from the rear axle.
2. Loosen the axle shaft nuts.
3. Raise and support the rear end on jackstands placed under the frame.
4. Remove the rear wheels.
5. Disconnect the rear stabilizer bar.
6. Disconnect the brake hose at the frame.
7. Disconnect the parking brake cable at the equalizer and remove the cables from the support brackets.
8. Matchmark the driveshaft-to-axle flange position.
9. Disconnect the driveshaft from the rear axle and move it out of the way.
10. Take up the weight of the axle with a floor jack.
11. Remove the nuts from the spring U-bolts and remove the spring seat caps.
12. Lower the axle and roll it from under the van.
13. Installation is the reverse of removal. Torque the spring U-bolt nuts to 160 ft. lbs. Bleed the brake system.

Conventional Differential Overhaul Ford 8.8 in. Ring Gear
DISASSEMBLY

Differential Carrier

1. Remove the cover and clean the lubricant from the internal parts.

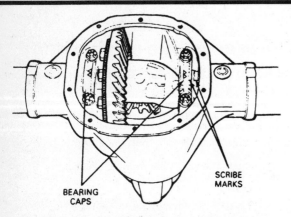

Bearing cap identification - Ford 8.8 in.

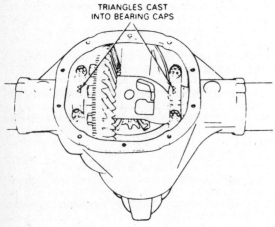

Bearing cap identification marks cast into caps - Ford 8.8 in.

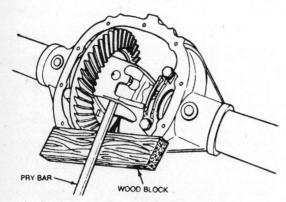

Prying out the case - Ford 8.8 in.

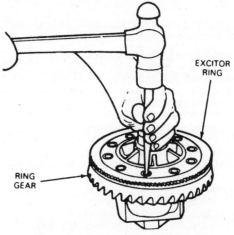

Ring gear removal - Ford 8.8 in.

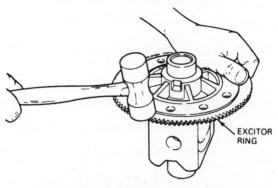

Exciter ring removal - Ford 8.8 in.

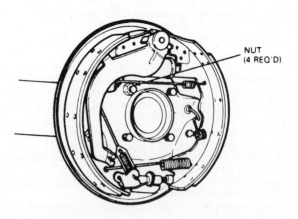

Backing plate removal - Ford 8.8 in.

2. Using a dial indicator, measure and record the ring gear backlash and the runout; the backlash should be 0.008–0.015 in. and the runout should be less than 0.004 in.

NOTE: On vans with anti-lock brakes, there is room provided between the exciter ring and the ring gear for measuring backface runout.

3. Mark 1 differential bearing cap to ensure it is installed its original position.

4. Loosen the differential bearing cap bolts.

5. Using a prybar, pry the differential carrier until the bearing cups and shims are loose in the bearing caps.

6. Remove the bearing caps and the differential assembly.

7. If necessary, remove ring gear-to-differential case bolts. Using a hammer and a punch, strike the alternate bolt holes around the ring gear to dislodge it from the differential.

8. If necessary, remove the exciter ring by striking it with a soft hammer.

9. Remove the pinion shaft lock bolt from the differential case. Remove the differential pinion shaft, the pinion gears and the thrust washers.

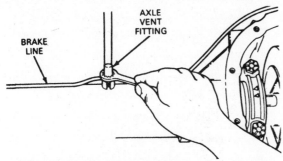

Disconnecting the vent hose - Ford 8.8 in.

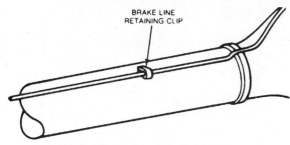

Brake line clip - Ford 8.8 in.

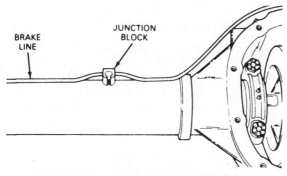

Junction block removal - Ford 8.8 in.

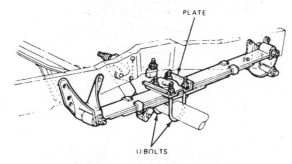

U-bolt removal - Ford 8.8 in.

10. Remove the side gears and thrust washers.
11. Using a bearing puller tool, press the bearings from the differential carrier.

Pinion Gear

1. Remove the differential carrier assembly.
2. Using a companion flange holding tool, remove the companion flange nut.

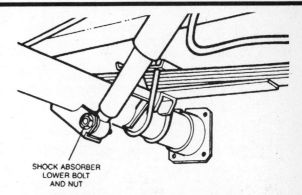

Lower shock mount - Ford 8.8 in.

3. Using a puller tool, press the companion flange from the pinion gear.
4. Using a soft hammer, drive the pinion gear from the housing.
5. Using a prybar, remove the pinion gear oil seal from the housing.
6. Remove the oil slinger and the front pinion bearing.
7. Using a shop press, press the bearing cone from from the pinion gear.
8. Remove and record the shim from the pinion gear.

INSPECTION

1. Clean the differential components in solvent and use compressed air to dry them; do not use compressed air on the bearings, only shop towels.
2. Check the components for wear or damage; replace them, if necessary.
3. Inspect the bearings and bearing cups for wear, cracks or scoring; replace them, if necessary.
4. Inspect the differential side and pinion gears for wear, cracks or chips; replace them, if necessary.
5. Inspect the ring and pinion gears for wear and/or damage; replace them, if necessary.
6. Inspect the differential case for cracks or damage; replace it, if necessary.

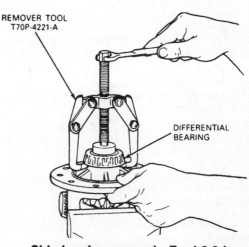

Side bearing removal - Ford 8.8 in.

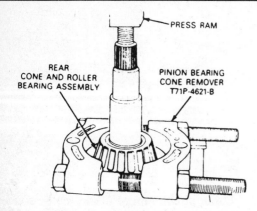

Drive pinion bearing removal - Ford 8.8 in.

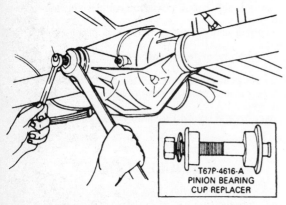

Removing the pinion mount - Ford 8.8 in.

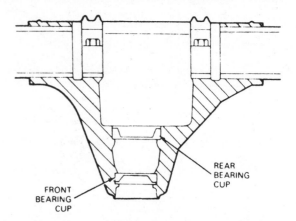

Bearing cup positioning - Ford 8.8 in.

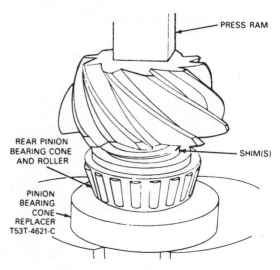

Pinion bearing shim installation - Ford 8.8 in.

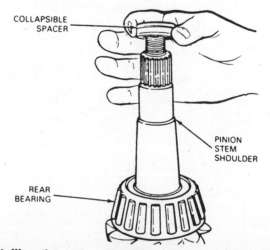

Installing the new collapsible spacer - Ford 8.8 in

ASSEMBLY

Pinion Gear

NOTE: When replacing the ring and pinion gear, the correct shim thickness for the new gear set to be installed is determined by following procedure using a pinion depth gauge tool set.

1. Assemble the appropriate aligning adapter, the gauge disc and gauge block to the screw.

2. Place the rear pinion bearing over the aligning tool and insert it into the rear portion of the bearing cup of the carrier. Place the front bearing into the front bearing cup and assemble the tool handle into the screw. Roll the assembly back and forth a few times to seat the bearings while tightening the tool handle, by hand, to 20 ft. lbs. (27 Nm).

NOTE: The gauge block must be offset 45 degrees to obtain an accurate reading.

3. Center the gauge tube into the differential bearing bore. Install the bearing caps and tighten the bolts to 70–85 ft. lbs. (96–115 Nm); be sure to install the caps with the triangles pointing outward.

4. Place the selected shim(s) on the pinion and press the pinion bearing cone and roller assembly until it is firmly seated on the shaft, using the pinion bearing cone replacer and the axle bearing/seal plate.

5. Place the collapsible spacer on the pinion stem against the pinion stem shoulder.

6. Install the front pinion bearing and oil slinger in the hous-

ing bore and install the pinion seal on the pinion seal replacer. Using a hammer, install the seal until it seats.

7. From the rear of the axle housing, install the drive pinion assembly into the housing pinion shaft bore.

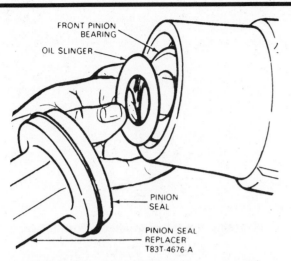

Installing the slinger and seal - Ford 8.8 in.

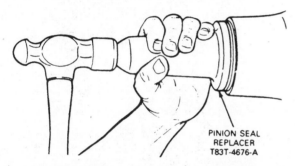

Driving the pinion into place - Ford 8.8 in.

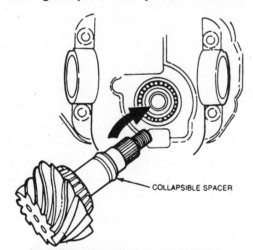

Installing the pinion - Ford 8.8 in.

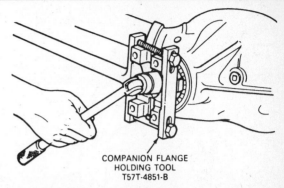

Tightening the pinion nut on the E-150 - Ford 8.8 in.

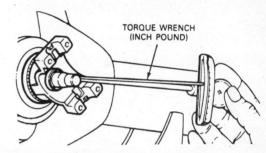

Checking rotational torque on the E-150 - Ford 8.8 in.

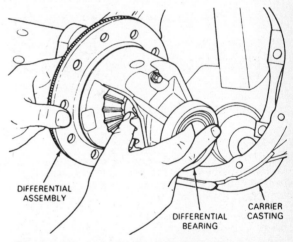

Placing the case in the housing - Ford 8.8 in

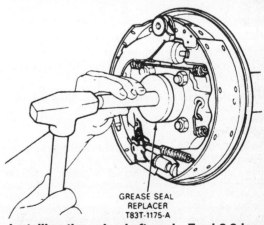

Installing the axle shaft seal - Ford 8.8 in.

8. Lubricate the pinion shaft splines and install the companion flange.

9. Using a companion flange holder tool, torque the pinion nut to 160 ft. lbs. (217 Nm); rotate the pinion gear, occasionally, to ensure proper bearing seating.

10. Using an inch pound torque wrench, frequently, measure the pinion bearing preload; it should be 8–14 inch lbs. for used bearings or 16–29 inch lbs. for new bearings.

NOTE: If the preload is higher than the specification, tighten to the original reading as recorded; never back off the pinion nut.

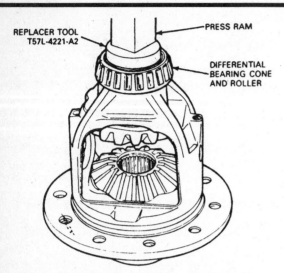

Installing the side bearing - Ford 8.8 in.

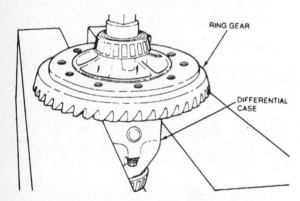

Installing the exciter ring - Ford 8.8 in.

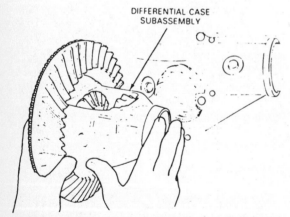

Placing the case in the housing - Ford 8.8 in.

Differential Carrier

1. If the bearings were removed, use a shop press to press them onto the differential case.

2. Install the side gears and thrust washers. Install the pinion gears, the thrust washer, the pinion shaft and the pinion shaft lock bolt.

3. Using a shop press, align the exciter ring tab with the differential case slot and press the ring gear and exciter ring onto

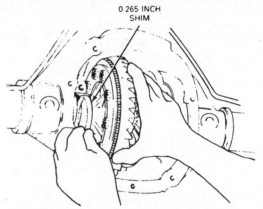

Installing the left side shim - Ford 8.8 in.

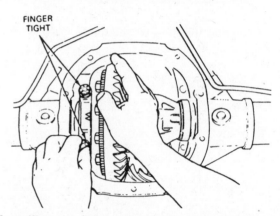

Installing the left bearing cap - Ford 8.8 in.

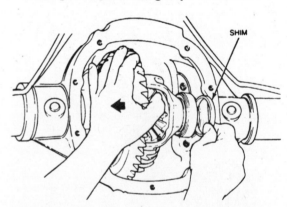

Installing the right side shim - Ford 8.8 in.

the differential case. Install the ring gear-to-differential case bolts and torque them to 100–120 ft. lbs. (135–162 Nm).

4. Place the differential case with the bearing cups into the housing.

5. On the left side, install a 0.265 in shim. Install the bearing cap and tighten the bolts finger tight.

6. On the right side, install progressively larger shims until the largest can be installed by hand. Install the bearing cap.

7. Torque the bearing cap-to-housing bolts to 70–85 ft. lbs. (95–115 Nm).

8. Rotate the assembly to ensure free rotation.

9. Adjust the ring gear backlash.

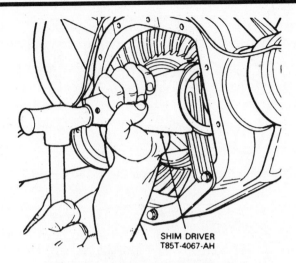

Final shim installation - Ford 8.8 in.

Shim driver
T85T-4067-AH

Backlash Change Required	Thickness Change Required	Backlash Change Required	Thickness Change Required
.001	.002	.009	.012
.002	.002	.010	.014
.003	.004	.011	.014
.004	.006	.012	.016
.005	.006	.013	.018
.006	.008	.014	.018
.007	.010	.015	.020
.008	.010		

Shim chart - Ford 8.8 in.

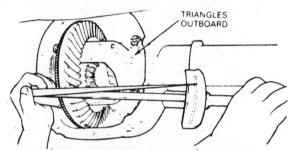

TRIANGLES OUTBOARD

Tightening the right side cap - Ford 8.8 in.

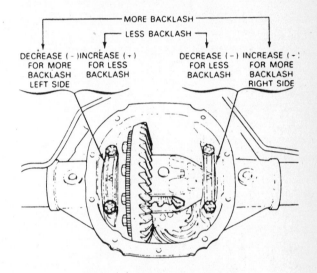

MORE BACKLASH

LESS BACKLASH

DECREASE (−) FOR MORE BACKLASH LEFT SIDE

INCREASE (+) FOR LESS BACKLASH

DECREASE (−) FOR LESS BACKLASH

INCREASE (−) FOR MORE BACKLASH RIGHT SIDE

Shim changes - Ford 8.8 in.

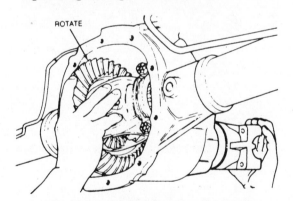

ROTATE

Checking for free rotation Ford 8.8 in.

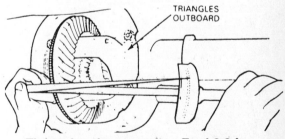

TRIANGLES OUTBOARD

Tightening the cap colts - Ford 8.8 in.

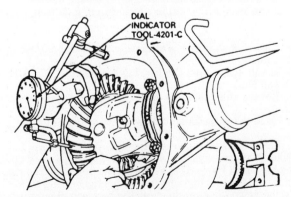

DIAL INDICATOR TOOL-4201-C

Checking ring gear backlash - Ford 8.8 in.

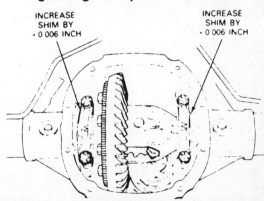

INCREASE SHIM BY + 0.006 INCH

INCREASE SHIM BY + 0.006 INCH

Shimming for bearing preload - Ford 8.8 in.

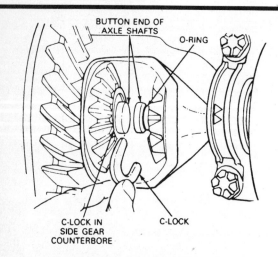

Installing C-locks - Ford 8.8 in.

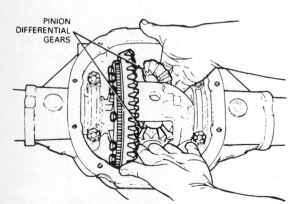

Installing pinion gears - Ford 8.8 in.

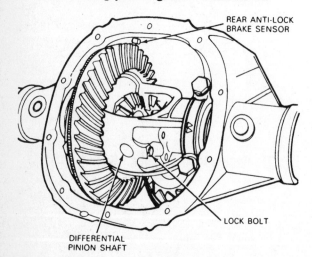

Pinion shaft and lockbolt installation - Ford 8.8 in

ADJUSTMENT

Ring Gear and Pinion Backlash

1. Using a dial indicator, measure the ring gear and pinion backlash; it should be 0.008–0.015 in. If the backlash is 0.001–0.007 in. or greater than 0.015 in. proceed to Step 3. If the backlash is zero, proceed to Step 2.

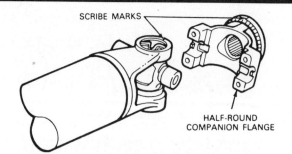

Connecting the driveshaft on the E-150 - Ford 8.8 in.

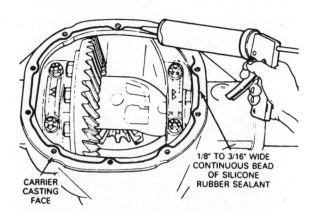

Rear cover sealer application - Ford 8.8 in.

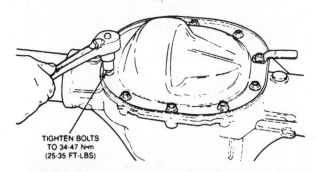

Tightening the rear cover bolts - Ford 8.8 in.

2. If the backlash is zero, add 0.020 in. shim(s) to the right side and subtract a 0.020 in. shim(s) from the left side.

3. If the backlash is within specification, go to step 7. If the backlash is 0.001–0.007 in. or greater than 0.015 in., increase the thickness of a shim on 1 side and decrease the same thickness of another shim on the other side, until the backlash comes within range.

4. Install and torque the bearing cap bolts to 80–95 ft. lbs. (109–128 Nm).

5. Rotate the assembly several times to ensure proper seating.

6. Recheck the backlash, if it is not within specification, go to step 7.

7. Remove the bearing caps. Increase the shim sizes, on both sides by 0.006 in.; make sure the shims are fully seated and the assembly turns freely. Use a shim driver to install the shims.

8. Install the bearing caps and torque the bearing caps to 80–95 ft. lbs. (109–128 Nm). Recheck the backlash; if not to specification, repeat this entire procedure.

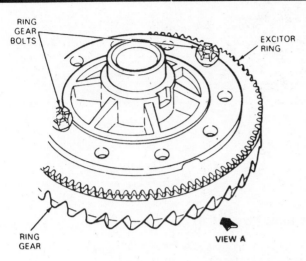

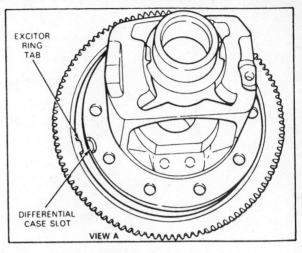

Exciter ring installation - Ford 8.8 in.

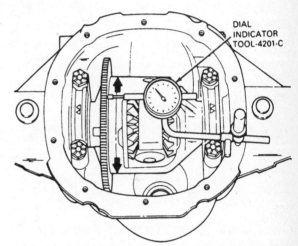

HOLD DOWN
BOLT-390356
TIGHTEN TO
34-40 N·m
(25-30 FT-LB)

Case flange runout check - Ford 8.8 in.

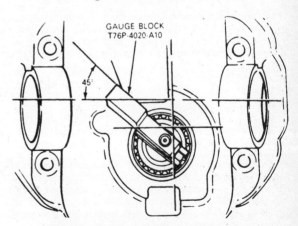

Installing the sensor - Ford 8.8 in.

Depth gauge checking - Ford 8.8 in.

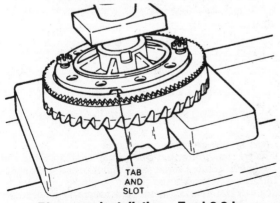

Ring gear installation - Ford 8.8 in.

Conventional Differential Overhaul Dana 60

The differential side bearing shims are located between the side bearing cup assembly and the differential case. The axle use

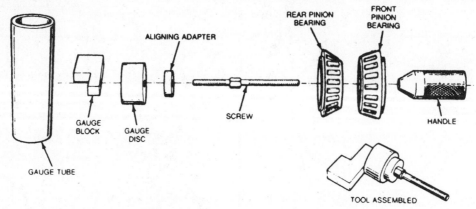

Pinion depth gauge tool - Ford 8.8 in.

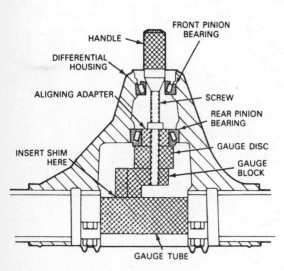

Shimming the differential - Ford 8.8 in.

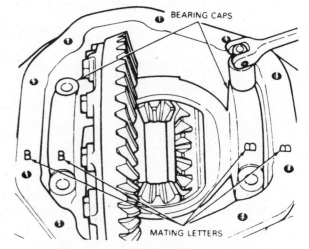

Bearing cap identification - Dana 60

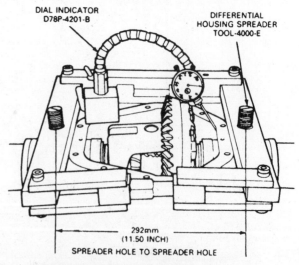

Spreading the differential - Dana 60

inner and outer shims on the pinion gear. The inner shims are used to control the pinion depth in the housing, while the outer shims are used to preload the pinion bearings. The axle uses a solid differential carrier with a removable side and pinion gear shaft.

DISASSEMBLY

Differential Carrier

1. The axle assembly can be overhauled either in or out of the vehicle. Either way, the free-floating axles must be removed.
2. Drain the lubricant and remove the rear cover and gasket.
3. Matchmark the bearing caps and the housing for reassembly in the same position. Remove the bearing caps and bolts.
4. Using a spreader tool mounted to the carrier housing, spread the housing a maximum of 0.015 in.

NOTE: Do not exceed this measurement. The housing could be permanently damaged. The use of a dial indicator is recommended to prevent over-stretching the housing.

5. Using a pry bar, remove the differential case from the housing. Remove the spreader tool from the housing.
6. Remove the differential side bearing cups and tag to identi-

fy the side, if they are to be used again.
7. Remove the differential gear pinion shaft lock pin and remove the shaft. Rotate the side and pinion gears to remove them from the carrier. Remove the thrust bearings.
8. Remove the bearing cones and rollers from the carrier, marking and noting the shim locations.

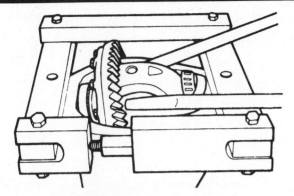

Prying out the case - Dana 60

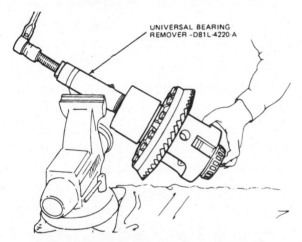

UNIVERSAL BEARING
REMOVER -D81L-4220-A

Differential bearing removal - Dana 60

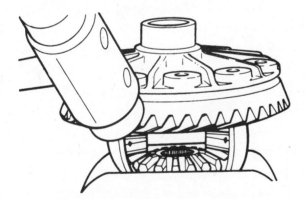

Removing the ring gear - Dana 60

9. Remove the ring gear bolts and tap the ring gear from the carrier housing.
10. Inspect the components.

Drive Pinion

1. Remove the pinion nut and flange from the pinion gear.
2. Remove the pinion gear assembly from the housing. It may be necessary to tap the pinion from the housing with a soft faced hammer. Catch the pinion so as not to allow it to drop on the floor.
3. With a long drift, remove the inner bearing cup, pinion seal, slinger, gasket, outer pinion bearing and the shim pack. Label the shim pack for reassembly.

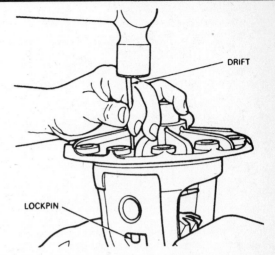

DRIFT

LOCKPIN

Driving out the pinion mate lockpin - Dana 60

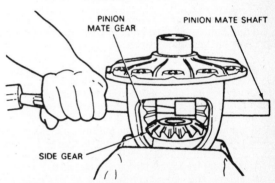

PINION MATE GEAR

PINION MATE SHAFT

SIDE GEAR

Driving out the pinion mate shaft - Dana 60

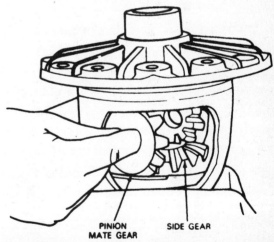

PINION MATE GEAR

SIDE GEAR

Removing the side gears and pinion mate gears - Dana 60

4. Remove the rear pinion bearing cup and shim pack from the housing. Label the shims for reassembly.
5. Remove the rear pinion bearing from the pinion gear with an arbor press and special plates.

INSPECTION

1. Clean the gears, bearings and component parts with solvent and inspect for scoring, chipping or excessive wear.

DRIVE TRAIN

Removing the pinion - Dana 60

2. Inspect the flanges and splines for excessive wear.
3. Replace the necessary parts as required.

PINION SHIM SELECTION

Ring gears and pinions are supplied in matched sets only. The matched numbers are etched on both gears for verification. On the rear face of the pinion, a plus (+) or a minus (−) number will be etched, indicating the best running position for each particular gear set. This dimension is controlled by the shimming behind the inner bearing cup. Whenever baffles or oil slingers are used, they become part of the adjusting shim pack. An example: If a pinion is etched +3, this pinion would require 0.003 in. less shims than a pinion etched 0. This means by removing shims, the mounting distance of the pinion is increased by 0.003 in., which is just what a plus (+) etching indicates. If a pinion is etched −3, it would be necessary to add 0.003 in. more shims than would be required if the pinion was etched 0. By adding the 0.003 in. shims, the mounting distance of the pinion is decreased 0.003 in., which is just what the minus (−) etching indi-

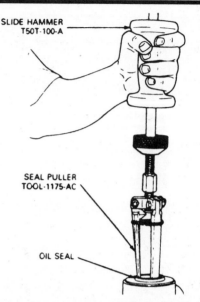

Removing the pinion seal - Dana 60

cates. Pinion adjusting shims are available in thicknesses of 0.003 in. (0.08mm), 0.005 in. (0.13mm), 0.010 in. (0.25mm) and 0.030 in. (0.76mm). An example: If a new gear set is used and the old pinion reads +2 and the new pinion reads −2, add 0.004 in. shims to the original shim pack.

ASSEMBLY

Drive Pinion

1. Select the correct pinion depth shims and install in the rear pinion bearing cup bore.

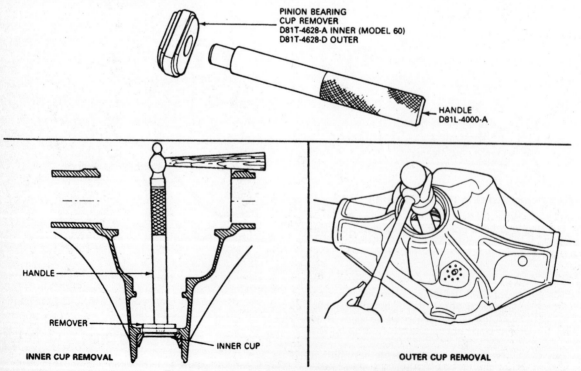

Removing the pinion bearing cups - Dana 60

7–66

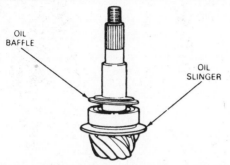

Oil baffle and slinger position - Dana 60

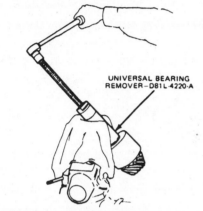

Removing the pinion bearing - Dana 60

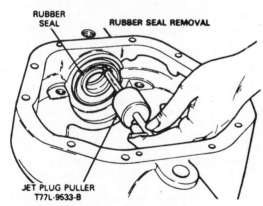

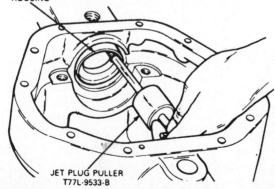

Removing the inner axle shaft seal and seal housing - Dana 60

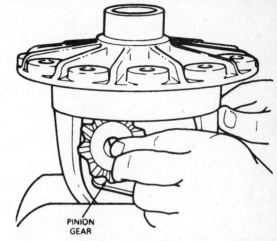

Placing the pinion gear in the case - Dana 60

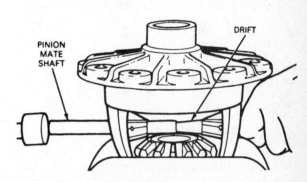

Installing the pinion mate shaft - Dana 60

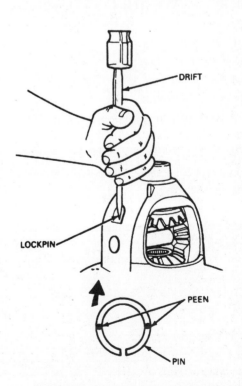

Installing the lockpin - Dana 60

7 DRIVE TRAIN

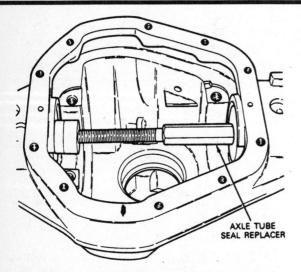

Installing the inner axle shaft seal - Dana 60

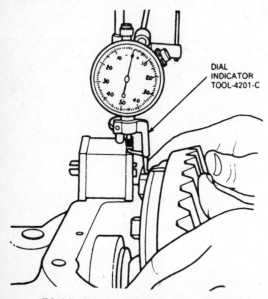

Dial indicator positioning - Dana 60

2. Install the rear bearing cup in the axle housing.
3. Add or subtract an equal amount of shim thickness to or from the preload or outer shim pack, as was added or subtracted from the inner shim pack.

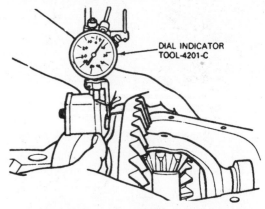

Measuring case endplay - Dana 60

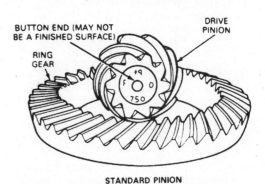

Ring and pinion matching - Dana 60

4. Install the front pinion bearing cup into its bore in the axle housing.
5. Press the rear pinion bearing onto the pinion gear shaft and install the pinion gear with bearing into the axle housing.
6. Install the preload shims and the front pinion bearing; do not install the oil seal at this time.
7. Install the flange with the holding bar tool attached, the washer and the nut on the pinion shaft end. Torque the nut to 220–280 ft. lbs. (298–379 Nm).
8. Remove the holding bar from the flange and with an inch lb. torque wrench, measure the rotating torque of the pinion gear. The rotating torque should be 10–20 inch lbs. with the original bearings or 15–35 inch lbs. with new bearings. Disregard the torque reading necessary to start the shaft to turn.
9. If the preload torque is not in specifications, adjust the shim pack as required.

PINION SETTING CHART — ENGLISH

Old Pinion Marking	New Pinion Marking								
	−4	−3	−2	−1	0	+1	+2	+3	+4
+4	+0.008	+0.007	+0.006	+0.005	+0.004	+0.003	+0.002	+0.001	0
+3	+0.007	+0.006	+0.005	+0.004	+0.003	+0.002	+0.001	0	−0.001
+2	+0.006	+0.005	+0.004	+0.003	+0.002	+0.001	0	−0.001	−0.002
+1	+0.005	+0.004	+0.003	+0.002	+0.001	0	−0.001	−0.002	−0.003
0	+0.004	+0.003	+0.002	+0.001	0	−0.001	−0.002	−0.003	−0.004
−1	+0.003	+0.002	+0.001	0	−0.001	−0.002	−0.003	−0.004	−0.005
−2	+0.002	+0.001	0	−0.001	−0.002	−0.003	−0.004	−0.005	−0.006
−3	+0.001	0	−0.001	−0.002	−0.003	−0.004	−0.005	−0.006	−0.007
−4	0	−0.001	−0.002	−0.003	−0.004	−0.005	−0.006	−0.007	−0.008

Pinion setting chart - English measure - Dana 60

PINION SETTING CHART — METRIC

Old Pinion Marking	New Pinion Marking								
	−10	−8	−5	−3	0	+3	+5	+8	+10
+10	+.20	+.18	+.15	+.13	+.10	+.08	+.05	+.03	0
+8	+.18	+.15	+.13	+.10	+.08	+.05	+.03	0	−.03
+5	+.15	+.13	+.10	+.08	+.05	+.03	0	−.03	−.05
+3	+.13	+.10	+.08	+.05	+.03	0	−.03	−.05	−.08
0	+.10	+.08	+.05	+.03	0	−.03	−.05	−.08	−.10
−3	+.08	+.05	+.03	0	−.03	−.05	−.08	−.10	−.13
−5	+.05	+.03	0	−.03	−.05	−.08	−.10	−.13	−.15
−8	+.03	0	−.03	−.05	−.08	−.10	−.13	−.15	−.18
−10	0	−.03	−.05	−.08	−.10	−.13	−.15	−.18	−.20

Pinion setting chart - Metric measure - Dana 60

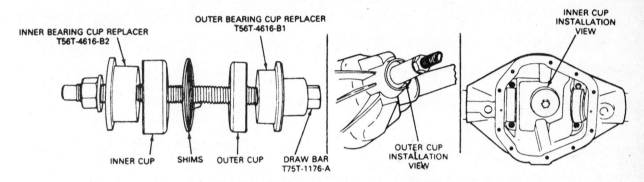

Pinion bearing race installation - Dana 60

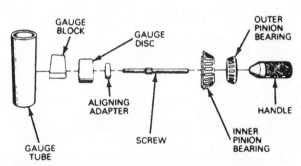

Description	Number
Handle	T76P-4020-A11
Screw	T80T-4020-F43
Gauge Block	T80T-4020-F42
Aligning Adapter	T76P-4020-A3
Gauge Disc	T78P-4020-A15
Gauge Tube	D80T-4020-F48

Depth gauge checking tools - Dana 60

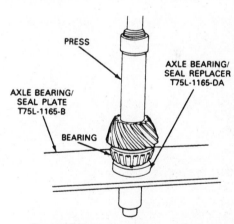

Assembling the pinion - Dana 60

a. To increase preload, decrease the thickness of the pre-load shim pack.

b. To decrease preload, increase the thickness of the pre-load shim pack.

10. When the proper preload is obtained, remove the nut, washer and flange from the pinion shaft.

11. Install a new pinion seal into the housing and reinstall the flange, washer and nut. Using the holder tool, torque the nut to 220–280 ft. lbs. (298–379 Nm).

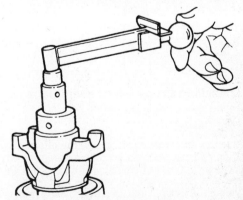

Checking pinion rotating torque - Dana 60

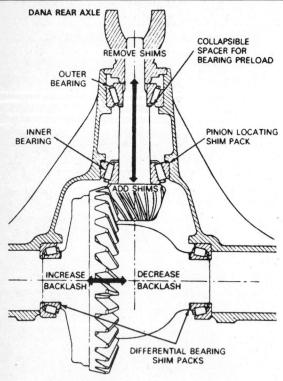

Adjusting the backlash - Dana 60

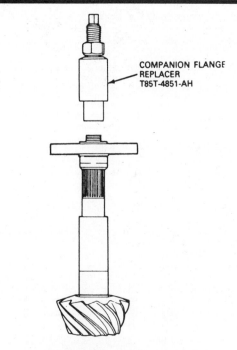

Installing the yoke - Dana 60

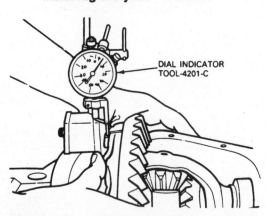

Checking ring and pinion backlash - Dana 60

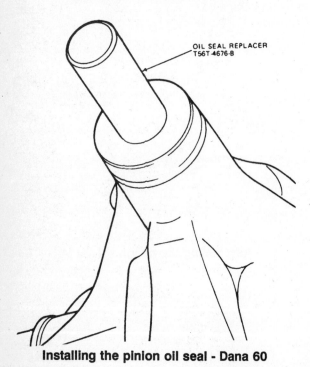

Installing the pinion oil seal - Dana 60

Differential Carrier

1. Install the differential side gears, the differential pinion gears and new thrust washers into the differential carrier.

2. Align the pinion gear shaft holes and install the pinion shaft into the carrier. Align the lock pin hole in the shaft and carrier. Install the lock pin and peen the hole to avoid having the pin drop from the carrier.

3. Install the differential case side bearings with the proper installation tools. Do not install the shims at this time.

4. Place the carrier assembly into the axle housing with the bearing cups on the bearing cones. Install the bearing caps in their original position and tighten the bearing cap bolts enough to keep the bearing caps in place.

5. Install a dial indicator on the housing so the indicator button contacts the carrier flange. Press the differential carrier to prevent sideplay and center the dial indicator. Rotate the carrier and check the flange for run-out. If the run-out is greater than 0.002 in. (0.05mm), the defect is probably due to the bearings or to the carrier and should be corrected.

6. Remove the assembly and install the ring gear. Torque the retaining bolts and reinstall the assembly into the housing. Install the bearing caps in their original position and tighten the cap bolts to keep the bearings caps in place.

7. Install the dial indicator and position the indicator button to contact the ring gear back surface. Rotate the assembly and the run-out should be less than 0.002 in. (0.05mm). If over 0.002 in. (0.05mm), remove the assembly and relocate the ring gear 180 degrees. Reinstall the assembly and recheck. If the

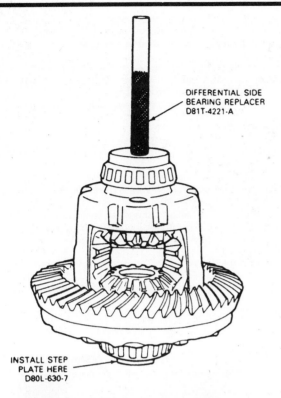

Installing the side bearings - Dana 60

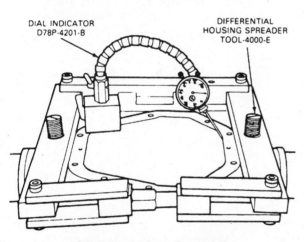

Case spreader - Dana 60

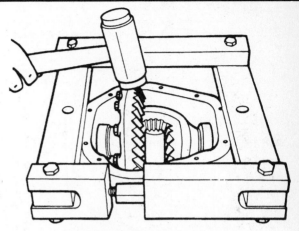

Installing the case - Dana 60

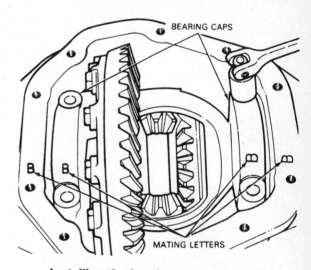

Installing the bearing caps - Dana 60

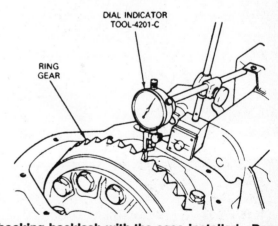

Checking backlash with the case installed - Dana 60

run-out remains over the 0.002 in. (0.05mm) tolerance, the ring gear is defective. If the measurement is within tolerances, continue on with the assembly.

8. Position 2 pry bars between the bearing cap and the housing on the side opposite the ring gear. Pull on the pry bars and force the differential carrier as far as possible towards the dial indicator. Rock the assembly to seat the bearings and reset the dial indicator to 0.

9. Reposition the prybars to the opposite side of the carrier and force the carrier assembly as far towards the center of the housing. Read the dial indicator scale. This will be the total amount of shims required for setting the backlash during the reassembly, less the bearing preload. Record the measurement.

10. With the pinion gear installed and properly set, position the differential carrier assembly into the axle housing and in-

stall the bearing caps in their proper positions. Tighten the cap bolts just to hold the bearing cups in place.

11. Install a dial indicator on the axle housing with the indicator button contacting the back of the ring gear.

12. Position 2 prybars between the bearing cup and the axle housing on the ring gear side of the case and pry the ring gear

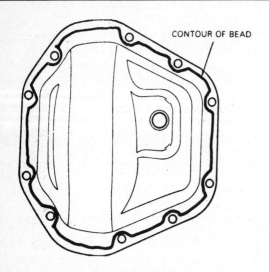

Applying case cover sealer bead - Dana 60

into mesh with the pinion gear teeth, as far as possible. Rock the ring gear to allow the teeth to mesh and the bearings to seat. With the pressure still applied by the prybars, set the dial indicator to 0.

13. Reposition the prybars on the opposite side of ring gear and pry the gear as far as it will go. Take the dial indicator reading. Repeat this procedure until the same reading is obtained each time. This reading represents the necessary amount of shims between the differential carrier and the bearing on the ring gear side.

14. Remove the bearing from the differential carrier on the ring gear side and install the proper amount of shims. Reinstall the bearing.

15. Remove the differential carrier bearing from the opposite side of the ring gear. To determine the amount of shims needed, use the following method.

    a. Subtract the size of the shim pack just installed on the ring gear side of the carrier from the reading obtained and recorded when measurement was taken without the pinion gear in place.

    b. To this figure, add an additional 0.015 in. to compensate for preload and backlash. An example: If the first reading was 0.085 in. and the shims installed on the ring gear side of the

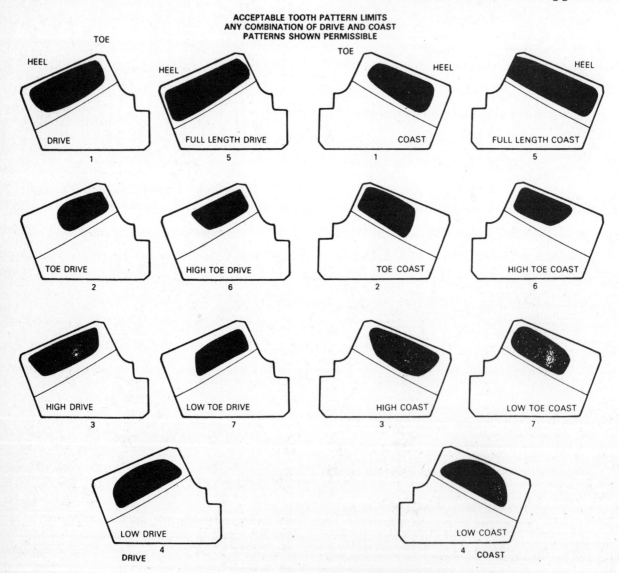

Acceptable tooth contact pattern limits - Dana 60

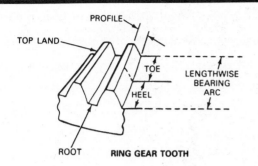

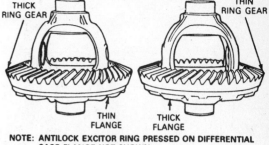

NOTE: ANTILOCK EXCITOR RING PRESSED ON DIFFERENTIAL CASE FLANGE NOT SHOWN.

Identifying the ring gears - Dana 60 axle

PATTERN INTERPRETATION (RING GEAR)

NORMAL OR DESIRABLE PATTERN. THE DRIVE PATTERN SHOULD BE CENTERED ON THE TOOTH. THE COAST PATTERN SHOULD BE CENTERED ON THE TOOTH, BUT MAY BE SLIGHTLY TOWARD THE TOE. THERE SHOULD BE SOME CLEARANCE BETWEEN THE PATTERN AND THE TOP OF THE TOOTH.

THE TOE OF THE GEAR TOOTH IS THE PORTION OF THE TOOTH SURFACE AT THE END TOWARDS THE CENTER. THE HEEL OF THE GEAR TOOTH IS THE PORTION OF THE TOOTH SURFACE AT THE OUTER END. THE TOP LAND OF A GEAR TOOTH IS THE SURFACE OF THE TOP OF THE TOOTH.

Pattern interpretation - Dana 60

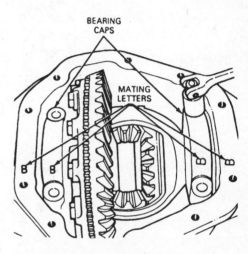

Bearing cap identification - Dana 60

carrier were 0.055 in., the correct amount of shims would be 0.085 in. − 0.055 in. + 0.015 in. = 0.045 in.

16. Install the required shims as determined under Step 15 and install the differential side bearing. The installation of the shims should give the proper preload to the bearings and the proper backlash to the ring and pinion gears.

17. Spread the axle housing with the spreader tool no more than 0.015 in. (0.38mm). Install the differential bearing outer cups in their correct locations and install the cups in their respective locations.

18. Install the bolts and tighten finger-tight. Rotate the differential carrier and ring gear and tap with a soft-faced hammer to insure proper seating of the assembly in the axle housing.

19. Remove the spreader tool and torque the cap bolts to 80–90 ft. lbs. (108–122 Nm).

20. Install a dial indicator and check the ring gear backlash at 4 equally spaced points of the ring gear circle. The backlash must be within a range of 0.005–0.009 in. (0.127–0.229mm) and must not vary more than 0.003 in. (0.076mm) between the points checked.

21. If the backlash is not within specifications, the shim packs must be corrected to bring the backlash within limits.

22. Check the tooth contact pattern and verify.

23. Install the cover and torque the bolts to 30–40 ft. lbs. (41–54 Nm). Refill to proper level with lubricant and operate to verify proper assembly.

DRIVE SIDE		COAST SIDE		
HEEL	TOE	TOE	HEEL	
				BACKLASH CORRECT. THINNER PINION POSITION SHIM REQUIRED.
				BACKLASH CORRECT. THICKER PINION POSITION SHIM REQUIRED.

THICKER PINION POSITION SHIM WITH THE BACKLASH CONSTANT MOVES THE PINION CLOSER TO THE RING GEAR.
DRIVE PATTERN MOVES DEEPER ON THE TOOTH (FLANK CONTACT) AND SLIGHTLY TOWARD THE TOE.
COAST PATTERN MOVES DEEPER ON THE TOOTH AND TOWARD THE HEEL.
THINNER PINION POSITION SHIM WITH THE BACKLASH CONSTANT MOVES THE PINION FURTHER FROM THE RING GEAR.
DRIVE PATTERN MOVES TOWARD THE TOP OF THE TOOTH (FACE CONTACT) AND TOWARD THE HEEL.
COAST PATTERN MOVES TOWARD THE TOP OF THE TOOTH AND SLIGHTLY TOWARD THE TOE.

Tooth pattern adjustment - Dana 60

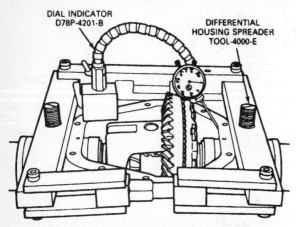

Spreading the differential - Dana 60

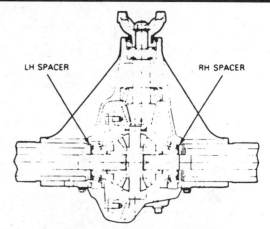

Spacer locations - Dana 60

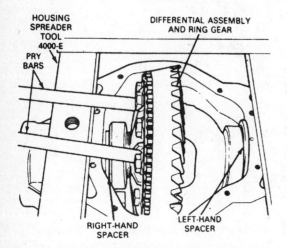

Prying out the case - Dana 60

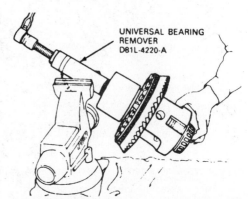

Differential bearing removal - Dana 60

Conventional Differential Overhaul Dana Model 70

DISASSEMBLY

Differential Carrier

NOTE: The axle assembly can be overhauled either in or out of the vehicle. Either way, the free-floating axles shafts must be removed.

1. Drain the lubricant.
2. Remove the rear cover and gasket.
3. Matchmark the bearing caps and the housing for reassembly in the same position. Remove the bearing caps and bolts.
4. Using a spreader tool mounted to the carrier housing, spread the housing a maximum of 0.015 in.

NOTE: Do not exceed this measurement. The housing could be permanently damaged. The use of a dial indicator is recommended to prevent over-stretching the housing.

5. Using a pry bar, remove the differential case from the housing. Separate the shims and record the dimensions. Remove the spreader tool from the housing.
6. Remove the differential side bearing cups and tag to identify the side, if they are to be used again.

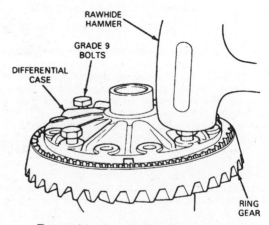

Removing the ring gear - Dana 60

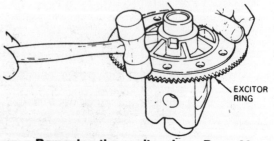

Removing the exciter ring - Dana 60

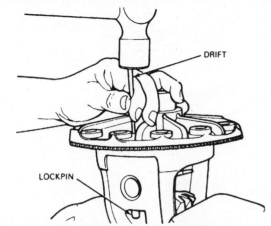

Driving out the pinion mate shaft lockpin - Dana 60

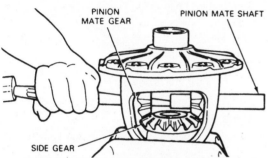

Driving out the pinion mate shaft - Dana 60

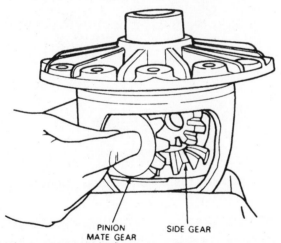

Removing the side gears and pinion mate gears - Dana 60

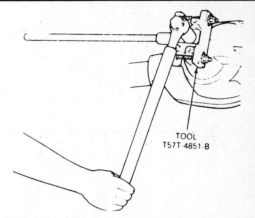

Removing the pinion yoke nut - Dana 60

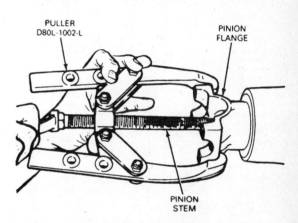

Removing the yoke - Dana 60

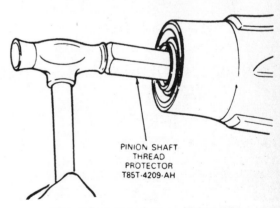

Removing the pinion - Dana 60

7. Remove the differential gear pinion shaft lock pin and remove the shaft. Rotate the side and pinion gears to remove them from the carrier. Remove the thrust bearings.

8. Remove the bearing cones and rollers from the carrier, marking and noting the shim locations.

9. Remove the ring gear bolts and tap the ring gear from the carrier housing.

10. Inspect the components.

Drive Pinion

1. Remove the pinion nut and flange from the pinion gear.

2. Remove the pinion gear assembly from the housing. It may be necessary to tap the pinion from the housing with a soft faced hammer. Catch the pinion so as not to allow it to drop on the floor.

3. With a long drift, remove the inner bearing cup, pinion seal, slinger, gasket, outer pinion bearing and the shim pack. Label the shim pack for reassembly.

4. Remove the rear pinion bearing cup and shim pack from the housing. Label the shims for reassembly.

5. Remove the rear pinion bearing from the pinion gear with an arbor press and special plates.

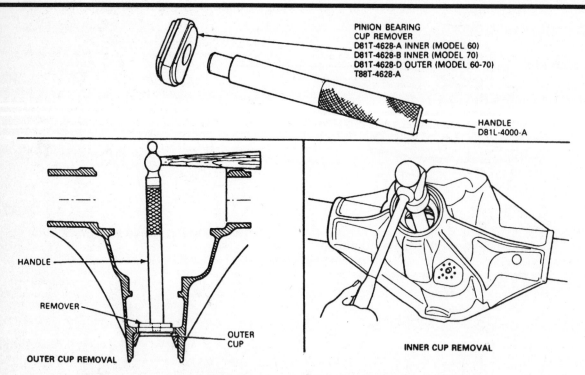

PINION BEARING
CUP REMOVER
D81T-4628-A INNER (MODEL 60)
D81T-4628-B INNER (MODEL 70)
D81T-4628-D OUTER (MODEL 60-70)
T88T-4628-A

HANDLE
D81L-4000-A

HANDLE

REMOVER

OUTER
CUP

OUTER CUP REMOVAL

INNER CUP REMOVAL

Bearing cup remover tool - Dana 60

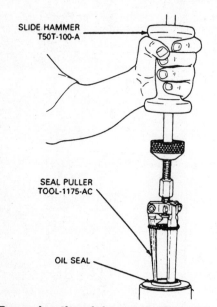

SLIDE HAMMER
T50T-100-A

SEAL PULLER
TOOL-1175-AC

OIL SEAL

Removing the pinion seal - Dana 60

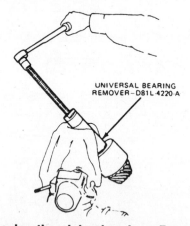

UNIVERSAL BEARING
REMOVER-D81L-4220-A

Removing the pinion bearing - Dana 60

INSPECTION

1. Clean the gears, bearings and component parts with solvent and inspect for scoring, chipping or excessive wear.
2. Inspect the flanges and splines for excessive wear.
3. Replace the necessary parts as required.

PINION SHIM SELECTION

Ring gears and pinions are supplied in matched sets only. The matched numbers are etched on both gears for verification. On the rear face of the pinion, a plus (+) or a minus (−) number will be etched, indicating the best running position for each particular gear set. This dimension is controlled by the shimming behind the inner bearing cup. Whenever baffles or oil slingers are used, they become part of the adjusting shim pack. An example: If a pinion is etched +3, this pinion would require 0.003 in. less shims than a pinion etched 0. This means by removing shims, the mounting distance of the pinion is increased by 0.003 in., which is just what a plus (+) etching indicates. If a pinion is etched −3, it would be necessary to add 0.003 in. more shims than would be required if the pinion was etched 0. By adding the 0.003 in. shims, the mounting distance of the pinion is decreased 0.003 in., which is just what the minus (−) etching indicates. Pinion adjusting shims are available in thicknesses of 0.003, 0.005 and 0.010 in. An example: If a new gear set is used and the old pinion reads +2 and the new pinion reads −2, add 0.004 in. shims to the original shim pack.

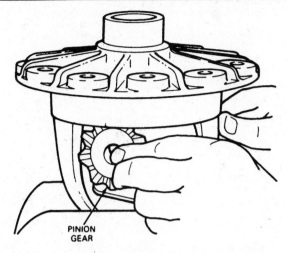

Placing the pinion gear in the case - Dana 60

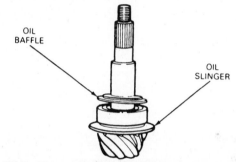

Oil baffle and slinger position - Dana 60

ASSEMBLY

Drive Pinion

1. Select the correct pinion depth shims and install in the rear pinion bearing cup bore.

2. Install the rear bearing cup in the axle housing.

3. Add or subtract an equal amount of shim thickness to or from the preload or outer shim pack, as was added or subtracted from the inner shim pack.

4. Install the front pinion bearing cup into its bore in the axle housing.

5. Press the rear pinion bearing onto the pinion gear shaft and install the pinion gear with bearing into the axle housing.

6. Install the preload shims and the front pinion bearing; do not install the oil seal at this time.

7. Install the flange with the holding bar tool attached, the washer and the nut on the pinion shaft end. Torque the nut to 440–500 ft. lbs. (271–298 Nm).

8. Remove the holding bar from the flange and with an inch lb. torque wrench, measure the rotating torque of the pinion gear. The rotating torque should be 10–20 inch lbs. with the original bearings or 20–40 inch lbs. with new bearings. Disregard the torque reading necessary to start the shaft to turn.

9. If the preload torque is not in specifications, adjust the shim pack as required.

   a. To increase preload, decrease the thickness of the preload shim pack.

   b. To decrease preload, increase the thickness of the preload shim pack.

10. When the proper preload is obtained, remove the nut, washer and flange from the pinion shaft.

11. Install a new pinion seal into the housing and reinstall the flange, washer and nut. Using the holder tool, torque the nut to 440–500 ft. lbs. (271–298 Nm).

Differential Carrier

1. Install the differential side gears, the differential pinion gears and new thrust washers into the differential carrier.

2. Align the pinion gear shaft holes and install the pinion shaft into the carrier. Align the lock pin hole in the shaft and carrier. Install the lock pin and peen the hole to avoid having the pin drop from the carrier.

3. Install the differential case side bearings with the proper installation tools. Do not install the shims at this time.

4. Place the carrier assembly into the axle housing with the bearing cups on the bearing cones. Install the bearing caps in their original position and tighten the bearing cap bolts enough to keep the bearing caps in place.

5. Install a dial indicator on the housing so the indicator but-

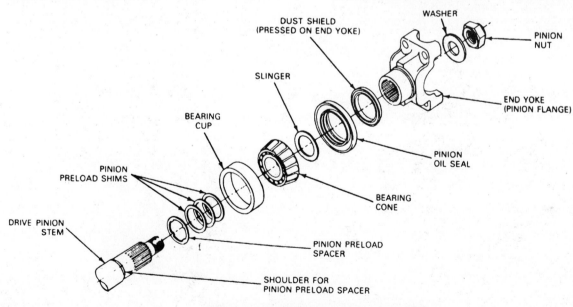

Pinion assembly sequence - Dana 60

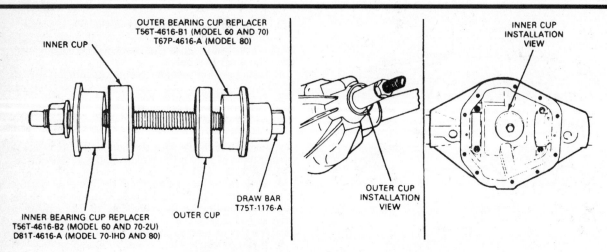

INNER CUP

OUTER BEARING CUP REPLACER
T56T-4616-B1 (MODEL 60 AND 70)
T67P-4616-A (MODEL 80)

DRAW BAR
T75T-1176-A

INNER BEARING CUP REPLACER
T56T-4616-B2 (MODEL 60 AND 70-2U)
D81T-4616-A (MODEL 70-IHD AND 80)

OUTER CUP

OUTER CUP
INSTALLATION
VIEW

INNER CUP
INSTALLATION
VIEW

Pinion bearing race installation - Dana 60

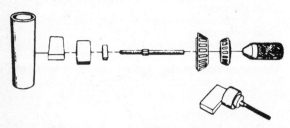

Description	Number	Model 60	Model 70-1HD	Model 70-2U	Model 80
Handle	T76P-4020-A11	X	X	X	T88T-4020-B
Screw	T80T-4020-F43	X	X	X	X
Gauge Block	T80T-4020-F42	X	X	X	X
Aligning Adapter	T76P-4020-A3	X			D80T-4020-R60
	T80T-4020-F48		X	X	
Gauge Disc	T78P-4020-A15	X			T88T-4020-A
	D80T-4020-F45		X	X	
Gauge Tube	D80T-4020-F48	X	X	X	D81T-4020-F51
Final Check (Not required with gear Gauge Block contact pattern method)	D81T-4020-F54	X			
	D81T-4020-F55		X	X	D81T-4020-F56

Depth gauge checking tools - Dana 60

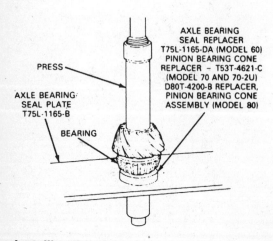

PRESS

AXLE BEARING
SEAL PLATE
T75L-1165-B

BEARING

AXLE BEARING
SEAL REPLACER
T75-1165-DA (MODEL 60)
PINION BEARING CONE
REPLACER – T53T-4621-C
(MODEL 70 AND 70-2U)
D80T-4200-B REPLACER,
PINION BEARING CONE
ASSEMBLY (MODEL 80)

Installing the pinion inner bearing - Dana 60

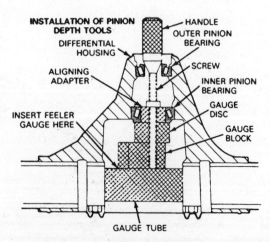

INSTALLATION OF PINION
DEPTH TOOLS

DIFFERENTIAL
HOUSING

ALIGNING
ADAPTER

INSERT FEELER
GAUGE HERE

HANDLE
OUTER PINION
BEARING

SCREW
INNER PINION
BEARING

GAUGE
DISC

GAUGE
BLOCK

GAUGE TUBE

Installation of pinion depth tools - Dana 60

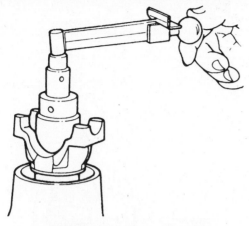

Installing the yoke - Dana 60

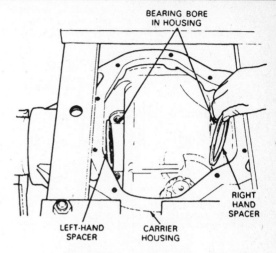

BEARING BORE IN HOUSING

LEFT-HAND SPACER

CARRIER HOUSING

RIGHT HAND SPACER

Adjusting the backlash - Dana 60

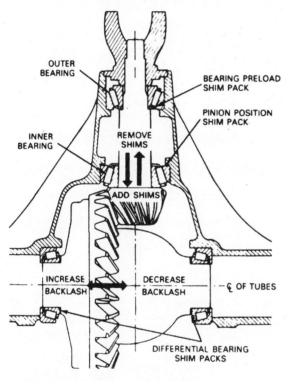

OUTER BEARING

BEARING PRELOAD SHIM PACK

PINION POSITION SHIM PACK

INNER BEARING

REMOVE SHIMS

ADD SHIMS

INCREASE BACKLASH

DECREASE BACKLASH

C OF TUBES

DIFFERENTIAL BEARING SHIM PACKS

Checking pinion rotating torque - Dana 60

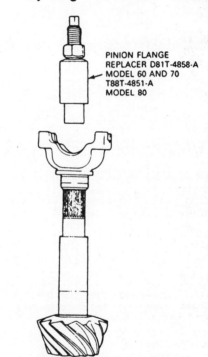

PINION FLANGE REPLACER D81T-4858-A MODEL 60 AND 70 T88T-4851-A MODEL 80

Installing the yoke - Dana 60

OIL SEAL REPLACER T56T-4676-B – MODEL 60 AND 70 T88T-4676-A MODEL 80

Installing the pinion oil seal - Dana 60

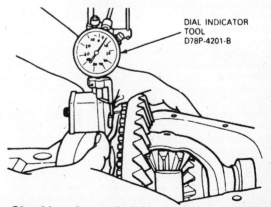

DIAL INDICATOR TOOL D78P-4201-B

Checking ring and pinion backlash - Dana 60

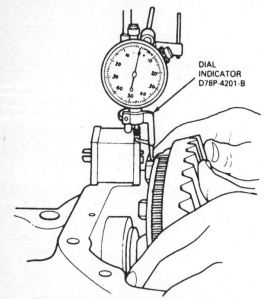

Dial indicator positioning - Dana 60

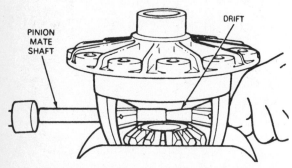

Installing the pinion mate shaft - Dana 60

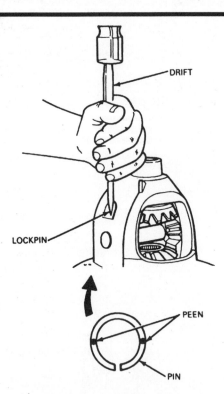

Installing the lockpin - Dana 60

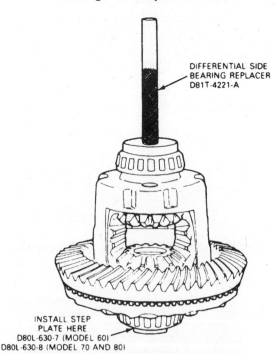

Installing the side bearings - Dana 60

ton contacts the carrier flange. Press the differential carrier to prevent sideplay and center the dial indicator. Rotate the carrier and check the flange for run-out. If the run-out is greater than 0.002 in., the defect is probably due to the bearings or to the carrier and should be corrected.

6. Remove the assembly and install the ring gear. Torque the retaining bolts and reinstall the assembly into the housing. Install the bearing caps in their original position and tighten the cap bolts to keep the bearings caps in place.

7. Install the dial indicator and position the indicator button to contact the ring gear back surface. Rotate the assembly and the run-out should be less than 0.002 in. If over 0.002 in., remove the assembly and relocate the ring gear 180 degrees. Reinstall the assembly and recheck. If the run-out remains over the 0.002 in. tolerance, the ring gear is defective. If the measurement is within tolerances, continue on with the assembly.

8. Position 2 pry bars between the bearing cap and the housing on the side opposite the ring gear. Pull on the pry bars and force the differential carrier as far as possible towards the dial indicator. Rock the assembly to seat the bearings and reset the dial indicator to zero.

9. Reposition the prybars to the opposite side of the carrier and force the carrier assembly as far towards the center of the housing. Read the dial indicator scale. This will be the total amount of shims required for setting the backlash during the reassembly, less the bearing preload. Record the measurement.

10. With the pinion gear installed and properly set, position the differential carrier assembly into the axle housing and install the bearing caps in their proper positions. Tighten the cap bolts just to hold the bearing cups in place.

11. Install a dial indicator on the axle housing with the indicator button contacting the back of the ring gear.

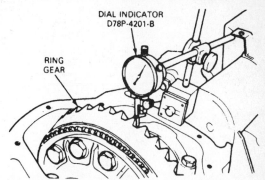

Case spreader - Dana 60

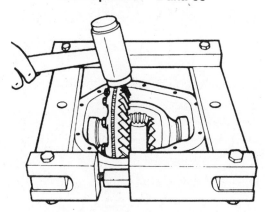

Installing the case - Dana 60

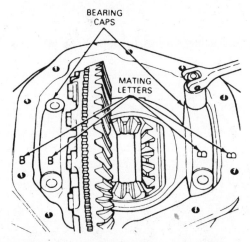

Installing the bearing caps - Dana 60

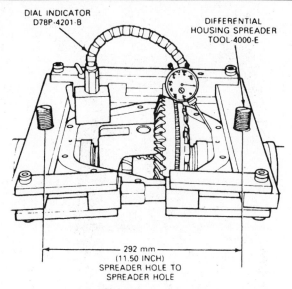

Checking backlash with the case installed - Dana 60

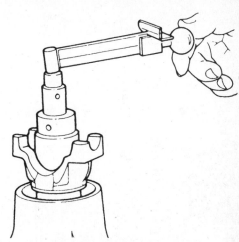

Checking preload - Dana 60

RING GEAR AND PINION TOOTH CONTACT PATTERN

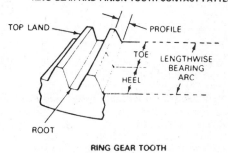

Pattern interpretation - Dana 60

12. Position 2 prybars between the bearing cup and the axle housing on the ring gear side of the case and pry the ring gear into mesh with the pinion gear teeth, as far as possible. Rock the ring gear to allow the teeth to mesh and the bearings to seat.

With the pressure still applied by the prybars, set the dial indicator to zero.

13. Reposition the prybars on the opposite side of ring gear and pry the gear as far as it will go. Take the dial indicator reading. Repeat this procedure until the same reading is obtained each time. This reading represents the necessary amount of shims between the differential carrier and the bearing on the ring gear side.

14. Remove the bearing from the differential carrier on the ring gear side and install the proper amount of shims. Reinstall the bearing.

15. Remove the differential carrier bearing from the opposite side of the ring gear. To determine the amount of shims needed, use the following method.

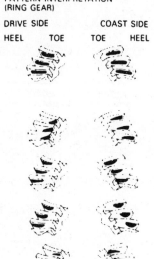

PATTERN INTERPRETATION
(RING GEAR)

DRIVE SIDE   COAST SIDE

HEEL   TOE   TOE   HEEL

NORMAL OR DESIRABLE PATTERN. THE DRIVE PATTERN SHOULD BE CENTERED ON THE TOOTH. THE COAST PATTERN SHOULD BE CENTERED ON THE TOOTH, BUT MAY BE SLIGHTLY TOWARD THE TOE. THERE SHOULD BE SOME CLEARANCE BETWEEN THE PATTERN AND THE TOP OF THE TOOTH.

BACKLASH CORRECT. THINNER PINION POSITION SHIM REQUIRED.

BACKLASH CORRECT. THICKER PINION POSITION SHIM REQUIRED.

PINION POSITION SHIM CORRECT. DECREASE BACKLASH.

PINION POSITION SHIM CORRECT. INCREASE BACKLASH.

Acceptable tooth contact pattern limits - Dana 70

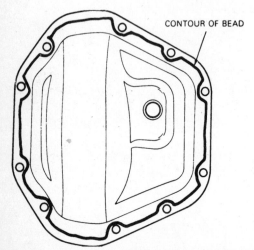

CONTOUR OF BEAD

Applying case cover sealer bead - Dana 60

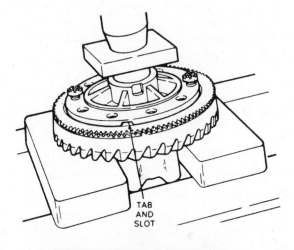

TAB AND SLOT

Installing the ring gear - Dana 70

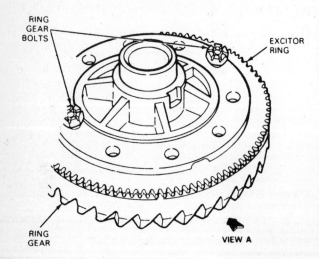

RING GEAR BOLTS

EXCITOR RING

RING GEAR

VIEW A

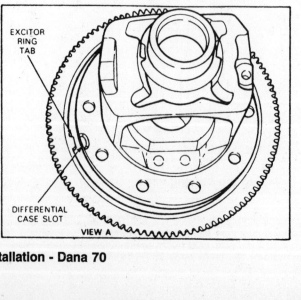

EXCITOR RING TAB

DIFFERENTIAL CASE SLOT

VIEW A

Exciter ring installation - Dana 70

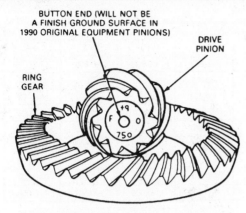

Ring and pinion matching - Dana 70

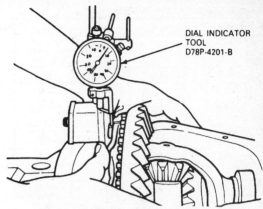

Measuring case endplay - Dana 70

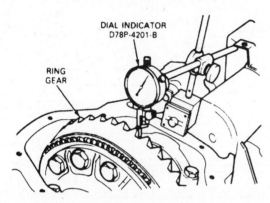

Checking ring gear backface runout - Dana 70

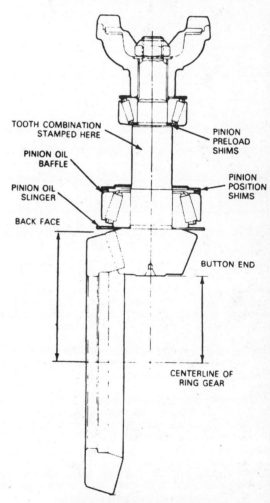

Pinion shimming - Dana 70

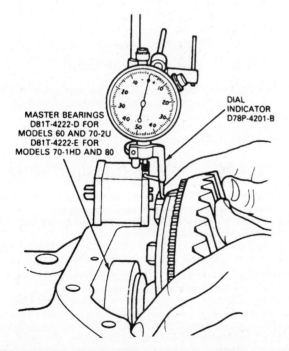

Mounting the dial indicator for case endplay - Dana 70

a. Subtract the size of the shim pack just installed on the ring gear side of the carrier from the reading obtained and recorded when measurement was taken without the pinion gear in place.

b. To this figure, add an additional 0.015 in. to compensate for preload and backlash. An example: If the first reading was 0.085 in. and the shims installed on the ring gear side of the carrier were 0.055 in., the correct amount of shims would be 0.085 in. − 0.055 in. + 0.015 in. = 0.045 in.

SHIM SELECTION CHART — INCHES

Old Pinion Marking	New Pinion Marking								
	−4	−3	−2	−1	0	+1	+2	+3	+4
+4	+0.008	+0.007	+0.006	+0.005	+0.004	+0.003	+0.002	+0.001	0
+3	+0.007	+0.006	+0.005	+0.004	+0.003	+0.002	+0.001	0	−0.001
+2	+0.006	+0.005	+0.004	+0.003	+0.002	+0.001	0	−0.001	−0.002
+1	+0.005	+0.004	+0.003	+0.002	+0.001	0	−0.001	−0.002	−0.003
0	+0.004	+0.003	+0.002	+0.001	0	−0.001	−0.002	−0.003	−0.004
−1	+0.003	+0.002	+0.001	0	−0.001	−0.002	−0.003	−0.004	−0.005
−2	+0.002	+0.001	0	−0.001	−0.002	−0.003	−0.004	−0.005	−0.006
−3	+0.001	0	−0.001	−0.002	−0.003	−0.004	−0.005	−0.006	−0.007
−4	0	−0.001	−0.002	−0.003	−0.004	−0.005	−0.006	−0.007	−0.008

Pinion setting chart - English measure - Dana 70

SHIM SELECTION CHART — METRIC

Old Pinion Marking	New Pinion Marking								
	−10	−8	−5	−3	0	+3	+5	+8	+10
+10	+.20	+.18	+.15	+.13	+.10	+.08	+.05	+.03	0
+8	+.18	+.15	+.13	+.10	+.08	+.05	+.03	0	−.03
+5	+.15	+.13	+.10	+.08	+.05	+.03	0	−.03	−.05
+3	+.13	+.10	+.08	+.05	+.03	0	−.03	−.05	−.08
0	+.10	+.08	+.05	+.03	0	−.03	−.05	−.08	−.10
−3	+.08	+.05	+.03	0	−.03	−.05	−.08	−.10	−.13
−5	+.05	+.03	0	−.03	−.05	−.08	−.10	−.13	−.15
−8	+.03	0	−.03	−.05	−.08	−.10	−.13	−.15	−.18
−10	0	−.03	−.05	−.08	−.10	−.13	−.15	−.18	−.20

Pinion setting chart - Metric measure - Dana 70

16. Install the required shims as determined under step 15 and install the differential side bearing. The installation of the shims should give the proper preload to the bearings and the proper backlash to the ring and pinion gears.

17. Spread the axle housing with the spreader tool no more than 0.015 in. Install the differential bearing outer cups in their correct locations and install the cups in their respective locations.

18. Install the bolts and tighten finger-tight. Rotate the differential carrier and ring gear and tap with a soft-faced hammer to insure proper seating of the assembly in the axle housing.

19. Remove the spreader tool and torque the cap bolts to specifications.

20. Install a dial indicator and check the ring gear backlash at 4 equally spaced points of the ring gear circle. The backlash must be within a range of 0.005–0.008 in. and must not vary more than 0.002 in. between the points checked.

21. If the backlash is not within specifications, the shim packs must be corrected to bring the backlash within limits.

   a. Low backlash is corrected by decreasing the shim on the ring gear side and increasing the opposite side shim an equal amount.

   b. High backlash is corrected by increasing the shim on the ring gear side and decreasing the opposite side shim an equal amount.

22. Check the tooth contact pattern and verify.

23. Complete the assembly, refill to proper level with lubricant and operate to verify proper assembly.

Limited Slip Differential Overhaul Ford. 8.8 in. Ring Gear

Other than the preload spring, pinion shaft and gears and the clutch packs, the overhaul of this unit is identical to that of the conventional 8.8 in. differential.

For removal of these components, see the Adjustment procedures immediately following.

CLUTCH PACK PRELOAD ADJUSTMENT

This adjustment can be made with the unit in the van. The axle shafts, however, must be removed completely.

1. Using a punch, drive the S-shaped preload spring half way out of the differential case.

2. Rotate the case 180°. Hold the preload spring with a pliers and tap the spring until it is removed from the differential.

— **CAUTION** —
Be careful! The preload spring is under tension!

3. Using gear rotator tool T80P-4205-A, or its equivalent, rotate the pinion gears until the can be removed from the differential. A 12 in. extension will be needed to remove the gears.

4. Remove the right and left side gear clutch pack along with any shims, and tag them for identification.

5. Clean and inspect all parts. Use only acid-free, non-flam-

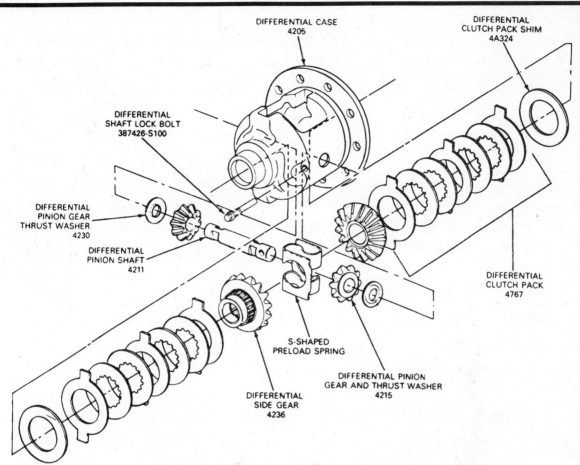

Ford 8.8 in. Traction-Lok differential case exploded view

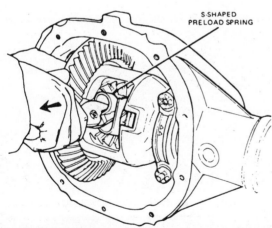

Removing the preload spring - Ford 8.8 in. Traction-Lok differential

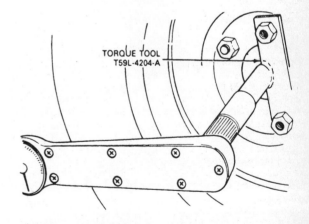

Checking axle shaft break-away torque - Ford 8.8 in. Traction-Lok differential

mable cleaning agents. Use a lint-free cloth to wipe the parts dry. Replace any damaged parts.

6. Assemble the clutch packs — without the shims — on their side gears. Coat all friction plates with limited slip lubricant, such as Ford Additive Friction Modifier, or equivalent meeting EST-M2C118-A specifications.

7. Place the base portion of the Traction-Lok Clutch Gauge T87T-4946-A, or equivalent, in a vise. Install the clutch pack and side gear — without the shims — over the base.

8. Install the tool's disc over the base and on top of the clutch pack.

9. Install the top portion of the tool over the disc and base stud.

10. Install the tool's nut and torque it to 60 inch lbs.

11. Using feeler gauges, determine the distance between the tool and the clutch pack. This will be the thickness of the necessary shim.

12. Install the right side gear, clutch pack and new shim into

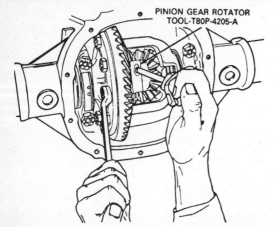

Removing the pinion gears - Ford 8.8 in Traction-Lok differential

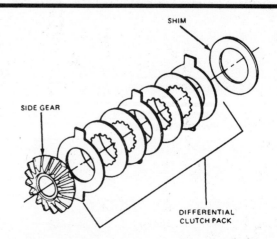

Clutch pack - Ford 8.8 in. Traction-Lok differential

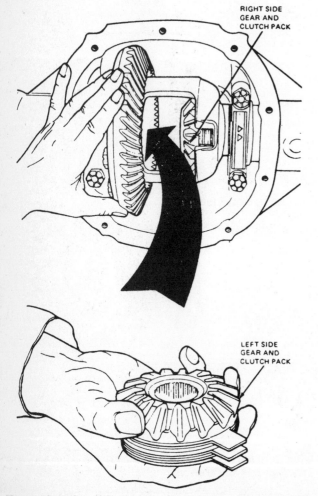

Removing the side gears - Ford 8.8 in. Traction-Lok differential

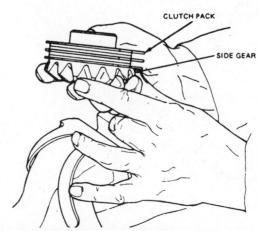

Clutch pack installed on the side gear - Ford 8.8 in. Traction-Lok differential

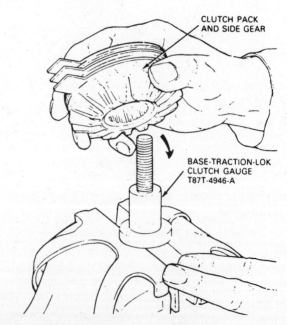

Clutch pack and side gear installation - Ford 8.8 in. Traction-Lok differential

the differential case. Repeat this for the left side.

13. Place the pinion gears and thrust washers 180° apart on the side gears. Install tool T80P-4205-A, or equivalent. A 12 in. extension should be used to install the gears.

14. Rotate the tool until the pinion gears are aligned with the pinion shaft hole. Remove the tool.

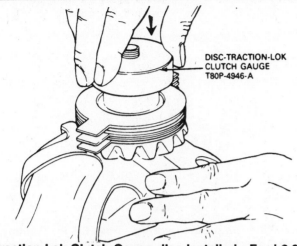

Traction-Lok Clutch Gauge disc installed - Ford 8.8 in. Traction-Lok differential

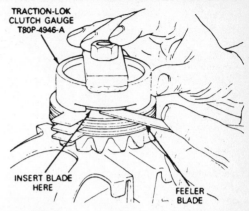

Determining shim thickness - Ford 8.8 in. Traction-Lok differential

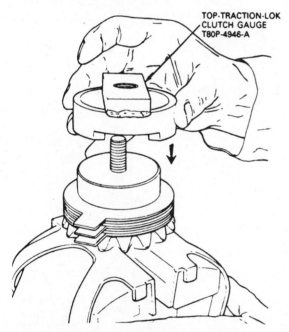

Traction-Lok Clutch Gauge top installation - Ford 8.8 in. Traction-Lok differential

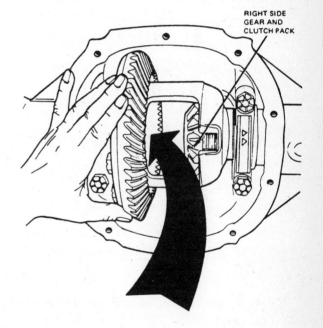

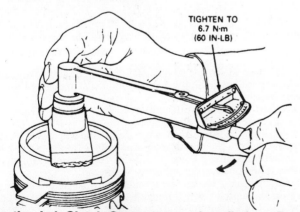

Traction-Lok Clutch Gauge top nut installation - Ford 8.8 in. Traction-Lok differential

Installing the right side gear - Ford 8.8 in. Traction-Lok differential

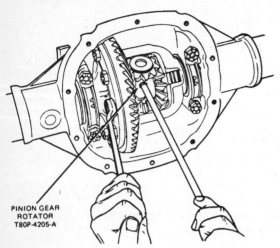

Installing the pinion gears - Ford 8.8 in. Traction-Lok differential

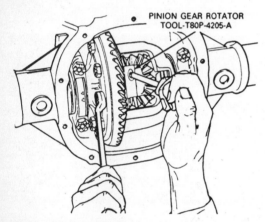

Aligning the pinion gears - Ford 8.8 in. Traction-Lok differential

15. Hold the S-shaped preload spring at the differential case window, and, with a plastic mallet, drive the spring into position. Check the spring for damage.

BENCH TORQUE TEST

This test must be made any time the differential has been removed, or adjustments have been made.

Using the locker tools in set T59L-4204-A, or equivalent, check the torque required to rotate one side gear while the other is held stationary.

The initial breakaway torque, if original clutch plates are used, should be at least 20 ft. lbs.

The rotating torque needed to keep the side gear turning, with new plates, will fluctuate.

Limited Slip Differential Overhaul Dana Axles

Overhaul of this differential, except for the differential case, is identical to that of the conventional differential.

1. Remove the ring gear.
2. Place the case on a holding fixture mounted in a vise.

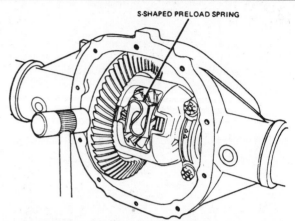

Installing the preload spring - Ford 8.8 in. Traction-Lok differential

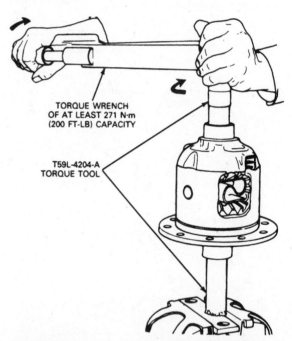

Bench torque test - Ford 8.8 in. Traction-Lok differential

3. For full floating axles, use a small punch to drive out the roll pin retaining the cross-shaft and drive out the cross-shaft.

On semi-floating axles, remove the lock screw retaining the cross-shaft. The cross-shaft is a slip fit.

4. Position the Step Plate T83T-4205-A4, or equivalent, into the bottom side gear. Apply a small amount of grease in the centering hole.

5. Insert the forcing nut and screw into the case. Guide the forcing screw onto the step plate.

6. Tighten the forcing screw securely. This will move the side gears away from the pinion gears and relieve the normally loaded condition. Using a piece of 0.03 in. (0.762mm) shim stock, push out the differential spherical washers.

7. Momentarily loosen the forcing screw to relieve the pressure on the clutch pack, then, tighten the screw until a slight movement of the pinion gears is seen.

8. Insert the tool handle into the pinion mating shaft bore and rotate the case until the pinion gears can be removed

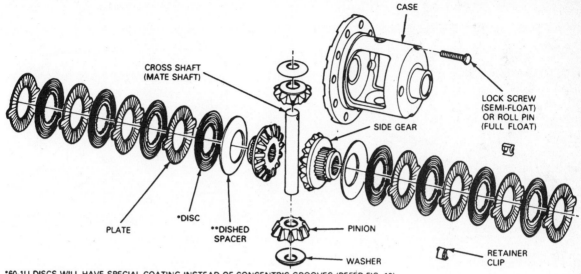

*60-1U DISCS WILL HAVE SPECIAL COATING INSTEAD OF CONCENTRIC GROOVES (REFER FIG. 13).
**MAY HAVE EXTERNAL LUGS, LIKE THE PLATE.

2-pinion Trac-Lok differential case exploded view - Dana

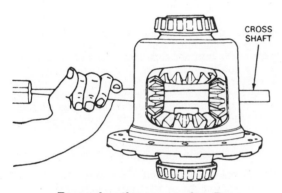

Removing the cross pin - Dana

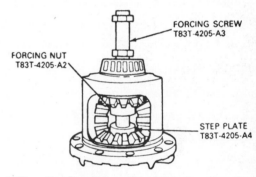

Installing the forcing nut and forcing screw - Dana

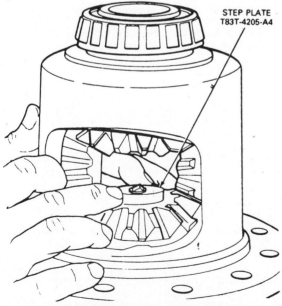

Installing the step plate - Dana

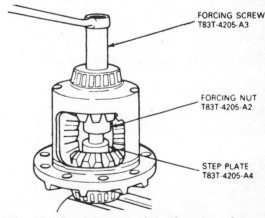

Guiding the forcing screw into the step plate - Dana

through the large openings in the case. Some tightening and loosening of the forcing screw will be required to permit gear movement.

9. Hold the top side gear and clutch pack in the case and remove the forcing screw and rotating tool. Then, remove the top side gear and clutch pack. Keep the stack of plates and discs in their exact order.

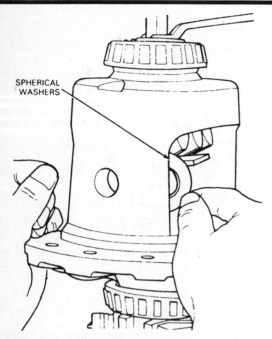

Removing the spherical washers - Dana

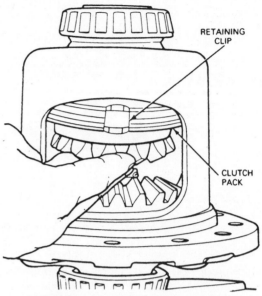

Holding the clutch pack - Dana

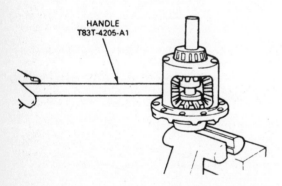

Installing the rotating tool handle - Dana

10. Turn the case so that the flange is up. Remove the step plate, side gear and clutch pack out of the case.

11. Remove the retainer clips from the clutch packs to allow separation of the discs and plates. Be sure to keep them in order!

To assemble:

12. Install the clutch packs, side gears and thrust washers. Assemble them is exactly the same order as the originals. Never replace just some of these parts. If any are damaged, replace the whole set.

13. Coat all parts with limited slip lubricant.

14. Assemble the plates and discs on the side gear splines.

NOTE: Discs for the model 60 axle that are of the newer, coated design — without concentric grooves — must be soaked for 20 minutes in limited slip friction additive before assembly.

15. Assemble the retainer clips on the plate ears. Make sure they are completely seated.

16. Assemble the clutch pack and side gear into the case. Make sure everything stays together and the clips stay in place.

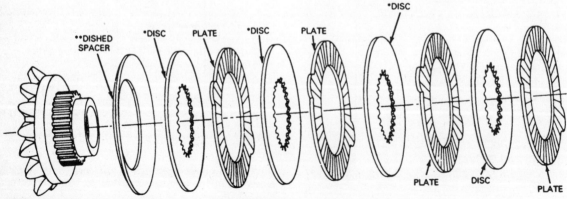

*DISCS HAVE SPECIAL COATING INSTEAD OF CONCENTRIC GROOVES.
**MAY HAVE EARS AS SHOWN ON PLATE.

Clutch plate and disc assembly sequence - Dana

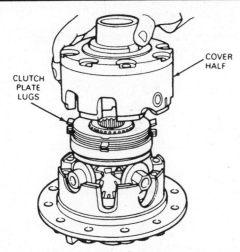

Removing the cover portion of the case - Dana

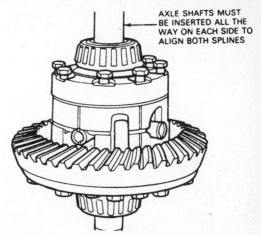

Aligning the side gear and side gear ring splines - Dana

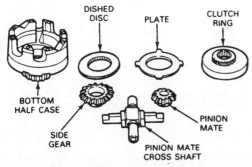

Check these parts for wear and/or damage - Dana

17. Position the step plate in the case on the side gear. Apply a small glob of grease in the hole.
18. Assemble the other clutch pack and side gear. Install the step plate.
19. Hold the side gear in place and install the forcing screw down through the top of the case. Thread the forcing nut on the screw. The tip of the forcing screw must contact the step plate.

20. Position the case on the holding fixture.
21. Position the pinion gears in the case, opposite each other. Be sure the holes in the gears are aligned.
22. Turn the forcing screw so that the side gears move away from the differential pinion gears and relieve the loaded condition.
23. Insert the tool handle into the pinion shaft mating hole and turn the case to allow the pinion gears to rotate themselves into the case.
24. Rotate the case until the holes of the pinion gears align with those of the case.
25. Apply force to the forcing screw to allow clearance for the spherical washers. DO NOT OVERTIGHTEN THE SCREW!
26. Assemble the washers in the case. Be sure the holes in the washers and gears are aligned.
27. Remove all special tools.
28. Install the pinion shaft.
29. Install the cross-shaft locking pin.
30. Install the ring gear.

NOISE DIAGNOSIS

The Noise Is	Most Probably Produced By
· Identical under Drive or Coast	· Road surface, tires or front wheel bearings
· Different depending on road surface	· Road surface or tires
· Lower as the car speed is lowered	· Tires
· Similar with car standing or moving	· Engine or transmission
· A vibration	· Unbalanced tires, rear wheel bearing, unbalanced driveshaft or worn U-joint
· A knock or click about every 2 tire revolutions	· Rear wheel bearing
· Most pronounced on turns	· Damaged differential gears
· A steady low-pitched whirring or scraping, starting at low speeds	· Damaged or worn pinion bearing
· A chattering vibration on turns	· Wrong differential lubricant or worn clutch plates (limited slip rear axle)
· Noticed only in Drive, Coast or Float conditions	· Worn ring gear and/or pinion gear

CHATTERS ON TURNS WITH NO LIMITED SLIP DIFFERENTIAL

TEST STEP		RESULT ▶	ACTION TO TAKE
1.0	DRIVE VEHICLE		
	Drive vehicle in fairly tight figure 8's — ten times total. (Five clockwise and five counterclockwise).	No Chatter ▶	STOP.
		Chatter still present ▶	GO to **2**.
2.0	CHANGE LUBRICANT		
	Siphon or drain lubricant from axle and refill with specified rear axle lubricant①. Drive vehicle in fairly tight figure 8's — ten times total. (Five clockwise and five counterclockwise).	No Chatter ▶	STOP.
		Chatter still present ▶	GO to **3**.
3.0	DRIVE VEHICLE		
	Drive vehicle 40-80 km (25-50 miles) in addition to figure 8's.	No Chatter ▶	STOP.
		Chatter still present ▶	REMOVE the differential and REPAIR as required.

① F-150, Bronco, E-150 with Ford 8.8 Limited Slip add 4 oz. of friction modifier (EST-M2C118-A) C8AZ-19B546-A.
E-250—350 with Dana Limited Slip or F-250-350 with Ford 10.25 Limited Slip add 8 oz. of friction modifier (EST-M2C118-A) C8AZ-19B546-A.

LIMITED SLIP DIFFERENTIAL DOES NOT OPERATE IN MUD OR SNOW OR ON ICE

TEST STEP		RESULT ▶	ACTION TO TAKE
1.0	ALL FORD AND DANA MODEL 60 AND 70		
	Starting with one wheel on an excessively slippery surface, slightly apply the parking brake. Gradually open throttle, if the vehicle moves, the axle is operating properly.	Vehicle moves ▶	Unit OK. STOP.
		Vehicle doesn't move ▶	REPAIR Unit as required.

Suspension and Steering

8

QUICK REFERENCE INDEX

GENERAL INDEX

WHEELS

> ### CAUTION
> *Some aftermarket wheels may not be compatible with these vehicles. The use of incompatible wheels may result in equipment failure and possible personal injury! Use only approved wheels!*

Front or Rear Wheels

REMOVAL AND INSTALLATION

E-150 and 250
E-350 with Single Rear Wheels

1. Set the parking brake and block the opposite wheel.
2. On trucks with an automatic transmission, place the selector lever in **P**. On trucks with a manual transmission, place the transmission in reverse.
3. If equipped, remove the wheel cover.
4. Break loose the lug nuts.
5. Raise the truck until the tire is clear of the ground.
6. Remove the lug nuts and remove the wheel.

To install:

7. Clean the wheel lugs and brake drum or hub of all foreign material.

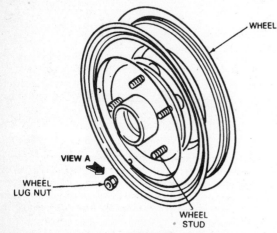

MAIN VIEW

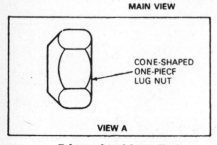

VIEW A

5-lug wheel installation

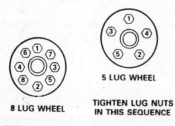

8 LUG WHEEL

5 LUG WHEEL

TIGHTEN LUG NUTS IN THIS SEQUENCE

Wheel lug torque sequence

8. Position the wheel on the hub or drum and hand-tighten the lug nuts. Make sure that the coned ends face inward.
9. Using the lug wrench, tighten all the lugs, in a criss-cross fashion until they are snug.
10. Lower the truck. Tighten the nuts, in the sequence shown, to 100 ft. lbs. for 5-lug wheels; 140 ft. lbs. for 8-lug wheels.

Front Wheels

REMOVAL AND INSTALLATION

E-350 with Dual Rear Wheels

> ### CAUTION
> *Use only integral 2-piece, swiveling lug nuts. Do not attempt to use cone-shaped, one-piece lugs. The use of cone-shaped nuts will cause the nuts to come loose during vehicle operation!*
>
> *Do not attempt to use older-style wheels that use cone-shaped lug nuts. This practice will also cause the wheels to come loose!*

1. Set the parking brake and block the opposite wheel.
2. On trucks with an automatic transmission, place the selector lever in **P**. On trucks with a manual transmission, place the transmission in reverse.
3. If equipped, remove the wheel cover.
4. Break loose the lug nuts.
5. Raise the truck until the tire is clear of the ground.
6. Remove the lug nuts and remove the wheel.

To install:

7. Clean the wheel lugs and brake drum or hub of all foreign material.
8. Position the wheel on the hub or drum and hand-tighten the lug nuts.

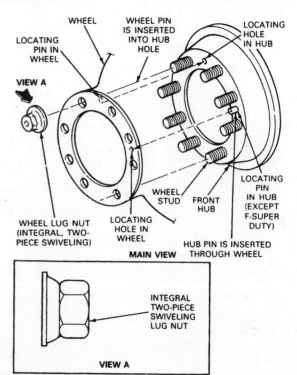

MAIN VIEW

VIEW A

Front wheel installation for E-350 w/dual rear wheels. The 10-lug wheel is identical except for the number of wheel lugs

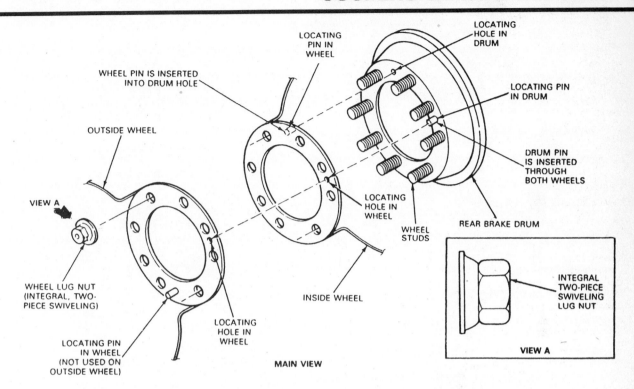

LOCATING
PIN IN
WHEEL

WHEEL PIN IS INSERTED
INTO DRUM HOLE

OUTSIDE WHEEL

VIEW A

WHEEL LUG NUT
(INTEGRAL, TWO-
PIECE SWIVELING)

LOCATING PIN
IN WHEEL
(NOT USED ON
OUTSIDE WHEEL)

LOCATING
HOLE IN DRUM

LOCATING PIN
IN DRUM

DRUM PIN
IS INSERTED
THROUGH
BOTH WHEELS

LOCATING
HOLE IN
WHEEL

WHEEL
STUDS

REAR BRAKE DRUM

INSIDE WHEEL

LOCATING
HOLE IN
WHEEL

MAIN VIEW

INTEGRAL
TWO-PIECE
SWIVELING
LUG NUT

VIEW A

Rear wheel installation for E-350 w/dual rear wheels

9. Using the lug wrench, tighten all the lugs, in a criss-cross fashion until they are snug.

10. Lower the truck. Tighten the nuts, in the sequence shown, to 140 ft. lbs.

Dual Rear Wheels

REMOVAL AND INSTALLATION

— CAUTION —

Use only integral 2-piece, swiveling lug nuts. Do not attempt to use cone-shaped, one-piece lugs. The use of cone-shaped nuts will cause the nuts to come loose during vehicle operation!

Do not attempt to use older-style wheels that use cone-shaped lug nuts. This practice will also cause the wheels to come loose!

1. Set the parking brake and block the opposite wheel.
2. On trucks with an automatic transmission, place the selector lever in **P**. On trucks with a manual transmission, place the transmission in reverse.
3. If equipped, remove the wheel cover.
4. Break loose the lug nuts.
5. Raise the truck until the tire is clear of the ground.
6. Remove the lug nuts and remove the wheel(s).

To install:

7. Clean the wheel lugs and brake drum or hub of all foreign material.
8. Mount the inner wheel on the hub with the dished (concave) side inward. Align the wheel with the small indexing hole — located in the wheel between the stud holes — with the alignment pin on the hub. Make sure that the wheel is flush against the hub.
9. Install the outer wheel so that the protruding (convex) side is flush against the inner wheel. Make sure that the alignment pin is protruding through the wheel index hole.
10. Hand-tighten the lug nuts.

11. Using the lug wrench, tighten all the lugs, in a criss-cross fashion until they are snug.

10. Lower the truck. Tighten the nuts, in the sequence shown, to 140 ft. lbs.

— CAUTION —

The lug nuts on dual rear wheels should be retightened after the first 100 miles of new-vehicle operation.

The lug nuts on dual rear wheels should be retightened at an interval of 500 miles after anytime a wheel has been removed and installed for any reason!

Failure to observe this procedure may result in the wheel coming loose during vehicle operation!

Wheel Lug Nut Stud

REPLACEMENT

Front Wheels

USING A PRESS

1. Remove the wheel.
2. Place the hub/rotor assembly in a press, supported by the hub surface. NEVER rest the assembly on the rotor!
3. Press the stud from the hub.
4. Position the new stud in the hub and align the serrations. Make sure it is sqaure and press it into place.

USING A HAMMER AND DRIVER

1. Remove the wheel.
2. Support the hub/rotor assembly on a flat, hard surface, resting the assembly on the hub. NEVER rest the assembly on the rotor!
3. Position a driver, such as a drift or broad punch, on the outer end of the stud and drive it from the hub.

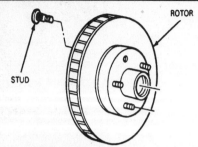

Front wheel stud

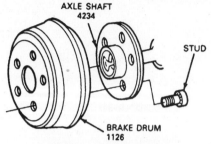

Brake drum and stud

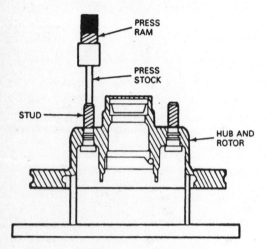

Pressing the stud from the hub

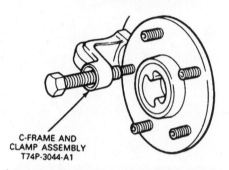

Pressing the stud out with a C-clamp

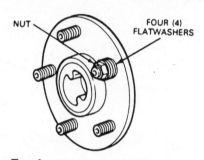

Forcing a new stud into place

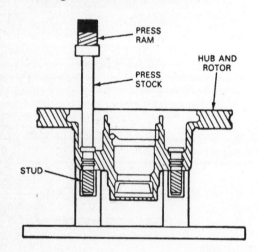

Pressing the new stud into the hub

4. Turn the assembly over, coat the serrations of the new stud with liquid soap, position the stud in the hole, aligning the serrations, and, using the drift and hammer, drive it into place until fully seated.

Rear Wheels

1. Remove the wheel.
2. Remove the drum or rotor from the axle shaft or hub studs.
3. Using a large C-clamp and socket, press the stud from the drum or rotor.
4. Coat the serrated part of the stud with liquid soap and place it in the hole. Align the serrations.
5. Place 3 or 4 flat washers on the outer end of the stud and thread a lug nut on the stud with the flat side against the washers. Tighten the lug nut until the stud is drawn all the way in.

WARNING: Do not use an impact wrench!

FRONT SUSPENSION

These vans use two I-beam type front axles; one for each wheel. One end of each axle is attached to the spindle and a radi- us arm, and the other end is attached to a frame pivot bracket on the opposite side of the truck. Coil spring are used.

Troubleshooting Basic Steering and Suspension Problems

Problem	Cause	Solution
Hard steering (steering wheel is hard to turn)	• Low or uneven tire pressure • Loose power steering pump drive belt • Low or incorrect power steering fluid • Incorrect front end alignment • Defective power steering pump • Bent or poorly lubricated front end parts	• Inflate tires to correct pressure • Adjust belt • Add fluid as necessary • Have front end alignment checked/adjusted • Check pump • Lubricate and/or replace defective parts
Loose steering (too much play in the steering wheel)	• Loose wheel bearings • Loose or worn steering linkage • Faulty shocks • Worn ball joints	• Adjust wheel bearings • Replace worn parts • Replace shocks • Replace ball joints
Car veers or wanders (car pulls to one side with hands off the steering wheel)	• Incorrect tire pressure • Improper front end alignment • Loose wheel bearings • Loose or bent front end components • Faulty shocks	• Inflate tires to correct pressure • Have front end alignment checked/adjusted • Adjust wheel bearings • Replace worn components • Replace shocks
Wheel oscillation or vibration transmitted through steering wheel	• Improper tire pressures • Tires out of balance • Loose wheel bearings • Improper front end alignment • Worn or bent front end components	• Inflate tires to correct pressure • Have tires balanced • Adjust wheel bearings • Have front end alignment checked/adjusted • Replace worn parts
Uneven tire wear	• Incorrect tire pressure • Front end out of alignment • Tires out of balance	• Inflate tires to correct pressure • Have front end alignment checked/adjusted • Have tires balanced

Coil Springs

REMOVAL AND INSTALLATION

1. Raise the front of the vehicle and place jackstands under the frame and a jack under the axle.
2. Remove the wheels.
3. Disconnect the shock absorber from the lower bracket.
4. Remove the two spring upper retainer attaching bolts from the top of the spring upper seat and remove the retainer.
5. Remove the nut attaching the spring lower retainer to the lower seat and axle and remove the retainer.

6. Place a safety chain through the spring to prevent it from suddenly coming loose. Slowly lower the axle and remove the spring.

To install:
7. Place the spring in position and raise the front axle.
8. Position the spring lower retainer over the stud and lower seat, and install the two attaching bolts.
9. Position the upper retainer over the spring coil and against the spring upper seat, and install the two attaching bolts.
10. Observe the following torques:
● Upper retaining bolts to 20-30 ft. lbs.
● Lower retainer attaching nuts: 70-100 ft. lbs.
● Shock absorber: 40-60 ft. lbs.

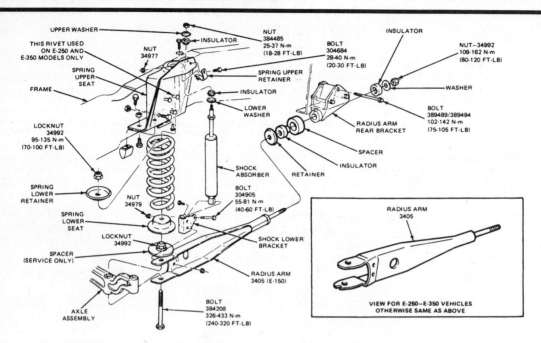

Front spring and shocker absorber

Shock Absorbers

TESTING

Bounce Test

Each shock absorber can be tested by bouncing the corner of the truck until maximum up and down movement is obtained. Let go of the truck. It should stop bouncing in 1-2 bounces. If not, the shock should be inspected for damage and possibly replaced.

Inspect the Shock Mounts

Check the shock mountings for worn or defective grommets, loose mounting nuts, interference or missing bump stops. If no apparent defects are noted, continue testing.

Inspecting Shocks for Leaks

Disconnect each shock lower mount and pull down on the shock until it is fully extended. inspect for leaks in the seal area. Shock absorber fluid is very thin and has a characteristic odor and dark brown color. Don't confuse the glossy paint on some shocks with leaking fluid. A slight trace of fluid is a normal condition; they are designed to seep a certain amount of fluid past the seals for lubrication. If you are in doubt as to whether the fluid on the shock is coming from the shock itself or from some other source, wipe the seal area clean and manually operate the shock (see the following procedure). Fluid will appear if the unit is leaking.

Manually Operating the Shocks

It may be necessary to fabricate a holding fixture for certain types of shock absorbers. If a suspected problem is in the front shocks, disconnect both front shock lower mountings.

NOTE: When manually operating air shocks, the air line must be disconnected at the shock.

Grip the lower end of the shock and pull down (rebound stroke) and then push up (compression stroke). The control arms will limit the movement of front shocks during the compression stroke. Compare the rebound resistance of both shocks and compare the compression resistance. Usually any shock showing a noticeable difference will be the one at fault.

If the shock has internal noises, extend the shock fully then exert an extra pull. If a small additional movement is felt, this usually means a loose piston and the shock should be replaced. Other noises that are cause for replacing shocks are a squeal after a full stroke in both directions, a clicking noise on fast reverse and a lag at reversal near mid-stroke.

REMOVAL AND INSTALLATION

To replace the front shock absorber, remove the self-locking nut, steel washer, and rubber bushings at the upper end of the shock absorber. Remove the bolt and nut at the lower end and remove the shock absorber.

When installing a new shock absorber, use new rubber bush-

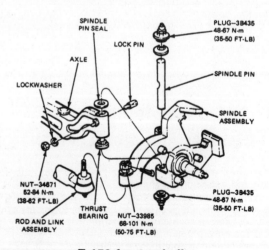

E-150 front spindle

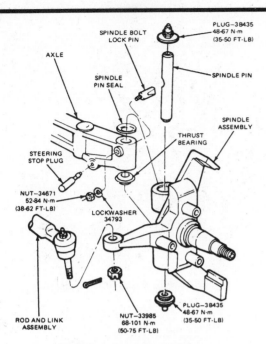

E-250/350 front spindle

ings. Position the shock absorber on the mounting brackets with the stud end at the top.

Install the rubber bushing, steel washer and self-locking nut at the upper end, and the bolt and nut at the lower end. Observe the following torques:

- Upper end: 18-28 ft. lbs.
- Lower end: 40-60 ft. lbs.

Front Wheel Spindle

REMOVAL AND INSTALLATION

1. Jack up the front of the truck and safely support it with jackstands.
2. Remove the wheels.
3. Remove the front brake caliper assembly and hold it out of the way with a piece of wire. Do not disconnect the brake line.
4. Remove the brake rotor from the spindle.
5. Remove the inner bearing cone and seal. discard the seal, as you'll be fitting a new one during installation.
6. Remove the brake dust shield.
7. Disconnect the steering linkage from the spindle arm using a tie rod removal tool.
8. Remove the nut and lockwasher from the lock pin and remove the lock pin.
9. Remove the upper and lower spindle pin plugs.
10. Drive the spindle pin out from the top of the axle and remove the spindle and thrust bearing.
11. Remove the spindle pin seal and thrust bearing.

NOTE: Always use new cotter pins! When aligning the cotter pin holes, NEVER back-off the nut; always advance the nut to align the holes!

12. Make sure that the spindle pin holes are clean and free from burrs and nicks. Lightly coat the bore with chassis lube.
13. Install a new spindle pin seal, with the metal backing facing upwards towards the bushing, into the spindle. Gently press the seal into position.
14. Install a new thrust bearing with the lip flange facing down, towards the lower bushing. Press it in until the bearing is firmly seated against the surface of the spindle.

15. Lightly coat the bushing surfaces with chassis lube and place the spindle into position on the axle.
16. Insert the spindle pin, with the **T** stamped on one end, facing the top, and the notch in the pin aligned with the lock pin hole in the axle. Insert the spindle pin through the bushings and the axle from the top, until the spindle pin notch and axle lock pin hole are aligned.
17. Install the lock pin with the threads pointing forward and the wedge groove facing the spindle pin notch. Firmly drive the lock pin into position and install the lockwasher and nut. Tighten the nut to 40-60 ft. lbs.
18. Install the spindle pin plugs into the threads at the top and bottom of the spindle. Tighten the plugs to 35-50 ft. lbs.
19. Lubricate the spindle pin and bushings with chassis lube through both fittings until grease is visible seeping past the upper seal and the thrust bearing slip joint. If grease does not escape at these top and bottom points, the spindle is installed incorrectly and rapid deterioration of the spindle components will result.
20. Install the brake dust shield.
21. Install the inner bearing cone and seal. Install the hub and rotor on the spindle.
22. Install the outer bearing cone, washer, and nut. Adjust the bearing end-play and install the nut retainer, cotter pin and dust cap.
23. Install the brake caliper. connect the steering linkage to the spindle. Tighten the nut to 70-100 ft. lbs. and advance the nut as far necessary to install the cotter pin.
24. Install the wheels. Lower the truck and adjust toe-in if necessary.

Spindle Bushings

REPLACEMENT

1. Remove the spindle.
2. On E-150, use the following tools:
- Reamer T53T-3110-DA
- Remover/Installer/Driver D82T-3110-G
- Driver Handle D82T-3110-C
3. On E-250/350, use the following tools
- Reamer D82T-3110-A

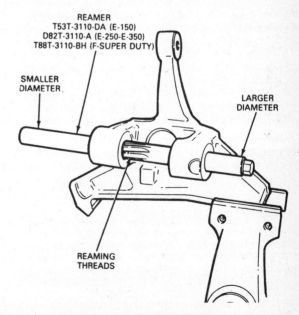

Reaming spindle bushings

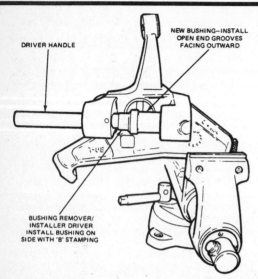

Bottom spindle bushing removal and installation

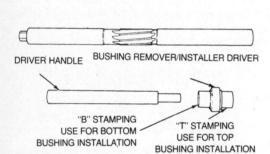

Spindle bushing removal/installation tools

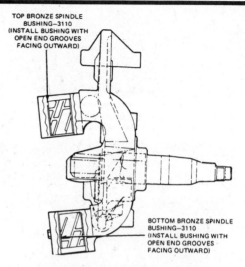

Spindle bushing installation

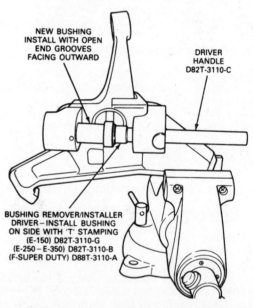

Top spindle bushing removal and installation

- Remover/Installer/Driver D82T-3110-B
- Driver Handle D82T-3110-C

NOTE: Each side of the Remover/Installer/Driver is marked with a T or a B. Use the side with the T to install the top spindle bushing; the side with the B to install the bottom spindle bushing.

4. Remove and discard the seal from the bottom of the upper bushing bore.

5. Remove and install the top spindle bushing first.
   a. Install the driver handle through the bottom bore.
   b. Position a new bushing on the **T** side stamping of the driver.
   c. The bushing must be installed so that the open end grooves will face outward when installed.
   d. Position the new bushing and driver over the old bushing, insert the handle into the driver and drive the old bushing out while driving the new bushing in. Drive until the tool is seated.
   e. The bushing will then be seated to the proper depth of 0.080 in. from the bottom of the upper spindle boss.

6. Remove and install the bottom spindle bushing.
   a. Insert the driver handle through the top bushing bore.
   b. Position a new bushing on the **B** side stamping of the driver. The bushing must be installed so that the open end grooves will face outward when installed.
   c. Position the new bushing and driver over the old bushing, insert the handle into the driver and drive the old bush-

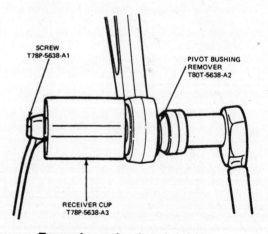

Removing axle pivot bushing

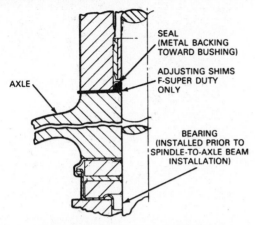

Spindle bearing seal installation

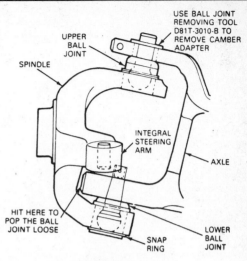

Spindle removal

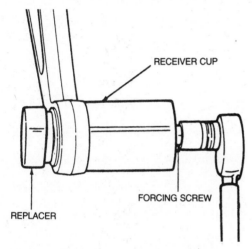

Installing the axle pivot bushing

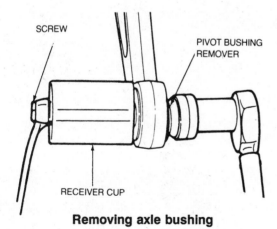

Removing axle bushing

ing out while driving the new bushing in. Drive until the tool is seated.

d. The bushing will then be seated to the proper depth of 0.130 in. from the bottom of the upper spindle boss.

7. Ream the new bushings to 0.001-0.003 in. larger than the diameter of the new spindle pin. Ream the top bushings first. Insert the smaller end of the reamer through the top bore and into the bottom bore until the threads are in position in the top bushing. Turn the tool until the threads exit the top bushing. Ream the bottom bushing. The larger diameter portion of the tool will act as a pilot in the top bushing to properly ream the bottom bushing.

8. Clean all metal shavings from the bushings. Coat the bushings with chassis lube.

9. Install a new seal on the driver on the side with the **T** stamping. Install the handle into the driver and push the seal into position in the bottom of the top bushing bore.

Radius Arm

REMOVAL AND INSTALLATION

NOTE: A torque wrench with a capacity of at least 350 ft. lbs. is necessary, along with other special tools, for this procedure.

1. Raise the front of the vehicle and place safety stands under the frame and a jack under the wheel or axle. Remove the wheels.

2. Disconnect the shock absorber from the radius arm bracket.

3. Remove the two spring upper retainer attaching bolts from the top of the spring upper seat and remove the retainer.

4. Remove the nut which attached the spring lower retainer to the lower seat and axle and remove the retainer.

5. Lower the axle and remove the spring.

6. Remove the spring lower seat and shim from the radius arm. The, remove the bolt and nut which attach the radius arm to the axle.

7. Remove the cotter pin, nut and washer from the radius arm rear attachment.

8. Remove the bushing from the radius arm and remove the radius arm from the vehicle.

9. Remove the inner bushing from the radius arm.

10. Position the radius arm to the axle and install the bolt and nut finger-tight.

11. Install the inner bushing on the radius arm and position the arm to the frame bracket.

12. Install the bushing, washer, and attaching nut. Tighten the nut to 120 ft. lbs. and install the cotter pin.

13. Tighten the radius arm-to-axle bolt to 269-329 ft. lbs.

14. Install the spring seat and insulator on the radius arm so that the hole in the seat fits over the arm-to-axle nut.

15. Install the spring.

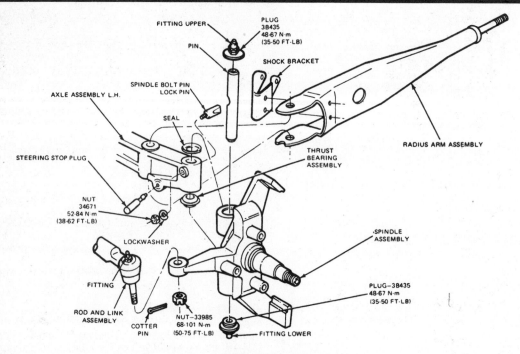

E-250/350 radius arm

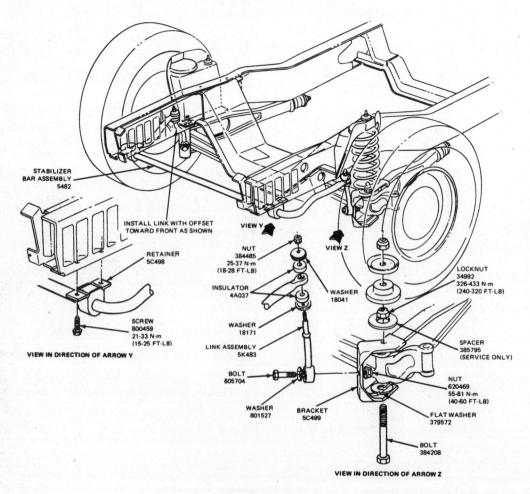

Stabilizer bar

16. Connect the shock absorber. Torque the nut and bolt to 40-60 ft. lbs.
17. Install the wheels.

Stabilizer Bar

REMOVAL AND INSTALLATION

1. Raise and support the front end on jackstands.
2. Disconnect the right and left stabilizer bar ends from the link assembly.
3. Disconnect the retainer bolts and remove the stabilizer bar.
4. Disconnect the stabilizer link assemblies by loosening the right and left locknuts from their respective brackets. on the I-beams.

To install:

5. Loosely install the entire assembly. The links are marked with an **R** and **L** for identification.
6. Tighten the link-to-stabilizer bar and axle bracket fasteners to 70 ft. lbs.
7. Check to make sure that the insulators are properly seated and the stabilizer bar is centered.
8. On the E-150, torque the 6 stabilizer bar to crossmember attaching bolts to 35 ft. lbs.

On the E-250 and E-350, torque the stabilizer bar-to-frame retainer bolts to 35 ft. lbs.

Torque the frame mounting bracket nuts/bolts to 65 ft. lbs.

Twin I-Beam Axles

REMOVAL AND INSTALLATION

NOTE: A torque wrench with a capacity of at least 350 ft. lbs. is necessary, along with other special tools, for this procedure.

1. Raise and support the front end on jackstands.
2. Remove the spindles.
3. Remove the springs.
4. Remove the stabilizer bar.
5. Remove the lower spring seats from the radius arms.
6. Remove the radius arm-to-axle bolts.
7. Remove the axle-to-frame pivot bolts and remove the axles.

To install:

8. Position the axle on the pivot bracket and loosely install the bolt/nut.
9. Position the other end on the radius arm and install the bolt. Torque the bolt to 269-329 ft. lbs.
10. Install the spring seats.
11. Install the springs.
12. Torque the axle pivot bolts to 150 ft. lbs.
13. Install the spindles.
14. Install the stabilizer bar.

FRONT END ALIGNMENT

WHEEL ALIGNMENT SPECIFICATIONS

Years	Ride Height (Inches)	E-150 Caster (deg.)	E-150 Camber (deg.)	E-250, 350 Caster (deg.)	E-250,350 Camber (deg.)
1989–91	3.75–4.00	$7^3/_4$P–9P	$^3/_4$N–$^1/_2$P	7P–$8^3/_4$P	$^3/_4$N–$1^1/_4$P
	4.00–4.25	$6^3/_4$P–$8^3/_4$P	$^3/_4$N–$^1/_2$P	$6^1/_4$P–$8^1/_4$P	$^1/_4$N–$1^1/_4$P
	4.25–4.50	$6^1/_2$P–$8^1/_4$P	$^1/_4$N–$1^1/_4$P	$5^3/_4$P–$7^3/_4$P	$^1/_4$P–$1^1/_2$P
	4.50–4.75	$5^1/_2$P–$7^1/_2$P	$^1/_4$P–$1^1/_2$P	$5^1/_4$P–$7^1/_4$P	1P–$2^1/_4$P
	4.75–5.00	$5^1/_4$P–$7^1/_4$P	$^7/_8$P–$2^1/_8$P	5P–7P	$1^1/_4$P–$2^1/_2$P
	5.00–5.25	$4^1/_4$P–$6^1/_4$P	2P–$3^1/_4$P	$4^1/_8$P–$6^1/_4$P	$2^1/_8$P–$3^1/_4$P
	5.25–5.50	4P–6P	$1^3/_4$P–3P	$3^3/_4$P–$5^3/_4$P	$2^1/_4$P–$3^1/_2$P
	5.50–5.75	$3^1/_2$P–$5^1/_4$P	$2^1/_4$P–$3^1/_4$P	$3^1/_8$P–$5^1/_8$P	$2^1/_2$P–$4^1/_4$P
	5.75–6.00	$3^1/_8$P–$5^1/_8$P	$2^5/_8$P–4P	—	—

Ride height is the measurement determined between the bottom of the spring tower and the top of the axle immediatley below.
toe-in: E-150—$^1/_{32}$ inch out
E-250, 350—$^1/_{32}$ inch in

Proper alignment of the front wheels must be maintained in order to ensure ease of steering and satisfactory tire life.

The most important factors of front wheel alignment are wheel camber, axle caster, and wheel toe-in.

Wheel toe-in is the distance by which the wheels are closer together at the front than the rear.

Wheel camber is the amount the top of the wheels incline in or out from the vertical.

From axle caster is the amount in degrees that the top of the steering pivot pins are tilted toward the rear of the vehicle. Positive caster is inclination of the top of the pivot pin toward the rear of the vehicle.

These points should be checked at regulator intervals, particularly when the front axle has been subjected to a heavy impact. When checking wheel alignment, it is important that the wheel bearings and knuckle bearings be in proper adjustment. Loose bearings will affect instrument readings when checking the camber and toe-in.

If you start to notice abnormal tire wear patterns and handling characteristics (steering wheel is hard to return to the straight ahead position after negotiating a turn), then front end misalignment can be suspected. However, toe-in alignment maladjustment, rather than cast or camber, is more likely to be the cause of excessive or uneven tire wear on vehicles with twin I-beam front axles. Seldom is it necessary to correct caster or camber. Hard steering wheel return after turning a corner is, however, a characteristic of improper caster angle. Nevertheless, the toe-in alignment should be checked before the caster and camber angles after making the following checks:

1. Check the air pressure in all the tires. Make sure that the pressures agree with those specified for the tires and vehicle model being checked.

2. Raise the front of the vehicle off the ground. Grasp each front tire at the front and rear, and push the wheel inward and outward. If any free-play is noticed between the brake drum and the brake backing plate, adjust the wheel bearings.

NOTE: There is supposed to be a very, very small amount of free-play present where the wheel bearings are concerned. Replace the bearing if they are worn or damaged.

3. Check all steering linkage for wear or maladjustment. Adjust and/or replace all worn parts.

4. Check the torque on the steering gear mounting bolts and tighten as necessary.

5. Rotate each front wheel slowly, and observe the amount of lateral or side run-out. If the wheel run-out exceeds ⅛ in., replace the wheel or install the wheel on the rear.

6. Inspect the radius arms to be sure that they are not bent or damaged. Inspect the bushings at the radius arm-to-axle attachment and radius arm-to-frame attachment points for wear or looseness. Repair or replace parts as required.

Caster

The caster angles are designed into the front axle and cannot be adjusted.

Camber

The camber angles are designed into the front axle and cannot be adjusted.

Toe-in Adjustment

All Models

Toe-in can be measured by either a front end alignment machine or by the following method:

With the front wheels in the straight ahead position, measure the distance between the extreme front and the extreme rear of the front wheels. In other words, measure the distance across the undercarriage of the vehicle between the two front edges and the two rear edges of the two front wheels. Both of these measurements (front and rear of the two wheels) must be taken at an equal distance from the floor and at the approximate centerline of the spindle. The difference between these two distances is the amount that the wheels toe-in or toe-out. The wheels should be always adjusted to toe-in according to specifications.

1. Loosen the clamp bolts at each end of the left tie rod, seen from the front of the vehicle. Rotate the connecting rod tube until the correct toe-in is obtained, then tighten the clamp bolts.

2. Recheck the toe-in to make sure that no changes occurred when the bolts were tightened.

NOTE: The clamps should be positioned ¹⁄₁₆ in. from the end of the rod with the clamp bolts in a vertical position in front of the tube, with the nut down.

REAR SUSPENSION

Semi-elliptic, leaf type springs are used at the rear axle. The front end of the spring is attached to a spring bracket on the frame side member. The rear end of the spring is attached to the bracket on the frame side member with a shackle. Each spring is attached to the axle with two U-bolts. A spacer is located between the spring and the axle on some applications to obtain a level ride position.

Springs

REMOVAL AND INSTALLATION

1. Raise the vehicle by the frame until the weight is off the rear spring with the tires still on the floor.

2. Remove the nuts from the spring U-bolts and drive the U-

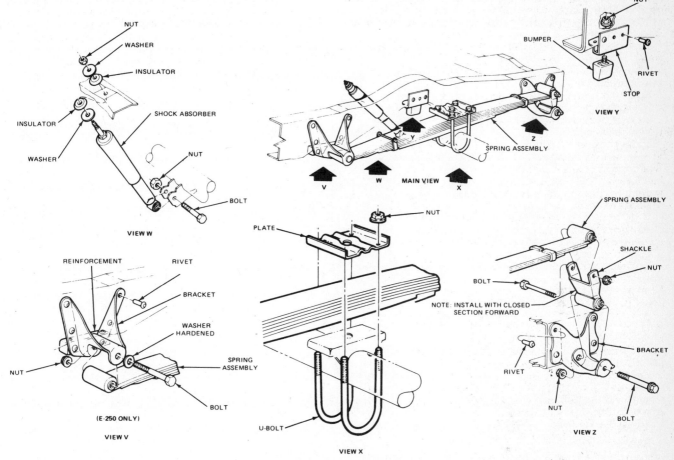

E-250/350 rear spring

bolts from the U-bolt plate. Remove the auxiliary spring and spacer, if so equipped.

3. Remove the spring-to-bracket nut and bolt at the front of the spring.

4. Remove the upper and lower shackle nuts and bolts at the rear of the spring and remove the spring and shackle assembly from the rear shackle bracket.

5. Remove the bushings in the spring or shackle, if they are worn or damaged, and install new ones.

NOTE: When installing the components, snug down the fasteners. Don't apply final torque to the fasteners until the truck is back on the ground.

6. Position the spring in the shackle and install the upper shackle-to-spring nut and bolt with the bolt head facing outward.

7. Position the front end of the spring in the bracket and install the nut and bolt.

8. Position the shackle in the rear bracket and install the nut and bolt.

9. Position the spring on top of the axle with the spring center bolts centered in the hole provided in the seat. Install the auxiliary spring and spacer, if so equipped.

10. Install the spring U-bolts, plate and nuts.

11. Lower the vehicle to the floor and tighten the attaching hardware as follows:

U-bolts nuts
- E-150, 250: 74-107 ft. lbs.
- E-250HD, 350: 150-180 ft. lbs.

Spring to front spring hanger:
- 150-204 ft. lbs.

Spring to rear spring hanger:
- 75-105 ft. lbs.

Shock Absorbers

TESTING

Check, inspect and test the rear shock absorbers in the same manner as outlined for the front shock absorbers.

REMOVAL AND INSTALLATION

To replace the rear shock absorber, remove the self-locking nut, steel washer, and rubber bushings at the upper and lower ends and remove the shock absorber.

When a new shock absorber is installed, use new rubber bushings. Position the shock on the mounting brackets with the large hole at the top.

Install the rubber bushings, steel washer, and self-locking nuts. Tighten the nut until it rests against the shoulder of the stud.

Observe the following torques:

Upper:
- 18-28 ft. lbs.

Lower:
- 40-60 ft. lbs.

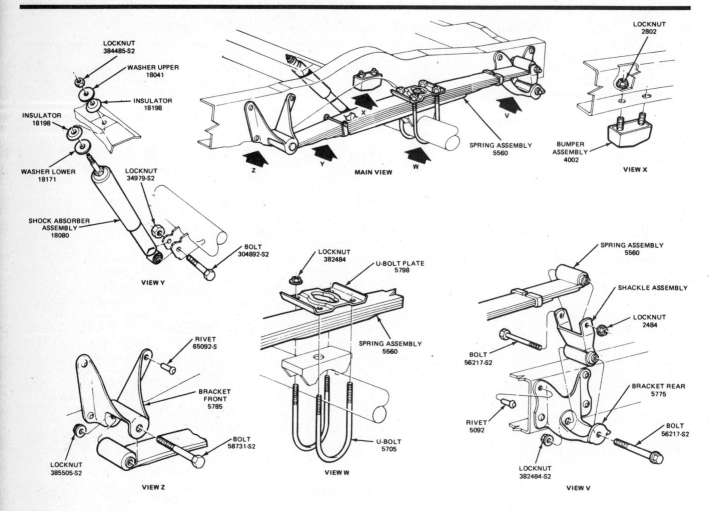

E-100/150 rear spring

STEERING

Troubleshooting the Steering Column

Problem	Cause	Solution
Will not lock	• Lockbolt spring broken or defective	• Replace lock bolt spring
High effort (required to turn ignition key and lock cylinder)	• Lock cylinder defective • Ignition switch defective	• Replace lock cylinder • Replace ignition switch

Troubleshooting the Steering Column (cont.)

Problem	Cause	Solution
High effort (required to turn ignition key and lock cylinder)	• Rack preload spring broken or deformed • Burr on lock sector, lock rack, housing, support or remote rod coupling • Bent sector shaft • Defective lock rack • Remote rod bent, deformed • Ignition switch mounting bracket bent • Distorted coupling slot in lock rack (tilt column)	• Replace preload spring • Remove burr • Replace shaft • Replace lock rack • Replace rod • Straighten or replace • Replace lock rack
Will stick in "start"	• Remote rod deformed • Ignition switch mounting bracket bent	• Straighten or replace • Straighten or replace
Key cannot be removed in "off-lock"	• Ignition switch is not adjusted correctly • Defective lock cylinder	• Adjust switch • Replace lock cylinder
Lock cylinder can be removed without depressing retainer	• Lock cylinder with defective retainer • Burr over retainer slot in housing cover or on cylinder retainer	• Replace lock cylinder • Remove burr
High effort on lock cylinder between "off" and "off-lock"	• Distorted lock rack • Burr on tang of shift gate (automatic column) • Gearshift linkage not adjusted	• Replace lock rack • Remove burr • Adjust linkage
Noise in column	• One click when in "off-lock" position and the steering wheel is moved (all except automatic column) • Coupling bolts not tightened • Lack of grease on bearings or bearing surfaces • Upper shaft bearing worn or broken • Lower shaft bearing worn or broken • Column not correctly aligned • Coupling pulled apart • Broken coupling lower joint • Steering shaft snap ring not seated • Shroud loose on shift bowl. Housing loose on jacket—will be noticed with ignition in "off-lock" and when torque is applied to steering wheel.	• Normal—lock bolt is seating • Tighten pinch bolts • Lubricate with chassis grease • Replace bearing assembly • Replace bearing. Check shaft and replace if scored. • Align column • Replace coupling • Repair or replace joint and align column • Replace ring. Check for proper seating in groove. • Position shroud over lugs on shift bowl. Tighten mounting screws.

Troubleshooting the Steering Column (cont.)

Problem	Cause	Solution
High steering shaft effort	• Column misaligned • Defective upper or lower bearing • Tight steering shaft universal joint • Flash on I.D. of shift tube at plastic joint (tilt column only) • Upper or lower bearing seized	• Align column • Replace as required • Repair or replace • Replace shift tube • Replace bearings
Lash in mounted column assembly	• Column mounting bracket bolts loose • Broken weld nuts on column jacket • Column capsule bracket sheared	• Tighten bolts • Replace column jacket • Replace bracket assembly
Lash in mounted column assembly (cont.)	• Column bracket to column jacket mounting bolts loose • Loose lock shoes in housing (tilt column only) • Loose pivot pins (tilt column only) • Loose lock shoe pin (tilt column only) • Loose support screws (tilt column only)	• Tighten to specified torque • Replace shoes • Replace pivot pins and support • Replace pin and housing • Tighten screws
Housing loose (tilt column only)	• Excessive clearance between holes in support or housing and pivot pin diameters • Housing support-screws loose	• Replace pivot pins and support • Tighten screws
Steering wheel loose—every other tilt position (tilt column only)	• Loose fit between lock shoe and lock shoe pivot pin	• Replace lock shoes and pivot pin
Steering column not locking in any tilt position (tilt column only)	• Lock shoe seized on pivot pin • Lock shoe grooves have burrs or are filled with foreign material • Lock shoe springs weak or broken	• Replace lock shoes and pin • Clean or replace lock shoes • Replace springs
Noise when tilting column (tilt column only)	• Upper tilt bumpers worn • Tilt spring rubbing in housing	• Replace tilt bumper • Lubricate with chassis grease
One click when in "off-lock" position and the steering wheel is moved	• Seating of lock bolt	• None. Click is normal characteristic sound produced by lock bolt as it seats.
High shift effort (automatic and tilt column only)	• Column not correctly aligned • Lower bearing not aligned correctly • Lack of grease on seal or lower bearing areas	• Align column • Assemble correctly • Lubricate with chassis grease
Improper transmission shifting—automatic and tilt column only	• Sheared shift tube joint • Improper transmission gearshift linkage adjustment • Loose lower shift lever	• Replace shift tube • Adjust linkage • Replace shift tube

Troubleshooting the Ignition Switch

Problem	Cause	Solution
Ignition switch electrically inoperative	• Loose or defective switch connector • Feed wire open (fusible link) • Defective ignition switch	• Tighten or replace connector • Repair or replace • Replace ignition switch
Engine will not crank	• Ignition switch not adjusted properly	• Adjust switch
Ignition switch wil not actuate mechanically	• Defective ignition switch • Defective lock sector • Defective remote rod	• Replace switch • Replace lock sector • Replace remote rod
Ignition switch cannot be adjusted correctly	• Remote rod deformed	• Repair, straighten or replace

Troubleshooting the Turn Signal Switch

Problem	Cause	Solution
Turn signal will not cancel	• Loose switch mounting screws • Switch or anchor bosses broken • Broken, missing or out of position detent, or cancelling spring	• Tighten screws • Replace switch • Reposition springs or replace switch as required
Turn signal difficult to operate	• Turn signal lever loose • Switch yoke broken or distorted • Loose or misplaced springs • Foreign parts and/or materials in switch • Switch mounted loosely	• Tighten mounting screws • Replace switch • Reposition springs or replace switch • Remove foreign parts and/or material • Tighten mounting screws
Turn signal will not indicate lane change	• Broken lane change pressure pad or spring hanger • Broken, missing or misplaced lane change spring • Jammed wires	• Replace switch • Replace or reposition as required • Loosen mounting screws, reposition wires and retighten screws
Turn signal will not stay in turn position	• Foreign material or loose parts impeding movement of switch yoke • Defective switch	• Remove material and/or parts • Replace switch
Hazard switch cannot be pulled out	• Foreign material between hazard support cancelling leg and yoke	• Remove foreign material. No foreign material impeding function of hazard switch—replace turn signal switch.

Troubleshooting the Turn Signal Switch (cont.)

Problem	Cause	Solution
No turn signal lights	• Inoperative turn signal flasher • Defective or blown fuse • Loose chassis to column harness connector • Disconnect column to chassis connector. Connect new switch to chassis and operate switch by hand. If vehicle lights now operate normally, signal switch is inoperative • If vehicle lights do not operate, check chassis wiring for opens, grounds, etc.	• Replace turn signal flasher • Replace fuse • Connect securely • Replace signal switch • Repair chassis wiring as required
Instrument panel turn indicator lights on but not flashing	• Burned out or damaged front or rear turn signal bulb • If vehicle lights do not operate, check light sockets for high resistance connections, the chassis wiring for opens, grounds, etc. • Inoperative flasher • Loose chassis to column harness connection • Inoperative turn signal switch • To determine if turn signal switch is defective, substitute new switch into circuit and operate switch by hand. If the vehicle's lights operate normally, signal switch is inoperative.	• Replace bulb • Repair chassis wiring as required • Replace flasher • Connect securely • Replace turn signal switch • Replace turn signal switch
Stop light not on when turn indicated	• Loose column to chassis connection • Disconnect column to chassis connector. Connect new switch into system without removing old.	• Connect securely • Replace signal switch
Stop light not on when turn indicated (cont.)	Operate switch by hand. If brake lights work with switch in the turn position, signal switch is defective. • If brake lights do not work, check connector to stop light sockets for grounds, opens, etc.	 • Repair connector to stop light circuits using service manual as guide
Turn indicator panel lights not flashing	• Burned out bulbs • High resistance to ground at bulb socket • Opens, ground in wiring harness from front turn signal bulb socket to indicator lights	• Replace bulbs • Replace socket • Locate and repair as required

Troubleshooting the Turn Signal Switch (cont.)

Problem	Cause	Solution
Turn signal lights flash very slowly	• High resistance ground at light sockets	• Repair high resistance grounds at light sockets
	• Incorrect capacity turn signal flasher or bulb	• Replace turn signal flasher or bulb
	• If flashing rate is still extremely slow, check chassis wiring harness from the connector to light sockets for high resistance	• Locate and repair as required
	• Loose chassis to column harness connection	• Connect securely
	• Disconnect column to chassis connector. Connect new switch into system without removing old. Operate switch by hand. If flashing occurs at normal rate, the signal switch is defective.	• Replace turn signal switch
Hazard signal lights will not flash— turn signal functions normally	• Blow fuse	• Replace fuse
	• Inoperative hazard warning flasher	• Replace hazard warning flasher in fuse panel
	• Loose chassis-to-column harness connection	• Conect securely
	• Disconnect column to chassis connector. Connect new switch into system without removing old. Depress the hazard warning lights. If they now work normally, turn signal switch is defective.	• Replace turn signal switch
	• If lights do not flash, check wiring harness "K" lead for open between hazard flasher and connector. If open, fuse block is defective	• Repair or replace brown wire or connector as required

Steering Wheel

REMOVAL AND INSTALLATION

1. Set the front wheel in the straight ahead position and make chalk marks on the column and steering wheel hub for alignment purposes during installation.
2. Disconnect the negative battery cable.
3. Remove the one screw from the underside of each steering wheel spoke, and lift the horn switch assembly (steering wheel pad) from the steering wheel. On vehicles equipped with the sport steering wheel option, pry the button cover off with a screwdriver.
4. Disconnect the horn switch wires at the connector and remove the switch assembly. On trucks equipped with speed control, squeeze the J-clip ground wire terminal firmly and pull it out of the hole in the steering wheel. Don't pull the wire out without squeezing the clip.
5. Remove the horn switch assembly.
6. Remove the steering wheel retaining nut and remove the steering wheel with a puller.

WARNING: Never hammer on the wheel or shaft to remove it! Never use a knock-off type puller.

7. Install the steering wheel in the reverse order of removal. Tighten the shaft nut to 40 ft. lbs.

Turn Signal Switch

REMOVAL AND INSTALLATION

1. Disconnect the battery ground cable.
2. Remove the steering wheel.
3. Remove the turn signal lever by unscrewing it from the steering column.
4. Disconnect the turn signal indicator switch wiring connector plug by lifting up the tabs on the side of the plug and pulling it apart.
5. Remove the switch assembly attaching screws.
6. On trucks with a fixed column, lift the switch out of the column and guide the connector plug through the opening in the shift socket.

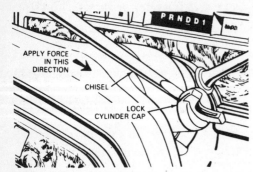

Breaking the cap away from the lock cylinder

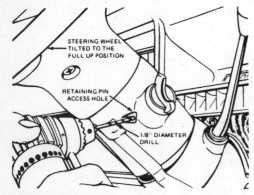

Drilling out the lock cylinder retaining pin

7. On trucks with a tilt column, remove the connector plug before removing the switch from the column. The shift socket opening is not large enough for the plug connector to pass through.

8. Install the turn signal switch in the reverse order of removal.

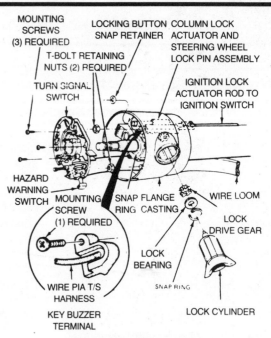

Non-tilting mechanism

Ignition Switch

REMOVAL AND INSTALLATION

1. Disconnect the battery ground cable.
2. Remove the steering column shroud and lower the steering column.
3. Disconnect the switch wiring at the multiple plug.
4. Remove the two nuts that retain the switch to the steering column.

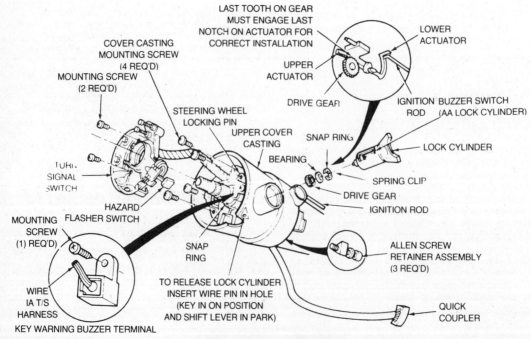

Tilt column mechanism

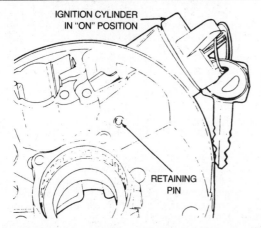

Lock retaining pin access slot on non-tilt columns

5. Lift the switch vertically upward to disengage the actuator rod from the switch and remove the switch.

6. When installing the ignition switch, both the locking mechanism at the top of the column and the switch itself must be in the LOCK position for correct adjustment.

   To hold the mechanical parts of the column in the LOCK position, move the shift lever into PARK (with automatic transmissions) or REVERSE (with manual transmissions), turn the key to the LOCK position, and remove the key. New replacement switches, when received, are already pinned in the LOCK position by a metal shipping pin inserted in a locking hole on the side of the switch.

7. Engage the actuator rod in the switch.

8. Position the switch on the column and install the retaining nuts, but do not tighten them.

9. Move the switch up and down along the column to locate the mid-position of rod lash, and then tighten the retaining nuts.

10. Remove the locking pin, connect the battery cable, and check for proper start in PARK or NEUTRAL.

   Also check to make certain that the start circuit cannot be actuated in the DRIVE and REVERSE position.

11. Raise the steering column into position at instrument panel. Install steering column shroud.

Ignition Lock Cylinder

REMOVAL AND INSTALLATION

With Key

1. Disconnect the battery ground.

2. On tilt columns, remove the upper extension shroud by unsnapping the shroud from the retaining clip at the 9 o'clock position.

3. Remove the trim shroud halves.

4. Unplug the wire connector at the key warning switch.

5. Place the shift lever in **PARK** and turn the key to **ON**.

6. Place a ⅛ in. wire pin in the hole in the casting surrounding the lock cylinder and depress the retaining pin while pulling out on the cylinder.

7. When installing the cylinder, turn the lock cylinder to the RUN position and depress the retaining pin, then insert the lock cylinder into its housing in the flange casting. Assure that the cylinder is fully seated and aligned in the interlocking washer before turning the key to the OFF position. This will allow the cylinder retaining pin to extend into the cylinder cast housing hole.

8. The remainder of installation is the reverse of removal.

Non-Functioning Cylinder or No Key Available
FIXED COLUMNS

1. Disconnect the battery ground.

2. Remove the steering wheel.

3. Remove the turn signal lever.

4. Remove the column trim shrouds.

5. Unbolt the steering column and lower it carefully.

6. Remove the ignition switch and warning buzzer and pin the switch in the LOCK position.

7. Remove the turn signal switch.

8. Remove the snapring and T-bolt nuts that retain the flange casting to the column outer tube.

9. Remove the flange casting, upper shaft bearing, lock cylinder, ignition switch actuator and the actuator rod by pulling the entire assembly over the end of the steering column shaft.

10. Remove the lock actuator insert, the T-bolts and the automatic transmission indicator insert, or, with manual transmissions, the key release lever.

11. Upon reassembly, the following parts must be replaced with new parts:
   - Flange
   - Lock cylinder assembly
   - Steering column lock gear
   - Steering column lock bearing
   - Steering column upper bearing retainer
   - Lock actuator assembly

12. Assembly is a reversal of the disassembly procedure. It is best to install a new upper bearing. Check that the truck starts only in PARK and NEUTRAL.

TILT COLUMNS

1. Disconnect the battery ground.

2. Remove the steering column shrouds.

3. Using masking tape, tape the gap between the steering wheel hub and the cover casting. Cover the entire circumference of the casting. Cover the seat and floor area with a drop-cloth.

4. Pull out the hazard switch and tape it in a downward position.

5. The lock cylinder retaining pin is located on the outside of the steering column cover casting adjacent to the hazard flasher button.

6. Tilt the steering column to the full up position and prepunch the lock cylinder retaining pin with a sharp punch.

7. Using a ⅛ in. drill bit, mounted in a right angle drive drill adapter, drill out the retaining pin, going no deeper than ½ in. (12.7mm).

8. Tilt the column to the full down position. Place a chisel at the base of the ignition lock cylinder cap and using a hammer break away the cap from the lock cylinder.

9. Using a ⅜ in. drill bit, drill down the center of the ignition lock cylinder key slot about 1¾ in. (44mm), until the lock cylinder breaks loose from the steering column cover casting.

10. Remove the lock cylinder and the drill shavings.

11. Remove the steering wheel.

12. Remove the turn signal lever.

13. Remove the turn signal switch attaching screws.

14. Remove the key buzzer attaching screw.

15. Remove the turn signal switch up and over the end of the column, but don't disconnect the wiring.

16. Remove the 4 attaching screws from the cover casting and lift the casting over the end of the steering shaft, allowing the turn signal switch to pass through the casting. The removal of the casting cover will expose the upper actuator. Remove the upper actuator.

17. Remove the drive gear, snapring and washer from the cover casting along with the upper actuator.

18. Clean all components and replace any that appear damaged or worn.

19. Installation is the reverse of removal.

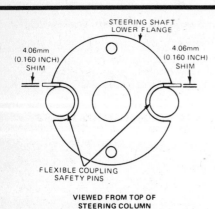

STEERING SHAFT
LOWER FLANGE

4.06mm
(0.160 INCH)
SHIM

4.06mm
(0.160 INCH)
SHIM

FLEXIBLE COUPLING
SAFETY PINS

VIEWED FROM TOP OF
STEERING COLUMN

Flexible coupling alignment

Steering Column

REMOVAL AND INSTALLATION

1. Set the parking brake.
2. Disconnect the battery ground cable.
3. Disconnect the flexible coupling from the steering shaft flange.
4. Disconnect the shift linkage rod(s) from the column.
5. Remove the steering wheel.

NOTE: If you have a tilt column, the steering wheel MUST be in the full UP position when it is removed.

6. Remove the floor cover screws at the base of the column.
7. Remove the steering column shroud by loosening the bottom screw and placing the shift lever in the No.1 position (on automatics) and pulling the shroud up and away from the column.
8. Remove the instrument cluster column opening cover.
9. Remove the 2 bolts securing the column support bracket to the pedal support bracket.

10. Disconnect the turn signal/hazard warning harness and the ignition switch harness.
11. Lift the column from the truck.

To install:
12. Position the column in the van.
13. Connect the wiring.
14. Insert the column through the floor so that the flange engages the flexible coupling, then, raise the column and loosely install the bracket bolts.
15. Loosely install the flexible coupling nuts and floor plate screws.
16. Install the steering wheel.
17. Adjust the steering column as follows:
    a. Tighten the flexible coupling nuts to 35 ft. lbs.
    b. Place the wheels in the straight-ahead position.
    c. Verify the safety pin-to-flange cut-out clearance of 0.160 in. with a feeler gauge.
    d. If necessary, loosen the flange nuts to adjust the clearance, then retighten the nuts when clearance is established.
    e. Tighten the column support bracket bolts to 20 ft. lbs.
    f. Tighten the cover plate screws to 10 ft. lbs.
    g. Tighten the lower clamp bolt to 10 ft. lbs.

Pitman Arm

REMOVAL AND INSTALLATION

1. Place the wheels in a straight-ahead position.
2. Disconnect the drag link at the pitman arm. You'll need a puller such as a tie rod end remover.
3. Remove the pitman arm-to-gear nut and washer.
4. Matchmark the pitman arm and gear housing for installation purposes.
5. Using a 2-jawed puller, remove the pitman arm from the gear.
6. Installation is the reverse of removal. Align the matchmarks when installing the pitman arm. Torque the pitman arm nut to 170-230 ft. lbs.; torque the drag link ball stud nut to 50-75 ft. lbs., advancing the nut to align the cotter pin hole. Never back off the nut to align the hole.

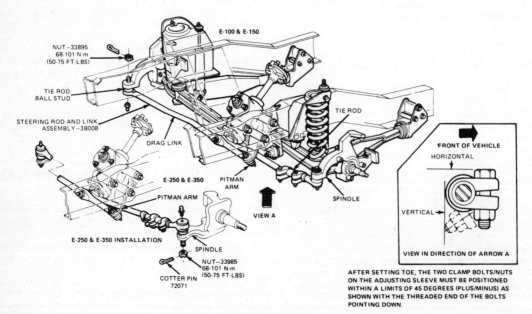

Steering linkage

Tie Rod and Link

REMOVAL AND INSTALLATION

Except Rubberized Ball Socket Linkage

1. Place the wheels in a straight-ahead position.
2. Remove the cotter pins and nuts from the drag link and tie rod ball studs.
3. Remove the drag link ball studs from the right hand spindle and pitman arm.
5. Remove the tie rod ball studs from the left hand spindle and drag link.
6. Installation is the reverse of removal. Seat the studs in the tapered hole before tightening the nuts. This will avoid wrap-up of the rubber grommets during tightening of the nuts. Torque the nuts to 70 ft. lbs. Always use new cotter pins.
7. Have the front end alignment checked.

Rubberized Ball Socket Linkage

1. Raise and support the front end on jackstands.
2. Place the wheels in the straight-ahead position.
3. Remove the nuts connecting the drag link ball studs to the connecting rod and pitman arm.
4. Disconnect the drag link using a tie rod end remover.
5. Loosen the bolts on the adjuster clamp. Count the number of turns it take to remove the drag link from the adjuster.
6. Installation is the reverse of removal. Install the drag link with the same number of turns it took to remove it. Make certain that the wheels remain in the straight-ahead position during installation. Seat the studs in the tapered hole before tightening the nuts. This will avoid wrap-up of the rubber grommets during tightening of the nuts. Torque the adjuster clamp nuts to 40 ft. lbs. Torque the ball stud nuts to 75 ft. lbs.
7. Have the front end alignment checked.

Spindle Connecting Rod (Tie Rod)

REMOVAL AND INSTALLATION

1. Raise and support the front end on jackstands.
2. Place the wheels in the straight-ahead position.
3. Disconnect the connecting rod from the drag link by removing the nut and separating the two with a tie rod end remover.
4. Loosen the bolts on the adjusting sleeve clamps. Count the number of turns it takes to remove the connecting rod from the adjuster sleeve and remove the rod.
5. Installation is the reverse of removal. Install the connecting rod the exact number of turns noted during removal. Torque the tie rod nuts to 40 ft. lbs.; the ball stud nut to 75 ft. lbs.
6. Have the front end alignment checked.

Tie (Connecting) Rod Ends

REMOVAL AND INSTALLATION

1. Raise and support the front end on jackstands.
2. Place the wheels in a straight-ahead position.
3. Remove the ball stud from the pitman arm using a tie rod end remover.
4. Loosen the nuts on the adjusting sleeve clamp. Remove the ball stud from the adjuster, or the adjuster from the tie rod. Count the number of turns it takes to remove the sleeve from the tie rod or ball stud from the sleeve.
5. Install the sleeve on the tie rod, or the ball in the sleeve the same number of turns noted during removal. Make sure that

the adjuster clamps are in the correct position, illustrated, and torque the clamp bolts to 40 ft. lbs.
6. Keep the wheels straight ahead and install the ball studs. Torque the nuts to 75 ft. lbs. Use new cotter pins.
7. Install the drag link and connecting rod.
8. Have the front end alignment checked.

Power Steering Gear

ADJUSTMENTS

Meshload

1. Raise and support the front end on jackstands.
2. Matchmark the pitman arm and gear housing.
3. Set the wheels in a straight-ahead position.
4. Disconnect the pitman arm from the sector shaft.
5. Disconnect the fluid RETURN line at the pump reservoir and cap the reservoir nipple.
6. Place the end of the return line in a clean container and turn the steering wheel lock-to-lock a few times to expel the fluid from the gear.
7. Turn the steering wheel all the way to the right stop. Place a small piece of masking tape on the steering wheel rim as a reference and rotate the steering wheel 45° from the right stop.
8. Disconnect the battery ground.
9. Remove the horn pad.
10. Using an inch-pound torque wrench on the steering wheel nut, record the amount of torque needed to turn the steering wheel 1/8 turn counterclockwise. The preload reading should be 4-9 inch lbs.
11. Center the steering wheel (1/2 the total lock-to-lock turns) and record the torque needed to turn the steering wheel 90° to either side of center. On a truck with fewer than 5,000 miles, the meshload should be 15-25 inch lbs. On a truck with 5,000 or more miles, the meshload should be 7 inch lbs. more than the preload torque.
   On trucks with fewer than 5,000 miles, if the meshload is not within specifications, it should be reset to a figure 14-18 inch lbs. greater than the recorded preload torque.
   On trucks with 5,000 or more miles, if the meshload is not within specifications, it should be reset to a figure 10-14 inch lbs. greater than the recorded preload torque.
12. If an adjustment is required, loosen the adjuster locknut and turn the sector shaft adjuster screw until the necessary torque is achieved.
13. Once adjustment is completed. hold the adjuster screw and tighten the locknut to 45 ft. lbs.
14. Recheck the adjustment readings and reset if necessary.
15. Connect the return line and refill the reservoir.
16. Install the pitman arm.
17. Install the horn pad.

REMOVAL AND INSTALLATION

1. Raise and support the front end on jackstands.
2. Place the wheels in the straight-ahead position.
3. Place a drain pan under the gear and disconnect the pressure and return lines. Cap the openings.
4. Remove the splash shield from the flex coupling.
5. Disconnect the flex coupling at the gear.
6. Matchmark and remove the pitman arm from the sector shaft.
7. Support the steering gear and remove the mounting bolts.
8. Remove the steering gear. It may be necessary to work it free of the flex coupling.

To install:

9. Place the splash shield on the steering gear lugs.
10. Slide the flex coupling into place on the steering shaft. Make sure the steering wheel spokes are still horizontal.

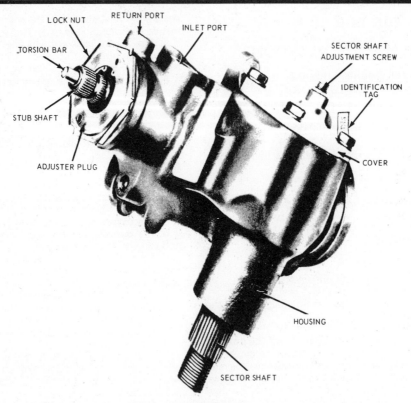

Power steering gear

11. Center the steering gear input shaft with the indexing flat facing downward.

12. Slide the steering gear input shaft into the flex coupling and into place on the frame side rail. Install the flex coupling bolt and torque it to 30 ft. lbs.

13. Install the gear mounting bolts and torque them to 65 ft. lbs.

14. Make sure that the wheels are still straight ahead and install the pitman arm. Torque the nut to 230 ft. lbs.

15. Connect the pressure, then, the return lines. Torque the pressure line to 25 ft. lbs.

16. Snap the flex coupling shield into place.

17. Fill the steering reservoir.

18. Run the engine and turn the steering wheel lock-to-lock several times to expel air. Check for leaks.

Power Steering Pump

REMOVAL AND INSTALLATION

1. Place a drain pan under the pump.

2. Disconnect the pressure and return lines and cap the ports and lines.

3. Remove the belt tension nut.

4. Remove the attaching bolts and take off the belt. Lift out the pump.

5. Installation is the reverse of removal. Adjust the belt. Torque all retainers to 40 ft. lbs. Torque the pressure line nut to 25 ft. lbs. Refill the pump. Start the engine and turn the wheel from lock-to-lock several times to expel any air. Refill the pump with power steering fluid.

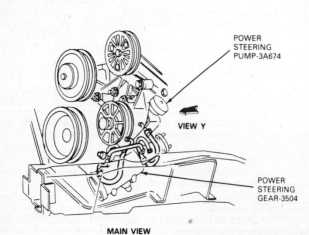

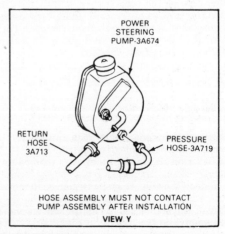

8-302 power steering pump installation

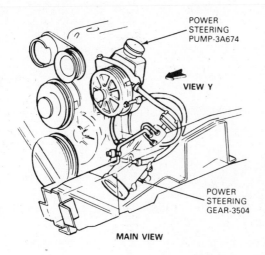
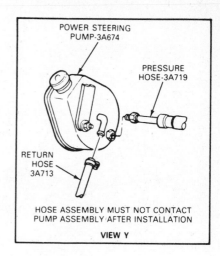

6-300 power steering pump installation

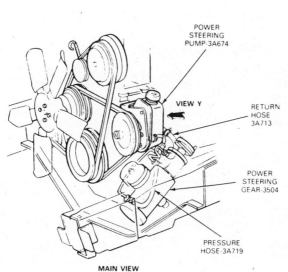
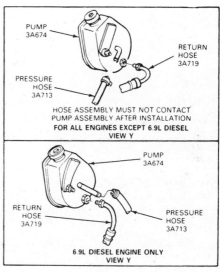

8-351 power steering pump installation

Quick-Connect Pressure Line

Some pumps will have a quick-connect fitting for the pressure line. This fitting may, under certain circumstances, leak and/or be improperly engaged resulting in unplanned disconnection.

The leak is usually caused by a cut O-ring, imperfections in the outlet fitting inside diameter, or an improperly machined O-ring groove.

Improper engagement can be caused by an improperly machined tube end, tube nut, snapring, outlet fitting or gear port.

If a leak occurs, the O-ring should be replaced with new O-rings. Special O-rings are made for quick-disconnect fittings.

Standard O-rings should never be used in their place. If the new O-rings do not solve the leak problem, replace the outlet fitting. If that doesn't work, replace the pressure line.

Improper engagement due to a missing or bent snapring, or improperly machined tube nut, may be corrected with a Ford snapring kit made for the purpose. If that doesn't work, replace the pressure hose.

When tightening a quick-connect tube nut, always use a tube nut wrench; never use an open-end wrench! Use of an open-end wrench will result in deformation of the nut! Tighten quick-connect tube nuts to 15 ft. lbs. maximum.

Swivel and/or endplay of quick-connect fittings is normal.

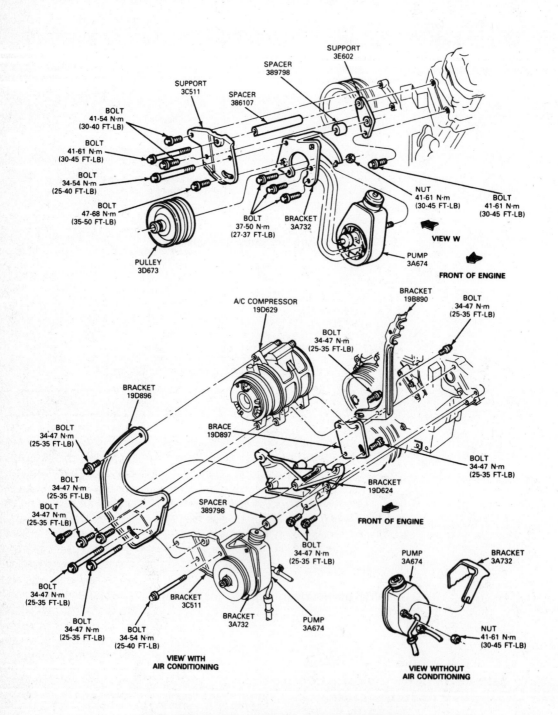

SUPPORT
3E602

SPACER
389798

SUPPORT
3C511

SPACER
386107

BOLT
41-54 N·m
(30-40 FT-LB)

BOLT
41-61 N·m
(30-45 FT-LB)

BOLT
34-54 N·m
(25-40 FT-LB)

BOLT
47-68 N·m
(35-50 FT-LB)

NUT
41-61 N·m
(30-45 FT-LB)

BOLT
41-61 N·m
(30-45 FT-LB)

VIEW W

BOLT
37-50 N·m
(27-37 FT-LB)

BRACKET
3A732

PULLEY
3D673

PUMP
3A674

FRONT OF ENGINE

A/C COMPRESSOR
19D629

BRACKET
19B890

BOLT
34-47 N·m
(25-35 FT-LB)

BRACKET
19D896

BOLT
34-47 N·m
(25-35 FT-LB)

BOLT
34-47 N·m
(25-35 FT-LB)

BOLT
34-47 N·m
(25-35 FT-LB)

BRACE
19D897

BOLT
34-47 N·m
(25-35 FT-LB)

BRACKET
19D624

BOLT
34-47 N·m
(25-35 FT-LB)

SPACER
389798

BOLT
34-47 N·m
(25-35 FT-LB)

FRONT OF ENGINE

BOLT
34-47 N·m
(25-35 FT-LB)

BOLT
34-54 N·m
(25-40 FT-LB)

BRACKET
3C511

BRACKET
3A732

PUMP
3A674

**VIEW WITH
AIR CONDITIONING**

PUMP
3A674

BRACKET
3A732

NUT
41-61 N·m
(30-45 FT-LB)

**VIEW WITHOUT
AIR CONDITIONING**

7.3L diesel power steering pump installation

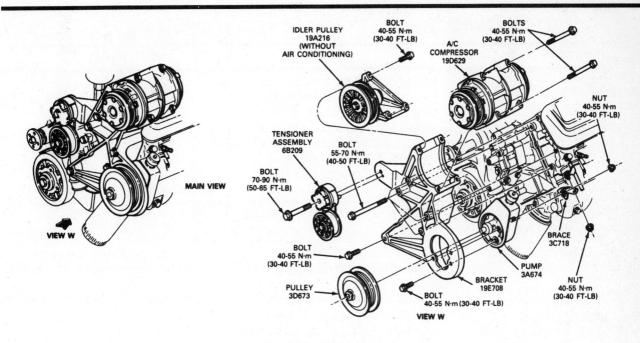

8-460 power steering pump installation

Troubleshooting the Power Steering Gear

Problem	Cause	Solution
Hissing noise in steering gear	• There is some noise in all power steering systems. One of the most common is a hissing sound most evident at standstill parking. There is no relationship between this noise and performance of the steering. Hiss may be expected when steering wheel is at end of travel or when slowly turning at standstill.	• Slight hiss is normal and in no way affects steering. Do not replace valve unless hiss is extremely objectionable. A replacement valve will also exhibit slight noise and is not always a cure. Investigate clearance around flexible coupling rivets. Be sure steering shaft and gear are aligned so flexible coupling rotates in a flat plane and is not distorted as shaft rotates. Any metal-to-metal contacts through flexible coupling will transmit valve hiss into passenger compartment through the steering column.
Rattle or chuckle noise in steering gear	• Gear loose on frame	• Check gear-to-frame mounting screws.
	• Steering linkage looseness	• Check linkage pivot points for wear. Replace if necessary.
	• Pressure hose touching other parts of car	• Adjust hose position. Do not bend tubing by hand.
	• Loose pitman shaft over center adjustment	• Adjust to specifications

Troubleshooting the Power Steering Gear (cont.)

Problem	Cause	Solution
	NOTE: A slight rattle may occur on turns because of increased clearance off the "high point." This is normal and clearance must not be reduced below specified limits to eliminate this slight rattle. • Loose pitman arm	 • Tighten pitman arm nut to specifications
Squawk noise in steering gear when turning or recovering from a turn	• Damper O-ring on valve spool cut	• Replace damper O-ring
Poor return of steering wheel to center	• Tires not properly inflated • Lack of lubrication in linkage and ball joints • Lower coupling flange rubbing against steering gear adjuster plug • Steering gear to column misalignment • Improper front wheel alignment • Steering linkage binding • Ball joints binding • Steering wheel rubbing against housing • Tight or frozen steering shaft bearings • Sticking or plugged valve spool • Steering gear adjustments over specifications • Kink in return hose	• Inflate to specified pressure • Lube linkage and ball joints • Loosen pinch bolt and assemble properly • Align steering column • Check and adjust as necessary • Replace pivots • Replace ball joints • Align housing • Replace bearings • Remove and clean or replace valve • Check adjustment with gear out of car. Adjust as required. • Replace hose
Car leads to one side or the other (keep in mind road condition and wind. Test car in both directions on flat road)	• Front end misaligned • Unbalanced steering gear valve NOTE: If this is cause, steering effort will be very light in direction of lead and normal or heavier in opposite direction	• Adjust to specifications • Replace valve
Momentary increase in effort when turning wheel fast to right or left	• Low oil level • Pump belt slipping • High internal leakage	• Add power steering fluid as required • Tighten or replace belt • Check pump pressure. (See pressure test)
Steering wheel surges or jerks when turning with engine running especially during parking	• Low oil level • Loose pump belt • Steering linkage hitting engine oil pan at full turn • Insufficient pump pressure • Pump flow control valve sticking	• Fill as required • Adjust tension to specification • Correct clearance • Check pump pressure. (See pressure test). Replace relief valve if defective. • Inspect for varnish or damage, replace if necessary

Troubleshooting the Power Steering Gear (cont.)

Problem	Cause	Solution
Excessive wheel kickback or loose steering	• Air in system	• Add oil to pump reservoir and bleed by operating steering. Check hose connectors for proper torque and adjust as required.
	• Steering gear loose on frame	• Tighten attaching screws to specified torque
	• Steering linkage joints worn enough to be loose	• Replace loose pivots
	• Worn poppet valve	• Replace poppet valve
	• Loose thrust bearing preload adjustment	• Adjust to specification with gear out of vehicle
	• Excessive overcenter lash	• Adjust to specification with gear out of car
Hard steering or lack of assist	• Loose pump belt	• Adjust belt tension to specification
	• Low oil level **NOTE:** Low oil level will also result in excessive pump noise	• Fill to proper level. If excessively low, check all lines and joints for evidence of external leakage. Tighten loose connectors.
	• Steering gear to column misalignment	• Align steering column
	• Lower coupling flange rubbing against steering gear adjuster plug	• Loosen pinch bolt and assemble properly
	• Tires not properly inflated	• Inflate to recommended pressure
Foamy milky power steering fluid, low fluid level and possible low pressure	• Air in the fluid, and loss of fluid due to internal pump leakage causing overflow	• Check for leak and correct. Bleed system. Extremely cold temperatures will cause system aeration should the oil level be low. If oil level is correct and pump still foams, remove pump from vehicle and separate reservoir from housing. Check welsh plug and housing for cracks. If plug is loose or housing is cracked, replace housing.
Low pressure due to steering pump	• Flow control valve stuck or inoperative	• Remove burrs or dirt or replace. Flush system.
	• Pressure plate not flat against cam ring	• Correct
Low pressure due to steering gear	• Pressure loss in cylinder due to worn piston ring or badly worn housing bore	• Remove gear from car for disassembly and inspection of ring and housing bore
	• Leakage at valve rings, valve body-to-worm seal	• Remove gear from car for disassembly and replace seals

Troubleshooting the Power Steering Pump

Problem	Cause	Solution
Chirp noise in steering pump	• Loose belt	• Adjust belt tension to specification
Belt squeal (particularly noticeable at full wheel travel and stand still parking)	• Loose belt	• Adjust belt tension to specification
Growl noise in steering pump	• Excessive back pressure in hoses or steering gear caused by restriction	• Locate restriction and correct. Replace part if necessary.
Growl noise in steering pump (particularly noticeable at stand still parking)	• Scored pressure plates, thrust plate or rotor • Extreme wear of cam ring	• Replace parts and flush system • Replace parts
Groan noise in steering pump	• Low oil level • Air in the oil. Poor pressure hose connection.	• Fill reservoir to proper level • Tighten connector to specified torque. Bleed system by operating steering from right to left— full turn.
Rattle noise in steering pump	• Vanes not installed properly • Vanes sticking in rotor slots	• Install properly • Free up by removing burrs, varnish, or dirt
Swish noise in steering pump	• Defective flow control valve	• Replace part
Whine noise in steering pump	• Pump shaft bearing scored	• Replace housing and shaft. Flush system.
Hard steering or lack of assist	• Loose pump belt • Low oil level in reservoir **NOTE:** Low oil level will also result in excessive pump noise • Steering gear to column misalignment • Lower coupling flange rubbing against steering gear adjuster plug • Tires not properly inflated	• Adjust belt tension to specification • Fill to proper level. If excessively low, check all lines and joints for evidence of external leakage. Tighten loose connectors. • Align steering column • Loosen pinch bolt and assemble properly • Inflate to recommended pressure
Foaming milky power steering fluid, low fluid level and possible low pressure	• Air in the fluid, and loss of fluid due to internal pump leakage causing overflow	• Check for leaks and correct. Bleed system. Extremely cold temperatures will cause system aeration should the oil level be low. If oil level is correct and pump still foams, remove pump from vehicle and separate reservoir from body. Check welsh plug and body for cracks. If plug is loose or body is cracked, replace body.

Troubleshooting the Power Steering Pump (cont.)

Problem	Cause	Solution
Low pump pressure	• Flow control valve stuck or inoperative • Pressure plate not flat against cam ring	• Remove burrs or dirt or replace. Flush system. • Correct
Momentary increase in effort when turning wheel fast to right or left	• Low oil level in pump • Pump belt slipping • High internal leakage	• Add power steering fluid as required • Tighten or replace belt • Check pump pressure. (See pressure test)
Steering wheel surges or jerks when turning with engine running especially during parking	• Low oil level • Loose pump belt • Steering linkage hitting engine oil pan at full turn • Insufficient pump pressure	• Fill as required • Adjust tension to specification • Correct clearance • Check pump pressure. (See pressure test). Replace flow control valve if defective.
Steering wheel surges or jerks when turning with engine running especially during parking (cont.)	• Sticking flow control valve	• Inspect for varnish or damage, replace if necessary
Excessive wheel kickback or loose steering	• Air in system	• Add oil to pump reservoir and bleed by operating steering. Check hose connectors for proper torque and adjust as required.
Low pump pressure	• Extreme wear of cam ring • Scored pressure plate, thrust plate, or rotor • Vanes not installed properly • Vanes sticking in rotor slots • Cracked or broken thrust or pressure plate	• Replace parts. Flush system. • Replace parts. Flush system. • Install properly • Freeup by removing burrs, varnish, or dirt • Replace part

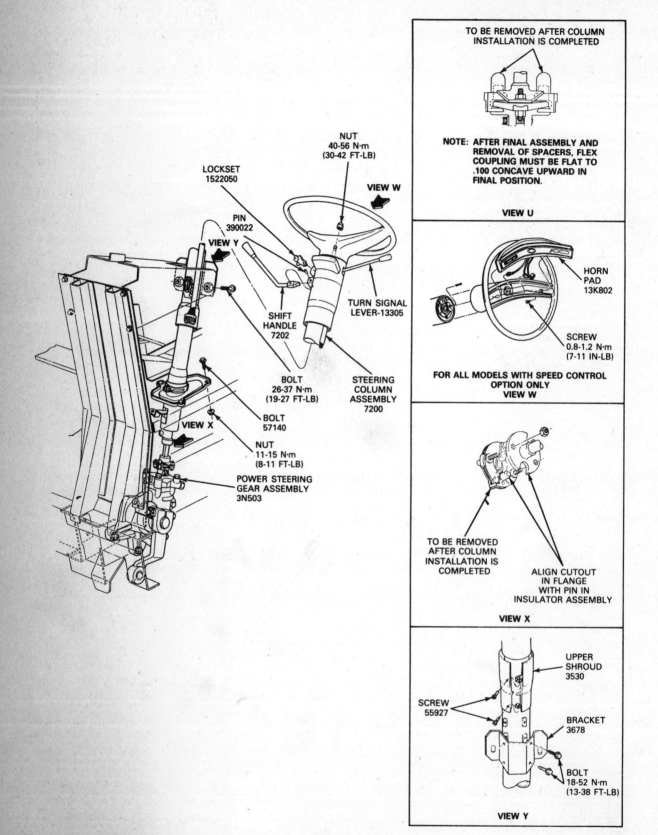

E-350 stripped chassis steering column

Brakes

BRAKE SPECIFICATIONS
All specifications in inches

| Years | Models | Master Cyl. Bore | Brake Disc | | Brake Drum | | Wheel Cyl. or Caliper Bore | |
			Minimum Thickness	Maximum Run-out	Orig. Inside Dia.	Max. Wear Limit	Front	Rear
1989–91	E-150	1.000	1.120	0.003	11.03	11.09	2.875	1.000
	E-250	1.062	1.180	0.003	12.00	12.06	2.180	1.000
	E-350	1.125	1.180	0.003	12.00	12.06	2.180	1.063

Troubleshooting the Brake System

Problem	Cause	Solution
Low brake pedal (excessive pedal travel required for braking action.)	• Excessive clearance between rear linings and drums caused by inoperative automatic adjusters	• Make 10 to 15 alternate forward and reverse brake stops to adjust brakes. If brake pedal does not come up, repair or replace adjuster parts as necessary.
	• Worn rear brakelining	• Inspect and replace lining if worn beyond minimum thickness specification
	• Bent, distorted brakeshoes, front or rear	• Replace brakeshoes in axle sets
	• Air in hydraulic system	• Remove air from system. Refer to Brake Bleeding.
Low brake pedal (pedal may go to floor with steady pressure applied.)	• Fluid leak in hydraulic system	• Fill master cylinder to fill line; have helper apply brakes and check calipers, wheel cylinders, differential valve tubes, hoses and fittings for leaks. Repair or replace as necessary.
	• Air in hydraulic system	• Remove air from system. Refer to Brake Bleeding.
	• Incorrect or non-recommended brake fluid (fluid evaporates at below normal temp).	• Flush hydraulic system with clean brake fluid. Refill with correct-type fluid.
	• Master cylinder piston seals worn, or master cylinder bore is scored, worn or corroded	• Repair or replace master cylinder
Low brake pedal (pedal goes to floor on first application—o.k. on subsequent applications.)	• Disc brake pads sticking on abutment surfaces of anchor plate. Caused by a build-up of dirt, rust, or corrosion on abutment surfaces	• Clean abutment surfaces
Fading brake pedal (pedal height decreases with steady pressure applied.)	• Fluid leak in hydraulic system	• Fill master cylinder reservoirs to fill mark, have helper apply brakes, check calipers, wheel cylinders, differential valve, tubes, hoses, and fittings for fluid leaks. Repair or replace parts as necessary.
	• Master cylinder piston seals worn, or master cylinder bore is scored, worn or corroded	• Repair or replace master cylinder

Troubleshooting the Brake System (cont.)

Problem	Cause	Solution
Decreasing brake pedal travel (pedal travel required for braking action decreases and may be accompanied by a hard pedal.)	• Caliper or wheel cylinder pistons sticking or seized • Master cylinder compensator ports blocked (preventing fluid return to reservoirs) or pistons sticking or seized in master cylinder bore • Power brake unit binding internally	• Repair or replace the calipers, or wheel cylinders • Repair or replace the master cylinder • Test unit according to the following procedure: (a) Shift transmission into neutral and start engine (b) Increase engine speed to 1500 rpm, close throttle and fully depress brake pedal (c) Slow release brake pedal and stop engine (d) Have helper remove vacuum check valve and hose from power unit. Observe for backward movement of brake pedal. (e) If the pedal moves backward, the power unit has an internal bind—replace power unit
Grabbing brakes (severe reaction to brake pedal pressure.)	• Brakelining(s) contaminated by grease or brake fluid • Parking brake cables incorrectly adjusted or seized • Incorrect brakelining or lining loose on brakeshoes • Caliper anchor plate bolts loose • Rear brakeshoes binding on support plate ledges • Incorrect or missing power brake reaction disc • Rear brake support plates loose	• Determine and correct cause of contamination and replace brakeshoes in axle sets • Adjust cables. Replace seized cables. • Replace brakeshoes in axle sets • Tighten bolts • Clean and lubricate ledges. Replace support plate(s) if ledges are deeply grooved. Do not attempt to smooth ledges by grinding. • Install correct disc • Tighten mounting bolts
Spongy brake pedal (pedal has abnormally soft, springy, spongy feel when depressed.)	• Air in hydraulic system • Brakeshoes bent or distorted • Brakelining not yet seated with drums and rotors • Rear drum brakes not properly adjusted	• Remove air from system. Refer to Brake Bleeding. • Replace brakeshoes • Burnish brakes • Adjust brakes

Troubleshooting the Brake System (cont.)

Problem	Cause	Solution
Hard brake pedal (excessive pedal pressure required to stop vehicle. May be accompanied by brake fade.)	• Loose or leaking power brake unit vacuum hose • Incorrect or poor quality brake-lining • Bent, broken, distorted brakeshoes • Calipers binding or dragging on mounting pins. Rear brakeshoes dragging on support plate.	• Tighten connections or replace leaking hose • Replace with lining in axle sets • Replace brakeshoes • Replace mounting pins and bushings. Clean rust or burrs from rear brake support plate ledges and lubricate ledges with molydisulfide grease. **NOTE:** If ledges are deeply grooved or scored, do not attempt to sand or grind them smooth—replace support plate.
	• Caliper, wheel cylinder, or master cylinder pistons sticking or seized • Power brake unit vacuum check valve malfunction	• Repair or replace parts as necessary • Test valve according to the following procedure: (a) Start engine, increase engine speed to 1500 rpm, close throttle and immediately stop engine (b) Wait at least 90 seconds then depress brake pedal (c) If brakes are not vacuum assisted for 2 or more applications, check valve is faulty
	• Power brake unit has internal bind	• Test unit according to the following procedure: (a) With engine stopped, apply brakes several times to exhaust all vacuum in system (b) Shift transmission into neutral, depress brake pedal and start engine (c) If pedal height decreases with foot pressure and less pressure is required to hold pedal in applied position, power unit vacuum system is operating normally. Test power unit. If power unit exhibits a bind condition, replace the power unit.

Troubleshooting the Brake System (cont.)

Problem	Cause	Solution
Hard brake pedal (excessive pedal pressure required to stop vehicle. May be accompanied by brake fade.)	• Master cylinder compensator ports (at bottom of reservoirs) blocked by dirt, scale, rust, or have small burrs (blocked ports prevent fluid return to reservoirs).	• Repair or replace master cylinder CAUTION: Do not attempt to clean blocked ports with wire, pencils, or similar implements. Use compressed air only.
	• Brake hoses, tubes, fittings clogged or restricted	• Use compressed air to check or unclog parts. Replace any damaged parts.
	• Brake fluid contaminated with improper fluids (motor oil, transmission fluid, causing rubber components to swell and stick in bores	• Replace all rubber components, combination valve and hoses. Flush entire brake system with DOT 3 brake fluid or equivalent.
	• Low engine vacuum	• Adjust or repair engine
Dragging brakes (slow or incomplete release of brakes)	• Brake pedal binding at pivot	• Loosen and lubricate
	• Power brake unit has internal bind	• Inspect for internal bind. Replace unit if internal bind exists.
	• Parking brake cables incorrrectly adjusted or seized	• Adjust cables. Replace seized cables.
	• Rear brakeshoe return springs weak or broken	• Replace return springs. Replace brakeshoe if necessary in axle sets.
	• Automatic adjusters malfunctioning	• Repair or replace adjuster parts as required
	• Caliper, wheel cylinder or master cylinder pistons sticking or seized	• Repair or replace parts as necessary
	• Master cylinder compensating ports blocked (fluid does not return to reservoirs).	• Use compressed air to clear ports. Do not use wire, pencils, or similar objects to open blocked ports.
Vehicle moves to one side when brakes are applied	• Incorrect front tire pressure	• Inflate to recommended cold (reduced load) inflation pressure
	• Worn or damaged wheel bearings	• Replace worn or damaged bearings
	• Brakelining on one side contaminated	• Determine and correct cause of contamination and replace brakelining in axle sets
	• Brakeshoes on one side bent, distorted, or lining loose on shoe	• Replace brakeshoes in axle sets
	• Support plate bent or loose on one side	• Tighten or replace support plate
	• Brakelining not yet seated with drums or rotors	• Burnish brakelining
	• Caliper anchor plate loose on one side	• Tighten anchor plate bolts
	• Caliper piston sticking or seized	• Repair or replace caliper
	• Brakelinings water soaked	• Drive vehicle with brakes lightly applied to dry linings
	• Loose suspension component attaching or mounting bolts	• Tighten suspension bolts. Replace worn suspension components.
	• Brake combination valve failure	• Replace combination valve

Troubleshooting the Brake System (cont.)

Problem	Cause	Solution
Chatter or shudder when brakes are applied (pedal pulsation and roughness may also occur.)	• Brakeshoes distorted, bent, contaminated, or worn • Caliper anchor plate or support plate loose • Excessive thickness variation of rotor(s)	• Replace brakeshoes in axle sets • Tighten mounting bolts • Refinish or replace rotors in axle sets
Noisy brakes (squealing, clicking, scraping sound when brakes are applied.)	• Bent, broken, distorted brakeshoes • Excessive rust on outer edge of rotor braking surface	• Replace brakeshoes in axle sets • Remove rust
Noisy brakes (squealing, clicking, scraping sound when brakes are applied.) (cont.)	• Brakelining worn out—shoes contacting drum of rotor • Broken or loose holdown or return springs • Rough or dry drum brake support plate ledges • Cracked, grooved, or scored rotor(s) or drum(s) • Incorrect brakelining and/or shoes (front or rear).	• Replace brakeshoes and lining in axle sets. Refinish or replace drums or rotors. • Replace parts as necessary • Lubricate support plate ledges • Replace rotor(s) or drum(s). Replace brakeshoes and lining in axle sets if necessary. • Install specified shoe and lining assemblies
Pulsating brake pedal	• Out of round drums or excessive lateral runout in disc brake rotor(s)	• Refinish or replace drums, re-index rotors or replace

BASIC OPERATING PRINCIPLES

The hydraulic system transports the power required to force the frictional surfaces of the braking system together from the pedal to the individual brake units at each wheel. A hydraulic system is used for two reasons.

First, fluid under pressure can be carried to all parts of an automobile by small pipes and flexible hoses without taking up a significant amount of room or posing routing problems.

Second, a great mechanical advantage can be given to the brake pedal end of the system, and the foot pressure required to actuate the brakes can be reduced by making the surface area of the master cylinder pistons smaller than that of any of the pistons in the wheel cylinders or calipers.

The master cylinder consists of a fluid reservoir and a double cylinder and piston assembly. Double type master cylinders are designed to separate the front and rear braking systems hydraulically in case of a leak.

Steel lines carry the brake fluid to a point on the vehicle's frame near each of the vehicle's wheels. The fluid is then carried to the calipers and wheel cylinders by flexible tubes and steel lines in order to allow for suspension and steering movements.

In drum brake systems, each wheel cylinder contains two pistons, one at either end, which push outward in opposite directions.

In disc brake systems, the cylinders are part of the calipers. The cylinders are used to force the brake pads against the disc.

All pistons employ some type of seal, usually made of rubber, to minimize fluid leakage. A rubber dust boot seals the outer end of the cylinder against dust and dirt. The boot fits around the outer end of the piston on disc brake calipers, and around the brake actuating rod on wheel cylinders.

The hydraulic system operates as follows: When at rest, the entire system, from the piston(s) in the master cylinder to those in the wheel cylinders or calipers, is full of brake fluid. Upon application of the brake pedal, fluid trapped in front of the master cylinder piston(s) is forced through the lines to the wheel cylinders. Here, it forces the pistons outward, in the case of drum brakes, and inward toward the disc, in the case of disc brakes. The motion of the pistons is opposed by return springs mounted outside the cylinders in drum brakes, and by spring seals, in disc brakes.

Upon release of the brake pedal, a spring located inside the master cylinder immediately returns the master cylinder pistons to the normal position. The pistons contain check valves and the master cylinder has compensating ports drilled in it. These are uncovered as the pistons reach their normal position. The piston check valves allow fluid to flow toward the wheel cylinders or calipers as the pistons withdraw. Then, as the return springs force the brake pads or shoes into the released position, the excess fluid reservoir through the compensating ports. It is during the time the pedal is in the released position that any fluid that has leaked out of the system will be replaced through the compensating ports.

Dual circuit master cylinders employ two pistons, located one behind the other, in the same cylinder. The primary piston is actuated directly by mechanical linkage from the brake pedal through the power booster. The secondary piston is actuated by fluid trapped between the two pistons. If a leak develops in front of the secondary piston, it moves forward until it bottoms against the front of the master cylinder, and the fluid trapped between the pistons will operate the rear brakes. If the rear brakes develop a leak, the primary piston will move forward until direct contact with the secondary piston takes place, and it will force the secondary piston to actuate the front brakes. In either case, the brake pedal moves farther when the brakes are applied, and less braking power is available.

All dual circuit systems use a switch to warn the driver when only half of the brake system is operational. This switch is located in a valve body which is mounted on the firewall or the frame below the master cylinder. A hydraulic piston receives pressure from both circuits, each circuit's pressure being applied to one end of the piston. When the pressures are in balance, the piston remains stationary. When one circuit has a leak, however, the greater pressure in that circuit during application of the brakes will push the piston to one side, closing the switch and activating the brake warning light.

In disc brake systems, this valve body also contains a metering valve and, in some cases, a proportioning valve. The metering valve keeps pressure from traveling to the disc brakes on the front wheels until the brake shoes on the rear wheels have contacted the drums, ensuring that the front brakes will never be used alone. The proportioning valve controls the pressure to the rear brakes to lessen the chance of rear wheel lock-up during very hard braking.

Warning lights may be tested by depressing the brake pedal and holding it while opening one of the wheel cylinder bleeder screws. If this does not cause the light to go on, substitute a new lamp, make continuity checks, and, finally, replace the switch as necessary.

The hydraulic system may be checked for leaks by applying pressure to the pedal gradually and steadily. If the pedal sinks very slowly to the floor, the system has a leak. This is not to be confused with a springy or spongy feel due to the compression of air within the lines. If the system leaks, there will be a gradual change in the position of the pedal with a constant pressure.

Check for leaks along all lines and at wheel cylinders. If no external leaks are apparent, the problem is inside the master cylinder.

Disc Brakes

BASIC OPERATING PRINCIPLES

Instead of the traditional expanding brakes that press outward against a circular drum, disc brake systems utilize a disc (rotor) with brake pads positioned on either side of it. Braking effect is achieved in a manner similar to the way you would squeeze a spinning phonograph record between your fingers. The disc (rotor) is a casting with cooling fins between the two braking surfaces. This enables air to circulate between the braking surfaces making them less sensitive to heat buildup and more resistant to fade. Dirt and water do not affect braking action since contaminants are thrown off by the centrifugal action of the rotor or scraped off the by the pads. Also, the equal clamping action of the two brake pads tends to ensure uniform, straight line stops. Disc brakes are inherently self-adjusting. There are three general types of disc brake:
1. A fixed caliper.
2. A floating caliper.
3. A sliding caliper.

The fixed caliper design uses two pistons mounted on either side of the rotor (in each side of the caliper). The caliper is mounted rigidly and does not move.

The sliding and floating designs are quite similar. In fact, these two types are often lumped together. In both designs, the pad on the inside of the rotor is moved into contact with the rotor by hydraulic force. The caliper, which is not held in a fixed position, moves slightly, bringing the outside pad into contact with the rotor. There are various methods of attaching floating calipers. Some pivot at the bottom or top, and some slide on mounting bolts. In any event, the end result is the same.

All the cars covered in this book employ the sliding caliper design.

Drum Brakes

BASIC OPERATING PRINCIPLES

Drum brakes employ two brake shoes mounted on a stationary backing plate. These shoes are positioned inside a circular drum which rotates with the wheel assembly. The shoes are held in place by springs. This allows them to slide toward the drums (when they are applied) while keeping the linings and drums in alignment. The shoes are actuated by a wheel cylinder which is mounted at the top of the backing plate. When the brakes are applied, hydraulic pressure forces the wheel cylinder's actuating links outward. Since these links bear directly against the top of the brake shoes, the tops of the shoes are then forced against the inner side of the drum. This action forces the bottoms of the two shoes to contact the brake drum by rotating the entire assembly slightly (known as servo action). When pressure within the wheel cylinder is relaxed, return springs pull the shoes back away from the drum.

Most modern drum brakes are designed to self-adjust themselves during application when the vehicle is moving in reverse. This motion causes both shoes to rotate very slightly with the drum, rocking an adjusting lever, thereby causing rotation of the adjusting screw.

Power Boosters

Power brakes operate just as non-power brake systems except in the actuation of the master cylinder pistons. A vacuum diaphragm is located on the front of the master cylinder and assists the driver in applying the brakes, reducing both the effort and travel he must put into moving the brake pedal.

BRAKE SYSTEM

─────── CAUTION ───────
WARNING:

Clean, high quality brake fluid is essential to the safe and proper operation of the brake system. You should always buy the highest quality brake fluid that is available. If the brake fluid becomes contaminated, drain and flush the system and fill the master cylinder with new fluid.

Never reuse any brake fluid. Any brake fluid that is removed from the system should be discarded.

Adjustments

DRUM BRAKES

The drum brakes are self-adjusting and require a manual adjustment only after the brake shoes have been replaced, or when the length of the adjusting screw has been changed while performing some other service operation, as i.e., taking off brake drums.

To adjust the brakes, follow the procedures given below:

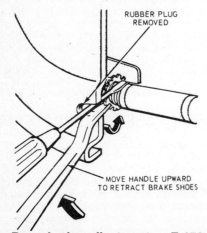

Drum brake adjustment — E-150

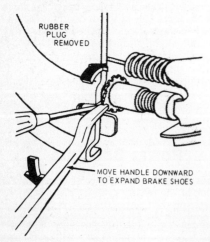

Drum brake adjustment — E-250/350

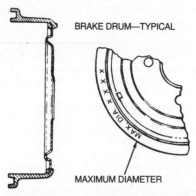

Brake drum oversize stamping

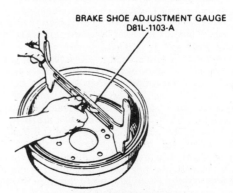

Measuring the drum

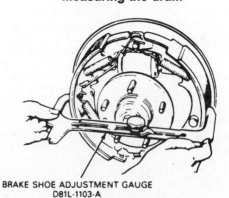

Measuring the shoes

Drum Installed

1. Raise and support the rear end on jackstands.
2. Remove the rubber plug from the adjusting slot on the backing plate.
3. Insert a brake adjusting spoon into the slot and engage the lowest possible tooth on the starwheel. Move the end of the brake spoon downward to move the starwheel upward and expand the adjusting screw. Repeat this operation until the brakes lock the wheels.
4. Insert a small screwdriver or piece of firm wire (coat hanger wire) into the adjusting slot and push the automatic adjusting lever out and free of the starwheel on the adjusting screw and hold it there.
5. Engage the topmost tooth possible on the starwheel with the brake adjusting spoon. Move the end of the adjusting spoon

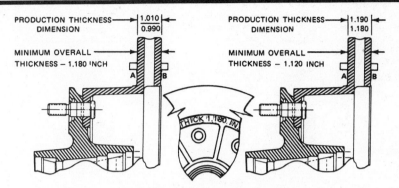

Brake rotor machining limits

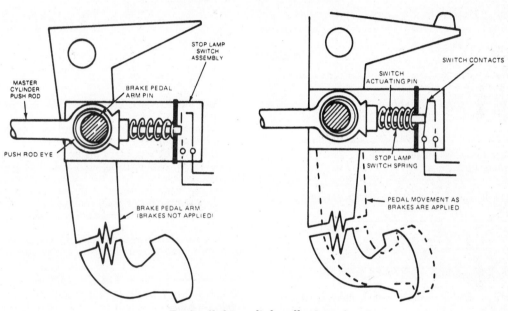

Brake light switch adjustment

upward to move the adjusting screw starwheel downward and contract the adjusting screw. Back off the adjusting screw starwheel until the wheel spins freely with a minimum of drag. Keep track of the number of turns that the starwheel is backed off, or the number of strokes taken with the brake adjusting spoon.

6. Repeat this operation for the other side. When backing off the brakes on the other side, the starwheel adjuster must be backed off the same number of turns to prevent side-to-side brake pull.

7. When the brakes are adjusted make several stops while backing the vehicle, to equalize the brakes at both of the wheels.

8. Remove the safety stands and lower the vehicle. Road test the vehicle.

Drum Removed

------------------------------ CAUTION ------------------------------
Brake shoes contain asbestos, which has been determined to be a cancer causing agent. Never clean the brake surfaces with compressed air! Avoid inhaling any dust from any brake surface! When cleaning brake surfaces, use a commercially available brake cleaning fluid.
----

1. Make sure that the shoe-to-contact pad areas are clean and properly lubricated.

2. Using and inside caliper check the inside diameter of the drum. Measure across the diameter of the assembled brake shoes, at their widest point.

3. Turn the adjusting screw so that the diameter of the shoes is 0.030 in. (0.76mm) less than the brake drum inner diameter.

4. Install the drum.

Brake Light Switch

REMOVAL AND INSTALLATION

1. Lift the locking tab on the switch connector and disconnect the wiring.

2. Remove the hairpin retainer, slide the stoplamp switch, pushrod and nylon washer off of the pedal. Remove the washer, then the switch by sliding it up or down.

NOTE: On vans equipped with speed control, the spacer washer is replaced by the dump valve adapter washer.

3. To install the switch, position it so that the U-shaped side is nearest the pedal and directly over/under the pin.

4. Slide the switch up or down, trapping the master cylinder pushrod and bushing between the switch side plates.

5. Push the switch and pushrod assembly firmly towards the brake pedal arm. Assemble the outside white plastic washer to the pin and install the hairpin retainer.

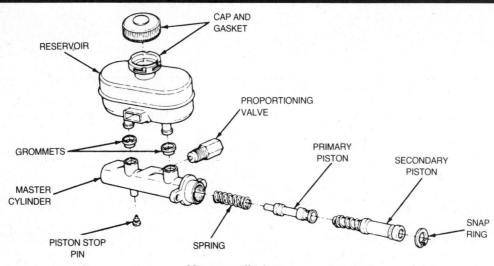

Master cylinder

---

6. Assemble the connector on the switch.
7. Check stoplamp operation.

Master Cylinder

REMOVAL AND INSTALLATION

1. With the engine off, depress the brake pedal several times to expel any vacuum.
2. Disconnect the fluid level warning switch wire.
3. Disconnect the hydraulic system brake lines at the master cylinder.
4. Remove the master cylinder retaining nuts and remove the master cylinder.
To install the master cylinder:
5. Position the master cylinder assembly on the booster and install the retaining nuts. Torque the nuts to 18–25 ft. lbs.
6. Connect the hydraulic brake system lines to the master cylinder.
7. Connect the wiring.
8. Bleed the master cylinder as described below.

OVERHAUL

The most important thing to remember when rebuilding the master cylinder is cleanliness. Work in clean surroundings with clean tools and clean cloths or paper for drying purposes. Have plenty of clean alcohol and brake fluid on hand to clean and lubricate the internal components. There are service repair kits available for overhauling the master cylinder.
1. Remove the master cylinder from the van and drain the brake fluid.
2. Using a large screwdriver, pry the reservoir off the master cylinder.
3. Mount the cylinder in a vise so that the outlets are up then remove the seal from the hub.
4. Remove the proportioning valve from the master cylinder.

5. Remove the stopscrew from the bottom of the master cylinder.
6. Depress the primary piston and remove the snapring from the rear of the bore.
7. Remove the secondary piston assembly using compressed air. Cover the bore opening with a cloth to prevent damage to the piston.
8. Using compressed air in the outlet port at the blind end and plugging the other port, remove the primary piston.
9. Clean metal parts in brake fluid and discard the rubber parts.
10. Inspect the bore for damage or wear, and check the pistons for damage and proper clearance in the bore.

11. If the master cylinder is not damaged, it may be serviced with a rebuilding kit. The rebuilding kit may contain secondary and primary piston assemblies instead of just rubber seals. In this case, seal installation is not required.
12. Clean all parts in isopropyl alcohol.
13. Install new secondary seals in the two grooves in the flat end of the front piston. The lips of the seals will be facing away from each other.
14. Install a new primary seal and the seal protector on the opposite end of the front piston with the lips of the seal facing outward.
15. Coat the seals with brake fluid. Install the spring on the front piston with the spring retainer in the primary seal.
16. Insert the piston assembly, spring end first, into the bore and use a wooden rod to seat it.
17. Coat the rear piston seals with brake fluid and install them into the piston grooves with the lips facing the spring end.
18. Assemble the spring onto the piston and install the assembly into the bore spring first. Install the snapring.
19. Hold the piston train at the bottom of the bore and install the stopscrew. Install a new seal on the hub.

NOTE: Whenever the reservoir or master cylinder is replaced, new reservoir grommets should be used.

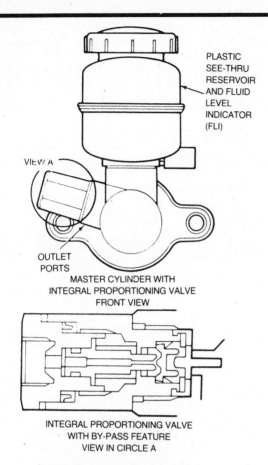

Integral proportioning valve

Proportioning valve

20. Coat the new grommet with clean brake fluid and insert them into the master cylinder. Bench-bleed the cylinder or install and bleed the cylinder on the car.

21. Press the reservoir into place. A snap should be felt, indicating that the reservoir is properly positioned.

Pressure Differential Valve

REMOVAL AND INSTALLATION

1. Disconnect the electrical leads from the valve.

2. Unscrew the valve from the master cylinder.
3. Install the valve in the reverse order of removal.
4. Bleed the master cylinder.

Height Sensing Proportioning Valve

REMOVAL AND INSTALLATION

E-250, 350

1. Raise and support the rear end on jackstands so that the suspension is fully extended.
2. Disconnect the linkage arm from the valve.
3. Disconnect the brake line from the valve.
4. Unbolt and remove the valve from its bracket.
5. Install the valve on its bracket and torque the bolts to 18 ft.lb.
6. Install the brake hose using NEW copper washers. Torque the bolt to 34 ft.lb.
7. Connect the brake line to the valve.
8. Connect the linkage arm to the valve. Torque the nut to 10 ft.lb.
9. Bleed the brakes.

Brake Pedal

REMOVAL AND INSTALLATION

1. Remove the brake light switch.
2. Slide the pushrod and spacer from the pedal pin.
3. If the van is equipped with speed control, you can leave the speed control bracket in place.
4a. On vans with manual transmission:
   a. Disconnect the clutch pedal return spring and remove the nut on the clutch rod lever.

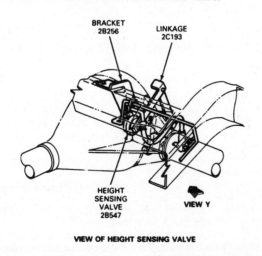

VIEW OF HEIGHT SENSING VALVE

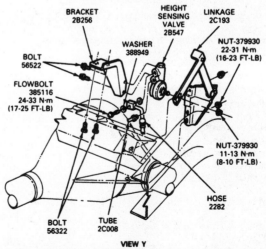

Height sensing proportioning valve installation

b. Remove the lever, spring washer and bushing.

c. Push the clutch pedal to the side far enough to allow the brake pedal to slide off the shaft.

d. Remove the pedal and bushings.

4b. On vans with automatic transmission:

a. Remove the spring retainer and bushing from the brake pedal shaft.

b. From the other end, pull out the shaft and remove the pedal.

c. Remove the bushings and spring washer from the pedal.

To install:

5a. On vans with automatic transmission:

a. Install the bushings and spring washer from the pedal.

b. Install the pedal.

c. Install the spring retainer and bushing on the brake pedal shaft.

5b. On vans with manual transmission:

a. Install the pedal and bushings.

b. Reposition the clutch pedal.

c. Install the lever, spring washer and bushing.

d. Connect the clutch pedal return spring and install the nut on the clutch rod lever.

6. Slide the pushrod and spacer on the pedal pin.

7. Install the brake light switch.

Brake Hoses and Lines

HYDRAULIC BRAKE LINE CHECK

The hydraulic brake lines and brake linings are to be inspected at the recommended intervals in the maintenance schedule. Follow the steel tubing from the master cylinder to the flexible hose fitting at each wheel. If a section of the tubing is found to be damaged, replace the entire section with tubing of the same type, size, shape, and length.

CAUTION

Copper tubing should never be used in the brake system! Use only SAE J526 or J527 steel tubing.

When installing a new section of brake tubing, flush clean brake fluid or denatured alcohol through to remove any dirt or foreign material from the line. Be sure to flare both ends to provide sound, leak-proof connections.

CAUTION

Double-flare the lines! Never single-flare a brake line!

When bending the tubing to fit the underbody contours, be careful not to kink or crack the line. Torque all hydraulic connections to 10–15 lbs.

Check the flexible brake hoses that connect the steel tubing to each wheel cylinder. Replace the hose if it shows any signs of softening, cracking, or other damage. When installing a new

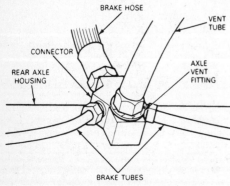

Brake hose junction

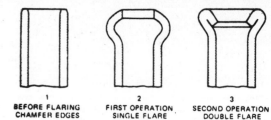

Brake pipe flaring sequence

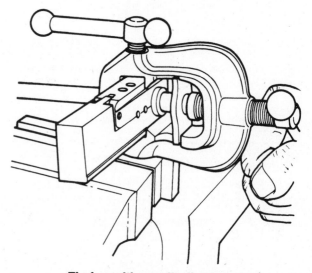

Flaring with a split die type tool

front brake hose, position the hose to avoid contact with other chassis parts. Place a new copper gasket over the hose fitting and thread the hose assembly into the front wheel cylinder. A new rear brake hose must be positioned clear of the exhaust pipe or shock absorber. Thread the hose into the rear brake tube connector. When installing either a new front or rear brake hose, engage the opposite end of the hose to the bracket on the frame. Install the horseshoe type retaining clip and connect the tube to the hose with the tube fitting nut.

Always bleed the system after hose or line replacement. Before bleeding, make sure that the master cylinder is topped up with high temperature, extra heavy duty fluid of at least SAE 70R3 (DOT 3) quality.

FLARING A BRAKE LINE

Using a Split-Die Type Flaring Tool

1. Using a tubing cutter, cut the required length of line.

2. Square the end with a file and chamfer the end.

3. Place the tube in the proper size die hole and position it so that it is flush with the die face. Lock the line with the wing nut.

4. The punches with most tools are marked to identify the sequence of flaring. Such marks are usually Op.1 and Op.2 or something similar.

5. Slide the Op.1 punch into position and tighten the screw to form a single flare.

6. Remove the punch and position the Op.2 punch. Tighten the screw to form the double flare.

7. Remove the punch and release the line from the die.

8. Inspect the finished flare for cracks or uneven flare form. If the flare is not perfect, cut it off and re-flare the end.

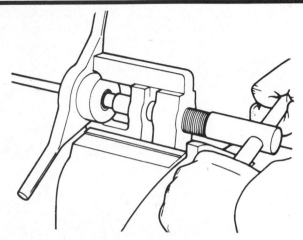

Flaring with a bar type tool

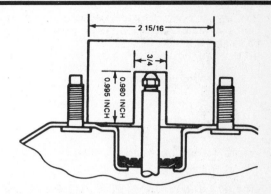

Booster pushrod gauge dimensions and adjustment

Using a Flaring Bar Type Tool

1. Using a tubing cutter, cut the required length of line.
2. Square the end with a file and chamfer the end.
3. Insert the tube into the proper size hole in the bar, until the end of the tube sticks out as far as the thickness of the adapter above the bar, or, depending on the tool, even with the bar face.
4. Fit the adapter onto the tube and slide the bar into the yoke. Lock the bar in position with the tube beneath the yoke screw.
5. Tighten the yoke screw and form the single flare.
6. Release the yoke screw and remove the adapter.
7. Install the second adapter and form the double flare.
8. Release the screw and remove the tube. Check the flare for cracks or uneven flaring. If the flare isn't perfect, cut it off and re-flare the line.

Power Booster

REMOVAL AND INSTALLATION

E-150 & E-250

NOTE: **On the E-150/250, make sure that the booster rubber reaction disc is properly installed if the master cylinder push rod is removed or accidentally pulled out. A dislodged disc may cause excessive pedal travel and/or extreme operation sensitivity. The disc is black compared to the silver colored valve plunger that will be exposed after the push rod and front seal is removed. The booster unit is serviced as an assembly and must be replaced if the reaction disc cannot be properly installed and aligned, or if it cannot be located within the unit itself.**

1. Disconnect the brake light switch wires.
2. Support the master cylinder from below, with a prop of some kind.
3. Loosen the clamp and remove the booster check valve hose.
4. Remove the master cylinder from the booster. Keep it supported. It will not be necessary to disconnect the brake lines.
5. Working inside the van below the instrument panel, disconnect the booster valve operating rod from the brake pedal assembly.
6. Remove the four bracket-to-dash panel attaching nuts.
7. Remove the booster and bracket assembly from the dash panel, sliding the valve operating rod out from the engine side of the dash panel.

To install:
8. Mount the booster and bracket assembly on the dash panel by sliding the valve operating rod in through the hole in the dash panel, and installing the attaching nuts. Torque the nuts to 18–25 ft. lbs.
9. Connect the manifold vacuum hose to the booster.
10. Install the master cylinder. Torque the nuts to 18–25 ft. lbs.
11. Connect the stop light switch wires.
12. Working inside the van below the instrument panel, connect the pushrod and stoplight switch.

E-250 HD
E-350

1. Disconnect the brake light switch wires.
2. Support the master cylinder from below, with a prop of some kind.
3. Loosen the clamp and remove the booster check valve hose.
4. Remove the wraparound clip from the booster inboard stud.
5. Remove the master cylinder from the booster. Keep it supported. It will not be necessary to disconnect the brake lines.
6. Working inside the van below the instrument panel, disconnect the booster valve operating rod from the brake pedal assembly.
7. Remove the four bracket-to-dash panel attaching nuts.
8. Remove the booster and bracket assembly from the dash panel, sliding the valve operating rod out from the engine side of the dash panel.

To install:
9. Mount the booster and bracket assembly on the dash panel by sliding the valve operating rod in through the hole in the dash panel, and installing the attaching nuts. Torque the nuts to 18–25 ft. lbs.
10. Connect the manifold vacuum hose to the booster.
11. Install the master cylinder. Torque the nuts to 18–25 ft. lbs.
12. Install the wraparound clip.
13. Connect the stop light switch wires.
14. Working inside the van below the instrument panel, connect the pushrod and stoplight switch.

BRAKE BOOSTER PUSHROD ADJUSTMENT

The pushrod has an adjustment screw to maintain the correct relationship between the booster control valve plunger and the master cylinder piston. If the plunger is too long it will prevent the master cylinder piston from completely releasing hydraulic pressure, causing the brakes to drag. If the plunger is too short it will cause excessive pedal travel and an undesirable clunk in the booster area. Remove the master cylinder for access to the booster pushrod.

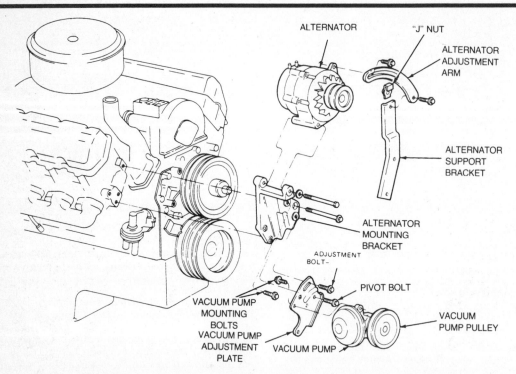

Brake booster vacuum pump installation for all diesel engines

To check the adjustment of the screw, fabricate a gauge (from cardboard, following the dimensions in the illustration) and place it against the master cylinder mounting surface of the booster body. Adjust the pushrod screw by turning it until the end of the screw just touches the inner edge of the slot in the gauge. Install the master cylinder and bleed the system.

Diesel Brake Booster Vacuum Pump

Unlike gasoline engines, diesel engines have little vacuum available to power brake booster systems. The diesel is thus equipped with a vacuum pump, which is driven by a single belt off of the alternator. This pump is located on the top right side of the engine.

Diesel vans are also equipped with a low vacuum indicator switch which actuates the BRAKE warning lamp when available vacuum is below a certain level. The switch senses vacuum through a fitting in the vacuum manifold that intercepts the vacuum flow from the pump. The low vacuum switch is mounted on the right side of the engine compartment, adjacent to the vacuum pump on E-250 and E-350 models.

NOTE: The vacuum pump cannot be disassembled. It is only serviced as a unit (the pulley is separate).

REMOVAL AND INSTALLATION

1. Remove the hose clamp and disconnect the pump from the hose on the manifold vacuum outlet fitting.
2. Loosen the vacuum pump adjustment bolt and the pivot bolt. Slide the pump downward and remove the drive belt from the pulley.
3. Remove the pivot and adjustment bolts and the bolts retaining the pump to the adjustment plate. Remove the vacuum pump and adjustment plate.
4. To install, install the pump-to-adjustment plate bolts and tighten to 11–18 ft. lbs. Position the pump and plate on the vacuum pump bracket and loosely install the pivot and adjustment bolts.

5. Connect the hose from the manifold vacuum outlet fitting to the pump and install the hose clamp.
6. Install the drive belt on the pulley. Place a ⅜ in. drive breaker bar or ratchet into the slot on the vacuum pump adjustment plate. Lift up on the assembly until the proper belt tension is obtained. Tighten the pivot and adjustment bolts to 11–18 ft. lbs.
7. Start the engine and make sure the brake system functions properly.

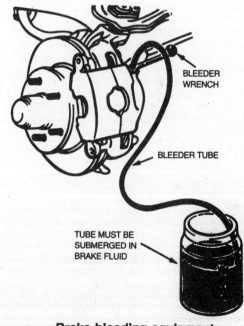

Brake bleeding equipment

NOTE: The BRAKE light will glow until brake vacuum builds up to the normal level.

Bleeding the Brakes

When any part of the hydraulic system has been disconnected for repair or replacement, air may get into the lines and cause spongy pedal action (because air can be compressed and brake fluid cannot). To correct this condition, it is necessary to bleed the hydraulic system after it has been properly connected to be sure that all air is expelled from the brake cylinders and lines.

When bleeding the brake system, bleed one brake cylinder at a time, beginning at the cylinder with the longest hydraulic line (farthest from the master cylinder) first. keep the master cylinder reservoir filled with brake fluid during bleeding operation. Never use brake fluid that has been drained from the hydraulic system, no matter how clean it is.

It will be necessary to centralize the pressure differential valve after a brake system failure has been corrected and the hydraulic system has been bled.

The primary and secondary hydraulic brake systems are individual systems and are bled separately. During the entire bleeding operation, do not allow the reservoir to run dry. Keep the master cylinder reservoirs filled with brake fluid.

WHEEL CYLINDERS AND CALIPERS

1. Clean all dirt from around the master cylinder fill cap, remove the cap and fill the master cylinder with brake fluid until the level is within ¼ in. (6mm) of the top of the edge of the reservoir.
2. Clean off the bleeder screws at the wheel cylinders and calipers.
3. Attach the length of rubber hose over the nozzle of the bleeder screw at the wheel to be done first. Place the other end of the hose in a glass jar, submerged in brake fluid.
4. Open the bleed screw valve ½–¾ turn.
5. Have an assistant slowly depress the brake pedal. Close the bleeder screw valve and tell your assistant to allow the brake pedal to return slowly. Continue this pumping action to force any air out of the system. When bubbles cease to appear at the end of the bleeder hose, close the bleed valve and remove the hose.

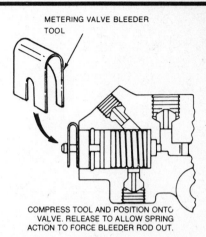

METERING VALVE BLEEDER TOOL

COMPRESS TOOL AND POSITION ONTO VALVE. RELEASE TO ALLOW SPRING ACTION TO FORCE BLEEDER ROD OUT.

A spring clip can be used to hold the pressure differential/metering/proportioning valve's bleeder valve out on E-150 disc brake systems

6. Check the master cylinder fluid level and add fluid accordingly. Do this after bleeding each wheel.
7. Repeat the bleeding operation at the remaining 3 wheels, ending with the one closest to the master cylinder. Fill the master cylinder reservoir.

MASTER CYLINDER

1. Fill the master cylinder reservoirs.
2. Place absorbant rags under the fluid lines at the master cylinder.
3. Have an assistant depress and hold the brake pedal.
4. With the pedal held down, slowly crack open the hydraulic line fitting, allowing the air to escape. Close the fitting and have the pedal released.
5. Repeat Steps 3 and 4 for each fitting until all the air is released.

FRONT DISC BRAKES

————— CAUTION —————

Brake shoes contain asbestos, which has been determined to be a cancer causing agent. Never clean the brake surfaces with compressed air! Avoid inhaling any dust from any brake surface! When cleaning brake surfaces, use a commercially available brake cleaning fluid.

There are two types of sliding calipers, the LD sliding caliper unit is operated by one piston per caliper. The caliper and steering arm are cast as one piece and combined with the spindle stem to form an integral spindle assembly.

The light duty system is used on all E-150 models.

The HD slider caliper unit contains two pistons on the same side of the rotor. The caliper slides on the support assembly and is retained by a key and spring.

The heavy duty system is used on all E-250, E-350 models.

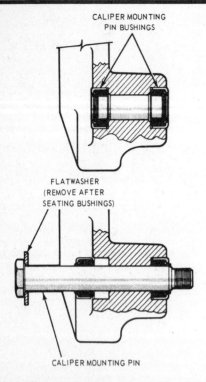

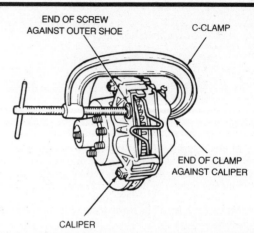

Bottoming the caliper piston on heavy duty calipers

Floating pin caliper mounting pin bushing installation

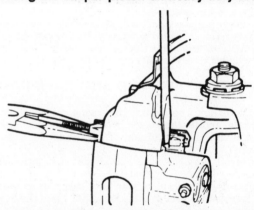

Compressing the pin tabs on light duty calipers

Disc Brake Pads

INSPECTION

Remove the brake pads as described below and measure the thickness of the lining. If the lining at any point on the pad assembly is less $1/16$ in. (1.5mm) for LD brakes or $1/32$ in. (0.8mm) for HD brakes, thick (above the backing plate or rivets), or there is evidence of the lining being contaminated by brake fluid or oil, replace the brake pad.

REMOVAL AND INSTALLATION

NOTE: NEVER REPLACE THE PADS ON ONE SIDE ONLY! ALWAYS REPLACE PADS ON BOTH WHEELS AS A SET!

LD Sliding Caliper (Single Piston)

1. To avoid overflowing of the master cylinder when the cali-

per pistons are pressed into the caliper cylinder bores, siphon or dip some brake fluid out of the larger reservoir.
2. Jack up the front of the van and remove the wheels.
3. Place an 8 in. (203mm) C-clamp on the caliper and tighten the clamp to bottom the caliper piston in the cylinder bore. Remove the C-clamp.
4. Clean the excess dirt from around the caliper pin tabs.
5. Drive the upper caliper pin inward until the tabs on the pin touch the spindle.
6. Insert a small prybar into the slot provided behind the pin tabs on the inboard side of the pin.
7. Using needlenosed pliers, compress the outboard end of the pin while, at the same time, prying with the prybar until the tabs slip into the groove in the spindle.

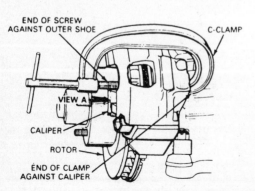

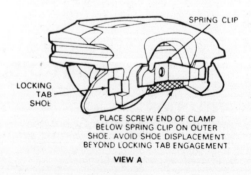

Bottoming the caliper piston on light duty calipers

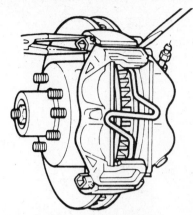

Compressing the pin tabs on heavy duty calipers

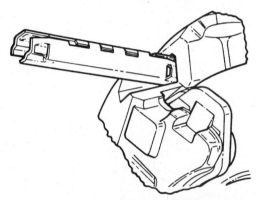

Caliper pin installation on light duty calipers

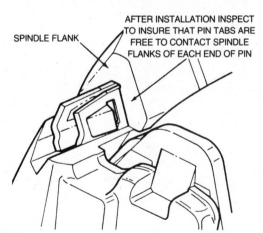

The caliper pin correctly installed on light duty calipers

8. Place the end of a $^7/_{16}$ in. (11mm) punch against the end of the caliper pin and drive the pin out of the caliper slide groove.
9. Repeat this procedure for the lower pin.
10. Lift the caliper off of the rotor.
11. Remove the brake pads and anti-rattle spring.

NOTE: Do not allow the caliper to hand by the brake hose.

12. Thoroughly clean the areas of the caliper and spindle as-

sembly which contact each other during the sliding action of the caliper.
13. Place a new anti-rattle clip on the lower end of the inboard shoe. Make sure that the tabs on the clip are positioned correctly and the loop-type spring is away from the rotor.
14. Place the lower end of the inner brake pad in the spindle assembly pad abutment, against the anti-rattle clip, and slide the upper end of the pad into position. Be sure that the clip is still in position.
15. Check and make sure that the caliper piston is fully bottomed in the cylinder bore. Use a large C-clamp to bottom the piston, if necessary.
16. Position the outer brake pad on the caliper, and press the pad tabs into place with your fingers. If the pad cannot be pressed into place by hand, use a C-clamp. Be careful not to damage the lining with the clamp. Bend the tabs to prevent rattling.
17. Position the caliper on the spindle assembly. Lightly lubricate the caliper sliding grooves with caliper pin grease.
18. Position the a new upper pin with the retention tabs next to the spindle groove.

NOTE: Don't use the bolt and nut with the new pin.

19. Carefully drive the pin, at the outboard end, inward until the tabs contact the spindle face.
20. Repeat the procedure for the lower pin.

WARNING: Don't drive the pins in too far, or it will be necessary to drive them back out until the tabs snap into place. The tabs on each end of the pin MUST be free to catch on the spindle sides!

21. Install the wheels.

HD Sliding Caliper (Two Piston)

1. To avoid overflowing of the master cylinder when the caliper pistons are pressed into the caliper cylinder bores, siphon or dip some brake fluid out of the larger reservoir.

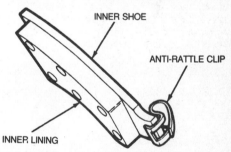

Installing the anti-rattle clip on the inner shoe on light duty calipers

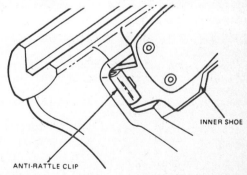

Installing the inner shoe and anti-rattle clip on light duty calipers

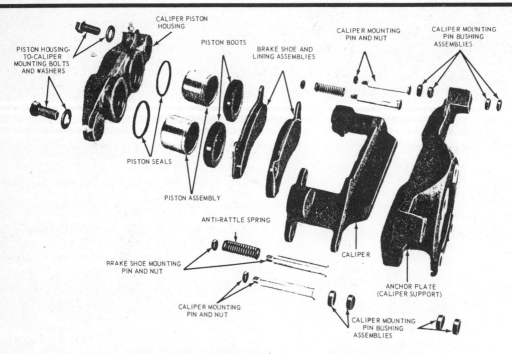

E-250, 350 floating caliper dual piston disc brake

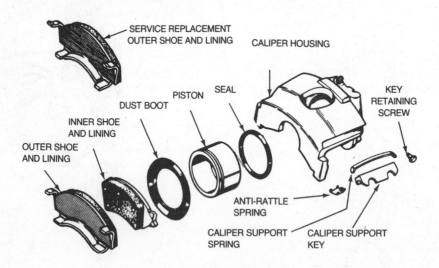

Light duty sliding caliper

2. Raise and support the front end on jackstands.

3. Jack up the front of the van and remove the wheels.

4. Place an 8 in. (203mm) C-clamp on the caliper and tighten the clamp to bottom the caliper pistons in the cylinder bores. Remove the C-clamp.

5. Clean the excess dirt from around the caliper pin tabs.

6. Drive the upper caliper pin inward until the tabs on the pin touch the spindle.

7. Insert a small prybar into the slot provided behind the pin tabs on the inboard side of the pin.

8. Using needlenosed pliers, compress the outboard end of the pin while, at the same time, prying with the prybar until the tabs slip into the groove in the spindle.

9. Place the end of a $7/16$ in. (11mm) punch against the end of the caliper pin and drive the pin out of the caliper slide groove.

10. Repeat this procedure for the lower pin.

11. Lift the caliper off of the rotor.

12. Remove the brake pads and anti-rattle spring.

NOTE: Do not allow the caliper to hand by the brake hose.

13. Thoroughly clean the areas of the caliper and spindle assembly which contact each other during the sliding action of the caliper.

14. Place a new anti-rattle clip on the lower end of the inboard shoe. Make sure that the tabs on the clip are positioned correctly and the loop-type spring is away from the rotor.

15. Place the lower end of the inner brake pad in the spindle assembly pad abutment, against the anti-rattle clip, and slide the upper end of the pad into position. Be sure that the clip is still in position.

16. Check and make sure that the caliper piston is fully bottomed in the cylinder bore. Use a large C-clamp to bottom the piston, if necessary.

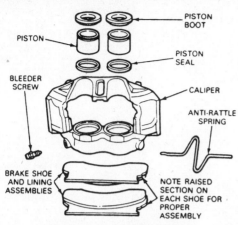

Heavy duty sliding caliper

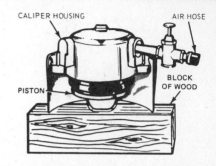

Removing piston using compressed air

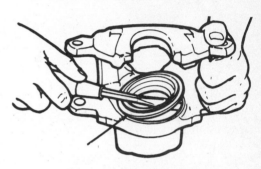

Removing the dust seal

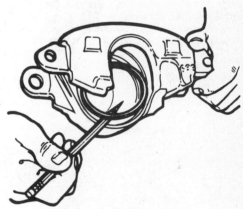

Removing the O-ring

17. Position the outer brake pad on the caliper, and press the pad tabs into place with your fingers. If the pad cannot be pressed into place by hand, use a C-clamp. Be careful not to damage the lining with the clamp. Bend the tabs to prevent rattling.

18. Position the caliper on the spindle assembly. Lightly lubricate the caliper sliding grooves with caliper pin grease.

19. Position the a new upper pin with the retention tabs next to the spindle groove.

NOTE: Don't use the bolt and nut with the new pin.

20. Carefully drive the pin, at the outboard end, inward until the tabs contact the spindle face.

21. Repeat the procedure for the lower pin.

WARNING: Don't drive the pins in too far, or it will be necessary to drive them back out until the tabs snap into place. The tabs on each end of the pin MUST be free to catch on the spindle sides!

22. Install the wheels.

Disc Brake Calipers

REMOVAL AND INSTALLATION

1. Raise and support the front end on jackstands.
2. Remove the wheels.
3. Remove the caliper and the brake pads as outlined under Disc Brake Pad Removal and Installation.
4. Disconnect the brake hose from the caliper.
5. When connecting the brake fluid hose to the caliper, it is recommended that a new copper washer be used at the connection of the brake hose and caliper.
6. Bleed the brake system and install the wheels. Lower the van.

OVERHAUL

LD Sliding Caliper (Single Piston)

1. Clean the outside of the caliper in alcohol after removing it from the vehicle and removing the brake pads.
2. Drain the caliper through the inlet port.
3. Roll some thick shop cloths or rags and place them between the piston and the outer legs of the caliper.
4. Apply compressed air to the caliper inlet port until the piston comes out of the caliper bore. Use low air pressure to avoid having the piston pop out too rapidly and possible causing injury.

5. If the piston becomes cocked in the cylinder bore and will not come out, remove the air pressure and tap the piston with a soft hammer to try and straighten it. Do not use a sharp tool or pry the piston out of the bore. Reapply the air pressure.
6. Remove the boot from the piston and seal from the caliper cylinder bore.
7. Clean the piston and caliper in alcohol.
8. Lubricate the piston seal with clean brake fluid, and position the seal in the groove in the cylinder bore.
9. Coat the outside of the piston and both of the beads of dust boot with clean brake fluid. Insert the piston through the dust boot until the boot is around the bottom (closed end) of the piston.
10. Hold the piston and dust boot directly above the caliper cylinder bore, and use your fingers to work the bead of dust boot into the groove near the top of the cylinder bore.
11. After the bead is seated in the groove, press straight down on the piston until it bottoms in the bore. Be careful not to cock the piston in the bore. Be careful not to cock the piston in the

Piston and dust boot

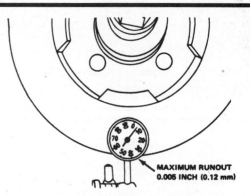

Checking the rotor lateral runout

MAXIMUM RUNOUT
0.005 INCH (0.12 mm)

bore. Use a C-clamp with a block of wood inserted between the clamp and the piston to bottom the piston, if necessary.

12. Install the brake pads and install the caliper. Bleed the brake hydraulic system and recenter the pressure differential valve. Do not drive the vehicle until a firm brake pedal is obtained.

HD Sliding Caliper (Two Piston)

1. Disconnect and plug the flexible brake hose.
2. Remove the front shoe and lining assemblies.
3. Drain the fluid from the cylinders.
4. Secure the caliper in a vise and place a block of wood between the caliper bridge and the cylinders.
5. Apply low pressure air to the brake hose inlet and the pistons will be forced out to the wood block.
6. Remove the block of wood and remove the pistons.
7. Remove the piston seals.
8. Lubricate the new piston seals with clean brake fluid and install them in the seal grooves in the cylinder bores.
9. Lubricate the retaining lips of the dust boots with clean brake fluid and install them in the grooves of the cylinder bores.
10. Apply a film of clean brake fluid to the pistons.
11. Insert the pistons into the dust boots and start them into the cylinders by hand until they are beyond the piston seals. Be careful not to dislodge or damage the piston seals.
12. Place a block of wood over one piston and press the piston into the cylinder. Be careful not to cock the piston in the cylinder bore.
13. Install the second piston in the same manner.
14. Install the brake shoe assemblies and anti-rattle clip in the caliper assembly.
15. Install the brake hose. Torque the fitting to 25 ft. lbs.
16. Install the caliper and bleed the system.

Brake Disc (Rotor)

REMOVAL AND INSTALLATION

1. Jack up the front of the van and support it with jackstands. Remove the front wheel.
2. Remove the caliper assembly and support it on the frame with a piece of wire without disconnecting the brake fluid hose.

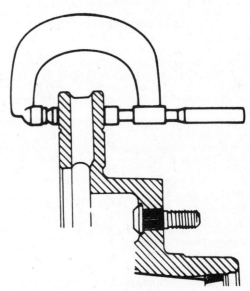

Measuring the rotor thickness with a micrometer

3. Remove the hub and rotor assembly as described in Section 1.
4. Install the rotor in the reverse order of removal, and adjust the wheel bearing as outlined in Section 1.

INSPECTION

If the rotor is deeply scarred or has shallow cracks, it may be refinished on a disc brake rotor lathe. Also, if the lateral run-out exceeds 0.010 in. (0.25mm) within a 6 in. (152mm) radius when measured with a dial indicator, with the stylus 1 in. (25mm) in from the edge of the rotor, the rotor should be refinished or replaced.

A maximum of 0.020 in. (0.5mm) of material may be removed equally from each friction surface of the rotor. If the damage cannot be corrected when the rotor has been machined to the minimum thickness shown on the rotor, it should be replaced.

The finished braking surfaces of the rotor must be parallel within 0.007 in. (0.18mm) and lateral run-out must not be more than 0.003 in. (0.076mm) on the inboard surface in a 5 in. (127mm) radius.

REAR DRUM BRAKES

Brake Drums

INSPECTION

Check that there are no cracks or chips in the braking surface. Excessive bluing indicates overheating and a replacement drum is needed. The drum can be machined to remove minor damage and to establish a rounded braking surface on a warped drum. Never exceed the maximum oversize of the drum when machining the braking surface. The maximum inside diameter is stamped on the rim of the drum.

REMOVAL AND INSTALLATION

E-150, and E-250 Light Duty

1. Raise the vehicle so that the wheel to be worked on is clear of the floor and install jackstands under the vehicle.
2. Remove the wheel. Remove the three retaining nuts and remove the brake drum. It may be necessary to back off the brake shoe adjustment in order to remove the brake drum. This is because the drum might be grooved or worn from being in service for an extended period of time.
3. Before installing a new brake drum, be sure to remove any protective coating with carburetor degreaser.
4. Install the brake drum in the reverse order of removal and adjust the brakes.

E-250HD, E-350

1. Raise the vehicle and install jackstands.
2. Remove the wheel. Loosen the rear brake shoe adjustment.
3. Remove the rear axle retaining bolts and lockwashers, axle shaft, and gasket.
4. Remove the wheel bearing locknut, lockwasher, and adjusting nut.
5. Remove the hub and drum assembly from the axle.
6. Remove the brake drum-to-hub retaining screws, bolts or bolts and nut. Remove the brake drum from the hub.
7. Place the drum on the hub and attach it to the hub with the attaching nuts and bolts.
8. Place the hub and drum assembly on the axle and start the adjusting nut.
9. Adjust the wheel bearing nut and install the wheel bearing lockwasher and locknut.
10. Install the axle shaft with a new gasket and install the axle retaining bolts and lockwashers.
11. Install the wheel and adjust the brake shoes. Remove the jackstands and lower the vehicle.

Brake Shoes

REMOVAL AND INSTALLATION

E-150, E-250 Light Duty

1. Raise and support the vehicle and remove the wheel and brake drum from the wheel to be worked on.

NOTE: If you have never replaced the brakes on a car before and you are not too familiar with the procedures

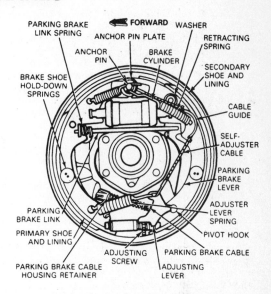

E-150 self-adjusting rear brakes

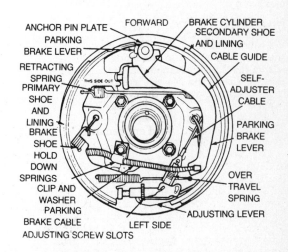

E-250/350 self-adjusting rear brakes

involved, only dissemble and assemble one side at a time, leaving the other side intact as a reference during reassembly.

2. Install a clamp over the ends of the wheel cylinder to prevent the pistons of the wheel cylinder from coming out, causing loss of fluid and much grief.
3. Contract the brake shoes by pulling the self-adjusting lever away from the starwheel adjustment screw and turn the starwheel up and back until the pivot nut is drawn onto the starwheel as far as it will come.

4. Pull the adjusting lever, cable and automatic adjuster spring down and toward the rear to unhook the pivot hook from the large hole in the secondary shoe web. Do not attempt to pry the pivot hook from the hole.
5. Remove the automatic adjuster spring and the adjusting lever.
6. Remove the secondary shoe-to-anchor spring with a brake

tool. (Brake tools are very common implements and are available to auto parts stores). Remove the primary shoe-to-anchor spring and unhook the cable anchor. Remove the anchor pin plate.

7. Remove the cable guide from the secondary shoe.

8. Remove the shoe holddown springs, shoes, adjusting screw, pivot nut, and socket. Note the color of each holddown spring for assembly. To remove the holddown springs, reach behind the brake backing plate and place one finger on the end of one of the brake holddown spring mounting pins. Using a pair of pliers, grasp the washer type retainer on top of the holddown spring that corresponds to the pin which you are holding. Push down on the pliers and turn them 90° to align the slot in the washer with the head on the spring mounting pin. Remove the spring and washer retainer and repeat this operation on the hold down spring on the other shoe.

9. Remove the parking brake link and spring. Disconnect the parking brake cable from the parking brake lever.

10. After removing the rear brake secondary shoe, disassemble the parking brake lever from the shoe by removing the retaining clip and spring washer.

11. Assemble the parking brake lever to the secondary shoe and secure it with the spring washer and retaining clip.

12. Apply a light coating of Lubriplate® at the points where the brake shoes contact the backing plate.

13. Position the brake shoes on the backing plate, and install the holddown spring pins, springs, and spring washer type retainers. On the rear brake, install the parking brake link, spring and washer. Connect the parking brake cable to the parking brake lever.

14. Install the anchor pin plate, and place the cable anchor over the anchor pin with the crimped side toward the backing plate.

15. Install the primary shoe-to-anchor spring with the brake tool.

16. Install the cable guide on the secondary shoe web with the flanged holes fitted into the hole in the secondary shoe web. Thread the cable around the cable guide groove.

17. Install the secondary shoe-to-anchor (long) spring. Be sure that the cable end is not cocked or binding on the anchor pin when installed. All of the parts should be flat on the anchor pin. Remove the wheel cylinder piston clamp.

18. Apply Lubriplate® to the threads and the socket end of the adjusting starwheel screw. Turn the adjusting screw into the adjusting pivot nut to the limit of the threads and then back off ½ turn.

NOTE: Interchanging the brake shoe adjusting screw assemblies from one side of the vehicle to the other would cause the brake shoes to retract rather than expand each time the automatic adjusting mechanism is operated. To prevent this, the socket end of the adjusting screw is stamped with an "R" or an "L" for "RIGHT" or "LEFT". The adjusting pivot nuts can be distinguished by the number of lines machined around the body of the nut; one line indicates left hand nut and two lines indicate a right hand nut.

19. Place the adjusting socket on the screw and install this assembly between the shoe ends with the adjusting screw nearest to the secondary shoe.

20. Place the cable hook into the hole in the adjusting lever from the backing plate side. The adjusting levers are stamped with an **R** (right) or a **L** (left) to indicate their installation on the right or left hand brake assembly.

21. Position the hooked end of the adjuster spring in the primary shoe web and connect the loop end of the spring to the adjuster lever hole.

22. Pull the adjuster lever, cable and automatic adjuster spring down toward the rear to engage the pivot hook in the large hole in the secondary shoe web.

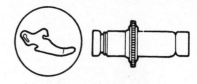

E-250-350 REAR; F-250, F-350

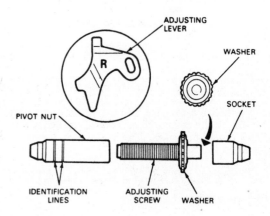

Adjusting screw and lever for self-adjusting brakes

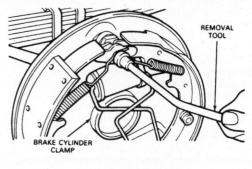

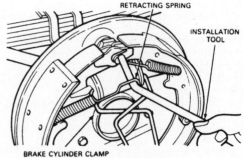

Brake spring replacement

23. After installation, check the action of the adjuster by pulling the section of the cable guide and the adjusting lever toward the secondary shoe web far enough to lift the lever past a tooth on the adjusting screw starwheel. The lever should snap into position behind the next tooth, and release of the cable should cause the adjuster spring to return the lever to its original position. This return action of the lever will turn the adjusting screw starwheel one tooth. The lever should contact the adjusting screw starwheel one tooth above the centerline of the adjusting screw.

If the automatic adjusting mechanism does not perform properly, check the following:

BOOT
2206

CUP
2201

CYLINDER
- 2261

CUP –
2201

BOOT –
2206

PISTON
2197

BLEEDER
SCREW –
2208

RETURN SPRING AND
CUP EXPANDER ASSY.
- 2204

PISTON
– 2197

Wheel cylinder

1. Check the cable and fittings. The cable ends should fill or extend slightly beyond the crimped section of the fittings. If this is not the case, replace the cable.

2. Check the cable guide for damage. The cable groove should be parallel to the shoe web, and the body of the guide should lie flat against the web. Replace the cable guide if this is not so.

3. Check the pivot hook on the lever. The hook surfaces should be square with the body on the lever for proper pivoting. Repair or replace the hook as necessary.

4. Make sure that the adjusting screw starwheel is properly seated in the notch in the shoe web.

E-250 HD, E-350

1. Raise and support the vehicle.

2. Remove the wheel and drum.

3. Remove the parking brake lever assembly retaining nut from behind the backing plate and remove the parking brake lever assembly.

4. Remove the adjusting cable assembly from the anchor pin, cable guide, and adjusting lever.

5. Remove the brake shoe retracting springs.

6. Remove the brake shoe holddown spring from each shoe.

7. Remove the brake shoes and adjusting screw assembly.

8. Disassemble the adjusting screw assembly.

9. Clean the ledge pads on the backing plate. Apply a light coat of Lubriplate® to the ledge pads (where the brake shoes rub the backing plate).

10. Apply Lubriplate® to the adjusting screw assembly and the holddown and retracting spring contacts on the brake shoes.

11. Install the upper retracting spring on the primary and secondary shoes and position the shoe assembly on the backing plate with the wheel cylinder pushrods in the shoe slots.

12. Install the brake shoe holddown springs.

13. Install the brake shoe adjustment screw assembly with the slot in the head
of the adjusting screw toward the primary shoe, lower retracting spring, adjusting lever spring, adjusting lever assembly, and

connect the adjusting cable to the adjusting lever. Position the cable in the cable guide and install the cable anchor fitting on the anchor pin.

14. Install the adjusting screw assemblies in the same locations from which they were removed. Interchanging the brake shoe adjusting screws from one side of the vehicle to the other will cause the brake shoes to retract rather than expand each time the automatic adjusting mechanism is operated. To prevent incorrect installation, the socket end of each adjusting screw is stamped with an **R** or an **L** to indicate their installation on the right or left side of the vehicle. The adjusting pivot nuts can be distinguished by the number of lines machined around the body of the nut. Two lines indicate a right hand nut; one line indicates a left hand nut.

15. Install the parking brake assembly in the anchor pin and secure with the retaining nut behind the backing plate.

16. Adjust the brakes before installing the brake drums and wheels. Install the brake drums and wheels.

17. Lower the vehicle and road test the brakes. New brakes may pull to one side or the other before they are seated. Continued pulling or erratic braking should not occur.

Wheel Cylinders

REMOVAL AND INSTALLATION

1. Remove the brake drum.

2. Remove the brake shoes.

3. Loosen the brake line at the wheel cylinder.

4. Remove the wheel cylinder attaching bolt and unscrew the cylinder from the brake line.

5. Installation is the reverse of removal.

OVERHAUL

Purchase a brake cylinder repair kit. Remove and disassemble the wheel cylinder. Follow the instructions in the kit. Never repair only one cylinder. Repair both at the same time.

PARKING BRAKE

NOTE: Before making any parking brake adjustment, make sure that the drum brakes are properly adjusted.

ADJUSTMENT

1. Raise and support the rear end on jackstands.

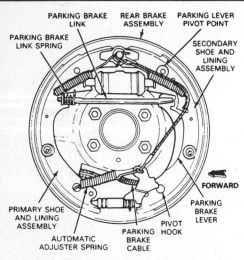

E-150 parking brake assembly

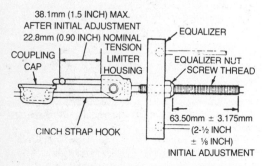

Parking brake cable tension limiter assembly

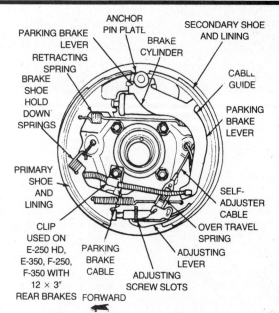

Rear brake shoes installed

REMOVAL AND INSTALLATION

Equalizer-to-Control Cable

1. Raise the vehicle on a hoist. Back off the equalizer nut and remove slug of front cable from the tension limiter.
2. Remove the parking brake cable from the retaining clips.
3. Lower the vehicle. Remove the forward ball end of the parking brake cable from the control assembly clevis.
4. Remove the cable and hair pin retainer from the control assembly.
5. Using a fish wire or cord attached to the control lever end of the cable, remove the cable from the vehicle.
6. Transfer the fish wire or cord to the new cable. Position the cable in the vehicle, routing the cable through the dash panel. Remove the fish wire and secure the cable to the control with the hair pin retainer.
7. Connect the forward ball end of the brake cable to the clevis of the control assembly and replace the hairpin clip around the conduit end fitting. Raise the vehicle on a hoist.
8. Route the cable and secure in place with retaining clips.
9. Connect the slug of the cable to the tension limiter connector. Adjust the parking brake cable at the equalizer.
10. Rotate both rear wheels to be sure that the parking brakes are not dragging.

Equalizer-to-Rear Wheel Cables

1. Raise the vehicle and remove the hub cap, wheel, tension limiter and brake drum. Remove the locknut on the threaded rod and disconnect the cable from the equalizer.
2. Compress the prongs that retain the cable housing to the frame bracket, and pull the cable and housing out of the bracket.
3. Working on the wheel side, compress the prongs on the cable retainer so they can pass through the hole in the brake backing plate. Draw the cable retainer out of the hole.
4. With the spring tension off the parking brake lever, lift the cable out of the slot in the lever, and remove the cable through the brake backing plate hole.
5. Pull the cable through the brake backing plate until the end of the cable is inserted over the slot in the parking brake lever. Pull the excess slack from the cable and insert the cable housing into the brake backing plate plate access hole until the retainer prongs expand.

2. The brake drums should be cold.
3. Make sure that the parking brake pedal is fully released.
4. While holding the tension equalizer, tighten the equalizer nut 6 full turns past its original position.
5. Fully depress the parking brake pedal. Using a cable tension gauge, check rear cable tension. Cable tension should be 350 lbs. minimum.
6. Fully release the parking brake. No drag should be noted at the wheels.
7. If drag is noted on E-250 and E-350 models, you'll have to remove the drums and adjust the clearance between the parking brake lever and cam plate. Clearance should be 0.015 in. (0.38mm). Clearance is adjusted at the parking brake equalizer adjusting nut.

If the tension limiter on the E-150 doesn't release the drag, the tension limiter will have to be replaced.

INITIAL ADJUSTMENT WHEN THE TENSION LIMITER HAS BEEN REPLACED

1. Raise and support the front end on jackstands.
2. Depress the parking brake pedal fully.
3. Hold the tension limiter, install the equalizer nut and tighten it to a point 2½ in. ± ⅛ in. (63.5mm ± 3mm) up the rod.
4. Check to make sure that the cinch strap has 1⅜ in. (35mm) remaining.

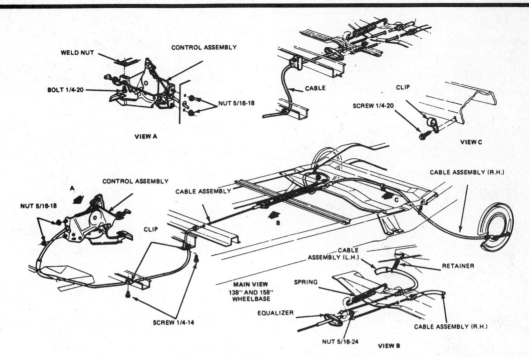

Pedal operated parking brake linkage

6. Insert the front end of the cable housing through the frame crossmember bracket until the prong expands. Insert the ball end of the cable into the key hole slots on the equalizer, rotate the equalizer 90 degrees and recouple the tension limiter threaded rod to the equalizer.

On vehicles with web ledge brakes, check the clearance between the parking brake operating lever and cam plate. The clearance should be 0.015 in. when the brakes are fully released.

7. Install the rear brake drum, wheel, and hub cap, and adjust the rear brake shoes.

8. Adjust the parking brake tension.

9. Rotate both rear wheels to be sure that the parking brakes are not dragging.

REAR ANTI-LOCK BRAKE SYSTEM (RABS)

Operation

The RABS system is found on all models.

The system constantly monitors rear wheel speed and, in the event of impending rear wheel lock-up in a sudden stop, regulates the brake fluid hydraulic pressure at the rear brakes to prevent total wheel lock-up, thus reducing the possibility of skidding.

Diagnosis and Service

Diagnosis is lengthy and complex and is best left to qualified service personnel.

Repair is limited to replacement of defective parts. No repairs to the parts are possible.

Computer Module

REMOVAL AND INSTALLATION

The module is located on the firewall just inboard of the master cylinder.

1. Disconnect the wiring harness.

2. Remove the 2 attaching screws and lift out the module.

3. Installation is the reverse of removal.

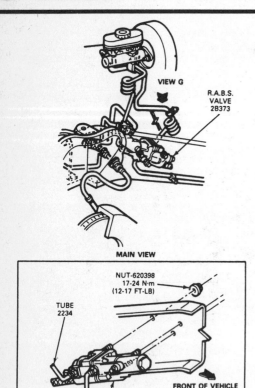

MAIN VIEW

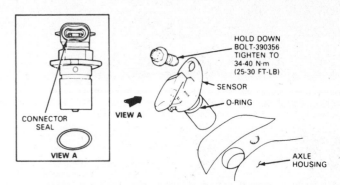

Rear anti-lock braking system sensor

Rear anti-lock braking system valve

RABS Valve

REMOVAL AND INSTALLATION

The valve is located in the brake lines, below the master cylinder.

1. Disconnect the brake lines from the valve and plug the lines.
2. Disconnect the wiring harness at the valve.
3. Remove the 3 nuts retaining the valve to the frame rail and lift out the valve.
4. Installation is the reverse of removal. Don't overtighten the brake lines. Bleed the brakes.

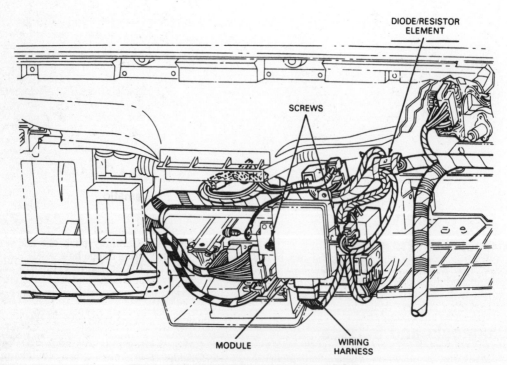

Rear anti-lock braking system module

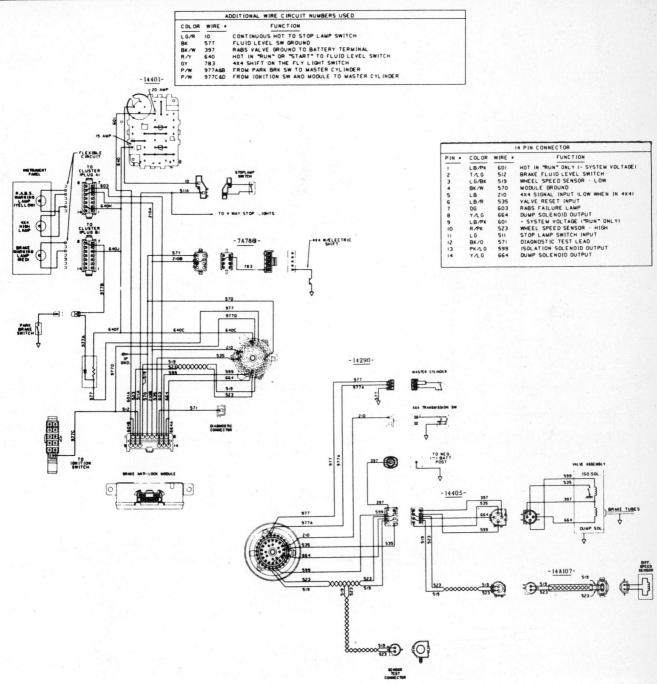

ADDITIONAL WIRE CIRCUIT NUMBERS USED		
COLOR	WIRE #	FUNCTION
LG/R	10	CONTINUOUS HOT TO STOP LAMP SWITCH
BK	57T	FLUID LEVEL SW GROUND
BK/W	397	RABS VALVE GROUND TO BATTERY TERMINAL
R/Y	640	HOT IN "RUN" OR "START" TO FLUID LEVEL SWITCH
GY	783	4X4 SHIFT ON THE FLY LIGHT SWITCH
P/W	977A&B	FROM PARK BRK SW TO MASTER CYLINDER
P/W	977C&D	FROM IGNITION SW AND MODULE TO MASTER CYLINDER

14 PIN CONNECTOR			
PIN #	COLOR	WIRE #	FUNCTION
1	LB/PK	601	HOT IN "RUN" ONLY (+ SYSTEM VOLTAGE)
2	T/LG	512	BRAKE FLUID LEVEL SWITCH
3	LG/BK	519	WHEEL SPEED SENSOR - LOW
4	BK/W	570	MODULE GROUND
5	LB	210	4X4 SIGNAL INPUT (LOW WHEN IN 4X4)
6	LB/R	535	VALVE RESET INPUT
7	DG	603	RABS FAILURE LAMP
8	Y/LG	664	DUMP SOLENOID OUTPUT
9	LB/PK	601	+ SYSTEM VOLTAGE ("RUN" ONLY)
10	R/PK	523	WHEEL SPEED SENSOR - HIGH
11	LG	511	STOP LAMP SWITCH INPUT
12	BK/O	571	DIAGNOSTIC TEST LEAD
13	PK/LG	599	ISOLATION SOLENOID OUTPUT
14	Y/LG	664	DUMP SOLENOID OUTPUT

1989 rear anti-lock braking system schematic

RABS Sensor

REMOVAL AND INSTALLATION

The sensor is located on the rear axle housing.
1. Remove the sensor holddown bolt.
2. Remove the sensor.
3. Carefully clean the axle surface to keep dirt from entering the housing.
4. If a new sensor is being installed, lubricate the O-ring with clean engine oil. Carefully push the sensor into the housing aligning the mounting flange hole with the threaded hole in the housing. Torque the holddown bolt to 30 ft. lbs.

If the old sensor is being installed, clean it thoroughly and install a new O-ring coated with clean engine oil.

Exciter Ring

The ring is located on the differential case inside the axle housing. Once it is pressed of the case it cannot be reused. This job should be left to a qualified service technician.

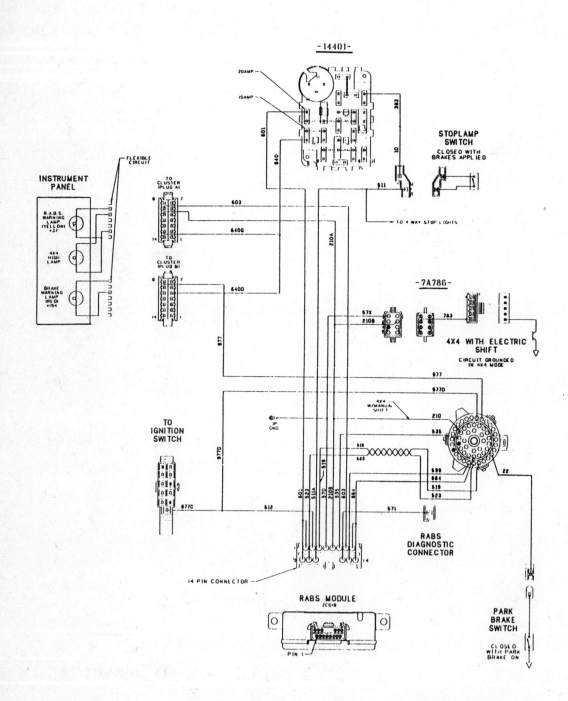

1990-91 rear wheel anti-lock braking system wiring diagram

ADDITIONAL WIRE CIRCUIT NUMBERS USED		
COLOR	WIRE NO.	FUNCTION
LG/R	10	CONTINUOUS HOT (STOP LAMP SWITCH)
R/LG	16	HOT IN RUN OR START
LB/BK	22	PARKING BRAKE SWITCH
BK	57T	FLUID LEVEL SW GROUND
R/W	383	STOP LIGHT SWITCH AT FUSE BOX
BK/W	397	RABS VALVE GROUND TO BATTERY TERMINAL
R/Y	640	HOT IN "RUN" OR "START"
GY	783	4X4 SHIFT ON THE FLY LIGHT SWITCH
P/W	977A&B	FROM PARK SWITCH TO MASTER CYLINDER
P/W	977C&D	FROM IG SW AND MODULE TO MASTER CYLINDER

14 PIN CONNECTOR			
PIN NO.	COLOR	WIRE NO.	FUNCTION
1	LB/PK	601	HOT IN "RUN" ONLY (+ SYSTEM VOLTAGE)
2	T/LG	512	BRAKE FLUID LEVEL SWITCH
3	LG/BK	519	WHEEL SPEED SENSOR - LOW
4	BK/W	570	MODULE GROUND
5	LB	210	4X4 SIGNAL INPUT (LOW WHEN IN 4X4)
6	LB/R	535	VALVE RESET INPUT
7	DG	603	RABS FAILURE LAMP
8	Y/LG	664	DUMP SOLENOID OUTPUT
9	LB/PK	601	+ SYSTEM VOLTAGE ("RUN" ONLY)
10	R/PK	523	WHEEL SPEED SENSOR HIGH
11	LG	511	STOP LAMP SWITCH INPUT
12	BK/O	571	DIAGNOSTIC TEST LEAD
13	PK/LG	599	ISOLATION SOLENOID OUTPUT
14	Y/LG	664	DUMP SOLENOID OUTPUT

NOTE : ALL VIEWS LOOKING INTO CONNECTOR

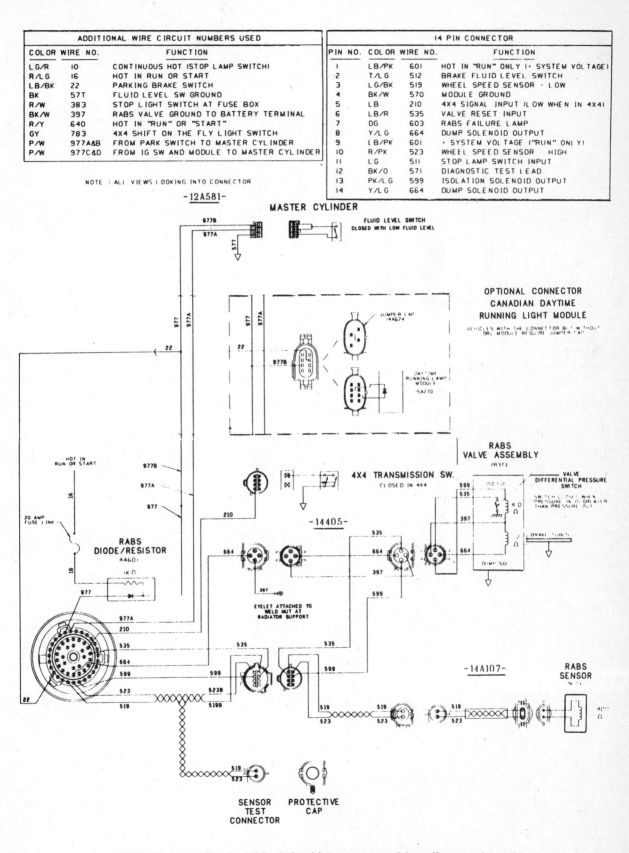

1990-91 rear wheel anti-lock braking system wiring diagram (cont.)

ADDITIONAL WIRE CIRCUIT NUMBERS USED		
COLOR	WIRE NO.	FUNCTION
LG/R	10	CONTINUOUS HOT TO STOP LAMP SWITCH
BK	57T	FLUID LEVEL SW GROUND
BK/W	397	RABS VALVE GROUND TO BATTERY TERMINAL
R/Y	640	HOT IN "RUN" OR "START" TO FLUID LEVEL SWITCH
P/W	977A&B	FROM PARK BRK SW TO MASTER CYLINDER
P/W	977C&D	FROM IGNITION SW AND MODULE TO MASTER CYLINDER
P/Y	128	BRAKE WARNING LAMP
LG/Y	547	PARK BRAKE SWITCH

NOTE: ALL VIEWS LOOKING INTO CONNECTOR

14 PIN CONNECTOR				OPER. CURRENT		OPER. VOLTAGE	
PIN NO.	COLOR	WIRE NO.	FUNCTION	MIN	MAX	MIN	MAX
1	LB/PK	601	HOT IN "RUN" ONLY (+ SYS. VOLTAGE)	0.1A	16A	11V	18V
2	T/LO	512	BRAKE FLUID LEVEL SWITCH	0	270mA	11V	18V
3	LO/BK	519	WHEEL SPEED SENSOR - LOW	0	10mA	-150V	-150V
4	BK/W	570	MODULE GROUND	0	620mA	0	1V
5			NO CONNECTION (4X4 ONLY)				
6	LB/R	535	VALVE RESET INPUT	0	10mA	0	18V
7	DG	603	RABS FAILURE LAMP	0	350mA	11V	18V
8	Y/LO	664	DUMP SOLENOID OUTPUT	0	13A	9V	18V
9	LB/PK	601	+ SYSTEM VOLTAGE ("RUN" ONLY)	0.1A	16A	11V	18V
10	R/PK	523	WHEEL SPEED SENSOR - HIGH	0	10mA	-150V	-150V
11	LO	511	STOP LAMP SWITCH INPUT	0	10mA	0	18V
12	BK/O	57I	DIAGNOSTIC TEST LEAD	0	10mA	0	18V
13	PK/LG	599	ISOLATION SOLENOID OUTPUT	0	3.6A	9V	18V
14	Y/LO	664	DUMP SOLENOID OUTPUT	0	13A	9V	18V
RABS MODULE PIN #5 CAN BE BLANK OR AT BATTERY - VOLTAGE IN 4X2 MODE							

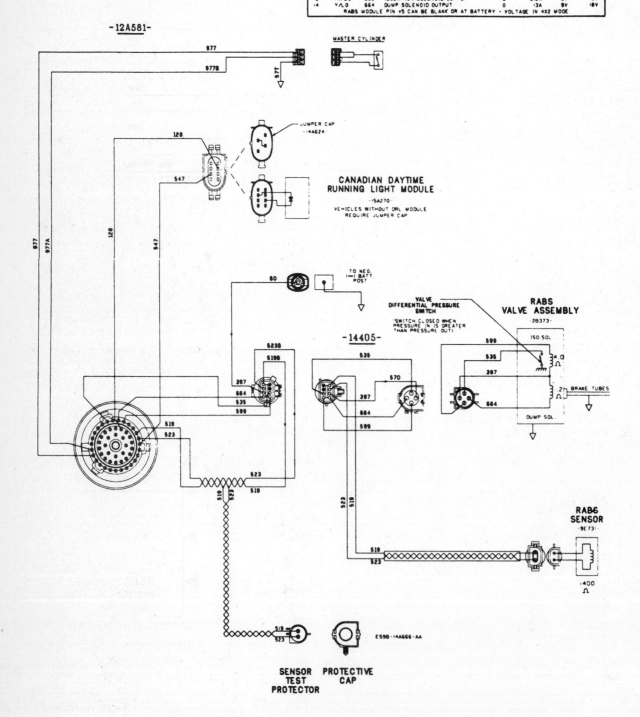

Diagnosis Charts

BRAKE AND ANTILOCK WARNING LAMPS CONDITION CHART

Condition	Action to Take
Yellow ANTILOCK Light Off and Does Not Self-Check	See Test A
Yellow ANTILOCK Light Off, and ANTILOCK Light Does Self-Check, Red BRAKE Light On	See Test B
Yellow ANTILOCK Light On and Red BRAKE Light On	See Test C
Yellow ANTILOCK Light On, Red BRAKE Light Off	See Test D
Yellow ANTILOCK Light Flashing, Red BRAKE Light Off	See Test E
Rear Wheels Lock with Hard Stops — Both Lamps Functioning Properly (Light Self-Checks are OK and Lights are OFF)	See Test F
Yellow ANTILOCK Light Self Checks, Red Brake Light Does Not Self Check	See Test G
Flashout Code is Known	See Flashout Codes Chart

CAUTION: WHEN CHECKING RESISTANCE IN THE ANTILOCK BRAKE SYSTEM, ALWAYS DISCONNECT THE BATTERY. IMPROPER RESISTANCE READINGS WILL OCCUR WITH THE VEHICLE BATTERY CONNECTED.

Yellow Anti-Lock Light Self Checks, Red Brake Light Does Not Self Check

Test G

TEST STEP	RESULT ▶	ACTION TO TAKE
G1 MASTER CYLINDER CONNECTOR		
• Check connector on master cylinder brake fluid level switch.	Connector is fully plugged in ▶	GO to Test **G2**.
	Connector is not fully plugged in ▶	CONNECT connector to master cylinder.
G2 RED BRAKE WARNING LIGHT		
• Apply parking brake to see if red brake warning light lights.	Red warning light lights ▶	GO to Test **D6**.
	Red warning light does not light ▶	REPAIR warning lamp circuit. CHECK for open bulb.

<table>
<tr><td colspan="2">Yellow ANTILOCK Light Off and Does Not Self-Check</td><td>Test A</td></tr>
</table>

TEST STEP	RESULT ▶	ACTION TO TAKE
A1 MODULE HARNESS CONNECTOR ● Check to make sure module harness is fully plugged into computer module.	Harness is fully plugged in ▶ Harness is not fully plugged in ▶	GO to Test **A2**. CONNECT harness to module.
A2 COMPUTER MODULE GROUND ● Check for good computer module ground: 1. Disconnect Battery 2. Remove harness connector from module. 3. Set ohmmeter on the 200 ohm scale. 4. Check for resistance between harness connector pin 4 and chassis ground PIN NO 4 MODULE HARNESS CONNECTOR — PIN VIEW **CAUTION: WHEN CHECKING RESISTANCE IN THE ANTILOCK SYSTEM, ALWAYS DISCONNECT THE POSITIVE (+) TERMINAL OF THE BATTERY. IMPROPER RESISTANCE MAY OCCUR WITH THE VEHICLE BATTERY CONNECTED.**	Resistance less than 1 ohm ▶ Resistance 1 ohm or greater ▶	GO to Test **A3**. CHECK for open in module ground wire. CHECK for loose, dirty or broken connector pins.
A3 ANTILOCK LIGHT POWER ● Check for voltage to ANTILOCK light: 1. Reconnect the battery. 2. Set voltmeter on 20 VDC scale position. 3. Turn ignition to the on position. 4. Check voltage between harness connector pin 7 and a known good chassis ground. PIN NO 7 MODULE HARNESS CONNECTOR — PIN VIEW	Voltage greater than 9V ▶ Voltage less than 9V ▶	REPLACE Module. GO to Test **A4**

Yellow ANTILOCK Light Off and Does Not Self-Check (Cont'd)

TEST STEP	RESULT ▶	ACTION TO TAKE
A4 RABS 15 AMP LIGHT FUSE		
• Remove and inspect RABS 15 amp light fuse.	Fuse is OK ▶	REPLACE fuse and GO to Test **A5**.
	Fuse is blown ▶	CHECK for short to ground between fuse panel and warning lamps. REPAIR short and replace 15 amp fuse.
A5 POWER TO RABS LIGHT FUSE		
• Check for voltage to fuse. 1. Set voltmeter to 20 VDC scale. 2. Turn ignition to the on position. 3. Check voltage between panel fuse connector and known good chassis ground.	Voltage greater than 9V ▶	GO to Test **A6**.
	Voltage less than 9V ▶	REPAIR fuse panel or vehicle electrical system.
A6 RABS LIGHT BULB		
• Check RABS light bulb.	Bulb is OK ▶	REPAIR open between RABS light fuse and pin 7 of the module wiring harness connector.
	Bulb is not OK ▶	REPLACE bulb.

<table>
<tr><td colspan="2">Red BRAKE Light On, Yellow ANTILOCK Light Off, and ANTILOCK Light Does Self-Check</td><td>Test B</td></tr>
</table>

TEST STEP	RESULT ▶	ACTION TO TAKE
B1 PARKING BRAKE • Check parking brake application: 1. Turn ignition key to the on position. 2. Check the parking brake pedal and release if applied.	BRAKE light goes off ▶ BRAKE light stays on ▶	PERFORM road test. If lockup occurs GO to Test **B2**. GO to Test **B2**.
B2 PARKING BRAKE SWITCH • Check parking brake switch: 1. Disconnect the parking brake switch connector.	BRAKE light goes off ▶ BRAKE light remains on ▶	ADJUST parking brake or REPLACE parking brake switch. Diesel vehicles GO to Test **B3**. Gas vehicles GO to Test **B4**.
B3 DIESEL LOW VACUUM SWITCH • Check for low brake vacuum: 1. Disconnect vacuum warning switch connector.	BRAKE light goes off ▶ BRAKE light stays on ▶	REFER to vacuum pump GO to Test **B4**.
B4 MODULE AND WIRING • Remove module harness connector from module.	BRAKE light goes off ▶ If BRAKE light remains on ▶	REPLACE the computer module. CHECK for short to ground in wiring from BRAKE light to the RABS diode/resistor.

Yellow ANTILOCK Light On and Red BRAKE Light On

TEST STEP	RESULT ▶	ACTION TO TAKE
C1 LOW BRAKE FLUID		
• Check the brake fluid level at the master cylinder reservoir.	Brake fluid level OK ▶	GO to Test **C2**.
	Brake fluid level low ▶	CHECK for fluid leaks in vehicle brake system and repair as required. Fill master cylinder to required level.
C2 MASTER CYLINDER FLOAT		
• Check master cylinder float for buoyancy: 1. Remove cap from master cylinder reservoir. 2. Using a clean steel implement, push down on float in reservoir.	Float moves down ▶	GO to Test **C3**.
	Float does not move down (sits at the bottom of the reservoir) ▶	REPLACE master cylinder reservoir.
C3 DIODE/RESISTOR ELEMENT		
• Check for proper functioning of the diode/resistor element. 1. Turn ignition key to the on position. 2. Check parking brake and release if applied.	Both the ANTILOCK and BRAKE warning lamps go off ▶	REPLACE RABS diode/resistor element.
	Both the ANTILOCK and BRAKE warning lamps stay on ▶	GO to Test **C4**.
C4 DIODE/RESISTOR ELEMENT CONTINUED		
• Continue to check for proper functioning of the diode/resistor element. 1. Remove the parking brake switch and the diesel low vacuum switch, if so equipped.	Both the ANTILOCK and BRAKE warning lamps go off ▶	REPLACE RABS diode/resistor element.
	Both the ANTILOCK and BRAKE warning lamps stay on ▶	GO to Test **C5**.

Yellow ANTILOCK Light On and Red BRAKE Light On — Cont'd | Test C

TEST STEP	RESULT	▶	ACTION TO TAKE
C5 ANTILOCK VALVE SWITCH			
• Obtain the flashout code as described in Diagnosis and Testing in this Section.	Flashout code is obtained	▶	REFER to Flashout Codes Charts in this Section.
	ANTILOCK and BRAKE warning lamps stay on steady	▶	GO to Test **C6**.
C6 MASTER CYLINDER SWITCH			
• Check for proper functioning of the master cylinder fluid level indicator switch: 1. Remove the connector from the master cylinder. 2. Connect a jumper wire between the two purple/white wires in the connector. 3. Turn the ignition key to the on position.	ANTILOCK and BRAKE warning lamps stay on	▶	GO to Test **C7**.
	ANTILOCK and BRAKE warning lamps go off	▶	REPLACE the master cylinder reservoir.
C7 BRAKE LIGHT WIRING			
• Check for shorts in brake light wiring. 1. Disconnect module harness connector from module. 2. Turn ignition key to the on position.	ANTILOCK light goes off and BRAKE light stays on	▶	CHECK for short to ground in the 977 circuit. REFER to wiring diagram in this Section.
	Both ANTILOCK and BRAKE warning lamps go off	▶	REPLACE module.

Yellow ANTILOCK Light On, Red BRAKE Light Off		Test D

TEST STEP	RESULT ▶	ACTION TO TAKE
D1 OBTAIN THE FLASHOUT CODE • Obtain the flashout code as described in Diagnosis and Testing in this Section. RABS DIAGNOSTIC CONNECTOR — PIN VIEW	Flashout code cannot ▶ be obtained Flashout code is ▶ obtained	GO to Test **D2**. Refer to the Flashout Code Charts in this Section.
D2 MASTER CYLINDER CONNECTOR • Make sure master cylinder connector is fully plugged in.	Master cylinder ▶ connector is not fully plugged in Master cylinder ▶ connector is plugged in	PLUG in the master cylinder connector. GO to Test **D3**.
D3 RABS 20 AMP FUSE • Remove and inspect the RABS 20 amp fuse.	Fuse is OK ▶ Fuse is blown ▶	REPLACE Fuse. GO to Test **D4**. Short to ground between the fuse panel and the module wiring harness connector. REPAIR short in the 601 circuit and REPLACE the 20 amp. fuse. REFER to the Wiring Diagrams in this Section.
D4 SHORTS IN MODULE HARNESS CONNECTOR WIRING • Check wiring for short to ground: 1. Turn ignition switch to the on position. 2. Remove the module harness connector from the module. 3. Observe the REAR ANTILOCK light.	Light goes off ▶ Light remains on ▶	GO to Test **D5**. CHECK for a short to ground in the 603 Circuit. REFER to Wiring Diagram in this Section.

9 BRAKES

Yellow ANTILOCK Light On, Red BRAKE Light Off (Cont'd)	Test D

TEST STEP	RESULT ▶	ACTION TO TAKE
D5 POWER TO THE MODULE • Check for an open in the circuit supplying power to the module: 1. Set the voltmeter on the 20 VDC scale. 2. Turn the ignition switch to the on position. 3. Measure the voltage between pin 1 (or pin 9) and chassis ground. PIN NO. 9 14 13 12 11 10 9 8 7 6 5 4 3 2 1 MODULE HARNESS CONNECTOR — PIN VIEW PIN NO. 1	Voltage less than 9V. ▶ Voltage greater than 9V. ▶	REPAIR the open in the 601 circuit or power to the fuse panel. See Wiring Diagram. GO to Test **D6**.
D6 VOLTAGE AT THE FLUID LEVEL CIRCUIT • Check the voltage from the fluid level switch circuit: 1. Set the voltmeter on the 20 VDC Scale. 2. Turn the ignition switch to the on position. 3. Measure the voltage between pin 2 and chassis ground. PIN NO. 2 14 13 12 11 10 9 8 7 6 5 4 3 2 1 MODULE HARNESS CONNECTOR — PIN VIEW	Voltage less than 8V. ▶ Voltage greater than 8V. ▶	GO to Test **D7**. GO to Test **D8**.
D7 FLUID LEVEL SENSOR AND WIRING • Check for voltage at the fluid level sensor: 1. Set voltmeter on the 20 VDC scale. 2. Turn the ignition switch to the on position. 3. Measure the voltage at each of the purple white wires at the back of the master cylinder fluid level switch connector without disconnecting the connector. PURPLE WHITE WIRES MASTER CYLINDER FLUID LEVEL SWITCH CONNECTOR	Voltage greater than 8V at both wires. ▶ Voltage less than 8V at both wires. ▶ Voltage greater than 8V at one wire and less than 8V at the other wire. ▶	CHECK for open in 977 circuit. REPLACE diode resistor element or open in 640 circuit. CHANGE the master cylinder reservoir.

Yellow ANTILOCK Light On, Red BRAKE Light Off (Cont'd)	Test D

TEST STEP	RESULT ▶	ACTION TO TAKE
D8 GROUNDED DIAGNOSTIC LEAD ● Check the voltage at the diagnostic lead. 1. Reconnect the module harness connector. 2. Set the voltmeter on the 20 VDC scale. 3. Turn the ignition to the on position. 4. Measure the voltage between the diagnostic lead and chassis ground. **RABS DIAGNOSTIC CONNECTOR PIN VIEW**	Voltage is less than 1V ▶ Voltage is greater than 1V ▶	CHECK for a short in the 571 diagnostic circuit. If no short is found, GO to Test **D9**. GO to Test **D9**.
D9 COMPUTER MODULE ● Replace computer module and retest.		

Yellow ANTILOCK Light Flashing, Red BRAKE Light Off	Test E

TEST STEP	RESULT ▶	ACTION TO TAKE
E1 INTERMITTENT POWER TO MODULE • Check for intermittent open in the 601 circuit, power to module. 1. Remove the module harness connector from the module. 2. Set the voltmeter on the 20 VDC scale. 3. Turn the ignition to the on position. 4. Shake the instrument panel harness. Check for battery voltage between pin 1 (or pin 9) and chassis ground. PIN 9 14 13 12 11 10 9 8 7 6 5 4 3 2 1 PIN NO. 1 **MODULE HARNESS CONNECTOR — PIN VIEW**	Voltage is steady and greater than 9V ▶ Voltage is intermittent or less than 9V ▶	GO to Test **E2**. REPAIR break in the 601 circuit. REFER to Wiring Diagram in this Section.
E2 GROUNDED DIAGNOSTIC LEAD • Check for an intermittent ground to chassis in the diagnostic lead circuit: 1. Turn the ignition switch off. 2. Disconnect the battery. 3. Set the ohmmeter on the 200K ohm scale. 4. Shake the instrument panel harness and check the resistance between pin 12 and chassis ground. PIN NO. 12 14 13 12 11 10 9 8 7 6 5 4 3 2 1 **MODULE HARNESS CONNECTOR — PIN VIEW**	Resistance is steady and greater than 100K ohms ▶ Resistance is below 100K ohms or fluctuates ▶	GO to Test **E3**. REPAIR short in the 571 circuit. REFER to Wiring Diagram in this Section.

	TEST STEP	RESULT ▶	ACTION TO TAKE
E3	FAULTY MODULE GROUND		
	• Check for intermittent or poor module ground: 1. Disconnect the battery. 2. Set the voltmeter on the 200 ohm scale. 3. Shake the instrument panel harness and check the resistance between pin 4 of the module harness connector and chassis ground.	Resistance is less than 1 ohm and steady ▶	REPLACE Module.
		Resistance is greater than 1 ohm or fluctuates ▶	REPAIR poor ground in the 570 circuit. REFER to Wiring Diagram in this Section.

Yellow ANTILOCK Light Flashing, Red BRAKE Light Off — Cont'd

Test E

PIN NO. 4

14 13 12   11 10 9
8 7 6 5 4 3 2 1

MODULE HARNESS CONNECTOR — PIN VIEW

Rear Wheels Lock with Hard Stops — Both Lamps Functioning Properly		Test F

TEST STEP	RESULT ▶	ACTION TO TAKE
F1 STOPLAMPS ● Check for stoplamp operation: 1. Apply the service brakes and observe the rear brakelamps.	Rear stoplamps not illuminated ▶ Rear stoplamps OK ▶	REPAIR the stoplamp circuit. GO to Test **F2**.
F2 VEHICLE ROAD TEST ● Perform a low speed vehicle road test: 1. At approximately 10 mph apply the service brakes in an attempt to lock all four wheels while observing the left rear wheel in the side mirror.	Rear wheels lock ▶ Rear wheels do not lock ▶	GO to Test **F3**. The system is now functioning OK. Consider a possible intermittent wiring problem or possibly a problem which only shows up during driving. REFER to Flashout Code 6 in this Section.

F3 WIRING FROM MODULE TO BRAKE SWITCH
 	
● Check for an open between the brake switch and the module:
  1. Turn the ignition off.
  2. Set the voltmeter on the 20 VDC scale.
  3. Remove the module harness connector.
  4. Measure the voltage between pin 11 and chassis ground while stepping on the brake pedal.
 	
PIN NO. 11
 	
14 13 12 11 10 9
8 7 6 5 4 3 2 1
 	
MODULE HARNESS CONNECTOR — PIN VIEW
	Voltage is less than 9V ▶
	
	Voltage is 9V or more ▶
		REPAIR the open in the 511 circuit.
		
		GO to Test **F4**.

F4 EXCITOR RING INSPECTION
 	
● Remove sensor from carrier and check for:
  1. Presence of the excitor ring
  2. Condition of the teeth.
	Ring is present with the teeth intact ▶
	
	Ring is not present or the teeth are damaged ▶
		REINSTALL the sensor and GO to Test **F5**.
		
		REPAIR axle.

Rear Wheels Lock with Hard Stops — Both Lamps Functioning Properly (Continued)

TEST STEP	RESULT ▶	ACTION TO TAKE
F5 SENSOR OUTPUT		
• Check for low sensor signal output: 1. Set the voltmeter on the 2000 mV AC scale. 2. Position the vehicle on the hoist and raise the rear wheels off the ground. 3. Remove the cap from the sensor test connector and connect the voltmeter across the connector leads. 4. Start the engine and turn the rear wheels at 5 mph. 5. Measure the voltage output of the sensor. CONNECTOR PINS **SENSOR TEST CONNECTOR – PIN VIEW**	Voltage is 650 mV (RMS) or greater ▶ Voltage is less than 650 mV (RMS) ▶	REINSTALL the sensor test connector cap and GO to Test **F7**. REPLACE the sensor, RETEST, and REINSTALL the sensor test connector cap. If the voltage is still low, GO to Test **F6**.
F6 SENSOR GAP		
• Determine the sensor gap: 1. Remove the sensor from the carrier. 2. Measure the height of the sensor pole piece from the mounting face of the sensor flange. Pole should be 27.18-27.43 mm (1.07-1.08 inch). 3. Measure the depth to the top of the excitor ring teeth from the sensor mounting face on the carrier. 4. Subtract the two measurements. This is the sensor gap.	Gap is less than 1.27 mm (0.050 inches) ▶ Gap is greater than 0.050 inches ▶	GO to Test **F7**. The gap is too large. CHECK for defective sensor or carrier housing.
F7 MECHANICAL PROBLEMS IN REAR BRAKES		
• Check the rear brakes for mechanical problems such as grabbing, locking or pulling.	Rear Brakes OK ▶ Rear brakes lock, grab or pull ▶	GO to Test **F8**. REPAIR and RETEST.
F8 COMPUTER MODULE		
• Replace computer module and retest.		

FLASHOUT CODES CHART

CONDITION	ACTION TO TAKE
No Flashout Code	See Flashout Code 0
Yellow REAR ANTILOCK Light Flashes 1 Time This Code Should Not Occur	See Flashout Code 1
Yellow REAR ANTILOCK Light Flashes 2 Times Open Isolate Circuit	See Flashout Code 2
Yellow REAR ANTILOCK Light Flashes 3 Times Open Dump Circuit	See Flashout Code 3
Yellow REAR ANTILOCK Light Flashes 4 Times Red Brake Warning Light Illuminated RABS Valve Switch Closed	See Flashout Code 4
Yellow REAR ANTILOCK Light Flashes 5 Times System Dumps Too Many Times in 2WD (2WD and 4WD vehicles) Condition Occurs While Making Normal or Hard Stops. Rear Brake May Lock	See Flashout Code 5
Yellow REAR ANTILOCK Light Flashes 6 Times (Sensor Signal Rapidly Cuts In and Out) Condition Only Occurs While Driving	See Flashout Code 6
Yellow REAR ANTILOCK Light Flashes 7 Times No Isolate Valve Self Test	See Flashout Code 7
Yellow REAR ANTILOCK Light Flashes 8 Times No Dump Valve Self Test	See Flashout Code 8
Yellow REAR ANTILOCK Light Flashes 9 Times High Sensor Resistance	See Flashout Code 9
Yellow REAR ANTILOCK Light Flashes 10 Times Low Sensor Resistance	See Flashout Code 10
Yellow REAR ANTILOCK Light Flashes 11 Times Stop Lamp Switch Circuit Defective. Condition Indicated Only When Driving Above 35 mph	See Flashout Code 11
Yellow REAR ANTILOCK Light Flashes 12 Times Fluid Level Switch Grounded During a RABS Stop	See Flashout Code 12
Yellow REAR ANTILOCK Light Flashes 13 Times Speed Processor Check	See Flashout Code 13
Yellow REAR ANTILOCK Light Flashes 14 Times Program Check	See Flashout Code 14
Yellow REAR ANTILOCK Light Flashes 15 Times Memory Failure	See Flashout Code 15
Yellow REAR ANTILOCK Light Flashes 16 Times or More 16 or More Flashes Should Not Occur	See Flashout Code 16

NOTE: Refer to Obtaining the Flashout Code in this Section for procedure to obtain flashout code.

CAUTION: WHEN CHECKING RESISTANCE IN THE RABS SYSTEM, ALWAYS DISCONNECT THE BATTERY. IMPROPER RESISTANCE READINGS MAY OCCUR WITH THE VEHICLE BATTERY CONNECTED.

No Flashout Code	Flashout Code 0

TEST STEP	RESULT ▶	ACTION TO TAKE
0a NO FLASHOUT CODE BUT RABS LIGHT IS ILLUMINATED		
• There are some faults that illuminate the REAR ANTILOCK light but will not provide a Flashout Code. Refer to Obtaining the Flashout Code in this Section for procedure. Also, be sure to make a good, momentary ground from the diagnostic lead.	No Flashout Code ▶	GO to Test **D2**.

9 BRAKES

Yellow REAR ANTILOCK Light Flashes 1 Time This Code Should Not Occur	Flashout Code 1

TEST STEP	RESULT ▶	ACTION TO TAKE
1a NO TEST • This code should not occur. Refer to Obtaining the Flashout Code in this Section for procedures involved in getting the code.	Flashout Code is 1 ▶	If after repeated attempts to take the Flashout Code, Code 1 is still obtained GO to Test **E**.

<table>
<tr><td colspan="2">**Yellow REAR ANTILOCK Light Flashes 2 Times
(Open Isolate Circuit)**</td><td>**Flashout
Code
2**</td></tr>
</table>

TEST STEP	RESULT ▶	ACTION TO TAKE
2a CHECK FOR OPEN RABS VALVE ISOLATION SOLENOID WIRING OR MODULE 1. Turn ignition switch to the OFF position. 2. Disconnect battery. 3. Set the ohmmeter to the 200 ohm scale. 4. Disconnect module harness connector from module. 5. Check for resistance between harness connector Pin 13 and chassis ground.	Resistance less than 6 ohms ▶ Resistance over 6 ohms ▶	REPLACE RABS module. GO to **2b**.
2b CHECK FOR OPEN RABS VALVE GROUND WIRE 1. Disconnect battery. 2. Disconnect RABS Valve harness connector from valve connector. 3. Set ohmmeter on the 200 ohm scale. 4. Check for resistance between ground pin of valve harness connector and chassis ground.	Resistance less than 1 ohm ▶ Resistance 1 ohm or more ▶	GO to **2c**. REPAIR open in 397 circuit, isolation solenoid wire. CHECK for dirty or loose connector pins.

PIN NO. 13 — 14 13 12 ... 11 10 9 / 8 7 6 5 4 3 2 1 — MODULE HARNESS CONNECTOR — PIN VIEW

GROUND PIN — RABS VALVE HARNESS CONNECTOR — PIN VIEW

<table>
<tr><td colspan="2">

Yellow REAR ANTILOCK Light Flashes 2 Times (Open Isolate Circuit) — Continued
</td><td>

Flashout Code 2
</td></tr>
</table>

TEST STEP	RESULT ▶	ACTION TO TAKE
2c CHECK FOR OPEN RABS VALVE ISOLATION SOLENOID OR WIRING 1. Disconnect battery. 2. Set ohmmeter to 200 ohm scale. 3. Check resistance between valve connector isolation solenoid pin and connector ground pin.	Resistance less than 6 ohms ▶ Resistance over 6 ohms ▶	REPAIR open in 599 circuit, isolation solenoid wire from valve to computer module. CHECK for dirty or loose connector pins. REPLACE RABS valve.

ISOLATION SOLENOID PIN

GROUND PIN

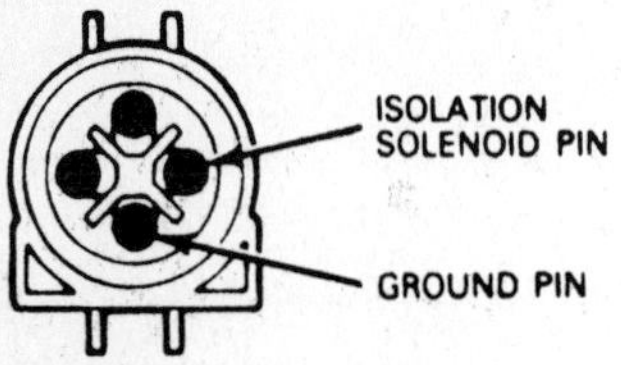

RABS VALVE CONNECTOR — PIN VIEW

Yellow REAR ANTILOCK Light Flashes 3 Times (Open Dump Circuit)	Flashout Code 3

TEST STEP	RESULT ▶	ACTION TO TAKE
3a CHECK FOR OPEN RABS VALVE DUMP SOLENOID WIRING OR COMPUTER MODULE 1. Turn ignition switch to the off position. 2. Disconnect the battery. 3. Disconnect module harness connector from module. 4. Place the ohmmeter on the 200 ohm scale. 5. Check resistance between pin 8 (or pin 14) and chassis ground. PIN NO. 14 14 13 12 11 10 9 8 7 6 5 4 3 2 1 PIN NO. 8 **MODULE HARNESS CONNECTOR — PIN VIEW**	Resistance less than 3 ohms ▶ Resistance greater than 3 ohms ▶	REPLACE computer module. GO to Test **3b**.
3b CHECK FOR OPEN RABS VALVE DUMP SOLENOID OR WIRING 1. Turn the ignition switch to the off position. 2. Disconnect the battery. 3. Disconnect RABS valve harness connector from valve connector. 4. Check resistance between valve connector dump solenoid pin and ground pin. DUMP SOLENOID PIN GROUND PIN **RABS VALVE CONNECTOR — PIN VIEW**	Resistance less than 3 ohms ▶ Resistance greater than 3 ohms ▶	REPAIR open in 664 circuit, dump solenoid wire, from valve to module. CHECK for loose or dirty connector pins. REPLACE RABS valve.

<table>
<tr><td colspan="2">Yellow REAR ANTILOCK Light Flashes 4 Times
Red Brake Warning Light Illuminated
RABS Valve Switch Closed</td><td>Flashout Code 4</td></tr>
</table>

TEST STEP	RESULT ▶	ACTION TO TAKE
4a CHECK FOR CLOSED RABS VALVE SWITCH 1. Disconnect RABS valve harness connector from valve connector. 2. Place ohmmeter on the 20K scale. 3. Check resistance between valve connector switch pin and valve body. RABS VALVE BODY GROUND — SWITCH PIN VALVE CONNECTOR — PIN VIEW	Resistance greater than 10K ohms ▶ Resistance less than 10k ohms ▶	GO to Test **4B**. REPLACE RABS valve.
4b CHECK FOR SHORT BETWEEN RABS VALVE SWITCH AND VALVE GROUND LEAD 1. Set the ohmmeter on the 20K ohm scale. 2. Check resistance between valve connector switch pin and valve solenoid ground pin. VALVE SWITCH PIN — VALVE SOLENOID GROUND PIN VALVE CONNECTOR — PIN VIEW	Resistance greater than 10K ohms ▶ Resistance less than 10K ohms ▶	GO to Test **4C**. REPLACE RABS valve.

<table>
<tr><td colspan="2">Yellow REAR ANTILOCK Light Flashes 4 Times
Red Brake Warning Light Illuminated
RABS Valve Switch Closed (Continued)</td><td>Flashout
Code
4</td></tr>
</table>

TEST STEP	RESULT ▶	ACTION TO TAKE
4c CHECK FOR RABS VALVE SWITCH WIRE SHORTED TO GROUND OR MODULE 1. Disconnect battery. 2. Set the ohmmeter on the 200K scale. 3. Disconnect the module harness connector from the module. 4. Check for resistance between harness connector pin 6 and chassis ground.	Resistance greater than 100K ohms ▶ Resistance less than 100K ohms ▶	REPLACE computer module. REPAIR short in 535 circuit, valve switch wire from valve to computer module.

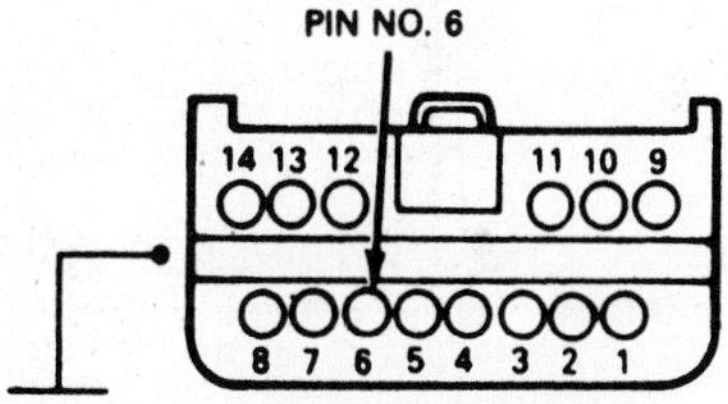

PIN NO. 6

14 13 12   11 10 9

8 7 6 5 4 3 2 1

**MODULE HARNESSS
CONNECTOR — PIN VIEW**

Yellow REAR ANTILOCK Light Flashes 5 Times System Dumps Too Many Times in 2WD (2WD and 4WD Vehicles) Condition Occurs While Making Normal or Hard Stops. Rear Brakes May Lock	Flashout Code 5

TEST STEP	RESULT ▶	ACTION TO TAKE
5a		
For 4x2 vehicles or 4x4 vehicles for which the problem was initiated in 4x2 mode		GO to Step **5b**.
For 4x4 vehicles for which the problem was initiated in 4x4 mode only		GO to Step **5c**.
5b CHECK FOR MECHANICAL PROBLEMS IN REAR BRAKE SYSTEM		
1. Disconnect the RABS module harness connector from the module to deactivate the RABS. 2. Drive the vehicle (in 4x2 mode). 3. Make normal stops in a safe area to determine the condition of the rear brake system.	Rear brakes are grabby or tend to lock up easily ▶ Rear brakes are satisfactory for normal braking ▶	REPAIR rear brake system and RETEST. REPLACE RABS valve.
5c CHECK FOR MISSING SIGNAL FROM 4 WD SWITCH TO COMPUTER MODULE		
1. Disconnect the RABS module harness from the module. 2. Turn ignition switch on. 3. Shift into 4x4 mode. 4. Set voltmeter to 20 VDC scale. 5. Measure voltage between pin 5 and chassis ground.	Voltage is less than 1 volt ▶ Voltage is greater than 1 volt ▶	REPLACE RABS valve. REPAIR 4x4 indicator switch.

PIN NO. 5

14 13 12   11 10 9
8 7 6 5 4 3 2 1

MODULE HARNESS CONNECTOR – PIN VIEW

Yellow REAR ANTILOCK Light Flashes 6 Times (Sensor Signal Rapidly Cuts In and Out) Condition Only Occurs While Driving	Flashout Code 6

TEST STEP	RESULT ▶	ACTION TO TAKE
6a CHECK FOR ERRATIC SENSOR SIGNAL AND LOOSE WIRE CONNECTIONS 1. Turn ignition off. 2. Disconnect battery. 3. Set ohmmeter on the 2000 ohm scale. 4. Check resistance between Pin 10 and Pin 3 of the harness connector while shaking the harness from sensor to module. PIN NO. 10 14 13 12 11 10 9 PIN NO. 3 8 7 6 5 4 3 2 1 MODULE HARNESS CONNECTOR – PIN VIEW	Constant reading of 1000 to 2000 ohms ▶ Reading is erratic ▶	GO to Step **6b**. REPAIR loose connection in the 519 or 523 circuits (sensor leads). CHECK for dirty or loose pins, frayed or shorted connectors.
6b CHECK FOR METAL CHIPS ON SENSOR MAGNET POLE PIECE ● Remove the sensor from the differential and inspect for a build-up of metal chips on sensor magnetic pole.	No metal chips are present ▶ Metal chips are present ▶	GO to Step **6c**. DRAIN and CLEAN differential. CHECK the excitor ring for broken or chipped teeth.
6c CHECK FOR EXCITOR RING DAMAGE 1. Remove sensor from carrier. 2. Rotate excitor ring and check for damage to teeth.	Teeth are intact and no visible lateral runout is observed ▶ Teeth are damaged or lateral runout of excitor ring is visible ▶	REINSTALL sensor and GO to Test **6d**. REPAIR axle.

9 BRAKES

Yellow REAR ANTILOCK Light Flashes 6 Times (Sensor Signal Rapidly Cuts In and Out) Condition Only Occurs While Driving (Cont'd)	Flashout Code 6

TEST STEP	RESULT ▶	ACTION TO TAKE
6d CHECK FOR ERRATIC OR LOW SENSOR OUTPUT ON COMPUTER MODULE 1. Locate the sensor test connector. 2. Position vehicle on a hoist and raise the rear wheels to clear the floor. 3. Start the engine and turn the wheels at 5 mph. 4. Place voltmeter on the 2000 mv AC scale. 5. Measure voltage at the two pins of the sensor test connector. CONNECTOR PINS **SENSOR TEST CONNECTOR — PIN VIEW**	Voltage greater than 650 mV RMS and steady ▶ Voltage less than 650 mV RMS or erratic ▶	REPLACE module. REPLACE sensor and recheck output and replace the sensor test connector cap.

Yellow REAR ANTILOCK Light Flashes 7 Times No Isolate Valve Self Test	Flashout Code 7

TEST STEP	RESULT ▶	ACTION TO TAKE
7a CHECK FOR RABS VALVE ISOLATION SOLENOID OR WIRING SHORTED TO GROUND 1. Turn ignition off. 2. Disconnect the valve harness connector from the valve connector. 3. Set the ohmmeter on the 200 ohm scale. 4. Measure the resistance between the valve isolation solenoid pin and the valve ground pin in the valve connector. ISOLATION SOLENOID PIN GROUND PIN **VALVE CONNECTOR PIN VIEW**	Resistance is greater than 3 ohms ▶ Resistance is less than 3 ohms ▶	GO to Test **7B**. REPLACE RABS valve.
7b CHECK FOR BLOWN INTERNAL FUSE IN THE MODULE 1. Turn ignition off. 2. Disconnect the battery. 3. Disconnect the valve harness connector from the valve. 4. Disconnect the module harness connector from the module. 5. Place the ohmmeter on the 20K ohm scale. 6. Measure the resistance between module harness connector pin 13 and chassis ground. PIN NO. 13 14 13 12 11 10 9 8 7 6 5 4 3 2 1 **MODULE HARNESS CONNECTOR — PIN VIEW**	Resistance greater than 20K ohms ▶ Resistance less than 20K ohms ▶	REPLACE module. REPAIR short in 599 circuit between RABS valve and module. RECONNECT module and valve.

Yellow REAR ANTILOCK Light Flashes 8 Times No Dump Valve Self Test	Flashout Code 8

TEST STEP	RESULT ▶	ACTION TO TAKE
8a CHECK FOR RABS VALVE SOLENOID OR WIRING SHORTED TO GROUND 1. Turn ignition switch off. 2. Disconnect valve harness connector from valve connector. 3. Set the ohmmeter on the 200 ohm scale. 4. Measure the resistance between the valve dump solenoid pin and the valve ground pin in the valve connector. DUMP SOLENOID PIN / GROUND PIN VALVE CONNECTOR — PIN VIEW	Resistance greater than 1 ohm ▶ Resistance is less than 1 ohm ▶	GO to Test **8b**. REPLACE RABS valve.
8b CHECK COMPUTER MODULE 1. Turn ignition off. 2. Disconnect battery. 3. Disconnect valve harness connector from valve connector. 4. Disconnect the module harness connector from the module. 5. Set the ohmmeter on the 20K ohm scale. 6. Measure the resistance between module harness connector pin 8 (or pin 14) and chassis ground. PIN NO. 14 14 13 12 11 10 9 8 7 6 5 4 3 2 1 PIN NO. 8 MODULE HARNESS CONNECTOR — PIN VIEW	Resistance greater than 20K ohm ▶ Resistance less than 20K ohm ▶	REPLACE module. REPAIR short in 664 circuit between RABS valve and RABS module. RECONNECT module and valve.

Yellow REAR ANTILOCK Light Flashes 9 Times High Sensor Resistance	**Flashout Code 9**

TEST STEP	RESULT ▶	ACTION TO TAKE
9a CHECK FOR OPEN SENSOR OR SENSOR WIRING		
1. Turn key off. 2. Disconnect sensor harness connector from the sensor on the differential. 3. Set the ohmmeter on the 20K ohm scale. 4. Measure the resistance at the two sensor pins. SENSOR PINS SENSOR — PIN VIEW	Resistance less than 2500 ohms ▶ Resistance greater than 2500 ohms ▶	GO to Test **9b**. REPLACE sensor.
9b CHECK FOR OPEN SENSOR HARNESS WIRING		
1. Turn key off. 2. Disconnect battery. 3. Reconnect sensor harness connector to sensor. 4. Disconnect module harness connector from module. 5. Set the ohmmeter on the 20K ohm scale. 6. Measure the resistance between harness connector pins 3 and 10. 14 13 12 11 10 9 — PIN NO. 10 8 7 6 5 4 3 2 1 — PIN NO. 3 MODULE HARNESS CONNECTOR — PIN VIEW	Resistance less than 2500 ohms ▶ Resistance greater than 2500 ohms ▶	REPLACE module. REPAIR open in circuits 519 or 523, sensor wires between the sensor and module. CHECK for loose or dirty pin connectors. If defect is found in 14A107 — Jumper Harness (from sensor to left frame rail), REPLACE with original equipment high flex wire.

<table>
<tr><td colspan="2">Yellow REAR ANTILOCK Light Flashes 10 Times
Low Sensor Resistance</td><td>Flashout
Code
10</td></tr>
</table>

TEST STEP	RESULT ▶	ACTION TO TAKE
10a CHECK FOR SHORTED SENSOR 1. Turn ignition off. 2. Disconnect the sensor harness from the sensor. 3. Place the ohmmeter on the 20K ohms scale. 4. Measure the resistance at the two sensor pins. SENSOR PINS SENSOR — PIN VIEW	Resistance less than 1000 ohms ▶ Resistance is greater than 1000 ohms ▶	REPLACE sensor. GO to Test **10b**.
10b CHECKING FOR GROUNDED SENSOR WIRING 1. Turn ignition off. 2. Disconnect the battery. 3. Disconnect the sensor harness connector from the sensor. 4. Disconnect the module harness connector from the module. 5. Set the ohmmeter on the 20K ohm scale. 6. Measure the resistance from pin 10 of the harness connector to chassis ground. PIN NO. 10 14 13 12 11 10 9 8 7 6 5 4 3 2 1 MODULE HARNESS CONNECTOR — PIN VIEW	Resistance less than 20K ohms ▶ Resistance is greater than 20K ohms ▶	REPAIR short to ground in 523 circuit, sensor HI lead to module. CHECK for frayed wires or shorted connectors. If defect is found in the 14A107 Jumper Harness (from sensor to left frame rail), REPLACE with original equipment high flex wire. GO to Test **10c**.

Yellow REAR ANTILOCK Light Flashes 10 Times Low Sensor Resistance (Continued)	Flashout Code 10

TEST STEP	RESULT ▶	ACTION TO TAKE
10c CHECK FOR SHORTED SENSOR WIRING 1. Turn ignition off. 2. Disconnect sensor harness connector from the sensor. 3. Disconnect the module harness connector from the module. 4. Place the ohmmeter on the 20K ohms scale. 5. Measure the resistance from pin 3 to pin 10 of the harness connector. 14 13 12 11 10 9 — PIN NO. 10 8 7 6 5 4 3 2 1 — PIN NO. 3 **MODULE HARNESS CONNECTOR — PIN VIEW**	Resistance less than 20K ohms ▶ Resistance greater than 20K ohms ▶	REPAIR short between the 523 and 519 sensor circuits. CHECK for frayed wires or shorted connectors. If defect is found in the 14A107 Jumper Harness (from sensor to left frame rail), REPLACE with original equipment high flex wire. REPLACE the RABS module.

Yellow REAR ANTILOCK Light Flashes 11 Times. Stop Lamp Switch Always Closed or Stop Lamp Switch Circuit Defective. Condition Indicated Only When Driving Above 35 mph.	Flashout Code 11

TEST STEP	RESULT ▶	ACTION TO TAKE
11a CHECK VEHICLE STOP LIGHTS		
• Apply the service brakes and observe the rear brake lamps.	Lamps illuminate ▶	GO to Test **11b**.
	Lamps do not illuminate ▶	REPAIR or REPLACE vehicle stop light switch. CHECK for blown stop light switch fuse. Investigate reason for blown fuse. CHECK for open stop light switch wiring or blown stop lamps. REPAIR as needed.
11b WIRING FROM MODULE TO BRAKE SWITCH		
• Check for an open between the brake switch and the module: 1. Turn the ignition off. 2. Set the voltmeter on the 20 VDC scale. 3. Remove the module harness connector. 4. Measure the voltage between pin 11 and chassis ground while stepping on the brake pedal.	Voltage is less than 9V ▶	REPAIR the open in the 511 circuit.
	Voltage is 9V or more ▶	CHECK 4 way flasher and directional wiring. This condition could create feedback through the stop light circuit. Also, cruise controls may not operate correctly

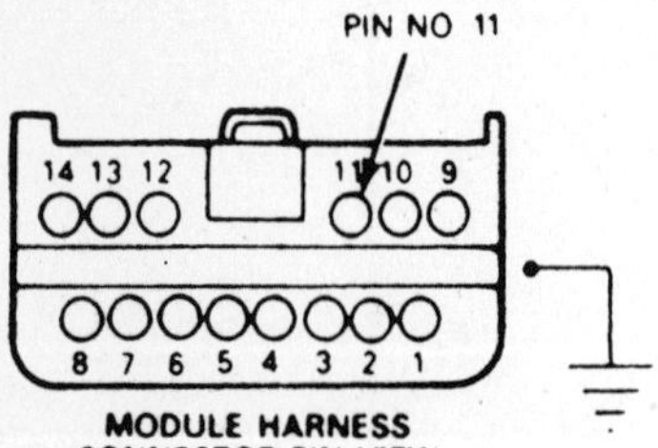

PIN NO 11

14 13 12   11 10 9

8 7 6 5 4 3 2 1

**MODULE HARNESS
CONNECTOR-PIN VIEW**

Yellow REAR ANTILOCK Light Flashes 12 Times. Red Brake Warning Light Illuminates. Fluid Level Switch Closed During a RABS Stop	Flashout Code 12

TEST STEP	RESULT ▶	ACTION TO TAKE
12a		
Follow the test procedure outlined in TEST C (but skip test C5).		

9 BRAKES

Yellow REAR ANTILOCK Light Flashes 13 Times Speed Processor Check	Flashout Code 13

TEST STEP	RESULT ▶	ACTION TO TAKE
13a NO TEST • RABS module speed circuit phase lock loop failure detected during module self test.	13 flashes are present ▶	REPLACE RABS module.

Yellow REAR ANTILOCK Light Flashes 14 Times Program Check	Flashout Code 14

TEST STEP	RESULT ▶	ACTION TO TAKE
14a NO TEST		
• RABS module program check sum failure detected during self test.	If 14 flashes are present ▶	REPLACE RABS module.

9 BRAKES

Yellow REAR ANTILOCK Light Flashes 15 Times
Memory Failure

Flashout Code 15

TEST STEP	RESULT ▶	ACTION TO TAKE
15a NO TEST		
• RABS module RAM failure detected during self test.	If 15 flashes are present ▶	REPLACE RABS module.

Yellow REAR ANTILOCK Light Flashes 16 Times or More
16 or More Flashes Should Not Occur

Flashout Code 16

TEST STEP	RESULT ▶	ACTION TO TAKE
16a NO TEST		
• This code should not occur. Refer to obtaining the Flashout Code in this Section for procedures involved in getting the code.	Flashout Code is 16 ▶	If after repeated attempts to take the Flashout Code, Code 16 is still obtained, REPLACE RABS module.

10 *Body*

QUICK REFERENCE INDEX

GENERAL INDEX

EXTERIOR

Front Doors

ADJUSTMENT

NOTE: Loosen the hinge-to-door bolts for lateral adjustment only. Loosen the hinge-to-body bolts for both lateral and vertical adjustment.

1. Determine which hinge bolts are to be loosened and back them out just enough to allow movement.
2. To move the door safely, use a padded pry bar. When the door is in the proper position, tighten the bolts to 24 ft. lbs. and check the door operation. There should be no binding or interference when the door is closed and opened.
3. Door closing adjustment can also be affected by the position of the lock striker plate. Loosen the striker plate bolts and move the striker plate just enough to permit proper closing and locking of the door.

REMOVAL AND INSTALLATION

NOTE: The hinges are bolted to the doors. Before removing the hinges from the doors, in either case, matchmark their location.

1. Matchmark the hinge-to-body locations. Support the door either on jackstands or have somebody hold it for you.
2. Remove the lower hinge-to-frame bolts.
3. Remove the upper hinge-to-frame bolts and lift the door off of the body.
4. If the hinges are being replaced, drill out the rivets using a 1 in. drill bit. New hinges are to be attached to the door with bolts, lockwashers and nuts. Use only hardened bolts of at least Grade 5.
5. Install the door and hinges with the bolts finger tight.
6. Adjust the door and torque the hinge bolts to 24 ft. lbs.

Sliding Side Doors

ADJUSTMENT

In or Out

1. Loosen the upper roller retaining nut and move the door in or out as required to obtain a flush fit. Tighten the nut.
2. Support the door so that no up or down movement can occur during the following adjustment:
3. Loosen the retaining screws on the lower guide and move the guide forward to obtain a closer fit to the body, or rearward to move it away from the body at the B-pillar. Tighten the screws.

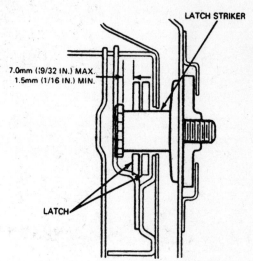

Door latch striker plate adjustment

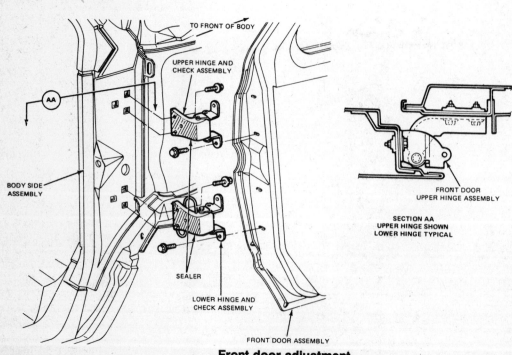

Front door adjustment